STRATEGIC MANAGEMENT and BUSINESS POLICY

eighth edition

Cases

Thomas L. Wheelen
University of South Florida

J. David Hunger
Iowa State University

Prentice
Hall

Upper Saddle River, New Jersey 07458

Library of Congress Cataloging-in-Publication Data

Wheelen, Thomas L.
   Strategic management and business policy. Cases / Thomas L. Wheelen, J. David
Hunger.—8th ed.
    p. cm.
   Includes bibliographical references and index.
   ISBN 0-13-065132-X
   1. Strategic planning—Case studies.   I. Hunger, J. David, 1941-II. Title

HD30.28.W43 2002b
658.4'012—dc21

                              2001036959

Executive Editor: David Shafer
Editor-in-Chief: Jeff Shelstad
Senior Managing Editor (Editorial): Jennifer Glennon
Assistant Editor: Melanie Olsen
Editorial Assistant: Kim Marsden
Media Project Manager: Michele Faranda
Marketing Manager: Shannon Moore
Marketing Assistant: Christine Genneken
Managing Editor (Production): Judy Leale
Production Editor: Cindy Spreder
Production Assistant: Dianne Falcone
Permissions Supervisor: Suzanne Grappi
Associate Director, Manufacturing: Vincent Scelta
Production Manager: Arnold Vila
Design Manager: Patricia Smythe
Designer: Steve Frim
Interior Design: Lee Goldstein
Cover Design: Steve Frim
Cover Illustration/Photo: Marjory Dressler
Illustrator (Interior): Electra Graphics
Manager, Print Production: Christy Mahon
Print Production Liaison: Ashley Scattergood
Composition: UG / GGS Information Services, Inc.
Full-Service Project Management: UG / GGS Information Services, Inc.
Printer/Binder: R.R. Donnelley-Willard

Credits and acknowledgments borrowed from other sources and reproduced, with permission, in this textbook appear on appropriate page within text.

Pearson Education LTD
Pearson Education Australia PTY, Limited
Pearson Education Singapore, Pte. Ltd
Pearson Education North Asia Ltd
Pearson Education, Canada, Ltd
Pearson Educación de Mexico, S.A. de C.V.
Pearson Education–Japan
Pearson Education Malaysia, Pte. Ltd

10 9 8 7 6 5 4 3 2 1
ISBN 0-13-065132-X

Dedicated to

Kathy, Richard, and Tom

Betty, Kari, Jeff, and Maddie, Suzi, Lori, Merry, and Smokey: Those for whom this book was written; and to Elizabeth Carey and Jackson S. Hunger—without whom there would be no book

And to the Prentice Hall sales representatives who work so hard to promote this book, we thank you!

Michael Ablassmeir	Mary Choi	Alli Gentile
Tara Algeo	Jody Coffey	Sybil Geraud
Peter Ancona	Catherine Colucci	Andrew Gilfillan
Larry Armstrong	Donna Conroy	David Gillespie
Tammy Arnold	Joy Costa	Keri Goldberg
Jonathan Axelrod	Candice Cotton	Brian Goldenberg
Hal Balmer	Lisa Coyle	Katherine Grassi
Alice Barr	Cyndi Crimmins	Doug Greive
Kelly Bell	Cary Crossland	Kirsten Hale
Lori Berman	Amanda Crotts	Edith Hall
Gretchen Bertani	Christine Culman	Julie Hildebrand
Jim Best	Kristin Cunningham	Kristen Hodge
Darcy Betts	Dan Currier	Devorah Hollwager
William Beville	Lisa Davis	Brett Holmes
Joan Blasco-Paul	Scott Day	Jane Hyatt
Melissa Blum	Matthew De Groat	Sandra Ivey
Marc Bove	Matt Denham	Susan Jacklson
Annette Bratcher	Kate Derrick	Connie James
Sara Bredbenner	Dennis DeValeria	Richard Jeffries
Jeanne Bronson	George Devenney	Jacqueline Johnson
Kimberly Brugger	Sue Dikun	Leah Johnson
Melissa Bruner	Scott Dustan	Glenn Johnston
Eleanor Bryant	Susan Fackert	Susan Joseph
Brian Buckley	James Farmer	Elizabeth Kaster
Kathleen Buhrow	Marissa Feliberty	Timothy Kent
Julie Burgmeier	Dennis Fernandes	Curtis Ketterman
Shauna Burgmeier	Mary Fernandez	Romayne Kilde
Janet Caffo	Steve Foster	Mary Beth Kodger
Ruth Cardiff	Yoliette Fournier	Kelly Lambing
Darrin Carr	Wayne Froelich	Sharon Lavoy
Brooke Cashion	Mary Gallagher	Tracey Leebrook
Meredith Chandler	Cheryle Gehrlich	Lisa Lehmann

Laura Less
Becky Lidard
Kristen Lindley
Tricia Liscio
James Lloyd
David Lopez
Amber Mackey
Patrick Mast
Carrie Mattaini
Nora Matthew
Jack Mayleben
Eileen McClay
Tabita McCaun
Brian McGarry
Milton McGowen
Lou McGuire
Jeff Mcilroy
Sally Mcpherson
Danielle Meier
Mary Meyer
Susan Miller
James Misenti
Paul Misselwitz
Becky Mitchell
Scott Montgomery
Kate Moore
Julie Morel
Therese Morgan
Kimberly Moran
Joseph Murray
Tom Nixon
Celeste Nossiter

Jessica Noyes
David Nurkiewicz
Meghan O'Donnell
Trisa O'Shea
Deborah Patterson
Emilia Pawlowski
Antoinette Payne
Mike Perman
Carol Pharo
Rebecca Poff
Andrew Pollard
Monica Proffitt
Catherine Ramsey
Jennifer Rehklau
Catherine Reynolds
Anne Riddick
Laura Roberts
Laura Rogers
Dorothy Rosene
Richard Rowe
Katharine Sandvoss
Corrina Schultz
Scott Shafer
Steven Shapiro
Roy Shaw
Kristi Shuey
Wayne Siegert
Phyllis Simon
Russell Slater
Jennifer Somerindyke
Stephen Soucy
Beth Spencer

Lois Stiller
Cindy Sullivan
Lori Sullivan
Pat Sullivan
Dan Sullivan
Robert Swan
Mark Templeman
David Theisen
Derek Thibodeau
Frank Timothy
David Ungerman
Paul Vaupel
David Visser
Dawn Vujevix
Marcie Wademan
Danielle Walsh
James Walsh
LeDawn Webb
Eric Weiss
Hannah Whitlock
Read Wickham
Jill Wiggins
Dennis Williams
Brian Williford
Alissa Wilmoth
Elizabeth Winter
Elizabeth Wood
Jennifer Woodle
Jacqueline Yeager
George Young
Sharon Young
Trina Zimme

Contents

section D General Issues in Strategic Management

INDUSTRY ONE INTERNET/SOFTWARE

INDUSTRY TWO INTERNET COMPANIES (DOT-COMS)

Preface

We wrote *Strategic Management and Business Policy* to introduce you to strategic management—a field of inquiry that focuses on the organization as a whole and its interactions with its environment. The corporate world is in the process of transformation driven by information technology (in particular the Internet) and globalization. Strategic management takes a panoramic view of this changing corporate terrain and attempts to show how large and small firms can be more effective and efficient not only in today's world, but in tomorrow's as well.

This text contains the latest theory and research currently available in strategic management. We sifted through the past 5 years' worth of articles from the following academic and business publications: *Academy of Management Journal, Strategic Management Journal, Academy of Management Review, Administrative Science Quarterly, Journal of Management, Long Range Planning, Organization Science, Academy of Management Executive, Organizational Dynamics, Journal of Business Strategy, SAM Advanced Management Journal, Journal of Business Strategies, Strategy and Leadership* (previously *Planning Review*), *Strategy and Business, Competitive Intelligence, Journal of Business Venturing, Entrepreneurship Theory and Practice, Harvard Business Review, Business Week,* and *The Economist.*

Both the concepts and the cases have been class-tested in strategy courses and revised based on feedback from students and instructors. The first 10 chapters are organized around a strategic management model that prefaces each chapter and provides a structure for both content and case analysis. We emphasize those concepts that have proven to be most useful in understanding strategic decision-making and in conducting case analysis. Our goal was to make the text as comprehensive as possible without getting bogged down in any 1 area. Endnote references are provided for those who wish to learn more about any particular topic. All cases in the combined text and the case text are about actual organizations. The firms range in size from large, established multinationals to small, entrepreneurial ventures, and cover a broad variety of issues. As an aid to case analysis, we propose the strategic audit as an analytical technique.

Objec

This book focuses on the following objectives, typically found in most strategic management and business policy courses:

- To develop an understanding of strategic management concepts, research, and theories.
- To develop a framework of analysis to enable a student to identify central issues and problems in complex, comprehensive cases; to suggest alternative courses of action; and to present well-supported recommendations for future action.
- To develop conceptual skills so that a student is able to integrate previously learned aspects of corporations.
- To develop an understanding of the global economy and the Internet and their current and potential impact on business activities in any location.
- To develop an understanding of the role of corporate governance in strategic management.

- To develop the ability to analyze and evaluate, both quantitatively and qualitatively, the performance of the people responsible for strategic decisions.

- To bridge the gap between theory and practice by developing an understanding of when and how to apply concepts and techniques learned in earlier courses on marketing, accounting, finance, management, production, and information systems.

- To improve research capabilities necessary to gather and interpret key environmental data.

- To develop a better understanding of the present and future environments in which corporations must function.

- To develop analytical and decision-making skills for dealing with complex conceptual problems in an ethical manner.

This book achieves these objectives by presenting and explaining concepts and theories useful in understanding the strategic management process. It critically analyzes studies in the field of strategy to acquaint the student with the literature of this area and to help develop the student's research capabilities. It also suggests a model of strategic management. It recommends the strategic audit as 1 approach to the systematic analysis of complex organization-wide issues. Through a series of special issue and comprehensive cases (available in the combined text and the cases text), it provides the student with an opportunity to apply concepts, skills, and techniques to real-world corporate problems. The book focuses on the business corporation because of its crucial position in the economic system of the world and in the material development of any society.

THIRTY-FIVE CASES

- **35 cases—21 new or revised & updated**
  - → **Sixteen new cases** (*Singapore Telecom, Hewlett-Packard in Vietnam, Waterford Crystal, Oracle, Sun Microsystems, drkoop.com, WingspanBank.com, Hewlett-Packard, Gardner Distribution, Amy's Bread, Guajilote Cooperativo Forestal, Carey Plant, Redhook Ale Brewery, Boeing, Mercedes-Benz,* and *A.W.A.R.E.)*
  - → **Five revised and updated cases** (*Apple Computer, Kmart, Wal-Mart, Home Depot,* and *Vermont Teddy Bear).*

- **Five special issue cases** dealing with Corporate Governance (*Reluctant Director at Byte Products* and *Wallace Group*), Environment (*The Audit* and *Brookstone Hospice*), and Not-for-profit Organizations (*A.W.A.R.E.*).

- **Twenty-six comprehensive strategy cases.** These cases are excellent to use in team analyses and presentations. These cases are grouped into 10 industries:
  - → Information Systems/Software (3 cases)
  - → Internet (2 cases)
  - → Computer (2 cases)
  - → Recreation & Leisure (3 cases)
  - → Major Home Appliances (1 industry note and 1 case)
  - → Mass Merchandising/Distribution (3 cases)
  - → Specialty Retailing (2 cases)
  - → Small/Medium Entrepreneurial Ventures (4 cases)

- → Beverage/Food (3 cases)
- → Aviation/Automobiles (2 cases)

- **Eighteen cases containing international issues**
  - → Six cases are of companies operating primarily outside North America (*Singapore Telecom, Hewlett-Packard in Vietnam, Body Shop, Waterford Crystal, Guajilote Cooperativo Forestal,* and *Mercedes Benz and Swatch*).
  - → Twelve cases are of North American-based companies with significant international operations and issues (*Oracle, Apple Computer, Cisco Systems, Sun Microsystems, Hewlett-Packard, Carnival, Harley-Davidson, Reebok, Major Home Appliance Industry, Maytag, Boeing,* and *Wal-Mart*).

- **Seven cases contain Internet-related issues**
  - → Two cases are of dot-com companies whose business model is the Internet (*drkoop.com* and *WingspanBank*).
  - → Five cases are of companies whose mission is tied to the Internet either directly (*Oracle, Cisco Systems,* and *Sun Microsystems*) or indirectly (*Apple Computer* and *Hewlett-Packard*).

- **Cases of companies at all stages of corporate development**
  - I. Entrepreneurial Companies with Founder as CEO (17)
    - A. Small / Medium Companies (10)
      Redhook Ale Brewery
      Inner-City Paint
      Brookstone Hospice
      Recalcitrant Director at Byte
      *Wallace Group**
      drkoop.com
      WingspanBank.com
      Amy's Bread
      Guajilote Cooperativo Forestal
      A.W.A.R.E.
    - B. Large / Very Large (7)
      Apple Computer
      Cisco Systems
      Sun Microsystems
      Oracle
      Reebok
      Home Depot
      Body Shop
  - II. **Established Companies Managed by Professional Managers** (14)
    Tasty Baking
    Hewlett-Packard
    Vermont Teddy Bear
    Singapore Telecom
    Carnival
    *Mercedes Benz and Swatch**
    Harley-Davidson

> *Major Home Appliance Industry*
> *Maytag**
> *Kmart*
> *Gardner Distribution*
> *Wal-Mart*
> *Arm & Hammer (Church & Dwight)**
> *Waterford Crystal*

III. **Business Units / Joint Ventures** (3)
> *Boeing Commercial Group*
> *Hewlett-Packard in Vietnam*
> *The Carey Plant*

> * *Note:* Diversified into multiple industries

ements

Supplemental materials are available to the instructor from the publisher. These include both Text and Case Instructor Manuals; an Instructor's Resource CD-ROM containing the Concepts IM, Computerized Test Manager, and PowerPoint Electronic Transparencies; New Part-Ending Video; and myPHLIP Web site. Also available are the following Standard Online Courses—Blackboard, Course Compass, and WebCT.

INSTRUCTOR'S MANUALS

Two comprehensive Instructor's Manuals have been carefully constructed to accompany this book. The first one accompanies the text chapters; the second one accompanies the cases.

Text Instructor's Manual

To aid in discussing the 14 chapters dealing with strategic management concepts, the Text Instructor's Manual includes:

(1) *Suggestions for Teaching Strategic Management*—discusses various teaching methods and includes suggested course syllabi.

(2) *Chapter Notes*—includes summaries of each chapter, suggested answers to discussion questions, suggestions for using end of chapter cases/exercises, plus additional discussion questions (with answers) and lecture modules.

(3) *Multiple choice test questions*—contains approximately 50 questions for each of the 14 chapters summing to over 700 questions from which to choose.

Case Instructor's Manual

To aid in case method teaching, the Case Instructor's Manual includes detailed suggestions for use, teaching objectives, and examples of student analyses for each of the 35 cases. This is the most comprehensive instructor's manual available in strategic management. A standardized format is provided for each case:

(1) Case Abstract

(2) Case Issues and Subjects

(3) Steps Covered in the Strategic Decision-Making Process

(4) Case Objectives

(5) Suggested Classroom Approaches

(6) Discussion Questions

(7) Case Author's Teaching Note

(8) Student-written Strategic Audit or Paper

(9) EFAS, IFAS, SFAS Exhibits

(10) Financial Analysis—ratios and common-size income statements

(11) Student Strategic Audit Worksheet

INSTRUCTOR'S RESOURCE CD-ROM

The Instructor's Resource CD-ROM includes the electronic Instructor's Manual, Win/PH Test Manager, and PowerPoint Electronic Transparencies. Containing all of the questions in the printed Test Item File, Test Manager allows educators to create and distribute tests for their courses easily, either by printing and distributing through traditional methods or by online delivery via a Local Area Network (LAN) server.

VIDEO: NEWBURY COMICS

New! The 8/e now offers all new part-ending footage shot at Newbury Comics, an exciting and current popular culture retail chain. Segments address key issues such as the company's basic model, mission and vision, and decision-making models. Accompanying case information can be found at the end of the parts in the text.

POWERPOINTS

The PowerPoint transparencies, a comprehensive package of text outlines and figures corresponding to the text and cases, are designed to aid the educator and supplement in-class lectures.

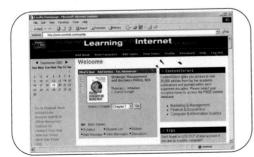

MYPHLIP WEB SITE

The new MyPHLIP provides professors with a customized course Web site including new communication tools, one-click navigation of chapter content, and great PHLIP resources such as Current Events and Internet Exercises. It also features an online Study Guide for students.
<**www.prenhall.com/wheelen**>

ONLINE COURSES

Courses are available in *Blackboard, Course Compass* and *WebCT*. These courses feature Companion Web Site and Test Item File Content in an easy-to-use system. Developed by educators for educators and their students, this online content and tools feature the most advanced educational technology and instructional design available today. The rich set of materials, communication tools, and course management resources can be easily customized to either enhance a traditional course or create the entire course online.

MASTERING STRATEGY

Mastering Strategy is the first product in the *Mastering Business* series. It offers students an interactive, multimedia experience as they follow the people and issues of CanGo, Inc., a small Internet startup. The text, video, and interactive exercises provide students an opportunity to simulate the strategic planning experience and chart the future activities for CanGo.

PRENTICE HALL GUIDE TO E-COMMERCE AND E-BUSINESS FOR MANAGEMENT

Free with any PH text, this guide introduces students to many aspects of e-business and the Internet, providing tips on searching out information, looking for jobs, continuing education, and using the Internet in Management courses.

FINANCIAL TIMES STUDENT SUBSCRIPTION

Participating students qualify for a $10.00, 15-week subscription to the *Financial Times*. **How It Works:** Wheelen/Hunger text + subscription package will contain a 16-page full-color *Financial Times* student guide shrinkwrapped to the text. Bound inside the student guide will be a postcard which entitles the student to claim a pre-paid 15-week subscription to the *Financial Times*. Free subscription for professors who choose to use this package! Contact your local Prentice Hall representative for more information.

We thank the many people at Prentice Hall who helped to make this edition possible. We are especially grateful to our editors, Jennifer Glennon and David Shafer, and their editorial assistant, Kim Marsden. We also thank Cindy Spreder, production editor, who took the book through the production process, and Melanie Olsen for coordinating the supplements package.

We are also very grateful to Kathy Wheelen for her first-rate administrative support and to Betty Hunger for her preparation of the subject and name indexes. We thank Dr. Patricia Ryan of Colorado State University for calculating ratios and common-sized statements for each case. We also thank Allan Afuah for acquiring the two Internet cases as part of his course on strategy, technology, and innovation at the University of Michigan's Graduate Business School. We are especially thankful to the many students who tried out the cases we chose to include in the combined book and the case book. Their comments helped us find any flaws in the cases before the books went to the printer.

In addition, we express our appreciation to Dr. Ben Allen, Dean, and Dr. Russ Laczniac, Management Department Chair, of Iowa State University's College of Business, for their support and provision of the resources so necessary to produce a textbook. We also recognize Dr. Robert L. Anderson, Dean, and Dr. Alan Balfour, Management Department Chair of the College of Business of the University of South Florida. Both of us acknowledge our debt to Dr. William Shenkir and Dr. Frank S. Kaulback, former Deans of the McIntire School of Commerce of the University of Virginia for the provision of a work climate most supportive to the original development of this book.

Lastly, to the many strategy/policy instructors and students who have expressed their problems with the strategy/policy course: We have tried to respond to your concerns as best we could by providing a comprehensive yet usable text coupled with recent and complex cases. To you, the people who work hard in the strategy/policy trenches, we acknowledge our debt. This book is yours.

T. L. W
Tampa, Florida

J. D. H.
Ames, Iowa

About the Contributors

Moustafa H. Abdelsamad, D.B.A. (George Washington University), is Dean of the College of Business at Texas A&M University–Corpus Christi. He previously served as Dean of the College of Business and Industry at University of Massachusetts–Dartmouth and as Professor of Finance and Associate Dean of Graduate Studies in Business at Virginia Commonwealth University. He is Editor-in-Chief of SAM *Advanced Management Journal* and International President of the Society for Advancement of Management. He is author of *A Guide to Capital Expenditure Analysis* and 2 chapters in the *Dow Jones–Irwin Capital Budgeting Handbook*. He is the author and coauthor of numerous articles in various publications.

Hitesh (John) P. Adhia, CPA, is currently the money manager for Adhia Twenty Fund and Adhia Investment Advisors, Inc. He resides in Tampa, Florida.

Philip H. Anderson, Ph.D. (University of Minnesota), is Chair and Professor of Management at the University of St. Thomas teaching strategic planning and organizational behavior in both the undergraduate and Masters of Business Administration programs. He also taught for 4 years, including 1 year on a Fulbright Scholars Fellowship, at the National University of Ireland, in Cork, Ireland while on leave from the University of St. Thomas. Dr. Anderson is coauthor of *Threshold Competitor: A Management Simulation* (2nd ed.) and *Threshold Entrepreneur: A New Business Venture Simulation* (1st ed.), computer-based management simulation exercises published by Prentice Hall. He has also published over 40 articles in the areas of educational pedagogy, small business growth, determinants of ethical behavior, quality systems (with special focus on the ISO 9000 International Quality Standard), and the use of personal computers as decision support tools. Before joining the University of St. Thomas, Dr. Anderson was a Senior Consultant with Tom Watson & Associates, Inc., a management assistance and business advisory firm, a manager with the Univac Corporation, and a professor at the University of Minnesota and at Bowling Green State University in Bowling Green, Ohio.

Stephen E. Barndt, Ph.D. (Ohio State University), is Professor of Management at the School of Business, Pacific Lutheran University. Formerly, he was head of a department in Graduate Education Division of the Air Force Institute of Technology's School of Systems and Logistics and taught at Central Michigan University. He has over 15 years of line and staff experience in operations and research and development. He has coauthored 2 fundamentals texts, *Managing by Project Management* and *Operations Management Concepts and Practices,* as well as numerous papers, articles, chapters, and cases addressing such subjects as organizational communication, project management, and strategic management. He serves on the Editorial Review Board of the *Business Case Journal.*

Ben M. Bensaou, Ph.D. (MIT Sloan School of Management), MA (Hitosubashi University, Tokyo), M.S. in Civil Engineering and D.E.A. in Mechanical Engineering from, respectively, Ecole National des TPE, Lyon and Institute National Polytechnique de Grenbole, 2 Grandes Ecoles in France. In 1998–1999 he was Visiting Professor at Harvard Business School. He was also a Visiting Professor in 1994 and 1997 at Aoyama Gakuin University in Tokyo. Dr. Bensaou is an Associate Professor of Technology Management and Asian Business at INSEAD, Fountainbleu, France. His publications include papers in *Management Science, Information Systems Research, Strategic Management Journal, Harvard Business Review,* the *European Journal of Information Systems,* book chapters, and conference proceedings. He has been consulting for Asian, European, and U.S. corporations since 1993. Professor Bensaou grew up in France and was educated in Japan. He and his wife, Masako, live in Belmont, Massachusetts, with their 3 sons.

Cathleen S. Burns, Ph.D. (New Mexico State University), CPA, is an Adjunct Assistant Professor of Management and Co-Chair of the AASCB Self-Study Team at the University of Missouri–Columbia. Dr. Burns currently teaches Contemporary Business Practices (interdisciplinary large lecture introductory course) and Management Policies and Problems (interdisciplinary senior capstone course). Dr. Burns has won 11 local, state, regional, and national teaching awards including the American Accounting Association's 1996 Award for Innovation in Accounting Education. *Amy's Bread* received the Curtis E. Tate Award from the North American Case Research Association in October 2000. Dr. Burns has been involved in numerous education and training projects with industry and has supervised 30 M.B.A. student-consulting teams working with major corporations, small business, education, and nonprofit organizations. Prior to returning to graduate school, Dr. Burns worked for Procter & Gamble, Honeywell, and in public accounting.

James W. Camerius, M.S. (University of North Dakota), is Professor of Marketing at Northern Michigan University. He is President of the Society for Case Research, Marketing Track Chair of the North American Case Research Association, and Workshop and Colloquium Director of the World Association for Case Method Research. He is a research grant recipient of the Walker L. Cisler College of Business at Northern Michigan University and also a 1995 recipient of the Distinguished Faculty Award of the Michigan Association of Governing Boards of State Universities. His cases appear in over 90 management, marketing, and retailing textbooks in addition to *Annual Advances in Business Cases,* a publication of the Society for Case Research. His studies of corporate situations include Kmart Corporation; Tanner Companies, Inc.; Mary Kay Cosmetics, Inc.; Sasco Products, Inc.; The Fuller Brush Company; Wal-Mart Stores, Inc.; Longaberger Marketing, Inc.; Encyclopaedia Britannica International; RWC, Inc.; and several others. His writings include several studies of the case method of instruction. He is an award and grant recipient of the Direct Selling Educational Foundation, Washington, D.C., and is listed in *Who's Who in the World, America, Midwest, American Education,* and *Finance and Industry.*

Thomas H. Cangley, B.S. (Florida Southern College), is Manager of e-Supply Chain Work Flow Deployment for Raytheon.

Roy A. Cook, D.B.A. (Mississippi State University), is Assistant Dean of the School of Business Administration and Professor of Management, Fort Lewis College, Durango, Colorado. He has written and published a textbook, numerous articles, cases, and papers based on his extensive experience in the hospitality industry and research interests in the areas of strategy, small business management, human relations, and communications. He serves on the editorial boards of the *Business Case Journal,* the *Journal of Business Strategies,* and the *Journal of Teaching and Tourism.* He is a member of the Academy of Management, Society for Case Research (past President), and the International Society of Travel and Tourism Educators. Dr. Cook teaches courses in Strategic Management, Small Business Management, Tourism and Resort Management, and Human Resource Management.

Laura W. Cooke, M.B.A. (University of Michigan), B.A. (Wittenberg University), is a Business Director at Metatec International, a disc manufacturing and supply chain solutions company located in Columbus, Ohio. Her responsibilities include sales, customer support, and marketing for publishing/media business unit. Prior to Metatec, Laura was President and Founder of Millennium Multimedia Publishing, a CD-ROM publishing company. Laura also serves on the Board of Trustees at the Wellington School, an independent K-12 school.

Richard A. Cosier, Ph.D. (University of Iowa), is Dean and Leeds Professor of Management at Purdue University. He formerly was Dean and Fred B. Brown Chair at the

University of Oklahoma and was Associate Dean for Academics and Professor of Business Administration at Indiana University. He served as Chairperson of the Department of Management at Indiana for 7 years prior to assuming his current position. He was formerly a Planning Engineer with Western Electric Company and Instructor of Management and Quantitative Methods at the University of Notre Dame. Dr. Cosier is interested in researching the managerial decision-making process, organization responses to external forces, and participative management. He has published in *Behavior Science, Academy of Management Journal, Academy of Management Review, Organizational Behavior and Human Performance, Management Science, Strategic Management Journal, Business Horizons, Decision Sciences, Personnel Psychology, Journal of Creative Behavior, International Journal of Management, The Business Quarterly, Public Administration Quarterly, Human Relations,* and other journals. In addition, Professor Cosier has presented numerous papers at professional meetings and has coauthored a management text. He has been active in many executive development programs and has acted as management-education consultant for several organizations. Dr. Cosier is the recipient of Teaching Excellence Awards in the M.B.A. Program at Indiana and a Richard D. Irwin Fellowship. He belongs to the Institute of Management Consults, Inc., Beta Gamma Sigma, the Academy of Management, Sigma Iota Epsilon, and the Decision Sciences Institute.

Andrew James Croll, B.A. (Appalachian State University), is currently teaching 4th grade in Boone, North Carolina. He previously resided in Charlottesville, Virginia.

David B. Croll, Ph.D. (Pennsylvania State University), is Professor of Accounting at the McIntire School of Commerce, the University of Virginia. He was Visiting Associate Professor at the Graduate Business School, the University of Michigan. He is on the editorial board of *SAM Advanced Management Journal.* He has published in the *Accounting Review* and the *Case Research Journal.* His cases appear in 12 accounting and management textbooks.

Gordon Paul Croll, B.A. (University of Alabama), is currently the Executive Vice President of Cavalier Reporting and the President of Cavalier Videography. He resides in Charlottesville, Virginia.

Dan R. Dalton, Ph.D. (University of California, Irvine), is the Dean of the Graduate School of Business, Indiana University, and Harold A. Polipl Chair of Strategic Management. He was formerly with General Telephone & Electronics for 13 years. Widely published in business and psychology periodicals, his articles have appeared in the *Academy of Management Journal, Journal of Applied Psychology, Personnel Psychology, Academy of Management Review,* and *Strategic Management Journal.*

Michael I. Eizenberg, M.A. (Tufts University), B.A. (Clark University), Honorary Doctorate (Richmond College), currently serves as President and CEO of Educational Travel Alliance (ETRAV), an organization he founded in 1999. ETRAV is the developer of Journey Milar, the Internet solution that provides support for educational travel programs worldwide and a broad range of other "value-added" travel services. From 1997 to 1999 Mr. Eizenberg served as "Entrepreneur in Residence" at Bentley College in Waltham, Massachusetts, where he divided his time between teaching, mentoring aspiring entrepreneurs, researching, and writing. Mr. Eizenberg cofounded America Council for International Studies (ACIS), an educational travel organization in 1978. He guided ACIS' growth from a tiny start-up with 7 employees to a leading international organization with offices in Boston, Atlanta, Chicago, Los Angeles, London, and Paris and 100 employees worldwide. In 1987, ACIS was acquired by AIFS, Inc., the publicly held company, with diversified holdings in the field of international education. Mr. Eizenberg stayed on as President of ACIS until 1997. During this time he also served as a member of the Board of Directors of AFIS, Inc., and the board of trustees of Richmond College.

Cathy A. Enz, Ph.D. (Ohio State University), is the Lewis G. Schaeneman Jr. Professor of Innovation and Dynamic Management at Cornell University's School of Hotel

Administration where she is also the Executive Director of the Center for Hospitality Research. Her doctoral degree is in organization theory and behavior. Professor Enz has written numerous articles, cases, and books on corporate culture, value sharing, change management, and strategic human resource management effects on performance. Professor Enz consults extensively in the service sector and serves on the Board of Directors for 2 hospitality related organizations.

Ellie A. Fogarty, M.L.S. (University of Pittsburgh), M.B.A. (Temple University), is the Business and Economics Librarian at the College of New Jersey. She is active in the American Library Association, where she serves on the Business Reference Committee; the Special Libraries Association, where she is President of the Princeton-Trenton chapter; and the New Jersey Library Association.

Donna M. Gallo, M.B.A. (Boston College), is a Ph.D. candidate at the University of Massachusetts, Amherst Isenberg School of Management, and is a Visiting Assistant Professor of Management at Bentley College in Waltham, Massachusetts. Her cases appear in several strategy textbooks. She is the coauthor of the following strategic management cases: "The Boston YWCA: 1991," "Chipcom," and "Cisco Systems."

Gamewell D. Gantt, JD, CPA, is Professor of Accounting and Management in the College of Business at Idaho State University in Pocatello, Idaho, where he teaches a variety of legal studies courses. He is a past President of the Rocky Mountain Academy of Legal Studies in Business and a past Chair of the Idaho Endowment Investment Fund Board. His published articles and papers have appeared in journals including *Midwest Law Review, Business Law Review, Copyright World,* and *Intellectual Property World.* His published cases have appeared in several textbooks and in *Annual Advances in Business Cases.*

Norman J. Gierlasinski, D.B.A., CPA, C.F.E., C.I.A., is Professor of Accounting at Central Washington University. He served as Chairman of the Small Business Division of the Midwest Business Administration Association. He has authored and coauthored cases for professional associations and the Harvard Case Study Series. He has authored various articles in professional journals as well as serving as a contributing author for textbooks and as a consultant to many organizations. He has also served as a reviewer for various publications.

Irene Hagenbuch, B.S. (Bentley College), is currently working as an Operations Specialist for Warburg Dillon Read in Stamford, Connecticut. Among her various roles at Warburg Dillon Read, Irene has spent time with the Precious Metals, Domestic Equities, and Fixed Income Groups. Some of her responsibilities have included the reduction of settlement risk through operational controls, new product development, design and testing, and general project management. Irene is an avid skier and runner. In her spare time, she enjoys foreign travel.

Loizos Heracleous, Ph.D. (University of Cambridge), is Associate Professor of Business Policy at the National University of Singapore. His research has been published in the *Academy of Management Journal, Human Relations, Journal of Applied Behavioral Science, Long Range Planning, Asia Pacific Journal of Management, Organization Development Journal, European Management Journal,* and several other journals. He serves on the Editorial Board of the *Asia Pacific Journal of Management.*

Nicole Herskowitz, M.B.A. (University of Michigan) B.A. (University of Texas at Austin), spent 3 years working as a business consultant for Arthur Anderson focusing on the telecommunications industry. She then returned to school to pursue an M.B.A. from the University of Michigan. After graduating, Nicole went to work for Agillion in CRM software solutions for small/mid-size businesses, as a Product Marketing Manager.

Tom Hinthorne, Ph.D. (University of Oregon), is a Professor of Management, Montana State University–Billings. He has published in the *Case Research Journal, Industrial Management,* the *Strategic Management Journal,* and *Thompson & Strickland's* textbook

Strategic Management: Concepts and Cases, 10th Edition. He has 15 years of management experience with a large multinational forest products company and has worked as a consultant, expert witness, and corporate director.

Alan N. Hoffman, D.B.A. (Indiana University), is Associate Professor of Management, Bentley College, Waltham, Massachusetts, and was formerly Assistant Professor of Business Environment and Policy at the University of Connecticut. He is coauthor of *The Strategic Management Casebook and Skill Builder,* with Hugh O'Neill. Recent publications have appeared in the *Academy of Management Journal, Human Relations,* the *Journal of Business Research, Business Horizons,* and the *Journal of Business Ethics.* His cases appear in more than 20 strategy textbooks. He is coauthor of the following strategic management cases: "Harley-Davidson: The Eagle Soars Alone," "The Boston YMCA: 1991," "Ryka, Inc.: The Athletic Shoe with a 'Soul,'" "Liz Claiborne: Troubled Times for the Women's Retail Giant," "Snapple Beverage," "NTN Communications: The Future Is Now!" "Ben and Jerry's Homemade: Yo! I'm Your CEO," "Chipcom, Inc.," "Cisco Systems," "Sun Microsystems," "Cognex, Inc.," and "ACIS."

Elizabeth B. Hovey, M.B.A. (University of Michigan), B.A. (College University), is an Associate Brand Manager at Kraft Foods North America. Her work at Kraft has included experiences managing the Toblerone and Milka Chocolate brands as well as the Ready to Eat Jell-O products as a part of these brand teams. Prior to joining Kraft, Elizabeth was the National Sales Manager for Safety 1st, Inc., a manufacturer of childcare products.

Fred Howard, M.B.A. (University of Michigan), B.S. (Yale University). Following Yale, Fred spent 5 years in the financial world primarily in consulting with Merrill Lynch. Fred is currently a Senior Consultant with DiamondCluster International. His consulting experiences have included the development of an overarching e-commerce strategy for a major international pharmaceutical company as well as the development of a corporate perspective on the wireless Internet market.

J. David Hunger, Ph.D. (Ohio State University), is Professor of Strategic Management at Iowa State University. He previously taught at George Mason University, the University of Virginia, and Baldwin-Wallace College. His research interests lie in strategic management, corporate governance, and entrepreneurship. He served as Academic Director of the Pappajohn Center for Entrepreneurship at Iowa State University. He worked in brand management at Procter & Gamble Company, as a selling supervisor at Lazarus Department Store, and served as a Captain in U.S. Army Military Intelligence. He has been active as consultant and trainer to business corporations, as well as to state and federal government agencies. He has written numerous articles and cases that have appeared in the *Academy of Management Journal, International Journal of Management, Human Resource Management, Journal of Business Strategies, Case Research Journal, Business Case Journal, Handbook of Business Strategy, Journal of Management Case Studies, Annual Advances in Business Cases, Journal of Retail Banking, SAM Advanced Management Journal,* and *Journal of Management,* among others. Dr. Hunger is a member of the Academy of Management North American Case Research Association (NACRA), Society for Case Research (SCR), North American Management Society, World Association for Case Method Research and Application (WACRA), Textbook and Academic Authors Association, and the Strategic Management Society. He is past President of the Society for Case Research and the Iowa State University Board of Directors. He also served as Vice President of the U.S. Association for Small Business and Entrepreneurship (USASBE). He is currently serving as NACRS's Vice President for the 2002 Program. He is currently serving on the editorial review boards of SAM *Advanced Management Journal, Journal of Business Strategies,* and *Journal of Business Research.* He is also a member of the Board of Directors of the North American Case Research Association and the Society for Case Research. He is coauthor with Thomas L.

Wheelen of *Strategic Management and Business Policy, Strategic Management, Essentials of Strategic Management, Cases in Strategic Management and Business Policy,* as well as *Strategic Management Cases (PIC: Preferred Individualized Cases),* and a monograph assessing undergraduate business education in the United States. His textbook *Strategic Management and Business Policy* received the McGuffey Award for Excellence and Longevity in 1999 from the Text and Academic Authors Association. Dr. Hunger received the *Best Case Award* given by the McGraw-Hill Publishing Company and the Society for Case Research in 1991 for outstanding case development. He is listed in various versions of *Who's Who,* including *Who's Who in the World.* He was also recognized in 1999 by the Iowa State University College of Business with its Innovation in Teaching Award and was elected a Fellow of the Teaching and Academic Authors Association in 2001.

George A. Johnson, Ph.D., is Professor of Management and Director of the Idaho State University M.B.A. program. He has published in the fields of management education, ethics, project management, and simulation. He is also active in developing and publishing case material for educational purposes. His industry experience includes several years as a Project Manager in the development and procurement of aircraft systems.

Edward R. Kasabov is a Ph.D. candidate in the School of Business Studies, University of Dublin, Trinity College, Dublin, Ireland. He is a Teaching Assistant at Trinity College (Marketing, International Business) and is lecturing at DIT (Consumer Behavior, Organization Development). His Ph.D. research focuses on sectoral model creation as well as on the application of the model to the field of Irish Biotechnology.

Michael J. Keeffe, Ph.D. (University of Arkansas), is Associate Professor of Management at Southwest Texas State University. He is the author of numerous cases in the field of strategic management, has published in several journals, and is an associate with the consulting firm of Hezel & Associates in San Antonio, Texas. He currently teaches and conducts research in the fields of strategic management and human resource management.

John A. Kilpatrick, Ph.D. (University of Iowa), is Professor of Management and International Business, Idaho State University. He has taught in the areas of business and business ethics for over 25 years. He served as Co-Chair of the management track of the Institute for Behavioral and Applied Management from its inception and continues as a board member for that organization. He is author of *The Labor Content of American Foreign Trade,* and coauthor of *Issues in International Business.* His cases have appeared in a number of organizational behavior and strategy texts and casebooks, and in *Annual Advances in Business Cases.*

Hyung T. Kim, M.D., M.B.A., B.A. (Johns Hopkins University, University of Michigan and Johns Hopkins University, respectively), is a consultant in the Detroit Office of McKinsey & Company, Inc., where his work has included post-merger management and strategy in banking, new economy, transportation, and healthcare. Prior to joining McKinsey, Kim was a Clinical Instructor of Internal Medicine at the University of Michigan Medical School where he taught and performed patient care. He earned an M.B.A. with High Distinction from the University of Michigan Business School; an M.D. from the Johns Hopkins University School of Medicine, where he was a Hartford Foundation Clinical Scholar in Geriatric Medicine; and a B.A. from Johns Hopkins in Natural Sciences with a concentration in the History of Science.

Eric G. Kirby, Ph.D. (University of Kentucky), is Assistant Professor of Strategic Management at Southwest Texas State University. He previously held a joint appointment on the faculties of the Colleges of Business Administration and Medicine at Texas Tech University. He has received numerous awards for his research in the areas of health care administration and sport management. He has published over a dozen articles in scholarly journals and presented many more at academic conferences. Most of his research examines how businesses understand and respond to their external environment. Prior to becoming an academic, he was a building contractor, technical writer, and information system manager. He can be contacted online at <www.EricKirby.com>.

Donald F. Kuratko is the Stoops Distinguished Professor of Entrepreneurship and Founding Director of the Entrepreneurship Program, College of Business, Ball State University. In addition, he is Executive Director of the Midwest Entrepreneurial Education Center. He has published 18 books, including the leading entrepreneurship book in American universities today, *Entrepreneurship: A Contemporary Approach,* 5th ed. (Harcourt College Publishers, 2001), as well as *Strategic Entrepreneurial Growth* (Harcourt College Publishers, 2001), and *Effective Small Management,* 7th ed. (Harcourt College Publishers, 2001). He has published over 150 articles on aspects of entrepreneurship, new venture development, and corporate entrepreneurship. His work has been published in journals such as *Strategic Management Journal, Academy of Management Executive, Journal of Business Venturing, Entrepreneurship Theory & Practice, Journal of Small Business Management, Journal of Small Business Strategy, Family Business Review,* and *Advanced Management Journal.* In addition, Dr. Kuratko has been consultant on Corporate Intrapreneurship and Entrepreneurial Strategies to a number of major corporations such as Anthem Blue Cross/Blue Shield, AT&T, United Technologies, Ameritech, The Associated Group (Acordia), Union Carbide Corporation, ServiceMaster, and TruServ.

The academic program in entrepreneurship that Kuratko developed at Ball State University has continually earned national ranking including: *Top 20 in Business Week Success* magazines; *Top 10 Business Schools for Entrepreneurship Research Over the Last 10 Years* (MIT study); and *Top 5* in *U.S. News & World Report's* elite ranking (including the No. 1 State University for Entrepreneurship). The program has also been honored with the NFIB Entrepreneurship Excellence Award (1993); The National Model Entrepreneurship Undergraduate Program Award (1990); The National Model Entrepreneurship Graduate Program Award (1998); and the National Model Innovative Pedagogy Award for Entrepreneurship (2001). In addition to earning the Ball State University College Business Teaching Award for 15 consecutive years, Kuratko holds the distinction of being the *only* professor in the history of Ball State University to achieve all 4 of the university's major lifetime awards, which include: Ball State University's *Outstanding Young Faculty* (1987); *Outstanding Teaching Award* (1990); *Outstanding Faculty Award* (1996); and *Outstanding Researcher Award* (1999). In 2000, he was honored with the Thomas W. Binford Memorial Award for Outstanding Contribution to Entrepreneurial Development by the Indiana Health Industry Forum. In 2001 Dr. Kuratko was named a *21st Century Entrepreneurship Research Fellow* by the National Consortium of Entrepreneurship Centers.

Geok Theng Lau, Ph.D. (Ivey School of Business, University of Western Ontario), is Associate Professor of Marketing at the National University of Singapore. His research interests are in B2B Marketing and Purchasing Management. His research has appeared in international journals such as *Industrial Marketing Management, Journal of Supply Chain Management,* and *European Journal of Purchasing and Supply Management.*

Janet Mehlhop, M.B.A. (University of Michigan), B.A. (UCLA), has worked and lived in Europe and Asia and specializes in International Business Development with focus on multilingual communications. She spent 4 years at the San Francisco Chamber of Commerce and 3 years working for a multilingual communications agency, based in New York. After business school, Janet joined Charles Schwab & Co., Inc. in a management training rotation program, focusing on affinity marketing and business development. In her spare time, Janet directs a Bay Area singing group called Global Voices.

Charles E. Michaels, Jr., Ph.D. (University of South Florida), is Associate Professor of Management at the University of South Florida, Sarasota. He has served on the editorial review board for *SAM Advanced Management Journal* and has authored articles appearing in the *Journal of Applied Psychology, Journal of Retail Banking,* and *Journal of Occupational Psychology,* as well as papers in the fields of business management and industrial psychology. He has developed a research and teaching interest in international business.

Bill J. Middlebrook, Ph.D. (University of North Texas), is Professor of Management at Southwest Texas State University. He has served as Acting Chair of the Department of Management and Marketing, published in numerous journals, served as a consultant in industry, and is currently teaching and researching in the fields of Strategic Management and Human Resources.

Nathan Nebbe, M.B.A. and M.A. (Iowa State University), has significant interests in the indigenous peoples of the Americas. With an undergraduate degree in Animal Ecology, he served as a Peace Corps Volunteer in Honduras, where he worked at the Honduran national forestry school ESNACIFORE (Escuela Nacional de Ciencias Forestales). After the Peace Corps, Nathan worked for a year on a recycling project for the Town of Ignacio and the Southern Ute Indian Tribe in southwestern Colorado. Following his experience in Colorado, Nathan returned to Iowa State University where he obtained his M.B.A. followed by an M.A. in Anthropology. He is currently studying how globalization of the Chilean forestry industry is affecting the culture of the indigenous Mapuche people of south central Chile.

Shirley F. Olson, D.B.A. (Mississippi State University), is Vice President of J.J. Ferguson Companies in Greenwood, Mississippi. She was formerly associated with Millsaps College–Jackson, Mississippi, as Professor with concentrations in strategic management and behavioral management. She has authored over 150 articles and numerous cases. She also has an active consulting practice focusing primarily on strategic planning.

Thomas M. Patrick, Ph.D. (University of Kentucky), is Professor of Finance at The College of New Jersey. He has also taught at Rider University and the University of Notre Dame. He has published widely in the areas of commercial banking and small business finance. His research appears in such journals as *Journal of Consumer Finance, Journal of International Business Studies, Journal of Small Business Management,* and *Banker's Monthly.* He also serves on the editorial review boards of a number of academic journals.

Paul Rakouski, M.B.A. (University of Michigan), B.S. (John Carroll University), is a Manager in the Strategy and Business Architecture service line in the Boston office of Accenture. His primary focus is the communications and high-technology industry where he works with clients in the areas of e-business strategy, marketing and channel strategy, new business development, and brand portfolio analysis. Prior to joining Accenture, Paul spent over 5 years at IBM Global Services and a software startup that developed enterprise applications for small to medium businesses.

John K. Ross, III, Ph.D. (University of North Texas), is Associate Professor of Management at Southwest Texas State University. He has served as SBI Director, Associate Dean, Chair of the Department of Management and Marketing, published in numerous journals, and is currently teaching and researching in the fields of strategic management and human resources.

Patricia A. Ryan, Ph.D. (University of South Florida), is an Assistant Professor of Finance at Colorado State University. She has published cases and articles in the *Business Case Journal, Journal of Accounting and Finance Research, Journal of Finance and Strategic Decisions, Educational and Psychological Measurement, Journal of Research in Finance, American Business Review,* and *Annual Advances in Business Cases.* Her work has also appeared in *Strategic Management and Business Policy, 6th, 7th, and 8th editions,* as well as *Research and Cases in Strategic Management.* She has served on multiple review boards and finance association program committees. She is currently serving as Track Chair for the Midwest Finance Association's 2002 meeting. Dr. Ryan is past Editor of *Annual Advances in Business Cases,* a publication of the Society for Case Research.

Richard C. Scamehorn, M.B.A. (Indiana University), B.S. in Aeronautical and Aerospace Engineering (University of Michigan), is Executive in Residence Emeritus at Ohio University's College of Business. Prior to Ohio University he was with Diamond Power Specialty Company, where he served as President, Vice President of Marketing, and Vice President of Manufacturing. He has conducted business and traveled in 52 countries and served on boards of directors of companies in Australia, Canada, China, Finland, Korea, Mexico, South Africa, Sweden, and the United Kingdom. He is listed in *Who's Who in Finance and Industry in America* and the *International Businessmen's Who's Who.*

Kulwant Singh, Ph.D. (University of Michigan), is Associate Professor of Business Policy at the National University of Singapore. He is Chief Editor of the *Asia Pacific Journal of Management* and serves on the Editorial Board of *Strategic Management Journal.* His research has been published in *Strategic Management Journal, Academy of Management Journal, Organization Science, Industrial and Corporate Change, Journal of Economic Behavior and Organization,* and other journals. He is coauthor of *Business Strategy in Asia: A Casebook* and *Surviving the New Millennium, Lessons from the Asian Crisis.* His cases have been published in the *Asian Case Research Journal* and in other case collections.

Stanley R. Sitnik, D.B.A. (George Washington University), M.B.A. (Seton Hall University), B.S. (Georgetown University), is currently teaching Advanced Business Financial Management to M.B.A. students. He was previously an Assistant Professor of Finance, a Securities Broker-Dealer, and a Founder and CEO of several companies engaged in the acquisitions, development, and operation of natural gas and coal producing properties. He is presently an associate of MLC S.A., an international consulting firm based in Geneva, Switzerland. He is actively engaged in financial management research but also explores the field of alternative energy.

Pilar Speer, M.B.A. (University of Michigan), B.A. (University of Colorado), is a Senior Consultant in Cap Gemini, Ernst & Young's Strategy & Transformation practice. While at the University of Colorado, she gained 5 years of advertising and sales experience in small business retail and print media. She then received her M.B.A. from the University of Michigan Business School with emphases in Corporate Strategy, Marketing, and Organizational Behavior and Design. Mrs. Speer also has business development, marketing and e-commerce experience. Within CGEY, she has worked in Consumer Products, High Tech for Middle Market clients, Mergers & Acquisitions in the energy sector, and B2B Private Exchange Strategy Evaluation.

Laurence J. Stybel, Ed.D. (Harvard University), is Cofounder of Stybel Peabody Lincolnshire, a Boston-based management consulting firm devoted to enhancing career effectiveness of executives who report to boards of directors. Services include search, outplacement, outplacement avoidance, and valued executive career consulting. Stybel Peabody Lincolnshire was voted "Best Outplacement Firm" by the readers of *Massachusetts Lawyers Weekly.* Its programs are the only ones officially endorsed by the Massachusetts Hospital Association and the Financial Executives Institute. He serves on the Board of Directors of the New England Chapter of the National Association of Corporate Directors and of the Boston Human Resources Association. His home page can be found at <www.stybelpeabody.com>. The "Your Career" department of the home page contains downloadable back issues of his monthly *Boston Business Journal* column, "Your Career."

Paul M. Swiercz, M.S., Ph.D. (Virginia Polytechnic Institute and State University), M.P.H. (University of Michigan), served on the faculty at Saginaw Valley State University from 1982 to 1984, where he was elected Chairman of the Department of Management/Marketing. From 1984 to 1986 he was a Visiting Professor at the Graduate School of Labor and Industrial Relations at Michigan State University. In 1986 he joined the faculty at Georgia State University, where he was a member of the Department of Management and a Senior Research Associate in the W.T. Beebe Institute of Personnel and

Employment Relations. In 1992 he joined the faculty at George Washington University as an Associate Professor of Human Systems and Employment Relations Policy. Dr. Swiercz is the Founder and Principal in the firm Executive Development Services International (EDSI). In his capacity as a consultant and trainer he has directed workshops for AT&T, General Motors, Management Science Associates, the State of Georgia, the Pentagon, and others. He has been a principal investigator on a number of research projects, including those sponsored by the State of Georgia, the Hewlett Foundation, and the Society for Human Resource Planning. Dr. Swiercz has published more than 30 articles; his case studies on *Home Depot* and *Delta Airlines* have appeared in the 6 best-selling strategy textbooks; and he has been interviewed by numerous news organizations, including CNN. He currently serves as Editor of the journal *Human Resource Planning* and is Director of the Strategic HRM Partnership Project at George Washington University.

Joyce P. Vincelette, D.B.A. (Indiana University), is Professor of Management and Division Head of Management, Marketing, Information Systems Management, and General Business at The College of New Jersey. She was previously a faculty member at the University of South Florida. She has published articles, professional papers, chapters, and cases in management journals and strategic management textbooks. She is also active as a consultant and trainer for a number of local and national business organizations as well as for a variety of not-for-profit and government agencies.

James E. Weber, Ph.D. (New Mexico State University), is an Assistant Professor of Business Computer Information Systems at St. Cloud State University. His cases have appeared in textbooks, the *Cases Research Journal,* and the *Thunderbird International Business Review.* Current research interests include the effect of e-commerce on small businesses.

Paula S. Weber, Ph.D., is a Professor of Strategic Management and International Management at St. Cloud State University. Dr. Weber formerly held positions as a Professor of Management at the University of Houston–Victoria and New Mexico Highlands University. Her publications include articles and cases in the *Journal of Applied Behavioral Science, Journal of Management Education, Case Research Journal,* and the *Leadership and Organizational Development Journal.* She serves as an Editor for the *Journal of Applied Business and Behavioral Sciences* and has been a reviewer for numerous publications. Dr. Weber's primary research interests are in the area of organizational change, organization development, and strategic decision-making.

Kathryn E. Wheelen, B.A. (University of Tampa), has worked as an Administrative Assistant for case and textbook development with the Thomas Wheelen Company (circa 1879). She is currently employed by Xerox Corporation.

Richard D. Wheelen, B.S. (University of South Florida), has worked as a Case Research Assistant. He is currently a buyer at Microserv, Inc., in Seattle.

Thomas L. Wheelen II, B.A. (Boston College), has worked as a Case Research Assistant.

Thomas L. Wheelen, D.B.A., M.B.A., B.S. Cum Laude (George Washington University, Babson College, and Boston College, respectively), Teaching Experience: Visiting Professor, Trinity College–University of Dublin (Fall 1999); Professor of Strategic Management, University of South Florida (1983–present); Ralph A. Beeton Professor of Free Enterprise, University of Virginia–McIntire School of Commerce (1985–1981); Professor (1981–1974); Associate Professor (1974–1971); and Assistant Professor (1971–1968); Visiting Professor— University of Arizona (1980–1979) and Northeastern University (Summer 1979, 1977, and 1975). Academic, Industry and Military Experience: University of Virginia College of Continuing Education: (1) Coordinator for Business Education (1983–1978, 1976–1971)— approve all undergraduate courses offered at 7 Regional Centers and approved faculty; (2) Liaison Faculty and Consultant to the National Academy of the FBI Academy (1983–1972); and (3) developed, sold, and conducted over 200 seminars for local, state, and national governments, and companies for McIntire School of Commerce and Continuing Education. *General Electric Company*—various management positions (1965–1961); *U.S. Navy Supply Corps (SC)*—Lt. (SC) USNR—Assistant Supply Officer Aboard Nuclear Support Tender (1960–1957). Publications: (1) *Monograph—An Assessment of Undergraduate Business Education in the United States* (with J. D. Hunger), 1980; (2) *Books*—coauthor with J. D. Hunger—5 active books: *Strategic Management and Business Policy*, 8th Ed. (2002); *Cases in Strategic Management*, 8th Ed. (2002); *Strategic Management*, 8th Ed. (2002); *Strategic Management*, 8th Ed. (2002); *Strategic Management and Business Policy*, 8th Ed., *International Edition* (2002); and *Essentials of Strategic Management*, 2nd Ed. (2001). (3) *Coeditor—Developments in Information Systems* (1974) *and Collective Bargaining in the Public Sector* (1977) and (4) *Codeveloper of software*—STrategic Financial ANalyzer (ST. FAN) (1993, 1990, 1989—different versions); (5) *Articles*—authored over 40 articles that have appeared in such journals as the *Journal of Management, Business Quarterly, Personnel Journal, SAM Advanced Management Journal, Journal of Retailing, International Journal of Management,* and the *Handbook of Business Strategy.* (6) *Cases*—about 186 cases appearing in over 65 text and case books, as well as the *Business Case Journal, Journal of Management Case Studies, International Journal of Case Studies and Research* and *Case Research Journal.* Awards: (1) *Fellow* elected by the Society for Advancement of Management in 2002; (2) *Fellow* elected by North American Case Research Association in 2000; (3) *Fellow* elected by Text and Academic Authors Association in 2000; *(4) 1999 Phil Carroll Advancement of Management Award in Strategic Management* from the Society for Advancement of Management; (5) 1999 McGuffey Award for Excellence and Longevity for Strategic Management and Business Policy—6th Edition from the Text and Academic Authors Association; (6) 1996/97 Teaching Incentive Program Award for teaching undergraduate strategic management; (7) Fulbright, 1996–97, to Ireland but I had to turn it down; (8) Endowed Chair, Ralph A. Beeton Professor, at University of Virginia (1981–1985); (9) Sesquicentennial Associateship research grant from the Center for Advanced Studies at the University of Virginia, 1979–80; (10) Small Business Administration (Small Business Institute) supervised undergraduate team that won District, Regional III, and Honorable Mention Awards; and (11) awards for 2 articles. Associations: Dr. Wheelen currently serves on the Board of Directors of Adhia Mutual Fund, Society for Advancement of Management, and on the Editorial Board and the Associate Editor of *SAM Advanced Management Journal.* He served on the Board of Directors of Lazer Surgical Software, Inc, and Southern Management Association and on the Editorial Boards of the *Journal of Management* and *Journal of Management Case Studies, Journal of Retail Banking, Case Research Journal,* and *Business Case Journal.* He was Vice President of *Strategic Management* for the *Society for the Advancement of Management,* and President of the *North American Case Research Association.* Dr. Wheelen is a member of the *Academy of Management, Beta Gamma Sigma, Southern Management Association, North American Case Research Association, Society for Advancement of Management, Society for Case Research, Strategic Management Association,* and *World Association for Case Method Research and Application.* He has been listed in *Who's Who in Finance and Industry, Who's Who in the South and Southwest,* and *Who's Who in American Education.*

Other Contributors:
Michael Iverson
Shirley F. Meadows
Eric Pfaffman

CONTENTS

Section A

Corporate Governance: Questions of Executive Leadership

Section B

Environmental Issues: Questions of Social Responsibility and Ethics

Section C

International Issues in Strategic Management

Section D

General Issues in Strategic Management

Industry One   Internet/Software

Industry Two   Internet Companies (Dot-Coms)

Industry Three Computers

Industry Four   Recreation and Leisure

Industry Five   Major Home Appliances

Industry Six   Mass Merchandising/Distribution

Industry Seven Specialty Retailers

Industry Eight Small/Medium Entrepreneurial Ventures

Industry Nine   Beverage/Food

Industry Ten   Aviation and Automobiles

Section E

Issues in Not-For-Profit Organizations

cases in strategic management

The Recalcitrant Director at Byte Products, Inc.: Corporate Legality Versus Corporate Responsibility

Dan R. Dalton, Richard A. Cosier, and Cathy A. Enz

Byte Products, Inc., is primarily involved in the production of electronic components that are used in personal computers. Although such components might be found in a few computers in home use, Byte products are found most frequently in computers used for sophisticated business and engineering applications. Annual sales of these products have been steadily increasing over the past several years; Byte Products, Inc., currently has total sales of approximately $265 million.

Over the past 6 years increases in yearly revenues have consistently reached 12%. Byte Products, Inc., headquartered in the midwestern United States, is regarded as 1 of the largest volume suppliers of specialized components and is easily the industry leader with some 32% market share. Unfortunately for Byte, many new firms—domestic and foreign—have entered the industry. A dramatic surge in demand, high profitability, and the relative ease of a new firm's entry into the industry explain in part the increased number of competing firms.

Although Byte management—and presumably shareholders as well—is very pleased about the growth of its markets, it faces a major problem: Byte simply cannot meet the demand for these components. The company currently operates 3 manufacturing facilities in various locations throughout the United States. Each of these plants operates 3 production shifts (24 hours per day), 7 days a week. This activity constitutes virtually all of the company's production capacity. Without an additional manufacturing plant, Byte simply cannot increase its output of components.

James M. Elliott, Chief Executive Officer and Chairman of the Board, recognizes the gravity of the problem. If Byte Products cannot continue to manufacture components in sufficient numbers to meet the demand, buyers will go elsewhere. Worse yet is the possibility that any continued lack of supply will encourage others to enter the market. As a long-term solution to this problem, the Board of Directors unanimously authorized the construction of a new, state-of-the-art manufacturing facility in the southwestern United States. When the planned capacity of this plant is added to that of the 3 current plants, Byte should be able to meet demand for many years to come. Unfortunately, an estimated 3 years will be required to complete the plant and bring it on line.

This case was prepared by Professors Dan R. Dalton and Richard A. Cosier of the Graduate School of Business at Indiana University and Professor Cathy A. Enz of Cornell University. The names of the organization, individual, location, and/or financial information have been disguised to preserve the organization's desire for anonymity. This case was edited for SMBP-8th Edition. Reprinted by permission.

Jim Elliott believes very strongly that this 3-year period is far too long and has insisted that there also be a shorter range, stopgap solution while the plant is under construction. The instability of the market and the pressure to maintain leader status are 2 factors contributing to Elliott's insistence on a more immediate solution. Without such a move, Byte management believes that it will lose market share and, again, attract competitors into the market.

Several Solutions

A number of suggestions for such a temporary measure were offered by various staff specialists, but rejected by Elliott. For example, licensing Byte's product and process technology to other manufacturers in the short run to meet immediate demand was possible. This licensing authorization would be short-term, or just until the new plant could come on line. Top management, as well as the board, was uncomfortable with this solution for several reasons. They thought it unlikely that any manufacturer would shoulder the fixed costs of producing appropriate components for such a short term. Any manufacturer that would do so would charge a premium to recover its costs. This suggestion, obviously, would make Byte's own products available to its customers at an unacceptable price. Nor did passing any price increase to its customers seem sensible, for this too would almost certainly reduce Byte's market share as well as encourage further competition.

Overseas facilities and licensing also were considered but rejected. Before it became a publicly traded company, Byte's founders decided that its manufacturing facilities would be domestic. Top management strongly felt that this strategy had served Byte well; moreover, Byte's majority stockholders (initial owners of the then privately held Byte) were not likely to endorse such a move. Beyond that, however, top management was reluctant to foreign license—or make available by any means the technologies for others to produce Byte products—as they could not then properly control patents. Top management feared that foreign licensing would essentially give away costly proprietary information regarding the company's highly efficient means of product development. There also was the potential for initial low product quality—whether produced domestically or otherwise—especially for such a short-run operation. Any reduction in quality, however brief, would threaten Byte's share of this sensitive market.

The Solution!

One recommendation that has come to the attention of the Chief Executive Officer could help solve Byte's problem in the short run. Certain members of his staff have notified him that an abandoned plant currently is available in Plainville, a small town in the northeastern United States. Before its closing 8 years before, this plant was used primarily for the manufacture of electronic components. As is, it could not possibly be used to produce Byte products, but it could be inexpensively refitted to do so in as few as 3 months. Moreover, this plant is available at a very attractive price. In fact, discreet inquiries by Elliott's staff indicate that this plant could probably be leased immediately from its present owners because the building has been vacant for some 8 years.

All the news about this temporary plant proposal, however, is not nearly so positive. Elliott's staff concedes that this plant will never be efficient and its profitability will be low. In addition, the Plainville location is a poor one in terms of high labor costs (the area is highly unionized), warehousing expenses, and inadequate transportation links to Byte's major markets and suppliers. Plainville is simply not a candidate for a long-term solution. Still, in the short run a temporary plant could help meet the demand and might forestall additional competition.

The staff is persuasive and notes that this option has several advantages: (1) there is no need for any licensing, foreign or domestic, (2) quality control remains firmly in the company's hands, and (3) an increase in the product price will be unnecessary. The temporary plant, then, would be used for 3 years or so until the new plant could be built. Then the temporary plant would be immediately closed.

CEO Elliott is convinced.

Taking the Plan to the Board

The quarterly meeting of the Board of Directors is set to commence at 2:00 P.M. Jim Elliott has been reviewing his notes and agenda for the meeting most of the morning. The issue of the temporary plant is clearly the most important agenda item. Reviewing his detailed presentation of this matter, including the associated financial analyses, has occupied much of his time for several days. All the available information underscores his contention that the temporary plant in Plainville is the only responsible solution to the demand problems. No other option offers the same low level of risk and ensures Byte's status as industry leader.

At the meeting, after the board has dispensed with a number of routine matters, Jim Elliott turns his attention to the temporary plant. In short order, he advises the 11-member board (himself, 3 additional inside members, and 7 outside members) of his proposal to obtain and refit the existing plant to ameliorate demand problems in the short run, authorized the construction of the new plant (the completion of which is estimated to take some 3 years), and plan to switch capacity from the temporary plant to the new one when it is operational. He also briefly reviews additional details concerning the costs involved, advantages of this proposal versus domestic or foreign licensing, and so on.

All the board members except 1 are in favor of the proposal. In fact, they are most enthusiastic; the overwhelming majority agree that the temporary plant is an excellent—even inspired—stopgap measure. Ten of the 11 board members seem relieved because the board was most reluctant to endorse any of the other alternatives that had been mentioned.

The single dissenter—T. Kevin Williams, an outside director—is, however, steadfast in his objections. He will not, under any circumstances, endorse the notion of the temporary plant and states rather strongly that "I will not be party to this nonsense, not now, not ever."

T. Kevin Williams, the senior executive of a major nonprofit organization, is normally a reserved and really quite agreeable person. This sudden, uncharacteristic burst of emotion clearly startles the remaining board members into silence. The following excerpt captures the ensuing, essentially one-on-one conversation between Williams and Elliott.

Williams: How many workers do your people estimate will be employed in the temporary plant?

Elliott: Roughly 1,200, possibly a few more.

Williams: I presume it would be fair, then, to say that, including spouses and children, something on the order of 4,000 people will be attracted to the community.

Elliott: I certainly would not be surprised.

Williams: If I understand the situation correctly, this plant closed just over 8 years ago and that closing had a catastrophic effect on Plainville. Isn't it true that a large portion of the community was employed by this plant?

Elliott: Yes, it was far and away the majority employer.

Williams: And most of these people have left the community presumably to find employment elsewhere.

Elliott: Definitely, there was a drastic decrease in the area's population.

Williams: Are you concerned, then, that our company can attract the 1,200 employees to Plainville from other parts of New England?

Elliott: Not in the least. We are absolutely confident that we will attract 1,200—even more, for that matter virtually any number we need. That, in fact, is 1 of the chief advantages of this proposal. I would think that the community would be very pleased to have us there.

Williams: On the contrary, I would suspect that the community will rue the day we arrived. Beyond that, though, this plan is totally unworkable if we are candid. On the other hand, if we are less than candid, the proposal will work for us, but only at great cost to Plainville. In fact, quite frankly the implications are appalling. Once again, I must enter my serious objections.

Elliott: I don't follow you.

Williams: The temporary plant would employ some 1,200 people. Again, this means the infusion of over 4,000 to the community and surrounding areas. Byte Products, however, intends to close this plant in 3 years or less. If Byte informs the community or the employees that the jobs are temporary, the proposal simply won't work. When the new people arrive in the community, there will be a need for more schools, instructors, utilities, housing, restaurants, and so forth. Obviously, if the banks and local government know that the plant is temporary, no funding will be made available for these projects and certainly no credit for the new employees to buy homes, appliances, automobiles, and so forth.

If, on the other hand, Byte Products does not tell the community of its "temporary" plans, the project can go on. But, in several years when the plant closes (and we here have agreed today that it will close), we will have created a ghost town. The tax base of the community will have been destroyed; property values will decrease precipitously; practically the whole town will be unemployed. This proposal will place Byte Products in an untenable position and in extreme jeopardy.

Elliott: Are you suggesting that this proposal jeopardizes us legally? If so, it should be noted that the legal department has reviewed this proposal in its entirety and has indicated no problem.

Williams: No! I don't think we are dealing with an issue of legality here. In fact, I don't doubt for a minute that this proposal is altogether legal. I do, however, resolutely believe that this proposal constitutes gross irresponsibility.

I think this decision has captured most of my major concerns. These along with a host of collateral problems associated with this project lead me to strongly suggest that you and the balance of the board reconsider and not endorse this proposal. Byte Products must find another way.

The Dilemma

After a short recess, the board meeting reconvened. Presumably because of some discussion during the recess, several other board members indicated that they were no longer inclined to support the proposal. After a short period of rather heated discussion, the following exchange took place.

Elliott: It appears to me that any vote on this matter is likely to be very close. Given the gravity of our demand capacity problem, I must insist that the stockholders' equity be protected. We cannot wait 3 years; that is clearly out of the question. I still feel that licensing—domestic or foreign—is not in our long-term interests for any number of reasons, some of which have been discussed here. On the other hand, I do not want to take this project forward on the strength of a mixed vote. A vote of 6–5 or 7–4, for example, does not indicate that the board is remotely close to being of 1 mind. Mr. Williams, is there a compromise to be reached?

Williams: Respectfully, I have to say no. If we tell the truth, namely, the temporary nature of our operations, the proposal is simply not viable. If we are less than candid in this respect, we do grave damage to the community as well as to our image. It seems to me that we can only go 1 way or the other. I don't see a middle ground.

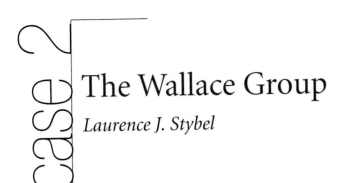

The Wallace Group

Laurence J. Stybel

Frances Rampar, President of Rampar Associates, drummed her fingers on the desk. Scattered before her were her notes. She had to put the pieces together in order to make an effective sales presentation to Harold Wallace.

Hal Wallace was the President of The Wallace Group. He had asked Rampar to conduct a series of interviews with some key Wallace Group employees, in preparation for a possible consulting assignment for Rampar Associates.

During the past 3 days, Rampar had been talking with some of these key people and had received background material about the company. The problem was not in finding the problem. The problem was that there were too many problems!

Background of The Wallace Group

The Wallace Group, Inc., is a diversified company dealing in the manufacture and development of technical products and systems (see **Exhibit 1**). The company currently consists of 3 operational groups and a corporate staff. The 3 groups include Electronics, Plastics, and Chemicals, each operating under the direction of a Group Vice President (see **Exhibits 2, 3,** and **4**). The company generates $70 million in sales as a manufacturer of plastics, chemical products, and electronic components and systems. Principal sales are to large contractors in governmental and automotive markets. With respect to sales volume, Plastics and Chemicals are approximately equal in size, and both of them together equal the size of the Electronics Group

Electronics offers competence in the areas of microelectronics, electromagnetic sensors, antennas, microwave, and minicomputers. Presently, these skills are devoted primarily to the engineering and manufacture of countermeasure equipment for aircraft. This includes radar detection systems that allow an aircraft crew to know that they are being tracked by radar units on the ground, on ships, or on other aircraft. Further, the company manufactures displays that provide the crew with a visual "fix" on where they are relative to the radar units that are tracking them.

In addition to manufacturing tested and proven systems developed in the past, The Wallace Group is currently involved in 2 major and 2 minor programs, all involving display systems. The Navy-A Program calls for the development of a display system for a tactical fighter plane; Air Force-B is another such system for an observation plane. Ongoing

Exhibit 1

An Excerpt from the Annual Report

To the Shareholders:

This past year was one of definite accomplishment for The Wallace Group, although with some admitted soft spots. This is a period of consolidation, of strengthening our internal capacity for future growth and development. Presently, we are in the process of creating a strong management team to meet the challenges we will set for the future.

Despite our failure to achieve some objectives, we turned a profit of $3,521,000 before taxes, which was a growth over the previous year's earnings. And we have declared a dividend for the fifth consecutive year, albeit one that is less than the year before. However, the retention of earnings is imperative if we are to lay a firm foundation for future accomplishment.

Currently, The Wallace Group has achieved a level of stability. We have a firm foothold in our current markets, and we could elect to simply enact strong internal controls and maximize our profits. However, this would not be a growth strategy. Instead, we have chosen to adopt a more aggressive posture for the future, to reach out into new markets wherever possible and to institute the controls necessary to move forward in a planned and orderly fashion.

The Electronics Group performed well this past year and is engaged in two major programs under Defense Department contracts. These are developmental programs that provide us with the opportunity for ongoing sales upon testing of the final product. Both involve the creation of tactical display systems for aircraft being built by Lombard Aircraft for the Navy and the Air Force. Future potential sales from these efforts could amount to approximately $56 million over the next five years. Additionally, we are developing technical refinements to older, already installed systems under Army Department contracts.

In the future, we will continue to offer our technological competence in such tactical display systems and anticipate additional breakthroughs and success in meeting the demands of this market. However, we also believe that we have unique contributions to make to other markets, and to that end we are making the investments necessary to expand our opportunities.

Plastics also turned in a solid performance this past year and has continued to be a major supplier to Chrysler, Martin Tool, Foster Electric, and, of course, to our Electronics Group. The market for this group continues to expand, and we believe that additional investments in this group will allow us to seize a larger share of the future.

Chemicals' performance, admittedly, has not been as satisfactory as anticipated during the past year. However, we have been able to realize a small amount of profit from this operation and to halt what was a potentially dangerous decline in profits. We believe that this situation is only temporary and that infusions of capital for developing new technology, plus the streamlining of operations, has stabilized the situation. The next step will be to begin more aggressive marketing to capitalize on the group's basic strengths.

Overall, the outlook seems to be one of modest but profitable growth. The near term will be one of creating the technology and controls necessary for developing our market offerings and growing in a planned and purposeful manner. Our improvement efforts in the various company groups can be expected to take hold over the years with positive effect on results.

We wish to express our appreciation to all those who participated in our efforts this past year.

Harold Wallace
Chairman and President

production orders are anticipated following flight testing. The other 2 minor programs, Army-LG and OBT-37, involve the incorporation of new technology into existing aircraft systems.

The Plastics Group manufactures plastic components utilized by the electronics, automotive, and other industries requiring plastic products. These include switches, knobs, keys, insulation materials, and so on, used in the manufacture of electronic equipment and other small made-to-order components installed in automobiles, planes, and other products.

The Chemicals Group produces chemicals used in the development of plastics. It supplies bulk chemicals to the Plastics Group and other companies. These chemicals are then injected into molds or extruded to form a variety of finished products.

Exhibit 2

Organizational Chart: The Wallace Group (Electronics)

President
- VP Finance
- VP Secretarial/Legal
- VP Marketing
- VP Industrial Relations
- VP Plastics Group
- VP Electronics Group
- VP Chemical Group

VP Electronics Group
- Director Industrial Relations
  - Personnel Services
  - Manpower Planning and Development
- Director Administration and Planning
  - Manager Contracts
  - Manager Cost and Schedule Administration
  - Controller
- Director Operations
  - Production Manager
  - Material Manager
  - Operations Control Manager
  - Plant Engineering Manager
  - Customer Service Manager
  - Quality Assurance Manager
- Director Engineering
  - Product Engineer Chief Engineer
    - Microwave Engineering Department
    - Digital Engineering Department
    - Mechanical Engineering Department
    - Electronic Engineering Department
  - Maintenance Engineer Chief Engineer
    - Engineering Services
    - Test Equipment Engineering Department
    - Drafting
- Director Advanced Engineering
  - Program Manager Navy-A
  - Program Manager Air Force-B
  - Program Manager Army-LG
  - Program Manager OBT-37

2-3

Exhibit 3

The Wallace Group (Chemicals)

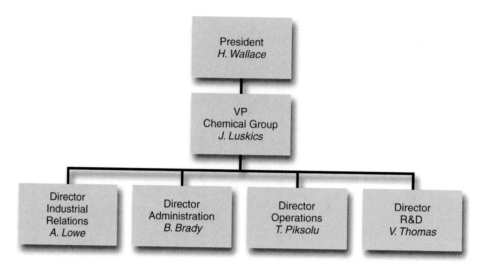

History of The Wallace Group

Each of the 3 groups began as a sole proprietorship under the direct operating control of an owner/manager. Several years ago, Harold Wallace, owner of the original electronics company, determined to undertake a program of diversification. Initially, he attempted to expand his market by product development and line extensions entirely within the electronics industry. However, because of initial problems, he drew back and sought other opportunities. Wallace's primary concern was his almost total dependence on defense-related contracts. He had felt for some time that he should take some strong action to gain a foothold in the private markets. The first major opportunity that seemed to satisfy his various requirements was the acquisi-

Exhibit 4

The Wallace Group (Plastics)

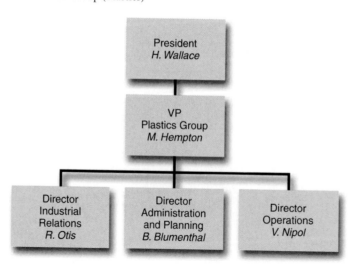

tion of a former supplier, a plastics company whose primary market was not defense-related. The company's owner desired to sell his operation and retire. At the time, Wallace's debt structure was such that he could not manage the acquisition and so he had to attract equity capital. He was able to gather a relatively small group of investors and form a closed corporation. The group established a Board of Directors with Wallace as Chairman and President of the new corporate entity.

With respect to operations, little changed. Wallace continued direct operational control over the Electronics Group. As holder of 60% of the stock, he maintained effective control over policy and operations. However, because of his personal interests, the Plastics Group, now under the direction of a newly hired Vice President, Martin Hempton, was left mainly to its own devices except for yearly progress reviews by the President. All Wallace asked at the time was that the Plastics Group continue its profitable operation, which it did.

Several years ago, Wallace and the Board decided to diversify further because two-thirds of their business was still defense-dependent. They learned that 1 of the major suppliers of the Plastics Group, a chemical company, was on the verge of bankruptcy. The company's owner, Jerome Luskics, agreed to sell. However, this acquisition required a public stock offering, with most of the funds going to pay off debts incurred by the 3 groups, especially the Chemicals Group. The net result was that Wallace now holds 45% of The Wallace Group and Jerome Luskics 5%, with the remainder distributed among the public.

Organization and Personnel

Presently, Harold Wallace serves as Chairman and President of The Wallace Group. The Electronics Group had been run by LeRoy Tuscher, who just resigned as Vice President. Hempton continued as Vice President of Plastics and Luskics served as Vice President of the Chemicals Group.

Reflecting the requirements of a corporate perspective and approach, a corporate staff has grown up, consisting of Vice Presidents for Finance, Secretarial/Legal, Marketing, and Industrial Relations. This staff has assumed many functions formerly associated with the group offices.

Because these positions are recent additions, many of the job accountabilities are still being defined. Problems have arisen over the responsibilities and relationships between corporate and group positions. President Wallace has settled most of the disputes himself because of the inability of the various parties to resolve differences among themselves.

Current Trends

Presently, there is a mood of lethargy and drift within The Wallace Group (see **Exhibits 1–11**). Most managers feel that each of the 3 groups functions as an independent company. And, with respect to group performance, not much change or progress has been made in recent years. Electronics and Plastics are still stable and profitable, but both lack growth in markets and profits. The infusion of capital breathed new life and hope into the Chemicals operation but did not solve most of the old problems and failings that had caused its initial decline. For all these reasons Wallace decided that strong action was necessary. His greatest disappointment was with the Electronics Group, in which he had placed high hopes for future development. Thus he acted by requesting and getting the Electronics Group Vice President's resignation. Hired from a computer company to replace LeRoy Tuscher, Jason Matthews joined The Wallace Group a week ago.

Last week, Wallace's annual net sales were $70 million. By group they were:

Electronics $35,000,000
Plastics $20,000,000
Chemicals $15,000,000

On a consolidated basis, the financial highlights of the last 2 years are as follows:

	Last Year	Two Years Ago
Net sales	$70,434,000	$69,950,000
Income (pre-tax)	3,521,000	3,497,500
Income (after-tax)	2,760,500	1,748,750
Working capital	16,200,000	16,088,500
Shareholders' equity	39,000,000	38,647,000
Total assets	59,869,000	59,457,000
Long-term debt	4,350,000	3,500,000
Per Share of Common Stock		
Net income	$.37	$.36
Cash dividends paid	.15	.25

Of the net income, approximately 70% came from Electronics, 25% from Plastics, and 5% from Chemicals.

Exhibit 5

Selected Portions of a Transcribed Interview with H. Wallace

Rampar: What is your greatest problem right now?

Wallace: That's why I called you in! Engineers are a high-strung, temperamental lot. Always complaining. It's hard to take them seriously.

Last month we had an annual stockholder's meeting. We have an Employee Stock Option Plan, and many of our long-term employees attended the meeting. One of my managers—and I won't mention any names—introduced a resolution calling for the resignation of the President—me!

The vote was defeated. But, of course, I own 45% of the stock!

Now I realize that there could be no serious attempt to get rid of me. Those who voted for the resolution were making a dramatic effort to show me how upset they are with the way things are going.

I could fire those employees who voted against me. I was surprised by how many did. Some of my key people were in that group. Perhaps I ought to stop and listen to what they are saying.

Businesswise, I think we're O.K. Not great, but O.K. Last year we turned in a profit of $3.5 million before taxes, which was a growth over previous years' earnings. We declared a dividend for the fifth consecutive year.

We're currently working on the creation of a tactical display system for aircraft being built by Lombard Aircraft for the Navy and the Air Force. If Lombard gets the contract to produce the prototype, future sales could amount to $56 million over the next 5 years.

Why are they complaining?

Rampar: You must have thoughts on the matter.

Wallace: I think the issue revolves around how we manage people. It's a personnel problem. You were highly recommended as someone with expertise in high-technology human resource management.

I have some ideas on what is the problem. But I'd like you to do an independent investigation and give me your findings. Give me a plan of action.

Don't give me a laundry list of problems, Fran. Anyone can do that. I want a set of priorities I should focus on during the next year. I want a clear action plan from you. And I want to know how much this plan is going to cost me!

Other than that, I'll leave you alone and let you talk to anyone in the company you want.

Exhibit 6

Selected Portions of a Transcribed Interview with Frank Campbell,
Vice President of Industrial Relations

Rampar: What is your greatest problem right now?

Campbell: Trying to contain my enthusiasm over the fact that Wallace brought you in!
   Morale is really poor here. Hal runs this place like a 1 man operation, when it's grown too big for that. It took a palace revolt to finally get him to see the depths of the resentment. Whether he'll do anything about it, that's another matter.

Rampar: What would you like to see changed?

Campbell: Other than a new President?

Rampar: Uh-huh.

Campbell: We badly need a management development program for our group. Because of our growth, we have been forced to promote technical people to management positions who have had no prior managerial experience. Mr. Tuscher agreed on the need for a program, but Hal Wallace vetoed the idea because developing such a program would be too expensive. I think it is too expensive *not* to move ahead on this.

Rampar: Anything else?

Campbell: The IEWU negotiations have been extremely tough this time around, due to excessive demands they have been making. Union pay scales are already pushing up against our foreman salary levels, and foremen are being paid high in their salary ranges. This problem, coupled with union insistence on a no-layoff clause, is causing us fits. How can we keep all our workers when we have production equipment on order that will eliminate 20% of our assembly positions?

Rampar: Wow.

Campbell: We have been sued by a rejected candidate for a position on the basis of discrimination. She claimed our entrance qualifications are excessive because we require shorthand. There is some basis for this statement since most reports are given to secretaries in handwritten form or on audio cassettes. In fact, we have always required it and our executives want their secretaries to have skill in taking dictation. Not only is this case taking time, but I need to reconsider if any of our position entrance requirements, in fact, are excessive. I am sure we do not want another case like this one.

Rampar: That puts The Wallace Group in a vulnerable position, considering the amount of government work you do.

Campbell: We have a tremendous recruiting backlog, especially for engineering positions. Either our pay scales are too low, our job specs are too high, or we are using the wrong recruiting channels. Kane and Smith [Director of Engineering and Director of Advanced Systems] keep rejecting everyone we send down there as being unqualified.

Rampar: Gee.

Campbell: Being head of human resources around here is a tough job. We don't act. We react.

Exhibit 7

Selected Portions of a Transcribed Interview with Matthew Smith, Director of Advanced Systems

Rampar: What is your greatest problem right now?

Smith: Corporate brass keeps making demands on me and others that don't relate to the job we are trying to get done. They say that the information they need is to satisfy corporate planning and operations review requirements, but they don't seem to recognize how much time and effort is required to provide this information. Sometimes it seems like they are generating analyses, reports, and requests for data just to keep themselves busy. Someone should be evaluating how critical these corporate staff activities really are. To me and the Electronics Group, these activities are unnecessary.

An example is the Vice President, Marketing (L. Holt), who keeps asking us for supporting data so he can prepare a corporate marketing strategy. As you know, we prepare our own group marketing strategic plans annually, but using data and formats that are oriented to our needs, rather than Corporate's. This planning activity, which occurs at the same time as Corporate's, coupled with heavy work loads on current projects, makes us appear to Holt as though we are being unresponsive.

Somehow we need to integrate our marketing planning efforts between our group and Corporate. This is especially true if our group is to successfully grow in nondefense-oriented markets and products. We do need corporate help, but not arbitrary demands for information that divert us from putting together effective marketing strategies for our group.

I am getting too old to keep fighting these battles.

Rampar: This is a long-standing problem?

Smith: You bet! Our problems are fairly classic in the high-tech field. I've been at other companies and they're not much better. We spend so much time firefighting, we never really get organized. Everything is done on an ad hoc basis.

I'm still waiting for tomorrow.

Exhibit 8

Selected Portions of a Transcribed Interview with Ralph Kane, Director of Engineering

Rampar: What is your greatest problem right now?

Kane: Knowing you were coming, I wrote them down. They fall into 4 areas:

1. Our salary schedules are too low to attract good, experienced EEs. We have been told by our Vice President (Frank Campbell) that corporate policy is to hire new people below the salary grade midpoint. All qualified candidates are making more than that now and in some case are making more than our grade maximums. I think our Project Engineer job is rated too low.
2. Chemicals Group asked for and the former Electronics Vice President (Tuscher) agreed to "lend" 6 of our best EEs to help solve problems it is having developing a new battery. That is great for the Chemicals Group, but meanwhile how do we solve the engineering problems that have cropped up in our Navy-A and OBT-37 programs?
3. As you know, Matt Smith (Director of Advanced Systems) is retiring in 6 months. I depend heavily on his group for technical expertise, and in some areas he depends heavily on some of my key engineers. I have lost some people to the Chemicals Group, and Matt has been trying to lend me some of his people to fill in. But he and his staff have been heavily involved in marketing planning and trying to identify or recruit a qualified successor long enough before his retirement to be able to train him or her. The result is that his people are up to their eyeballs in doing their own stuff and cannot continue to help me meet my needs.
4. IR has been preoccupied with union negotiations in the plant and has not had time to help me deal with this issue of management planning. Campbell is working on some kind of system that will help deal with this kind of problem and prevent them in the future. That is great, but I need help now—not when his "system" is ready.

Exhibit 9

Selected Portions of a Transcribed Interview with Brad Lowell, Program Manager, Navy-A

Rampar: What is your . . .?

Lowell: . . . great problem? I'll tell you what it is. I still cannot get the support I need from Kane in Engineering. He commits and then doesn't deliver, and it has me quite concerned. The excuse now is that in "his judgment," Sid Wright needs the help for the Air Force program more than I do. Wright's program is 1 week ahead of schedule, so I disagree with "his judgment." Kane keeps complaining about not having enough people.

Rampar: Why do you think Kane says he doesn't have enough people?

Lowell: Because Hal Wallace is a tight-fisted S.O.B. who won't let us hire the people we need!

Exhibit 10

Selected Portions of a Transcribed Interview with Phil Jones, Director, Administration and Planning

Jones: Wheel spinning—that's our problem! We talk about expansion, but we don't do anything about it. Are we serious or not?

For example, a bid request came in from a prime contractor seeking help in developing a countermeasure system for a medium-range aircraft. They needed an immediate response and concept proposal in 1 week. Tuscher just sat on my urgent memo to him asking for a go/no go decision on bidding. I could not give the contractor an answer (because no decision came from Tuscher), so they gave up on us.

I am frustrated because (1) we lost an opportunity we were "naturals" to win, and (2) my personal reputation was damaged because I was unable to answer the bid request. Okay, Tuscher's gone now, but we need to develop some mechanism so an answer to such a request can be made quickly.

Another thing, our MIS is being developed by the Corporate Finance Group. More wheel spinning! They are telling us what information we need rather than asking us what we want! E. Kay (our Group Controller) is going crazy trying to sort out the input requirements they need for the system and understanding the complicated reports that came out. Maybe this new system is great as a technical achievement, but what good is it to us if we can't use it?

Exhibit 11

Selected Portions of a Transcribed Interview with Burt Williams, Director of Operations

> **Rampar:** What is your biggest problem right now?
>
> **Williams:** One of the biggest problems we face right now stems from corporate policy regarding transfer pricing. I realize we are "encouraged" to purchase our plastics and chemicals from our sister Wallace groups, but we are also committed to making a profit! Because manufacturing problems in those groups have forced them to raise their prices, should *we* suffer the consequences? We can get some materials cheaper from other suppliers. How can we meet our volume and profit targets when we are saddled with noncompetitive material costs?
>
> **Rampar:** And if that issue was settled to your satisfaction, then would things be O.K.?
>
> **Williams:** Although out of my direct function, it occurs to me that we are not planning effectively our efforts to expand into nondefense areas. With minimal alteration to existing production methods, we can develop both end-use products (e.g., small motors, traffic control devices, and microwave transceivers for highway emergency communications) and components (e.g., LED and LCD displays, police radar tracking devices, and word processing system memory and control devices) with large potential markets.
>
> The problems in this regard are:
>
> 1. Matt Smith (Director, Advanced Systems) is retiring and has had only defense-related experience. Therefore, he is not leading any product development efforts along these lines.
> 2. We have no marketing function at the group level to develop a strategy, define markets, and research and develop product opportunities.
> 3. Even if we had a marketing plan and products for industrial/commercial application, we have no sales force or rep network to sell the stuff.
>
>   Maybe I am way off base, but it seems to me we need a Groups/Marketing/Sales function to lead us in this business expansion effort. It should be headed by an experienced technical marketing manager with a proven track record in developing such products and markets.
>
> **Rampar:** Have you discussed your concerns with others?
>
> **Williams:** I have brought these ideas up with Mr. Matthews and others at the Group Management Committee. No one else seems interested in pursuing this concept, but they won't say this outright and don't say why it should not be addressed. I guess that in raising the idea with you I am trying to relieve some of my frustrations.

The Problem Confronting Frances Rampar

As Rampar finished reviewing her notes (see **Exhibits 5–11**), she kept reflecting on what Hal Wallace had told her:

> Don't give me a laundry list of problems, Fran. Anyone can do that. I want a set of priorities I should focus on during the next year. I want a clear action plan from you. And I want to know how much this plan is going to cost me!

Fran Rampar again drummed her fingers on the desk.

case 3

The Audit

*John A. Kilpatrick, Gamewell D. Gantt,
and George A. Johnson*

Sue was puzzled as to what course of action to take. She had recently started her job with a national CPA firm, and she was already confronted with a problem that could affect her future with the firm. On an audit, she encountered a client who had been treating payments to a large number, but by no means a majority, of its workers as payments to independent contractors. This practice saves the client the payroll taxes that would otherwise be due on the payments if the workers were classified as employees. In Sue's judgment this was improper as well as illegal and should have been noted in the audit. She raised the issue with John, the senior accountant to whom she reported. He thought it was a possible problem but did not seem willing to do anything about it. He encouraged her to talk to the partner in charge if she didn't feel satisfied.

She thought about the problem for a considerable time before approaching the partner in charge. The ongoing professional education classes she had received from her employer emphasized the ethical responsibilities that she had as a CPA and the fact that her firm endorsed adherence to high ethical standards. This finally swayed her to pursue the issue with the partner in charge of the audit. The visit was most unsatisfactory. Paul, the partner, virtually confirmed her initial reaction that the practice was wrong, but he said that many other companies in the industry follow such a practice. He went on to say that if an issue was made of it, Sue would lose the account, and he was not about to take such action. She came away from the meeting with the distinct feeling that had she chosen to pursue the issue she would have created an enemy.

Sue still felt disturbed and decided to discuss the problem with some of her coworkers. She approached Bill and Mike, both of whom had been working for the firm for a couple of years. They were familiar with the problem because they had encountered the same issue when doing the audit the previous year. They expressed considerable concern that if she went over the head of the partner in charge of the audit, they could be in big trouble since they had failed to question the practice during the previous audit. They said that they realized it was probably wrong, but they went ahead because it had been ignored in previous years and they knew their supervisor wanted them to ignore it again this year. They didn't want to cause problems. They encouraged Sue to be a "team player" and drop the issue.

This case was prepared by Professors John A. Kilpatrick, Gamewell D. Gantt, and George A. Johnson of the College of Business, Idaho State University. The names of the organization, individual, location, and/or financial information have been disguised to preserve the organization's desire for anonymity. This case was edited for SMBP-8th Edition. Presented to and accepted by the refereed Society for Case Research. All rights reserved to the authors and the SCR. Copyright © 1995 by John A. Kilpatrick, Gamewell D. Gantt, and George A. Johnson. Reprinted by permission.

Brookstone Hospice: Heel or Heroine?

Shirley F. Olson and Sharon Meadows

"To be profit oriented is acceptable for any business but when that profit is given priority over a patient's life . . . well—I've got problems with that," Kathy Bennett tearfully declared. Kathy's anger stemmed from an incident that had taken place earlier in the month. As the nursing supervisor for a large hospice located in the northeastern United States, she had seen many things that she questioned but nothing quite like this latest occurrence.

The hospice with which she was associated employed 35 people and operated under the same philosophy as that of all other hospices—its goal was to ensure that the terminally ill patient was as comfortable as possible during the last days of life. Its reason for existence was therefore not to cure in the traditional medical sense but to ensure the patient a relatively pain-free, dignified death. Its mission and purpose as outlined in the company manual was (a) to provide a holistic approach to the dying patients and their significant others (family, friends), (b) to help the surviving significant others back to an optimal level of functioning, and (c) to assist health care professionals dealing with dying patients and their significant others.

To achieve that purpose, Brookstone's stated strategy was to offer care in the last 6 months of the terminally ill patient's life, with 24-hour, hands-on care if needed, for up to 7 days. Otherwise care was limited to 2 visits per week by the RN and weekly visits from the chaplain and social worker. The hospice doctor made visits as needed. The organization also offered a hot line that patients' families could use for discussing their concerns with the chaplain and for preplanning the funeral. Brookstone's home health aides were available as the family required for daily duties—patient baths, trips to and from the doctor and the grocery, and light housework. Thus, not only the patient but also the family received services in the form of support from the team. Unlike traditional care, the group members—with the exception of the doctor—continued to visit the family after the death of the patient and thus assured their well-being, as noted in the organization's mission/purpose statement. Team members always attended the funeral and even visited families on the first anniversary of the death, which was a very painful time.

This case was prepared by Professor Shirley F. Olson, Vice President of J. J. Ferguson Companies, and Ms. Sharon Meadows, Nurse Practitioner. It was presented at the North American Case Research Association Meeting, 1986. Distributed by the North American Case Research Association. All rights reserved to the authors and the North American Case Research Association. The names of the organization, individual, location, and/or financial information have been disguised to preserve the organization's desire for anonymity. Reprinted by permission of the authors and the North American Case Research Association. This case was edited for SMBP-8th Edition.

The structure of the organization was quite loose, as was required by the very nature of the work being done. Essentially all employees were part of matrix-type structures with each patient constituting the center of that matrix. Needless to say, the nurses, chaplains, and so on were associated with more than 1 patient at any 1 time, but because the patients' needs were always changing, the components in the matrix also changed rapidly as different members were needed for their particular expertise.

The matrixes were coordinated by an overall administrator, Jim Cole, who prided himself on the organization's flexibility. Cole went so far as to indicate, "Our people are top-level professionals and need very little managing. I like to leave decisions—to the extent possible—to their discretion. Of course, I still see myself as the final authority. My nurse supervisor coordinates all the RNs, and the doctors are coordinated similarly by our in-house physician. The social worker and chaplain also work through the nurse supervisor. My job essentially then is to watch all this happen. So far I've been pretty successful. Just this last year Brookstone grossed $2.5 million. And we are projecting $3.2 million this year."

Despite Cole's quick overview of the hospice's structure, Kathy Bennett was 1 of many to note that although the company procedures manual had a segment devoted to structure, that page was blank. "My team director told me not to ask too many questions about who reported to whom. She said Cole liked the feeling of flexibility and did not want anything about Brookstone to appear bureaucratic. However, I do know that our Chief Team Operator, the Executive Medical Director, and the Marketing Director all answered to Cole. Answering to the Team Operator were the 2 team directors who directly supervised the RNs, aides, chaplains, and social workers. The hospice MDs reported to the Executive Medical Director, and the marketing representative reported to the Marketing Director." As Kathy noted, "The very nature of the work we do makes us such a close knit group. When you are faced with death every day and sometimes several times a day, you have a much greater appreciation for life and family, and people in general. I've been with this group almost 7 years and up until this incident a few days ago, Brookstone has been ideal—not just for me as an employee but for our patients also. Their needs are so great and their time so short. When I leave here every night, I never have to wonder what we accomplished that day. At least that was the case until now."

The Episode

The incident to which Kathy continued to refer involved an 86-year-old man, Sam Gardner, suffering from a malignancy of the kidney. Mr. Gardner had been accepted by Brookstone 3 weeks earlier and was being visited regularly. On Sunday, February 18, Gardner's daughter, Beverly, had contacted Brookstone's duty nurse saying that her father seemed to be bleeding profusely internally. Although the family had been told that this would happen in the latter stages of the illness, the bleeding was much worse than they had expected and had gone on for almost 16 hours.

In response, Bennett sent the on-call nurse to the Gardner home to assess the patient's condition. Within minutes of her arrival, the nurse phoned Kathy, the nursing supervisor, and indicated that Mr. Garner needed to be admitted to a hospital's acute-care in-patient unit. While the nurse was on the phone with Kathy, the family became increasingly hysterical. At 1 point during the phone conversation, Kathy heard Beverly scream out, "I'll call an ambulance myself and take him. We just can't sit here and let him bleed to death while your bureaucratic organization has us on hold."

Realizing the urgency in the duty nurse's voice, Kathy immediately began the procedure for admitting Gardner to Covington General Hospital, the hospital with which Brookstone contracted. The procedure required by Brookstone Hospice was quite lengthy if Gardner was to be admitted to the Hospice Inpatient Unit at Covington General. Specifically:

1. The patient's primary doctor had to be contacted and had to approve admission.

2. The hospice doctor had to be contacted to act as the attending physician; if the patient's primary doctor refused the case, the hospice physician then performed as the primary doctor.

3. The hospital admissions office had to be notified of the incoming patient.

Although Kathy was more than familiar with the required procedure, several factors prevented it from being followed. First, the primary doctor refused to care for Gardner if he were transported to Covington General, stating that he would treat the patient if and only if he were taken to Catholic Charities Hospital. Brookstone had no contractual agreement with Catholic Charities.

As Kathy attempted to reason with the physician, the patient meanwhile had been placed in an ambulance that sat in the Gardners' driveway and waited for instructions from the duty nurse as to where the patient was to be taken. Kathy desperately continued her telephoning as she sought to follow established procedure, which required that no action on a hospice patient be taken without approval from a hospice's MD. Despite the efforts she was not able to contact any of the 4 hospice doctors who were on call that weekend. "I called every answering service, home, and golf course I could think of at the time but to no avail. That went on for at least 45 minutes while my poor patient lay in the ambulance waiting on our 'procedure.' You can only imagine how I felt. Finally in my desperation I gave permission to transport Gardner to the nearest hospital—Covington General (C.G.H.)—and the story goes on from there," Kathy noted.

After Gardner was taken to C.G.H., he went directly to the emergency room where he was assessed by the E.R. physician, C. Wallace. Wallace immediately set Gardner up for urological surgery the following Monday morning. On that Monday, the urologist contacted 1 of Brookstone's team doctors to discuss the so-called "curative surgery." Brookstone had well-defined policies about how hospice patients were to be treated. Once a patient signed with the hospice, no other health care professional could take any action whatsoever without contacting the hospice. As the procedure manual noted, a paramedic could not even resuscitate a nonbreathing hospice patient until contact was made with Brookstone. Realizing these rules, Wallace knew he faced a battle when he made the call.

Because the hospice discouraged curative measures—surgical or otherwise—the hospice physician was forced to discuss the proposed surgery with his superior in the hospice office before giving the urologist his approval to go ahead with the procedure. Immediately the supervisor vigorously discouraged the proposal—primarily on the grounds that the urologist stated that the surgery would extend the patient's life. Kathy overheard 1 of the team doctors state, "The man is 86 years old and has cancer. Can't you people understand the situation? That surgery will cost the hospice a minimum of $7,800. We—you and me—will pay for that right out of our pockets. We don't want to do that, do we? After all, Gardner will be dead anyway in 3 months. Our purpose is not to extend life but to assure quality life even until death."

Needless to say Kathy could not believe what she was hearing. Affiliated with an organization that she perceived as 1 of the best in the nation, she suddenly saw Brookstone quite differently in just those few split seconds of that comment.

The Aftermath

"At least something good finally came out of all the madness. Despite the discouragement from the hospice doctors, the Covington General urologist operated anyway. Five days later, the 86-year-old Gardner, who had been diagnosed as having only 3 months to live, was discharged from the hospital—with a prognosis of 3 years or more. Somehow he got my name from his duty nurse and called me here at the hospice yesterday. Gardner's voice was a bit weak, but his message was extremely clear. He told me in no uncertain terms that he credited me with saving his life and with giving him 3 years instead of 3 months. Gardner said he knew the chance I took by sending him to Covington General. His call meant everything to me, and I could use some good news. The same day he called, I was fired. A medical team doctor and Jim Cole called me in, showed me the surgical bill Brookstone received on Gardner, and informed me that I had seriously violated numerous policies and procedures. As a result, my termination was effective immediately. One of the doctors went so far as to remind me of the financial constraints facing the hospice and said, 'Kathy, you know as well as anyone the money difficulty we've been having. Only 2 weeks ago, our payroll was held up to 2 days because of our cash flow difficulties. That $7,800 we had to pay on Gardner would have gone a long way here in the organization. Yet you saw fit to spend it on a guy who is old and going to die anyway.'"

Case 5

Singapore Telecom: Strategic Challenges in a Turbulent Environment

Loizos Heracleous and Kulwant Singh

The financial year 1998/1999 has been a difficult and challenging year for the Singapore Telecom Group. We operated in a difficult business environment as a result of the regional economic crisis. We also faced increasing competition both locally and abroad (Koh Boon Hwee, Singapore Telecom Chairman).[1]

Singapore Telecom is preparing for battle. Having successfully met the challenge of changing from a government department to becoming the largest listed firm in Singapore, it is now facing its next major challenge—competition in its primary market. Its stated goal is to maintain its exceptional record of profitability and as much market share as possible, after StarHub, a full-service telecom provider starts operating in Singapore on April 1, 2000. StarHub will be the first competitor that Singapore Telecom will have in the fixed-line telecommunications (telecom) sector, having faced initial competition in the mobile sector with the entry of MobileOne in April 1997. The effects of StarHub's entry on the competitive landscape will be dramatic. StarHub is backed by some of the largest global telecom providers such as British Telecom and Nippon Telecom and Telegraph. Technologies Telemedia and Singapore Power will try to capture a significant part of the lucrative International Direct Dialing (IDD) market as well as of the large corporate business segment.

In addition to the intensifying competitive arena, the Asian crisis is taking its toll on Singapore Telecom's performance, and technological advancements such as Internet telephony mean that it is increasingly possible to bypass the networks of local telecom providers to make overseas calls, depriving telecom firms of an important source of income. The barriers that protected Singapore Telecom's market appear to be in danger of collapse.

It is no surprise that Singapore Telecom's chairman warned that earnings growth for the year ending March 2000 would be "negative and if I'm lucky, flat," unless there is a "significant recovery in the region's real economy."[2] For some observers, this warning foretold of more difficult times to come for Singapore Telecom.

This case was prepared by Dr. Loizos Heracleous of the National University of Singapore and Dr Kulwant Singh of the National University of Singapore as a basis for class discussion rather than to illustrate either effective or ineffective handling of an administrative or business situation. Copyright © 2000 by Loizos Heracleous, Kulwant Singh and *Asian Case Research Journal (ACRJ)*. This case appeared in *Asian Research Journal*, Vol. 4, Number 1, pp. 49–77. This case was edited for SMBP-8th Edition. All rights reserved to the authors and the ACRJ. Reprinted by permission.

The National Context: Singapore's National Development and Infrastructure Policy

To promote a vibrant environment for the development of a worldclass infocommunication industry to enhance Singapore's economic competitiveness and quality of life ... Singapore is a fully networked knowledge based society, connected to the world, connecting to the future.[3]

Singapore's strategic goals have largely focused on achieving rapid economic development through closely integrating its economy with global trade and development, accepting heavy foreign investments and attracting multinational corporations. These goals evolved from a mindset of survival in the 1960s, to the drive for efficiency in the 1970s, to the focus on people development, productivity, and value-added investments in the 1980s, to anticipating and embracing continuous change in the 1990s,[4] and lastly to the need to develop a "learning nation" in the late 1990s and beyond.

Singapore's broad strategic actions have focused on leveraging its natural advantage of having a strategic location by establishing worldclass transportation and materials handling facilities; extending this concept to the manufacturing, financial, and service domains by developing a sophisticated telecommunications and IT infrastructure; continuously improving workforce skills; and lastly, monitoring and absorbing global technological developments[5] through acting as a rapid adopter of tried and tested technologies to minimize the risk of adoption.[6] These strategies were guided by a sophisticated industrial policy that was developed and closely monitored by the government.

Singapore's economy has performed exceptionally well. Between 1960 and 1997, Singapore achieved real annual growth in GDP exceeding 8%, which in 1998 amounted to S$133 billion. Per capita GDP of S$27,480 is among the highest in Asia and matches or exceeds most developed countries. However, economic growth slowed drastically to 1.5% in 1998 from 8% in 1997 as the effects of the Asian economic crisis took their toll.[7] At the end of 1998, Singapore was in recession for only the second time since the early 1960s.

National infrastructure has played a key part in Singapore's development. Recognizing that infrastructure quality has a major positive impact on national economic development,[8] major resources were committed to developing the country's physical infrastructure. Singapore has placed particular importance on developing its information infrastructure, which it views as a national asset, and has implemented a number of forward-looking national plans. The "IT2000 Report: A Vision of an Intelligent Island," for example, was published in 1992, advocating the creation of a National Information Infrastructure aimed at making Singapore a more efficient switching center for goods, capital, information, and people, and at achieving further improvements in productivity.[9] In some respects, Singapore has about the most advanced information technology hardware infrastructure in the world. The Singapore government has invested in its rapid development by providing financial support, protection from market forces, and managerial talent, while urging the adoption of competitive rates and standards. In recent years, it has taken a more free market approach to the telecommunications industry, introducing a program to gradually privatize Singapore Telecom and to introduce competition into the industry.

The Industry Context: Trends in the Telecommunications Industry

For most of the 100 or so years the industry has been in existence, the big operators have provided mostly basic services on a take-it-or-leave-it basis, protected by the barriers of their monopoly status. Now, stripped of this protection and facing competition at home and abroad, the telecommunications industry is rapidly becoming one of the most competitive and turbulent industries. Operators are seeking ways to secure new customers and to hold on to as many existing customers as possible. It is clear that only a few years after the opening of telecom markets to full competition, the gloves are off and no holds are barred.[10]

THE GLOBAL COMPETITIVE ENVIRONMENT

Trends of deregulation, technological advancement and privatization, and more sophisticated and demanding consumers are causing turmoil in a once stable and highly profitable industry. The advent of competition is exerting continuous downward pressure on prices with margins falling as a result, and necessitating the introduction of value-added services by telecom providers in an effort to sustain volume and profitability. Asia has not been spared these trends, which are global and sweeping in scope.

The rulings of global organizations such as the World Trade Organization and the European Union, and a general movement toward more open and competitive markets, are having an unprecedented effect on the global telecom environment. In Asia, Japan and Hong Kong were among the first countries to liberalize their telecom markets. Though in 1990 only 35% of outgoing international telecom traffic was open to competition, by 1998 this amount had risen to 74%.[11] In 1990, only 3 countries (Japan, the United Kingdom, and the United States) permitted competition in basic telecom services; by 1998 over 30 countries did so, a number that continues to grow (see **Exhibit 1**).[12]

RAPID TECHNOLOGICAL CHANGE

The convergence of the technologies underlying telecommunications, computers, television, movies, and publishing is increasingly leading to overlapping products, markets, and competition and to firms moving among these industries. During the 1990s, there has also been a pronounced movement toward wireless communications, with mobile phones representing the fastest growth segment in almost all national markets and 1 of the fastest growing markets in the world. Such technological advancements are a huge threat for telecom companies, but they are also an opportunity for entrepreneurial, innovative firms to invest in and develop new technologies, products, and services. The telecommunications industry is shifting from proprietary to open standards, much as the computer industry did in the 1980s. Telecom technology is progressing so fast that forecasts of more than a few years are seldom attempted. In this industry, the long term is often viewed as the period beyond 3 years. Arguably, only the computer industry is experiencing the same rate of technological change as the telecommunications industry.

To become effective competitors in such conditions would require a cultural change for most telecommunication companies, which have historically operated in a slow-moving, monopolistic, and protectionist world. "The idea is to create a company run by people who think in terms of a world where the ratio of performance to price doubles every 18 months, and where deals have to be snapped up at once."[13]

New services such as Internet telephony or Virtual Private Networks, which are forecasted to be widely adopted in Singapore,[14] are threatening to gain substantial market share in

Exhibit 1
Countries Allowing Competition in Basic Telecom Services in 1998

Australia	Germany	Netherlands
Austria	Ghana	Norway
Belgium	Hong Kong	Philippines
Canada	Israel	Russia
Chile	Italy	Spain
China	Ireland	Sweden
Denmark	Japan	Switzerland
El Salvador	Korea	Uganda
Finland	Mexico	United Kingdom
France	New Zealand	United States

domestic and international voice traffic at the expense of established telecommunication companies. A major feature of these new services is that they often bypass the existing infrastructure, allowing providers to deal directly with customers. In time, these services will challenge the importance of national boundaries, regulatory constraints, licensing approval, and domestic telecommunications providers.

The pressure of Internet telephony will be felt most in international traffic, which produces an estimated 12 to 15% of the revenues of large international operators but 30 to 40% of profits.[15] In Singapore Telecom's case, international calls account for around 38% of total revenues. Internet telephony is forecasted to account for as much as 15 to 30% of the global market for voice and fax calls within 5 years. Internet telephony is inexpensive for users and allows closer customization of services, where consumers can choose the level of service they require and be charged accordingly. It also enables the provision of several value-added services to consumers, for example real-time billing, cheaper videoconferencing and unified messaging. In Asia, Internet telephony is said to be a "regulatory minefield," with some countries banning it, others embracing it, and some unsure as to how to handle it.[16]

In addition to deregulation and the effects of technology, another major force for change are consumers themselves, who expect consistently high quality of services and support the liberalization of telecom markets and the global harmonization of technological and regulatory standards.[17]

MERGERS AND ACQUISITIONS

The greater financial and competency resources required to deal with rapidly changing technology, the growing pressures of globalization and increased competition, and the convergence between industries led to a wave of mergers, acquisitions, and alliances in the industry from the mid-1990s. The resulting large firms are believed to be more likely to have the resources and strength to survive in the new environment. Consequently, there was a clear move toward larger, more global, and better endowed firms in the industry. Many of these industry-leading organizations emerged from mergers that combined firms that were unknown even months before. Many incumbents merged with firms not traditionally viewed to be part of the industry, to integrate new skills, or to pool their resources. The growing belief is that only a relatively few large global firms will prosper in the future, with the bulk of the industry serving as their local partners or suppliers. Mergers and acquisitions are greatly accelerating the pace of change and consolidation in the industry, with each megamerger being exceeded by a bigger one. According to the CEO of Cable and Wireless,

> We had 10 years in which every operator was suppressed because they were regulated and government-owned. While industries like the oil business were consolidating, telecom was not. Suddenly, 10 years' activity is being squeezed into 24 months. Sometimes it feels like 24 weeks.[18]

THE ASIAN COMPETITIVE ENVIRONMENT

The huge telecom overcapacity in certain Asian markets, such as mobile telecommunications in Malaysia and fixed-line services in Hong Kong, intensifying competition in general, and the Asian economic crisis of the late 1990s, are increasing competition and pressures for industry consolidation. Downward pricing pressures in Asia have been intense. The average reduction in the cost of a basket of business telecom services in Asia for the year ending April 30, 1998, was 16%. Some countries experienced high reductions, such as Indonesia with a decrease of 65% and South Korea with a decrease of 57%. Singapore was relatively buffered, with a reduction of only 6% for the same period (Singapore's cost for this basket of telecom services was US$2,657, lower than the Asian average of US$3,685).[19]

Analysts believe, moreover, that mergers and acquisitions will radically restructure the industry in the near future, especially in countries that have awarded too many telecom licenses and whose telecom companies have massive overcapacity. Telecom companies that are cash rich and have limited growth opportunities domestically, such as Hong Kong Telecom and Singapore Telecom, are believed to be scouting for good investment opportunities. One interesting outcome of the economic crisis is that it gives some "breathing space" to the established players since newer and smaller challengers are finding it much harder to realize their expansion plans.[20]

Large telecom companies such as British Telecom (BT) are investing heavily in the Asian region. In the 6 months leading up to April 1999, BT has invested a total of around S$1.8 billion to acquire various stakes in the region.[21] These ventures have immediately made it 1 of the major players on the continent, 1 of very few firms with multicountry operations. BT's longer term goal is to invest as much in Asia as it has in Europe; current investments in Europe are 5 times as large as those in Asia. According to the CEO of BT Worldwide,

> There's no question that over the long term, Asia has to be the engine for growth in telecoms worldwide. At the moment, Asia probably accounts for 22% of the total market . . . Within 10 years, most of the projections say Asia will be 60% of the market.[22]

The Asian competitive climate in telecommunications differs from the global climate in some respects. For example, major investments are needed in many Asian countries such as China and India, as their telecommunications infrastructure is relatively undeveloped, in contrast with Western Europe, which has a mature infrastructure. For example, China has in recent years been adding as many new telephone lines *each year* as are available in the whole of Switzerland. However, service availability and quality in many parts of Asia lag significantly behind those of developed countries. Key characteristics of and trends in Asian telecommunications are shown in **Exhibit 2**.[23]

While the characteristics and trends described in **Exhibit 2** apply to many Asian countries, companies such as Singapore Telecom and Hong Kong Telecom operate under very different conditions, illustrating the contrast between national competitive environments within Asia. With regard to industry characteristics for example, Singapore has high teledensity, high quality fixed-line services, higher demand for specialized features, lower vulnerability to credit risks, and falling tariffs. Hong Kong, while similar to Singapore in many of these characteris-

Exhibit 2
Characteristics and Trends in Asian Telecommunications

Characteristics
- Extremely low teledensity
- Lower quality and availability of fixed-line services
- Higher concentration of residential users
- Less demand for specialized features
- Higher vulnerability to credit risks
- Highly regulated tariffs
- Relatively limited competition among service providers

Trends
- Strong emphasis on telecommunications infrastructure development by most governments
- Strong growth of fixed line and mobile telecommunications networks
- Acceleration of deregulation and privatization
- Increased competition from entry of Western telecommunications firms
- Concession/licensing periods of 15–25 years utilizing the Build-Transfer-Operate model or a variation thereof
- Strong demand for debt and equity capital to finance expansion
- Industry rationalization through mergers and acquisitions
- Upgrading of telecommunications technology, with significant pricing impact

Exhibit 3

Penetration Rates in Singapore and Developed Countries (%)

	Singapore (Sept. 1999)	Developed Countries Average
Fixed lines	57.6	50.0
Mobile phones	41.4	9.7
Paging lines	39.1	15.3

tics, is a highly competitive market with many firms competing in every segment of the industry. **Exhibit 3** shows the penetration rate per 100 people of fixed phone lines, mobile phones, and pagers in Singapore, as well as the average figures for developed countries.[24] A more detailed look at the size and growth of telecommunications in various countries is provided in **Exhibit 4** (figures denote lines per 100 inhabitants).

Exhibit 4

Telecommunications Growth in Selected Countries

	Number of Fixed Lines (2000)			Lines Per 100 People		
	1990	1995	2000F	1990	1995	2000F
Australia	7,787	9,200	10,870	45.7	50.7	57.2
Belgium		8,850	11,044		49.6	58.1
China	6,850	40,706	241,884	0.6	3.4	19.3
Denmark		3,123	3,494		60.4	69.9
Hong Kong	2,475	3,278	4,342	43.4	53.0	72.2
India	5,074	11,978	28,272	0.6	1.3	2.8
Indonesia	1,066	3,291	10,157	0.6	1.7	4.9
Japan	54,528	61,106	68,477	44.1	48.8	53.9
South Korea	13,276	18,600	26,059	31.0	41.5	55.4
Malaysia	1,588	3,332	7,003	9.0	16.6	31.8
Norway		2,392	2,838		55.4	71.0
Philippines	610	1,410	3,257	1.0	2.1	4.2
Singapore	1,053	1,429	1,938	39.0	47.9	64.6
Sweden		5,967	6,357		68.3	70.7
Thailand	1,325	3,482	9,154	2.4	5.9	14.1
Vietnam	96	775	6,095	0.2	1.1	7.5
United Kingdom		28,389	33,770		48.9	57.2
United States	136,337	164,624	198,781	54.6	62.6	72.0
Asia	109,759	182,454	459,954	3.5	5.4	12.7
World	519,203	692,101	1,107,094	9.9	12.1	18.1

Note: F means forecasted information.

Source: K. Singh, 1999. Singapore Telecom in Europe. *ASEAN-EU Management Centre* cases series.

Exhibit 5

Penetration Figures in Various Regions in 1998 (%)

	Africa	Americas	Asia	Europe	Oceania	World
Fixed lines	2.24	32.33	7.34	37.25	40.29	14.26
Mobile phones	0.45	12.09	3.05	13.15	24.87	5.39

The penetration rates of fixed and cellular lines in Asia as a whole, however, are considerably lower than for other continents (other than Africa) and for the world as a whole (see **Exhibit 5**; figures denote lines per 100 inhabitants).[25] The lower penetration rates suggest high potential for growth, particularly when economic growth resumes after the economic crisis of the late 1990s.

Some industry observers believe that mobile phone penetration rates in developed markets and in some high growth developing countries could reach as high as 70% in the near term. This growth will be fueled, it is thought, by new third generation phones and technologies that will be capable of linking to the Internet, thus providing a whole range of additional information and video services.[26] Even more conservative observers estimate that cellular penetration in Singapore could reach 50% by 2001.[27]

Singapore's domestic telecom environment is more similar to those of developed countries than to most of Asia in areas such as service quality and penetration levels. Singapore has therefore experienced a higher intensity of global trends such as deregulation and privatization, technological advancement, and increased sophistication of consumers who increasingly demand higher standards of quality and service, as well as a greater choice of telecom providers.

Singapore Telecom's Strategy, Performance, and Local Competitive Context

EARLY DAYS AND PRIVATIZATION

Singapore Telecom traces its roots to the introduction of telephone services in Singapore in 1879, just 3 years after Alexander Graham Bell's invention. The amalgamation of many private and government service providers over the following decades ultimately resulted in a single organization providing telephone and postal services in Singapore. After many permutations in its administrative structure and product portfolio, Singapore Telecom in 1972 became the monopoly government-owned postal and telecommunications services provider. Following a global trend, the government announced plans in 1986 to privatize Singapore Telecom.

Privatization is often carried out to raise private capital for infrastructural development, to ease the fiscal burden of the state, to improve the quality of service, and to reduce prices for consumers.[28] In Singapore's case, however, these traditional objectives of privatization were not the primary motivating factors, as Singapore Telecom has been performing to world standards even without privatization. Instead, the privatization of Singapore Telecom was part of a wider effort aimed at reducing the state's involvement in business.[29] The main aims were to increase Singapore Telecom's flexibility, to prepare it for the challenges of global competition and technological advancements,[30] and to stimulate the development of the Singapore stock market, which lacked depth and scope.[31]

However, as a small country that lacks natural resources and that has a strategic interest in ensuring the development and control of its telecommunications sector, the government endorsed only limited privatization. This would allow it to retain control of the telecommunications infrastructure[32] while achieving the broader objectives. An additional advantage would be control over the potentially negative social implications from the uncontrolled flow of information into Singapore. Consequently, despite privatization, the government continues to own about 80% of Singapore Telecom.[33]

SINGAPORE TELECOM'S STRATEGY

The main elements of Singapore Telecom's strategy have been a focus on the achievement of short- and medium-term profitability, pursuit of globally competitive service and efficiency standards, high investments in proven technologies, and the establishment of a worldclass telecom infrastructure. More recently, Singapore Telecom has initiated foreign investments in several countries, has engaged in strategic alliances in order to gain market entry and acquire technological skills, and has undertaken diversification into IT and value-added services in order to sustain its growth and profitability levels.[34]

According to Singapore Telecom's Chairman, in the area of e-commerce Singapore Telecom "intends to exploit synergies and capabilities to offer total solutions."[35] Singapore Telecom Mobile, SingNet, and Singapore Post are major partners in the recently formed Asia Mobile Electronic Services alliance aiming to provide various cross-border mobile electronic services through mobile phones. These services include mobile banking, electronic bill payment, electronic ticketing, secure postal services, e-mail, and information access. According to Singapore Telecom's CEO, "This is truly a convergence between e-commerce, Internet, and mobile services."[36] New services initiated over the last 5 years, such as maintenance of cable chips and ownership of Singapore Telecom's own satellite, contribute to about 12–15% of revenues (around $700 million).[37]

Some investors believe that the addition of Internet services will be an important growth platform for Singapore Telecom. According to the managing director of Bear Sterns Singapore, "You've got the prospect that Singapore Telecom will start to be looked at by investors not as a rusty telecom company but an Internet stock."[38]

Singapore Telecom's internationalization strategy began in the late 1980s. This effort was driven by several trends, including the increasing maturity of the small Singapore market, the prospective entry of competitors into Singapore Telecom's previously closed domestic market, the globalization of business and telecommunications, the emergence of major opportunities globally, and the need to find productive uses for Singapore Telecom's large cash reserves. By June 1999, Singapore Telecom had invested $2.3 billion in 55 overseas ventures and operations in 19 countries.[39] Though initial efforts were in Asian countries such as Thailand, Vietnam, and Sri Lanka, the focus of international efforts quickly switched to Europe. Most investments were made in cable television and mobile communications services in England and Western Europe. With few exceptions these were not profitable and Singapore Telecom has so far been unable to achieve its target of drawing 15 to 20% of total sales from its foreign ventures.[40] As a consequence, Singapore Telecom disposed of all of its significant investments in Europe, most of these less than 5 years after the initial investments, unusual in an industry with fairly long gestation periods. Many observers viewed these ventures as expensive lessons for Singapore Telecom, which taught it that success in the protected domestic market did not necessarily prepare it for success in distant and competitive markets against large and technologically sophisticated firms. Results have been improving, however, and in financial year 1999, overseas investments contributed 11% of pre-tax profits at S$292 million. Singapore Telecom is on track to achieve its target of 20% foreign sales by 2005.

More recently, Singapore Telecom has refocused its overseas investments on Asia. Significant investments include S$55.6 million in AAPT of Australia, which provides switched and leased-line communications services; S$47.1 million in PT Bukaka Singapore Telecom International in Indonesia, which operates fixed public switch telephone services; S$155.7 million in Globe Telecom in the Philippines, which provides mobile phone, international, and fixed-line services; S$36.9 million in Shinawatra Datacom and Shinawatra Paging, which provide data communication and paging services; and S$551 million in Advanced Info Services of Thailand, a cellular phone operator.[41] In November 1999, Singapore Telecom and KDD, Japan's largest international telecommunications operator established an equity joint venture to integrate their services. However, it also pulled back from some regional ventures, as it became clear that these were too minor to significantly impact Singapore Telecom's profitability.

Faced with competition from foreign callback services, Singapore Telecom has continually reviewed and reduced its international direct dialing rates in order to retain globally competitive standards and continuously introduced newer and cheaper pricing packages. The average international call charge declined by 42% between 1993 and 1998.[42] Several new value-added services for private and business users were also introduced to improve the quality of services, to provide new streams of revenue, and to meet customer demands. Yet the challenges ahead probably dwarf those that Singapore Telecom has faced to date:

> With the rapid advancement in communications technology, Singapore Telecommunications may have no option but to offer a fixed monthly charge to those who use its service for international calls in 2 years' time. In 5 years, it might even have to offer long-distance calls for free . . . bandwidth is growing by leaps and bounds, tripling annually by some estimates. In 5 years, the amount of information that can be carried through a network could be some 250 times that of the current level. In 2004, a "phone" call could include real-time video of the 2 (or more) parties conversing. It could also feature pictures and graphics, and at the same time link the many users to the Internet. Faced with a huge bandwidth, it makes no sense for a telco to charge for a specific service.[43]

Perhaps in anticipation of the prospective entry of more competition, Singapore Telecom launched a new effort in 1999 to establish long-term service agreements with its major commercial customers. These efforts locked major customers into multiyear service agreements in Singapore and in the region in return for preferential rates. By this means, Singapore Telecom appears to be preventing defection among its existing customers to new service providers.

The turnover composition of Singapore Telecommunications' various services is shown below in **Exhibit 6**.[44]

Exhibit 7 contains Singapore Telecom Chairman's 1999 statement to shareholders, giving more information on the various aspects of Singapore Telecom's strategy.

Exhibit 6

Group Turnover Composition

	FY 98/99		FY 97/98	
	S$ million	%	S$ million	%
International telephone	1,843.7	37.8	2,057.9	41.6
Mobile communications	880.0	18.0	805.9	16.3
Public data and private network	620.6	12.7	561.6	11.4
National telephone	546.6	11.2	539.2	10.9
Postal services	307.9	6.3	311.8	6.3
IT and engineering services	262.3	5.4	157.5	3.2
Sale of equipment	216.8	4.4	275.0	5.6
Directory advertising	125.8	2.6	130.2	2.6
Public messages	37.3	0.8	54.4	1.1
Others	42.5	0.8	48.7	1.0
Total	4,883.5	100.0	4,942.2	100.0

Exhibit 7

Singapore Telecom Chairman's Statement to Shareholders, 1998/1999

Dear Shareholder,

Financial year 1998/1999 has been a difficult and challenging year for the Singapore Telecom Group. We operated in a difficult business environment as a result of the regional economic crisis. We also faced increasing competition both locally and abroad.

Corporate Reorganisation

As the business landscape and market environment change, Singapore Telecom must also evolve to meet the company's and customers' changing needs. To this end, Singapore Telecom reorganized in April 1999 to increase our focus on the people that matter most to us—our customers. Specific customer units have been set up to manage the diverse telecommunications needs of our different customer segments including corporate clients, small and medium sized enterprises, and residential consumers. In addition, the new organisational structure also emphasises new growth areas such as our overseas ventures and new businesses like e-commerce, systems integration, multimedia, and Internet-based services.

Growth

Singapore Telecom has identified e-commerce and Internet-based activities as areas where there are significant growth opportunities. The Singapore Telecom Group of companies is uniquely positioned to offer services throughout the e-commerce value chain, from providing terminals to end users to fulfilling the orders of consumers. For example, Singapore Telecom, Singapore Telecom Mobile, and SingNet provide the infrastructure for e-commerce, NCS can provide the systems integration capabilities, and SingPost can support the physical fulfilment of orders. Singapore Telecom will also take advantage of the growing trend towards the convergence of telecommunications, IT, and media to introduce new services. Our broadband multimedia service, Singapore Telecom Magix, is a good example.

Infrastructure Development

Despite an already extensive domestic and international infrastructure, we continue to invest heavily in infrastructure to ensure that we have sufficient capacity to meet the growing demands of our customers. At the same time, we actively implement the latest technologies to offer innovative services.

For the financial year 1998/1999, our capital expenditure amounted to approximately S$1 billion. In the current year, we expect to spend another S$900 million to build and improve our networks, particularly to support mobile and e-commerce services. For example, Singapore Telecom Mobile is currently conducting a wideband CDMA trial. It will also be introducing various high speed data services (e-ideas) to give our customers the convenience of e-commerce applications such as mobile stock trading, banking, and ticketing services.

To provide our corporate customers with the global connectivity that is essential in today's competitive business environment, we will continue to invest in international network and cable systems. This also ensures that there will always be sufficient capacity to support increasing demand for bandwidth. Singapore Telecom has invested a total of more than US$500 million in digital submarine cable networks. An extensive international infrastructure provides our multinational customers with the redundancy and diversity they require. This is a strategic advantage that new entrants to the market cannot offer.

Overseas Investments

Our overseas investments have done well, contributing 11.2% to our pre-tax profit this year. In fact, the success of our internationalisation efforts has contributed significantly to

Exhibit 7
(*continued*)

our earnings growth this year. Belgacom in Belgium and Globe Telecom in the Philippines are the Group's two most successful overseas investments. We target contributions from our overseas investments to increase to 20% of pre-tax profit by 2005.

It is our strategy to participate actively in the companies in which we invest and to add value through our expertise. Of the S$2.5 billion that we have invested in 19 countries, S$1.3 billion are now in listed companies. Today, the value of these companies is more than double the invested amount.

Besides the financial returns we receive from our overseas projects and ventures, Singapore Telecom also seeks to maximise synergies from its investments. For example, Singapore Telecom Mobile is exploring the feasibility of launching regional mobile products and services jointly with our partners, Advanced Info Service of Thailand and Globe Telecom. Such products and services, which include local SIM cards and preferred roaming, offer significant value to frequent travellers in the region. The three cellular companies are also looking at bulk purchasing of handsets and network equipment to achieve greater savings through economies of scale. Singapore Telecom will continue to look for investment opportunities overseas that will make meaningful contributions to our bottom line.

Looking Forward
Singapore Telecom's businesses are closely linked to economic activities in Singapore and the region. Although the worst seems to be over for the regional economies, the outlook nonetheless remains uncertain. The impact of significant rate cuts implemented in the first quarter of this year will be fully realised in the financial year 1999/2000. However, we expect contributions from our associated companies overseas to continue to improve, which will mitigate the expected weaker operating results.

Singapore Telecom commemorates 120 years of telecommunications services in Singapore this year. We are proud to have contributed to Singapore's success as a telecommunications hub for the region. Our many years of experience and expertise in providing telecommunications services to Singapore homes and businesses will put us in good stead notwithstanding the introduction of competition next year.

We will strive, through innovation and continued customer service improvements, to build on the relationships we have established with our customers so that we can continue to serve them in the years ahead.

Enhancing shareholder value is one of Singapore Telecom's key objectives. To achieve this, we intend to create a more efficient capital structure through various measures, including a share buyback programme, if and when appropriate, and the payment of special dividends. Our aim is to work towards a debt to equity ratio of 20 to 30%. This will, however, not inhibit the Group's ability to continue with its expansion plans and overseas investments.

I would like to thank my fellow Directors of the Singapore Telecom Board for their contributions to the success and development of the Group. I also thank the Management, Union, and Staff of the Group. Through their unstinting efforts, Singapore Telecom has been able to perform well given the difficult circumstances. With their continued support and dedication, Singapore Telecom will be more than able to meet the demands of the coming year.

KOH BOON HWEE
Chairman

SINGAPORE TELECOM'S STRUCTURE

Singapore Telecom's subsidiaries include National Computer Systems, Singapore Aeradio, Singapore Post, Singapore Telecom International, Singapore Telecom Investments, Singapore Telecom Mobile, Singapore Telecom Paging, Singapore Telecom Yellow Pages Pte Ltd, and Telecom Equipment. Singapore Telecom provides fixed-line, mobile, Internet and satellite services, as well as systems integration through its wholly owned subsidiary National Computer Systems, and aspires to be "a total service provider with a range that covers the entire spectrum of the telecom business."[45]

Singapore Telecom's organizational structure up to early 1999 involved the grouping of businesses into international, domestic mobile, and domestic fixed-line businesses. In March 1999, Singapore Telecom announced a major restructuring, whose primary aim was to focus on growth areas such as overseas ventures and new business areas such as e-commerce, systems integration, multimedia, and Internet-based services.[46]

The restructuring involves the creation of 3 new units: the consumer business unit, covering residential customers and small and medium-sized enterprises; the corporate business unit dealing with corporate accounts; and the global business unit concerned with Singapore Telecom's overseas investments. A new Chief Operating Officer (COO) position and 3 customer units under the COO were also created. This new post is intended to relieve the Chief Executive Officer from running day-to-day operations and allow him to focus on growth areas such as overseas ventures and new business areas such as e-commerce, systems integration, multimedia, and Internet-based services.

THE ADVENT OF COMPETITION

Despite Singapore Telecom's success in building Singapore's telecommunications infrastructure, the government embarked on a program of gradually introducing competition. This decision reflected global trends of deregulation and increased competition and the government's belief that competitive pressures would prepare Singapore Telecom for increased international competition and expansion, thus ensuring the competitiveness of Singapore's telecommunications infrastructure and services.[47] Competition was introduced in phases to allow Singapore Telecom to prepare.

The first direct competitor to Singapore Telecom, MobileOne, commenced mobile phone services in April 1997. MobileOne (M1) is a consortium of 2 foreign firms (Cable & Wireless of UK and its partially owned subsidiary HongKong Telecoms) and 2 local firms (Singapore's sole newspaper publisher SPH and the diversified, government-linked Keppel Corporation). MobileOne's entry had the usual dramatic results associated with the introduction of competition in a previously protected market: MobileOne captured significant market share, prices declined by between 50 and 70% within a year, the range and quality of services improved significantly, and the market expanded rapidly. In the process, the mobile phone penetration rate rose from 14% at the start of 1997 to 33% by the end of 1998. According to analysts,

> M1's success—it grabbed 32% of the market share within 2 years, a phenomenal achievement by world standards—was largely due to its marketing savvy, attention to customer service, and network quality.[48]

As an example of the price wars that erupted with the entry of MobileOne, in January 1999, Singapore Telecom was forced to cut its rates twice in 1 day, by a total of 18%, when MobileOne responded to its first rate cut. In the next few days Singapore Telecom also reduced some monthly subscriptions by 35 to 40%.[49] According to the *Business Times*, it is a "monumental task" to compare which package would offer the best value, given that Singapore Telecom and MobileOne have different peak hours and denominate free talk time differently, in dollars or in minutes. After a comparison of the competitive packages, it concluded that:[50]

> Singapore Telecom is the bigger culprit in trying to 'confuse' consumers. Besides different charges for the different times of the day, it also has separate rates for incoming and outgoing calls.

The 2 competitors in the mobile market constantly monitor each others' performance and make countermoves. In January 1999, for example, about 90% of the 15,000 new mobile phone subscribers signed on with M1.[51] Singapore Telecom immediately carried out a promotion and announced that it had attracted more than 50% of new mobile subscribers for February as a result of this promotion. Advertising in the telecom industry is intense and growing in value. In financial year 1996 it was S$27.4 million, which rose sharply in 1997 to S$70 million with the entry of MobileOne. In 1998 advertising spending rose to S$76.4 million, and it is expected to surpass S$100 million in financial year 1999, with the entry of StarHub, which announced:

> StarHub's advertising and promotion budget will be significant—in the double-digit, multi-million-dollar region—to enable us to create a strong presence in the marketplace.[52]

Although Singapore's mobile market may appear saturated, given global levels of mobile phone penetration, industry analysts forecast that the penetration may rise to about 50 to 60% in the short run. It is also forecasted that the Asia-Pacific region's number of mobile subscribers would nearly treble by 2003, from 109 million to 296 million, while the average monthly revenue per subscriber would decline from US$41 to US$29. This will lead to an increase in annual mobile subscriber revenue from US$69.4 billion to US$104 billion.[53] In the medium term, mobile phone penetration rates are forecasted to exceed fixed-line rates. In the longer term, mobile communications will become a part of many types of home and office devices, and the industry will lose its identity as a distinct industry primarily offering voice telecommunications services.

Continuing with its plan for introducing competition, the government in 1998 issued 2 more licenses for mobile phone services and 1 for fixed telephone services to start operations in April 2000. All license winners were consortia that comprised at least 1 government-linked corporation. The primary factor driving this liberalization was the recognition that competition would bring the same positive benefits to the fixed-line market as it did in the mobile phone market. The failure to do this would, on the other hand, handicap the country with higher telecommunications costs and older technology than in competitor economies with more effective telecommunications industries.

SINGAPORE TELECOM'S PERFORMANCE

Singapore Telecom's performance in the 1990s has been spectacular, with profitability being unmatched in Singapore, and arguably, in much of the global telecom industry. Operating returns are high enough to replace net fixed assets in less than 2 years, while shareholders' funds can be repaid with about 3 years' profits. **Exhibit 8** shows Singapore Telecom's financial summary for the period 1990–1999. Despite intensifying competition and falling international call rates, Singapore Telecom has continued to deliver in terms of service quality and financial returns.

The quality of Singapore's telecommunications infrastructure ranked first in a survey of 10 Southeast Asian countries in 1997.[54] Its telecom infrastructure in particular has also ranked first in the Asia-Pacific Telecommunications Index 1999, compiled by the National University of Singapore's Centre for Telemedia Studies. However, Singapore's telecom infrastructure scored poorly in the "choice" and "regulation" subindex of this survey, where it was perceived as offering limited choice of service providers and having a regulator that was not responsive

Exhibit 8
Singapore Telecom's Financial Performance

	1999	1998	1997	1996	1995	1994	1993	1992	1991	1990
Turnover	4,883.5	4,942.2	4,240.9	3,999.0	3,516.0	3,190.8	2,759.3	2,479.7	2,221.7	1,998.6
Operating expenses	2,910.4	2,738.1	2,337.9	2,029.6	1,791.2	1,677.1	1,526.6	1,390.8	1,351.2	1,266.5
Operating profit	1,973.1	2,204.1	2,083.0	1,969.4	1,724.8	1,513.7	1,232.7	1,088.9	870.5	732.1
Profits and losses of associated firms	291.7	180.8	47.6	(87.8)	(38.7)	(15.6)	(0.9)	3.3	(1.8)	(0.7)
Restructuring costs	—	(154.0)	—	—	—	—	—	—	—	—
Net profit	1,955.4	1,886.1	1,687.5	1,501.4	1,333.0	1,205.8	1,005.3	—	—	—
Fixed assets	4,549.1	4,005.3	3,535.0	3,341.1	3,100.3	2,908	2,559.3	2,449.5	1,684.5	1,498.4
Cash and bank deposits	‡	4,112.0	3,987.5†	1,481.4	2,153.2	1,106.1	1,621.3	‡	‡	‡
Net current assets	4,438.7	3,998.6	2,970.9	441.4	602.5	192.0	(410.7)*	3,351.7	3,161.1	2,634.9
Noncurrent liabilities	503.6	418	255.7	468.4	396.0	522.4	190.9	31.2	32.2	30.8
Shareholders' funds	7,967.9	6,873.2	5,558.1	4,188.5	4,123.1	3,297.1	2,450.0	6,273.3	5,266.1	4,374.0
Turnover growth (%)	–1.2	16.5	6.0	13.7	10.2	15.6	11.2	11.6	11.1	—
Net profit growth (%)	3.7	11.8	12.4	12.6	10.5	19.9	—	‡	‡	‡
Earnings per share (¢)	12.82	12.37	11.07	9.85	8.74	7.91	6.59	‡	‡	‡
Net tangible asset per share (¢)	52.25	45.07	36.45	27.47	27.04	21.62	16.02	‡	‡	‡
Dividends (¢)	5.5	5.0	4.5	4.0	3.5	3.0	5.2	‡	‡	‡
Return on shareholders funds (%)	26.4	30.3	34.6	36.1	35.9	32.8	27.4	‡	‡	‡
Return on total assets (%)	15.1	17.5	20.3	22.3	22.5	23.2	22.2	‡	‡	‡
Operating return on turnover (%)	40.4	44.6	47.1	49.2	49.1	47.4	44.7	43.9	39.2	36.6
Operating return on net fixed assets (%)	‡	58.5	60.6	61.1	57.4	55.4	50.2	52.7	54.7	48.6
Turnover per employee ($,000)	‡	434.6	414.1	359.5	316.5	292.1	255.3	230.9	207.0	177.9

*Singapore Telecom transferred large funds back to the government prior to its public listing.
†Includes a $1.5 billion cash compensation from the government for bringing forward the end of Singapore Telecom's exclusive license by 7 years.
‡Figures are not available or not comparable due to its then status as a government department.

Source: Singapore Telecom annual reports 1990–1998.

or transparent.[55] Singapore Telecom was also ranked 7th out of 26 international carriers in a 1999 Data Communications survey that rated telecom providers on value, quality reliability, speed of repairs, billing, and general responsiveness for frame relay and leased-line services.[56]

In terms of absolute profit figures, Singapore Telecom remains the most profitable Singapore firm, with a profit of S$1.88 billion for financial year 1998 and S$1.95 billion for 1999.[57] Although the company managed to go through the worst of the Asian crisis relatively unscathed in 1988, the outlook appears gloomy. According to Singapore Telecom's Chairman, growth earnings were flat.[58] Group revenue in 1999 fell by 1.2%, operating profits fell by 10.5%, and operating expenses increased by 6% from 1998. Singapore Telecom's IDD (international direct dialing) revenue, its largest revenue contributor, fell by 10.4% in 1999, largely due to lower call rates, which fell by 13%. Singapore Telecom's growth rate in recent years has become relatively unstable (see **Exhibit 8**).

What Does the Future Hold?

The competitive environment will become more intense with the entry of StarHub in April 2000. StarHub aims to be "the first infocommunications company in Asia-Pacific to offer total convergence of fixed and mobile communications on a single, integrated platform. This means your home, office, and mobile phones can all be linked, so you can be reached anywhere with just one number."[59]

The relative contribution of IDD revenues has been declining over the years, from 50% at the time of Singapore Telecom's listing in 1993, to 38% in financial year 1999.[60] StarHub's entry is expected to spell even steeper decline as market share is inevitably lost to the new competitor. Singapore Telecom expects to lose between 20 and 40% of the fixed-line and IDD markets to StarHub within the next 2 to 3 years.[61] According to Singapore Telecom's Vice-President for Corporate Products, the decrease in IDD's revenue contribution will depend on StarHub's price aggressiveness, the growth of new revenue streams, and new technological advancements and industry trends.[62] Corporate customers account for about 80% of Singapore Telecom's S$5 billion revenue; StarHub's CEO believes that once StarHub enters the market in April 2000, it can attract a significant amount of business from these customers:

> Corporate customers were quite keen to talk to us . . . and we haven't come across a locked door yet . . . You hear things like why can't I get this particular kind of service in Singapore. I can get that in the U.S., why does it cost me so much, why does it take 2 months to get this installed.[63] . . . our strength is that Singapore Telecom can't imagine where we're coming from.[64]

Singapore Telecom stresses that it will match or surpass all offers StarHub makes when it begins operations:

> We will never let our competitor get the better of us.[65]
>   . . . firstly, we want to ensure that we are price-competitive, that we offer value-for-money. We also need to deliver appropriate levels of customer service. There we have been continuously trying to improve the service delivery . . . The other area is, we will continuously look for new products and services . . . I think there is always a problem that you are an incumbent, you are large and people feel that therefore they favor the underdog.[66]

According to the Minister for Communications, Mah Bow Tan, the Telecommunications Authority of Singapore will continue to ensure high service standards and a sustainable competitive environment; but when the playing field is more even, it will adopt a more relaxed regulatory attitude. They will also ensure that customers are free to switch between providers and that there will be no penalty involved in the switch.[67] In the past, charges for switching have been finely balanced to avoid penalizing or encouraging switching between providers.[68]

The newly appointed head of Singapore Telecom Mobile, however, fears that public sympathy is not with Singapore Telecom, as it was a former monopoly in the mobile market and has a current monopoly in the fixed-line market until April 2000. Consumer response to new offerings by MobileOne since April 1997 demonstrated that consumers were glad to have a choice of mobile providers and may have felt that prices were maintained at an artificially high level before the opening of the market to competition:[69]

When I took the job, I really felt the public sympathy was not with us, it was with the newcomer. People will not be very forgiving if Singapore Telecom makes a mistake . . . We need to go back to tell the customers that first of all, we are sorry for all the things that we've done to you in the past . . . .

A recent event in which SingNet (a Singapore Telecom subsidiary) subscribers' computers were secretly scanned suggests that improvements are needed. According to the Asian *Wall Street Journal*:

At the request of an Internet service provider, Singapore's internal-security agency secretly scanned 200,000 computers last month to trace a virus that allows hackers to steal computer passwords and credit-card numbers. The action came to light last week only after a law student who had installed antihacking software filed a police report, alleging that her computer had been entered into by the Ministry of Home Affairs on 10 different occasions in mid-April. The revelation has caused such a controversy in the island-state that this week the Internet service provider involved, SingNet, issued a public apology headed, "We should have informed you first." SingNet insisted that the scanning was only for the purpose of identifying computers susceptible to hackers, and that no computers were actually entered to access confidential information . . . But SingNet's reassurance did little to calm computer users in Singapore . . . Online discussion groups have been filled with protests charging invasion of privacy and expressing suspicions of hidden motives for the intrusion.[70]

In March Singapore Telecom said that it was searching for the identity of an Internet user who claimed in a newsgroup posting that Singapore Telecom Mobile's users had not benefited from the company's recent price cuts, and threatened to sue him.[71] Singapore Telecom's stern reaction to this Internet user's allegedly libelous comments about its packages is a telling indication of the intense rivalry in this industry sector.

The outlook for the near term is seen to be negative by Singapore Telecom. Downward trends are expected to continue in its "key business drivers," international telephone traffic, mobile subscribers, and business lines. Singapore Telecom intends to implement stricter cost control measures to protect its bottom line.[72] Cost cutting measures included reducing the salaries of senior managers by 10% and management flying economy instead of business class. According to the Singapore Telecom Group Director of Human Resources:

The wage cuts will help SingTel to better manage its costs in the current economic slowdown . . . Being leaders in the company, we must show our staff that we are willing to live through good and bad times with them together . . . .[73]

In the most recent announcement of Singapore Telecom's planned competitive strategy, Singapore Telecom's Chairman explained how the company would focus on the competition and on growth:

SingTel has consistently regarded competition as a regional challenge . . . . In the Asia Pacific, we continue to outperform our competitors . . . . Besides getting ready for the competition, our other focus is to develop our growth strategy. We have a 4-pronged approach. Firstly, we will take advantage of the business opportunities that come with the convergence of telecommunications, IT, and media. Our broadband multimedia service, Singapore Telecom Magix, is a good example of a "convergent service." Secondly, we will seek new business opportunities as they emerge and synergize them with our existing services and operations. Examples of these include e-commerce and Internet hubbing. Thirdly, we will pursue global and regional expansion through investments overseas. Finally, we will also take advantage of our existing assets, such as our billing systems, telecom networks, and real estate, to generate new revenues through services such as facility management and billing services.[74]

Notes

1. *Annual Report 1998/99*, Chairman's statement.
2. H. L. Teh, "Singapore Telecom Warning Even as Its Profits Rise 3.7%," *Business Times* (June 5, 1999).
3. Telecommunications Authority of Singapore, *1998/1999 Annual Report* (1999).
4. S. G. Lim, "Sustaining Excellence in Government: The Singapore Experience," *Public Administration and Development* 17 (1997), pp. 167–174.
5. R. S. Sisodia, "Singapore Invests in the Nation-Corporation," *Harvard Business Review* (May–June, 1992), pp. 5–11.
6. K. Singh, 1995.
7. Ministry of Trade and Industry, *Economic Survey of Singapore, 1998* (Singapore: SNP Publishers, 1999).
8. S. Durchslag, T. Puri, and A. Rao, "The Promise of Infrastructure Privatisation," *McKinsey Quarterly* 1 (1994), pp. 3–19.
9. C. I. Knoop, L. M. Applegate, B. S. Neo, and J. L. King, "Singapore Unlimited: Building the National Information Infrastructure," *Harvard Business School Case 9-196-012* (1996).
10. *Financial Times* (September 30, 1999).
11. International Telecommunications Union <www.itu.int>.
12. International Telecommunications Union <www.itu.int>.
13. "Managing Telecoms: Old Champions, New Contenders," *The Economist* (October 11, 1997).
14. "Virtual Private Network Posed for Big Take-off Here," *The Business Times* (April 12, 1999).
15. "Telecommunications: The Death of Distance," *The Economist* (September 30, 1995).
16. "Asian Telecommunications," *Asian Wall Street Journal* (June 2, 1998).
17. *BT World Communications Report 1998/9.*
18. *Financial Times* (September 30, 1999).
19. *Asian Wall Street Journal* (1998).
20. *Asian Wall Street Journal* (1998).
21. C. Ong, "Another British Invasion of Asia," *Business Times* (April 7, 1999).
22. "British Tel Still Hungry for More Asian Acquisitions," *Business Times* (March 11, 1999).
23. Bank of America, *Guide to Telecommunications in Asia* (Hong Kong: Euromoney Publications, 1996) pp. 1–6.
24. Telecommunications Authority of Singapore <www.tas.gov.sg>.
25. International Telecommunications Union <www.itu.int> (data dated October 4, 1999).
26. "Mobile Phone Penetration Seen Hitting 70%," *Business Times* (February 13–14, 1999).
27. C. Ong, "Corporate Customers Willing to Give Business to Us: StarHub Chief," *Business Times* (April 9, 1999).
28. L. Heracleous, "Privatisation: Global Trends and Implications of the Singapore Experience," *Research Paper Series*, Faculty of Business Administration, National University of Singapore, RPS #98–45 (1998).
29. L. Low, "Privatisation in Singapore: The Big Push," paper for Symposium on Privatisation organised by the Asian Productivity Organisation, Bangkok, July 4–6; C. H. Tan, "Singapore Telecom: From Public to Private Sector," *International Journal of Public Sector Management* 5, 4 (1995), pp. 4–14.
30. K. Singh, 1995.
31. Kuo, Low, and Toh, 1989; L. Low, 1995; M. H. Toh and L. Low, "Towards Greater Competition in Singapore's Telecommunications," *Telecommunications Policy* (August, 1990), pp. 303–314; M. H. Toh and L. Low, "Privatisation of Telecommunications Services in Singapore," in J. Pelkmans and N. Wagner (eds.), *Privatisation and Deregulation in ASEAN and EC: Making Markets More Effective* (1990), pp. 82–93.
32. E. C. Y. Kuo, L. Low, and M. H. Toh, "The Singapore Telecommunications Sector and Issues Affecting Its Competitive Position in the Pacific Region," *Colombia Journal of World Business* (Spring, 1989), pp. 59–71.
33. K. Singh, "Guided Competition in Singapore's Telecommunications Industry," presented at 4th Annual Conference of the Consortium for Research on Telecommunications Policy and Strategy, University of Michigan, Ann Arbor (June 1998).
34. K. Singh, 1995.
35. "Group Wants Bigger Role in E-Commerce," *Business Times* (June 5, 1999).
36. "E-Commerce, Internet and Mobile Services Coverage," *Keylines* (June 7, 1999).
37. T. Tan, "Singapore Telecom Reaps $700m from New Services," *Straits Times* (April 12, 1999).
38. "Singapore Telecom Seen Growing on Internet, Asian Expansion," *Business Times* (April 28, 1999).
39. "Singapore Telecom's Overseas Earnings on the Rise," *Business Times* (June 5, 1999) <www.Singtel.com>.
40. K. Singh, 1998; K. Singh, "Singapore Telecom in Europe," *ASEAN-EU Management Centre Cases Series*, 1999.
41. T. Tan, "Singapore Telecom to Pay $551m for Thai Stake," *Business Times* (January 7, 1999).
42. K. Singh, 1998.
43. H. S. Lee, "Singapore Telecom's Cash Cow Could Turn into a Free Service," *Business Times* (September 30, 1999).
44. Singapore Telecom Annual Report, 1998/99.
45. "Singapore Telecom's Competitive Strategy," *Keylines* (May 8–9, 1999).
46. H. L. Teh, "Singapore Telecom Unveils Major Restructuring," *Business Times* (March 12, 1999); T. Tan, "Major Shake-Up at Singapore Telecom," *Straits Times* (March 12, 1999).
47. K. T. Leong, "Lessons of Regulatory Changes for Asian Needs," in Proceedings of Special Session on Effective Transition Through Regulation, World Telecommunications Forum, Singapore (May 1993), pp. 113–116.
48. C. Ong, "Pro-Choice, Pro-Competition," *Business Times* (May 6, 1999).
49. H. L. Teh, "Singapore Telecom Mobile Cuts Rates Twice in a Day to Fend Off M1 Challenge," *Business Times* (January 30–31, 1999); T. Tan, "Singapore Telecom, M1 Slug It Out in Price War," *Straits Times* (January 30, 1999).
50. H. L. Teh, "Packing a Punch: Hi and Low of Handphone Packages," *Business Times* (February 19, 1999).
51. T. Tan, "M1 Gains on Singapore Telecom Mobile," *Business Times* (March 10, 1999).
52. H. L. Teh, "Telcos' Advertising Tab Seen Topping $100m in '99," *Business Times* (April 28, 1999).
53. H. L. Teh, "US$450b to Be Made in Region's Mobile Market," *Business Times* (June 5, 1999).

54. "Singapore Is Tops for Business," *Straits Times* (August 22, 1997).

55. "S'pore Is Tops Again in Telecoms Ranking," *Straits Times* (January 19, 1999).

56. "Singapore Telecom Shines in Telecom Survey," *Straits Times* (May 14, 1999).

57. J. Chia, "Singapore Telecom Takes the Lead with $1.88b Net Profit," *Straits Times* (March 2, 1999).

58. H. L. Teh, "Singapore Telecom Warning Even as Its Profits Rise 3.7%," *Business Times* (June 5, 1999).

59. <www.StarHub.com.sg>

60. W. Choong and T. Tan, "IDD Revenue Drops for the First Time," *Straits Times* (June 5, 1999).

61. "20%–40% Loss in Market Share Expected," *Business Times* (June 5, 1999).

62. T. Tan, "Singapore Telecom to Reap Less from IDD Calls," *Straits Times* (June 14, 1999).

63. C. Ong, "Corporate Customers Willing to Give Business to Us: StarHub Chief," *Business Times* (April 9, 1999).

64. T. Tan, "StarHub Eyes 25% of IDD Market," *Straits Times* (April 9, 1999).

65. T. Tan, "Singapore Telecom to Match Prices," *Straits Times* (April 12, 1999).

66. C. Ong and H. L. Teh, "Standing Above the Fray," *Business Times* (May 6, 1999).

67. "TAS Will 'Step Back' Once Market Opens Up," *Business Times* (February 12, 1999); C. Ong, "New TAS Rule May Spell End of Handphone Subscription Perks," *Business Times* (November 27, 1998).

68. K. Singh, 1998.

69. C. Ong, "Singapore Telecom Mobile Takes Battle to the Competition," *Business Times* (January 11, 1999).

70. S. Sesser, "SingNet Apologizes for Virus Scanning," *Asian Wall Street Journal* (May 7, 1999).

71. T. Tan, "Singapore Telecom Mobile May Sue Net User," *Business Times* (March 22, 1999).

72. <www.SingaporeTelecom.com>

73. T. Tan, "Singapore Telecom's Top Earners Take Extra Pay Cut," *Straits Times* (January 19, 1999).

74. Transcript of comments by Mr. Koh Boon Hwee, Singapore Telecom Chairman, at news conference of June 4, 1999.

Hewlett-Packard Company in Vietnam

Dr. Geok Theng Lau

In September 1995, John Peter, a Marketing Manager of Hewlett-Packard Asia Pacific (HPAP) was evaluating HPAP's long-term strategic investment options for doing business in Vietnam. HPAP was a subsidiary of the Hewlett-Packard (HP) Company and its headquarters was located in Singapore. Vietnam had recently adopted an open door policy after the United States lifted its embargo on the country in February 1994. The country had a population of over 70 million with a literacy rate of over 90%. Foreign investment in the country had climbed steadily and had reached almost US$12 billion by the end of 1994.

An environmental and market analysis revealed that the information technology (IT) market in Vietnam had potential. However, the market was currently small and market growth was uncertain. Several business units within HP had begun to distribute some HP products in Vietnam. John needed to make a recommendation on whether the HPAP should enter the Vietnam market in a more strategic fashion, that is, to give serious consideration to Vietnam as a major market for HP. If so, what form should the market entry take and how should it be done?

The Country of Vietnam and Its Business Environment

Vietnam is situated in the east of the Indochina Peninsula with a total land area of 330,363 square kilometers (see **Exhibit 1**). It shares borders with China in the north, Laos in the west, and Cambodia in the southwest. The coastline in the east stretches 3,400 km. The country has 56 provinces. Its major cities included the capital city of Hanoi, Ho Chi Minh City (formerly Saigon), and the port cities of Haiphong and Danang. The official language is Vietnamese.

This case was prepared by Dr. Geok Theng Lau. This case was written as a basis for class discussion rather than to illustrate effective or ineffective handling of an administrative situation. Names of individuals were disguised. The author wishes to acknowledge the cooperation of Hewlett-Packard Asia Pacific Limited in the writing of this case and especially to thank Mr. Dennis Khoo, who provided the main structure and the information for this case. The involvement and advice of Dr. A. N. Hakam in this case development project is also recognized. This case was edited for SMB-8th Edition. All other rights reserved jointly to the author and the North American Case Research Association (NACRA). This case appeared in *Case Research Journal*, Summer, 2000, pp. 115–138. Copyright © 2000 by *Case Research Journal* and Geok Theng Lau. Reprinted by permission of author.

Exhibit 1

Map of Vietnam

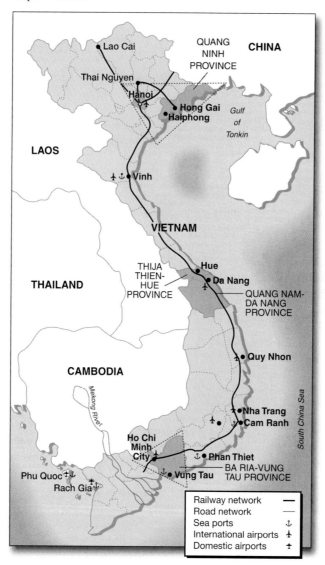

HISTORY

For over a thousand years, from 111 B.C. to 939 A.D., Vietnam was governed as a Chinese province, Giao Chia. After it liberated itself, Vietnam frequently had to resist Chinese invasions. The country remained free from foreign control until 1885 when France brought all of Vietnam under its rule. After the Japanese surrender in August 1945, Ho Chi Minh, founder of the Vietminh, proclaimed the independence of the Provisional Democratic Republic of Vietnam.

France's refusal to give up its colony led to a protracted war. China and the Soviet Union backed the Vietminh, while the United States backed the French. In subsequent years, the United States-backed Ngo Dinh Diem took power in the South. A united front organization called the National Front for the Liberation of South Vietnam was formed to oppose Diem.

The conflict escalated and turned into an American war, with the United States deploying 500,000 troops in Vietnam by 1968. The Southern forces collapsed after the U.S. withdrawal and on April 30, 1975, the communists entered Saigon and Vietnam's 30-year war of independence was over.

After the fall of Saigon, the North proceeded to reunify the country. Vietnam subsequently found itself treated with suspicion and, after its invasion of Cambodia in late 1978, was isolated by the international community. After the final withdrawal of Vietnamese troops from Cambodia in late 1989, the process of normalization of economic ties with ASEAN (Association of South East Asian Nations), Western Europe, Northeast Asia, Australia, and New Zealand began to gather pace. In late 1991, after the Paris agreement on Cambodia, diplomatic and economic relations with many countries, including China, were fully normalized.

POLITICAL ENVIRONMENT

The supreme organ of state power in Vietnam was the National Assembly, which performed functions such as promulgation of laws; ratification of the annual and long-term plans for economic and social development; budget planning; election of top officials; and selection of the cabinet members. The Government was the executive body responsible for the enforcement of the laws of the country issued by the National Assembly.

Until the mid-to-late 1980s, the leadership of the Vietnamese Communist Party (VCP) held orthodox Marxist-Leninist beliefs, which viewed the world as a mortal struggle between imperialist and revolutionary camps. In the late 1980s to early 1990s, due partly to the end of the Cold War, the Vietnamese Political Bureau acknowledged the need for Vietnam to participate actively in the global capitalist economy, since the socialist organization for economic cooperation (COMECON) was becoming less relevant. The leadership sought to achieve a breakthrough in trade with the capitalist countries and an expansion of external cooperation, including taking out loans for capital investment and promoting joint venture projects.

Elements of the old world view, however, continued to coexist with the new one. The aging leadership continued to adopt an autocratic political system, and there was conflict between a closed political system and the economy opening up. This resulted in continuing debates and shifts in emphasis from struggle against imperialism to economic interdependence.

THE PEOPLE AND WORKFORCE

The population of Vietnam was approximately 71 million people, 70% of them under 35 years old. The annual population growth was 2.2%. The population was basically rural and was concentrated in the two main rice-growing deltas: the Red River in the north and the Mekong in the south. The river delta population was almost entirely ethnic Vietnamese (Kinh), who made up 87% of the total population. The minority groups (including Khmer, Cham, Muong, and Thai peoples), whose cultures and languages were quite distinct from those of the Kinh Vietnamese, were found in the upland areas. The overseas Chinese community, which was largely concentrated in the south, was depleted by the decision of many to leave the country, often as "boat people." This community had partly recouped its position in the economy since the late 1980s, largely on the strength of its links with Hong Kong and Taiwan.

Vietnam was underurbanized in comparison with many other developing countries in Southeast Asia. The largest city was Ho Chi Minh (Saigon) with a population of well over 4 million. The capital, Hanoi, had a registered population of 3.1 million. The level of primary education was comparatively high. The population, especially in the north, was basically literate, with a literacy rate of over 90%. The average wages in Vietnam and some neighboring countries are shown in **Exhibit 2**.

Exhibit 2

Monthly Minimum Wage Rates of Selected Countries in Asia

Country	Monthly Wage Rates (US$)
China	50
Hong Kong	525
Indonesia	80
Malaysia	290
Philippines	95
Singapore	600
Taiwan	650
Thailand	165
Vietnam	35

Source: World Bank, Trends in Developing Countries.

ECONOMIC ENVIRONMENT

Vietnam was the largest of the 3 Indo-Chinese nations, accounting for about 44% of total land area and 75% of the combined population of the region. The country was endowed with oil reserves and extensive mineral resources. It was an agro-based economy with the agricultural sector absorbing 70% of the workforce (numbering about 32 million people) and contributing some 40% to the GNP and nearly 40% to total exports. Since 1989, Vietnam had become an important rice exporter and was the world's third largest rice exporter, after Thailand and the United States.

Light industries, including textiles, garments, footwear, paper, food processing, electrical, and electronics, though scattered throughout the country, were more concentrated in the south. Heavy industries, including iron and steel, power generation, cement, mining, chemicals, fertilizers, and machine tools were mainly concentrated in the north. The number of industrial establishments in Vietnam is shown in **Exhibit 3**.

In the past, Vietnam relied mainly on the former Soviet Union and Eastern European countries for trade and economic cooperation and assistance. All of its foreign aid and one-half of its export markets vanished with the collapse of the Eastern bloc in 1991. The country, however, survived this crisis and economic growth rebounded to an official 8.3% in 1992 after a mild slowdown to around 5% in 1990. Inflation eased from about 700% in 1986 to 17.5% in 1992. Foreign investment approvals rose by 73% in 1992 and accounted for 26.2% of total investments. Exports rose by 19% to US$2.5 billion, while imports climbed by 9% during the same year. For the first time in several decades, Vietnam was estimated to have registered a trade and current account surplus in 1992. **Exhibit 4** shows some key economic indicators for Vietnam from 1991 to 1994.

The government encouraged greater exports and imports. Exports were encouraged and only a few items were subject to export duty, which had been kept low. The import of capital goods and materials for domestic production was encouraged, while the import of consumer goods, which could be produced at home or were considered luxurious, were discouraged. The list of items subjected to export and import prohibition or quota had been substantially cut down. Greater autonomy had been given to companies and enterprises in their export and

Exhibit 3
Number of Industrial Establishments in Vietnam

| Year | State | | | Nonstate | | |
	Central	Local	Total	Cooperatives	Private Enterprises	Private Household
1985	711	2,339	3,050	35,629	902	–
1986	687	2,454	3,141	37,649	567	–
1987	682	2,457	3,139	33,962	490	–
1988	681	2,430	3,111	32,034	318	318,557
1989	666	2,354	3,020	21,901	1,248	333,337
1990	589	2,173	2,762	13,086	770	376,900
1991	546	2,053	2,599	8,829	959	446,771
1992	537	1,731	2,268	5,723	1,114	368,000

Source: General Statistical Office (Vietnam).

import business. State subsidies and price controls on export and import had ended except for some major items. The country established its first Export Processing Zone named Tan Thuan in Ho Chi Minh City in 1991.

Vietnam had diversified its export and import markets to other parts of the world. As a result, about 80% of total trade were now with Asia-Pacific countries, with Singapore, Japan, Hong Kong, South Korea, Taiwan, Australia, and Thailand as the main trade partners. Meanwhile, widespread tax reforms and improved collection had raised government revenue by 82%. Reflecting these strengths, the Vietnamese currency, the Dong, appreciated almost 5% against the U.S. dollar in 1993, in contrast to 1991, when its value was almost halved (see exchange rates of the Dong in **Exhibit 5**). Vietnam had normalized relations with the World Bank, the International Monetary Fund (IMF), and the Asian Development Bank (ADB) and had attracted many sources of bilateral and multilateral financial support. Vietnam joined ASEAN in July 1995.

Exhibit 4
Some Key Economic Indicators for Vietnam (1991–1994)

Year	GDP Growth	Industrial Growth	Services Growth	Agricultural Growth
1991	6.0%	10.0%	2.2%	8.2%
1992	8.6%	15.0%	7.2%	8.3%
1993	8.1%	12.0%	4.4%	13.0%
1994	8.5%	13.5%	4.5%	12.5%

Source: General Statistical Office (Vietnam).

Exhibit 5

Exchange Rates of the Dong

Year	Exchange Rates (Dong per US$)
1989	4,000
1990	5,200
1991	9,390
1992	11,181
1993	10,641
1994	11,080

Source: Economic Intelligence Unit, Business in Vietnam.

Exhibit 6 shows the distribution of foreign investments by sectors. **Exhibit 7** shows the foreign investments from the top 10 countries. Joint ventures accounted for about 74% of the foreign investments, totally foreign-owned companies accounted for 11%, and business cooperation contracts accounted for 15%.

The lifting of the U.S. trade embargo on Vietnam in February 1994 brought benefits such as direct access to U.S. technology and investment and smoother access to soft loans and aids from multilateral institutions. A survey of 100 American companies by the US-ASEAN council (reported in the *Business Times* of Singapore on February 5, 1994) indicated that trade and investment opportunities in Vietnam were worth US$ 2.6 billion in the first 2 years following the lifting of the embargo. Foreign investment had climbed steadily and reached US$11.05 billion (from 1,201 projects) as of the beginning of January 1995.

The government had set the target growth rates of 3.5 to 4% for the agriculture, aqua-culture, and livestock husbandry sectors and 7 to 8% for the industrial sector. The food processing indus-

Exhibit 6

Foreign Direct Investments by Economic Activities

Activity	(as of January 4, 1995)	
	Number of Projects	Investment Capital (US$ million)
Industry (manufacturing)	548	4,334
Oil and gas	26	1,303
Agriculture and forestry	74	369
Aqua- and mariculture	21	62
Transportation and communication	128	951
Tourism and hotels	113	2,235
Services	134	1,254
Finance and banking	15	177
Housing	14	71
Others	8	14
Export processing zone	29	109
Industrial zone	2	167
Total	1,201	11,046

Source: State Committee for Cooperation and Investment in Vietnam.

Exhibit 7
Foreign Direct Investments In Vietnam—Top Ten Countries

Country	(as of January 4, 1995)	
	Number of Projects	Investment Capital (US$ million)
Taiwan	179	1,968
Hong Kong	171	1,796
Singapore	76	1,028
Korea, Republic of	98	889
Japan	73	789
Australia	42	861
Malaysia	32	585
France	58	510
Switzerland	14	463
United Kingdom	15	376

Source: State Committee for Cooperation and Investment in Vietnam.

try would give priority to the development of the Mekong and Red River Delta regions in order to upgrade the quality of processed agro-products and aquatic products to export standards. In the production of consumer goods, attention would be paid to the rehabilitation of current equipment and installation of new ones to improve the quality of manufactured products. Electronics assembling and manufacturing facilities would be established. Oil and gas exploitation on the continental shelf would be carried out and an oil refinery would be constructed. The mining, cement production, steel and mechanical industries were also targeted for development.

Despite the preceding positive economic outlook, some economic observers had pointed out several problems. The low savings rate and lack of hard currency constrained investment growth. Vietnam had an estimated US$15 billion of foreign debt, and the foreign exchange reserve constituted only about 1 month of imports. Three-quarters of export revenues were generated from only 2 sources—unprocessed farm products and crude oil. The annual inflation rate in Vietnam had ranged from a high of 400% in 1988 to a low of 15% in 1992. The annual inflation forecast for 1994 to 1998 was 40%. The Vietnam currency, the Dong, was not a fully convertible currency. The official exchange rate had depreciated from 5,200 dong per U.S. dollar to 9,390 dong per U.S. dollar in 1991 (see **Exhibit 5**). The state-owned enterprises appeared inefficient. They used 85% of the total fixed capital, 80% of total credit volume, 100% of savings, 60% of forestry output, and 90% of trained and high-school educated people, but they contributed less than 15% of total GDP in 1992.

FOREIGN EXCHANGE AND INVESTMENT REGULATIONS

Prior to 1980, in Vietnam, all transactions had to pass through the state export and import corporations. Beginning in 1980, however, provinces, cities, and individual enterprises were given some freedom to sign contracts with foreign traders. Exchange control was administered by the State Bank, which had branches in Hanoi and Ho Chi Minh City.

On January 1, 1988, a new Foreign Investment Law was promulgated to supersede the one dating from 1977. The new code allowed foreigners to own up to 100% of a venture, against a previous maximum of 49%. The old requirement that foreign investors should take a minimum 30% stake in joint ventures was retained. Priority areas for investment specified in the code were production for export and import substitution. Investors were expected to meet their own foreign exchange needs. The duration of a venture with foreign capital generally might not exceed 20 years, but it could be extended in special cases.

The corporate income tax rate had been reduced from between 30% and 50% in the old code to between 15% and 25% in the new one. There was provision for tax holidays of up to 2 years after the company made a profit. A statute governing labor relations and remuneration in foreign-invested companies was issued in 1990. Some main provisions in the statute specified the minimum wages, working hours, day of rest and holidays, minimum working age, rights to join a union, and labor arbitration process. The State Committee for Cooperation and Investment was created to manage and administer all foreign direct investment in 1988.

Land in Vietnam could not be purchased, only leased for a period, which depended on the duration of investment. The cost of land lease ranged from US$0.50 to US$18.00 per square meter per year in 1995.

INFRASTRUCTURE AND BANKING SYSTEM

The existing telecommunications system in Vietnam was found by many to be expensive and inefficient. The country relied mainly on waterways for transportation. The port facilities were felt to be backward, and it was thought that they might hinder the distribution system, especially when volume increased with the expected surge in economic activities. Many observers from the financial sector felt that the banking system, though reformed, was still far from those in capitalist countries, and might cause delays and confusion, especially in the handling of foreign exchange remittances.

The Vietnamese government had directed the state to invest in the construction of infrastructures, such as water supply and drainage systems in big cities, in-town traffic projects, highway network connecting the big cities, North-South railway network, restoration and improvement of sea ports, and upgrading of airports in major cities. There were plans to construct new hydropower plants and thermopower plants with a target production of 16 to 17 billion KWH (kilowatt hours) for 1995.

Information Technology Market in Vietnam

MARKET CHARACTERISTICS

The computer industry in Vietnam was in its infancy. The 18-year-old trade embargo imposed by the United States had effectively prevented computer technology from being transferred into the country by any of the major computer manufacturers and restricted heavily any capital inflow. Since the number of computer installations currently was small and located mostly in Ho Chi Minh City, many businessmen viewed the computer industry as an emerging industry with good market potential. There were not many competitors in the market, and there were no clear leaders in the market yet. Distribution channels for the industry were also not fully developed.

An analysis of Vietnam's IT end-user market showed that the government, together with its related agencies and institutions, made up 35% of the market, followed by multinationals (35%), small and medium enterprises (25%), and small home or office users making up the remaining market. The buyers in the foreseeable future would be the public sector and major foreign companies. The deal sizes were forecast to be large as the government departments and foreign companies made initial investments in information technology infrastructure.

Different types of computers, such as personal computers, minicomputers, RISC based workstations, and mainframes, could be used by businesses in their operation in Vietnam. The price differences among them would be an important consideration for these different business customers in their buying decision. Skilled local expertise in IT in Vietnam was somewhat limited. The Vietnamese workforce, however, was hardworking and well-educated and could possibly be trained quickly.

Computer products had limited intrinsic proprietary attributes and most innovations were easily imitated. Computer products, thus, were increasingly becoming less differentiated. The market, especially the low-end segment, tended to have fierce price competition and switching costs from 1 manufacturer to another was low. The Vietnamese users tended to favor U.S. brands of computers, even though brand loyalty for the product area was currently not strong.

There were problems associated with the lack of normalized ties between the United States and Vietnam, although the trade embargo had been lifted. As a result, American banks were not able to provide credit, although financing for their operation was a necessity in doing business in Vietnam. This was because hard currency was still hard to come by. American IT companies such as UNISYS had invested heavily in at least 2 large IT bids, only to find that their European and Japanese competitors had the edge against them when it came to extending credit. This problem might be resolved in the near future, as U.S. Secretary of State Warren Christopher had recommended that ties with Vietnam be normalized.

As in other Asian countries, "guanxi" was an important factor in doing business in Vietnam. "Guanxi" is a Chinese term denoting the use of personal connections, relationships, or networks to win business deals, forge business ventures, or to get business approvals for government authorities. Local and regional competitors could have a better understanding of such culture and practices, and they could have built up their own networks since they entered the market before the trade embargo was lifted.

VIETNAM'S IT-2000 PROGRAM

Vietnam planned to propel itself into the twenty-first century through a billion-dollar program called IT-2000. It was based on a similar development model created in Singapore. The IT-2000 called for expenditures of up to U.S. $2 billion over the next 5 years to set up the hardware necessary to create a national data communications network, establish a domestic industry in component manufacturing, and educate over 5,000 Vietnamese in the use of computer technology. The government adopted the IT-2000 on August 4, 1993, designating it a national initiative. The Ministry of Science Technology and Environment had been given the formidable task to oversee the plan.

Part of this plan was to create online computer networks for almost all government agencies and the financial sector, build the Vietnam Education Research and Development Network (VERDNet), and provide each secondary school and university student in Vietnam with access to an integrated computer complete with Vietnamese educational software. The IT-2000 also addressed government policies for financial management and support. The State Bank of Vietnam and the Ministry of Finance were desperately in need of an integrated nationwide data processing network to manage the chaos of transactions in banking, financial markets, and tax collection.

The Minister of Science, Technology and the Environment, and Chairman of IT-2000, Dr. Dang Hua, was quoted as saying:

> The purpose of IT-2000 is to build a foundation for basic information demands in the management of government and socioeconomic activities, and to develop the IT industry to a level where it can help in national development. We have stated very clearly in the masterplan for IT-2000 that an integrated system of different computing networks must be built, with strong enough software and database systems which are able to service the Government and other key essential activities. Some domestic services will be integrated with international systems.

Customer Groups in the IT Market

Two segmentation approaches, by industry and by benefits, were adopted to examine customer groups in the IT market. The industry segmentation identified the high growth business segments of the Vietnamese economy which, from HP's experience in other countries, might be heavy and early adopters of IT. The benefit segmentation further defined the characteristics and needs of these segments.

INDUSTRY SEGMENTATION

Financial Services

The Vietnam government had increasingly liberalized foreign bank participation. As of the beginning of 1995, investments totaling US$1.77 billion had been made in financial and commercial services. Apart from the lucrative trade finance business, which was forecast to expand rapidly, other financial services, especially venture capital, leasing, and project financing, had potential, too. In the short- to medium-term, this was generally the segment most Vietnam watchers and experts deemed likely to experience explosive growth. Funds from lenders were desperately needed to fuel the growth of the economy. In addition, the government was trying to encourage savings to create a pool of investment money. The financial industry had long viewed IT as a competitive advantage and, thus, IT investment in this segment was expected to pick up strongly. Due to the mission critical nature of financial applications, financial customers demanded a high level of support services.

Telecommunications

Vietnam's telecommunications infrastructure was still in its infancy. Explosive growth was expected here as well, especially in mobile communications and high-speed data communications links for businesses. The postal and telecommunications sectors were still very much a monopoly in Vietnam in 1995, so any investor wanting to offer a public telecommunications service would have to work with VNPT, the Vietnam Post and Telecommunications Department. Some announcements of foreign joint ventures in the telecommunications sector are shown in **Exhibit 8**.

Exhibit 8

Foreign Joint Ventures in the Telecommunications Sector

> **France:** Alcatel Alsthom said it had been selected by the Ministry of the Interior to supply the first private national communications network in Vietnam. The contract covered the supply, installation, implementation, and maintenance of a service integration network, which would eventually cover the entire country and represent 50,000 lines. The first part of the network was to be operational in March 1995.

> **Sweden:** Three Swedish companies and Vietnam's Posts and Telecommunications Department had applied for a license to set up a US$340 million mobile phone network covering the whole of Vietnam. They hoped to install and operate a cellular telephone and paging system connected by hubs in Hanoi in the north, Danang in the center, and Saigon in the south by the end of 1995. The Swedish companies were reported to be Industriforvaltings, Kirnevik, and Comvik International, and they said their combined investment would be US$159 million.

> **Canada:** Montreal-based Teleglobe, Inc., said its cable systems arm and Telesystem International Wireless Services, Inc., had signed a deal to study the feasibility of a multiregional wireless and communication service and coastal submarine fiberoptic cable system in Vietnam. The study would cost US$720,000 and the project itself would cost US$100 million.

Source: Internal company file—extracted from various sources.

Hotels and Tourism

Vietnam had increasingly become a new tourist destination and business travels continued to surge. This would create demand for hotel facilities, as well as spark the growth of a retail sector. Some international hotel groups, such as the Accor Group and Pullman International Hotels, and some Singapore companies, had begun a number of hotel projects in Vietnam. As of the beginning of 1995, foreign investment projects totaling US$2.235 billion had been made in this sector.

Manufacturing

Vietnam was an attractive location for labor-intensive industries due to low wages and a relatively skilled and productive workforce. The government encouraged export-oriented and resource- or agricultural-based manufacturing, such as assembly operations for electronic goods, garment, and food-processing industries.

Utilities

There would be explosive growth in this area as Vietnam sought to build its power infrastructure to cope with the demands of a modern economy. The Phu My thermal power plant project, worth US$900 million, was expected to provide 600 megawatts of power.

Oil and Gas

There were extensive offshore crude extraction activities going on. The Vietnamese government wished to promote local refining of crude oil. Many joint ventures with the various international and regional oil extraction and refining companies like BHP, Mobil, Shell, and Petronas were already in place. Total foreign investments as of the beginning of 1995 in this sector totaled US$1.3 billion.

Government

The government was expected to play a major role in influencing the use and penetration of IT in the Vietnamese economy. With its IT-2000 plan, the Vietnamese government hoped to follow in Singapore's footsteps and accelerate the country's entry into high technology.

BENEFIT SEGMENTATION

The benefit segmentation of IT customers is shown in **Exhibit 9**. Benefit segmentation distinguishes customers by choice criteria, technology requirements, and primary needs. Four benefit segments were identified.

The Economy Segment

This segment used IT mainly for productivity gains. PCs, simple networks, and off-the-shelf software were generally preferred because of cost reasons. Price-to-performance ratio was an important buying criterion, and these customers were extremely cost sensitive and also did not require high-quality, round-the-clock support.

The Technology Segment

This segment planned IT implementation so that they could be seen as technology leaders. Customers here generally had deep pockets and were willing to pay for the latest and the best technology.

The Mission Critical–Mission Sensitive Segment

This segment used IT for competitive advantage. The failure of its information systems would interrupt business operations, sometimes bringing it to a standstill, thus affecting revenue and profit. Hence, these customers looked for high availability, near-zero downtime, round-the-

Exhibit 9
Benefit Segments

Segments	Some Customers	Choice Criteria	Technology Requirements	Primary Needs
Economy (low price)	Consumer products; retail sector	Low price; low design content	Simple	Low costs; productivity gains
Technology	Oil and gas utilities	Leading edge solution	Complex	Technology leadership
Mission critical, mission sensitive	Banking and finance; couriers	High reliability; good and fast service	Proven and tested	Maximum uptime; performance
Geographical coverage	MNCs	Regional or worldwide presence	Wide area requirement	Branch connectivity; consistent support

clock support, and reliable solutions. They might also be uncomfortable with new technologies and view them as risky unless they saw a distinct competitive advantage in implementing them.

The Geographical Coverage Segment

This segment consisted of multinational corporations who operated worldwide or regionally and had a need to connect their dispersed operations together to ensure that information was disseminated quickly and reliably. Consistent, global support was critical when serving this segment.

Some Players in the IT Market in Vietnam

Exhibit 10 shows selected information on some major players in the IT market.

Exhibit 10
Some Players in the IT Market

(Dollar amounts in millions, except employee revenues per employees)					
Company	**1994 Annual Revenue**	**1994 Net Income**	**1993 Net Income**	**Number of Employees**	**Revenue per Employee**
IBM	$62,716.0	$(8,101.0)	$(4,965.0)	267,196	$234,719
Hewlett-Packard	24,991.0	1,599.0	1,177.0	98,400	253,974
DEC	13,450.8	(2,156.1)	(251.0)	78,000	172,466
Unisys	7,742.5	565.4	361.2	49,000	158,010
Compaq	7,191.0	462.0	213.0	10,043	716,021

Source: Software Asia Magazine (June/July, 1995).

DIGITAL EQUIPMENT CORPORATION (DEC)

Digital Equipment Corporation or DEC was a leading supplier of networked computer systems, software, and services. Its areas of differentiation were open systems, client-server knowledge and experiences, and multivendor experiences. Its strategy was to invest in technical research, build up technical capabilities, and to focus on training.

Over the past few years, DEC's financial results had been poor and DEC had a net loss of US$2 billion in 1994. DEC's poor performance caused the ouster of DEC's founder and CEO, Ken Olsen. His replacement from within was Robert Palmer, who had since sold off a number of DEC's noncore divisions, such as the disk drive operation, database software, and the consulting unit. He sought to focus on DEC's core hardware business and increase margin by adding value in networking. Palmer had positioned DEC to take advantage of key trends, such as mobile computing and video on demand. Palmer had also shifted most sales to indirect distribution channels and sought to slash costs by signing on computer resellers as key partners. Salomon Brothers, Inc., expected DEC's new Alpha system sales to soar in 1995 by 84% to US$1.7 billion and by another 55% in 1996.

In 1992, DEC had 45% of its turnover in the United States, 40% in Europe, 10% in Asia-Pacific (including Japan), and 5% in Canada. Alpha still faced a long-term problem: The chip had not won a single influential convert among computer makers. That could ultimately prove fatal when it came time to fund the mind-boggling cost of succeeding generations of chips. Most industry analysts believed that Palmer's accomplishments of the past year had merely brought DEC to the point where it was ready to compete again. If Palmer could not make DEC stand out with his networking strategy, the company risked following the path of another former industry, number 2, Unisys Corp., which now served mostly its old customers, and its revenue was shrinking slowly. Digital had a strong client base in government, banking and finance, insurance, and telecommunications. DEC had also done projects in health care, transportation, utilities, and retail. DEC currently had a representative office in Hanoi. So far, their main area of activity seemed to be on large internationally funded tenders. They had appointed 3 distributors in Vietnam as sales outlets and as service providers.

INTERNATIONAL BUSINESS MACHINES (IBM)

Despite losses amounting to over US$8 billion in 1994, IBM was still the world's largest information systems and services company. In 1995, IBM CEO Lou Gertsner had engineered a turnaround. Recently, IBM purchased Lotus Corporation for US$3.5 billion. IBM's worldwide revenues had declined since 1990, slipping to US$62.7 billion in 1994. In 1992, IBM had 1,500 consultants worldwide. While these consultants provided support to all industries, their key focus was on finance, retail, and manufacturing.

IBM's key area of differentiation was its ability not only to provide insights, experience, and specialized skills to its customers, but also to deliver results and increase the value of IBM products and services to customers. Its strategy was to focus on customer relationship and develop account presence. Its global organization allowed IBM to bring its best intellectual capabilities to bear on any project. IBM, however, was still encumbered by a mainframe image it might never completely shake. Still in recovery mode and uncertain about its strategic directions, IBM supported more than a half dozen operating systems as well as dual desktop hardware platforms with PowerPC and X86.

IBM had set up IBM Vietnam in Hanoi in 1995. The operation provided sales and marketing support to distributors and dealers as well as customers. They had also appointed their dealers as service providers for hardware repair and support.

UNISYS

In 1994, Unisys was the ninth largest systems and PC vendor in the world. Unisys manufactured and marketed computer-based networked information systems and software. The company also offered related services, such as systems integration and IT outsourcing. As such, its strategy was to provide a full spectrum of services and solutions. It sought to develop leading edge hardware and technology in open systems.

Unisys specialized in providing business-critical solutions based on open information networks for organizations that operated in transaction-intensive environments. In 1992, Unisys generated 49% of its revenue from the United States, 30% from Europe, 9% from Canada, 5% from Asia-Pacific, and 7% from Japan. For international projects, local resources were normally relied upon. Vertically, Unisys focused on airlines, public sectors, financial services, and telecommunications. Horizontally, they focused on networking and online transaction processing. Unisys had also established a representative office in Vietnam. With 15 marketing staff based in the country, it appeared that they had adopted an aggressive strategy in Vietnam. In 1995, they installed their equipment for the banking sector in the country for SWIFT (Society for Worldwide Interbank Financial Telecommunications) transactions. Unisys was targeting to set up an operation (subsidiary) in Vietnam in 1996.

COMPAQ

In 1995, Compaq completed yet another record year with sales of US$10.9 billion, up 51% from the previous year. Net income grew by a healthy 88% to reach US$867 million. As the leading manufacturer of PC systems (desktops, portables, and servers), Compaq was currently positioned to tackle both the consumer and corporate computing markets and was now a major player in the commercial server market.

The reasons for Compaq's success to date included aggressive expansion of distribution channels, efficient manufacturing, ability to bring new products and technologies into the market early, ability to deliver top-quality products, and ability to include added-value features in its products.

Hewlett-Packard Businesses in Southeast Asia

THE HEWLETT-PACKARD COMPANY

In January 1939, in a garage in Palo Alto, California, 2 graduates from nearby Stanford University, William Hewlett and David Packard, set up a company called the Hewlett-Packard (HP) Company with an initial capital of US$538. They marketed their first product (invented by Bill), a resistance-capacity audio oscillator. HP's initial emphasis was on instrumentation. It was not until 1972 that the company finally acknowledged that it was in the computer field, with the introduction of its first business computer, the HP3000.

In 1995, HP was a sprawling corporate giant with annual sales in excess of US$25 billion and about 90,000 employees worldwide. It was involved principally in the manufacture, supply, marketing, and distribution of computer-based products, test and measurement products, medical and analytical products, electronic components and Information Technology related service and support. In 1985, HP was ranked by a *Fortune* magazine survey as 1 of the 2 most admired companies in America. In 1995, the bulk of the company's business, a good 76.6% of the net revenue, came from computational products and services.

Years ago, Bill Hewlett and Dave Packard developed a set of management objectives for the company. With only slight modification, these became the corporate objectives of HP and were first published in 1957. These objectives gave a clear idea as to how the company viewed itself and its position in society. The HP Statement of Corporate Objectives (October 1986) is shown in **Exhibit 11**.

Exhibit 11

Objectives: Hewlett-Packard

> a. **Profit.** To achieve sufficient profit to finance our growth and to achieve corporate objectives through self-generated resources.
>
> b. **Customers.** To provide products and services of the highest quality and the greatest possible value to customers, thereby gaining and holding their respect and loyalty.
>
> c. **Fields of Interest.** To participate in those fields of interest that build upon our technology and customer base, that offer opportunities for continuing growth, and that enable us to make a needed and profitable contribution.
>
> d. **Growth.** To let growth be limited only by our profits and ability to develop and produce innovative products that satisfy real customer needs.
>
> e. **People.** To help HP people share in the company's success which they make possible; to provide employment security based on their performance; to ensure them a safe and pleasant work environment; to recognize their individual achievements; and to help them gain a sense of satisfaction and accomplishment from their work.
>
> f. **Management.** To foster initiative and creativity by allowing the individual great freedom of action in attaining well-defined objectives.
>
> g. **Citizenship.** To honor our obligations to society by being an economic, intellectual, and social asset to each nation and each community in which we operate.

These corporate objectives formed the basis of what was known as "The HP Way," which sought to create a work environment geared to produce capable, innovative, well-trained, and enthusiastic people who could give their best to the company. HP's guiding strategic principle had been to provide customers with devices superior to any competitive offering in performance, quality, and overall value. To this day, HP corporate strategy was pursued with 3 measures in mind:

1. Getting the highest return out of the company's most important asset, its people.

2. Getting the best output from a given technology.

3. Giving the customer the best performance for price paid.

Around the world, Hewlett-Packard was organized broadly into several strategic business units as shown in **Exhibit 12**. Each business unit was represented at HP's top management and was more or less run as an independent entity within HP.

Exhibit 12

Strategic Business Units: Hewlett-Packard

> a. **Computer Systems Organization (CSO)** which manufactured and marketed HP minicomputers and workstations.
>
> b. **Computer Products Organization (CPO)** which manufactured and marketed PCs, PC peripherals, and networking products.
>
> c. **Tests and Measurements Organization (TMO)** which manufactured, marketed, and serviced test and measurement products.
>
> d. **Analytical Products Group (APG)** which manufactured, marketed, and serviced analytical chemical compound products.
>
> e. **Medical Products Group (MPG)** which manufactured, marketed, and serviced products, such as defibrillators, ECG, and monitoring equipment, that were used in the medical industry.
>
> f. **Components Group** which manufactured and marketed opto-electronic components.
>
> g. **Worldwide Customer Support Organization (WCSO)** which provided services for HP's computer-related business (i.e., the CSO and CPO).

HP'S MARKET POSITION AND CAPABILITIES

HP had established its presence in countries like Hong Kong, Singapore, Japan, Taiwan, and Korea for more than 25 years. It had extensive experience in entering into emerging Asian markets such as China, Indonesia, and the Philippines. Though a subsidiary of an American company, HP Southeast Asia had a largely Asian management team. They shared similar norms, practices, beliefs, customs, and languages with many local markets. Nevertheless, HP was still an American company with its own stringent code of business and the requirement to comply with American laws.

HP had, over the years, built up many major customer accounts, some of which were multinational corporations with offices worldwide. It had developed a strong reputation and brand identity. The HP name was often synonymous with quality products and high technology, albeit at a premium price. HP could not be as aggressive in product pricing due to its higher cost structure and overhead. HP had, for many years, come up tops in many independent customer satisfaction surveys conducted by organizations such as Datapro and IDC.

HP had a large network of subsidiaries and associated companies in different countries in the Asia Pacific. It was, thus, able to source for raw materials and parts in these countries at the cheapest prices, manufacture at locations with the lowest costs, and establish an efficient distribution and warehousing network to transport products from manufacturing sites to markets.

Exhibit 13 shows some information related to the turnover and earnings of HP from 1989 to 1994. In the brutal, fast-paced world of IT, customers looked for financial stability to ensure that vendors would still be around when their projects were completed, especially for large multiyear, infrastructural projects.

HP was a diversified company and had products and services in computation, measurement, and communications. This gave it a breadth that few computer vendors could match. The autonomous units dealing with measurement, communications, and computers in the HP setup, however, often acted as separate companies and, thus, created functional silos that might not effectively leverage HP's knowledge and diversity.

Exhibit 13
Income and Earnings (1994–1989): Hewlett-Packard

	\(U.S. Dollar amounts in millions\)					
	1994	**1993**	**1992**	**1991**	**1990**	**1989**
Revenue	$24,991	$20,317	$16,410	$14,494	$13,233	$11,889
Cost of revenue	15,490	12,123	9,152	7,858	6,993	6,091
Gross profit	9,501	8,194	7,258	6,636	6,240	5,808
R&D	2,027	1,761	1,619	1,463	1,367	1,269
Mktg, gen, & admin	4,925	4,554	4,224	3,963	3,711	3,327
Operating income	2,549	1,879	1,415	1,210	1,162	1,212
Other income/exp	(126)	(96)	(79)	(83)	(106)	(61)
Pre-tax income	2,423	1,783	1,336	1,127	1,056	1,151
Income tax	824	606	449	372	317	322
Net income	1,599	1,177	887	755	739	829

Source: Salomon Brothers.

HP was the industry leader in open systems technology and solutions and it had a specialized knowledge and extensive experience in this area. HP moved into RISC Technology long before DEC, IBM, and other rivals and was now collecting the dividends. HP was strong in client/server computing involving PCs, workstations, and large systems and servers. HP opened up its proprietary HP3000 systems and it had become a whirlwind of success.

While HP served a cross-section of the IT industry, it had in particular established significant presence in 3 industry groups: manufacturing, telecommunications, and financial services. In addition, HP also had large installed bases in industries such as retail, hospitality, government, and health services. In manufacturing, HP was the dominant worldwide supplier of UNIX systems accounting for 45% of this market. HP had a wide range of customers in the manufacturing sector, which remained HP's largest vertical market.

HP sought to use the distribution channel as a means to support its customers. In 1988, HP sold its products primarily through a direct sales force. HP foresaw the rapid fall in gross margins as standardization, volumes, and competitiveness increased, and so developed 2 distinct sales strategies, 1 for volume sales where sales was indirect and took place through sales channels, and the other direct, providing value sales to large HP target accounts around the world. While many high-tech companies viewed distribution channels as their customers, HP had identified end users as its customers. HP recognized that the computer industry had become a demand-driven (pull) environment, and HP had sought to create demand for its products among end users. HP tracked very closely consumer buying preferences and responded quickly to changes in the market.

HP'S BUSINESSES IN SOUTHEAST ASIA

Hewlett-Packard Southeast Asia had its headquarters in Singapore with fully owned subsidiaries in Singapore, Malaysia, and Thailand. In Indonesia, the Philippines, and Brunei, HP appointed distributors. In addition, HP had a joint venture in Indonesia with its distributor, Berca, called HPSI which was primarily an IT services company.

In Southeast Asia, HP's Worldwide Customer Support Organization (WCSO) was represented by the Southeast Asia (SEA) Customer Support Organization, whose role was to provide services and support in satisfying customers' needs in financing, implementing and operating their IT operations. The SEA Customer Support Organization managed the following product lines:

PL72	Hardware Support for Computer Systems and Networks
PL3D	Software Support for Computer Systems
PL71	Support for Personal Computers and Peripherals
PL6N	Outsourcing Services
PL6L	Network Integration Services

Product Lines 72, 3D, and 71 were the traditional maintenance services that HP had provided for buyers and users of its computer systems and was primarily focused on post-sales maintenance. In recent years, these businesses had experienced declining growth rate. Prices of computer products continued to drop, even as their performance improved. This trend was especially prevalent in the hardware maintenance business. Support expenditure, typically capped at a percentage of total IT expenditure, was thus greatly affected by this trend.

Product Lines 6N and 6L were the newer businesses WCSO had set up to counter the slower growth of the traditional maintenance businesses. They required higher investment and typically had lower profitability. The selling model for these product lines was also different, requiring more direct selling as it was not always possible to leverage support revenues off computational product sales as was more often the case in the traditional maintenance businesses.

CURRENT STATUS OF HP'S BUSINESS IN VIETNAM

Since the lifting of the U.S. embargo on February 3, 1994, different business units in HP had taken initial and ad hoc steps to develop their businesses in Vietnam in response to the current changes taking place in the country. The HP business units Customer Systems Organization (CSO), Computer Products Organization (CPO), and Test and Measurements Organization (TMO) had signed up distributors in Vietnam to distribute their products. The CSO currently had 1 main distributor, the High Performance Technology Corporation (HiPT). HiPT was 100% privately owned. One of the owners, Dr. Binh, had good contacts with the Vietnamese government. CSO was ready to appoint a second distributor (the Peregrine Group) for the south of Vietnam. TMO had also appointed a distributor, Systems Interlace, while CPO had appointed several wholesalers and resellers in Vietnam. Projected orders from these product organizations were expected to hit US$10 million at the end of October 1995. HP's computer support business, WCSO, was not represented in Vietnam in 1994.

Hewlett-Packard and its CSO distributor in Vietnam, the HiPT, officially opened a Center for Open Systems Computing Expertise in Hanoi on July 1, 1995. Its establishment was part of a formal memorandum of understanding that HP and the Ministry of Science, Technology and the Environment (MOSTE) had signed in March 1995. MOSTE was the body responsible for the promotion and development of information technology in Vietnam. The center would assist MOSTE's goal of developing a pool of qualified IT professionals to implement the Vietnam IT-2000 plan, based on the open systems concept.

Field Trip To Vietnam

In January 1995, John made a business visit to Vietnam to assess first hand the business climate and investment opportunities and to provide ideas on how WCSO in Southeast Asia should plan its overall investment strategy in Vietnam, rather than the current ad-hoc involvement of its CSO, CPO, and TMO in the Vietnamese market. The first stop was Ho Chi Minh City, a bustling city of 5 million people, 1 hour and 25 minutes from Singapore by air.

MEETING WITH DR. VO VAN MAI (MANAGING DIRECTOR OF HiPT)

Dr. Vo Van Mai was the Managing Director of High-Performance Technology (HiPT), HP's distributor in Vietnam. He was educated in Hungary. Dr. Mai expected the IT market in Vietnam to hit US$300 million by the year 2000. The market size had doubled each year for the past few years and Dr. Mai expected the IT market to grow even more rapidly in the next 2 years. Currently, IT took the form of mainly personal computers (PCs) with some limited local area networks. Vietnam, being an IT greenfield, looked likely to adopt client-server technology in a big way, bypassing legacy and proprietary systems common in most developing and developed countries. The PC brands available in Vietnam included Compaq, HP, ACER, Wearnes, AST, Digital, Unisys, and IBM.

Dr. Mai felt that the most attractive segments of the IT market would be finance, utilities, telecommunications, petrochemicals, and airlines. Currently, within Vietnam, the primary means of data transmission was using phone lines and modems. Between Hanoi and Ho Chi Minh City, more sophisticated and higher bandwidth transmission methods were available through fiber optic links and X.25.

IBM had representative offices in Hanoi and Ho Chi Minh City, with staff strength of 10. They had 6 to 7 distributors in Vietnam, and it was known that they had applied for a license to operate a service operation in Vietnam.

Dr. Mai's conclusions were that it would be 3 to 4 years before the Vietnamese market became really significant in IT revenues. He felt that the next 2 years would be critical in establishing a presence and building relationships and awareness of products and services. Obtaining budgets for IT expenditure was still a problem. The government's IT-2000 plan, however, was a clear indication of the government's commitment to IT.

MEETING WITH ROSS NICHOLSON (GENERAL MANAGER OF DHL WORLDWIDE EXPRESS)

Nicholson felt that he had access to good market information as DHL had been operating in Vietnam since 1988. DHL worked through the Vietnam Post Office as the Vietnamese government still controlled the provision of mail and postal services tightly. Nicholson was assigned to Vietnam as a Technical Advisor in April 1994. He told John that things had not boomed as expected since the American embargo was lifted. Some obstacles like chaotic taxation laws and investment risks still plagued potential investors. In the short term, the fluctuating Mexican peso incident was likely to affect investor outlook, especially in emerging economies like Vietnam. In his opinion, the Asians, especially Japanese, were moving in very quickly. Hotels in Hanoi were usually full of Japanese.

In Nicholson's opinion, the finance industry had the highest prospects for growth in the immediate future. Presently, agriculture was DHL's biggest customer for the provision of shipping facilities. In time, more technologically advanced production activity would take place. DHL would then have the opportunity to sell logistics services to these new entrants, leveraging on their long experience in the Vietnamese market. DHL would like to get itself integrated into these companies, which would be very happy to listen because they were in startup mode.

Nicholson believed that there would not be anything spectacular until 2 to 3 years later. He cited the lack of skilled IT personnel as 1 of the obstacles to IT growth. Still, he felt that it was well worth the investment of establishing a presence in Vietnam now, so that when the boom came, companies like DHL would be well positioned to capitalize on the ensuing growth. DHL currently used a stand-alone PC for its IT needs. This was certainly not suitable for the anticipated growth. Nicholson intended to upgrade to a nationwide system comprising 2 HP9000 E45s.

MEETING WITH DR. TRUENE GIA BINH (MANAGING DIRECTOR OF FPT)

The Corporation for Financing and Promoting Technology (FPT) was a wholly government-owned company incorporated under the auspices of the Ministry of Science, Technology and the Environment (MOSTE). Dr. Binh, the Managing Director of FPT and son-in-law of a prominent general in Vietnam, elaborated on the difference in status between a representative office and an operating office. Basically, a representative office could only acquire goods required for the operation of the office. It was not allowed to receive payment for any products or services rendered but could provide marketing and support services as part of its distributor support service. Commenting on the attractiveness of the IT market, Dr. Binh felt that the financial sector would be very attractive due to the high growth prospects and the prominence placed on it by the Vietnamese economy in the next 3 to 4 years.

MEETING WITH HAI CHAO DUY (DIRECTOR OF TECHNICAL SERVICES AND OPERATIONS, VIETNAM MOBILE TELECOMMUNICATION SERVICES)

Hai Chao Duy expressed that he looked forward to a long-term relationship with HP. He mentioned the tremendous opportunities in Vietnam Mobile Telecom Services (VMS) to build networks. Today, VMS supplied cellular services to 9,000 subscribers in Ho Chi Minh City and Hanoi. The IT projects needed to facilitate the provision of cellular services were in operation, transmission, business support, finance, end-user computing, and e-mailing. He also mentioned that the next project would involve some management system software for the telecommunication network.

MEETING WITH NGUYEN TRANG (CHAIRMAN OF HCMC COMPUTER ASSOCIATION)

Nguyen Trang was a very influential personality in IT and was the Chairman of the Ho Chi Minh City Computer Association. The Vietnam IT-2000 plan would be driven centrally from Hanoi. The city also had a board that would oversee the implementation of the IT-2000 plan. That plan had been approved, and Nguyen revealed details regarding 2 other projects.

One project was IT applications for municipal and government administration in the areas of transportation and traffic control, financial control, industrial administration, land property, city planning, trade services, and manpower development.

The other project was governmental IT infrastructural development. This included the setup of units such as the Center for System Analysis and Design and the Center for Manpower Development, and projects such as the feasibility study for Ho Chi Minh EDI, a museum for IT development, and an Internet gateway for Vietnam. In his estimate, the market size of the Vietnamese IT industry would be US$500 million by the year 2000.

Market Entry Decisions

Vietnam represented a promising market with untapped potential. There were, however, risks. Despite all the recent rapid progress toward a free economy, the basic political structure in Vietnam had not changed. Although Vietnam had recently adopted an open-door policy, economic development in the country was only beginning to take off and the pace and direction of reform was still uncertain. Although economic growth was robust, the economy recently suffered from high inflation, and the dong was expected to depreciate against the U.S. dollar. There were gaps in Vietnam's legal framework with 2 instances where business firms were subjected to different interpretations of the law by authorities at different levels in the government, which resulted in different applications of the same law. This had caused uncertainties and delay in the business setup.

Although the information technology (IT) market in Vietnam had potential, the market was currently small and market growth was uncertain. HPAP management needed to weigh the positive and negative factors before deciding if the company should enter the Vietnam market in a more strategic manner.

POSSIBLE MODES OF ENTRY

The following are some possible entry strategies available to HP to set up its presence in Vietnam if it decides to enter the market.

Majority Joint Venture with Local Partner

HP could use the joint venture strategy to enter the Vietnam market. In Southeast Asia, a HP joint venture existed in Indonesia where an agreement was entered into with Berca, a distributor, to set up a service company, HPSI. Berca retained the primary responsibility for the sale of HP products, while HPSI was charged with providing HP services to the marketplace. This option required less initial investment, compared to the direct presence strategy, thus reducing the risk involved. A local joint-venture partner could be a valuable resource where "guanxi" was vital for doing business.

Distribution (Independent Partner)

HP could appoint 1 or more independent organizations as distributors, as well as service and support providers. In the initial years, it was likely that products from each business unit would be sold only through 1 distributor, although the same distributor might be chosen for the products of more than 1 business unit.

This strategy offered a quick start-up for HP and was especially suited for the off-the-shelf, mass-market, plug-and-play type of products offered by CPO. To be successful, HP needed to commit resources to train and develop the distributor to build up their service capability. The disadvantage of this strategy was that it would result in the cultivation of future competitors for support services. Where services in many other markets were concerned, HP had not found a way to provide support to its mission-sensitive and mission-critical end users through channel members and still maintain the high quality and responsiveness that customers required. In addition, the margins on services were high and services contributed significantly to HP's profit. The profit was likely to drop if HP allowed its channels to sign support contracts directly with the end users.

Distribution (Ex-HP Employee Start-Up)

A modified form of the entry strategy was to appoint a start-up company founded by ex-HP employees as its distributor. These ex-HP employees could be trusted to deliver quality service. In the future, this company would probably be more obliged to pay off the goodwill shown by HP in giving it the opportunity to be HP's service provider in Vietnam. When HP decided to establish a direct presence in Vietnam, the former employees could also be rehired as key managers in the new subsidiary.

Cooperative Venture/ Franchising

Investment in the form of a cooperative venture was also viable. HP could initially franchise the support services and provide advisory services to a partner on how to establish and manage a support business. HP could act as a supplier of spares to its Vietnamese partner. HP would not have to take the risks incurred in direct investment, and trade ties could still be forged because of the special relationship with a local firm. At present, Singapore firms like Rothmans of Pall Mall (cigarettes) and Cold Storage (retail supermarkets) had established such ventures with Vietnam firms Agrex Saigon and Saigon-Intershop, respectively.

Direct Presence

HP could have a direct presence in Vietnam by setting up a subsidiary or representative office to provide marketing, sales support, and management services. This strategy required the largest investment and commitment of resources. It also offered maximum control and flexibility and the best payoff. HP's direct presence in the market would allow it to keep in touch with customers. HP would gain invaluable access to markets and customers. To reduce the risk, uncertainty, and investment requirement, it was possible to start off with limited staff on a smaller scale and increase staffing as required.

The Body Shop International PLC: Anita Roddick, OBE

Ellie A. Fogarty, Joyce P. Vincelette, and Thomas L. Wheelen

I am not taking a back seat. I have no intention of marginalizing myself from this business as a nonworking director. I just can't see myself retiring. I will still do what I do best—that's marketing, styling, image, store design and so on.

—Comment from Anita Roddick on the prospect of handing over the reins at the company she founded.[1]

Asked what her new role as Co-Chairman would actually mean, she said: "I have no bloody idea."[2]

On May 12, 1998, Anita Roddick announced that she would cede her post of Chief Executive Officer of The Body Shop International PLC to Patrick Gournay. She admitted she was bored with basic retail disciplines such as distribution. Anita would rather spend time with the Dalai Lama, whom she met the day before stepping down. Anita moved alongside her husband Gordon as Executive Cochairman. She said titles are meaningless and "tomorrow's job is exactly the same as yesterday's."[3]

Patrick Gournay, an experienced international business manager, had worked 26 years with Groupe Danone, the multiproduct food group headquartered in Paris with sales of £8 billion. He was the Executive Vice President of Danone's North and South American division, with strategic responsibilities for 8 companies in 5 countries.[4] Gournay had never heard of The Body Shop until he was approached by headhunters (executive recruiters). He met Anita and Gordon to ask them if they really wanted to change." It was important to me to establish that Anita in particular was ready for a change, for someone to come in and take responsibility for the business. We spent a lot of time talking about that and the conclusion is clear."[5] Although he admitted he was not an activist, he realized that The Body Shop "is not just an average cosmetics company, it is something unique."[6]

Gournay was granted options of over 2.5 million shares that may be exercised at £123 British. Half the performance-related options were exercisable between May 2001 and May 2008. The other half were exercisable between May 2003 and May 2008. These options may be exercised only if normalized earnings per share over any 3 consecutive years exceed growth in the retail prices index for the same period by at least 4%.[7]

On July 14, 1998 (Bastille Day), Gournay began his work at The Body Shop. He planned to focus on defining the roles and processes within the company. He felt the operations needed to be made more flexible and more innovative. Gournay thought the expansion program should continue with South America as an obvious starting point, based on his previous experience. His long-term targets included India and China. He and Anita agreed that due to high store rents, more emphasis should be placed on direct selling operations, perhaps even replacing some stores with this effective new method. Gournay's future plans included tackling the issue of extending the Body Shop brand. Anita was interested in directing that expansion to include leisure services such as weekend retreats.

Also in 1998, The Body Shop shareholders approved a joint venture with Bellamy Retail Group LLC to manage the operations of The Body Shop, Inc., in the United States, giving the owner up to 51% of the company at a future date.

Anita admitted that several previous senior appointments from outside failed to work. But she promised this time would be different. "It will have to work. There is no option."[8]

Anita Roddick: The Entrepreneur

> I certainly had no ambition to start a big international company. I did not want to change the world; I just wanted to survive and be able to feed my children.
>
> —Anita Roddick, OBE

In 1942, Anita Perellas was born to Italian immigrant parents and grew up working in the family-owned cafe, the Clifton Cafe, in Littlehampton, West Sussex, England. She wanted to be an actress, but her mother, Gilda, wanted her to be a teacher. Her mother told her to "be special" [and] "be anything but mediocre."[9] She received a degree in education from Newton Park College of Education at Bath. In 1963, her senior year, she received a 3-month scholarship to Israel, which enabled her to do research for her thesis, "The British Mandate in Palestine."

After graduation, she taught for a brief time at a local junior school. She then accepted a position in Paris with the *International Herald Tribune* in its library. Her next position was with the United Nations International Labour Organization in Geneva. She worked on women's rights in Third World countries. She said of her United Nations experience that she learned "the extraordinary power of networking, but I was appalled by the money that was squandered on red tape and all the wining and dining that was going on with no apparent check on expenses. I found it offensive to see all of those fat cats discussing problems in the Third World over 4-course lunches at the United Nations Club."[10]

With the money saved from her United Nations position, she decided to satisfy her quest to travel. She boarded a boat bound for Tahiti via the Panama Canal. She went on to visit Africa. During her travels, she developed a deep interest in and curiosity about the beauty practices of women that she encountered. She focused on the effectiveness and simplicity of these beauty practices.

After returning to England, she met Gordon Roddick at El Cubana, her family-owned club. He was an adventurer who loved to travel and write poetry. They got married in Reno, Nevada, on a trip to San Francisco to visit friends in 1970. After the birth of their 2 daughters, Justine in 1969 and Samantha in 1971, they decided to settle down. They purchased a Victorian hotel, St. Winifred Hotel, in Littlehampton, which required substantial renovations. They resided in part of the hotel while renovating the guest quarters. The next Roddick enterprise was the Paddington's restaurant in the center of Littlehampton. They borrowed £10,000 from the bank to lease and renovate the restaurant.[11] This was a time-consuming enterprise for the couple. They had no social or family life while running the Paddington and residing in and staffing the hotel, St. Winifred. Anita said, "We did not have time for each other and our marriage was beginning to suffer as a result, exacerbated by the fact we had no privacy; being at St. Winifred's was like living in a commune with a lot of elderly people. And despite all the leisure time we had sacrificed, we were not making much money. All we were doing was surviving."[12] Paddington became the most popular place in the town, especially on a Saturday night. Gordon crawling into bed one night said, "This is killing us," . . . [and] "I can't cope with it any more. Let's pack it in."[13]

In 1976, Gordon and Anita agreed that Gordon should fulfill his dream of riding horseback across the Americas from Buenos Aires to New York City. The 5,300-mile horseback trek would take about 2 years to complete. Anita said, "I have admired people who want to be remarkable, who follow their beliefs and passions, who make grand gestures."[14] Anita wanted a real home life, which as entrepreneurs they had never had, and she wanted to spend some time with her children, who were 4 and 6. She needed a business to survive and feed the children, so they decided she needed to open a shop.

The Body Shop

Anita decided to sell naturally based cosmetics in 5 sizes so that her customers had a choice. She felt that "people tend not to trust their gut instincts enough, especially about those things that irritate them, but the fact is that if something irritates you it is a pretty good indication that there are other people who feel the same. Irritation was a great source of energy and creativity."[15] She had been dissatisfied with the purchase of body lotion because most stores sold only 1 size.[16] Her dissatisfaction led her to question why she could not buy cosmetics by weight or bulk, like groceries or vegetables, and why a customer could not buy a small size of a cream or lotion to try it out before buying a big bottle. These were simple enough questions, but at the time there were no sensible answers.[17] She and Gordon discussed her concept for a shop where she could sell cosmetic products in a cheap container and in different sizes. He liked the concept. Anita decided to sell products made from "natural ingredients." The environmental green movement had not yet started.

She obtained a £4,000 bank loan (approximately $6,000) to open the first Body Shop at 22 Kensington Gardens, Brighton. The shop opened Saturday, March 26, 1976, at 9:00 A.M. By noon, Anita had to call Gordon and ask him to come to the shop and work. At 6:00 P.M., they closed the shop and counted the daily receipts of exactly £130. She had a goal of £300 of weekly receipts to cover her living costs.[18]

Just before she opened the shop, she had encountered opposition over the shop name, The Body Shop. The name came from the generic name for auto repair shops in the United States. Two nearby funeral homes threatened to sue her over the shop's name. She contacted the local newspaper about the pending lawsuits. The article on her plight helped draw attention to her new shop. Based on this experience, she developed a company policy of never spending a cent on advertising.[19] It has been estimated that The Body Shop receives £2,000,000 of free publicity each year based on the company's and Anita's position on key social problems. The shop's logo was designed by a local art student at a cost of £25.

In developing the design of The Body Shop, Anita based it on "a Second World War mentality (shortages, utility goods, and rationing) imposed by sheer necessity and the fact that I had no money. But I had a very clear image in my mind of the kind of style I wanted to create: I wanted it to look a bit like a country store in a spaghetti western."[20]

The first products—all 25 of them—were composed of natural ingredients that Anita could gather and mix together herself rather inexpensively. The cheapest bottles she could find were those used by hospitals to collect urine samples and she offered to fill any bottle the customer would bring in. The labels were plain and simple, as they still are today, and handwritten. The store also carried knickknacks to fill space, including cards, books, and jewelry; sometimes this merchandise accounted for 60% of the turnover. She developed loyal clients.

Perhaps because Anita sprayed Strawberry Essence on the sidewalks in the hopes that potential customers would follow it, the first store did well. After a successful summer, Anita

Exhibit 1

A Timeline: The Body Shop

1976	Anita Roddick opens the first branch of The Body Shop in Brighton on England's south coast.
1977	The first franchise of The Body Shop opens in Bognor Regis, England.
1978	The first branch opens outside the United Kingdom in Brussels, Belgium.
1984	The Body Shop goes public. With a placing of 95p ($1.38), shares close at £1.65 ($2.39) on the first day of dealing.
1985	The Body Shop runs its first in-shop campaign, "Save the Whale" with Greenpeace.
1986	The Body Shop launches its cosmetic range, called Colourings, and Mostly Men, a skin care line for men.
1987	The Body Shop establishes its first Trade Not Aid initiative in Nepal.
1988	The first U.S. branch of The Body Shop opens in New York.
	Soapworks, a soap-making plant for The Body Shop, opens in Easterhouse, Scotland.
	Queen awards Anita Roddick the Order of the British Empire (OBE).
1989	One million people sign The Body Shop's petition to "Stop the Burning" in the Amazon Rainforest.
	Anita receives the United Nations' Global 500 Environment Award.
1990	2.6 million people sign The Body Shop's "Against Animal Testing" petition.
	The Body Shop launches its Eastern European Drive of volunteers to renovate 3 orphanages in Halaucesti, Romania.
	The Body Shop opens in Tokyo, Japan.
1991	*The Big Issue*, a paper sold by and for the homeless, is launched by The Body Shop in London.
	Anita is awarded the World Vision Award by the Centre for World Development Education in recognition of Trade Not Aid initiative.
	The Body Shop marks Amnesty International's 30th anniversary with a campaign to increase membership.
1992	The Body Shop's voter registration drive in the United States signs up more than 33,000 voters.
	The Company publishes the results of the first environmental audit, *The Green Book*, in the United Kingdom.
	The Body Shop opens its first American community-based shop on 125th Street, Harlem, New York.
1993	The Body Shop opens its 1,000th shop.
	The American "Reuse/Refill/Recycle" campaign increases awareness of the refill and recycling services available at The Body Shop.
	The Body Shop USA joins with other corporations in signing the CERES Principles, an environmental code of conduct.
	The Body Shop USA joins forces with the Ms. Foundation to support the first annual Take Our Daughters to Work Day.
	The Body Shop USA is honored by the NAACP for excellence in minority economic development.
	"Protect & Respect" project, on AIDS education and awareness, is launched.
1994	The Body Shop launches its biggest ever international campaign in 30 markets and more than 900 shops to gain public support influencing the U.N. Convention on International Trade in Endangered Species to enforce regulations governing trade in endangered species.
1995	The Body Shop introduces The Body Shop Direct home selling operation.
1996	The first shop in the Philippines opens.
	First social audit published.
	The Body Shop is recognized in the 1996 PR Week award categories for Best International Campaign and Best Overall PR Campaign in the United Kingdom for the Ogoni people of Nigeria campaign.
	Largest ever petition on animal testing—over 4 million signatures from 16 countries—was presented to the European Parliament and Commission in Brussels in November.
1997	Created an international Franchisee Advisory Board.
	Won the Retail Week Store Design of the Year Award for its new format stores.
1998	With Amnesty International, launched Make Your Mark on May 11 in Atlanta, Georgia, with the Dalai Lama.
	Published *Naked Body*, a 50-page magazine featuring articles on hemp, beauty tips, a photo of a woman's naked lower body, and an interview with a London prostitute.

Source: The Body Shop, "This Is the Body Shop" (November 1994), pp. 3–4, and author's additions.

decided to open a second store in Chichester and approached the bank for a £4,000 loan. She was turned down because she had no track record. So, she turned to a friend, Ian McGlinn, who owned a local garage. Ian received a 50% interest in the company for his investment.[21] In 1998, he owned 45,666,768 (23.5%) of the ordinary shares. The Roddicks owed 48,237,136 shares. Ian played no role in the management of the company. Anita felt, "To succeed you have to believe in something with such a passion that it becomes a reality.[22] This was 1 of the 2 principal reasons for the company's initial success. The other was that Anita had to survive while Gordon was away. **Exhibit 1** shows a timeline of the key highlights of the company.

Franchising as a Growth Strategy

A friend's daughter, Chris Green, wanted to open her own shop in Hove. The Roddicks agreed and thought it was a great idea. Their only interest was in her selling their products. There were no fees or contracts. Another friend, Aidre, wanted to open a shop with her parents in Bognor Regis. They gave her the same deal.

Gordon had returned home before the 2 shops were opened. He could see the potential of the business to grow, but no bank wanted to lend them money.

Gordon hired a lawyer to develop a franchising contract. The formula was based on a license to use The Body Shop name and to sell its products, and the franchisee would put up the money. In 1978, the first franchise outside the United Kingdom was opened in Brussels. The franchise fee was £300.[23] Women owned all the initial franchises. Anita felt that "men were good at the science and vocabulary of business, at talking about economic theory and profits and loss figures (some women are, too, of course). But I could also see that women were better at dealing with people, caring, and being passionate about what they are doing."[24]

During this time, the company was developing its own style of "respond[ing] to needs rather than creating them."[25] The company was run in an informal way as an extended big family. Anita understood the concept of developing a niche around a competitive advantage. She said, "A true key to success is knowing what features set you apart from the competitor."[26] And also, "We had stuck closely to a policy of being open and honest about our products, and it was paying dividends among our customers who were increasingly irritated by the patently dishonest advertising of the cosmetics industry. Women in the 1980s were less and less inclined to fall for the 'buy this mixture of oil and water and you will be a movie star' pitch dreamed up in the expensive offices of advertising agencies."[27]

By 1982, the Roddicks were exercising much stricter control over what could and could not be done in the shop. They had learned, from experience, that it was absolutely essential to maintain a strong identity.[28] The company opened shops at the rate of 2 a month. They had shops in Iceland, Denmark, Finland, Holland, and Ireland.

During these early franchising years, the biggest mistake management made was offering 3 choices of shop styles to franchisees—dark green, dark mahogany stain, or stripped pine. Anita quickly recognized that the shops looked different, and as such the shops lost their distinctiveness. So she persuaded all the shops to return to the dark green.[29]

Anita kept strict control over the franchising process. At times, 5,000 franchise applications were in process. The franchise process included a home visit, a personality test, and an assessment of the applicant's attitude toward people and the environment. The process could take 3 years to complete. In the final interview with Anita, she was known to ask unexpected questions ("How would you like to die?" "Who is your favorite heroine in literature?") This type of applicant process could ensure that the franchisee would adhere to the principles and image of The Body Shop. After being selected to own a franchise, owners underwent extensive training on products, store operations, and merchandising techniques.

In 1985, The Body Shop Training School opened. The curriculum focused on human development and consciousness-raising. Anita said, "Conventional retailers trained for a sale; we

Exhibit 2

Shop Locations by Regions: The Body Shop[1]

	Number of Shops			First Shop Opening
	February 1998	February 1997	February 1996	
Europe				
Austria	17	17	15	1979
Belgium	18	18	18	1978
Cyprus	3	3	3	1983
Denmark	19	20	19	1981
Eire	11	11	10	1981
Finland	24	23	21	1981
France	23	32	34	1982
Germany	72	67	60	1983
Gibraltar	1	1	1	1988
Greece	51	46	44	1979
Holland	50	51	50	1982
Iceland	3	2	2	1980
Italy	53	50	46	1984
Luxembourg	2	2	2	1991
Malta	3	1	1	1987
Norway	24	24	21	1985
Portugal	12	11	9	1986
Spain	65	63	59	1986
Sweden	48	44	42	1979
Switzerland	28	28	27	1983
Total Shops	**527**	**514**	**484**	
United Kingdom				
Total Shops	**263**	**256**	**252**	1976
Asia				
Bahrain	2	2	2	1985
Brunei	3	3	3	1993
Hong Kong	16	13	11	1984
Indonesia	17	13	8	1990
Japan	116	87	58	1990
Korea	5	0	0	1997
Kuwait	9	8	3	1986
Macau	3	2	2	1993
Malaysia	25	22	21	1984
Oman	4	4	2	1986
Philippines	7	3	0	1996
Qatar	1	1	1	1987
Saudi Arabia	33	25	21	1987
Singapore	16	15	12	1983
Taiwan	34	21	14	1988
Thailand	12	9	8	1993
UAE	5	5	4	1983
Total Shops	**308**	**233**	**170**	

(*Continued*)

Exhibit 2
Shop Locations by Regions: The Body Shop (*continued*)

	Number of Shops			First Shop
	February 1998	February 1997	February 1996	Opening
Australia and New Zealand				
Australia	62	59	57	1983
New Zealand	14	12	11	1989
Total Shops	**76**	**71**	**68**	
America Excluding USA				
Antigua	1	1	1	1987
Bahamas	3	3	3	1985
Bermuda	1	2	2	1987
Canada	119	119	115	1980
Cayman Islands	1	1	1	1989
Mexico	5	4	4	1993
Total Shops	**130**	**130**	**126**	
USA				
Total Shops	**290**	**287**	**273**	1988
Grand Total Shops	**1,594**	**1,491**	**1,373**	

Note:
1. The Company shops (1998) are located as follows:
   - USA 210, UK 67, Singapore 16, France 15
   - Number of countries: 47
   - Number of languages company traded in: 24

Source: The Body Shop, *1998* and *1997 Annual Reports*, pp. 68 and 48.

trained for knowledge. They trained with an eye on the balance sheet; we trained with an eye on the soul."[30] The courses centered on "educating" the participant, not training. In the customer care course, the teacher "encouraged the staff to treat customers as potential friends, to say hello, smile, make eye contact and to offer advice if it was wanted, to thank them and always to invite them back."[31] She viewed money spent on staff training as an investment and not as an expense.

Franchisees had mixed feelings over developments at The Body Shop to pursue direct selling at home parties through Body Shop Direct and sales of products over the Internet. Some felt threatened and wanted to sell back their stores. They felt customers would bypass their shops and order on the Web. Others felt these new distribution channels would help them rather than take sales away.

In 1998, The Body Shop had over 1,594 shops in 47 countries (see **Exhibit 2**) and traded in 24 languages worldwide. The Body Shop expected to open 70 new stores in 1999, almost all of which would be franchised.[32]

Anita Roddick's Philosophy and Personal Values Translate into Corporate Culture and Citizenship

Below are some of Anita's most salient quotes on the issues of our time:

It is immoral to trade on fear. It is immoral to make women feel dissatisfied with their bodies. It is immoral to deceive a customer by making miracle claims for a product. It is immoral to use a photograph of a glowing 16-year-old to sell a (beauty) cream aimed at preventing wrinkles in a 40-year-old.[33]

I think all business practices would improve immeasurably if they were guided by "feminine" principles—qualities like love and care and intuition.[34]

I honestly believe I would not have succeeded if I had been taught about business.[35]

We communicate with passion, and passion persuades.[36]

I learned there was nothing more important to life than love and work.[37]

Passion persuades, and by God I was passionate about what I was selling.[38]

In a society in which politicians no longer lead by example, ethical conduct is unfashionable, and the media does not give people real information on what is happening in the world, what fascinates me is the concept of turning our shops into centers of education.[39]

You can be proud to work for The Body Shop and boy, does that have an effect on morale and motivation.[40]

I have never been able to separate Body Shop values from my personal values.[41]

I think the leadership of a company should encourage the next generation not just to follow, but to overtake.[42]

When you take the high moral road, it is difficult for anyone to object without sounding like a fool.[43]

Whenever we wanted to persuade our staff to support a particular project we always tried to break their hearts.[44]

You have to look at leadership through the eyes of the followers and you have to live the message. What I have learned is that people become motivated when you guide them to the source of their own power and when you make heroes out of employees who personify what you want to see in the organization.[45]

I do not believe women have a chance in hell of achieving their desired status and power in business within the foreseeable future. My daughters might see it, but I won't.[46]

If you have a company with itsy-bitsy vision, you have an itsy-bitsy company.[47]

The thought that every day might be my last, and the desire to make the most of every moment, drives me on.[48]

These were the statements of a unique woman who had a strong personal value system that she clearly articulated. She saw herself as a concerned citizen of the world, who continuously searched and developed solutions for its problems; a leader in the green political movement; a very successful business leader; a spokesperson for those without a voice in the world arena; a wife; a mother; and a daughter. She served the needs of the underprivileged and the environment. Anita was a trader. She said, "I am not rushing around the world as some kind of loony do-gooder; first and foremost I am a trader looking for a trade."[49]

In 1988, Anita was knighted by Queen Elizabeth into the Order of the British Empire (OBE).

United States Market

HISTORY

By 1987, the company received about 10,000 letters from the United States inquiring about franchising opportunities and asking when stores would be opened so they could purchase products.

Before opening the first U.S. store, the Roddicks negotiated for the trademark to The Body Shop. Two companies, owned by the Saunders and Short families, held the rights between them to "The Body Shop" name. Their trademark covered the United States and

Japan, which represented 40% of the world's consumers. Gordon negotiated to buy the rights in both countries for $3,500,000.

The first shop was opened in New York on Broadway and 8th Street on July 1, 1988. A few weeks before opening, there was much questioning whether The Body Shop could succeed in the United States without advertising. A Harvard Business School professor was quoted in the *Wall Street Journal* saying that the company needed, "at minimum," a major launch advertising campaign. Anita had the quote reprinted on a postcard with her response: "I'll never hire anyone from the Harvard Business School."[50]

The first shop was an instant success, and over the next 2 years, 13 more company-owned shops were opened. Initially the company had a hard time trying to locate in malls because it was an unknown. Management asked their mail-order customers, who lived within a 110-mile radius of a proposed shop, for a letter-writing campaign. It was very successful. The first franchised store in the United States was opened in Washington, DC, in 1990.

After this successful start in the United States, The Body Shop began to run into trouble. Unsuccessful managers, too many product lines, copycat rivals who discounted, and too few products created specifically for the U.S. consumer were some of the biggest problems. Many U.S. stores were located in expensive major cities that led to high real estate costs. By 1995, critics were saying that U.S. consumers no longer bought into the company's political message. Price-driven consumers did not rate The Body Shop as a premium brand. Instead, they enjoyed the aggressive discounting by Body Shop rivals Garden Botanica and Bath & Body Works. Turnover in Body Shop U.S. leadership and low brand recognition due to lack of advertising contributed to the problem.

JOINT VENTURE

In January 1997, Adrian Bellamy became a Non-Executive (outside member of The Body Shop's Board of Directors). From 1983 until he retired in1995, Bellamy had served as Chairman and CEO of DFS Group Limited—the U.S.-based global duty-free and luxury goods retailer. He also served as a Non-executive Director of GAP Inc., Gucci Group NV, and Williams-Sonoma. He approached The Body Shop board with the idea for a joint venture. The terms of the deal were as follows:

- Bellamy Retail Group (BRG) LLC would pay The Body Shop a nonrefundable $1 million to acquire options over the U.S. business.
- BRG would immediately take over management responsibility of The Body Shop in the United States with options to buy 49% of the company at its net asset value between 2000 and 2002, provided it met performance targets.

Bellamy had a further option to acquire another 2% of the company at a later date. The targets were to reach breakeven by 2000, a profit of $1 million in 2001, and $4 million in 2002. The option lapsed if aggregate losses of $4 million or more occurred in the United States in 2000 and 2001.[51]

At the June 19, 1998, shareholders' meeting, only a handful of shareholders voted against the management.[52] Bellamy planned to focus the new U.S. regime on boosting sales per square foot by improving retail operations and marketing and also by cutting operating costs. He planned to focus on better customer service, improved promotions, and a balanced product range.[53]

As of February 1998, there were 290 shops in the U.S. Retail sales were £98.5 million ($161.6 million) and £100.6 million ($165.0 million) for 1998 and 1997, respectively. As of June 1998, The Body Shop U.S. was not taking applications for new franchises.

Mission Statement

The company's mission statement dedicated its business to the pursuit of social and environmental change:

To creatively balance the financial and human needs of our stakeholders: employees, customers, franchisees, suppliers, and shareholders.

To courageously ensure that our business is ecologically sustainable, meeting the needs of the present without compromising the future.

To meaningfully contribute to local, national, and international communities in which we trade, by adopting a code of conduct which ensures care, honesty, fairness, and respect.

To passionately campaign for the protection of the environment and human and civil rights, and against animal testing within the cosmetics and toiletries industry.

To tirelessly work to narrow the gap between principle and practice, while making fun, passion, and care part of our daily lives.[54]

Corporate Governance

BOARD OF DIRECTORS

The *Annual Report* stated the Directors' responsibilities. The Directors were required by company law to prepare financial statements for each financial year that give a true and fair view of the state of affairs of the company and the group and of the profit or loss of the group for that period.

In preparing those financial statements, the Directors were required to:

- Select suitable accounting policies and then apply them consistently.
- Make judgments and estimates that are reasonable and prudent.
- State whether applicable accounting standards have been followed, subject to any material departures disclosed and explained in the financial statements.
- Prepare the financial statements on the going concern basis unless it is inappropriate to presume that the company will continue in business.

The Directors were responsible for maintaining proper accounting records that disclosed with reasonable accuracy at any time the financial position of the company and to enable them to ensure that the financial statements comply with the Companies Act. They were also responsible for safeguarding the assets of the company and hence for taking reasonable steps for the prevention and detection of fraud and other irregularities.[55]

There were 10 board members, of which 7 were Executive and 3 Non-Executive Directors. The first Non-Executive Directors had been appointed in 1995.

The board members were as follows:[56]

Anita L. Roddick, OBE	Chief Executive
T. Gordon Roddick	Chairman
Stuart A. Rose	Managing Director
Eric G. Helyer	Executive
Ivan C. Levy	Executive
Jane Reid	Executive
Jeremy A. Kett	Executive
Terry G. Hartin	Executive
Penny Hughes	Non-Executive
Aldo Papone	Non-Executive
Adrian D. Bellamy	Non-Executive

Remuneration for the Executive Directors in 1998 was as follows:[57]

(British pound amounts in thousands)

Name	Salary	Benefits	Total
A. L. Roddick	140	22	162
T. G. Roddick	140	22	162
S. A. Rose	250		250
E. G. Helyer	161		161
J. Reid	220		220
J. A. Kett	155		155
T. G. Hartin	286	7	293
I. C. Levy	198	56	254

The Remuneration Committee recommended that the total salaries of both Anita and Gordon Roddick be at a rate of £300,000 per annum, but the Roddicks have chosen to be remunerated at the level set out in the preceding table (an increase of £5,000 each).

Directors' share holdings in 1998 were as follows:[58]

A. L. Roddick	24,010,456
T. G. Roddick	24,226,680
E. G. Helyer	10,000
I. C. Levy	300
T. G. Hartin	15,785
A. Papone	3,000

Ian McGlinn, who had loaned £6,000 to Anita to open her second shop, owned 45,666,768 (23.5%) ordinary shares. The Prudential Corporation owned 6,911,146 (3.6%) ordinary shares, and the Aeon Group had an interest in 6,700,000 (3.5%).

TOP MANAGEMENT

Anita said about Gordon and her roles that "Gordon rarely accompanies me on shop visits because we are each more comfortable in our chosen roles of high profile and low profile. Outsiders often think of Gordon as a shadowy figure, but that is certainly not how he is viewed within The Body Shop. He is well known to everyone, much loved, and deeply respected as the real strength of the company. Our relationship bequeathed a very distinct management style to the company—loosely structured, collaborative, imaginative, and improvisatory, rather than by the book—which matured as the company expanded. I think Gordon provides a sense of constancy and continuity, while I bounce around breaking the rules, pushing back the boundaries of possibility, and shooting off my mouth. We rarely argue . . . it is never about values. His calm presence and enormous influence are rarely taken into account by critics who see The Body Shop as a flaky organization led by a madwoman with fuzzy hair."[59]

Group Structure and Organization

The Body Shop International PLC had stakes in 6 principal subsidiaries as of February 28, 1998 (see **Exhibit 3**). The operating structure is shown in **Exhibit 4.**

Marketing and Advertising

The company had no marketing or advertising department. In 1979, Janis Raven was hired to handle public relations. She helped to publicize the company for its image and stances on public social issues. An analyst felt that the lack of an advertising and marketing budget con-

Exhibit 3

Principal Subsidiaries: The Body Shop International PLC

> **The Body Shop Inc. (90% owned, USA)[1]**
> Responsible for U.S. retail activities.
> **The Body Shop (Singapore) Pte Limited (100% owned, Singapore)[1]**
> Responsible for The Body Shop retail outlets in Singapore.
> **Soapworks Limited (100% owned, Great Britain)[1]**
> Manufactures soap and related products.
> **Skin & Hair Care Preparations Inc. (100% owned, USA)[1]**
> U.S. holding company. Does not trade.
> **The Body Shop Direct Limited (100% owned, Great Britain)[1]**
> Makes direct sales through a home-selling program.
> **The Body Shop (France) SARL (100% owned, France)[1]**
> Operates The Body Shop retail outlets in France.

Note:

1. Shows % holding ordinary shares and country of incorporation and operation.

Source: The Body Shop, *1998 Annual Report*, p. 52.

tributed to low repeat customer sales. Customers came in looking for a gift for a friend or out of curiosity. Once the customer satisfied his or her need, there seemed to be little incentive for the customer to come back. Product Information Manuals (PIMs) were available to all customers and staff to increase their knowledge or answer questions about every Body Shop product. These manuals contained information about how the products were made, a listing of product ingredients, and the uses for each product. Many potential customers were not sure what products the company offered.

Anita Roddick used regular visits by regional managers to keep tight control over shop layout, window displays, PIM handouts, and operating style. Anita viewed marketing as hype;

Exhibit 4

Operating Structure

*Group-owned.

Source: The Body Shop, *1996 Annual Report*.

instead she wanted to establish credibility by educating the customer. She viewed the shop as the company's primary marketing tool. In 1990, The Body Shop was nominated to the United Kingdom Marketing Hall of Fame.

By 1997, Body Shop products were regularly accused of being "tired" and "lacking innovation."[60] One critic went so far as to say that the product mix would not be out of place in Woolworth's.[61] Recognizing this, The Body Shop placed a high priority on reorganizing the product range. The goal was to refocus on core lines and values, communicate effectively with consumers, and create new products that were young, funky, energizing, and marketed efficiently.[62]

Packaging also received a new look in 1997. Instead of continuing with dark green labels, clear labels were phased in to create a more sophisticated look. Colorings of makeup cases went from gun metal gray to metallic green.[63]

Complaints of cluttered, dark, uninviting shops led The Body Shop to design a new store format. The new store format performed well in the United Kingdom during the first year, 1997. The Body Shop planned to open up to 150 new format stores within 2 years.[64] Five U.S. stores scheduled to undergo face lifts in 1998 were straying from the signature green look of old stores. Brighter lighting, hardwood floors, a bolder storefront logo, and light green, bright orange, and yellow colors were intended to help consumers locate products more easily.[65]

In 1997, The Body Shop launched a self-esteem campaign featuring Ruby Rubenesque, a plus-sized doll, as the spokeswoman. A strategic alliance formed with British Airways provided amenity kits from The Body Shop to over 2 million passengers who flew Club World each year.

Product Development and Production

In 1998, the company introduced 3 major new lines of products: Hemp, Aromatherapy, and Bergamot. In May 1998, The Body Shop unveiled a 5-product body care line for dry skin formulated with hemp. It featured hand protector, lip conditioner, soap, elbow grease, and 3-in-1 oil for dry skin sold in metal tins with hemp leaf designs on the packaging. The Body Shop developed educational pamphlets to distribute in stores describing the essential fatty acids and amino acids found in the herb. Support of hemp farmers at the local level was begun immediately. In the United States, the 1970 Controlled Substance Act made it illegal to grow marijuana. The difference between drug-grade marijuana and industrial hemp is the level of tetrahydrocannabinol (THC). Marijuana contains high levels of THC, which is psychoactive, whereas hemp has so little THC that it's virtually drug-free.[66]

Anita handed out packets of hemp seeds that carried the message: "Do not attempt to use this plant as a narcotic. You would need to smoke a joint the size of a telegraph pole to get high." Within a week of going on sale, the Hemp range accounted for 5% of total sales.[67]

Aromatherapy—the use of essential oils to enhance physical and mental well-being—fit in well with the value of The Body Shop. Products in this range included shower gel, massage oils, foaming milk bath, and bath oils organized into 4 collections: Energizing, Balancing, Relaxing, and Sensual.

Products made with Bergamot oil were a key component of the Aromatherapy range. A bergamot is a small bitter, yellow-green citrus fruit grown in Calabria, Italy. Bergamot oil was reputed to have a stimulating effect that reinvigorated the mind and imparted a feeling of well-being. Because its oil could be produced synthetically at very low cost, the bergamot orchards in Italy had been cleared, destroying the local economy. Anita was trying to reverse the decline in the region by increasing the demand for the fruit and thereby bringing jobs and income to the area. This Community Trade relationship had been developed from the collaboration between Simone Mizzi, the Italian Head Franchisee of The Body Shop, The Body Shop International, and the Calabrian authorities. The Body Shop's Trading Charter and Mission are included in **Exhibit 5**.

Exhibit 5
Trading Charter and Mission: The Body Shop

A. OUR TRADING CHARTER

The way we trade creates profits with principles.

We aim to achieve commercial success by meeting our customers' needs through the provision of high quality, good value products with exceptional service and relevant information which enables customers to make informed and responsible choices.

Our trading relationships of every kind—with customers, franchisees, and suppliers—will be commercially viable, mutually beneficial, and based on trust and respect.

Our trading principles reflect our core values.

We aim to ensure that human and civil rights, as set out in the Universal Declaration of Human Rights, are respected throughout our business activities.

We will establish a framework based on this declaration to include criteria for workers' rights embracing a safe, healthy working environment, fair wages, no discrimination on the basis of race, creed, sex or sexual orientation, or physical coercion of any kind.

We will support long-term, sustainable relationships with communities in need.

We will pay special attention to those minority groups, women, and disadvantaged peoples who are socially and economically marginalized.

We will use environmentally sustainable resources wherever technically and economically viable. Our purchasing will be based on a system of screening and investigation of the ecological credentials of our finished products, ingredients, packaging, and suppliers.

We will promote animal protection throughout our business activities. We are against animal testing in the cosmetics and toiletries industry. We will not test ingredients or products on animals, nor will we commission others to do so on our behalf. We will use our purchasing power to stop suppliers' animal testing.

We will institute appropriate monitoring, auditing, and disclosure mechanisms to ensure our accountability and demonstrate our compliance with these principles.

B. DIRECT TRADING: OUR MISSION
The Body Shop believes that all trading should be viewed as an exercise in ethics. This is the attitude we seek to apply to all goods and services within the company and its retail shops.

Our ethical trading program helps create livelihoods for economically stressed communities, mostly in the majority world. Although trading with such communities is currently just a small percentage of all our trade, we intend to increase this practice wherever possible.

Fair Prices. The Body Shop will pay for the products it purchases. While our program aims to benefit the primary producers directly, we also recognize the value of commercial intermediaries. Where world market prices are applicable, we commit ourselves to pay these prices or more.

Partnership. Both sides must benefit commercially. We aim to develop long-term relationships if possible, and plan to work in partnership to solve potential problems. We aim to help our trade partners achieve self-reliance.

Community Benefits. The company will work with a variety of trading partners—cooperatives, family businesses, tribal councils—with the intention of benefiting the individual worker as much as possible. We can't control the dispersal of community benefits that we provide. That process is determined by local needs, which may mean anything from funds managed by consensus to direct payments to individual producers.

(Continued)

Exhibit 5
Trading Charter and Mission: The Body Shop *(continued)*

Respect. Our trading relationships are based on respect. The guidelines we are developing for sustainable development ensure that we respect all environments and cultures that may be affected by our trade. Wherever possible, we use renewable natural materials and skills that are appropriate to local cultures.

Cooperation. The Body Shop is committed to an open relationship with other fair trade organizations and places great emphasis on maintaining dialogue with organizations that are helping to define the path to sustainable development.

Accountability. We believe it is essential that our trading policy be measurable, audited, and open to scrutiny, and we are energetically seeking the mechanisms to achieve that goal. We already use an open approach to assess our impact on the environment and to promote our opposition to animal testing in the cosmetics industry by monitoring our suppliers.

Our trading practices are not the solution to everyone's needs. We simply see them as 1 component of the help we feel qualified to give. We will also help trading partners to broadly assess the likely social and environmental impact of developing trade.

In committing itself to the above aims, The Body Shop believes it is creating a trading policy that will satisfy the needs of our business, our trading partners, and our customers. Letting consumers know that neither places nor peoples have been exploited in getting our products to market helps The Body Shop customer make informed, responsible choices.

Source: The Body Shop, handouts.

In-house manufacturing facilities at Littlehampton, Glasgow, and Wake Forest in the United States produced approximately 60% of The Body Shop products, excluding accessories. Bulk production of toiletries rose 13% to 9,427 tons from 1997 at the Watersmead plant. The U.S. facility filled 11.8 million units, up 4% from 1997.

Soapworks, a wholly owned subsidiary of The Body Shop, manufactured soap and essential oil filling for the Aromatherapy range. Anita opened the facility in Easterhouse, Scotland, an area with historically high unemployment. When Soapworks was founded, the company made a commitment to donate 25% of its cumulative after-tax profits to local community projects. Between 1989 and 1998, the group had made or provided for donations of £274,810. Soapworks manufactured 30 million units in 1998, which was an increase of 4% over 1997.

Anita spent up to 5 months a year traveling the world looking for new product ideas and ingredients. Her samples were brought back to Watersmead where they were analyzed for their potential and durability. The department was backed up by anthropological and ethnobotanical research in traditional uses of plants, herbs, fruits, flowers, seeds, and nuts.

Human Resources Management

Most of the employees in the company were women under 30. Anita constantly worked at communications within the company. Each shop had a bulletin board, a fax machine, and a video player with which she provided the staff a continuous stream of information concerning new products, causes that she supported, or status reports on her latest trip. The in-house video production company produced "Talking Shop," which was a monthly multilingual video magazine. It also produced training tapes and documentaries on social campaigns.

Anita encouraged upward communication through a suggestion system, DODGI (The Department of Damned Good Ideas), and through regularly scheduled meetings of a cross-section of staff, often at her home. She set up the "Red Letter" system so an employee could directly communicate with a director and bypass the normal chain of communications.

She believed in educating her employees and customers. In 1985, The Body Shop Training Center was opened in London and began offering courses on the company's products and philosophy, customer services, and hair and skin care problems. Sessions were held on key social issues such as AIDS, aging, management by humor, drug and alcohol abuse, and urban survival. She discussed the idea of opening a business college. She said, "You can train dogs and you can train horses, but we wanted to educate and help the people realize their potential."[68]

The Body Shop empowered its staff. It encouraged debate, encouraged employees to speak out and state their views. Anita wanted her staff to be personally involved in social campaigns. She said, "One of the risks of corporate campaigning is that the staff start to fall in love with doing good and forget about trading."[69]

Anita had problems recruiting staff for the U.S. headquarters, located in New Jersey, because employees were not willing or able to embrace the company's culture. She went on to say, "Most of them came from conventional, moribund jobs and seemed confused by the idea of a company being quirky or zany or contemptuous of mediocrity. I could never seem to get their adrenaline surging. We are a company in which image, design, style, and creativity are of paramount importance, but we were unable to find employees who appreciate these qualities."[70] Headquarters for the United States were moved to Wake Forest (Winston-Salem), North Carolina, in 1993. Although in 1998, in the face of the troubled U.S. market, Anita admitted that it had been a mistake to move the U.S. headquarters to North Carolina instead of a big city like New York or San Francisco.

The company created "the Company Care Team, a 5-person group that is taking responsibility for The Body Shop's performance as a caring employer. The team coordinated child care through the company's Family Centre and through the launch in April 1994 of programs offering financial help with child care for all company staff. A counselor service provided 24-hour confidential counseling services for employees and their families."[71]

Global Corporate Citizenship

The company clearly stated its position on the key global issue of corporate citizenship in its publication, *This Is the Body Shop*:[72]

Human and Civil Rights

The Body Shop is committed to supporting and promoting social and environmental change for the better. We recognize that human and civil rights are at the very heart of such change.

We're All in This Together

Working with organizations like Amnesty International, Human Rights Watch, the Unrepresented Nations and Peoples Organization, and the Foundation for Ethnobiology, The Body Shop has tried to promote awareness of our responsibility as human beings. What happens to one of us affects us all. We can no longer pretend it is none of our business if people suffer, whether they're on the other side of the world or in our own backyards. Here are a few successful examples of work by The Body Shop in both those areas:

- In 1990, The Body Shop started a relief drive to fund volunteers to renovate orphanages in Romania, where thousands of children had been abandoned under the regime of dictator Nicolae Ceacescu. The Project has been so successful that we've now extended it to Albania.

- In 1993, the Body Shop Foundation donated £162,000 ($234,900) to "Rights and Wrongs," a weekly human rights television series created by Globalvision Inc. on a nonprofit basis. By focusing on the human rights revolution around the world, the series explained how interrelated many of our problems are.

■ In 1993, our biggest campaign in the U.S. focused attention on people living with HIV and AIDS. Working with groups like the American Red Cross, the San Francisco AIDS Foundation, the Gay Men's Health Crisis, and the National Leadership Coalition on AIDS, we developed a multifaceted campaign, focusing particularly on women and teenagers who are the fastest growing risk groups for HIV infection. Using the theme "Protect & Respect," our campaign included a new corporate policy on life threatening illness; training for all our employees; educational materials on safer sex and living with HIV and AIDS for distribution in our shops; outreach to local community groups; and funding support for organizations which assist people with HIV and AIDS.

■ The Body Shop Foundation was founded in 1989. The company donated £0.9 million to the foundation in 1997/98, up from £0.75 million in 1996/97.[73]

Against Animal Testing

The Body Shop is against animal testing of ingredients and products in the cosmetics industry. We do not test our products or ingredients on animals. Nor do we commission others to test on our behalf. We never have and we never will.

We will never endorse the use of animal tests in the cosmetics or toiletries industry. However, no cosmetics company can claim that its manufactured ingredients have never been tested on animals by somebody at some stage for someone. We support a complete ban on the testing of both finished cosmetic products and individual ingredients used in cosmetic products.

We work with leading animal welfare organizations to lobby for a complete ban on animal testing of cosmetic ingredients and products. We also encourage our ingredient suppliers and those who want to become our suppliers to stop animal testing by making our position on animal testing clear to them. We require our suppliers of raw materials to provide written confirmation every 6 months that any material they supply to us has not been tested by them for the cosmetics industry for the last 5 years.

The "5-year rolling rule" is the most effective mechanism for change. Every 6 months, our technical information specialists send out hundreds of declarations requiring all our suppliers to certify the last date of any animal testing they have conducted on behalf of the cosmetics industry on any ingredient which they supply to us.

If a supplier fails to complete the form, the company is pursued until we get the information we need. If no declaration is forthcoming, or if the company reports conducting an animal test for any part of the cosmetics industry within the last 5 years, we immediately stop buying the ingredient from that supplier and look for alternative suppliers who have not tested on animals within the previous 5 years. If no supplier can be found who meets the 5-year rule, we will try to reformulate the product without that ingredient. If we cannot reformulate, we will stop making the product.

Some companies who adopt an against-animal-testing policy take a "fixed cut off date" stance, declaring they will not use an ingredient which comes into existence after a specific date. This position does little to persuade ingredient suppliers, who continue to develop new ingredients, to stop animal testing. A "fixed cut off date" company provides no market for new ingredients, forcing suppliers to continue dealing with those cosmetic companies which require tests. In addition, the extent to which a company's suppliers adhere to its rule may be questionable since most "cut-off" date companies never recheck with their suppliers to see if previously untested ingredients have been retested.

The Body Shop polices the 5-year rule. It's not just the rule itself that provokes the changes we want. It's the policing with regard to each ingredient. As our ingredient suppliers trade with new customers and in new markets, they are confronted by additional demands for animal testing. Our twice yearly declarations ensure they continue to meet our requirements.

We rely upon a number of alternative techniques to help assess a product's safety. At The Body Shop, customer safety is paramount. We believe (as do many experts) that the reliability of animal testing is questionable. In developing products we use natural ingredients, like bananas and Brazil nut oil, as well as others with a long history of human usage. Our ingredients and/or finished products are subject to in-vitro testing methods such as Eytex, human patch testing, SPF testing, and analytical procedures.

Working for the World's Wildlife

All around the world animals are in danger of extinction as their food sources are threatened, their natural habitats diminish, and environmental degradation takes its toll. The Body Shop takes action on several fronts to keep this critical issue in the public eye.

The Body Shop has a long established commitment to helping endangered species. Over the years, The Body Shop and its franchisees have raised hundreds of thousands of dollars, locally, nationally, and internationally, to support a host of campaigns and projects. We also work hard to inform the public and influence governments the world over to protect the environment and stop the illegal trade in endangered species.

Care for the Environment

The Body Shop believes it just isn't possible for any business to claim to be environmentally friendly because all commerce involves some environmental impact. But at The Body Shop, we take responsibility for the waste we create. We aim to avoid excessive packaging, to refill our bottles, and to recycle our packaging and use raw ingredients from renewable sources whenever technically and economically feasible.

The most accessible aspect of our environmental practice for customers is our refill service. Customers bring back their empty, clean containers and we refill them with the same product at a discount. This conserves resources, reduces waste, and saves money. We also accept our packaging back for recycling. At the same time, we're always searching for new ways to reduce our impact on the environment. In the United Kingdom, we are investing in wind energy with the ultimate aim of putting back into the national grid as much electricity as we take out.

In the United States, we've yet to achieve the level of environmental management reached in the United Kingdom and, unsurprisingly, we've had some growing pains which we've done our best to minimize. For instance, we discovered that because of regulations in some states, our larger bottles required special labels to comply with the state's recycling program. So we used a special stick-on label while we phased out stock of that particular bottle.

A New Kind of Audit

To create a framework for our environmental commitment, we have introduced an annual environmental audit pursuant to European Community Eco-management and Audit Regulation at our U.K. headquarters. The results of the audit are publicly available. [See **Exhibit 6** for results of first social audit.] By setting targets to meet on a yearly basis, the audit process is a constant challenge to our commitment, as well as a campaigning platform for us and a role model for other companies. And it's a constant reminder to staff that good environment housekeeping is everyone's business.

Having relocated our headquarters to Wake Forest, NC, from Cedar Knolls, NJ, we are now committed to publishing a comprehensive and externally verified environmental audit statement like "The Green Book," which is published annually in the United Kingdom. Our internal reviews have helped us identify problems to work on and get our staff more involved in environmental management as well.

We are beginning to execute environmental reviews at our principal subsidiaries, retail outlets, and overseas franchises. All will be subject to independent examinations which will eventually result in separately accountable environmental management procedures.[74]

In 1995, the company commissioned Professor Kirk Hanson, a leading American professor in business ethics and social responsibility at the Graduate School of Business of Stanford University, to conduct an independent evaluation of the company's social performance and make recommendations for improvements.[75]

A Brief Summary of Our Environmental Policy

1. Think Globally as a constant reminder of our responsibility to protect the environment.

2. Achieve Excellence by setting clear targets and time scales within which to meet them.

3. Search for Sustainability by using renewable resources wherever feasible and conserving natural resources where renewable options aren't available.

Exhibit 6

Results of Social Audit—The Good News and *The Bad News*: The Body Shop

Employees	Franchisees	Customers
93% agreed or strongly agreed that The Body Shop lives up to its mission on the issues of environmental responsibility and animal testing.	94% of U.K. and 73% of U.S. franchisees agreed or strongly agreed that The Body Shop campaigns effectively on human rights, environmental protection, and animal testing.	The Body Shop scored an average of 7.5 out of 10 for campaigning effectively on human rights, environmental protection, and animal protection.
79% agreed or strongly agreed that working for The Body Shop has raised their awareness of pressing global issues.	90% of U.K. and 80% of U.S. franchisees felt that the company provides reliable and honest information to them on social issues.	The Body Shop scored an average of 9 out of 10 for its stance against animal testing among British customers.
23% felt the best way for them to develop their career was to change companies.	*More than one-fifth of U.K. and U.S. franchisees expressed no opinion on the majority of issues related to doing business with The Body Shop.*	*Many customers in the U.K. and U.S. are still confused by what is natural.*
53% disagreed or strongly disagreed that the behavior and decision making of managers was consistent throughout the company.	*43% of U.K. and 64% of U.S. franchisees disagreed that The Body Shop's sales divisions communicated their long-term strategy clearly to the franchisees.*	*U.K. customer complaints rose from 18.3 per 100,000 transactions in 1992/93 to 20.9 per 100,000 transactions in 1994/95.*

Suppliers	Shareholders	Community Involvement
95% agree or strongly agree that The Body Shop takes active steps to make its business more environmentally responsible.	90% agreed or strongly agreed that The Body Shop takes active steps to make its business more environmentally responsible.	In 1994/95 The Body Shop's directly employed staff gave an estimated 19,500 hours to projects in the community.
Prompt payment, clarity of delivery and purchase order requirements, and fairness of quality assurance arrangements were all recognized by 80% or more.	78% were satisfied with the information they receive on The Body Shop's financial performance.	87% of recipients of funding from The Body Shop Foundation agreed or strongly agreed that The Body Shop takes active steps to make its business more environmentally responsible.
One-fifth disagreed or strongly disagreed that The Body Shop's purchasing and logistics functions are well structured and efficient.	*29% disagreed or strongly disagreed that the company enjoys the trust of the financial community.*	*75% of The Body Shop employees do not participate actively in the community volunteering program.*
8% claimed to have experienced ethically corrupt behavior in their dealings with individual members of The Body Shop staff.	*33% had no opinion or disagreed that The Body Shop has a clear long-term business strategy.*	*Nearly half the recipients of funding disagreed or strongly disagreed that it was easy to identify the right decision makers in The Body Shop Foundation.*

Source: The Body Shop.

4. Manage Growth by letting our business decisions be guided as much by their environmental implications as by economics.

5. Manage Energy by working towards replacing what we must use with renewable resources.

6. Manage Waste by adopting a 4-tier approach: reduce, reuse, recycle, and as last resort, dispose by the safest and most responsible means possible.

7. Control Pollution by protecting the quality of land, air, and water on which we depend.

8. Operate Safely by minimizing risk at every level of our operations: for staff, for customers, and for the community in which the business operates.

9. Obey the Law by complying with environmental laws at all times.

10. Raise Awareness by continuously educating our staff and our customers.

Community Outreach

The Body Shop believes that businesses should give something back to the communities in which they trade. We try to do that in a number of different ways.

Harlem

We opened our 120th American shop on 125th Street in Harlem in 1992. Staffed in part by residents of the community, this shop is helping to contribute to the economic revitalization of the Harlem community. Fifty percent of the post-interest, pre-tax profits from the shop are placed in a fund which will be used to open other community-based shops around the country, while the other 50% is given to a fund (monitored by an advisory group of local community leaders) for Harlem community projects.

Community Projects

We encourage all of our employees to do volunteer work and allow them 4 hours each month of paid time to do it! Community projects are as diverse as our staff and the communities in which we trade. They range from Adopt-a-Highway clean-ups, to delivering meals to homebound people with AIDS, to working with children who have been physically abused, to serving meals to the homeless.

Local Events

In addition to regular community projects work, our employees frequently help out with local events. Recent projects have included a Harlem street fair, participation in AIDS walkathons, and benefit dances to raise money for the Kayapo Indians in Brazil. Many shops do makeovers, foot and hand massages, and aromatherapy massages and donate the proceeds to local organizations. And staff also frequently give talks to various community groups on a wide range of topics—from endangered species to how The Body Shop does business to the rights of indigenous people.[76]

Global Operations and Financial Results

RETAIL SALES

Worldwide retail sales grew by 5% to £604.4 million in 1998. This reflected growth of 14% in Asia, 9% in the Americas (excluding the United States), 6% in Europe, 4% in Australasia, 3% in the United Kingdom, and a decline of 2% in the United States. The retail sales by region are shown below, with prior year figures restated at comparable exchange rates:[77]

Retail Sales by Region
(British pound amounts in millions)

Region	1998	1997	% Change	% of Operating Profit
United Kingdom	£165.0	£161.0	3	27
Europe	148.0	139.5	6	25
United States	98.5	100.6	(2)	16
Americas (excluding USA)	50.0	45.9	9	8
Asia	108.3	95.2	14	18
Australia and New Zealand	33.8	32.6	4	6
Total	£603.6	£574.8		

Worldwide, comparable shop sales growth was unchanged year to year, reflecting a combination of 7% growth in the Americas (excluding the United States), 2% growth in the United Kingdom, 1% growth in Europe, an unchanged position in Australia, a 5% decline in the United States, and a 6% decline in Asia. Japan was the major influence on the performance in Asia where comparable store sales declined by 19%.

Customer transactions showed a 1% decrease during 1998 to 86.5 million. The average transaction per customer increased by 5% to £6.84. Customer transactions in 1998 by geographic region were: United Kingdom—37%; Europe—24%; United States—12%; Americas (excluding the United States)—9%; Asia—13%; and Australia and New Zealand—5%.

TURNOVER

Turnover (a term used in the United Kingdom) was a combination of retail sales (excluding sales taxes) through company-owned shops and wholesale revenue for goods sold to franchisees.[78]

The *1998 Annual Report* stated "Group turnover for the year increased by 8% to £293.1 million, of which 60% relates to international markets. Of the total turnover, 60% represented wholesale sales to franchisees and 40% was achieved in retail sales through company-owned stores, mail order, and The Body Shop Direct. The change reflects the higher proportion of company-owned stores, with retail sales of £117.7 million being 24% higher than in the previous year. The growth in 1998 turnover also reflects higher exports, which, including sales to overseas subsidiaries, increased by 7% to £107.8 million."[79]

OPERATING PROFITS

The operating profits of the company's 6 geographic regions were as follows:[80]

Operating Profit (Loss) by Region
(British pound amounts in millions)

Region	1998	1997	% Change	% of Operating Profit
United Kingdom	£11.2	£13.6	−18	37
Europe	8.0	8.1	−1	20
United States	(1.7)	(3.0)	—	—
Americas (excluding USA)	3.4	3.0	13	16
Asia	15.4	14.7	5	8
Australia and New Zealand	1.8	2.0	−10	5
Total	£38.1	£38.4		

MANAGEMENT ANALYSIS BY REGIONS

This section is management analyses of operations by geographic regions as reported in the Company's *1998 Annual Report.*[81]

United Kingdom

The company acted as the head franchisee in the United Kingdom, managing wholesale and retail activities. Seven new shops were opened during the 1998 financial year, giving a total of 263 stores at year's end of which 67 were company-owned. In line with the company's strategy to operate stores located in large cities, 10 shops were purchased from franchisees during the year.

Region: United Kingdom	1998	1997	
Shops at year end	263	256	
Shop openings	7	4	
Category	**£m**	**£m**	**Change**
Retail sales	£165.8	£161.2	+3%
Turnover	116.2	103.1	10%
Operating profit	11.2	13.6	−18%

Total retail sales grew by 3% in the year to February 1998, with comparable store sales up by 2% from the previous year. The comparable store sales excluded sales realized though The Body Shop Direct, the home selling program, which were included in the total retail sales figure. The Body Shop Direct continued to move forward, with over 1,100 registered consultants at the year's end. More than 60,000 parties were held during the year, reaching some 625,000 customers.

The testing of the new store design progressed, with 7 of these stores operating by the year's end. The Body Shop anticipated that up to 15 of these new designs would be fitted in existing and new stores during 1998.

Turnover in the United Kingdom grew by 10%, ahead of the growth in retail sales due to the larger number of company-owned stores. Operating profit was 18% lower, with the profit from the additional company-owned stores being offset by an increase in marketing expenses and higher costs associated with The Body Shop Direct.

United States

The company's subsidiary, The Body Shop Inc., functioned as the head franchisee for the United States. The head office, filling facilities, and main distribution center were based in Wake Forest, North Carolina.

Store openings were minimal, with a net increase of 3 stores during the year. Of the 290 stores at the period's end, 210 were company-owned with 68 stores that were purchased from franchisees during the year. This number included 16 shops that were acquired with the southeastern distributorship. Once most of the lowest performing franchised stores had been bought, The Body Shop anticipated few store buy-backs in 1998.

Region: USA	1998	1997	
Shops at year end	290	287	
Shop openings	3	14	
Category	**$m**	**$m**	**Change**
Retail sales	161.6	165.0	−2%
Turnover	128.1	119.6	+7%
Category	**£m**	**£m**	**Change**
Retail sales	98.5	100.6	−2%
Turnover	78.0	73.1	+7%
Operating profit	(1.7)	(3.0)	

Total retail sales in the United States were 2% lower than in the previous year, reflecting the low number of new store openings together with a comparable store sales decline of 5%. Other than Manhattan, which performed slightly better than the average, sales performances were similar across the regions.

Fewer new product introductions, poor retailing, and competitive pressures continued to affect sales performance.

Turnover in the United States was 7% higher given the larger number of company-owned stores. The U.S. operating results were a combination of the margin realized in the United Kingdom on supplying goods to the United States, together with the margin arising from wholesale and retail activities within the United States. The operating loss of £1.7 million showed an improvement on the 1997 result although the result was similar year to year if the effect of currency changes were excluded.

Europe

The 13 net store openings in Europe reflected 41 openings and 28 closures, with 9 closures in France. The 6% total retail sales growth achieved in Europe reflected the store openings and a 1% increase in comparable store sales.

Region: Europe United	1998	1997	
Shops at year end	527	514	
Shop openings	13	30	
Category	**£m**	**£m**	**Change**
Retail sales	148.0	139.5	+6%
Turnover	42.0	39.3	+7%
Operating profit	8.0	8.1[1]	−1%

Note: 1. Excluding the exceptional item relating to France. The exceptional item related to a provision of £6.5 million (£4.3 million after tax) in respect of facilities extended to the former head franchisee in France prior to the acquisition of the French business in November 1997.

Comparable store sales performance varied across the region with markets such as Holland, Sweden, Finland, and Ireland showing the strongest underlying growth. Other markets, such as France, Germany, and Spain, showed improving trends with negative comparable store sales reversing in the second 6 months. The improvements being achieved in France reflected a rationalization of the store base there and the successful introduction of a stronger retail agenda following the acquisition of the business during the year.

Turnover in Europe grew by 7%, with operating profit similar to the previous year.

Asia

Of the 75 new store openings in Asia, 29 were in Japan. The Body Shop anticipated fewer store openings in Asia during the current year given the economic difficulties in a number of Southeast Asian Countries.

Region: Asia	1998	1997	
Shops at year end	308	233	
Shop openings	75	63	
Category	**£m**	**£m**	**Change**
Retail sales	108.3	95.2	+14%
Turnover	37.5	35.7	+5%
Operating profit	15.4	14.7	+5%

Retail stores in the Asian region showed growth of 14%, with comparable store sales declining by 6%. Excluding the impact of Japan, where comparable store sales declined by 19%, comparable store sales in the region grew by 4%. Although Taiwan, Malaysia, Indonesia, and Saudi Arabia all showed strong positive underlying growth, other markets such as Singapore and Thailand saw comparable store sales declines. The first shop opened in Korea at the end of March 1997, with 5 stores opening by the year's end.

Americas (excluding the United States)

Total retail sales grew by 9%, with comparable store sales growth of 7%. These results were mainly influenced by the sales performance in Canada, which continued to benefit from a focused marketing and retail program.

Region: Americas (excluding the United States)	1998	1997	
Shops at year end	130	130	
Shop openings	—	4	
Category	**£m**	**£m**	**Change**
Retail sales	50.0	45.9	+9%
Turnover	12.8	9.9	+29%
Operating profit	3.4	3.0	+13%

Turnover was 29% higher, with operating profit 13% up from the previous year.

Exhibit 7

Balance Sheets: The Body Shop[1,2]
(British pounds in millions)

Year Ending February 28	Group		Company	
	1998	**1997**	**1998**	**1997**
Fixed Assets				
Tangible assets	78.4	74.9	50.7	52.7
Investments	2.0	0.5	50.5	15.8
	80.4	75.4	101.2	68.5
Current Assets				
Stocks	47.7	34.8	28.5	21.2
Debtors	47.0	45.0	59.5	65.6
Cash at bank and in hand	29.6	47.1	21.3	39.0
	124.3	126.9	109.3	125.8
Creditors: amounts falling due within 1 year	70.4	59.0	59.3	44.9
Net current assets	53.9	67.9	50.0	80.9
Total assets less current liabilities	134.3	143.3	151.2	149.4
Creditors: amounts falling due after more than 1 year	2.9	13.0	0.0	0.1
Provisions for liabilities and charges				
Deferred tax	1.1	0.2	1.9	0.6
Total assets	£130.3	£130.1	£149.3	£148.7
Capital and Reserves				
Called up share amount	9.7	9.7	9.7	9.7
Share premium account	42.8	42.1	42.8	42.1
Profit and loss account	77.8	78.3	96.8	96.9
Shareholders' funds	£130.3	£130.1	£149.3	£148.7

Notes:
1. These financial statements were approved by the Board on May 13, 1998.
2. Notes were deleted.

Source: The Body Shop, *1998 Annual Report*, p. 39.

Australia and New Zealand

Total retail sales in Australia and New Zealand increased by 4%, with comparable store sales unchanged from the previous year.

Region: Australia and New Zealand	1998	1997	
Shops at year end	76	71	
Shop openings	5	3	
Category	**£m**	**£m**	**Change**
Retail sales	33.8	32.6	+4%
Turnover	6.6	6.7	−1%
Operating profit	1.8	2.0	−10%

Turnover was down 1% and operating profit was down 10% from the previous year mainly due to the timing of product shipments.

Exhibits 7 and **8** show the company's balance sheets and consolidated profit and loss accounts.

Exhibit 8

Consolidated Profit and Loss Accounts: The Body Shop[2]
(British pounds in millions, except per ordinary share data)

Year Ending February 28	1998	1997
Turnover[1]	£293.10	£270.80
Cost of sales	115.90	111.90
Gross Profit	177.20	158.90
Operating expenses—excluding exceptional item	139.10	120.50
Operating expenses—exceptional item	0	6.50
Operating Profit	38.10	31.90
Interest payable (net)	0.10	0.20
Profit on Ordinary Activities Before Tax	38.00	31.70
Tax on profit on ordinary activities	15.20	14.10
Profit for the Financial Year	22.80	17.60
Dividends paid and proposed	10.80	9.10
Retained profit	£ 12.00	£ 8.50
Earnings per ordinary share including exceptional item	11.8p	9.2p
Earnings per ordinary share excluding exceptional item	11.8p	11.4p

Notes:
1. Turnover represents the total accounts receivable in the ordinary course of business for goods sold and services provided and excludes sales between companies in the Group, discount given, Value Added Tax (VAT), and other sales taxes.
2. Other notes were deleted.

Source: The Body Shop, *1998 Annual Report*, p. 38.

Notes

1. Nigel Cope, "Roddick Quits Helm at Body Shop," *Independent* (May 21, 1998), p. 21.
2. *Ibid.*
3. "They Said It," *Daily Telegraph* (May 16, 1998), p. 33.
4. "Body Shop, Capitalism and Cocoa Butter," *The Economist* (May 16, 1998), p. 66.
5. Rufus Olins, "Body Shop Calls in Corporate Man," *The Sunday Times* (May 17,1998).
6. *Ibid.*
7. Sarah Cunningham, "Body Shop Offers Golden Handcuffs," *Times* (May 15, 1998).
8. Rufus Olins, "Body Shop."
9. Anita Roddick, *The Body Shop* (NY: Crown Publishers, Inc.), 1991, p. 43.
10. *Ibid.*, p. 52.
11. *Ibid.*, pp. 55–62.
12. *Ibid.*, p. 66.
13. *Ibid.*
14. *Ibid.*, p. 67.
15. *Ibid.*, p. 68.
16. *Ibid.*
17. *Ibid.*
18. *Ibid.*, p. 77.
19. *Ibid.*, p. 68.
20. *Ibid.*, p. 74.
21. *Ibid.*, pp. 85–86.
22. *Ibid.*, p. 86.
23. *Ibid.*, p. 92.
24. *Ibid.*, pp. 94–95.
25. *Ibid.*, pp. 96–97.
26. *Ibid.*, p. 101.
27. *Ibid.*
28. *Ibid.*, p. 100.
29. *Ibid.*
30. *Ibid.*, p. 143.
31. *Ibid.*, p. 144.
32. The Body Shop, *1998 Annual Report*, p. 25.
33. The Body Shop, *1995 Annual Report*, p. 15.
34. *Ibid.*, p. 17.
35. *Ibid.*, p. 20.
36. *Ibid.*, p. 25.
37. *Ibid.*, p. 49.
38. *Ibid.*, p. 81.
39. *Ibid.*, p. 108.
40. *Ibid.*, p. 115.
41. *Ibid.*, p. 123.
42. *Ibid.*, p. 226.
43. *Ibid.*, p. 158.
44. *Ibid.*, p. 178.
45. *Ibid.*, p. 214.
46. *Ibid.*, p. 217.
47. *Ibid.*, p. 223.
48. *Ibid.*, p. 231.
49. *Ibid.*, p. 181.
50. *Ibid.*, p. 137.
51. James Fallon, "Body Shop Shakeup Brings New CEO," *WWD* (May 13, 1998), p. 3.
52. Robert Wright, "Body Shop U.S. Venture Approved," *Financial Times* (June 23, 1998), p. 28
53. Ernest Beck, "Body Shop Founder Roddick Steps Aside as CEO," *Wall Street Journal* (May 13, 1998), p. B14.
54. The Body Shop. *Our Reason for Being* (handout).
55. The Body Shop. *1998 Annual Report*, p. 25.
56. *Ibid.*, p. 32.
57. *Ibid.*, p. 36.
58. *Ibid.*
59. Anita Roddick, pp. 235–236.
60. "Loosening One's Grip," *Cosmetic Insiders' Report*, no. 11, vol. 17.
61. Ruth Nicholas, "New Age Finds a New Face," *Marketing* (May 21, 1998), p. 15.
62. *Ibid.*
63. Diane Seo, "Body Shop Hopes Hemp Will Plant Seeds of Recovery," *LA Times* (February 26, 1998), p. D1.
64. Fallon, p. 3.
65. Seo, p. D1.
66. Alev Aktar, "Hemp: A Growing Controversy," *WWD* (February 13, 1998), p. 8.
67. Nicholas, p. 15
68. *Ibid.*, p. 143.
69. *Ibid.*, p. 125.
70. *Ibid.*, p. 135.
71. The Body Shop. *1994 Annual Report*, p. 22.
72. The Body Shop. *This Is The Body Shop*, (November 1994), p. 57. All 5 paragraphs below are directly taken from this source.
73. The Body Shop. *1998 Annual Report*, p. 67.
74. The Body Shop. *This Is The Body Shop* (November 1994), pp. 6–8. All 15 paragraphs below are directly taken from this source.
75. The Body Shop. *1995 Annual Report*, p. 3.
76. The Body Shop. *This Is The Body Shop* (November 1994), pp. 8–9.
77. The Body Shop. *1998 Annual Report*, pp. 25–29.
78. *Ibid.*
79. *Ibid.*
80. *Ibid.*, pp. 18–20.
81. *Ibid.*

Waterford Wedgwood Plc (2000): The Millennium

Thomas L. Wheelen, Edward Kasabov, Philip Anderson, and Kathryn E. Wheelen

On March 14, 2000, P. Redmond O'Donoghue, Chief Executive Officer (CEO), of Waterford Crystal Limited was chairing a meeting. The focus of the meeting was on the sale of Millennium products. A Millennium Waterford crystal ball, the "Star of Hope," was used in Times Square, New York, to ring in the New Year and the Millennium. The 500-pound Waterford crystal ball was lowered down a 77-foot flag pole that was 22 stories above the ground. It took a team of 40 designers and 10 months to assemble the 6-foot diameter geodesic sphere. O'Donoghue was curious about the impact the Millennium crystal ball had on the sale of the company's products.

Overview of the Crystal Business and the History of Waterford Crystal[1]

MANUFACTURING OF CRYSTAL

The crystal manufacturing business was labor intensive. Each piece of crystal had gone through the processes of mixing, blowing, cutting, and polishing. Mixing involved heating raw materials in a furnace to temperatures in excess of 1400 degrees centigrade to create molten crystal. Blowing formed the molten crystal into a basic item such as a wine goblet or vase. The cutting process etched a design pattern into the blank piece. Finally, each piece was polished to smoothen the edges of the cuts and give the piece the luster and sparkle for which crystal was known. Labor costs typically represented 50 to 55% of the cost of manufacturing crystal.

Blowing was done either by machine or was mouth-blown by a skilled craftsman. Similarly, crystal pieces could be cut by machine or hand-cut. Three different technologies were used in the crystal cutting process. They were (1) fully hand-cut, (2) semiautomated and slow speed-automated, and (3) high speed-automated. Crystal pieces that were both mouth-blown and hand-cut had the highest image of quality of all crystal products.

Developing craft skills was a key element in a manufacturer's ability to increase its production output. This was particularly critical in the case of mouth-blown and hand-cut products. In addition to the wages paid to craftsmen (i.e., blowers and cutters), an intensive

This case was prepared by Visiting Professor Thomas L. Wheelen at University of Dublin at Trinity College and Edward Kasabov, doctoral student at the University of Dublin at Trinity College and Professor Philip H. Anderson at the University of St. Thomas, St. Paul, Minnesota, and Visiting Professor at the University of Cork, Ireland, and Kathryn E. Wheelen, Research Associate, of Wheelen Associates. This case was edited for SMBP-8th edition. This case may not be reproduced in any form without written permission of the copyright holder, Thomas L. Wheelen. Copyright © 2001 by Thomas L. Wheelen. Reprinted by permission.

apprenticeship program had to be maintained. Apprenticeships typically lasted for 4 or more years. Each craftsman usually oversaw several apprentices. The availability of craft and design skills was a major factor in establishing and maintaining competitive advantage. Relative to the labor component involved in manufacturing crystal, raw materials were inexpensive and readily available.

Labor cost efficiency was not a significant issue until the late 1970s. At that time, pressure on prices forced manufacturers to focus on costs in order to maintain gross profit margins. The pressure on prices came from multiple sources. Primary among these were general economic conditions, an increasing number of competitors (most of them European), and new technology. The technology of glass blowing had changed little since crystal making began. The traditional tools, hollow irons and wooden templates, were still used by glass blowers to create the crystal pieces that were then passed on to cutters who hand-cut the design patterns. Recently, improved processing of machine-cut crystal had been introduced into the industry.

While the quality of machine-cut crystal had improved, its level varied and it was not equal to hand-cut crystal. Machine-cut crystal was lower in price relative to hand-cut crystal.

Lead crystal manufacturing was not a fixed capital-intensive business. However, it did require a significant level of investment and its working capital needs were high. High-valued finished inventories had to be maintained throughout the distribution channels. In addition, work-in-progress inventories contained a high value-added component that had to be financed, reflecting significant cash requirements.

The technology differences used in the manufacture of crystal products translate into 3 market segments: *high-end*, *medium*, and *low-end*. These 3 segments were based on price and brand-name recognition.

HISTORY OF WATERFORD

In 1783, businessmen George and William Penrose founded the Waterford Glass House in the busy port of Waterford, Ireland, and began to make crystal "as fine a quality as any in Europe . . . in the most elegant style." The Penroses knew the secret of mingling minerals and glass to create crystal with beauty and mystery. When tapped, it sang sweetly. When touched, it felt warm and soft. Yet it possessed strength and durability and, most wonderful of all, the crystal shone with a romantic, silvery brilliance. Patience, skill, and artistry had forged a triumph.

In 1851, Waterford Crystal won several gold medals and universal acclaim at the Great Exhibition in London. But just as Waterford's art was reaching its full bloom, the financial climate turned grim. In the same year, the Waterford factory was forced to close, largely due to heavy excise duties.

Waterford Crystal's great tradition lay dormant for a hundred years. But when Irish independence rekindled a passion for the Irish arts in the 1940s and 1950s, a group of businessmen resolved to bring back to life the legacy that had made Waterford synonymous with the finest crystal in the world.

In 1947, they recruited a small group of artisans and, under the guidance of these masters, young apprentices learned the art of Waterford Crystal made famous by their skilled countrymen decades before. By 1951, Waterford Crystal was again launched on the world market. When, in the early 1960s, demand began to exceed supply, a larger glass works was built. This was later expanded until, by the 1980s, Waterford Crystal was the largest producer of hand-crafted crystal in the world.

In 1991, Waterford launched Marquis by Waterford Crystal, the first new brand in the company's 200-year history fine enough to carry the name Waterford Crystal. Marquis by Waterford Crystal became the most successful new entry in the tabletop industry, and it was the number 4 brand. Marquis offered innovative crystal patterns ranging from contemporary to traditional design, designed by Waterford and brought to life by the great crystal makers in Europe.

In 1992, after extensive consumer research, Waterford learned that many consumers desired Waterford Crystal in less formal designs. In a move to broaden Waterford's design and consumer appeal, some new products were successfully introduced from the finest crystal facilities in Europe—all manufactured to the same exacting standards of Waterford, Ireland.

Each piece of Waterford Crystal stands today as a testament to the traditions and standards of excellence that have survived with the Waterford name for more than 200 years ". . . to be enjoyed and displayed now. . . to be cherished as an heirloom for generations to come."

Corporate Governance Board of Directors

The *Annual Report* states the Directors' responsibilities:

> The Directors are required by Irish company law to prepare financial statements for each financial year which give a true and fair view of the state of affairs of the Company and the Group and of the profit or loss of the Group for that financial year.
>
> In preparing those financial statements the Directors are required to:

- select appropriate accounting policies and apply them consistently;
- make reasonable and prudent judgments and estimates; and
- state that all accounting standards which they consider to be applicable have been followed.

> The Directors have responsibility for ensuring that the Group keeps accounting records which disclose with reasonable accuracy the financial position of the Group at any time and which enable them to ensure that the financial statements are prepared in accordance with accounting standards generally accepted in Ireland and comply with Irish statute, comprising the Companies Acts 1963 to 1999 and the European Communities (Companies: Group Accounts) Regulations, 1992. The Directors confirm that the financial statements comply with the above requirements. The Directors also have responsibility for taking such steps as are reasonably open to them to safeguard the assets of the Group and to prevent and detect fraud and other irregularities.[2]

Exhibit 1 provides the names of the 17 Board Members. Eight are internal members. Eight are classified as Nonexecutive Independent Directors. Dr. O'Reilly announced that Lord Wedgwood would join the Board as an Executive Director at next board meeting. Lord Wedgwood was a direct descendant of Josiah Wedgwood, founder of Wedgwood, and has served for years as Wedgwood's International Ambassador.

In February, 2000, Dr. O'Reilly announced the appointment of Peter John Goulandris as Executive Chairman of Ceramics. Goulandris was a major shareholder (see **Exhibit 2**) and Deputy Chairman of Waterford Wedgwood since 1999. He was the Chairman's brother-in-law.

R. A. Barnes, O. C. Küsel, C. J. McGillivary, K. C. McGoran, and F. A. Wedgwood were reelected at the 2000 Annual Meeting.

Exhibit 2 shows the stock ownership of Dr. A. J. F. O'Reilly; Mrs. C. J. O'Reilly; P. J. Goulandris, Mrs. O'Reilly's brother; and other substantial ordinary shareholders.

TOP MANAGEMENT

The Executive Directors are P. J. Goulandris, Richard A. Barnes, P. R. O'Donoghue, B. D. Patterson, O. C. Küsel, C. J. McGillivary, S. Michaels, and C. J. S. Johnson (see **Exhibit 1**).

Exhibit 1

Board of Directors: Waterford Wedgwood plc

Dr. Anthony J. F. O'Reilly[1]
Chairman, had been a Director of the Group since 1990 and was appointed Chairman on 1 January 1994. He was Chairman of H.J. Heinz Company and Executive Chairman of Independent News & Media plc.

Peter John Goulandris
Joined the Group as a Director in 1996. He was Deputy Chairman of the Group and Executive Chairman, Ceramics. His other directorships included Fitzwilton Limited.

Chryssanthie J. O'Reilly[1]
Joined the Group as a Director in 1995. She was also Chairperson of the Irish National Stud Company Limited.

Richard A. Barnes
Joined the Group in 1988. He was appointed a Director in 1993. He was Waterford Wedgwood Group Finance Director and a Director of West Midlands Regional Development Agency, a U.K. Government appointment.

P. Redmond O'Donoghue
Joined the Group as a Director in 1985. He was Chief Executive Officer of Waterford Crystal Limited. Additionally he was Nonexecutive Chairman of Bord Failte (Irish Tourist Board) and Nonexecutive Director of Greencore plc.

Brian D. Patterson
Joined the Group in 1987. He was appointed a Director in 1992. He is Chief Executive Officer of Wedgwood and Chairman of Competitiveness Council of Ireland, a Government appointment.

Ottmar C. Küsel
Is Chief Executive Officer of Rosenthal AG. He was appointed a Director of the Group in 1997. He was Chairman of the Ceramics Industry Association in Germany and of the Ambiente/Tendence Trade Show Committee in Frankfurt.

Christopher J. McGillivary
Joined the Group in 1990. He was appointed a Director in 1996. He was Chief Executive Officer of Waterford Wedgwood U.S.A., Inc. He was also Co-Chairman of All-Clad Holdings, Inc.

Sam Michaels
Joined the Group as a Director on 2 July 1999. He was Co-Chairman and Chief Executive Officer of All-Clad Holdings, Inc., and Chairman of Pittsburgh Annealing Box Company.

Robert H. Niehaus[1]
Joined the Group as a Director in 1990. He was Chairman of Waterford Wedgwood U.K. plc. He was also Chairman and Managing Partner of Greenhill Capital Partners, a private equity investment fund in New York. His other directorships included the American Italian Pasta Company.

David W. Sculley[1]
Is a partner in the New York based investment firm, Sculley Brothers. He joined the Group as a Director in 1997. He serves on the board of a number of private companies.

Tony O'Reilly, Jr.[1]
Joined the Group as a Director in 1998. He was a Director and Chief Executive Officer of Arcon International Resources plc. His other directorships included Tedcastle Holdings Limited, Lockwood Financial Group, Inc. (U.S.A.), Providence Resources plc, and Independent News & Media plc.

Dr. F. Alan Wedgwood[1]
Joined the Group as a Director in 1986 and before that was a Director of Josiah Wedgwood & Sons Limited since 1966. He was also a Director of Waterford Wedgwood U.K. plc.

Kevin C. McGoran[1]
Joined the Group as a Director in 1990. He was Deputy Chairman of Fitzwilton Limited, and Chairman of Waterford Crystal Limited.

Gerald P. Dempsey[1]
Joined the Group as a Director in 1986. His other directorships included UNM Financial Services Ireland and Design and Project Management Limited.

Christopher J. S. Johnson
Joined Wedgwood in 1968. He was appointed a Group Director in 1988. He was Manufacturing and Technical Director of Wedgwood.

Lewis L. Glucksman[1]
Joined the Group as a Director in 1998. He acted as a senior adviser at Salomon Smith Barney, New York, and was a member of the Advisory Committee of the National Treasury Management Agency in Ireland—a Government appointment. His directorships included Risk Capital Holdings (U.S.A.).

Note:
1. Nonexecutive Independent Director.

Source: Waterford Wedgwood plc, *1999 Annual Report*, p. 11.

Exhibit 2

Substantial Ordinary Shareholders: Waterford Wedgwood plc
March 7, 2000

A. General Ownership

Name	Holding	Percentage
Greater than 10%		
Stoneworth Investment Ltd.	119,666,795	16.20%
Bank of Ireland Nominees Ltd.	112,016,276	15.17%
Between 5% and 10%		
Allied Irish Banks plc & its subsidiaries	42,136,373	5.71%
Ulster Bank Markets (Nominees) Ltd.	37,293,695	5.05%
Between 3% and 5%		
Irish Life Assurance plc	29,541,431	4.00%
Araquipa International Ltd.	27,111,201	3.67%
Albany Hill Ltd.	26,778,362	3.63%

B. A. J. F. O'Reilly, Mrs. C. J. O'Reilly, and P. J. Goulandris (Mrs. O'Reilly's brother) Stock Ownership

Name	Stock Owner	Percentage	Shares
Indexia Holdings Ltd.	A. J. F. O'Reilly	100%	250,000
Mystic Investments (Cayman) Ltd.			420,097
Albany Hill Limited	A. J. F. O'Reilly	100%	26,778,362
	Mrs. C. J. O'Reilly combined		
	P. J. Goulandris		
Stoneworth Investments Ltd.	A. J. F. O'Reilly	49%	119,666,795
	P. J. Goulandris	49%	
	L. L. Glucksman	2%	

Source: Waterford Wedgwood plc, *1999 Annual Report*, pp. 7, 10.

GROUP STRUCTURE AND ORGANIZATION

Exhibit 3 shows the 4 product lines for the company. The principal executives of these units are:

Name	Title	Unit
P. R. O'Donoghue	CEO	Waterford Crystal Ltd.
B. D. Patterson	CEO	Wedgwood
O. C. Küsel	CEO	Rosenthal
C. J. McGillivary	CEO	Waterford Wedgwood, U.S.A., Inc.
S. Michael	CEO Co-Chairman	All-Clad Holdings
C. J. S. Johnson	Manufacturing and Technical Director	Wedgwood
P. J. Goulandris	Deputy Chairman Executive Chairman	Ceramics

Exhibit 4 shows principal subsidaries of the company.

Exhibit 3

Product Lines: Waterford Wedgwood plc

Source: Waterford Wedgwood plc, *1999 Annual Report*, backside of cover page.

Strategic Group Units

WATERFORD CRYSTAL: CEO'S STRATEGIC REPORT

Group Crystal sales increased by 31.5% in 1999, an all time record year for the peerless Waterford and our other luxury crystal brands.[3]

P. R. O'Donoghue, CEO

I am delighted to report that Group Crystal operating profit in 1999 was €57.0 million, an increase of no less than 39% (see **Exhibit 5**). Sales were €395.2 million, up 31.5% (€395.2 million [IR £501.8 million]). Our record 1999 performance was based on many things, but most particularly on our successful design and marketing of exciting new products, on reaping the benefits of investments over the past several years, in reducing unit costs, and on manufacturing and logistics skills.

Waterford Crystal is the only truly global luxury crystal brand. Last year's success was repeated in all of our major international markets, with the sole exception of Japan where consumer demand remained depressed. In the world's largest market, the United States, our outstandingly professional team, under the inspired leadership of Chris McGillivary, increased sales by 37%. Working closely with Ireland, the products development effort in America has gone from strength to strength. At home in Ireland sales increased by 28%, while the United Kingdom showed 17% growth and Europe grew 8%. Furthermore we achieved strong growth in Australia and Canada with sales up by 42% and 39%, respectively.

Exhibit 4

Principal Subsidiaries, 2000: Waterford Wedgwood plc

Company	Registered office and country of incorporation	Nature of business
A. Manufacturing		
Waterford Crystal (Manufacturing) Ltd.	Kilbarry, Waterford, Ireland	Crystal glass manufacturer
Josiah Wedgwood & Sons Ltd.	Barlaston, Stoke-on-Trent, England	Ceramic tableware/giftware manufacturer
Rosenthal AG	Selb, Germany	Ceramic tableware/giftware manufacturer
All-Clad Metalcrafters LLC	Delaware, U.S.A.	Kitchenware manufacturer
Stuart & Sons Ltd.	Stourbridge, West Midlands, England	Kitchenware manufacturer
B. Distribution		
Waterford Crystal Ltd.	Kilbarry, Waterford, Ireland	Distributor
Waterford Crystal Gallery Ltd.	Kilbarry, Waterford, Ireland	Product display and sales center
Waterford Wedgwood Australia Ltd.	Barlaston, Stoke-on-Trent, England	Distributor
Waterford Wedgwood Canada, Inc.	Toronto, Canada	Distributor
Waterford Wedgwood U.S.A., Inc.	New York, U.S.A.	Distributor
Waterford Wedgwood Japan Ltd.	Tokyo, Japan	Distributor
Waterford Wedgwood Retail Ltd.	Barlaston, Stoke-on-Trent, England	Retailer
Josiah Wedgwood & Sons (Exports) Ltd.	Barlaston, Stoke-on-Trent, England	Exporter
Josiah Wedgwood (Malaysia) Sdn Bhd.	Kuala Lumpur, Malaysia	Retailer
Waterford Wedgwood Trading Singapore Pte. Ltd.	Singapore	Distributor
Waterford Wedgwood (Taiwan) Ltd.	Taipei, Taiwan	Distributor
Wedgwood GmbH	Selb, Germany	Sales office
C. Finance		
Statum Limited	Barlaston, Stoke-on-Trent, England	Finance
Waterford Wedgwood International Financial Services	Dublin, Ireland	Finance
D. Other		
Waterford Wedgwood U.K. plc	Barlaston, Stoke-on-Trent, England	Subsidiary holding company
Wedgwood Ltd.	Barlaston, Stoke-on-Trent, England	Subsidiary holding company
Waterford Wedgwood, Inc.	Delaware, U.S.A.	Subsidiary holding company
Waterford Glass Research and Development Ltd.	Kilbarry, Waterford, Ireland	Research and development
Dungarvan Crystal Ltd.	Kilbarry, Waterford, Ireland	Dormant
Waterford Wedgwood Employee Share Ownership Plan (Jersey) Ltd.	St. Helier, Jersey	Trustee company
Waterford Wedgwood GmbH	Dusseldorf, Germany	Subsidiary holding company
All-Clad Holdings, Inc.	Canonsburg, Pennsylvania, U.S.A.	Subsidiary holding company

One of the key factors in our success in recent years has been the continuous introduction of innovative, market-led new products, which have attracted new consumers to our brands at the same time as keeping existing consumers loyal. On top of the success of new products we have been able to maintain and increase sales of existing products. This unique combination of new contemporary products and traditional products has been the driving force behind our sales growth rate, which has been so dramatic year after year since the early 1990s. In 1999, however, we elevated our performance onto an entirely new plane with a range of Waterford Crystal Millennium products. These were a particular success for 2 main reasons. Firstly, they

Exhibit 5

Segment Information: Waterford Wedgwood plc
(Stated in pounds)

Year Ending December 31	1999			1998				
	Turnover	Operation Profit	1999 Net Assets	Turnover	Operating Profit Before Exceptional Cost	Exceptional Costs	Operating Profit/(Loss)	1998 Net Assets Restated
Crystal	£ 395.2	£ 57.0	£ 213.5	£ 300.5	£ 41.0	(£ 4.5)	£ 36.5	£ 182.8
Ceramics	396.8	14.0	227.2	382.1	13.9	(26.7)	(12.8)	186.9
Other	87.6	11.9	110.2	47.9	8.8	—	8.8	4.9
Group Net Borrowings	—	—	(311.8)	—	—	—	—	(190.8)
Minority Interests	879.6	82.9	239.1	730.5	63.7	(31.2)	32.5	183.8
Total Group	579.6	82.9	236.0	730.5	63.7	(31.2)	32.5	180.0

Note:

1. The segmental analysis provided has been changed from business segment to product category analysis reflecting the greater integration of the Group's ceramic businesses and the acquisition of All-Clad. Crystal includes the manufacture and distribution of the Group's crystal products. Ceramics includes the manufacture and distribution of the group's ceramic products. "Other" includes products manufactured and distributed by All-Clad together with the Group's other non-crystal and ceramic products.

Source: Waterford Wedgwood plc, *1999 Annual Report*, p. 19.

appealed to gift buyers by providing attractively packaged, well-priced gift solutions. Secondly, they were linked by a series of related themes, and collectors were delighted to own several pieces or, indeed, the whole collection.

In addition to the growth in our core crystal business, line and brand extensions have continued to expand and are now making a valuable contribution to our overall performance. Thus a combination including John Rocha at Waterford, Waterford China, Waterford Holiday Heirlooms, the newly launched Waterford Jewelry, and our licensed products (table linen, cutlery and writing instruments) accounted for retail sales in 1999 of €70 million. And none of these products existed before mid 1997! The John Rocha line was particularly strong showing 1999 growth of 75%.

Marquis and Stuart Crystal brands also had a successful year. Stuart launched the Jasper Conran at Stuart range designed to appeal to more contemporary taste and attract younger consumers. It was greeted with acclaim and immediate sales success. The 'livery' and identity of the core Stuart brand were tastefully rejuvenated and have already won a national U.K. design award. At home in Waterford the Visitor Center remained 1 of Ireland's most popular tourist attractions with 315,000 visitors and sales up 24%.

Waterford has continued its strategy of investing in appropriate manufacturing technology, together with maintaining the largest team of traditional craftspeople in our industry. Our 3 Waterford plants have now been smoothly consolidated into 2, the Kilbarry tank furnace rebuilt, while the Stuart plant in Stourbridge has been fully integrated into Waterford's manufacturing organization. As a result of this streamlining, we were able to meet last year's record consumer demand and so achieve our remarkable sales and profit results.

Waterford's greatest public highlight of last year—indeed of the last century—was, of course, the Times Square Millennium crystal ball, which received front page coverage in hundreds of newspapers and was watched by 1.4 billion television viewers around the world. The visual excitement of this spectacular event was literally overwhelming for every member of the Waterford family and a source of pride for Irish people everywhere. It was the emotional zenith of a stunningly successful year and I want to thank everyone, both in Ireland and in

America, who worked on the ball and, in doing so, met a near impossible challenge—in terms of crystal making, engineering, and logistics—in record time and to glorious effect. At the same time, my sincere thanks go to all of Waterford's employees everywhere whose talent, determination, and skill produced the finest year in our company's history.

The next challenge is to use the platform of our 1999 achievements as a base for further innovation, more growth, and ever wider Waterford brand awareness. Even though our Millennium products remain on sale in 2000 (and are selling well), we already have in the pipeline a broad range of exciting new products to maintain and extend sales momentum. These will replicate the key attributes of the Millennium Collection and will appeal to consumers looking for the ideal gift and to collectors who enjoy owning a series of beautiful pieces of crystal linked by a theme or story. Additionally there is significant potential for further expansion of line and brand extensions which are still at an early stage of their lives. Our recently launched Waterford Jewelry is a particularly exciting prospect. Given the proven creativity of our people and the responsiveness of our organization to market trends, we are sure of continued success.

Waterford Crystal has been a great brand for a long time. In the past decade, we have nurtured and promoted our brand with the utmost care and thoughtfulness. We have made it more accessible to many more consumers. We continue to refuse to sell seconds and we discourage discounting, while insisting that we distribute only in the finest stores. We have extended the brand carefully, protectively, intelligently. We have invested in effective advertising and wonderful, indeed spectacular, public relations. We have maintained the highest standards of craftsmanship which, allied to the most suitable technology available, assures the breathtaking beauty and quality of our products. We have transformed a brand that was once heavily identified with stemware, (i.e., drinking glasses) into a multifaceted brand that today provides our consumers all over the world with perfect solutions to gift giving challenges. We have made a great international luxury brand even greater, which allows us to look forward with confidence to the continuing profitable growth of Waterford in the years ahead.[4]

We have extended the brand carefully, protectively, intelligently.

Waterford Crystal Products: Waterford Crystal product offerings are crystal and table lamps, ceiling and wall fixtures, crystal chandeliers, table items, candle sticks, cutlery, hurricane lamps, collectibles (baby, sport, religious), vanity (picture frames, vanity items, bridal items), executive desk items, crystal animals, clocks and time pieces, vases, and bowls.[5]

Waterford Linens: In spring, 1996, Waterford Linens were introduced. W-C Design of New York manufactured these linens. The label bore Waterford name and W-C Design name in smaller letters. The initial linens were tested in the Irish market before being sold in the United States. The prices varied from $450 for a tablecloth to $8 for napkins. These linens were sold through selected department stores with limited advertising.

Waterford Writing Instruments: In April 1996, Lodis Corporation of Los Angeles was granted exclusive rights to manufacturer and distribute writing instruments with Waterford name.

Waterford Holiday Heirlooms: In December 1996, the company introduced a line of crystal and glass holiday ornaments and tree toppers. Each Christmas (dated-year) new items offered.[6]

WEDGWOOD: CEO'S STRATEGIC REPORT

Happily, Wedgwood today stands more firmly than ever at the top of its league, leaner, hungrier, stronger, the world's pre-eminent luxury ceramic brand.[7]

B. Patterson, CEO

In a tough global ceramics industry, Wedgwood is doing well. Several years ago, we determined that our prime strategic goal was to increase and maintain our international competitiveness in the face of an industry increasingly under pressure from overcapacity, widespread discounting, and cheap, imported products. We recognized that the Wedgwood brand was unique in its international appeal, its centuries-old reputation for quality and craftsmanship and because of its symbolic stature as 1 of the greatest of all English brands.

In order to generate the oxygen to power the Wedgwood brand, we initiated early action—starting in 1997—to take substantial costs out of our business. This included further investment in—and radical restructuring of—our manufacturing and supply-chain operations. We are now the leader in applying appropriate technology in manufacturing, while preserving the traditional hand-crafted element that makes Wedgwood so desirable to discerning consumers. Our restructuring program included over 100 different projects.

I am pleased to report this is now virtually complete. It has not been easy. We now manufacture in 5 rather than 8 factories and we employ 1,800 fewer people, as a result of restructuring, than we did at the end of 1996. Our costs of manufacturing have decreased greatly, while our customer service is more efficient and cost-controlled than ever before in the company's history. We know that had we not acted decisively and in time, Wedgwood might be in a similar unfortunate position to some of our competitors. Happily, Wedgwood today stands more firmly than ever at the top of its league, leaner, hungrier, stronger, the world's pre-eminent luxury ceramic brand.

Total sales in 1999 increased by 5.4%. Our sales in the United Kingdom increased by an encouraging 6.2%. In the widest context, Wedgwood remains the number 1 premium ceramic brand in the nation. We continue to have wonderful relationships with the best British and Irish retailers and we are confident the success of recently launched product lines like Sarah's Garden and Contrasts will be repeated with new lines such as Time for Wedgwood, Fruit Symphony, and the exclusive ceramic creations of leading designers Nick Munro and Paul Costelloe.

Japan's prolonged recession did not abate during 1999, although there were several encouraging signs. In common with overall retail sales, Wedgwood sales in Japan were down 4% year on year. The effect of the recession is felt far beyond the national boundaries of Japan itself, for Japanese tourists have in the past spent considerable sums on Wedgwood products in foreign markets from Hong Kong to London, from Singapore to Hawaii. However, research shows that these same consumers continue to hold the Wedgwood brand in the highest esteem, which has allowed us over the past decade to extend our brand into food, crystal, cutlery, and linen. But the Japanese consumer is changing as well and, as a result, the traditional gifting market is evolving too. Hence we have taken a number of major steps to strengthen our brand—and our distribution efforts—in Japan, aimed at encouraging consumers to self-buy our products as well as purchase for gifts. To this end, we have an outstanding team in place, led by company President Hanspeter Kappeler. Our network of retail shops is being focused and strengthened and our advertising and promotion reinvigorated. The prestige accorded to Wedgwood in Japan continues to flourish, most recently evident in a series of exclusive high-end gift items—some costing £15,000 [IR £19,046]—currently being produced for Takashimaya, the leading department store chain. We are confident that the economy will continue to improve in Japan during the course of 2000 and, as a result of our wide-ranging efforts in 1999, we will be ideally placed to meet the rise in consumer demand.

We made excellent sales progress in the United States, up 14.5%. In this market, which still holds enormous potential for Wedgwood, our brand is perceived in more traditional terms than in either the United Kingdom or Europe, hence the continuing success of our formal bone china lines. During the year we introduced ranges of specially designed giftware along with new tableware lines at more affordable price points. Plans for 2000 include innovative marketing initiatives, improved merchandising, and the penetration of new distribution channels. The dedicated efforts of our Wedgwood spokesperson, Sarah, Duchess of York, paid handsome dividends for us throughout America in both brand awareness and customer loyalty. I continue to receive a stream of letters from Americans who admire and respect the Duchess of York and who are impressed by Wedgwood's association with her.

Outside our 3 main markets, Wedgwood achieved some outstanding results. In Australia, sales increased by a record 13% in 1999. As one of the official licensees for the Sydney Olympic Games, opening in September 2000, we foresee even greater rewards ahead in Australia where our brand has been virtually adopted by a nation, which first started trading with Josiah Wedgwood back in the eighteenth century. In Canada, too, we enjoyed a second great year of sales in a market that ranks Wedgwood at the very highest level of premium desirability.

In Continental Europe, despite the difficult conditions in the German market, we achieved some important new sales breakthroughs. Italy, thanks to our integration with the highly successful existing Rosenthal marketing and distribution team, saw Wedgwood firmly establish itself as 1 of the best-selling brands of premium ceramics. In Holland, always a strong national market for Wedgwood, we saw sales grow significantly. We developed new distribution in the Scandinavian countries—which hold great promise—and we re-established our position in the promising Spanish market, through our relationship with leading retail chain El Corte Ingles.

During 1999 we made an important step into Taiwan—a sophisticated market of 22 million people with high disposable income. Setting up our own operation under Michael Boyle in Taipei, we already operate 8 stores with more to come. The results so far are very encouraging.

The world of distribution and retailing is being shaken by rapid developments in e-commerce. We already use the Internet for business-to-business transactions with our key customers and in 1999, Wedgewood opened its own e-commerce site promoting initially a limited range of giftware items.

Wedgwood is now emerging from some years of rationalization and investing in manufacturing and supply chain operations—making us the least cost manufacturer with leading customer service. In the years ahead the focus of investment can now shift to the front end of the business—our retail partners and our consumers.

In the last year we have carried out some important work on the Wedgwood brand. Working with the London consultancy, The Partners, we sought to refresh our emotional conviction about its consumer appeal—and to renew ourselves with the qualities that make Wedgwood so special. Working through a "right brain" process of visualization and emotional cues, we arrived at a 3-word summation that epitomizes for all of us the essence of our brand—"Authentic English Style."

- *Authentic*—because in the age of "hype," consumers increasingly value things that are real. And with its roots going back nearly 250 years to the founder Josiah Wedgwood, our brand has a heritage and tradition which is truly genuine. For Wedgwood, authenticity is a given.

- *English*—because Englishness is aspirational in all of our markets—from the United States to Germany to Japan.

- *Style*—has within it a dynamic which can embrace both the traditional and the modern, and English style has a unique capability of taking an old idea and re-expressing it in a modern way, often with a twist of humor or surprise. Style then, is dynamic, and it positions us as highly desirable in today's fashion-conscious world.

"Authentic English Style" is the message which Wedgwood will consistently communicate to our consumers as we advance as 1 of the world's leading luxury lifestyle brands in the century ahead.[8]

We plan to increase our brand advertising in lifestyle magazines and other media, in keeping with our long-term strategy of being a global luxury brand.

If we look at recent Wedgwood brand achievements, there are a number of outstanding success stories. At home, British Airways has chosen Wedgwood to provide the special gift which all Concorde passengers will receive as they fly through the Millennium date change and Wedgwood is the sole licensee for premium ceramics in the U.K.'s Millennium

Experience. Also in the United Kingdom, we have embarked on a major study of our national retailing perspectives.

In the United States, Sarah, Duchess of York, has begun her active association with Wedgwood to very favorable press reaction. We are confident that she will bring to our brand the same kind of excellent U.S. consumer awareness that she achieved for Weight Watchers through her energetic, high-profile endorsement.

In Australia, Wedgwood—like Waterford—has been selected as an official licensee for next year's Olympic Games in Sydney. While such licenses were open only to Australian companies, our innovative enterprise—and the strong historical links with Wedgwood, dating back to the eighteenth century (when Joseph Banks sent back to Josiah Wedgwood clay from Sydney Cove)—resulted in the manufacturing processes incorporating Australian materials in a line of luxury gifts, thus opening the door to a unique Australian-U.K.-Irish partnership, in keeping with the international Olympic spirit.

Wedgwood sells 35% of its products worldwide through its own 320 retail shops, outlets, and shops-in-shops. We have embarked on a program of refurbishment to ensure that the Wedgwood shopping environment will appeal to the affluent, younger consumer targeted by our marketing strategy.

In Tokyo, our flagship store in the Ginza will be used to test future retail environments for the Japanese market, including "super boutiques" and other new concepts.

Our strategy calls for increased "relationship" marketing of our products, with direct marketing in appropriate areas, including the Internet, and through expanding our presence in lifestyle retail shops. We plan to increase our brand advertising in lifestyle magazines and other media, in keeping with our long-term strategy of being a global luxury brand.

It would be remiss not to mention the dedication and energy of Lord Wedgwood, our international ambassador, who has travelled the globe for week after week to promote the brand with his own unique combination of knowledge, eloquence, and conviction. His appearances on television and radio and in the press around the world have won many new friends for Wedgwood. In addition to his efforts, our public relations achievements include numerous craft events, the Wedgwood Chef & Potter competition in Ireland and the United Kingdom, and a host of other PR successes.

In July, Wedgwood Brand Director, Gavin Haig, and I met in Barlaston, together with other Wedgwood marketing colleagues from around the world, for the Strategic Marketing and International Marketing Meetings. Held over a 3-day period, this was a most constructive series of reporting and planning sessions. We were particularly encouraged by the support and direction provided over the entire 3 days by Deputy Chairman Peter John Goulandris.

All the above can be seen in the context of our 3-part strategy to achieve our medium- and long-term goals for the Wedgwood brand. First, we have been working hard to develop new products, which will reach the right markets at the optimum price. Second, we have been concentrating on enhancing our existing retail distribution network and on expanding in a manner consistent with a successful modern premium lifestyle brand. Finally, we have taken a number of important steps to communicate directly with consumers the contemporary excitement and appeal of today's Wedgwood products—and the relevance to their lives of the great Wedgwood brand.[9]

Rosenthal: CEO's Strategic Report

Last year was a very exciting one for us at Rosenthal.[10]
O. C. Küsel, CEO

Though conditions in our home consumer market of Germany were difficult, particularly in the first half of the year, there were definite signs of improvement in the second half. At the same time, we increased our leading market share in Germany, crossing the significant 25%

hurdle for the first time in our history. Overall the German ceramics market was down about 13%, while Rosenthal managed to hold its sales decrease to just 2.5%.

The forecasts for the German economy in 2000 are good, predicting double the growth of last year, and we know from past history that, if correct, this should make a substantial impact on Rosenthal's sales, particularly in the second half of this year.

Looking at our other markets offers a more comprehensive and realistic view of where Rosenthal truly stands some 2 years after joining the Waterford Wedgwood group. Thanks to the successful integration which has been achieved, Rosenthal saw double-digit sales growth in the United States and in Continental Europe (outside Germany). In Japan, where conditions remain difficult, sales growth was less dramatic but this should improve in 2000 as that market improves and as major steps are completed in our integration with the powerful Wedgwood marketing organization in that country.

Italy, in particular, is 1 market that stood out as a major success story for Rosenthal in 1999. Not only are we market leader in Italy, but now that we have completed integration with Wedgwood, we find ourselves on-par in the Italian ceramics rankings and, collectively, miles ahead of any other challenger. This is a model that I am confident we will see repeated in many other European countries in the next few years.

Our single proudest achievement of last year, of course, came with the overwhelming success of the new Bvlgari luxury tableware and gifts lines. Following much the same trajectory as our earlier phenomenally successful partnership with Versace, the elegant new Bvlgari range sold a total of DM10 million [German marks] by year end, which was 2.5 times more than we had forecast. Not only have discerning consumers in the major markets around the world taken our Bvlgari products to their hearts, but they have also received fantastic coverage in the most important lifestyle publications.

We fully intend to develop the Bvlgari range in the future as we have done with the Versace range and look forward to many years of handsome returns from both partnerships. Naturally, we are also currently exploring other possible collaborative relationships with a handful of the world's leading luxury goods designers.

"Design Your Life" remains our corporate and consumer rallying cry and nowhere in our product range is this better expressed than in both our medium-market Thomas line of products and the distinguished new additions to our famous Rosenthal Studio Line. The latter is in brilliant accord with an international consumer trend today towards what is to be called "emotional purism": simple, elegant, functional and highly desirable. The reception to these products has been very favourable, most particularly in Germany, and as the consumer market recovers there, we are confident that we have the exciting new products to take full advantage of improved conditions.

I am pleased to report that our major restructuring efforts are now almost 100% completed. The strategy set out in 1997 called for a number of goals to be achieved: reduction in capacity, a re-focus on our key businesses, and an improvement in the profitability of our retail business. To these ends, 4 factories have either been closed or sold; we have disposed of our other non-ceramics-related businesses and completed the high-tech modernization of our Rothbuhl factory. The program at our factory at Thomas am Kulm, including new cup and plate lines, will be completed in a matter of weeks as I write this.

Our 1997 strategy called for an investment of DM65.8 million in our manufacturing process to effect cost savings of DM 17.6 million per annum. By last summer, having invested slightly more—DM66.9 million—we had achieved our goal and were saving at a rate of DM17.6 million. Our strategy also called for us to outsource 20% of our production in order to increase our global competitiveness and maintain maximum production and price-structure flexibility. We have now achieved that goal as well.

By the end of 1999, I was very pleased by the progress Rosenthal had made in reaching the above and many other goals, first set 2 years earlier. The restructuring program has been successfully implemented with immediately conclusive results. Our concept of Rosenthal 'meets' some of the world's leading luxury designer brands—Bvlgari and Versace—has been an absolute triumph, and will continue to be developed.

Finally, and above all, Rosenthal has traveled an immense distance in a very short time towards becoming 1 of the world's leading premium lifestyle brands in table and giftware. As our reputation begins to soar ever higher in markets like the United States and the Far East, and together with our Waterford Wedgwood partners, I look forward to the next century as 1 that offers almost unlimited opportunity to our company and our great brand.[11]

WATERFORD WEDGWOOD AND ROSENTHAL: CHAIRMAN O'REILLY'S FINANCIAL REPORT

Waterford Wedgwood's operating profit increased by 19.7% to a record-breaking 21.3 million (IR £27.0 million) up from €17.8 million (IR £22.6 million) in 1998. Total Group sales increased 5.5% to €342.6 million (from €324.7 million [IR £435.2 million] in 1998), with Waterford sales growing particularly strongly. Interest costs were up by 23.3% on 1998, reflecting the cash out-flow of the Rosenthal acquisition, restructuring and capital expenditure. Our group pre-tax profits increased by 17.5% to €13.4 million (IR £17.0 million), from €11.4 million (IR £14.4 million) in 1998. The Group ROS of 6.2% showed a gain of 0.7 percentage points on 1998.

Earnings per share before goodwill amortization increased by 13.8% to 1.73¢; this represents a compound growth of 18% in the past 5 years. The Directors are proposing an interim dividend of 0.5714¢ (IR 0.45p) up 12.5%, to be paid to shareholders on the register on 15 October 1999. A scrip dividend alternative will be available to shareholders.[12]

ACQUISITION OF ALL-CLAD

In June 1999, the management acquired All-Clad, which was a premier U.S. luxury cookware company. The acquisition price was $100 million, which was more than double last year's sales of $51.6 million, and 11.2 times operating profits. The goodwill cost was estimated to be $80 million. All-Clad sales had increased more than 3-fold from 1993 to $51.5 million in 1998.[13]

Waterford Wedgwood provided figures to show All-Clad's premium sector growth rate of more expensive cookware and kitchen was about 18% from 1990 to 1998, while overall sector grew about 7% during same period.[14]

Chairman O'Reilly said, "The single most important strategic decision by Waterford Wedgwood last year [1999] was the acquisition of All-Clad."[15] He further stated, "At the heart of any successful luxury brand, of course, are truly great products."[16]

At acquisition time, 97% of All-Clad sales were in the United States. An executive said, "All-Clad is an important brand in the United States and we are going to make it important elsewhere, be that United Kingdom or Japan, Australia or Italy."[17]

Chairman O'Reilly said, "Our strategy is based firmly on a long tradition of quality, style and confidence—embodied in our existing luxury brands in all the world's markets—and on a dynamic approach to promoting and strengthening them in future."[18] This became a crucial criteria for the selection of companies to acquire or invest in.

ALL-CLAD: CO-CHAIRMAN'S STRATEGIC REPORT

Record sales in 1999 continued the outstanding growth which has made All-Clad the envy of the rest of its industry.

C. McGillivary, Co-Chairman

On behalf of my Co-Chairman, Sam Michaels, I [C. McGillivary] am delighted to report that All-Clad's total sales reached US$69.2 million in 1999, representing a rise in our cookware sales of 39%. With the overall U.S. cookware industry growing by between 4 and 6% per year,

All-Clad has averaged 32% a year growth over the past 5 years. This truly outstanding achievement is a result of All-Clad's success in distinguishing and separating itself from the rest of its market. Indeed, the company has virtually created its own category at the very top end of the market.

Innovative new products, strong relationships with leading U.S. retailers, and a distinct vision of its future: these are the 3 key elements which first attracted Waterford Wedgwood to All-Clad and, subsequently, have produced another record year in 1999. It is remarkable but true that, while averaging 32% sales growth, we see enormous promise for All-Clad to sustain and advance its growth in the U.S. market—at an even faster rate. Having already taken so much market share from our competitors, the All-Clad team is full of enthusiasm, ideas, and determination.

I strongly dispute those who say that the gourmet cookware sector is a trend that will peak in a few years. In fact, it seems clear that if you take the sales trend of All-Clad over the past 5 years together with the huge popularity of celebrity chefs on television, the high sales of cookbooks, and the continuing expansion of fine restaurants around the world, you must conclude that this category is on the upside of the bell curve, far from having peaked.

Breaking down our sales in terms of product lines, Stainless increased by 34%, LTD by 24%, and Master Chef was up 20%. In its first year, our All-Clad Kitchen Tools range sold $2.90 million worth of product. When Waterford Wedgwood acquired All-Clad in June 1999, the strategy was to enhance its growth capabilities and improve its ability to better service the U.S. market. Thereafter, in careful stages, we look to expand into selected foreign markets where Waterford Wedgwood already has a strong presence. One of our first decisions was to invest about $5 million in order to increase the manufacturing capacity of the Pittsburgh plant by 33%. Second, we decided to expand the shopping warehouse in order to increase its capacity by 50%. Both of these programs are on track, with the manufacturing increase due to be completed by the summer of 2000.

We fully expected to find a great deal of synergy between All-Clad and the Waterford Wedgwood group, and we have not been disappointed. Distribution and purchasing are 2 of the most important areas in which we have already begun to merge our efforts. However, the Waterford Wedgwood philosophy is firm in its determination to allow each brand considerable independence. We don't want to homogenize a new business. On the other hand, both Waterford Wedgwood and All-Clad have considerable influence on major U.S. retailers and, working together, expect this influence only to increase.

For instance, both Waterford and Wedgwood have outstanding relations with the leading U.S. department stores' bridal registry departments. Brides are, above all, seeking information. Surely there is no better company to advise a new bride on setting up her first home kitchen than All-Clad. We foresee marketing several starter kits of All-Clad cookware that will enable a bride to receive, along with her heirloom bone china and crystal tableware, the finest cookware available in the land. Our WW group clout with bridal registry departments will enable this marketing plan to become reality.

I believe that new ideas are what really drive successful businesses, and I have been very pleased by the quality of innovative thinking that I have found within All-Clad. I am particularly optimistic about the launch of the new line of Emeril Ware in co-partnership with America's leading gourmet television chef, Emeril Lagasse. When the idea was first presented to us at Waterford Wedgwood, it met our own thinking exactly, based on our previous success in launching the Marquis sub-brand for Waterford Crystal. Just as Marquis has been an outstanding success and allowed Waterford to move into the middle market without in any way tarnishing its own prestige value, so I believe the Emeril Ware product line can rapidly and profitably expand All-Clad's market presence.

When it comes to the great opportunities for foreign expansion outside the United States, we are determined to make this move in a manner that will ensure a solid, long-term success for our brand. Rather than leak product into a market, we will have full business plans, full marketing strategies and, when we enter a market, it will be with a splash. All-Clad is an important brand in the United States and we are going to make it equally important elsewhere, be that the United Kingdom or Japan, Australia or Italy. No doubt we will look to All-Clad's previously successful strategy of seeding its products with top professionals who recognize that this is truly an outstanding, high-performance range of cookware. These professionals have gone on to be our most loyal and enthusiastic advocates.

Ideally, we want to make All-Clad a very strong supplier to a number of categories of housewares. The outstanding thing about the All-Clad brand is that it carries a real emotion with the consumer. Its strongest advocate is the user, whether a professional chef or an enthusiastic amateur, who actually owns All-Clad products, who endorses them to friends, who shows them off in the kitchen. This emotional strength residing in the All-Clad brand—the same kind of emotional strength possessed by Waterford Crystal and Wedgwood—should enable a carefully planned and innovative expansion into new categories and, as a result, even higher levels of growth in sales and profits in what is already a lucrative business.

Finally, I want to thank all of the people at both All-Clad and Waterford Wedgwood who have worked hard and intelligently to make this union between the 2 companies a success. I have discovered that the All-Clad team, led by my Cochairman and CEO Sam Michaels, is very similar to the Waterford Wedgwood team: highly professional, thoughtful, not easily satisfied, aggressive, and excellent at working together. I am confident that, thanks to our new products, the new resources brought by Waterford Wedgwood, and our new strategic thinking, All-Clad has only just begun its journey towards becoming 1 of the world's leading home lifestyle brands.[19]

At All-Clad, each and every item of cookware is individually built and finished. As part of the process, we have recently installed in our Canonsburg, Pennsylvania, facility state-of-the-art buffing equipment. These buffers enhance our staff's productivity; at the same time this new technology helps our experienced team to hone and perfect All-Clad's finished quality, already renowned as the best in the world.[20]

ALL-CLAD: CHAIRMAN O'REILLY'S FINANCIAL REPORT

All-Clad, Inc., is the leading premium cookware brand in the United States. Its acquisition was another major step towards achieving Waterford Wedgwood's strategic goals. Not only is All-Clad a company with a strong reputation and unique products, its financial performance over the past 5 years has been outstanding. Sales have gone up more than 300% in that period, to US$51.5 million in 1998. The company has 300 employees at its 2 plants outside Pittsburgh, Pennsylvania. All-Clad has superb relationships with the top premium lifestyle retail groups in the United States.

All-Clad's products are based on a special process of metal bonding. Its high-quality cookware has been widely hailed by the top U.S. professional chefs and food writers and is the fastest growing product range in a very fast-growing sector in the United States. We see enormous opportunities to take it to new markets in the United Kingdom, Continental Europe, and the Far East markets where Waterford Wedgwood has great presence and expertise.

In specific terms, Waterford Wedgwood currently derives 46% of its sales in Europe, 12% in Australia, and 40% in North America. All-Clad has no significant market presence outside the United States. With Continental Europe the fastest growing market in the world for cookware, there is an enormous opportunity for our Group, particularly Rosenthal and Wedgwood, to bring All-Clad into this dynamic new European market. In Japan, Wedgwood's great brand strength will lend a very important helping hand to All-Clad. At the same time, All-Clad's market share in the United States will further strengthen all our Group's brands in that important retail arena. Adding All-Clad products to our Waterford, Wedgwood, and Rosenthal contemporary ranges will extend our Group's presence across a fuller spectrum of the premium lifestyle marketplace.

The European launch of All-Clad is scheduled for the year 2000, with other world markets to follow.

Sam Michaels will continue as Chairman and CEO of All-Clad—a role which he has held since 1988. I am very pleased that he has also joined the main Board of Waterford Wedgwood plc as an Executive Director. His past success and vast business experience will be extremely valuable in guiding the future development of All-Clad within our Group.

All-Clad sales and profits are not included in these interim results, as All-Clad was acquired on 30 June 1999.[21]

OTHER IRISH CRYSTAL COMPANIES

Galway Crystal Ltd. was part of Fermanagh-based Belleek Pottery Group. Galway Crystal was established over 25 years ago. In June 1993, Belleek Galway Irish Crystal was purchased by the Belleek Pottery Group. At the time of purchase, Galway Crystal ". . . was struggling with 35 employees and heavy financial losses." The company went into receivership on April 17, 1993. George Moore, who owned Belleek, turned the company round. It now employed 80 and was profitable. Moore purchased Belleek Pottery in 1990, when it was losing money. Moore established ". . . strong links with U.S. distributors, aggressive marketing and improved brand image were the ingredients which led to a turnaround in that business."[22] These are basically the same strategies he employed in the mid-1990s.

Tipperary Crystal was purchased in 1992 by Ray Stafford and had a debt of 1 million Irish pounds in 1996. The company was sold. From October through December of 1997, the business was at breakeven. In 1998, Yeoman International Holdings reduced their 100% stake to 52%. Two minority partners, Irelandia Investments and Nial Wall, acquire 30% and 18%, respectively. In September, 1999, Louise Kennedy, noted Irish designer, agreed to create a new range of products. Kennedy was compared with John Rocha, who design a modern line of products for Waterford Crystal. Kennedy said, my work will be ". . . a different look and appeal to a different consumer."[23]

Some 60,000 visitors come yearly to the thatched cottage-style showroom in the Tipperary Crystal plant. There are several small regional crystal companies.

Royal Doulton Investment

On November 19, 1999, Waterford Wedgwood management bought 12,380,000 shares of Royal Doulton at 90 p sterling. The shares opened on the previous day at 78 p. The shares were garnered from 5 institutions.

Royal Doulton expected losses for 1999 to be £16 million; the company had recorded a £14.4 million tax loss for the first half of the year. A new software system delivery was delayed for 10 weeks. This caused Royal Doulton to lose about 5% of its annual turnover, the estimated loss was between £10 to £12 million.[24]

Royal Doulton has been undergoing ". . . a major rationalization program, announcing the laying off of 1,200 employees, a fifth of its workforce, last December [1998]."[25] Royal Doulton raised £31 million by issuing shares.

Royal Doulton generated £225 million in sales. The company's primary products are Royal Crown Derby, Minton, Royal Doulton, and Royal Albert. The company had 3 plants in Stoke-on-Trent and 1 in Indonesia.

Richard Barnes, Group Finance Director for Waterford Wedgwood, said, "the purchase represented 'good value,' provided closer cooperation between the 2 companies and gave it 'flexibility'. [Barnes was] . . . adamant the group had 'no intention' of making a bid for the whole company." He further stated, "We are pursuing our strategy of becoming the world's largest luxury lifestyle group."[26]

Royal Doulton management remained neutral on their reaction to the purchase of 14.9% equity stake by Waterford Wedgwood.

Royal Doulton management stressed that the company had "outstanding brand portfolio and strong positions in major markets worldwide and stressed its determination to realize the values of those brands and strategic market positions to the benefit of all its shareholders, employees and customers."[27]

Waterford Wedgwood management did not seek board representation and described the investment as a "strategic investment."

An analyst said Waterford Wedgwood and Royal Doulton brands have each suffered from "grandmother's inheritance syndrome." A young bride or couple will not purchase these brands since the couple will inherit these family treasures. This has been hurting these brands for a decade or more. This has acted as a stimulant for these companies to make new designs (Jasper Conran by Stuart, John Rocha by Waterford). This is their future—new brands and products for the modern couple who want luxury.

Technology, Research, and Product Development

How had advanced technology been adapted to Waterford Crystal's requirements? For centuries glass was formed by pot-melting, then hand-gathered. This method resulted in wastage of up to 75%, and glass pulled from the surface was of necessity marred with impurities. At Waterford we have installed 3 of the most advanced continuous-melt, automatically gathered furnaces in the world, at a cost of tens of millions of euros. Operating this state-of-the-art technology we have more than doubled our previous yield. More importantly, special gathering equipment (inelegantly called "gob-feeders") pulls glass from the purest part of the molten stream of liquid crystal—eliminating all inclusions, air or foreign matter—and delivers it to Waterford's master blowers and cutters. As a benefit of our investment in sophisticated technology, our craftspeople are therefore not only more productive, but they are today creating crystal pieces unprecedented in their quality and purity, each one a masterwork.

But our application of technology is much more than a mathematical exercise. At Waterford Wedgwood we also assure that the science to be applied is befitting of our product, consistent with our traditions, supportive of our craftspeople, and enhancing of quality. This is 1 of our Group's true marks of genius. Building upon a heritage of several centuries, our Irish, English, German, and American engineers, a brilliant team, are without rival in adapting the latest technology to ensure that it is appropriate to the Group's special production needs.

Rosenthal's facility on the outskirts of Selb in southern Bavaria, designed by Walter Gropius, is architecture of great sensitivity—a work environment of harmony and light. Here, Ralf Kuhn and his team have put in place state-of-the-art mechanical handling equipment. This equipment eliminates tedious and heavy manual work, avoids breakage and other handling damage, and frees up Rosenthal's superb manufacturing craftspeople to concentrate their full attention on the making of their product. The result is greater efficiency with improved production quality.[28]

The company spent £5.6 million on design and development in 1999.[29]

Internet Strategy

With the market for business-to-business e-commerce predicted to rise from US$145 billion in 1999 to $7.29 trillion in 2004, Waterford Wedgwood's excellent corporate Web sites are a vital asset for safeguarding the future of the leading luxury home lifestyle brand company in the twenty-first century.

Since the launch of <www.wwreview.com> last year, Waterford Wedgwood has expanded its corporate presence on the Internet to 2 more sites: <www.wwinterim.com> and www.wwelegance.com. All have proved extremely popular.

As any visitor can quickly see, the Waterford Wedgwood group sites contain highly useful information in a very stylish format for both investors and consumers alike. As well as the most up-to-date Waterford Wedgwood financial news, including annual and interim reports, analyst presentations, statements from Chairman Dr. Tony O'Reilly, fascinating features about our products and our co-partners like Bvlgari and Versace, users can access detailed information on each individual brand within the WW group.

Waterford Crystal, Wedgwood, Rosenthal, and All-Clad: if you are searching for company history, product information, and news on the latest happenings for each of these brands, check out the group sites first. Visitors can also watch video footage of special statements and events, access the latest press releases, and e-mail a request for corporate literature or any comments or inquiries. Soon other useful information including contact details for retail stocklists in each market, details of regional or national Waterford Wedgwood headquarters, and even advice on caring for your product will be available.

Click us up today and soon you will be a regular visitor to 1 of the Internet's most informative, exciting, and easy-to-use corporate sites.

KEY FACTS ABOUT THE INTERNET AND TODAY'S BUSINESS

- Britain is the market leader for e-commerce in Europe, accounting for an amazing 95% of EU companies claiming a Web site, and more than half of business leaders using the Net for buying and selling.

- Total global sales transactions will reap $105 trillion in revenue by 2004, with e-commerce accounting for 7% of those.

- The Internet grows by 10,900 people a day in the United Kingdom. Currently, there are 10.6 million people with Internet access in the United Kingdom.

- By 2004, 58.5 million people in the United States will have access to the Internet. (That's 55% of all households and 89% of PC-owning households.)

- Three million people in the United Kingdom search for financial information on the Net every year.

- Spending on Internet infrastructure is expected to quadruple to $41.5 trillion by 2003, surpassing the $1.3 trillion spent on e-commerce that year.[30]

The Internet site has proved extremely popular with <www.wwreview.com> registering over half a million users in just 4 months.[31]

Financial Report by Chairman O'Reilly

REGIONAL FINANCIAL INFORMATION

North America—40% of Group Sales

Waterford continues to make great gains in the United States with sales up 26% over the same period in 1998 (see **Exhibit 6**). As the American economy continues to thrive, Waterford Crystal has increased its U.S. market share to well over 50% of the premium crystal market.

The Times Square New Year's Eve ball by Waterford Crystal, which will be lowered to mark the Millennium celebrations, has already captured the imagination of the American people and hundreds of millions of people around the world will observe, via television and other media, the start of the new Millennium in New York City, focusing on the magnificent Waterford Crystal ball.

Exhibit 6

Selected Financial Information: Waterford Wedgwood plc
(Geographical segment by country of operation. Amounts stated in millions of pounds)

Year Ending December 31	Turnover by Destination	Turnover by Country of Operation	Operating Profit/(Loss)	1999 Net Assets	Destination	Turnover by Country of Operation	Operating Profit Before Exceptional Costs	Exceptional Costs	Operating Profit/(Loss)	1998 Net Assets Restated
Europe	£356.8	£651.6	£68.1	£421.7	£354.9	£579.4	£55.5	(£28.4)	£27.1	£288.6
North America	406.9	399.8	14.3	96.8	283.4	276.2	7.1	(1.1)	6.0	58.8
Asia Pacific	79.8	63.2	(1.1)	24.4	58.7	54.8	—	(1.3)	(1.3)	21.4
Rest of World	36.1	25.2	1.6	8.0	33.5	20.7	1.1	(0.4)	0.7	5.8
	879.6	1,139.8	82.9	550.9	730.5	931.1	633.7	(31.2)	32.5	374.6
Inter Segment Sales[1]	—	(260.2)	—	—	—	(200.6)	—	—	—	—
Group Net Borrowings	—	—	—	(311.8)	—	—	—	—	—	(190.8)
	879.6	879.6	82.9	239.1	730.5	730.5	63.7	(31.2)	32.5	183.8
Minority Interest	—	—	—	(3.1)	—	—	—	—	—	(3.8)
Total Group	879.6	879.6	82.9	236.0	730.5	730.5	63.7	(31.2)	32.5	180.0

Exchange rates used between the euro and the principal foreign currencies in which the Group does business were as follows:

	Profit and Loss Transactions		Balance Sheet	
	1999	1998	1999	1998
U.S. Dollar	$1.06	$1.13	$1.00	$1.17
Sterling	£0.66	£0.68	£0.62	£0.71
Yen	¥121.33	¥146.91	¥102.93	¥132.80

Note:
1. All inter segment sales originate from Europe.

Source: Waterford Wedgwood plc, *1999 Accounts*, p. 19.

This momentous event, and the imaginative new crystal products created to celebrate it, are winning huge numbers of new customers for the Waterford brand—seed corn for new sales opportunities in the years ahead.

I am glad to report that Wedgwood's sales in the United States have reached double-digit growth rates, up by 11%. In April we appointed Sarah, Duchess of York, as our official Wedgwood ambassador in the United States. As her program of events begins in Fall 1999, we expect further growth arising from this exciting alliance. I am also pleased to report that Rosenthal's sales in the United States have increased by 5%.

I have already discussed the benefits that All-Clad's strong position in its sector of the premium homewares market will bring to our Group. I am sure these benefits will lead not only to increased sales for our Waterford, Wedgwood, and Rosenthal brands, but also to a further increase in All-Clad's advancing market share in the United States.

Were All-Clad sales consolidated into the first half, sales in the continuingly robust North American market would be close to 45% of the worldwide total.

U.K. and Ireland—24% of Group Sales

Wedgwood's sales remained steady during the first 6 months and a growth trend is already apparent for the second half of 1999. Highly successful product lines like Sarah's Garden, Variations, and our new Weekday Weekend, have enjoyed steady sales increases. The upcoming launch of a new Paul Costelloe range of ceramic tableware, new giftware and jewelry lines, and Wedgwood's appointment as sole premium ceramics licensee for the U.K.'s Millennium Experience will underpin the growth trend. The completion and launch of our state-of-the-art Global Processing Center (distribution facility) in Staffordshire is already bringing significant benefits to our cost efficiency and customer service.

Waterford Crystal had an excellent year in the United Kingdom and Ireland, echoing its success in the United States, with sales up 18%. With the John Rocha range continuing to grow strongly and the imminent launch of the superb new Jasper Conran-designed range of crystal from Stuart, Waterford's subsidiary in the U.K., we expect even greater returns by the end of 1999.

Continental Europe—22% of Group Sales

The Group's sales in Europe, particularly Rosenthal in Germany, reflected difficult market conditions there. Despite this, several of our new product launches were very successful. The Bvlgari collection from Rosenthal has been a fantastic success and has already sold €2.6 million in 3 months, the figure originally estimated for its first year's sales, and Versace remains strong. The lower cost Benetton range, designed to introduce the Rosenthal brand to a new younger consumer group, has begun to take off—all indications show that sales will exceed our expectations.

Wedgwood sales in Europe were affected by restructuring of distribution in order to change from third party distribution to joint Rosenthal/Wedgwood distribution to our customers. In Holland, Scandinavia, and Spain, Wedgwood continued to report strong growth.

Australia—12% of Group Sales

Overall Australian sales declined by 3.6%, continuing to recognize the slowdown in Japan but gaining in the rest of this region.

In Australia, our Waterford Wedgwood team achieved a considerable triumph with the appointment of both Waterford and Wedgwood brands as licensees for the creation of commemorative ranges for the next Olympic Games in Sydney. I am proud that Waterford and Wedgwood will both be linked to the Olympics in 2000.

In the difficult Japanese economy of recent years, Wedgwood has held market share and is continuing to invest in the brand, to develop new products—both ceramic and licensed non-ceramic ranges—and to position at price points to meet customer needs. The economy in

Japan is now showing signs of picking up momentum, and we are looking to an expanding market in 2000.

Wedgwood is planning 2 major exhibitions of prestige products in Japan in the year 2000: the first with leading store group Takashimaya and the second with 1 of Japan's top daily newspapers, Sankei Shimbun.[32]

Chairman O'Reilly believes people who come to the Olympic games will want true heirlooms to remember them by, not just tee-shirts or caps.[33]

Overall

During the first half the Group has invested €25 million [IR £31.7 million] in advertising and marketing its brands. This represents 7.3% of revenue, maintaining the 1998 standard. Gross capital investment at €16.7 million [IR £21.2 million] primarily reflects the completion of the Rosenthal capital expenditure programs. At both Wedgwood and Rosenthal the extensive restructuring is nearing completion. We have now, we believe, the 3 most modern and progressive ceramic manufacturing locations in the world. The Group has again shown its growth capability in both sales and profits, as well as through acquisition. Our Group today is twice the size it was in 1994 in sales and profitability, and our brand portfolio is more widely spread by category and these brands are more widely known for their "luxury living" qualities. We shall continue this strategy.

The sustained nature of the Group's growth encourages me for the future. The opportunity for top line improvements presented by All-Clad, the strong performance of our brands in the U.S., the global exposure of the Times Square New Year's Eve Ball by Waterford Crystal for the Millennium, the success of our wide ranging new product development, and the easing of the Asian economies all point to the Group increasing its momentum.[34]

Other Selected Financial Information

Exhibits 7 and **8** are consolidated profit and loss accounts. **Exhibit 7** was stated in millions of euros (€) for 1999–1995, and **Exhibit 8** was stated in millions of Irish pounds (IRE) for 1998–

Exhibit 7

Consolidated Profit and Loss Account (1999–1995): Waterford Wedgwood plc
(Amounts stated in millions of Euros, except per share data)

Year Ending December 31	1999	1998	1997	1996	1995
Turnover	€879.6	€730.5	€529.7	€477.8	€437.4
Operating profit before exceptional charge	82.9	63.7	57.4	49.8	42.3
Operating profit after exceptional charge	82.9	32.5	22.1	49.8	42.3
Share of profits of associated undertaking	—	—	0.6	—	—
Net interest cost	(17.4)	(13.6)	(7.2)	(5.5)	(6.6)
Profit on ordinary activities before taxation	65.5	18.9	15.5	44.3	35.7
Taxation on profit on ordinary activities	(9.4)	(2.5)	(7.4)	(7.5)	(5.1)
Profit on ordinary activities after taxation	56.1	16.4	8.1	36.8	30.6
Minority interests	0.9	(0.3)	—	—	—
Profit attributable to members of parent company	57.0	16.1	8.1	36.8	30.6
Dividends	(19.1)	(16.1)	(14.1)	(12.8)	(11.2)
Retained profit/(loss) for the year	37.9	—	(6.0)	24.0	19.4
Earnings per share (cents)	7.82¢	2.21¢	1.12¢	5.08¢	4.30¢
Diluted earnings per share (cents)	7.80¢	2.18¢	1.10¢	5.03¢	4.23¢
Earnings per share (before exceptional charge and goodwill amortization)—(cents)	8.26¢	6.59¢	5.97¢	5.08¢	4.30¢

Source: Waterford Wedgwood plc, *1999 Annual Report*, p. 34.

Exhibit 8

Consolidated profit and loss account (1998–1995): Waterford Wedgwood plc
(Amounts stated in millions of Irish pounds (IR£), except per share data)

Year Ending December 31	1998	1997	1996	1995
Turnover	IR£575.3	IR£417.2	IR£376.3	IR£344.5
Operating profit before exceptional charge	50.2	45.2	39.2	33.3
Operating profit after exceptional charge	25.6	17.4	39.2	33.3
Share of profits of associated undertaking	—	0.5	—	—
Net interest cost	(10.7)	(5.7)	(4.3)	(5.2)
Profit on ordinary activities before taxation	14.9	12.2	34.9	28.1
Taxation on profit on ordinary activities	(2.0)	(5.8)	(5.9)	(4.0)
Profit on ordinary activities after taxation	12.9	6.4	29.0	24.1
Minority interests	(0.2)	—	—	—
Profit attributable to members of parent company	12.7	6.4	29.0	24.1
Dividends	(12.7)	(11.1)	(10.1)	(8.8)
Retained profit/(loss) for the year	0.0	(4.7)	18.9	15.3
Earnings per share	1.74p	0.88p	4.00p	3.39p
Diluted earnings per share	1.72p	0.87p	3.96p	3.33p
Earnings per share (before exceptional charge and goodwill amortization)	5.19p	4.70p	4.00p	3.39p

Source: Waterford Crystal plc, *1999 Accounts*, p. 32.

1995. In 1999, the company started stating its financial statements in Euros (€); **Exhibit 9** shows the company's consolidated profit and loss account in millions of Euros (€). **Exhibit 10** shows the company's consolidated balance sheet in millions of Euros (€), **Exhibit 11** provides selected financial information in 3 currencies—Euros (€), British pound sterling (STG) (£), U.S. dollars ($).

Exhibit 9

Consolidated Profit and Loss Account: Waterford Wedgwood plc
(Amounts stated in millions of Euros (€), except per share data)

Year Ending December 31	Continuing Operations 1999	Acquisitions All-Clad 1999	Total 1999	1998 Restated
Turnover	€842.9	€36.7	€879.6	€730.5
Cost of sales	(425.4)	(20.1)	(445.5)	(389.7)
Gross profit	417.5	16.6	434.1	340.8
Distribution costs	(250.6)	(7.5)	(258.1)	(233.5)
Administrative expenses	(89.7)	(4.7)	(94.4)	(74.9)
Other operating income	1.3	—	1.3	0.1
	(339.0)	(12.2)	(351.2)	(308.3)
Operating profit	78.5	4.4	82.9	32.5
Net interest payable			(17.4)	(13.6)
Profit on ordinary activities after taxation			65.5	18.9
Taxation on profit on ordinary activities			(9.4)	(2.5)
Profit on ordinary activities after taxation			56.1	16.4
Minority interests			0.9	(0.3)
Profit attributable to members of the parent company			57.0	16.1

(continued)

Exhibit 9

(continued)

Year Ending December 31	Continuing Operations 1999	Acquisitions All-Clad 1999	Total 1999	1998 Restated
Dividends			(19.1)	(16.1)
Retained profit for the year			37.9	0.0
Transfer to/(from) reserves and translation adjustments			16.9	(17.8)
Increase/(decrease) in balance during year			54.8	(17.8)
Balance at beginning of year			(62.9)	(45.1)
			(8.1)	(62.9)
Earnings per share			7.82¢	2.21¢
Diluted earnings per share			7.80¢	2.18¢
Earnings per share before exceptional charge and goodwill amortization			8.26¢	6.59¢

Note: Notes were deleted.

Source: Waterford Wedgwood plc, *1999 Annual Report*, p. 14.

Exhibit 10

Consolidated Balance Sheet: Waterford Wedgwood plc
(Amounts stated in millions of Euros [€])

Year Ending December 31	1999 €m	1998 Restated €m
Fixed assets		
Intangible assets	104.8	16.8
Tangible assets	259.5	226.6
Financial assets	22.6	6.7
Total of fixed assets	386.9	250.1
Current assets		
Stocks	238.8	203.9
Debtors	167.0	132.9
Cash and deposits	87.4	68.2
Total of current assets	493.2	405.0
Creditors (amount falling due within 1 year)	(202.3)	(171.6)
Net current assets	290.9	233.4
Total assets less current liabilities	677.8	483.5
Creditors (amounts falling due after more than 1 year)	(430.1)	(291.5)
Provisions for liabilities and charges	(8.6)	(8.2)
Total assets	239.1	183.8
Capital and reserves		
Called up share capital	56.6	56.5
Share premium account	176.7	175.6
Revaluation reserve	10.8	10.8
Revenue reserves	(8.1)	(62.9)
Shareholders' funds—equity interests	236.0	180.0
Minority interests—equity interests	3.1	3.8
Shareholders' funds	239.1	183.8

Note: Notes were deleted.

Source: Waterford Wedgwood plc, *1999 Annual Report*, p. 15.

Exhibit 11

Summary Financial Statements: Waterford Wedgwood plc

To assist overseas investors, the consolidated financial statements of Waterford Wedgwood plc are presented in summary form below prepared in accordance with generally accepted accounting principles applicable in the Republic of Ireland ('Irish GAAP') translated at the year-end exchange rates of €1 = STG £0.62 and US$1.00.

Statement stated in Irish pounds (IR £), pounds sterling (STG £), and U.S. dollars ($):
Waterford Wedgwood plc

A. Consolidated income statement	1999 €mils	1999 STG £mils	1999 US $mils
Net sales	879.6	545.4	879.6
Net income before taxes	65.5	40.6	65.5
Taxes on income	(9.4)	(5.8)	(9.4)
Minority interests	0.9	0.6	0.9
Net income	57.0	35.4	57.0
Income per ordinary share	7.82c	4.85p	7.82c
Diluted income per ordinary share	7.80c	4.84p	7.80c
Income per ordinary share before exceptional charge and goodwill amortization	8.26c	5.12p	8.26c

B. Consolidated balance sheet	1999 €mils	1999 STG £mils	1999 US $mils
Fixed assets	386.9	239.9	386.9
Current assets	493.2	305.8	493.2
Total assets	880.1	545.7	880.1
Current Liabilities	202.3	125.4	202.3
Long term liabilities	438.7	272.1	438.7
Shareholders' funds	236.0	146.3	236.0
Minority interests	3.1	1.9	3.1
Total liabilities, shareholders' funds, and minority interests	880.1	545.7	880.1

Special Note: 1998 conversion rates were based on IR£ (not € as in 1999). The exchange rates were IR£ 1 = U.S. $1.43 and STG£0.86.

Source: Waterford Wedgwood plc, *Accounts 1999*, p. 36.

Notes

1. Parts of this case were written in the present tense to directly represent the quoted materials of Waterford Wedgwood executives. This Overview portion of this section is from Philip H. Anderson's case "Waterford Crystal Ltd." These sections were directly quoted with minor editing. The History section is from ⟨www.wwreview.com⟩.
2. Waterford Wedgwood plc, *1999 Accounts*, p. 9. The above paragraphs were directly quoted with minor editing.
3. Waterford Wedgwood plc, *Interim Review 1999*, p. 22. Just this sentence.
4. Waterford Wedgwood plc, *Review of 1999*, pp. 72, 74, and 75. The above 9 paragraphs were directly quoted with minor editing.
5. Waterford Crystal, 2000 *Give the Gift You Love To Receive*, back side of the cover.
6. *Ibid.*
7. Waterford Wedgwood plc, *Review of 1999*, p. 81. Just this sentence.
8. Waterford Wedgwood plc, *Review of 1999*, pp. 81–83. The above 16 paragraphs were directly quoted with minor editing.
9. Waterford Wedgwood plc, *Interim Review 1999*, p. 19. The above 9 paragraphs were directly quoted with minor editing.
10. *Ibid.*, *Review of 1999*, p. 89. Just this sentence.
11. *Ibid.*, pp. 89–90. The above 11 paragraphs are directly quoted with minor editing.
12. Waterford Wedgwood plc, *Interim Review 1999*, p. 1 of the Chairman's Statement. These 2 paragraphs were directly quoted with minor editing.
13. "All-Clad Has Right Ingredient for Waterford," *Irish Times* (May 31, 1999), p. 12.

14. "All-Clad Has Right Ingredient for Waterford," p. 10.

15. Waterford Wedgwood plc, *Review of 1999*, p. 9.

16. Waterford Wedgwood plc, *Review of 1999*, p. 10.

17. *Ibid.*, p. 95.

18. *Ibid.*, p. 12.Waterford Wedgwood plc, *Review 1999*, p. 1 of the Chairman's Statement. The above 6 paragraphs were directly quoted with minor editing.

19. *Ibid.*, p. 93.

20. *Ibid.*, pp. 93–96. The above 11 paragraphs were directly quoted with minor editing.

21. Waterford Wedgwood plc, *Interim Review 1999*, p. 1 of the Chairman's Statement. The above 6 paragraphs were directly quoted with minor editing.

22. Alex Meehan, "Hordes Expected at Galway Crystal Centre," *Sunday Business* (May 5, 1996), and Eddie Doyle, "Moore Plans £2.5m Galway Centre," *Sunday Business* (May 8, 1994).

23. "Crystal Firm Hoping Things Will Take Shape with Louise Kennedy Designs," *Irish Times* (September 16, 1999).

24. Bill Murdock, "Waterford Wedgwood Takes 14.9% Equity Stake in Royal Doulton," *Irish Times* (November 20, 1999).

25. *Ibid.*

26. *Ibid.*

27. *Ibid.*

28. Waterford Wedgwood plc, *Review of 1999*, p. 65. The above 4 paragraphs were directly quoted with minor changes.

29. Waterford Wedgwood plc, *Accounts 1999*, p. 10.

30. Waterford Wedgwood plc, *Review 1999*, pp. 34–35. The above 6 paragraphs were directly quoted with minor editing.

31. *Ibid.*, 35.

32. Waterford Crystal plc, *Interim Review 1999*, pp. 1–2 of the Chairman's Statement. The above 14 paragraphs were directly quoted with minor editing.

33. Waterford Wedgwood plc, *Review of 1999*, p. 25.

34. Waterford Crystal plc, *Interim Review 1999*, p. 2 of the Chairman's Statement. The above 2 paragraphs were quoted with minor editing.

Case 9

Larry J. Ellison—Entrepreneurial Spirit at Oracle Corporation (2000)

Joyce P. Vincelette, Ellie A. Fogarty, and Thomas L. Wheelen

Larry J. Ellison has been Chief Executive Officer (CEO) since he cofounded Oracle in 1977, and he became Chairman in June 1995. His business philosophy is "to heck with cooperation, this means war." He is obsessed with toppling the number 1 software company (Microsoft and Bill Gates) from its perch, but occasionally trains his guns on other competitors as well."[1]

He was known as a loose cannon among industry leaders. His best friend, Steve Jobs, Chairman and CEO of Apple Computer, calls Ellison the "outrageous poster child."[2]

He has been accused of company bashing of competitors and their products. Some executives felt that some of Oracle's advertising sometimes goes overboard. Scott McNeally, Chairman of Sun Microsystems, said with some admiration, "There's a bit of P. T. Barnum in him."[3]

Jim Barksdale, CEO of Netscape, said, Ellison ". . . is talking down Netscape's stock because he wants to acquire the company."[4] AOL acquired Netscape.

Ellison was very competitive in all aspects of his life. He had a passion for ocean yachting and competed once in the Trans Pacific race and won it. His other passions were piloting jets, fitness, fine art, Asian culture, and women. He was frequently listed among the most eligible bachelors in Silicon Valley.

Ellison's management style was that he was a big-picture individual all the way. He delegated the day-to-day management to 2 of his trusted lieutenants. Others said that he had centralized decision making over the past few years.

Ellison's Internet strategy was "To be the company that makes the software that runs e-commerce. The largest retail sites are all powered by Oracle, most large Web sites use Oracle's database products, and the company was investing heavily in ventures for wireless data devices. Ellison was creating a network within Oracle as well, linking international offices and sharing sales, marketing, and other data. The effort has already saved the company about $1 billion."[5]

His personal strengths were "A rare blend of technology savvy and super salesmanship."[6] His personal weaknesses were "Not the most popular guy in the Valley. Loquacious, opinionated, abrasive, given to missing product-introduction. Until last year's [1999] decision to work 50-hour weeks, rarely had he showed at the office before 10 A.M."[7]

His stockholders had about 300% increase in their stock in 1999. The stock was scheduled to split 2 for 1 in October, 2000. Ellison was ranked the 15th Best CEO by *Worth* magazine.[8]

His passion for Asian culture and art led him to build a $40 million palace, which was modeled after a sixteenth century imperial Japanese residence, on his San Francisco property.

In 2000, he was ranked number 2 in the world with a net worth of $52 billion. Only Bill Gates', his arch rival, fortune exceeded Ellison's net worth. In late 2000, he passed Gates as the richest man in the world. This was during the slump in high-tech stocks.

Corporate Governance

TOP MANAGEMENT

On June 30, 2000, Raymond Lane, President and Chief Operating Officer (COO) resigned but remained on the Board of Directors until the Annual Meeting on October 16, 2000. No one was appointed to these positions. Raymond Lane joined Oracle in 1992, when Oracle ". . . was still struggling to rebound from a downturn caused by lax financial controls and hyperaggressive sales practices." In 1990, Oracle ". . . almost floundered . . . when auditors discovered that its sales force had been concocting sales in pursuit of commissions."[9] Oracle had to restate its earnings, which resulted in a loss from previously stated earnings with a profit. This re-statement resulted in the stock falling 80%.

This resulted in Ellison hiring Raymond Lane, in 1992, who became President and received many accolades for the company's recovery strategy. Lane had been a top executive at consulting firm Booz-Allen & Hamilton. Ellison said, "Ray's job had changed dramatically [and] he has gradually been decommissioning himself."[10] During Lane's tenure, Ellison focused mainly on product development, and Ellison reasserted his influence to overhaul many of the company's operations. He was able to harness the potentials of the Internet to cut costs by $1 billion and increased efficiencies. These changes according to Ellison, ". . . also reduced Mr. Lane's authority over sales and other operations."[11] Ellison further stated, "He [Lane] used to be more autonomous," and "The line had always been that Ray wanted to run his own show, and there is 1 show at Oracle."[12] During this time, 2 executive Vice Presidents, Safra Catz and Gary Bloom, had been granted more responsibilities. David Roux, former Oracle executive, said, "Ray was the keel to Larry's sail, [and] the fact is the boat would have flipped over without him."[13]

Lane said he was concerned about "Larrygate." He further stated, "Larry intruded on my duties and made it difficult for me to fit into the system the past year; I had no choice but to leave."[14]

Charles Fitzgerald, Director of Business Development at Microsoft, said "without Ray, there is no adult supervision."[15]

The Lane announcement came 2 days (June 28, 2000) after Ellison admitted that Oracle had hired a Washington, DC detective agency, Investigative Group International, ". . . to help prove that archrival Microsoft Corp. had given financial support to groups expressing opposition to a federal antitrust against the dominant software maker."[16] The detectives offered money [up to $1,200] for the garbage of Microsoft allies."[17] A former Oracle executive said ". . . the 2 episodes reinforce a stereotype of Oracle as a brash company that hadn't been to college."[18]

Charles Fitzgerald said, "Make Oracle to be your trusted technology adviser? You can't even trust them to take out the trash."[19] Some observers called the incident "cash for trash," or "Larrygate."

The executive officers of Oracle were:[20]

Lawrence J. Ellison, 54, had been Chief Executive Officer since he cofounded the company in May 1977. Mr. Ellison had been Chairman of the Board since June 1995 and served as Chairman of the Board from April 1990 until September 1992. He also served as President of the company from May 1977 to June 1996. Mr. Ellison was Co-Chairman of California's Council on Information Technology. He was also a Director of Apple Computer, Inc.

Jeffrey O. Henley, 55, had been Executive Vice President and Chief Financial Officer of the company since March 1991 and had been a Director since June 1995. Prior to joining Oracle, he served as Executive Vice President and Chief Financial Officer of Pacific Holding Company, a privately held company with diversified interests in manufacturing and real estate, from August 1986 to February 1991.

Gary L. Bloom, 39, had been Executive Vice President (currently responsible for server development, platform technologies, marketing, education, customer support, and corporate development) of the company since May 1999 and the Executive Vice President of the System Products Division from March 1998 to May 1999. He had held various positions at Oracle, including Senior Vice President of the System Products Division from November 1997 to March 1998, Senior Vice President of the Worldwide Alliances and Technologies Division from May 1996 to May 1997, Vice President of the Mainframe and Integration Technology Division, and Vice President of the Massively Parallel Computing Division from May 1992 to May 1996. Prior to joining Oracle, Mr. Bloom worked at IBM and at Chevron Corporation where he held various technical positions in their mainframe system areas.

Safra Catz, 38, had been Executive Vice President (currently responsible for global business practices) of the company since November 1999 and was a Senior Vice President between April 1999 and October 1999. Prior to joining Oracle, Ms. Catz was at Donaldson, Lufkin & Jenrette, a global investment bank, where she was Managing Director from February 1997 to March 1999 and a Senior Vice President from January 1994 until February 1997 and had previously held various investment banking positions since 1986.

Sergo Giacoletto, 50, had been Executive Vice President for Europe, Middle East and Africa, since June 2000, and Senior Vice President, Business Solutions, since November 1998. He was Vice President of Alliances and Technology of the company from March 1997 to November 1998. Before joining Oracle, he was President, AT&T Solutions for Europe, since August 1994. Previously, he spent 20 years with Digital Equipment Corporation in various positions in marketing and services in the European unit.

Jay H. Nussbaum, 56, had been Executive Vice President, Oracle Service Industries, since October 1998, and Senior Vice President and General Manager of the company's Federal group since 1992. Prior to joining Oracle, Mr. Nussbaum worked at Xerox Corporation where he held various management roles during his 24-year tenure, including President of Integrated Systems Operations. Mr. Nussbaum had served on several key advisory boards for George Mason University, James Madison University, and the University of Maryland.

George J. Roberts, 43, had been Executive Vice President, North American Sales, since June 1999 and served as Senior Vice President, North American Sales from June 1998 to May 1999. Mr. Roberts served as Senior Vice President, Business Online, from March 1998 to June 1998. He took a leave of absence from July 1997 to March 1998. Mr. Roberts joined Oracle in March 1990 and from June 1990 to June 1997, he served as Group Vice President, Central Commercial Sales.

Charles A. Rozwat, 52, had been Executive Vice President, Database Server, since November 1999 and served as Senior Vice President, Database Server from December 1996 to October 1999. Mr. Rozwat served as Vice President of Development from May 1995 to November 1996.

Edward J. Sanderson, 51, had been Executive Vice President, Consulting and Latin American Division, since June 1999, and Senior Vice President of Consulting and the Latin American Division of the company from July 1998 to May 1999. He served as Senior Vice President of Americas Consulting for the company from July 1995 to July 1998. Before joining Oracle, Mr. Sanderson served as President of Worldwide Information Services for Unisys Corporation from February 1994 to June 1995. Prior to Unisys, he spent 18 years in the consulting industry at McKinsey & Company and Andersen Consulting.

Frank Varasano, 54, had been Executive Vice President, Oracle Product Industries since October 1999. Before joining Oracle, Mr. Varasano was a Senior Partner at Booz Allen & Hamilton from October 1998 to September 1999. Mr. Varasano held several positions at Booz Allen & Hamilton, including Managing Officer United States, Global Managing Officer Engineering and Manufacturing Industries, and Managing Officer, New York office. He also served on Booz Allen & Hamilton's Executive Committee and Board of Directors.

Ronald Wohl, 39, had been Executive Vice President, Applications Development, since November 1999 and served as Senior Vice President, Applications Development, from December 1992 to October 1999. From September 1989 until December 1992, Mr. Wohl was Vice President and Assistant General Manager of the Systems Product Division.

Daniel Cooperman, 49, had been Senior Vice President, General Counsel, and Secretary of the company since February 1997. Prior to joining Oracle, Mr. Cooperman had been associated with the law firm of McCutchen, Doyle, Brown & Enersen since October 1977, and had served there as a partner since June 1983. From September 1995 until February 1997, Mr. Cooperman was Chair of the law firm's Business & Transactions Group, and from April 1989 through September 1995, he served as the Managing Partner of the law firm's San Jose Office.

Jennifer L. Minton, 39, had been Senior Vice President and Corporate Controller of the company since April 2000, and Vice President and Corporate Controller since November 1998. From May 1989 to November 1998, Ms. Minton held various positions in Oracle's finance organization including Assistant Corporate Controller, and was a Vice President of the Company since August 1995. Prior to joining Oracle, Ms. Minton held various positions in the Audit Division of Arthur Andersen firm since December 1983.

Ellison had relinquished his $200,000 salary and bonuses through May 2003 for 20 million stock options, worth potentially $1.4 billion. **Exhibit 1** shows the salaries and stock own-

Exhibit 1

Executive Compensation: Oracle Corporation
Summary Compensation Table

Name and Principal Position	Fiscal Year	Annual Compensation		Long-Term Compensation Awards Securities Underlying Options/ SARs (#)
		Salary ($)	Bonus ($)	
Lawrence J. Ellison	2000	$ 208,000		20,000,000[1]
Chairman and	1999	1,000,000	$ 2,752,000	3,000,000
Chief Executive Officer	1998	999,987	$ 530,000	1,500,000
Raymond J. Lane[2]	2000	1,000,000	2,180,000	1,500,000
President and Chief	1999	1,000,000	2,250,000	2,250,000
Operating Officer	1998	974,991	$ 206,250	0
Gary L. Bloom	2000	1,000,000	1,915,000	2,400,000
Executive Vice President	1999	888,864	2,352,919	3,600,000
	1998	334,713	200,000	2,100,000
Jeffrey O. Henley	2000	806,250	1,361,250	1,000,000
Executive Vice President	1999	727,500	1,334,609	1,200,000
and Chief Financial Officer	1998	645,000	113,437	0
Jay Nussbaum	2000	742,897	1,772,069	800,000
Executive Vice President	1999	525,000	1,151,730	1,500,000
Oracle Service Industries	1998	345,600	386,996	360,000
George Roberts	2000	643,182	4,020,158	800,000
Executive Vice President	1999	406,458	357,967	875,000
	1998	106,831	115,844	180,000

Notes:

1. All figures in this column reflect options to purchase common stock and adjustments, to the extent applicable, for two 3-for-2 stock splits and one 2-for-1 stock split effective August 15, 1997, February 26, 1999, and January 18, 2000, respectively. Mr. Ellison's option grant is intended to be the only option grant that he receives in the 4-year period from fiscal year 2000 to fiscal year 2003.
2. Mr. Lane is no longer an employee of the company.

Source: Oracle Corporation *Annual Stockholders Meeting,* September 11, 2000, p. 7.

Exhibit 2

Executives' Stock Ownership: Oracle Corporation

Name and Address of Beneficial Owner	Amount and Nature of Beneficial Ownership	Percent of Class
Lawrence J. Ellison	696,356,050	24.16%
500 Oracle Parkway, Redwood City, CA 94065		
Raymond J. Lane	10,104,298	1*
Gary L. Bloom	3,007,982	1*
Jeffrey O. Henley	7,534,010	1*
Jay Nussbaum	618,954	1*
George Roberts	695,178	1*
Donald L. Lucas	439,815	1*
Michael J. Boskin	477,060	1*
Jack Kemp	18,351	1*
Jeffrey Berg	179,250	1*
Richard A. McGinn	13,500	1*
Kay Koplovitz	79,300	1*
All current executive officers and directors as a group (19 persons)	725,171,403	25.16%

* Means less than 1%.
Note: Original notes were deleted.

Source: Oracle Corporation *Annual Stockholders Meeting,* September 11, 2000, p. 5.

erships of 25.16% by Oracle's executives. **Exhibit 2** shows stock options. Ellison owned 696,356,050 shares (24.16%), so the other 18 executives owned 1.0% of the stock. Institutions owned 44.5%, and insiders owned 46.7%.

BOARD OF DIRECTORS

The 8 directors were:[21]

> **Mr. Ellison**, 56, had been Chief Executive Officer and a Director of the company since he cofounded it in May 1977. Mr. Ellison had been Chairman of the Board since June 1995 and served as Chairman of the Board from April 1990 until September 1992. He also served as President of the company from May 1977 to June 1996. Mr. Ellison was Co-Chairman of California's Council on Information Technology. He was also a Director of Apple Computer, Inc.

> **Mr. Lucas**, 70, had been a Director of the company since March 1980. He had been Chairman of the Executive Committee since 1986 and Chairman of the Finance and Audit Committee since 1987. Mr. Lucas had been a member of the Committee on Compensation and Management Development (the "Compensation Committee") since 1989 and a member of the Nominating Committee since December 1996. He was Chairman of the Board from October 1980 through March 1990. He had been a venture capitalist since 1960. He also served as a Director of Cadence Design Systems, Inc., Coulter Pharmaceutical, Inc., Macromedia, Inc., Transcend Services, Inc., Preview Systems, Inc., and Tricord Systems, Inc.

> **Dr. Boskin**, 54, had been a Director of the company since May 1994. He had been a member of the Finance and Audit Committee and the Nominating Committee since July 1994 and a member of the Compensation Committee since July 1995. He was appointed Chairman of the Compensation Committee by the Board in July 1997. Dr. Boskin had been a Professor of Economics at Stanford University since 1971 and was Chief Executive Officer and President of

Boskin & Co., Inc., a consulting firm. He was Chairman of the President's Council of Economic Advisers from February 1989 until January 1993. Dr. Boskin also served as a Director of Exxon Mobil Corporation, First Health Group Corp., and Vodafone AirTouch Public Limited Company.

Mr. Henley, 55, had been Executive Vice President and Chief Financial Officer for the company since March 1991 and had been a Director since June 1995. Prior to joining Oracle, he served as Executive Vice President and Chief Financial Officer of Pacific Holding Company, a privately held company with diversified interests in manufacturing and real estate, from August 1986 to February 1991.

Mr. Kemp, 65, had served as a Director of the company since February 1997 and previously served as a Director for the company from February 1995 until September 1996. Mr. Kemp had been Co-director of Empower America from 1993 to the present. Mr. Kemp served as a member of Congress for 18 years and as Secretary of Housing and Urban Development from February 1989 until January 1992. In 1996, Mr. Kemp was the Republican candidate for Vice President of the United States. Mr. Kemp also served as a Director of Hawk Corporation, JumpMusic.com, Inc., Proxicom, Inc., Speedway Motorsports, Inc., and ZapMe! Corporation. He was a former quarterback for the Buffalo Bills football team.

Mr. Berg, 53, had been a Director of the company since March 1997. He had been a member of the Finance and Audit Committee since April 1997. Mr. Berg had been an agent in the entertainment industry for over 25 years and the Chairman and Chief Executive Officer of International Creative Management, Inc., a talent agency for the entertainment industry, since 1985. He served as Co-Chair of California's Council on Information Technology and was President of the Executive Board of the College of Letters and Sciences at the University of California at Berkeley.

Mr. McGinn, 53, had been a Director of the company since March 1997. Mr. McGinn had served as the Chairman of the Board of Lucent Technologies, Inc., since February 1998 and had been its Chief Executive Officer since October 1997. He had been President since February 1996, and was Chief Operating Officer from February 1996 to October 1997. Lucent Technologies was the communications and technology subsidiary of AT&T and was spun off in April 1996. Mr. McGinn served as Executive Vice President of AT&T and Chief Executive Officer of AT&T Network Systems from October 1994 to April 1996. He served as President and Chief Operating Officer of AT&T Network Systems from August 1993 to October 1994 and as a Senior Vice President from August 1992 to August 1993. Mr. McGinn also served as a Director of the American Express Company.

Ms. Koplovitz, 55, had been a Director of the company since October 1998. She had been a member of the Nominating Committee since July 1999. Since January 2000, she had been CEO of Working Woman Network, Inc., which operated a Web site aimed at women and provides business tools. From June 1998 to January 2000, she served as Chief Executive Officer of Koplovitz & Co., a company specializing in media start-up ventures. She was the Founder of USA Networks, and served as its Chairman and Chief Executive Officer from its premiere in 1977 as television's first advertiser-supported basic cable network until June 1998. In 1992, Ms. Koplovitz launched the Sci-Fi Channel, which had become one of the industry's fastest growing networks. Ms. Koplovitz was also a director of Liz Claiborne, Inc. In June 1998, Ms. Koplovitz was appointed by President Clinton to Chair the National Women's Business Council.

The outside directors, Kemp, Berg, McGinn, Lane, and Koplovitz, were paid an annual retainer of $40,000 each. Dr. Boskin was paid $100,000 and Mr. Lucas was paid $160,000 in connection with their additional board committee duties. Nonemployee members of the Board also receive directors fees of (1) $1,500 for each Board meeting attended; (2) $3,000 for each meeting of the Finance and Audit Committee attended, and (3) $2,000 per day for each special meeting or committee attended. Nonemployee members are granted stock option (30,000 to 90,000) depending on specific time constraints.

The Organization

Oracle Corporation was the world's leading supplier of software for information management. The company developed, manufactured, marketed, and distributed computer software that helped corporations manage and grow their businesses. The company's software products were categorized into 2 broad areas: *Systems software* and *Internet business applications software*. Systems software was a complete Internet platform to develop and deploy applications on the Internet and corporate intranets, and included database management software and development tools that allowed users to create, retrieve, and modify the various types of data stored in a computer system. Internet business applications software allowed users to access information or use the applications through a simple Internet browser on any client computer, and automates the performance of specific business data processing functions for financial management, procurement, project management, human resources management, supply chain management, and customer relationship management. The company's software ran on a broad range of computers, including mainframes, minicomputers, workstations, personal computers, laptop computers, and information appliances (such as hand-held devices and mobile phones) and was supported on more than 85 different operating systems, including UNIX, Windows, Windows NT, OS/390, and Linux. In addition to computer software products, the company offered a range of consulting, education, and support services for its customers. Also, for customers who choose not to install their own applications, Oracle's Business On-Line offered an online service that hosted and delivered Internet business applications across a network that could be accessed via any standard Web browser.[22]

Product Development Architecture

ORACLE INTERNET PLATFORM

Oracle's product development platform was based on an Internet computing architecture. The Internet computing architecture was comprised of data servers, application servers, and client computers or devices running a Web browser. Internet computing centralized business information and applications allowed them to be managed easily and efficiently from a central location. End users were provided with ready access to the most current business data and applications through a standard Internet browser. Database servers managed all business information, while application servers ran all business applications. These servers were managed by professional information technology managers. By contrast, the traditional, client-server computing architecture required that each client computer ran and managed its own applications, and also be updated every time an application changed. The company believed that the design of its software for Internet computing improved network performance and data quality and helped organizations decrease installation, maintenance, and training costs associated with information technology.

ELECTRONIC BUSINESS

Oracle believed that electronic commerce (the exchange of goods and/or services electronically over the Internet) was revolutionizing business by providing a relatively low cost means of distributing products and expanding markets globally, increased efficiencies, and provided better, more personalized customer services. Because organizations were changing the way employees work, communicate, share knowledge, and deliver value, the company believed that to remain competitive, they needed to develop and deploy Web-based business and commerce applications on the Internet.[23]

Major Product Groups

Oracle had 3 major product groups.[24]

1. SYSTEMS SOFTWARE

The Oracle relational database management system (DBMS)—the key component of Oracle's Internet platform—enabled storing, manipulating, and retrieving relational, object-relational, multidimensional, and other types of data.

- Oracle Version 8*i* was a database specifically designed as a foundation for Internet development and deployment, extending Oracle's technology in the areas of data management, transaction processing, and data warehousing to the new medium of the Internet. Built directly inside the database, Internet features such as Java Server (Jserver), Internet File System (iFS), Internet Directory, Internet Security, and Intermedia, allowed companies to build Internet applications that lower costs, enhance customer and supplier interaction, and provide global information access across different computer architectures and across the enterprise.

- *Oracle Lite Version 8i* was the company's mobile database for Internet computing. The Oracle Lite database management system could be used to run applications on portable devices and to temporarily store data on these devices, which could be replicated back to Oracle. Oracle Lite was a complete and comprehensive platform for building, deploying, and managing mobile applications that principally ran on laptops and information appliances such as hand-held devices, cell phones, smart phones, pagers, smart cards, and television set-top boxes.

- *Oracle Internet Application Server Version 8i* was introduced in June 2000, which was an open software platform for developing, deploying, and managing distributed Internet software application programs. Oracle Internet application *Server 8i* provided the infrastructure necessary to run Internet computing applications, and it enabled customers to build and deploy portals, transactional applications, and business intelligence facilities with a single product.

- *Internet Application Server (IAS) Wireless Edition* was formerly Portal-to-Go, which enabled information and services to be accessed through wireless and other devices. These devices included smart phones, wireless personal digital assistants, standard phones connected to Interactive Voice Recognition systems, modem-equipped personal organizers and television set-top boxes. Using *IAS Wireless Edition*, mobile operators, content providers, and wireless Internet service providers could quickly implement wireless portals (access hubs offering content formatted for small devices) for providing personalized services and content through wireless devices.

2. APPLICATION DEVELOPMENT TOOLS

The company's Oracle Internet Developer Suite contained application development tools, enterprise portal tools, and business intelligence tools.

The company's application development tools supported different approaches to software development. For a model-based approach to development, Oracle offered 2 products: *Oracle Designer* and *Oracle Developer*. *Oracle Designer* allowed business processes to be visually modeled and enterprise database applications to be generated. *Oracle Developer* was a development tool for building database applications that can be deployed, unchanged, in both Internet and client/server based environments. For Java programmers, Oracle offered *Oracle JDeveloper*, a

Java development tool suite for building enterprise applications for use on the Internet. The *Oracle JDeveloper* suite provided a complete Java development environment for developing and deploying applications from Java and HTML clients to server based business components across the enterprise.

Oracle offered *Oracle iPortal* to build portal sites that provided access to database applications. *Oracle iPortal* features a unique browser-based interface and allowed portal sites to be rapidly assembled from "portlets"—reusable information components that wrap commonly accessed pieces of information and application services. Portal sites built with *Oracle iPortal* may be personalized by role and customized by end users.

Oracle's Business Intelligence tools were designed for the Internet and provided a comprehensive and integrated suite of products that enabled companies to address the full range of user requirements for information publishing, data exploration, advanced analysis, and data mining. *Oracle Warehouse Builder* was an extensible data warehouse design and deployment environment that automated the process of creating a single database for business analysis. *Oracle Warehouse Builder* could quickly and easily integrate historical data with the massive, daily influxes of online data from Web sites. After collecting the data, *Oracle Warehouse Builder* cleaned, transformed, and loaded the data into an *Oracle8i*-based data warehouse.

3. INTERNET BUSINESS APPLICATIONS AND ONLINE BUSINESS EXCHANGES

- *E-Business Suite Version 11i* was a fully integrated and Internet-enabled set of Enterprise Resource Planning (ERP), Supply Chain and Customer Relationship Management (CRM) software applications for the enterprise. Oracle was the only company to offer a fully integrated suite of Internet business applications. This integrated suite, which also was available on a component basis, provided integrated enterprise information so that companies can manage their entire business cycle, from initial contact with customers through planning, production, and delivery, to postsale service and support (see **Exhibit 3**). This allowed companies to better align strategic and tactical goals across the entire organization. Available in approximately 30 languages, Oracle's Internet business applications allowed companies to operate in multiple currencies and languages, support local business practices and legal requirements, and handle business-critical operations across borders.

- *Oracle's ERP* applications consisted of integrated software modules to automate business functions such as financial management, supply chain management, procurement, manufacturing, project systems, and human resources for large and mid-sized commercial and public sector organizations throughout the world. These applications combined business functionality with innovative technologies, such as workflow and self-service applications, and enabled customers to lower the cost of their business operations by providing their customers, suppliers, and employees with self-service access to both transaction processing and selected business information using the Internet platform. Self-service applications automated a variety of business functions such as procuring and managing inventories of goods and services and employee expense reporting and reimbursement.

- *Oracle's CRM* applications helped automate and improve the business processes associated with managing customer relationships in the areas of sales, marketing, customer service and support, and call centers. Oracle's CRM applications allowed multichannel customer interactions over the Internet, such as through a call center. *I-store* (an Internet-based storefront used for selling products and services directly to customers over the Web), helped to maximize the use of technology to improve customer relationships. Integrated with Oracle's ERP applications, Oracle's CRM products also allowed enterprises to coordinate global sales forecasting and lead generation with order capture capabilities to help increase the overall efficiency of running a business.

- *OracleExchange.com* was an Internet marketplace that allowed contract and spot buying capabilities, online auctioning, and reverse auctioning. Branded exchanges were company specific versions of *OracleExchange.com,* allowing businesses to take control of their supply chain. Major corporations in the same industry were partnering to bring all their suppliers online with the goal of reducing supply chain costs through increased visibility into demand. Demand that could be fulfilled using their existing supply chain plans could be auctioned out to exchanges. In addition to the exchange platform, Oracle provided procurement software to allow businesses to collect demand from within their organization. Oracle also provided supply-chain planning software so businesses can check and reconfigure their supply chains based on demand.

Services

The company offered the following 3 services:

- **Consulting:** In most of Oracle's sales offices around the world, the company had trained consulting personnel who offer consulting services. Consultants supplemented the company's product offerings by providing services to assist customers in the implementation of applications based on the company's products. Consulting revenues represented approximately 22%, 27%, and 25% of total revenues in fiscal years 2000, 1999, and 1998, respectively.
- **Support:** The company offered a wide range of support services that included on-site, telephone, or Internet access to support personnel, as well as software updates. Telephone support was provided by local offices as well as Oracle's 5 global support centers located around the world. Support revenues represented approximately 29%, 27%, and 25% of total revenues in fiscal years 2000, 1999, and 1998, respectively.
- **Education:** The company offered both media-based and instructor-led training to customers on how to use the company's products. Education revenues represented approximately 5%, 5%, and 6% of total revenues in fiscal years 2000, 1999, and 1998, respectively.[25]

Marketing and Sales

KEY MARKET SEGMENTS

The Company had identified 2 key market segments where its products were sold; the *enterprise business market* and the *general business market.* The enterprise business market segment was defined by the company as those businesses with total revenues of $500 million and above. In the enterprise business market segment, the company believed that the most important considerations for customers were performance, functionality, product reliability, ease of use, quality of technical support, and total cost of ownership, including the initial price and deployment costs as well as ongoing maintenance costs. The general business market segment was defined by the company as those businesses with total revenues of less than $500 million. In the general business market segment, the company believed that the principal competitive factors are strength in distribution and marketing, brand name recognition, price/performance characteristics, ease of use, ability to link with enterprise systems, and product integration. The company believed that it competed effectively in each of these markets, although the competition was intense.

SALES DISTRIBUTION CHANNELS

In the United States, Oracle marketed its products and services primarily through its own direct sales and service organization. The sales and service group was based in the company's headquarters in Redwood City, California, and in field offices that, as of May 31, 2000, were located in approximately 90 metropolitan areas within the United States.

Outside the United States, the company marketed its products primarily through the sales and service organizations of approximately 60 subsidiaries. These subsidiaries licensed and supported the company's products both within their local countries and in certain other foreign countries where the company did not operate through a direct sales subsidiary.

The company also marketed its products through indirect channels, which were called Oracle Alliance partners. The partners included value-added relicensors, value-added distributors, hardware providers, systems integrators, and independent software vendors that combined the Oracle relational DBMS, application development tools, and business applications with computer hardware, software application packages, or services for redistribution.

The company also marketed its products through independent distributors in international territories not covered by its subsidiaries' direct sales organizations.

As of May 31, 2000, in the United States, the company employed 12,485 sales, service, and marketing employees, while the international sales, service, and marketing groups consisted of 18,224 employees.

Revenues from international customers (including end users and resellers) amounted to approximately 48%, 49%, and 50% of the company's total revenues in fiscal years 2000, 1999, and 1998, respectively.

ORACLE PARTNER PROGRAM

The Oracle Partner Program allowed Oracle to pursue new business opportunities with partners as well as direct customers. The types of partners in the Oracle Partner Program were consultants, education providers, Internet service providers, network integrators, resellers, independent software vendors, and system integrators. Partners could join the Oracle Technology Network (OTN), a program specifically designed for the Internet developer community. Oracle provided the technology, education, and technical support that enabled a partner to effectively integrate Oracle products into its business. The combination of Oracle technology and a partner's expertise broadened the company's exposure in new markets, such as the Internet.

HOSTED ONLINE SERVICES

Oracle offered Oracle Business OnLine, a service that delivered enterprise applications and technology across a network from a server that was hosted in a professionally managed environment at a remote data center. With a simple browser and network connections, companies could access Oracle's Internet business applications at costs significantly lower than a traditional deployment. While the customer owned the applications, Oracle owned the hardware, managed the application and server architecture, maintained and upgraded the software, and provided technical support for the customer's operations.[26]

Competition

The computer software industry was intensely competitive and rapidly evolving. Historically, the company had competed in various markets including the database, application development tools, business applications, and services sectors. The principal software competitors in the enterprise DBMS marketplace were International Business Machines Corporation, Sybase, Inc., and Informix Corporation. In the workgroup and personal DBMS marketplace, the company competed with several desktop software vendors, including Microsoft Corporation. In the data warehousing market, the company's OnLine Analytical Processing ("OLAP") products competed with those of Business Objects, S.A., Cognos, Inc., and Hyperion Solutions. In the application server market, competitors included IBM, and BEA Systems, Inc. In the business applications software market, competitors included J. D. Edwards, Peoplesoft Inc., and SAP Aktiengeschellschaft. The company continued to compete in these traditional markets as well as in some new, rapidly expanding marketed like the CRM, procurement and supply-chain marketplaces where the competition includes Siebel Systems, Ariba, Inc., Commerce One, and 12 Technologies.[27]

Product and Services Revenues

The Oracle's standard end-user license agreement for the company's products provided for an initial fee to use the product in perpetuity up to a maximum number of power units (processing power of the computers in the customer's network) or a maximum number of named users. The company also entered into other license agreement types, which allowed for the use of the company's products, usually restricted by the number of employees or the license term. Fees from licenses were recognized as revenue upon shipment, provided fees were fixed and determinable and collection were probable. Fees from licenses sold together with consulting services were generally recognized upon shipment, provided that the above criteria had been met, payment of the license fees was not dependent upon the performance of the consulting services, and the consulting services were not essential to the functionality of the licensed software. In instances where the aforementioned criteria had not been met, both the license and consulting fees were recognized under the percentage of completion method of contract accounting.

The company received sublicense fees from its Oracle Alliance Partners (value-added relicensors, value-added distributors, hardware providers, systems integrators, and independent software vendors) based on the sublicenses granted by the Oracle Alliance partner. Sublicense fees were typically based on a percentage of the company's list price and were generally recognized as they were reported by the reseller.

Support revenues consisted of 2 components: (1) updates for software products and end-user documentation; and (2) technical product support services that included on-site, telephone, or Internet access to support personnel. The company priced technical product support services as a percentage of the license price while on-site support services were based on the level of support services provided. Software subscription update rights were also priced as a percentage of the license price and can be purchased separately from technical product support. Most customers purchased support initially and renew their support agreements annually. The company generally billed support fees at the beginning of each support period. Support revenues were recognized ratably over the contract period.

Revenues related to consulting and education services to be performed by the company generally were recognized over the period during which the applicable service was to be performed or on a services-performed basis.

The company's quarterly revenues and expenses reflected distinct seasonality.[28]

Employees

As of May 31, 2000, the company employed 41,320 full-time persons, including 29,564 in sales and services, 1,145 in marketing, 6,650 in research and development, and 3,961 in general and administrative positions. Of these employees, 19,771 were located in the United States and 21,549 were employed in approximately 60 other countries.

None of the company's employees were represented by a labor union. The company had experienced no work stoppages and believes that its employee relations are good.[29]

E-Business Suite (Oracle 11i)

In May, 2000, Ellison introduced e-business suite, Oracle 11i, which was the most important new product introduced by the company in years. It ". . . was a suite of business applications that worked seamlessly with one another to handle everything from customer service on 1 end to relationships with suppliers on the other. And it's all rejiggered to run on the Web."[30]

Ellison's vision of the e-business suite was to make it as popular as Microsoft's Office Desktop Suite. Ellison figured this allowed every size business, from giant corporations to small dot-coms, to buy a single package from Oracle to run their e-business, instead of buying software from many competitors and then trying to merge and integrate these different softwares (see **Exhibit 3**).

David Yockelson, Director of E-business Strategies of Mesa Group, Inc., said that he believed there's no way Oracle can build all this technology itself and match the capabilities of its rivals."[31] He further stated that ". . . building it all themselves is going to be too slow."[32] Oracle's e-business suite was already a year behind in delivery. Yockelson warned his corporate customers that Oracle's e-business suite wouldn't be stable enough until the end of the year to

Exhibit 3
Seamless e-business Suite Software: Oracle Corporation

Seamless e-business
demands
seamless software.

E-business Kit		E-business Suite
Microsoft	Database	**Oracle**
Epiphany	Marketing	**Oracle**
Siebel	Sales	**Oracle**
Clarify	Support	**Oracle**
IBM	Webstore	**Oracle**
Commerce One	Procurement	**Oracle**
SAP	Manufacturing	**Oracle**
i2	Supply Chain Mgnt	**Oracle**
SAP	Financials	**Oracle**
PeopleSoft	Human Resources	**Oracle**

**A complete e-business
suite from Oracle.
Or an e-business kit
from lots of vendors.
The choice is yours.**

ORACLE
SOFTWARE POWERS THE INTERNET

Source: Oracle Corporation.

handle a company's most crucial jobs. Another analyst wondered how Yockelson felt with the e-commerce suite announcement.

Ellison conceded that the development of Oracle's e-business suite had been devilish. "It's a huge job," he said, "but it's the right strategy for Oracle."[33] Ellison insisted that Oracle Release 11i was on target for a May launch. Ellison vowed that "You ain't seen nothin' yet!" and further stated, "If this e-business suite plan works, we're going to be an extraordinary company."[34]

Exhibit 4 shows Oracle's e-business strengths in data storage, business applications, and e-market places, and prospects for each market.

An analyst remembered that Ellison had 3 years ago predicted that the personal computer (PC) was finished. He predicted it would be replaced by the network computer or NC, which Oracle had just built. The new machine would be like an ordinary appliance—cheap, reliable, and solid state. It would not be dependent on Intel chips or Microsoft software. Ellison made this announcement at a gala press conference at Radio City Music Hall in New York City. Pablo Galarza and Brian L. Clark said, "The NC . . . was a spectacular failure . . . "[35] They said, "We are undoubtedly entering a new age of computing dominated by the Internet, where having a PC is no longer a requirement. Welcome to the post-PC era."[36] These analysts wonder if Oracle's e-business suite would be a major success or be like the NC.

Projects for the Internet needed to be done at Internet speed. Wolfgang Kenna, CEO, SAP Americas, said "Our old projects took 18 months or 2 years. Internet speed means 4

Exhibit 4

Assembling an E-Business Powerhouse: Oracle Corporation

Oracle Corp.'s software is the foundation for Web sites, e-commerce, and corporate networks. Here are its most crucial markets:

Data Storehouses	Business Applications	E-Marketplaces
Database software for storing and analyzing corporate data, inventories, and customer info.	*For running everything from accounting to customer management to Web sales.*	*Web-site and internal software for transactions between companies, including auctions.*
Market Size: $10.5 billion in 1999 for software and maintenance; heading for $16.6 billion in 2003.	**Market Size:** $26 billion in 1999; heading for $33 billion this year.	**Market Size:** $3.9 billion in 1999; heading for $18.6 billion in 2003.
Oracle's Third-Quarter Sales: Software-license sales grew 32%, to $778 million.	**Oracle's Third-Quarter Sales:** Up 35%, to $199 million.	**Oracle's Third-Quarter Sales:** $26 million for supply-chain and procurement software.
Market Share: 40%, compared to 18% for IBM, 5.7% for Informix, and 5.1% for Microsoft.	**Market Position:** Oracle is a distant second behind SAP in the market for core corporate applications. Siebel Systems leads in customer-management software.	**Market Position:** The procurement market is expanding into e-exchanges, and Oracle is an early leader along with Commerce One, Ariba, and i2.
Prospects: Oracle dominates the database-software realm on both Unix and Windows NT operating systems. Analysts predict it will hold off the competition indefinitely, thanks to its strong technology and new cachet with dot-coms.	**Prospects:** In May, Oracle plans to release the most comprehensive package of business applications available. It has a good chance to gain market share because its applications are integrated, while others offer pieces that have to be stitched together.	**Prospects:** Oracle has deals to power exchanges for Ford, Sears, and Chevron and is expected to have staying power, thanks to its army of 7,000 software programmers.

Source: Steve Hamm, "Why It's Cool Again," *Business Week* (May 8, 2000), p. 120.

weeks, 6 weeks."[37] Many executives referrred to Internet planning in terms of "dog years." Internet executives did 6 to 7 years of strategic planning for every 1 year of planning done by old brick and mortar companies. This was due to the dynamic changing environment of the Internet.

Oracle's 1-stop-shopping approach appeared to have strong appeal to start-up and mid-market companies because of the ". . . tantalizing prospects of more seamless automation."[38] Doug Allen, CIO of Hostcentric, which was a Web-hosting company in Houston, said, the suite's up-front cost wasn't any less than buying the pieces from different providers. "But it's the ongoing cost of ownership where you don't have to manage different releases from different vendors that is going to make us more successful."[39] Allen's company acquired Oracle's e-commerce suite in the spring and were working its way through the modules. They were installing 1 at a time. Allen thought Ellison's vision "of automating most of a company's customer interaction isn't a pipe dream."[40] He further stated, "If we can automate 85%, that would be pretty good."[41]

Ellison felt the balance of power in software and computing began to shift from desktop computers linked by small servers, which he viewed as Microsoft's market, to giant servers and databases that ran the Internet and electronic-commerce platforms, which was Oracle's market.[42] Ellison felt with this shift in the market, that "I actually believe now we will pass Microsoft." In a recent interview, he said, "I think they [Microsoft] are so late."[43]

Oracle Practices What It Practices

In 1997, Ellison decided to take a few months to find out why Oracle's application business—mainly accounting, ordering, and software sales that ran on Oracle's databases—was having problems. He didn't understand at the time, he admitted, because he had never used his own applications. Ellison said, "The earliest revelations were that I've never even see the applications, because the applications don't provide any information."[44] He was shocked to find the purchasing system could not ". . . identify who the best suppliers were by price, quality, and other metrics."[45] The information was scattered among 70 different computer systems and 70 databases in 70 different countries. He found the same type of problems existed for sales data and human-resources data.[46]

Ellison found the knowledge gaps from his investigation to be "galling." "I'm the CEO of the number 1 company in the world providing technology to manage information," he said. "Well, this is insane. We've got to build a global system, we've got to unfragment our data."[47] Ellison blamed Gates for the fragmentation and complexity issues that existed in the industry.

After Ellison's investigation, he ". . . discovered that there were huge holes in our applications."[48] So he said, "It was very clear to me that we had to build complete suite applications; we had to build a sales system, a marketing system; we had to build it so it is a global system, put it on the Internet; and then we had to roll it out inside of Oracle."[49]

Ellison quickly realized that the first step was to dismantle his country managers. Each manager had his/her own e-mail, human resource, and financial reporting systems, which were supported by 43 data centers around the world. Ellison said, "Not only did we have to separate accounting systems into different countries, but all of these countries hired IT departments to change them in different ways."[50] Ellison decreed that there be only 2 data centers—headquarters and a backup one in Colorado Springs—and only 1 global database for each major function, such as sales and accounting. Ellison realized that knowledge was power and he was asking his managers to give up their power. Many of the units used passive resistance to stop or slow down the changes. Ellison recalls, laughing, that "we had to make numerous management changes. I mean, we had to send a Navy Seal team to blow up the Canadian data center."[51]

Other findings before the complete changeover were:

1. Oracle prices varied from country to country. This made financial forecasts more difficult to develop.[52]

2. Oracle had 250 people whose sole job was to review requests for discounts. This group has been cut to 4. There was 1 global Web store price for each product. The customer goes to Oracle's Web store and gets prices and specifications.[53]

3. Each sales person cut their own compensation plan. Ellison felt vast amounts of time were wasted by the salespeople on this issue. In 2000, headquarters decreed all compensation plans were to be distributed via the Internet. This change was not well received by the managers or the salespeople. Two thirds of the plans were held up by the managers. Ellison said, "I said, the managers don't need to approve them . . . we can bypass the managers."[54]

4. Ellison discovered that by centralizing information and automating relationships with employees and customers, he could cut out a huge amount of costs. He became so enthused about the rewards of "management-by-computer" that he was able to eliminate Lane's $100 million headquarters budget. Ellison was able to wipe out most of the headquarters functions and distribute some of it to division heads. This could be why Lane resigned.[55]

Some specific results of implementing the e-commerce suite were:

1. Oracle estimated that each customer call handled by an employee cost about $350 to process. The new customer service system required customers to enter their own complaints on products. Mike Javis, Oracle's Vice President, said, "We make our customers enter their own bug reports [on problems with software]. That saves us money because we don't have people sitting by telephones." Using the global-sales database, says Javis, "Customers buy Oracle products themselves by going online. That improves the accuracy of everything we do and lowers our costs." Handling a customer "call" on the new Web site was estimated to cost $20, "and twice as likely to be resolved without more follow-up."[56]

2. Gary Roberts, Senior Vice President, cited the tangible benefits as "250 IT staffers; 2,000 fewer servers (which will be auctioned off using Oracle's business-exchange software); 80% reduction in leased space for computer operations when the 2 data centers come online in December, 2000."[57] In 1999, Oracle saved $200 million in IT costs. By the end of 2000, he expected to cut the 450 staff to 50 who supported Oracle's desktop computers.

3. The company was able to expand its online store, which opened in the summer of 1999, to sell all Oracle products to thousands of businesses. The e-business suite allowed Oracle to build a Web-based store operation. Ellison predicted that 100% of revenue in 2000 would be from online sales. It was 10 to 15% in the fall of 1999.[58]

Craig Conway, CEO of PeopleSoft, said that Ellison ran ". . . a sociopathic company" addicted to "lying."[59] He doubted the cost-cutting claims as marketing hype. Conway was a former executive of Oracle.

Other benefits of the new system were:

1. Oracle's aggressive marketing campaigns, which cost $30 million. These campaigns focused on conferences and seminars on Internet computing that had drawn legions of developers. An analyst said, "Oracle will be a monster in this market." And, they are doing it "by winning the hearts and minds of the developers."[60]

2. Oracle forged partnerships with *Fortune 500* giants and small businesses that were moving into e-commerce. Ford and Oracle developed Auto X-Changed, an online exchange for Ford's 30,000 suppliers. Jim Pickert, an analyst at Hambrecht & Quist, said, "They make a great partner for companies trying to figure out their e-business strategies."[61]

Ellison said, "We couldn't beat Microsoft in PC or IBM in mainframes, but we can be number 1 software provider on the Internet. We're the odds-on favorite."[62]

Neil Herman of Lehman Bros. said "Oracle is one of the key Internet infrastructure companies, along with Sun, Cisco, and EMC." Another analyst said, "with all the emphasis on the e-business suite don't forget Oracle had 40% of the global market for database software. IBM was in second place with 18%; followed by Informix with 6%; in fourth place Microsoft with 5%; then Sybase with 4% and all others with 27%."[63]

Oracle Venture Fund

In 1999, Oracle management established an in-house venture-capital fund with a $100 million authorization from the company's Board of Directors. During 2000, the fund attained a rate of return of 504%, thanks in part to a stake in Red Hat Inc., which was a popular Linux operating system. Red Hat went public in August, 1999.[64]

In 2000, the Board of Directors approved quintupling the size of the fund. The company anticipated having stakes in about 70 companies by the end of 2000.

Only 2 of Oracle's companies have gone public. Broom, Executive Vice President, said ". . . he expected the number to grow to 8 by the end of the year."[65]

General Electric Company was the number 1 investor in new companies. In 1999, General Electric invested in 100 companies, and Microsoft was second with 44 investments.[66]

Ellison had invested more than $500 million of his money in approximately 30 companies (biotech, e-commerce, and network appliance companies). A few of his investments were (1) Salesforce.com—$2 million investment—which will replace desktop software for salespeople; (2) Supergen Inc.—$23 million investment—which was working on treatment for the cancer that killed his mother; and (3) New Internet Computer Co.—$10 million investment—which produces a device to replace the PC for the Internet.[67]

In-house investment funds have become somewhat controversial, since some companies (Microsoft, Cisco, etc.) have used the capital gains from their investments to enhance their earnings. Broom said Oracle had not engaged in this practice. On cable finance channels (NBC, Bloomberg, Tech Channel, CNN), the analyst will usually note the earnings per share derived from this type of investment, and state what the company's actual earnings were less the income derived by these types of investments.

Management's Discussion and Analysis of Financial Condition and Results of Operations

RESULTS OF OPERATIONS

Total revenues grew 15%, 24%, and 26% in fiscal years 2000, 1999, and 1998, respectively (see **Exhibit 5**). The lower overall revenue growth rates in both fiscal 2000 and fiscal 1999 as compared to the prior corresponding periods were primarily due to lower consulting services revenue growth rates than those experienced in prior years, partially offset by higher license revenue growth. Sales and marketing expenses continued to represent a significant portion of operating expenses, constituting 26%, 30%, and 33% of revenues in fiscal 2000, 1999, and 1998, respectively, while cost of services as a percentage of total revenues decreased to 29% in fiscal year 2000 from 35% in fiscal year 1999 and 32% in fiscal year 1998 (see **Exhibit 6**). The decline in the sales and marketing and cost of services percentages in fiscal year 2000 was primarily the result of increased license revenues and productivity improvements that reduced headcount and related expenditures. The company's investment in research and development amounted to 10% of revenues in fiscal years 2000, 1999, and 1998. General and administrative expenses as a percentage

Exhibit 5

Revenues by Licensing and Services: Oracle Corporation

	(Dollar amounts in thousands)				
	Fiscal Year 2000	**Change**	**Fiscal Year 1999**	**Change**	**Fiscal Year 1998**
Licenses and other	$4,446,795	21%	$3,688,366	15%	$3,193,490
Percentage of revenues	43.9%		41.8%		44.7%
Services	$5,683,333	11%	$5,138,886	30%	$3,950,376
Percentage of revenues	56.1%		58.2%		55.3%
Total revenues	**$10,130,128**	15%	**$8,827,252**	24%	**$7,143,866**

Source: Oracle Corporation, *Form 10-K* (May 31, 2000), p. 11.

of revenues were 5% in fiscal years 2000, 1999, and 1998. Overall, operating income as a percentage of revenues was 30%, 21%, and 17% (20% prior to the charges for acquired in-process research and developments), in fiscal years 2000, 1999, and 1998, respectively.

Domestic revenues increased 17% in fiscal year 2000 and 27% in fiscal year 1999, while international revenues increased 12% and 21% in fiscal years 2000 and 1999, respectively. International revenues were unfavorably affected in both fiscal years 2000 and 1999 when compared to the corresponding prior year periods as a result of the strengthening of the U.S. dollar against certain major international currencies. International revenues expressed in local currency increased by approximately 17% and 24% in fiscal years 2000 and 1999, respectively. Revenues from international customers were approximately 48%, 49%, and 50% of revenues in fiscal years 2000, 1999, and 1998, respectively. Management expected that the company's international operations would continue to provide a significant portion of total revenues. However, international revenues could be adversely affected if the U.S. dollar continued to strengthen against certain major international currencies.

Exhibit 6

Operating Expenses: Oracle Corporation

	(Dollar amounts in thousands)				
Operating Expenses	**Fiscal Year 2000**	**Change**	**Fiscal Year 1999**	**Change**	**Fiscal Year 1998**
Sales and marketing	$2,616,749	0%	$2,622,379	11%	$2,371,306
Percentage of revenues	258%		29.7%		33.2%
Cost of services	$2,942,679	(4)%	$3,064,148	35%	$2,273,607
Percentage of revenues	29.0%		34.7%		31.8%
Research and development	$1,009,882	20%	$841,406	17%	$719,143
Percentage of revenues	10.0%		9.5%		10.1%
General and administrative	$480,658	13%	$426,438	16%	$368,556
Percentage of revenues	4.7%		4.8%		5.2%
Acquired in-process research and development	—		—		$167,054
Percentage of revenues	—		—		2.3%

Source: Oracle Corporation, *Form 10-K* (May 31, 2000), p. 121.

Licenses and Other Revenues

License revenues represented fees earned for granting customers licenses to use the company's software products. License and other revenues also included documentation revenues and other miscellaneous revenues, which constituted 3% of total license and other revenues in fiscal years 2000, 1999, and 1998. License revenues, excluding other revenues, grew 20% and 16% in fiscal year 2000 and fiscal year 1999. Systems software license revenues, which included server and development tools revenues, grew 15% and 16% in fiscal year 2000 and fiscal year 1999, respectively. Business applications license revenues grew 42% and 16% in fiscal year 2000 and fiscal year 1999, respectively. The higher license revenue growth rate experienced in fiscal year 2000 was primarily due to stronger demand for the company's business applications products, and the introduction and market positioning of new Internet business application products and versions, which had stimulated demand for the company's products.

SERVICES REVENUES

Services revenues consisted of support, consulting, and education services revenues, which comprised 52%, 40%, and 8% of total services revenues, respectively, during fiscal year 2000 (see **Exhibit 9-5**). Support revenues grew 27% and 31% in fiscal year 2000 and fiscal year 1999, respectively, reflecting an increase in the overall customer installed base. The support revenue growth rate will continue to be affected by the overall license revenue growth rates. Consulting revenues declined 4% in fiscal year 2000, as compared to a 34% growth rate in fiscal year 1999. The decline in the consulting services revenues experienced in fiscal year 2000 was primarily due to a decrease in the demand for these services as a result of the following: (1) a slowdown in the business applications market in fiscal year 1999; (2) the company's strategy to focus only on profitable business; (3) a push toward a partner model, leveraging third-party consulting firms who provided consulting services to the company's customers; and (4) shorter implementation engagements for Oracle's newer generation of products. Education revenues, which grew 4% and 12% in fiscal year 2000 and fiscal year 1999, respectively, were also affected by the lower business applications growth rate experienced in fiscal year 1999 and will continue to be affected by the overall mix in the systems and applications license revenue growth rates. Consulting and education revenue growth rates were expected to increase in fiscal year 2001 as compared to the prior year corresponding period due to the increased demand for the company's business applications products experienced in fiscal year 2000.

International expenses were favorably affected in both fiscal years 2000 and 1999 when compared to the corresponding prior year periods due to the strengthening of the U.S. dollar against certain major international currencies. The net impact on operating margins, however, was unfavorable, since the negative effect on revenues was greater than the positive effect on expenses.[68]

SALES AND MARKETING EXPENSES

Oracle continued to place significant emphasis, both domestically and internationally, on direct sales through its own sales force. However, the company also continued to market its products through indirect channels as well. Sales and marketing expenses as a percentage of both total revenues and license revenues decreased in both fiscal year 2000 and fiscal year 1999 as compared to the corresponding prior year periods. As a percentage of license and other revenues, sales and marketing expenses decreased to 59% in fiscal year 2000 from 71% in fiscal year 1999 and 74% in 1998. These decreases were primarily related to increased license revenues and productivity improvements that favorably affected headcount and related expenditures.[69]

Sales and marketing expenses were 25.8%, 29.7%, and 33.2% of total revenue in fiscal years 2000, 1999, and 1998 respectively (see **Exhibit 6**).

COST OF SERVICES

The cost of providing services consisted largely of consulting, support, and education personnel expenses. As a percentage of services revenues, cost of services decreased to 52% in fiscal year 2000 from 60% in fiscal year 1999. The decrease in cost of services as a percentage of services revenues in fiscal year 2000 was due primarily to support revenues, which have relatively higher margins; constituting of higher percentage of total services revenues; improved consulting utilization rates; increased productivity efficiencies; and controls over headcount and related expenditures as the company continued to focus on margin improvement. As a percentage of services revenues, cost of services increased to 60% in fiscal year 1999 from 58% in fiscal year 1998, primarily due to lower consulting and education utilization rates as a result of lower than anticipated revenue growth.[70] Cost of services expenses were 29.0%, 34.7%, and 31.8% of total revenue in fiscal years 2000, 1999, and 1998, respectively (see **Exhibit 6**).

RESEARCH AND DEVELOPMENT EXPENSES

Research and development expenses were 10.0%, 9.5%, and 10.1% for fiscal year 2000, 1999, and 1998 (see **Exhibit 6**). Research and development expenses increased 20% and 17% in fiscal years 2000 and 1999, respectively, when compared to corresponding prior year periods. The higher expense growth rate in fiscal year 2000 was due to planned increases in research and development headcount in fiscal year 2000. The company believed that research and development expenditures were essential to maintaining its competitive position and expected these costs to continue to constitute a significant percentage of revenues.[71]

GENERAL AND ADMINISTRATIVE EXPENSES

General and administrative expenses as a percentage of revenues were 4.7%, 4.8% and 5.2% in fiscal years 2000, 1999, and 1998, respectively (see **Exhibit 6**).

Financial Performance

Oracle's Board of Directors had approved the repurchase of up to 548,000,000 shares of common stock to reduce the dilutive effect of the company's stock plans. Pursuant to this repurchase program, the company had repurchased a total of 467,182,575 shares for approximately $7,725,489,000. In fiscal years 2000 and 1999, shares outstanding were 2,807,572,142 and 2,862,267,300 respectively.

The company's stock had two 3-for-2 stock splits and two 2-for-1 stock splits in August 15, 1997, February 26, 1999, January 18, 2000, and 1 scheduled for fall of 2000.

Exhibits 7 and **8** are the company's consolidated statement of operations and the consolidated balance sheets.

In early May, 2000, Lawrence J. Ellison, Chairman, CEO, and Founder of Oracle met with his executive officers to review and discuss the company's new ad to introduce its new e-business suite. The advertisement focused on Oracle's potential competitive advantage of 1-stop shopping; buying e-business suite versus buying software from many sources. Multisourcing means the e-business must integrate these different software packages into 1 package and deal with each supplier when a problem arises. **Exhibit 3** shows the proposed advertisement.

Exhibit 7

Consolidated Statements of Operations: Oracle Corporation
(Dollar amount in thousands, except per share data)

Year Ending May 31	2000	1999	1998
Revenues			
Licenses and other	$ 4,446,795	$ 3,688,366	$ 3,193,490
Services	5,683,333	5,138,886	3,950,376
Total revenues	10,130,128	8,827,252	7,143,866
Operating expenses			
Sales and marketing	2,616,749	2,622,379	2,371,306
Cost of services	2,942,679	3,064,148	2,273,607
Research and development	1,009,882	841,406	719,143
General and administrative	480,658	426,438	368,556
Acquired in-process research and development	—	—	167,054
Total operating expense	7,049,968	6,954,371	5,899,666
Operating income	3,080,160	1,872,881	1,244,200
Other income (expenses)			
Net investment gains related to marketable securities	6,936,955	24,457	4,300
Interest income	141,904	118,486	85,986
Interest expense	(18,894)	(21,424)	(16,658)
Other	(16,691)	(12,322)	9,991
Total other income (expense)	7,043,274	109,197	83,619
Income before provision for income taxes	10,123,434	1,982,078	1,327,819
Provision for income taxes	3,826,631	692,320	514,124
Net income	$ 6,296,803	$ 1,289,758	$ 813,695
Earnings per share			
Basic	$2.22	$0.45	$0.28
Diluted	$2.10	$0.43	$0.27
Shares outstanding			
Basic	2,839,419	2,891,176	2,932,798
Diluted	2,997,921	2,968,450	2,999,176

Source: Oracle Corporation, *Form 10-K* (May 31, 2000), p. 31.

Exhibit 8

Consolidated Balance Sheets: Oracle Corporation
(Dollar amount in thousands, except per share data)

	2000	1999
Assets		
Current assets		
Cash and cash equivalents	$ 7,429,206	$1,785,715
Short-term cash investments	332,792	777,049
Trade receivables, net of allowance for doubtful accounts of $272,203 in 2000 and $217,096 in 1999	2,533,964	2,238,204
Other receivables	256,203	240,792
Prepaid and refundable income taxes	212,829	299,670
Prepaid expenses and other current assets	118,340	105,844
Total current assets	10,833,334	5,447,274
Long-term cash investments	110,000	249,547
Property, net	934,455	987,482
Intangible and other assets	1,148,990	575,351
Total assets	**$13,076,779**	**$7,259,654**

(*continued*)

Exhibit 8
(continued)

	2000	1999
Liabilities and stockholders' equity		
Current liabilities		
Notes payable and current maturities of long-term debt	$ 2,691	$ 3,638
Accounts payable	287,495	283,896
Income taxes payable	2,821,776	277,700
Accrued compensation and related benefits	725,860	693,525
Customer advances and unearned revenues	1,133,482	1,007,149
Value added tax and sales tax payable	165,304	128,774
Other accrued liabilities	725,630	651,741
Total current liabilities	5,862,238	3,046,423
Long-term debt	300,770	304,140
Other long-term liabilities	186,178	77,937
Deferred income taxes	266,130	135,887
Commitments (Note 5)		
Stockholders' equity	—	—
Preferred stock, $0.01 par value—authorized, 1,000,000 shares; outstanding: none	—	—
Common stock, $0.01 par value, and additional paid in capital—authorized, 11,000,000,000 shares; outstanding 2,807,572,142 shares in 2000 and 2,862,267,330 shares in 1999	3,112,126	1,475,763
Retained earnings	3,343,857	2,266,915
Accumulated other comprehensive income (loss)	5,480	(47,411)
Total stockholders' equity	6,461,463	3,695,267
Total liabilities and stockholders' equity	**$13,076,779**	**$7,259,654**

Source: Oracle Corporation, *Form 10-K* (May 31, 2000), p. 30.

Notes

1. Larry Olmsted, "The Best CEOs," *Worth* (May 2000). He was ranked 14th.
2. Janice Maloney, "Larry Ellison Is Captain Ahab and Bill Gates Is Moby Dick," *Fortune* (October 28, 1996), p. 120.
3. *Ibid.*
4. *Ibid.*, pp. 120–121.
5. Olmsted, "The Best CEOs."
6. *Ibid.*
7. *Ibid.*
8. *Ibid.*
9. G. Christian Hill, "Dog Eats Dog Food and Damn If It Ain't Tasty," *e-company* (November, 2000), p. 170.
10. Don Clark and Lee Gomes, "Oracle President, Operations Chief Quits," *Wall Street Journal* (September 30, 2000).
11. *Ibid.*
12. *Ibid.*
13. *Ibid.*
14. Jon Swartz, "Put Up Your Dukes, Microsoft," *USA Today* (September 28, 2000), p. 2B.
15. *Ibid.*
16. *Ibid.*
17. *Ibid.*
18. *Ibid.*
19. *Ibid.*
20. Oracle Corporation, *Form 10-K* (May 31, 2000), pp. 7–8. This section was directly quoted, except for minor editing.
21. Oracle Corporation, *Annual Stockholders Meeting Announcement* (September 11, 2000), pp. 2–3. This section was directly quoted, except for minor editing.
22. *Form 10-K* (May 31, 2000), pp. 2–3. This section was directly quoted, except for minor editing.
23. *Ibid.*, pp. 2–3. This section was directly quoted, except for minor editing.
24. *Ibid.*, pp. 2–4. This section was directly quoted, except for minor editing.
25. *Ibid.*, p. 4. This section was directly quoted, except for minor editing.
26. *Ibid.*, pp. 4–5. This section was directly quoted, except for minor editing.
27. *Ibid.*, pp. 5–6. This section was directly quoted, except for minor editing.
28. *Ibid.*, p. 6.

29. *Ibid.* This section was directly quoted, except for minor editing.
30. Steve Hamm, "Why It's Cool Again," *Business Week* (May 8, 2000), p. 115.
31. *Ibid.*, p. 188.
32. *Ibid.*
33. *Ibid.*
34. *Ibid.*
35. Pablo Galarza and Brian L. Clark, "Winners & Losers Investing in the Post PC Era," *Money* (May 2000), p. 76.
36. *Ibid.*
37. Stephen Baker and Spencer E. Ante, "Can SAP Swim with the Swiftest?" *Business Week* (June 26, 2000), p. 188.
38. Hill, "Dog Eats Dog Food and Damn If It Ain't Tasty," p. 178.
39. *Ibid.*
40. *Ibid.*
41. *Ibid.*
42. *Ibid.*, p. 171.
43. *Ibid.*
44. *Ibid.*
45. *Ibid.*, p. 172.
46. *Ibid.*
47. *Ibid.*
48. *Ibid.*, p. 172.
49. *Ibid.*, p. 174.
50. *Ibid.*
51. *Ibid.*
52. *Ibid.*, p. 178.
53. *Ibid.*
54. *Ibid.*
55. *Ibid.*
56. *Ibid.*, p. 174.
57. *Ibid.*
58. Edward Iwata, "Oracle Sees Future as No. 1 Software Source on Net," *USA Today* (December 27, 1999), p. 4B.
59. Hill, "Dog Eats Dog Food and Damn If It Ain't Tasty," p. 176.
60. Iwata, "Oracle Sees Future as No. 1 Software Source on Net," p. 4B.
61. *Ibid.*
62. *Ibid.*
63. Jon Swartz, "Put Up Your Dukes, Microsoft," p. 2B.
64. Lee Gomes, "Oracle, After a Good Year, Quintuples Size of In-House Venture-Capital Fund," *Wall Street Journal* (February 4, 2000), p. B4.
65. *Ibid.*
66. *Ibid.*
67. Jim Kerstetter, "Putting His Money Where His Passion Is," *Business Week* (May 8, 2000), p. 124.
68. *Form 10-K* (May 31, 2000), pp. 10–11. The above sections were directly quoted, with minor editing.
69. *Ibid.*, p. 12. This section was directly quoted, with minor editing.
70. *Ibid.* This section was directly quoted, with minor editing.
71. *Ibid.* This section was directly quoted, with minor editing.

Cisco Systems, Inc.

Michael I. Eizenberg, Donna M. Gallo, Irene Hagenbuch, and Alan N. Hoffman

Company Background

Internet giant Cisco Systems, Inc., had its humble beginnings in 1984 as the brainchild of Leonard Bosack and Sandy Learner, a husband and wife team, both of whom were computer scientists at Stanford University. Together, they had designed a new networking device that made it dramatically easier for computers to communicate data with each other. It was their plan to integrate this technology into local area and wide area networks (LANs and WANs). Their vision was to bring the ideas and technology they had used in developing the campus-wide computer network at Stanford to a broader marketplace.

Cisco's original customers were universities, the aerospace industry, and government agencies. Bosack and Learner hired John P. Morgridge to run their growing company. Morgridge, now Chairman of the Board, established a culture at Cisco that stressed frugality and rapid, ongoing innovation. In 1986, the company shipped its first multiprotocol router; in 1987, revenues reached $1.5 million.

Since 1987, Cisco had pioneered the development of router and switch technology that enabled the development and connectivity of larger and larger computer networks, which in a few short years combined to form the burgeoning World Wide Web of today. Throughout a period of rampant Internet and intranet development, Cisco had remained the market leader and held either number 1 or number 2 market share in almost every segment in which it participated. In 1998, Cisco stood at the threshold of a sea of unparalleled opportunities as all forms of communication, whether data, voice, or video, were converging on the Internet as the multimedia superhighway of the future.

Cisco's key to growth was its position as the innovative leader in providing an ever broader and more powerful range of intranet and Internet products, primarily routers, switches, and related services. Expandability was a critical aspect as customers moved from small office networks to huge intranet- and Internet-based network solutions that transmit data as well as voice and full motion video. Potential prospects now saw Cisco Systems as forming the strategic backbone of their enterprises with completely integrated end-to-end solutions capable of expanding as business requirements changed or networking capabilities increased.

This case was prepared by Michael I. Eizenberg, Donna M. Gallo, Irene Hagenbuch, and Professor Alan N. Hoffman of Bentley College. This case was edited for SMBP-8th Edition. Copyright © 1998 Michael I. Eizenberg, Donna M. Gallo, Irene Hagenbuch, and Professor Alan N. Hoffman. Reprinted by permission.

Corporate Governance

JOHN CHAMBERS, CEO

Within 1 year of Cisco's going public, Morgridge hired John T. Chambers as Senior Vice President of Worldwide Operations. Chambers was the son of 2 physicians and had thoughts of entering the medical field himself, but opted for "running his own business." He held a JD (law degree) as well as BS and BA degrees in business from West Virginia University and an MBA from Indiana University. His career in the computer industry began with IBM in 1977 where he spent 6 years. Subsequently he worked at Wang Laboratories for 8 years. Since 1994, Chambers had been President and CEO of Cisco Systems, Inc. He led Cisco through a period of huge expansion in the face of extremely tough competition. His personal and corporate business philosophy remained customer oriented.

Chambers spent as much as 40% of his working hours dealing directly with Cisco's customers. He saw at least 2 and as many as 12 customers every day. He said, "The 2 things that get companies into trouble is that they get too far away from their customers and too far away from their employees." Chambers was committed to staying close to customers and employees. His method was simple. Every employee associated with a Cisco account marked an account as critical when it was associated with an upcoming decision that might go against Cisco. Chambers still personally checked out each of the company's critical accounts every day, always with the employee, and often with the company itself.

Exhibit 1 lists other corporate executives. **Exhibit 2** provides a biographical sketch of the company's Board of Directors.

JOHN CHAMBERS GOES TO CHINA

In September 1998, John Chambers embarked on a 5-day tour of Asia that included meetings with Prime Minister Goh Chok Tong of Singapore, Prime Minister Mahathir Mohamad of Malaysia, and Chief Executive Tung Chee Hwa of the Hong Kong SAR. On September 21, 1998, Chambers met with China's President Jiang Zemin at the Diaoyutai State Guesthouse in Beijing, the final stop of his Asian tour.

During the 90-minute meeting, President Jiang and Chambers exchanged views on a broad range of topics, including the development of the China market economy, the importance of IT and education on the future development of China, the impact of networking technology on the globalization of economies, and China's leadership role during the Asian financial crisis.

President Jiang expressed his desire to see more multinational companies such as Cisco Systems cooperate with, and invest in, China. However, he further stressed that although investment in manufacturing is important, even greater synergy would arise from intellectual exchange. To this end, he said the Chinese government would set legislation and policies to create a beneficial environment to facilitate the technology transfer process.

Said Chambers, "Rapid innovations in networking and telecommunications technologies have accelerated the pace of globalization of the emerging Internet economy. These technological innovations have created unprecedented opportunities for companies in emerging nations such as China to compete globally by leveling the playing field."

He continued, "At a time [1998] when multinational corporations are withdrawing from Asia due to the recent financial crisis, Cisco Systems is taking a long-term view and increasing our investment in Asia, leveraging our position as the worldwide leader in networking for the Internet and the converging telecommunications market."

Chambers further noted, "As a business leader I would like to express my thanks to President Jiang for his leadership role in the recent Asian financial crisis. I would also like to reaffirm Cisco Systems' long-term commitment to China, with continued investments in the form of technol-

Exhibit 1

Corporate Executives: Cisco Systems, Inc.

A. Officers	B. Other Senior Vice Presidents
Larry R. Carter Senior Vice President, Finance and Administration Chief Financial Officer and Secretary	**Douglas C. Allred** Senior Vice President, Customer Advocacy
John T. Chambers President and Chief Executive Officer	**Barbara Beck** Senior Vice President, Human Resources
Gary J. Daichendt Executive Vice President Worldwide Operations	**William Carrico** Senior Vice President Small/Medium Business Line of Business
Judith Estrin Senior Vice President, Business Development Chief Technology Officer	**Howard S. Charney** Senior Vice President, Office of the President
Edward R. Kozel Senior Vice President, Corporate Development	**Charles H. Giancarlo** Senior Vice President, Global Alliances
Donald J. Listwin Executive Vice President Service Provider and Consumer Lines of Business	**Richard J. Justice** Senior Vice President, Americas
Mario Mazzola Senior Vice President Enterprise Line of Business	**Kevin J. Kennedy** Senior Vice President Service Provider Line of Business
Carl Redfield Senior Vice President Manufacturing and Logistics	**Clifford B. Meltzer** Senior Vice President/General Manager IOS Technology and Engineering Operations
	James Richardson Senior Vice President, EMEA/AN Operations
	F. Selby Wellman Senior Vice President/General Manager InterWorks Business Unit and RTP Site Executive

Source: Cisco Systems, Inc., 1998 Annual Report.

ogy laboratories, Cisco Networking Academy education program, joint research and development programs, and local manufacturing alliances. Through these investments, we aim to cooperate with the Chinese government in training a new generation of knowledge workers who can take on the challenges of the emerging Internet economy." In conclusion, President Jiang Zemin wished Cisco continued success in China, and reemphasized his desire to see further cooperation between the Chinese government and Cisco Systems, as part of his government's efforts to strengthen the IT industry and further accelerate the pace of modernization.

Cisco, the largest networking company in China, enjoyed tremendous growth in this market, achieving a year-on-year revenue growth of over 100% for 2 years. In a 12-month period, Cisco increased its China staff by 500% and continued to invest heavily in this country.

CISCO'S BUSINESS PLAN

During 3½ years as President and CEO of Cisco Systems, Chambers grew Cisco Systems revenue from $1.2 billion to more than $8.5 billion in annual revenues. Cisco became the fastest growing company in the history of the computer industry.

Unlike most technology companies, Cisco had never taken a restrictive approach that favored 1 technology over another. The company's philosophy was to pay close attention to its customers' requests, monitor all technological alternatives, and provide customers a range of options from which to choose. Cisco designed and developed its products to encompass all widely accepted industry standards. Some of its technological solutions were so broad that they became industry standards themselves.

Exhibit 2

Board of Directors: Cisco Systems, Inc.

Ms. Bartz, 50, has been a member of the Board of Directors since November 1996. She has been Chairman and Chief Executive Officer of Autodesk, Inc., since September 1996. From April 1992 to September 1996 she was Chairman, Chief Executive Officer, and President of Autodesk, Inc. Prior to that, she was with Sun Microsystems from August 1983 to April 1992, most recently as Vice President of Worldwide Field Operations. Ms. Bartz also currently serves on the Board of Directors of Airtouch Communications, Inc., BEA Systems, Inc., Cadence Design Systems, Inc., and Network Appliance, Inc.

Mr. Chambers, 49, has been a member of the Board of Directors since November 1993. He joined the company as Senior Vice President in January 1991 and became Executive Vice President in June 1994. Mr. Chambers became President and Chief Executive Officer of the Company as of January 31, 1995. Prior to his services at Cisco, he was with Wang Laboratories for 8 years, most recently as Senior Vice President of U.S. Operations.

Ms. Cirillo, 51, has been a member of the Board of Directors since February 1998. She has been at Bankers Trust as Executive Vice President and Managing Director since July 1997. Prior to joining Bankers Trust, she was with Citibank for 20 years, most recently as Senior Vice President. Ms. Cirillo also currently serves on the Board of Directors of Quest Diagnostics, Inc.

Dr. Gibbons, 67, has been a member of the Board of Directors since May 1992. He is a Professor of Electrical Engineering at Stanford University and also Special Consul to the Stanford President for Industrial Relations. He was Dean of the Stanford University School of Engineering from 1984 to 1996. Dr. Gibbons also currently serves on the Board of Directors of Lockheed Martin Corporation, Centigram Communications Corporation, El Paso Natural Gas Company, and Raychem Corporation.

Mr. Kozel, 43, has been a member of the Board of Directors since November 1996. He joined the Company as Director, Program Management in March 1989. In April 1992, he became Director of Field Operations, and in February 1993, he became Vice President of Business Development. From January 1996 to April 1998, he was Senior Vice President and Chief Technical Officer. In April 1998, Mr. Kozel became Senior Vice President, Corporate Development of the Company. Mr Kozel currently serves on the Board of Directors of Centigram Communications Corporation.

Mr. Morgan, 60, has been a member of the Board of Directors since February 1998. He has been Chief Executive Officer of Applied Materials, Inc., since 1977 and also Chairman of the Board since 1987. He was President of Applied Materials, Inc., from 1976 to 1987. He was previously a senior partner with West Ven Management, a private venture capital partnership affiliated with Bank of America Corporation.

Mr. Morgridge, 65, joined the Company as President and Chief Executive Officer and was elected to the Board of Directors in October 1988. Mr Morgridge became Chairman of the Board on January 31, 1995. From 1986 to 1988 he was President and Chief Operating Officer at GRiD Systems, a manufacturer of laptop computer systems. Mr. Morgridge currently serves on the Board of Directors of Polycom, Inc.

Mr. Puette, 56, has been a member of the Board of Directors since January 1991. He has been President, Chief Executive Officer, and on the Board of Directors of Centigram Communications Corporation since September 1997. Prior to this, he was Chairman of the Board of Directors of NetFRAME Systems, Inc., from January 1996 to September 1997 and was President, Chief Executive Officer, and on the Board of Directors of NetFRAME Systems, Inc., from January 1995 to September 1997. He was a consultant from November 1993 to December 1994. Prior to that, he was Senior Vice President of Apple Computer, Inc., and President of the Apple USA Division from June 1990 to October 1993. Mr. Puette also currently serves on the Board of Directors of Quality Semiconductor, Inc.

Mr. Son, 41, has been a member of the Board of Directors since July 26, 1995. He has been the President and Chief Executive Officer of SOFTBANK Corporation since September 1981.

Mr. Valentine, 66, has been a member of the Board of Directors of the company since December 1987 and was elected Chairman of the Board of Directors in December 1988. He became Vice Chairman of the Board on January 31, 1995. He has been a general partner of Sequoia Capital since 1974. Mr. Valentine currently serves as Chairman of the Board of Directors of C-Cube Microsystems Inc., a semiconductor video compression company, and as Chairman of the Board of Network Appliance, Inc., a company in the network file server business.

Mr. West, 43, has been a member of the Board of Directors of the company since April 1996. He has been President and Chief Executive Officer of Hitachi Data Systems, a joint venture computer hardware services company owned by Hitachi, Ltd., and Electronic Data Systems Corporation, since June 1996. Prior to that, Mr. West was at Electronic Data Systems Corporation from 1984 to June of 1996, most recently as President of Electronic Data Systems Corporation Infotainment Business Unit.

Source: Cisco Systems, Inc., *1998 Form 10-K.*

Cisco was the world's largest supplier of high-performance computer Internet working systems. Its routers and other communication products connected and managed local and wide area networks (LANs and WANs). The work entailed many protocols, media interfaces, network topologies, and cabling systems, which allowed customers to connect different computer networks by using a variety of hardware and software across offices, countries, and continents. Cisco's products were sold in 90 countries through a direct sales force, distributors, and value-added resellers (VARs). They were supported through a worldwide network of direct sales representatives and business partners. Their products included backbone and remote access routers, LAN and asynchronous transfer mode (ATM) switches, dial-up access servers, and network management software.

All these products upheld multiprotocol multiple media connectivity in a multitude of vendor environments. Cisco's Gigabit Switch Router (GSR), which provided Internet routing and switching at gigabit speed, was introduced to answer criticism that routers created bottlenecks in the Internet backbone, the network's core. It was targeted at the Internet–service provider market and was designed to substantially outperform Ascend Technologies' GRF high-speed router. The GSR supported several hundred thousand routes compared to the GRF, which was limited to supporting about 150,000 routes.

Cisco's Target Market

Cisco sold to 3 target markets: large enterprises, service providers (SPs) and small/medium businesses. Enterprises that used Cisco's products were large corporations, government agencies, utilities, and educational institutions that had complex networking requirements. In these environments, Cisco's products connected multiple locations and types of computer systems into one large network. SPs were companies that provided information services such as telecommunications carriers, Internet service providers, cable companies, and wireless communication providers. The small and medium-sized businesses that Cisco targeted needed data networks for connections to the Internet and their business partners.

Selling to these target markets had become more complex as technology developed. The industry trend during the mid 1990s had been for high-tech companies to provide consultation services when selling their products. For Cisco this meant that each sale had the potential of becoming a technical consulting assignment. This often resulted in a system integration issue to be addressed from the level of overall business strategy. Cisco consultants would become an integral part of this process. Selling became a highly value added service where a company could not solely depend "on selling the box." In response to this demand, Cisco began to build its network application consulting service. This service, headed by Sue Bostrom, who came to Cisco with extensive consulting experience from McKinsey, consisted of the Networked Application Group of 12 people that began expanding in late 1997.

Cisco's Stock

Cisco's stock had been a strong point of the company's history. Cisco Systems went public on February 16, 1990, in an initial public offering underwritten by Morgan Stanley & Co. with Smith Barney, Harris Upham & Co., of 90.4 million shares at a split-adjusted price of $0.5625 per share. Cisco's annual revenues increased from $69 million in 1990 to $6.44 billion in fiscal 1997. This represented a nearly 100-fold growth in 7 years. Cisco was the third largest company on NASDAQ and among the top 40 in the world measured by market capitalization. The stock had split 6 times since the initial public offering. A share of Cisco common stock sold on February 16, 1990, for $18.00. That single share of stock on November 18,1997, was worth $53.42, and the split history would yield 48 shares of stock for a total value of $2,564.16. In short, an investment of $1,000 in 1990 grew nearly 150 times to a value of slightly more than

$142,000 by 1997. The fundamental challenge for Cisco's management was to maintain the phenomenal growth rate in revenue as well as profitability in the future. Where would the continuing growth opportunities come from?

Globally Networked Businesses

In the 1990s, the rapid emergence of networking technologies had changed the pace at which individuals and companies communicated. The speed of conducting business accelerated daily. A dynamic environment like this forced companies to vastly increase accessibility to all its relevant information in order to remain competitive.

Chris Sinton, Director of Cisco Connection, was convinced that, "The first challenge is moving beyond viewing the network only as an information-sharing tool to using the network as a foundation for applications linked to core business systems that serve all business constituents."

Cisco transformed itself using its own technology to its fullest advantage into a leading example of a globally networked business. Cisco positioned its network, together with its core business systems and operational information, and opened this information to prospects, customers, partners, suppliers, and employees. The company worked in an open, collaborative environment that transcended the traditional corporate barriers in business relationships. There were no communication channels for customers, employees, or suppliers to make their way through. Virtually all operational and business information was open to everybody online all the time, no matter what their geographic location or business relationship to Cisco. Through being globally networked, Cisco saved $250 million in 1997 business expenses by reducing servicing costs and improving customer/supplier relationships.

According to John Chambers, the globally networked business model was based on 3 core assumptions:

- The relationships a company maintains with its key constituencies can be as much of a competitive differentiation as its core products or services.
- The manner in which a company shares information and systems is a critical element in the strength of its relationships.
- Being "connected" is no longer adequate. Business relationships and the communications that support them must exist in a "networked" fabric.

John Chambers believed that globally networked business would set new standards on efficiency and productivity within business relationships by simplifying network infrastructures and deploying a unifying software fabric that supports end-to-end network services. This would allow companies to automate the fundamental ways in which they work together.

Global network applications provided Cisco Systems with a wide range of business opportunities. Cisco's prospects were presented with several attractive alternatives when they considered the purchase of a network system. Cisco noted that a key competitive differentiator was the ease with which prospects could access company information that simplified and facilitated the purchasing processes. Hence Cisco provided its prospects with the Cisco Connection Online (CCO) Web site. CCO was the foundation of the Cisco Connection suite of interactive, electronic services that provided immediate, open access to Cisco's information, resources, and systems any time, anywhere, allowing all constituents to streamline business processes and improve their productivity. Using CCO, prospects had immediate access to information on Cisco's products, services, and partners. CCO allowed potential customers to buy promotional merchandise and Internet software, read technical documentation, and download public software files. Almost one quarter of a million prospects logged on to CCO monthly.

Cisco's fast growth forced the company to find alternatives to traditional sales ordering methods. With rising expenses and a shortage in qualified sales people in the industry, Cisco created the Internetworking Product Center (IPC), part of CCO. IPC served as an online ordering system for direct customers as well as partners. It created better access to support capabilities that enabled the customers to solve problems in less time. Within 6 months of operation, IPC processed more than $100 million in orders. It led to an immense increase in the percentage of orders that Cisco received via the Web. Between September 1996 and September 1997, the percentage of orders increased by 800%. At the same time, the annualized dollar run rate of orders received climbed from $30 million to $2.734 billion, a 9,013% increase. In 1998, the company was receiving more than $9 million in orders per day. Through IPC, Cisco also assisted their direct customers and partners to configure equipment. This led to shorter delivery intervals and more precise orders than would have been the case if Cisco used traditional sales methods. In short, customers received exactly what they wanted in less time.

Cisco also assisted its worldwide clientele through the CCO with technical support. The online support service looked at over 20,000 support cases each month. The service hastened the resolution of problems, improved the support process, and gave immediate global access to Cisco's engineers and support systems around the clock.

For its partners, Cisco had a Partner-Initiated Customer Access (PICA) program. Partners had access to information and interactive applications that supported them in selling more effectively. PICA helped partners to in turn provide their customers with real-time access to the latest software releases. It lifted the resources of Cisco's partners and increased customer satisfaction and loyalty. Through CCO, partners could quickly address difficult customer questions and problems by using the self-help support solutions.

Being a globally networked company, Cisco relied heavily on successful partnerships with suppliers. To do that, Cisco created the Cisco Supplier Connection. This was an extranet application that increased the productivity and efficiency in the supply function. The Cisco Supplier Connection enabled suppliers and manufacturers to dial into Cisco's manufacturing resource planning. It allowed them to use this connection to reduce the order fulfillment cycle. Through the link, they could monitor orders and see them almost at the same time Cisco's customers placed them. The suppliers then could assemble the parts needed from stock and ship them right to the specific customer. After that, the system reminded Cisco to pay for the parts used. Through the Cisco Supplier Connection, the company was able to reduce the time- and labor-intensive functions of purchase ordering, billing, and delivery. The application allowed suppliers to better manage their manufacturing schedules, improve their cash management, and respond more quickly to Cisco's needs, which in turn benefited Cisco's customers. Cisco gained real-time access to suppliers' information, experienced lower business costs in processing orders (an estimated $46 per order), improved the productivity of its employees involved in purchasing (78% increase), and saw order cycles reduced substantially.

For its employees, Cisco created Cisco Employee Connection (CEC), an intranet Web site that allowed them to fulfill their tasks more proficiently. The site contained the unique needs of its 10,000 networked employees and provided users with immediate access to current services and information and instant global communications. All of Cisco's employees could access the same information simultaneously through the power of networking regardless of where they were located. The CEC had been the primary mechanism for decreasing Cisco's communication cost and time to market.

Overall, by becoming a globally networked business, Cisco was able to react more quickly and compete more effectively. Becoming a globally networked business provided Cisco with a scalable (the ability to add on to), manageable business system that enabled them to do more with less. The technology allowed Cisco to reach the goals of improved productivity, reduced time to market, greater revenue, lower expenses, and stronger relationships. They would prosper as other businesses adopt the model it has successfully pioneered. As indicated by the market researcher International Data Corporation (IDC), sales on the Internet would grow to $116 billion by the year 2000. More than 70% of that amount would be from business-to-business transactions, which indicated that the Internet would become 1 of the key distribution channels for companies. Ultimate business success depended on the ability of companies to become online businesses, leveraging their networks and cultivating their interactive relationships with prospects, customers, partners, suppliers, and employees.

The Convergence of Data, Voice, and Video

In 1994, there were 3,000 Web sites in the world, 3.2 million host computers, and 30 million Internet users. Four short years later, there were 2.5 million sites, 36.7 million hosts, and 134 million Internet users. During this time of rapid expansion, the question of which communication protocol would be the standard for linking the increasingly vast numbers of computer systems and networks was resolved. Internet Protocols (IP) have become the 1 fundamental language used in every type of interconnected computing. Two important questions remained unresolved: How pervasive will Internet-based communication become? Will it become the predominant means of converging data, voice, and video? That public communications in the year 2002 will be synonymous with the Internet, at this juncture, seems more realistic than strained.

The world is now experiencing exponential growth of communication via the Internet. This rapid rate of growth is accelerating because of the daily increase in the number of Internet users and because transmissions over the Internet have evolved from just text and data to include multimedia, audio, and full motion video.

Traditional phone companies, using proven and highly stable circuit switching, continue to make impressive technological gains. Northern Telecom's DMS stored program switch has been able to double its performance every 6½ years without any increase in cost. IP routers and frame relay packet switches, such as the ones Cisco provides, have been able to double their performance every 10 to 20 months without cost increases. IP routers and switches can now transfer a higher number of bits per second at a lower cost than traditional circuit switches.

Tom Steinert-Threlkeld stated in his "Internet 2002" article that if you follow this trend to its most reasonable conclusion, the Internet will soon provide the underlying structure for all communication networks, including multimedia transmissions between individuals and businesses, local and long-distance phone service, and television broadcasts via cable or satellite. Given this perspective, we are barely at the beginning of the growth cycle in the networking industry.

Cisco executives are already talking about the day when the cost of moving data, voice, and video along IP networks will be so inexpensive that the price of bundled IP data services will include both long distance and local phone calls at a price substantially lower than what customers pay now for telephone services alone. Other included features will be as diverse as video conferencing, feature film and audio downloading, and voice mail messaging, including lengthy video and audio clips.

Cisco itself continued to provide fundamental solutions that would enable data to move more efficiently along IP networks. Its new Tag Switching technology allowed data packets of various sizes to flow substantially faster and more reliably through routers directly past switches using the same unique Tag. This new technology enabled networks to handle more traffic, users, media-rich data, and bandwidth-intensive applications.

The opportunities in the networking industry were becoming vast as the Internet took its place as the platform for all forms of traditional and innovative communication. Cisco was positioned to be a major innovative force in the future generations of Internet technology. Many experts predicted a 100-fold increase in Internet usage within the next 5 years.

Key Competitive Issues

Customers of the computer networking industry are seeking access to information that will set higher standards of efficiency and productivity, leading to higher profits. Their objective is to heighten their competitive capabilities and give them a competitive advantage over their rivals. Central to this is the ability to manage constituent relationships through the sharing of critical information and the open exchange of resources and services. The need for seamless transmission of data and voice is important to the customer base. Accomplishing this necessitates broad-based suppliers of networking products. Competitors in the networking industry are shifting their focus toward becoming full-service providers in this rapidly growing industry in order to meet the needs of their growing customer base. Correctly assessing the current and, most importantly, the future informational needs of customers is a key factor to a firm's survival or extinction. Cisco Systems, Lucent Technologies, 3Com, Ascend Communications, and Bay Networks are the strongest forces in the push to dominate the market.

Industry growth is so dramatic that analysts and investors are having difficulty determining continuing and future growth rates. This leaves competitors scrambling to gain as much market share as their organizations can maintain and manage. High growth and profitability lead to intense competitive challenges. New entrants are possible from many segments of the high-tech community. New competitors could be from the telecommunications, data networking, software, and semiconductors industries. Companies from these industries are likely to enter based on their strengths in brand name recognition, technological knowledge and capabilities, and a strong financial background. Globalization and the growing strength of both domestic and foreign competitors in all these industries makes the competitive pressure even greater for existing companies.

The Challengers

Commanding approximately 80% of its market put Cisco in an enviable competitive position. However, formidable competitors existed, and as the industry growth rates continued to accelerate, maintaining this market share could be a daunting task. As the industry moved toward the convergence of voice and data systems, competitors were expected to be positioning for growth through merger, acquisition, and/or joint venture partnering. End users were driving industry competitors to provide a full range of services as well as a high level of customization. The ability to create a total system that enabled customers to access information and enhanced their ability to efficiently facilitate their own business and communication processes with their vendors and customers would be a key factor for success. Escalating industry growth left Cisco faced with deciding how much internal growth it could sustain in order to hold its current percentage of a growing market. Its top competitors were sure to be opportunistic of any weakness within Cisco.

ASCEND COMMUNICATIONS

Founded in 1989, Ascend Communications was the leading supplier of remote access solutions, supporting in excess of 30 million Internet connections daily. The company operated in over 30 countries worldwide through a distribution system that included direct sales, OEM relationships, strategic alliances, distributors, and VARs. Ascend's extensive service program, Ascend Advantage Services, was enhanced through an alliance with IBM's Availability Services, a segment of IBM Global Services. This allowed Ascend and its participating resellers to use the resources of IBM's worldwide service network to support Ascend products. Quality was an important strength for Ascend. The company held the prestigious Quality System Certificates ISO 9000 and ISO 9001 covering design, manufacture, sale, and service of data networking products.

Fiscal year 1997 proved to be prosperous for Ascend. Net sales increased 31% from $890.3 million in 1996 to $1.167 billion in 1997. Strengthening the company's competitive position and maintaining a leadership status in networking products and technologies was a high priority for top management. Several acquisitions throughout the year supported the company's transition from a recognized leading supplier of remote access solutions to a broad-based supplier of wide area networking products. The acquisition of Cascade Communications proved to be a significant link to becoming a full-service provider for global communications. Cascade's strength as a leader in broadband data communications products enabled Ascend to extensively broaden its product base. The company also acquired Whitetree, Inc., a pioneer in local area network switching technology, and InterCon, a developer of client software products for both the corporate and ISP markets. These 2 smaller acquisitions filled gaps in building a seamless networking system for their customers. Strong research and development, strategic alliances, and key acquisitions were the strategies Ascend used to position itself as a strong competitor in providing integrated networking solutions for its service provider customers and its enterprise customers.

LUCENT TECHNOLOGIES

On February 1, 1996, AT&T transformed Lucent Technologies into a stand-alone entity by separating it from the parent corporation. The independent organization competed in 3 core businesses. The largest was network operating systems followed by business communications systems and microelectronics products. Lucent's technologies connect, route, manage, and store information across networks. In 1997, net income was reported as $541 million, compared to a net loss of $793 million for the previous 12 months.

Lucent faced serious challenges from both the intense competitive nature of the industry and its internal organization. Two significant factors played a role in the company's performance. The first was its heavy reliance on a limited number of large customers for a material portion of their revenues. One of its largest customers was the former parent AT&T. Increasingly Lucent's customer base was purchasing from fewer suppliers. Therefore, the contracts from these buyers were very large and tended to be highly seasonal, which was the second significant factor impacting Lucent's performance. Delaying capital expenditures until the fourth quarter of the calendar was typical purchasing behavior for Lucent's large customers. With a fiscal year ended September 30, the result was that a disproportionate share of Lucent's revenue stream was recognized in its first quarter. On a calendar-year basis, profitability was lower in each of the first 3 quarters than in the fourth quarter. Consequently investors may have concerns regarding the value of the stock throughout the year. In addition to fluctuations in its revenue stream, Lucent faced stringent demands from its large customers in terms of favorable pricing, financing, and payment terms that extend over multiyear contracts. Recognition of revenue from large cost outlays in the development of large-scale systems for its customers reflected harshly on the company's financial statements. The company encountered a material risk factor should any of its large purchasers reduce orders or move to a competitor.

To reduce the overall risk of dependence on a few large buyers, Lucent began to diversify its customer base by pursuing customers from other industries such as cable television network operators, access providers, and computer manufacturers. However, management did not anticipate that the company's customer base would broaden significantly in the near future. Beginning in fiscal year 1997, the company embarked on an acquisition strategy aimed at strengthening its core businesses and smoothing out the revenue stream. The first transaction in October 1996 was for Agile Networks, Inc., a provider of advanced intelligent data switching products that support both ethernet and ATM technology. In September 1997, Lucent embarked on a major transaction with the $1.8 million purchase of Octel Communications Corporation, a provider of voice, fax, and electronic messaging technologies. The products of Octel were viewed as complementary to the products and services Lucent was offering. Fiscal year 1998 began with 2 transactions. The company sought to further enhance and broaden R&D knowledge and the capabilities gained from the previous transactions. The acquisition of Livingston Enterprises, Inc., a global company that provided connection equipment to Internet service providers was a strategic step in this direction. Lucent continued to follow its strategy of strengthening its core businesses in a joint venture with Philips Electronics N.V. The joint venture, 40% owned by Lucent, was a global conveyor of personal communications products. The complete range of products included digital analog wireless phones, corded and cordless phones, answering machines, screen phones, and pagers.

In an effort to focus on its core businesses, Lucent sold off some of its businesses. The subsidiary Paradyne and the company's interconnect products and Custom Manufacturing Services were sold in 1996. The company's Advanced Technology Systems unit was sold in October 1997. By the end of fiscal 1997, Lucent had positioned itself as a leader in the design, development, and manufacture of integrated systems and software applications for network operators and business enterprises.

3COM

3Com Corporation was the first organization to develop technology for networking personal computers. In the 20 years following its introduction of this new technology, the industry grew to be 1 of the largest in the world. 3Com remained 1 of the top industry competitors. Revenues in 1997 were approximately $3.2 billion, up from $2.3 billion in 1996. Net income rose from $177 million in 1996 to $373 million in 1997. Growth in fiscal 1997 focused on the introduction of new products to expand and strengthen its product breadth and establish the company in emerging market segments. New products were developed in its systems business, switching technology, client access business, and networking software. The new product introductions were supported through the bolstering of the company's sales and support functions and acquisition activity.

The first acquisition of 1997 was OnStream Networks, a leading provider of solutions for integrated video, voice, and data. This addition to 3Com's business portfolio strengthened its ATM/broadband wide-area focus. The most significant event of 1997 was the announcement of a merger between 3Com and U.S. Robotics, creating a $5.6 billion company. U.S. Robotics was a leader in remote access concentrators, modems, and connected handheld organizers. The addition of U.S. Robotics' products and technology to 3Com's product portfolio gave it strong representation in key business areas. Once the transaction was completed in early fiscal 1998, it was 1 of 2 networking companies with revenues over $5 billion. These acquisitions enabled 3Com to gain leverage as a full-service provider in each of the 4 key markets of the networking industry: enterprise networks, Internet service providers, business systems, and the consumer market. Further, the combined companies constituted a wider distribution channel, allowing for greater reach to the customer base.

3Com's management believed that flexible, faster, and simpler access to networks would be the most important features a networking company could offer and believed that through these acquisitions, the company was in a superior competitive position to its nearest competitors. They saw that the way to achieve this was by providing low-cost solutions to customers for fully integrated end-to-end connectivity that extends across local and wide area networks. 3Com was solidly positioned to provide that extensive service to the networking market.

BAY NETWORKS

Bay Networks was a global company offering networking solutions to enterprise networks and Internet and telecommunications service providers. The company's fiscal position remained steady from 1996 to 1997 with little growth. Revenues in each year were just over $2.0 billion. The company adopted a strategy called Adaptive Networking to meet the changes and challenges of the high growth Internet services and networking segments of the industry. Its focus was on key technologies in switching/ATM services and network management. As with most of its competitors, Bay Networks used a merger and acquisition strategy to bolster its competitive position and become a full-service provider. However, the strategy failed to change the company's position. By the end of fiscal 1997, net income fell with a loss of $1.46 per share. A few months later, the company made a blockbuster announcement that would have a drastic effect on the competitive environment in the industry. Executives of the communications giant Northern Telecom and of Bay Networks announced a merger of the 2 organizations, to be called Nortel. This merger would combine telecommunications with the data equipment used to move information across networks, giving the combined entity a significant competitive advantage that no other competitor comes close to matching. Estimates set the value of Nortel at almost $18 billion, by far the largest company in the industry.

NICHE COMPETITORS

Cisco also faced competition from smaller networking companies specializing in specific niches of the industry. Company estimates placed the number of competitors in the ATM switching, frame relay, and workgroups segments to be between 30 and 50 in each segment. Customers with the need for specialties in these areas might find doing business with a small expert organization to be advantageous. However, as the industry moved toward mergers and consolidations, competitors from this segment were not a formidable threat.

The key challenge for Cisco Systems would be its ability to remain on top of a critical and growing industry in light of increasing competitive challenges and continuing weakness from foreign markets.

Financial Performance

Exhibits 3 and **4** are the company's consolidated statement of operations, consolidated balance sheets, and selected financial information, respectively.

Exhibit 3

Consolidated Statements of Operations: Cisco Systems, Inc.
(Dollar amounts in thousands, except per share data)

Year Ending	July 25, 1998	July 26, 1997	July 28, 1996
Net sales	$8,458,777	$6,440,171	$4,096,007
Cost of sales	2,917,617	2,241,378	1,409,862
Gross margin	5,541,160	4,198,793	2,686,145
Expenses			
Research and development	1,020,446	698,172	399,291
Sales and marketing	1,564,419	1,160,269	726,278
General and administrative	258,246	204,661	159,770
Purchased research and development	593,695	508,397	—
Total operating expenses	3,436,806	2,571,499	1,285,339
Operating income	2,104,354	1,627,294	1,400,806
Realized gains on sale of investment	5,411	152,689	
Interest and other income, net	192,701	108,889	64,019
Income before provision for income taxes	2,302,466	1,888,872	1,464,825
Provision for income taxes	952,394	840,193	551,501
Net income	$1,350,072	$1,048,679	$ 913,324
Net income per share—basic	$ 0.88	$ 0.71	$ 0.64
Net income per share—diluted	$ 0.84	$ 0.68	$ 0.61
Shares used in per-share calculation—basic	1,533,869	1,485,986	1,437,030
Shares used in per-share calculation—diluted	1,608,173	1,551,039	1,490,078

Source: Cisco Systems, Inc., *1998 Annual Report*, p. 28.

Exhibit 4

Consolidated Balance Sheets: Cisco Systems, Inc.
(Dollar amounts in thousands, except par value)

Year Ending	July 25, 1998	July 26, 1997
Assets		
Current assets		
Cash and equivalents	$ 534,652	$ 269,608
Short-term investments	1,156,849	1,005,977
Accounts receivable, net of allowances for doubtful		
accounts of $39,842 in 1998 and $22,340 in 1997	1,297,867	1,170,401
Inventories, net	361,986	254,677
Deferred income taxes	344,905	312,132
Prepaid expenses and other current assets	65,665	88,471
Total current assets	3,761,924	3,101,266
Investments	3,463,279	1,267,174
Restricted investments	553,780	363,216
Property and equipment, net	595,349	466,352
Other assets	542,373	253,976
Total assets	$8,916,705	$5,451,984
Liabilities and shareholders' equity		
Current liabilities		
Accounts payable	$ 248,872	$ 207,178
Income taxes payable	410,363	256,224
Accrued payroll and related expenses	390,542	263,269
Other accrued liabilities	717,203	393,438
Total current liabilities	1,766,980	1,120,109
Commitments and contingencies		
Minority interest	43,107	42,253
Shareholders' equity		
Preferred stock, no par value, 5,000 shares authorized:		
none issued or outstanding in 1998 and 1997		
Common stock and additional paid-in capital,		
$0.001 par value (no par value—July 26, 1997)		
2,700,000 shares authorized: 1,562,582 shares issued		
and outstanding in 1998 and 1,509,252 shares in 1997	3,220,205	1,763,200
Retained earnings	3,828,223	2,487,058
Unrealized gain on investments	78,314	49,628
Cumulative translation adjustments	(20,124)	(10,264)
Total shareholders' equity	7,106,618	4,289,622
Total liabilities and shareholders' equity	$8,916,705	$5,451,984

Source: Cisco Systems, Inc., *1998 Annual Report*, p. 29.

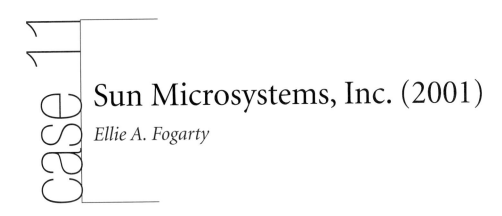

case 11

Sun Microsystems, Inc. (2001)

Ellie A. Fogarty

Sun's overall goal: to develop the infrastructure that enables the Internet.[1]

Sun: Coming into Focus

Scott McNealy, Sun's Chairman and CEO and a long-time admirer of GE's Jack Welch, learned about focus as his company grew from just over 10,000 to almost 43,000 employees in 10 years.

> The bigger the boat gets, the more crisp, clear, and sparing you need to be about picking strategies and ideas to pursue . . . . There have been just 5 companywide initiatives in Jack's whole career. My folks will tell you that I've got 5 initiatives per meeting. So 1 thing I'm learning to do is to step back from spewing an idea a minute to focus on driving higher level issues . . . . I'm going to pick very few fights going forward, and I'm going to win them. That's the best thing I've learned from Jack.[2]

This theme reappeared in Sun's *2000 Annual Report* as an equation: Vision + Focus + Execution = Success. McNealy wrote, in the Letter from the Chairman, "The key to our success? Focus."[3] The Annual Report also included other "focus" quotes from the top 3 executives at Sun: from McNealy, "Some companies change directions more often than I change the oil in my car. Sun's focus is right where it's always been: the Net"; from Ed Zander, President and Chief Operating Officer, "Our focus is simple: Be the number 1 provider of technologies, products, and services that drive the Net economy"; and from Bill Joy, Cofounder and Chief Scientist, "From Unix to NFS (Network File System) to Java technology—it's all about the network. First, last, and always, that's our focus."[4]

This focus came to Sun's leadership at a crucial time in an industry that faced intense competition and a slowing economy. During fiscal year 2000, Sun reduced the number of system configurations it sold from thousands to under 200 models, continuing efforts to simplify the manufacturing process by reducing the diversity of system configurations offered and increasing the standardization of components across product types.

On July 1, 2000, McNealy reorganized Sun, consolidating sales and operation functions into 2 new groups, Global Sales Operation, to manage most field sales organizations and all

---

field marketing organizations, and Worldwide Operations, to manage all operations, supply-chain activities, and purchasing. At the same time, Sun focused on the product and service lines of business described in **Exhibit 1**.

ACQUISITIONS

Merger and acquisition activity was high in the computer industry. Companies sought to enter new markets, expand geographically, and increase revenue growth. By acquiring another firm, a company could augment its own technical skills by gaining skilled workers without the need for extensive training. Some companies actively pursued acquisition strategies as a way to increase the breadth of their product offerings, saving the months or years required to develop all of their products from scratch.

From August 1997 to December 2000, Sun completed 18 acquisitions (see **Exhibit 2**). In 1999, Sun completed its merger with Forte Software, Inc., a software company that designed, developed, marketed, and supported a set of products for developing, deploying, and managing production applications in distributed environments including client/server and the Internet. The stock-swap transaction was valued at $540 million. Sun began negotiations to acquire 2 storage software companies, HighGround Systems Inc., and LSC Inc., in fiscal year 2001 for $400 million and $74 million, respectively. Sun hoped to ensure that customers purchasing its servers would also buy its storage systems.

Exhibit 1
Products and Services: Sun Microsystems, Inc.

System Products and Network Storage: Designs, develops, and brings to market a broad range of desktop system, servers, storage and network switches, incorporating the UltraSPARC microprocessors and the Solaries Operating Environment. This organization also designs and develops high performance UltraSPARC and MAJC microprocessors, computer board platforms, processor modules, chip sets and logic products for Sun systems products and OEM customers.

Enterprise Services: Provides a full range of global services and support for heterogeneous network computing environments, including system/network management, systems integration, and support, education, and professional services.

Software Systems: Designs, develops, and brings to market Sun's Solaris Operating Environment, the Java platform and Sun's core technologies for consumer and embedded markets including implementations that utilize the Java technology, Jini connection technology, XML technology, software development tools, and Sun's StarOffice application software.

Network Service Provider: Designs, develops, and brings to market carrier-grade software, systems, and storage that are designed to meet the needs of traditional telecommunications customers as well as the increasing demands of service providers. This organization focuses on the needs of network-based telecommunications companies, cable operators, and the network equipment suppliers who develop products and technologies for the broader service provider industry.

Sun-Netscape Alliance: Through the alliance with America Online, Inc. (AOL), the Sun-Netscape Alliance, Sun designs, develops, markets, and sells enterprise and E-commerce software for consumers and businesses under the iPlanet brand. These software products and technologies, commonly referred to as middleware, complement Sun's enterprise servers, storage and workstation products. Combined, these products provide customers with comprehensive solutions to their enterprise and Internet computing needs.

Source: Sun Microsystems, Inc., *2000 Form 10-K.*

Exhibit 2

Acquisitions: Sun Microsystems, Inc.

Date	Company Name	Description of Business	Consideration
Fiscal 2001 Acquisitions			
12/00	Cobalt Networks, Inc.	Maker of Linux-based server appliances	$2,000,000,000
11/00	grapeVINE Technologies, LLC	Portal software	$9,000,000
7/00	Gridware, Inc.	Resource management software	$20,000,000
7/00	Dolphin Interconnect Solutions	Infiniband interconnect architecture	$19,000,000
Fiscal 2000 Acquisitions			
6/00	Ed Learning Systems, Inc. and eTech, Inc.	Dot-com learning solutions	$10,300,000
3/00	Innosoft International Inc.	Internet mail, directory and messaging services	$42,400,000
1/00	Trustbase Limited and JCP Computer Services Limited	Financial e-commerce applications	$20,500,000
10/99	NetBeans Cesta Republica a.s.	Java technology-based development environment	$9,000,000
8/99	Star Division Corporation and Star Division Software– Entwicklung und Vertriebs GmbH	Office productivity applications	$75,500,000
Fiscal 1999 Acquisitions			
1/99	Maxstrat Corporation	Network storage hardware/software	$101,500,000
10/98	Beduin Communications Inc.	Java technology-based consumer applications	$8,400,000
9/98	i-Planet, Inc.	Java technology-based Internet applications	$30,000,000
8/98	NetDynamics, Inc.	Enterprise Application Platform	$148,200,000
Fiscal 1998 Acquisitions			
5/98	Red Cape Software, Inc.	Policy-based storage management software	$16,700,000
11/97	Encore Computer Corporation	Open systems storage	$186,200,000
10/97	Chorus Systems S.A.	JavaOS kernel technology	$26,500,000
9/97	Integrity Arts	Java Card application programming interface	$30,200,000
8/97	Diba, Inc.	Turnkey information appliance software	$29,700,000

Source: Sun Microsystems, Inc., *2000 Annual Report*, p. 43; and Sun Microsystems, Inc., *Form 10-Q*, October, 1, 2000.

Sun was not always able to bring the technologies made by acquired firms to market. Some were still in development years later and other product lines were canceled in the development stage. By the end of 2000, Sun began to look at acquisitions in a more methodical and disciplined way, searching for companies that fit its strategic goals rather than financial ones. Previously, Sun looked internally to develop products and services.[5]

Corporate Governance

BOARD OF DIRECTORS

Exhibit 3 lists the company's Board of Directors and the number of shares owned by each. Scott G. McNealy, Chairman and CEO, was the only executive officer to own more than 1% of outstanding shares. As of June 30, 2000, McNealy owned 2.23% of outstanding shares.

TOP MANAGEMENT

Exhibit 4 lists the company's corporate officers and outlines the worldwide corporate structure.

Scott G. McNealy

The story behind Sun's current Chairman of the Board and Chief Executive Officer Scott G. McNealy was not very typical for a Silicon Valley entrepreneur. He didn't drop out of college to realize his idea for the PC business nor did he work his way up through engineering. His background in manufacturing made McNealy a fierce competitor who knew his business funda-

Exhibit 3

Board of Directors: Sun Microsystems, Inc.

Name, Age, Director Since	Principal Occupation	Number of Shares Owned [1]
Scott G. McNealy, 45 1982	Chairman of the Board of Directors and Chief Executive Officer, Sun Microsystems, Inc.	27,837,597
James L. Barksdale, 57 1999	Managing Partner, The Barksdale Group	0
L. John Doerr, 49 1982	General Partner/Managing Director, Kleiner Perkins Caufield & Byers	1,359,248
Judith L. Estrin, 45 1995	Chief Executive Officer, Packet Design, Inc.	320,000
Robert J. Fisher, 46 1995	Member, Board of Directors, The Gap, Inc.	384,400
Robert L. Long, 63 1988	Independent Management Consultant	96,206
M. Kenneth Oshman, 60 1988	Chairman of the Board of Directors, President, and Chief Executive Officer, Echelon Corporation	1,301,600
Naomi O. Seligman, 67 1999	Senior Partner, Ostriker von Simson, Inc.	0

Note:
1. Excludes shares that may be acquired through option exercises.

Source: Sun Microsystems, Inc., *2000 Proxy Statement,* pp. 5, 9.

Exhibit 4

Corporate Officers and Worldwide Corporate Structure: Sun Microsystems, Inc.

Corporate Officers

Scott G. McNealy
Chief Executive Officer

William T. Agnello
Senior Vice President, Workplace Resources

Crawford W. Beveridge
Executive Vice President and Chief Human Resources Officer

Mel Friedman
Senior Vice President, Customer Advocacy

Lawrence W. Hambly
Executive Vice President, Enterprise Services

H. William Howard
Senior Vice President, Chief Information Officer

Masood A. Jabbar
Executive Vice President, Global Sales Operations

William N. Joy
Cofounder and Chief Scientist

Michael L. Lehman
Executive Vice President, Corporate Resources and Chief Financial Officer

John P. Loiacono
Senior Vice President, Chief Marketing Officer

John S. McFarlane
Executive Vice President, Network Service Providers

Michael H. Morris
Senior Vice President, General Counsel and Secretary

Gregory M. Papadopoulos
Senior Vice President and Chief Technology Officer

Janpieter T. Scheerder
Executive Vice President, Storage Products

Jonathan I. Schwartz
Senior Vice President, Corporate Strategy and Planning

John C. Shoemaker
Executive Vice President, System Products Group

Patricia C. Sueltz
Executive Vice President, Software Products and Platforms

Mark E. Tolliver
Executive Vice President and President, iPlanet, Sun-Netscape Alliance

Edward J. Zander
President and Chief Operating Officer

Sun Worldwide

Manufacturing
2 countries

International Research and Development
8 countries

International Sales, Service, and Support
53 countries

International Distributors
More than 170 countries

Source: Sun Microsystems, Inc., *2000 Annual Report*, p. 60.

mentals, always kept score, and had good moves. He was smart, complex, and fiercely ambitious. Over the many years at Sun, McNealy had become 1 of the industry's most respected managers. Those talents, plus a competitive instinct and nonstop drive, kept Sun rolling through a decade of tremendous change in the computer industry.

McNealy grew up in a house where hard work and a fast-paced environment were part of everyday life. As a child, Scott learned a great deal about manufacturing. His curiosity in his father's work as Vice Chairman of American Motors Corp., led the grade-schooler to look into his dad's briefcase at night to inspect its contents. Many Saturdays, young McNealy went along to the plant and snooped around while his father caught up on paperwork. By the time he was a teenager, Scott was spending evenings with his father reading over memos and playing golf with industry leaders such as Lee Iacocca.

After graduating from Harvard University with a degree in economics, McNealy took a job for 2 years as a foreman at a Rockwell International Corp. plant in Ashtabula, Ohio, that made body panels for semitractors. In 1978, he enrolled in Stanford University's business school where he focused on manufacturing at a time when finance and information technologies were the ways to the top. Although many of his classmates wanted to launch a Digital Age business, McNealy signed on as a manufacturing trainee for FMC Corp. The company assigned him to a factory in Silicon Valley where it was building Bradley fighting vehicles for the U.S. Army. McNealy's career in the computer world started in 1981 when his mentor from Harvard asked him for help in the troubled production department of a workstation company called Onyx Systems. After only 10 months at Onyx, a former Stanford classmate, Vinod Khosla, contacted McNealy to join him and Bechtolsheim in starting Sun. In 1982, he joined Sun to head up manufacturing and operations. McNealy's manufacturing skills enabled the new company to keep up with the high demand as sales went from $9 million in 1983 to $39 million in 1984. Nonetheless, the high amount of new orders surpassed the cash available for expansion. McNealy then asked Sun's customer Eastman Kodak Co. to invest $20 million. As a condition of the investment, Kodak insisted that McNealy take over as President. In 1984, McNealy was officially named CEO of the company only after a Board-directed search turned up no one better.

McNealy showed his ability as a CEO over the coming years. After the company went public in 1986, it took 2 years for Sun to outgrow its production capacities, which led to the company's first quarterly loss. Its troubled production facilities were reason enough for McNealy to move from Sun's executive suite to the floor of Sun's biggest factory and revamp the company's manufacturing. In the months after production was rolling again, he showed skills nobody expected. He deliberately pruned the product line, sharpening Sun's focus to workstations built around a high-powered processor of its own design. Realizing that fixing problems on the factory floor was no job for the CEO of a company of Sun's size led McNealy to reorganize the company. He pushed profit-and-loss responsibility down to individual product organizations, called planets, that let them feel the trouble if things went wrong.[6]

McNealy served as Chairman, CEO, and President of Sun from December 1984 to April 1999 and as Chairman and CEO since April 1999. His salary was $103,846 in fiscal year 2000, with a bonus $4,767,500 (see **Exhibit 5**). McNealy also served as a Director of General Electric Company. He was invited to join after developing a friendship with legendary CEO Jack Welch

Exhibit 5

Executive Compensation, 2000: Sun Microsystems, Inc.

Name and Principal Position	Annual Compensation		Securities Underlying Options (#)	All Other Compensation
	Salary	Bonus		
Scott G. McNealy Chairman and CEO	$103,846	$4,767,500	500,000	$6,923
Edward J. Zander President and Chief Operating Officer	$778,846	$2,145,375	200,000	$6,800
William N. Joy Cofounder and Chief Scientist	$433,654	$808,761	100,000	$6,846
Michael L. Lehman EVP, Corporate Resources and Chief Financial Officer	$623,077	$1,144,200	550,000	$6,800
Lawrence W. Hambly EVP, Enterprise Services	$429,423	$515,361	100,000	$7,142

Source: Sun Microsystems, Inc., *2000 Proxy Statement*, p. 10.

on the golf course. Welch encouraged McNealy in his efforts to transform Sun from something of a seat-of-the-pants operation to a more disciplined organization that, like GE, was obsessed with product quality and customer service. McNealy inflamed discussion on the GE board and helped GE recognize ways to incorporate e-commerce practices into their business.

William N. Joy

William N. Joy, Cofounder and Chief Scientist, risked losing touch with Silicon Valley and Sun's senior management when he moved to Aspen, Colorado, from Palo Alto in 1991 to avoid traffic jams, back-to-back meetings, and constant interruptions from his next-door office neighbor, McNealy. Joy graduated high school at 15, studied computing at University of Michigan, and began graduate work at University of California at Berkeley in 1975. There Joy and his classmates began working with AT&T's Unix operating system, adapting it for use on the University's Digital Equipment computer called a VAX. In 1978, Joy's Unix team won a contract from the Pentagon to develop software to enable VAXes to connect to the Internet (started as Advanced Research Projects Agency Network or ARPAnet). Six years into his work toward a Ph.D., Joy agreed to join Vinod Khosla, Scott McNealy, and Andreas Bechtolsheim to develop a cheap but powerful desktop computer called a Stanford University Network workstation. Admired for his 20-year record of technological innovation, McNealy said "AT&T has Bell Labs, and we have Bill Joy. We get a lot more for our money."[7] His salary was $433,654 in fiscal year 2000, with a bonus of $808,761. Joy also served on the Board of Directors for Novell, working again with old graduate school buddy Eric Schmidt, Sun's former Chief Technology Officer and currently Novell's CEO.

Edward J. Zander

Edward J. Zander, President and Chief Operating Officer, had over 25 years of experience in the computer industry. Born and raised in Brooklyn, he earned his B.S. from the Rensselaer Polytechnic Institute in New York and his M.B.A. from Boston University. Prior to joining Sun, Zander spent 9 years at Data General (now a unit of Sun's rival EMC Corp.) and 5 years at Apollo Computers (acquired by Hewlett-Packard), where he was Vice President of Marketing. He joined Sun in October 1987 as Vice President of Corporate Marketing. To ensure that Zander would not be tempted to leave Sun when both Compaq and Hewlett-Packard were searching for a CEO, McNealy promoted Zander to President and Chief Operating Officer in April 1999. He was responsible for the day-to-day business operation, for overseeing all of Sun's 7 product divisions and for the SunLabs Research and Development Group. Zander felt "the thing that makes Sun really unique in the industry is that the vision and the focus stay consistent. We don't flinch, and we've got the courage to stay the course. And that's what makes this company special."[8] His salary for fiscal year 2000 was $778,846, with a bonus of $2,145,375. He served on the directing boards of the Jason Foundation for Education, Documentum Inc., Multilink Technology Corp., Portal Software, Inc., Rhythm Netconnection, and the Science Advisory Board of RPI.

Competition

Sun competed in the intensely competitive hardware and software products and services markets for customers in 2 major categories: enterprise customers—large corporations, government and educational organizations, and utilities—and service providers—firms that provide data communication services including telecommunication carriers, cable companies, wireless communication providers, and Internet service providers.

In the industry's formative years, most companies specialized in 1 product area. By the turn of the century, however, the increasing complexity of networks meant that customers were demanding that computer firms provide not only an end-to-end product solution, but also a product strategy to handle future networking needs. While committed to open source solutions that performed well regardless of platform, Sun hoped to offer enough hardware, software, and services that customers would not have to look elsewhere for any of their computing needs.

SERVERS

In the server market, Sun competed with Compaq, Hewlett-Packard (HP), and IBM. The market was divided into 3 segments—entry-level servers, usually defined as servers priced below $100,000 including PC servers; mid-range servers used in Internet-related functions such as database hosting and support of e-commerce applications by Internet service providers (ISPs) and application service providers (ASPs); and high-end servers/mainframes, systems prices above $1 million.

In 2000, all the major computer hardware companies released higher-end computer systems. HP introduced its new Superdome server, which filled a gap in HP's high-end Unix line. HP was hoping to gain share in data-intensive markets with this powerful system. Around the same time, IBM announced its new G7 (seventh generation S/390) mainframe that could handle up to 9 billion transactions per day. The new system, called the z900, was targeted for e-business-intensive operations like applications service providers, Internet service providers, and technology hosting companies. Compaq also launched a new server named Wildfire for the mid-range ($100,000) and high-end market ($1.5 million). For Compaq, the key to success with this product was to get software developers' support for the platform. Different versions of Sun's Netra Internet Servers and its Sun Enterprise Servers competed in all 3 segments. Both lines were powered by Sun's UltraSPARC processors and contained Solaris, Sun's Unix operating system.

UltraSPARC III, manufactured by Texas Instruments, was Sun's first major new processor in almost 4 years when it debuted, 2 years late, in 2000. Intel's Itanium microprocessor, designed for the server market, was introduced in September 2000. Combined with Windows 2000, Microsoft's new operating system, it posed a serious threat to the Unix market. Wintel, the combination of Windows operating systems and Intel processors, competed with Sun at the entry-level and mid-range server market. Analysts anticipated that the delay in introducing UltraSPARC III would cause customers to choose a Wintel solution. In the high-end market, Sun's Enterprise 10000 was the first server to rival IBM's RS/6000 S80 mainframe. IBM followed Sun's lead by simplifying its product offerings and unifying its 4 server lines under the "eServer" brand name in early 2001. IBM's focus was to move aggressively to recapture the Unix server market.

Sun led in the market for Unix servers in the third quarter of calendar year 2000. According to International Data Corporation's report, Sun led in worldwide Unix server revenue with 39% market share, beating out Hewlett-Packard (23%), IBM (23%), and Compaq (9%).[9] In the entry-level Unix server market, Sun had 44% market share in the third quarter of 2000. In the mid-range and high-end Unix server markets, Sun had 27% and 56% respectively.[10]

STORAGE

The storage segment of the computer hardware industry was growing rapidly. All major computer hardware vendors altered or augmented their storage product offerings from 1999 to 2001. Sales of storage systems were expected to increase 12% a year through 2003, to $46 billion, according to International Data Corporation.[11]

The Sun StorEdge line of disk storage, tape backup, management software and data services competed with EMC Corporation, the storage market's leading manufacturer. Sun introduced StorEdge T3, a computer storage system the size of a VCR, in June 2000 and offered a better price ($155,000) and more flexibility than rival EMC product ($400,000). T3 storage boxes do not have to be near a server, lined up in huge storage racks, and wired to servers the way most storage farms operate. IBM introduced its new Shark storage line in 1999. In 2000, Compaq and IBM announced they had entered into an agreement under which IBM would use Compaq as a reference account for customers' low-end storage needs, while Compaq would refer its customers to IBM for their higher-end storage needs. In March 2000, HP reorganized its storage group, consolidating 6 separate product divisions into a single storage organization and increasing its sales force by 25% to 30%. Previously, HP had a joint-selling agreement with EMC for its customers' storage needs.[12]

SOFTWARE

Solaris, Sun's version of the Unix operating system, grew out of William Joy's work at Berkeley as a graduate student. Solaris, with version 8.0 released in 2000, earned the trust of information technology managers and gained a reputation of being the safest and most reliable choice in a wide range of business environments, similar to IBM's hardware in the 1960s. Solaris competed with other versions of Unix, such as IBM's AIX and Hewlett Packard's HP-UX, and Windows 2000 (formerly known as Windows NT 5.0). In early 2001, Solaris was facing a challenge from Linux, the Unix operating system collectively developed by volunteer programmers from around the world. At the time, Linux was mostly run on Intel microprocessors and could not rival Solaris for high-end applications. However, many in the industry felt that after tackling Microsoft's Windows 2000, Linux would move on to challenge Sun's well-regarded operating environment within 2 to 3 years.[13] For more information on Linux, see the Future Considerations section below.

In 1995, Sun introduced Java, a new programming language developed to allow programmers to write a single Internet application that could run on almost any device. The importance of Java to Sun was 3-fold: it gave substance to the firm's vision of computing—many devices connected to powerful servers sitting in data centers dispensing applications; it eroded the primacy of Windows as the only platform that programmers wanting to reach a large audience could write for; and it made Sun seem hip and glamorous.[14] Sun released the technical specifications for rivals to use and revise, but Sun controlled the standards. Sun planned to create an open source license for Java to foster wider adoption and ongoing improvements. Open source is software code that is freely distributed and modified across the Internet.

Sun tried to persuade Microsoft to incorporate a Java interpreter right into the Windows operating systems. After 4 months of negotiations, Sun received a fax from Microsoft in March 1996 agreeing to license Java on Sun's terms. On October 7, 1997, however, Sun announced that the company had filed a lawsuit accusing Microsoft of violating the agreement by shipping a version of Java that could be made to run exclusively on Windows. Although later overshadowed by Microsoft's antitrust case, Sun's lawsuit was at that time 1 of the most significant challenges to Microsoft's dominance of software. The Java case itself never went to trial, but the suit had developed into a public fight between Sun and Microsoft leaders. By January 2001, the 2 companies settled, with Microsoft agreeing to pay Sun $20 million and terminating its license to use Sun's Java software technology. In the settlement, Microsoft did win the right to continue to distribute an older, Sun-compatible version of Java for 7 years.[15]

SERVICES

According to International Data Corporation, the global technology services market was expected to grow at a compound annual growth rate of 14% to reach $701 billion in 2004. As with servers and storage, all major computer hardware companies focused on new services offerings for their customers in 2000.

HP produced strong growth in services in fiscal 2000. In September 2000, HP tried to acquire the PricewaterhouseCoopers information technology consulting unit in order to augment its staff with 31,500 consultants and to enhance its service offerings. While unsuccessful, it demonstrated that HP was committed to growing its services capabilities in house or by acquiring other firms. Compaq took the acquisitions route in 1998 by taking over Digital Equipment for its worldwide services organization. In September 2000, Compaq announced that it would narrow the set of services it offered to focus on better service delivery and customer satisfaction. IBM was the clear leader in the information technology services industry, with $40 billion in annual revenues, more than twice the size of Sun's, HP's, and Compaq's services revenues combined.

Sun provided support services (systems support for hardware and software), educational services (classroom, CD-ROM- or Web-based training), and professional services (IT consulting and systems integration). Sun was concentrating on increasing staff in all 3 service areas. In fiscal year 2000, Sun hired 2,700 people into its Enterprise Services organization, bringing the total to 10,200 service professionals. Services accounted for 14.6% of total net revenues in fiscal 2000.

Company Profile

CORPORATE CULTURE

In the early years at Sun's headquarters, McNealy, who had an image in the industry of being brash, built a corporate culture based on his own motto: "Kick butt and have fun." Soon after that, the company became known for its aggressive marketing, featuring Network, McNealy's Greater Swiss Mountain dog, and various juvenile antics taking place within Sun's headquarters, including the most elaborate April Fool's Day pranks imaginable. This humor had an important effect on the culture. During the competitive times in the computer industry, when good positions and good workers were hard to find, it helped employees live with their demanding jobs and bound employees together. Using humor and a tremendous amount of energy, McNealy had the ability to raise employees enthusiastically to their feet.[16]

By the year 2000, Sun was no longer a start-up firm and McNealy could no longer gather his employees in the lunchroom, stand on a chair, and present ideas like he used to. Even as the organization grew, Sun tried to hold on to the feeling of the old days. Ed Zander, President and Chief Operating Officer, described the culture as a place to be very innovative, creative, fun, very open door, very participatory management. He said it was "really a place to market your ideas, try to keep bureaucracy to a minimum, lots of information around every day for anybody and everybody . . . we're very hungry, very aggressive. Market share's important. Winning is important. Customer satisfaction is very important. We try to make it a place where employees can have fun every day because we ask them to work hard."[17]

Sun enjoyed a spot on *Fortune* magazine's list of the 100 Best Companies to Work For, rising from number 83 in 1999 to number 60 in the 2000 ranking. Factors such as Sun's 45 hours of professional training per year, 35% minority employees, 34% women employees, and voluntary turnover of only 6% were considered in the survey. Eighty-five percent of Sun's employees said they were paid fairly for the work they do and all employees were eligible for stock options.[18]

MARKETING

In 1988, John Gage, director of Sun's science office, coined the slogan "The network is the computer," meaning the network you're connected to, not the box on your desk, will do the job you want done.[19] While this vision held true during the boom in the Internet economy, Sun moved on to other themes. In 1998, advertising agency Lowe Lintas launched Sun's "We're the dot in .com" campaign. Due to mergers in the advertising industry, Lowe Lintas found itself representing both Sun and 1 of Sun's newest competitors in the low-end server market, Dell Computer Corporation. When a Dell ad ran in August 2000 with the headline "It's time to focus less on The Dot and more on The Commerce," Sun left Lowe Lintas and gave its $100 million account to J. Walter Thompson. Sun advertised in computer publications and the business press, direct mailings to customers and prospects, televised programs, and attendance at trade shows. Sun continued to take jabs at Microsoft, referring in ads to the millions of dollars Microsoft had to pay Sun, for Sun's Java software in early 2001.

Sun used both direct and indirect distribution methods to sell its products and services. The newly organized Global Sales Operations group managed most field sales organizations and all field marketing organizations. Sun's indirect methods included partnering with systems integrators, value-added resellers (VARs), original equipment manufacturers (OEMs), and independent distributors in 150 foreign countries. More than half of Sun's revenue was derived through reseller channels.

Sun experimented with a new marketing channel, online auctions, using eBay, Mercata, and TekSell auction Web sites. Introduced in December 1999, Sun generated only a small fraction of its annual sales from auctions (0.1% of sales in 2000, and projections of 0.5% of sales in 2001). Auctions were used to establish pricing for older and overstocked products, and as a quick way to test prices for newer products.[20] Sun committed to the channel when it announced that the 600 MHz version of the Sun Blade 1000 (a low-end server) would be offered only on eBay's auction site. Depending on its success, more auction-only items would be considered.[21]

RESEARCH AND DEVELOPMENT

Compared with most other U.S. manufacturing industries, computer companies typically invested more in research and development, often 10% or more of revenues. Such outlays were crucial in that they enabled companies to identify new product opportunities and bring products to market in a timely manner. Given the computer industry's rapid technological change, companies had to support consistently high levels of R&D expenditures to remain competitive. These investments were necessary to develop new products and to upgrade and enhance existing ones.

R&D expenses as a percentage of net revenues were 10.4% in 2000. The total amount, $1,630,000, was an increase of 27% over fiscal 1999. Sun expected to continue to increase R&D spending in the future to remain in the 10 to 11% range. The high levels of R&D spending reflected Sun's belief that "to maintain our competitive position in a market characterized by rapid rates of technological advancement, we must continue to invest significant resources in new systems, software, and microprocessor development, as well as continue to enhance existing products."[22] Sun conducted research and development in the United States, France, United Kingdom, Ireland, Japan, India, and Israel.

SUPPLY CHAIN

Sun's newly reorganized operation functions, Worldwide Operations, managed all operations, supply-chain activities, and purchasing. Sun had manufacturing operations in California, Oregon, and Scotland, and distributed from California, the Netherlands, and Japan. Sun's manufacturing operations consisted primarily of final assembly, test and quality control of systems, materials, and components. Sun purchased some types of monitors from Sony and had its SPARC microprocessors built by Texas Instruments.

Firmly grounded in Sun's competitive strategy was the goal to create a virtual logistics network for the movement of service parts. This was part of a promise to establish collaborative relationships with suppliers. Previously, the parts delivery process was too complex. Once a part was requested, the order was routed through an obstacle course of different parties that included remote stocking locations, distribution centers, and repair suppliers. The process time was in excess of 36 days and required more than 12 receipt-shipping points. With the introduction of a Web-based management system, the supply-chain cycle time for parts was reduced to less than a week. In addition, Sun accrued savings of "tens of millions" of dollars and customer satisfaction ratings rose.[23] The next challenge for the Worldwide Operations division was to combine all of Sun's operations into a single global ERP system.

Most of Sun's procurement was EDI-based and some Internet procurement was carried out in Europe and Asia-Pacific. In 2000, Sun spent about $1 billion in procurement via Internet auctions such as the business-to-business hub FreeMarkets.[24] Sun held annual Supplier Performance Awards Ceremony, presenting companies with recognition such as the Outstanding Performance and the Meritorious Performance awards.

FINANCIAL PERFORMANCE

Over the past decade, Sun's revenues had grown an average of 20% annually. For fiscal year 2000 (ended June 30, 2000), Sun reported revenues of $15,721 million, an increase of 33% over the previous fiscal year (see **Exhibit 6**). Products net revenue accounted for 85.4% of total net revenues in 2000. This included revenue from sales of computer systems and storage, high-speed microprocessors, and software for operating network computing equipment. Services

Exhibit 6

Consolidated Statements of Income: Sun Microsystems, Inc.
(Dollar amounts in millions, except per share data)

Year Ending June 30	2000	1999	1998
Net revenue:			
Products	$13,421	$10,171	$8,675
Services	2,300	1,635	1,187
Total net revenues	15,721	11,806	9,862
Cost of sales:			
Cost of sales—products	6,096	4,696	3,992
Cost of sales—services	1,453	974	721
Total cost of sales	7,549	5,670	4,713
Gross margin	8,172	6,136	5,149
Operating expenses:			
Research and development	1,630	1,280	1,029
Selling, general and administrative	4,137	3,215	2,830
Purchased in-process research and development	12	121	176
Total operating expenses	5,779	4,616	4,035
Operating income	2,393	1,520	1,114
Gain on sale of investments, net	208		
Interest income, net	170	85	48
Income before income taxes	2,771	1,605	1,162
Provision for income taxes	917	575	407
Net income	$ 1,854	$ 1,030	$ 755
Net income per common share—basic	$ 1.18	$ 0.67	$ 0.50
Net income per common share—diluted	$ 1.10	$ 0.63	$ 0.47
Shares used in the calculation of net income per common share—basic	1,576	1,544	1,507
Shares used in the calculation of net income per common share—diluted	1,689	1,641	1,590

Source: Sun Microsystems, Inc., *2000 Annual Report*, p. 34.

net revenue, 14.6% of total net revenues, came from sales of support, education and professional services. Sales to General Electric Company accounted for approximately 19% of fiscal year 2000 net revenues.

In the computer hardware and software industries, U.S. companies generated a significant proportion of their sales and profits from outside the United States. Foreign markets were large and rapid growth was expected for the coming years. In fiscal year 2000, nearly 50% of Sun's revenue came from non-North American sales. European sales represented 27.3% and sales to Japan accounted for 8.6% of revenue. **Exhibits 6** and **7** provide financial information for Sun.

Exhibit 7

Consolidated Balance Sheets: Sun Microsystems, Inc.
(Dollar amounts in millions, except par value)

Year Ending June 30	2000	1999
Assets		
Current assets:		
Cash and cash equivalents	$ 1,849	$ 1,101
Short-term investments	626	1,591
Accounts receivable, net of allowances of $534 in 2000 and $340 in 1999	2,690	2,310
Inventories	557	308
Deferred tax assets	673	506
Other current assets	482	372
Total current assets	6,877	6,188
Property, plant and equipment, net	2,095	1,614
Long-term investments	4,496	
Other assets, net	684	697
Total assets	$14,152	$ 8,499
Liabilities and stockholders' equity		
Current liabilities:		
Short-term borrowings	$ 7	$ 2
Accounts payable	924	756
Accrued payroll-related liabilities	751	520
Accrued liabilities and other	1,366	991
Deferred revenues and customer deposits	1,289	576
Income taxes payable	422	403
Total current liabilities	4,759	3,248
Deferred income taxes	364	192
Long-term debt and other obligations	1,720	192
Commitments and contingencies		
Stockholders' equity:		
Preferred stock, $0.001 par value, 10 shares authorized (3 shares of which have been designated as Series A Preferred participating stock); no shares issued and outstanding		
Common Stock and additional paid-in-capital, $0.00067 par value, 3,600 shares authorized; issued: 1,748 shares in 2000 and 1,746 shares in 1999	2,728	1,816
Treasury stock, at cost: 151 shares in 2000 and 180 shares in 1999	(1,438)	(1,046)
Deferred compensation	(15)	
Retained earnings	5,959	4,107
Accumulated other comprehensive income (loss)	75	(10)
Total stockholders' equity	7,309	4,867
Total liabilities and stockholders' equity	$14,152	$ 8,499

Source: Sun Microsystems, Inc., *2000 Annual Report*, p. 35.

Future Considerations

Linux was a clone of the Unix operating system collectively developed by Linus Torvalds and countless other programmers that grew into a serious product endorsed by some of the biggest computer makers. IBM Corp., 1 of the strongest Linux advocates, said it would spend $1 billion on Linux development in 2001. Linux was a free operating system that could run on almost any manufacturer's hardware.

Stacey Quandt, analyst at Giga Information Group and author of the report "Linux—The Dark Side of Sun," said Sun would hurt itself financially in the long-term by failing to recognize Linux as a threat and not supporting the operating system in Sun servers. Also affecting Sun in the long term was the switch in training at universities, once Sun's stronghold, from Solaris to Linux.[25] Anyone studying computer science in the eighties and nineties trained on Solaris and then ordered Solaris for the workplace after graduation.

Ed Zander, President and COO, was quoted in August 2000 saying that Sun would never adopt Linux as a part of its main business although he was happy for Sun applications to run on Linux.[26] By September 2000, Sun announced that it was planning to acquire Cobalt Networks Inc., an unprofitable maker of appliance servers that run on Linux software, for $2 billion. Zander held his ground, saying "We don't want to do Linux across the board like these other companies. We've got the greatest operating system on the planet, and that's Solaris."[27]

Notes

1. Brent Shearer, "A More Deal-Friendly Mood at Sun," *Mergers & Acquisitions* (September 2000).
2. Brent Schlender, "The Odd Couple," *Fortune* (May 1, 2000), p. 126.
3. Sun Microsystems, Inc., *2000 Annual Report*, p. 9.
4. Sun Microsystems, Inc., *2000 Annual Report*, p. 5.
5. Shearer.
6. Irene Hagenbuch and Alan N. Hoffman, "Sun Microsystems, Inc. (1998)," in Thomas L. Wheelen and J. David Hunger, *Strategic Management and Business Policy*, 7th edition (2000), pp. 10–4 to 10–7. All four paragraphs about Scott McNealy are taken from this source.
7. Brent Schlender, "The Edison of the Internet," *Fortune* (February 15, 1999), pp. 86–90.
8. Patti Ziemke, "Microsoft and Other Hot Topics," *Upside* (September 2000), p. 88.
9. April Jacobs, "Competitors Aim to Give Sun a Run in the Server Market," *Network World* (December 18, 2000), p. 16.
10. Charles Babcock, "Sun Says It's King of Unix," *Interactive Week* (December 13, 2000).
11. Peter Burrows, "Sun Takes Another Shot at Storage," *Business Week* (June 26, 2000), p. 192.
12. Megan Graham-Hackett, "Computers: Hardware," Standard & Poor's Industry Surveys (December 14, 2000), pp. 5–6.
13. David Kirkpatrick, "The New Player," *Fortune* (April 17, 2000), p. 168.
14. "Sun Microsystems: Bright, Some Clouds," *The Economist* (August 19, 2000), p. 58.
15. David P. Hamilton, "Microsoft Will Pay $20 Million to Sun, End Java License," *Wall Street Journal* (January 24, 2001), p. B8.
16. Hagenbuch, p. 10–8.
17. Ziemke, p. 90.
18. Robert Levering, "100 Best Companies to Work For," *Fortune* (January 8, 2001), p. 162.
19. Schlender, "The Edison of the Internet."
20. Mitch Wagner, "Sun Turns Net Focus Inward," *Internetweek* (September 4, 2000), p. 1.
21. Scott Campbell, "Auctions IRE Sun Partners," *Computer Reseller News* (October 16, 2000), pp. 3–4.
22. Sun Microsystems, Inc., *2000 Annual Report*, p. 21.
23. Ken Cottrill, "Rewiring the Supply Chain," *Traffic World* (October 9, 2000), p. 18.
24. Wagner.
25. Antone Gonsalves, "Sun Needs to Warm Up to Linux, Analyst Says," *TechWeb News* (September 5, 2000).
26. "Sun Microsystems: Bright, Some Clouds," p. 58.
27. Mitch Wagner, "Sun Moves into Appliances—$2B Cobalt Buy Also Pushes Unix Titan into Linux for the First Time," *Internetweek* (September 25, 2000), p. 12.

case 12

drkoop.com

Nicole Herskowitz, Fred Howard, Michael Iversen, Janet Mehlhop, and Pilar Speer

As Dennis Upah, Cofounder of drkoop.com, sat in his small, dimly lit office sipping a glass of water, he thought back to his conversation the previous day with his partner C. Everett Koop, former Surgeon General of the United States. He kept coming back to the comment that Everett had made.

> "I am excited about how the Web has greatly enhanced consumers' abilities to access healthcare information," Everett had said. "I firmly believe that empowered consumers make better, more informed decisions with their physicians. Our new Web site gives Americans 1 premier location on the Net to find trusted, quality healthcare information."[1]

Since the drkoop.com launch less than a year ago, the company had quickly grown to be the largest Web-based health information service, but it had yet to make a profit. Although Dennis and Everett's focus was on providing healthcare information, Dennis knew the site had to make a profit to keep its shareholders happy and to ensure that the business would survive. He thought to himself, "This tap water is terrible. I hope we soon turn a profit so we can afford a water cooler!" But more importantly, he wrestled with the question: What is the right strategy for drkoop.com to ensure that its early success will be sustainable in the long run?

The History of Medical Advice

People have always sought to obtain knowledge about their ailments. One can go back to ancient civilizations when medicine men performed spells and advised people on their spiritual and mental health. In the more modern world, people have relied on doctors for medical advice. For sicknesses like the flu or the common cold, this is still the case. There are also numerous books available for the "home doctor." In the case of more serious illnesses or prolonged illness such as cancer or diabetes, there is a wealth of support organizations available to the afflicted individual. These organizations not only offer support, but in many cases also give advice and support research.

The pharmaceutical industry plays an important role as a major contributor to these organizations. Bristol-Myers Squibb, for example, donated $23 million through the Bristol-Myers Squibb foundation in 1997. A large portion of this money went to organizations such as

This case was prepared by Nicole Herskowitz, Fred Howard, Michael Iversen, Janet Mehlhop, and Pilar Speer for class discussion in Professor Alan Afuah's Corporate Strategy Lecture on Strategy, Technology, and Innovations at the University of Michigan. This case was edited for SMBP-8th Edition. Reprinted by permission.

the National Cancer Foundation and the National Diabetes Foundation. The industry also does a great deal to inform patients of new treatment options through advertising, Web sites, and other forms of publications. Another important characteristic of the industry is that firms continue R&D efforts not only into broad areas of medicine that affect many consumers, but also into more obscure areas that affect only a small population.

In addition, all pharmaceutical companies today have extensive Web sites with numerous links and information options that address their primary treatment areas. Companies like Medtronic and Guidant have Web sites with specific areas dedicated to various types of cardiovascular problems. On Medtronic's site, for example, there are pages dedicated to ventricular fibrillation, which feature not only medical advice, but also contain many links to associated sites such as the American Heart Association. Beyond this, they work extensively with various patient support and prevention groups.

Medical Web Site History

The first Web sites to appear that pertained to the medical industry were those by pharmaceutical firms, which began to conduct business-to-business e-commerce with their customers. Most firms began their online presence by advertising their services in an effort to attract more business. However, those firms neglected to examine the aspect of the Internet that actually attracts most users: information. The sites that provided a free wealth of content were the ones that began seeing thousands and then millions of unique hits each quarter. This is where medical information sites got their start.

Medical information sites formed with the original purpose of providing the public with as much information as they could find in 1 place. Instead of having to try to call or get an appointment with a physician (or specialist, in many cases), patients could read everything on their own. Founders of these sites espoused a desire to foster a public environment for people to have access to trusted healthcare information. Through these sites, "the public has open access to tens of thousands of pages of reliable healthcare information." Site leaders embrace "the value of the Internet as a viable tool for educating the public . . ."[2] World-class sources of information include well-known physicians, information partners, a medical advisory board, and various authors and experts.

Medical information Web sites are popping up left and right. With competition on the rise, sites have been forced to add services to their sites in order to maintain growth in number of hits and unique viewers. Following the business models from other content provider Internet companies, the idea of "chat rooms" emerged into the healthcare scene. Due to the importance of accurate, timely information, which is often jeopardized by these "chat rooms," most medical sites added an "Ask the Expert" feature. Experts including physicians and specialists have joined the sites as partners who give feedback and advice to its questioners. Additionally, most sites ensure accuracy by setting up "stringent rules governing the ethics of the sites, including how advertising and editorial content should be addressed."[3]

Who Is Dr. Koop?

C. Everett Koop, M.D., is best known as the controversial Surgeon General who served under President Ronald Reagan. He built awareness of the destructive effects of tobacco and the AIDS virus. Today, Dr. C. Everett Koop continues his mission of encouraging good health. His latest effort is the launch of a health Web site, www.drkoop.com.

Dr. Koop was born in Brooklyn in 1916. After earning his M.D. from Cornell University in 1941, he worked at Children's Hospital at the University of Pennsylvania for 35 years. During his tenure, he built a reputation as 1 of the nation's best pediatric surgeons.

From 1981 to 1989, Dr. Koop served as Surgeon General of the United States Public Health Service and Director of International Health. Today, Dr. Koop continues to lead an active role in the health community and health education through writings, electronic media, public appearances, and personal contacts. He teaches medical students at Dartmouth College, where the Koop Institute is based. He is chairman of the National Safe Kids Campaign, Washington, D.C., and is producing 75 point-of-diagnosis videos over the next 2 years for Time-Life Medical, of which he is Chairman of the Board.

Why name a Web site after the 83-year-old Cofounder? The name provides credibility in a highly competitive and controversial environment. "It's an incredible asset," say Cofounder Dennis Upah. "He's the most trusted man in healthcare. He's an icon. With that comes a tremendous responsibility and scrutiny."[4] "In a recent survey by Bruskin-Goldring, almost 60% of consumers recognize Dr. Koop, and of those, nearly 50% percent believe him to be a top authority on healthcare issues," noted Donald Hackett, President and Chief Executive Officer of drkoop.com.[5]

drkoop.com Is Born

On July 20, 1998, Empower Health Corporation launched drkoop.com. Key to this new company was the name and guidance of C. Everett Koop, the former U.S. Surgeon General and the Chairman of Empower. "I am excited about how the Web has greatly enhanced consumers' abilities to access healthcare information," said Dr. Koop. "I firmly believe that empowered consumers make better, more informed decisions with their physicians. Our new Web site gives Americans 1 premier location on the Net to find trusted, quality healthcare information."[6]

To build drkoop.com brand awareness, they partnered with USWeb Corporation. Together they devised a strategy implementing innovative banner advertising and media placement, search engine optimization, and online public relations and promotions.[7] The strategies paid off with more than 1 million visitors in the first 90 days of operation. "The success of drkoop.com demonstrates the effectiveness of audience development techniques and reflects the strong demand for branded healthcare content on the Web," said Keith Schaefer, Managing Partner of the USWeb Audience Development Practice.[8]

The initial success that drkoop.com had during the first 90 days of existence continued over the next year. drkoop.com drew over 15 million page views for the month of October in 1999 according to Nielsen I/PRO.[9] In November 1999, both PC Data and Media Metrix ranked the site as the number 1 health Web site. According to PC Data's December 1999 records, drkoop.com held this position for the past 8 months. Media Metrix also recognized drkoop.com as the number 25 site in its News/Information/ Entertainment category.

drkoop.com Web Site

The Web site is designed to better inform consumers about their health. The site has over 70,000 pages of health information and tools for users. The header of the site quotes Dr. Koop's philosophy, "The best prescription is knowledge." Currently, the site serves as a content and community portal that provides links to other information sources. The site includes the following categories:

- News
- Family
- Resources
- Wellness
- Community
- Conditions

Users can join as drkoop.com members, enabling them to access interactive tools, community bulletin boards, and chat rooms. The site allows members to customize their own drkoop.com homepage to cover topics, health issues, and diseases relevant to them.

NEWS

drkoop.com puts the latest and most critical information about health in the hands of consumers. Users can locate information about recalls, editorials, health events, polls, special reports, and sports medicine. The site includes reports and press releases from credible sources including the American Council on Science and Health (ACSH) and Occupational Safety and Health Administration (OSHA). Users also have searchable access to archived articles related to their health concerns. drkoop.com's HealthSearch™ provides access to a variety of resources for credible information. The search function not only scans the drkoop.com site, but also searches the MedLine database of medical journals and the National Cancer Institute's bibliographic database for relevant articles or abstracts.

Family

The Family section of the drkoop.com Web site is divided into categories including Children, Men, Women, and Elderly. The Web site has received accolades as a superior healthcare destination for women and children. On November 8, 1999, eHealthCare World awarded drkoop.com a gold medal for the "Best Site for Women" based on meeting women's needs for its health and medical news, information, education, advice, support, and community events.[10]

RESOURCES

drkoop.com includes a variety of content and tools that provide consumers with convenience and knowledge to make better-informed decisions.

drkoop.com's Personal Drugstore is a central location where consumers can refill their prescriptions, find drug information, and check drug interactions. The site provides links to pharmacy sites where consumers can order and reorder their prescriptions with doctor approval. Consumers can not receive prescriptions from the Web site. When asked if prescriptions will be given almost exclusively online, Donald Hackett, president and CEO of drkoop.com expresses his viewpoint as,

> Absolutely not. Although I'm a technologist at heart, there's a tremendous amount of human interaction that needs to take place. But even when the consumer needs to schedule the appointment, you can eliminate waste from the system with new technology. This technology is about streamlining the screening process.[11]

One of the most outstanding features on the site is the Drug Checker™, a proprietary drkoop.com technology that enables consumers to ensure that their medications do not interact with each other or with food to cause an adverse reaction in their bodies. Drug Checker™ provides users with critically vital information, considering the fact that the American Medical Association reported that adverse drug interactions are the fourth leading cause of death in the United States. Over 100,000 deaths in 1997 were attributed to these adverse affects.[12] The Drug Checker™ technology received a gold medal for the "Best Interactive Assessment Tool" in eHealthcare World awards.[13] drkoop.com allows its customers to download the tool and add it to their Web site, free of charge. Currently, over 9,500 Web sites provide this unique tool to their users.[14]

drkoop.com's Personal Insurance Center helps consumers evaluate insurance plans through access to an insurance library, glossary of terms and expert advice. Users can review frequently asked questions, search archived questions, and send their questions to insurance expert, Jim Perry, the Director of State Affairs for the Council for Affordable Health Insurance. The site includes direct links/advertisements to several health insurance sites, eHealthInsurance.com and Quotesmith.com, which provide online policy information and quotes. drkoop.com won a silver medal at the eHealthcare World Awards for the "Best Managed Care Site." The site was recognized for its extensive library of insurance articles, information on insurance programs by state, Medicare and Medicaid information, and an insurance policy chooser.[15]

Prior to the proliferation of the Internet, information about clinical trial results and registration was limited for patients. drkoop.com has taken initial steps to provide consumers with information about clinical studies such as patient information, trial procedures, how research is conducted, and how consumers can participate in a Quintiles clinical study. drkoop.com formed a partnership with Quintiles, the world's leading provider of healthcare services to the pharmaceutical industry and largest clinical trials management organization, in which drkoop.com is compensated for successfully recruiting qualified participants into clinical trials.

The strength of the Dr. Koop name in healthcare sets the stage for well-perceived recommendations. For example, the site provides drkoop.com's rankings of other health sites; however, it does not include major competitors such as WebMD and OnHealth.com. drkoop.com includes a list of books recommended by drkoop.com experts and community leaders. A partnership with Amazon.com provides online content and purchase capabilities. To buy a book, users are transferred to the Amazon.com site from drkoop.com.

drkoop.com provides consumers with information about health resources in their local communities. A regional directory helps consumers locate hospitals; however, it is limited to hospitals that participate in the drkoop.com Community Partner Program.[16] The site also includes a Physician Locator, provided by the American Board of Medical Specialties (ABMS). This service allows consumers to search and verify the location and specialty of any physician certified by the Member Boards of the ABMS. When accessing this portion of the site, users exit the drkoop.com and enter ABMS's site.

WELLNESS

The fourth section of drkoop.com focuses on personal wellness. The primary topics in this section are fitness and prevention. Consumers can access pages that help plan a workout routine to match a specified diet and time constraints. The section's theme is that by staying healthy and fit, one can prevent many illnesses.

To support this theme, there are pages that address 1 of C. Everett Koop's favorite subjects: smoking. Here one can find extensive information on the effects of smoking on the body, along with information on quitting programs and support groups. The Web site carries the banner for the most ardent issues during Dr. Koop's term in office as Surgeon General. Although most consumers may agree that smoking is bad for one's health, many of the drkoop.com claims could be considered biased, as this part of the Web site is clearly tainted by his personal views.

Finally, the *Wellness* section offers advice on weight loss. Through online chat rooms, users can design diet plans and obtain recipes for diet foods.

Community

drkoop.com's underlying philosophy of getting people together and giving them tools to help themselves is clear in this portion of the Web site, which is dedicated to health information and interactive chat boards. Here, one has the ability to select a specific affliction and log onto a message board or participate in online chat rooms. This portion of the Web site boasts more than 140 interactive information opportunities. In addition, there are daily topics of discussion where participants can "listen in" on discussions not only with other patients, but also with doctors. Visitors to the site can also find numerous stories of other patients who share the same affliction.

In this *Community* section, advertising is constant in the form of banners and large side-bars with ads from sites such as drugemporium.com. The ads often focus on the particular disease that one is currently examining.

Conditions

The last of the 6 main pages is designed to function as an online encyclopedia of medical advice. Visitors can come to this section and look up almost any disease or mental health issue they have questions about. It also offers shortcuts to advice pages for first aid and for common symptoms such as back pain or insomnia. The first aid section is particularly helpful in that it gives advice on anything from animal bites to sunburn. As in the *Community* section, the focus here is to provide people with information to help them help themselves.

Marketing

To build brand awareness and traffic, drkoop.com advertises on high frequency Web sites such as Yahoo!. Competitors also follow similar strategies. For example, WebMD.com advertises on NetZero, a free ISP for consumers, and OnHealth.com also advertises on Yahoo!.

drkoop.com has arrangements with local TV stations, which give the stations content for their Web sites in exchange for a drkoop.com "plug" at the end of a news story on a health issue.

In late 1999, drkoop.com is expected to launch a $10 million to $15 million advertising campaign supported by Lowe & Partners/SMS, New York.[17] The competitive market increasingly requires higher spending to build brand name recognition in the medical information industry. drkoop.com's planned marketing expenditures are shown in **Exhibit 1**.

Recently, drkoop.com established an exclusive relationship with Creative Artists Agency (CAA).[18] Dan Adler who is heading up the CAA's effort on drkoop.com stated, "We are excited by the opportunity to help broaden the reach of the most respected and recognized eHealth brand. We are confident that the strategic partnerships we help to build will secure drkoop.com's preeminent position in the eHealth category and will help it in its mission to revolutionize healthcare for consumers."[19]

drkoop.com Revenue Sources

drkoop.com is well positioned to take advantage of the mass amounts of money spent around the health care industry. This is further enhanced due to drkoop.com's broad positioning throughout the medical world. **Exhibits 2** and **3** show current financial information. **Exhibit 4** is an estimate of the market size to which drkoop.com has access.

ADVERTISING

drkoop.com generates most of its revenues through advertisements on its site. DrugEmporium is the only "sponsor" of the Web site. The site is covered with DrugEmporium advertisements and direct links to allow for over-the-counter medication purchases. drkoop.com also generates advertising revenues from Community Partners (i.e., hospitals) and health insurance companies. drkoop.com also receives advertising rates for Web banners by selling banner space to advertisers.

Exhibit 1

drkoop.com: Annual Statement of Earnings, 1997–2001
(Dollar amounts in millions, except for share data)

Year Ending December 31	1997	1998	1999¹	2000E¹	2001E¹	Revenue Analysis 1997	1998	1999	2000E	2001E
Revenues										
Advertising	$ —	$ —	$ 7.0	$ 23.3	$ 42.3	N/A	N/A	77.2%	72.7%	63.4%
Content Licensing	$ —	$ —	$ 1.9	$ 6.7	$ 17.1	N/A	N/A	21.2%	20.8%	25.6%
Other	$ —	$ —	$ 0.1	$ 2.1	$ 7.4	N/A	N/A	1.6%	6.5%	11.0%
Total revenues	**$ —**	**$ 0.04**	**$ 9.0**	**$ 32.1**	**$ 66.7**	**N/A**	**N/A**	**100.0%**	**100.0%**	**100.0%**
Cost of operations										
Production, content and Product Development	$ 0.5	$ 4.4	$ 13.7	$ 20.8	$ 23.5	N/A	N/A	151.5%	64.9%	35.2%
Sales and Marketing		$ 2.0	$ 29.5	$ 34.6	$ 35.8	N/A	N/A	326.5%	107.7%	53.6%
Total cost of sales	**$ 0.5**	**$ 6.4**	**$ 43.2**	**$ 55.4**	**$ 59.3**	**N/A**	**N/A**	**478.0%**	**172.6%**	**88.8%**
Gross income	**$ (0.5)**	**$ (6.4)**	**$ (34.1)**	**$ (23.3)**	**$ 7.4**					
Gross Margin %	*NM*	*NM*	*NM*	*(72.6%)*	*(11.1%)*					
G & A Expense	$ 0.2	$ 2.6	$ 8.8	$ 10.6	$ 12.2	N/A		97.7%	33.0%	18.3%
Operating income	**$ (0.6)**	**$ (9.0)**	**$ (42.9)**	**$ (33.9)**	**$ (4.8)**					
Operating Margin	*NM*	*NM*	*NM*	*(105.6%)*	*(7.2%)*					
Nonoperating income and expenses										
Interest (Net)	$ —	$ —	$ 1.1	$ 1.7	$ 1.7	N/A	N/A	12.6%	5.3%	2.5%
Other	$ —	$ —	$ —	$ —	$ —	N/A	N/A	0.0%	0.0%	0.0%
Pretax income	**$ (0.6)**	**$ (9.0)**	**$ (41.8)**	**$ (32.2)**	**$ (3.1)**	**N/A**	**N/A**	**(463.1%)**	**(100.3%)**	**(4.6%)**
Pretax Margin	*NM*	*NM*	*NM*	*(100.3%)*	*(4.6%)*					
Provision for Income Taxes	$ —	$ —	$ —	$ —	$ 0.6					
Tax Rate	*0%*	*0%*	*0%*	*0%*	*(18.0%)*					
Income	**$ (0.6)**	**$ (9.0)**	**$ (41.8)**	**$ (32.2)**	**$ (3.6)**	**N/A**	**N/A**	**(463.1%)**	**(100.3%)**	**(5.4%)**
Nonrecurring items	$ —	$ —	$ (26.4)							
Net income	**$ (0.6)**	**$ (9.0)**	**$ (68.2)**	**$ (32.2)**	**$ (3.6)**	**N/A**	**N/A**	**(755.8%)**	**(100.3%)**	**(5.4%)**

Note:
1. Rounding error(s) in columns 1999, 2000E, and 2001E.

Source: Company reports; Bear, Stearns & Co. Inc. estimates.

12-7

Exhibit 2

Balance Sheet, 1998–2001E
(Dollar amounts in millions, except for share data)

Year Ending December 31	1998	1999[1]	2000E[1]	2001E[1]
Assets				
Current assets				
Cash and Equivalents	$ —	$ 56.6	$ 19.9	$ 11.1
Accounts Receivable	$ —	$ 4.7	$ 9.6	$ 14.5
Other	$ —	$ 5.9	$ 5.9	$ 5.9
Total current assets	$ 0.1	$ 67.1	$ 35.4	$ 31.5
Property, plant, and equipment	$ 0.3	$ 0.6	$ 1.0	$ 2.2
Investment	$ —	$ 5.0	$ 5.0	$ 5.0
Licenses	$ —	$ 3.0	$ 2.1	$ 1.2
Other	$ —	$ —	$ —	$ —
Total assets	$ 0.4	$ 75.8	$43.6	$ 39.9
Liabilities				
Current liabilities				
Accounts Payable	$ 2.0	$ 5.0	$ 5.0	$ 5.0
Accrued Liabilities	$ 0.5	$ 2.7	$ 2.7	$ 2.7
Deferred Revenue	$ —	$ 0.7	$ 0.7	$ 0.7
Notes Payable	$ 0.5	$ 0.3	$ 0.3	$ 0.3
Total current liabilities	$ 3.0	$ 8.7	$ 8.7	$ 8.7
Other	$ —	$ —	$ —	$ —
Redeemable Preferred Stock	$ 12.8	$ —	$ —	$ —
Stockholder's Equity				
Preferred Stock	$ —	$ —	$ —	$ —
Common Stock	$ —	$ —	$ —	$ —
Capital in Excess of par	$ (0.3)	$133.5	$133.5	$129.9
Retained Earnings (Deficit)	$ (15.2)	$ (62.6)	$ (94.8)	(94.9)
Other	$ —	$ (3.8)	$ (3.8)	$ (3.9)
Total stockholders' equity	$ (15.4)	$ 67.0	$ 34.8	$ 31.2
Total liabilities and stockholders' equity	$ 0.4	$ 75.8	$ 43.6	$ 39.9

	Dec–98	Dec–99	Dec–00E	Dec–01E
Current Ratio	0	7.7	4.1	3.6
Days Sales Outstanding	N/A	94	80.4	65.2
Book Value/Share	N/A	$ 2.23	$ 1.14	$ 0.99
Return on Equity	N/A	N/A	N/A	N/A
Cash Flow per Share	$(0.32)	$(0.41)	$(1.00)	$(0.06)
Free Cash Flow per Share	$(0.33)	$(0.41)	$(1.04)	$(0.12)
Long-Term Debt/Total Capital	0%	0%	0%	0%

Note:
1. Rounding error(s) in columns 1999, 2000E, and 2001E.

Source: Company reports; Bear, Stearns & Co. Inc. estimates.

PARTNERSHIPS

drkoop.com has revenues from numerous partnership agreements. These range from the arrangement with Quintiles, for which drkoop.com receives revenue for every referral generated, to the agreements that generate licensing fees for products and services that drkoop.com co-develops with partners.

Exhibit 3

Statement of Cash Flows, 1998–2001E
(Dollar amounts in millions, except for share data)

Year Ending December 31	1998[1]	1999[1]	2000E[1]	2001E[1]
Net income	$ (9.0)	$ (68.2)	$ (32.2)	$ (3.6)
Depreciation and amortization	$ 0.1	$ 1.4	$ 1.8	$ 1.8
Other	$ 0.1	$ 26.5	$ —	$ —
Change in current account				
Accounts receivable	$ —	$ (4.7)	$ (4.9)	$ (4.9)
Increase in other assets	$ —	$ —	$ —	$ —
Accounts payable	$ 2.1	$ (0.1)	$ —	$ —
Accrued liabilities and other assets	$ —	$ (0.2)	$ —	$ —
Deferred revenue	$ —	$ 0.5	$ —	$ —
Other	$ —	$ (6.0)	$ —	$ —
Cash provided by operating activities	**$ (6.8)**	**$ (50.7)**	**$ (35.4)**	**$ (6.7)**
Cash flows from investing activities				
Capital expenditures	$ (0.3)	$ (0.6)	$ (1.3)	$ (2.1)
Net cash used in investing activities	**$ (0.3)**	**$ (0.6)**	**$ (1.3)**	**$ (2.1)**
Cash flows from financing activities				
Net long-term financing	$ 0.5	$ —	$ —	$ —
Preferred stock issuances	$ 6.6	$ 5.8	$ —	$ —
Common stock issuances	$ —	$ 90.0	$ —	$ —
Other	$ —	$ 12.0	$ —	$ —
Net cash provided in financing activities	**$ 7.1**	**$ 107.8**	**$ —**	**$ —**
Net increase (decrease) in cash	$ —	$ 56.6	$ (36.7)	$ (8.8)
Cash beginning of year	$ —	$ —	$ 56.6	$ 19.9
End of year	**$ —**	**$ 56.6**	**$ 19.9**	**$ 11.1**
Cash flow/share	$ (0.3)	$ (2.25)	$ (1.00)	$ (0.06)
Free cash flow (FCF) per share	$ (0.3)	$ (2.27)	$ (1.04)	$ (0.12)
	1998	**1999**	**2000 E**	**2001 E**
CFFO-NI	$ 2.2	$ 17.5	$ (3.1)	$ (3.1)
EBITDA	$ (9.0)	$ (41.6)	$ (32.1)	$ (3.0)
Free cash flow (FCF)	$ (6.5)	$ (50.1)	$ (34.1)	$ (4.6)

Note:
1. Rounding error(s) in columns 1998, 1999, 2000E, and 2001E.

Source: Company reports; Bear, Stearns & Co. Inc. estimates.

CONTENT PROVIDER

drkoop.com has signed numerous deals with hospitals, for $50,000 to $100,000 a year, and the firm provides them with content to support their own hospital Web sites. drkoop.com also receives fees as a content provider for various other entities, such as the GO! Network and America Online.

Strategic Partnerships

One of the major strategies drkoop.com has employed since inception is that of partnerships. These partnerships have focused on numerous areas including those that broaden the firm's service offerings, expand its viewing base, and further expand its business model into traditional areas of the healthcare industry. drkoop.com currently has over 1 dozen portal agree-

Exhibit 4

1999 Potential Annual Market Size (in billions)

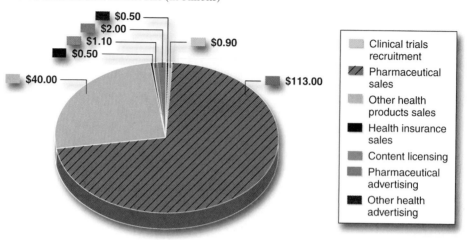

$0.50	
$2.00	
$1.10	
$0.50	
$40.00	
$0.90	
$113.00	

Clinical trials recruitment

Pharmaceutical sales

Other health products sales

Health insurance sales

Content licensing

Pharmaceutical advertising

Other health advertising

ments where drkoop.com is the exclusive or preferred provider of health care information. These partnerships range from The Dartmouth Medical School to the American Council on Science and Health.

Some of the most beneficial strategies are described below.

ADVENTIST HEALTH SYSTEMS

In January of 1999, drkoop.com exchanged 2,615,677 shares of preferred stock for $3.5 million in cash plus a 10% share of HealthMagic. HealthMagic is a subsidiary of Adventist Health Systems and a developer of a personal medical record application.[20] This was a key partnership for drkoop.com in that it allowed the firm access to and use of a personal medical record application and secured Adventist as a customer in its community partner program.

FHC INTERNET

FHC purchased $10 million of drkoop.com common stock at the offering price. FHC Internet is a subsidiary of Foundation Health Systems that specializes in the outsourcing of disease management programs for local health care organizations. FHC and drkoop.com have entered into an agreement whereby FHC is sponsoring drkoop.com's mental health center.[21]

QUINTILES TRANSNATIONAL

Quintiles purchased $5 million worth of shares of drkoop.com at the IPO price of $9. Quintiles is currently the world's largest provider of clinical research services to pharmaceutical companies. The firm has entered into an agreement with drkoop.com to jointly develop a clinical trials information center. This center allows drkoop.com visitors to view information about clinical trials that are currently going on across the country, to fill out an online prescreen form for various clinical trials, and then refers these prescreens to study sites. drkoop.com receives approximately $100 for each referral. Quintiles receives an expectation of realizing faster recruiting of patients, lower prescreening costs, and a larger pool of potential candidates for clinical trials.[22]

AMERICA ONLINE

drkoop.com entered into an agreement with America Online to offer services to its Internet Service Providers, America Online and CompuServe, as well as to its portals, AOL.com, Netscape.com, and DigitalCity.com. While all of the details of the deal have not been released, drkoop.com will pay AOL $89 million over the next 4 years and give the firm 1.6 million warrants with an exercise price of $15.94. In exchange, drkoop.com has access to over 70.3 million users from the 5 entities combined. In addition, drkoop.com receives an $8 million license fee for the use of a co-developed personal medical record as well as the use of AOL's salesforce.

PHAR-MOR

A cross partnership has been established between Phar-Mor, an online drugstore, and drkoop.com. Phar-Mor will sponsor a monthly drkoop.com pharmacy newsletter. Users of Phar-Mor's Web site will be directed to drkoop.com to gain further necessary information. In return, visitors to drkoop.com will be able to access Phar-Mor's Web site directly from drkoop.com's site. "Our relationship with drkoop.com allows us to provide our on line shoppers with the best health care content available so they can make sound purchasing decisions," said Phar-Mor president and CEO David Schwartz.[23]

DRUGEMPORIUM.COM

DrugEmporium.com and drkoop.com signed an agreement on October 4, 1999, to work together. Under the agreement drkoop.com visitors have access to over 20,000 discounted products sold by DrugEmporium.com. Shoppers at DrugEmporium.com can now go directly to drkoop.com for further information on products they are considering. Further, drkoop.com's Drug Checker™ has been integrated into the purchase of all prescription drugs, automatically checking for any potential problems.

Some of the additional drkoop.com selected affiliations include:

- ABC Television Affiliates (through the GO! Network)
- Dell Computer Corporation
- Element Media
- GO! Network (GO! Health Center, ESPN.com training room and Family.com Health Channel)
- Highmark
- iSyndicate
- MemorialCare
- Physicians' Online
- Salon Magazine
- Scott and White Hospital and Clinic
- Tallahassee Memorial HealthCare
- The Weather Channel

drkoop.com has numerous partnerships with various health care providers and HMOs including: Highmark (1 of the 10 largest insurers in the United States); MemorialCare (a large health care system serving more than 14 million residents in Los Angeles and Orange County); Scott and White Hospital and Clinic (1 of the largest multispecialty hospitals in the U.S.); Promina Health Systems (a nonprofit health care organization serving 4.3 million residents in the Atlanta area); the Cleveland Clinic (with a staff of over 850 physicians); and the Baptist Health System (serves the 3.5 million residents in the Miami area).

Competition

Many would argue that drkoop.com is the leader in the online healthcare industry, yet the competition is intense. Hundreds of new medical sites have emerged over the past year and it is difficult to distinguish between the leaders in the market. All of the most popular sites provide extensive consumer health information, chat rooms, expert advice, links to products and comprehensive, fully tailored health care publications for professionals of all specialties.

In addition to the companies that specialize primarily in online health information, large medical companies are establishing an Internet presence by acquiring information and service firms such as insurance or drug products. Most pharmaceutical companies have portions of their corporate Web sites dedicated to consumer health information. One big player in this area is Merck, which publishes an online "medical bible." These pharmaceutical companies are not direct competitors of drkoop.com because their main focus is to sell products, but they are still "players" in the market.

In October 1999, PC Data ranked drkoop.com as the number 1 dedicated healthcare site for the seventh consecutive month.[24] According to PC Data, the site is the forty-third most popular site on the Internet overall. See **Exhibit 5** for the ranking for unique users for healthcare sites.

The following is a brief overview of some of the leading sites and how they position themselves in the competitive marketplace.

HEALTHEON/WEBMD.COM—REVENUES FOR QUARTER ENDING SEPTEMBER 1999: $28.7 M

drkoop.com's top competitor is Healtheon/WebMD, which claims to be the first comprehensive, online healthcare portal.[25]

Following the trend in consolidation, Healtheon and WebMD announced their merger in May 1999 to form Healtheon WebMD Corporation (HLTH). As a part of this merger, the companies combined their consumer Web sites, MyHealtheon.com and MyWebMD.com, into 1 site, www.webmd.com.

Exhibit 5

Traffic on competitive Web sites

Company	No. of Unique Hits 9/99
drkoop.com	5,539,000
onhealth.com	2,262,000
discoveryhealth.com	1,077,000
webmd.com	765,000
thriveonline.com	753,000
healthyideas.com	714,000
intelihealth.com	675,000
allhealth.com	596,000
AOLhealth.com	568,000
healthcentral.com	532,000
medscape.com	415,000
ama-assn.org	404,000
mediconsult.com	225,000

In early December 1999, Rupert Murdoch's News Corp. formed a $1 billion partnership with Healtheon/WebMD. According to CBS Market Watch's Barbara Kollmeyer, it's being "billed as the largest media and Internet deal to date."[26]

News Corp. is taking a 10.8% stake in Healtheon/WebMD, providing $700 million in "branding services" over 10 years, purchasing $100 million of Healtheon/WebMD, investing $100 million cash in the Internet company and signing a $62.5 million 5-year licensing deal to syndicate WebMD's daily broadcast content.

The licensing part of the deal is innovative because it changes the way media content is ordinarily used across media. Reuters quoted News Corp. President and Chief Operating Officer Peter Chernin, "Companies traditionally re-purpose print or broadcast content for the Web. With this deal, we're using the Web as a source for original, unique programming which will be leveraged across all media owned by News Corp."[27]

The goal of this partnership is to drive television viewers to medical Web sites and vice versa, creating single health care information brands across all media. The News Corp. partnership could give Healtheon/WebMD an advantage in internationalizing online health care.

The company is building a system of software and services to automate such tasks as HMO enrollment, referrals, data retrieval, and claims processing for use by insurers, doctors, pharmacies, and consumers. The site also offers physician communications services, physician references, medical information and news, and personalized content to its users.

The company has high aspirations for success, but whether it can surmount the daunting technological and economic challenges in rewiring the health-care industry remains to be seen.

MEDICONSULT.COM—REVENUES FOR QUARTER ENDING SEPTEMBER 1999: $3.1 M

The company's mission is to provide timely, comprehensive, and accessible information on chronic medical conditions, utilizing the latest available to deliver information efficiently. It features a fee-based service, *MediXpert*, which lets visitors present a case to a medical specialist who responds with a confidential report.

The company is completely independent of another company, HMO, hospital, or other healthcare organization in order to ensure unbiased, objective, credible information. All information that appears on the site "must pass a rigorous clinical review process before we deem it worthy" of the consumer.[28]

On September 7, Mediconsult.com acquired Physicians Online in a stock deal valued at $180 million. The acquisition could help Mediconsult.com take advantage of the recent introduction of online medical records and other services designed to connect doctors and patients and deliver health care.[29]

The site also has a powerful search engine, "Medisearch" which allows quick keyword inquiries.

AHN.COM (THE HEALTH NETWORK)—QUARTERLY REVENUES NOT AVAILABLE

Los Angeles based The Health Network, or ahn.com, is the 1-stop television and Internet site where consumers can find information and motivation about leading a healthy life. Twenty-four hours a day, 7 days a week, doctors and other medical experts provide credible, relevant information in a clear, interesting and easy-to-understand manner.

A 50/50 partnership between FOX Entertainment Group and AHN Partners, LP, The Health Network combines the leading health cable television network with 1 of the most visited health information sites on the Internet. The site is the premier source of live medical events, such as the first live Internet birth and the first live Internet triplet birth.

MEDSCAPE—REVENUES FOR QUARTER ENDING SEPTEMBER 1999: $3.1 M

The site's homepage is comprehensive, well organized, and more user-friendly than many competitors. It features the *Medscape Network* (for student, nurses, physicians), *Medscape Resources, My Medscape* (records personalized info from previous visits) and an *Editorial Board.*

In July 1999, CBS (CBS) took a 35% stake in Medscape, in exchange for $157 million in advertising and branding services. The company produces the consumer oriented CBS *HealthWatch* and provides information through AOL. In addition, Medscape publishes *Medscape General Medicine,* an online, peer-reviewed medical journal, and it offers a database of continuing medical education programs, an online bookstore, and physician Web sites for its members.

The company recently announced a content agreement with America Online. The 3-year arrangement calls for Medscape to develop co-branded health sites for AOL's 18 million subscribers. In exchange, Medscape will pay AOL $33 million for 2 years.

WWW.AMA-ASSN.ORG—QUARTERLY REVENUES NOT AVAILABLE

The American Medical Association is primarily a membership organization. Its core objective is to be the world's leader in obtaining, synthesizing, integrating, and disseminating information on health and medical practice. It publishes numerous journals and its Web site provides valuable online information, which is accessible to "members only."

In addition to providing valuable information to its members, the AMA's corporate Web site contains a large variety of information available to the public. Consumers can use the site to look for medical groups and physician locators, to get medical advice about injuries, illnesses and specific conditions, and to read about general health information. Consumers can also learn about the Association's advocacy and legislative initiatives and read about topics on medical ethics and education.

Membership has been declining: the AMA represents about 35% of U.S. doctors (down from 50% in 1975). Most likely this decline will continue due to the emergence of medical information Web sites. Therefore, the AMA may devote time and funding to developing its consumer site and look for new revenue sources in addition to membership fees and publication sales.

ONHEALTH.COM—REVENUES FOR QUARTER ENDING SEPTEMBER 1999: $1 M

OnHealth Network Co. is a consumer health information company based in Seattle. Its site is not tied to a particular doctor, health system, or insurance company.

The site is supported by advertising, but the authors claim to keep the ads and the articles separate from each other—both behind the scenes and on the pages one sees. Information about a topic is not influenced by the advertisements displayed on that page. Authors write, "If it ever appears otherwise to you, please let us know."[30]

OnHealth Network offers both proprietary and syndicated content, and the company has negotiated many distribution deals with entities ranging from America Online to WebTV, as well as advertising deals with companies such as Johnson & Johnson and Pfizer.

In December 1999, OnHealth.com signed an agreement with Ask Jeeves, Inc., a leading provider of natural-language question answering services on the Web for consumers and businesses. This deal will provide OnHealth with prominent brand positioning.[31]

Most information comes from the publishers of the *New England Journal of Medicine,* from Cleveland Clinic, from Beth Israel Deaconess Medical Center, and from physicians who teach at Harvard, Columbia, and Stanford. A unique feature on the site's homepage is the Herbal Index, which contains 140 descriptions of alternative health remedies. About 80% of OnHealth's audience is female. Affiliates of Van Wagoner Capital Management own about 39% of the company.

iVILLAGE'S WWW.ALLHEALTH.COM—REVENUES FOR QUARTER ENDING SEPTEMBER 1999: $10.7 M

iVillage's Web site targets women aged 25 to 49 through more than 15 "channels" focusing on topics such as health, food, parenting, relationships, and shopping. The health sections of the site can be found at <betterhealth.com> or <allhealth.com>. The underlying themes of the site are "Take Charge of Your Health!" and "Information you need from a Community you can trust."[32] The site also features extensive chat rooms, weekly polls and shopping, and allows iVillage members to "ask the experts" for medical advice.

CEO Candice Carpenter recently commented on the merger between Healtheon and WebMD by saying, "I think it's pretty obvious there needs to be some (more) consolidation. We've got to clean this up a little. I don't know who's going to do it, but somebody should step up to the plate to do that job."[33]

iVillage generates more than 80% of its revenue from advertising, but the company is looking to enlarge its e-commerce presence with offerings such as its iBaby.com online baby products retailer. Perhaps the allhealth.com section will follow this trend.

Other Considerations

DISCLAIMERS/ LIABILITY

Similar to the competition, the drkoop.com site includes a disclaimer that states, "This information is not intended to be a substitute for professional medical advice. You should not use this information to diagnose or treat a health problem or disease without consulting with a qualified healthcare provider. Please consult your healthcare provider with any questions or concerns you may have regarding your condition."[34]

HIGH-ETHICS ALLIANCE/ LEGALITY

The growing concern of potential conflicts of interests related to inaccurate information, diagnosis, and prescribing drugs online resulted in the formation of a coalition of 16 companies including Healtheon/WebMD, Medscape Inc., America Online Inc., and drkoop.com. Dr. C. Everett Koop called this group together to develop an ethical code of conduct for consumers. Alliance members include 27% of total Internet audience traffic according to PC Data.[35] The committee will create policies for advertising, privacy and content and ensure the reliability of health information that consumers access through e-health providers. Donald Kemper, the chairperson of Hi-Ethics states that, "our ultimate goal is to guide a future of consumer confidence in healthcare information."[36]

On November 4, 1999, drkoop.com won the most awards of any e-healthcare Web site at eHealthcare World Awards in New York. The site received 2 Gold and 2 Silver awards, honoring the site for its trusted content and healthcare information for consumers. However, the drkoop.com Web site has been criticized by the American Medical Association for not providing sufficient information related to sponsorship and commerce relationships.

Conclusion

Dennis Upah knew the challenges were numerous, and the competitive field seemed to increase daily. He wondered which business model was the correct choice. Companies like Healtheon/WebMD, who were partnering with hospitals to provide other services, were definitely on the right track. In addition, WebMD and News Corp's recent announcement to put more than $1 billion into developing their site was also worrying. Although he felt drkoop.com had a significant advantage in its brand name, he knew this was not enough. How, then, could he continue to build on the important partnerships he had helped establish, such as the one with Quintiles? And how could he leverage the important innovations the firm had made, such as Drug Checker™? It was obvious to him that there were many opportunities out there, and his task was now to identify the best ones to pursue.

Notes

1. "Dr. Koop's Community" *1998 Business Wire, Inc.* (July 20, 1998).
2. <www.drkoop.com/aboutus/koop/>
3. *Ibid.*
4. "i:20 drkoop.com's Dennis Upah," *Crain Communications,* November 1999.
5. PR Newswire Association, Inc. March 29, 1999.
6. "Dr. Koop's Community" *1998 Business Wire, Inc.* (July 20, 1998).
7. "USWeb Audience Development Practice Helps Establish Success of Leading Consumer Healthcare Site," *1998 Business Wire, Inc.* (November 19, 1998).
8. "USWeb Audience Development Practice Helps Establish Success of Leading Consumer Healthcare Site," *1998 Business Wire, Inc.* (November 19, 1998).
9. "drkoop.com Breaks 15 million Page Views for October," *PR Newswire* (November 22, 1999).
10. "drkoop.com Web Site Dominates Awards at eHealthcareWorld," *PR Newswire* (November 8, 1999).
11. "Posts," *The Standard* (June 28, 1999).
12. "Dr. Koop's Community," *Business Wire, Inc.* (July 20, 1998).
13. "drkoop.com Web Site Dominates Awards at eHealthcareWorld," *PR Newswire* (November 8, 1999).
14. *Ibid.*
15. *Ibid.*
16. Hospitals that participate in the Community Partner pay $50,000 to $100,000 per year to license drkoop.com healthcare information to use on their Web sites. In addition, direct links are provided from the drkoop.com site to their individual Web sites.
17. "i:20 drkoop.com's Dennis Upah," *Crain Communications* (November 1999).
18. CAA provides strategic consulting services in marketing and technology areas and holds alliances with Internet incubator, idealab! And communications consulting and advertising company, Shepardson, Stern and Kaminsky.
19. "CAA to Provide Exclusive eHealth Representation to drkoop.com," *PR Newswire* (November 10, 1999).
20. Bear Stearns Equity Research, Health Care Industry, July 27, 1999.
21. *Ibid.*
22. Bear Stearns Equity Research, Health Care Industry, July 27, 1999.
23. "Phar-Mor, drkoop.com Enter Pact," FirstSearch database MMR, vol.16, no. 17, 990823, p. 19.
24. PR Newswire Association, Oct. 7, 1999, Financial News section.
25. <www.ixl.com/success/webmd/index.html>
26. <www.thestandard.com/article/display/0,1151,6224,00.html>
27. <thestandard.com>
28. <www.mediconsult.com>
29. <www.thestandard.com/article/display/0,1151,6224,00.html>
30. <nhealth.com/ch1/info/item.asp>
31. <www.askjeeves.com. Investor Relations>
32. <www.allhealth.com>
33. <www.thestandard.com/article/display/0,1151,4839,00.html>
34. Disclaimer present on every page of the drkoop.com Web site.
35. "Leading E-Healthware Companies Form Alliance to Benefit Internet Consumers," *Business Wire* (November 4, 1999).
36. *Ibid.*

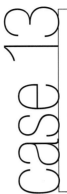

CASE 13

WingspanBank.com

Laura Cooke, Liza Hovey, Hyung Kim, and Paul Rakouski

W*ingspanBank cannibalize[s] existing business to build new business.*[1]

—John B. McCoy, President and CEO
BANK ONE CORPORATION

It was Monday, November 15, 1999, and John B. McCoy already felt like it had been a long week. The *Wall Street Journal* had announced the impending departure of James Stewart,[2] Chief Executive of Wingspan, and investors and media hounds alike were clamoring for more details.

McCoy remembered the beginning, when he worried about the many Internet start-ups beginning to offer a wide array of financial services. Reasoning that bankone.com was insufficient to stem the tide, he launched WingspanBank.com as a freestanding Internet bank.[3] After all, he thought, if customers were going to abandon bricks and mortar banks in favor of Internet banks, BANK ONE should offer the best choice: WingspanBank.com.

Thus, WingspanBank.com was launched on June 24, 1999, under the auspices of the First USA division of BANK ONE. Unfortunately, the First USA division had performed poorly since then, and analysts had been questioning whether the excitement of launching WingspanBank.com had distracted management from its core business—credit cards.[4]

As McCoy considered the situation, several questions came to mind: Had he been right about permitting cannibalization? What is the role of Wingspan at BANK ONE? What is the future of BANK ONE in the era of e-commerce?

Background

There was a lot for McCoy to consider. The final decades of the twentieth century had brought changes to every possible dimension of banking. From changes in government regulations to the emergence of the Internet, the ever-changing landscape for financial service companies brought difficult challenges and uncertain opportunities.

MBA candidates Laura Cooke, Liza Hovey, Paul Rakouski, and Hyung Kim prepared this case under the supervision of Professor Allan Afuah as the basis for discussion in University of Michigan Business School class "Strategy, Technology and the Management of Innovation," not to demonstrate effective or ineffective handling of an administrative situation. Some data, names, and situations have been disguised to maintain confidentiality. Copyright ©1999 by Laura Cooke, Elizabeth Hovey, and Hyung Kim. This case was edited for SMBP-8th Edition. All rights reserved. Reprinted by permission.

HISTORY OF BANK ONE

Just as its all-caps name BANK ONE CORPORATION (hereinafter Bank One) proclaims, this financial institution thinks big, and its recent history (see **Exhibit 1**) shows that it embraces innovations. Among them are the first Visa (then called BankAmericard) credit card service outside California in 1966, and the first cash management account in 1977, which combined the higher interest rates of a brokerage account with the flexibility of checking services.

The bank—founded in 1868 and called City National Bank after the merger of two Columbus, Ohio, banks in 1929—also has a strong history of acquisitions. In 1967, its management created a holding company to enable expansion and named it First Banc Group of Ohio to skirt legal restrictions on the use of the word "bank." Its acquisition of a bank in neighboring Mansfield, Ohio, initiated a string of intrastate acquisitions. When restrictions on interstate banking were removed in 1984, BANC ONE (changed from First Banc in 1979) expanded into Arizona, Illinois, Indiana, Kentucky, Michigan, Texas, Utah, and Wisconsin—primarily through stock swaps.

Following its "merger of equals" (under BANC ONE leadership) with First Chicago NBD in 1998, Bank One (so renamed after the merger) was the fourth largest banking company in

Exhibit 1

Milestones: BANK ONE

1999	Becomes world's largest issuer of Visa credit cards
	Launches WingspanBank.com (as unit of First USA division), which offers wide array of financial services—including insurance, mortgage, mutual fund services
1998	Acquires First Chicago NBD in $30 billion stock swap
	Changes name to BANK ONE CORPORATION, based in Chicago, Illinois
	BANK ONE is number 4 banking company in United States
	Launches <bankone.com>, which offers traditional banking services to current customers (and general information about BANK ONE CORPORATION)
1997	Acquires number 4 credit card issuer First USA
	Buys Liberty Bancorp of Oklahoma
1996	Buys Premier Bancorp., Louisiana's #3 bank
1994	Begins major consolidation effort
1992	Enters Arizona and Utah
1991	Enters Illinois
1989	Enters Texas market with acquisition of 20 failed Mcorp and other banks
1984	John (B.) McCoy becomes third (and present) bank president
	Federal government relaxes restrictions on interstate banking
	BANC ONE expands into Indiana, Kentucky, Michigan, and Wisconsin
1979	Changes name to BANC ONE; all affiliated banks renamed Bank One
1977	Introduces first cash management account in partnership with Merrill Lynch
1967	First Banc Group of Ohio formed as holding company for City National
	Buys Farmers Savings and Trust of Mansfield, Ohio
1966	Introduces first Visa (then BankAmericard) credit card outside California
1958	John (G.) McCoy becomes second bank president
1935	John (H.) McCoy becomes first bank president
1929	Commercial National and National Bank of Commerce combine to form City National Bank and Trust
1868	F. C. Session founds Commercial National Bank in Columbus, Ohio

Sources: BANK ONE CORPORATION 1998 Annual Report, Hoover's Company Capsules, WingspanBank Marketing.

Exhibit 2

Summary Balance Sheet: BANK ONE
(Dollar amounts in millions)

Year Ending December 31	1998	1997
Assets		
Cash and due from banks	$ 19,878	$ 15,380
Interest-bearing due from banks	4,642	6,910
Funds and securities under resale agreements	9,862	9,168
Trading and derivative products	12,299	9,869
Investment securities	44,852	26,039
Loans, net	153,127	156,762
Bank premises and equipment, net	3,340	3,426
Other assets	13,496	11,818
Total assets	$261,496	$239,372
Liabilities		
Deposits, total	$161,542	$153,726
Short-term borrowings, total	40,101	33,152
Long-term debt	21,295	20,543
Other liabilities	17,998	12,901
Total liabilities	$240,936	$220,322
Stockholders' equity		
Preferred stock	190	326
Common stock, $0.01 par value	12	12
Surplus	10,769	12,584
Retained earnings	9,528	8,063
Other	61	(1,935)
Total stockholders' equity	$ 20,560	$19,050
Total liabilities and stockholders' equity	$261,496	$239,372

Sources: BANK ONE CORPORATION 1998 Annual Report.

the United States (see **Exhibits 2** and **3**). In addition, the recent acquisition of credit card issuer First USA made Bank One the largest issuer of Visa credit cards in the world.

First USA featured a more entrepreneurial culture and also brought significant e-commerce expertise in the form of its Internet Marketing Group. In its efforts to develop an e-commerce strategy for First USA and implement <firstusa.com>, this group had learned important lessons and forged useful relationships. The Internet Marketing Group made it possible for Bank One to take fuller advantage of the mounting Internet explosion than its current presence. BankOne.com (see **Exhibit 4**) was meant simply to offer online services to current customers of Bank One and to serve as the corporation's online information presence.

Explosion of the Internet

By the late 1990s, the Internet had already transformed itself from a convenience for academics and curiosity for intellectuals to a viable commercial force and powerful business tool. Three primary phenomena converged to spur this emergence:

1. **More people had access to the Internet**. Personal computers (PCs) and Internet access became increasingly affordable and reliable. Frenetic competition, learning effects, and scale economies in the PC and Internet industries even made it possible for some com-

Exhibit 3

Summary Income Statement: BANK ONE
(Dollar amounts in millions, except share data)

Year Ending December 31	1998	1997
Interest income		
Interest income, total	$17,524	$17,545
Interest expense, total	8,177	8,084
Less provision for credit losses	1,408	1,988
Net interest income after credit losses	$ 7,939	$ 7,473
Noninterest revenue		
Market-driven revenue	546	552
Fee-based revenue	6,728	5,645
Other	797	497
Total noninterest revenue	$ 8,071	$ 6,694
Noninterest expense		
Salaries and benefits	4,477	4,224
Net occupancy and equipment	845	739
Depreciation and amortization	680	693
Outside service fees and processing	1,349	1,145
Marketing and development	1,024	837
Communication and transportation	781	711
Merger-related and restructuring charges	1,062	337
Other	1,327	1,054
Total	$11,545	$ 9,740
Earnings before income taxes	$ 4,465	$ 4,427
Applicable income taxes	$ 1,357	$ 1,467
Net income	$ 3,108	$ 2,960
Earnings per share, basic	$ 2.65	$ 2.48
Earnings per share, diluted	$ 2.61	$ 2.43

Source: BANK ONE CORPORATION 1998 Annual Report.

panies to offer free PCs to consumers willing to purchase Internet access (and vice versa). In addition, the network software offered security and ease of use. By 1998, over 50% of U.S. households had personal computers (PCs), and over 30% had Internet access (see **Exhibit 5**).

2. **The Internet offered something for everyone**. Internet companies were enjoying extraordinary market valuations, and no one wanted to be left out. For instance, the market value of online toy merchant eToys surpassed the market value of Toys 'R' Us within its first day of trading. As a result, seemingly every business looked for ways to offer its products and services on the Internet, and consumers invested what they could. With this infusion of capital and labor, the Internet grew, and the number of online destinations grew 6-fold between 1996 and 1999.[5]

3. **People became comfortable with e-commerce**. Consumers were doing more and more business on the Internet. Advances in Internet security assuaged fears, and peoples' familiarity with and the affordability of the Internet meant people could and would spend more time "surfing" and buying. As a result, the $7.8 billion online retail market of 1998 is projected to reach $108 billion by 2003 (see **Exhibit 6**).

With the longest economic expansion in the history of the United States as a backdrop, the Internet was real, and e-commerce was an undeniable force.

Exhibit 4

BankOne.com Start Page, Wednesday, December 31, 1999

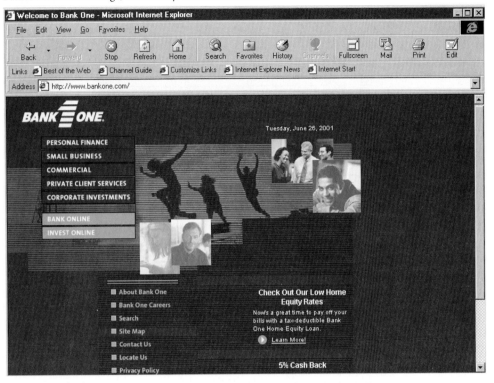

Source: <www.bankone.com>

Exhibit 5

Number of U.S. Consumers with PCs and Internet Access

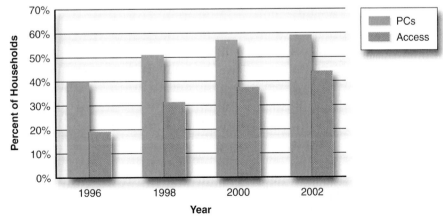

Source: Forrester Research.

Exhibit 6

U.S. Online Retail Spending

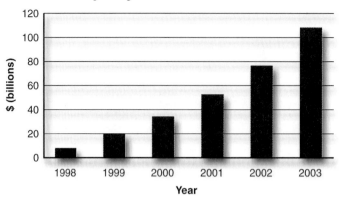

Source: Forrester Research.

Internet Banking

As the Internet achieved greater prominence, online banking emerged. Early Internet-only entrants included Telebank, Netb@nk (see **Exhibits 7** and **8**) and Security First Network Bank. Offering cost savings to suppliers and convenience to consumers, Internet banking appeared poised for tremendous growth. In addition to the lack of overhead expenses from bricks and mortar locations, an online transaction cost only $0.01, compared to $1.07 for a traditional

Exhibit 7

Start Page: NetB@nk.com

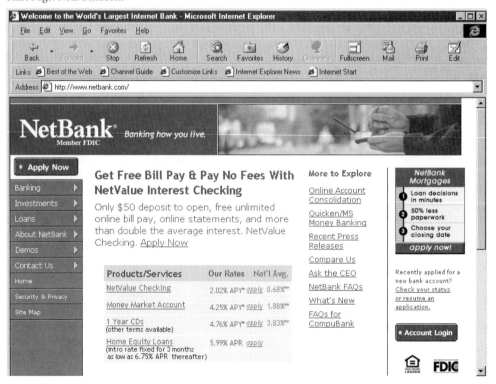

Source: <www.netbank.com>

Exhibit 8

Summary Income Statement: NetB@nk
(Dollar amount in millions)

Six Months Ending June 30	1999	1998
Interest income		
Interest income, total	$17,979	$ 6,459
Interest expense, total	10,290	4,017
Net interest income	$ 7,689	$ 2,442
Noninterest income		
Noninterest income, total	477	226
Noninterest income, total	5,851	2,570
Net noninterest income	$(5,374)	$(2,344)
Provision for loan loss	$ 105	$ 10
Earnings before income taxes	$ 2,210	$ 88
Income tax (expense) benefit	$ (751)	$ (30)
Tax benefit of loss	$ —	$ 3,059
Net income	$ 1,459	$ 3,117

Source: NetB@nk Investor Relations.

face-to-face bank teller transaction (see **Exhibit 9**). Internet banks could pass these cost savings onto customers as higher interest rates and lower service fees (see **Exhibits 10** and **11**).

In the mid-1990s, the industry began its climb despite Federal banking regulations that limited its growth. For instance, unlike other Internet ventures, online banks had to generate sufficient revenue to cover such expenses as marketing and administration. Nevertheless, pure play Internet banks continued to appear, and in October 1998, CompuBank became the first national virtual bank to receive a charter from the Office of the Comptroller of the Currency and approval from the FDIC.

With interest rates rising and fees falling at online banks, Internet banking burgeoned in the late 1990s. In 1998 alone, the number of households using online banking nearly doubled to 7 million, and estimates suggested that this number would reach 24 million by 2002.[6] Ominously, this growth, while rapid, paled in comparison to that of other financial services like online brokerage.

Witnessing this growth, traditional "bricks and mortar" banks began to acknowledge the importance of this new channel and worked to develop Internet strategies. Among the first were large national banks like Bank of America, Citibank, and Wells Fargo. Their initial

Exhibit 9

Estimated Banking Transaction Costs

Transaction Type	Per unit Cost
Face-to-face (with teller)	$1.07
Mail-in	$0.73
Telephone*	$0.54
Automatic teller machine	$0.27
Internet	$0.01

*Balance inquiry or money transfer.

Source: "Cyber-Banking Breaks New Ground Expands Towards Mainstream," *Bank Rate Monitor* (January 12, 1999).

Exhibit 10

Banks' Interest Rates

Bank	Checking[1]	Savings[1]
AmEx Membership Bank	2.00%	2.00%
Bank One	1.49%	1.49%
Bank of America	0%	1.00%
Chase.com	0.75%	2.13%
Citi f/I	0%	2.47%
CompuBank	3.00%	3.50%
NetB@nk	Up to 3.93%	N/A
Telebank	Up to 3.68%	Up to 4.88%
WingspanBank	Up to 4.5%	N/A
Mean	**0.84%**	**2.13%**

Note:
1. For balances of $0-$15,000.

Source: Company Web sites as of December 13, 1999.

Internet attempts meant limited services such as the ability to check balances and transfer funds. The primary purpose of their Internet sites was to retain existing customers and provide information about retail products at bricks and mortar locations. Soon, however, such other banking giants as Citibank, American Express, and Bank One would work to create separate entities under which to develop true online offerings (see **Exhibit 12**).

Traditional banks had many assets to leverage in developing Internet products. Customers could use pre-existing ATM networks without "per-use" transaction fees. In addition, individuals could make deposits at bank locations, electronically or by "snail mail." Finally, traditional banks' strong brand recognition meant virtually instant trust with potential online clientele.

Exhibit 11

Online Banks' Fees

	Savings Account	Bill Payment Services	Out-network ATM	Monthly Service Fee	Minimum Account Balance	Online Brokerage Link	Instant Credit Access
AmEx Membership B@nking	Free	Free	Free[1]	None	Yes	Yes	
Bankofamerica.com	Free				Yes		
Bankone.com	Free						Yes
Citi f/I	Free	Free	Free	None		Yes	
Chase.com	Free						Yes
CompuBank	Free	Free	Free[1]	None	Yes		
Net.B@nk		Free		None		Yes	
Telebank	Free	Free		None	Yes[2]	Yes	
Wellsfargo.com	Free	Free[3]			Yes	Yes	
WingspanBank.com		Free	Free[4]	None		Yes	Yes

Notes:
All offer free Interest Checking and In-network ATM use.
1. Maximum 4 surcharges per month reimbursed.
2. Interest not paid on balance below $1,000.
3. With minimum balance.
4. Up to $5 per month.

Source: Company Web sites as of December 6, 1999.

Exhibit 12

Internet Only Divisions of Established Banks

	Internet-only Division	**Launch Date**
BANK ONE	WingspanBank.com	June, 1999
Citibank	Citi f/I	August, 1999
American Express	Membership B@nking	July, 1999
Central Bank USA	USAccess Bank	Pending
Texas Capital Bank	BankDirect	Pending

Source: Team Research.

Established banks faced special challenges, too. General concerns about online privacy and security took on heightened importance when considering individuals' finances. In addition, the considerable investments were unlikely to bring short-term returns. Indeed, this new channel could cannibalize existing business. Furthermore, their conservative outlook coaxed most traditional banks to view the Internet as a revenue source—not as another "branch" location—and many actually charged customers for online transactions.

Quickly, however, online banks began to recognize that banking services—not venue—would continue to provide most of the revenue. Pete Kight, CEO of CheckFree Corporation, the premier bill payment and presentment service for online banks, sums it up:

> *You don't open a new branch and ask your customers to pay to bank there. You need to open a branch online because that's where your customers are.*

By November 1999, the landscape looked fragmented, and the competition fierce. Already there were more than 500 online banks,[7] and another 1000 were predicted to launch in the next year. The Federal government further spurred competition in November with the repeal of the Glass-Steagall Act, removing barriers among banks, brokerages, and insurance companies (see **Exhibit 13**). E*Trade quickly announced its intention to pur-

Exhibit 13

Glass-Steagall Act

On November 12, 1999, United States President Bill Clinton signed a new financial modernization bill into law, the Gramm-Leach Act, thus repealing the significant restrictions that had been placed on financial institutions in the United States by the Depression-era legislation, the Glass-Steagall Act. That bill had regulated the industry by preventing banks, insurance companies, and brokerage firms from entering into each other's lines of business.

The essence of the Glass-Steagall Act had been to separate commercial and investment banking. Its intention was to protect the commercial customers since it was born out of the concept that the investing activities of bankers in the 1920s had led to the stock market crash and resulting Great Depression of the 1930s. As financial markets have become more accessible to the consumer through such means as the Internet and the Securities and Exchange Commission has been diligent in keeping the markets transparent, such protection no longer was relevant.

While for the most part individual consumers were unaware of the restrictions caused by Glass-Steagall, much infighting had resulted over the years between various financial institutions desiring to offer a wider variety of services to their customers. It is anticipated that with the Act's repeal, many mergers will take place in the financial services industry and that competition will increase significantly. The lines between banks, brokerage firms, and insurance companies have certainly been blurred.

Source: Dee DePass, *The Minneapolis Star Tribune* (November 13, 1999).

chase Telebank, an early Internet-only bank. Bill Wallace, CIO of Wingspan, describes an even more chaotic scenario:

> *The other potential competitors that keep me up at night are the Yahoo's and AOL's of the world. They have the customer base, but currently face a barrier to entry in being unable to secure charters. If this [barrier] opens up, . . .*

New entrants vying for space would simply overrun the online banking industry.

WingspanBank.com

Making 119 acquisitions in the past 15 years had helped make Bank One the fourth largest bank in the U.S. For the twenty-first century, however, CEO John McCoy looked to another avenue for growth—the Internet.[8]

THE DECISION TO LAUNCH

This fundamental shift in strategy came during a Fall 1998 trip which McCoy took with Dick Vague, then head of the First USA Division and a Bank One Executive Vice President. McCoy and Vague visited Internet companies like Yahoo!, Excite, and America Online. The ostensible purpose was for Vague to negotiate marketing deals for First USA's credit cards.[9] Importantly, however, McCoy began to see the power of the Internet in general and of online banking in particular.

This exposure served as the foundation for a new type of bank within Bank One and a new growth strategy. McCoy quipped that Bank One might never buy another bank because of the tremendous growth potential he saw in the Internet.

After the trip, McCoy gathered key Bank One executives in February 1999 to discuss what type of online bank to create. The result was WingspanBank.com—a broad-based, Internet-only bank that met all of a customer's financial service needs through 1 integrated user I.D.

THE VISION

> *If your bank could start over, this is what it would be.*
>
> —WingspanBank.com slogan

To herald this new Internet-only bank, senior management wanted to create a new brand. James Stewart, the original CEO of Wingspan, explains:

> *We wanted something that was unique to online and financial services. We wanted a name that was not necessarily a literal name like Internet bank.com but something that could ultimately come to mean something. Like Amazon didn't mean "books online" and Excite didn't mean "search engine" —but now they do.*[10]

The team looked to the market for this new name. After a series of focus groups, potential customers and senior management agreed upon Wingspan. Wingspan symbolized the breadth of new products and emphasized the fresh start. With their early entry into the market, the team hoped that WingspanBank would soon become synonymous with "Internet banking."

WingspanBank should be more than simply Bank One online—indeed, bankone.com already existed. WingspanBank should be a "1-stop shop" for financial services: checking, savings, direct deposit, credit cards, installment and other loans, investments, bill payment, financial planning, CDs, mortgages, insurance, and more. Multiple "best in class" vendors would provide these services, permitting WingspanBank customers to use a variety of financial institutions through 1 channel.

Michael Cleary, President of Wingspan comments:

Bank One has a multibrand strategy on the Internet. Our goal is to create different products for different customers with different needs. Bank One is for the bricks and mortar customer with a regional focus. Wingspan is for an Internet-customer with a national focus. To make a consumer products analogy, you may not know whether a customer wants Tide or Wisk, but either way, P&G will make sure to provide it.

The essence of WingspanBank, however, would be convenient, comprehensive, and objective solutions to customers' problems at competitive prices—not products. Wingspan committed to becoming a "trusted advisor" to its customers. Cleary notes:

Offline banks have promised for years to be the trusted advisor for customers. The Internet provides us with the tools to do that. [But] only time will tell whether people will provide the information we need to deliver that value.

The scope was national—extending beyond the 14 states where Bank One operated. The primary target market for WingspanBank.com was a segment that bankone.com could not reach—the growing core group of Internet users who disdain the bricks and mortar of traditional banks. Wingspan wanted both present and future users of Internet banks, especially those who currently bank with Bank One competitors. Even taking Bank One's own customers was deemed acceptable.

IMPLEMENTATION

Jim Stewart was selected to be CEO of Wingspan and an "iBoard of Directors" of technology leaders was created. Together, they set a timeframe of 90 days to launch, but where should WingspanBank be born in order to foster creativity, innovation and speed to market?

The answer was First USA. According to Cleary:

Bank One bought First USA for its speed and marketing savvy. First USA has the entrepreneurial spirit and acts quickly. I never thought it could move so fast, but indeed it is a fast company.

First USA understood direct marketing and lived to "test and learn." In addition, its Internet Marketing Group had recent experience in the Internet world, and its culture appeared to align well with the goals of Wingspan.

Over 30 external vendors were selected to speed launch and expand product offerings in keeping with the Wingspan vision. These partners comprised the best service providers for each product area. Though invisible in most cases to WingspanBank customers, they directly represented the brand and were thus crucial to the success of the venture. All partners began work based on verbal agreements—time constraints prevented legal negotiations. The work required to implement so much functionality in so little time meant 18-hour days for Wingspan employees and partner staff alike.

Meanwhile Carol Knight, a former First USA consultant, had been selected to head up the marketing and PR efforts. Within the first month, her group conducted over 60 focus groups! These groups clarified what consumers wanted from an Internet bank and helped refine the Wingspan goals.

For instance, consumers were most concerned about trustworthiness of the site (followed closely by price). Ease of use and customer service became paramount, increasing the importance of site design and seamless integration of the multiple vendors. Thorough testing before launch was essential—any technical difficulty with the site could sabotage the new brand. A customer's first impression of WingspanBank.com was critical.

Customers also believed putting all of their assets in 1 place was risky, but using multiple vendors made them feel more secure. This sentiment reassured Wingspan management that partnerships and offerings of non-Bank One products on the site were keys to success.

Customers also desired Personal Financial Management (PFM). Although these checking and bill payment services offered no profit margin, customized PFM could ultimately generate revenue by permitting targeted products such as loans to be "pushed" to consumers.

The marketing team of 30—including Wingspan's advertising and PR agencies, First USA staff and external consultants—was also developing a plan in keeping with the Wingspan vision. The perceived importance of marketing shows in the nearly $100 million allocated from a total annual operating budget for Wingspan of approximately $150 million.[11] The plan included network TV spots, radio ads, celebrity personalities, press releases, and news features. Each of these activities was critical to the establishment of a stand-alone brand.

Unlike traditional Bank One advertising, which was regional, this campaign demanded national exposure, especially in markets where Bank One did not have a presence (to minimize cannibalization). Cities such as Boston, Seattle, and Philadelphia were ideal. However, the campaign also had a presence in California and Texas, existing Bank One markets.

The timeliness was critical to the plan:

> The ad agency had 8 weeks to design a campaign and shoot a commercial. The actors practiced a script with no bank name because it was not yet determined. The day of the commercial shoot when the name was revealed, the biggest concern was whether the actors would be able to make this change.[12]

WingspanBank.com was launched on June 24, 1999 (see **Exhibit 14**)—just 123 days from kick-off. McCoy was very visible during this time, including an interview for the *Wall Street Journal* where he announced the financial impact to Bank One. In the first year, WingspanBank was expected to dilute the value of Bank One's stock by 5¢ per share; in the second year, to add 5¢ per share; and in the third year, to add 20¢ per share.

Exhibit 14
Start Page: WingspanBank.com

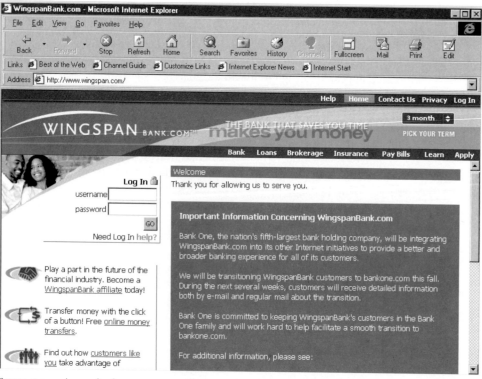

Source: <www.wingspanbank.com>

CURRENT STATE (1999)

By most measures, Wingspan succeeded in meeting its goals.

Culture

Being an Internet start-up within a larger organization offered both opportunities and challenges. Kevin Watters, Wingspan's Marketing Senior Vice President, summarized the advantages:

> Compared to other Internet banks Wingspan has the cash resources of Bank One and First USA, which means enormous marketing dollars. In addition, we are able to mine data from First USA to provide better offers via direct mail and e-mail than competitors. That's a 70 million cardholder database to pull from. There is also shared learning across the 3 organizations (Bank One, First USA and Wingspan).

Cleary noted the challenges:

> It's sometimes hard to act like an Internet company. There is no currency like an E-Trade—currency for marketing deals, advertising, and talent. Businesses are about people and if we don't have what Internet savvy people want, we're handcuffed. We're also responsible for part of an earnings stream at Bank One, and we all know that at Internet start-ups, earnings don't drive success. We're forced to look at profitability [earlier].

Customer Base

Within its first 90 days of operations, Wingspan had signed up 50,000 customer accounts. By comparison, Net.B@nk, which has been operating for over 3 years, had only 35,000 customers. On the other hand, bankone.com had 350,000 customers, nearly 8 million people were online, and 200,000 of them used Internet-only banks.

Wingspan wanted to know whether their customers will switch among banks or remain loyal. Wingspan's "stickiest" products so far included online bill payment and direct deposit. With these products, customers spent a great deal of time and provided specific information to the bank, thus increasing their switching costs. In fact, Wells Fargo research indicated that online customers using bill payment services were 16 times more likely than bricks and mortar customers to stay with the bank and be profitable.[13]

In terms of "mindshare" and general awareness, Wingspan had hit its goals, but hoped to target better the core Internet banking consumer through both traditional and Internet advertising. In addition, a recent alliance with Lycos through which Lycos customers can bank through a co-branded Wingspan and Lycos site may represent future direction.

Services

Customers can use Bank One's ATM machines for free—but not the tellers and other face-to-face branch services. Customers can complete applications online, get approved, and start banking in the same online session, which is unusual—most online banks make customers wait for passwords received via e-mail. Customers can also receive virtually instant decisions on products ranging from credit cards to installment loans—the response to an online home equity loan application took only 50 seconds! Many WingspanBank services and rates were not available to Bank One customers. For example, they paid $4.95 per month for the same bill payment services Wingspan customers got for free.

Since the launch, Wingspan continued to demonstrate its commitment to its vision through continual spending and maintenance of product quality. For example, in its commitment to maintain the best portfolio of products and services, management added CheckFree Corporation, the leading supplier of bill payment services, to the list of vendors. According to CIO Wallace, "Wingspan will continue to look at all vendors in the marketplace and select the best ones."

The original plan added novel, meaningful functionality to the site every 4 to 6 weeks. Wingspan ran at a 6- to 8-week time frame, but continued to innovate. According to Cleary, there was still much to do:

> *We launched quickly to beat Citibank and American Express, to test and to learn. There are many things not done at launch that we must complete in order to reach our goals. For example, we have not yet implemented many of our cross-selling techniques. Wingspan needs to recognize customers when they come to the site using CRM (Customer Relationship Management) tools to deepen the relationship.*

Wallace reflected on the future as well:

> *The model for Wingspan must change from product- to relationship-focused. In the past 25 years, banks created complicated views of banking and took away customers' control over their finances. Wingspan can erase the complexity and give customers back this control. For example, if there is $10,000 in a checking account, we can automatically issue a CD for the unused portion so that customer earns an extra $25. This adds value to the relationship.*

Wingspan planned to continue its furious growth and use its flexibility and size to its advantage. Relative to other Internet banks, Wingspan had higher brand awareness, better prices and leaner operations, meaning it could provide customer enhancements that other companies could not match.

The Dilemma

John McCoy liked what Wingspan had achieved, but was concerned. Shares of Bank One had fallen more than 40% since May. The First USA division suffered $70 billion in outstanding receivables, and expensive advertising campaigns had yet to deliver predicted returns.[14] Furthermore, the press unrelentingly included Wingspan in their criticism of Bank One even though Wingspan revenues meant little to a banking behemoth with $260 billion in assets. Was it because several executives at Wingspan—including Dick Vague and now James Stewart—had departed?

It's ironic, McCoy thought, that Wingspan had met virtually all of its goals and leads the industry, yet remains underappreciated outside—and maybe even inside—Bank One. Given all this, he had to ask himself: Now what?

Notes

1. "Internet Defense Strategy: Cannibalize Yourself," *Fortune* (September 6, 1999), p. 122.
2. "Bank One Says CEO of Internet Venture, Wingspan, Will Resign at Year's End," *Wall Street Journal* (Monday, November 15, 1999), p. B11.
3. "Internet Defense Strategy: Cannibalize Yourself," *Fortune* (September 6, 1999), pp. 121–134.
4. "WingspanBank: Losing Its Wings?" <www.thestandard.com/article/display/0,1151,7658,00.html?05>, *The Industry Standard*.
5. <Forrester.com> (October 15, 1999).
6. "Take Your Banking Online," <cnnfn.com/1999/05/21/banking/q_online_banks/> (May 21, 1999).
7. "True U.S. Internet Banks," *Online Banking Report* (November 29, 1999).
8. "Taking Flight with Wingspan," *Crain's Chicago Business* (August 2, 1999).
9. "Bank One: Nothing but Net," *Business Week* (August 2, 1999).
10. *Crain's Chicago Business* (August 2, 1999).
11. "Bank One Says CEO of Internet Venture, Wingspan, Will Resign at Year's End," *Wall Street Journal* (Monday, November 15, 1999), p. B11.
12. Telephone interview with Michael Cleary, President, Wingspan (December 6, 1999).
13. Telephone Interview with Peter Kight, Chief Executive Officer, CheckFree Corporation (December 1, 1999).
14. *Ibid.*

Apple Computer, Inc. (2000): Here We Go Again

David B. Croll, Gordon P. Croll, and Andrew J. Croll

The Warm Glow of Success

It was 10 days before the July 19, 2000, Macworld trade show in New York, when Apple Computer, Inc., Chief Executive Steven P. Jobs once again wowed the masses with his P.T. Barnum-style product introductions. First came the small stuff: a see-through plastic keyboard and a sleek mouse. Then, off came the covers from new versions of Apple's popular iMac computer—now in 4 rich new colors, including ruby and indigo. Finally the climax—an 8-inch cube-shaped Mac that packed Apple's most powerful technology into a clear plastic case about the size of a toaster.

The reporter *Business Week* sent to the trade show gushed "Since returning 3 years ago to the company he founded, Jobs, 44, has worked the most unlikely comeback since the 1969 Amazin' Mets."[1] Close to death in 1997 with mounting losses and shriveling market share, Apple was back to making the most stylish products. Revenues were up 17% to $1.8 billion in the quarter reported on July 18. The stock was up 8-fold since Jobs returned. Stock analysts expected 25% plus revenue growth in the year that ended September 30, 2001 (see **Exhibits 1** and **2**).[2]

Thanks to the coolness factor of Apple's products, they had gotten away with charging up to 25% more than their competitors for a machine with similar capabilities. That helped Apple gain a gross profit margin of 29.8% in the quarter ending June 30. More amazing is that in a company known for its free-spirited, free-spending ways Apple had become a master of operating efficiencies. Jobs slashed expenses from $8.1 billion in 1997 to $5.7 billion in 1999. This was accomplished by outsourcing manufacturing, trimming inventories, shifting 25% of sales to an online store, and slicing the number of distributors from the double digits to 2.[3]

Three Months Later

Under the headline "Apple Computer Plunges 52%, Drags Down Rest of Market"[4] the *Wall Street Journal* noted that on Friday, September 30, 2000, the value of a share of Apple Computer, Inc., dropped from $53.00 to $25.75 a share in heavy trading on the Nasdaq

This case was prepared by Professor David B. Croll of the McIntire School of Commerce at the University of Virginia; Gordon P. Croll, President and Founder of Cavalier Videography of Charlottesville; and Andrew J. Croll of The Discovery School of Virginia. This case was edited for SMBP-8th Edition. This case may not be reproduced in any form without written permission of the copyright holder, David B. Croll. Copyright © 2001 by David B. Croll.

Exhibit 1
Yes, Steve, You Fixed It. Congrats!

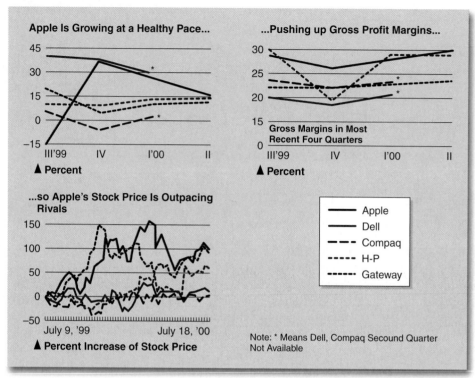

Source: *Business Week* (July 31, 2000), pp. 104, 105.

Stock Market (see **Exhibit 3**).[5] The loss came after the Cupertino, California, personal-computer maker issued a warning late Thursday 9/29 that its fiscal fourth quarter profits were predicted to be far less than expected. Apple Computer's fiscal year 2000 ended on September 30. By contrast when an embattled Apple released a far more dire news release prompting 1 analyst at the time to question "the viability of the whole turnaround plan." Apple's shares fell just 18% that day.[6] What was it about Apple now that had the market spooked?

The Stock Market in Year 2000

In the year 2000 investors lived through 1 of the most extraordinary years in stock-market history. The rapid drop of technology and Internet stocks marked the end of what many consider the U.S.'s biggest financial mania of the last 100 years. Yet it was a drop that left much of the market relatively unscathed.

The Nasdaq Composite Index plunged 39.3%, the worst year since it was created in 1971, giving back almost all of 1999's record increase. Its peak-to-trough 54% plunge represented a loss of $3.3 trillion in paper wealth, equivalent, in dollars, to one third of the houses in America sliding into the ocean. But the Dow Jones Industrial Average fell only 6.2% for the year. Though that broke a 9-year winning streak and represented its worst calendar year since 1981, the Dow's peak-to-trough decline of just 16% was less than that of 1990. The Standard

Exhibit 2
Steve Job's Unfinished Business

Apple has been winning back U.S. market share since 1997. Still, it's nowhere near its peak as a leader in home and education products.
(All based on U.S. unit sales)

Home Market

Maker	1994	Maker	1997	Maker	1999
Packard Bell	32.4%	Packard Bell NEC	23.3%	Compaq	19.0%
Apple	**14.7**	Compaq	18.8	H-P	16.1
Compaq	11.5	Gateway	11.1	Gateway	15.3
IBM	6.1	IBM	7.0	Emachine	11.0
Gateway	5.5	Acer	5.9	Packard Bell NEC	7.3
		Apple	**5.0**	**Apple**	**7.1**
Others	29.8	Others	28.9	Others	24.2

Business Market

Maker	1994	Maker	1997	Maker	1999
Compaq	14.2%	Compaq	15.7%	Dell	22.4%
IBM	10.1	Dell	12.8	Compaq	15.0
Apple	**6.4**	IBM	9.5	IBM	9.2
Dell	5.9	H-P	8.0	H-P	6.0
Gateway	5.3	Toshiba	5.6	Toshiba	4.7
		Apple	**1.4**	**Apple**	**1.3**
Others	58.1	Others	47.0	Others	41.4

Education Market

Maker	1994	Maker	1997	Maker	1999
Apple	**47.0%**	**Apple**	**27.2%**	Dell	21.4%
IBM	8.5	Compaq	13.2	**Apple**	**16.5**
Dell	4.3	Dell	10.7	Gateway	13.6
Gateway	3.3	Gateway	7.8	Compaq	9.2
Compaq	3.2	IBM	6.9	IBM	3.8
Others	33.7	Others	34.2	Others	35.5

Source: Business Week (July 31, 2000), p. 108.

& Poor's 500-stock index lost 10.1% in 2000, its worst since 1977. But excluding its technology components, the index was down just 4% (see **Exhibit 4**).[7]

By contrast, the 1973–74 bear market affected all stocks. The Nasdaq's 60% slide then was the only time it had fallen further than the previous year. The Dow lost 45% and the S&P 500 ended 1974 at its lowest levels since 1963. Year 2001 began with investors wondering if Nasdaq's drop was the vanguard of a broad-based bear market. The answer depended mostly on whether the economy's downshift in the end of 2000 was a pause in the longest expansion in a century or the first stage of a recession. UBS Warburg strategist Edward Kerschner thought Apple was 1 of the 5 most attractive opportunities to own stocks in 20 years, and he predicted the S&P 500 would gain 30% in 2001. Strategists as a group were the most bullish they had been in the 16 years Merrill Lynch surveyed them. Merrill's head

Exhibit 3
Apple's Unseasonable Fall

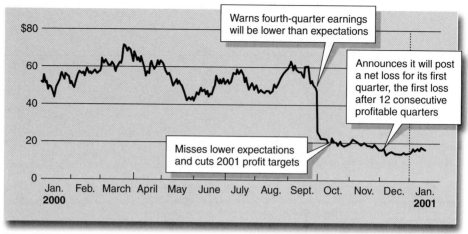

Source: *Wall Street Journal* (January 18, 2000), p. B8.

of quantitative research, Richard Bernstein, found this enthusiasm ironic, given that cash and bonds both performed better than stocks in 2000, and that markets usually bottom at the point of maximum pessimism, not optimism.[8]

Historical Background

Founded in a California garage in 1976, Apple created the personal computer revolution with powerful, yet easy-to-use, machines for the desktop. Steve Jobs sold his Volkswagen van and Steve Wozniak hocked his programmable calculator to raise seed money to begin the business.

Exhibit 4
Tale of the Tickers

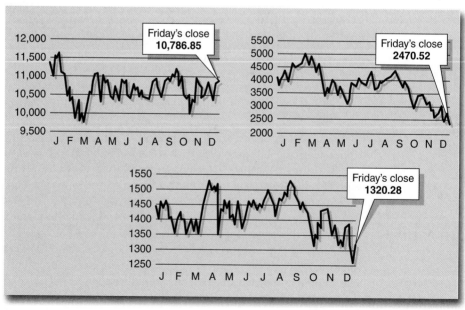

Source: *Washington Post* (Sunday, December 31, 2000).

Not long afterward, a mutual friend helped recruit A. C. "Mike" Markkula to help market the company and give it a million-dollar image. All 3 founders had left the company's management team in the 1980s but Mike Markkula remained as a member of the Board of Directors until August 1997.

The early success of Apple was attributed largely to marketing and technological innovation. In the high growth industry of personal computers in the early 1980s, Apple grew quickly. It stayed ahead of its competitors by contributing key products that stimulated the development of software specifically for their computers. Landmark programs such as Visicalc (forerunner of Lotus 1-2-3 and other spreadsheet programs) were developed first for the Apple II. Apple also secured early dominance in the education and consumer markets by awarding hundreds of thousands of dollars in grants to schools and individuals for the development of education software.

Even with enormous competition, Apple's revenues continued to grow at unprecedented rates, reaching $583.1 million by fiscal 1982. The introduction of the Macintosh graphical user interface in 1984, which included icons, pull-down menus, and windows, became the catalyst for desktop publishing and instigated the second technological revolution attributable to Apple. Apple kept the architecture of the Macintosh proprietary, i.e., it could not be cloned like the "open system" IBM PC. This allowed the company to charge a premium for its distinctive "user-friendly" features.

A shakeout in the personal computer industry began in 1983, when IBM entered the PC market, first affecting companies selling low-priced machines to consumers. Companies that made strategic blunders or that lacked sufficient distribution or brand awareness of their products disappeared. By 1985, only the largest computer and software companies survived.

In 1985, amid a slumping market, Apple saw the departure of its founders, Jobs and Wozniak, and instituted a massive reorganization to streamline operations and expenses. Under the leadership of John Sculley, Chief Executive Officer and Chairman of the Board, the company engineered a remarkable turnaround. Macintosh sales gained momentum throughout 1986 and 1987. Sales increased 40% from $1.9 billion to $2.7 billion in fiscal 1987, and earnings jumped 41% to $217 million.

In the early 1990s, Apple sold more personal computers than any other computer company. Net sales grew to over $7 billion, net income to over $540 million, and earnings per share to $4.33. The period from 1993 to 1995 was a time of considerable change in the management of Apple. In June 1993, John Sculley was forced to resign and Michael H. Spindler was appointed CEO of the company. Many of the company's executives advocated Apple's merging with another company, and when that didn't happen left Apple.

Spindler was forced out and Gilbert Amelio was hired from outside of Apple to serve as CEO. Amelio's regime presided over an accelerated loss of market share, deteriorating earnings, and stock that had lost half of its value. Apple had failed to license the Mac operating system to other manufacturers early enough that it might today be as ubiquitous as Windows. Both Amelio and his immediate predecessor, Michael Spindler, failed to accept any of the buyout offers proposed to Apple. By the end of Amelio's tenure, Apple seemed to be in utter disarray. In July of 1997 Gilbert Amelio resigned and was replaced by Steve Jobs, 1 of the 2 founders of the company. Jobs was back 14 years after being replaced as CEO by John Sculley.

Corporate Governance

Exhibit 5 lists the 6 members of Apple's Board of Directors, a board that has not changed since the profound change that took place when Steve Jobs returned as CEO in 1997. Mr. Jobs was the only internal member of Apple's Board of Directors. Apple's top management as of October 1, 2000, is listed in Exhibit 6.[9]

Exhibit 5

Board of Directors: Apple Computer, Inc.

William V. Campbell has been Chairman of the Board of Directors of Intuit, Inc., since August of 1998. From September 1999 to January 2000, Mr. Campbell acted as Chief Executive Officer of Intuit.

Gareth C.C. Chang is the Chief Executive Officer and Chairman of the Board of PingPong Technology. He is also the Executive Chairman of click2Asia.com. Formally, Mr. Chang served as Chairman and Chief Executive Officer of STAR TV and Executive Director of News Corporation. He is currently a member of the Advisory Council of Nike, Inc., and serves on the board of SRS Labs Inc.

Millard S. Drexler has been Chief Executive Officer of Gap, Inc., since 1995, and President since 1987. Mr. Drexler has been a member of the Board of Directors of Gap, Inc., since November 1983. He also served as the President of the Gap Division from 1983 to 1987.

Lawrence J. Ellison has been Chief Executive Officer and a Director of Oracle Corporation since he cofounded Oracle in May 1977, and was President of Oracle until June 1996. Mr. Ellison has been Chairman of the Board of Oracle since June 1995.

Steven P. Jobs is 1 of the company's Cofounders and currently serves as its Chief Executive Officer. Mr. Jobs is also the Chairman and Chief Executive Officer of Pixar Animation Studios. In addition, Mr. Jobs cofounded NeXT Software, Inc. and served as the Chairman and Chief Executive Officer of NeXT from 1985 until 1997 when NeXT was aquired by the Company. Mr Jobs is currently a Director of Gap, Inc.

Arthur D. Levinson, Ph.D., has been President, Chief Executive Officer, and a Director of Genentech, Inc., since July 1995. He joined Genentech in 1980 and served in a number of executive positions, including Senior Vice President of R&D from 1993 to 1995.

Jerome B. York is Chairman and Chief Executive Officer of Micro Warehouse, Inc. Previously, he was Vice Chairman of Tracinda Corporation from September 1995 to October 1999. In May 1993 he joined International Business Machines Corporation as Senior Vice President and Chief Financial Officer, and served as a Director of IBM from January 1995 to August 1995. Prior to joining IBM, Mr. York served in a number of executive positions at Chrysler Corporation, including Executive Vice President–Finance and Chief Financial Officer from May 1990 to May 1993. Mr. York is also a Director of MGM Mirage, Inc., Metro-Goldwyn-Mayer, Inc., and National TechTeam, Inc.

Apple Computer, Inc.'s head of worldwide sales announced his retirement 2 weeks after the company warned of slowing product sales. Mitch Mandich, a longtime member of the management team of Apple's Chief Executive, Steve Jobs, announced he would retire at the end of December 2000.

Mr. Mandich temporarily was replaced by Tim Cook, Apple's Senior Vice President of Operations. The unexpected retirement of Mandich hints at trouble at the computer maker. "If Mitch is taking the fall for this, it's undeserved," said Steven Fortuna, a First Vice President at Merrill Lynch & Co.[10] Mitch Mandich was the first member of Apple's current executive team to leave since Mr. Jobs assembled the team in 1997.

Mr. Mandich, who previously worked with Mr. Jobs at NeXT Software, Inc., followed him to Apple in 1997. He was quickly promoted from Vice President of Apple's North America Business Division to Senior Vice President of North American Sales before taking responsibility for worldwide sales.

Current Situation in the Education Market

Many schools and universities, the mainstays of Apple's customer base for years, were phasing out their Macs in favor of personal computers based on the rival Windows operating system. The trend accelerated over the 12-month period ending September 30, 2000. In 1999, Dell moved ahead of Apple and became the largest supplier to education claiming 15.1% of the

Exhibit 6

Executive Officers: Apple Computer, Inc.

Fred D. Anderson, Executive Vice President and Chief Financial Officer (age 56), joined the Company in April 1996. Prior to joining the Company, Mr. Anderson was Corporate Vice President and Chief Financial Officer of Automatic Data Processing, Inc., a position he held from August 1992 to March 1996.

Timothy D. Cook, Senior Vice President, Worldwide Operations, and interim Senior Vice President, Worldwide Sales, Service & Support (age 40), joined the Company in February. Prior to joining the Company Mr. Cook held the position of Vice President, Corporate Materials, for Compaq Computer Corporation. Previous to his work at Compaq, Mr. Cook was the Chief Operating Officer of the Reseller Division at Intelligent Electronics. Mr. Cook also spent 12 years with IBM, most recently as Director of North American fulfillment.

Nancy R. Heinen, Senior Vice President, General Counsel, and Secretary (age 44), joined the Company in September. Prior to joining the Company, Ms. Heinen held the position of Vice President, General Counsel, and Secretary of the Board of Directors at NeXT from February 1994 until the acquisition of NeXT by the Company in February 1997.

Ronald B. Johnson, Senior Vice President, New Business Development (age 42), joined the Company in February 1997. Before joining the Company, Mr. Johnson was Executive Vice President and Chief Operating Officer of FirePower Systems Incorporated, from May 1993 to August 1996. Mr. Johnson also serves as member of the Board of Directors of Immersion Corporation.

Avadis Tevanian, Jr., Ph.D., Senior Vice President, Software Engineering (age 39), joined the Company in February 1997 upon the Company's acquisition of NeXT. With NeXT, Dr. Tevanian held several positions, including Vice President, Engineering, from April 1995 to February 1997. Prior to April 1995, Dr. Tevanian worked as an engineer with NeXT and held several management positions.

Sima Tamaddon, Senior Vice President, Applications (age 43), joined the Company in September 1997. Mr. Tamaddon has also served with the Company in the position of Senior Vice President Worldwide Service and Support, and Vice President and General Manager, Newton Group. Before joining the Company, Mr. Tamaddon held the position of Vice President, Europe with NeXT from September 1996 through March 1997. From August 1994 to August 1996, Mr. Tamaddon held the position of Vice President, Professional Services with NeXT.

Mitchell Mandich, Senior Vice President, Worldwide Sales (age 52) joined the Company in February 1997 upon the Company's acquisition of NeXT. Mr. Mandich has also served the Company in the position of Vice President, North American Business Division. Prior to joining the Company, Mr. Mandich held the position of Vice President, Worldwide Sales and Service, with NeXT from December 1995 through February 1997.

market (see **Exhibit 7**).[11] Apple dropped to a 12.5% market share, down from its 14.6% share in 1998 and its 16.5% share in 1999.

The shift hurt Apple's bottom line. Education had accounted for 40% of Apple's total U.S. sales over the past few quarters. Apple machines, however, were still used in 40% of the schools across the country, according to market tracker Quality Education Data, and the computer maker continued to make numerous education sales.

"Apple has done well in the past to show they're on the side of education," said Wayne Grant, Chief Executive of the educational software company ImagiWorks, Inc.[12] When the big push to wire classrooms more than a decade ago started, Apple jumped on the market and Macs became educators' top choice because of their ease of use and friendly graphical interface. The company deluged the market with special marketing programs, often at a discount, and created a widespread network of education sales agents. "But Apple has come under more pressure in pricing and ease of use recently as Windows 98 has come on board. It's more difficult for Apple to differentiate itself now," said Charles Smulders, an analyst at Garter Group.[13]

Exhibit 7

Apple Crunch

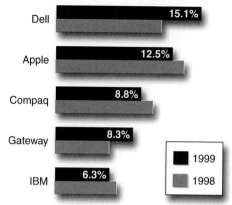

Top education PC vendors, by market share

Dell — 15.1%
Apple — 12.5%
Compaq — 8.8%
Gateway — 8.3%
IBM — 6.3%

■ 1999
▦ 1998

Source: Wall Street Journal (October 17, 2000), pp. B1, B4.

In addition, many educational software developers have migrated away from the Mac platform over the past few years, analysts say. "Software developers now develop for Windows only because they don't think the Mac market is big enough anymore," said Roger Kay, research manager at International Data Corp. "That's a crushing economic reality."[14]

Apple was doing what it could to hold onto the education niche. It hoped to sell iMacs with preloaded software, such as its popular iMovie video-editing program. It planned to launch its next generation operating system OS X to attract new software developers to the Mac platform.

Since the start of fiscal year 2000, Apple's education sales team had also undergone confusing changes, many schools complained. Mike Lorion, an Apple executive overseeing education sales, left the company and joined hand-held device maker Palm, Inc. After his departure, Apple eliminated its contracted education sales force and brought the team in-house. This resulted in Apple having far less direct contact with schools than it had. Instead, the company trained schools to deal with Apple primarily through the Internet. That left many educational districts displeased.

Such stumbles have given rivals like Dell and Gateway, Inc., an opportunity. Bill Rodrigues, Dell's Vice President in charge of education and health care, said Dell's sales to schools had grown so much over the previous 2 years that it split its education operations into a higher education unit and a K–12 division. Dell also boosted its education field operatives to more than 100 people across the United States, and it was partnering with software developers such as Computer Curriculum Corp. and Compass Learning Corp. to provide educational software solutions to schools.

Competition[15]

The personal computer industry was highly competitive and was characterized by aggressive pricing practices, downward pressure on gross margins, frequent introduction of new products, short product life cycles, continual improvement in product price/performance characteristics, price sensitivity on the part of consumers, and a large number of competitors. Rapid technological advances in software performance features based on existing or emerging industry standards had also characterized the personal computer industry. As the personal computer industry and its customers placed more reliance on the Internet, an increasing number of Internet devices that were smaller and simpler than traditional personal computers competed for market share with Apple's existing products. Further, several competitors have either targeted or announced their intention to target certain of the company's key market segments, including consumer, education, and design and publishing. These competitors had greater financial, marketing, manufacturing, and technological resources, as well as broader product lines and larger installed customer bases than those of Apple.

Apple was the only maker of hardware using the Mac OS. The Mac OS had a minority market share in the personal computer market, which was dominated by makers of computers utilizing Microsoft Windows operating systems. Apple's future operating results and financial condition were substantially dependent on its ability to continue to develop improvements in the Macintosh platform in order to maintain perceived design and functional advantages over competing platforms.

Computer and Peripherals Industry

The computer and peripherals industry did not turn in quite as good a performance in year 2000 as had been expected. The sector's prospects for the next year, and at least through mid-decade, were good. It was widely expected by analysts that the industry would get off to a slow start in year 2000 because many businesses spent heavily in 1999 so they would correctly handle dates in the new century.

The second half of the year 2000 was expected to be better than the first half. However there were reports of slowing demand from some chipmakers, notably Intel, which raised fears that personal computer sales might be slowing. The strong dollar could trim overseas sales figures especially from Europe.

Over the next 3 to 5 years there should be continued growth in the industry. Businesses were going to continue to spend on computer gear to increase their efficiency and become more competitive. They were increasingly using the Internet to hook up with their customers and suppliers to cut costs and to speed up business processes. The increasing computerization of operations also meant more data were generated and stored electronically, which boosted demand for storage devices and printers to turn the digital data into hardcopy.[16]

COMPAQ COMPUTER

Compaq Computer Corp. was the second largest computer company in the world in 1999. It manufactured mainframes, servers, and workstations. Compaq also provided professional services that accounted for 52% of 1999 revenue, with commercial desktops and portables accounting for 32%, and personal computers for the consumer market 16%.

Compaq computer's effort to increase earnings growth was working. The commercial personal computer group returned to profitability after several periods of deficit results. New products with simpler designs and higher margins helped, as did lower costs aided by a shift to more direct sales. Whereas the commercial PC unit's focus in the past year has been on profitability rather than market share, management planned to also emphasize market share growth in the future. In Compaq's industry standard server business, sales benefited from shipments of a new ultra thin 2-way server, as well as from companies building their Internet infrastructures.

However, Compaq still faced a number of challenges. The operating climate no doubt had become more difficult since mid-2000, especially in Europe, which together with the Middle East and Africa, accounted for about a third of their sales. It was also unclear whether the component shortages that held back shipments of Compaq's new AlphaServer in the June period will continue to restrain sales. At mid-year, there were over $200 million of orders for the AlphaServer in the backlog. Although Compaq now appeared on the recovery track, it still had a lot of work ahead of it.[17]

DELL COMPUTER

Dell Computer Corp. was the world's largest direct computer systems company in 1999. Dell made notebook and desktop computers, network servers, storage products, workstations, peripheral hardware, and computing software. They marketed their products via sales teams to corporate and institutional customers, as well as via the telephone and Internet. The majority of Dell's sales, 71%, were to the Americas; with 22% in Europe, Middle East, and Africa; and 7% in the Asia/Pacific market.

Dell Computer's top-line growth was slowing down. Management attributed the slow-down in sales to weak demand in Europe, lower sales to the U.S. government, and below-projected sales to small businesses worldwide. To recharge sales growth Dell announced price reductions across many product lines.

Dell's direct-to-consumer business model and efficient supplier alliances allowed it to keep its costs low. A continued shift in the sales mix from workstations to higher margined products was expected to enhance margins. The growth in Dell's cash flow seemed to be accelerating while its capital spending requirements were moderating, leaving it room to buy back stock, invest in promising technology ventures, and perhaps use some for acquisitions. The company expected to be successful in implementing its plans to expand overseas as well as in the storage systems market.[18]

GATEWAY, INC.

Gateway, Inc., manufactured, marketed, and supported a product line of Windows-compatible desktop, notebook, and subnotebook personal computers. The company marketed directly to businesses, individuals, government agencies, and educational institutions. Only 14.6% of their total sales were outside the United States.

While Dell computer saw its sales growth falter, Gateway's revenues rose by mid-year 2000. Strong consumer demand and "Gateway's limited exposure to the slowing corporate market" was given credit for this strong showing. Also, the move by management into products other than personal computers has been more profitable than even Gateway's management expected.

Gateway was no longer relying on processor chips from only 1 supplier. Using chips from both AMD and Intel broadened the company's product line and partially protected it from the processor shortages that occurred in the fall of 1999. Analysts predicted that dollar sales in the future would not rise as fast as earlier projected, due to falling prices not unit sales.[19]

INTERNATIONAL BUSINESS MACHINES CORPORATION

IBM Corporation was the world's largest supplier of advanced information processing technology and communication systems and services in 1999. The revenue breakdown was 43% hardware, 37% global services, 14% software, and 6% other. Business outside of the United States accounted for 58% of total revenue.

IBM had some positive and negative results in year 2000. On the minus side, unfavorable currency trends were having a negative impact on revenues. During the year, the hard disk drives—the company's new 10,000 RPM drives—were not ready when they were expected to be, causing personal computers to be a drag on total sales.

A new generation system, 309s, that was introduced in 2000 was expected to provide an increase in sales with a greater increase in year 2001. Also on the plus side, the amount of new service contract signings had picked up, thanks in part to strong demand for the company's e-business services. The demand for the company's servers, especially Web servers, and high-end hard disk drives improved.

IBM was positioning itself for further growth. For one thing, management expected the company's new G7 mainframes to sell extremely well, since they would be much more powerful than the older G6 generation. However, the major increase in growth was likely to be in the services area. IBM was also investing in Web products and services and such growth areas as customer relation and supply-chain management. What's more, IBM was providing services, such as storage, Web hosting, and facilities for application service providers, on a rental basis.[20]

HEWLETT-PACKARD COMPANY

Hewlett-Packard Company was a leading provider of computing and imaging solutions and services for business and home. Its 1999 revenue breakdown was 43.7% imaging and printing systems, 42.6% computing systems, and 13.7% IT services. Business outside of the United States accounted for 55% of total revenue.

Year 2000 got off to a slow start, as a number of factors, including a sales mix shift to low-end home personal computers and printers, a drop in the yen–dollar exchange rate, and costs associated with an early retirement program dragged net income down. Growth increased in July thanks to strong demand for home personal computers, laptops, printers, and supplies and services.

The company was positioning itself to post good gains over the next 5 years. A new family of high-end servers that would round out that product line and was expected to boost sales. A shift to color printing in offices lifted sales of the company's color laser printers and the move to digital photography fueled demand for H-P's color inkjet printers. Analysts thought that the company's emphasis on the fast-growing Internet infrastructure market would lead to good demand for its servers, storage products, and consulting and services. Finally, Hewlett-Packard was in talks to acquire the consulting business of PricewaterhouseCoopers for roughly $18 billion of cash and stock.[21]

Semiconductor Industry

In year 2000 some factors changed in the semiconductor industry. A considerable number of companies in the chip industry, including industry leader Intel, announced they were about to encounter earnings or revenue shortfalls. It appeared that most of the disappointment was stemming from the personal computer area, but there was also some concern about the wireless handset market.

Intel's management blamed their lower gains almost entirely on its European exposure. Indeed the company sold its personal computer chips in Europe in U.S. dollars, which made its products much more expensive due to a weak euro.

Many stocks in the semiconductor universe had experienced significant price erosion over the past few months. It appeared that there might be some potential signs that the boom in the chip market could be coming to an end. However this drop seemed to be almost entirely on the personal computer side of the industry.[22]

INTEL CORPORATION

Intel Corporation was a leading manufacturer of integrated circuits. These they marketed primarily to makers of personal computers. Their main products were microprocessors and memory chips. They also sold computer modules and boards and network products. Foreign business represented 57% of total revenue.

Intel achieved only modest 3% to 5% growth during 2000. Lackluster European demand was the primary reason for the low growth rate. Intel has canceled plans for the Timna microprocessor, which was targeted toward computers in the sub-$600 price category. Intel's management cited design delays and lackluster demand by personal computer makers. Furthermore, the introduction of the company's high-end Pentium 4 chip was delayed until the fourth quarter of 2000.

Analysts warned that Intel was subject to a high degree of volatility. The current decrease in growth that had occurred in the industry was mostly personal computer related. Intel's efforts to increase its stake in the communications arena was expected to help it diversify beyond the traditional computer market and add some stability to their earnings.[23]

MOTOROLA, INC.

Motorola, Inc., was a leading manufacturer of electronic equipment and components. Their product mix in 1999 was 39% personal communications; 19% semiconductor products; 21% network systems; 13% commercial, government, and industrial systems; and 8% other. Foreign business represented 63% of total sales.

Motorola's handset business had some problems, causing orders to be down 23% compared to 1999. The company stated that concerns over the previous year's supply problems led customers to preorder at very high levels, but since component shortages were no longer an issue, orders had consequently fallen. Motorola was intent on revitalizing the phone unit sales. It rolled out low-tier products and began the transition to mid- and high-tier digital devices.

The broadband communications sector of Motorola was achieving record results. This segment continued to exceed expectations due to surging demand for digital set-top terminals and cable modems. Additionally, momentum was building outside of North America for large sales.[24]

Computer Software and Services

Year 2000 was not a good year for the computer software and services industry. Businesses had spent heavily on new computer gear and software in 1999 to be sure that their systems could handle dates after the turn of the century. This overhang of equipment purchase had to be worked off before new systems were needed. The fall of the dot-com boom also restricted growth in software sector. Many of these ventures have shut down as profits failed to materialize and funds ran out.

Some analysts thought that spending on computer services and equipment would rise at a faster rate than the economy as a whole. There were some signs that demand was accelerating in Europe. If that were true, that drag on sales would be eliminated.

The trend to move more activities to computers wasn't likely to end any time soon. Now that the most basic business functions, such as accounting and human resources, were computerized, companies were moving additional activities, such as ordering, billing, and customer relationship management on to computers. These trends should continue to drive strong demand for software and services.[25]

MICROSOFT CORPORATION

Microsoft Corporation was the largest independent maker of software. Its fiscal year 2000 revenue breakdown was 41% Windows platforms (operating systems and server applications and Internet products); 46% productivity applications and development (desktop applications, server applications, and developer tools); 13% consumer, commerce, and other (learning and entertainment software and PC input devices).

The company suffered a big loss in June when the presiding judge in the antitrust suit ruled that the company had violated antitrust laws. He proposed that as a remedy the company should be broken into 2 parts and that restrictions should be placed on its operations.

But then, in September of 2000, the Supreme Court decided against accepting the case directly without having it go through the appeals process. That was expected to be good for Microsoft, because the appeals court previously ruled in the company's favor on other matters.

Microsoft continued to broaden and upgrade its product line it rolled out. In early 2000 the Windows 2000 Datacenter Server, its high-end server software for businesses. Coupled with new versions of its database offering and its messaging server, that was expected to enable it to make inroads against UNIX-based products. The Windows 2000 operating system was gaining ground in the corporate world and that should also boost sales of its applications product suite, Office 2000.

Microsoft's efforts to move into new areas, such as television set-top boxes and Internet access appeared to be paying off. The company was working to expand its Web-based offerings such as providing access to applications on a subscription basis over the Internet.[26]

Foreign and Domestic Operations and Geographic Data[27]

The United States represented Apple's largest geographic marketplace. Approximately 54% of the company's net sales in fiscal 2000 came from operations inside the United States. Sales margins on Apple products in foreign countries, and on sales of products that include components obtained from foreign suppliers, could be adversely affected by foreign currency exchange rate fluctuations.

Apple managed its business primarily on a geographic basis. There were 4 geographic segments within the Company, the Americas, Europe, Japan, and Asia-Pacific. Each geographic operating segment provided similar hardware and software products and similar services. The European segment included European countries as well as the Middle East and Africa. The Japan segment included only Japan, while the Asia-Pacific segment included Australia and Asia except for Japan.

Net sales and unit sales in the Americas segment increased 22% and 24%, respectively, during fiscal 2000. The growth of the Americas' net sales in 2000 was indicative of strong growth in unit sales of iMac and iBook and relatively flat unit sales of professionally oriented Macintosh systems.

Net sales in the Europe segment increased 38% during 2000 driven by a 53% increase in Macintosh unit sales. Growth in unit sales resulted from a 96% increase in combined unit sales of iMac and iBook and an increase of 19% in combined unit sales of the company's professionally oriented Macintosh systems.

Net sales in the Japan segment increased 57% to $1.345 billion in fiscal 2000 with Japan's Macintosh unit sales increased 39%. The fact that Japan's net sales rose at a higher rate than its unit sales reflects several factors. First iMac unit sales in Japan were relatively flat. Second, unit sales of iBook, which generally carry a higher price than iMac units, accounted for approximately 17% of Japan's total Macintosh unit sales. Third, Japan saw a 43% increase in combined unit sales of the company's professionally oriented Macintosh systems.

The majority of the increase in both net sales and unit sales in the Asia Pacific segment can be attributed to sales of the G4 Cube and iBook, both of which were introduced in the region during fiscal 2000. Macintosh unit sales in the Asia Pacific segment increased 37% due in large part from the general economic recovery experienced in the region.

Product Introductions[28]

Due to the highly volatile nature of the personal computer industry, which was characterized by dynamic customer demand patterns and rapid technological advances, Apple needed to continually introduce new products and technologies and enhance existing products in order to remain competitive. The success of new product introductions was dependent on a number of factors, including market acceptance, Apple's ability to manage the risks associated with product transitions, the availability of products in appropriate quantities to meet anticipated demand, and the risk that new products might have quality or other defects in the early stages of introduction.

During fiscal 2001 Apple planned to introduce a new client operating system, Mac OS X, which would offer advance functionality based on Apple and NeXT software technologies. Inability to successfully introduce Mac OS X on a timely basis, gain customer acceptance, obtain the commitment of developers to transition existing applications to run on Mac OS X, or ensure adequate backward compatibility of Mac OS X with applications authored for previous versions of the Mac OS, might have an adverse impact on Apple's operating results.

Inventory and Supply[29]

Apple has recorded a write-down of inventories of components and products that have become obsolete or are in excess of anticipated demand. Apple ended fiscal year 2000 with substantially more inventory in its distribution channels than planned due to the lower than expected unit sales of products in September. Apple currently anticipated a significant sequential decline in quarterly net sales during the December quarter of year 2000, due in part to the company's plan to reduce substantially the level of inventory in its distribution channels.

Although certain components essential to Apple's business were generally available from multiple sources, other key components (including microprocessors and application specific integrated circuits) were currently obtained from single sources. In addition, new products introduced by Apple often utilized custom components obtained from only 1 source until Apple evaluated whether there was a need for additional suppliers. Apple's ability to produce and market competitive products was dependent on the ability and desire of IBM and Motorola, the sole suppliers of the PowerPC RISC based microprocessor for the Macintosh computers.

Support from Third-Party Software Developers[30]

Apple Corporation believed that decisions by customers to purchase its personal computers, as opposed to a Windows based system, were often based on the availability of particular applications. Management believed the availability of software for its hardware products depended in part on third-party developers' perception of the relative benefits of developing, maintaining, and upgrading such software versus software for the larger Windows market. To the extent that financial losses in prior years and the minority market share held by Apple in the personal computer market had caused software developers to question Apple's prospects in the personal computer market, developers might not develop new application software or upgrade existing software.

In August 1997, Apple and Microsoft Corporation entered into patent cross-licensing and technology agreements. For a period of 5 years from August 1997, Microsoft would make future versions of its Microsoft Office and Internet Explorer products for the Mac OS. Although Microsoft had announced its intention to do so, these agreements did not require Microsoft to produce future versions of its products that were optimized to run on Mac OS X. While Apple's management believed its relationship with Microsoft had been and would continue to be beneficial, the relationship was for a limited term and did not cover many of the areas in which they competed. Accordingly, Microsoft's interest in producing application software for the Mac OS, including Mac OS X, might be influenced by Microsoft's perception of its interests as the vendor of the Windows operating system.

Education Market[31]

Several competitors of Apple have announced their intention to target the education market for personal computers. As a result, Apple's overall share of this market has declined. Additionally, net sales in the company's education market fell short of expectations by approximately $60 million during the September quarter of year 2000, the quarter most school purchases are made. This may have been the result of Apple's transition to a more direct sales model from a model heavily dependent on third-party sales agents. Failure to increase or maintain market share in Apple's traditionally strong education market could have serious impact on operating results.

Markets and Distribution[32]

Apple's customers were primarily in the education, creative, consumer, and business markets. Certain customers were attracted to Macintosh computers for a variety of reasons, including the reduced amount of training resulting from the intuitive ease of use, advanced graphics capabilities, industrial design features of the hardware products, ability of the computers to network and communicate with other computer systems, and availability of application software. Apple was 1 of the major suppliers of personal computers for both elementary and secondary school customers.

Apple distributed its products through wholesalers, resellers, national and regional retailers, and cataloguers. During fiscal 2000, a single distributor, Ingram Micro, Inc., accounted for approximately 11.5% of Apple's net sales. Apple also sold many of its products to consumers, certain education customers, and certain resellers either directly or through 1 of its online stores around the world. During fiscal 2000, net sales attributable to the company's online stores totaled approximately $1.7 billion.

Two years after practically disappearing from many U.S. retail stores, Apple Computer, Inc., was back on the shelves. This store invasion signaled a marked turnaround in Apple's rocky relationships with retailers. In the early to mid-1990s, many stores complained about inventory problems and battled over Apple's rigid sales rules. The company, for example, once set a $500,000 annual sales cap for dealers, cutting many small distributors on strong growth tracks out of much needed business. Apple, in the past, would often change its mind about who could sell to the big education market, causing turmoil among dealers while keeping them in the dark on fast changing product strategies. "Apple used to be among the worst companies to deal with for a long time," said Larry Mondry, chief operating officer of CompUSA, Inc. "Apple is a different company today."[33]

For retail outlets such as the Wiz, a 41-store northeastern electronics chain, this translated into a revived give-and-take with Apple. Three years ago, the Wiz stopped selling Apple products after demand for the computers stalled at the same time that Apple began trimming its retail presence. Then in 1999, after Apple posted strong sales increases led by strong sales of its PowerBook laptops and its G4 high-end desktop model, Wiz executives called the computer company back. Unlike before when Apple didn't respond to many retailers' requests, the company was "very receptive" and "wanted us badly," says Tasso Koken, the Wiz's Executive Vice President of Merchandising.[34]

Behind this latest change was a renewed focus on giving customers a particular experience when they shop for Apple computers, an issue brought to the forefront by Steve Jobs. By improving the shopping environment for Apple buyers, marketing experts said, the company hoped to attract more of the first-time computer buyers. In a market inundated with lower-cost machines, Apple needed to capitalize on its successful iMac line, which had set milestones in computer design and offered candy-colored hardware that made for an attractive store display.

Besides renewing ties with the likes of the Wiz, Apple recruited department store chain Sears Roebuck & Co. in May 1999 to carry its computers. Apple then added new distributors, middlemen that sold to a variety of retailers, including mom-and-pop shops. The retail push was also going global to Europe and Japan, where Apple traditionally enjoyed strong sales. Stores such as Japan's DeoDeo Corp. and Comp Mart Company Ltd. boasted distinct Apple spaces.

Legal Proceedings[35]

Apple Corporation was subject to certain legal proceedings and claims, which have arisen in the ordinary course of business and had not been fully adjudicated. In the opinion of management, the company did not have a potential liability related to any existing legal proceedings and claims that will have a material adverse effect on its financial condition or operating results.

Financials[36]

During the fiscal year 2000, Apple experienced a 30% increase in net sales the result of a 32% increase in Macintosh unit sales. This increase in Macintosh unit sales was primarily attributable to increased sales of iMac, the company's moderately priced desktop Macintosh system designed for the education and consumer markets, and the introduction of iBook, the company's consumer and education oriented notebook computer introduced at the beginning of year 2000. Growth in net sales and unit sales was strong in fiscal 2000 in all of Apple's geographic operating segments with particular strength in Europe and Japan.

Apple experienced improved profitability in fiscal 2000 as well. Operating income before special charges rose 61% to $620 million. Improved profitability was driven by the 30% increase in net sales and stable overall gross margins. Special charges included both restructuring actions and executive bonuses. During the first quarter of fiscal 2000 Apple initiated restructuring actions resulting in recognition of an $8 million restructuring charge. This charge comprised $3 million for the write-off of various operating assets and $5 million for severance payments to approximately 95 employees associated with various domestic and international sales and marketing functions. Also during the first quarter of fiscal 2000, Apple's Board of Directors approved a special executive bonus for the company's Chief Executive Officer for past services in the form of an aircraft with the total cost to the Company of $90 million dollars (see **Exhibits 8, 9,** and **10**).[37]

Despite overall increases during fiscal 2000 in net sales, unit sales and profitability, Apple's performance in the fourth quarter ending in September of year 2000 was disappointing. Net sales during this quarter fell short of the company's expectations by approximately $180 million causing operating margin before special charges to fall to 4% for the quarter. The fourth-quarter revenue shortfall was primarily the result of 3 factors. First, fourth-quarter net sales of the G4 Cube, a new Macintosh system announced and introduced by the company during the fourth quarter, did not meet the company's expectations. G4 sales were approximately $90 million short of expectations. Second, net sales in the company's education market fell short of expectations by approximately $60 million. Third, although total fourth quarter Power Mac unit sales were close to expectations, the company experienced an unanticipated mix shift toward lower priced Power Mac configurations resulting in lower than anticipated net sales of approximately $30 million. Apple ended fiscal 2000 with substantially more inventory in its distribution channels than planned due to the lower than expected sell-through of the company's products during the fourth quarter.

Exhibit 8

Consolidated Balance Sheets: Apple Computer, Inc.
(Dollar amounts in millions, except share amounts)

	Sept 30, 2000	Sept 25, 1999
Assets		
Current assets:		
Cash and cash equivalents	$1,191	$1,326
Short-term investments	2,836	1,900
Accounts receivable, less allowances of $64 and $68, respectively	953	681
Inventories	33	20
Deferred tax assets	162	143
Other current assets	252	215
Total current assets	5,427	4,285
Property, plant, and equipment, net	313	318
Non-current debt and equity investments	786	339
Other assets	277	219
Total assets	6,803	5,161
Liabilities and shareholders' equity		
Current liabilities:		
Accounts payable	1,157	812
Accrued expenses	776	737
Total current liabilities	1,933	1,549
Long-term debt	300	300
Deferred tax liabilities	463	208
Total liabilities	2,696	2,057
Commitments and contingencies		
Shareholders' equity:		
Series A nonvoting convertible preferred stock, no par value; 150,000 shares authorized, 75,750 and 150,000 issued and outstanding, respectively	76	150
Common stock, no par value; 900,000,000 shares authorized; 335,676,889 and 321,598,122 shares issued and outstanding, respectively	1,502	1,349
Retained earnings	2,285	1,499
Accumulated other comprehensive income	244	106
Total shareholders' equity	4,107	3,104
Total liabilities and shareholders' equity	6,803	5,161

Future

Apple Computer anticipated a significant sequential decline in quarterly net sales during the first quarter of fiscal 2001(the quarter ending December 31, 2000) of approximately $1.0 billion. This decline was anticipated because of a perceived continued deterioration in demand, price cuts and a plan to reduce substantially the level of inventory in the Company's distribution channels.

For all of fiscal 2001, Apple anticipated net sales would decline as compared to fiscal 2000. Apple's future operating results and financial condition were dependent upon general economic conditions, market conditions within the PC industry, and the company's ability to successfully develop, manufacture, and market technologically innovative products within the highly competitive market for personal computers.[38]

Exhibit 9

Consolidated Statements of Operations: Apple Computer, Inc.
(Dollar amounts in millions, except share and per share amounts)

Fiscal Years Ending September 30	2000	1999	1998
Net sales	$7,983	6,134	5,941
Cost of sales	5,817	4,438	4,462
Gross margin	2,166	1,696	1,479
Operating expenses:			
Research and development	380	314	303
Selling, general, and administrative	1,166	996	908
Special charges:			
Executive bonus	90	—	—
Restructuring costs	8	27	—
In-process research and development	—	—	7
Total operating expenses	1,644	1,337	1,218
Operating income	552	359	261
Gains from sales of investment	367	230	40
Interest and other income, net	203	87	28
Total interest and other income, net	507	317	68
Income before provision for income taxes	1,092	676	329
Provision for income taxes	306	75	20
Net income	786	601	309
Earnings per common share:			
Basic	2.42	2.10	1.17
Diluted	2.18	1.81	1.05
Shares used in computing earnings per share (in thousands):			
Basic	324,568	286,314	263,948
Diluted	360,324	348,328	335,834

Apple was in the process of changing its message. The company decided to try to remake its image into a purveyor of "killer applications" or groundbreaking software programs that computer users can't live without. The Apple executives believed that new Apple applications would give Wintel users a reason to supplement their existing Windows-based systems with Apple hardware.

Apple's focus on applications was the latest effort by the computer company to reinvent itself. Following an unexpected profit warning in September of 2000, the company began offering rebates on several of its hardware lines to boost sales. The rebates had little effect, and Apple issued another profit warning in December.

The Company knew that lowering prices wasn't enough. The company hadn't managed to gather very much business from non-Mac users. For the first 3 fiscal quarters of 2000, Apple derived only 15% of its revenue from former Wintel customers. While an additional 28% of the company's sales came from first-time computer buyers, the majority of sales were generated by repeat Mac customers.

Hardware remained a core business for Apple. Steve Jobs has been highlighting Apple software applications for the past year, especially as the company readied its next generation operating system, Mac OS X, for release. Steven Jobs was a vocal champion of iMovie, Apple's home-movie editing software. He once said iMovie was at the heart of the company's philosophy of being at "the intersection of art and technology."

Exhibit 10

Consolidated Statements of Cash Flows: Apple Computer, Inc.
(Dollar amounts in millions)

Fiscal Years Ending September 30	2000	1999	1998
Cash and cash equivalents, beginning of the year	$1,326	$1,481	$1,230
Operating:			
Net income	786	601	309
Adjustments to reconcile net income to cash generated by operating activities:			
Depreciation and amortization	84	85	111
Provision for deferred income taxes	163	(35)	1
Loss on sale of property, plant, and equipment	3	—	—
Gains from sales of equity investment	(367)	(230)	(40)
In-process research and development	—	—	7
Changes in operating assets and liabilities:			
Accounts receivable	(272)	274	72
Inventories	(13)	58	359
Other current assets	(37)	(32)	31
Other assests	(15)	(3)	83
Accounts payable	345	93	34
Accrued restructuring costs	(27)	2	(107)
Other current liabilities	176	(15)	(85)
Cash generated by operating activities	826	798	775
Purchase of short-term investments	(4,267)	(4,236)	(2,313)
Proceeds from maturities of short-term investments	3,331	3,155	1,723
Purchases of long-term investments	(232)	(112)	—
Proceeds from sale of property, plant and equipment	11	23	89
Purchase of property, plant, and equipment	(107)	(47)	(46)
Proceeds from sales of equity investment	372	245	24
Other	(38)	8	(20)
Cash used for investing activities	(930)	(964)	(543)
Financing:			
Decrease in notes payable to banks	—	—	(22)
Proceeds from issuance of common stock	85	86	41
Cash used for repurchase of common stock	(116)	(75)	—
Cash generated by (used for) financing activities	(31)	11	19
Increase (decrease) in cash and cash equivalents	(135)	(155)	251
Cash and cash equivalents, end of the year	$1,191	$1,326	$1,481
Supplemental cash flow disclosures:			
Cash paid during the year for interest	$10	$58	$59
Cash paid (received) for income taxes, net	$47	$33	$(15)
Noncash transactions:			
Issuance of common stock for redemption of long-term debt	—	654	—
Issuance of common stock for acquisition of PCC assets	—		80
Issuance of common stock for conversion of Series A Preferred Stock	74	—	—

"Apple has needed to change its marketing for a long time," says Mark Macgillivray, a consultant at H&M Consulting, a market-research firm in Sunnyvale, California, that has worked with Apple in the past. "It's when Apple has focused on solutions that they've done reasonably well, because they've given customers a distinctive reason to buy a Mac."[39]

As Apple prepared in January of 2001 to hold the latest of the twice-annual expos in San Francisco, did Steven Jobs have enough flash left to rejuvenate Apple once again? Apple's stock was trading near its 52-week low. It wouldn't even come close to meeting its earnings projections for its most recent quarter. To top it all off, Apple was even losing some of its tiny share of the personal computing market.

All eyes were on the expo. Some who watched the company closely said they expected Apple to introduce new lines of laptops and desktops, perhaps a wireless gadget or 2, and maybe expound more on its fledgling plans for a line of retail stores. Jobs, in his keynote address, also would likely disclose more details about the long awaited release of Mac OS X operating system, slated for February 2001, which would contain new Internet features. At some point, Jobs probably would feel compelled to address the company's financial condition.

Jobs and his associates are still running Apple, and they've never failed to rejuvenate the company. When Apple couldn't get a foothold in the consumer desktop market in the early 1980s, they came up with the revolutionary Macintosh that helped build the foundations of desktop publishing. When Apple found itself being devastated by Windows-based computers in the early 1990s, it came up with the Power PC, and later the iMac and the iBook. In 1996, when tired and flagging Apple and its partners were badly in need of some new flash and some profits, Steve Jobs was the one who arrived on the scene to provide it. "The Apple Corporation and Steve Jobs personally have been masters at repositioning that company," said John Kortier, Vice President of channel sales for Atlanta-based EarthLink Inc.[40]

Notes

1. Peter Burrows, "Yes, Steve, you fixed it. Congrats! Now What's Act Two? Apple," *Business Week* (July 31, 2000), p. 102.
2. *Ibid.*, pp. 105, 108.
3. *Ibid.*, p. 104.
4. Robert O'Brien, "Apple Computer Plunges 52%, Drags Down Rest of the Market," *Wall Street Journal* (October 2, 2000), p. C2.
5. Pui-Wing Tam, "Apple Reports First Loss in 3 Years; Stock Slips," *Wall Street Journal* (January 18, 2000), p. B6.
6. O'Brien, "Apple Computer Plunges 52%, Drags Down Rest of the Market," p. C2.
7. Terrence O'Hara, "It Was the Best of Times and the Worst of Times, and the Difference Was All in the Numbers," *The Washington Post* (December 31, 2000), p. H18.
8. Greg Ip, "A Year of Living Dangerously," *Wall Street Journal* (January 2, 2001), p. R1.
9. Apple Computer Inc., *Form 10-K* (2000), pp. 63, 64.
10. Staff reporter, "Apple Sales Executive Says He Is Leaving Post at End of Year," *Wall Street Journal* (October 11, 2000), p. B23.
11. Pui-Wing Tam, "Dwindling Education Sales Take a Bite Out of Apple's Bottom Line," *Wall Street Journal* (October 17, 2000), p. B1.
12. *Ibid.*, p. B4.
13. *Ibid.*, p. B4.
14. *Ibid.*, p. B4.
15. Apple Computer Inc., *Form 10-K* (2000), p. 4.
16. "Computer and Peripherals Industry," *Value Line* (October 20, 2000), p. 1095.
17. "Compaq Computer," *Value Line* (October 20, 2000), p. 1101.
18. "Dell Computer," *Value Line* (October 20, 2000), p. 1102.
19. "Gateway, Inc.," *Value Line* (October 20, 2000), p. 1105.
20. "International Business Machines," *Value Line* (October 20, 2000), p. 1110.
21. "Hewlett-Packard," *Value Line* (October 20, 2000), p. 1109.
22. "Semiconductor Industry," *Value Line* (October 20, 2000), p. 1051.
23. "Intel," *Value Line* (October 20, 2000), p. 1067.
24. "Motorola," *Value Line* (October 20, 2000), p. 1075.
25. "Computer Software & Services," *Value Line* (December 1, 2000), p. 2171.
26. "Microsoft," *Value Line* (December 1, 2000), p. 2202.
27. Apple Computer, Inc., *Form 10-K* (2000), p. 6. The material in this section, Foreign and Domestic operations and Geographic Data, was directly abstracted. The verb tense was changed and some material altered.
28. *Ibid.*, p. 21. The material in this section, Product Introductions, was directly abstracted. The verb tense was changed and some material altered.
29. *Ibid.*, p. 21. The material in this section, Inventory and Supply, was directly abstracted. The verb tense was changed and some material altered.
30. *Ibid.*, p. 24. The material in this section, Support from Third-Party Software Developers, was directly abstracted. The verb tense was changed and some material altered.
31. *Ibid.*, p. 23. The material in this section, Education Market, was directly abstracted. The verb tense was changed and some material altered.
32. *Ibid.*, p. 4. The material in this section, Markets and Distribution, was directly abstracted. The verb tense was changed and considerable additional material was added.

33. Pui-Wing Tam, "Apple Computer Tries Courting Retailers Again," *Wall Street Journal* (July 7, 2000), p. B1.
34. *Ibid.*
35. Apple Computer, Inc., *Form 10-K* (2000), p. 8. The material in this section, Legal Proceedings, was directly abstracted. The verb tense was changed.
36. *Ibid.*, p. 12. The material in this section, Financials, was directly abstracted. The verb tense was changed and some material altered.
37. *Ibid.*, pp. 33–36.
38. *Ibid.*, p. 13. The material in this section, Future, was directly abstracted. The verb tense was changed and considerable material was added.
39. Pui-Wing Tam, "Apple Seeks New Image as Producer of Killer Apps," *Wall Street Journal* (Jan 5, 2001), pp. B1, B4.
40. Bob Keefe, "Steve Jobs to Carry Extra Burden at Expo," *The Atlanta Constitution* (January 7, 2001), p. 5G.

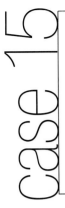

Carly Fiorina: The Reinvention of Hewlett-Packard

Patricia A. Ryan

. . . we owe you . . . 3 things. We owe you a clear vision and a sense of direction, how we are going to help you be successful in the next millennium. We owe you enough focus and leverage to execute well, each and every time. And we owe you an understanding of the total experience that we provide and an understanding on our part of how to make that experience a competitive advantage for you as well as for us.

Carleton (Carly) Fiorina, CEO and President of HP
San Francisco, August 17, 1999[1]

It was July 19, 1999, and Carleton (Carly) Fiorina, spoke with exuberance and confidence as she thanked Lewis (Lew) Platt, a 33-year company veteran for his leadership as the former President and CEO of Hewlett-Packard (HP) from 1992 through July 1999. Fiorina was the first female CEO of 1 of America's largest companies, the only female heading the ranks at a Dow 30 company. She did not believe in a glass ceiling; rather argued that competence would prevail. It certainly seemed she was right; 2 of the 4 finalists for the job were women, and Fiorina was the only one without significant computer industry experience. How did she move into the coveted position with the magnum computer company? She convinced the Board of Directors that computer experience was not what HP lacked; rather it was the ability to pick up quickly and help the struggling HP develop a stronger strategic vision. She shrewdly convinced the Board their skills were complementary, turning what some thought to be a negative into a positive. Fiorina was confident and poised at the helm; however, she realized that as a newcomer to HP, she needed to work diligently to maintain alignment of internal forces while at the same time move the company forward in a new direction. The former President of Lucent Technologies, a global service provider business, Fiorina led the Lucent spin-off from AT&T and ran the largest IPO at that time, totaling more than $3 billion. Fiorina saw a unique opportunity in Hewlett-Packard; she saw an opportunity to rethink HP's approach to the market, structure, and resources the company needed to achieve its objectives.[2]

Hewlett-Packard designs and manufactures computing and imaging solutions and services for both business and home use. There are 3 major businesses within HP. The first is Imaging and Printing Systems, which provides laser and inkjet printers, scanners, all-in-1 devices, personal color copiers and faxes, digital senders, large format and wide printers, printer servers, network management software, networking solutions, digital photography,

This case was prepared by Professor Patricia A. Ryan, Colorado State University. This case may not be reproduced in any form without written permission of the copyright holder. This case was presented to and accepted by the Society for Case Research. This case will appear in a 2001 issue of the *Business Case Journal*. This case was edited for SMBP-8th Edition. Copyright © 2001 Patricia A. Ryan. Reprinted by permission.

imaging and printing supplies and software, and other professional and consulting services. The second arm of HP is the Computing Systems, which provides computing systems for both commercial and consumer use. The third arm is Information Technology Services, which provides consulting, education, design and installation services, ongoing support and maintenance, outsourcing, and utility computing capabilities.[3] She knew she needed to transform HP into a fast, customer-focused maker of computers and printers and place heavy emphasis on the company's commitment to e-services.

In recent years, price competition in printers, servers, workstations, and personal computers caused growth rates to slow. On March 2, 1999, then President and CEO Lew Platt made 2 critical announcements: first that Hewlett-Packard would spin off their Test and Measurement division later that year, and second that he would retire after a new CEO was recruited. When Carly joined HP, Platt agreed to stay on as Chairman until December 31, 1999, to assist in the spin-off of the Test and Measurement division (soon to be known as Agilent Technologies) and to assist Fiorina with her transition.

Hewlett-Packard was in need of reinvention; Carly Fiorina was the person hired to lead the charge. The company was at a pivotal point; poised to take full advantage of the Internet age, yet steadfast in its traditional core values.

> Reinvention to me is about 4 things. It's about culture, it's about strategy, it's about what you measure and how you reward those measurements, and it's about business process. All of those levers need to be pulled.

Carly Fiorina, President and CEO, HP[4]

Hewlett-Packard had become too slow to react and position itself in the global economy of the twenty-first century. Platt worked hard to maintain a consensus spirit. Fiorina needed to preserve the core values that have made the company successful.

History of Hewlett-Packard

Hewlett-Packard became the foundation for the entrepreneurial fountain of American innovation now known as Silicon Valley.[5] Two Stanford electrical engineering graduates, Dave Packard and Bill Hewlett set out on a small business venture upon the advice of their professor, Fred Terman. Professor Terman told them to "make a run for it." After a 2-week camping trip to the Colorado mountains, Packard and Hewlett decided to join forces to form the seedling of what was to become known to the world as Hewlett-Packard. They soon found there was a demand for a lower priced audio oscillators similar to the type they developed while at Stanford. Interestingly, the ordering of their names was determined by a coin toss in a small Palo Alto, CA, garage. In 1940, total revenues were $34,000 and Dave and Bill had 3 employees. Business was boosted significantly by the war effort and high defense spending; HP was able to internally finance all its growth through World War II. Their expertise in microwave technology developed through the war years, and HP had little difficulty expanding its product line to meet the burgeoning electronics industry in the postwar boom. It was not until 1957 that the company went public with 10% of its shares. At that time, 4 divisions were created, divisions that remained up to the spin-off of the Test and Measurement division in 1999. In 1962, Hewlett-Packard joined the Standard & Poor's 500 where the company remains today. In 1999, revenue topped $47.1 billion, and HP employed over 124,000 throughout the world. (See **Exhibit 1** for historical milestones.)

Walt Disney was 1 of their first customers with the purchase of 8 audio oscillators to test the sound equipment in the movie *Fantasia*. In the 1950s, Hewlett-Packard developed their corporate objectives and began globalization of HP. The philosophy that was to become known as the "HP Way," depictive of the innovative and generous relationships with employ-

Exhibit 1

Historical Milestones in the History of Hewlett-Packard

Date	Event
Mid-2000	Agilent's independence is achieved when Hewlett-Packard distributes its remaining Agilent stock holdings to Hewlett-Packard shareholders.
July 17, 1999	Carly Fiorina joined HP as the new President and CEO; Platt would remain on board 6 months.
March 2, 1999	Hewlett-Packard announces strategic realignment into 2 companies.
1998	Sales reach $47.1 billion with 124,600 employees. The company's Pavilion PC reached its peak in the U.S. market.
1997	Acquired Verifone, the industry leader in electronic-payments systems, through a stock-for-stock merger valued at $1.29 billion.
1996	Cofounder David Packard dies of pneumonia.
1995	Introduced HP Pavilion PC for the home computing market.
1994	Sales topped $25 billion with 98,400 employees. Introduced HP Color LaserJet printer and HP OfficeJet printer/fax machine/copier.
1993	Dave Packard retired as Chairman. Lew Platt named Chairman, President, and CEO. Shipped 10 millionth LaserJet printer. Company sales were $20.3 billion with 96,200 employees.
1992	CEO John Young retires; Lew Platt named President and CEO.
1990	Opened research lab in Tokyo. Company sales were $13.2 billion with 91,500 employees.
1989	Listed on 4 European stock exchanges: London, Zurich, Paris, and Frankfurt. Acquired Apollo Computer, workstation manufacturer. Original HP garage was designated a California State Historical Landmark in this fiftieth anniversary year.
1988	Company sales reached $10 billion, were listed on the Tokyo Stock Exchange, and were ranked #49 on the *Fortune 500*.
1987	Bill Hewlett retired as Vice Chairman of the Board of Directors. His son, Walter Hewlett, along with Dave Packard's son, David Woodley Packard, were elected to the Board.
1985	HP Laboratories opened research facility in Bristol, England. HP sales reached $6.5 billion with 85,000 employees.
1980	Sales reached $3 billion with 57,000 employees. Introduced first personal computer, HP-85.
1977	John Young named President (appointed CEO in 1978).
1970	Sales reached $365 million with 16,000 employees.
1969	Dave Packard was appointed U.S. Deputy Secretary of Defense (1969–71)
1966	HP Laboratories formed as the company's central research facility. It went on to become 1 of the world's leading electronics industry research centers.
1965	HP entered analytical-instrumentation field with acquisition of F&M Scientific Corporation, located in Avondale, PA. HP sales totaled $165 million with 9,000 employees.
1964	Dave Packard elected Chairman; Bill Hewlett elected President.
1963	First joint venture in Japan.
1962	First HP Listing on *Fortune's* list of largest U.S. industrial companies at #460.
1961	Listed on the New York and the Pacific Stock Exchanges.
1960	Established first U.S. manufacturing facility outside Palo Alto, in Loveland, CO.
1959	Established first presence overseas in Switzerland and West Germany.
1958	Sales topped $30 million with 1,778 employees and 373 products.
November 6, 1957	First public offering, wrote first corporate objectives. Company began manufacturing in new facilities in Palo Alto, CA.
1951	Sales were $5.5 million with 215 employees.
August 18, 1947	Incorporated, annual sales were $679,000 with 111 employees.
1940	Sales: $34,000, employees: 3, products: 8.
1938	Bill Hewlett and Dave Packard began working part time in a garage at 367 Addison Avenue, Palo Alto, CA, with an initial investment of $538.

ees, was formally developed in this decade of change and growth. The company went public on November 6, 1957, with 373 products, $30 million in net revenue, and 1,778 employees. In the late 1950s, marketing emphasis was placed on European markets in Switzerland and West Germany. In the 1960s, the computing division bloomed and the Test and Measurement division became known for its progressive position in the market. Hewlett-Packard was respected as a well-managed company. The 1960s brought joint ventures in Japan and Germany. John Young was named CEO in 1978 and served in that capacity until 1992. Young succeeded in growing the company into a major computer giant. By the 1980s, the increasing global presence of HP was partially due to the onslaught of personal computers and peripherals. Hewlett-Packard strove to provide high performance at reasonable cost. In the early 1990s, Young's efforts to corral the company's independent units led to bureaucracy that bogged the company down. In 1992, the popular engineer Lew Platt was named President and CEO of the computing and measurement giant. That same year, Hewlett-Packard introduced a new atomic clock that became the world's most precise timekeeper. The remainder of the 1990s brought accelerated Web-based information and increased focus on the computing side of the company. In the very fast growth period of that decade, Hewlett-Packard struggled to keep up with all the new technological breakthroughs while operating in multiple industries. It became clear that some action would now have to be taken to streamline the company. Platt succeeded in managing HP's growth in the 1990s, but missed the Internet revolution in the late 1990s.

Corporate Culture: The HP Way

Hewlett-Packard, from its early beginnings, was a company that emphasized invention, innovation, and work–life balance. However, along the road, work–life balance appeared to take a stronger position in the triad, leaving innovation and invention to suffer in a rapidly changing technological environment.

> The most important thing about HP's culture is the assumption it is built upon, namely, that people want to do a good job, a creative job, and will do so if given the right environment.
>
> Bill Hewlett, referenced by Lew Platt[6]

Hewlett's statement was central to the culture at Hewlett-Packard. This culture operated with 5 basic values:

- We have trust and respect for individuals.
- We focus on a high level of achievement and contribution.
- We focus on a high level of business with uncompromising integrity.
- We achieve our common objectives through teamwork.
- We encourage flexibility and innovation.[7]

Lew Platt was proud of HP's positions as 1 of America's favorite employers and spoke frequently about work–life balance, the need for a company to assist employees to maintain the appropriate balance between their work life and home life. He felt strongly that work–life balance was important to maintain happy, creative employees and believed the employees were the most significant assets HP had.

The HP Way, as defined by top management, included 6 key elements. They are

1. **Profit**: To achieve sufficient profit to finance our company growth and to provide the resources we need to achieve our other corporate objectives.

2. **Customers:** To provide products and services of the highest quality and the greatest possible value to our customers, thereby gaining and holding their respect and loyalty.

3. **Fields of Interest**: To participate in those fields of interest that build upon our technologies, competencies, and customer interests, that offer opportunities for continuing growth, and that enable us to make a needed and profitable contribution.

4. **Growth**: To let our growth be limited only by our profits and our ability to develop and produce innovative products that satisfy real customer needs.

5. **Our People**: To help HP people share in the company's success which they make possible; to provide them employment security based on performance; to create with them an injury-free, pleasant, and inclusive work environment that values their diversity and recognizes individual contributions; and to help them gain a sense of satisfaction and accomplishment from their work.

6. **Management**: To foster initiative and creativity by allowing the individual great freedom of action in attaining well-defined objectives.[8]

These corporate objectives form the basis of the "HP Way"—an ideology that sought to create a work environment designed to allow well-trained, innovative, enthusiastic, and competent people to give their all for the company.

With new leadership comes change, and Carly would do just that. Carly Fiorina saw the HP culture needed to be reshaped more along the revolutionary and radical lines developed by Hewlett and Packard in 1939. In order to see revolution, the culture had to accept radical and not always popular decisions. For example, HP created the first handheld calculator, a revolutionary change; HP also created flexible work hours on the factory floor, a revolutionary change. Fiorina saw her challenge to reignite the spirit of HP and focus on the inventive nature of the original core business.

In a speech on November 15, 1999, Fiorina emphasized the need to maintain balance while focusing on innovation, invention, and change. "In many ways we are truly returning to our roots" she emphasized the changes were necessary to maintain a competitive position in the marketplace.

Top Management

The main executive offices in Palo Alto, CA, serve as corporate headquarters. (See **Exhibit 2** for Executive Officers and Board of Directors and **Exhibit 3** for Selected Executive Compensation and Stock Options.)

Carleton (Carly) S. Fiorina, 45, President and CEO of Hewlett-Packard. She assumed that position on July 17, 1999, and on July 23, 1999, was elected to the Board of Directors. Prior to joining HP, Fiorina spent nearly 20 years with AT&T and Lucent, most recently as the President of the Global Services Provider Business of Lucent Technologies after having worked her way up the executive ranks. Perhaps her most successful accomplishment at Lucent was spearheading Lucent's initial public offering and subsequent spin-off from AT&T. In addition to leading HP into the new millennium, Fiorina served as a member of the Board of Directors of the Kellogg Company and Merck and Company and was recently appointed to the U.S. China Board of Trade.

Ann M. Livermore, 41, President of the Enterprise and Commercial Business Division. One of the frontrunners to succeed Lew Platt as President and CEO, Fiorina worked quickly to maintain Livermore as an ally, naming her to her current position in October 1999. This highly visible division would be responsible for many of the e-business initiatives HP would like to take on in the immediate future. Livermore also served on the Board of Directors for the United Parcel Service and on the Board of Visitors of the Kenan-Flagler Business School at the University of North Carolina in Chapel Hill.

Antonio M. Perez, 54, President of Consumer Business. Appointed by Fiorina in November 1999, Perez had previously served HP in the capacity of General Manager and later President of Inkjet Imaging Solutions.

Exhibit 2
Executive Officers and Board of Directors

Name	Title	Executive Since
Carleton S. Fiorina, 45	President and Chief Executive Officer	1999
Ann M. Livermore, 41	President, Enterprise and Commercial Business	1995
Antonio M. Perez, 54	President, Consumer Business	1995
Carolyn M. Ticknor, 52	President, Imaging and Printing Systems	1995
Duane E. Zitzner, 52	Computing Systems	1996
Robert P. Wayman, 54	Executive Vice President, Finance, and CFO	1984
Raymond W. Cookington, 56	Vice President and Controller	1986
Susan D. Bowick, 51	Vice President, Human Resources	1993
Debra L. Dunn, 43	Vice President and General Manager, Strategy and Corporate Operations	1999
William V. Russell, 47	Vice President, Enterprise Systems and Software	1998
Stephen L. Squires	Vice President, Chief Science Officer	
Joshi Vyomesh	President of Imaging and Printing Systems Business	1980

Board of Directors

Name	Inside or Outside Director	Affiliation
Carleton S. Fiorina, 45	Inside	President and CEO, HP
Robert P. Wayman, 54	Inside	CFO, HP
Philip M. Condit, 57	Outside	Chairman and CEO, The Boeing Company
Patricia C. Dunn, 46	Outside	Chairman and Co-CEO, Barclays Global Investors
Sam Ginn, 62	Outside	Vodafone AirTouch
Richard A. Hackborn, 62	Outside	Designated Chairman, HP, effective January 2000
Walter B. Hewlett, 55	Outside	Chairman, Vermont Telephone
George A. Keyworth II, 60	Outside	Chairman and Senior Follow, The Progress & Freedom Foundation
Susan Packard Orr, 53	Outside	President, Technology Resource Assistance Center
Lewis E. Platt, 58	Inside	Retiring Chairman as of December 31, 1999
Thomas E. Everhart, 67	Outside	President Emeritus, California Institute of Technology, retired September 1999
David M. Lawrence, M.D.	Outside	Chairman and CEO, Kaiser Foundation Health Plans, Inc, Kaiser Foundation Hospitals
John B. Fery, 70	Outside	Retired Chairman and CEO, Boise Cascade Corporation, retiring from the Board February 2000
Jean-Paul G. Gimon	Outside	Retired General Representative in North America Credit Lyonnais S. A., retiring February 2000

Source: 1999 10-K, pp. 55–56, and *1999 Annual Report.*

Exhibit 3

Hewlett-Packard's Executive Compensation and Stock Options for the Fiscal Year Ending October 31, 1999

Name	Year	Annual Compensation		Long-Term and Other Compensation	
		Salary	Bonus	Restricted Stock Award	Other Compensation[5]
Carleton S. Fiorina, President, CEO, Director[1]	1999	$287,933	$366,438	$65,557,400[4]	$3,223,867
Lewis E. Platt, Former Chairman, President, and CEO[2]	1999	$1,000,000	$3,114,721	$1,298,501	$600,089
	1998	$1,000,000	$910,700	$2,265,258	$6,491
	1997	$1,700,000	$111,435	$2,712,071	$6,427
Robert P. Wayman, Executive Vice President, CFO, Director	1999	$930,000	$471,590	$4,208,840	$264,384
	1998	$997,625	$147,804	$1,289,516	$6,491
	1997	$968,750	$63,550	$1,360,426	$6,427
Antonio M. Perez, President, Consumer Business	1999	$530,875	$431,066	$1,301,374	$6,485
	1998	$600,875	$33,055	$926,250	$6,491
	1997	$517,500	$33,964	$679,936	$6,427
Carolyn M. Ticknor, President, Imaging and Printing Systems	1999	$603,125	$310,773	$1,897,088	$9,303
	1998	$629,250	$34,612	$1,185,025	$6,283
	1997	$538,750	$35,364	$654,834	$6,427
Edward W. Barnholt, Former Executive Vice President[3]	1999	$920,635	$474,684	$416,589	$313,892
	1998	$759,488	$115,754	$967,581	$6,491
	1997	$702,500	$46,092	$1,083,627	$6,427

Notes:
1. Ms. Fiorina was elected President and CEO effective July 17, 1999, and a Director effective July 23, 1999.
2. Mr. Platt resigned as President and CEO effective July 31, 1999, and as Chairman effective December 31, 1999.
3. Mr. Barnholt resigned as Executive Vice President effective October 31, 1999, and was appointed CEO of Agilent Technologies effective May 4, 1999.
4. Ms. Fiorina received 290,000 shares of restricted stock and 290,000 shares of unrestricted stock units, which vest annually over a 3-year period with an aggregate value of $65,557,400 at the time of the grant. These shares were provided in order to partially compensate her for stock and options she forfeited upon her departure from Lucent Technologies.
5. These amounts include a $3 million signing bonus for Ms. Fiorina, mortgage assistance of $36,343, relocation allowance of $187,500, and $24,000 for term life insurance for Ms. Fiorina. Other executives received compensation in 401(k) retirement plans, term life insurance, and accrued sick leave payments.

Source: 1999 Notice of Annual Meeting and Proxy Statement, pp. 27–31.

Carolyn M. Ticknor, 52, President of Imaging and Printing Systems. Ticknor was known as a take-no-prisoners operations whiz. Her goal was to pioneer e-publishing, the ability to manipulate images in cyberspace.[9]

Duane E. Zitzner, 52, President of the Computer Products division. Zitzer served HP as General Manager of the Personal Information Products Group since 1996. The most recent promotion came 1 month after Platt announced the spin-off of the Test and Measurement business into what became known as Agilent Technologies.

Robert P. Wayman, 54, Executive Vice President of Finance and Administration and Chief Financial Officer (CFO). Additionally, Wayman has served on HP's Board of Directors since 1993. He has held the position as CFO since 1984. Wayman was an outside member of the Board of Directors of Sybase, Inc,. and CNF Transportation. Finally, he was active in academia, serving as a member of the Kellogg Advisory Board to Northwestern University School of Business.

Raymond W. Cookington, 56, Controller. Cookington has served as Controller since 1986 and was elected a Vice President in 1993.

Susan D. Bowick, 51, Vice President of Human Resources. Bowick was elected a Vice President in November 1999. She previously served as Business Personnel Manager for the Computer Organization and Personnel Manager for the San Diego site.

Debra L. Dunn, 43, Vice President and General Manager, Strategy and Corporate Operations. Dunn was elected Vice President in November 1999. Prior to that, she served as General Manager of HP's Executive Staff and Manager of Video Communications Division. She joined HP in 1994.

William V. Russell, 47, Vice President of Enterprise Systems and Software. Russell was appointed to his current position in October 1999. Prior to that, he was the General Manager of Europe, Asia, and the Middle East for the Computer Systems organization and later the General Manager for the Enterprise Systems Group.

Stephen L. Squires, Vice President, Chief Science Officer. Squires was well known as an architect of the Strategic Computing and High Performance Computing programs that work with the Internet, maximizing performance and speed. He had also worked on long-term strategic issues that involved joint issues in biology, information technology, and the physical sciences. An accomplished scientist, Squires worked to provide technical leadership in information security.

Joshi Vyomesh, President of Imaging and Printing Systems Business. Vyomesh joined HP in 1980 as a Research and Development scientist and had worked his way up the ranks mainly through the Inkjet business. He led the team that developed the first HP color inkjet cartridge and, in 1995, led HP's entry into the digital imaging business. More recently, Vyomesh led the company's Inkjet Systems business as well as the latest efforts in digital imaging including the development of the digital camera, photo scanner, and photo printer offerings.

Board of Directors

Hewlett-Packard's Board of Directors consisted of 14 members with the majority of them outside directors. Inside directors include President and CEO Fiorina and CFO Wayman. Other board members are listed in **Exhibit 2**. The Board of Directors represents a widely diverse group of industries including aircraft manufacturing, financial services, technology, medical, and education. Family members Walter Hewlett, son of Cofounder Bill Hewlett, and Susan Packard Orr, daughter of Bill Packard, sit on the board.

The Tightening Computer Hardware Industry

The computer hardware industry was very competitive throughout the 1990s. The main PC players in 1999 were Dell, Compaq, Gateway, IBM, and HP. In 1999, Dell enjoyed the largest market share of PC shipments of 17.1%, up from 13.4 % in 1998. Compaq was second with a

15.3% market share in 1999 compared to 15% in 1998. Gateway came in third, accruing a market share of 9.3% in 1999, up from 8.2% in 1998. And Hewlett-Packard came in fourth with 8.2% market share in 1999, down from 8.4% in 1998. Finally, IBM dropped market share from 8.9% in 1998 to 7.6 % in 1999. In sum, both Hewlett-Packard and IBM lost market share, while Dell, Compaq, and Gateway gained. All 5 companies saw unit sales increase in 1999 over 1998 with Dell enjoying a 56.5% increase, Compaq a 24.9% increase, Gateway a 40.1% increase, Hewlett-Packard a 19.4% increase, and IBM a 5.3% increase.[10] These numbers show that significant increases in unit sales translate to small changes in market share; for example, Compaq saw a 24.9% increase in unit sales, but only a 0.3% increase in market share. Hewlett-Packard and IBM both saw unit sale increases, but market shares losses. These numbers reflect a growing industry and indicate that it was difficult to increase market share via increased sales. There were more smaller competitors entering the market each year, making market share points harder and harder to come by; however, Hewlett-Packard had good name recognition as did the other leaders in the market. Therefore, they had the opportunity to leverage their brand name into increased revenue and market share if they operated efficiently and strategically in this ever-tightening market.

Lew Platt's Era

Lew Platt was not HP's first choice to replace John Young as CEO in 1992. Their first choice was Dick Hackborn who had built their industry-leading printer business from scratch. Hackborn declined the position, and HP then chose Platt, a competent yet low-key manager and conservative dresser who some believed lacked the innovation of Hackborn. Platt was a competent leader but did not catch on to the Internet revolution until too late, which left HP in a secondary position in the Internet market in 1999.[11] Platt was wise to see the need to split HP into 2 divisions, divesting the company of the Test and Measurement division that they started years earlier. Platt was able to make this decision with the clarity and foresight that few top CEO's would recognize, shrinking the size of his empire down to allow a new CEO to come in and reinvigorate the company.

After 2 years of spotty growth, Platt's move to separate the 2 companies and leave HP was seen as a bold move, one that placed HP ahead of personal goals. Clearly a successful CEO, he would have other opportunities, and at 58, he appeared interested in moving toward a slightly lower profile company with fewer internal pressures. At HP, there was a lot of money and market share at risk. Demand was booming in the United States and wireless communications were expanding rapidly through Latin America and Asia. During Platt's first 6 years as CEO, HP succeeded in tripling revenues and increasing profits 5-fold.

Platt was a strong advocate of work–life balance, recognizing the difficulties many of today's working families had in maintaining the proper balance between work and home life. He attributed part of his consideration to the passing of his first wife and the realization of how difficult it was to maintain a career and be a good parent to his children. He recognized this challenge was greater in the Silicon Valley than in many other areas because of the sheer speed of business development and the demand on employees to commit more than full time to their job. Along these lines, Platt expanded HP's level of absence policies to allow for greater flexibility, developed an HP financed insurance program for elder care to assist employees caring for aging parents, provided assistance with dependent care, implemented alternative work schedules including telecommuting for employees—all with the thought of assisting the employee to better balance their work and home life. Platt clearly saw that a happy employee was an empowered employee and worked more effectively.

From an analysts' perspective, Platt agreed HP was hard to analyze since the company was involved in so many diverse areas. Known worldwide for computers and printers, HP started as a test and measurement company and kept that division until 1999. Platt was not a media personality, but rather a relatively quiet man who spoke when he had something to say. He recognized HP was now in a position in which they needed someone with more flash, a more outgoing personality, and most likely an outsider to the company. HP needed a fearless leader, one without bias, without inside allegiances, commitments, or relationships.

> In retrospect, I wish I was more rebellious. We live in a world where visibility and what you say have become more important. Leaders in the industry—Michael Dell, Scott McNealy [of Sun Microsystems]—generate a lot of interest. There's a positive aura that surrounds their companies because they're upfront. I was brought up in a world that said, "Do great things and the world will notice."[12]
>
> Lew Platt, former CEO, Hewlett-Packard

Under Platt, the vision for developing HP's presence on the Internet was developed. He believed HP's future was tied to the tremendous growth of the Internet. In a speech at Edison Electric Institute Annual Convention in Long Beach, California on June 13, 1999, he spoke about this exponential growth. In the past 5 years, approximately $70 billion of business was conducted on the Internet. Platt estimated that $2.7 trillion of business would be done via the Internet between 1999 and 2004. Platt emphasized that by 2003, 10% of all U.S. business would be conducted over the Internet.

The Current Situation and Industry Trends

Hewlett-Packard's main geographic offices are located in Cupertino, CA, Geneva, Switzerland, and Hong Kong with suboffices and manufacturing facilities in Colorado, Delaware, Oregon, Texas, Washington, Idaho, and Utah. International facilities include Canada, France, Germany, India, China, Japan, Malaysia, Ireland, Netherlands, United Kingdom, Korea, Taiwan, and Israel.[13]

Hewlett-Packard's computer business, which constituted 84% of revenues, included personal computers, servers, workstations, and printers. Additionally, they provided service and support in each area. Their servers and workstations run both HP's version of the Unix operating system and Windows NT. Unix sales have lagged in recent years, but printer sales remained a strong point. HP was especially well known for its position in the printer market with the popular HP LaserJet and DeskJet family of printers. Hewlett-Packard dominates the printer market despite very aggressive pricing from competitors such as Lexmark. Printers were 1 area where the HP brand name appeared to dominate.

While enjoying annual revenue growth in the 20% range in the mid-1990s, growth slowed significantly in 1998 and 1999. Really facing a somewhat uncertain future, HP suffered through months of sluggish growth after the burgeoning mid 1990s, all of which placed tremendous pressure on Lew Platt. After all, the country was still in 1 of the largest bull markets in American history, yet HP was stagnating. Faced with inconsistent financial performance, HP needed a jump start and a strong sense of direction.

Hewlett-Packard's industry is one that demands constant change and innovation. Market share and customer base may be easily lost if the company cannot keep up with ever-changing demand. Furthermore, product life cycles are short and investment commitments are generally long term. Often management will have to accept the risk and move forward on a particular path while still uncertain about the outcome. Such decisions involve large capital investments. Transition from 1 product to another must be smooth and with 36,000 products in the business, HP faces enormous challenges to maintain the competitive edge in the marketplace.

Inventory management is complex and requires constant updating to maintain accurate database control.

Hewlett-Packard uses third-party distributors to market and sell their products, especially personal computers and printers. The reliance on these third-party vendors is significant and HP is reliant on the financial strength of each distributor to maximize market access. While the company has maintained third-party distributorship to accommodate changing customer preferences, Fiorina realizes there are risks inherent in this decision.

Hewlett-Packard relies heavily on patent, copyright, and trade secret laws in the United States and around the world, as well as agreements with employees, partners, and customers to establish and maintain proprietary intellectual property rights for technology and products. Since intellectual property provides companies such as HP with significant competitive advantage, it is critical these rights not be violated. Clearly, management faces substantial costs if such a violation would occur and must protect intangible and intellectual property as much as possible.

Over half of Hewlett-Packard's revenues are generated outside of the United States. Additionally, significant manufacturing occurs abroad. In this light, Hewlett-Packard must carefully watch international issues such as other country's political and economic conditions, trade protection measures, import or export licensing requirements, multinational tax structures, regulatory requirements, different technology standards, foreign currency exchange rate risk, as well as unavoidable natural disasters.

Gordon Moore, founder of Intel, was the first to quantify the speed of improvement and the microprocessor. In what became known as Moore's Law, he has shown how the functionality and performance of a microprocessor and similar technology doubles roughly every 18 months. While the speed of change may present its own problems, there are significant business opportunities for Hewlett-Packard because of the new challenges in the computer and peripheral market not to mention electronic commerce. In this environment, invention must remain a top priority and HP must fund their research labs. It is common for businesses to decrease the funds allocated to research and development during economic downturns since much of these expenditures are intangible. HP cannot afford to do this; rather it must do the opposite. Research funding must remain a top priority for management because of the sheer speed of product improvement.

The Repositioning of Hewlett-Packard

In her October 1, 1999, presentation to security analysts, Fiorina outlined what was working well for HP and what areas needed improvement. She first mentioned printers and imaging products, noting that color LaserJets had done especially well over the past year. Increased market share in this area was an important focus point. Also faring well was the PC business, both home and business. Market share was improved in Europe and in the Asia-Pacific. Previously weak, the Unix server line was doing much better in Europe and Asia. Finally, Fiorina noted increased strength in e-services.

When discussing areas of concern, Fiorina first spoke of North American sales of the Unix server product line. To improve sales in this area, HP recently changed their compensation system for the North American sales staff and planned to implement an incentive-based compensation system in November 1999. She felt this system would work better than the salary structure many were used to and would reward and provide direction for top performers.

Second, Fiorina discussed the earthquake in Taiwan in mid-1999. While this was not an event HP could control, it had a significant impact on revenue since many of the semiconductor products were manufactured in the now destroyed facilities. This situation created a backlog problem for HP and their competitors alike. Fiorina noted the disruption was temporary, albeit significant for 1999.[14]

> Hewlett-Packard was started over 60 years ago as a company of inventors. Today, they are reinventing themselves again. They also believe the future knows no limits and guiding this vision is a CEO who perfectly represents the bold and groundbreaking spirit. If her new position makes headlines, and yes, even history, it's the history she's about to make that is the most exciting thing of all.
>
> Eric Chappt, Chairman and CEO, Ziff Davis
> Introducing Carly Fiorina as a speaker at COMDEX, November 15, 1999

Hewlett-Packard faces aggressive competition in all areas of business. Competitors range from the large, multinational firms like Compaq and Dell to small, high technology specialized start-ups that sought a competitive edge in 1 or 2 product lines. Product life cycles are short, which forces constant innovation at HP. Furthermore, the consumer base is price sensitive, which can easily cut into profit margins.

> In the last quarter, HP did a good job increasing unit shipment of its Unix servers—they were up 16%. But because of price pressures, revenue increased only 5%.
>
> Kelly Sprang, Industry Analyst, Technology Business Group[15]

Fiorina faced a challenge unlike what she had faced earlier with Lucent. She successfully took Lucent public for over $3 billion, now she needed to define Hewlett-Packard in the Internet age. Unlike previous technological advances, the Internet age promised to be different. Successfully taming this animal meant reaching out to consumers with products that use the Internet. The future of information technology was to bring information technology to the masses, not the select.

The Financial Situation

Fiorina saw HP's respect and service to customers and the community as the shining soul of the company—so much so that she believed it was this that provided HP with its competitive edge.[16] Analysts have had concern about HP's asset intensity compared to many of their competitors. Wayman noted that 1 benefit from spinning off Agilent would be to gain 2 distinct business models. Capital expenditures dropped in 1999 when Agilent was taken out of the equation. Balance Sheet, Income Statement, Statement of Cash Flows, and Selected Industry Ratios are shown in **Exhibits 4, 5, 6,** and **7** respectively. **Exhibit 8** shows the stock price history from January 1998 through the spin-off in November 1999. Wall Street rewarded HP with an appreciating stock price through October 1999, when the price dropped because management stated they might not make analysts' earnings estimates for the year ending October 31. Additionally, Agilent Technologies was receiving much media attention as the largest Silicon Valley initial public offering in history, scheduled the next month. After the spin-off, HP's employee base dropped from 123,000 to 85,000.

Immediate goals for HP included aggressive profitable growth and increased consistency of financial results. Fiorina also planned to work hard to improve the total customer experience, which, if done successfully, should transfer to the bottom line. HP would also have to aggressively seek to improve U.S. sales of its Unix server line. In his address to security analysts, CFO Robert Wayman commented that the "New" HP would be more focused on growth by

- Defending and growing our key printing and server businesses.
- Investing in carefully chosen growth opportunities.
- Continuing to demand and reward superior performance.
- Accelerating key operational initiatives.
- Eliminating redundant activities.[17]

Exhibit 4

Hewlett-Packard Balance Sheets, 1989–1999

(Dollar amounts in millions)

	1999	1998	1997	1996	1995	1994	1993	1992	1991	1990	1989
Assets											
Cash and equivalents	$ 5,590	$ 4,067	$ 4,569	$ 3,327	$ 2,616	$ 2,478	$ 1,644	$ 1,035	$ 1,120	$ 1,077	$ 926
Net receivables	7,847	7,752	8,173	7,126	6,735	5,028	4,208	3,497	2,976	2,883	2,494
Inventories	4,863	6,184	6,763	6,401	6,013	4,273	3,691	2,605	2,273	2,092	1,947
Other current assets	3,342	3,581	1,442	1,137	875	730	693	542	347	458	364
Total current assets	$21,642	$21,584	$20,947	$17,991	$16,239	$12,509	$10,236	$ 7,679	$ 6,716	$ 6,510	$ 5,731
Gross plant, property, and equipment	8,920	12,570	11,776	10,198	8,747	7,938	7,527	6,592	5,961	5,565	4,982
Accumulated depreciation	4,587	6,212	5,464	4,662	4,036	3,610	3,347	2,943	2,616	2,364	2,089
Net plant, property, and equipment	$ 4,333	$ 6,358	$ 6,312	$ 5,536	$ 4,711	$ 4,328	$ 4,180	$ 3,649	$ 3,345	$ 3,201	$ 2,893
Intangibles	189	174	165	288	398	528	623	620	0	0	403
Other assets	9,133	5,557	4,325	3,884	3,079	2,202	1,697	1,752	1,912	1,684	1,048
Total assets	$35,297	$33,673	$31,749	$27,699	$24,427	$19,567	$16,736	$13,700	$11,973	$11,395	$10,075
Liabilities											
Long term debt due in one year	$ 468	$ 1,007	$ 254	$ 85	$ 0	$ 0	$ 20	$ 36	$ 24	$ 387	$ 51
Notes payable	2,637	238	972	2,040	3,214	2,469	2,170	1,348	1,177	1,509	1,290
Accounts payable	3,517	3,203	3,185	2,375	2,422	1,466	1,223	925	686	660	642
Taxes payable	2,152	2,796	1,515	1,514	1,494	1,245	922	490	381	257	309
Accrued expenses	2,823	4,776	4,141	3,658	3,032	2,452	2,026	1,846	1,420	1,283	1,195
Other current liabilities	2,724	1,453	1,152	951	782	598	507	449	375	347	256
Total current liabilities	$14,321	$13,473	$11,219	$10,623	$10,944	$ 8,230	$ 6,868	$ 5,094	$ 4,063	$ 4,443	$ 3,743
Long term debt	$ 1,764	$ 2,063	$ 3,158	$ 2,579	$ 663	$ 547	$ 667	$ 425	$ 188	$ 139	$ 474
Deferred taxes	NA	NA	NA	NA	NA	NA	31	49	243	261	248
Other liabilities	917	1,218	1,217	1,059	981	864	659	633	210	189	164
Total liabilities	$17,002	$16,754	$15,594	$14,261	$12,588	$ 9,641	$ 8,225	$ 6,201	$ 4,704	$ 5,032	$ 4,629
Equity											
Common stock	$ 10	$ 10	$ 1,041	$ 1,014	$ 510	$ 255	$ 253	$ 251	$ 252	$ 244	$ 238
Capital surplus	0	0	146	0	361	778	684	623	758	495	221
Retained earnings	18,285	16,909	14,968	12,424	10,968	8,893	7,574	6,625	6,259	5,624	4,987
Total equity	$18,295	$16,919	$16,155	$13,438	$11,839	$ 9,926	$ 8,511	$ 7,499	$ 7,269	$ 6,363	$ 5,446
Total liabilities and equity	$35,297	$33,673	$31,749	$27,699	$24,427	$19,567	$16,736	$13,700	$11,973	$11,395	$10,075
Number of shares outstanding (mil.)	1,005	1,015	1,041	1,014	1,020	1,019	1,011	1,003	1,006	976	951

Source: Standard & Poor's Compustat database.

Exhibit 5

Hewlett-Packard Income Statement, 1989–1999
(Dollar amounts in millions, except per share data)

	1999	1998	1997	1996	1995	1994	1993	1992	1991	1990	1989
Sales	$42,370	$47,061	$42,895	$38,420	$31,519	$24,991	$20,317	$16,410	$14,494	$13,233	$11,899
Cost of goods sold	28,404	29,943	26,763	24,202	18,875	14,484	11,380	8,519	7,253	6,505	5,673
Gross profit	$13,966	$17,118	$16,132	$14,218	$12,644	$10,507	$8,937	$7,891	$7,241	$6,728	$6,226
SG&A expense	8,962	11,148	10,237	9,195	7,937	6,952	6,315	5,785	5,351	5,078	4,596
Operating income before depreciation	$5,004	$5,970	$5,895	$5,023	$4,707	$3,555	$2,622	$2,106	$1,890	$1,650	$1,630
Depreciation and amortization	1,316	1,869	1,556	1,297	1,139	1,006	743	596	555	488	435
Operating profit	$3,688	$4,101	$4,339	$3,726	$3,568	$2,549	$1,879	$1,510	$1,335	$1,162	$1,195
Interest expense	202	235	215	327	206	155	121	96	130	172	126
Non-operating income/expense	708	485	331	295	270	29	25	48	72	66	91
Special items	0	(260)	0	0	0	0	0	(137)	(150)	0	(9)
Pretax income	$4,194	$4,091	$4,455	$3,694	$3,632	$2,423	$1,783	$1,325	$1,127	$1,056	$1,151
Total income taxes	1,090	1,146	1,336	1,108	1,199	824	606	444	372	317	322
Income before extraordinary Items and discontinued operations	$3,104	$2,945	$3,119	$2,586	$2,433	$1,599	$1,177	$881	$755	$739	$829
Extraordinary items	0	0	0	0	0	0	0	0	0	0	0
Discontinued operations	387	0	0	0	0	0	0	(332)	0	0	0
Net income	$3,491	$2,945	$3,119	$2,586	$2,433	$1,599	$1,177	$549	$755	$739	$829
Earnings per share basic — excluding extra items & disc op	3	3	3	2	2	2	1	1	1	1	1
Earnings per share basic — including extra items & disc op	3	3	3	2	2	2	1	1	1	1	1
Earnings per share diluted — excluding extra items & disc op	3	3	3	2	2	2	1	1	1	1	1
Earnings per share diluted — including extra items & disc op	3	3	3	2	2	2	1	1	1	1	1
EPS basic from operations	3	3	3	2	2	2	1	1	1	1	1
EPS diluted from ops	3	3	3	2	2	2	1	1	1	1	1
Dividends per share	1	1	1	0	0	0	0	0	0	0	0
Common shares for basic EPS	1,009	1,034	1,057	1,052	1,052	1,042	1,013	1,010	1,001	967	942
Common shares for diluted EPS	1,052	1,072	NA	NA	NA	NA	NA	NA	NA	NA	NA
Closing stock price, October 31	$74.19	$60.25	$61.63	$44.13	$92.63	$97.88	$73.63	$56.88	$50.38	$26.00	$47.75

Source: Standard & Poor's Compustat database.

Exhibit 6

Hewlett-Packard Statement of Cash Flows, 1989–1999
(Dollar amounts in millions)

	1999	1998	1997	1996	1995	1994	1993	1992	1991	1990	1989
Indirect operating activities											
Income before extraordinary items	$3,104	$2,945	$3,119	$2,586	$2,433	$1,599	$1,177	$881	$755	$739	$829
Depreciation and amortization	1,316	1,869	1,556	1,297	1,139	1,006	846	673	624	566	462
Extraordinary items and discontinued operations	(62)	0	0	0	0	0	0	0	0	0	0
Deferred taxes	(171)	(1,263)	(232)	(284)	(102)	(156)	(137)	(35)	(41)	78	(6)
Funds from operations—other	0	0	(249)	(94)	(220)	57	86	(69)	48	(43)	(181)
Receivables—decrease (increase)	(1,637)	(1,019)	(752)	(293)	(1,696)	(848)	(709)	(480)	(117)	(409)	(385)
Inventory—decrease (increase)	(171)	563	(279)	(356)	(1,740)	(582)	(1,056)	(267)	(181)	(145)	(324)
Accounts payable & accrued Liabilities—inc (decrease)	751	1	775	(55)	956	243	283	226	26	18	134
Income taxes—accrued—Increase (decrease)	(639)	1,216	(63)	102	180	320	452	31	124	(52)	(130)
Other assets and liabilities—Net change	543	1,130	446	553	663	585	200	328	314	47	97
Operating activities—net cash flow	3,034	5,442	4,321	3,456	1,613	2,224	1,142	1,288	1,552	799	496
Investing activities											
(−)Investments—increase	$8	$762	$0	$734	$308	$332	$22	$53	$394	$157	$0
(+)Sale of investments	0	0	0	0	0	47	22	4	145	6	0
(+)Short-term investments—change	41	1,476	(1,055)	422	478	(366)	(351)	101	(466)	11	116
(−)Capital expenditures	1,134	1,997	2,338	2,201	1,601	1,257	1,405	1,032	862	955	857
(+)Sale of property, plant, and	542	413	333	316	294	291	215	183	163	159	120
(−)equipment acquisitions	0	0	0	0	0	62	86	411	0	0	486
(+)Investing activities—other	(69)	75	48	22	(38)	69	23	(58)	0	(30)	(45)
(=)Investing activities—net cash flow	(628)	(795)	(3,012)	(2,175)	(1,175)	(1,610)	(1,604)	(1,266)	(1,414)	(966)	(1,152)
Financing activities											
(+)Sale of common and preferred stock	$660	$467	$419	$363	$361	$300	$308	$293	$251	$220	$223
(−)Purchase of common and preferred stock	2,643	2,424	724	1,089	686	325	314	530	79	0	140
(−)Cash dividends	650	625	532	450	358	280	228	183	120	102	85
(+)Long-term debt—issuance	240	223	1,182	1,989	434	64	387	309	131	90	31
(−)Long-term debt—reduction	1,047	580	273	0	0	0	0	0	(778)	0	0
(+)Current debt—changes	2,399	(734)	(1,194)	(1,178)	423	91	579	107	5	111	704
(+)Financing activities—other	0	0	0	(4)	4	4	(22)	(2)	0	19	15
(=)Financing activities—net cash flow	(1,041)	(3,673)	(1,122)	(369)	178	(146)	710	(6)	(590)	338	748
Cash and equivalents—change	1,365	974	187	912	616	468	248	16	(452)	171	92
Direct operating activities											
Interest paid—net	$1,866	$205	$325	$267	$187	$143	$109	$84	$137	$162	$108
Income taxes paid	224	1,039	1,488	1,159	1,058	626	293	459	335	283	484

Source: Standard & Poor's Compustat database.

Exhibit 7

Selected Industry Financial Ratios

Ratio	Formula	Industry
Liquidity		
Current	$\dfrac{\text{Current assets}}{\text{Current liabilities}}$	1.24
Quick	$\dfrac{\text{Current assets} - \text{Inventory}}{\text{Current liabilities}}$	0.75
Asset Management		
Inventory Turnover	Sales/Inventory	4.65
Days Sales Outstanding	Receivables/(Annual sales/360)	77.00
Fixed Asset Turnover	Sales/Net fixed assets	4.79
Total Asset Turnover	Sales/Total assets	1.32
Debt Management		
Total Debt to Assets	Total liabilities/Total assets	37.74%
Times Interest Charged	Operating profit/ Interest changes	4.68
Profitability		
Profit Margin on Sales	Net income/Sales	2.27%
Return on Assets	Net income/Total assets	3.30%
Return on Equity	Net income/Total equity	5.55%
Market Value		
Price to Earnings	Price per share/Earnings per share	18.5

Source: Industry data from Standard & Poor's Compustat database, 1999 edition.

Exhibit 8

Hewlett-Packard Closing Stock Prices:
January 2, 1998, through November 2, 1999

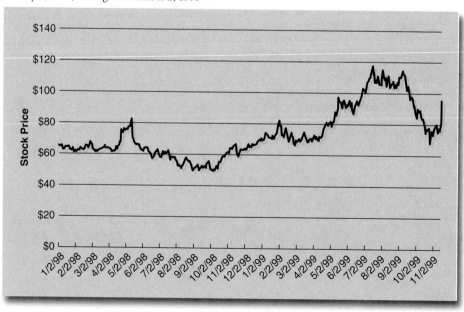

Finally, Wayman commented that the initial ratios would likely reflect the diseconomies caused by developing 2 separate infrastructures, but HP planned to offset some of these expenses with reduced infrastructure costs in information technology, operations procurement, human resources, as well as real estate and site services. Financial management must also manage risk by carefully hedging with derivatives, covering exposed positions, and holding a diversified portfolio.

Marketing

Hewlett-Packard was not known for its marketing expertise. Rather than be vocal about their products and services, HP tended to be modest and unassuming, a strategy that caused the company to slip in world markets. The company was reactive rather than proactive, defensive rather than offensive. Recently, the company had begun to consolidate their sales and challenge management activities to focus on emerging markets and better capitalize on their growth. For example, in electronic commerce, HP merged with Verifone in a $1.3 billion stock-for-stock transfer. The intent of this agreement was to leverage the power of the Internet to offer new products and services.[18] Fiorina referred to the early marketing programs as modest and unassuming, and indicated the need to become more vocal about the company's abilities.[19]

Fiorina planned to institute a $200 million brand campaign in December 1999 to promote the spirit of HP. Since many of their competitors appeared to do a much better job of tooting their horns, Fiorina set out to improve HP's marketing program. The goal was to reinvigorate and relaunch the HP brand name in the marketplace as a symbol of a new, energized company that is moving forward into the new millennium, rather than stagnating. The essence of the campaign went back to the "Rules of the Garage" where Bill Hewlett and Dave Packard started in 1939. The campaign was designed to be a reminder of the inventive capability of the employees. Fiorina set out to build an organization where roles and responsibilities are clear, but there is also a strong demand for interdependence and collaboration. The spirit she intended to present was that the company and its people were unbeatable by leveraging the human resource capabilities the company had.

Carly Fiorina: Reinventing the HP Way

One of Fiorina's first decisions was to change the salary structure for HP salespeople. She instituted pay for performance rather than set salary, a move that pleased analysts such as Michael Kwatinetz of Credit Suisse First Boston Advisory Partner. "Let's face it: if you're an aggressive salesperson and you think you can blow out your numbers, you want to work in a place where you'll be rewarded for that."[20] A new logo was adopted in November 1999 consisting of a single lower case word, "invent" by the lowercase graphic of the initials "hp." The intent of this logo was partially to remind employees, customers, and investors of the company's creative roots and frugal beginnings.

Fiorina promoted Duane Zitzner to President and CEO of HP's Computer Products, leading the company's Unix and NT server products, enterprise storage, and software initiatives. She kept Ann Livermore as a strong ally by leaving her in charge of all e-service initiatives as well as HP's services, financing, and consulting businesses.

Ann Livermore, Chief Executive and President of HP's Enterprise Computing Solution commented, "Quality of service will be 1 key factor in whether a company wins or loses on the Internet. The companies that win have technical innovation and business model innovation. We're creating loyalty to HP when we help businesses create their wealth."[21]

Fiorina made aggressive revenue and earnings growth goals of 12 to 15% for fiscal year 2000. She made it clear that she wanted to reopen Hewlett and Packard's garage philosophy and reminded staffers that the founders "didn't operate a democracy and they made very fast decisions."

Separation for Hewlett-Packard and Formation of Agilent Technologies

Hewlett-Packard wanted to revitalize its stifled business. On March 2, 1999, the company announced a strategic realignment that would essentially spin-off the Test and Measurement division of the business while maintaining the computing divisions. Test and Measurement, with an estimated $7.6 billion in annual sales, or 16% of revenues, consisted of several business lines including Chemical Analysis, Healthcare Solutions, and Semiconductors and would go public in November 1999 as Agilent Technologies. The new company went unnamed for 4 months as Hewlett-Packard attempted to realign with a new "HP Way," one that would and could keep up with the lightning fast speed of change. At the same time, Lew Platt announced that he would retire after the spin-off, allowing a new chief executive to start with the revitalized Hewlett-Packard. Hewlett-Packard would continue to focus on computing, imaging, and peripherals, and the new company would take the other business units and operate independently of Hewlett-Packard. Hewlett-Packard believed this transition would allow better focus on the remaining businesses since growth rates had slowed significantly since the mid 1990s. The stock market reacted cautiously to this news with HP earning a modest gain of 19¢ on the day of the announcement to close at $68.81.

In 1966, when HP entered the computer business, few would have believed the company would 1 day split and the HP name would go with the computer business rather than Test and Measurement. It was 25 years after the introductions of the HP 3000 series that HP would formally reorganize and acknowledge the computer division to be its core business.[22] Times change; technology changes even faster. Hewlett-Packard opted to spin off the Test and Measurement division to enable the remaining HP businesses to place greater strategic focus on core computing, imaging, and printing businesses. As with any major change, however, it remained uncertain as to whether or not HP would retain all the benefits the company perceived. In other words, would they regret the decision to realign, or would they gain from the decision? The key to that issue was only to become available as the future unraveled.

When asked about the spin-off, Fiorina spoke in favor of it.

> Focus is crucial for a company, especially a large one. I believe it was a wise decision to spin off Agilent—making up HP's former test and measurement, medical products, chemical analysis and semiconductor businesses. What continues under the HP name—computers, printing and imaging products, information technology services and software—has a rich history in innovation, outstanding people and technologies, and world-class partnerships. We're confident both companies will be able to innovate better and faster as separate entities. And there's no reason we can't partner on certain things.
>
> Carly Fiorina, President and CEO, HP[23]

Historically, Hewlett-Packard tended to have slowdowns every 6 to 7 years, usually matching the business cycle. However, the Internet revolution presents a much more radical shift in the way HP will need to operate. It is about speed, agility, and the ability to change direction. The Internet economy provides a lot of uncertainty, which makes 5- to 10-year business plans difficult and of limited value. While the core of HP did not need significant change, the HP Way could hamper progress. While the HP Way made the company successful, it also could hamper growth, especially as the HP moves into the new millennium. The HP Way does not promote the change that would be necessary in the Internet revolution. HP was reluctant to take risks, and carefully calculated risks were exactly what HP would need to undertake to succeed. HP would need to grow faster, sell more, and do so more profitably. Not an easy task for managers used to the HP Way.

> Ten years may sound like a lot in "Internet time," but it's not in reality—not when you're talking about something as fundamental as replacing a technology, like silicon, that will finally reach its physical and financial limits. You've got to start now or risk being left behind or missing out altogether. Basically high-tech companies have to do both: continue their efforts to extend current technologies, and to work on "disruptive" technologies that show great promise for the future. There are very few companies in the world that have the resources to do both successfully. HP is 1 of them.

> Carly Fiorina, President and CEO, HP[24]

The Future of Hewlett-Packard: To Keep the Best ... and the Rest?

With a bachelor's degree in medieval history and philosophy from Stanford, an MBA from the University of Maryland and an MS degree from MIT, 20 years of experience in the communications industry, 2 years heading *Fortune* magazine's list of the most powerful women in America, Fiorina accepted the challenge to reinvent Hewlett-Packard. She moved quickly to institute changes immediately upon her arrival. She utilized HP talent and expected her people to work as hard as she did. After 4 months on the job, HP announced they had narrowly beat analysts' earnings estimates for the fourth quarter 1999, which ended on October 31, 1999. On November 18, 1999, HP announced that net income for the last quarter rose 7% to $760 million or 73¢ per diluted share from the $710 million of 68¢ per diluted share from the same quarter in 1998. The financial results excluded those of the spun-off Test and Measurement division, Agilent Technologies, and were a pleasant boost to Fiorina's fifth month on the job. Y2K problems remained a concern, as did the uncertainty about the success of Fiorina's changes yet to be fully implemented. However, she appeared to be off to a cautiously optimistic start. "Pieces are in place, there are no holes in the solution, but mindshare counts for a lot," commented Tony Iams, Senior Analyst, D. H. Brown Associates.[25]

The spin-off of the Test and Measurement Division, to be known as Agilent Technologies, posed certain risks for HP shareholders. The spin-off allowed HP shareholders to retain 84% ownership in Agilent Technologies. Agilent was scheduled to go public in November 1999 and distribute the 84% ownership to HP shareholders in June 2000. Since stock prices can fluctuate wildly, especially around an initial public offering (IPO), there was considerable uncertainty as to the value HP shareholders would receive in June 2000.

> Exponential growth is based on the principle that the state of change is proportional to the level of effort expended. The level of effort will be far greater in the twenty-first century than it has been in the twentieth century.

> Bill Hewlett
> Cofounder Hewlett-Packard[26]

Where does the future lie for HP? Hewlett-Packard must work hard to capitalize in e-services and digital imaging while continuing to aggressively defend and develop their core business. The company needs to maintain and grow its positions as a global provider of computing and imaging solutions, but must focus heavily on the opportunities the Internet provides with the proliferation of e-business and e-services. The Asia-Pacific region remained a concern as did the struggling Unix server lines. Marketing would be revamped. E-services would be revolutionized. If they can do that and earn more, faster, and more efficiently, they will succeed. Otherwise, Fiorina may find it difficult to justify her $65 million in stock options to an employee base many of whom she demands work on a pay-for-performance basis.

> . . . see your life as a journey, pause at moments like this to see life's markers and the patterns that emerge, know yourself, be true to yourself, engage your whole self in everything you do. Remember that leadership is not in fact about you, but about the people you are trying to inspire by unleashing their talents, their hopes, their aspirations. Remember that leadership comes in small acts as well as bold strokes. And last, if technology is your passion, then make sure people are at the heart of your endeavors. And finally, remember that throughout this journey, the only limits that really matter are the ones that you place on yourself, and that those crucial moments of your life, when you know what you need to, but others advise against what they perceive to be a detour from your path, know yourself, trust your whole self, and don't blink.

> Carly Fiorina[27]

Blinking would not allow Hewlett-Packard to regain its power, grow to its potential, maximize e-service, or grow at 12 to 15% in 2000. Blinking was not an option for Carly in November 1999.

Notes

1. HP World, San Francisco, August 17, 1999. Carly Fiorina's incoming speech as President and CEO of Hewlett Packard.
2. Presentation to Security Analysts, July 19, 1999.
3. Marketguide at <yahoo.marketguide.com>
4. "Wake-Up Call for HP," *Technology Review 103*, no. 3 (May/June 2000), pp. 94–100.
5. "Best Practices at Hewlett-Packard," *Dealerscope 42*, no. 3 (March 2000), p. 57.
6. Lew Platt speech, Managing Innovation: An Oxymoron?, Speech at Yale University Sheffield School, February 28, 1997.
7. *Ibid.*
8. Hewlett Packard Corporate Objectives, Corporate Literature, 1996.
9. Peter Burrows and Peter Elstrom, "The Boss," *Business Week* (August 2, 1999), pp. 76–84.
10. David P. Hamilton, "Dell Beat Compaq in 3rd-Period U.S. PC Sales," *Wall Street Journal* (October 25, 1999), pp. A3, A10.
11. Eric Nee, "Lew Platt: Why I Dismembered HP," *Fortune 139*, no. 6 (March 29, 2000), pp. 167–70.
12. Hal Lancaster, "Managing Your Career: An Ex-CEO Reflects: H-P's Platt Regrets He Wasn't a Rebel," *Wall Street Journal* (November 16, 1999), p. B1.
13. *Moody's Industrial Manual*, Volume 1 (1999), pp. 3579–3580.
14. Carly Fiorina's Presentation to Security Analysts, October 1, 1999.
15. Paul Korzenowski, "Hewlett Packard's Makeover Starts Turning Heads," *Informationweek* no. 761 (November 15, 1999), pp. 189–192.
16. "Wake-Up Call for HP," *Technology Review 103*, no. 3 (May/June 2000), pp. 94–100.
17. Robert Wayman, Executive Vice President and CFO, Presentation to Security Analysts, September 21, 1999.
18. Standard & Poor's Compustat database, 1999 edition.
19. Christina Torode, "CRN Business Close-Up: An Interview with Carly Fiorina—Hewlett Packard," *Computer Reseller* no. 863, (October 11, 1999), p. 176.
20. *Ibid.*
21. *Ibid.*
22. Leslie Goff, "HP's Radical Move," *Computerworld 33*, no. 18 (May 3, 1999), p. 80.
23. "Wake-Up Call for HP," *Technology Review 103*, no. 3 (May/June 2000), pp. 94–100.
24. *Ibid.*
25. *Ibid.*
26. Tim Gouldson, "Realignment: The HP Way," *Canadian Electronics 14*, no. 3 (May 1999), p. 6.
27. Commencement Address, Massachusetts Institute of Technology (June 2, 2000)

CASE 16

Harley-Davidson, Inc.: The 95th Anniversary

Thomas L. Wheelen, Kathryn E. Wheelen, Thomas L. Wheelen II, and Richard D. Wheelen

On March 5, 1998, the Committee of the 95th Celebration met to discuss the route kickoffs for Canada, Mexico, the United States, and Latin America. The starting cities for the United States motorcycle routes were: Riverside, CA (June 2); Dallas, TX (June 5); Orlando, FL (June 5); York, PA (June 5); and Spokane, WA (June 3). The Canadian, Mexican, and Latin American starting cities were: Dartmouth, Nova Scotia (June 3); Vancouver, British Columbia (June 3); Edmonton, Alberta (June 4); Ottawa, Ontario (June 5); Mexico City, Mexico (June 1); and Miami, FL (June 5). **Exhibit 1** shows the motorcycle routes for the United States participants. The riders were to meet on June 9 in Milwaukee. Over 100,000 were expected to participate in the 95th celebration on June 13. An analyst said, "this is the ultimate in customer loyalty." At the end of the meeting, the committee for the analysis of new competition was to meet to discuss how their individual research was progressing.

History[1]

In 1903, William Harley (age 21), a draftsman, and his friend, Arthur R. Davidson, began experimenting with ideas to design and build their own motorcycles. They were joined by Arthur's brothers, William, a machinist, and Walter, a skilled mechanic. The Harley-Davidson Motor Company started in a 10 × 15 foot shed in the Davidson family's backyard in Milwaukee, Wisconsin.

In 1903, 3 motorcycles were built and sold. The production increased to 8 in 1904. The company then moved to Juneau Avenue, which is the site of the company's present offices. In 1907, the company was incorporated.

In 1969, AMF Inc., a leisure and industrial product conglomerate, acquired Harley-Davidson. The management team expanded production from 15,000 in 1969 to 40,000 motorcycles in 1974. AMF favored short-term profits instead of investing in research and development and retooling. During this time, Japanese competitors continued to improve the quality of their motorcycles, while Harley-Davidson began to turn out noisy, oil-leaking, heavily

This case was prepared by Professor Thomas L. Wheelen of the University of South Florida, Kathryn E. Wheelen, Thomas L. Wheelen II, and Richard D. Wheelen of Wheelen Associates. This case may not be reproduced in any form without the written permission of the copyright holder, Thomas L. Wheelen. This case was edited for SMBP-8th Edition. Copyright © 1998 by Thomas L. Wheelen. Reprinted by permission.

Exhibit 1

Motorcycle Routes for the 95th anniversary Celebration in Milwaukee: Harley-Davidson, Inc.

Source: Harley-Davidson, Inc., *1997 Annual Report*, pp. 75–76.

vibrating, poorly finished, and hard-to-handle machines. AMF ignored the Japanese competition. In 1975, Honda Motor Company introduced its "Gold Wing," which became the standard for large touring motorcycles. Harley-Davidson had controlled this segment of the market for years. There was a $2,000 price differential between Harley's top-of-the-line motorcycles and Honda's comparable Gold Wing. This caused American buyers of motorcycles to start switching to Japanese motorcycles. The Japanese companies (Suzuki and Yamaha) from this time until the middle 1980s continued to enter the heavyweight custom market with Harley lookalikes.

During AMF's ownership of the company, sales of motorcycles were strong, but profits were weak. The company had serious problems with poor quality manufacturing and strong Japanese competition. In 1981, Vaughn Beals, then head of the Harley Division, and 13 other managers conducted a leveraged buyout of the company for $65 million.

New management installed a Materials As Needed (MAN) system to reduce inventories and stabilize the production schedule. Also, this system forced production to work with marketing for more accurate forecasts. This led to precise production schedules for each month, allowing only a 10% variance. The company forced its suppliers to increase their quality in order to reduce customer complaints.

The management team invested in research and development. Management purchased a Computer-Aided Design (CAD) system that allowed the company to make changes in the entire product line and still maintain its traditional styling. These investments by management had a quick payoff in that the break-even point went from 53,000 motorcycles in 1982 to 35,000 in 1986.

In June 1993, over 100,000 members of the worldwide Harley-Davidson family came home (Milwaukee) to celebrate the company's 90th anniversary. Willie G. Davidson, Vice President—Styling, grandson of the founder, said, "I was overwhelmed with emotion when our parade was rolling into downtown Milwaukee. I looked up to heaven and told the founding fathers, 'Thanks, guys.'"[2]

During 1993, the company acquired a 49% interest in Buell Motorcycle Company, a manufacturer of sport/performance motorcycles. This investment in Buell offered the company the possibility of gradually gaining entry into select niches within the performance motorcycle market. In 1998, Harley-Davidson owned most of the stock in Buell. Buell began distribution of a limited number of Buell motorcycles during 1994 to select Harley-Davidson dealers. Buell sales were:

Year	Sales	Units
1994	$ 6 million	576
1995	$14 million	1,407
1996	$23 million	2,762
1997	$40 million	4,415

Buell's mission "is to develop and employ innovative technology to enhance 'the ride' and give Buell owners a motorcycle experience that no other brand can provide." The European sport/performance market was 4 times larger than its U.S. counterpart. In 1997, there were 377 Buell dealers worldwide. In February 1998, Buell motorcycles placed first and third in the inaugural Pro Thunder series of racing; Buell had been racing motorcycles since 1996. The Buell motorcycles were priced at $5,245 and $8,399.

On November 14, 1995, the company acquired substantially all of the common stock and common stock equivalents of Eaglemark Financial Services, Inc., a company in which it held a 49% interest since 1993. Eaglemark provided credit to leisure product manufacturers, their dealers, and customers in the United States and Canada. The transaction was accounted for as a step acquisition under the purchase method. The purchase price for the shares and equivalents was approximately $45 million, which was paid from internally generated funds and short-term borrowings. The excess of the acquisition cost over the fair value of the net assets purchased resulted in approximately $43 million of goodwill, which was amortized on a straight-line basis over 20 years.

On January 22, 1996, the company announced its strategic decision to discontinue the operations of the Transportation Vehicles segment in order to concentrate its financial and human resources on its core motorcycle business. The Transportation Vehicles segment comprised the Recreational Vehicles division (Holliday Rambler trailers), the Commercial Vehicles division (small delivery vehicles), and B & B Molders, a manufacturer of custom or standard tooling and injection-molded plastic pieces. During 1996, the company completed the sale of the Transportation Vehicles segment for an aggregate sales price of approximately $105 million; approximately $100 million in cash and $5 million in notes and preferred stock.[3]

In the fall of 1997, GT Bicycles manufactured and distributed a 1,000 Harley Limited Edition at a list retail price of $1,700. The pedal-powered bike had a real Harley paint job, signature fenders, a fake gas tank, and chrome of a Harley Softail motorcycle. GT Bicycles manufactured the Velo Glide bikes and was licensed by Harley to produce the limited version. The 4-speed bike weighed 40-plus pounds. Ken Alder, cycle shop owner, said, "It's a big clunker that no one would really want to ride." Nevertheless, the bicycles sold out in less than 4 months to buyers. The resale price for the Limited Edition jumped to $3,500, and 1 collector advertised his for $5,000. In contrast, a person could purchase an actual Harley XHL 883 Sportster motorcycle for $5,245.[4]

Corporate Governance

BOARD OF DIRECTORS

The Board of Directors consisted of 10 members, of which 3 were internal members—Richard E. Teerlink, Chairman; Jeffrey E. Bleustein, President and Chief Executive Officer (CEO); and Vaughn L. Beals, Jr., Chairman Emeritus (see **Exhibit 2**).

Exhibit 2

Board of Directors: Harley-Davidson, Inc.

Barry K. Allen, Executive Vice-President, Ameritech Corporation

Barry has been a member of the Board since 1992. His distinguished business career has taken him from the telecommunications industry to leading a medical equipment and systems business and back again. Barry's diverse experience has been particularly valuable to the Board in the areas of marketing and organizational transformation.

Vaughn L. Beals, Jr., Chairman Emeritus, Harley-Davidson, Inc.

This Senior Director joined the company in 1975. He served as President, Chief Executive Officer, and Chairman during his years with the company. Vaughn led the group of 13 employees who took the company back to private ownership in 1981 and engineered the now famous "turnaround" following the LBO. Without Vaughn Beals, it is extremely unlikely that Harley-Davidson would exist today.

Richard I. Beattie, Chairman of the Executive Committee, Simpson Thacher & Bartlett

Dick has been a valued advisor to Harley-Davidson for nearly 20 years. His contributions evolved and grew with the company over time. In the early 1980s, he provided legal and strategic counsel to the 13 leaders who purchased Harley-Davidson from AMF, taking it back to private ownership. He also advised the team when it was time to take the company public again in 1986. Dick was elected to the Board in 1996.

Jeffrey L. Bleustein, President and Chief Executive Officer, Harley-Davidson, Inc.

Jeff began his association with Harley-Davidson in 1975 when he was asked to oversee the engineering group. During his tenure as Vice President—Engineering, Harley-Davidson developed the Evolution engine and established the foundations of our current line of cruiser and touring motorcycles. Jeff has demonstrated creativity and vision across a wide range of senior leadership roles. In 1996 he was elected to the Board, and in June 1997 he was appointed to his current position.

Richard J. Hermon-Taylor, Group Vice President, Abt Associates, Inc., President, BioScience International, Inc.

Richard joined the Board in 1986 and has been advising on marketing and manufacturing strategy for Harley-Davidson for nearly 20 years. His association with the company began when he was with the Boston Consulting Group in the mid-1970s and has been valued through the intervening years.

Donald A. James, Vice Chairman, Chief Executive Officer, Fred Deeley Imports Ltd.

Don's wisdom and knowledge of the motorcycle industry have guided the Board since 1991. As a 31-year veteran of Harley-Davidson's exclusive distributor in Canada, he has a strong sense for our core products. Don has a particularly keen understanding of the retail issues involved with motorcycles and related products and the competitive advantage inherent in strong, long-lasting dealer relationships.

Richard G. Lefauve, President, GM University, Senior Vice President, General Motors Corporation

Skip joined the Board in 1993. He has generously shared his vehicle industry experience with Harley-Davidson, including learning from his prior role as President of Saturn. Parallels in durable goods manufacturing, consumer trends, and life-long customer marketing strategy have provided considerable creative stimuli for Board discussion.

Sara L. Levinson, President, NFL Properties, Inc.

Sara joined the Board in 1996. She understands the value and power of strong brands, and her current senior leadership role in marketing and licensing, together with her previous experience at MTV, give her solid insights into the entertainment industries and younger customer segments.

James A. Norling, President and General Manager, Messaging, Information and Media Sector, Motorola, Inc.

Jim has been a Board member since 1993. His career with Motorola has included extensive senior leadership assignments in Europe, the Middle East, and Africa, and he has generously shared his international experience and understanding of technological change to benefit Harley-Davidson.

Richard F. Teerlink, Chairman of the Board, Harley-Davidson, Inc.

Rich joined Harley-Davidson in 1981 and was elected to the Board in 1982. In 1988 he was appointed President of the company; in 1989, Chief Executive Officer. In 1996 he was named Chairman of the Board. Rich is credited with the financial restructuring of Harley-Davidson from private to public during the mid 1980s. His leadership was instrumental in creating a values-based culture at the company, which revolves around developing mutually beneficial relationships with all stakeholders.

Source: Direct quotation, Harley-Davidson, Inc., *1997 Annual Report*, p. 70.

The terms of the Board of Directors were a 3-year stagger system: (a) terms expiring in 2000 were Vaughn L. Beals, Jr. (69), Donald A. James (53), and James A. Norling (55); (b) terms expiring in 1999 were Richard J. Hermon-Taylor (53), Sara L. Levinson (48), and Richard F. Teerlink (60); and (c) terms expiring in 1998 were Barry K. Allen (48), Richard I. Beattie (57), and Richard G. LeFauve (62). Sara L. Levinson, President of NFL Properties, Inc., joined the board in 1996.[5]

The company's vision was that: "Harley-Davidson, Inc., is an action-oriented, international company—a leader in its commitment to continuously improve the quality of profitable relationships with stakeholders (customers, dealers, employees, suppliers, shareholders, government, and society). Harley-Davidson believed the key to success was to balance stakeholders' interests through the empowerment of all employees to focus on value-added activities."[6]

Directors who were employees of the company did not receive any special compensation for their services as Directors. Except for Beals, Directors who were not employees of the company received in 1996 an annual fee of $25,000 plus $1,500 for each regular meeting of the Board, $750 for each special meeting of the Board, and $750 for each Board committee meeting, provided that Directors did not receive any additional compensation for more than 2 Board committee meetings in connection with any Board meeting. The company reimbursed Directors for any travel expenses incurred in connection with attending Board or Board committee meetings.

The company had a consulting contract with Beals pursuant to which Beals was paid $242,240 per year. The consulting term was to expire on June 30, 1998. The consulting contract also provided for supplemental retirement benefits of $159,840 per year after the consulting term expired until his death. In the event of Beals's death prior to the end of the consulting term, the consulting agreement provided, as a death benefit, the continuation of certain payments under the consulting agreement through July 1, 1999.

All directors and executive officers as a group (14 individuals) owned 2,126,498 shares (2.8%). Richard F. Teerlink owned 1,059,923 shares (1.4%), Jeffrey L. Bleustein owned 352,000 shares, and Vaughn L. Beals, Jr., owned 401,076 shares. Both the Bleustein and Beals ownership of shares was less than 1%. Ruane, Cunniff & Co., Inc. owned 4,284,345 shares (5.7%). This company was the largest owner of stock.[7]

Top Management

Richard F. Teerlink has been a director of the company since 1982. He has been Chairman of the Board of the company since May 1996, Chief Executive Officer of the company since 1989, and President of the company since 1988. He was also a Director of Johnson Controls, Inc. and Outboard Marine Corporation. His salary was $518,751, $486,303, and $440,901 and bonuses were $715,000, $500,000, and $700,000 for 1996, 1995, and 1994, respectively.

Jeffrey L. Bleustein has been a director of the company since December 1996. He has been Executive Vice President of the company since 1991 and President and Chief Operating Officer of the Motor Company since 1993. He was also a director of Rexworks, Inc. His salary was $370,227, $318,183, and $283,257 and bonuses were $362,082, $269,183, and $265,297 for 1996, 1995, and 1994, respectively.[8]

Exhibit 3 shows the corporate officers for Harley-Davidson and its 2 business segments—Motorcycles and Related Products and Financial Services.

Harley Owners Group (HOG)

A special kind of camaraderie marked the Harley Owners Group rallies and other motorcycle events. At events and rallies around the globe, members of HOG came together for fun, adventure, and a love of their machines and the open road. As the largest motorcycle club in the

Exhibit 3

Corporate Officers: Harley-Davidson, Inc.

1. Corporate Officers, Harley-Davidson, Inc.

Richard F. Teerlink
Chairman

Jeffrey L. Bleustein
President and
Chief Executive Officer

James M. Brostowitz
Vice President,
Controller and Treasurer

C. William Gray
Vice President,
Human Resources

Gail A. Lione
Vice President, General
Counsel and Secretary

James L. Ziemer
Vice President and
Chief Financial Officer

2. Motor Company Leadership

Jeffrey L. Bleustein
President and
Chief Executive Officer

Garry S. Berryman
Vice President, Purchasing

Joanne M. Bischmann
Vice President, Marketing

James M. Brostowitz
Vice President and Controller

William B. Dannehl
General Manager, York Operations

William G. Davidson
Vice President, Styling

Kathleen A. Demitros
Vice President,
Communications

Karl M. Eberle
Vice President, General Manager,
Kansas City Operations

Clyde Fessler
Vice President, Business
Development

Jon R. Flickinger
General Sales Manager,
North America

John D. Goll
Vice President,
Quality and Reliability

C. William Gray
Vice President,
Human Resources

John A. Hevey
Vice President, General
Manager, Asia-Pacific
and Latin American Regions

Timothy K. Hoelter
Vice President, International Trade
and Regulatory Affairs

Ronald M. Hutchinson
Vice President, Parts, Accessories,
and Customer Service

Michael D. Keefe
Director, Harley Owners Group

Brian P. Lies
Vice President,
General Merchandise

Gail A. Lione
Vice President and General Counsel

James A. McCaslin
Vice President,
Continuous Improvement

Steven R. Phillips
General Manager,
Tomahawk Operations

John K. Russell
Vice President, Managing
Director, Europe

David J. Storm
Vice President, Planning
and Information Services

W. Kenneth Sutton, Jr.
Vice President, General Manager
Powertrain Operations

Earl K. Werner
Vice President, Engineering

Jerry G. Wilke
Vice President

3. Eaglemark Financial Services Leadership

Steven F. Deli
Chairman and
Chief Executive Officer

Christopher J. Anderson
Vice President, Bankcards

Mark R. Budde
Vice President, Insurance

Michael G. Case
Vice President, Operations

Al C. Ely
Vice President, Wholesale Operations

Glen J. Villano
Vice President, Sales and Marketing

Donna F. Zarcone
Vice President and
Chief Financial Officer

4. Buell Motorcycle Company Leadership

Jeffrey L. Bleustein
Chief Executive Officer

Erik F. Buell
Chairman and
Chief Technical Officer

Jerry G. Wilke
President and Chief Operating Officer

Source: Harley-Davidson, Inc., *1997 Annual Report*, p. 76.

Exhibit 4
1997 Profile of the HOG: Harley-Davidson, Inc.

HOG Sponsored Events: In 1997, U.S. national rallies were held in Portland, Maine; Oklahoma City, Oklahoma; and Portland, Oregon. There were 2 touring rallies and 46 state rallies in the U.S. HOG also participated in events at Daytona and Sturgis Bike Weeks, factory open houses, and numerous motorcycle races. Internationally HOG held rallies in Norway, France, Japan, Canada, Australia, New Zealand, Brazil, and Mexico. There were also 5 state rallies in Australia, 2 provincial rallies in Canada, 4 touring rallies in Europe, and 1 touring rally in South Africa.

HOG Membership: Any Harley-Davidson motorcycle owner could become a member of HOG In fact, the first year of membership was included with the purchase of a new Harley-Davidson motorcycle. The number of HOG members had grown rapidly since the motorcycle organization began in 1983 with 33,000 members in the United States and Canada. There were 380,000 HOG members worldwide in more than 100 countries. Sponsorship of HOG chapters by Harley-Davidson dealers grew from 49 chapters in 1985 to 988 chapters at the close of 1997. Worldwide membership renewal increased to 71% in 1997.

A Snapshot of HOG

Worldwide members	380,000
Worldwide dealer-sponsored chapters	988
Countries with members	105
Worldwide rallies	70
Worldwide attendance at rallies	127,00
Miles logged by members attending U.S. rallies and events	41 million

Source: Harley-Davidson, Inc., *1997 Annual Report*, pp. 22–23.

world, HOG offered customers organized opportunities to ride. HOG rallies and events visibly promoted the Harley-Davidson experience to potential new customers and strengthened the relationships among members, dealers, and Harley-Davidson employees.

Exhibit 4 provides a profile of the HOG clubs. As of 1997, there were about 380,000 members of the HOG clubs worldwide.

Other Key Relationships[9]

DEALERSHIP RELATIONSHIPS

- **The Americas:** There were 595 Harley-Davidson dealerships in the United States and 41 MotorClothes apparel and collectible retail stores. In 1997, 35 dealerships were relocated; 71 dealerships were modernized or expanded; 6 new dealerships and 11 new apparel and collectibles retail stores were added to the U.S. network. In Canada, there were 76 Harley-Davidson dealerships serviced by the independent Canadian distributor, Fred Deeley Imports. In Latin America and Mexico, there were 16 dealerships and 7 MotorClothes apparel and collectible retail stores.

- **Europe/Middle East/Africa:** In 1997 there were 305 Harley-Davidson dealerships in the European Region, up from 253 dealerships in 1996. Growing the business in the European Region meant helping dealers there develop relationships with new customers. In 1998, Harley introduced 2 new motorcycle models for this market, specifically designed to appeal to the preferences of European cruiser motorcycle riders. Saudi Arabia and Oman were established as new markets in 1997.

- **Asia-Pacific:** Building relationships like the one between Tokyo dealership manager Masatoshi Ohtsubo and his customers was 1 of the keys to expanding Harley-Davidson's business in the Asia-Pacific region. There were 43 authorized dealers and 77 smaller "Live to Ride" shops serviced by the Japanese subsidiary. There were also 55 dealers in Australia and New Zealand that were serviced by 3 independent distributors, and direct deals in Malaysia, Singapore, Taiwan, and Thailand.

SUPPLIER RELATIONSHIPS

More than 250 of Harley-Davidson's largest suppliers gathered at the annual supplier conference to share a vision of growing together. Through these meetings, the Supplier Advisory Council, and other efforts such as regular visits to suppliers by senior management, Harley-Davidson was successful in continuously reducing costs and increasing quality.

FAMILY RELATIONSHIPS

Since the beginning of the Harley-Davidson Motor Company in 1903, Davidson family members have always been involved in the business. Many other families were also represented within the ranks of employees, like Alvin Burnett and his daughter Lynn Rhody, both of Tomahawk, Wisconsin.

EMPLOYEE RELATIONSHIPS

According to management, all Harley-Davidson employees across the company worked to grow the business by delivering continuous improvements and first-rate quality. Harley-Davidson and their union partners developed long-lasting relationships to ensure continued success. For example, in 1996 the company and Lodge 175 of the International Association of Machinist and Aerospace Workers ratified a progressive long-term operating agreement for the York facility.

ONLINE

Harley-Davidson's Web site ⟨www.harley-davidson.com⟩ has been affectionately called the "anti-Web site" because it encourages visitors to get off-line and onto their Harleys. Nearly 1.5 million visitors in 1997 said the Web site provided easy access to information about the company and its national events.

Business Segments and Foreign Operations[10]

The company operated in 2 business segments (excluding discontinued operations): Motorcycles and Related Products and Financial Services. The company's reportable segments were strategic business units that offered different products and services. They were managed separately, based on the fundamental differences in their operations.

Motorcycles and Related Products ("Motorcycles") (referred to as the Motor Company) consisted primarily of the company's wholly owned subsidiary, H-D Michigan, Inc., and its wholly owned subsidiary, Harley-Davidson Motor Company. The Motorcycles segment designed, manufactured, and sold primarily heavyweight (engine displacement of 651+ cc) touring and custom motorcycles and a broad range of related products that included motorcycle parts and accessories and riding apparel. The company, which was the only major American motorcycle manufacturer, had held the largest share of the United States heavyweight motorcycle market since 1986. The company held a smaller market share in the European market, which was a larger market than that of the United States, and in the Japanese market, which was a smaller market than that of the United States. In 1997, 132,300 motorcycles shipped and 147,000 were expected to ship in 1998.

Financial Services ("Eaglemark") consisted of the company's majority-owned subsidiary, Eaglemark Financial Services, Inc. Eaglemark provided motorcycle floor planning and parts and accessories financing to the company's participating North American dealers. Eaglemark also offered retail financing opportunities to the company's domestic motorcycle customers. In addition, Eaglemark had established the Harley-Davidson Chrome VISA Card for customers in the United States. Eaglemark also provided property and casualty insurance for motorcycles as well as extended service contracts. A smaller portion of its customers were in other leisure products businesses. Prior to 1995, Eaglemark carried on business only in the United States. In 1995, Eaglemark extended its operations to include Canada.

Exhibit 5 provides financial information on the company's 2 business segments.

Exhibit 5

Information by Industry Segments: Harley-Davidson, Inc.
(Dollar amounts in thousands)

A. Revenues and Income from Operations

Year Ending December 31	1997	1996	1995
Net sales	$1,762,569	$1,531,227	$1,350,466
Motorcycles and related products	—	—	—
Financial services[1]	$1,762,569	$1,531,227	$1,350,466
Income from operations			
Motorcycles and related products	$ 265,486	$ 228,093	$ 184,475
Financial services[1]	12,355	7,801	3,620
General corporate expenses	(7,838)	(7,448)	(7,299)
Operating income	$ 270,003	$ 228,446	$ 180,796

B. Assets, Depreciation, and Capital Expenditures

	Motorcycles and Related Products	Transportation Vehicles[2]	Financial Services[2]	Corporate	Consolidated
1997					
Identifiable assets	$856,779	—	$598,514	$143,608	$1,598,501
Depreciation and amortization	66,426	—	3,489	263	70,178
Net capital expenditures	183,194	—	2,834	143	186,171
1996					
Identifiable assets	$770,271	—	$387,666	$142,048	$1,299,985
Depreciation and amortization	51,657	—	3,367	258	55,282
Net capital expenditures	176,771	—	1,994	6	178,771
1995					
Identifiable assets	$575,118	$111,556	$269,461	$ 24,535	$ 980,670
Depreciation and amortization	41,754	—	320	255	42,329
Net capital expenditures	112,579	—	221	185	112,985

Notes:
1. The results of operations for the majority-owned financial services subsidiary are included as operating income from financial services in the statements of operations.
2. The results of operations for the Transportation Vehicles segment are classified as discontinued operations in the statements of operations.

Source: Harley-Davidson, Inc., *1997 Annual Report*, p. 67.

Motorcycles and Related Products Segment

PRESIDENT AND CEO'S COMMENTS[11]

Jeffrey L. Bleustein said in the *1997 Annual Report*, "At Harley-Davidson we are focused on growing our business, and I am very confident about our continued success. Consider these strengths:

- Our distinctive Harley-Davidson motorcycles are among the most admired in the world. These products, and those that come out of our new Product Development Center in the future, will continue to define leadership in our chosen market segments and enable us to reach out to new customers and new markets.

- Last year marked the sixth consecutive year of continued growth for the worldwide heavy-weight motorcycle market. From the U.S. to Asia-Pacific, Europe to South America, the opportunities for Harley-Davidson have never been better. (See **Exhibits 6** and **7**.)

- We have developed long-lasting relationships, built on trust and mutual respect, with our customers, dealers, suppliers, and the employees of Harley-Davidson.

- We have a strong and widely admired brand that begins with the passion that our customers have for their Harley-Davidson motorcycles. This translates into unparalleled brand loyalty and a remarkably high repurchase intent.

- We have a proven management team with an excellent track record and a committed work-force dedicated to growing the business.

- We have demonstrated for 12 consecutive years that we can deliver sustained revenue growth and earnings growth at the levels of the finest high-performing companies.

No one can accurately predict the future. What I can predict with the utmost confidence are the things that won't change at Harley-Davidson—namely, our commitment to providing more great motorcycles; to enhancing the unparalleled Harley lifestyle experience; and to continuing to provide excellent financial performance.

Undoubtedly there will be some bumps in the road ahead as there have been in the road just traveled, but we will always seek to deliver a smooth ride."

OVERVIEW[12]

The primary business of the Motorcycles segment was to design, produce and sell premium heavyweight motorcycles. The Motor Company's motorcycle products emphasized traditional styling, design simplicity, durability, ease of service, and evolutionary change. Studies by the company indicated that the typical U.S. Harley-Davidson motorcycle owner was a male in his mid-forties, with a household income of approximately $68,000, who purchased a motorcycle for recreational purposes rather than to provide transportation, and who was an experienced motorcycle rider. Over two thirds of the Motor Company's sales were to buyers with at least 1 year of higher education beyond high school, and 34% of the buyers had college degrees. Approximately 9% of the Motor Company's U.S. retail sales were to female buyers. (See **Exhibit 8**.)

The heavyweight class of motorcycles comprised 4 types: *standard*, which emphasized simplicity and cost; *performance*, which emphasized handling and acceleration; *touring*, which emphasized comfort and amenities for long-distance travel; and *custom*, which emphasized styling and individual owner customization. The Motor Company manufactured and sold 20 models of touring and custom heavyweight motorcycles, with suggested domestic retail prices

Exhibit 6

Selected U.S. and World Financial and Sales Information: Harley-Davidson, Inc.

A. Motor Company Revenue, 1997
(Dollar amounts in millions)

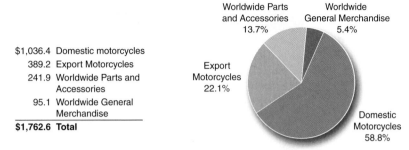

$1,036.4	Domestic motorcycles
389.2	Export Motorcycles
241.9	Worldwide Parts and Accessories
95.1	Worldwide General Merchandise
$1,762.6	**Total**

Worldwide Parts and Accessories 13.7%

Worldwide General Merchandise 5.4%

Export Motorcycles 22.1%

Domestic Motorcycles 58.8%

B. Worldwide Motorcycle Shipments
(Units in thousands)

Total Worldwide	36.7	43.3	50.5	58.9	62.5	68.6	76.5	81.7	95.8	105.1	118.8	132.3
Export	6.8	8.6	11.6	15.3	19.3	21.6	23.3	24.5	29.3	32.1	34.7	36.1
Export Percentage	18.5%	19.9%	23.0%	26.0%	30.9%	31.5%	30.5%	30.0%	30.6%	30.5%	29.2%	27.3%

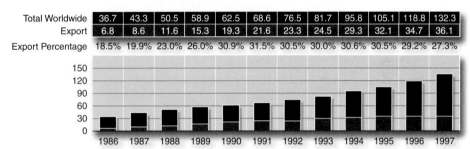

C. Worldwide Parts & Accessories and General Merchandise Revenue
(Dollar amounts in millions)

Parts and Accessories	35.0	42.2	51.4	63.2	80.2	94.3	103.6	127.8	162.0	192.1	210.2	241.9
General Merchandise[1]	9.4	13.6	19.2	23.0	29.8	36.0	52.1	71.2	94.3	100.2	90.7	95.1

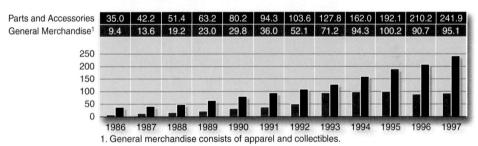

1. General merchandise consists of apparel and collectibles.

D. Operating Income
(Dollar amounts in millions)

21.3	30.6	50.4	63.2	90.2	89.6	102.3	136.2	163.5	184.5	228.1	265.5

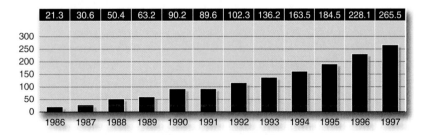

Exhibit 7

World Registrations: Harley-Davidson, Inc.

A. North American 651 + cc Motorcycle Registrations[1]
(Units in thousands)

100.7	112.0	132.8	150.4	163.1	178.5	205.4	Total Industry
48.3	56.0	63.4	69.5	77.0	85.1	99.3	Harley-Davidson
48.0%	50.0%	47.7%	46.2%	47.2%	47.6%	48.3%	Harley-Davidson Market Share

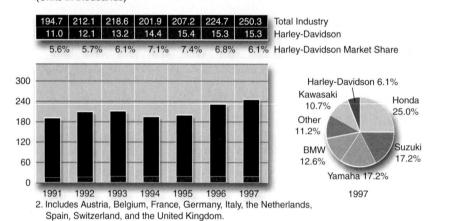

1. Includes the United States and Canada

B. European 651 + cc Motorcycle Registrations[2]
(Units in thousands)

194.7	212.1	218.6	201.9	207.2	224.7	250.3	Total Industry
11.0	12.1	13.2	14.4	15.4	15.3	15.3	Harley-Davidson
5.6%	5.7%	6.1%	7.1%	7.4%	6.8%	6.1%	Harley-Davidson Market Share

2. Includes Austria, Belgium, France, Germany, Italy, the Netherlands, Spain, Switzerland, and the United Kingdom.

C. Asia/Pacific 651 + cc Motorcycle Registrations
(Units in thousands)

27.0	37.5	35.7	39.1	39.4	37.4	58.9	Total Industry
5.3	6.0	6.7	7.6	7.9	8.2	9.7	Harley-Davidson
19.5%	16.1%	18.7%	19.4%	20.1%	21.9%	16.5%	Harley-Davidson Market Share

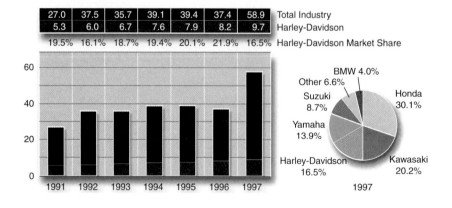

Exhibit 8

Purchaser Demographic Profile: Harley-Davidson, Inc.

Demographic	1985	1987	1988	1989	1990	1991	1992	1993	1994	1995
Gender (%)										
Male	98%	98%	96%	96%	96%	95%	95%	93%	93%	91%
Female	2	2	4	4	4	5	5	7	7	9
Median age										
Years	34.1	34.7	34.6	34.6	36.7	38.5	38.4	41.6	42.1	42.5
Marital Status (%)										
Married	54%	55%	59%	56%	56%	62%	59%	65%	68%	67%
Single	29	25	25	27	27	23	23	19	18	17
Widowed/Divorced	17	16	16	17	17	15	18	16	14	16
No answer	—	4	—	—	—	—	—	—	—	—
Children living at home (%)										
None	41%	55%	54%	57%	58%	57%	57%	53%	54%	53%
1–2	34	37	37	36	35	36	36	38	38	39
3+	6	7	8	7	7	7	7	9	8	9
No Answer	19	1	1	—	—	—	—	—	—	—
Median income (dollars in thousands)										
Personal	$28.0	$30.7	$31.3	$36.4	$38.5	$40.3	$42.7	—	—	—
Household	35.3	38.4	40.0	44.7	47.3	50.5	53.7	61.9	65.2	66.4
Education level (%)										
Non-high school grad	8%	9%	8%	8%	7%	6%	6%	5%	5%	4%
High school grad	41	32	34	33	34	27	28	26	25	24
Some college/trade school	31	41	37	38	38	40	38	39	39	38
College grad/post grad	19	18	20	21	22	26	29	31	31	34

Source: Harley-Davidson, Inc., *Background and History* (company document), p. 3.

ranging from approximately $5,200 to $19,300. (See **Exhibit 9**.) The touring segment of the heavyweight market was pioneered by the company and included motorcycles equipped for long-distance touring with fairings, windshields, saddlebags, and Tour Paks®. The custom segment of the market included motorcycles featuring the distinctive styling associated with classic Harley-Davidson motorcycles. These motorcycles were highly customized through the use of trim and accessories. The Motor Company's motorcycles were based on variations of 4 basic chassis designs and were powered by 1 of 3 air-cooled, twin cylinder engines of "V" configuration which had displacements of 883 cc, 1200 cc, and 1340 cc. The Motor Company manufactured its own engines and frames.

Although there were some accessory differences between the Motor Company's top-of-the-line touring motorcycles and those of its competitors, suggested retail prices were generally comparable. The prices for the high end of the Motor Company's custom product line ranged from being competitive to 50% more than its competitors' custom motorcycles. The custom portion of the product line represented the Motor Company's highest unit volumes and continued to command a premium price because of its features, styling, and high resale value. The Motor Company's smallest displacement custom motorcycle (the 883 cc Sportster®) was directly price competitive with comparable motorcycles available in the market. The Motor Company's surveys of retail purchasers indicated that, historically, over three-quarters of the purchasers of its Sportster model came from competitive-brand

Exhibit 9

1998 Motorcycles Product Line: Harley-Davidson, Inc.

	Suggested Selling Price ($)	
Motorcycle	**States**	**California**
XLH Sportster 1200	$ 7,610	$ 7,730
XL 1200S Sportster 1200 Sport	8,395	8,515
XL 1200C Sportster 1200 Custom	8,670	8,790
XLH Sportster 883	5,245	5,365
XLH Sportster 883 Hugger	5,945	6,065
FXDL Dyna Low Rider	13,750	14,035
FXD Dyna Super Glide	10,865	11,150
FXDS-CONV Dyna Convertible	14,100	14,385
FXDWG Dyna Wide Glide	14,775	15,060
FLSTC Heritage Softail Classic	15,275	15,565
FXSTC Softail Custom	14,125	14,145
FXSTS Heritage Springer	17,145	17,435
FLSTF Fat Boy	14,595	14,885
FXSTS Springer Softail	14,765	15,055
FLTR/FLTRI Road Glide	14,850	15,095
FLHT Electra Glide Standard	12,275	12,990
FLHTC/FLHTCI Electra Glide Classic	14,975	15,220
FLHTCUI Ultra Classic Electra Glide	18,065	18,165
FLHR Road King	14,725	14,990
FLHRCI Road King Classic	15,960	16,080
FLHRCI Road King with Sidecar	N/A	N/A

Source: Harley-Davidson, Inc., *Harley-Davidson 1998 Motorcycles.*

motorcycles, were people completely new to the sport of motorcycling, or were people who had not participated in the sport for at least 5 years. Since 1988, the Motor Company's research had consistently shown a repurchase intent in excess of 92% on the part of purchasers of Harley-Davidson motorcycles, and the Motor Company expected to see sales of its 833 cc Sportster model partially translated into sales of its higher priced products in the normal 2- to 3-year ownership cycle. The Motor Company's worldwide motorcycle sales generated 78.5%, 78.3%, and 76.9% of revenues in the Motorcycles segment during 1997, 1996, and 1995, respectively.

The major product categories for the Parts and Accessories (P&A) business were replacement parts (Genuine Motor Parts™) and mechanical accessories (Genuine Motor Accessories™). Worldwide net P&A sales comprised 13.7%, 13.7%, and 14.2% of net sales in the Motorcycles segment in 1997, 1996, and 1995, respectively. Worldwide P&A net sales had grown 49.3% over the last 3 years (since 1994).

Worldwide net sales of the General Merchandise business, which included Motor-Clothes® apparel and collectibles, comprised 5.4%, 5.9%, and 7.4% of net sales in the Motorcycles segment in 1997, 1996, and 1995 respectively.

The Motor Company also provided a variety of services to its dealers and retail customers, including service training schools, customized software packages for dealers, delivery of its motorcycles, membership in an owners club, and a Fly and Ride™ program through which a member could rent a motorcycle through a dealer at a vacation destination.

Exhibit 10 shows that motorcycle sales in units (excluding Buell) increased by 11.4% in 1997 and net sales for this business segment were up 15.1% in 1997.

Exhibit 10

Motorcycle Unit Shipments and Net Sales: Harley-Davidson, Inc.

	1997	1996	Increase	% Change
Motorcycle Units (excluding Buell)	132,285	118,771	13,514	11.4%
Net sales (in millions)				
Motorcycles (excluding Buell)	$1,382.8	$1,199.2	$183.6	15.3%
Motorcycle parts and accessories	241.9	211.2	30.7	14.5
General merchandise	95.1	90.7	4.4	4.8
Other	42.8	30.1	12.7	42.2
Total motorcycles and related products	$1,762.5	$1,531.2	$231.4	15.1%

Source: Harley-Davidson, Inc., *Form 10-K* (December 31, 1997), p. 20.

Licensing[13]

In recent years, the company has endeavored to create an awareness of the Harley-Davidson brand among the nonriding public and provide a wide range of product for enthusiasts by licensing the name "Harley-Davidson" and numerous related trademarks owned by the company. The company had licensed the production and sale of a broad range of consumer items, including tee-shirts, jewelry, small leather goods, toys, and numerous other products. In 1993, the licensed Harley-Davidson Café opened in Manhattan, New York. In 1995, the company entered into an agreement to license 3 additional restaurants with the New York Café's owners. Under this agreement, a new Café in Las Vegas, Nevada, was opened in September 1997. Although the majority of licensing activity occurred in the United States, the company continued to expand into international markets.

The company's licensing activity provided it with a valuable source of advertising and goodwill. Licensing also had proven to be an effective means for enhancing the company's image with consumers and provided an important tool for policing the unauthorized use of the company's trademarks, thereby protecting the Harley-Davidson brand and its use. Royalty revenues from licensing, included in motorcycle revenue, were approximately $24 million, $19 million, and $24 million during 1997, 1996, and 1995, respectively. Although royalty revenues from licensing activities were relatively small, the profitability of this business was relatively high.

Marketing and Distribution[14]

The company's basic channel of U.S. distribution for its motorcycles and related products consisted of approximately 600 independently owned, full-service dealerships to whom the company sold direct. With respect to sales of new motorcycles, approximately 77% of the U.S. dealerships sold the company's motorcycles exclusively. All dealerships carried the company's genuine replacement parts and aftermarket accessories and performed servicing of the company's motorcycle products.

The company's marketing efforts were divided among dealer promotions, customer events, magazine and direct mail advertising, public relations, and cooperative programs with Harley-Davidson dealers. The company also sponsored racing activities and special promotional events and participated in all major motorcycle consumer shows and rallies. In an effort to encourage Harley-Davidson owners to become more actively involved in the sport of motorcycling, the Motor Company formed a riders club in 1983. The Harley Owners Group, or HOG, was the industry's largest company-sponsored motorcycle enthusiast organization.

The Motor Company's expenditures on domestic marketing, selling, and advertising were approximately $85.2 million, $75.4 million, and $71.5 million during 1997, 1996, and 1995, respectively.

Retail Customer and Dealer Financing[15]

The company believed Eaglemark and other financial services companies provided adequate retail and wholesale financing to the Motor Company's domestic and Canadian dealers and customers. In addition, to encourage its dealers to carry sufficient parts and accessories inventories and to counteract the seasonality of the parts and accessories business, the Motor Company, from time to time, offered its domestic dealers quarterly special discounts and/or 120-day delayed payment terms through Eaglemark. Eaglemark also began to provide wholesale financing to dealers supported by the company's European subsidiaries through a joint venture agreement with Transamerica Distribution Finance Corporation. Previously the company offered extended winter terms to certain European customers.

International Sales[16]

International sales were approximately $458 million, $421 million, and $401 million, accounting for approximately 26%, 27%, and 30% of net sales of the Motorcycles segment during 1997, 1996, and 1995, respectively. The international heavyweight (651+ cc) market was growing and was significantly larger than the U.S. heavyweight market. The Motor Company ended 1997 with an approximate 6.1% share of the European heavyweight (651+ cc) market and an approximate 16.5% share of the Asia/Pacific (Japan and Australia) heavyweight (651+ cc) market (see **Exhibit 7**).

In total, the Motor Company was represented internationally by 577 independent dealers in 55 countries. Japan, Germany, and Canada, in that order, represented the company's largest export markets and accounted for approximately 51% of export sales.

In the European Region (Europe/Middle East/Africa), there were currently 305 independent dealers serving 30 country markets. This network of dealers was served by 9 independent distributors and 4 wholly owned subsidiaries in France, Germany, the Netherlands, and the United Kingdom. The company had continued to build infrastructure in Europe, following the establishment of its United Kingdom–based European Headquarters in 1995. New information systems, linking all the European subsidiary markets, were successfully installed and began operating in early 1997. The European management team was continuing to build and develop distributor, dealer, and customer relationships. The company's focus was to expand and improve the distribution network, tailor product development to market needs, and attract new customers through coordinated Europe-wide and local marketing programs.

In the Asia-Pacific Region, there were currently 179 independent dealers serving 8 country markets. During 1996, the company began to implement a strategic plan for the Asia-Pacific Region, which outlined growth objectives and strategies for achieving them. Although the economic crisis in Southeast Asia had currently curtailed the company's plans to open new markets in Southeast Asia, according to management, short-term growth should continue to come from existing markets in Japan and Australia. Long-term growth opportunities were expected to come from existing markets in Japan, Australia, and Southeast Asia and from new markets in the region.

The Americas market included Canada and a separate Latin American distribution network. The Latin American market consisted of 16 country markets managed from Milwaukee. The Latin American market had a diverse dealer network including 17 full-line dealers, as well as 7 resort and mall stores focusing on selling General Merchandise. During 1997, the company's distribution network was expanded in Mexico and Argentina. In the future, the focus will be on improving distribution and volumes within the 2 largest Latin American markets, Mexico and

Brazil. Management intended to expand advertising and promotion, and to investigate regional sourcing of General Merchandise to extend the customer reach of branded products in the region. In Canada, there were currently 76 full-line dealerships served by a single independent distributor.

Competition[17]

The U.S. and international heavyweight (651+ cc) motorcycle markets were highly competitive. The company's major competitors generally had financial and marketing resources that were substantially greater than those of the company. They also had larger overall sales volumes and were more diversified than the company. Harley management believed the heavyweight motorcycle market was the most profitable segment of the U.S. motorcycle market. During 1997, the heavyweight segment represented approximately 54% of the total U.S. motorcycle market (on- and off-highway motorcycles and scooters) in terms of new units registered. (See **Exhibit 11.**)

Domestically, the Motor Company competed in the touring and custom segments of the heavyweight motorcycle market, which together accounted for 80%, 80%, and 78% of total heavyweight retail unit sales in the United States during 1997, 1996, and 1995, respectively. The custom and touring motorcycles were generally the most expensive and most profitable vehicles in the market.

For the last 10 years, the Motor Company had led the industry in domestic (United States) sales of heavyweight motorcycles. The Motor Company's share of the heavyweight market was 49.1% in 1997, up from 48.2% in 1996. This was significantly greater than the company's largest competitor (Honda) domestically, which had an 18.5% market share at the end of 1997. (See **Exhibit 12.**)

Exhibit 11

Worldwide Heavyweight Motorcycle Registration Data
(Engine displacement of 651+ cc; units in thousands)

	1997	1996	1995
North America[1]			
Total registrations	205.4	178.5	163.1
Harley-Davidson registrations	99.3	85.1	77.0
Harley-Davidson market share percentage	48.3%	47.6%	47.2%
Europe[2]			
Total registrations	250.3	224.7	207.2
Harley-Davidson registrations	15.3	15.3	15.4
Harley-Davidson market share percentage	6.1%	6.9%	7.4%
Japan/Australia[3]			
Total registrations	58.9	37.4	39.4
Harley-Davidson registrations	9.7	8.2	7.9
Harley-Davidson market share percentage	16.5%	21.9%	20.1%
Total			
Total registrations	514.6	440.6	409.7
Harley-Davidson registrations	124.3	108.6	100.3
Harley-Davidson market share percentage	24.2%	24.6%	24.5%

Notes:
1. Includes the United States and Canada.
2. Includes Austria, Belgium, France, Germany, Italy, the Netherlands, Spain, Switzerland, and United Kingdom. (Data provided by Giral S.A.)
3. Data provided by JAMA and ABS.

Source: Harley-Davidson, Inc., *Form 10-K* (December 31, 1997), p. 9.

Exhibit 12

Shares of U.S. Heavyweight Motorcycle Market
(Above 750 cc engine displacement)

Year Ending December 31	1997	1996	1995	1994	1993
New U.S. registrations (thousands of units)					
Total new registrations	190.2	165.7	151.2	140.8	123.8
Harley-Davidson new registrations	93.5	79.9	72.1	65.2	59.3
Percentage market share (%)					
Harley-Davidson	49.1%	48.2%	47.7%	46.3%	47.9%
Buell	1.0	1.0	0.5	0.1	0.0
Honda	18.5	18.8	20.2	22.5	20.1
Suzuki	10.1	8.7	9.6	10.6	12.1
Kawasaki	10.4	12.2	10.6	9.8	9.7
Yamaha	5.4	5.9	5.8	5.6	5.8
Other	5.5	5.2	5.6	5.1	4.4
Totals	100%	100%	100%	100%	100%

Note: Information in this report regarding motorcycle registrations and market shares has been derived from data published by R. L. Polk & Co.

Source: Harley-Davidson, Inc., *1997 Form 10-K*, p. 8.

On a worldwide basis, the Motor Company measured its market share using the heavyweight classification. Although definitive market share information did not exist for many of the smaller foreign markets, the Motor Company estimated its worldwide competitive position using data reasonably available to it. (See **Exhibit 11**.)

Competition in the heavyweight motorcycle market was based on several factors, including price, quality, reliability, styling, product features, customer preference, and warranties. The Motor Company emphasized quality, reliability, and styling in its products and offered warranties for its motorcycles. The Motor Company regarded its support of a motorcycling lifestyle in the form of events, rides, rallies, and HOG as a competitive advantage. In general, resale prices for used Harley-Davidson motorcycles, as a percentage of prices when new, were significantly higher than resale prices for used motorcycles of the company's competitors.

Domestic heavyweight registrations increased 15% and 10% during 1997 and 1996, respectively. The company believed its ability to maintain its market share would depend primarily on its ability to increase its annual production capacity as discussed in the Motorcycle Manufacturing section of this case.

New Competitors

New competitors have entered the marketplace because Harley-Davidson has not been able to fully meet the demand for its heavyweight motorcycles. This backlog of customers was the primary reason that Harley-Davidson had increased units shipped from 81,696 in 1993 to 132,285 in 1997, which represented an increase of 50,589 motorcycles (61.9%) over the past 5 years. Over the past 7 years, the demand for Harley-Davidson motorcycles had exceeded production. A few years ago, a potential customer would have to wait 1 or more years to purchase his or her new motorcycle. Some potential customers, who did not want to wait for their turn on the waiting list for a new motorcycle, would offer thousands of dollars to acquire another person's motorcycle allotment. How lists were set up and maintained was solely the dealer's responsibility.

This backlog caused new entrants to start manufacturing cruiser motorcycles. These were:

1. *Big Dog Motorcycles* was expected to produce 2,000 motorcycles in 1998 and double that in 1999. These motorcycles should cost upward of $22,000 versus about $16,000 for Harley-Davidson. In 1997, the company had 55 employees who turned out 300 motorcycles. Sheldon Coleman, President, said, "When you buy a Harley, the factory bike is an anemic motorcycle." He further stated, "You have to put several thousands into it to get it up to real-world standards."[18]

2. *Polaris* was one of the largest manufacturers of all-terrain vehicles, snowmobiles, and personal watercraft. In 1997, the company introduced the Polaris Victory with a price tag of about $12,500. Polaris selected about 200 of its 2,000 dealers to sell the Victory. Matt Parks, General Manager of Polaris' Victory Motorcycle Division, said, "We're going to be a major player in the business."[19]

3. *Excelsior Supply* bought Henderson Co. in 1917, 1 of the "big 3" U.S. manufacturers, along with Harley and Indian. Excelsior went bankrupt in 1931 but reappeared recently as Excelsior-Henderson. In 1993, Excelsior-Henderson decided to reintroduce the Excelsior motorcycles. The first motorcycle was scheduled to be out in October 1998 and expected to retail between $16,000 and $20,000. The company was moving into new production facilities with a yearly 20,000 motorcycle capacity.

Industry analysts expected the cruiser sales to grow 12 to 15% a year for several years.

Ducati SpA, an Italian maker of deluxe motorcycles, was "mounting an ambitious push to market its bikes as a passport to a fast-paced lifestyle."[20] CEO Federino Minoli said, "That is not a mechanical industry thing. That is about exclusivity, luxury, having fun." He went on to say, "We want to create a Ducati way of life."[21] Neiman Marcus featured a limited-series Ducati 748 in its 1997 "wish list" catalog for men, along with other luxury merchandise such as a Porsche bicycle, Emporio Armani watches, and Gucci shoes. New York's Solomon R. Guggenheim Museum featured several Ducatis in its 1997 exhibit, "The Art of Motorcycling." Ducati's 2 top sellers were the $8,000 Monster and the $17,000 top-of-the-line 916. An analyst said, "The Ducati owners tended to be speed and racing fanatics, while Harley owners seek a custom look and comfortable ride." He further stated, "Still, as Ducati's strategy evolves, it's looking more and more like its Milwaukee-based cousin."[22]

A Tampa dealer for Polaris, Moto Guzzi, and other competitive foreign motorcycle said "about 35% of his customers are female." He further stated that the "average male buyer makes about 8 visits to his store before purchasing his motorcycle, while the female buyer made only 1 or 2 visits." A car dealer of pre-owned Jaguars found these comments to be the opposite of his business. Men will call about the car advertisement in the paper and ask several questions about price, color, and model. About 90% of the men buyers come to his dealership and purchase the car after 1 or 2 visits. The majority of the men buyers come to the dealership and purchase on the first visit, and many never drive the car. Women usually make 2 to 3 visits before purchasing the car.[23]

Motorcycle Manufacturing[24]

To achieve cost and quality parity with its competitors, the company had incorporated manufacturing techniques to continuously improve its operations. These techniques, which included employee involvement, just-in-time inventory principles, and statistical process control, had significantly improved quality, productivity, and asset utilization.

The Motor Company's use of just-in-time inventory principles allowed it to minimize its inventories of raw materials and work-in-process as well as scrap and rework costs. This system also allowed quicker reaction to engineering design changes, quality improvements, and market demands. The Motor Company had trained the majority of its manufacturing employees in problem solving and statistical methods.

For the past 2 years, the Motor Company had been implementing a comprehensive motorcycle manufacturing strategy designed to, among other things, significantly increase its motorcycle production capacity. "Plan 2003" called for the enhancement of the Motor Company's ability to increase capacity, increase flexibility to adjust to changes in the marketplace, improve product quality, and reduce costs. The strategy called for the achievement of the increased capacity at the existing facilities combined with some new additions. The transition into a new engine plant in Milwaukee and the construction of a new assembly plant in Kansas City, Missouri, were both completed in 1997. The Motor Company believed the worldwide heavyweight (651+ cc) market would continue to grow and planned to continue to increase its motorcycle production capacity to be able to sustain its annual double-digit unit growth. For 1998, the Motor Company's production target was 147,000 units.

In 1997, the Motor Company and Dr. Ing. h.c. Porsche AG of Stuttgart, Germany, formed a joint venture to source and assemble powertrain components for use in potential new motorcycle products. The joint venture planned to operate out of 1 of the Motor Company's U.S. manufacturing facilities.

Raw Material and Purchase Components[25]

The Motor Company was proceeding aggressively to establish long-term mutually beneficial relationships with its suppliers. Through these relationships the Motor Company was gaining access to technical and commercial resources for application directly to product design, development, and manufacturing initiatives. This strategy was resulting in improved product technical integrity, application of new features and innovations, reduced lead times for product development, and smoother/faster manufacturing ramp-up of new vehicle introductions.

The Motor Company purchased all of its raw material, principally steel and aluminum castings, forgings, sheets and bars, and certain motorcycle components, including carburetors, batteries, tires, seats, electrical components, and instruments. The Motor Company anticipated no significant difficulties in obtaining raw materials or components for which it relied on a limited source of supply.

Research and Development[26]

The Motor Company believed research and development were significant factors in the Motor Company's ability to lead the market definition of touring and custom motorcycling. As a result, the Motor Company completed construction of a new 213,000-square-foot Product Development Center (PDC) in 1996. The PDC brought together employees from styling, purchasing, and manufacturing with regulatory professionals and supplier representatives to create a concurrent product and process development methodology. The Motor Company incurred research and development expenses of approximately $53.3 million, $37.7 million, and $27.2 million during 1997, 1996, and 1995, respectively.

The $40 million Product Development Center was headed by Willie G. Davidson, Vice President—Styling. Davidson was the grandson of 1 of the founders.

Patents and Trademarks[27]

The company owned certain patents that related to its motorcycles and related products and processes for their production. Management had increased its efforts to patent its technology and to enforce those patents. The company saw such actions as important as it moved forward with new technologies. The company's goal was to make all of its intellectual property assets work together to achieve the greatest effect.

Trademarks were important to the company's motorcycle business and licensing activities. The company had a vigorous global program of trademark registration and enforcement to strengthen the value of the trademarks associated with its products, prevent the unauthorized use of those trademarks, and enhance its image and customer goodwill. Management believed the "Harley-Davidson®" trademark was highly recognizable by the general public and a very valuable asset. The Bar and Shield Design trademark was also highly recognizable by the general public. Additionally, the company used numerous trademarks, trade names, and logos, which were registered both in the United States and abroad. The "Harley-Davidson" trademark had been used since 1903 and the Bar and Shield trademark since 1907.

Seasonality

The company, in general, had not experienced significant seasonal fluctuations in motorcycle production. This had primarily been the result of a strong demand for the Motor Company's motorcycles and related products as well as the availability of floor plan financing arrangements for its North American independent dealers. Dealers had to pay for the motorcycles when they were delivered. Thus they needed "floor plan" financing to pay for inventory until they sold it. Floor plan financing allowed dealers to build their inventory levels in anticipation of the spring and summer selling seasons. The lack of floorplanning had caused foreign accounts receivable to be an issue of concern. Beginning in 1998, floorplanning for dealers supported by the company's European subsidiaries was made available.[28]

December 31	1997	1996
(Dollar amounts in thousands)		
Accounts receivable		
Domestic	$ 15,189	$ 49,888
Foreign	87,608	91,427
	$102,797	$141,315

Domestic motorcycle sales were generally floorplanned by the purchasing dealers. Foreign motorcycle sales were sold on open account, letter of credit, draft, and payment in advance. Effective September 1, 1997, Eaglemark became responsible for all credit and collection activities for the Motorcycles segment's domestic receivables. As such, approximately $69 million of accounts receivable were classified as finance receivables as of December 31, 1997. The presentation of finance receivables had been changed to classify receivables representing wholesale motorcycle and parts and accessories receivables and retail finance receivables with maturities of less than 1 year as current.

The allowance for doubtful accounts deducted from accounts receivable was $1.5 million and $1.9 million at December 31, 1997, and 1996, respectively.[29]

Regulations[30]

Both U.S. federal and state authorities had various environmental control requirements relating to air, water, and noise pollution that affected the business and operations of the company. The company endeavored to ensure that its facilities and products complied with all applicable environmental regulations and standards.

European Union Certification procedures ensured that the company's motorcycles complied with the lower European Union noise standards (80 dba). At the beginning of the next decade, there may be a further reduction of European Union noise standards. Accordingly, the company expected that it should continue to incur some level of research and development costs related to this matter over the next several years.

The company's motorcycles were subject to certification by the U.S. Environmental Protection Agency (EPA) for compliance with applicable emissions and noise standards and by the State of California Air Resources Board (ARB) with respect to the ARB's more stringent emissions standards. The company's motorcycles were subjected to the additional ARB tailpipe and evaporative emissions standards that required the company to build unique vehicles for sale exclusively in California. The company's motorcycle products had been certified to comply fully with all such applicable standards. The company anticipated there will be further reductions in the ARB's, and potentially in the EPA's, motorcycle emissions standards in the coming years. Accordingly, the company expected to incur some level of research and development costs related to this matter over the next several years.

The company, as a manufacturer of U.S. motorcycle products, was subject to the National Traffic and Motor Vehicle Safety Act (Safety Act), which was administered by the National Highway Traffic Safety Administration (NHTSA). The company had acknowledged to NHTSA that its motorcycle products complied fully with all applicable federal motor vehicle safety standards and related regulations.

In accordance with NHTSA policies, the Motor Company had, from time to time, initiated certain voluntary recalls. During the last 3 years, the Motor Company had initiated 5 voluntary recalls at a total cost of approximately $3.7 million. The company fully reserved for all estimated costs associated with recalls in the period that they are announced.

Federal, state, and local authorities had adopted various control standards relating to air, water, and noise pollution that affected the business and operations of the Motorcycles segment. Management did not anticipate that any of these standards would have a materially adverse impact on its capital expenditures, earnings, or competitive position.

Employees[31]

As of December 31, 1997, the Motorcycles segment had approximately 5,700 employees. Production workers at the motorcycle manufacturing facilities in Wauwatosa, Menomonee Falls, and Tomahawk, Wisconsin, and Kansas City, Missouri, were represented principally by the United Paperworkers International Union (UPIU) of the AFL-CIO as well as by the International Association of Machinist and Aerospace Workers (IAM). Production workers at the motorcycle manufacturing facility in York, Pennsylvania, were represented principally by the IAM. The collective bargaining agreement with the Wisconsin-UPIU and IAM will expire on March 31, 2001, the collective bargaining agreement with the Kansas City-UPIU and IAM will expire on December 31, 2003, and the collective bargaining agreement with the Pennsylvania-IAM will expire on February 2, 2002.

Commitments and Contingencies[32]

The company was involved with government agencies in various environmental matters, including a matter involving soil and groundwater contamination at its York, Pennsylvania, facility. The facility was formerly used by the U.S. Navy and AMF (the predecessor corporation of Minstar). The company purchased the facility from AMF in 1981. Although the company was not certain as to the extent of the environmental contamination at the facility, it was working with the Pennsylvania Department of Environmental Resources in undertaking certain investigation and remediation activities. In March 1995, the company entered into a settlement agreement with the Navy. The agreement called for the Navy and the company to contribute amounts into a trust equal to 53% and 47%, respectively, of future costs associated with investigation and remediation activities at the facility (response costs). The trust will administer the payment of the future response costs at the facility as covered by the agreement. In addition, in March 1991 the company entered into a settlement agreement with Minstar related to certain indemnification obligations assumed by Minstar in connection with the company's purchase of the facility. Pursuant to this settlement, Minstar was obligated to reimburse the company for a portion of its response costs at the facility.

Although substantial uncertainty existed concerning the nature and scope of the environmental remediation that will ultimately be required at the facility, based on preliminary information then available to the company and taking into account the company's settlement agreement with the Navy and the settlement agreement with Minstar, the company estimated that it will incur approximately $6 million of net additional response costs at the facility. The company had established reserves for this amount. The company's estimate of additional response costs was based on reports of environmental consultants retained by the company, the actual costs incurred to date, and the estimated costs to complete the necessary investigation and remediation activities. Response costs were expected to be incurred over a period of approximately 10 years.

Under the terms of the sale of the Commercial Vehicles Division, the company had agreed to indemnify Utilimaster Corporation for 12 years for certain claims related to environmental contamination present at the date of sale, up to $20 million. Based on the environmental studies performed as part of the sale of the Transportation Vehicles segment, the company did not expect to incur any material expenditure under this indemnification.

Since June 1996, the company self-insured its product liability losses in the United States up to $2.5 million ($3.0 million between June 1995 and June 1996). Catastrophic coverage was maintained for individual claims in excess of $2.5 million ($3.0 million between June 1995 and June 1996) up to $25 million. Prior to June 1995, the company was self-insured for all product liability losses in the United States. Outside the United States, the company was insured for product liability up to $25 million per individual claim and in the aggregate. The company accrued for claim exposures that were probable of occurrence and could be reasonably estimated.

At December 31, 1997, the company was contingently liable for $15.9 million related to letters of credit. The letters of credit typically act as a guarantee of payment to certain third parties in accordance with specified terms and conditions.

Lawsuit

A New Jersey jury awarded $9.9 million to a Harley-Davidson motorcyclist who claimed his cruise control stuck and caused him serious injury. This award was believed to be the largest one ever against a motorcycle company for product liability. He still rode his modified motorcycle with a sidecar.[33]

Properties

The Motor Company had 5 facilities that performed manufacturing operations: Wauwatosa and Menomonee Falls, Wisconsin, suburbs of Milwaukee (motorcycle powertrain production); Tomahawk, Wisconsin (fiberglass parts production and painting); York, Pennsylvania (motorcycle parts fabrication, painting, and assembly). The construction of a new 330,000-square-foot manufacturing facility in Kansas City, Missouri, was completed in 1997 and was expected to be producing all Sportster motorcycles by the end of the second quarter of 1998. As a result of the February acquisition of the remaining interest in BMC, the company had a manufacturing facility in East Troy, Wisconsin, dedicated to the production of Buell motorcycles.

Expansion had also taken place at the company's powertrain operations in the Milwaukee area, its motorcycle assembly operations in York, Pennsylvania, and its fiberglass products plant in Tomahawk, Wisconsin, to enable the company to achieve its long-term goal of increased motorcycle production capacity.

The principal properties of the Motorcycles and Related Products segment as of March 20, 1998, are shown in **Exhibit 13**.[34]

Exhibit 13

Motorcycles and Related Products Segment Properties: Harley-Davidson, Inc.

Type of Facility	Location	Square Feet	Status
Office and Warehouse	Milwaukee, WI	512,100	Owned
Product Development Center	Wauwatosa, WI	213.000	Owned
Manufacturing	Wauwatosa, WI	443,000	Owned
Manufacturing	Menomonee Falls, WI	448,000	Owned
Manufacturing	Tomahawk, WI	112,250	Owned
Manufacturing	York, PA	1,033,060	Owned
Manufacturing	Kansas City, MO	330,000	Owned
Manufacturing	East Troy, WI	40,000	Lease expiring 1999
Distribution Center	York, PA	84,000	Lease expiring 2004
Distribution Center	Franklin, WI	250,000	Owned
Motorcycle Testing	Talladega, AL	23,500	Lease expiring 1998–1999
Office	Kansas City, MO	23,600	Lease expiring 1998
Office	Mukwanago, WI	4,800	Lease expiring 1998
Office	Ann Arbor, MI	2,300	Lease expiring 1999
Office and Warehouse	East Troy, WI	8,044	Lease expiring 1998
Office and Service Area	Morfelden-Walldorf, Germany	25,840	Lease expiring 2001
Office	Tokyo, Japan	13,048	Lease expiring 1999
Warehouse	Yokohama, Japan	10,652	Lease expiring 1999
Office	Brackley, England	2,845	Lease expiring 2005
Warehouse	Brackley, England	1,122	Lease expiring 2005
Office	Windsor, England	10,147	Lease expiring 2006
Office	Liederdorp, The Netherlands	8,400	Lease expiring 2001
Office	Paris, France	5,650	Lease expiring 2005

Source: Harley-Davidson, Inc., *Form 10-K* (December 31,1997), p. 14.

Harley-Davidson Cafés

In 1997, the second Harley-Davidson Café opened in Las Vegas. The first café had opened in New York City. These 2 restaurants represented another opportunity for riders and nonriders to immerse themselves in the energy and excitement of Harley-Davidson. These cafés were among the most visible brand-building tools the company had, and they generated licensing income for Harley-Davidson as they created an entertaining dining experience for customers. Road Burnin' Bar-B-Que, Big Bowl Roadside Greens, and some classic motorcycles and memorabilia were all part of the scene. Hundreds of thousands of diners had already savored the experience.[35]

Financial Services Segment[36]

Eaglemark provided financial services programs to leisure product manufacturers and their dealers and customers in the United States and Canada. The company had acquired a 49% interest in Eaglemark in 1993 and subsequently acquired substantially all of the remaining shares in 1995. Eaglemark commenced doing business in 1993 with the purchase of the Harley-Davidson wholesale financing portfolio from ITT Commercial Finance Corporation. In January 1998, Eaglemark entered the European market through a joint venture agreement with Transamerica Distribution Finance Corporation to provide wholesale financing to dealers supported by the Company's European subsidiaries.

HARLEY-DAVIDSON

Eaglemark provided both wholesale and retail financial services to Harley-Davidson dealers and customers and operated under the trade names Harley-Davidson Credit and Harley-Davidson Insurance. Wholesale financial services included floorplan and open account financing of motorcycles, trade acceptance financing of motorcycle parts and accessories, computer loans, showroom remodeling loans, and the brokerage of a range of commercial insurance products, including property and casualty, general liability, and special events insurance policies. Eaglemark's wholesale financial services were offered to all Harley-Davidson dealers in the United States and Canada, and during 1997 were used 1 or more times by approximately 95% of such dealers. Eaglemark's wholesale finance operations were located in Plano, Texas.

Retail financial services included installment lending for new and used Harley-Davidson motorcycles; the Harley-Davidson Chrome® VISA® Card; the brokerage of a range of motorcycle insurance products, including liability, casualty and credit life and disability insurance policies; and extended service agreements. Eaglemark acted only as an insurance agent and did not assume any underwriting risk with regard to the various insurance policies and extended service agreements that it sold. Eaglemark's retail financial services were available through virtually all Harley-Davidson dealers in the United States and Canada. Eaglemark's retail finance operations were located in Carson City, Nevada.

OTHER MANUFACTURERS

Eaglemark also provided wholesale and retail financial services through manufacturer participation programs to certain aircraft, marine, and recreational vehicle dealers and customers. These programs were similar to the Harley-Davidson program described above.

FUNDING

Eaglemark's growth had been funded through a combination of capital contributions from the company, unsecured commercial paper borrowings, revolving credit facilities borrowings, senior subordinated notes borrowing, and the securitization of its retail installment loans. Future growth was expected to be financed by using similar sources as well as internally generated funds.

COMPETITION

Eaglemark believed that its ability to offer a package of wholesale and retail financial services using the name of the manufacturer provided a significant competitive advantage over its competitors. Its competitors competed for business based largely on price and, to a lesser extent, service. Eaglemark competed based on convenience, service, and, to a lesser extent, price.

The only significant national retail financing competitor for Harley-Davidson motorcycle installment loans was Greentree Financial. During 1997, Eaglemark financed 19% of new Harley-Davidson motorcycles retailed in the United States, up from 17% in 1996. In contrast, competition to provide retail financial services to aircraft, recreational vehicle, and watercraft dealers was substantial, with many competitors being much larger than Eaglemark. These competitors included The CIT Group, NationsCredit, BankOne, and KeyBank USA. Credit unions, banks, other financial institutions, and insurance agencies also competed for retail financial services business in their local markets.

Eaglemark faced little national competition for the Harley-Davidson wholesale financial business. Competitors were primarily banks and other financial institutions that provided wholesale financing to Harley-Davidson dealers in their local markets. In contrast, competition to provide wholesale financial services to aircraft, recreational vehicle, and watercraft dealers was substantial, with many competitors being much larger than Eaglemark. These competitors included Deutche Financial, NationsCredit, Bombardier, and Transamerica. They typically offered manufacturer-sponsored programs similar to Eaglemark's programs.

PATENTS AND TRADEMARKS

Eaglemark had registered trademarks for the name "Eaglemark" and the Eaglemark logo. All the other trademarks or trade names used by Eaglemark, such as Harley-Davidson Credit, were licensed from the manufacturer.

SEASONALITY

The leisure products for which Eaglemark currently provided financial services were used only during the warmer months of the year in the northern United States and Canada, generally March through August. As a result, the business experienced significant seasonal variations. From September until mid-March, dealer inventories increased and turned more slowly, increasing wholesale financing volume substantially. During this same time there was a corresponding decrease in the retail financing volume. Customers typically did not buy motorcycles, watercraft, and recreational vehicles until they could use them. From about mid-March through August, retail financing volume increased and wholesale financing volume decreased.

EMPLOYEES

As of December 31, 1997, the Financial Services segment had approximately 360 employees. None of Eaglemark's personnel was represented by labor unions.

OPERATING INCOME

Exhibit 14 shows the operating income and identifiable assets of Eaglemark under Financial Services.

Exhibit 14
Revenues, Operating Income, and Assets: Harley-Davidson, Inc.

	Motorcycles and Related Products	Transportation Vehicles[1]	Financial Services[2]	Corporate
1997				
Revenue	$1,762,569	—	—	—
Operating income (loss)	265,486	—	$ 12,355	$ (7,838)
Identifiable assets as of December 31	856,779	—	598,514	143,608
1996				
Revenue	$1,531,227	—	—	—
Operating income (loss)	228,093	—	$ 7,801	$ (7,448)
Identifiable assets as of December 31	770,271	—	387,666	142,048
1995				
Revenue	$1,350,466	—	—	—
Operating income (loss)	184,475	—	$ 3,620	$ (7,299)
Identifiable assets as of December 31	595,118	$111,556	269,461	24,535

Notes:
1. The Transportation Vehicles segment was reported as discontinued operations commencing in 1995.
2. The Financial Services segment's results of operations are included in operating income.

Source: Harley-Davidson, Inc., *Form 10-K* (December 31, 1997), p. 3.

Impact of Year 2000[37]

The company had completed an assessment and was modifying or replacing portions of its software so that its computer systems would function properly with respect to dates in the year 2000 and thereafter. The company also had initiated discussions with its significant suppliers and financial institutions to ensure that those parties had appropriate plans to remediate year 2000 issues where their systems interfaced with the company's systems or otherwise impacted its operations. The company was assessing the extent to which operations were vulnerable should those organizations fail to properly remediate their computer systems.

The company's comprehensive year 2000 initiative was being managed by a team of internal staff with the assistance of outside consultants. The team's activities were designed to ensure that there was no adverse effect on the company's core business operations and that transactions with suppliers and financial institutions were fully supported. The company was well underway with these efforts, which were scheduled to be completed by mid 1999. While the company believed its planning efforts were adequate to address its year 2000 concerns, there could be no guarantee that the systems of other companies on which the company's systems and operations relied would be converted on a timely basis and would not have a material effect on the company. The cost of the year 2000 initiatives was estimated to be approximately $11 million, of which $2 million was incurred in 1997.

The costs of the project and the date on which the company believed it would complete the year 2000 modifications were forward-looking statements and were based on management's best estimates, which were derived using numerous assumptions of future events, including the continued availability of certain resources and other factors. However, there could be no guarantee that these estimates would be achieved, and the actual results could differ materially from those anticipated. Specific factors that might cause such material differences included, but were not limited to, the availability and cost of personnel trained in this area, the ability to locate and correct all relevant computer codes, and similar uncertainties.

Corporate

HUMAN RESOURCES AND SOCIAL RESPONSIBILITY

Harley-Davidson employed approximately 6,060 people in 1997. This was approximately a 9% reduction from 6,700 employees in 1995. This reduction was principally due to the sale of the Transportation Segment. The employment details for the Motorcycles and Related Products segment and the Financial Services segment were discussed earlier in this case.

Some of the highlights and growth initiatives in community affairs according to management were:

1. In its 16 years as a national corporate sponsor of MDA, the Harley-Davidson family of employees, dealers, customers, and suppliers had raised more than $25 million for the fight against neuromuscular disease. Not included in that figure were hundreds of thousands of dollars raised for MDA through the European and Asian-Pacific families. In 1997, more than $2.6 million was raised for MDA.

2. Harley-Davidson dealers and HOG chapters had adopted many local charitable or civic organizations around the world.

3. Through the Motor Company's Volunteer Matching Hours Program, employees were encouraged to volunteer and become involved in charitable organizations. Harley-Davidson then matched volunteer hours with monetary grants to those organizations, giving all employees a voice in how the company invested in its communities.

Richard F. Teerlink said, "The employees of Harley-Davidson are committed to identifying new opportunities that will perpetuate our growth. And they're committed to developing these opportunities because it's fun! They want the excitement of remaining a growth company that is focused on continuously improving the mutually-beneficial relationships we have with all of our stakeholders over the long term. Their adherence to this simple philosophy has created positive results and a solid foundation for continued growth."[38]

CORPORATE FINANCIAL PERFORMANCE

The net sales of the company had increased annually for the last 5 years. The net sales for the company were $1,762,569,000, $1,531,227,000, $1,350,446,000, $1,158,887,000, and $932,262,000 for 1997, 1996, 1995, 1994, and 1993, respectively.

The net income for the company were $174,070,000, $166,028,000, $112,480,000, $104,272,000, and $(11,885,000) for 1997, 1996, 1995, 1994, and 1993, respectively. The 1993 loss was the result of a $55,600,000 (after-tax) write-down of goodwill and certain other assets at Holiday Rambler Corporation and a $30,300,000 (after-tax) 1-time charge for accounting

Exhibit 15

Consolidated Statements of Operations: Harley-Davidson, Inc.
(Dollar amounts in thousands, except per share data)

Year Ending December 31	1997	1996	1995
Net Sales	$1,762,569	$1,531,227	$1,350,466
Cost of goods sold	1,176,352	1,041,133	939,067
Gross profit	586,217	490,094	411,399
Operating income from financial services	12,355	7,801	3,620
Selling, administrative, and engineering	(328,569)	(269,449)	(234,223)
Income from operations	270,003	228,446	180,796
Interest income	7,871	3,309	1,446
Interest expense	—	—	(1,350)
Other—net	(1,572)	(4,133)	(4,903)
Income from continuing operations before provision for income taxes	276,302	227,622	175,989
Provision for income taxes	102,232	84,213	64,939
Income from continuing operations	174,070	143,409	111,050
Discontinued operations			
Income from operations, net of applicable income taxes	—	—	1,430
Gain on disposition of discontinued operations, net of applicable income taxes	—	22,619	—
Net income	$ 174,070	$ 166,028	$ 112,480
Basic earnings per common share:			
Income from continuing operations	$ 1.15	$ 0.95	$ 0.74
Income from discontinued operations	$ —	$ 0.15	$ 0.01
Net income	$ 1.15	$ 1.10	$ 0.75
Diluted earnings per common share:			
Income from continuing operations	$ 1.13	$ 0.94	$ 0.73
Income from discontinued operations	$ —	$ 0.15	$ 0.01
Net income	$ 1.13	$ 1.09	$ 0.74
Cash dividends per common share	$ 0.135	$ 0.11	$ 0.09

Source: Harley-Davidson, Inc., *1997 Annual Report*, p. 49.

changes related to post-retirement health care benefits and income taxes. Net sales and earnings for 1997 and 1996 were at record levels.

The board had authorized the repurchasing of 8 million shares of common stock. In 1995, 3.3 million shares were purchased. The company was still able to repurchase another 4.7 million shares. As of March 20, 1998, there were approximately 52,578 shareholders of record.

On August 20, 1997, the company's Board of Directors declared a 2-for-1 stock split for shareholders of record on September 12, 1997. On December 31, 1997, the company had 157,241,441 shares of common stock issued.

Exhibit 16

Consolidated Balance Sheets: Harley-Davidson, Inc.
(Dollar amounts in thousands, except per share data)

Year Ending December 31	1997	1996
Assets		
Current assets		
Cash and cash equivalents	$ 147,462	$ 142,479
Accounts receivable, net	102,797	141,315
Finance receivables, net	293,329	183,808
Inventories	117,475	101,386
Deferred income taxes	24,941	25,999
Prepaid expenses	18,017	18,142
Total current assets	704,021	613,129
Finance receivables, net	249,346	154,264
Property, plant, and equipment—net	528,869	409,434
Deferred income taxes	3,001	4,691
Goodwill	38,707	40,900
Other assets	74,957	77,567
Total assets	$1,598,901	$1,299,985
Liabilities and shareholders' equity		
Current liabilities		
Accounts payable	$ 106,112	$ 100,699
Accrued and other liabilities	164,938	142,334
Current portion of finance debt	90,638	8,065
Total current liabilities	361,688	251,098
Finance debt	280,000	250,000
Long-term liabilities	62,131	70,366
Post-retirement healthcare benefits	68,414	65,801
Commitments and contingencies		
Shareholders' equity		
Series A Junior Participating preferred stock, none issued	—	0
Common stock, 157,241,441 and 156,252,182 shares		
issued in 1997 and 1996, respectively	1,572	1,562
Additional paid-in capital	187,180	174,371
Retained earnings	683,824	530,782
Cumulative foreign currency translation adjustment	(2,835)	(566)
	869,741	706,149
Less		
Treasury stock (4,916,488 and 4,914,368 shares in		
1997 and 1996, respectively), at cost	(41,959)	(41,933)
Unearned compensation	(1,114)	(1,496)
Total shareholders' equity	826,668	662,720
Total liabilities and shareholders' equity	$1,598,901	$1,299,985

Source: Harley-Davidson, Inc., *1997 Annual Report*, p. 50.

The stock price ranged from $31.25 to $16.875 and $24.75 to $13.185 for 1997 and 1996. The company paid its first dividend in 1993. The dividends were 13.5¢, 11¢, 9¢, 7¢, and 3¢ for 1997, 1996, 1995, 1994, and 1993, respectively (see **Exhibit 16**).

Exhibits 15, 16, and **17** are the company's income statement, balance sheet, and selected financial data. **Exhibit 18** provides geographic revenues and assets.

Exhibit 17

Selected Financial Data: Harley-Davidson, Inc.
(Dollar amounts in thousands, except per share data)

Year Ending December 31	1997	1996	1995	1994	1993
Income Statement Data					
Net sales	$1,762,569	$1,531,227	$1,350,466	$1,158,887	$ 933,262
Cost of goods sold	1,176,352	1,041,133	939,067	800,548	641,248
Gross profit	586,217	490,094	411,399	358,339	292,014
Operating income from financial services	12,355	7,801	3,620	—	—
Selling, administrative, and engineering	(328,569)	(269,449)	(234,223)	(204,777)	(162,675)
Income from operations	270,003	228,446	180,796	153,562	129,339
Interest income, net	7,871	3,309	96	1,682	994
Other income (expense), net	(1,572)	(4,133)	(4,903)	1,196	(3,249)
Income from continuing operations before provision for income taxes and accounting changes	276,302	227,622	175,989	156,440	127,084
Provision for income taxes	102,232	84,213	64,939	60,219	50,765
Income from continuing operations before accounting changes	174,070	143,409	111,050	96,221	76,319
Income (loss) from discontinued operations, net of tax	—	22,619	1,430	8,051	(57,904)
Income before accounting changes	174,070	166,028	112,480	104,272	18,415
Cumulative effect of accounting changes, net of tax	—	—	—	—	(30,300)
Net income (loss)	$ 174,070	$ 166,028	$ 112,480	$ 104,272	$ (11,885)
Weighted average common shares					
Basic	$ 151,650	$ 150,683	$ 149,972	$ 150,440	$ 149,048
Diluted	153,948	152,925	151,900	153,365	152,004
Earnings per common share from continuing operations					
Basic	$ 1.15	$ 0.95	$ 0.74	$ 0.64	$ 0.51
Diluted	1.13	0.94	0.73	0.63	0.50
Dividends paid	$ 0.135	$ 0.11	$ 0.09	$ 0.07	$ 0.03
Balance sheet data					
Working capital	$ 342,333	$ 362,031	$ 288,783	$ 189,358	$ 142,996
Currant finance receivables, net	293,329	183,808	169,615	—	—
Long-term finance receivables, net	249,346	154,264	43,829	—	—
Total assets	1,598,901	1,299,985	980,670	676,663	527,958
Short-term debt, including current maturities of long-term debt	—	2,580	2,691	1,431	4,190
Long-term debt, less current maturities	20,934	25,122	18,207	9,021	2,919
Short-term finance debt	90,638	8,065	—	—	—
Long-term finance debt	280,000	250,000	164,330	—	—
Total debt	391,572	285,767	185,228	10,452	7,109
Shareholders' equity	$ 826,668	$ 662,720	$ 494,569	$ 433,232	$ 324,912

Note: The notes were deleted.

Source: Harley-Davidson, Inc., *1997 Annual Report*, p. 40.

Exhibit 18
Geographic Information: Harley-Davidson, Inc.
(Dollar amounts in thousands)

	1997	1996	1995
Revenues[1]			
United States	$1,304,748	$1,110,527	$ 949,415
Canada	62,717	58,053	48,046
Germany	81,541	82,800	102,638
Japan	90,243	79,401	69,350
Other foreign countries	223,320	200,446	181,017
Total revenues	**$1,762,569**	**$1,531,227**	**$1,350,466**
Long-lived assets[2]			
United States	$ 607,363	$ 492,054	$ 353,801
Other foreign countries	7,073	7,508	5,325
Total	**$ 614,436**	**$ 499,562**	**$ 359,126**

Notes:
1. Revenues are attributed to geographic regions based on location of customer.
2. Long-lived assets include all long-term assets except those specifically excluded under SFAS No. 131 such as deferred income taxes and financial instruments, including finance receivables.

Source: Harley-Davidson, Inc., *Form 10-K* (December 31, 1997), p. 53.

Notes

1. Stuart C. Henricks, Charles B. Shrader, and Allan N. Hoffman, "The Eagle Soars Alone," in *Strategic Management and Business Policy*, 3rd Ed., by Thomas L. Wheelen and J. David Hunger (Reading, Mass.: Addison-Wesley Publishing Company, 1989), pp. 453–458. Parts of this case were abstracted and rewritten from the case "The Eagle Soars Alone." Harley-Davidson, Inc., *1997 Annual Report*, pp. 9, 27, and 32; and Harley-Davidson, Inc., *Form 10-K* (December 31, 1997), p. 40.
2. Harley-Davidson, Inc., *1993 Annual Report*, p. 23.
3. Harley-Davidson, Inc., *Form 10-K* (December 31, 1997), p. 40. These above 2 paragraphs were directly quoted with minor editing.
4. Roy Furchgott, "Rebel Without an Engine," *Business Week* (September 15, 1997), p. 8.
5. Harley-Davidson, Inc., *1997 Notice of Annual Meeting*, pp. 3–5. Some paragraphs were directly quoted with minor editing.
6. Harley-Davidson, Inc., *1997 Annual Report*, p. i.
7. Harley-Davidson, Inc., *1997 Notice of Annual Meeting*, p. 2.
8. *Ibid.*, pp. 3, 4, and 6.
9. Harley-Davidson, Inc., *1997 Annual Report*, pp. 18–19. These 3 paragraphs were directly quoted with minor editing.
10. Harley-Davidson, Inc., *1997 Form 10-K*, p. 51. These 2 paragraphs were directly quoted with minor editing.
11. Harley-Davidson, Inc., *1997 Annual Report*, p. 3. The following section was directly quoted with minor editing.
12. Harley-Davidson, Inc., *1997 Form 10-K*, pp. 6–7. The following 6 paragraphs were directly quoted with minor editing.
13. *Ibid.* The following 2 paragraphs were directly quoted with minor editing.
14. *Ibid.* The following 2 paragraphs were directly quoted with minor editing.
15. *Ibid.*, pp. 6–7. The following paragraph was directly quoted with minor editing.
16. *Ibid.*, p. 7. The following 5 paragraphs were directly quoted with minor editing.
17. *Ibid.*, pp. 7–9. The following 6 paragraphs were directly quoted with minor editing.
18. Ken Stevens and Dale Kurschner, "That Vroom! You Hear May Not Be a Harley," *Business Week* (October 20, 1997), p. 160.
19. *Ibid.*
20. Maureen Kline, "An Italian Motorcycle Maker Revs Up Luxury Image," *Wall Street Journal* (December 26, 1997), p. B1.
21. *Ibid.*
22. *Ibid.*, p. B3.
23. Case author's conversation with these 2 dealers.
24. *Ibid.*, pp. 9–10. The below 4 paragraphs were directly quoted with minor editing.
25. *Ibid.*, p. 10. The below 2 paragraphs were directly quoted with minor editing.
26. *Ibid.* The below paragraph was directly quoted with minor editing.
27. *Ibid.*, pp. 10–11. The below 2 paragraphs were directly quoted with minor editing.
28. *Ibid.*, p. 11. The above paragraphs were directly quoted with minor editing.
29. *Ibid.*, p. 38. The table and above 2 paragraphs were directly quoted with minor editing.
30. *Ibid.*, p. 11. The below 6 paragraphs were directly quoted with minor editing.
31. *Ibid.*, p. 12. This paragraph was directly quoted with minor editing.
32. *Ibid.*, p. 44. The below 4 paragraphs were directly quoted with minor editing.
33. Richard Gibson, "Jury Finds Against Harley-Davidson in Accident Case," *Wall Street Journal* (February 2, 1997), p. B2.
34. *Ibid.*, pp. 14–15. The above 3 paragraphs were directly quoted with minor editing.
35. *Ibid.*
36. Harley-Davidson, Inc., *1997 Form 10-K*, pp. 12 and 13. The operating income paragraph was added. All other paragraphs were directly quoted with minor editing. Harley-Davidson, Inc., *1997 Annual Report*, p. 28.
37. *Ibid.*, p. 26. The below 3 paragraphs were directly quoted with minor editing.
38. Harley-Davidson, Inc., *1994 Annual Report*, p. 39.

Carnival Corporation

Michael J. Keeffe, John K. Ross III, and Bill J. Middlebrook

Carnival Corporation, in terms of passengers carried, revenues generated, and available capacity, was the largest cruise line in the world and considered the leader and innovator in the cruise travel industry. Given its inauspicious beginnings, Carnival had grown from 2 converted ocean liners to an organization with 2 cruise divisions (and a joint venture to operate a third cruise line) and a chain of Alaskan hotels and tour coaches. Corporate revenues for fiscal 1997 reached $2.4 billion with net income from operations of $666 million. The growth continued, with May 1998 revenues up $100 million over the same quarter in 1997 to $1.219 billion. Carnival had several "firsts" in the cruise industry: the first cruise line to carry over 1 million passengers in a single year and 5 million total passengers by fiscal 1994. In 1998, its market share of the cruise travel industry stood at approximately 26% overall.

Carnival Corporation CEO and Chairman Micky Arison and Carnival Cruise Lines President Bob Dickinson were prepared to maintain the company's reputation as the leader and innovator in the industry. They assembled 1 of the newest fleets catering to cruisers, with the introduction of several "superliners" built specifically for the Caribbean and Alaskan cruise markets, and expected to invest over $3.0 billion in new ships by the year 2002. Additionally the company had expanded its Holland America Lines fleet to cater to more established cruisers and planned to add 3 of the new ships to its fleet in the premium cruise segment. Strategically, Carnival Corporation seemed to have made the right moves at the right time, sometimes in direct contradiction to industry analysts and cruise trends.

The Cruise Lines International Association (CLIA), an industry trade group, tracked the growth of the cruise industry for over 25 years. In 1970, approximately 500,000 passengers took cruises for 3 consecutive nights or more, reaching a peak of 5 million passengers in 1997, an average annual compound growth rate of approximately 8.9% (this growth rate declined to approximately 2% per year over the period from 1991 to 1995). At the end of 1997, the industry had 136 ships in service, with an aggregate berth capacity of 119,000. CLIA estimated that the number of passengers carried in North America would increase from 4.6 million in 1996 to 5 million in 1997, or approximately 8.7%. CLIA expected the number of cruise passengers to increase to 5.3 million in 1998; and with new ships to be delivered, the North American market would have roughly 144 vessels with an aggregate capacity of 132,000 berths.

Carnival exceeded the recent industry trends, and the growth rate in the number of passengers carried was 11.2% per year over the 1992 to 1996 period. The company's passenger

This case was prepared by Professors Michael J. Keeffe, John K. Ross III, and Bill J. Middlebrook of Southwest Texas State University. The case was edited for SMBP-8th Edition. Copyright © 1998 by Michael J. Keeffe, John K. Ross III, and Bill J. Middlebrook. Reprinted by permission.

capacity in 1991 was 17,973 berths and had increased to 31,078 at the end of fiscal 1997. Capacity was added with the delivery of several new cruise ships, such as the Elation, which went into service in early 1998 and increased passenger capacity by 2,040.

Even with the growth in the cruise industry, the company believed that cruises represented only 2% of the applicable North American vacation market, defined as persons who travel for leisure purposes on trips of 3 nights or longer, involving at least 1 night's stay in a hotel. The Boston Consulting group, in a 1989 study, estimated that only 5% of persons in the North American target market have taken a cruise for leisure purposes and estimated the market potential to be in excess of $50 billion. Carnival's management believed that by 1996 only 7% of the North American population has ever cruised. Various cruise operators, including Carnival Corporation, had based their expansion and capital spending programs on the possibility of capturing part of the 93% of the North American population who had yet to take a cruise vacation.

The Evolution of Cruising

With the replacement of ocean liners by aircraft in the 1960s as the primary means of transoceanic travel, the opportunity for developing the modern cruise industry was created. Ships that were no longer required to ferry passengers from destination to destination became available to investors with visions of a new vacation alternative to complement the increasing affluence of Americans. Cruising, once the purview of the rich and leisure class, was targeted to the middle class, with services and amenities similar to the grand days of first-class ocean travel.

According to Robert Meyers, Editor and Publisher of *Cruise Travel* magazine, the increasing popularity of taking a cruise as a vacation can be traced to 2 serendipitously timed events. First, television's "Love Boat" series dispelled many myths associated with cruising and depicted people of all ages and backgrounds enjoying the cruise experience. This show was among the top 10 shows on television for many years, according to Nielsen ratings, and provided extensive publicity for cruise operators. Second, the increasing affluence of Americans and the increased participation of women in the work force gave couples and families more disposable income for discretionary purposes, especially vacations. As the myths were dispelled and disposable income grew, younger couples and families "turned on" to the benefits of cruising as a vacation alternative, creating a large new target market for the cruise product, which accelerated the growth in the number of Americans taking cruises as a vacation.

Carnival History

In 1972, Ted Arison, backed by American International Travel Services, Inc. (AITS), purchased an aging ocean liner from Canadian Pacific Empress Lines for $6.5 million. The new AITS subsidiary, Carnival Cruise Line, refurbished the vessel from bow to stern and renamed it the *Mardi Gras* to capture the party spirit. (Also included in the deal was another ship later renamed the *Carnivale.*) The company start was not promising, however. On its first voyage, the *Mardi Gras*, with over 300 invited travel agents aboard, ran aground in Miami Harbor. The ship was slow and guzzled expensive fuel, limiting the number of ports of call and lengthening the minimum stay of passengers on the ship to break even. Arison then bought another old ocean vessel from Union Castle Lines to complement the *Mardi Gras* and the *Carnivale* and named it the *Festivale*. To attract customers, Arison began adding on-board diversion such as planned activities, a casino, nightclubs, discos, and other forms of entertainment designed to enhance the shipboard experience.

Carnival lost money for the next 3 years, and in late 1974, Ted Arison bought out the Carnival Cruise subsidiary of AITS, Inc., for $1 cash and the assumption of $5 million in debt. One month later, the *Mardi Gras* began showing a profit and through the remainder of 1975 operated at more than 100% capacity. (Normal ship capacity is determined by the number of fixed berths available. Ships, like hotels, can operate beyond this fixed capacity by using roll-away beds, pullmans, and upper bunks.)

Ted Arison (then Chairman), along with Bob Dickinson (who was then Vice President of Sales and Marketing) and his son Micky Arison (then President of Carnival), began to alter the current approach to cruise vacations. Carnival went after first-time and younger cruisers with a moderately priced vacation package that included air fare to the port of embarkation and home after the cruise. Per diem rates were very competitive with other vacation packages, and Carnival offered passage to multiple exotic Caribbean ports, several meals served daily with premier restaurant service, and all forms of entertainment and activities included in the base fare. Items of a personal nature, liquor purchases, gambling, and tips for the cabin steward, table waiter, and busboy were not included in the fare. Carnival continued to add to the ship-board experience with a greater variety of activities, nightclubs, and other forms of entertainment and varied ports of call to increase its attractiveness to potential customers.

Carnival was the first modern cruise operator to use multimedia advertising promotions and to establish the theme of "Fun Ship" cruises, primarily promoting the ship as the destination and ports of call as secondary. Carnival told the public that it was throwing a shipboard party and everyone was invited. The "Fun Ship" theme still permeated all Carnival Cruise ships.

Throughout the 1980s, Carnival was able to maintain a growth rate of approximately 30%, about 3 times that of the industry as a whole, and between 1982 and 1988, its ships sailed with an average of 104% capacity (currently they operate at 104% to 105% capacity, depending on the season). Targeting younger, first-time passengers by promoting the ship as a destination proved to be extremely successful. Carnival's 1987 customer profile showed that 30% of the passengers were between the ages of 25 and 39 with household incomes of $25,000 to $50,000.

In 1987, Ted Arison sold 20% of his shares in Carnival Cruise Lines and immediately generated over $400 million for further expansion. In 1988, Carnival acquired the Holland America Line, which had 4 cruise ships with 4,500 berths. Holland America was positioned to the higher income travelers, with cruise prices averaging 25 to 35% more than similar Carnival cruises. The deal also included 2 Holland America subsidiaries, Windstar Sail Cruises and Holland America Westours. This success, and the foresight of management, allowed Carnival to begin an aggressive "superliner" building campaign for its core subsidiary. By 1989, the cruise segments of Carnival Corporation carried over 750,000 passengers in 1 year, a "first" in the cruise industry.

Ted Arison relinquished the role of Chairman to his son Micky in 1990, a time when the explosive growth of the 1980s began to subside. Higher fuel prices and increased airline costs began to affect the industry as a whole. The Persian Gulf War caused many cruise operators to divert ships from European and Indian ports to the Caribbean area of operations, increasing the number of ships competing directly with Carnival. Carnival's stock price fell from $25 in June 1990 to $13 late in the year. The company also incurred a $25.5 million loss during fiscal 1990 for the operation of the Crystal Palace Resort and Casino in the Bahamas. In 1991, Carnival reached a settlement with the Bahamian government (effective March 1, 1992) to surrender the 672-room Riviera Towers to the Hotel Corporation of the Bahamas in exchange for the cancellation of some debt incurred in constructing and developing the resort. The corporation took a $135 million write-down on the Crystal Palace for that year.

The early 1990s, even with industry-wide demand slowing, were still a very exciting time. Carnival took delivery of its first 2 "superliners"; the *Fantasy* (1990) and the *Ecstasy* (1991), which were to further penetrate the 3- and 4-day cruise market and supplement the 7-day market. In early 1991, Carnival took delivery of the third "superliner," *Sensation* (inaugural sailing November 1, 1993), and later in the year contracted for the fourth "superliner" to be named the *Fascination* (inaugural sailing 1994).

In 1991, Carnival attempted to acquire Premier Cruise Lines, which was then the official cruise line for Walt Disney World in Orlando, Florida, for approximately $372 million. The deal was never consummated because the involved parties could not agree on price. In 1992, Carnival acquired 50% of Seabourn, gaining the cruise operations of K/S Seabourn Cruise Lines, and formed a partnership with Atle Byrnestad. Seabourn serves the ultra-luxury market with destinations in South America, the Mediterranean, Southeast Asia, and the Baltics.

The 1993 to 1995 period saw the addition of the "superliner" *Imagination* for Carnival Cruise Lines and the *Ryndam* for Holland America Lines. In 1994, the company discontinued operations of Fiestamarina Lines, which attempted to serve Spanish-speaking clientele. Fiestamarina was beset with marketing and operational problems and never reached continuous operations. Many industry analysts and observers were surprised at the failure of Carnival to successfully develop this market. In 1995, Carnival sold a 49% interest in the Epirotiki Line, a Greek cruise operation, for $25 million, and it purchased $101 million (face amount) of senior secured notes of Kloster Cruise Limited, the parent of competitor Norwegian Cruise Lines, for $81 million. Kloster was having financial difficulties and Carnival could not obtain common stock of the company in a negotiated agreement. If Kloster were to fail, Carnival Corporation would be in a good position to acquire some of the assets of Kloster.

Carnival Corporation expanded through internally generated growth, as evidenced by the number of new ships on order (**Exhibit 1**). Additionally Carnival seemed to be willing to continue with its external expansion through acquisitions if the right opportunity arose.

In June 1997, Royal Caribbean made a bid to buy Celebrity Cruise Lines for $500 million and assumption of $800 million in debt. Within a week, Carnival had responded by submit-

Exhibit 1

Carnival and Holland America Ships Under Construction

Vessel	Expected Delivery	Shipyard	Passenger Capacity[1]	Cost (millions)
Carnival Cruise Lines				
Elation	03/98	Masa-Yards	2,040	$ 300
Paradise	12/98	Masa-Yards	2,040	300
Carnival Triumph	07/99	Fincantieri	2,640	400
Carnival Victory	08/00	Fincantieri	2,640	430
CCL Newbuild	12/00	Masa-Yards	2,100	375
CCL Newbuild	2001	Masa-Yards	2,100	375
CCL Newbuild	2002	Masa-Yards	2,100	375
Total Carnival Cruise Lines			15,660	$2,555
Holland America Line				
Volendam	6/99	Fincantieri	1,440	274
Zaandam	12/99	Fincantieri	1,440	286
HAL Newbuild	9/00	Fincantieri	1,440	300
Total Holland America Line			4,320	$ 860
Windstar Cruises				
Wind Surf	5/98	Purchase	312	40
Total all vessels			20,484	$3,337

Note:
1. In accordance with industry practice, all capacities indicated are calculated based on 2 passengers per cabin even though some cabins can accommodate 3 or 4 passengers. (*Form 10-Q, 5/31/98*).

ting a counter offer to Celebrity for $510 million and the assumption of debt, then 2 days later raising the bid to $525 million. However, Royal Caribbean seemed to have had the inside track and announced the final merger arrangements with Celebrity on June 30, 1997. The resulting company had 17 ships with approximately 30,000 berths.

However, not to be thwarted in their attempts at continued expansion, Carnival announced in June 1997 the purchase of Costa, an Italian cruise company and the largest European cruise line, for $141 million. External expansion continued when, on May 28, 1998, Carnival announced the acquisition of Cunard Line for $500 million from Kvaerner ASA. Cunard was then merged with Seabourn Cruise Line (50% owned by Carnival) with Carnival owning 68% of the resulting Cunard Line Limited.

The Cruise Product

Ted and Micky Arison envisioned a product in which the classical cruise elegance along with modern convenience could be had at a price comparable to land-based vacation packages sold by travel agents. Carnival's all-inclusive package, when compared to resorts or a theme park such as Walt Disney World, often was priced below these destinations; especially when the array of activities, entertainment, and meals was considered.

A typical vacation on a Carnival cruise ship starts when the bags are tagged for the ship at the airport. Upon arriving at the port of embarkation, passengers are ferried by air-conditioned buses to the ship for boarding, and luggage is delivered by the cruise ship staff to the passenger's cabin. Waiters dot the ship offering tropical drinks to the backdrop of a Caribbean rhythm, while the cruise staff orients passengers to the various decks, cabins, and public rooms. In a few hours (most ships sail in the early evening), dinner is served in the main dining rooms, where wine selection rivals the finest restaurants and the variety of main dishes are designed to suit every palate. Diners can always order double portions if they decide not to save room for the variety of desserts and after-dinner specialties.

After dinner, cruisers can choose between many forms of entertainment, including live music, dancing, nightclubs, and a selection of movies; or they can sleep through the midnight buffet until breakfast. (Most ships have 5 or more distinct nightclubs.) During the night, a daily program of activities arrives at the passengers' cabins. The biggest decisions to be made for the duration of the vacation will be what to do (or not to do), what to eat and when (usually 8 separate serving times, not including the 24-hour room service), and when to sleep. Service in all areas from dining to housekeeping is upscale and immediate. The service is so good that a common shipboard joke says that if you leave your bed during the night to visit the head (sea talk for bathroom), your cabin steward will have made the bed and placed chocolates on the pillow by the time you return.

After the cruise, passengers are transported back to the airport in air-conditioned buses for the flight home. Representatives of the cruise line are on hand at the airport to help cruisers meet their scheduled flights. When all amenities are considered, most vacation packages would be hard pressed to match Carnival's per diem prices that range from $125 to $250 per person/per day, depending on accommodations. (Holland America and Seabourn are higher, averaging $300 per person/per day.) Occasional specials allow for even lower prices and special suite accommodations can be had for an additional payment.

Carnival Operations

Carnival Corporation, headquartered in Miami, was composed of Carnival Cruise Lines, Holland America Lines (which included Windstar Sail Cruises as a subsidiary), Holland America Westours, Westmark Hotels, Airtours, and the newly created Cunard Line Limited.

Carnival Cruise Lines, Inc., was a Panamanian corporation, and its subsidiaries were incorporated in Panama, the Netherlands Antilles, the British Virgin Islands, Liberia, and the Bahamas. The ships were subject to inspection by the U.S. Coast Guard for compliance with the Convention for the Safety of Life at Sea (SOLAS), which required specific structural requirements for the safety of passengers at sea, and by the U.S. Public Health Service for sanitary standards. The company was also regulated in some aspects by the Federal Maritime Commission.

At its helm, Carnival Corporation was led by CEO and Chairman of the Board Micky Arison and Carnival Cruise Lines President and COO Bob Dickinson. A. Kirk Lanterman was the President and CEO of the Holland America cruise division, which included Holland America Westours and Windstar Sail Cruises. (A listing of corporate officers is presented in **Exhibit 2.**)

The company's product positioning stemmed from its belief that the cruise market actually comprises 3 primary segments with different passenger demographics, passenger characteristics, and growth requirements. The 3 segments were the *contemporary, premium,* and *luxury* segments. The contemporary segment was served by Carnival ships for cruises that are 7 days or shorter in length and featured a casual ambiance. The premium segment, served by Holland America, served the 7-day and longer market and appealed to more affluent consumers. The luxury segment, although considerably smaller than the other segments, catered to experienced cruisers for 7-day and longer sailings and was served by Seabourn. Windstar Sail Cruises, a subsidiary of Holland America, provided specialty sailing cruises.

Corporate structure was built around the "profit center" concept and updated periodically when needed for control and coordination purposes. The cruise subsidiaries of Carnival gave the corporation a presence in most of the major cruise segments and provided for worldwide operations.

Carnival always placed a high priority on marketing in an attempt to promote cruises as an alternative to land-based vacations. It wanted customers to know that the ship in

Exhibit 2
Corporate Officers of Carnival Corporation

Micky Arison Chairman of the Board Chief Executive Officer Carnival Corporation	**Lowell Zemnick** Vice President and Treasurer Carnival Corporation
Gerald R. Cahill Senior Vice President—Finance and CFO Carnival Corporation	**Meshulam Zonis** Senior Vice President—Operations Carnival Cruise Lines
Robert H. Dickinson President and COO Carnival Cruise Lines	**A. Kirk Lanterman** Chairman of the Board Chief Executive Officer Holland America Lines
Howard S. Frank Vice Chairman and Chief Operating Officer Carnival Corporation	**Peter T. McHugh** President and COO Holland America Lines
Roderick K. McLeod Senior Vice President—Marketing Carnival Corporation	

Source: Carnival Corporation, 1998.

itself was the destination and the ports of call were important, but secondary, to the cruise experience. Education and creation of awareness were critical to corporate marketing efforts. Carnival was the first cruise line to successfully break away from traditional print media and use television to reach a broader market. Even though other lines had followed Carnival's lead in selecting promotional media and were near in total advertising expenditures, the organization still led all cruise competitors in advertising and marketing expenditures.

Carnival wanted to remain the leader and innovator in the cruise industry and intended to do so with sophisticated promotional efforts and by gaining loyalty from former cruisers, by refurbishing ships, varying activities and ports of call, and being innovative in all aspects of ship operations. Management intended to build on the theme of the ship as a destination given the historical success with this promotional effort. The company capitalized and amortized direct-response advertising and expenses other advertising costs as incurred. Advertising expense totaled $112 million in 1997, $109 million in 1996, $98 million in 1995, and $85 million in 1994.

Financial Performance

Carnival retained Price Waterhouse as independent accountants, the Barnett Bank Trust Company–North America as the registrar and stock transfer agent, and its Class A Common stock traded on the New York Stock Exchange under the symbol CCL. In December 1996, Carnival amended the terms of its revolving credit facility primarily to combine 2 facilities into a single $1 billion unsecured revolving credit facility due in 2001. The borrowing rate on the One Billion Dollar Revolver is a maximum of LIBOR[1] plus 14 basis points and the facility fee is 6 basis points. Carnival initiated a commercial paper program in October 1996, which is supported by the One Billion Dollar Revolver. As of November 30, 1996, the company had $307 million outstanding under its commercial paper program and $693 million available for borrowing under the One Billion Dollar Revolver.

The consolidated financial statements for Carnival Cruise Lines, Inc., are shown in **Exhibits 3** and **4** and selected financial data are presented in **Exhibit 5**.

Customer cruise deposits, which represent unearned revenue, are included in the balance sheet when received and recognized as cruise revenues on completion of the voyage. Customers also are required to pay the full cruise fare (minus deposit) 60 days in advance, with the fares being recognized as cruise revenue on completion of the voyage.

---

[1]"LIBOR Rate" means, for an Interest Period for each LIBOR (London Interbank Offer Rate) Rate Advance comprising part of the same Borrowing, the rate determined by the Agent to be the rate of interest per annum rounded upward to the nearest whole multiple of 1/100 of 1% per annum, appearing on the Telerate screen 3750 at 11:00 A.M. (London time) 2 business days before the first day of such interest period for a term equal to such interest period and in an amount substantially equal to such portion of the loan, or if the agent cannot so determine the LIBOR rate by reference screen 3750, then (ii) equal to the average (rounded upward to the nearest whole multiple of 1/100 of 1% per annum, if such average is not such a multiple) of the rate per annum at which deposits in United States dollars are offered by the principal office of each of the reference lenders in London, England, to prime banks in the London Interbank market at 11:00 A.M. (London time) 2 business days before the first day of such interest period for a term equal to such interest period and in an amount substantially equal to such portion of the loan. In the latter case, the LIBOR rate for an interest period shall be determined by the agent on the basis of applicable rates furnished to and received by the agent from the reference lenders 2 business days before the first day of such interest period, subject, however, to the provisions of Section 2.05. If at any time the agent shall determine that by reason of circumstances affecting the London Interbank market (i) adequate and reasonable means do not exist for ascertaining the LIBOR rate for the succeeding interest period or (ii) the making or continuance of any loan at the LIBOR rate has become impracticable as a result of a contingency occurring after the date of this agreement which materially and adversely affects the London Interbank market, the agent shall so notify the lenders and the borrower. Failing the availability of the LIBOR rate, the LIBOR rate shall mean the base rate thereafter in effect from time to time until such time as a LIBOR rate may be determined by reference to the London Interbank market.

Seabourn targeted the luxury market with 3 vessels providing 200 passengers per ship with all-suite accommodations. Seabourn was considered the "Rolls Royce" of the cruise industry and in 1992 was named the "World's Best Cruise Line" by the prestigious Condé Naste *Traveler's* Fifth Annual Readers' Choice poll. Seabourn cruised the Americas, Europe, Scandinavia, the Mediterranean, and the Far East.

AIRTOURS

In April 1996, Carnival acquired a 29.5% interest in Airtours for approximately $370 million. Airtours and its subsidiaries was the largest air-inclusive tour operator in the world and was publicly rated on the London Stock Exchange. Airtours provided air-inclusive packaged holidays to the British, Scandinavian, and North American markets. Airtours provided holidays to approximately 5 million people per year and owned or operated 32 hotels, 2 cruise ships, and 31 aircraft.

Airtours operated 19 aircraft exclusively for its U.K. tour operators, providing a large proportion of their flying requirements. In addition, Airtours' subsidiary Premiair operated a fleet of 14 aircraft, which provided most of the flying requirements for Airtours' Scandinavian tour operators.

Airtours owned or operated 32 hotels (6,500 rooms), which provided rooms to Airtours' tour operators principally in the Mediterranean and the Canary Islands. In addition, airtours had a 50% interest in Tenerife Sol, a joint venture with Sol Hotels Group of Spain, which owned and operated 3 additional hotels in the Canary Islands providing 1,300 rooms.

Through its subsidiary Sun Cruises, Airtours owned and operated 3 cruise ships. Both the 800-berth *MS Seawing* and the 1,062-berth *MS Carousel* commenced operations in 1995. Recently Airtours acquired a third ship, the *MS Sundream*, which was the sister ship of the *MS Carousel*. The ships operated in the Mediterranean, the Caribbean, and around the Canary Islands and were booked exclusively by Airtours' tour operators.

COSTA CROCIERE S.P.A

In June 1997, Carnival and Airtours purchased the equity securities of Costa from the Costa family at a cost of approximately $141 million. Costa was headquartered in Italy and was considered Europe's largest cruise line with 7 ships and a 7,710-passenger capacity. Costa operated primarily in the Mediterranean, Northern Europe, the Caribbean, and South America. The major market for Costa was in southern Europe, mainly Italy, Spain, and France. In January 1998, Costa signed an agreement to construct an eighth ship with a capacity of approximately 2,100 passengers.

CUNARD LINE

Carnival's most recent acquisition had been the Cunard Line, announced on May 28, 1998. Comprised of 5 ships, the Cunard Line was considered a luxury line with strong brand name recognition. Carnival purchased 50% of Cunard for an estimated $255 million, with the other 50% being owned by Atle Brynestad. Cunard was immediately merged with Seabourn and the resulting Cunard Cruise Line Limited (68% owned by Carnival) with its now 8 ships, was to be headed by the former President of Seabourn, Larry Pimentel.

JOINT VENTURE WITH HYUNDAI MERCHANT MARINE CO. LTD.

In September 1996, the Carnival and Hyundai Merchant Marine (HMM) Co. Ltd. signed an agreement to form a 50/50 joint venture to develop the Asian cruise vacation market. Each contributed $4.8 million as the initial capital of the joint venture. In addition, in

November 1996, Carnival sold the cruise ship *Tropicale* to the joint venture for approximately $95.5 million cash. Carnival then chartered the vessel from the joint venture until the joint venture was ready to begin cruise operations in the Asian market, targeting a start date in or around the spring of 1998. The joint venture borrowed the $95.5 million purchase price from a financial institution, and Carnival and HMM each guaranteed 50% of the borrowed funds.

This arrangement was, however, short lived as in September 1997, the joint venture was dissolved, and Carnival repurchased the *Tropicale* for $93 million.

Future Considerations

Carnival's management had to continue to monitor several strategic factors and issues for the next few years. The industry itself was expected to see further consolidation through mergers and buyouts, and the expansion of the industry could negatively affect the profitability of various cruise operators. Another factor of concern to management was how to reach the large North American market, of which only 5% to 7% have ever taken a cruise.

With the industry maturing, cruise competitors were becoming more sophisticated in their marketing efforts and price competition was the norm in most cruise segments. (For a partial listing of major industry competitors, see **Exhibit 7.**) Royal Caribbean Cruise Lines had also instituted a major shipbuilding program and was successfully challenging Carnival Cruise Lines in the contemporary segment. The announcement that the Walt Disney Company was entering the cruise market with two 80,000-ton cruise liners in 1998 was expected to significantly impact the "family" cruise vacation segment.

With competition intensifying, industry observers believed the wave of failures, mergers, buyouts, and strategic alliances would increase. Regency Cruises ceased operations on October 29, 1995, and filed for Chapter 11 bankruptcy. American Family Cruises, a spin-off from Costa Cruise Lines, failed to reach the family market, and Carnival's Fiestamarina failed to reach the Spanish-speaking market. EffJohn International sold its Commodore Cruise subsidiary to a group of Miami-based investors, which then chartered 1 of its 2 ships to World Explorer Cruises/Semester At Sea. Sun Cruise Lines merged with Epirotiki Cruise Line under the name of Royal Olympic Cruises, and Cunard bought the Royal Viking Line and its name from Kloster Cruise Ltd., with 1 ship of its fleet being transferred to Kloster's Royal Cruise Line. All of these failures, mergers, and buyouts occurred in 1995, which was not an unusual year for changes in the cruise line industry.

The increasing industry capacity was also a source of concern to cruise operators. The slow growth in industry demand was occurring during a period when industry berth capacity continued to grow. The entry of Disney and the ships already on order by current operators was expected to increase industry berth capacity by over 10,000 per year for the next 3 years, a significant increase. The danger lay in cruise operators using the "price" weapon in their marketing campaigns to fill cabins. If cruise operators could not make a reasonable return on investment, operating costs would have to be reduced (affecting quality of services) to remain profitable. This would increase the likelihood of further industry acquisitions, mergers, and consolidations. A worst case scenario would be the financial failure of weaker lines.

Still, Carnival's management believed that demand should increase during the remainder of the 1990s. Considering that only 5% to 7% of the North American market had taken a cruise vacation, reaching more of the North American target market would improve industry profitability. Industry analysts stated that the problem was that an "assessment of market potential" was only an "educated guess"; and what if the current demand figures were reflective of the future?

Exhibit 7

Major Industry Competitors

Celebrity Cruises, 5200 Blue Lagoon Drive, Miami, FL 33126
Celebrity Cruises operates 4 modern cruise ships on 4-, 7-, and 10-day cruises to Bermuda, the Caribbean, the Panama Canal, and Alaska. Celebrity attracts first-time cruisers as well as seasoned cruisers. Purchased by Royal Caribbean on July 30, 1997.

Norwegian Cruise Lines, 95 Merrick Way, Coral Gables, FL 33134
Norwegian Cruise Lines (NCL), formally Norwegian Caribbean Lines, was the first to base a modern fleet of cruise ships in the Port of Miami. It operates 10 modern cruise liners on 3-, 4-, and 7-day Eastern and Western Caribbean cruises and cruises to Bermuda. A wide variety of activities and entertainment attracts a diverse array of customers. NCL just completed reconstruction of 2 ships and is building the Norwegian Sky, a 2,000-passenger ship to be delivered in the summer of 1999.

Disney Cruise Line, 500 South Buena Vista Street, Burbank, CA 91521
Disney has just recently entered the cruise market with the introduction of the *Disney Magic* and *Disney Wonder*. Both ships cater to both children and adults and feature 875 staterooms each. Each cruise includes a visit to Disney's private island, Castaway Bay. Although Disney currently has only 2 ships and the cruise portion of Disney is small, the potential for future growth is substantial, with over $22 billion in revenues and $1.90 billion net profits in 1997.

Princess Cruises, 10100 Santa Monica Boulevard, Los Angeles, CA 90067
Princess Cruises, with its fleet of 9 "Love Boats," offers 7-day and extended cruises to the Caribbean, Alaska, Canada, Africa, the Far East, South America, and Europe. Princess's primary market is the upscale 50-plus experienced traveler, according to Mike Hannan, Senior Vice President for Marketing Services. Princess ships have an ambiance best described as casual elegance and are famous for their Italian-style dining rooms and onboard entertainment.

Royal Caribbean Cruise Lines, 1050 Caribbean Way, Miami, FL 33132
RCCL's 9 ships have consistently been given high marks by passengers and travel agents over the past 21 years. RCCL's ships are built for the contemporary market, are large and modern, and offer 3-, 4-, and 7-day as well as extended cruises. RCCL prides itself on service and exceptional cuisine. With the purchase of Celebrity, RCCL becomes the largest cruise line in the world with 17 ships and a passenger capacity of over 31,100. Plans include the introduction of 6 additional ships by the year 2002. In 1997, RCCL had net income of $175 million on revenues of $1.93 billion.

Other Industry Competitors (Partial List)

American Hawaii Cruises	(2 Ships–Hawaiian Islands)
Club Med	(2 Ships–Europe, Caribbean)
Commodore Cruise Line	(1 Ship–Caribbean)
Cunard Line	(8 Ships–Caribbean, Worldwide)
Dolphin Cruise Line	(3 Ships–Caribbean, Bermuda)
Radisson Seven Seas Cruises	(3 Ships–Worldwide)
Royal Olympic Cruises	(6 Ships–Caribbean, Worldwide)
Royal Cruise Line	(4 Ships–Caribbean, Alaska, WW)

Source: Cruise Line International Association, *1996 Form 10-K* and *Annual Report.*

Reebok International, Ltd.: Customer Revolt

Thomas L. Wheelen, Moustafa H. Abdelsamad, Stanley R. Sitnik, and Charles E. Michaels, Jr.

Paul Fireman, Chairman, President, and Chief Executive Officer (CEO) of Reebok, spelled out the company's situation in his letter to the shareholders in the *1997 Annual Report.*

This isn't going to be a traditional shareholders' letter. I'm not going to spend a lot of time telling you what went up, down or sideways in 1997. Despite difficult market conditions, we improved our earnings per share but fell short of our financial goals for the year.

Instead, I'd like to focus on the big picture. I'd like to talk with you about shifting consumer preferences. I'd like to share with you our multiple-brand strategy for achieving growth across a variety of market segments. But most importantly, I'd like to tell you about the future—my personal vision for where our company is headed—and why that should be important to you as an investor.

A Significant Market Shift

If you follow our business, you've probably read stories about a "worldwide product glut" plaguing the athletic footwear and apparel industry—the primary market for our Reebok® brand, which accounts for approximately 84% of our revenues. I can tell you first-hand these reports are not exaggerated. It's tough out there, and we believe it is unlikely that conditions will improve significantly until the end of the year or later.

Here's what I think is happening: Every 10 years or so, consumers get bored with the status quo. People change, fashions change, sports trends change. Without much warning, a fundamental market shift occurs. And things are never the same again.

In the 60s, canvas sneakers were king. In the 70s, track and field and tennis footwear grabbed the spotlight. This was followed by an explosion in running shoes and apparel. Reebok's heyday during the 80s was defined by fitness and aerobics. Throughout the past decade basketball shoes and big-name sport stars have dominated the industry.

Now a new change is underway—a rebellion. Consumers appear to be turning their backs on marketing hype and superheroes. Prices are coming down; close-outs are common. Retail distribution channels are clogged with unsold inventory.

This case was prepared by Professor Thomas L. Wheelen of the University of South Florida, Dean Moustafa H. Abdelsamad of Texas A&M University at Corpus Christi, Dr. Stanley R. Sitnik, private financial consultant, and Professor Charles E. Michaels, Jr. of the University of South Florida at Sarasota. This case may not be reproduced in any form without the written permission of the copyright holder, Thomas L. Wheelen. This case was edited for SMBP-8th Edition. Copyright ©1998 by Thomas L. Wheelen. Reprinted by permission.

While we haven't experienced excessive inventories or the need for major markdowns to date, the events surrounding the industry are having a significant impact on our business, and things could get worse before getting better. The market is being saturated with discounted products, making it difficult to increase market share. It could take retailers the rest of the year or longer to whittle down their excess inventories.

But Here's the Good News . . .

Change is good. The disruption in the marketplace provides an opportunity for us to separate ourselves from the competition. Retailers and consumers are looking for fresh ideas and new products. And Reebok has built a diversified portfolio of footwear, apparel, and lifestyle brands that we think will allow us to capitalize on the opportunity.

I'm not suggesting a "right time, right place" scenario, by any means. But many factors are working in our favor. The market influences are moving away from tough, in-your-face urban culture, and clean-cut, all-American styles are enjoying popularity. Upscale, casual lifestyle brands are surging. Sleek running shoes are back in vogue. Classic styles have re-emerged. Outdoor and adventure shoes are hot, as are many alternative sport products. Customers are choosing product quality and performance over flash.

We believe these trends play to our company's strengths. Over the past 2 years, we have worked tirelessly to revitalize our products, technologies, and marketing strategy. We've gone back to the fundamentals of developing distinctive products that make a real difference for our customers. We think our new DMX and 3D Ultralite athletic footwear technologies deliver unparalleled benefits to athletes, and our research shows a significant "intent to repurchase" among initial buyers. We have plans to incorporate these breakthrough technologies into many new products over the coming years.

Our multiple-brand strategy is also coming to the forefront. Our Rockport®, Ralph Lauren® Footwear, and Greg Norman® brands are now beginning to reap the rewards of changing consumer demands for comfortable, stylish "brown shoes" and fashionable sportswear. And our Ralph Lauren Polo Sport® brand, which will be expanded over the course of 1998 and 1999, will continue to bring an exciting high-end fashionable athletic element to the mix. These valuable brands provide us with a diversified portfolio of products to pursue growth across a variety of markets and consumers.

Getting Our Internal House in Order

We haven't been sitting around waiting for conditions to change. We have taken aggressive actions to maintain our profitability despite market challenges. Our Reebok® brand has improved inventory management, credit management, and customer service while reducing general and administrative type expenses. We have initiated a plan to consolidate our warehouse facilities and improve efficiencies throughout our supply chain. These initiatives should be enhanced with the installation of an enterprise-wide global management information system, which will be substantially completed during 1999.

We have also announced a number of actions to increase efficiency in the near-term. We will be simplifying our organizational structure by eliminating management layers, combining business units, and centralizing operations, beginning in the first quarter of 1998. This is an effort to become more focused and to free up resources which can be allocated to near-term projects that we believe can generate immediate results.

One Customer at a Time

So what's the missing ingredient? What must we do to achieve success? Simply put: We have to get out there and tell our story more effectively. We need to have more consumers "try on the future" and experience the Reebok difference. We need to re-establish the Reebok® brand as a major influence in its marketplace, a brand which people can trust and rely upon.

I want consumers to buy the quality and value of our products, not the hype which surrounds them. We must win respect 1 customer and retailer at a time. To supplement our benefits-driven advertising, we will deploy a mobile marketing tour of our new technologies utilizing both try-on vans and special mall kiosks. These efforts are expected to result in millions of new customer "try-ons" worldwide in 1998.

We will reposition the Reebok® brand around creating possibilities 1 athlete at a time. Our product will be the hero, enabling the customer to fulfill his or her dreams. Rather than creating sports stars, we will create the products and technologies of the future which sports stars choose to wear. We must separate ourselves from our competition, create a clear brand identity, and continually demonstrate and market the performance-enhancing benefits of our products.

I recognize that short-term difficulties lie ahead. But I feel confident that positive opportunities line our path. We will work to rise above the noise and clatter to be a company that provides enduring value—both for our customers and our shareholders. And we will continue to refocus our resources to take greater advantage of opportunities among our complete portfolio of brands. That is our strategy; that is our commitment; that is our formula for high-quality growth.[1]

An analyst said of Fireman's letter to the shareholders, "He didn't mention that Nike has increased its market share of 31.7% in 1993 to 47.0% in 1997, while Reebok's has decreased from 20.6% in 1993 to 16.0 in 1997; the Asian financial crisis and potential impact on athletic shoe sales; and the concern over cheap labor and human rights in Southeast Asia." Nike has received the most publicity over the Southeast Asia human rights concerns. **Exhibit 1** shows Reebok's Human Rights Production Standards. Nike had taken a similar position and published it. Reebok, also, had stockholder unrest by large institutional investors over Paul Fireman's management style and turnover of executives, which they felt affected company performance.

Exhibit 1

Human Rights Production Standards: Reebok International, Ltd.

Nondiscrimination
Reebok will seek business partners that do not discriminate in hiring and employment practices on grounds of race, color, national origin, gender, religion, or political or other opinion.

Working Hours/Overtime
Reebok will seek business partners who do not require more than 60-hour work weeks on a regularly scheduled basis, except for appropriately compensated overtime in compliance with local laws, and we will favor business partners who use 48-hour work weeks as their maximum normal requirement.

Forced or Compulsory Labor
Reebok will not work with business partners that use forced or other compulsory labor, including labor that was required as a means of political coercion or as punishment for peacefully expressing political views, in the manufacture of its products. Reebok will not purchase materials that were produced by forced prison or other compulsory labor and will terminate business relationships with any sources found to utilize such labor.

Fair Wages
Reebok will seek business partners who share our commitment to the betterment of wage and benefit levels that address the basic needs of workers and their families so far

as possible and appropriate in light of national practices and conditions. Reebok will not select business partners that pay less than the minimum wage required by local law or that pay less than prevailing local industry practices (whichever was higher).

Child Labor
Reebok will not work with business partners that use child labor. The term "child" generally refers to a person who was less than 14 years of age, or younger than the age for completing compulsory education if that age was higher than 14. In countries where the law defines "child" to include individuals who were older than 14, Reebok will apply that definition.

Freedom of Association
Reebok will seek business partners that share its commitment to the right of employees to establish and join organizations of their own choosing. Reebok will seek to assure that no employee was penalized because of his or her nonviolent exercise of that right. Reebok recognizes and respects the right of all employees to organize and bargain collectively.

Safe and Healthy Work Environment
Reebok will seek business partners that strive to assure employees a safe and healthy workplace and that do not expose workers to hazardous conditions.

Source: Reebok International, Ltd., "Reebok Human Rights Production Standards," company document.

Background and History

The history of Reebok began in England in the 1890s. Athletes wanted to run faster. To meet this demand, Joseph William Foster developed cleated running shoes. By 1895, he had formed J.W. Foster and Sons, which made hand-stitched athletic shoes for many of the top athletes of that time.

In 1958, 2 of J. W. Foster's grandsons started a companion company that they named Reebok International after an African gazelle. In time this new company would absorb the parent company.

In 1979, Paul Fireman purchased an exclusive North American distribution license from Reebok. That year he marketed 3 running shoes in the United States, and at $60 a pair they were the most expensive on the market. Sales increased slowly, exceeding $1.3 million in 1981, and eventually outgrew the production capacity of the U.K. plant. In 1981, needing financing for expansion, Reebok USA swapped 56% of its stock for $77,500 with Pentland Industries, a British shoe distributor, and established production facilities in Korea. That year, in a move that was to characterize the company, Reebok noted the popularity of a new fitness craze called aerobic dancing. It also noted that no one was making a shoe for this purpose. Thus it was the first company to market an athletic shoe just for women. Shortly, the "Freestyle" line, a fashion-oriented aerobic shoe, was introduced and sales took off. Company sales were $3.5 million, $13 million, and $3.6 billion in 1982, 1983, and 1997, respectively.

In 1985, Reebok USA and Reebok International merged to become Reebok International, Ltd. Four million shares of stock were offered to the public, and Pentland became a large shareholder. Paul Fireman continued as CEO and Chairman. This share offering was used to finance the company's growth strategy.

Reebok pursued a strategy of line extensions and acquisitions. In 1986, it acquired The Rockport Company for $118.5 million in cash. In 1987, Reebok purchased the outstanding common stock of Avia Group International for $181.0 million in cash and 194,000 shares of Reebok common shares. It also acquired ESE Sports for $18 million in cash. Rockport purchased John A. Frye Co. for $10 million cash. In 1988 and 1989, it acquired Ellesse USA, Inc. (for $25 million in cash) and Boston Whaler, respectively. In 1981, it purchased a large portion of Pentland Group's holdings in Reebok (Pentland still had an ownership interest of about 13% after the Reebok purchase) and acquired the assets of Above the Rim International. The following year, Reebok acquired Perfection Sports Fashions, which marketed under the Tinley brand name. In 1993, Reebok sold Ellesse USA, and Boston Whaler, Inc.

In the late 1980s, after 5 years of phenomenal growth in the United States, the decision was made to aggressively pursue expansion into overseas markets and achieve an objective of 50% sales internationally. In 1997, Reebok products were available in 140 countries, and about 45.1% of total shares were generated from international shares.

In 1992, Paul Fireman had set a bold goal for the company: to displace Nike as the top sports and fitness brand and become number 1 by 1995. By the end of 1994, Reebok's market share was 21.3%, a 3.4% increase over 1993. Nike's market share decreased by 6.3% from 31.7% to 29.7% during the same time. Since Fireman established this goal to be number 1, public perceptions of the brand had noticeably changed. Reebok started out as a brand that focused on aerobics, walking, and women. Eventually, it began to receive real credence by serious athletes—but not to the extent received by Nike. "We've lost the Michael Jordan generation. That battle has been lost—Nike owns them,"[2] said Tom Carmody, Reebok's General Manager—North America. The next step was a 2-year marketing offensive designed to bump Nike from number 1. The project included more inspired and focused advertising, expansion of the apparel, business, and more cross-promotion with other marketers, like Wheaties, to enhance Reebok's image as a leading sports brand.[3] Reebok intended to establish a worldwide reputation in sports as a supplier of innovative, high-performance athletic footwear, apparel, and equipment.

In late 1995, Reebok was facing an open revolt by a group of institutional shareholders who owned about 15% of Reebok's stock. This group included Warren Buffet's Government Employees Insurance Company (GEICO) and Chieftain Capital Management. These groups "were fed up with management missteps, rising costs, earning disappointments, and a sagging stock."[4] Some of the groups wanted Fireman to resign as CEO. Fireman said that he "isn't opposed to a new chief executive officer or chief operating officer." He further stated, "Titles don't mean anything."[5] Earlier in 1995, both Joint Presidents had resigned. Fireman announced that there had been "a consolidation of leadership and a focus."[6] Glenn Greenberg, Money Manager of Chieftain Capital, indicated that Chieftain had dumped 4.5 million shares of Reebok. Warburg Pincus Asset Management and GEICO had reportedly sold Reebok shares. Over the next year, the management team stabilized.

On June 7, 1996, Reebok sold its subsidiary, Avia Group International, Inc. The company recorded a special charge of $54,064,000 in the fourth quarter of 1995 for this sale. In 1987, Reebok had paid $181 million in cash and 194,000 shares of Reebok stock for Avia. The company sold the Avia Group to refocus the company's strategies back to its core brands. As part of this strategy, the company discontinued its Bok Division in November 1996. Bok products were aimed at 4 segments and targeting the 16- to 24-year-old market: "Freesport," characterized by activities such as skateboarding, surfing, snowboarding; "Clubsport," a fashion-oriented line; "Utility," with worker-boot influence; and "Classic," updated popular designs from earlier seasons.

On July 28, 1996, the Board of Directors authorized the repurchase of up to 24.0 million shares of the company's common stock. The offer to repurchase commenced on July 30, 1996, and expired on August 27, 1996, and the price range for repurchasing stock was $30.00 to $36.00 net per share in cash. The company repurchased approximately 17.0 million common stock at a price of $36.00. Reebok's Board of Directors also suspended the quarterly dividend.[7] An analyst felt these measures resulted from the earlier revolt by the institutional shareholders.

Corporate Governance

BOARD OF DIRECTORS

The Board of Directors of Reebok International, Ltd., as of December 31, 1997, were:[8]

Name	Company
Paul B. Fireman	Chairman, President, and CEO Reebok International, Ltd.
Paul R. Duncan	Executive Vice President Reebok International, Ltd.
M. Katherine Dwyer	President Revlon Consumer Products, USA Revlon, Inc.
William F. Glavin	President Emeritus Babson College
Mannie L. Jackson	Chairman and Chief Executive Officer Harlem Globetrotters International, Inc.
Bertram M. Lee, Sr.	Chairman of the Board Albimar Communications, Inc.

Name	Company
Richard G. Lesser	Executive Vice President and Chief Operating Officer TJX Companies, Inc.
William M. Marcus	Executive Vice President and Treasurer American Biltrite, Inc.
Robert Meers	Executive Vice President Reebok International, Ltd. President and Chief Executive Officer Reebok Division
Geoffery Nunes	Retired Senior Vice President and General Counsel Millipore Corporation

During 1997, each Director who was not an officer or employee of the company received $25,000 annually plus $2,000 for each committee chairmanship held, $2,000 for each directors' meeting, and $1,000 for each committee meeting attended, plus expenses. Beginning in 1998, as a part of a new policy adopted by the Board of Directors that required each director to own Reebok Common Stock with a market value of at least four times the amount of the annual retainer within 5 years from the date of the director's first election to the Board, a minimum of 40% of the annual retainer was paid to the Directors in Reebok's common stock.[9]

TOP MANAGEMENT

In 1995, both Joint Presidents, John H. Duerden and Roberto Muller, had resigned: John H. Duerden resigned on April 7 and Robert Muller resigned on May 26. On August 22, 1995, John Watson was named Senior Vice President and General Manager of the company's Apparel Division. He previously worked for Espirit De B mgH of Duesseldorf, Germany, as head of European operations.[10] This was what partially caused the unrest of institutional investors in the fall of 1995.

The company's executives as of December 31, 1997, were:[11]

Paul B. Fireman (54) founded the company and served as its Chief Executive Officer and a Director since the company's founding in 1979 and its Chairman of the Board since 1986. With the exception of 1988, Fireman served as President of the company from 1979 to the present.

In the mid and late 1980s, Fireman was 1 of the highest paid executives in the country. His salary package included base pay of $357,200 plus 5% of the amount by which Reebok's pretax earnings topped $20 million. He averaged $13.6 million a year. In 1990, the Board of Directors decided that Mr. Fireman's compensation should be more closely tied to increases in value for Reebok shareholders. Fireman has a new employment contract that determines his annual salary, plus an annual bonus based on the company's earnings, with a maximum of $1 million. He also was given a 1-time grant of options to purchase 2.5 million Reebok common shares. The options will become exercisable over a period of 5 years at exercise prices ranging from $17.32 to $18.37 per share and remain exercisable until July 24, 2000. In 1991, Reebok paid a $513,601 premium on a $50 million life insurance policy for Mr. Fireman and his wife, Phyllis. This was reduced to only $46,162 in 1996. Mr. Fireman paid the remainder of the premiums. There had been some shareholder criticism of the high level of Fireman's compensation.

Paul Fireman and his wife, Phyllis, have sold some of their stock through secondary offerings, lowering their ownership to 7.7 million and 5.0 million shares, respectively. This represented about a 21.04% ownership interest, worth approximately $383 million at $30 per share. This left the company insiders (other than Fireman) with a 2.1% ownership interest.

Fireman was known to have a problem in delegation, which contributed to management turnover. A former executive who was highly recruited and lasted less than a year said that "Paul was the sort of fellow who would make a great neighbor . . . But he was absolutely convinced that no one can do a job better than he can."[12] The institution investment groups felt that this caused some of the turmoil in the company management team.

Fireman was a strong advocate of "est training," the human-potential program founded by Werner Erhart in the 1970s. The Forum was the current version of est. His admiration for est was best summarized when he said, "I believe in anything that allows you to look at yourself and see what's possible."[13] A former Reebok executive said that "the company sometimes divides up between those who buy into the est message and those who don't." He further said, "Key employees, even top management, at times seem to be kept out of the loop, denied crucial new research or excluded from strategy meetings unless they accept the est outlook and methods. Fervent est adherents, meanwhile, form a sort of subculture with its own attitudes and jargon."[14]

Paul R. Duncan (54) was appointed Executive Vice President in February 1990, with responsibility for special projects since November 1996. Prior to that, Duncan was President of the company's Specialty Business Group from October 1995 to November 1996, and Chief Operating Officer for the Reebok Division from June 1995 to October 1995. Previously, from 1985 to June 1995, he was Chief Financial Officer. He had served as a Director since March 1989.

Arthur I. Carver (47) has been the Senior Vice President of Sourcing and Logistics of the Reebok Division since January 1996. Prior to that, Carver was Vice-President of Operations Development Worldwide for the Reebok Division since February 1994. Previously, from June 1992 through February 1994, he was Vice President of North American Operations. Prior to that, he was Director of Sales Operations. Carver joined the company in 1990.

Roger Best (45) has been Senior Vice President of the Reebok Division since February 1996. In July 1997, he became the General Manager of the Reebok Division's European Region. Prior to that, he was General Manager of Reebok North America since February 1996. Previously, from April 1995 through February 1996, he was Regional Vice President of the Reebok Division's Northern Europe Operations and Managing Director of Reebok U.K. and, from January 1992 through April 1995, he was Managing Director of Reebok U.K. Best joined the company in 1992.

William M. Sweeney (40) has been Senior Vice President of the Reebok Division and General Manager of Reebok North America since August 1997. Prior to that, Sweeney was Regional Vice President of the Reebok Division's Asia-Pacific Region and President of Reebok Japan since November 1995. He joined Reebok in 1991 as Marketing Director for the Asia/Pacific Region and was based at the regional headquarters in Hong Kong.

James R. Jones III (53) has been Senior Vice President of Human Resources for the Reebok Division since April 1997. Prior to that, Jones was Vice President of Human Resources of Inova Health System from May 1996 through April 1997. From July 1995 through May 1996, Jones was the Senior Vice President of Human Resources of Franciscan Health System. Prior to that, since 1991, Jones was the Vice President of Human Resources of The Johns Hopkins University.

Barry Nagler (41) has been Senior Vice President of the company since February 1998 and General Counsel since September 1995. Nagler was previously a Vice President of the company since May 1995. Prior to that, Nagler was divisional Vice President and Assistant General Counsel for the company since September 1994. He joined the company in June 1987 as Counsel.[15]

The directors and executive officers owned 9,022,592 shares (14.96%) of the company. William Marcus owned 612,373 shares, and is the only corporate person to own more than 1.0% beside Paul Fireman.

EXECUTIVE COMPENSATION

Exhibit 2 shows the aggregate compensation paid or accrued by the company for service rendered during the years ended December 1995, 1996, and 1997 for the Chief Executive Officer and the company's 4 other most highly compensated executive officers.[16]

Exhibit 2

Summary Compensation Table: Reebok International, Ltd.

Name and Principal Position	Year	Annual Compensation			Long-Term Compensation Awards			All Other Compensation ($)
		Salary ($)	Bonus ($)	Other Annual Compensation	Restricted Stock Awards	Options (#)	
Paul B. Fireman	1997	$1,038,474	$562,500	—	None	111,150	$ 54,112
Chairman, President and	1996	1,000,012	None	—	None	500,000	100,913
Chief Executive Officer	1995	1,000,000	None	—	None	87,300	96,645
Robert Meers	1997	769,227	365,625	—	None	35,000	39,749
Executive Vice President;	1996	699,978	None	—	None	250,000	41,066
President and CEO,	1995	591,325	None	—	None	140,000	31,041
Reebok Division							
Angel Martinez	1997	467,328	325,078	—	None	None	29,001
Executive Vice President;	1996	425,022	201,354	—	None	187,500	31,776
President and CEO	1995	400,010	60,000	$62,000	$21,483	25,000	28,889
The Rockport Company							
Kenneth I. Watchmaker	1997	509,600	281,250	—	None	None	29,769
Executive Vice President and	1996	440,387	None	—	None	150,000	30,750
Chief Financial Officer	1995	400,000	60,000	—	$21,483	25,000	29,003
Roger Best	1997	379,972	85,000	—	None	None	17,875
Senior Vice President	1996	344,515	100,000	—	None	220,550	17,883
of the Reebok Division	1995	195,000	75,075	—	None	6,950	30,389

Note: All notes were deleted

Corporate Organization

The 3 principal business group units of Reebok were Reebok Division, Rockport Company, Inc., and Greg Norman Division.

THE REEBOK DIVISION

The Reebok Division designed, produced, and marketed sports and fitness footwear, apparel, and accessories as well as related sports and fitness products that combined the attributes of athletic performance and style. The Division's products included footwear for basketball, running, soccer, rugby, tennis, golf, track and field, volleyball, football, baseball, aerobics, cross training, outdoor and walking activities, and athletic apparel and accessories. The Division continued to expand its product scope through the development and marketing of related sports and fitness products and services, such as sports and fitness videos and programming, and through its strategic licensing program, pursuant to which the company's technologies and/or trademarks were licensed to third parties for fitness equipment, sporting goods, and related products and services.

The Reebok Division had targeted, as its primary customer base, athletes and others who believed that technical and other performance features were the critical attributes of athletic footwear and apparel. Over the past few years, the company had sought to increase Reebok's on-field presence and establish itself as an authentic sports brand. Through such effort, Reebok had gained increased visibility on playing fields worldwide through endorsement arrangements with such prominent athletes as NBA Rookie of the Year Allen Iverson of the Philadelphia 76ers, and with various sports and event sponsorships. Recently, given the diminishing influence of sports "icons" on consumer buying preferences and the increasing consumer appeal of "brown shoe" or "casual" footwear products, the company had been reevaluating its substantial investment in sports marketing deals and was in the process of eliminating or restructuring certain of its underperforming marketing contracts that the company believed no longer reflected the company's brand positioning. In 1998, the Reebok Division intended to focus its efforts on the performance of its products and, in particular, its proprietary technologies, and on bringing its message, both product and brand essence, directly to the consumer. Consistent with this focus, in 1998 the Reebok Division implemented a new direct-to-the-consumer campaign called "Try on the Future," a nationwide, mobile tour designed to give consumers the opportunity to experience and "try on" Reebok's new products and technologies.

As part of its commitment to offer leading athletic footwear technologies, the Division engaged in product research, development, and design activities in the company's Stoughton, Massachusetts, headquarters, where it had a state-of-the-art 50,000-square-foot product development facility that was dedicated to the design and development of technologically advanced athletic and fitness footwear, and in its various Far East offices. Recently, Reebok had opened development centers in the Far East to enable its development activities to be more closely integrated with production. Development centers were opened in Korea in May 1996 and in China in June 1997. New development centers were also scheduled to open in Taiwan and Thailand during 1998.[17]

The Reebok Division's worldwide sales (including Greg Norman) were $3.131 billion in 1997, an increase of 5.0% for comparable sales of $2.982 billion in 1996. The stronger U.S. dollar adversely impacted 1997 sales and profits for this division. In constant dollars, the sales for Reebok brand increased 8.3% in 1997, when compared with 1996. The increase in U.S. sales was attributed primarily to increases in running, walking, and men's cross-training categories. These increases were partially offset by decreasing sales of basketball, outdoor, and women's fitness shoes.

The Reebok Division U.S. apparel sales increased by 37.2% to $431.9 million from $314.9 million in 1996. The increase resulted primarily from increases in branded core basics, licensed, and graphic categories. Total international sales for Reebok Division were $1.471 billion and $1.474 billion, respectively, for 1997 and 1996. International sales in constant dollars showed a gain of 6.4%, and all regions generated sales increases over the prior year on a constant dollar basis.

THE ROCKPORT COMPANY

The company's Rockport subsidiary, headquartered in Marlborough, Massachusetts, designed, produced, and distributed specially engineered comfort footwear for men and women worldwide under the Rockport® brand, as well as apparel through a licensee. Rockport also developed, marketed, and sold footwear under the Ralph Lauren® brand pursuant to a license agreement entered into in May 1996.

Rockport Brand

Designed to address different aspects of customers' lives, the Rockport product line included casual, dress, outdoor performance, golf, and fitness walking shoes. In 1997, Rockport focused on its men's business with the introduction of its Bourbon Street™ collection, refined footwear combining comfort with style and targeting an expanded customer base including younger consumers. Rockport also solidified its success with its ProWalker® World Tour Shoe, with an expanded product line.

Internationally, the Rockport brand continued to grow. In 1997, the Rockport brand's international revenues grew by 46%.

Rockport expanded its retail presence in 1997 with the opening of a "concept" shop in San Francisco, California, and an increase in the United States in the number of its Rockport shops—independent retail shops dedicated exclusively to the sale of Rockport products—from 15 to 21 (see discussions under "Retail Stores"). In addition, Rockport emphasized retail in its international business by opening additional "concept" or retail shops outside of the United States, operated by Rockport distributors or third-party retailers.

Rockport introduced an integrated marketing campaign in 1997 using the directive, "Be Comfortable. Uncompromise. Start with your feet."™ The campaign featured real individuals, unique for their nonconformity, wearing Rockport shoes with a statement of their unique comfort level. The "Uncompromise" campaign was used as the major marketing platform for the brand in the fall of 1997, encompassing television advertising, print advertising, public relations, and retail promotions. In 1997, Rockport continued to expand its offerings on its Internet Web site including the establishment of a business-to-business direct purchase program enabling employees at participating companies to purchase Rockport products through Rockport's Web site.

Rockport marketed its products to authorized retailers throughout the United States primarily through a locally based employee sales staff, although Rockport used independent sales agencies for certain products. Internationally Rockport marketed its products through approximately 30 locally based distributors in approximately 50 foreign countries and territories. A majority of the international distributors were either subsidiaries of the company or joint venture partners or independent distributors that also sold Reebok brand products.

Rockport distributed its products predominantly through select higher quality national and local shoe store chains, department stores, independent shoe stores, and outdoor outfitters, emphasizing retailers that provided substantial point-of-sale assistance and carried a full product line. Rockport also sold its products through independently owned Rockport dedicated retail shops as well as Rockport concept or company stores (see discussion under "Retail Stores"). Rockport had not pursued mass merchandisers or discount outlets for the distribution of its products.

Ralph Lauren Brand

In 1997, Rockport continued to develop the Ralph Lauren footwear business, which was acquired in May 1996. The Ralph Lauren footwear line was expanded in 1997 to include men's English dress shoes. In addition, Collection Classics were introduced for women's shoes and the Refined Casual segment for both men's and women's shoes was expanded. Also in 1997, Polo Sport athletic footwear products were offered. The Polo Sport athletic footwear product line was expected to expand over the next 2 years with the introduction of new product categories.

Ralph Lauren footwear was marketed to authorized retailers though a locally based employee staff. Products were distributed primarily through higher quality department stores. Products were also sold through space licensing and merchandising arrangements at Ralph Lauren Polo retail stores.

Rockport's sales increased by 14.5% to $512.5 million from $447.6 million in 1996. Exclusive of the Ralph Lauren footwear business, which was acquired in May 1996, Rockport's sales increased 7.3% in 1997. International revenues, which grew by 46.0%, accounted for approximately 21% of Rockport sales (excluding Ralph Lauren footwear) in 1997, as compared with 16.0% in 1996. Increased sales in the walking and men's categories were partially offset by decreased sales in women's lifestyle category. The decrease in the women's lifestyle category was the result of a strategic initiative to refocus the women's business around an outdoor, adventure, and travel positioning and reduce the product offerings in the refined women's dress shoe segment. Rockport continued to attract young customers to the brand with the introduction of a wider selection of dress and casual products. The Ralph Lauren footwear business performed well in 1997 and was beginning to generate sales growth in its traditional segments, reflecting the benefits of improved product design and development and increased distribution. Rockport planned to expand the current product line of Ralph Lauren Polo Sport athletic footwear during 1998 with additional products to be available at retail during 1999.[18]

GREG NORMAN DIVISION

The company's Greg Norman Division produced a collection of apparel and accessories marketed under the Greg Norman® name and logo. The Greg Norman Collection had grown from a golf apparel line to a broader line of men's casual sportswear. The Greg Norman product line had been expanded to include a wide range of apparel products—from leather jackets and sweaters to activewear—at a variety of upper-end price points. The Greg Norman Division intended to grow the Greg Norman brand further by offering a variety of lifestyle products and expanding into international markets. It was anticipated that the Division would accomplish such expansion through various licensing and distribution arrangements. In 1997, Greg Norman footwear, leather, and hosiery products were sold through licensees of the company. The Division anticipated entering into a number of new agreements that would broaden the scope of products offered and expand distribution internationally.

The Greg Norman brand was marketed though its endorsement by pro golfer Greg Norman and a marketing and advertising campaign designed to emphasize his aggressive, bold, charismatic, and "winning" style. The current tag line for the brand and marketing focus was "Attack Life."

Greg Norman products were distributed principally at department and men's specialty stores, on-course pro shops, and golf specialty stores and were sold by a combination of independent and employee sales representatives. The Greg Norman Collection was also sold in Greg Norman dedicated shops within independently owned retail stores as well as Greg Norman concept or company stores.[19]

Reebok's strategy was to challenge the men's super brands. Greg Norman, celebrity golfer, finished 1997 ranked number 1 in The Official World Golf Rankings. But Reebok's Greg Norman Collection may have had an even better year. Sales for the operating unit approximated $80 million, an increase of more than 50% compared with 1996. While remaining a strong leadership position within the golf industry, the Greg Norman Collection had expanded its retail distribution to 750 department stores, up from 550 the year before. With its high-quality product and bold styling, the brand continued to pursue a larger share of the growing upscale collection sportswear market. Three broad-based market trends were working in Reebok's favor: the maturing of the baby-boomer generation, strong growth in casual lifestyle apparel, and golf's surging popularity. In 1998, Reebok planned to build on its success by introducing new lines of clothing—from swimwear and volleyball apparel to high-fashion outerwear. Reebok also planned to continue to expand its retail presence and advertising to challenge the men's apparel super brands for increased floor space and market share.[20]

International Operations

The Reebok Division's international sales were coordinated from the company's corporate headquarters in Stoughton, Massachusetts, which was also where the Division's regional operations responsible for Latin America were located. There were also regional offices in Luesden,

Holland, which was responsible for Europe; in Hong Kong, which was responsible for Far East operations; and in Denham Lock, England, which was responsible for the Middle East and Africa, although this office moved to Delhi, India, in March 1998. The Canadian operations of the Division were managed through a wholly owned subsidiary headquartered outside of Toronto. The Division marketed Reebok products internationally through wholly owned subsidiaries in Austria, Belgium, Canada, France, Germany, Ireland, the Netherlands, Italy, Poland, Portugal, Russia, Switzerland, and the United Kingdom, and through majority-owned subsidiaries in Japan, India, South Korea, Spain, and South Africa. Reebok products were also marketed internationally through 29 independent distributors and joint ventures in which the company held a minority interest. The company or its wholly owned U.K. subsidiary held partial ownership interests in 6 of these international distributors, with its percentage of ownership ranging from 30 to 35%. Through this international distribution network, products bearing the Reebok brand were actively marketed internationally in approximately 170 countries and territories. The Division's International operations unit also had small design staffs that assisted in the design of Reebok apparel.

In 1997, Reebok finalized its plans to restructure its international logistics over the next several years. This global restructuring effort included reducing the number of European warehouses in operation from 19 to 3, establishing a shared services company to centralize European administrative operations, and implementing a global management information system. The global restructuring initiative, which was expected to be completed in 1999, should enable the company to achieve operational efficiencies and to manage its business on a global basis more cost effectively. In connection with such restructuring, the company recorded a special pre-tax charge of $33.2 million in 1997.

During 1997, the contribution of the division's International operations unit to overall sales of Reebok products (including Greg Norman apparel) decreased to $1.471 billion from $1.474 billion in 1996. The Division's 1997 international sales were negatively impacted by changes in foreign currency exchange rates. In addition, these sales figures did not reflect the full wholesale value of all Reebok products sold outside the United States in 1997 because some of the division's distributors were not subsidiaries and thus their sales to retailers were not included in the calculation of the Division's international sales. If the full wholesale value of all international sales of Reebok products were included, total sales of Reebok products outside the United States would represent approximately $1.779 billion in wholesale value, consisting of approximately 33.2 million pairs of shoes totaling approximately $1.098 billion in wholesale value of footwear sold outside the United States in 1997 (compared with approximately 35.7 million pairs totaling approximately $1.189 billion in 1996) and approximately $680.5 million in wholesale value of Reebok apparel (including Greg Norman apparel) sold outside the United States in 1997 (compared with approximately $613.8 million in 1996).[21] On a constant dollar basis, international sales increased by 6.4%.

INTERNATIONAL SALES AND PRODUCTION

A substantial portion of the company's products were manufactured abroad, and approximately 40% of the company's sales were made outside the United States. The company's footwear and apparel production and sales operations were thus subject to the usual risks of doing business abroad, such as currency fluctuations, longer payment terms, potentially adverse tax consequences, repatriation of earnings, import duties, tariffs, quotas, and other threats to free trade, labor unrest, political instability, and other problems linked to local production conditions and the difficulty of managing multinational operations. If such factors limited or prevented the company from selling products in any significant international market or prevented the company from acquiring products from its suppliers in China, Indonesia, Thailand, or the Philippines, or significantly increased the cost to the company of such products, the company's operations could be seriously disrupted until alternative suppliers were found or alternative markets were developed, with a significant negative impact.[22]

TRADE POLICY

For several years, imports from China to the United States, including footwear, have been threatened with higher or prohibitive tariff rates, either through statutory action or intervention by the Executive Branch, due to concern over China's trade policies, human rights, foreign weapons sales practices, and foreign policy. Further debate on these issues was expected to continue in 1998. However, the company did not anticipate that restrictions on imports from China would be imposed by the United States during 1998. If adverse action was taken with respect to imports from China, it could have an adverse effect on some or all of the company's product lines, which could result in a negative financial impact. The company had put in place contingency plans that would allow it to diversify some of its sourcing to countries other than China if any such adverse action occurred. In addition, the company did not believe that it would be more adversely impacted by any such adverse action than its major competitors. The actual effect of any such action, however, depended on several factors, including how reliant the company, as compared to its competitors, was on production in China and the effectiveness of the contingency plans put in place.

The European Union (EU) imposed quotas on certain footwear from China in 1994. The effect of such quota scheme on Reebok had not been significant because the quota scheme provided an exemption for certain higher priced special technology athletic footwear. Such exception was available for most Reebok products. This exemption did not, however, cover most of Rockport's products. Nevertheless, the volume of quota available to Reebok and Rockport in 1998 was expected to be sufficient to meet the anticipated sales for Rockport products in EU member countries. However, an insufficient quota could adversely affect Rockport's international sales.

In addition, the EU had imposed antidumping duties against certain textile upper footwear from China and Indonesia. A broad exemption from the dumping duties was provided for athletic textile footwear, which covered most Reebok models. If the athletic footwear exemption remained in its current form, few Reebok product lines would be affected by the duties; however, Rockport products would be subject to these duties. Nevertheless, the company believed that those Reebok and Rockport products affected by the duties could generally be sourced from other countries not subject to such duties. If, however, the company was unable to implement such alternative sourcing arrangements, certain of its product lines could be adversely affected by these duties.

The EU also had imposed antidumping duties on certain leather upper footwear from China, Thailand, and Indonesia. These duties applied only to low-cost footwear, below the import prices of most Reebok and Rockport products. Thus the company did not anticipate that its products would be impacted by such duties.

The EU continued to review the athletic footwear exemption that applied to both the quota scheme and antidumping duties discussed above. The company, through relevant trade associations, was working to prevent imposition of a more limited athletic footwear exception. If revisions were adopted narrowing such exemption, certain of the company's product lines could be affected adversely, although the company did not believe that its products would be more severely affected than those of its major competitors.

Various other countries had taken or were considering steps to restrict footwear imports or impose additional customs duties or other impediments, which actions would affect the company as well as other footwear importers. The company, in conjunction with other footwear importers, was aggressively challenging such restrictions. Such restrictions had, in some cases, had a significant adverse effect on the company's sales in some of such countries, most notably Argentina, although they had not had a material adverse effect on the company as a whole.[23]

GLOBAL RESTRUCTURING ACTIVITIES

The company currently was undertaking various global restructuring activities designed to enable the company to achieve operating efficiencies, improve logistics, and reduce expenses. There could be no assurance that the company would be able to effectively execute its restructuring plans or that such benefits would be achieved. In addition, in the short term, the company could experience difficulties in product delivery or other logistical operations as a result of its restructuring activities, which could have an adverse effect on the company's business. In the short term, the company could also be subject to increased expenditures and charges from such restructuring activities. The company was also in the process of eliminating or restructuring certain of its underperforming marketing contracts. There could be no assurance that the company would be able to successfully restructure such agreements or achieve the cost savings anticipated.[24]

Industry and Competition

CHANGING MARKETS

In 1997, U.S. athletic footwear sales were about $8 billion, and they had experienced little growth over the past few years. In 1997, Nike had 47.0% of the U.S. market, which was a growth of 48.3% over its market share of 31.7% in 1993 (see **Exhibit 3**). Reebok had 16.0% of the U.S. market and had seen its market share decrease by 22.3% from 20.6% in 1993. The 2 companies combined had 63.0% and 52.3% of the U.S. market in 1997 and 1993, respectively. A major shift was Others at 30.5% in 1993 to 14.0% (a drop of 54.1%). New companies among the "top 8" were New Balance and Airwalk, both with 3.0% market share. Fila's market share had increased by 50% from 4.0% in 1993 to 6.0% in 1997. Adidas had the highest increase of 93.5% for this period. Keds was the biggest loser with a 65.5% decrease (5.8% to 2.0%) over these 5 years. Converse also suffered a 30.2% loss of market share (see **Exhibit 3**).

Adidas, a German corporation, had 6.0% and 3.1% of the U.S. market in 1997 and 1993, respectively. The potential customer liked the classic Adidas styling. In the mid 1990s, Adidas controlled more than 70% of the global market for soccer shoes and apparel. Both Nike and Reebok had made serious financial commitments to enter this market and to become number 1. In 1997, Nike agreed to pay $120 million over 8 years to sponsor the U.S. Soccer Foundation, the governing body for the top men's, women's, and youth teams. Nike had 12% of the U.S. soccer shoe market, and Adidas had 42%. In soccer apparel sales, Adidas led with 32%, Britain's Umbro was second with 24%, and Nike was third with 12%. During the past 2 years, Nike locked up the marketing rights to several multinational soccer foundations, including Brazil, Italy, Russia, Nigeria, Holland, and South Korea. Nike was paying about $200 million over 10 years to Brazil. Robert Muller, former Reebok International President, said, "Nike is saying 'Let's get the top teams that we can win on a consistent basis and pay whatever it takes.'" He further stated, "By not letting anyone else in, they can maximize their global exposure."[25]

The women's market has been a growth market for athletic footwear companies. In 1994, women, for the first time, purchased more athletic footwear than men. This segment of the market had become the battleground because men's sales seemed to be flat. Women basketball players were a large segment of this market. High school girls played basketball more than other sports. Walking shoes, 1 of the biggest categories of women's sales, was also 1 of the fastest growth areas.[26]

Exhibit 3

Share of the U.S. Athletic Footwear Market

	1997	1994	1993	% Change 1993–1997
Nike	47.0%	29.7%	31.7%	48.3%
Reebok	16.0	21.3	20.6	(22.3)
Adidas	6.0	5.1	3.1	93.5
Fila	6.0	4.7	4.0	50.0
Converse	3.0	4.6	4.3	(30.2)
New Balance	3.0	—	—	—
Airwalk	3.0	—	—	—
Keds	2.0	4.6	5.8	(65.5)
Others[1]	14.0	30.0	30.5	(54.1)

Note:
1. Other balances total to 100% for 1994 and 1993.

Sources: Business Week (March 13, 1995), p. 7; and Bill Sporito, "Can Nike Get Unstuck?" *Time* (March 30, 1998), p. 51.

In 1997, PCH Investments LLC purchased a 42% stake in L.A. Gear. A new board was elected and the board announced a restructuring that eliminated about 60% of the company's roughly 100 employees at headquarters. L.A. Gear had 5.1% and 3.1% market share in 1994 and 1993, respectively. PCH Investments' filing with the Security and Exchange Commission noted that the board was considering a number of measures to keep the company afloat. The filing also included "a merger, reorganization or liquidation" strategies as strategic choices for the board. Trefoil Investment, Disney family's investment group, had invested $100 million in the company in 1990 and had received some $25 to $30 million in dividends over the next 7 years. Trefoil sold PCH Investments' controlling interest for $230,000. This was 3 weeks after PCH Investments acquired its 42% stake in L.A. Gear.[27]

Teenage Research Unlimited did its latest 1997 survey and found that 40% of teens named Nike as 1 of the "coolest" brands, but this was down from 52% (or 30% decrease) from just 6 months earlier. Kim Hastrieter of *Paper*, a New York magazine, said, "the coolest things around now are brilliantly colored suede sneakers by New Balance." Adidas, which was torpedoed by Reebok and Nike in the 80s, was staging a comeback. Candie's, a small maker of women's shoes, was running ads featuring former MTV star Jenny McCarthy with the slogan, "Just Screw It," while Nike had the slogan, "Just Do It." So, the new competitors (New Balance, Airwalk, and others; see **Exhibit 3**) were attacking Nike and Reebok straight on.[28]

In the fall of 1997, a new trend emerged as schools reopened—teens were turning their noses up at the "white shoe" that they had wanted in past years; instead, they were opting for "brown shoes." The 1997 casual footwear included clunky, huge, and Caterpillar boots. So, the big winners could be: Wolverine, which made Caterpillar and Wolverine boots, and Hush Puppies—the latter 2 had strong fall sales—and Timberland, which made popular outdoor and casual brown-shoe styles. Reebok's Rockport division could supply some of the demand for this change in consumer buying preferences.

Susan Pulliam and Laura Bird, *Wall Street Journal* reporters, felt the big losers would be Nike, Fila, and Woolworth's Foot Locker unit. Brenda Gall, a Merrill Lynch analyst, wrote to her clients that "feedback from industry contacts suggests that basketball shoe sales have gotten off to a sluggish start for the important back-to-school season, and stronger demand for running models has not been enough of an offset."[29]

John Stanley, a retail analyst at Genesis Merchant Group Securities, predicted "that Woolworth's athletic shoe group will record another decline for August [1997] in sales at stores open at least a year, following an 8% decline in July."[30] Woolworth reported a same-store companywide sales decline of 5.8% in July 1997. In early 1998, sales trends had not reversed.

The "Asian Economic Crisis" started in the fall of 1997 and lasted for several years. The impact of the crisis on Reebok and Nike were 2-fold. First, the cost of manufacturing athletic footwear was greatly reduced as the currencies in these countries devaluated and it could take several years or more to fully rebound. Second, the Asian consumer did not have sufficient funds to buy athletic footwear as they had in past years. Nike seemed to be taking a bigger hit from the Asian Economic Crisis. In 1997, Nike's revenues from the Asia-Pacific market were $1,245,217,000 (13.6% of total revenues), $735,094,000 (11.3%), and $515,652,000 (10.8%), and operating income was $174,997,000 (13.3% of total operating revenue), $123,585,000 (13.7%), and $64,168,000 (9.9%) for 1997, 1996, and 1995, respectively. See **Exhibit 4** for Reebok's sales, net income, and identifiable assets. The Asia-Pacific region was included in the geographic heading "Other countries." Other countries' revenues were 12.9% in 1997.

THE Y GENERATION REBELLION

A survey of the U.S. Y generation found 6.5 million skateboarders, 4.5 million snowboarders, 1.5 million stunt bikers, 2 million wakeboarders, and 1 million all-terrain boarders, die-hards who rode down off-season ski slopes or other hills on 3½-foot-long boards with 6-inch wheels that looked like little inner-tubes.[31]

Over the next 3 years, experts expected the wakeboarders to increase 6-fold and skateboard and snowboard users to double. Terry Dorner, World Sports & Marketing, said, "You ain't seen nothing yet."[32]

Exhibit 4

Operations by Geographical Area: Reebok International, Ltd.
(Dollar amounts in thousands)

	1997		1996		1995		1994	
	Amount	**%**	**Amount**	**%**	**Amount**	**%**	**Amount**	**%**
Net sales								
United States	$2,000,883	54.9	$1,935,724	55.6	$2,027,080	58.2	$1,974,904	60.3
United Kingdom	661,358	18.2	566,196	16.3	492,843	14.2	506,658	15.4
Europe	510,981	14.0	623,209	17.9	642,622	18.4	502,029	15.3
Other countries	470,377	12.9	353,475	10.2	318,905	9.2	296,827	9.0
Total	$3,643,599	100.0	$3,478,604	100.0	$3,481,450	100.0	$3,280,418	100.0
Net income								
United States	$ 83,894	62.1	$ 41,522	29.9	$ 52,314	31.7	$ 126,916	49.9
United Kingdom	50,441	37.3	60,050	43.2	74,175	45.0	62,949	24.7
Europe	(567)	(0.4)	21,854	15.6	28,138	17.1	28,290	11.1
Other countries	1,351	1.0	15,524	11.3	10,171	6.2	36,323	14.3
Total	$ 135,119	100.0	$ 138,950	100.0	$ 164,798	100.0	$ 254,478	100.0
Identifiable assets								
United States	$ 938,027	53.4	$ 887,217	49.7	$ 813,935	49.3	$ 963,462	58.5
United Kingdom	372,526	21.2	391,865	21.9	291,825	17.7	282,795	17.1
Europe	278,606	15.8	282,057	15.8	311,903	18.9	221,771	13.4
Other countries	166,938	9.6	225,045	12.6	233,956	14.1	181,433	11.0
Total	$1,756,097	100.0	$1,786,184	100.0	$1,651,619	100.0	$1,649,461	100.0

Source: Reebok International, Ltd. *1997 Annual Report*, p. 36.

This shift by the Y generation had seen companies like Vans, Airwalk, Etonic, and DC have their annual sales increase by 20% to 50% over the previous 2 years. During this time, these niche companies' sales increased to $500 million, or 6.3% of the $8 billion U.S. sneaker market.

Their shoes were cheap. A pair of Vans cost $45 to $50, underpricing Nike's retail average of $70 to $75. The shoes had dimpled rubber soles, instead of waffled ones, and simple colors and designs. The logos were discreet versus the boisterous swoosh of Reebok's logo.

PepsiCo Inc.'s Mountain Dew sales increased 13% in 1996, and moved from No. 6 to No. 4, behind Coke, Pepsi-Cola, and Diet Coke, by featuring snowboarding in its advertisements. In fiscal 1997, Van's sales were up 26% to $159 million. In fiscal 1998, Van's sales were hit by the collapse of its Japanese distribution system, but analysts still predicted sales to be up 13% to $180 million. Much of the sales growth should come from footwear chains that in the past have not given its products much exposure. In 1998, Foot Locker was featuring Van shoes in window displays and started selling them in more than 1,000 stores, up from a few the previous year.

Van's had a cadre of 236 athletic endorsers. The endorsers were relatively unknown, compared with Nike's endorsers.

Van's had competed for years against Reebok and Nike in the basketball and running shoe segments of the market. The company was started in 1966, and had sales of only $35 million in 1995. Walter Schoenfeld, former owner of the Seattle Mariners and founder of Brittania jeans, and his son, Gary Schoenfeld, CEO, said, "I figure the most we could make do is $750 million in annual sales." He further stated, "After that, we run the risk of losing our core customers who do not want us to get too big."[33]

For Reebok's star athletes, ESPN was raising their profiles with shows featuring boarding sports in its twice-a-year X-Games competition. MTV ran an extreme-sports festival in November 1997 and planned more such programming.

Snow Valley, formerly a struggling ski resort, changed its name to Mountain of Youth and doubled its attendance to 200,000. Snowboarders made up 70% of the customers.[34]

COMPETITORS

Nike

Nike was the world's top marketer of high-quality footwear and sports apparel. The Foot Locker, a Woolworth's division, was Nike's largest customer (about 14%). The company's U.S. market share for athletic footwear was 47.0%, and up 48.2% (31.7% to 47.0% from 1993 (see **Exhibit 3**). Sales were $9,186.5 million (up 42.0%), $6,470.6 million (up 35%) and $4,760.8 million, and operating income was $1,295.2 million (up 44.1%), $899.1 million (up 38.3%), and $649.9 million for 1997, 1996, and 1995, respectively (see **Exhibit 5**).

On September 10, 1997, Nike announced that Michael Jordan would head his own Nike Division, Jordan, Inc. Jordan discussed this with Phil Knight, Chairman and CEO, about 10 years ago, but at that time Knight scoffed at the notion. Jordan has been the heart and soul of Nike's presence in athletic footwear (Air Jordan) and athletic sportswear. Jordan saw the new company as part of his opportunity to stay with the game after he retired. Asked about his title and role he would play with the new division, Jordan said, "I don't have a title. They call me CEO, but my responsibilities are to help create the product, implement my feelings and my style."[35] The apparel suggested retail prices ranged from $30 to $140. Air Jordan would cost about $150.

Nike's company culture was based on dedicated corporate loyalty and fierce competition from its 9,700 employees. The company was located on a 74-acre corporate campus in Beaverton, Oregon. Phil Knight, Founder and Chairman, was a former University of Oregon track star and Stanford MBA. Knight wanted to base his company's culture on the deep loyalty

Exhibit 5
Athletic Shoe Industry

A. Revenues (millions of dollars)

	Estimated			Actual		
Company	2000–2002	1998	1997	1996	1995	1994
Nike	$13,000.0	$ 9,750.0	$ 9,186.5	$6,470.6	$4,760.8	$3,789.7
Reebok	4,500.0	3,700.0	3,643.6	3,478.6	3,481.5	3,280.4
Stride Rite	800.0	565.0	516.7	448.3	496.4	523.9

B. Net Profits (millions of dollars)

	Estimated			Actual		
Company	2000–2002	1998	1997	1996	1995	1994
Nike	$ 950.0	$ 565.0	$ 795.8	$ 553.2	$ 406.7	$ 298.8
Reebok	240.0	135.0	134.3	139.0	209.7	254.5
Stride Rite	60.0	26.0	19.8	2.5	1.5	19.8

C. Operating Profit Margin (%)

	Estimated			Actual		
Company	2000–2002	1998	1997	1996	1995	1994
Nike	15.0%	12.5%	16.5%	16.6%	15.9%	15.3%
Reebok	10.5	8.5	8.8	8.9	11.6	13.9
Stride Rite	13.5	8.7	7.9	2.5	3.1	7.7

D. Net Profits Margins (%)

	Estimated			Actual		
Company	2000–2002	1998	1997	1996	1995	1994
Nike	7.3%	5.8%	8.7%	8.5%	8.5%	8.0%
Reebok	5.3	3.3	3.7	4.0	6.0	7.8
Stride Rite	7.5	4.6	3.8	0.6	0.3	3.8

Source: Value Line (February 20, 1998), pp. 1669, 1671, and 1672.

that he had seen in Japan, and he wanted his employees to feel the adrenaline rush of athletes performing at their highest levels. Nike still had this culture 30 years later. When entering his office, Knight removed his shoes, Japanese style.[36]

Knight found that consumers responded best "to athletes who combined passion to win with a maverick disregard for convention. Outlaws with morals!"[37] Some of his rules of business were: "Play by the rules, but be ferocious," and "It's all right to be Goliath, but always act like David."[38] Employees took 2-hour workouts at midday at the Bo Jackson Sports and Fitness Center on campus, then worked late into the night at a relentless pace. Paul Fireman stated that "I think Nike was more of a cult, where people have to give up their individuality."[39]

On March 16, 1998, Nike announced the lay-off of about 450 employees. This was in addition to 300 temporary workers announced earlier. The lay-offs were caused by sales weakness in U.S. and Asian markets.

New Balance

New Balance had total sales of $560 million in 1997. This was an increase of 16% over 1996. The company ranked fifth with a market share of 3.0% (see **Exhibit 3**). The company's athletic footwear sales were $260 million.

Mike Kormas, President of Footwear Market Insights, said that New Balance "is becoming the Nike of the baby-boomer generation."[40] His company surveyed 25,000 households every 4 months on footwear purchasing preferences. He reckoned that "the average age of a Nike consumer is 25, the average age of a Reebok consumer is 33, and the average age of a New Balance consumer is 42."[41] New Balance offered 5 widths of shoes, from a narrow AA to an expansive EEEE. About 20 to 30% of the population had narrower or wider foot size than average. Most other companies offered 2 widths—medium and wide. Retailers for New Balance said they sold more EE or EEEE than the other 3 sizes.

The company in the past competed for the basketball shoe market, but efforts were disappointing. Jim Davis, President and CEO, said, "We chose not to be in a position where we live and die by basketball. We'd just as soon pass the $10 to $15 a pair we need in superstar endorsements to the consumer."[42] New Balance spent $4 million in advertising and promotion to generate sales of $560 million. The $4 million was less than 1% of Nike's or Reebok's budgets. In 1998, the company planned to increase the marketing budget to $13 million.

Stride Rite

Stride Rite was the leading marketer of quality children's footwear in the United States and 1 of the major marketers of boating and outdoor recreational shoes and athletic and casual footwear for children and adults. Major brand names included Stride Rite, Sperry Top-Sider, Keds, Pro-Keds, and Tommy Hilfiger lines for men and women. The company stabilized its previously falling Keds. Sales were down 10% from 1996 in the Keds lines, but profitability improved by approximately 50%, due primarily to fewer markdowns and aggressive cost cutting. The company's margins improved in 1997, which was primarily the result of shifting manufacturing overseas. The company operated 204 retail stores and leased children's shoe departments.[43] The company's market share dropped from 5.8% in 1994 to 2.0% (65.5%) in 1997 (see **Exhibits 3 and 5**).

Adidas AG

Adidas AG had seen its market share increase from 3.1% in 1993 to 6.0% in 1997. (See **Exhibit 3**.) Adidas's sales were $500 million. The German company had been founded in 1920. The company's profits had been squeezed by intense competition from Reebok and Nike on its home territories during the 1990s. Nike and Reebok had entered the soccer shoe segment of the world market to attack Adidas's dominance of this market. Joachim Bernsdorff, a consumer-goods expert with Bank Julius Bear in Frankfurt, said, "The basic mistake was Adidas's insistences on making athletic gear." He further stated, "They felt above selling style, colorful clothes—without seeing that's what young people want."[44] The company had restarted production of old models, as teenagers and trendsetters around the world rediscovered sneakers made by Adidas 20 years ago. It was being called the revival of a classic!

Fila

Fila had sales of $484 million and a market share of 6.0%, which was a 50% increase over 1993 (see **Exhibit 3**).

Converse

Converse was a sneaker company before Nike and Reebok were founded. The company's sales were $280 million, and it ranked tied for third place with 3.0% market share and down 30.2% since 1993 (see **Exhibit 3**).

Puma AG

Puma AG had suffered almost a decade of losses, but had profitable years beginning in 1994.

Marketing and Promotional Activities

The Reebok Division devoted significant resources to advertising its products to a variety of audiences through television, radio, and print media and used its relationships with major sports figures in a variety of sports to maintain and enhance visibility for the Reebok brand. The Reebok Division's advertising program in 1997 was directed toward both the trade and the ultimate consumers of Reebok products. The major advertising campaigns in 1997 included an ad campaign featuring real-life portraits of rookies Allen Iverson of the National Basketball Association (NBA) and Saudia Roundtree of the American Basketball League (ABL) depicting their adjustment to professional sports, as well as real-life portraits of Reebok endorsers Shawn Kemp and Shaquille O'Neal, and a marketing campaign for the DMX® Run shoe featuring Spencer White, Reebok's Director of Research Engineering.[45]

Advertising expense (including cooperative advertising) amounted to $164,870,000, $201,584,000, and $157,573,000 for 1997, 1996, and 1995, respectively. Advertising production costs were expensed the first time the advertisement was run. Selling, general, and administrative expenses decreased as a percentage of sales from 30.6% ($1,065,792,000) in 1996 to 29.4% ($1,069,433,000) in 1997.

Substantial resources were devoted to promotional activities in 1997, including endorsement agreements with athletes, teams, leagues, and sports federations; event sponsorships; in-store promotions; and point-of-sale materials. In 1997, the Reebok Division gained visibility for the Reebok brand through endorsement arrangements with such athletes as 1997 Rookie of the Year Allen Iverson of the Philadelphia 76ers, with whom Reebok marketed a signature line of footwear and apparel. Other endorsements in basketball in 1997 came from professional players such as Shaquille O'Neal, Shawn Kemp, Clyde Drexler, Nick Van Exel, and Steve Smith. In 1997, Reebok entered into a multiyear agreement with NBA Properties for a comprehensive licensed merchandise, marketing, and basketball development program in Latin America. In addition, Reebok sponsored a number of college basketball programs and had a sponsorship agreement with the Harlem Globetrotters. Reebok was also the founding sponsor of the ABL and the official footwear and apparel sponsor of the league. Reebok was the exclusive supplier of uniforms and practice gear to the league's 9 teams and an official ABL licensee and had entered into endorsement agreements with a number of ABL players including Saudia Roundtree, Jennifer Azzi, and Carolyn Jones. Reebok was also an official footwear supplier to the Women's National Basketball Association (WNBA).

To promote the sale of its cross training footwear in 1997, Reebok used endorsements by prominent athletes such as National Football League (NFL) players Emmitt Smith, Derrick Thomas, John Elway, Ken Norton, Jr., Herman Moore, and Ben Coates, as well as Major League Baseball (MLB) players Frank Thomas, Mark McGwuire, Juan Gonzalez, and Roger Clemens. To promote its cleated football and baseball shoes, the company also had endorsement contracts with numerous MLB and NFL players, and sponsored a number of college football programs.

The company had a multiyear agreement with NFL Properties under which Reebok had been designated a "Pro Line" licensee for the U.S. and international markets with the right to produce and market uniforms and sideline apparel bearing NFL team logos. Pursuant to this agreement, in 1997 Reebok supplied uniforms and sideline apparel to the San Francisco 49ers, Detroit Lions, New York Giants, New Orleans Saints, Kansas City Chiefs, and Atlanta Falcons. In addition to the Pro Line license, Reebok had an agreement with the NFL under which Reebok was 1 of only 3 brands authorized to provide NFL players with footwear that had visible logos, and all NFL on-field game officials wore Reebok footwear exclusively.[46]

Jerry Jones, owner of the Dallas Cowboys, signed an exclusive contract with Nike. This contract had to be approved by the President of the NFL. Under current NFL rules, only a company licensed by the NFL to sell NFL's Pro Line products can do so for NFL teams. So the NFL sued Jerry Jones. He countersued the NFL. The NFL and Jerry Jones subsequently dropped their suits, allowing Jones to proceed.

In soccer, Reebok had a number of endorsement arrangements including contracts with Gabriel Batistuta of Fiorentina and the Argentinean national team, Ryan Giggs of Manchester United and Wales, Dennis Bergkamp of Arsenal and the Netherlands, and Guiseppe Signori of Lazio and Italy, as well as U.S. national team members Eric Wynalda, Brad Friedel, Michelle Akers, and Julie Foudy. The company also had major sponsorship agreements with the Liverpool Football Club, 1 of the world's best known soccer teams, and with the Argentina National Football Association, which took effect in 1999. In addition, Reebok had entered into sponsorship agreements with such soccer teams as Aston Villa, Borussia Moenchengladbach of Germany, Bastia of France, Palmeiras of Brazil, Brondby of Denmark, and IFK Gothenburg of Sweden. In 1997, the company extended its sponsorship of the Bolton Wanderers of England to include naming rights to the team's new soccer arena, the Reebok Stadium. Reebok was also the official uniform supplier of 2 U.S. major league soccer teams: the New England Revolution and the Colorado Rapids. In July 1997, the first-ever Reebok Cup, an international soccer tournament featuring 4 of the world's most powerful club teams, was held in the United States. In rugby, the company sponsored the national rugby teams of Australia and Italy.

Tennis promotions in 1997 included endorsement contracts with well-known professionals including Michael Chang, Venus Williams, Patrick Rafter, and Arantxa Sanchez-Vicario. Promotional efforts in running included endorsement contracts with such well-known runners as Ato Boldon, Derrick Adkins, Kim Batten, and Marie Jose Perec.

In February 1997, Reebok apologized for naming a shoe "Incubus." Incubus, according to legend, was a demon that had sex with sleeping women. The name received national media coverage and complaints from customers. Dave Fogelson, a Reebok spokesman, said, "Someone should have looked it [Incubus] up." He further stated, "There are no excuses, and we apologize." Reebok management hired a name consultant to avoid future mistakes.[47]

To promote its women's sports and fitness products, Reebok sponsored athletes such as Rebecca Lobo of the WNBA as well as Michelle Akers and Julie Foudy of the U.S. national soccer team, Lisa Fernandez of the U.S. national softball team, and Liz Masakayan, pro beach volleyball player. In addition, Reebok sponsored a variety of college basketball and volleyball teams and such organizations as the ABL and the WNBA.

In 1997, the Reebok Division also continued its promotional efforts in the fitness area. Reebok fitness programming was featured on Fit-TV, a 24-hour cable network, pursuant to a programming agreement. Through an agreement with Channel One Communications, in 1997 Reebok provided the programming for P.E. TV, an award-winning program designed to educate kids about physical fitness. Reebok had developed numerous fitness programs, such as its Versa Training program, designed to help consumers meet their varied fitness goals with aerobic, strength, and flexibility workouts, the Walk Reebok program, which promoted walking; its Cycle Reebok program that featured the Cycle Reebok studio cycle; and the Reebok Flexible Strength program that developed strength and flexibility simultaneously. These pro-

Exhibit 6
Sales by Quarter

Year Ending December 1997	First Quarter	Second Quarter	Third Quarter	Fourth Quarter
Net sales	$930,041	$841,059	$1,009,053	$863,446
Gross profit	356,229	323,511	370,211	299,599
Net income	40,184	20,322	73,968	645
Basic earnings per share	.72	.36	1.32	.01
Diluted earnings per share	.69	.35	1.26	.01

grams were complemented by the marketing and sale of a line of Reebok fitness videos, as well as the marketing and sale of Reebok fitness equipment products such as the Step Reebok exercise platform and the Cycle Reebok studio cycle.

To gain further visibility for the Reebok brand, Reebok had also entered into several key sport sponsorships such as an arrangement under which Reebok was designated the official footwear and apparel sponsor of the Russian Olympic Committee and approximately 25 individual associated Russian sports federations. This arrangement was recently extended through the Sydney 2000 Summer Olympic Games. Reebok will also be an official sponsor of the Sydney 2000 Olympic Games and the official sports brand of the 1998 and 2000 Australian Olympic teams, as well as an official sponsor and supplier of sports footwear and apparel to the national Olympic teams from Brazil, New Zealand, Poland, and South Africa. In addition, as an extension of its commitment to provide athletes with technologically advanced products, Reebok had entered into sponsorship agreements with the Team Scandia and Cristen Powell, a top fuel drag racer on the National Hod Rod Association circuit, as well as with Eliseo Salazar, 1 of the top drivers on the Indy Car racing circuit, and the R&S Indy Racing League (IRL) TEAM on the 1998 IRL circuit. Reebok also had school-wide sponsorship arrangements with colleges such as U.C.L.A., University of Texas, University of Virginia, and University of Wisconsin. In 1997, the Reebok Division also ran marketing promotions on its Internet Web site.[48]

Sales of the following categories of products contributed more than 10% to the company's total consolidated revenue in the years indicated: 1997, footwear (approximately 72%) and apparel (approximately 27%); 1996, footwear (approximately 75%) and apparel (approximately 24%); 1995, footwear (approximately 81%) and apparel (approximately 18%).[49]

Sales by the company of athletic and casual footwear tended to be seasonal in nature, with the strongest sales occurring in the first and third quarter. Apparel sales also generally varied during the course of the year, with the greatest demand occurring during the spring and fall seasons. **Exhibit 6** shows sales by quarters.[50]

Sports and Fitness Equipment and Licensing

The company had continued to pursue its strategic trademark and technology licensing program begun in 1991. This program was designed to pursue opportunities for licensing the company's trademarks, patents, and other intellectual property to third parties for sporting goods, apparel, and related products and services. The licensing program was focused on expanding the Reebok brand into new sports and fitness markets and enhancing the reputation of the company's brands and technologies. The company had pursued strategic alliances with licensees who Reebok believed were leaders and innovators in their product categories and who shared Reebok's commitment to offering superior, innovative products. The company believed that its licensing program reinforced Reebok's reputation as a market leader.

The company's licensing program included such products as a full line of athletic gloves, including baseball batting gloves, football gloves, running gloves, court/racquetball gloves, fitness/weightlifting gloves, cycling gloves, golf gloves, and winter gloves, all featuring the Reebok trademark and Reebok's Vector Logo; a collection of Reebok performance sports sunglasses; the Watch Reebok collection of sport watches, and a line of heart rate monitors and a pedometer and stopwatch; Reebok weight belts, both with and without Reebok's Instapump technology; and a line of gymnastic apparel including replicas of the U.S. gymnastics team uniforms. Reebok also had license agreements with Mead for a line of Reebok school supplies and with Haddad Apparel for a line of Reebok infant and toddler apparel. In addition, in 1997, Reebok entered into a licensing agreement with Fab-Knit, Ltd., to manufacture and sell a new line of Reebok team uniforms and jackets.

In 1997, Reebok entered into a new video license agreement with BMG Video, a unit of BMG Entertainment, to produce, market, and sell a line of Reebok fitness videos. Through a licensee, Reebok also sold Reebok fitness audio tapes. In the equipment area, in January 1998, the company signed a license agreement with industry leader Icon Health & Fitness, Inc. to develop, market, and sell a complete line of Reebok fitness equipment products for the home market. The initial home fitness products from this license debuted at the Super Show in Atlanta in February 1998. Reebok also had a license agreement with Cross Conditioning Systems under which Cross Conditioning Systems sold a line of Reebok fitness equipment products designed for use in health clubs and other institutional markets. In 1997 under this relationship the Reebok Body Mill, Reebok Body Tree, Reebok Body Peak, Reebok Studio Cycle, and Reebok Cycle Plus were sold to health clubs and other institutions.

In addition, as part of the company's licensing program, WEEBOK infant and toddler apparel and accessories and a line of WEEBOK footwear were sold by licensees. WEEBOK is a fashion-oriented, kid-specific brand that offered apparel in sizes 0–7 and footwear in sizes 0–12.[51]

Retail Stores

Woolworth's athletic division included Foot Locker, Lady Foot Locker, Kid Foot Locker, Champs, and Eastbay catalog, which had sales of $3.6 billion. In 1996, sales soared by 10.2% but grew at half this rate in 1997. Foot Locker was the hardest hit chain in 1997. Foot Locker's same-store sales for 1996 and 1997 had an 11.2% decrease. The decrease was attributed to the Y Generation shift in shoe purchasing and the brown versus white shoe rebellion by students.

In the summer of 1996, management of Woolworth decided to shut down its Woolworth retail chain. Roger N. Farah, CEO, decided to make Foot Locker the linchpin of his turnaround plan for the $7.1 billion retailer. Kurt Bernard, who published Bernard's Retail Trend Report, said, "They gave up a dead industry in favor of putting all the eggs in 1 basket."[52] He further stated, "And the basket is getting shaken up. They're going to have scrambled eggs."[53] To make things a little worse, Woolworth could not account for $43 million in inventory at its Woolworth stores. This shrinkage was 5.82%, which was 3 times the companywide average.

Foot Locker was also losing ground to newcomers that had superstores, which were as much as 10 times larger than its stores. At some competitors' stores, Just For Feet, Inc., and Sneaker Stadium, kids could try out gear on a real basketball court. Foot Action had sport shows on big-screen TVs and racks of spandex and sweats. Thomas E. Clark, President of Nike, said of the new competitors, "These larger formats give the retailer the opportunity to romance products better."[54]

CEO Roger N. Farah's response was to create 1,500 Foot Locker superstores by pushing back the storeroom walls. In late 1998, he expected to convert 100 of the old Woolworth stores into superstores that combined all the company's athletic products in 1 store.[55]

Reebok and Nike have been battling over dominance in sales in the Foot Locker. Tensions between Reebok and Foot Locker went back to the 1980s. At that time, Reebok's aerobic shoe sales were not in the stores. So, Foot Locker management asked Reebok to turn out a specialty line for Foot Locker. Josie Esquivel, an analyst at Morgan Stanley, said that "Reebok basically thumbed its nose" at the retailer. Reebok "was selling to whomever it wanted, including the discounter down the street from Foot Locker."[56] Foot Locker's strategy was to offer exclusive lines as a weapon against discounters and was receiving exclusive lines from other athletic shoe manufacturers. Nike agreed to make exclusive lines for Foot Locker. In 1996, Nike introduced Flight 65 and Flight 67, which were high-priced basketball shoes that sold only at Foot Locker. These shoes came in Nike's trademark black and white. Earlier in the year, Reebok had agreed to make shoes exclusively for Foot Locker, but none of the shoes had reached the store.

Fireman's views on the rocky relations with Foot Locker were that "Reebok wasn't as good a listener to [Foot Locker], which happens to have a good ear as to what's happening on the street and consumers."[57] Fireman was trying to repair the relationship, so he recently spent a few days with buyers of Woolworth's foot units, "trying to discern their needs."[58]

Over the past few years, "Reebok had hired an army of testers at Woolworth's shoe chains . . . to find out whether Reebok was getting equal treatment with other brands."[59] Reebok was disappointed with their findings. They found that Reebok had the most shoes on display in the stores but got little positive help from the stores' salespeople. A salesperson told one 17-year-old customer that "Nikes were hip."[60]

Reebok recognized that Foot Locker's customers were not Reebok's core clients, who were older customers and preteens unable to spend $80 to $90 for shoes. Foot Locker's target market were teens and Generation X customers, who spent $80 to $90 for shoes. Fireman said, "There's no question Nike owns that market," and "there's no one really in that market to compete against them in the high-end niche."[61]

Nike had a special salesforce, Elkins, which called on stores and spread the gospel of Nike. They were enthusiastic sponsors of Nike's product lines. They provided the company with excellent information on market trends and competition.

William DeVrues, who headed Woolworth's footwear units, dismissed talk about bad relations with Reebok. He said, "We're only selling what the customer wants."[62]

REEBOK'S RETAIL STORES

The company operated approximately 150 factory direct stores, including Reebok, Rockport, and Greg Norman stores which sold a variety of footwear, apparel, and accessories marketed under the company's various brands. The company intended to continue to open additional factory direct stores, although its policy was to locate and operate those retail outlets in such a way as to minimize disruption to its normal channels of distribution.

The company also operated Reebok "concept" or company retail stores located in New York City and King of Prussia, Pennsylvania. The company envisioned its concept stores as a model for innovative retailing of its products and as a potential proving ground for testing new products and marketing/merchandising techniques. The stores sold a wide selection of in-line Reebok footwear and apparel. Internationally, the company, its subsidiaries, or its independent distributors owned several Reebok retail stores. The company continued to open retail stores either directly or through its distributors in numerous international markets. Reebok retail shops were expected to be an important means of presenting the brand in relatively new markets such as China, India, and Russia and in other international markets.

The company was working to develop a retail store concept to showcase the Reebok brand at retail and was expected to incorporate this design into independently owned retail stores dedicated exclusively to the sale of Reebok products. In 1998, the company planned to test this concept in a few stores to be opened in markets around the world.

Rockport had concept or company retail stores in San Francisco, California; Boston, Massachusetts; Newport, Rhode Island; King of Prussia, Pennsylvania; and New York City. In addition, there were a number of Rockport shops—independent stores that sold Rockport products exclusively—in the U.S. as well as internationally. There were 2 Greg Norman concept or company retail stores in New York City. Rockport's Ralph Lauren footwear subsidiary operated "concept" footwear departments in Ralph Lauren/Polo stores in a number of locations in the United States, including New York City and Beverly Hills, California. In addition, the Ralph Lauren footwear subsidiary had footwear retail operations in approximately 19 Ralph Lauren/Polo factory direct stores and operated 1 factory direct store in Tannersville, Pennsylvania.

Reebok was also a partner in the Reebok Sports Club/NY, a premier sports and fitness complex in New York City featuring a wide array of fitness equipment, facilities, and services in a luxurious atmosphere. The club used approximately 125,000 square feet and occupied 5 floors of the Lincoln Square project. A Reebok concept store as well as Rockport and Greg Norman concept stores were also located in the building.[63]

Manufacturing and Production

Virtually all of the company's products were produced by independent manufacturers, almost all of which were outside the United States, except that some of the company's apparel and some of the component parts used in the company's footwear were sourced from independent manufacturers located in the United States. Each of the company's operating units generally contracted with its manufacturers on a purchase order basis, subject in most cases to the terms of a formal manufacturing agreement between the company and such manufacturers. All contract manufacturing was performed in accordance with detailed specifications furnished by the operating unit, subject to strict quality control standards, with a right to reject products that did not meet specifications. To date, the company had not encountered any significant problem with product rejection or customer returns. The company generally considered its relationships with its contract manufacturers to be good.

As part of its commitment to human rights, Reebok had adopted human rights standards and a monitoring program that applied to manufacturers of its products (see **Exhibit 1**). In conjunction with this program, the company required its supplier of soccer balls in Pakistan to end the use of child labor by centralizing all production, including ball stitching, so that the labor force could be adequately monitored to prevent the use of child labor. Reebok soccer balls were sold with a guarantee that the balls were made without child labor.

China, Indonesia, Thailand, and the Philippines were the company's primary sources for footwear, accounting for approximately 39%, 28%, 15%, and 8%, respectively, of the company's total footwear production during 1997 (based on the number of units produced). The company's largest manufacturer, which had several factory locations, accounted for approximately 13% of the company's total footwear production in 1997.

Reebok's wholly owned Hong Kong subsidiary, and a network of affiliates in China, Indonesia, India, Thailand, Taiwan, South Korea, and the Philippines, provided quality assurance, quality control, and inspection services with respect to footwear purchased by the Reebok Division's U.S. and international operations. In addition, this network of affiliates inspected certain components and materials purchased by unrelated manufacturers for use in footwear production. The network of affiliates also facilitated the shipment of footwear from the shipping point to point of destination, as well as arranging for the issuance to the unrelated footwear manufacturers of letters of credit, which were the primary means used to pay manufacturers for finished products. The company's apparel group used the services of independent third parties, as well as the company's Hong Kong subsidiary and its network of affiliates in the Far East, to assist in the placement, inspection, and shipment of apparel and accessories orders internationally. Production of apparel in the United States was through independent contractors that the company's apparel group retained and managed. Rockport products were produced by independent contractors that were retained and managed through country managers employed by Rockport. The remainder of the company's order placement, quality control, and inspection work abroad was handled by a combination of employees and independent contractors in the various countries in which its products were made.[64]

When Reebok began manufacturing in a new location, it started with the simplest and least expensive lines. This procedure allowed the workers to learn the trade and Reebok to establish acceptable standards. The company had 480 employees involved in production who worked closely with the factories to provide detailed specifications for production and quality control. These employees also facilitated the shipment of footwear and arranged for the issuance of letters of credit. Some of the apparel and some of the component parts of the footwear were sourced in the United States.

Since 1983, Reebok had used production facilities in South Korea (1983), Taiwan (1985), Philippines (1986), China (1987), Indonesia (1987), Thailand (1987), India (1994), and Vietnam (1995). Some of the plants in these countries had been closed.

TECHNOLOGY

Reebok placed a strong emphasis on technology and had continued to incorporate various proprietary performance technologies in its products, focusing on cushioning, stability, and lightweight features.

In 1995, Reebok introduced its propriety DMX® technology for superb cushioning. DMX® used a 2-pod system that allowed air to flow from the heel to the forefoot. This technology continued to be used successfully in several Reebok walking shoes. In April 1997, the company debuted its DMX® 10 technology at retail with the introduction of the DMX Run shoe. This advanced technology incorporated a 10-pod, heel to forefoot, active air transfer system delivering cushioning when and where it was needed. The DMX® 10 technology was also introduced at retail in November 1997 in The Answer, an Allen Iverson signature basketball shoe. In February 1998, Reebok debuted at retail DMX® 6, a 6-pod, heel to forefoot, active air transfer system, in a running shoe, Run DMX® 6. In addition, DMX® 6 was available at retail in February 1998 in The Lightning, a signature basketball shoe to be worn by NBA player Nick Van Exel and as a team shoe to be worn by many college athletes. The company also introduced a DMX® Sockliner, which was expected to debut at retail in a golf shoe in March 1998 and in a soccer shoe in April 1998.

3D Ultralite™ technology was Reebok's approach to lightweight performance footwear. 3D Ultralite was a proprietary material that allowed the midsole and outsole to be combined in 1 injection molded unit composed of foam and rubber, thus making the shoe lightweight, flexible, and durable. In 1997, the company introduced this technology in running, walking, basketball, and women's fitness shoes. In 1998, the company planned to continue to introduce 3D Ultralite technology at retail in additional footwear categories, including women's sports training and men's cross-training.

Reebok continued to incorporate Hexalite®, a honeycomb-shaped material, which provided stability and cushioning, in many of its shoes and in many different applications. Radial Hexalite®, 1 application of this technology, combined under-the-foot cushioning and lateral stabilization and was first available at retail in early 1997. Hexliner™, a PU foam sockliner that included reengineered Hexalite® material in the heel for a softer feel close to the foot, was first available at retail in June 1997.

Finally, Reebok has incorporated advanced technology into its apparel products with the introduction of Hydromove™ technology in certain performance apparel. This moisture management system helps keep athletes warm in cold weather and dry and cool in hot weather. Performance apparel incorporating the Hydromove™ technology first became available at retail at the end of 1996.[65]

SOURCES OF SUPPLY

The principal materials used in the company's footwear products were leather, nylon, rubber, ethylvinyl acetate, and polyurethane. Most of these materials could be obtained from a number of sources, although a loss of supply could temporarily disrupt production. Some of the components used in the company's technologies were obtained from only 1 or 2 sources, and thus a loss of supply could disrupt production. The principal materials used in the company's apparel products were cotton, fleece, nylon, and spandex. These materials could be obtained from a number of sources.

The footwear products of the company that were manufactured overseas and shipped to the United States for sale were subject to U.S. Customs duties. Duties on the footwear products imported by the company ranged from 6% to 37.5% (plus a unit charge, in some cases, of $.90), depending on whether the principal component was leather or some other material and on the construction.

As with its international sales operations, the company's footwear and apparel production operations were subject to the usual risks of doing business abroad, such as import duties, quotas and other threats to free trade, foreign currency fluctuations and restrictions, labor unrest, and political instability. Management believed that it had the ability to develop, over time, adequate substitute sources of supply for the products obtained from present foreign suppliers. If, however, events should prevent the company from acquiring products from its suppliers in China, Indonesia, Thailand, or the Philippines, or significantly increase the cost to the company of such products, the company's operations could be seriously disrupted until alternative suppliers were found, with a significant negative impact.[66]

BACKLOG

The company's backlog of orders at December 31, 1997 (many of which were cancelable by the purchaser), totaled approximately $1.224 billion, compared to $1.198 billion as of December 31, 1996. The company expected that substantially all of these orders would be shipped in 1998, although, as noted above, many of these orders were cancelable. The backlog position was not necessarily indicative of future sales because the ratio of future orders to "at once" shipments and sales by company-owned retail stores may vary from year to year.[67]

Information Systems

YEAR 2000

The company had conducted a global review of its computer systems to identify the systems that could be affected by the technical problems associated with the year 2000 and had developed an implementation plan to address the "year 2000" issue. As part of its global restructuring, in 1997 the company began its global implementation of SAP software, to substantially replace all legacy systems. The company believed that, with modifications to existing software and converting to SAP software, the year 2000 would not pose significant operational problems for the company's computer systems. The cost of such modifications was not expected to be material. The company expected its SAP programs to be substantially implemented by 1999 and the implementation was currently on schedule. However, if the modifications and conversions were not implemented or completed in a timely or effective manner, the year 2000 problem could have a material impact on company operations. In addition, in converting to SAP software, the company was relying on its software partner to develop new software applications, and there could be problems in successfully developing such new applications.[68]

Human Rights

REEBOK HUMAN RIGHTS AWARD

Reebok explained its stand on human rights in its *1997 Annual Report*.[69]

> Reebok International has a long-held commitment to human rights, and we require our partners and vendors to abide by an internationally recognized standard of human rights.
>
> In 1992 we adopted a worldwide code of conduct mandating the fair treatment of workers involved in making Reebok products. This code rejects the use of child labor, unsafe working conditions, unfair wages, and other threats to basic human rights. In addition, our commitment has resulted in a number of important human rights initiatives [cited below] of which we are proud.
>
> ### Guarantee: "Manufactured Without Child Labor"
>
> In November 1996, Reebok announced a program to label its soccer balls with a guarantee that the balls are made without child labor. This was believed to be the first time a guarantee of this kind was placed on a widely distributed consumer product. We used a stringent monitoring program at a new soccer ball facility in Sialkot, Pakistan, to ensure that children did not enter the workplace and that soccer balls are not distributed to children for stitching. In addition, Reebok will commit $1,000,000 from the sale of soccer balls toward the educational and vocational needs of children in the Sialkot region, where the majority of the world's soccer balls are produced. The Reebok Educational Assistance to Pakistan program, together with the Pakistan-based group, Society for the Advancement of Education (SAE), opened a school for former child workers, the first in a series of initiatives in this region.
>
> ### Witness
>
> In 1993, the Reebok Foundation joined the Lawyers Committee for Human Rights and musician Peter Gabriel to create Witness, a program which supplies activists with communications equipment to document and expose human rights abuses.
>
> ### Reebok Human Rights Award
>
> Since 1988, we have sponsored the annual Reebok Human Rights Awards to recognize young people who, early in their lives and against great odds, join the struggle for human rights. It is unique for being a human rights award sponsored by a corporation that recognizes activists 30 years of age and younger.

HUMAN RIGHTS INCIDENTS AND RESOLVES

In 1996 and 1997, both Reebok and Nike were accused by activists of worker abuse in Southeast Asian countries and China. Most of the heat was on Nike. Some of the accusations and resolves were:

- **Incident 1**: Teenage girls were paid 20 cents an hour to make $180 Nike sneakers in Vietnam factories. At 1 plant, sex abuses were reported. Thuyen Nguyen, founder of Vietnam Labor Watch, issued the report. He said about 35,000 workers at 5 Vietnamese plants—almost all young women—put in 12-hour days making Nike shoes. Though labor costs amount to less than $2 a pair, the shoes retail up to $180 in the United States. So, the Vietnamese workers earn $2.40 a day, which was slightly more than the $2 it costs to buy 3 meals a day. McLain Ramsey, Nike spokeswoman, reported that the manager at that plant was suspended and that an accounting firm had been hired to inspect the factories for abuses. She asked, "What is Nike's responsibility?" and further stated, "But we have put in the time and energy to make what are in many cases good factories into better factories."[70]

- **Incident 2**: Subcontractors making shoes in China for Nike and Reebok used workers as young as 13 who earned as little as 10 cents an hour toiling up to 17 hours a day in enforced silence (a violator could be fined $1.20 to $3.60), the independent observers charged. The watchdog group, Global Exchange, provided a study of the Chinese factories to the Associated Press. The report described the companies' motives this way: "Where in the world can we find the cheapest labor, even if in the most repressed circumstances."[71] Nike said the report was erroneous. Reebok said it monitored work records at these plants. Global Exchange stated that the subcontractors at all 4 sites with about 80,000 employees violated not only "the most basic tenets of Chinese labor law, they're also flagrantly violating [Nike and Reebok's] own code of conduct,"[72] which the companies formulated to regulate their practices overseas.

- **Resolve 1**: Nike hired former U.N. Ambassador Andrew Young to review its labor practices in Asia. He acknowledged some incidents of worker abuse, such as forced overtime. But, he said, he found no pattern of widespread mistreatment.[73]

- **Resolve 2**: In September 1997, Chairman Phil Knight announced at the company's shareholders' meeting that Nike had severed contracts with 4 factories in Indonesia where wages being paid workers were the government minimum wage.[74]

- **Resolve 3**: In January 1998, Mike hired Maria Eitel, a former Microsoft public relations executive, to the newly created position of Vice President, Corporate and Social Responsibility. Eitel would be responsible for Nike's labor practices, environmental affairs, and "global community involvement." Thomas Clarke, Nike's President and CEO, said the hiring of Eitel "signals Nike's commitment from the top to be a leader not only in developing footwear, apparel and equipment, but in global corporate citizenship."[75] Eitel said, "Nike has been an easy target [for critics] because of its high profile." She further stated, "we have to put this into perspective," and "This isn't just Nike's issue. It's an industry and government issue as well."[76]

- **Resolve 4**: On May 12, 1998, Phil Knight "pledged to raise the minimum worker age and let human rights groups help monitor its foreign plants, which employ half a million workers."[77] Nike used U.S. safety and health standards in these plants. Nike would also summarize the human rights groups' conclusion. An analyst felt Phil Knight's new labor policies would put pressure on other U.S. companies operating in developing nations.

Financial Performance

MANAGEMENT REPORT ON 1997 OPERATING RESULTS

Net sales for the year ended December 31, 1997, were $3.644 billion, a 4.7% increase from the year ended December 31, 1996, sales of $3.479 billion, which included $49.4 million of sales from the company's Avia subsidiary that had been sold in June 1996. The Reebok Division's worldwide sales (including Greg Norman) were $3.131 billion in 1997, a 5.0% increase from comparable sales of $2.982 billion in 1996.The stronger U.S. dollar had adversely impacted Reebok Brand worldwide sales comparisons with the prior year. On a constant dollar basis, sales for the Reebok Brand worldwide increased 8.3% in 1997 as compared to 1996. The Reebok Division's U.S. footwear sales increase of 3.0% to $1.229 billion in 1997 from $1.193 billion in 1996. The increase in the Reebok Division's U.S. footwear sales was attributed primarily to sales increases in the running, walking, and men's cross-training categories. The increase in sales in these categories was partially offset by decreases in Reebok's basketball, outdoor, and women's fitness categories. The underlying quality of Reebok footwear sales in the United States improved from 1996. Sales to athletic specialty accounts increased approximately 31%, and the amount of off-price sales declined from 7.6% of total Reebok footwear sales in 1996 to 3.2% of total Reebok footwear sales in 1997. The Reebok Division's U.S. apparel sales increased by 37.2% to $431.9 million from $314.9 million in 1996. The increase resulted primarily from increases in branded core basics, licensed, and graphic categories. The Reebok Division's international sales (including footwear and apparel) were $1.471 billion in 1997, approximately equal to the Division's international sales in 1996 of $1.474 billion. The international sales comparison was negatively impacted by changes in foreign currency exchange rates. On a constant dollar basis, for the year ended December 31, 1997, the international sales gain was 6.4%. All international regions generated sales increases over the prior year on a constant dollar basis. For international sales, increases in the running, classic, and walking categories were offset by decreases in the basketball and tennis categories. Generally in the industry there was in 1998 a slowdown in branded athletic footwear and apparel at retail, and there was a significant amount of promotional product offered across all distribution channels. As a result of this situation and the expected ongoing negative impact from currency fluctuations, it would be difficult to increase reported sales for the Reebok Brand in 1998.

Rockport's sales for 1997 increased by 14.5% to $512.5 million from $447.6 million in 1996. Exclusive of the Ralph Lauren footwear business, which was acquired in May 1996, Rockport's sales increased 7.3% in 1997. International revenues, which grew by 46.0%, accounted for approximately 21.0% of Rockport's sales (excluding Ralph Lauren Footwear) in 1997, as compared to 16.0% in 1996. Increased sales in the walking and men's categories were partially offset by decreased sales in the women's lifestyle category. The decrease in the women's lifestyle category was the result of a strategic initiative to refocus the women's business around an outdoor, adventure, and travel positioning and reduce the product offerings in the refined women's dress shoe segment. Rockport continued to attract younger customers to the brand with the introduction of a wider selection of dress and casual products. The Ralph Lauren footwear business performed well in 1997 and was beginning to generate sales growth in its traditional segments, reflecting the benefits of improved product design and development and increased distribution. Rockport planned to expand the current product line of Ralph Lauren Polo Sport athletic footwear during 1998 with additional products available at retail during 1999.

The company's gross margin declined from 38.4% in 1996 to 37.0% in 1997. Margins were being negatively impacted by both start-up costs and initially higher manufacturing costs on the company's new technology products (DMX 2000 and 3D Ultralite). In addition, the decline reflected a significant impact from currency fluctuations as a result of the stronger U.S. dollar and a decrease in full-margin, at-once business as a result of an over-inventoried promotional retail environment. The company estimated that 100 basis points of the margin decline was due to currency. Looking forward, the company expected margins to continue to be under pressure through at least the first half of 1998. However, the company believed that if the technology product line expanded and gained greater critical mass and with improving production capabilities, the new technology products were capable of generating margin improvement.

Selling, general, and administrative expenses decreased as a percentage of sales from 30.6% in 1996 to 29.4% in 1997. The reduction was primarily due to the absence of certain advertising and marketing expenses associated with the 1996 Summer Olympics. In addition, nonbrand building general and administrative infrastructure expenses declined. Research, design, and development expenses increased 27.0% for the year and retail operating expenses increased in support of new store openings. At December 31, 1997, the company operated 157 Reebok, Rockport, and Greg Norman retail stores in the United States as compared to 141 at the end of 1996.

Interest expense increased as a result of the additional debt the company incurred to finance the shares acquired during the 1996 Dutch Auction share repurchase.[78]

Exhibits 7 and **8** are Reebok's Consolidated Statement of Income and Balance Sheets. The highlights of the Reebok report of first quarter 1998 results are shown below.[79]

- Net sales in the 1998 first quarter were $880.1 million, a decrease of 5.4% from 1997's first quarter net sales of $930.0 million. Worldwide sales for the Reebok brand in the 1998 first quarter were $750.5 million, a decrease of 7.5% from 1997's first quarter sales of $811.6 million. Approximately half of the decline in the Reebok brand sales is due to currency fluctuations, primarily as a result of the strength of the U.S. dollar and the devaluation of certain Asian currencies.

- In the U.S., Reebok footwear sales in the current year quarter were $293.7 million, a decrease of 12.2% from 1997 U.S. footwear sales of $334.6 million. Reebok apparel sales in the United States were $96.8 million for the quarter, as compared with 1997's first quarter apparel sales of $97.9 million.

Exhibit 7

Consolidated Statements of Income: Reebok International, Ltd.
(Dollar amounts in thousands, except per share data)

Year Ending December 31	1997	1996	1995
Net sales	$ 3,643,599	$ 3,478,604	$ 3,481,450
Other income (expense)	(6,158)	4,325	3,126
Total income	3,637,441	3,482,929	3,484,576
Costs and expenses			
Cost of sales	2,294,049	2,144,422	2,114,084
Selling, general, and administrative expenses	1,069,433	1,065,792	999,731
Special charges	58,161	—	72,098
Amortization of intangibles	4,157	3,410	4,067
Interest expense	64,366	42,246	25,725
Interest income	(10,810)	(10,609)	(7,103)
Total costs and expenses	3,479,356	3,245,261	3,208,602
Income before income taxes and minority interest	158,085	237,668	275,974
Income taxes	12,490	84,083	99,753
Income before minority interest	145,595	153,585	176,221
Minority interest	10,476	14,635	11,423
Net income	$ 135,119	$ 138,950	$ 164,798
Basic earnings per share	$ 2.41	$ 2.06	$ 2.10
Diluted earnings per share	$ 2.32	$ 2.03	$ 2.07
Dividends per common share	$ —	$ 0.225	$ 0.300
Common shares issued	93,115,835	92,556,295	111,015,133

Source: Reebok International, Ltd., *1997 Annual Report,* pp. 26–27.

Exhibit 8

Consolidated Balance Sheets: Reebok International, Ltd.
(Dollar amounts in thousands, except per share data)

Year Ending December 31	1997	1996
Assets		
Current assets		
Cash and cash equivalents	$ 209,766	$ 232,365
Accounts receivable, net of allowance for doubtful accounts		
(1997: $44,003; 1996: $43,527)	561,729	590,504
Inventory	563,735	544,522
Deferred income taxes	75,186	69,422
Prepaid expenses and other current assets	54,404	26,275
Total current assets	1,464,820	1,463,088
Property and equipment, net	156,959	185,292
Non-current assets		
Intangibles, net of amortization	65,784	69,700
Deferred income taxes	19,371	7,850
Other	49,163	60,254
	134,318	137,804
Total assets	$1,756,097	$1,786,184
Liabilities and shareholders' equity		
Current liabilities		
Notes payable to banks	$ 40,665	$ 32,977
Current portion of long-term debt	121,000	52,684
Accounts payable	192,142	196,368
Accrued expenses	219,386	169,344
Income taxes payable	4,260	65,588
Total current liabilities	577,453	516,961
Long-term debt, net of current portion	639,355	854,099
Minority interest	32,132	33,890
Shareholders' equity		
Common stock, par value $.01; authorized 250,000,000 shares;		
issued 93,115,835 shares in 1997; 92,556,295 shares in 1996	931	926
Retained earnings	1,145,271	992,563
Less 36,716,227 shares in treasury at cost	(617,620)	(617,620)
Unearned compensation	(140)	(283)
Foreign currency translation adjustment	(21,285)	5,648
Total shareholders' equity	507,157	381,234
Total liabilities and shareholders' equity	$1,756,097	$1,786,184

Source: Reebok International, Ltd., *1997 Annual Report*, p. 28.

- Sales of the Reebok brand outside the United States—including both footwear and apparel—decreased 5.0% in the 1998 first quarter to $360.0 million from $379.1 million in 1997. On a constant dollar basis, international revenues grew approximately 2.0% in the first quarter of 1998 as compared to the first quarter of 1997.

- Sales for the company's Rockport subsidiary grew 9.5% to $129.6 million from $118.4 million in the first quarter of 1997.

- The company reported that its total backlog of open customer orders to be delivered from April 1998 through September 1998 for the Reebok brand was down 3.8%. North American backlog was down 9.0%, and international backlog increased 5.7%. On a constant dollar basis, worldwide Reebok brand backlog was down 2.6%, and international backlog was up 9.5%.

- As previously announced, the company recorded a special pre-tax charge of $35.0 million in the first quarter of 1998 for personnel-related expenses in connection with ongoing business re-engineering efforts and the restructuring of certain underperforming marketing contracts. As a result of this charge, the company reported a first quarter 1998 net loss of $3.4 million, or $0.06 per share. In 1997, the company had reported a profit of $40,184,000 or $0.72 per share.

Commenting on these poor first quarter results, Paul Fireman said,

The company's overall results were in line with our expectations and reflect the continuing difficult conditions in the athletic footwear and apparel industry, which is experiencing an over-inventoried and highly promotional environment. Despite these difficulties, however, we did achieve strong sell-throughs on several of our marquis product introductions during the quarter, including our 3D Ultralite product, the Shroud, and our new DMX 6 running shoe. We think these successes are indicative of our ability to apply our 2 new proprietary technologies, DMX and 3D Ultralite, and we will continue our efforts to market these technologies through unique direct-to-the-consumer campaigns that allow customers to experience our products first-hand. During the quarter we started the Reebok "Try on the Future" Tour using vans and kiosks in major malls to take our products direct to the consumer. Our experience is that when consumers try on our technologies, they are much more likely to buy our product. In addition to this marketing campaign, we will launch a brand image advertising campaign which will debut during the second quarter, and we are optimistic that this along with our product specific advertising will begin to generate excitement and momentum for the Reebok brand.[80]

Notes

1. Reebok International, Ltd., *1997 Annual Report*, pp. 7–11. This letter was directly quoted and 1 sentence deleted.
2. *Footwear News*, May 8, 1995.
3. *Ibid.*
4. Joseph Pereira, "In Reebok–Nike War, Big Woolworth Chain Was a Major Battleground," *Wall Street Journal* (September 22, 1995), p. A-1.
5. *Ibid.*
6. *Ibid.*
7. Reebok International, Ltd., *1996 Annual Report*, p. 36.
8. Reebok International, Ltd., *1997 Annual Report*, p. 39.
9. Reebok International, Ltd., *1998 Notice of Annual Meeting of Shareholders*, p. 5. This was directly quoted.
10. *Wall Street Journal* (August 23, 1995), p. B-7.
11. Reebok International, Ltd., *Form 10-K* (December 31, 1997), pp. 18–20.
12. Kenneth Labich, "Nike vs. Reebok," *Fortune* (September 18, 1995), p. 104.
13. *Ibid.*
14. *Ibid.*
15. Reebok International, Ltd., *Form 10-K* (December 31, 1997), p. 20
16. Reebok International, Ltd., *1998 Notice of Annual Meeting of Shareholders*, p. 8.
17. Reebok International, Ltd., *Form 10-K* (December 31, 1997), pp. 2–3. The above 3 paragraphs were directly quoted with minor editing.
18. *Ibid.*, pp. 8–9. The above 10 paragraphs were directly quoted with minor editing.
19. Reebok International, Ltd., *Form 10-K* (December 31, 1997), p. 9. The above 3 paragraphs were directly quoted with minor editing.
20. Reebok International, Ltd., *1997 Annual Report*, p. 17. The above paragraph was directly quoted with minor editing.
21. Reebok International, Ltd., *Form 10-K* (December 31, 1997), pp. 6–7. The above 3 paragraphs were directly quoted with minor editing.
22. *Ibid.*, p. 16. The above paragraph was directly quoted with minor editing.
23. *Ibid.*, pp. 11–12. The above 6 paragraphs were directly quoted with minor editing.
24. *Ibid.*, p. 18. The above paragraph was directly quoted with minor editing.
25. Stefan Fatsis, "Nike Kicks in Millions to Sponsor Soccer in U.S.," *Wall Street Journal* (October 22, 1997), p. B-1.
26. Joseph Pereira, "Women Jump Ahead of Men in Purchase of Athletic Shoes," *Wall Street Journal* (May 26, 1995), p. B-1.
27. Kathryn Kranhold, "L.A. Gear Plans to Restructure, Cutting Jobs," *Wall Street Journal* (November 4, 1997), p. 6.
28. J. Solomon, "When Cool Goes Cold," *Newsweek* (March 30, 1998), p. 37.
29. Susan Pulliam and Laura Bird, "Season's Casual Shoe Trend Means Some Firms Will Get Stomped. . . ," *Wall Street Journal* (August 27, 1997), p. C-1.
30. *Ibid.*
31. "A Fast Ride Uphill," *St. Petersburg Times* (April 14, 1998), p. 10-A.
32. *Ibid.*

33. *Ibid.*, pp. 9A–10A.

34. *Ibid.*, p. 10A.

35. Bill Meyers, "Jordan Inc.," *USA Today* (September 9, 1997), p. 1A, and Oscar Dixon, "Air Apparent Executive," *USA Today* (September 9, 1997), p. 3C.

36. Kenneth Labich, "Nike vs. Reebok," *Fortune* (September 18, 1995), pp. 14–16.

37. *Ibid.*, p. 92.

38. *Ibid.*

39. *Ibid.*, p. 100

40. Joseph Pereira, "Sneaker Company Tag Out-of-Breath Baby Boomers," *Wall Street Journal* (January 1, 1998), p. B-1.

41. *Ibid.*

42. *Ibid.*

43. Jonathan B. Chappell, "Stride Rite," *Value Line* (February 20, 1998), p. 1672.

44. Cecile Rohwedder and Matt Marshall, "Germany's Adidas Was Seen Sprinting Toward Making Initial Public Offering," *Wall Street Journal* (September 18, 1995), p. A7B.

45. Reebok International, Ltd., *Form 10-K* (December 31, 1997), p. 4. The above paragraph was directly quoted with minor editing.

46. *Ibid.* The above 2 paragraphs were cited directly with minor editing.

47. "Reebok Issues Apology for Naming Shoe 'Incubus,'" *Wall Street Journal* (February 26, 1997), p. B12.

48. *Ibid.*, pp. 4–5. The above 5 paragraphs, not including note 47, were cited directly with minor editing.

49. *Ibid.*, p. 12.

50. *Ibid.*, p. 13, and *1997 Annual Report*, p. 39.

51. *Ibid.*, p. 7. The above 4 paragraphs were cited directly with minor editing.

52. I. Jeanne Dugan, "Why Foot Locker Is in a Sweat," *Business Week* (October 27, 1997), p. 52.

53. *Ibid.*

54. *Ibid.*

55. *Ibid.*

56. Joseph Pereira, "In Reebok–Nike War," p. A-1.

57. *Ibid.*, p. A-5.

58. *Ibid.*

59. *Ibid.*

60. *Ibid.*

61. Labich, p. 104.

62. Pereira, "In Reebok–Nike War," p. A-1.

63. Reebok International, Ltd., *Form 10-K* (December 31, 1997), pp. 9–10. The above 5 paragraphs were directly quoted with minor editing.

64. *Ibid.*, pp. 10–11. The above 4 paragraphs were directly quoted with minor editing.

65. *Ibid.*, pp. 3–4. The above 5 paragraphs were directly quoted with minor editing.

66. *Ibid.*, p. 11. The above 3 paragraphs were directly quoted with minor editing.

67. *Ibid.*, p. 13. The above paragraph was directly quoted with minor editing.

68. *Ibid.*, p. 18. The above paragraph was directly quoted with minor editing.

69. Reebok International, Ltd., *1997 Annual Report*, p. 18. The 4 below paragraphs were directly quoted with minor editing.

70. "Activist: Nike-makers Abused," *St. Petersburg Times* (March 28, 1997), p. 6-E.

71. "Report Blasts Nike, Reebok Subcontractors," *St. Petersburg Times* (July 21, 1997), p. 3-A.

72. *Ibid.*

73. "Nike Factory Manager Sentenced," *St. Petersburg Times* (June 29, 1997), p. E1.

74. "Nike Cancels Pacts with Indonesia Plants Over Wage Policies," *Wall Street Journal* (September 23, 1997), p. B-6.

75. Bill Richards, "Nike Hires an Executive from Microsoft for New Post Focusing on Labor Policies," p. B-14.

76. *Ibid.*

77. Aaron Bernstein, "Nike Finally Does It," *Business Week* (May 25, 1998), p. 46.

78. Reebok International, Ltd., *1997 Annual Report*, pp. 20–21. The above 5 paragraphs were directly quoted with minor editing.

79. Reebok International, Ltd., *Reebok Report First Quarter 1998 Results* (April 22, 1998), pp. 1–2. The below 6 paragraphs were directly quoted with minor editing.

80. *Ibid.*, p. 3. The above paragraph was directly quoted with minor editing.

case 19

The U.S. Major Home Appliance Industry: Domestic Versus Global Strategies

J. David Hunger

The U.S. major home appliance industry in 1996 was an example of a very successful industry. Contrasted with the U.S. automobile and consumer electronics industries, U.S. major appliance manufacturers had been able to ward off Japanese competition and were actually on the offensive internationally. Imports to the United States of major home appliances (primarily microwave ovens and small refrigerators) were only a small proportion of total sales. For "white goods"—refrigerators, freezers, washing machines, dryers, ranges, microwave ovens, and dishwashers—over 84% of those sold in the United States were made domestically.[1] The industry had been very successful in keeping prices low and in improving the value of its products. Compared to 1982, major home appliance prices had increased more slowly than the increase in U.S. earnings and the consumer price index (CPI). Thus the average American consumer in 1996 could earn a new appliance in 80% fewer hours on the job than a half-century ago. For example, although the price of a Maytag automatic washing machine had risen from $280 in 1949 to $440 in 1995, it had actually declined when inflation was considered. In addition, the energy efficiency of the most common major appliances had increased every year since 1972. Sales had also been increasing. More appliances were made and sold in the United States in 1994 than in any preceding year. (See **Exhibits 1** and **2**.) Although shipments for 1995 were down slightly, most industry analysts predicted that 1996 shipments should be fairly stable.

Nevertheless, the major home appliance industry faced some significant threats, as well as opportunities, as it moved through the last decade of the twentieth century. After 50 years of rising sales in both units and dollars, the North American market had reached maturity. Aside from some normal short-term fluctuations, future unit sales were expected to grow only 1% to 2% annually on average for the foreseeable future. Operating margins had been dropping as appliance manufacturers were forced to keep prices low to be competitive, even though costs kept increasing. In Western Europe, however, a market already 25% larger than the mature North American appliance market, unit sales were expected to grow 2% to 3% annually on average. This figure was expected to increase significantly as Eastern European countries opened their economies to world trade. Economies in Asia and Latin America were becoming more important to world trade as more countries moved toward free-market economies. Industry analysts expected appliance markets in these areas to grow at a

This industry note was prepared by Professor J. David Hunger of Iowa State University. This case was edited for SMBP-8th Edition. All rights reserved to the author. Copyright © 1996 by J. David Hunger. Reprinted by permission.

Exhibit 1

U.S. Manufacturers' Unit Shipments of Major Home Appliances
(Unit amounts in thousands)

Product	2000[1]	1995	1994	1993	1992	1991	1990	1985	1980
Compactors	128	98	130	125	126	129	185	177	235
Dishwashers									
Built-in	4,713	4,327	4,326	3,891	3,619	3,360	3,419	3,327	2,354
Portable	243	226	254	208	201	211	217	248	384
Disposers	4,945	4,519	4,798	4,436	4,195	4,002	4,137	4,105	2,962
Dryers									
Compact	258	160	220	275	275	268	275	189	207
Electric	4,252	4,020	4,036	3,853	3,563	3,295	3,318	2,891	2,287
Gas	1,381	1,205	1,303	1,221	1,154	1,018	1,002	834	682
Freezers									
Chest	979	933	960	871	1,005	794	723	634	963
Compact	350	357	340	368	360	355	351	237	310
Upright	730	756	731	735	686	620	573	602	789
Microwave Ovens									
Comb. ranges[2]	88	80	86	94	110	128	146	314	265
Countertop	7,946	7,760	7,830	7,130	6,990	7,233	8,193	9,727	3,320
Microwave/Convect.	129	115	125	130	280	300	303	256	NA
Over-the-range	1,087	1,100	924	778	625	674	780	900	NA
Range/Oven Hoods	3,029	2,740	2,725	2,650	2,522	2,342	2,450	2,588	2,400
Ranges, Electric									
Built-in	740	619	699	659	624	568	631	574	555
Free-standing	3,234	3,004	3,024	2,731	2,508	2,332	2,358	2,567	1,975
Glass/Ceramic[2]	575	450	400	320	257	150	85	86	155
Surface units	466	425	446	458	442	409	455	409	NA
Ranges, Gas									
Built-in	95	86	87	90	91	92	106	84	102
Free-standing	2,671	2,490	2,534	2,343	2,221	2,041	2,061	1,729	1,437
Surface units	368	278	337	322	301	268	262	NA	NA
Refrigerators									
Built-in	NA	123	122	115	100	NA	NA	NA	NA
Compact[2]	1,325	1,032	950	1,030	950	925	932	783	543
Standard	8,851	8,670	8,652	8,109	7,761	7,273	7,101	6,080	5,124
Washers									
Automatic	7,190	6,901	7,035	6,792	6,515	6,197	6,192	5,278	4,426
Compact	295	200	275	365	365	358	344	303	266
Water Heaters									
Electric	4,034	3,917	3,897	3,609	3,399	3,170	3,226	3,452	2,451
Gas	5,098	4,453	4,750	4,470	4,241	3,936	3,906	3,529	2,818
Total Appliances[3]	66,200	60,159	61,174	57,396	54,759	51,814	53,152	51,268	37,010

Notes:
1. Estimated.
2. Duplications, not included in total. Numbers have been rounded off.
3. Data for major electric appliances include all imports and exports.

Source: Appliance (April 1990), p. 33; (April 1995), p. 45; (January 1996), p. 42; (April 1996), p. 43.

Exhibit 2
U.S. Manufacturers' Unit Shipments of Floor Care Appliances
(Unit amounts in thousands)

Product	1995	1994	1993	1992	1991	1990	1989	1988	1985
Polishers	180	185	NA	NA	NA	NA	NA	NA	NA
Shampooers	1,825	2,300	1,950	1,600	1,200	1,000	NA	NA	NA
Vacuum Cleaners									
Canisters	1,840	1,963	1,700	2,100	2,385	2,741	3,010	3,177	2,998
Central	174	157	141	134	129	130	NA	NA	NA
Handheld electric	3,140	3,750	3,810	3,610	2,900	2,500	1,900	1,050	564
Handheld rechargeable	2,380	2,500	2,640	2,740	3,500	5,000	5,125	5,300	5,440
Stick	2,320	2,060	1,825	1,600	1,500	1,644	1,893	1,725	1,077
Upright	10,737	10,215	9,250	8,330	6,960	6,578	6,470	5,750	4,438
Total Floor Care	22,596	23,130	21,316	20,114	18,574	19,593	18,398	17,002	14,517

Source: Appliance (April 1990), p. 35; (April 1995), p. 46; (January 1996), p. 44; (April 1996), p. 44.

rate of 5% to 6% annually.[2] The industry was under pressure from governments around the world to make environmentally safe products and significantly improve appliance energy efficiency.

Development of the U.S. Major Home Appliance Industry

In 1945, there were approximately 300 U.S. major appliance manufacturers in the United States. By 1996, however, the "big 5" of Whirlpool, General Electric, Maytag, A.B. Electrolux (*no* relation to Electrolux Corporation, a U.S. company selling Electrolux brand vacuum cleaners), and Raytheon controlled over 98% of the U.S. market. The consolidation of the industry over the period was a result of fierce domestic competition. Emphasis on quality and durability coupled with strong price competition drove the surviving firms to increased efficiencies and a strong concern for customer satisfaction.

INDUSTRY HISTORY

All of the major U.S. automobile firms except Chrysler had participated at 1 time in the major home appliance industry. Giants in the consumer electronics industry had also been involved heavily in appliances. Some of the major auto, electronics, and diversified companies active at 1 time in the appliance industry were General Motors (Frigidaire), Ford (Philco), American Motors (Kelvinator), Studebaker (Franklin), Bendix, International Harvester, General Electric, RCA, Emerson Electric, Westinghouse, McGraw Edison, Rockwell, United Technologies, Raytheon, Litton, Borg-Warner, and Dart & Kraft. Only General Electric, Raytheon, and Emerson Electric remained in major home appliances in 1996. Emerson Electric continued through its In-Sink-Erator line of disposers and dishwashers, as well as being a major supplier of electronic parts to the remaining appliance makers. Most of the other firms divested their appliance business units, many of which were acquired by White Consolidated Industries, which itself was acquired by the Swedish firm A.B. Electrolux in 1986 and subsequently renamed Frigidaire.

Prior to World War II, most appliance manufacturers produced a limited line of appliances derived from 1 successful product. General Electric made refrigerators. Maytag focused on washing machines. Hotpoint produced electric ranges. Each offered variations of its basic product, but not until 1945 did firms begin to offer full lines of various appliances. By 1955, the major appliance industry began experiencing overcapacity, leading to mergers and acquisitions and a proliferation of national and private brands.

The industry almost doubled in size during the 1960s as sales of several products grew rapidly. Dishwasher unit sales almost quadrupled. Unit sales of clothes dryers more than tripled. Product reliability improved even though real prices (adjusted for inflation) declined by about 10%.

Although the 1970s were a time of high inflation and high interest rates, the major home appliance industry continued to increase its unit sales. Profit margins were squeezed even more, and the industry continued to consolidate around fewer firms. Although antitrust considerations prevented GE and Whirlpool from acquiring other appliance units, White was able to buy the troubled appliance divisions of all the automobile manufacturers, along with Westinghouse's, as they were put up for sale.

The market continued to expand in the 1980s, thanks partially to the acceptance by the U.S. consumer of the microwave oven. By the 1990s, U.S. appliance manufacturers offered a full range of products even if they did not make the item themselves. A company would fill the gaps in its line by putting its own brand name on products it purchased from another manufacturer. For example, Whirlpool made trash compactors for Frigidaire (A.B. Electrolux), In-Sink-Erator (Emerson Electric), Jenn-Air, Magic Chef (Maytag), and Sears. Caloric (Raytheon) not only made gas ranges for its in-house Amana Brand, but also for Whirlpool. General Electric made some microwave ovens for Caloric (Raytheon), Jenn-Air, Magic Chef (Maytag), and its own Hotpoint and RCA brands.

PRODUCT AND PROCESS DESIGN

Innovations in the industry tended to be of 3 types: (1) new products that expanded the appliance market, (2) new customer-oriented features, and (3) process improvements to reduce manufacturing costs. New products that had strongly increased industry unit sales were dishwashers in the 1960s and microwave ovens in the 1980s. The combination washer-dryer and compact versions of other appliances, such as refrigerators and washers, were not very popular in the United States but had been successful in Europe and Asia where household space was at a premium and cultural norms favored daily over weekly food shopping. One potential new product was the microwave clothes dryer. The use of microwave energy for drying meant that clothes could be dried faster at a lower temperature (thus less shrinkage and damage) with less energy use than a conventional dryer. Unfortunately, the technology needed further development before it could be marketed; microwaves have a tendency to heat metal objects to such a point that they cause fabric damage.

Customer-oriented features included the self-cleaning oven, pilotless gas range, automatic ice cube-making refrigerator, and others. In most cases, features were introduced on top-of-the-line models and made available on lower priced models later. Manufacturers' own brands usually had the newest and most elaborate features, followed by national retailers such as Sears, Roebuck and Co. and Montgomery Ward whose offerings usually copied the most successful features from the previous year. In this competitive industry, aside from patented features, no one producer could successfully keep a new innovation to itself for more than a year.

In the mid 1990s, 3 trends were evident. First, European visual product design was having strong impact on appliance design worldwide. Frigidaire, for example, introduced a "Euroflair" line of appliances. A soft, rounded appearance was replacing the block, sharp-cornered look. Second, manufacturers were introducing "smart" appliances with increasingly sophisticated electronic controls and self-diagnostic features. The Japanese firms of Matsushita, Hitachi, Toshiba, and Mitsubishi had pioneered the use of "fuzzy logic" computer software to replace the many selector switches on an appliance with 1 start button. By 1996, all of the major U.S. home appliance manufacturers were using fuzzy logic to some extent in making and marketing their products. Whirlpool's new "Sixth Sense" oven could determine the necessary settings for reheating or defrosting food with no guesswork from the cook. The user simply pressed a single button for defrost; the oven then calculated on its own the correct time and power output. The third trend was the increasing emphasis on environmentally safe products, such as the use of CFC-free refrigerant, and on greater efficiency in the use of water and energy. Maytag, among others, was actively involved in developing a "horizontal axis" washing machine that would use significantly less water and electricity than its typical "vertical axis" washer.

Process improvements for more efficient manufacturing of current products (compared to new-product development) has tended to dominate research and development efforts in the U.S. major home appliance industry. Although modern appliances were much more effective and efficient, a refrigerator or a washing machine in the 1990s still looked and acted very much the same as it did in the 1950s. It was built in a far different manner, however. Richard Topping, director of the Center for Product Development of the consulting firm Arthur D. Little, indicated that the appliance industry historically had been characterized by low intensity in research and development because of intense cost competition and demand for higher reliability. Topping went on to stress that the basis for effective competition in the future would be in producing the fewest basic components necessary in the most efficient plants. Although individual designs might vary, the components inside the appliances would become more universal and would be produced in highly automated plants, using computer integrated manufacturing processes.[3] Examples of this emphasis on product simplification were Maytag's "Dependable Drive" and Whirlpool's frame fabrication for its "Eye Level" ranges. Maytag's new washer transmission was designed to have 40.6% fewer parts than the transmission it replaced. Fewer parts meant simplified manufacturing and less chance of a breakdown. The result was lower manufacturing costs and higher product quality.

Most industry analysts agreed that continual process improvements had kept U.S. major home appliance manufacturers dominant in their industry. The emphasis on quality and durability, coupled with a reluctance to make major design changes simply for the sake of change, resulted in products with long average life expectancy. With the average useful life of a refrigerator or range approaching 18 years and those of washers and dryers approaching 15 years, it was easy to see 1 reason why the Japanese manufacturers had been less successful in entering the U.S. appliance market than with automobiles. (See **Exhibit 3**.) another reason was a constant unrelenting pressure to reduce costs or be driven from the marketplace.

Exhibit 3
Average Life Expectancy of Major Home
Appliances (in years)

Compactors	8
Dishwashers	9
Disposers	9
Dryers—electric	13
Dryers—gas	14
Freezers	12
Microwave ovens	10
Ranges—electric	15
Ranges—gas	18
Refrigerators	15
Washers	13
Vacuum cleaners	10
Floor polishers	12
Water heaters—electric	10
Water heaters—gas	9

Source: Appliance (September 1992), pp. 46–47; (September 1995), p. 73.

MANUFACTURING AND PURCHASING

Although many manufacturing operations took place in an appliance factory, much of the process focused on proper preparation of the metal frame within which the washing, drying, or cooking components and elements would be attached. Consequently, appliance manufacturers could be characterized as "metal benders" who fabricated different shapes of metal boxes out of long coils of metal. Sophisticated machines would form and even weld the frames, and automated assembly lines and robots would add porcelain to protect the metal and add color to the finish. People were usually still needed to install the internal components in the frame and to wire sophisticated electronic controls. Quality control was often a combination of electronic diagnostics and personal inspection by employees.

Manufacturing costs were generally in the range of 65% to 75% of total operating cost. (See **Exhibit 4**.) Although direct labor costs were still an important part of the cost of completed goods (about 10%), most companies were carefully examining material costs, general administration, and overhead for cost reduction. Traditionally, the optimal size of an assembly plant was considered to be an annual capacity of 500,000 units for refrigerators, ranges, washers, dryers, and dishwashers. Even though production costs were believed to be 10% to 40% percent higher in smaller sized plants, the use of robots suggested that the optimal plant could be even smaller than previously believed.[4]

During the 1990s, the trend continued toward dedicated manufacturing facilities combining product line production in fewer larger plants to gain economies of scale. Although a dedicated production line for washing machines could be adjusted to make many different models, it could still only be used to make washing machines. Each product category required its own specialized manufacturing equipment.

All of the major home appliance manufacturers were engaged in renovating and building production facilities to gain economies of scale, improve quality, and reduce labor and materials costs. Frigidaire had just finished spending over $600 million upgrading its current factories and building new refrigerator and dishwasher plants. General Electric was investing some $1 billion over a 4-year period in appliance product development and capital equipment—a

Exhibit 4
The Major Home Appliance Value Chain

Sales		100%
Manufacturing costs		65–75
Fully integrated		
raw materials	30–40%	
labor	6–10	
plant and equipment	12–20	
general administration	12–20	
Not integrated		
components	35–45	
labor and overhead	30–40	
Transportation and warehousing		5–7
Advertising		1–2
Sales and marketing		4–8
Service		2–5
Product research and development		2–5
Overhead		2–10

Source: C. R. Christensen, K. R. Andrews, J. L. Bower, R. G. Hamermesh, and M. E. Porter, "Note on the Major Home Appliance Industry in 1984 (Condensed)," *Business Policy*, 6th ed. (Homewood, IL: Irwin, 1987), p. 339.

50% increase over previous spending levels. Whirlpool had completely renovated the manu-facturing processes and its labor management system in its aging tooling and plating factory in Benton Harbor—thus increasing productivity more than 19%.

As the major home appliance industry had consolidated, so too had their suppliers. The purchasing function and relationship with suppliers changed considerably in the 1980s as more companies used fewer suppliers and more long-term contracts to improve quality and ensure just-in-time (JIT) delivery. Along with its global orientation, Whirlpool was also putting emphasis on working with global suppliers. Appliance companies used certification programs to ensure that their smaller supplier bases were able to supply both the needed quantity and quality of materials, parts, and subassemblies when they were needed. Full-line, full-service suppliers had an advantage over 1-dimensional suppliers. Appliance makers con-tinued to put pressure on their suppliers to institute cost-saving productivity improvements. On the other hand, they were much more willing to involve suppliers earlier in the design stage of a product or process improvement. Joe Thomson, Vice President of Purchasing at Maytag's Galesburg Refrigeration Products unit, provides 1 example:

> We made an arrangement with a large steel supplier that led to a team effort to establish hard-ness specifications on our cabinet and door steel to improve fabrication. This team was very suc-cessful and the quality improvement and reduction in cost reached all our expectations. The company is now supplying all of our steel requirement.[5]

These alliances between appliance makers and their suppliers were one way to speed up the application of new technology to new products and process. For example, Maytag Company was approached by one of its suppliers who offered its expertise in fuzzy logic tech-nology—a technology Maytag did not have a that time. The resulting partnership in product development resulted in Maytag's new IntelliSense™ dishwasher. Unlike previous dishwash-ers, which had to be set by the user, Maytag's fuzzy logic dishwasher automatically selected the proper cycle to get the dishes clean based on a series of factors, including the amount of dirt and presence of detergent.

Some of the key materials purchased by the U.S. appliance industry were steel (primarily in sheets and coils from domestic suppliers), plastics, coatings (paint and porcelain), motors, glass, insulation, wiring, and fasteners. By weight, major appliances consisted of about 75% steel. Sales to the major home appliance industry of steel and aluminum together accounted for 10% of total industry sales.[6]

MARKETING AND DISTRIBUTION CHANNELS

Due to relatively high levels of saturation in the United States, the market for major home appliances was driven primarily by the demand for replacements. Washers, ranges, refrigera-tors, and even microwave ovens were in more than 70% of U.S. households. (See **Exhibit 5.**) Generally speaking, replacements accounted for 75% of sales, new housing for 20%, and new household formation for about 5% of sales of major home appliances. Replacement demand was usually driven by existing housing turnover, remodeling, changes in living arrangement trends, introduction of new features, and price levels in the economy. Although each new house had the potential to add 4 to 6 new appliances, the sale of an existing house also had an impact. According to J. Richard Stonesifer, President and CEO of GE Appliances, "About 4 mil-lion existing homes are sold each year, and approximately 1 new appliance is sold for every existing home that changes hands."[7] The National Kitchen and Bath Association estimated that about $4 billion of the total $25 billion spent annually on kitchen remodeling was for home appliances. Both the new housing and remodeling markets in the 1990s tended to emphasize more upscale appliances in contrast to the previous tendency for builders to econ-omize by buying the cheapest national brand appliances.[8] A study by Simmons Market

Exhibit 5

Major Home Appliance Saturation in the United States, Western Europe, and Japan
(Households with at least 1 of a particular appliance)

Appliance	United States	Western Europe[1]	Japan
Dishwashers	52%	29%	NA
Freezers	40	47	NA
Microwave ovens	89	43	87%
Ranges/ovens	99	95	NA
Refrigerators	99	97	98
Dryers	70	21	19
Washers	75	90	99
Vacuums	97	86	98
Water heaters	99	NA	30
Floor polishers	7	NA	NA
Floor shampooers	9	NA	NA

Note:
1. Composite of Austria, Belgium/Luxembourg, Switzerland, Germany, Denmark, Spain, France, Great Britain (U.K.), Greece, Italy, Ireland, Norway, the Netherlands, Portugal, Sweden, and Finland.

Source: Appliance (September 1995), pp. 74–75; (June 1995), p. 46; (February 1996), p. 73.

Research Bureau for New Home magazine revealed that more than $13 billion was spent annually by new-home owners on household goods, especially appliances. In order of importance, the appliances typically bought within the first 3 months of owning a new home were the refrigerator, washer, dryer, microwave oven, vacuum cleaner, dishwasher, coffee-maker, and range.[9] This phenomenon provided sales opportunities for well-positioned appliance makers because brand loyalty in the appliance industry was only 35%.[10]

Changes in U.S. demographics in the 1990s favored the highly profitable, high-end, high-profile segment of the business. This trend was detrimental to the mass market business, which emphasized cost over features. The aging of the baby boomers and the increase of 2-income families had increased the upscale market, which demanded more style and costly features. Appliance manufacturers were responding by expanding product lines that emphasized quality and features. Those brands most identified in customers' minds with high product quality were most likely to do well. (See **Exhibit 6**.)

Exporting was reasonably strong for high-quality U.S.-made refrigerators, vacuum cleaners, and laundry appliances, but was much less than the importing of microwave ovens from Asia. For a number of reasons, exporting was not a significant factor for the U.S. major home appliance industry. The weight of most of these appliances meant high transportation costs, which translated into higher prices to the consumer. In addition, U.S.-made major appliances tended to be fairly large, whereas European and Asian markets preferred smaller appliances. As a result, most people around the world tended to buy appliances made locally, if they were available. Thus, appliance companies wanting a significant presence in other parts of the world were either acquiring local companies, engaging in joint ventures, or building new manufacturing facilities in those regions in order to have a local presence.

There were 2 major distribution channels for major home appliances in the United States: contract and retail. A third, but less important, distribution channel was the commercial market, comprising laundromats and institutions.

Contract sales were made to large home builders and to other appliance manufacturers. Direct sales accounted for about 80% of contract sales. Firms sold appliances to the contract segment both directly to the large builders and indirectly through local builder suppliers. Since builders were very cost conscious, they liked to buy at the middle to low end of a well-known appliance brand. Consequently, appliance manufacturers with strong offerings in this

Exhibit 6

Rating of Brands by Retailers in Terms of Customer Perception
of Quality[1]

Brand	Excellent	Very Good
Maytag	90%	9%
KitchenAid	84	14
Jenn-Air	61	35
Amana	54	40
Monogram	44	26
Whirlpool	39	56
GE	28	59
Speed Queen	8	52
Frigidaire	6	56
RCA	6	41
Tappan	2	42
Magic Chef	2	41
Hotpoint	2	39
Caloric	1	31
White–Westinghouse	1	28
Roper	1	25
Gibson	1	20
Kelvinator	0	11
Admiral	0	11

Note:
1. Responses were by 536 appliance dealers that were members of the North American Retail Dealers Association.
   Each brand was evaluated as excellent, very good, good, and poor. Only the percentages of excellent and very good
   responses are shown here.

Source: J. Jancsurak, "In Their Opinion," *Appliance Manufacturer* (April 1995), p. 45.

range, such as Whirlpool and General Electric, tended to do very well in this market. In contrast, companies such as Maytag, which traditionally emphasized high-end products, sold little (except for the lower priced Magic Chef brand) to home builders. Whirlpool and GE designed whole kitchen concepts and sold the entire package—including their appliances—to builders. To further its advantage, Whirlpool opened a 35,000-square-foot customer center at its Benton Harbor headquarters in 1993 to demonstrate its offerings to retailers and contractors—the first such customer center in the industry.

Retail sales in the United States were made to 3 major kinds of outlets: (1) national chain stores and mass merchandisers; (2) department, furniture, and discount stores; and (3) appliance dealers. Sales to national chain stores and mass merchandisers were usually private brands promoted by the retailers. For example, Whirlpool had traditionally been a heavy supplier of Sears and Kenmore brand appliances to Sears, Roebuck and Co. Magic Chef sold similar private brand appliances to Montgomery Ward. Some 30% to 40% of white goods were traditionally sold through this channel. Sears, Roebuck had been so strong in major home appliance sales that it alone sold 1 of 4 major appliances sold in the United States.

Department stores, furniture stores, and discount stores were another important channel for major appliances—selling some 20% of white goods sold in the United States. These stores usually purchased well-known brands to offer their customers. As department stores tended to alter their product offerings to more soft goods (clothing items) and less hard goods (furniture and appliances) during the 1980s, discount stores became more important in major home appliance sales. Their concern with price, however, put even more pressure on manufacturers to sell in large quantity at low price.

Appliance dealers had traditionally been an important retail outlet for white goods. About 30% to 40% of major home appliances were sold through this channel. In the late 1980s and early 1990s, many locally owned stores were being replaced by national chains. Richard Haines, Executive Vice President of Maytag Corporation, explained the impact of changes in distribution channels on his firm:

> When we [Maytag Company] decided to expand our offerings beyond laundry and dishwashers, 1 of the reasons we did so was the changing marketplace. What we saw happening was a significant decrease in the number of independent Mom and Pop dealerships that used to be the mainstay of the retail appliance business. The field was becoming increasingly dominated by national power retailers and by regional super stores.
>
> These new age marketers make their livings on high volume sales with relatively low unit margins. To maintain profitability, they must seek out the lowest wholesale prices possible from manufacturers on large volume buys. By purchasing only a few full lines of major appliances, today's retailers develop the clout they need with individual appliance producers to get the best pricing at wholesale and, therefore, the best margins at retail.
>
> Manufacturers who wish to compete in this new arena need a full line of products plus the capacity and manufacturing efficiency to make the volume sales mass merchants require.[11]

By the 1990s, the so-called "power retailers"—Sears, Montgomery Ward, and regional appliance chains, such as Circuit City—were selling over 60% of all retail appliances in the United States.

The *commercial market* was an additional distribution channel. Never as important to manufacturers as the contract and retail channels, this market nevertheless was an important set of customers for sales of washing machines and dryers. Laundromats and institutions, such as colleges for their dormitories, typically bought the most durable appliances made for the home market. Manufacturers simply added coin meters to the top of the washers and dryers destined for use in these commercial or public establishments. Although these home laundry appliances adapted for the commercial market comprised over 50% of sales to this channel, there were some indications that this market might be moving to commercial washers built to last 2 to 3 times longer than would a home washer used commercially. With regard to the makers of freezers, refrigerators, and ranges for use in business establishments such as restaurants, these were usually a different group of U.S. manufacturers (for example, Traulsen, Hobart, and Glenco) from those manufacturing home appliances.

Appliance manufacturing in 1996 was shifting from a primary emphasis on quality and reliability to speed and agility as well. This meant that manufacturers were working to improve their use of logistics in order to provide better service to their distributors. The JIT concept had been introduced during the 1980s in order to improve manufacturing efficiency. Similar concepts were now being applied in the 1990s to distribution and marketing. For example, Whirlpool introduced "Quality Express" in 1992 as part of its revamped distribution system. Quality Express used dedicated trucks, personnel, and warehousing to deliver Whirlpool, KitchenAid, Roper, and Estate brand appliances to 90% of all dealer and builder customers within 24 hours and to 100% within 48 hours. As part of the service, drivers delivering product unloaded units from the truck and put them where the customer wanted them. This service even included uncrating, customizing, and installation if desired. Other appliance companies were following Whirlpool's lead. A 1995 survey of 2,000 North American appliance dealers reported the following ranking of appliance manufacturers in terms of how well they serviced retailers:

1. Whirlpool Corporation
2. Maytag Corporation
3. General Electric Appliances
4. Amana Refrigeration Company (Raytheon's appliance unit)
5. Frigidaire Group (AB Electrolux's U.S. appliance unit)[12]

ENVIRONMENTAL ISSUES AND GOVERNMENT REGULATION

The major home appliance industry had rarely been a key target for criticism regarding safety or pollution as had the U.S. steel and automobile industries, among others. By the 1980s, however, this situation had changed. Chlorofluorocarbons (CFCs) used in refrigerator and freezer insulation and in refrigerant had been linked by the early 1980s to the depletion of the earth's ozone layer. A 1987 meeting of the developed nations in Montreal resulted in a Montreal Protocol signed by 46 countries. In November 1992, the members of the Montreal Protocol and others met to firm up the agreements concerning the elimination of the use of chlorine-containing, ozone-depleting CFCs and to create a schedule for the elimination of hydrochlorofluorocarbons (HCFCs), which had substantially lower ozone-depleting potential. By 1996, CFCs had been effectively eliminated from use in appliances. Although the schedule for the phaseout of HCFCs called for similar elimination by January 1, 2030, the European Union wanted a halt by 2015.[13]

Thus, U.S. refrigerator and freezer manufacturers faced a serious dilemma. On the 1 hand, governments were requiring less use of chemicals crucial to cooling. On the other hand, the U.S. Department of Energy (DOE) was requiring energy conservation improvements for refrigerators and freezers. These appliances had traditionally been notorious energy hogs, consuming about 20% of the electricity used in the American home. The appliance industry had worked significantly to make products more energy efficient over the decades. For example, from 1972 to 1990, for a typical top-mount, automatic defrost refrigerator (the most popular U.S. refrigerator), the amount of energy consumed dropped from 1,986 kilowatt hours per year to 950 kilowatt hours per year (kwh/yr). Chest freezer energy consumption dropped during the same period from 1,268 kwh/yr to 575 kwh/yr. Nevertheless, the DOE mandated further energy reductions for all refrigerators and freezers. Its standards required that the average residential refrigerator/freezer manufactured after 1998 use no more energy than that used by a 60-watt light bulb. Units imported into the United States were also required to meet the regulations. The dilemma being faced by the industry in the 1990s was that a reduction in the use of CFCs and HCFCs for cooling tended to reduce the efficiency of the appliance—thus increasing energy consumption.

Another issue facing appliance manufacturers was the presence of widely different standards for major appliances in countries around the world. These standards for quality and safety were drafted by such bodies as the British Standards Institute (BSI) in the United Kingdom, Japanese Industrial Standards Committee (JISC), AFNOR in France, DIN in Germany, CSA in Canada, and UL in the United States. These standards had traditionally created entry barriers that served to fragment the major home appliance industry by country. In 1986, the Canadian Standards Association (CSA) signed a memorandum with UL, Inc. (Underwriters Laboratories) to harmonize the Canadian and U.S. standards. The UL also signed an agreement in 1993 with Mexico's ANCE to accredit electrical products in Mexico. The International Electrotechnical Commission (IEC) standards were created to harmonize standards in the European Union and eventually to serve as worldwide standards with some national deviations to satisfy specific needs. The emergence of a true global market in major home appliances required the development of common world standards. By 1996, such standards were beginning to emerge.

Products

Major home appliances, or white goods, as they were commonly called, were generally classified as laundry (washers and dryers), refrigeration (refrigerators and freezers), cooking (ranges and ovens), and other (dishwashers, disposals, and trash compactors) appliances. In addition to making white goods, a number of appliance manufacturers also made and sold floor care appliances, such as vacuum cleaners, carpet shampooers, and floor polishers. (See **Exhibits 7**, **8**, **9** and **10** for detailed information by appliance category on market share, average retail price, and reliability.)

Exhibit 7

U.S. Market Shares in Percentage by Category

Category	1983	1992	1995
A. White Goods			
Compactors			
Whirlpool	48	70[1]	92[1]
GE	26	14	—
Broan	NA	14	8
Emerson Contract	NA	—	—
Thermador/Waste King	4	1	—
Others	22[2]	1	—
Disposers			
In-Sink-Erator	61	65	64
Electrolux (Anaheim)	—	17	17
Thermador/Waste King	8	10	10
Watertown Metal Products	—	2	6
Maytag	—	2	1
KitchenAid	—	2	2
Others	31[3]	2	—
Dishwashers			
GE	22	40	36
Whirlpool	13	31[4]	36[4]
Electrolux (Frigidaire)	7	20[5]	12[5]
Maytag	7	8	14
Thermador	—	1	1
Design & Manufacturing	36	—	—
Emerson Contract	13	—	—
Others	2	—	1
Dryers, electric			
Whirlpool	47	52	52
GE	17	18	19
Maytag	15	15	15
Electrolux (Frigidaire)	15	12	10
Raytheon (Speed Queen)	5	3	4
Others	1	—	—
Dryers, gas			
Whirlpool	47	53	53
Maytag	12	17[6]	14[6]
GE	16	14	15
Electrolux (Frigidaire)	15	10	12
Raytheon (Speed Queen)	5	4	6
Norge	4	—	—
Others	1	2	—
Freezers			
Electrolux (Frigidaire)	30	76	70
W. C. Wood	NA	14	29
Whirlpool	34	5	1
Raytheon (Amana)	6	5	—
Maytag (Admiral)	22	—[8]	—[8]
Others	8[7]	—	—
Microwave ovens			
Sharp	11	20	24
Samsung	7	18	13

Exhibit 7
U.S. Market Shares in Percentage by Category *(continued)*

Category	1983	1992	1995
Matsushita (Panasonic, Quasar)	5	17	14
Electrolux (Frigidaire)	9	10	7
Goldstar	1	10	9
Sanyo	13	7	6
MCD (previously Maytag)	4	6	6
Raytheon (Amana)	11	4	3
Whirlpool	4	3	5
Toshiba	3	1	—
Others	20[9]	4	13
Range hoods			
Broan	30	51[10]	52[10]
Nutone	20	14	9
Rangaire	18	12	19
Watertown Metal Products	NA	12	11
Fasco	NA	4	—
Aubrey	12	—	—
Others	20[11]	7	9
Ranges, electric			
GE	32	30	41
Whirlpool	12	30[12]	22[12]
Maytag	—	17	14
Electrolux (Frigidaire)	16	15[13]	14[13]
Raytheon (Caloric)	8	7	7
Thermador/Waste King	—	1	—
Roper	10	—	—
Tappan	6	—	—
Others	1	—	2
Ranges, gas			
Maytag	—	27	22
Electrolux (Frigidaire)	6	25[14]	22[14]
Raytheon (Caloric)	18	22	20
GE	—	19[15]	26[15]
Brown	7	3	3
Peerless-Premier	—	3	3
Tappan	NA	—	—
Roper	14	—	—
Others	7	1	4
Refrigerators, full-size, stand-alone			
GE	31	35	38
Whirlpool	30	25	27
Electrolux (Frigidaire)	23	17	15
Maytag (Admiral)	12	13	10
Raytheon (Amana)	7	8	9
Others	—	2	1
Refrigerators, compact			
Sanyo	NA	62[16]	63[17]
GE/MABE	NA	16	21
Wanbao	NA	8	10
Whirlpool/Consul	NA	2	2
Others	NA	12	4
Refrigerators, built-in			
U-Line	NA	54[18]	58[19]
Marvel Industries	NA	27	27

(continued)

Exhibit 7

U.S. Market Shares in Percentage by Category *(continued)*

Category	1983	1992	1995
Sub-Zero Freezer	NA	10	12
Others	NA	9	3
Washers			
Whirlpool	48	52	53
GE	18	16	17
Maytag	15	17	17
Electrolux (Frigidaire)	15	11	11
Raytheon (Speed Queen)	4	4	2
Others	—	—	—
B. Floor Care: Vacuum Cleaners			
Upright, Canister, Stick			
Hoover	40	34	35
Eureka	21	16	37
Royal	—	13	7
Regina	—	9	1
Whirlpool	4	9	—
Electrolux	10	6	2
Ryobi (Singer)	16	5	2
Kirby	8	4	3
Matsushita (Panasonic)	—	2	9[20]
Others	1	2	4[21]
Handheld			
Royal	NA	43[22]	43
Black & Decker	NA	40	31
Hoover	NA	6	10
Eureka	NA	3	4
Bissel	NA	—	3
Ryobi (Singer)	NA	—	3
Douglas	NA	2	3
Regina	NA	4	1
Others	NA	2	2

Notes:
1. Includes Emerson Contract, a Whirlpool unit.
2. Includes 12 for Hobart's KitchenAid, 6 for Tappan, and 4 for Amana.
3. Includes 12 for Tappan, 11 for GE, and 7 for Hobart's KitchenAid.
4. Includes Emerson Contract, a Whirlpool unit.
5. Includes Design and Manufacturing, an Electrolux unit.
6. Includes Norge, a Maytag unit.
7. Includes 5 for GE.
8. No longer makes freezers.
9. Includes 16 for GE.
10. Includes Aubrey, now part of Broan.
11. Includes 10 for GE.
12. Includes Roper, a Whirlpool unit.
13. Includes Tappan, an Electrolux unit.
14. Includes Tappan, an Electrolux unit.
15. Includes Roper, a GE unit.
16. Second column of data is 1991 data.
17. Third column of data is 1994 data.
18. Second column of data is 1991 data.
19. Third column of data is 1994 data.
20. Produces for Whirlpool
21. Includes 1 for Bissel and 1 for Rexaire (Rainbow).
22. Second column of data is 1991 data.

Source: Appliance Manufacturer (February 1989), pp. 32–34; (September 1995), pp. 70–71; (April 1996), pp. 29–31.

Exhibit 8

Average Price of Selected U.S. Major Home Appliances
(In U.S. dollars)

Type of Product	Average Price	Highest Price	Lowest Price
Washer	$422	$496 (Maytag)	>$400 (GE, Hotpoint, Roper, Speed Queen)
Dryer	365	440 (Maytag)	NA
Refrigerator	840	NA	NA
Dishwasher	396	519 (KitchenAid)	284 (Caloric)
Microwave Oven	201	283 (Whirlpool)	120 (Emerson)
Disposer	99	NA	NA

Source: K. Edlin, "Demand Performance," *Appliance* (July 1995), p. 90.

Competitors

In 1996, 5 appliance manufacturers controlled over 98% of the U.S. major home appliance market, led by Whirlpool with 35% and General Electric with 29%. (See **Exhibits 10** and **11**.) Of these 5, only A.B. Electrolux, Whirlpool, and GE appeared to be in good position to similarly dominate other world markets. Whirlpool was gaining share in both the United States and Europe. Although A.B. Electrolux was rapidly gaining market share in Europe, its Frigidaire unit was just as rapidly losing share in the United States. General Electric's joint venture with GEC of the United Kingdom (General Domestic Appliances) was successful in Great Britain, but so far had only minimal sales to the European continent. Its U.S. market share was increasing by about the same percentage that its European share was slipping. Nevertheless, GE had a significant presence in Mexico and in other world markets. Maytag's acquisition of Hoover in 1989 failed to provide Maytag Corporation with the desired international presence in major home appliances. Its sale of Hoover's major appliance units in 1995 left Maytag with no foothold in markets outside North America. Nevertheless, Maytag was successful in slightly raising its share of the U.S. market. Thanks to Frigidaire's declining market share, Maytag moved into third place in U.S. shipments and market share for 1995. Raytheon continued to improve its U.S. market share by emphasizing its Amana division, but—like Maytag—was only active in North America.

As the major home appliance industry increasingly became more global, industry analysts wondered if purely domestic companies like Maytag and Raytheon would continue to be successful in the future. The January 1996 announcement by the powerful German-based Bosch-Siemens Hausgerate GmbH that it was planning to build a 200,000-unit-capacity dishwasher plant in North Carolina with production to commence in 1997 to serve the North American market signalled that the U.S. major home appliance industry was about to change significantly. As the European market leader in dishwashers, Bosch-Siemens intended to expand sales of its high-end dishwashers from the 40,000 units it was exporting to North America in 1995 to a projected 100,000 units in 1998 and a 5% dishwasher market share.[14] Until now, the only foreign appliance manufacturing presence had been in floor care. Whirlpool Corporation had arranged a joint venture in 1990 with Matsushita Electric Industrial Company, Ltd., to own and operate Whirlpool's current manufacturing plant in Danville, Kentucky, to provide vacuum cleaners for Sears. Matsushita was expected to use the Kentucky facilities to expand its manufacturing and marketing base in North America.

Exhibit 9

Ratings of Major U.S. Home Appliance Reliability
(Listed in order from most to least reliable in terms of repairs)

Washers	Dryers (electric)	Dryers (gas)
KitchenAid	KitchenAid—tied 1st	Whirlpool
Whirlpool—tied 2nd	Whirlpool—tied 1st	Sears
Hotpoint—tied 2nd	Maytag—tied 3rd	Hotpoint—tied 3rd
Sears—tied 4th	Sears—tied 3rd	Maytag—tied 3rd
Maytag—tied 4th	Amana—tied 4th	GE
Amana	Hotpoint—tied 4th	
GE—tied 7th	GE—tied 4th	
Speed Queen—tied 7th	Speed Queen—tied 4th	
White-Westinghouse—tied 7th	White-Westinghouse	
Frigidaire—tied 10th	Frigidaire	
Magic Chef—tied 10th	Magic Chef	

Top-Freezer Refrigerators (no icemakers)	Top Freezer Refrigerators (w/icemakers)	Microwave Ovens
Magic Chef	Hotpoint—tied 1st	Panasonic—tied 1st
Sears—tied 2nd	Sears—tied 1st	Goldstar—tied 1st
Whirlpool—tied 2nd	Whirlpool—tied 1st	Sanyo—tied 3rd
White-Westinghouse	GE	Sharp—tied 3rd
Frigidaire—tied 5th	Frigidaire	Emerson—tied 3rd
Hotpoint—tied 5th	Amana	Magic Chef—tied 6th
GE		Quasar—tied 6th
Amana		Sears—tied 6th
		Tappan—tied 6th
		Samsung—tied 6th
		GE—tied 11th
		Amana—tied 11th
		Whirlpool

Ranges (electric)	Ranges (gas)	Dishwashers
Whirlpool	Whirlpool	Magic Chef—tied 1st
GE—tied 2nd	Sears—tied 2nd	Whirlpool—tied 1st
Hotpoint—tied 2nd	GE—tied 2nd	Hotpoint—tied 1st
Frigidaire—tied 4th	Tappan	GE—tied 4th
Sears—tied 4th	Magic Chef	In-Sink-Erator—tied 4th
	Caloric	Amana
		KitchenAid—tied 7th
		Jenn-Air—tied 7th
		Maytag—tied 9th
		Sears—tied 9th
		Caloric
		Tappan
		White-Westinghouse
		Frigidaire

Note: Ratings based on repair history from 29,000 to 130,000 (number varies by appliance category) responses to 1994 Consumers Union Annual Questionnaire regarding appliances purchased between 1986 and 1994.

Source: "1996 Buying Guide," *Consumer Reports* (December 15, 1995), pp. 20–23.

Exhibit 10

Shares of U.S. and Western European Market in White Goods
(Refrigerators, washing machines, dryers, ranges, and dishwashers)

Company	United States Market Share		Brands
	1991	1995	
Whirlpool	33.8%	35.0%	Whirlpool, KitchenAid, Roper
General Electric	28.2	29.3	GE, Hotpoint, RCA, Monogram
Maytag	14.2	14.4	Maytag, Hardwick, Jenn-Air, Magic Chef, Admiral, Norge
A.B. Electrolux (Frigidaire)	15.9	13.5	Frigidaire, Gibson, Kelvinator, Tappan, White-Westinghouse
Raytheon	5.6	6.2	Amana, Speed Queen, Caloric
Others	2.3	1.6	In-Sink-Erator, Brown, Peerless-Premier, Sub-Zero, W. C. Wood, etc.

Company	Western Europe Market Share		Brands
	1990	1994	
A.B. Electrolux (Sweden)	19%	23.9%	Electrolux, AEG, Buderus, Zanker, Zanussi, Thorn-EMI, Cobero
Bosch-Siemens (Germany)	13	16.0	Bosch, Siemens, Neff, Constructa, Balay, Pitsos
Whirlpool (U.S.)	10	10.7	Philips, Whirlpool, Bauknecht, Ignis
Miele (Germany)	7	6.2	Miele, Imperial
Group Brandt (France/Spain)	1	6.1	Ocean, Thomson
Liebherr (Austria/Germany)	NA	3.6	Liebherr
Temfa (France/Spain)	6	1	Thomson, Fagor, DeDetriech, Ocean
AEG (Germany)	5	2	AEG
Merloni (Italy)	4	3.1	Merloni, Ariston, Indesit, Scholtes
General Domestic App. (U.S./U.K.)	4	3.0	Hotpoint, Creda, General Electric
Candy (Italy)	4	3.1	Candy, Rosieres, Kelvinator, Gasfire
Others	28	24.0	Hoover, Crosslee, Vestfrost, etc.

Notes:
1. Group Brandt in 1994 included both the Ocean and Thomson groups (and thus Temfa).
2. AEG acquired by A.B. Electrolux.

Sources: Appliance (September 1995), p. 71; (June 1995), p. 48. *Appliance Manufacturer* (April 1996), p. 29.

WHIRLPOOL

Whirlpool and General Electric had traditionally dominated the U.S. major home appliance industry. Whirlpool owed its leadership position to its 50-plus years' relationship with Sears, which historically accounted for some 40% of the company's North American sales. Sears stocked Whirlpool's own brand and Whirlpool's Kenmore and Sears brands. Sears' movement away from a heavy reliance on its private Sears and Kenmore brands toward its new Brand Central concept in the late 1980s had serious implications for whirlpool. Nevertheless, even though it no longer dominated Whirlpool's sales, Sears continued to be Whirlpool's largest single customer in 1996 and accounted for about 20% of Whirlpool's sales. Like Maytag, major home appliances was Whirlpool's primary business.

Exhibit 11

Major Home Appliance Operating Results for Primary U.S. Competitors
(Dollar and Swedish kronor amounts in millions)

Company	Category	1993	1994	1995
General Electric	Revenue	$5,555	$5,965	$5,933
	Operating income	372	683	697
	Assets	2,193	2,309	2,304
Whirlpool	Revenue	$7,368	$7,949	$8,163
	Operating income	504	370	366
	Assets	4,654	5,240	6,168
Electrolux[1]	Revenue	SEK58,888	SEK66,272	SEK75,209
	Operating income	SEK869	SEK2,555	SEK2,581
	Assets	NA	NA	NA
Maytag	Revenue	$2,830	$3,181	$2,845
	Operating income	163	334	296
	Assets	2,147	2,053	1,594
Raytheon	Revenue	$1,285	$1,454	$1,473
	Operating income	45	87	81
	Assets	806	998	992

Note: Figures for Electrolux given in Swedish kronor (SEK). One U.S. dollar equals approximately 7 Swedish krona.

Source: Annual reports of respective companies.

Whirlpool revealed its excellence in product development when it successfully built a prototype to win the Super Efficient Refrigerator Program (SERP) award. The competition was sponsored by 24 utilities and offered a $30 million award (in the form of a $100 rebate to the manufacturer for each unit sold) to the manufacturer that successfully developed a CFC-free refrigerator with at least 25% more energy efficiency than current DOE standards. To win the award, Whirlpool had to produce a prototype in 5 months—half the usual time. The first model was introduced to the public during Earth Week in April 1994 and was 30% more efficient than DOE standards.[15]

With the completion of its purchase of Dutch-based Philips Electronics' appliance operations in 1991, Whirlpool became a serious global competitor in the emerging worldwide major home appliance industry. Sales and market share consistently increased annually in every geographic section of the company—North America, Europe, Latin America, and Asia. Whirlpool usually competed with General Electric to be the most profitable U.S. major home appliance company (in terms of appliance operating profit). It was first in North America and third in Western Europe in terms of market share. The company's marketing strategy was to focus on making the Whirlpool name a global brand. (Even though the company ranked only third in Europe in terms of overall market share of its Philips, Whirlpool, Bauknecht, and Ignis brands, management liked to point out that the Whirlpool brand by itself had the highest share of any brand in Europe.) It had developed a series of joint ventures and equity arrangements with appliance manufacturers throughout Asia and South America. Although its share of the Asian market was still fairly small, Whirlpool together with its affiliates in Argentina and Brazil had the largest manufacturing base and market share in South America. Whirlpool in cooperation with its affiliates in Brazil and joint venture partners in India and Mexico built facilities in those countries to produce what the company called the "world washer." Debuting in 1992 in Mexico, production of the new compact washing machine was intended to meet the increasing consumer demand in developing countries.

GENERAL ELECTRIC

General Electric, with a U.S. major home appliance market share of 29%, was a strong and profitable competitor in many industries. As a business unit, GE Appliances accounted for 14% of the corporation's total sales. General Electric had a powerful name and brand image and was the most vertically integrated of the major home appliance manufacturers. Like others, it manufactured some of its components, but it was the only appliance producer to own its entire distribution and service facilities. Realizing that GE's manufacturing facilities at its 40-year-old Appliance Park near Louisville, Kentucky, were slowly losing their competitiveness, management modernized the washing machine plant at a cost of $100 million. This resulted in the 1995 introduction of GE's new Maxus washer containing a floating suspension system to reduce vibration and 40% fewer parts to reduce cost and increase reliability. The Park's refrigerator plant was next in line for a $70 million makeover. Overall the company was investing some $1 billion over a 4-year period in appliance product development and capital equipment, a 50% increase over previous spending levels.

With relatively slow growth in the North American market, GE Appliances planned to continue moving into faster growing international locations. In 1989, GE paid $580 million for a joint appliance venture and other ventures with the U.K.'s General Electric Corporation (GEC). GEC was known for its mass market appliances in Europe, whereas GE was known in Europe for its high-end appliances. Named General Domestic Appliances (GDA), the joint venture was a leading (and profitable) competitor in the U.K. market with its GE, Hotpoint, and Creda Brands, but was only a minor competitor on the continent. General Electric was interested in gaining a stronger position in Europe, particularly in Eastern Europe. The company was also involved with international partners in Mexico (MABE), Venezuela (Madosa), India (Godrej & Boyce Mfg. Co.), the Philippines (Philacor), and Japan (Toshiba). Appliances manufactured by the joint ventures were primarily sold in the country of origin, with small amounts going into contiguous markets.

A.B. ELECTROLUX

A.B. Electrolux of Sweden, with its purchase of White Consolidated Industries in 1986, became part of the U.S. major home appliance industry. Electrolux sold approximately 17 million appliances with over 40 brand names in countries around the world. After acquiring Zanussi in Italy, Tricity and Thorn EMI in the United Kingdom, WCI in the United States, and AEG in Germany, Electrolux passed Whirlpool to become the world's largest major home appliance manufacturer. Electrolux had a strong presence in every European country from Finland to Portugal and extended eastward with production facilities in Hungary, Estonia, and Russia. Leif Johansson, President and CEO, explained the corporation's growth strategy:

> We always make acquisitions to gain synergy, never just to hold the share. We normally go for short-term synergies like purchasing, speed, productivity, cost efficiency—things we can accomplish with the industrial structure that is already there, and by bringing in our expertise on how to run factories and our ability to do a great deal of internal benchmarking because of our size. Then we enter the restructuring phase, where we are investing capital and giving factories specific assignments in a Group context . . . . The entire strategy is based on turning these units into something that is worth more as part of an integrated, global group than they were as standalone units, and it has meant increased market shares for us.[16]

The household appliance area (including white goods and floor care, air conditioners, and sewing machines) accounted for slightly over 60% of total corporation sales. As of 1996, Electrolux was first in market share in Western Europe and fourth in North America. Europe accounted for about 65% of its major home appliance sales. North America accounted for approximately 30%. The rest was scattered throughout Asia, Latin America, Oceania, and Africa. Careful planning was needed by Electrolux to properly take advantage of a proliferation of brands worldwide without getting bogged down with competing internal demands for attention to each brand. After noticing Whirlpool's success with 1 brand across all of Europe, the company began the introduction of its own pan-European brand using the Electrolux name. The company was in the process of spending about SEK600 million over a 5-year period to market the Electrolux products throughout Europe. It was also investing $50 million in Southeast Asia with an objective of becoming 1 of the top 3 suppliers of white goods in the ASEAN region by the year 2000. Leif Johansson, Electrolux President and CEO, stated how well global integration had progressed at the company:

> The integration, after 10 years, has gone so far that it's difficult to assess what is really Italian, what is really Swedish, and what is really American. We are working in multinational teams. On a team going to China, for example, very often you will find Italians, Spaniards, Swedes, and Americans working together.[17]

In 1991, the WCI Major Appliance Group was renamed Frigidaire Company in order to provide A.B. Electrolux's U.S. subsidiary the recognition earned by its pioneering namesake brand. Previously the company's brands had competed against one another and had not been designed for automated manufacturing. Consequently the quality of many of its well-known branded products had deteriorated over time. To reverse this situation, the company had invested more than $600 million to upgrade its existing plants and build new refrigerator and dishwasher plants. Top management also introduced its Vision 2000 program, using benchmarking and total quality management to boost production quality and efficiency. It was aggressively advertising its products. Nevertheless, its share of the U.S. market dropped significantly from 16.9% in 1994 to 13.5% in 1995 and had caused the company to drop from its traditional third place in the U.S. market to fourth place behind Maytag.

MAYTAG

Maytag Corporation, with a U.S. market share of 14%, was in a position in 1996 of having to work hard to keep from being outdistanced globally by the 3 powerhouses of Whirlpool, Electrolux, and GE. Realizing that the company could not successfully compete in the major home appliance industry as just a manufacturer of high-quality laundry products, the company embarked during the 1980s in the acquisition of Hardwick Stoves, Magic Chef, and Jenn-Air. These acquisitions provided Maytag the full line of appliances it needed to compete effectively in the U.S. market. Realizing that the industry was going global as well, Maytag purchased Hoover Company, a successful floor-care company in the United States and a strong white goods producer in the United Kingdom and Australia. In acquiring Hoover, Maytag unfortunately also acquired a significant amount of debt. This debt, coupled with the heavy amount of investment needed to upgrade and integrate its newly acquired facilities and operations, put a big strain on Maytag's profitability. Like Whirlpool, Maytag operated primarily in major household appliances. Not until 1994 did Hoover's European appliance business become profitable. Nevertheless, Maytag sold Hoover Australia in 1994 to Southcorp Holdings, Ltd., of Australia and Hoover Europe in 1995 to Candy S.p.A., an Italian-based appliance maker. Even though Maytag accepted losses of $16.4 million and $130 million, respectively, on the sales, the corporation was able to use the proceeds to reduce its debt. According to Chairman and CEO Leonard Hadley, "This is a strategic decision to focus on growing our core North American appliance and floor-care businesses, which include Hoover North America."[18] It was somewhat ironic that just 1 month after the sale, a survey in the United Kingdom revealed that of 173 household names Hoover ranked at the top of major appliance producers![19]

In 1995, Maytag invested $13.7 million to expand its recently completed state-of-the-art dishwasher plant in Tennessee. According to Joseph Fogliano, Executive Vice President and President of Maytag's North American Appliance Group, dishwashers were the fastest growing major appliance in the United States. He added that the growth of the corporation's dishwasher sales was approximately twice that of the industry.[20] This investment plus the corporation's decisions to spend $160 million upgrading its Admiral refrigerator plant and $50 million to build a new horizontal-axis washer plant indicated that Maytag had no intention of being outmaneuvered by others on its own territory. Now that Maytag had shed its European Hoover "money pit" and had greatly improved its financial situation, industry analysts worried that the corporation would soon be a takeover target by another international appliance company. Other analysts wondered what kind of future faced a purely domestic Maytag Corporation, given the globalization of the industry.

RAYTHEON

Raytheon Company, an electronics, as well as an appliances firm, was the fifth important player in the U.S. major home appliance industry. Raytheon's Appliances Group constituted 14% of the total corporation's sales and was composed of Amana Home Appliance division (including Caloric brands) and Speed Queen Company. Operating under the belief that its technological leadership in the electronics and defense industries could drive innovations in the appliance industry, Raytheon acquired enough appliance companies to assemble the full line of products necessary to compete effectively in the U.S. market. Because it was interested in broadening its offerings in home and commercial appliances, in 1995 the company purchased Unimac Company, a global leader in the front-load washer and dryer coin laundry markets. This supplemented its commercially oriented Huebsch, Menumaster, and Speed Queen lines. Given the actual and threatened cutbacks in the U.S. defense budget during the 1990s, Raytheon might need a strong appliance business to make up for any reduction in its defense-related electronics and aircraft divisions. Unfortunately Raytheon's major home appliance sales and operating profits declined every year from 1989 through 1991. Of its 3 home appliance brands, only Amana continued to show increasing sales and income from strong refrigerator sales.

To reverse its declining appliance fortunes, Raytheon invested $173 million into new appliance plants and equipment. All operations of the Caloric division were then combined under Amana. Speed Queen now focused on serving the commercial laundry market and on producing home laundry products for Amana to market. To support its home appliance business further, in 1994 Raytheon moved its New Product Center from Burlington, Massachusetts, to its new home appliance headquarters in Amana, Iowa, and renamed it the Appliance Technology Center. The Center was no longer to serve other Raytheon business units but to expand Amana's existing R&D by focusing exclusively on the Raytheon Appliance Group. As a result of Raytheon's investments in and restructuring of its appliance business, both sales and profits showed positive growth from 1992 forward. Nevertheless, the trend toward global acquisitions and consolidation in the appliance industry left analysts wondering if Raytheon's domestic-only home appliance division would be able to compete successfully in the coming world appliance market.

The Future: A Global Appliance Market?

The U.S. major home appliance industry was composed of 5 major manufacturers with 35 to 40 factories and 19 major brands. Volume in the 1990s was at an all-time high. Although product quality was judged to be good, but not excellent, the products provided excellent consumer value.[21] In the short run, the outlook for major home appliance sales was conservatively positive. In North America, sales for 1996 were expected to be slightly above those for 1995 but not quite as high as the exceptionally good sales in 1994. Analysts expected a slight upturn in new U.S. single-family home construction and a 2.4% increase in home and commercial remodeling activity. Economists predicted a "rather tranquil" U.S. economy through 1997 with a 2% to 2.5% increase in real gross domestic product (GDP). Consumer prices were expected to rise 2% to 3% annually through 1997. Although Canadian home appliance sales dropped 8% in 1995 (coinciding with a 42% drop in home sales), the Canadian Appliance Manufacturers Association predicted a steady growth of approximately 2.3% per year, reaching an annual volume of 3.9 million units in sales by the year 2000. With a weak peso continuing to dampen economic prospects in Mexico, economists were predicting a meager 2% economic improvement in 1996.

MEXICO AND NAFTA

The 2 full-line major home appliance makers in Mexico, Vitromatic and MABE, were involved in joint ventures with U.S. firms. Whirlpool had a joint venture with Vitromatic S.A., which included 3 facilities in Mexico. General Electric had a joint venture with MABE, a consortium of Mexican appliance producers. This was beginning to affect the competitiveness of those U.S. firms without Mexican white goods operations: Maytag, Raytheon, and Frigidaire. Appliances exported to Mexico from the United States were subject to a 20% tariff, whereas Mexican appliances going to the United States were assessed no tariffs. The original North American Free Trade Agreement (NAFTA) allowed the Mexican tariff to continue for a 10-year period (ending in 2003) to keep Mexican businesses from being immediately overwhelmed by larger U.S. companies. One result was escalating imports into the United States of low-priced gas ranges from a MABE plant, forcing Maytag to lay off workers at its Magic Chef plant in Cleveland, Tennessee. Under NAFTA, tariffs were being phased out for various items over 5-year and 10-year periods but only for products that satisfied Rules of Origin. For example, if the Rules of Origin call for 50% regional value content (RVC), but 51% of a company's product is sourced from Asia or Europe, the company would be forced to pay the full tariff. According to Serge Ratmiroff, senior manager of international services for Deloitte & Touche in Chicago, "Mexico is not only a market just beginning to boom, but it is the front door to a potential Latin American free trade bloc."[22]

EUROPE

The economic climate of Western Europe was similar to that of the United States. Analysts were predicting a 2% to 3% unit volume sales growth in appliances during 1996. Although no countries of the former Eastern Bloc had yet returned to 1989 levels of prosperity, continued improvement was likely. For example, the economy of the Commonwealth of Independent States was expected to grow by 1% in 1996. Because Western Europe was going through a demographic shift similar to that of the United States—toward a more middle-aged society coupled with lower overall saturation levels (see **Exhibit 5**) of major home appliances—sales over the long run were predicted to grow faster annually than the 1% to 2% growth rate predicted for the United States. Europeans as a whole were much more concerned that their appliances be "environmentally friendly" than were consumers in North America. The continuing economic integration of the 15-member countries of the European Union—Austria, Belgium, Denmark, Finland, France, Germany, Greece, Ireland, Italy, Luxembourg, the Netherlands, Portugal, Spain, Sweden, and the United Kingdom—was providing the impetus for a series of mergers, acquisitions, and joint ventures among major household appliance manufacturers. The barriers to free trade among Western European countries were steadily being eliminated. The requirement of at least 60% local content to avoid tariffs made a

European manufacturing presence imperative for any U.S. or Japanese major home appliance manufacturer.

The European appliance industry was in the final stages of consolidation. It was home to approximately 30 appliance producers, down from over 150 in the 1960s. The big 3 of Electrolux, Bosch-Siemens, and Whirlpool controlled over half of the market in Western Europe and were making strong inroads into Eastern Europe via joint ventures and acquisitions. Small- and medium-sized manufacturers, such as Gaggenau, Kuppersbusch, and Seppelfricke in Germany, have managed to maintain their independence by specializing in built-in appliances. Overall, product quality was good, but not excellent.[23] As distribution shifted from being solely through furniture and kitchen studios to specialty chains and discount stores (especially in Germany), price competition was becoming increasingly important. The primary markets in Europe were Germany with 37%, Italy with 22%, and France and the United Kingdom with 10% each. Spain was the next largest market.

With its acquisitions of the powerful Italian Zanussi company, the U.K.'s Thorn-EMI, the U.S.'s White Consolidated Industries (Frigidaire), and Germany's AEG, along with 3 Spanish companies, Electrolux was in a good position to control the coming global market. Germany's largest domestic appliance maker, Bosch-Siemens Hausgerate GmbH, was forging a course to overtake Electrolux in Europe as well as elsewhere. It acquired a washing machine factory in Poland, the third largest domestic appliance producer in Brazil, a minority stake in the second largest appliance maker in Turkey, and majority control of a leading Chinese laundry appliance manufacturer. The company had formed an alliance with Maytag in 1993 to exchange information on new product technologies and design, but it was discontinued when Maytag sold Hoover Europe. According to CEO Hans-Peter Haase, "Today it is certainly conceivable that worldwide operating companies such as BSHG can convert a washing machine based on European technology to U.S. dimensions and sell it in America." Explaining the rationale for building a dishwasher plant in the United States in 1996, Haase said, "Once Americans accept stainless-steel interiors and we offer our product at an acceptable price, we will be able to achieve sales volumes comparable to European levels."[24] Upon acquiring Philips, the second largest European producer of white goods, Whirlpool became a key player throughout Europe and the world. It was actively involved in strategic alliances with appliance companies in Slovakia and Hungary, among other countries. It was the first company to market a pan-European brand. According to company sources, Whirlpool was the number 1 recognized brand name throughout Western and Central Europe by 1995. General Domestic Appliances (GDA), a joint venture by the British General Electric Corporation (GEC) and General Electric (GE) of the United States, was performing well in Britain but was only a minor player on the continent. The purchase of Hoover Europe from Maytag by the Italian-based Candy gave it immediate access to the United Kingdom to complement its presence on the continent and was a signal that it did not intend to be left behind by the "big 3."

Unlike the U.S. appliance market, the European market was heavily segmented into a series of national markets. In cooking appliances, for example, over 90% of the ranges purchased in Germany were electric, whereas gas prevailed through the rest of Europe. Also, 65% of German ranges were built-in, while the percentage of built-ins outside Germany was considerably less. Top loading washers, long dominant in the United States, commanded 80% of the market in France, but front loaders dominated the rest of Europe, where washers and dryers must fit into a kitchen under a work surface or in a bathroom. Although built-in refrigerators formed only a small part of refrigerator sales in most of Europe, they constituted over 50% of the German market. The large, freestanding home appliances preferred by Americans were much less popular in Europe where smaller, energy efficient units were generally preferred. Hans G. Backman, President of Frigidaire Company and Vice President of AB Electrolux, commented on this situation:

Globalization of the product and globalization of the company are 2 different things. The appliance industry is becoming global, but the products and the consumers are still local. The more the world comes together, the more that national differences get emphasized.[25]

SOUTH AMERICA

Regional trade agreements and the lowering of tariffs made it easier to sell products such as home appliances in South America in the 1990s. The establishment of the Mercosur free-trade area among Argentina, Brazil, Uruguay, and Paraguay meant that a manufacturing presence within these countries was becoming essential to avoid tariffs. Whirlpool, with its Brazilian and Argentine affiliates, had a very strong presence in the area. AB Electrolux formed an alliance with Refrigeracao Parana S.A., the second-largest white goods company in Brazil. It also established a wholly-owned subsidiary in Argentina to market its Electrolux, Zanussi, and Frigidaire brands. Through its purchase of Continental 2001, Brazil's third-largest domestic appliance manufacturer, Bosch-Siemens was also a force in the region. General Electric held part ownership of Madosa, a leading appliance maker in Venezuela. According to the consulting firm Datamonitor, the predicted primary markets in 1998 for washers, dryers, vacuum cleaners, and dishwashers would be Argentina at $344 million (compared to $457 million for Mexico), Brazil at $250 million, Chile at $167 million, Venezuela at $150 million, Columbia at $73 million, and Peru at $50 million. Washers should constitute the largest segment for these figures as the markets for dryers, dishwashers, and vacuum cleaners were still small.[26] In Brazil, for example, the percentage of saturation was about 80% for ranges and refrigerators, 20% for washing machines, 15% for freezers and dryers, and 10% for dishwashers and microwave ovens.

ASIA

In 1996, Asia was already the world's second largest home appliance market, and opportunities were still emerging. According to Roger Merriam, Vice President of Sales and Marketing for Whirlpool Overseas Corporation, "In the U.S., we talk of households equipped with between 7 and 9 major appliance products. In Asia, which already accounts for 40% of the world market, it's more like 4 appliances per home." The saturation level of clothes washers in India and China, for example, was about 10%, compared to 54% in Mexico. About 27% of the roughly 190 million units sold worldwide were sold in Asia—more than in North America and fewer only than in Europe. The combined economies of the Asian region were expected to grow by about 6% to 8% annually through the 1990s, with industry shipments of appliances likely to grow at a more rapid pace.

Although Japanese and Korean manufacturers dominated the Asian home appliance market in the 1990s, the industry was still fragmented with no single dominant company in terms of market share. The top Asian players included Hitachi, Matsushita, Mitsubishi, Sharp, and Toshiba of Japan plus Goldstar, Samsung, and Daewoo of Korea. Matsushita was the overall market leader in Asia, but had a market share of less than 10% outside Japan. Asian distribution was rapidly moving away from small retailers to power retailer organizations. A.B. Electrolux was establishing a full line of appliance facilities in China and India, among other Asian locations. One of the company's objectives was to be 1 of the top 3 white goods suppliers in Southeast Asia by the year 2000.[27] In purchasing Philips, Whirlpool obtained key distributors in Australia, Malaysia, Japan, Singapore, Thailand, and Taiwan. In addition, Whirlpool established joint ventures in China and India. General Electric held part ownership of Philcor in the Philippines and had a joint venture with Godrej & Boyce, India's largest appliance maker. According to Jeff Immelt, Vice President of Worldwide Marketing and Product Management at GE Appliances, the Asian market was still young enough to justify building one's own brand instead of acquiring someone else's established brands as was done in Europe.[28]

Nevertheless, much of Asia, Africa, and significant parts of South America were not yet sufficiently developed economically to be significant markets for major home appliances. For 1 thing, electricity and natural gas service were not yet widely available in most developing countries. Even in those locations where electricity was available, it was not always provided consistently—power outages were a common occurrence in some countries.

THE FUTURE

Hans G. Backman, President of Frigidaire Company, predicted that domestic appliance brands would continue to dominate the U.S. market, but that both domestic and multinational brands would dominate Europe. Asia would continue to be a market share battleground dominated by multinational appliance companies from the United States, Europe, Japan, and Korea. In Asia, according to Backman, "The products will be smaller and simpler than in the U.S. or Europe, but the technologies and components will be the same. Manufacturing will be local, but may serve as a low-cost base for exporting basic low-end products to the U.S. and Europe."[29]

Robert L. Holding, President of the Association of Home Appliance Manufacturers, predicted that even though the American industry had a strong base from which to operate, it would face continuing pressures on profits. He predicted that in 25 years the number of global appliance makers would be in the 5 to 10 range. In terms of important considerations, Holding predicted that environmental issues and product quality would be crucial. "Creating a basic design that can be manufactured into a 'family' of brands or models will be important."[30] Because retailers had been gaining increasing leverage over manufacturers, "speed to market" and flexible low-cost manufacturing would be key to future success. In addition to energy use and air pollution laws, governments would probably enact recycled-content legislation and disposal fees for appliances. Led by the trend to locate more appliances in main living areas of the house instead of in the basement, consumers would demand quieter appliances. According to Holding, the future of individual major home appliance manufacturers would depend on their ability to provide value to the consumer.

Notes

1. David Hoyte, Executive Vice President of Operations, Frigidaire, as quoted by M. Sanders, "ISO 9000: The Inside Story," *Appliance* (August 1994), p. 43. ("White goods" is the traditional term used for major home appliances. The contrasting term "brown goods" refers to home electronics products such as radios and televisions.)
2. J. Jancsurak, "Global Trends for 1995–2005," *Appliance Manufacturer* (June 1995), p. A-6.
3. S. Stevens, "Finessing the Future," *Appliance* (April 1990), pp. 42–43.
4. C. R. Christensen, K. R. Andrews, J. L. Bower, R. G. Hammermesh, and M. E. Porter, "Note on the Major Home Appliance Industry in 1984 (Condensed)," *Business Policy*, 6th ed. (Homewood, IL.: Irwin, 1987), p. 340.
5. M. Sanders, "Purchasing Power," *Appliance* (June 1993), pp. 45–46.
6. "For Appliances, Coated Coil Grows by 14.6%," *Appliance Manufacturer* (June 1993), p. 10.
7. D. Davis, "1996: A Soft Landing," *Appliance* (January 1996), p. 52.
8. R. Holding, "1990 Shipment Outlook," p. 64.
9. "Buying Power—Home Purchase Triggers Sales of Appliances," *Appliance Manufacturer* (February 1989), p. 31.
10. Chuck Miller, Vice President of Marketing, North American Appliance Group, Whirlpool Corporation, as quoted by R. J. Babyak and J. Jancsurak in "Product Design & Manufacturing Process for the 21st Century," *Appliance Manufacturer* (November 1994), p. 59.
11. R. J. Haines, "Appliance Newsquotes," *Appliance* (June 1989), p. 21.
12. J. Jancsurak, "In Their Opinion," *Appliance Manufacturer* (April 1995), p. 48.
13. M. Sanders, "The Next Generation," *Appliance* (September 1995), p. 59.
14. "BSCH to Build U.S. Plant," *Appliance* (January 1996), p. 17; "Bosch Targets U.S. Niche," *Appliance Manufacturer* (April 1996), p. 26.
15. "Designing a Winner," *Appliance Manufacturer* (May 1994), pp. W-20–W-23.
16. S. Stevens, "An Appliance Arsenal," *Appliance* (February 1995), p. F-25.

17. "Zanussi Celebrates 10 Years With Electrolux," *Appliance* (November 1994), p. 9.
18. R. Brack, "Hoover Europe Sold at Loss," *Des Moines Register* (May 31, 1995), p. 10S.
19. "Hoover Tops Quality Charts," *Appliance* (August 1995), p. 10.
20. "Maytag to Expand Dishwasher Plant," *Appliance* (December 1994), p. 29.
21. Jancsurak, "Global Trend for 1995–2005," p. A-6.
22. J. R. Stevens, "Exporting to Mexico? Take Another Look," *Appliance Manufacturer* (August 1994), p. 6.
23. Jancsurak, "Global Trend for 1995–2005," p. A-6.
24. J. Jancsurak, "Big Plans for Europe's Big Three," (April 1995), p. 28.
25. Jancsurak, "Global Trends for 1995–2005," p. A-3.
26. J. R. Stevens, "Appliance Market Grows in South America," *Appliance Manufacturer* (September 1994), p. 8.
27. S. Stevens, "An Appliance Arsenal," p. E-28.
28. "Global Growth Strategies," *Appliance Manufacturer* (January 1992), p. GEA-13.
29. Jancsurak, "Global Trends for 1995–2005," pp. A-3–A-6.
30. N. C. Remich, Jr., "AHAM: The Next 25 Years," *Appliance Manufacturer* (March 1993), p. 71.

Maytag Corporation: Back to Basics

J. David Hunger

Leonard Hadley, CEO and Chairman of the Board of Maytag Corporation, looked up and smiled briefly as his secretary handed him the completed 1995 financial statements along with his morning cup of coffee. Warm in his office, Hadley took a moment to gaze from his second floor window at the thick blanket of snow surrounding the building. He used the steaming cup of coffee to warm his still-numb hands. Even though he lived less than a mile from the office, it had been cold driving into work today. Only 30 miles east of Des Moines, Newton shared the sub-zero temperatures of the upper Midwest in early February 1996. Hadley wasn't sure which he dreaded most: the blustery winter weather or having to explain less than expected financial results to the media and shareholders.

Hadley thought back to April 27, 1993, when he chaired his very first shareholders' meeting. He had looked forward to his promotion to Chairman of the Board that January. Accepting the gavel from his mentor, the much-respected Daniel Krumm, had been a great honor. It should have been a great year because 1993 marked Maytag's 100th birthday. Unfortunately it was overshadowed by the fact that in 1992 the company suffered its first loss since the early 1920s! As the new Chairman, Hadley's first key task had been to explain this loss to increasingly antagonistic shareholders and cynical investment bankers. The reverence that people had shown Krumm as Chairman seemed to evaporate when Hadley stood at the podium to open the floor to questions. Hadley still winced when he remembered some of those questions from that day in 1993. One person—a very angry man standing in the back right of the auditorium—still stood out in his mind. Speaking into the microphone held by an usher, but looking straight at Hadley, he asked: "How long will it be before earnings get back to the 1988 level of $1.77 per share from continuing operations? And along with that," he added, "why should we have any confidence in your answer, given the performance of the past 5 years?" The hush in the auditorium had been unbearable. The bittersweet nature of Maytag's 100th birthday year had not been helped by Daniel Krumm's death from cancer on November 22, 1993.

The financial reports for 1993 and 1994 had shown significant improvement. Although net income still had not reached the 1988 figure of $158 million, 1994 had been a very good year for everyone in the home appliance industry, including Maytag. As he skimmed through the financial reports for 1995, Hadley couldn't help but wonder how the shareholders and

This case was prepared by Professor J. David Hunger of Iowa State University. This case was edited for SMBP-8th Edition. All rights reserved to the author. Copyright © 1996 by J. David Hunger. Reprinted by permission. The author thanks Susan J. Martin, Director of Internal Communications of Maytag Corporation, for helpful comments on an earlier draft of this case.

financial analysts would respond to another net loss. Maytag's management had worked hard to boost the stock price from its low of about $13 in 1993 to the current $19, but the price was still below the $29 value estimated by 1 financial analyst.[1]

The decisions to sell Hoover Australia and Hoover Europe had not been easy ones. Hadley had supported Daniel Krumm and the rest of the Executive Committee in their 1988 decision to acquire Chicago Pacific in order to obtain Hoover with its Australian and European operations. In retrospect, it was clear that they had paid far too much for a very marginal European business. The movie *The Money Pit* seemed to be an appropriate title for Hoover Europe. Selling off the overseas operations had meant big after-tax book losses, but they had provided the corporation cash to reduce its heavy debt load. After all, if you excluded the $9.9 million after-tax settlement of the Dixie-Narco workers' lawsuit, the $5.5 million extraordinary item for early debt retirement, and the $135.4 million after-tax loss on the sale of Hoover Europe, Maytag Corporation would have shown a healthy profit in 1995.

History of the Company

The history of Maytag Corporation falls into 4 distinct phases. The first phase included the entrepreneurial days at the turn of the century when the company was founded by F. L. Maytag and the company became the U.S. market leader in washing machines. The second phase was the company's retreat from market leadership in the 1950s to focus on a high-quality niche in laundry products. During the third phase, the company was revitalized under Daniel Krumm in the 1980s to become a full-line globally oriented major home appliance manufacturer through acquisitions. The fourth phase included the attempts to stabilize and refocus the corporation during the 1990s.

ENTREPRENEURIAL ENERGY CREATES MARKET LEADER

Fred L. Maytag (or F. L., as he was commonly called), who came to Newton, Iowa, as a farm boy in a covered wagon, joined 3 other men in 1893 to found the Parsons Band Cutter and Self Feeder Company. The firm produced attachments invented by 1 of the founders to improve the performance of threshing machines. The company built its first washing machine, the "Pastime," in 1907 as a sideline to its farm equipment. The founders hoped that this product would fill the seasonal slumps in the farm equipment business and enable the company to have year-round production.

In 1909, F. L. Maytag became sole owner of the firm and changed its name to The Maytag Company. Farm machinery was soon phased out as the company began to focus its efforts on washing machines. With the aid of Howard Snyder, a former mechanic whose inventive genius had led him to head Maytag's development department, the company generated a series of product and process improvements. Its gasoline powered washer (pioneered by Maytag), for example, became so popular with rural customers without electricity that Maytag soon dominated the small-town and farm markets in the United States.

Under the leadership of Lewis B. Maytag, a son of the founder, the company expanded from 1920 to 1926 into a national company. Using a radically new gyrator to move clothes within its tub, the Model 80 was introduced in 1922. F. L. Maytag, then serving as Chairman of the Board, was so impressed with the new product that he personally took 1 of the first 4 washers on a western sales trip. Sales of the Model 80 jumped from 16,000 units in 1922 to more than 258,000 units in 1926! The company went from a $280,000 loss in 1921 to profits exceeding $6.8 million in 1926. Throughout the 1920s and 1930s, Maytag Company had an average U.S. market share of 40% to 45% in washing machines. During the Great Depression of the 1930s, Maytag never suffered a loss.

FROM MARKET LEADER TO NICHE MANAGER

Unfortunately the innovative genius and entrepreneurial drive of the company's early years seemed to fade after the death of its founder. Top management became less interested in innovation and marketing than with quality and cost control practices. Bendix, a newcomer to the industry, introduced an automatic washing machine at the end of World War II that used a spin cycle instead of a wringer to squeeze excess rinse water out of clothes. Maytag, however, was slow to convert to automatic washers. Management felt that the automatic washer needed more research before it could meet Maytag quality standards. The company still had a backlog of orders for its wringer washer, and management was reluctant to go into debt to finance new manufacturing facilities. This reluctance cost the company its leadership of the industry. Even with automatics, Maytag's share of the U.S. washer market fell to only 8% in 1954. Nevertheless, the company continued to be a profitable manufacturer of high-quality, high-priced home laundry appliances.

During the 1960s and 1970s, Maytag reaped the benefits of its heavy orientation on quality products and cost control. *Consumer Reports* annually ranked Maytag washers and dryers as the most dependable on the market. Maytag washers lasted longer, needed fewer repairs, and had lower service costs when they did require service. The Leo Burnett advertising agency dramatized the concept of Maytag brand dependability by showing that Maytag products were so good that repairmen had nothing to do and were thus "lonely." The company's "Ol' Lonely" ads, which first aired in 1967 and featured the lonely Maytag repairman, were consistently ranked among the most effective on television. Profit margins were the highest in the industry. The company invested in building capacity, improved its dishwasher line, and changed the design of its clothes dryers. Maytag's plants were perceived at that time to be the most efficient in the industry. By the end of the 1970s, Maytag's share of the market had increased to approximately 15% in both washers and dryers.

REVITALIZATION: GROWTH THROUGH ACQUISITIONS

In 1978, top management, under the leadership of CEO Daniel Krumm, decided that the company could no longer continue as a specialty manufacturer operating only in the higher priced end of the laundry market. Consequently Maytag adopted a strategy to become a full-line manufacturer and develop a stronger position in the U.S. appliance industry. Up to this point, the company had been able to finance its growth internally. The strategic decision was made to grow by acquisition within the appliance industry through debt and the sale of stock.

In 1981, Maytag purchased Hardwick Stove Company, a low-priced manufacturer of gas and electric ranges with an estimated 5% share of the range market. In 1982, the company acquired Jenn-Air, a niche manufacturer of high-quality built-in electric grill ranges. In 1986, Maytag acquired Magic Chef, Inc., a successful manufacturer of mass marketed appliances in the mid-price segment of the market. The acquisition included not only Magic Chef's best-selling ranges and other products, but also appliances sold under the Admiral, Norge, and Warwick labels, and Dixie-Narco, a leading manufacturer of soft drink vending equipment. Maytag Company and the Magic Chef family of companies were then merged under a parent Maytag Corporation on May 30, 1986, headed by Chairman and CEO Daniel Krumm.

In 1988, realizing that the U.S. home appliance market had reached maturity, top management of the new Maytag Corporation decided to extend the corporation's growth strategy to the international arena. Maytag offered close to $1 billion in cash and Maytag stock for Chicago Pacific Corporation (CP), the owner of Hoover Company. In this 1 step Maytag Corporation moved into the international home appliance marketplace with 9 manufacturing operations in the United Kingdom, France, Australia, Mexico, Colombia, and Portugal. Hoover was known worldwide for its floor care products and throughout

Europe and Australia for its washers, dryers, dishwashers, microwave ovens, and refrigerators. Prior to the acquisition, Maytag's international revenues had been too small to even report.

RELUCTANT RETRENCHMENT

By 1995, Maytag Corporation had achieved its goal of becoming an internationally oriented, full-line major home appliance manufacturer. However, its profits had deteriorated significantly. Although Hoover's North American operations had always been very profitable, Hoover Europe had not shown a profit since being acquired by Maytag until 1994 when it earned a modest one. Hoover Australia had also incurred significant losses during this time. Unknown to Maytag Corporation's top management before the acquisition, Hoover's U.K. facilities were in desperate need of renovation and the product line needed to be upgraded. Some weaknesses at the South Wales facility were apparent before the purchase, but the corporation was too preoccupied with learning about the vacuum cleaner business to investigate further. Once it realized the need to modernize the U.K. facilities, Maytag's top management committed millions of dollars to renovate the laundry and dishwasher plant in South Wales and its floor care plant in Scotland.

Although some former executives talked of a culture clash between the collegial Hoover and the more rigid Maytag executives, CEO Leonard Hadley blamed Hoover's woes purely on the poor U.K. business environment. However, industry analysts concluded that the Hoover acquisition had been a strategic error. To pay for the acquisition, management not only increased long-term debt to its highest level in the company's history, but it also had to sell more stock. These actions combined with a high level of investment in the unprofitable overseas facilities to lower corporate profits and decrease earnings per share. Since other major home appliance companies continued to operate profitably, some analysts were beginning to question management's ability to run an international corporation.

After concluding that there was no way the corporation could recoup its overseas investments, Maytag sold its Hoover operations in Australia and New Zealand in December 1994 and Hoover Europe in May 1995. The sale of the Australian/New Zealand operations for $82 million resulted in a 1994 after-tax loss of $16.4 million. The sale of Hoover Europe to Candy S.p.A. of Monza, Italy, for $180 million resulted in a more significant 1995 after-tax loss of $135.4 million. In evaluating the strength of both Hoover Europe and Hoover Australia, Chairman Hadley commented, "Each lacked the critical mass alone to be strong players in their respective global theaters. As a result, we sold both businesses to focus on growth from our North American-based businesses." The sales enabled the corporation to reduce the long-term debt it had acquired in the Chicago Pacific purchase. Hadley further commented in a July 1995 letter to the shareowners that Maytag was now a much more focused corporation than it had been for the past few years.

> After the sale of Hoover Europe and Hoover Australia, we are focused clearly on our core North American-based businesses: major appliances, floor care, and vending—all businesses that we know well, have managed well, and have grown successfully into strong brand positions. We also have regained much needed financial strength and flexibility over the past 2 years, reducing our debt by more than $300 million.[2]

Major Home Appliance Industry: White Goods

In 1996, the U S major home appliance industry was a very successful industry. Unlike other industries (such as automobiles and consumer electronics) that had been unable to compete against aggressive Japanese competition, U.S. major home appliance manufacturers dominated the North American market. For "white goods"—refrigerators, freezers, washing machines, dryers, ranges, microwave ovens, and dishwashers—over 84% of those sold in the United States were made domestically.[3] The industry had been very successful in keeping prices low and in improving the value of its products. Compared to 1982, major home appliance prices had increased more slowly than the increase in U.S. earnings and the consumer price index. Thus the average American consumer in 1996 could earn a new appliance in 80% fewer hours on the job than a half-century ago. For example, although the price of a Maytag automatic washing machine had risen from $280 in 1949 to $440 in 1995, it had actually declined when inflation was considered.[4] In addition, the energy efficiency of the most common major appliances had increased every year since 1972.[5] Sales had also been increasing. More appliances were made and sold in the United States in 1994 than in any preceding year. Although shipments for 1995 were slightly down, most industry analysts predicted that 1996 would be another good year for appliance makers.

Nevertheless, the major home appliance industry was facing some significant threats as well as opportunities as it moved through the last decade of the twentieth century. The North American market had reached maturity. Future unit sales were expected to grow only 1% to 2% annually on average for the foreseeable future. Operating margins had been dropping as appliance manufacturers were forced to keep prices low to be competitive, even through costs kept increasing. In Western Europe, however, a market already 25% larger than the mature North American appliance market, unit sales were expected to grow 2% to 3% annually on average. This figure was expected to increase significantly as Eastern European countries opened their economies to world trade. Appliance markets in Asia and Latin America were expected to grow at a rate of 5% to 6% annually.[6] The industry was under pressure from governments around the world to make environmentally safe products and significantly improve appliance energy efficiency.

In 1945, there were approximately 300 major appliance manufacturers in the United States. By 1996, however, the "big 5" of Whirlpool (35.0%—up from 33.8% in 1991), General Electric (29.3%—up from 28.2% in 1991), Maytag (14.4%—up from 14.2% in 1991), Frigidaire, owned by A.B. Electrolux (*no* relation to Electrolux Corporation, a U.S. company selling Electrolux brand vacuum cleaners) (13.5%—down from 15.9% in 1991), and Raytheon (6.2%—up from 5.6% in 1991) controlled over 98% of the U.S. market. The consolidation of the industry over the period was a result of fierce domestic competition. Emphasis on quality and durability coupled with strong price competition drove the surviving firms to increased efficiencies and a strong concern for customer satisfaction. The European appliance industry was in the final stages of consolidation. It was home to approximately 30 appliance producers, down from over 150 in the 1960s.[7] The big 3 of Electrolux (24%), Bosch-Siemens (16%), and Whirlpool (11%) controlled over half of the market in Western Europe and were making strong inroads into Eastern Europe via joint ventures and acquisitions. These 3 giants plus General Electric were also building a dominant presence in Latin America via acquisitions and joint ventures. Although Japanese and Korean manufacturers were important competitors in the Asian home appliance market in the 1990s, the Asian market was still fragmented with no single dominant company in terms of market share. The top Asian players included Hitachi, Matsushita, Mitsubishi, Sharp, and Toshiba of Japan and Goldstar, Samsung, and Daewoo of Korea. Matsushita was the overall market leader in Asia, but had a market share of less than 10% outside Japan.

(*For additional industry information, see* **Case 19**, *"The U.S. Major Home Appliance Industry: Domestic Versus Global Strategies."*)

Maytag Corporation Business Segments and Products

In early 1996, Maytag Corporation was organized into 3 business units: North American Appliance Group (all major home appliances), Hoover North America (all floor care appliances), and Dixie-Narco (vending machines). Previous to their sale, Hoover Europe and Hoover Australia had been managed as separate business units.

NORTH AMERICAN MAJOR APPLIANCES

North American major appliances contained the original Maytag Company plus the plants of Admiral, Magic Chef, and Jenn-Air, in addition to the Jackson Dishwasher plant, Maytag Customer Service, Maytag International, Inc., and Maytag Financial Services Corporation. Maytag and Admiral appliances were administered through the Maytag and Admiral Products Unit in Newton, Iowa. Jenn-Air and Magic Chef appliances were administered through the Jenn-Air and Magic Chef Products Unit in Indianapolis, Indiana. Given the corporation's interest in obtaining synergy in production and marketing among the various products, there was no attempt to identify or isolate Admiral, Jenn-Air, or Magic Chef as separate profit centers. Admiral made refrigerators for all the brands, Magic Chef made cooking products for Maytag, and so on.

Compared to its competition, Maytag's North American Major Appliance group generally ranked third or fourth in U.S. market share in each major home appliance category—usually far behind either Whirlpool or General Electric—except in washers, dryers, and gas ranges. Washers and dryers were Maytag's traditional strength. Market surveys consistently found Maytag brand laundry appliances to be not only the brand most desired by consumers (when price was not considered), but also the most reliable. Refrigeration was a traditional strength of Admiral. Although Admiral quality had been allowed to decline under previous management, it was reemphasized after the Maytag acquisition. Gas ranges had always been a particular strength of Magic Chef and were perceived as very reliable in surveys.

Exhibit 1 compares Maytag's 1995 share of the U.S. market, by home appliance category, to that of the market leader. Contrasted with 1992, a number of changes occurred to Maytag's market share. Its share of disposers dropped from 2% to 1% and to sixth place. Its share in dishwashers increased dramatically from 8% to 14%, thanks to new product designs and the Jackson plant. Its share in electric dryers was stable at 15%. Its share in gas dryers dropped from 17% to 14% and out of second place. Its share in electric ranges dropped from 17% to 14% but remained in third place. Its share in gas ranges dropped significantly from 27% to

Exhibit 1

Maytag Corporation's Share of U.S. Market Compared to Market Leaders' Share by Home Appliance Category in 1995

Appliance Category	Market Leader	Leader Share	Maytag Share	Maytag Rank
Disposers	In-Sink-Erator	64%	1%	6
Dishwashers	GE and Whirlpool	36	14	3
Dryers, electric	Whirlpool	52	15	3
Dryers, gas	Whirlpool	53	14	3
Freezers	Electrolux	70	—[1]	—
Microwave ovens	Sharp	24	—[1]	—
Ranges, electric	GE	41	14	3 (tie w/Electrolux)
Ranges, gas	GE	26	22	2 (tie w/Electrolux)
Refrigerators	GE	38	10	4
Washers	Whirlpool	53	17	2 (tie w/GE)
Vacuums, regular	Eureka	37	35	2
Vacuums, hand-held	Royal	43	10	3

Note:
1. Maytag no longer makes freezers or microwave ovens.

Source: Appliance Manufacturer (April 1996), pp. 29–31.

22% and out of first place to second place. Competition from GE's joint venture with MABE in Mexico contributed to GE's taking over market leadership in gas ranges from Maytag. Maytag's share in full-sized refrigerators dropped from 13% to 10% but remained in fourth place. Hoover increased its market share in upright, canister, and stick vacuum cleaners (from 34% in 1991 to 35% in 1995), but lost its first-place position in vacuum cleaners to Eureka, whose share grew more rapidly. Hoover's share in handheld vacuums increased from 6% in 1991 to 10% in 1995.

Maytag and Admiral Products

Headquartered in Newton, Iowa, the original Maytag Company was the flagship of the corporation and manufactured Maytag brand washing machines and dryers in its Newton plant. It also marketed Maytag and Admiral brand cooking products made by Magic Chef and Jenn-Air, a refrigerator line manufactured by Admiral, and dishwashers manufactured at the Jackson facility. Market emphasis was on the premium-price segment and the upscale builder market. A survey of Americans found the Maytag brand to be fifteenth in a list of the strongest brand names, based on consumer recognition and perception of quality.

Located in Galesburg, Illinois, the Admiral plant manufactured refrigerators for Maytag, Jenn-Air, Admiral, and Magic Chef brands. Admiral products were marketed to the mid-price segment in conjunction with Maytag brand products. Admiral marketed private-label products, predominantly the Signature 2000 line to Montgomery Ward.

The Maytag and Admiral products unit sold Maytag and Admiral brand appliances through over 9,000 retail dealers in the United States and Canada. A relatively small number of appliances were sold overseas through Maytag Corporation's international sales arm, Maytag International. Maytag appliances were also sold through Montgomery Ward, but not through Sears. According to Leonard Hadley, Maytag/Admiral refused to join the Sears Brand Central concept because it did not want to antagonize its carefully nurtured dealers. Maytag/Admiral dealers accepted distribution through Montgomery Ward because Ward had not traditionally been as dominant a force in appliance retailing as had Sears with its strong Kenmore brand. Maytag/Admiral dealers, in turn, were very loyal and appreciated the company's emphasis on quality.

Prior to Maytag's purchase of Magic Chef (and thus Admiral) in 1986, Admiral had been owned by 3 different corporations. Very little had been invested into the operation by these previous owners and production quality had dropped significantly. The corporation had invested $60 million in Admiral to improve production efficiencies, enhance product quality, and increase capacity and another $160 million in 1995 to further upgrade the facility.

Jenn-Air and Magic Chef Products

The Magic Chef facilities manufactured gas and electric ranges for the Admiral, Magic Chef, and Maytag brands in Cleveland, Tennessee. As part of the Jenn-Air and Magic Chef Products unit, Magic Chef also marketed refrigerators, dishwashers, laundry equipment, and microwave ovens under the Magic Chef brand to the mid-price segment and to certain private label businesses (primarily Montgomery Ward). Prior to its purchase by Maytag, Magic Chef had been a small, family run business. Its product development strategy had been to be a very fast follower. Maytag Corporation had invested $50 million in the Cleveland facilities. From this investment came new lines of Magic Chef and Maytag brand ranges.

In conjunction with Jenn-Air, the company sold Magic Chef and Norge brands directly to dealers. The 2 additional lower price brands of Hardwick and Crosley were sold through distributors. Like Maytag and Admiral, Magic Chef worked with Jenn-Air to use selected dealers for its Magic Chef and Norge brands. The company's medium to low price orientation had enabled it to sell successfully to builders.

The North American Free Trade Agreement (NAFTA) had created some problems for Magic Chef's range business. Under NAFTA, U.S. tariffs on Mexican imports were eliminated immediately while Mexican tariffs of 20% on U.S. imports were scheduled to be slowly phased out over a 10-year period. Escalating imports of low-priced gas ranges from a Mexican MABE plant (part of a joint venture between GE and MABE) had forced Magic Chef to lay off workers. It was estimated that imports from this and other U.S. and Mexican joint venture plants were some 500,000 units annually—close to one-third of the U.S. market. In a statement addressed to the U.S. government, Leonard Hadley urged that negotiators eliminate the tariffs on U.S.-built appliances:

> This is causing appliance manufacturers who are heavily invested in U.S. facilities to be faced with a rising volume of duty-free imports from Mexico. The high Mexican appliance tariffs make it extremely difficult for Maytag to sell its high-quality, large capacity U.S. products to consumers in Mexico.[8]

Located in Indianapolis, Indiana, as part of the Jenn-Air and Magic Chef Products Unit, Jenn-Air specialized in the manufacture of electric and gas downdraft grill-ranges and cooktops. The unit marketed Jenn-Air brand refrigerators, freezers, dishwashers, and disposers manufactured by Admiral, the corporation's Jackson plant, and other non-Maytag appliance manufacturers, such as Emerson Electric. Jenn-Air billed itself as "The Kitchen Equipment Expert" and believed that its high-quality cooking expertise complemented Maytag Company's high-quality image in laundry appliances. In 1992. Jenn-Air canceled its marketing agreements with its distributors and combined its marketing with that of Magic Chef. Magic Chef dealers were now able to sell the high-quality Jenn-Air brand in conjunction with the medium-quality Magic Chef brand, combining both brands' solid connections with home builders. Interestingly, Jenn-Air was the only Maytag Corporation brand distributed through Sears' Brand Central. This was an important consideration because Sears typically sold 1 of every 4 major home appliances sold in the United States.

Jackson Dishwashing Products

Located in Jackson, Tennessee, was a $43 million, 400,000-square-foot, state-of-the-art manufacturing facility dedicated to producing dishwashers for the Maytag, Admiral, Jenn-Air, and Magic Chef brands. It was designed as a "team plant," with little distinction made between hierarchical levels. Upon the completion of this plant in 1992, dishwasher production was phased out at Maytag's Newton plant and the company no longer had to purchase dishwashers from GE for Magic Chef or Jenn-Air.

The dishwasher had become the fastest growing major home appliance category in North America. Maytag's U.S. market share had jumped significantly from 8% in 1992 to 14% in 1995. This growth was approximately double that of the industry. After only 2 years of operation, the corporation invested $13.7 million to add 2 more assembly lines at the Jackson plant.

Unfortunately, half the Maytag brand dishwashers produced during 1994 were later discovered to have a potentially defective component, which in some cases started fires. After receiving 140 complaints, Maytag informed the U.S. Consumer Product Safety Commission of the problem and started a program in October 1995 to notify, inspect, and repair the 231,000 potentially defective dishwashers (out of 553,000) made during that time. The defective component had been made by a long-term Maytag supplier. According to Dick Haines, President of Maytag Company, "Although the likelihood of a component failure is small, we believe the inspection program being undertaken by Maytag is another expression of our commitment to dependability."[9] With the Jackson expansion coming on line in early 1996, management hoped that publicity about the defective component would not affect 1996 dishwasher sales.

Maytag Customer Service

Headquartered in Cleveland, Tennessee, Maycor handled all parts and service for Maytag Corporation appliance brands. A consolidated and automated warehouse facility in Milan, Tennessee, replaced the 4 separate parts distribution operations of Maytag, Admiral, Jenn-Air, and Magic Chef.

HOOVER NORTH AMERICA

Headquartered in North Canton, Ohio, Hoover North America manufactured and marketed to all price segments upright and canister vacuum cleaners, stick and handheld vacuum cleaners, disposable vacuum cleaner bags, floor polishers and shampooers, central cleaning systems, and commercial vacuum cleaners—and washing machines in Mexico under the Hoover brand name. It heavily advertised to the consumer. The company was almost totally integrated. In addition to the North Canton headquarters and 3 Stark County, Ohio, manufacturing plants, Hoover North America controlled 4 other facilities in El Paso, Texas, Ciudad Juarez, Mexico (a maquiladora assembly plant), Burlington, Ontario (Hoover Canada), and Industrial Vallejo, Mexico (Hoover Mexicana). Praised by industry experts as 1 of the best manufacturing facilities in the United States, the new North Canton "factory within a factory" was designed by an interdisciplinary team to reduce costs and improve quality.

In the United States, Hoover held 35% share of the very competitive market for residential full-sized vacuum cleaners and over half of the floor polisher market. Nevertheless, its share of the market for full-sized vacuum cleaners had dropped from 40% in 1983 when it led the industry. It only had 10% of the handheld vacuum cleaner market compared to Royal's 43% and Black & Decker's 31%. Eureka (now part of A.B. Electrolux of Sweden) was first in 1995 full-sized cleaner sales, with a U.S. market share of 37% (up dramatically from only 16% in 1992). Royal was third in full-sized cleaner sales in 1995, with a declining market share of 7%. Growth in the U.S. floor care market exceeded that of many other appliance segments. Over 22 million vacuum cleaners were sold in the United States in 1995. Continued growth was predicted. Although over 97% of U.S. households had at least 1 vacuum cleaner, many homes had 2 or 3 full-sized vacuums plus handheld vacuums. Like major home appliances, the average life expectancies of full-sized vacuum cleaners were over 10 years.

DIXIE-NARCO

Dixie-Narco, Inc., was a subsidiary of Maytag Corporation that made canned and bottled soft drink and juice vending machines sold to soft drink syrup bottlers and distributors, canteen owners, and others. Headquartered in Williston, South Carolina, the group manufactured vending machines in its factory there. It also had an Electronics Division (previously called Ardac, Inc.) outside Cleveland in Eastlake, Ohio. The Eastlake facility made dollar-bill acceptors, changers, and foreign banknote acceptors for soft drink vending machines. Dixie-Narco had spent $31 million in 1990 to convert the Admiral freezer and refrigerator factory in Williston into the largest and most highly automated vending machine producing facility of its type in the country. Maytag Corporation had decided in 1989 to stop manufacturing home freezers and compact refrigerators because of decreasing profit margins and low sales and to buy whatever it needed from others. This conversion enabled Dixie-Narco to move all of its vending machine production from its old plant in Ranson, West Virginia, to the new Williston plant.

The company sold vending equipment directly to independent bottlers and full-service operators who installed banks of vending machines in offices and factories. It also marketed through bottlers directly to syrup company–owned bottlers. In 1994, Dixie-Narco introduced a new glass-front merchandiser for use by convenience stores. Instead of inserting coins into the machine to buy a product, the customer opened the machine's glass door to select a product—then paid a clerk. According to Maytag Corporation management, sales of vending machines continued to be relatively flat in the United States, but due to strong demand for Dixie-Narco products, the company was able to hold its solid share of the U.S. market. International sales had been increasing thanks to the introduction of the glass-front merchandiser. Traditional coin-fed vending machines have not been well accepted outside North America.

On November 2, 1995, Maytag Corporation announced that management had entered into a letter of intent to sell Dixie-Narco's Eastlake, Ohio, Electronics Division for a noncash book loss in the $6–$7 million range. According to Dixie-Narco President Robert Downing, "Going forward, Dixie-Narco's management resources and capital investments will be focused on our core business of designing, manufacturing, and marketing vending machines and glass front merchandisers."[10]

When asked why Dixie-Narco remained a part of Maytag Corporation, Leonard Hadley responded:

> Mechanically, a vending machine is a refrigerator, and we build thousands of refrigerators per day at our plant in Galesburg, Illinois. . . . As a marketing assignment, our Dixie-Narco customers have the same needs as our Maytag commercial laundry customers. . . . Dixie-Narco's great value to us is that it has a different set of competitors than the major home appliance business or the floor care industry. It allows us an important earnings stream from a business that our largest 2 major appliance competitors don't have. . . . It provides us with an important supplement to our U.S. business by allowing us an international export opportunity.[11]

HOOVER EUROPE

Overseas, where close to 70% of its total revenues had been generated prior to joining Maytag, Hoover had become successful, not only in manufacturing and marketing upright and canister vacuum cleaners, but also (especially in Great Britain and Australia) in washing machines, dryers, refrigerators, dishwashers, and microwave ovens. Headquartered in Merthyr Tydfil, South Wales, Hoover Europe manufactured washers, dryers, and dishwashers in a nearby factory. Upright vacuum cleaners, motors for washers and dryers, and disposable vacuum cleaner bags were produced in a facility in Cambuslang (near Glasgow), Scotland. A plant in Portugal manufactured canister-type vacuums, most of which were sold on the continent. Hoover Europe marketed its products to the mid-priced segment of European markets.

British consumers accounted for 75% of Hoover's $600 million European sales. Its market position in the United Kingdom was 34% in washers (second place), 5% in dryers (third place), and 19% in dishwashers (second place). Although Hoover vacuum cleaners were big sellers in continental Europe, its major appliances were not. This concentration in Great Britain became a serious problem for Hoover in the late 1980s and early 1990s when a combination of a recession and high interest rates acted to reduce sharply Hoover's European sales.

To boost sales, Hoover Europe initiated a promotion during late 1992 and early 1993, offering customers free international airline tickets when they bought appliances for as little as $150. The overly generous offer resulted in such an overwhelming response that Maytag Corporation was forced to pay a total of more than $72 million over the 3-year period 1992–1994 for sales and administrative expenses related to the promotion. The promotion also became a public relations nightmare because people complained about having trouble getting their free flights. Three British representatives from the "Hoover Holiday Pressure Group" attended Maytag's 1994 annual shareholders' meeting in Newton. They labeled the fiasco "Hoovergate" and threatened to go to Ralph Nader's group if the problem was not settled to their satisfaction. The corporation fired 3 top Hoover Europe executives and established a task force to examine the situation and to deal with the issue of control versus autonomy.[12]

With only $400 million in revenues, Hoover Europe was at a significant disadvantage against established European competitors such as Electrolux, Whirlpool, and GE–GEC who counted their revenues in billions. This was a big reason why Maytag Corporation decided to sell Hoover Europe to Italian-based Candy, S.p.A. in May 1995. Included in the sale were Hoover Europe's headquarters, 2 manufacturing sites in Britain, a plant in Portugal, and the rights to the Hoover trademark in Europe, parts of the Middle East, and North Africa. Hoover North America continued selling floor care products to the rest of the world.

HOOVER AUSTRALIA

Hoover Pty, Ltd., located near Sydney, manufactured vacuum cleaners, washers, and dryers. Hoover Appliances, Ltd. produced refrigerators and freezers near Melbourne. The Melbourne plant had earlier been purchased from Philips and was producing Admiral and Norge refrigerators in addition to the Hoover brand. Prior to the decision to sell Hoover Australia at the end of 1994, Maytag Corporation had been considering the possibility of manufacturing Admiral and/or Norge laundry equipment at the Sydney plant. Hoover Australia marketed its products to the mid-priced segment of the Australian and New Zealand markets.

Marketing

Of the 3 brands—Maytag, Magic Chef, and Jenn-Air—only the Maytag brand had been heavily advertised to consumers. The Magic Chef and Jenn-Air brands received only cooperative advertising and promotions through dealers. Since Maytag Corporation had used Admiral primarily as a manufacturing facility to make refrigerators for other brands and for private labels (for example, Montgomery Ward's Signature line), it did little advertising of Admiral as a brand. Corporate advertising expenses had risen from $113.4 million in 1992 and $136.5 million in 1993 to $153.2 million in 1994 but fell to $134 million in 1995.

Until 1993, Maytag, Magic Chef, and Jenn-Air brands had been sold through separate dealer networks. The decision was made in late 1992 to reorganize the corporation's marketing into 2 major channels. The Admiral brand was positioned as a mid-priced product to be sold through Maytag dealers. This gave Maytag dealers a lower priced product to complement the relatively high-priced Maytag brand. Jenn-Air, known for its high quality, merged its dealer network into that of Magic Chef in order to make available to Magic Chef Jenn-Air's historically strong relationship with small, quality builders. The goal was to increase sales to builders—something Maytag brand appliances had traditionally been unable to do. As a result, the newly combined Magic Chef/Jenn-Air sales organization had 4 brands to market and could cover all quality and price levels: Norge and Hardwick as the low-end brands for special opportunities; Jenn-Air as the mid-range to high-end brand with unique styling and innovative features; and Magic Chef as the mid-range to low-end brand with less innovative but more value-oriented features.

Both Jenn-Air and Magic Chef moved their advertising business to Leo Burnett USA, the same agency responsible for Maytag's "lonely repairman" ads. No longer would the 2 brands focus only on dealer ads and promotions to market their products. Magic Chef planned to take some of the money it had been spending on dealer ads to spend on consumer ads to build market awareness.

In 1995, Maytag and the Leo Burnett USA advertising agency were honored by the New York chapter of the American Marketing Association with a gold "EFFIE" award for the Maytag brand's "Growing the Legend" advertising campaign. The campaign featured the Maytag repairman, "Ol' Lonely," and included TV commercials, print advertising, and point-of-purchase materials.[13] (See **Exhibit 2** for The Real Maytag Repairman.)

Exhibit 2

The Real Maytag Repairman

The "Ol' Lonely" Maytag repairman created for television ads in 1967 had little to do with the actual daily life of a real Maytag repairman. Michael Headlee of Michael's Maytag Home Appliance Center in Des Moines, Iowa, repairs approximately 40 malfunctioning machines per week. On average, only 3 of them are Maytags. Although Headlee sells only Maytag, he services all brands. No one exclusively repairs Maytag brand appliances. "You won't find one because he would starve," explained Headlee. Headlee had been working as an independent service contractor until 1991, when Maytag Company asked him to open a Maytag store.

Headlee enjoys doing stunts to show off the quality built into Maytag brand appliances. In 1992, he started a Maytag and a Kenmore washer after rigging both to run continuously. Although Maytag officials weren't too excited about his project, Headlee went ahead to see for himself which product would last longer. The Kenmore died in 6 months; the Maytag continued for 2 years.

When a customer walked into Headlee's store 1 day to look at refrigerators. Headlee showed him the fine points of a floor model. According to Headlee, Maytag builds for the "what ifs." For example, what if a neighbor boy uses the door as a step ladder and knocks out 1 of the storage bins? No problem, says Headlee. The bins are removable and adjustable. No need to replace the $180 liner or the $35 bin—only a $2 breakaway clip. "The hinges are heavier than any other in the industry. . . . Rollers? We've got the fattest rollers in the industry." To demonstrate, Headlee took out the meat–cheese drawer, turned it over on the floor, and jumped on it. According to Headlee, a person could do aerobics on the meat–cheese drawer!

Competition from "super stores" keeps profit margins low, so Headlee depends on repair work to stay in business. "We got a deck of cards. We got a cribbage board. And that keeps us pretty well occupied when we're not working on . . . a Kenmore or a Whirlpool," joked Headlee.

Source: M. A. Lickteig, "A Real Repairman Juggles Calls and Sales," *Des Moines Register* (November 1, 1994), p. M1.

Hoover floor care products had traditionally received strong advertising in all the media. The company continued its successful "Nobody does it like Hoover" consumer-oriented advertising. After noting that 70 dealers accounted for approximately 80% of Hoover's North American floor care sales, management restructured the sales organization in 1992 to serve these "power retailers" better.

Strategic Managers

BOARD OF DIRECTORS

One-third of the 14-member Board of Directors was elected every year for a 3-year term. From 1989 to 1994, the same members had served on the Board continuously. Three had come from the Chicago Pacific (and thus Hoover) acquisition. Of these, Lester Crown and Neele Stearns still served in early 1996. New to the board in 1994 were Wayland Hicks, a former Executive Vice President of Xerox Corporation and CEO of Nextel Communications (a satellite cellular company), and Bernard Rethore, President of Phelps Dodge Industries (a manufacturer of truck wheels and specialty chemicals). New to the board in 1995 were Barbara Allen, Executive Vice President at Quaker Oats Company, and Carole Uhrich, Group Vice President at Polaroid Corporation. Leonard Hadley, CEO, served as Chairman of the Board. (See **Exhibit 3** for a complete list of the Board of Directors.)

Exhibit 3

Board of Directors: Maytag Corporation

Director	Joined Board	Position	Term Expires	Shares Owned
Barbara R. Allen (43)[1]	1995	Executive Vice President Quaker Oats	1996[2]	100
Edward Cazier, Jr. (71)[1]	1987	Counsel to law firm of Morgan, Lewis, & Bockius	1997	11,900
Howard L. Clark, Jr. (52)[1]	1986	Vice Chairman Shearson, Lehman, Hutton Holdings, Inc.	1996[2]	13,836
Lester Crown (70)[3]	1989	Chairman Material Service Corporation	1997	4,503,565
Leonard A. Hadley (61)	1985	Chairman and CEO Maytag Corporation	1996[2]	211,920
Wayland R. Hicks (53)	1994	CEO and Vice Chair Nextel Corporation	1998	6,000
Robert D. Ray (67)[3]	1983	CEO IASD Health Services Corporation	1996[2]	15,600
Bernard G. Rethore (54)	1994	President Phelps Dodge Industries	1997	4,000
Dr. W. Ann Reynolds (58)[3,4]	1988	Chancellor City University of N.Y.	1998	12,300
John A. Sivright (67)[3,4]	1976	Senior Relationship Executive Harris Bankcorp, Inc.	1998	23,712
Neele Stearns, Jr.[1,4](60)	1989	CEO CC Industries	1997	14,090
Fred G. Steingraber (57)	1989	Chair and CEO A.T. Kearney, Inc.	1998	15,000
Peter S. Willmott (58)	1985	Chair and CEO Willmott Services	1996[2]	35,000
Carole J. Uhrich (52)	1995	Group Vice President Polaroid Corporation	1997	—

Notes:
1. Member of audit committee.
2. Up for reelection at April, 1996 annual meeting.
3. Member of nominating committee.
4. Member of compensation committee.

Source: Maytag Corporation, *Notice of Annual Meetings & Proxy Statement* (1996), pp. 3–8.

Counting only personally owned shares, the executive officers and directors owned only 4.8% of Maytag's outstanding shares. (Lester Crown was the largest holder of stock with 4.27% plus 0.79% in trusts or owned by family members.) More than 60% of Maytag's stock was owned by individual shareholders. The only significant blocks of stock owned by institutional investors were the 11% owned by FMR Corporation and the 6% owned by Delaware Management Holdings, Inc.

TOP MANAGEMENT

Many of the Maytag Corporation Executive Officers had worked their way up through the corporation and had spent most of their careers immersed in the Maytag Company culture. This was certainly the case for Leonard Hadley, Chairman and CEO, who had served the company continuously since joining the company 34 years ago as a cost accountant. (See **Exhibit 4** for a listing of corporate executives.)

In a move to diversify top management backgrounds, the corporation in mid 1993 hired John Cunningham to serve as Corporate Executive Vice President and Chief Financial Officer and Joseph Fogliano to serve as Corporate Executive Vice President and President of North American Operations. These were the second and third, respectively, most powerful corporate executive officers after Hadley. Cunningham had previously been Vice President and Assistant General Manager of IBM's Main Frame Division. Fogliano previously had served as President and CEO of Thomson Electronics. In addition, David D. Urbani was hired in 1994 to serve as Corporate Vice President and Treasurer. Previously, he had been Assistant Treasurer at Air Products and Chemicals.

In a surprise move, North American President Fogliano resigned from the corporation in August 1995. In an interview, Fogliano (age 55) stated that he had joined the corporation with the understanding that he would be a leading candidate to replace Leonard Hadley. As time went by, according to Fogliano, it became apparent that this was not to be. His decision to leave Maytag developed in discussions with Leonard Hadley. "These things are a matter of fit, and Len has to make a decision on that," commented Fogliano. He further explained that there may have been a lack of fit between himself and the Maytag culture.[14] Donald Lorton, President of the corporation's diversified operations, was then named acting President of the North American Appliance Group until a national search could find a replacement for Fogliano.

Four months later, John Cunningham announced that he was leaving the corporation to take a similar position with Whirlpool Corporation. Hadley commented that Cunningham had "implemented the strategy to restructure our balance sheet that I outlined to him when he arrived here 2 years ago, and he did an excellent job."[15] Gerald Pribanic, Vice President of

Exhibit 4

Executive Officers: Maytag Corporation

Officer	Office	Became an Officer
Leonard A. Hadley (61)	Chairman and CEO	1979
Donald M. Lorton (65)	Executive VP and President of Maytag Appliances (acting)	1995
Gerald J. Pribanic (52)	Executive VP and Chief Financial Officer	1996
Brian A. Girdlestone (62)	President, Hoover Company	1996
Robert W. Downing (59)	President, Dixie-Narco	1996
Edward H. Graham (60)	Senior VP, General Counsel, and Asst. Secretary	1990
Jon O. Nicholas (56)	VP, Human Resources, Maytag Appliances	1993
Carleton F. Zacheis (62)	Senior VP, Administrative	1988
John M. Dupuy (39)	VP, Strategic Planning	1996
David D. Urbani	VP and Treasurer	1994
Steven H. Wood (38)	VP, Financial Reporting and Audit	1996

Source: Maytag Corporation, *Form 10-K* (December 31, 1995), p. 7.

Finance and Controller for Hoover North America, took over Cunningham's position in January 1996 as acting Corporate Vice President and Chief Financial Officer.

In January 1996, John Dupuy joined Maytag as Corporate Vice President of Strategic Planning. Previously, he had been a consultant with Booz, Allen & Hamilton and with A. T. Kearney.

Corporate Culture

Much of Maytag Corporation's corporate culture derived from F. L. Maytag's personal philosophy and from lessons the founder had learned when starting the Maytag Company at the turn of the century. His greatest impact was still felt in Maytag's (1) commitment to quality, (2) concern for employees, (3) concern for the community, (4) concern for innovation, (5) promotion from within, (6) dedication to hard work, and (7) emphasis on performance.

- **Commitment to Quality**: Concerned when almost half the farm implements sold were defective in some way, F. L. Maytag vowed to eliminate all defects. Maytag's employees over the years had taken great pride in the company's reputation for high-quality products and being a part of "the dependability company."

- **Concern for Employees**: Long before it was required to do so by law, Maytag Company established safety standards in the workplace and offered its employees accident and life insurance policies. Wages have traditionally been some of the highest in the industry.

- **Concern for the Community**: Following F. L. Maytag's example, Maytag management had been active in community affairs and concerned about pollution. The decision to build its new automatic washer plant in Newton after World War II indicated the company's loyalty to the town.

- **Concern for Innovation**: From its earliest years, the company was not interested in cosmetic changes for the sake of sales, but in internal improvements related to quality, durability, and safety.

- **Promotion from Within**: F. L. Maytag was very concerned about building company loyalty and trust. The corporation's policy of promoting from within was an extension of that concern.

- **Dedication to Hard Work**: In tune with the strong work ethic permeating the midwestern United States, F. L. Maytag put in huge amounts of time to establish and maintain the company. His fabled trip West, while Chairman of the Board, to personally sell a train carload of washers set an example to his salesforce and became a permanent part of company lore.

- **Emphasis on Performance**: Preferring to be judged by his work rather than by his words, F. L. Maytag was widely regarded as a good example of the Midwest work ethic.

In 1996, the Maytag Corporation still reflected its strong roots in the Maytag Company culture. Corporate headquarters were housed on the second floor of a relatively small building (compared to Maytag Company's Plant 1 and the Research and Development building surrounding it). Built in 1961, the Newton, Iowa, building still housed Maytag Company administrative offices on its first floor. Responding to a question in 1990 regarding a comment from outside observers that the corporation had "spartan" offices, Leonard Hadley, then–Chief Operating Officer, looked around at his rather small office with no windows and said, "See for yourself. We want to keep corporate staff to a minimum." Hadley felt that the headquarters location, and the fact that most of the corporate officers had come from Maytag Company resulted in an overall top management concern for quality and financially conservative management. This supported then–CEO Daniel Krumm's position that the corporation's competitive edge was its *dedication to quality*. According to Krumm: "We believe quality and reliability are, ultimately, what the consumer wants." This devotion to quality was exemplified by a corporate policy that no cost reduction proposal would be approved if it reduced product quality in any way.

R&D and Purchasing

Research and Development (R&D) at Maytag had always been interested in internal improvements related to quality, durability, and safety. This orientation traditionally dominated the company's view of product development. One example was the careful way the company chose in 1989 to replace the venerable Helical Drive transmission with a new Dependable Drive™ transmission for its automatic washers. The new drive was delivered in 1975, patented in 1983, and put into test market in 1985, after it had been demonstrated that the drive would contribute to a 20-year product life. The Dependable Drive contained only 40 parts, compared to the previous drive's 65, and allowed the agitator to move 153 strokes a minute, compared to only 64 previously.

However, this methodical approach to R & D meant that Maytag Corporation might miss out on potential innovations. Realizing this dilemma, the corporation began to emphasize closer relationships with its key suppliers in both product development and process engineering. Joe Thomson, Vice President of Purchasing at Galesburg Refrigeration Products (Admiral plant), provided 1 example:

> We made an arrangement with a large steel supplier that led to a team effort to establish hardness specifications on our cabinet and door steel to improve fabrication. This team was very successful and the quality improvement and reduction in cost reached all our expectations. The company is now supplying all of our steel requirements.[16]

These strategic alliances between appliance makers and their suppliers were 1 way to speed up the application of new technology to new products and processes. For example, Maytag Company was approached by 1 of its suppliers, Honeywell's Microswitch Division, offering its expertise in fuzzy logic technology—a technology Maytag did not have at that time. The resulting partnership in product development resulted in Maytag's new IntelliSense™ dishwasher. Unlike previous dishwashers, which had to be set by the user, Maytag's fuzzy logic dishwasher automatically selected the proper cycle to get the dishes clean, based on a series of factors, such as the amount of dirt, presence of detergent, and other factors.[17] According to Paul Ludwig, Business Development Manager for Honeywell's Microswitch Division, "Had Maytag not included us on the design team, we don't believe the 2 companies would have achieved the same innovative solution, nor would we have completed the project in such a short amount of time."[18] Terry Carlson, Vice President of Purchasing for Maytag Corporation, stressed the importance of close relationships with suppliers:

> Strategic partnerships are a developing reality in our organization. . . . By paring our supplier base down by more than 50% in the past 3 years, we are encouraging greater supplier participation in our product design and production-planning processes. We're making choices to establish preferred supplier directions for our technical groups. These groups interact with their supplier counterparts. We are assigning joint task teams to specific projects, be they new-product-design oriented or continuous improvement of current products or processes.[19]

The corporation's R&D expenses were $44 million in 1992, $42.7 million in 1993, $45.9 million in 1994, and $47 million in 1995. According to Doug Ringger, Director of Product Planning for Maytag and Admiral products, the use of cross-functional teams had helped cut development time in half from what it used to be. He stated, "By having input from all areas early in the development cycle, issues are resolved before becoming problems."[20]

Manufacturing

Like other major home appliance manufacturers, Maytag Corporation was in the midst of investing millions of dollars in upgrading its plants and other facilities. Once considered to be the most efficient in the nation, Maytag's Newton, Iowa, plant was beginning to show its age by the late 1980s. Consequently, top management made a controversial decision to move dishwasher production from its Newton plant to a new plant in Jackson, Tennessee. This new plant was dedicated to the manufacturing of dishwashers for all the corporation's brands. This was in line with the industry trend to build "dedicated," highly efficient plants to produce only 1 product line with variations for multiple brands and price levels. Previously, only Maytag brand dishwashers had been made in Newton. Dishwashers had been purchased from General Electric for the Jenn-Air and Magic Chef brands.

Community leaders and union officials, who had been discouraged by the corporation's dishwasher decision, were jubilant in January 1994, when top management announced that it had chosen Newton as the production site for its new line of "horizontal axis" clothes washing machines. (The Iowa Department of Economic Development had offered Maytag a $1 million forgivable loan if it built the plant in Newton.[21]) A front-loader, the new washer would be similar to those currently popular in most of Europe. This type of washer was expected to use some 40% less water than comparable top loaders (vertical axis) and significantly less electricity. Like Frigidaire, Maytag concluded that only a horizontal-axis washer would meet future U.S. Department of Energy standards. In contrast, GE and Whirlpool were still unsure about the superiority of this design and were attempting to design a more efficient vertical-axis washer.

The corporation was also investing $160 million in the old Admiral refrigeration plant in Galesburg, Illinois, during the 3-year period beginning 1995. As mentioned earlier, after only 2 years of operation, Maytag was spending $13.7 million to add 2 more assembly lines to its successful Jackson dishwasher plant.

Human Resources and Labor Relations

Throughout the corporation, employees were organized into various labor unions. The bargaining unit representing Maytag and Admiral Products' unionized employees in Newton, Iowa, was the United Auto Workers. The unions representing employees at other U.S. Maytag Corporation companies were the Sheet Metal Workers International Association (Jenn-Air facilities), the International Brotherhood of Electrical Workers (Hoover North America), and the International Association of Machinists and Aerospace Workers (Admiral and Magic Chef facilities). All the presidents of union locals belonged to a Maytag Council, which met once a year to discuss union issues.

Traditionally, the Maytag Company had had cordial relations with its local unions, but the change to a large corporation seemed to alter that union relationship. Nevertheless, the corporation had not had any strikes by any of its unions since a 1-day walkout at Maytag Company in 1974. This was worthy of note, considering that during the 3-year period 1990–1992 the corporation reduced employment by 4,500 people. Newton's UAW Local 997 supported a 6-year contract extension in December 1993 to help entice the corporation to locate its planned horizontal-axis washing machine facility in Newton rather than at the washer plant in Herrin, Illinois, originally owned by Magic Chef. Members of the International Association of Machinists and Aerospace Workers at the Galesburg (Admiral) refrigeration plant overwhelmingly approved a 5-year agreement in November 1994 that would allow the company to expand production during the peak summer months instead of closing down for 2 weeks for vacations. This was done partially to encourage the corporation to invest further in the plant. Mike Norville, President of Local 2063 in Galesburg, said that, although automation could result in short-term job losses, in the long-run "there will be more jobs. We're going to make a lot more (refrigerators) because we want a bigger piece of the market."[22]

In August 1995 Maytag Corporation agreed to a $16.5 million (pre-tax) settlement with 800 workers who had lost their jobs when the corporation closed Dixie-Narco's plant in Ranson, West Virginia. Although the workers had been nonunion and not subject to a written contract, they claimed that Maytag officials had repeatedly told them that the new Williston factory would supplement, not replace, production at the Ranson plant. Although agreeing to the settlement, Maytag officials did not admit any wrongdoing. "The original plant closing was not what we desired, but it's what was required by economic and business realities," explained Edward Graham, Vice President and General Counsel of Maytag. "We reluctantly agreed to settle this case even though we believe our actions in closing the plant were lawful, prudent, and reasonable."[23]

Strategic Planning

Strategic planning had led to many of the recent changes in Maytag Corporation. In 1978, when Leonard Hadley was working as Maytag Company's Assistant Controller, CEO Daniel Krumm asked him and 2 others from manufacturing and marketing to serve as a strategic planning task force. Krumm asked the 3 people the question: "*If we keep doing what we're now doing, what will the Maytag Company look like in 5 years?*" The question posed a challenge—considering that the company had never done financial modeling, and none of the 3 knew much of strategic planning. Hadley worked with a programmer in his MIS section to develop "what if" scenarios. The task force presented its conclusion to the Board of Directors: A large part of Maytag's profits (the company had the best profit margin in the industry) was coming from products and services with no future: repair parts, portable washers and dryers, and wringer washing machines.

Looking back to 1978, Hadley felt that this was yet another crucial time for the company. The Board of Directors was becoming less conservative as more outside directors came from companies that were growing through acquisitions. With the support of the Board, Krumm promoted Hadley to the new position of Vice President of Corporate Planning. Hadley was given the task of analyzing the industry to search for acquisition candidates. Until that time, most planning had been oriented internally with little external analysis.

In 1990, then–Chairman Daniel Krumm had presented Maytag Corporation's strategic plan at the annual shareholders meeting. In addition to stressing quality, synergy, and globalization as keys, Krumm had said:

> Increasing *profitability* is essential. . . . Our objective is to be the profitability leader in the industry for each product line we manufacture. We intend to out-perform the competition in the next 5 years striving for a 6.5% return on sales, a 10% return on assets, and a 20% return on equity. . . . However, . . . we must not emphasize market share at the expense of profitability.

It was clear by the end of 1992 that these objectives were not going to be met anytime soon. In his speech to the 1993 annual meeting, newly promoted Chairman Hadley updated the strategic plan by presenting the corporation's 3 current goals:

- Increased profitability
- Become number 1 in total customer satisfaction
- Become the third largest appliance manufacturer (in unit sales) in North America.

Profitability would be increased by growing market share in the "core" North American major appliance and floor care businesses. Hadley pointed out that "Maytag Corporation wants all its brands to beat the competition in satisfying the customer, be that customer a dealer, builder, or end user of the product."

Financial Situation

Return on equity (ROE) has been a weak spot of the corporation since it first embarked on the strategy of growth through acquisitions. The ROE was over 25% before the Magic Chef merger in 1986, peaked at over 30% in 1988, was nearly cut in half to 18.3% in 1989 after the Chicago Pacific acquisition, and fell to 8% in 1991. In 1992, the annual report showed a net loss for the first time since the 1920s. In 1993 and 1994, net income showed real improvement, but in 1995 it dropped again. (See **Exhibits 5, 6,** and **7** for the company's financial statements.) Profits declined from $147.6 million in 1994 to a $20.5 million loss in 1995.

Exhibit 5

Statements of Consolidated Income (Loss): Maytag Corporation
(Dollar amounts in thousands, except per share data)

Year Ending December 31	1995	1994	1993	1992	1991	1990
Net sales	$3,039,524	$3,372,515	$2,987,054	$3,041,223	$2,970,626	$3,056,833
Cost of sales	2,250,616	2,496,065	2,262,942	2,339,406	2,254,221	2,309,138
Gross profit	788,908	876,450	724,112	701,817	716,405	747,695
Selling, general and administrative expenses	500,674	553,682	515,234	528,250	524,898	517,088
Reorganization expenses	—	—	—	95,000	—	—
Special charge	—	—	50,000	—	—	—
Operating income	288,234	322,768	158,878	78,567	191,507	230,607
Interest expense	(52,087)	(74,077)	(75,364)	(75,004)	(75,159)	(81,966)
Loss on business dispositions	(146,785)	(13,088)	—	—	—	—
Settlement of lawsuit	(16,500)	—	—	—	—	—
Loss of guarantee of indebtedness	(18,000)	—	—	—	—	—
Other—net	4,942	5,734	6,356	3,983	7,069	10,764
Income before income taxes, extraordinary item, and accounting changes	59,804	241,337	89,870	7,546	123,417	159,405
Income taxes	74,800	90,200	38,600	15,900	44,400	60,500
Income before extraordinary item and effect of accounting changes	(14,996)	151,137	51,270	(8,354)	79,017	98,905
Extraordinary item—loss on early retirement of debt	(5,480)	—	—	—	—	—
Effect of accounting changes for postretirement benefits other than pensions and income taxes	—	—	—	(307,000)	—	—
Cumulative effect of accounting change	—	(3,190)	—	—	—	—
Net income (loss)	$(20,476)	$147,947	$51,270	$(315,354)	$79,017	$98,905
Average number of shares of common stock	107,062,000	106,795,000	106,252,000	106,077,000	105,761,000	105,617,000
Per share data						
Income (loss) before extraordinary item and effect of accounting changes	$(0.14)	$1.42	$ 0.48	$(0.08)	$0.75	$0.94
Extraordinary item	(0.05)					
Cumulative effect of accounting change	—	0.03	—	(2.89)	—	—
Net income (loss) per share	$(.19)	$1.39	$ 0.48	$(2.97)	$0.75	$0.94

Source: Maytag Corporation, *Annual Reports.*

Exhibit 6

Statements of Consolidated Financial Condition: Maytag Corporation
(Dollar amounts in thousands)

Year Ending December 31	1995	1994	1993	1992	1991	1990
Assets						
Current assets						
Cash and cash equivalents	$141,214	$110,403	$31,730	$57,032	$48,752	$69,587
Accounts receivable, less allowance						
(1995, $12,540; 1994, $20,037;						
1993, $15,629; 1992, $16,380;						
1991, $14,119; 1990, $17,600)	417,457	567,531	532,353	476,850	457,773	487,726
Inventories—finished goods	163,968	254,345	282,841	249,289	314,493	335,417
Inventories—raw materials and supplies	101,151	132,924	146,313	151,794	174,589	200,370
Deferred income taxes	42,785	45,589	46,695	52,261	24,858	22,937
Other current assets	43,559	19,345	16,919	28,309	56,168	52,484
Total current assets	910,134	1,130,137	1,056,851	1,015,535	1,076,633	1,168,521
Noncurrent assets						
Deferred income taxes	91,610	72,394	68,559	71,442	—	—
Pension investments	1,489	112,522	163,175	215,433	232,231	235,264
Intangible pension asset	91,291	84,653	4,928	—	—	—
Other intangibles less amortization allowance						
(1995, $65,039; 1994, $56,250;						
1993, $46,936; 1992, $37,614; 1991, $28,295;						
1990, $18,980)	300,086	310,343	319,657	328,980	338,275	347,090
Miscellaneous	29,321	44,979	35,266	35,989	52,436	45,209
Total noncurrent assets	513,797	624,891	591,585	651,844	622,942	627,563
Property, plant, and equipment						
Land	24,246	32,600	46,149	47,370	51,147	50,613
Buildings and improvements	260,394	284,439	288,590	286,368	296,684	282,828
Machinery and equipment	1,030,233	1,109,411	1,068,199	962,006	895,025	828,464
Construction in progress	97,053	30,305	44,753	90,847	92,954	61,775
	1,411,926	1,456,755	1,447,691	1,386,591	1,335,810	1,223,680
Less allowances for depreciation	710,791	707,456	626,629	552,480	500,317	433,223
Total property, plant, and equipment	701,135	749,299	821,062	834,111	835,493	790,457
Total assets	$2,125,066	$2,504,327	$2,469,498	$2,501,490	$2,535,068	$2,586,541
Liabilities and shareholders' equity						
Current liabilities						
Notes payable	$ —	$45,148	$157,571	$19,886	$ 23,504	$ 56,601
Accounts payable	142,676	212,441	195,981	$218,142	273,731	266,190
Compensation to employees	61,644	61,311	84,405	89,245	63,845	53,753
Accrued liabilities	156,041	146,086	178,015	180,894	165,384	154,369
Income taxes payable	3,141	26,037	16,193	11,323	17,574	13,736
Current maturities of long-term debt	3,201	43,411	18,505	43,419	23,570	11,070
Total current liabilities	366,703	534,434	650,670	562,909	567,608	555,719
Noncurrent liabilities						
Deferred income taxes	14,367	38,375	44,882	89,011	75,210	71,548
Long-term debt	536,579	663,205	724,695	789,232	809,480	857,941
Postretirement benefits—not pensions	428,478	412,832	391,635	380,376	—	—
Pension liability	88,883	59,363	17,383	—	—	—
Other noncurrent liabilities	52,705	64,406	53,452	80,737	72,185	86,602
Total noncurrent liabilities	1,121,012	1,238,181	1,232,047	1,339,356	956,875	1,016,091

Exhibit 6
Statements of Consolidated Financial Condition: Maytag Corporation *(continued)*

Year Ending December 31	1995	1994	1993	1992	1991	1990
Shareholders' equity						
Common stock						
Authorized: 200,000,000 shares (par = $1.25)						
Issued: 117,150,593 shares in treasury	146,438	146,438	146,438	146,438	146,438	146,438
Additional paid-in capital	472,602	477,153	480,067	478,463	479,833	487,034
Retained earnings	344,346	420,174	325,823	328,122	696,745	670,878
Cost of common stock in treasury						
(1995, 11,745,395 shares;						
1994, 9, 813,893 shares;						
1993, 10,430,833 shares;						
1992, 10,545,915 shares;						
1991, 10,808,116 shares;						
1990, 11,424,154 shares)	(255,663)	(218,745)	(232,510)	(234,993)	(240,848)	(254,576)
Employee stock plans	(57,319)	(60,816)	(62,342)	(65,638)	(66,711)	(63,590)
Minimum pension liability adjustment	(5,656)	—	—	—	—	—
Foreign currency translation	(7,397)	(32,492)	(70,695)	(53,167)	(4,872)	28,547
Total shareholders' equity	637,351	731,712	586,781	599,225	1,010,585	1,014,731
Total liabilities and shareholders' equity	$ 2,125,066	$ 2,504,327	$ 2,469,498	$2,501,490	$2,535,068	$2,586,541
Number of employees	16,595	19,772	20,951	21,407	22,533	24,273
Stock price/share (high–low)	$21.5–$14.5	$20.125–$14	$18.625–$13	$ 21–$13	$ 17–$10	$ 21–$10

Source: Maytag Corporation, *Annual Reports.*

Exhibit 7
Principal Business Groups: Maytag Corporation
(Dollar amounts in thousands)

Performance	North American Appliances	Vending Equipment	European Appliances
1995			
Sales	$2,663,611	$194,713	$181,200
Operating income	295,400	23,466	406
1994			
Sales	2,639,834	191,749	398,966
Operating income	321,021	21,866	420
1993			
Sales	2,311,777	156,597	390,761
Operating income	233,384	17,944	(73,581)
1992			
Sales	2,242,270	165,321	501,857
Operating income	129,680	16,311	(67,061)
1991			
Sales	2,182,567	149,798	495,517
Operating income	186,322	4,498	(865)
1990			
Sales	2,212,335	191,444	496,672
Operating income	221,164	25,018	(22,863)

Source: Maytag Corporation, *Annual Reports.*

If special charges were ignored, however, net income for 1995 would have been $144.7 million—down only 2% from 1994. Sales had actually increased 0.9% from 1994. In analyzing the figures, Hadley noted that each of the product lines—major appliances, floor care, and vending—had performed well, even with increasing materials costs and lower industry-wide sales.

At its October 1995 meeting, the Board of Directors had authorized the repurchase of up to 10.8 million shares of the corporation's common stock, which represented 10% of the outstanding shares. The directors had also approved an increase of 12% in the December dividend, raising the quarterly dividend from 12.5¢ to 14¢ per share. Hadley explained the decisions:

> Our balance sheet is significantly stronger than it has been at any time since 1989, and we've reduced debt by some $400 million in the past 18 months. We've shed underperforming assets, operating performance has improved, and our capital investment remains strong. As a result, we are well-positioned to increase shareholder value as we go forward. The share repurchase and dividend increase are 2 important steps we are able to take now. Both signal our confidence in Maytag's future and our commitment to improve the value shareowners receive from their continued investment in Maytag.[24]

Alex Silverman of *Value Line* agreed with Hadley that Maytag seemed to be turning its operations around at last. Even though he predicted that, due to the divestitures of Hoover Europe and part of Dixie-Narco, Maytag's 1996 sales would probably drop 10% from 1995, lower labor expenses, greater plant efficiencies, and reduced interest costs would more than offset rising raw materials costs and lower sales volume, resulting in increased profits. Silverman projected the stock price for the time period 1998–2000 to have a high of $35 and a low of $25 per share.[25]

In early February 1996, Maytag Corporation stock was selling at a little over $19. Nicholas Heymann, an analyst with NatWest Securities in New York, had earlier concluded that the corporation was worth up to $29 per share (when it still owned Hoover Europe).[26] Some analysts were wondering if the corporation might have no choice but to sell to a competitor by the end of the decade. The major players in the U.S. industry, such as A.B. Electrolux, Whirlpool, and General Electric, were moving forward through successful acquisitions to become successful global competitors. Even Bosch-Siemens, the number 2 appliance maker in Europe, had begun making the transition to global operations with its decision to build a dishwasher plant in North Carolina. Could a purely domestic appliance manufacturer such as Maytag survive in the coming global industry? It had been widely rumored that Maytag's purchase of Chicago Pacific in 1988 had not just been to acquire Hoover, but to become a less tempting takeover target. Although there was currently no talk on Wall Street about any interest in acquiring the corporation, the sale of Maytag's overseas operations and improved cash position could make the firm a tempting takeover target.

Maytag's New Strategic Posture

As Leonard Hadley began outlining his letter to the shareholders for the upcoming *1995 Annual Report*, he wondered how the past year's developments would be received. Cynics might point out that Hadley's big accomplishment since becoming CEO was to return the company to 1988, when Maytag had no foreign operations. Some might be very pleased, especially the current workforce. He hoped that the impact of the corporation's second net loss since the 1920s would be softened by the sale of Hoover Europe. Net income should increase significantly in the coming years. Retired shareholders would probably applaud the recent increase in dividends. Financial analysts would probably agree that the decision to buy back stock would help raise the stock price and perhaps reduce any interest in a hostile takeover.

Industry analysts would probably wonder how Maytag would be able to compete in the future against globally integrated competitors in a fiercely competitive, mature U.S. industry. Now that Maytag Corporation was back on solid footing, the financial community would want some sort of strategic plan to justify any rosy predictions.

Maytag Corporation's mission statement was clearly stated on the inside front cover of the *1994 Annual Report*:

> To improve the quality of home life by designing, building, marketing, and servicing the best appliances in the world.

Hadley thought back to Daniel Krumm's list of objectives at the 1990 shareholders' meeting and his own listing of 3 primary goals at the 1993 meeting. Although net income was negative in 1995, the sales of Hoover Europe and Hoover Australia should pave the way for solid profits, beginning in 1996. Although it could be argued that consumer surveys consistently placed the Maytag brand in the most desired category (when price was not considered), the same could not always be said of the corporation's other brands. Could a company be number 1 in consumer satisfaction if none of its products were first in market share? Nevertheless, Maytag Corporation did pass Frigidaire during 1995 in overall U.S. shipments and market share to move into third place in North America—a real accomplishment. Unfortunately, it was more a case of Frigidaire losing market share rather than Maytag gaining it. (Frigidaire's market share had plummeted from 16.9% in 1994 to 13.5%, whereas Maytag's market share remained at 14.4%.) The real question now seemed to be: What objectives and strategies were now appropriate? Before Hadley and the Executive Committee could propose a revised set of objectives to the board, he needed to develop a new strategic vision for the corporation to take it through the turn of the century.

Notes

1. R. Brack, "Is Maytag Preparing for a Sale?" *Des Moines Register* (June 1, 1995), p. 8S.
2. L. Hadley, "To Our Shareowners," *Maytag Corporation Second Quarter Report* (1995), p. 2.
3. David Hoyte, Executive Vice President of Operations, Frigidaire, as quoted by M. Sanders, "ISO 9000: The Inside Story," *Appliance* (August 1994), p. 43. ("White goods" is the traditional term used for major home appliances. The contrasting term "brown goods" refers to home electronics products such as radios and televisions.)
4. Kevin Lanning, Director of Market Research, Maytag Company, in "A Real Bargain," *Appliance Manufacturer* (November, 1993), p. M-21; K. Edlin, "Demand Performance," *Appliance* (July 1993), p. 90.
5. T. Somheil, "The Incredible Value Story—Part 3," *Appliance* (June 1992), pp. 25–32.
6. J. Jancsurak, "Global Trends for 1995–2005," *Appliance Manufacturer* (June 1995), p. A-6.
7. D. Davis, "The Value of World Leadership," *Appliance* (December 1994), p. E-6.
8. N. C. Remich, Jr., "Mexico, Drop Tariffs," *Appliance Manufacturer* (December 1994), p. 7.
9. "Maytag Announces In-Home Inspection: Will Voluntarily Replace Component," Press Release, *Maytag Corporation* (October 17, 1995).
10. "Maytag Corp. to Exit Currency Validator Business," *Maytag Corporation News Release* (November 1, 1995).
11. Interview with Leonard Hadley, Maytag Corporation, *1994 Annual Report*, p. 10.
12. W. Ryberg, "Cost of Maytag Ad Fiasco Climbs," *Des Moines Register* (April 21, 1995), p. 10S; W. Ryberg, "'Hoovergate' Winding Down," *Des Moines Register* (April 27, 1994), p. 10S.
13. Maytag Corporation News Release, 1995.
14. W. Ryberg, "Maytag's No. 2 Officer Resigns," *Des Moines Register* (August 12, 1995), p. 10S.
15. W. Ryberg, "Maytag Executive Resigns," *Des Moines Register* (December 14, 1995), p. 8S.
16. M. Sanders, "Purchasing Power," *Appliance* (June 1993), pp. 45–46.
17. A. Baker, "Intelligent Dishwasher Outsmarts Dirt," *Design News* (April 10, 1995), pp. 69–73.
18. S. Stevens, "Speeding the Signals of Change," *Appliance* (February 1995), p. 7.
19. N. C. Remich, Jr., "The Power of Partnering," *Appliance Manufacturer* (August 1994), p. A-1.
20. R. Dzierwa, "The Permanent Press," *Appliance* (September 1995), p. 48.
21. "Maytag, Fawn, Lennox, Parsons Get State Aid," (Ames, Iowa) *Daily Tribune* (June 23, 1995), p. 1A.
22. "Maytag Keeps Jobs in Galesburg," (Ames, Iowa) *Daily Tribune* (November 12, 1994), p. A4.
23. "Maytag Announces Out-of-Court Settlement in Class-Action Suit," Maytag Corporation News Release (August 3, 1995); K. Pins, "Maytag Settles Plant-Closing Case," *Des Moines Register* (August 4, 1995), p. 8S.
24. "Maytag Will Repurchase Shares; Increase Dividend," Maytag Corporation News Release (October 19, 1995).
25. A. Silverman, "Maytag Corporation," *Value Line* (December 15, 1995).
26. Brack, "Is Maytag Preparing for a Sale?" p. 8S.

CASE 21

Kmart Corporation (2000): Seeking Customer Acceptance and Preference

James W. Camerius

On June 1, 2000, the search for the new Chairman and Chief Executive Officer of Kmart Corporation was over. Charles C. Conaway, a 39-year-old drugstore chain executive, was selected to fill the position. His appointment meant that the strategic direction of the Kmart would come from a man who was previously unknown outside of the drugstore industry. He would have to provide an answer to a crucial question: How can Kmart respond to the challenges of industry leader Wal-Mart Stores, Inc., in the extremely competitive arena of discount retailing?

As President and Chief Operating Officer of CVS Corporation, Mr. Conaway was the number 2 executive at the nation's largest drugstore chain, whose annual sales were about half those of Kmart's annual revenue of $36 billion. By all accounts, Mr. Conaway had made a sizable contribution in sales, earnings, and market value at CVS, Inc., headquartered in Woonsocket, Rhode Island. CVS had 1999 sales of $18 billion with 4,100 stores. Mr. Conaway, who became President and Chief Operating Officer of CVS in 1998, was responsible for merchandising, advertising, store operations, and logistics. After joining the firm in 1992, he helped engineer the restructuring of the then parent Melville Corporation, a diversified retailer, into a successful drugstore chain. Mr. Conaway said in an interview upon assuming his new position with Kmart that his primary task would be to improve customer service, productivity of resources, and problems with out-of-stock merchandise. Setting the stage for a new direction, Mr. Conaway said, "Customer service is going to be at the top. We're going to measure it and we're going to tie incentives around it."

Floyd Hall, the previous Chairman, President, and Chief Executive Officer of Kmart since June of 1995, appeared pleased with the appointment. He had announced 2 years earlier that he had wanted to retire, and now he would be able to do so. Mr. Hall in the last 5 years had restored Kmart profitability and made improvements in store appearance and merchandise selection. Analysts had noted, however, that the firm was without a definable niche in discount retailing. Studies had shown that number 1 ranked Wal-Mart, originally a rural retailer, had continued to be known for lower prices. Target Corporation, number 3 in sales, had staked out a niche as a merchandiser of discounted upscale products. Kmart was left without a feature that would give it competitive distinction in the marketplace.

This case was prepared by Professor James W. Camerius of Northern Michigan University. This case was edited for SMBP-8th Edition. All rights reserved to the author. Copyright © 2000 by Professor James W. Camerius. Reprinted by permission.

Kmart's financial results reported in the first quarter of 2000 noted that net income fell 61% to $22 million. The decline ended a string of 15 consecutive quarters of profit increases that Floyd Hall felt had signaled a turnaround at the discount chain. Hall, however, was very optimistic about the company's future. The financial information over the previous periods had convinced him that a new corporate strategy that he introduced would revitalize Kmart's core business, its 2,171 discount stores, and put the company on the road to recovery. Industry analysts had noted that Kmart, once an industry leader, had posted 11 straight quarters of disappointing earnings prior to 1998 and had been dogged by persistent bankruptcy rumors. Analysts cautioned that much of Kmart's recent growth reflected the strength of the consumer economy and that uncertainty continued to exist about the company's future in a period of slower economic growth.

Kmart Corporation was 1 of the world's largest mass merchandise retailers. After several years of restructuring, it was composed largely of general merchandise businesses in the form of traditional Kmart discount department stores and Big Kmart (general merchandise and convenience items) stores as well as Super Kmart Centers (food and general merchandise). It operated in all 50 of the United States and in Puerto Rico, Guam, and the U.S. Virgin Islands. It also had equity interests in Meldisco subsidiaries of Footstar, Inc., that operated Kmart footwear departments. Measured in sales volume it was the third largest retailer and the second largest discount department store chain in the United States.

The discount department store industry was perceived by many to have reached maturity. Kmart, as part of that industry, had a retail management strategy that was developed in the late 1950s and revised in the early 1990s. The firm was in a dilemma in the terms of corporate strategy. The problem was how to lay a foundation to provide a new direction that would reposition the firm in a fiercely competitive environment.

The Early Years

Kmart was the outgrowth of an organization founded in 1899 in Detroit by Sebastian S. Kresge. The first S. S. Kresge store represented a new type of retailing that featured low-priced merchandise for cash in low-budget, relatively small (4,000 to 6,000 square foot) buildings with sparse furnishings. The adoption of the "5 & 10" or "variety store" concept, pioneered by F. W. Woolworth Company in 1879, led to rapid and profitable development of what was then the S. S. Kresge Company.

Kresge believed it could substantially increase its retail business through centralized buying and control, developing standardized store operating procedures, and expanding with new stores in heavy traffic areas. In 1912, the firm was incorporated in Delaware. It had 85 stores with sales of $10,325,000, and, next to Woolworth's, was the largest variety chain in the world. In 1916 it was reincorporated in Michigan. Over the next 40 years, the firm experimented with mail-order catalogues, full-line department stores, self-service, a number of price lines, and the opening of stores in planned shopping centers. It continued its emphasis, however, on variety stores.

By 1957, corporate management became aware that the development of supermarkets and the expansion of drug store chains into general merchandise lines had made inroads into market categories previously dominated by variety stores. It also became clear that a new form of store with a discount merchandising strategy was emerging.

The Cunningham Connection

In 1957, in an effort to regain competitiveness and possibly save the company, Frank Williams, then President of Kresge, nominated Harry B. Cunningham as General Vice President. This maneuver was undertaken to free Mr. Cunningham, who had worked his way up the ranks in the organization, from operating responsibility. He was being groomed for the presidency and was given the assignment to study existing retailing businesses and recommend marketing changes.

In his visits to Kresge stores, and those of the competition, Cunningham became interested in discounting—particularly a new operation in Garden City, Long Island. Eugene Ferkauf had recently opened large discount department stores called E. J. Korvette. The stores had a discount mass-merchandising emphasis that featured low prices and margins, high turnover, large free-standing departmentalized units, ample parking space, and a location typically in the suburbs.

Cunningham was impressed with the discount concept, but he knew he had to first convince the Kresge Board of Directors, whose support would be necessary for any new strategy to succeed. He studied the company for 2 years and presented Kresge with the following recommendation:

> We can't beat the discounters operating under the physical constraints and the self-imposed merchandise limitations of variety stores. We can join them—and not only join them, but with our people, procedures, and organization, we can become a leader in the discount industry.

In a speech delivered at the University of Michigan, Cunningham made his management approach clear by concluding with an admonition from the British author, Sir Hugh Walpole: "Don't play for safety, it's the most dangerous game in the world."

The Board of Directors had a difficult job. Change is never easy, especially when the company has established procedures in place and a proud heritage. Before the first presentation to the board could be made, rumors were circulating that 1 shocked senior executive had said:

> We have been in the variety business for 60 years—we know everything there is to know about it, and we're not doing very well in that, and you want to get us into a business we don't know anything about.

The Board of Directors accepted H. B. Cunningham's recommendations. When President Frank Williams retired, Cunningham became the new President and Chief Executive Officer and was directed to proceed with his recommendations.

The Birth of Kmart

Management conceived the original Kmart as a conveniently located 1-stop shopping unit where customers could buy a wide variety of quality merchandise at discount prices. The typical Kmart had 75,000 square feet, all on 1 floor. It generally stood by itself in a high-traffic, suburban area, with plenty of parking space. All stores had a similar floor plan.

The firm made an $80 million commitment in leases and merchandise for 33 stores before the first Kmart opened in 1962 in Garden City, Michigan. As part of this strategy, management decided to rely on the strengths and abilities of its own people to make decisions rather than employing outside experts for advice.

The original Kresge 5 & 10 variety store operation was characterized by low gross margins, high turnover, and concentration on return on investment. The main difference in the Kmart strategy would be the offering of a much wider merchandise mix.

The company had the knowledge and ability to merchandise 50% of the departments in the planned Kmart merchandise mix, and contracted for operation of the remaining departments. In the following years, Kmart took over most of those departments originally contracted to licensees. Eventually all departments, except shoes, were operated by Kmart.

By 1987, the twenty-fifth anniversary year of the opening of the first Kmart store in America, sales and earnings of Kmart Corporation were at all-time highs. The company was the world's largest discount retailer with sales of $25,627 million and operated 3,934 general merchandise and specialty stores.

On April 6, 1987, Kmart Corporation announced that it agreed to sell most of its remaining Kresge variety stores in the United States to McCrory Corporation, a unit of the closely held Rapid American Corporation of New York.

Corporate Governance

Exhibit 1 shows the 12 members of the Board of Directors of Kmart. The 1 internal member was Charles C. Conaway, Chairman and CEO of Kmart. Seven board members had joined the board since 1995: (1) James B. Adamson, (2) Richard G. Cline, (3) Charles C. Conaway, (4) Robert D. Kennedy, (5) Robin B. Smith, (6) Thomas T. Stallkamp, (7) James O. Welsh, Jr. **Exhibit 2** lists the corporate officers.

The Nature of the Competitive Environment

A CHANGING MARKETPLACE

The retail sector of the United States economy went through a number of dramatic and turbulent changes during the 1980s and early 1990s. Retail analysts concluded that many retail firms were negatively affected by increased competitive pressures, sluggish consumer spending, slower-than-anticipated economic growth in North America, and recessions abroad. As 1 retail consultant noted:

> The structure of distribution in advanced economies is currently undergoing a series of changes that are as profound in their impact and as pervasive in their influence as those that occurred in manufacturing during the nineteenth century.

Exhibit 1

Board of Directors: Kmart Corporation

James B. Adamson[1*]
Chairman, President and CEO of Advantica Restaurant Group
Director of Kmart since 1996

Lilyan H. Affinito[1,3,5]
Former Vice Chairman of the Board of Maxxam Group, Inc.
Director of Kmart since 1990

Joseph A. Califano, Jr.[4]
Chairman and President, The National Center on Addiction and Substance Abuse at Columbia University
Director of Kmart since 1990

Richard G. Cline[2,3,5]
Chairman, Hawthorne Investors, Inc.
Director of Kmart since 1995

Charles C. Conaway[3*]
Chairman of the Board and CEO of Kmart Corporation
Director of Kmart since 2000

Willie D. Davis[2]
President of All Pro Broadcasting, Inc.
Director of Kmart since 1986

Joseph P. Flannery[3,4,5]
Chairman, President, and CEO of Uniroyal Holding, Inc.
Director of Kmart since 1985

Robert D. Kennedy[2*]
Former Chairman of the Board of Union Carbide Corporation
Director of Kmart since 1996

J. Richard Munro[3,4,5]
Former Cochairman of the Board and Co-CEO of Time Warner, Inc.
Director of Kmart since 1990

Robin B. Smith[1,5*]
Chairman and CEO of Publishers Clearing House
Director of Kmart since 1996

Thomas T. Stallkamp[4*]
Vice Chairman and CEO of MSX International
Director of Kmart since September 1999

James O. Welch, Jr.[2]
Former Vice Chairman of RJR Nabisco, Inc., and Chairman of Nabisco Brands, Inc.
Director of Kmart since 1995

Committees:
1 = Audit   4 = Finance
2 = Compensation & Incentives   5 = Nominating
3 = Executive   * = Committee Chair

Source: Kmart Corporation, *2000 Annual Report.*

Exhibit 2

Corporate Officers: Kmart Corporation

Charles C. Conway
Chairman of the Board,
Chief Executive Officer

Michael Bozic
Vice Chairman

Andrew A. Giancamilli
President and General Merchandise
Manager, U.S. Kmart

Donald W. Keeble
President, Store Operations,
U.S. Kmart

Warren F. Cooper
Executive Vice President,
Human Resources and Administration

Ernest L. Heether
Senior Vice President,
Merchandise Planning and
Replenishment

Paul J. Hueber
Senior Vice President, Store
Operations

Cecil B. Kearse
Senior Vice President,
General Merchandise
Manager—Home

Jerome J. Kuske
Senior Vice President,
General Merchandise
Manager—Hardlines

James P. Mixon
Senior Vice President, Logistics

Joseph A. Osbourn
Senior Vice President and Chief
Information Officer

E. Jackson Smailes
Senior Vice President,
General Merchandise Manager—Apparel

Martin E. Welch III
Senior Vice President and Chief
Financial Officer

Larry E. Carlson
Vice President, Real Estate Market
Strategy

Ronald J. Chomiuk
Vice President, General Merchandise
Manager—Pharmacy/HBC/Cosmetics/
Photo Finishing

Timothy M. Crow
Vice President, Compensation, Benefits,
Workers Compensation
and HRIS

Larry C. Davis
Vice President, Advertising

David R. Fielding
Vice President, Northwest Region

Larry J. Foster
Vice President, Training and
Organizational Development

G. William Gryson, Jr.
Vice President, Special Projects

Walter E. Holbrook
Vice President, Southeast Region

Shawn M. Kahle
Vice President, Corporate Affairs

Lorrence T. Kellar
Vice President, Real Estate

Nancie W. LaDuke
Vice President and Secretary

Ronald Lalla
Vice President, Merchandise Controller

Thomas W. Lemke
Vice President, Data Base Marketing

Michael P. Lynch
Vice President, Southwest Region

Michael T. Macik
Vice President, Human Resources and
Labor and Associate Relations

Leo L. Maniago
Vice President, Mideast Region

David R. Marsico
Vice President, Store Operations

Harry Meeth, III
Vice President, Design and
Construction

Douglas M. Meissner
Vice President, Northeast Region

James L. Misplon
Vice President, Taxes

Ann A. Morgan
Vice President, Field Human
Resources

Lorna E. Nagler
Vice President, General Merchandise
Manager—Kidsworld and Menswear

Gary J. Ruffing
Vice President, Merchandise
Presentation and Communication

Lucinda C. Sapienza
Vice President,
General Merchandise
Manager—Ladieswear, Fashion
Accessories and Lingerie

David L. Schuvie
Vice President, Electronic Sales
and Services

Brent C. Scott
Vice President, Grocery Operations

Stephen E. Sear
Vice President, Facilities Management
and Corporate Purchasing

Stephen W. St. John
Vice President, Great Lakes Region

E. Anthony Vaal
Vice President, Global Operations,
Corporate Brands and Quality
Assurance

John S. Valenti
Vice President, Southern Region

Leland M. Viliborghi
Vice President, Central Region

Michael J. Viola
Vice President and Treasurer

Francis J. Yanak
Vice President, General Merchandise
Manager—Food and Consumables

Source: Kmart Corporation, *2000 Annual Report*, and company announcement of new Chairman and CEO.

This changing environment affected the discount department store industry. Nearly a dozen firms like E. J. Korvette, W. T. Grant, Arlans, Atlantic Mills and Ames passed into bankruptcy or reorganization. Some firms like Woolworth (Woolco Division) had withdrawn from the field entirely after years of disappointment. St. Louis based May Department Stores sold its Caldor and Venture discount divisions, each with annual sales of more than $1 billion. Venture announced liquidation in early 1998.

Senior management at Kmart felt that most of the firms that had difficulty in the industry faced the same situation. First, they were very successful 5 or 10 years ago but had not changed and, therefore, had become somewhat dated. Management that had a historically successful formula, particularly in retailing, was perceived as having difficulty adapting to change, especially at the peak of success. Management would wait too long when faced with a threat in the environment and then would have to scramble to regain competitiveness.

Wal-Mart Stores, Inc., based in Bentonville, Arkansas, was an exception. It was especially growth orientated and had emerged in 1991 and continued in that position through 2000 as the nation's largest retailer as well as largest discount department store chain in sales volume. Operating under a variety of names and formats, nationally and internationally, it included Wal-Mart stores, Wal-Mart Supercenters, and SAM's Warehouse Clubs. The firm found early strength in cultivating rural markets, merchandise restocking programs, "everyday low-pricing," and the control of operations through companywide computer programs that linked cash registers to corporate headquarters.

Sears, Roebuck & Co., in a state of stagnated growth for several years, completed a return to its retailing roots by spinning off to shareholders its $9 billion controlling stake in its Allstate Corporation insurance unit and the divestment of financial services. After unsuccessfully experimenting with an "everyday low-price" strategy, management chose to refine its merchandising program to meet the needs of middle market customers, who were primarily women, by focusing on product lines in apparel, home, and automotive.

Many retailers such as Target Corporation (formerly Dayton Hudson), which adopted the discount concept, attempted to go generally after an upscale customer. The upscale customer tended to have a household income of $25,000 to $44,000 annually. Other segments of the population were served by firms like Ames Department Stores of Rocky Hill, Connecticut, which appealed to outsize, older, and lower income workers, and by Shopko Stores, Inc., of Green Bay, Wisconsin, which attempted to serve the upscale rural consumer.

Kmart executives found that discount department stores were being challenged by several other retail formats. Some retailers were assortment-oriented, with a much greater depth of assortment within a given product category. To illustrate, Toys "R" Us was an example of a firm that operated 20,000-square-foot toy supermarkets. Toys "R" Us prices were very competitive within an industry that was very competitive. When the consumers entered a Toys "R" Us facility, there was usually no doubt in their minds if the product wasn't there, no one else had it. In the late 1990s, however, Toys "R" Us was challenged by Wal-Mart and other firms that offered higher service levels, more aggressive pricing practices, and more focused merchandise selections.

Some retailers were experimenting with the "off price" apparel concept where name brands and designer goods were sold at 20 to 70% discounts. Others, such as Home Depot and Menards, operated home improvement centers that were warehouse-style stores with a wide range of hard-line merchandise for both do-it-yourselfers and professionals. Still others opened drug supermarkets that offered a wide variety of high turnover merchandise in a convenient location. In these cases, competition was becoming more risk oriented by putting 3 or 4 million dollars in merchandise at retail value in an 80,000-square-foot facility and offering genuinely low prices. Jewel-Osco stores in the Midwest, Rite Aid, CVS, and a series of independents were examples of organizations employing the entirely new concept of the drug supermarket.

Competition was offering something that was new and different in terms of depth of assortment, competitive price image, and format. Kmart management perceived this as a threat because these were viable businesses and hindered the firm in its ability to improve and maintain share of market in specific merchandise categories. An industry competitive analysis is shown in **Exhibit 3**.

Exhibit 3

An Industry Competitive Analysis, 1999

	Kmart	Wal-Mart	Sears	Target
A. Company Data				
Sales (millions)	$35,925	$165,013	$41,071	$33,702
Net Income (millions)	403	5,575	1,453	1,144
Sales growth	6.6%	20%	2.7%	10%
Profit margin	1.1%	3.4%	2.8%	3.4%
Sales/sq ft	233	374	318	242
Return/equity	6.4%	22.9%	23%	19.5%

Number of stores:
  Kmart Corporation
    Kmart Traditional Discount Stores—202
    Big Kmart—1,860
    Super Kmart Centers—105
  Wal-Mart Stores, Inc. (includes international)
    Wal-Mart Discount Stores—2,373
    Supercenters—1,104
    SAM's Clubs—512
  Sears, Roebuck & Company
    Full-line stores—858
    Hardware stores—267
    Sears dealer stores—738
    Sears automotive stores:
      Sears Auto Centers—798
      National Tire & Battery stores—310
    Contract sales
    The Great Indoors (prototype decorating)—2
  Target Corporation
    Target—912
    Mervyn's—267
    Department Store Division—64

B. How the Stores Did

DISCOUNTERS	SALES 2000 (millions)	TOTAL LATEST MONTH Change from year earlier	COMPARABLE STORES Change from year earlier	SALES 2000 (millions)	TOTAL YEAR-TO-DATE Change from year earlier	COMPARABLE STORES Change from year earlier
Wal-Mart	$14,140.0	+28.4%	+10.9%	$44,011.0	+23.6%	+ 6.6%
Kmart	2,770.0	+ 0.8	− 0.8	8,195.0	+ 1.5	+ 0.0
Target	2,460.0	+17.0	+11.1	7,612.0	+ 8.2	+ 3.2
Costco	2,270.0	+13.0	+ 9.0	20,610.0	+16.0	+12.0
Dollar General	305.0	+17.9	+ 3.6	996.7	+18.1	+ 4.0
Ames	256.7	−6.2	+ 4.1	830.7	+ 1.8	+ 1.2

Source: A. Company Annual Reports. *B. Wall Street Journal* (February 4, 2000), p. 2B.

Expansion and Contraction

When Joseph E. Antonini was appointed chairman of Kmart Corporation in October 1987 he was charged with the responsibility of maintaining and eventually accelerating the chain's record of growth, despite a mature retail marketplace. He moved to string experimental formats into profitable chains. As he noted:

> Our vision calls for the constant and never-ceasing exploration of new modes of retailing, so that our core business of U.S. Kmart stores can be constantly renewed and reinvigorated by what we learn from our other businesses.

In the mid-1970s and throughout the 1980s, Kmart became involved in the acquisition or development of several smaller new operations. Kmart Insurance Services, Inc., acquired as Planned Marketing Associates in 1974, offered a full line of life, health, and accident insurance centers located in 27 Kmart stores primarily in the South and Southwest.

In 1982, Kmart initiated its own off-price specialty apparel concept called Designer Depot. A total of 28 Designer Depot stores were opened in 1982, to appeal to customers who wanted quality upscale clothing at a budget price. A variation of this concept, called Garment Rack, was opened to sell apparel that normally would not be sold in Designer Depot. A distribution center was added in 1983 to supplement them. Neither venture was successful.

Kmart also attempted an unsuccessful joint venture with the Hechinger Company of Washington, D.C., a warehouse home center retailer. However, after much deliberation, Kmart chose instead to acquire, in 1984, Home Centers of America of San Antonio, Texas, which operated 80,000-square-foot warehouse home centers. The new division, renamed Builders Square, had grown to 167 units by 1996. It capitalized on Kmart's real estate, construction, and management expertise and Home Centers of America's merchandising expertise. Builders Square was sold in 1997 to the Hechinger Company. On June 11, 1999, Hechinger filed for Chapter 11 bankruptcy protection. As a result, Kmart recorded a noncash charge of $354 million that reflected the impact of lease obligations for former Builders Square locations that were guaranteed by Kmart.

Waldenbooks, a chain of 877 bookstores, was acquired from Carter, Hawley, Hale, Inc., in 1984. It was part of a strategy to capture a greater share of the market with a product category that Kmart already had in its stores. Kmart management had been interested in the book business for some time and took advantage of an opportunity in the marketplace to build on its common knowledge base. Borders Books and Music, an operator of 50 large-format superstores, became part of Kmart in 1992 to form the "Borders Group," a division that would include Waldenbooks. The Borders Group, Inc., was sold during 1995.

The Bruno's, Inc., joint venture in 1987 formed a partnership to develop large combination grocery and general merchandise stores or "hypermarkets" called American Fare. The giant, 1-stop-shopping facilities of 225,000 square feet traded on the grocery expertise of Bruno's and the general merchandise of Kmart to offer a wide selection of products and services at discount prices. A similar venture, called Super Kmart Center, represented later thinking on combination stores with a smaller size and format. In 2000, Kmart operated 105 Super Kmart Centers, all in the United States.

In 1988, the company acquired a controlling interest in Makro, Inc., a Cincinnati-based operator of warehouse "club" stores. Makro, with annual sales of about $300 million operated "member only" stores that were stocked with low priced fresh and frozen groceries, apparel and durable goods in suburbs of Atlanta, Cincinnati, Washington, and Philadelphia. PACE Membership Warehouse, Inc., a similar operation, was acquired in 1989. The "club" stores were sold in 1994.

PayLess Drug Stores, a chain that operated super drug stores in a number of western states was sold in 1994 to Thrifty PayLess Holdings, Inc., an entity in which Kmart maintained a significant investment. Interests in The Sport Authority, an operator of large-format sporting goods stores, which Kmart acquired in 1990, were disposed of during 1995.

On the international level, an interest in Coles Myer, Ltd., Australia's largest retailer was sold in November, 1994. Interests in 13 Kmart general merchandise stores in the Czech and Slovak Republics were sold to Tesco PLC at the beginning of 1996, 1 of the United Kingdom's largest retailers. In February, 1998, Kmart stores in Canada were sold to Hudson's Bay Co., a Canadian chain of historic full-service department stores. The interest in Kmart Mexico, S.A.de C.V. was disposed of in FY 1997.

Founded in 1988, OfficeMax with 328 stores was 1 of the largest operators of high-volume, deep discount office products superstores in the United States. It became a greater than 90% owned Kmart unit in 1991. Kmart's interest in OfficeMax was sold during 1995. In November 1995, Kmart also sold its auto service center business to a new corporation controlled by Penske Corporation. In connection with the sale, Kmart and Penske entered into a sublease arrangement concerning the operation of Penske Auto Service Centers.

During 1999, Kmart signed agreements with SUPERVALU, Inc., and Fleming Companies, Inc., under which they would assume responsibility for the distribution and replenishment of grocery-related products to all of Kmart stores. Kmart also maintained an equity interest in Meldisco subsidiaries of Footstar, Inc., operators of footwear departments in Kmart stores.

The Maturation of Kmart

Early corporate research revealed that on the basis of convenience, Kmart served 80% of the population. One study concluded that 1 out of every 2 adults in the United States shopped at a Kmart at least once a month. Despite this popular appeal, strategies that had allowed the firm to have something for everybody were no longer felt to be appropriate for the new millennium. Kmart found that it had a broad customer base because it operated on a national basis. Its early strategies had assumed the firm was serving everyone in the markets where it was established.

Kmart was often perceived as aiming at the low-income consumer. The financial community believed the Kmart original customer was blue collar, low income, and upper lower class. The market served, however, was more professional and middle class because Kmart stores were initially in suburban communities where that population lived.

Although Kmart had made a major commitment in more recent years to secondary or rural markets, these were areas that had previously not been cultivated. The firm, in its initial strategies, perceived the rural consumer as different from the urban or suburban customer. In readdressing the situation, it discovered that its assortments in rural areas were too limited and there were too many preconceived notions regarding what the Nebraska farmer really wanted. The firm discovered that the rural consumer didn't always shop for bib overalls and shovels but shopped for microwave ovens and the same things everyone else did.

One goal was not to attract more customers but to get the customer coming in the door to spend more. Once in the store the customer was thought to demonstrate more divergent tastes. The upper income consumer would buy more health and beauty aids, cameras and sporting goods. The lower income consumer would buy toys and clothing.

In the process of trying to capture a larger share of the market and get people to spend more, the firm began to recognize a market that was more upscale. When consumer research was conducted and management examined the profile of the trade area and the profile of the person who shopped at Kmart in the past month, they were found to be identical. Kmart was predominantly serving the suburban consumer in suburban locations. In 1997 Kmart's primary target customers were women, between the ages of 25 and 45 years old, with children at home and with household incomes between $20,000 and $50,000 per year. The core Kmart shopper averaged 4.3 visits to a Kmart store per month. The purchase amount per visit was $40. The purchase rate was 95% during a store visit. The firm estimated that 180 million people shopped at Kmart in an average year.

In lifestyle research in markets served by the firm, Kmart determined there were more 2-income families, families were having fewer children, there were more working wives, and customers tended to be homeowners. Customers were very careful how they spent their money and were perceived as wanting quality. This was a distinct contrast to the 1960s and early 1970s, which tended to have the orientation of a "throw away" society. The customer had said, "What we want is products that will last longer. We'll have to pay more for them but will still want them and at the lowest price possible." Customers wanted better quality products but still demanded competitive prices. According to a Kmart Annual Report, "Consumers today are well educated and informed. They want good value and they know it when they see it. Price remains a key consideration, but the consumers' new definition of value includes quality as well as price."

Corporate management at Kmart considered the discount department store to be a mature idea. Although maturity was sometimes looked on with disfavor, Kmart executives felt that this did not mean a lack of profitability or lack of opportunity to increase sales. The industry was perceived as being "reborn." It was in this context, in the 1990s, that a series of new retailing strategies, designed to upgrade the Kmart image, were developed.

The 1990 Renewal Program

The strategies that emerged to confront a changing environment were the result of an overall reexamination of existing corporate strategies. This program included accelerated store expansion and refurbishing, capitalizing on dominant lifestyle departments, centralized merchandising, more capital investment in retail automation, an aggressive and focused advertising program, and continued growth through new specialty retail formats.

The initial 1990, 5-year, $2.3 billion program involved virtually all Kmart discount stores. There would be approximately 250 new full-size Kmart stores, 620 enlargements, 280 relocations, and 30 closings. In addition 1,260 stores would be refurbished to bring their layout and fixtures up to new store standards. Another program, introduced in 1996, resulted in an additional $1.1 billion being spent to upgrade Kmart stores. By year-end 1999, 1,860 new "Big Kmart" stores offered more pleasant shopping experiences thanks to the updated and easy-to-shop departmental adjacencies, better signing, lighting, wider aisles, and more attractive in-store presentation.

One area receiving initial attention was improvement in the way products were displayed. The traditional Kmart layout was by product category. Often these locations for departments were holdovers from the variety store. Many departments would not give up prime locations. As part of the new marketing strategy, the shop concept was introduced. Management recognized that it had a sizable "do-it-yourself" store. As planning management discussed the issue, "nobody was aware of the opportunity. The hardware department was right smack in the center of the store because it was always there. The paint department was over here and the electrical department was over there." "All we had to do," management contended, "was put them all in 1 spot and everyone could see that we had a very respectable 'do-it-yourself' department." The concept resulted in a variety of new departments such as "Soft Goods for the Home," "Kitchen Korners," and "Home Electronic Centers." The goal behind each department was to sell an entire lifestyle-orientated concept to consumers, making goods complementary so shoppers would want to buy several interrelated products rather than just 1 item.

Name brands were added in soft and hard goods as management recognized that the customer transferred the product quality of branded goods to perceptions of private label merchandise. In the eyes of Kmart management, "if you sell Wrangler, there is good quality. Then the private label must be good quality." The company increased its emphasis on trusted national brands such as Rubbermaid, Procter & Gamble, and Kodak, and put emphasis on major strategic vendor relationships. In addition it began to enhance its private label brands in apparel such as Kathy Ireland, Jaclyn Smith, Route 66, and Sesame Street. Additional private label merchandise included K Gro in home gardening, American Fare in grocery and consumables, White-Westinghouse in appliances and Penske Auto Centers in automotive services. Some private labels were discontinued following review.

Kmart hired Martha Stewart, an upscale Connecticut author of lavish best-selling books on cooking and home entertaining, as its "lifestyle spokesperson and consultant." Martha Stewart was featured as a corporate symbol for housewares and associated products in advertising and in store displays. Management visualized her as the next Betty Crocker, a fictional character created some years ago by General Mills, Inc., and a representative of its interest in "lifestyle" trends. The "Martha Stewart Everyday" home fashion product line was introduced in 1995 and expanded in 1996 and 1997. A separate division was established to manage strategy for all Martha Stewart label goods and programs. Merchandise was featured in the redesigned once-a-week Kmart newspaper circular that carried the advertising theme: "The quality you need, the price you want."

Several thousand prices were reduced to maintain "price leadership across America." As management noted, "it is absolutely essential that we provide our customers with good value—quality products at low prices." Although lowering of prices hurt margins and contributed importantly to an earnings decline, management felt that unit turnover of items with lowered prices increased significantly to "enable Kmart to maintain its pricing leadership that will have a most positive impact on our business in the years ahead."

A "centralized merchandising system" was introduced to improve communication. A computerized, highly automated replenishment system tracked how quickly merchandise sold and just as quickly, put fast-moving items back on the shelves. Satellite capability and a Point-of-Sale (POS) scanning system were introduced as part of the program. Regular, live satellite communication from Kmart headquarters to the stores would allow senior management to communicate with store managers and allow for questions and answers. The POS scanning system allowed a record of every sale and transmission of the data to headquarters. This enabled Kmart to respond quickly to what's new, what's in demand, and what would keep customers coming back.

The company opened its first Super Kmart Center in 1992. The format combined general merchandise and food with emphasis upon customer service and convenience and ranged in size from 135,000 to 190,000 square feet with more than 40,000 grocery items. The typical Super Kmart operated 7 days a week, 24 hours a day, and generated high traffic and sales volume. The centers also featured wider shopping aisles, appealing displays, and pleasant lighting to enrich the shopping experience. Super Kmarts featured in-house bakeries, USDA fresh meats, fresh seafood, delicatessens, cookie kiosks, cappuccino bars, in-store eateries and food courts, and fresh carry-out salad bars. In many locations, the center provided customer services like video rental, dry cleaning, shoe repair, beauty salons, optical shops, express shipping services, as well as a full line of traditional Kmart merchandise. To enhance the appeal of the merchandise assortment, emphasis was placed on "cross merchandising." For example, toasters were featured above the fresh baked breads, kitchen gadgets were positioned across the aisle from produce and baby centers featured everything from baby food to toys. At the end of 1999, the company operated 105 Super Kmart stores.

The Planning Function

Corporate planning at Kmart was the result of executives, primarily the senior executive, recognizing change. The role played by the senior executive was to get others to recognize that nothing is good forever. "Good planning," was perceived as the result of those who recognized that at some point they would have to get involved. "Poor Planning," was done by those who didn't recognize the need for it. When they did, it was too late to survive. Good planning, if done on a regular and timely basis, was assumed to result in improved performance. Kmart's Michael Wellman then Director of Planning and Research contended, "planning, as we like to stress, is making decisions now to improve performance tomorrow. Everyone looks at what may happen tomorrow, but the planners are the ones who make decisions today. That's where I think too many firms go wrong. They think they are planning because they are writing reports and are aware of changes. They don't say, 'because of this, we must decide today to spend this money to do this to accomplish this goal in the future.'"

Kmart management believed that the firm had been very successful in the area of strategic planning. "When it became necessary to make significant changes in the way we were doing business," Michael Wellman suggested, "that was accomplished on a fairly timely basis." When the organization made the change in the 1960s, it recognized there was a very powerful investment opportunity and capitalized on it—far beyond what anyone else would have done. "We just opened stores," he continued, "at a great, great pace. Management, when confronted with a crisis, would state, 'It's the economy, or it's this, or that, but it's not the essential way we are doing business.'" He noted, "Suddenly management would recognize that the economy may stay like this forever. We need to improve the situation and then do it." Strategic planning was thought to arise out of some difficult times for the organization.

Kmart had a reasonably formal planning organization that involved a constant evaluation of what was happening in the marketplace, what competition was doing, and what kinds of opportunities were available. Management felt a need to diversify because it would not be a viable company unless it was growing. Management felt it was not going to grow with the Kmart format forever. It needed growth and opportunity, particularly for a company that was able to open 200 stores on a regular basis. Michael Wellman, Director of Planning and Research, felt that, "Given a 'corporate culture' that was accustomed to challenges, management would have to find ways to expend that energy. A corporation that is successful," he argued, "has to continue to be successful. It has to have a basic understanding of corporate needs and be augmented by a much more rigorous effort to be aware of what's going on in the external environment."

A planning group at Kmart represented a number of functional areas of the organization. Management described it as an "in-house consulting group" with some independence. It was made up of (1) financial planning, (2) economic and consumer analysis, and (3) operations research. The Chief Executive Officer (CEO) was identified as the primary planner of the organization.

Reorganization and Restructuring

Kmart financial performance for 1993 was clearly disappointing. The company announced a loss of $974 million on sales of $34,156,000 for the fiscal year ended January 26, 1994. Chairman Antonini, noting the deficit, felt it occurred primarily because of lower margins in the U.S. Kmart stores division. "Margin erosion," he said, "stemmed in part from intense industry-wide pricing pressure throughout 1993." He was confident, however, that Kmart was on track with its renewal program to make the more than 2,350 U.S. Kmart stores more "competitive, on-trend, and cutting merchandisers." Tactical Retail Solutions, Inc., estimated that during Mr. Antonini's 7-year tenure with the company, Kmart's market share in the discount arena fell to 23% from 35%. Other retail experts suggested that because the company had struggled for so long to have the right merchandise in the stores at the right time, it had lost customers to competitors. An aging customer base was also cited.

In early 1995, following the posting of its eighth consecutive quarter of disappointing earnings, Kmart's Board of Directors announced that Joseph Antonini would be replaced as Chairman. It named Donald S. Perkins, former chairman of Jewel Companies, Inc., and a Kmart Director, to the position. Mr. Antonini relinquished his position as President and Chief Executive Officer in March. After a nationwide search, Floyd Hall, 57, and former Chairman and CEO of the Target discount store division of the Dayton-Hudson Corporation, was appointed Chairman, President and Chief Executive Officer of Kmart in June of 1995.

The company concluded the disposition of many noncore assets in 1996, including the sale of the Borders group, OfficeMax, the Sports Authority, and Coles Myer. During the 1990s, it also closed a large number of underperforming stores in the United States and cleared out $700 million in aged and discontinued inventory in the remaining stores.

In 1996, Kmart converted 152 of its traditional stores to feature a new design that was referred to as the high-frequency format. These stores were named Big Kmart. The stores emphasized those departments that were deemed that most important to core customers and offered an increased mix of high frequency, everyday basics and consumables in the pantry area located at the front of each store. These items were typically priced at a 1 to 3 percentage differential from the leading competitors in each market and served to increase inventory turnover and gross margin dollars. In an addition to the pantry area, Big Kmart stores featured improved lighting, new signage that was easier to see and read, and adjacencies that created a smoother traffic flow. In 1999, 588 stores were converted to the new Big Kmart format bringing the total to 1,860. Other smaller stores would be updated to a "best of Big Kmart" prototype.

Kmart launched its first e-commerce site in 1998. The initial Kmart.com offered a few products and was not considered a successful venture. In 1999, it partnered with SOFTBANK Venture Capital, who provided technical expertise, experienced personnel, and initial capital to create an Internet site 60% owned by Kmart. BlueLight.com increased the number of Kmart products it offered online to about 65,000 from 1,250. It planned to boost the number to 100,000 by year-end 2000 and possibly to millions of items in the future.

Major changes were made to the management team. In total, 23 of the company's 37 corporate officers were new to the company's team since 1995. The most dramatic restructuring had taken place in the merchandising organization where all 4 of the general merchandise managers responsible for buying organizations joined Kmart since 1995. In addition, 15 new divisional vice presidents joined Kmart during 1997. Significant changes also were made to the Board of Directors with 9 of 15 directors new to the company since 1995. A list of the Board of Directors and corporate officers at the beginning of 2000 is shown in **Exhibits 1** and **2.**

At the end of his tenure, Floyd Hall announced that the company mandate in the year and century ahead was to create sustained growth that would profitably leverage all of the core strengths of the firm. The corporate mission in 2000 was "to become the discount store of choice for low- and middle-income households by satisfying their routine and seasonal shopping needs as well as, or better than, the competition." Management believed that the actions taken by Charles Conaway, the new president, would have a dramatic impact on how customers perceived Kmart, how frequently they shopped in the stores, and how much they would buy on each visit. Increasing customer's frequency and the amount they purchased each visit were seen as having a dramatic impact on the company's efforts to increase its profitability.

Financial Situation

Kmart's financial position is shown in **Exhibits 4**, **5**, **6** and **7**. A 5-year (2000–1996) record of financial performance of Kmart is shown in **Exhibit 6**. In FY 1990, Kmart's sales were $32,070,000,000, and Wal-Mart's sales were $32,601,594,000. In FY 1991, Kmart's sales were up $35,925,000,000 (an increase $3,855,000,000 or 12.02%), while Wal-Mart's sales increased to $165,013,000,000 (an increase of $132,411,406,000 or 406.15%). Wal-Mart's sales increase was 34.347 times larger than Kmart's sales increase. Wal-Mart's FY 1999, net income was $5,575,000,000 compared with Kmart's net income of $403,000,000. Kmart had 1,860 Big Kmart stores, 105 Super Kmart Centers, and 202 Discount stores for a total of 2,167. Wal-Mart had 2,373 Wal-Mart stores, 512 SAM's Clubs, and 1,104 Supercenters, for a total of 3,989 stores.

Exhibit 4

Consolidated Operating Statements: Kmart Corporation, 1998–99
(Dollar amounts in millions, except per share data)

Fiscal Years Ending	2000	1999	1998
Sales	$35,925	$33,674	$32,183
Cost of sales, buying and occupancy	28,102	26,319	25,152
Gross margin	7,823	7,355	7,031
Selling, general and administrative expenses	6,523	6,245	6,136
Voluntary early retirement programs	—	19	114
Continuing income before interest, income taxes and dividends on convertible preferred securities of subsidiary trust	1,300	1,091	781
Interest expense, net	280	293	363
Income tax provision	337	230	120
Dividends on convertible preferred securities Of subsidiary trust, net of income taxes of $27, $27, and $26	50	50	49
Net income from continuing operations	633	518	249
Discontinued operations, net of income taxes of $(124)	(230)	—	—
Net income	$ 403	$ 518	$ 249
Basic earnings per common share			
Net income from continuing operations	$ 1.29	$ 1.05	$ .51
Discontinued operations	(.47)	—	—
Net income	.82	1.05	.51
Diluted earnings per common share			
Net income from continuing operations	$ 1.22	$ 1.01	$ .51
Discontinued operations	(.41)	—	—
Net Income	$ .81	$ 1.01	$ .51
Basic weighed average shares (millions)	491.7	492.1	487.1
Diluted weighted average shares (millions)	561.7	564.9	491.7

Note:
1. The company's fiscal year is February through January.

Source: Kmart Corporation, *1999 Annual Report.*

Exhibit 5

Consolidated Balance Sheet: Kmart Corporation
(Dollar amounts in millions)

Fiscal Year Ending January 31[1]	2000	1999	1998	1997	1996
Assets					
Current Assets					
Cash and Equivalents	$ 344.0	$ 710.0	$ 498.0	$ 406.0	$ 1,095.0
Receivables	0.0	0.0	0.0	0.0	0.0
Inventories	7,101.0	6,536.0	6,367.0	6,354.0	6,635.0
Other Current Assets	715.0	584.0	611.0	973.0	1,092.0
Total current assets	8,160.0	7,830.0	7,476.0	7,733.0	8,822.0
Non-Current Assets					
Property, Plant & Equipment, Gross	11,554.0	10,778.0	10,402.0	10,768.0	10,052.0
Accum. Depreciation & Depletion	5,144.0	4,864.0	4,659.0	5,028.0	4,751.0
Property, Plant & Equipment, Net	6,410.0	5,914.0	5,743.0	5,740.0	5,301.0
Intangibles	0.0	0.0	0.0	0.0	0.0
Other Non-Current Assets	534.0	422.0	339.0	813.0	1,274.0
Total Non-Current Assets	6,944.0	6,336.0	6,082.0	6,553.0	6,575.0
Total assets	**$15,104.0**	**$14,166.0**	**$13,558.0**	**$14,286.0**	**$15,397.0**
Liabilities & shareholder's equity					
Current Liabilities					
Accounts Payable	$ 2,204.0	$ 2,047.0	$ 1,923.0	$ 2,009.0	$ 1,993.0
Short Term Debt	66.0	77.0	78.0	156.0	7.0
Other Current Liabilities	1,806.0	1,567.0	1,273.0	1,437.0	1,264.0
Total Current Liabilities	4,076.0	3,691.0	3,274.0	3,602.0	3,264.0
Non-Current Liabilities					
Long Term Debt	2,773.0	2,629.0	2,904.0	3,599.0	5,564.0
Deferred Income Taxes	0.0	0.0	0.0	0.0	0.0
Other Non-Current Liabilities	965.0	883.0	965.0	1,013.0	1,289.0
Minority Interest	986.0	984.0	981.0	980.0	0.0
Total Non-Current Liabilities	4,724.0	4,496.0	4,850.0	5,592.0	6,853.0
Total Liabilities	8,800.0	8,187.0	8,124.0	9,194.0	10,117.0
Shareholder's Equity					
Preferred Stock Equity	0.0	0.0	0.0	0.0	0.0
Common Stock Equity	6,304.0	5,979.0	5,434.0	5,092.0	5,280.0
Total liabilities & stock equity	**$15,104.0**	**$14,166.0**	**$13,558.0**	**$14,286.0**	**$15,397.0**

Note:
1. The company's fiscal year is February through January.

Source: Kmart Corporation, *1999 Annual Report.*

Exhibit 6

Consolidated Selected Financial Data: Kmart Corporation
(Dollar amounts in millions, except per share data)

Fiscal Year Ending January 31	2000	1999	1998	1997	1996
Sales	$35,925.0	$33,674.0	$32,183.0	$31,437.0	$34,389.0
Cost of Sales	27,332.0	25,648.0	24,492.0	23,736.0	26,267.0
Gross Operating Profit	8,593.0	8,026.0	7,691.0	7,701.0	8,122.0
Selling, General & Admin. Expense	6,523.0	6,264.0	6,136.0	6,274.0	7,554.0
Other Taxes	0.0	0.0	0.0	0.0	0.0
EBITDA	2,070.0	1,762.0	1,555.0	1,427.0	568.0
Depreciation & Amortization	770.0	671.0	660.0	654.0	729.0
EBIT	1,300.0	1,091.0	895.0	773.0	(161.0)
Other Income, Net	0.0	0.0	0.0	10.0	303.0
Total Income Avail for Interest Exp.	1,300.0	1,091.0	781.0	783.0	(266.0)
Interest Expense	280.0	293.0	363.0	453.0	446.0
Minority Interest	50.0	50.0	49.0	31.0	0.0
Pre-tax Income	970.0	748.0	369.0	299.0	(712.0)
Income Taxes	337.0	230.0	120.0	68.0	(222.0)
Special Income/Charges	0.0	0.0	(114.0)	0.0	(408.0)
Net Income from Cont. Operations	633.0	518.0	249.0	231.0	(490.0)
Net Income from Discont. Opers.	(230.0)	0.0	0.0	(451.0)	(30.0)
Net Income from Total Operations	403.0	518.0	249.0	(220.0)	(520.0)
Normalized Income	633.0	518.0	363.0	231.0	(82.0)
Extraordinary Income	0.0	0.0	0.0	0.0	0.0
Income from Cum. Eff. of Acct. Chg.	0.0	0.0	0.0	0.0	0.0
Income from Tax Loss Carryforward	0.0	0.0	0.0	0.0	0.0
Other Gains (Losses)	0.0	0.0	0.0	0.0	(51.0)
Total net income	**403.0**	**518.0**	**249.0**	**(220.0)**	**(571.0)**
Dividends Paid per Share	0.00	0.00	0.00	0.00	0.61
Preferred Dividends	0.00	0.00	0.00	0.00	0.00
Basic EPS from Cont. Operations	1.29	1.05	0.51	0.48	(0.51)
Basic EPS from Discont. Operations	(0.47)	0.00	0.00	(0.94)	(0.63)
Basic EPS from Total Operations	0.82	1.05	0.51	(0.46)	(1.14)
Diluted EPS from Cont. Operations	1.22	1.01	0.51	0.48	(0.51)
Diluted EPS from Discont. Operations	(0.41)	0.00	0.00	(0.94)	(0.63)
Diluted EPS from Total Operations	0.81	1.01	0.51	(0.46)	(1.14)

Note:
1. The company's fiscal year is February through January.

Source: <moneycentral.msn.com/investor/invsub/results/statemnt.asp?Symbol=km> (June 21, 2001).

Exhibit 7

Comparison of Financial Performance: Kmart Corporation and Wal-Mart Stores, Inc.
(For Fiscal Year February 1–January 31)
(Dollar amounts in thousands)

A. Kmart Financial Performance

Fiscal Year	Sales	Assets	Net Income	Net Worth
2000	35,925,000	15,104,000	403,000	7,290,000
1999	33,674,000	14,166,000	518,000	6,963,000
1998	32,183,000	13,558,000	249,000	6,445,000
1997	31,437,000	14,286,000	(220,000)	6,146,000
1996	34,389,000	15,397,000	(571,000)	5,280,000
1995	34,025,000	17,029,000	296,000	6,032,000
1994	34,156,000	17,504,000	(974,000)	6,093,000
1993	37,724,000	18,931,000	941,000	7,536,000
1992	34,580,000	15,999,000	859,000	6,891,000
1991	32,070,000	13,899,000	756,000	5,384,000

B. Wal-Mart Financial Performance

Fiscal Year[1,2]	Sales	Assets	Net Income	Net Worth
2000	165,013,000	70,349,000	5,377,000	25,834,000
1999	137,634,000	49,996,000	4,430,000	21,112,000
1998	117,958,000	45,384,000	3,526,000	18,503,000
1997	104,859,000	39,604,000	3,056,000	17,143,000
1996	93,627,000	37,541,000	2,740,000	14,756,000
1995	82,494,000	32,819,000	2,681,000	12,726,000
1994	67,344,000	26,441,000	2,333,000	10,753,000
1993	55,484,000	20,565,000	1,995,000	8,759,000
1992	43,886,900	15,443,400	1,608,500	6,989,700
1991	32,601,594	11,388,915	1,291,024	5,365,524

Notes:
1. After taxes and extraordinary credit or charges.
2. Data from 1996, 1997, and 1998 reflect disposition of subsidiaries.

Sources: (A) *Fortune* financial analysis and Kmart Annual Reports. (B) Wal-Mart annual reports/*Fortune* financial analysis.

Notes

Robert Berner, "Kmart's Earnings More Than Tripled in First Quarter," *Wall Street Journal* (May 14, 1998), p. A13.

Molly Brauer, "Kmart in Black 'in 6 Months,'" *Detroit Free Press* (January 26, 1996), p. E1.

"Where Kmart Goes Next Now That It's No. 2," *Business Week* (June 2, 1980), pp. 109–110, 114.

John Bussey, "Kmart Is Set to Sell Many of Its Roots to Rapid-American Corp's McCrory," *Wall Street Journal* (April 6, 1987), p. 24.

Eleanore Carruth, "Kmart Has to Open Some New Doors on the Future," *Fortune* (July 1977), pp. 143–150, 153–154.

Calmetta Coleman, "BlueLight.com Aims to Coax Kmart Shoppers Online," *Wall Street Journal* (June 19, 2000), p. B4.

Calmetta Coleman, "Kmart Lease Pledge May Slow Rebound," *Wall Street Journal* (May 24, 1999), p. A3.

Calmetta Coleman, "Kmart's New CEO Outlines Plans for Fast Changes," *Wall Street Journal* (July 27, 2000), p. B4.

Calmetta Coleman, "Kmart Sees $740 Million Pretax Charge from Closing 72 Stores, Other Changes," *Wall Street Journal* (July 26, 2000), p. B10.

Calmetta Coleman, "Kmart Selects CVS President to Be Its CEO," *Wall Street Journal* (June 1, 2000).

Calmetta Coleman, "Kmart's Wave of Insider Sales Continues Amid Questions About Retailer's Plans," *Wall Street Journal* (June 23, 1999), p. A4.

Robert E. Dewar, "The Kresge Company and the Retail Revolution," *University of Michigan Business Review* (July 2, 1975), p. 2.

Christina Duff and Joann S. Lubin, "Kmart Board Ousts Antonini as Chairman," *Wall Street Journal* (January 18, 1995), p. A3.

Vickie Elmer and Joann Muller, "Retailer Needs Leader, Vision," *Detroit Free Press* (March 22, 1995), pp. 1A, 9A.

Mark Frankel, "Attention, Kmart Grocery Shoppers," *Business Week* (August 2, 1999), p. 49.

Melinda G. Guiles, "Attention, Shoppers: Stop That Browsing And Get Aggressive," *Wall Street Journal* (June 16, 1987), pp. 1, 21.

Melinda G. Guiles, "Kmart, Bruno's Join to Develop 'Hypermarkets'," *Wall Street Journal* (September 8, 1987), p. 17.

Paul Ingrassia, "Attention Non Kmart Shoppers: A Blue-Light Special Just For You," *Wall Street Journal* (October 6, 1987), p. 42.

Kmart Corporation, *Annual Report*, Troy, Michigan, 1990.

Kmart Corporation, *Annual Report*, Troy, Michigan, 1995.

Kmart Corporation, *Annual Report*, Troy, Michigan, 1996.

Kmart Corporation, *Annual Report*, Troy, Michigan, 1997.

Kmart Corporation, *Annual Report*, Troy, Michigan, 1999.

Kmart Corporation, *Kmart Fact Book*, Troy, Michigan, 1997.

Kathryn Kranhold, "Kmart Hopes to Steer Teens to Route 66," *Wall Street Journal* (July 27, 2000), p. B14.

Jerry Main, "Kmart's Plan to Be Born Again," *Fortune* (September 21, 1981), pp. 74–77, 84–85.

Faye Rice, "Why Kmart Has Stalled," *Fortune* (October 9, 1989), p. 79.

Francine Schwadel, "Kmart to Speed Store Openings, Renovations," *Wall Street Journal* (February 27, 1990), p. 3.

Bill Saporito, "Is Wal-Mart Unstoppable?," *Fortune* (May 6, 1991), pp. 50–59.

Patrica Sternad, "Kmart's Antonini Moves Far Beyond Retail 'Junk' Image," *Advertising Age* (July 25, 1988), pp. 1, 67.

Karen Talaski, "Kmart to Invest $2 Billion," *The Detroit News* (August 11, 2000), p. 1C.

Karen Talaski, "Kmart Profits Plunge Sharply," *The Detroit News* (May 12, 2000), p. 1B.

Michael Wellman, Interview with Director of Planning and Research, Kmart Corporation (August 6, 1984).

David Woodruff, "Will Kmart Ever Be a Silk Purse?," *Business Week* (January 22, 1990), p. 46.

CASE 22

Gardner Distributing Co.—"Providing Products for Plants and Pets"

Tom Hinthorne

It was May 1999 and the end of another beautiful day in Montana's Big Sky Country as the Delta flight descended into its final approach to the Logan International Airport in Billings, Montana (population 85,000). Butch Tonigan, 54 years of age, President and sole shareowner of the Gardner Distributing Co., was idly contrasting the 5 weeks he had just spent vacationing in Puerto Vallarta, Mexico, with his business situation:

> The people were so friendly and the pace of life was so slow and easy . . . I could easily retire there . . . 2 years ago I was mired in the daily problems of a struggling business . . . trying to form a management team that would allow me to gradually disengage from the business . . . now the team's in place . . . we have a mission statement and objectives, but we *must* define our strategies . . . things are changing so fast . . . we're still vulnerable, and vulnerable is 1 step away from dead!

In 1998, Gardner reported sales of $13.2 million (**Exhibit 1**) on assets of $1.8 million (**Exhibit 2**). The company employed 37 people. Gardner purchased, sold, and distributed products in 3 businesses:

1. **Iams (pronounced "eyems") premium pet food products** accounted for 68% of sales. Gardner was a regional distributor for Iams and operated under Iams's direction in a very competitive market. Iams's directive to its distributors was to reduce operating costs. Yet its strategy from the distributors' perspective was unclear. Moreover, distributors' profit margins were being squeezed.

2. **Pet supplies** accounted for 14% of sales. (The pet supplies were not Iams's products.) The entry of specialty retailers into Gardner's market (e.g., PETsMART and PETCO) was expected to eliminate many of the independent pet supply retailers—Butch's customers.

3. **Lawn and garden supplies** accounted for 18% of sales and might have the greatest potential for growth, but this was also a seasonal business segment.

This case was prepared by Professor Tom Hinthorne of Montana State University—Billings. This case was published in the *Case Research Journal* (Spring 2000), pp. 1–24. All other rights reserved jointly to the author and the North American Case Research Association (NACRA). Copyright © 2000 by the *Case Research Journal* and Tom Hinthorne. Reprinted by permission. The author would like to acknowledge the support of several anonymous reviewers; Professors William Cunningham, Howard Feldman, Donald Howard, Charles Matthews, Marilyn Okleshen, John Seeger, and Joanne Sheridan; Todd Vralsted, Account Executive, Morgan Stanley-Dean Witter; and many students, including Daniel Cahill. Special thanks go to Butch Tonigan, Glen Brown, Rob Chouinard, Milan Cook, Mike Hofferber, and Don Hefner at the Gardner Distributing Co. and Professor Deborah Ettington at Eastern Michigan University.

Exhibit 1

Income Statement: Gardner Distribution Co.
(Dollar amounts in millions)

Year Ending December 31	1998	1997	1996	1995	1994
Sales—Billings					
Iams pet food	$ 5,082	$ 5,140	$ 5,062	$ 4,453	$ 3,206
Pet supplies	1,839	2,011	2,208	2,408	2,017
Lawn & garden	2,336	2,151	1,902	2,156	2,038
Total Billings	9,257	9,302	9,172	9,017	7,261
Sales—Spokane					
Iams pet food	2,305	2,334	2,584	2,756	3,115
Iams national accts.	1,595	1,241	951	486	*
Pet supplies	*	*	*	*	*
Total Spokane	3,900	3,575	3,535	3,242	3,115
Total sales	13,157	12,877	12,707	12,259	10,376
Cost of goods sold	10,356	10,140	9,964	9,495	7,893
Gross profit	2,801	2,737	2,743	2,764	2,483
Operating expenses—Billings					
Warehouse	333	343	348	373	335
Delivery	450	439	478	384	311
Sales	727	699	441	359	331
Administration	339	476	594	597	501
Total	1,849	1,957	1,861	1,713	1,478
Operating expenses—Spokane					
Warehouse	76	94	92	106	88
Delivery	187	178	175	195	158
Sales	–	–	140	125	94
Administration	93	104	86	73	70
Total	356	376	493	499	410
Total Operating Expenses	2,205	2,333	2,354	2,212	1,888
Net income (pre tax)	596	404	389	552	595
Estimated income tax					
U.S. tax	225	149	143	208	225
State tax	66	44	43	61	65
Net income	305	211	203	283	305
Return on sales					
Pre-tax	4.53%	3.14%	3.06%	4.50%	5.73%
After-tax (est.)	2.32%	1.64%	1.60%	2.31%	2.94%
Average tax rate	48.8%	47.8%	47.8%	48.7%	48.7%

* Indicates amount is relatively small and included in the Billings amount.

Source: Company records except for estimation of taxes and net income.

Exhibit 2

Balance Sheet: Gardner Distributing Co.

Year Ending December 31	1998	1997	1996	1995	1994
Assets					
Accounts receivable	$ 693	$ 595	$ 996	$1,077	$ 860
Inventory					
Iams—Billings	289	276	250	181	141
Spokane	184	199	280	168	165
Pet supplies	290	447	572	589	497
Lawn and garden	222	192	267	229	372
Total inventory	985	1,114	1,369	1,167	1,175
Current assets	1,678	1,709	2,365	2,244	2,035
Fixed assets (net)	74	195	208	203	46
Total assets	$1,752	$1,904	$2,573	$2,447	$2,081
Liabilities and equity					
Accounts payable	$ 287	$ 230	$ 335	$ 290	$ 186
Notes payable					
Bank		71	300	200	120
Officers[1]	383	618	826	568	294
Other	55	60	97	102	102
Current liabilities	725	979	1,558	1,160	702
Long-term liabilities		78	212	327	358
Stockholders' equity					
Common stock	104	104	104	104	104
Retained earnings					
C corporation	82	82	82	82	82
S corporation	245	257	257	257	257
Accumulated S corp. net income	596	404	360	517	578
Total equity	1,027	847	803	960	1,021
Total liabilities and **shareholders' equity**	$1,752	$1,904	$2,573	$2,447	$2,081

Note:
1. The note payable to officers is money that Butch lent the corporation.

Source: Company records.

Most Iams distributors sold only Iams products. Gardner was the only Iams distributor that sold lawn and garden supplies. The pet supplies and lawn and garden businesses gave Gardner options and created synergies.

As Butch headed for the baggage claim area, he met Rob Chouinard, General Manager of Gardner Distributing Co. (**Exhibit 3**). Rob had worked for Colgate-Palmolive and Supervalu. Supervalu was a large wholesaler and retailer of grocery products. When he arrived in December 1996, there was no strategic planning and minimal budgeting. By 1998, the team was operating to a budget. By 1999, the team had developed a statement of purpose, mission, and objectives (**Exhibit 4**). The team members worked well together and shared common expectations about the business, but they had yet to define Gardner's strategies.

Rob's greeting was enthusiastic. In March 1999, he and Butch had attended the Iams distributors meeting in Cancun, Mexico; and Rob had fond memories of that trip. Rob was also enthusiastic because he had been getting calls from other distributors. They had heard from Iams about Gardner's success in opening new accounts, and they wanted to know how Gardner was doing it.

At the Iams meeting in Cancun, Butch had told the Iams people, "We are aggressively looking for more volume in our region. We also want to expand our business territory, and we hope Iams will support this." The Iams people were very receptive to these comments.

Background

Butch grew up in the small town of Aberdeen, South Dakota. He graduated from the University of North Dakota in 1967 with a degree in marketing, and he worked part-time for Sears, Roebuck and Co. while he was at the university. His father was the store manager for Sears in Aberdeen.

After graduation, Butch went to work for Sears as a management trainee in Grand Forks, North Dakota. In 1970, he was promoted to Assistant Store Manager in Butte, Montana. In 1972, he was promoted to Merchandise Manager in Great Falls, Montana. By 1976, the Sears culture was changing. The store managers were losing their autonomy, so Butch left Sears. As he explained, "I was single. I toured the western U.S. for 3 months and sort of lived like a hobo."

Exhibit 3
Gardner Distributing Co., Organizational Chart and Biographies

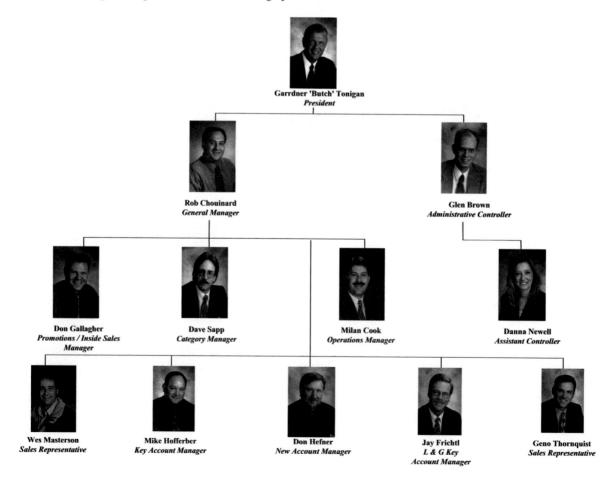

Exhibit 3
Gardner Distributing Co., Organizational Chart and Biographies (*continued*)

Butch Tonigan – President
After 14 years in management with Sears, Roebuck & Co. followed by several years as a managing partner of a predecessor company, Graham and Ross, Butch started Gardner Distributing Co. with the aid of "smoke and mirrors" and very little liquid capital. Butch graduated from the University of North Dakota in 1967 with a Bachelor of Science in Business Administration (BSBA) degree. Butch likes to think of himself as a good judge of people and recognizes that his employees are the most valuable asset of Gardner Distributing Co. Focusing his efforts on developing the capacity of the company's management and capital resources in preparation for triggering Gardner's next growth stage is his primary current objective, all while planning for the succession of his company.

Rob Chouinard – General Manager
Hired in 1996 as a key candidate in the company's succession planning strategy, Rob brings to the company those leadership skills important to directing the company's management toward meeting the company's strategic plans. Rob graduated from Eastern Montana College in 1987 while learning the distribution business from the bottom up by working part-time in the Supervalu distribution warehouse. In 1988 Rob began his career as a Territory Sales Manager for Colgate Palmolive followed by a position as a Sales Consultant for the Supervalu Corporation. In 1990 Rob was promoted to a management position with Supervalu as a Category Buyer, which led to yet another promotion to that of Category Merchandise Manager. Rob works closely with Butch as President and Glen as Administrative Controller developing and executing the company's strategic plans.

Glen Brown – Administrative Controller
Glen truly created his own position with Gardner. Joining Gardner in 1988 while still a student at Eastern Montana College, Glen juggled his work and student time to earn a Bachelor of Science in Business Administration (BSBA) degree in 1990 and then go on to receive his CPA certification in 1994. Starting as an invoicing clerk, Glen proved his prowess at number crunching and computer skills to advance to Controller and eventually to Administrative Controller. Self taught in RPG computer programming, Glen creates in-house software to provide the company management with information to excel at their work. Glen works closely with Butch as President and Rob as General Manager in developing company strategy and planning.

Milan Cook – Operations Manager
A graduate of North Dakota State University with an Urban Forestry Degree, it didn't take long for Milan to realize that there weren't many trees in North Dakota. Milan started his career as a warehouse manager in a lawn and garden distributor's branch warehouse in Fargo, ND and then moved to Montana as a retail store manager of a lawn and garden, and pet supplies center. Recruited by Gardner in 1994 to manage its new branch distribution facility in Spokane, WA, Milan quickly demonstrated his ability to squeeze a dime out of a nickel and his management and personnel skills. In the newly created position as Operations Manager, Milan is transferring to the Billings headquarters where he will be responsible for meeting and exceeding vendor and industry standards of the company's operations in its present and future locations.

Don Gallagher – Promotions / Inside Sales Manager
Approaching the challenge of his job with the "can do" attitude from his training as an Army MP, Don supervises the inside sales team and develops marketing programs to grow incremental sales for the company. Joining Gardner in 1995, it didn't take long to see Don's "take no enemies" approach. Don works with vendors, inside and outside sales people and buyers to develop and administer sales promotions that work.

Danna Newell – Assistant Controller
The newest member to the Gardner team, Danna joined the company in 1998. After earning a degree in Finance from the University of Montana in 1991, Danna continued balancing a full-time job and school to pass the uniform CPA exam soon after joining Gardner. Danna quickly demonstrated her ability to collect past due receivables while keeping satisfied customers. As the Assistant Controller, Danna is training in all functions of the Administrative Controller position including accounting and information systems.

(*continued*)

Exhibit 3

Gardner Distributing Co., Organizational Chart and Biographies (*continued*)

Dave Sapp – Category Manager

Determined never to lose a sale because of an out of stock, Dave is responsible for buying more than 200 vendor lines and maintaining the best fill-rate and inventory turn-over ratios in our industries and throughout the history of the company. Dave joined Gardner in 1984 serving his stint in the warehouse and delivery before his promotion as a category buyer. With a Forestry Technician degree from the Montana University System and his customer service skills, Dave is responsible for much of the company's sales growth of professional horticultural products to commercial growers.

Jay Frichtl – L & G Key Account Manager

A true professional sales consultant to the professional horticultural customer, Jay joined Gardner in 1990 after over 9 years experience in retail lawn and garden center sales where he supervised the landscape division and learned garden center, nursery, and greenhouse management. Jay has been largely responsible for Gardner's dominating the horticulture grower and garden center market in the geographical markets Gardner serves.

Don Hefner – New Account Manager

Considered "bullet-proof" in his ability to win over new customers, Don's position as New Account Manager focuses nearly exclusively on adding retail distribution for the company by seeking and opening new independent retail dealers. Don grew up in retail sales, selling pet supplies before he was old enough to drive a car and going on to work in retail pet supplies sales until he joined Gardner in 1987. He draws on his retail experience, enthusiasm, and warm personality necessary to develop the rapport with a retail owner or manager and open them as a Gardner account.

Mike Hofferber – Key Account Manager

Mike and Butch first became acquainted when Butch hired Mike as a high school student to work his first job as part-time sales at Sears. Their careers parted and Mike went on to earn a B. S. degree in Business Management from Montana State University in 1978. Mike was hired as a Key Account Manager to assist Gardner's entry into serving the grocery, drug, and hardware multiple store chain accounts. Mike's past employment and management experience with Osco Drug, Coast to Coast Hardware, and over 10 years as Retail Sales Manager and General Manager of a regional food brokerage firm bring the insight, skills and knowledge required to enter this class of retailer customer trade.

Geno Thornquist – Sales Representative

Give him a program to sell and he draws on his previous training as a Pitney Bowes salesman to close the sale time after time. Geno is responsible for developing sales growth with assigned existing customers by increasing the number of product lines they purchase from Gardner and by creating enthusiasm for, and the execution of sales promotions and programs. After earning his BSBA degree from Eastern Montana College in 1991, Geno gained valuable experience in merchandising, promotional execution, and retail shelf management as a Retail Account Manager for Hershey. Geno joined Gardner in 1993 as a sales representative based out of Billings for Iams pet foods and pet supplies.

Wes Masterson – Sales Representative

Wes joined Gardner in 1994 as a distributor sales representative responsible for the new Iams territory served by the Spokane, WA branch facility. Graduating with both a B. A. in Business Administration and a B. A. in Psychology from the University of Washington, Wes has the educational background to assist the future growth of Gardner. With his sales and merchandising training from previous employment as a sales representative with Gallo Wine, Wes demonstrates his training by repeatedly gaining choice merchandise positioning and incremental shelf space in retail dealer locations. Never afraid to get his hands dirty, Wes is quick to reset retail shelf racks and displays to grow visibility and retail shelf position.

Exhibit 4
Purpose, Mission, and Objectives, May 1999: Gardner Distributing Co.

Purpose: The purpose of Gardner Distributing Co. is the distribution of premium pet foods, pet supplies, and horticultural supplies while improving the economic well being and quality of life of all stakeholders.

Mission: We will be the leading regional marketing and distributing company of premium pet foods, pet supplies, and horticultural products.

We will achieve a growth rate consistent with the expectations of our vendors and shareholders.

We will continuously improve employee performance and company processes.

We will earn the loyalty of our customers by consistently meeting their performance expectations.

We will create a sense of pride and long-term commitment for everyone associated with our company.

In all we do, we will be guided by the following principles:

We will act professionally and with integrity in all circumstances.
We will honor the intent of all our commitments, contracts, and governing laws.
We will build an environment of individual trust and respect.
We will provide an environment for employees to realize professional growth and development.
We will expect and reward excellence in all aspects of our business.

Objectives:
1. Achieve a minimum 15% increase each year in cash flow from company operations.

    (This objective was set in 1999. The reductions in accounts receivable and incentory increased Gardner's cash flow from operations, but this was a 1-time-only increase. As of May 1999, Gardner had not established a measure of historical cash flows against which it could measure the future cash flow performance of the management team.)

2. Expand retail distribution by achieving no less than a 15% annual increase each year in the number of A, B, and C class customer locations.

3. Develop and maintain to the satisfaction of the stockholder, contingent plans of action which assure the company's future viability is independent of any individual owner, employee, vendor, or customer.

Source: Company records.

In 1976, Butch returned to Great Falls and went to work for Graham and Ross, a family-owned retailer and wholesaler of farm supplies, pet supplies, and lawn and garden supplies in Montana and Wyoming. The company's sales grew from $2.5 million in 1976 to $4.6 million in 1980. Butch received stock options and purchased stock in the company. In 1980, he had the opportunity to spin off the pet supplies and lawn and garden businesses.

In the spin off, Butch received a small warehouse in Billings that was worth $40,000. Billings was growing much faster than Great Falls, so Butch decided to locate in Billings. Graham and Ross's Norwest Bank manager in Great Falls introduced Butch to the Norwest manager in Billings. As Butch explained:

In August 1980, I presented my business plan. I asked for a $330,000 credit line to finance sales of $1 million. I had $64,000 in inventory and trucks, but it was the $40,000 of real estate that the bank wanted for collateral. The oil and gas industry was booming in Billings. The banks had money, and I got the $330,000.

I used the loan to finance the spring lawn and garden inventory. We moved into the warehouse with 6 employees from Graham and Ross and started ordering merchandise for the spring. Then Ortho, my largest supplier, decided my financing wasn't good enough. They jerked the contract and gave it to another local distributor. Then I faced the possibility of losing other lines. Ortho was the key player in lawn and garden and an entry into many of the retailers. If you didn't have Ortho, you weren't a full-line lawn and garden distributor.

My plan was unraveling, but I didn't tell the bank. I convinced an Ortho distributor in Denver to sell to me at 3% over cost, and for 5 years I supplied my retailers with Ortho products from Denver and kept my business alive. Ortho gained market coverage with no credit risk. The other local distributor didn't like it. In 1986, they gave up the Ortho line, and we got it.

We plugged along in the first 6 years. In 1980, my equity was $104,000. The first year we lost $100,000. The second year we lost $30,000. I was afraid the bank was going to call the loan; but they stuck with me. In the third year, we made a profit. It was the sixth year before my equity was back where I started!

In 1987, we were in the right place at the right time. We got the Iams distributorship for eastern Montana. Iams had a distributor in Missoula that went belly-up, and they came to us. In the spring of 1994, we took on the distribution of Iams products in northern Idaho and eastern Washington with a warehouse and 8 people in Spokane.

By 1996, I was thinking about reducing my time involvement in the company. But I felt that Iams seemed to want distributors who managed the day-to-day operations, 50 weeks a year. A lot of guys were trying to do succession planning. They were nervous about it because Iams didn't seem to reinforce it. Yet all of us realized that for the survival of our companies that was what we had to do. We didn't want to be managing our businesses day-to-day all of our lives.

Everyone always came to me with his or her problems. What should I do about the flat tire on the truck? Can I have Friday off? What should I do about this customer's order? I loved to make these decisions, but it was becoming overwhelming, so I began to appoint some managers from within the company. Then, my biggest problem was learning to let the managers solve the problems!

In 1996, I decided to hire a Chief Operating Officer. I developed a case study of the company and asked the best candidates to analyze it. A local man talked to my customers and employees and carefully analyzed the business. I offered him the job in December, but he didn't want to move until after his March bonus was paid.

Then, as I thought about it, I realized I was not ready to make the move. In March, I withdrew the offer. I was nervous about turning the business over to someone else. Ironically, Rob had joined us in December 1996; and it was soon evident that he had the leadership skills we needed. I feel so fortunate! Rob came in and earned the respect of the employees!

In May 1999, Gardner's Iams territory spanned a sparsely settled area of rolling grasslands and mountains that included Montana (population 860,000), northern Idaho, eastern Washington, northern Wyoming, and western North and South Dakota. The other 2 businesses operated within this area. Billings was the largest city in Montana, and the largest city in the market was Spokane, Washington (population 200,000). The Continental Divide bisected the region. The summers were warm and pleasant, but the winters could be formidable, with temperatures ranging to 30 or 50 degrees below zero Fahrenheit. In the winter of 1996–1997, Billings received a record snowfall of 8.5 feet. As Butch noted:

> Part of our success is attributable to the fact that we operate in a part of the country that until recently hasn't been attractive to the competition. Most distributors don't like it here, it's too vast, there's too little business, and it's too hard to operate.

Gardner leased a 41,000-square-foot warehouse in Billings and a small warehouse in Spokane. The office facilities in the Billings warehouse were functional. The atmosphere was friendly and casual. The people were variously dressed—shorts, bib overalls, jeans, sports casual, and the occasional tie. The fixed assets included office and warehouse equipment. The trucks were leased from a company owned by Butch. The statements, "Gardner Distributing Co." and "Providing Products for Plants & Pets" were positioned prominently on the sides of the trailers.

Gardner was Subchapter S corporation. Originally, it was incorporated as an S corporation. It was then changed to a C corporation and then back to an S corporation. Butch later attributed the firm's stint as a C corporation to bad advice.

An S corporation did not pay income taxes. Pre-tax net income and losses were allocated to the shareowners based on the number of shares held. The pre-tax net income was taxed as personal income in the year it was incurred, even if it was not withdrawn from the business. Thus, the pre-tax net income from Gardner was combined with Butch's personal income and losses from other sources, and the total was taxed at the personal income tax rates.

Societal Forces

Gardner operated in 2 industries: (1) the pet supplies industry and (2) the lawn and garden industry. Several societal forces were affecting these industries in North America:

1. In 1999, economic conditions were supporting business development and consumer spending. The economy was growing; interest rates, unemployment rates, and inflation rates were relatively low; and personal discretionary income was rising. However, acquisitions, alliances, and mergers on a global scale were leading to consolidation and economies of scale in many industries.

2. Computer and communications technology was enabling small firms to compete effectively against larger rivals.

3. The rising level of discretionary income was enabling people to give their pets a better lifestyle and to improve their lawns and gardens.

4. The pet industry and particularly the lawn and garden industry were benefiting from the increasing number of retired people who had the money and the time to have and to pamper pets, lawns, and gardens. Marketing strategies recognized pets, lawns, and gardens created rewarding experiences for retired people.

5. The premium pet food industry was benefiting from people's desire to eat healthier foods, which carried over into pet foods. Some people wanted their pets to eat healthier foods too, and the premium pet food industry promoted an increasing awareness of this need.

6. Environmental consciousness had established a "green is good" mentality that benefited the lawn and garden industry. People expected firms and institutions to attractively landscape their facilities.

7. The increasing number of institutions that catered to retired people (e.g., country clubs, golf courses, retirement communities, etc.) were expected to be attractively landscaped and appropriately maintained.

8. Innovations in gardening (e.g., hydroponics, personal greenhouses, patio gardens, etc.) were increasing the size of the lawn and garden market.

9. The "1-stop-shopping" strategies of the mass retailers were making lawn and garden products more accessible to buyers. Special trips to a nursery were often unnecessary and more expensive than going to, say, a Wal-Mart or Home Depot.

The Competition

PREMIUM PET FOOD MANUFACTURERS

The Iams Company was a private firm located in Dayton, Ohio. Iams's annual sales were about $800 million. Iams targeted the premium dog and cat food markets with its Iams and Eukanuba (pronounced "you-caa-new-baa") brands. Iams had about 27% of the market.

Iams's primary competitor was Hill's Pet Nutrition, Inc., with its Science Diet brand. Hill's had about 33% of the market. Hill's was a subsidiary of Colgate-Palmolive. The Ralston Purina Co., the leader in mass-market pet-food sales, had about 15% of the premium pet food business. There were about 6 smaller competitors in the premium market. While all of the competitors promoted their products, Hill's in particular invested heavily in developing early brand loyalty among veterinarian students; and the retail profit margins on premium pet foods were significant. As Parker-Pope (1997) explained:

> Borrowing a page from pharmaceuticals companies, which routinely woo doctors to prescribe their drugs, Hill's has spent a generation cultivating its professional following. It spends hundreds of thousands of dollars a year funding university research and nutrition courses at every one of the 27 U.S. veterinary colleges. Once in practice, vets who sell Science Diet and other premium foods directly from their offices pocket profits of as much as 40%.

Iams had tried to establish its brands in the veterinary schools but had been only moderately successful. Butch felt that Hill's did a better job of marketing its "prescription diet" specialty products to veterinarians than Iams did.

Iams and Hill's monitored each other's actions closely. Hill's owned its distribution channels. Iams's policy was to use independent distributors, but its actions suggested that this policy might be changing. Iams had recently acquired the operations of a bankrupt distributor in California and Arizona. Iams's operating expenses in these operations were less than 10% of sales, and it was pressuring its distributors to reduce their operating expenses accordingly. However, as Rob pointed out, "The figures [operating expenses] weren't directly comparable."

Iams's strategy toward its distributors was unclear. As Butch explained:

> This is the mystery to us. We [the distributors] sensed that Iams sees a further consolidation of distributors, and maybe Iams is purposely leaving an environment where only the strongest will survive. I'm not sure we know where they're going. The market is changing so fast.

PET FOOD & PET SUPPLIES RETAILERS

The competition in premium pet foods and pet supplies was intensifying. For example, in Gardner's market, PETsMART, a specialty retailer of premium pet foods and animal supplies, was opening stores in Billings and Missoula, Montana. PETCO, a similar competitor, was opening a store in Great Falls, Montana. Both companies had recently opened stores in Spokane, Washington.

Iams sold direct to the "national accounts" (e.g., PETsMART and PETCO), and its distributors were paid a delivery fee to deliver the products. The national accounts were large-volume accounts, and there were no associated sales expenses for Gardner. So in this sense the accounts were attractive. However, Iams's sales to PETsMART and PETCO in Montana would reduce Gardner's gross profit percentage in the Iams business because the PETsMART and PETCO sales were low-margin volumes. Moreover, the entry of the specialty retailers was expected to reduce the number of independent pet stores who were currently Gardner's relatively higher-margin Iams customers. The margin on Iams sales was generally lower than in pet supplies and lawn and garden.

The independent pet store faced increasing competition from the specialty retailers—also known as "big box" stores—and the mass merchandisers (e.g., Wal-Mart was the largest pet food retailer). The independent pet store averaged 1,000–3,000 square feet and carried 1,000 to 2,000 stock keeping units (SKUs). The specialty retailers carried 10,000 to 12,000 SKUs. The mass merchandisers carried about 500 high-volume SKUs.

PETsMART—"where pets are family"—had about 550 stores in the U.S., Canada, and the U.K. Its stores averaged 25,000 square feet and carried about 12,000 SKUs. Pet owners were encouraged to shop with their pets. PETsMART was aggressively acquiring competitors and opening new stores.

PETCO had over 482 stores in 37 states and the District of Columbia. Most of its stores averaged 13,000 square feet, carried more than 10,000 SKUs, and were located in sites coanchored by strong consumer-oriented retailers. PETCO was also aggressively acquiring competitors and opening new stores.

PETsMART and PETCO were the largest survivors of a decade of consolidation in the pet supplies industry. Both companies had experienced difficulties absorbing some of their acquisitions; and by May 1999, their common shares were trading well below their 1996–1997 highs.

LAWN AND GARDEN RETAILERS

In the lawn and garden industry, independent retailers, such as flower and gift retailers and nurseries, specialty retailers, and mass merchandisers sold lawn and garden supplies. The buyers included individuals and organizations, such as golf courses, government agencies, hospitals, landscaping firms, and universities.

CENTRAL GARDEN & PET

Central Garden & Pet was Gardner's primary competitor and the leading U.S. distributor of lawn and garden and pet supplies. It offered 45,000 brand-name products from 1,000 manufacturers to mass merchants, warehouse clubs, nurseries, and grocery store chains through its 41 distribution centers and affiliated distributors. About 32% of its revenues came from sales of the Solaris Group's Ortho, Round-Up, and Green Sweep lawn products. (In 1994, Gardner once again lost the Ortho line when Ortho signed a national contract with Central Garden & Pet.)

Gardner's Operations Strategy

By 1996, it was apparent that the company's financial performance was slipping; and Butch and his managers were groping for an explanation. As Butch explained:

> We'd been going along for 16 years making our numbers and growing about as fast as I could afford to. Suddenly, we were leveling out. We had to find out what forces were driving us. We had to find out what was going to work for us in the future.

Gardner's information system provided some of the answers. It was developed by Glen Brown, the administrative controller, and it was used to manage accounts payable and receivable, billing, the general ledger (i.e., income statements, balance sheets, and cash flow statements), inventory, order entry, payroll, purchasing, and warehousing. EDI (electronic data interchange) was used for credit checks and some supplier transactions.

As the system came online in 1997, Butch was surprised at the response of his employees:

> It was amazing! As people realized they could access information, they'd download it to their PCs from the mainframe and use it to help them manage their part of the business. They became empowered, and they loved it!

Most of the North American Iams distributors (about 25 in early 1999) participated in an annual data exchange that was facilitated by an independent firm. The data exchange gave Butch benchmark data, but they were aggregated, so the identity of the distributors was unknown (**Exhibits 5** and **6**). The data reflected a median sales level of $14 million and a median return on assets of 22% (i.e., pre-tax profit divided by total assets). Given the time lags inherent in data collection and dissemination, the data were from the 1996–1997 period.

ACCOUNTS RECEIVABLE

By early 1997, accounts receivable were under scrutiny. Gardner's billing cycle closed on the 25th of each month so all credit sales from the 26th of one month through the 25th of the next month were due on the 10th of the following month. Thus, purchases on the 26th of the prior

Exhibit 5

Survey Sample, Common-Size Income Statement (percent)

	Median[1]
Total net sales	100.0
Cost of goods sold	81.4
Gross profit	18.6
Operating expenses	
Wages	5.5
Salaries—owners	0.8
Payroll taxes, benefits, etc.	1.0
Total labor	8.6
Advertising and promotion	0.4
Bad debts	0.1
Building rent	0.9
Depreciation and amortization	0.6
Freight	0.1
Insurance	0.4
Legal and professional fees	0.2
Office and postage expense	0.3
Repairs and maintenance	0.4
Supplies (warehouse & delivery)	0.2
Taxes and licenses	0.2
Telephone and utilities	0.4
Travel and entertainment	0.3
Delivery truck expense (rental, fuel, maintenance)	1.2
Other	0.2
Total operating expenses	15.7
Operating profit	3.0
Interest expense	0.2
Other income	0.1
Net income before taxes	2.9

Note:

1. Due to the proprietary nature of the data, the data are approximate and generally representative of the 1996–1997 period. Median values do not add to 100%.

Source: Company records.

month were outstanding for 45 days; purchases on the 25th of the current month were outstanding for 15 days. If people paid on the 10th, the average age of the receivables would be 30 days. Glen charted the collections and found they peaked around the 13th—extending the receivables by 10%.

Glen also monitored the seasonal pattern in receivables and aged them. The receivables ranged from a high of 40 days in April and May to a low of 25–30 days in July. On the average, 24% of the receivables were 30–90+ days in arrears. Given his knowledge of other distributors' operations, Butch knew that Gardner's credit terms were relatively liberal. The benchmark data showed accounts receivable averaging 30.2% of current assets (**Exhibit 6**). Gardner's accounts receivable were a significantly higher proportion of current assets (e.g., 42% in 1996). Butch was concerned that reducing the availability of credit would reduce sales, but the

Exhibit 6
Survey Sample, Common-Size Balance Sheet (percent)

	Median[1]
Current assets	
Accounts receivable	30.2%
Inventory	42.1
Prepaid expenses, etc.	0.8
Total current assets	84.1
Fixed assets	
Buildings	0.0
Furniture, fixtures, and equipment	27.0
Leasehold improvements	0.6
(−) Accumulated depreciation	−14.8
Total fixed assets	13.2
Other assets	1.7
Total assets	100.0%
Liabilities and shareholders' equity	
Accounts payable	17.6%
Accrued liabilities	3.0
Notes payable	2.3
Other current liabilities	1.0
Total current liabilities	43.4
Long-term debt (less current portion)	10.5
Total liabilities	58.3
Shareholders' equity	
Common stock	0.4
Retained earnings	36.4
Total shareholders' equity	41.7
Total liabilities and shareholders' equity	100.0%

Note:
1. Due to the proprietary nature of the data, the data are approximate and generally representative of the 1996–1997 period. Median values do not add to 100%.

Source: Company records.

reduction in net income had reduced the cash flow from operations. With cash flows contracting, Butch had to act. As Glen explained:

> We implemented delivery-to-delivery terms. The customer pays the driver for the prior week's delivery before the new delivery is off-loaded. This avoids delays for mail time, and it gives us closer control over the customer because we can hold the delivery hostage. There are still some delays because the driver may be on the road for a week, and chains with multiple stores and central disbursement won't pay until they receive the invoice from the store.

INVENTORY

In early 1997, inventory levels also came under scrutiny. As Rob explained:

> Iams sets the buying configurations. They tell me where to buy from, what kinds of configurations to buy in, and things like that. It's not a problem. The Iams inventory turns quickly.
>
> When I arrived, we carried about 10,000 items in pet supplies. When the items were ranked in descending order of sales, we found the top 1,000 items accounted for 67% of the sales and

32% of the inventory value [**Exhibit 7**]. The last 3,500 items accounted for 34% of the inventory and 1% of the sales. We set aggressive targets, closed out a lot of inventory, and freed up a lot of cash.

The strategy is to limit the number of lines and optimize the SKUs. The pet retailers need to carry products that turn quicker, or they won't be competitive with PETsMART and PETCO.

When I started, the average fill rate in pet supplies was 82%. Now we're at 92 to 94% in pet. (The fill rate was the average percent of customers' orders that was filled at the time the orders were placed.) As we shrink our SKUs, we may be able to raise the fill rate. On Iams it is 99%, and our lawn and garden fill rate is 96 to 97%.

NOTES PAYABLE AND LONG-TERM LIABILITIES

In 1997, action was also taken to reduce notes payable and long-term liabilities. By October 1998, the debt/equity ratios had improved. As Glen stated, "We want to be positioned to take advantage of the opportunities."

TRUCKING AND WAREHOUSE EQUIPMENT

In April 1999, the management team decided to move Milan Cook, the Spokane branch manager, to Billings and make him Operations Manager for all of Gardner's operations. Rob in particular felt this was an important move and noted, "When Milan was in Spokane, we didn't have any problems! Milan took care of things. Milan is extremely important to the future of this company." As Milan explained:

> I'll be taking some of the day-to-day work off Rob, so he can concentrate on marketing. We need to develop a real efficient warehouse and order picking system. I also need to get a program going for buying new trucks and replacing warehouse equipment.

Exhibit 7

Comparison of April 8, 1997, Inventory and January–March Sales for Pet Supplies: Gardner Distributing Co.

Item Ranking Descending Order of Sales	Sales	Percent of Sales %	Inventory	Percent of Inventory %
0–1000	$315,959	67	$174,364	32
1001–1500	46,612	10	40,264	7
1501–2000	31,533	7	28,756	5
2001–2500	23,547	5	24,955	5
2501–3000	17,348	4	23,035	4
3001–3500	9,502	2	20,619	4
3501–4000	8,898	2	21,415	4
4001–4500	7,052	1	15,642	3
4501–5000	5,358	1	13,720	2
5001–8491	6,902	1	185,749	34
Totals	$472,711	100	$548,519	100

Additional Closeout Items	Sales		Inventory	
2,634	$ 20,348		$132,970	

Source: Company records.

GARDNER'S MARKETING STRATEGY

In the early 1990s, Iams began to take over the marketing and sales for the distributors' high-volume accounts. Gardner turned over 31 accounts (42% of its Iams business) and reduced its staff. It delivered the product, but the gross profit percentage was much lower than on the smaller Iams accounts. The role of the distributor changed accordingly. As Butch explained:

> Recently, I visited 3 distributors' operations. They sold only Iams products. Their warehouse and delivery operations were very efficient. There was very little sales, service, or marketing.
>
> What I like best is the buying and selling. Even when I was a kid, I was buying and selling things. Dad would bring home old lawn mowers he'd taken in on trade at Sears; and I'd clean them up, paint them, and get them running good. Then, I'd take them door-to-door and sell them. When I was in high school, I'd buy and sell cars. I don't like the office work. I like to be out in the field finding business opportunities!

In 1996, Gardner segmented its customers by contribution to gross profit (**Exhibit 8**) and, as Butch explained, focused on 4 issues:

> How can we get more products into each store? How can we increase our share of each store's purchases? How do we grow each customer's business? How do we grow our customer base?
>
> We separated our customer accounts into 4 categories according to each account's annual contribution to gross profit. Then, we identified about 250 key accounts with potential for growth, given their resources and attitudes. A key account might be a C account, but we'd treat them as a B account to help them grow.
>
> It was costing us about $100 to make a sales call. We couldn't afford to call on a C or D account, so inside sales serviced them by telephone. C accounts that had the potential to become B accounts within 1 year were serviced by outside sales. (Inside sales people operated from Gardner's office. Outside sales people traveled the region and called on existing and potential customers.) We're finding that the big accounts are getting bigger and the small accounts are holding their own or getting smaller, and we can't change the small account mentality.
>
> We have 5 outside sales people. We assigned them 40 to 50 accounts and are holding them accountable for the growth of those accounts. The inside sales people are also accountable for their accounts.
>
> We have other customers that are not regular customers; but they are key accounts, for example, a nursery that needs a new green house or a landscaper that is putting in a golf course.
>
> Most of our customers don't know how to stock their stores. They don't have good inventory controls. They can't identify their best-selling items. And their floor and shelf space management concepts are rudimentary. It's scary! But it also creates an opportunity for us. We are becoming more of a consultant to our customers, and this may help us promote our products and build our customer base.

Exhibit 8

Classification of Customer Accounts: Gardner Distributing Co.

Customer Accounts	Annual Contribution To Gross Profit	Personal Sales Contacts
A (40)	$15,000–$100,000	Two–four personal visits/month
B (93)	$ 5,000–$ 14,999	One–two personal visits/month
C (202)	$ 1,000–$ 4,999	One telephone call/week
D (162)	$<1,000	Two+ telephone calls/month

Source: Company records.

In September 1998, Butch hired a key account manager, Mike Hofferber, to develop large volume accounts through the central purchasing operations of multistore businesses. Heretofore, the strategy had been to sell to 1 store at a time. Mike had the knowledge and interpersonal skills to bundle and sell multiple products and lines (e.g., in lawn and garden) to knowledgeable buyers.

Mike arrived in November 1998. He began his career in retail management with OSCO Drug after college, and he worked for OSCO for 6 years. During this time, he worked with Gardner who was supplying Ortho to the OSCO store. After that, he managed a Coast-to-Coast store in Billings for 3 years. Then, he worked for a food broker for 11 years where he worked with clients such as Albertsons, Buttreys, Smiths, and Supervalu. As he explained in May 1999:

> I sold to Rob when he was at Supervalu. He contacted me in the summer of 1998. Gardner didn't have the know-how to develop the drug, hardware, and mass customers. The goal was to make Gardner the everyday supplier to some of the key multioutlet retailers, like Albertsons, OSCO Drug, Smiths, Costco, Tidymans, County Market, and owners of multiple Ace Hardware stores. We wanted to be the go-to distributor for these major players!
>
> In pet supplies and lawn and garden, we are putting programs in place, so we can get the stores doing the same thing. For example, the average hardware store doesn't understand pet, so we show them how to set it up. We have also designed systems for them, so they can fax their orders, and we can deliver every week.
>
> That was the real key for us at Albertsons! We put a program in front of them, and all the buyer had to do was sign his name to it. At Albertsons, we started with 12 SKUs. Now we're looking at putting whole lines in there! Robinson Pottery is a good example. We tested this in 2 of their stores in Great Falls. When this settles in, and it varies by season, we'll have about 50 SKUs in 10 stores! Next year I want Albertsons to come to us and say, "Okay, design our program for us."
>
> We have hydraulic lifts on all of our semitruck trailers. The lifts cost about $12,000 each, but this allows us to off-load pallets at the store and put them where the store wants them. The store's labor is nonexistent. Albertsons loves it!
>
> This strategy is going to put us into a hundred accounts that we weren't in a year ago, and a third of those might be Albertsons! There are so many opportunities; we physically can't get to all of them! Our trucks are full, and that's becoming a bottleneck for us, even though this is our busy time of year.
>
> Shortly after I came to Gardner, Iams made a policy change that has really helped us, although it has received a negative reaction from some of the independents and PETsMART. For years, Iams had been telling its buyers, "You'll never see Iams in grocery or mass." They built their business on this! But in the last 3 years, Iams has lost 5,000 independent accounts with the entry of PETsMART and PETCO. It's been a brutal eye-opener for Iams!
>
> We now have Iams's permission, on a case-by-case basis, to sell Iams products to "rural and upscale" [Iams's terms] grocery stores in areas where Iams products are not available. Traditionally, the premium pet foods have not been available in grocery stores. Iams still does not want to sell direct to the chains other than PETsMART and PETCO.
>
> We are 1 of the lead distributors doing this, and it opens up tremendous opportunities for us! Rural grocers are trying to keep people from driving to larger places to shop. For example, Columbus is 40 miles from Billings; and we now have an agreement to put Iams products in the IGA grocery in Columbus. I can open 60 grocery stores in the next 6 months! Moreover, when we go in with our Iams presentations, we do pet supplies and lawn and garden presentations too. The Iams products pull the other product lines and underwrite the cost of developing them!

Butch felt Hill's would not follow Iams's "rural and upscale" grocery store strategy. He felt Hill's and the other competitors in premium pet foods would exploit the opportunity and tell their independent pet store customers that, unlike Iams, they weren't going to abandon them!

In May 1999, a presentation of Gardner's marketing strategy to the Iams people emphasized 3 objectives:

1. Expand retail availability and increase product exposure to more consumers.
   a. Focus Don Hefner, our senior sales representative, on opening new independent retail accounts.
   b. Utilize the extensive talent and experience of Mike Hofferber and Rob Chouinard in grocery, hardware, and mass merchants to aggressively develop our pet supplies, premium pet foods, and lawn and garden categories in those industries.
2. Dominate retail store presence with store resets, e.g.:
   a. Planograms (product display layouts).
   b. Backtagging (This was an adhesive shelf tag in a plastic clip that was supplied by Gardner. It had an item description and a bar code for reordering.)
   c. Promotional and seasonal displays.
   d. Merchandising aids, e.g., clipstrips (cross-merchandising displays, e.g., chew toys hung in the pet food section).
3. Execute vendor and in-house promotions, e.g., Iams national promotions, Iams regional promotions, monthly sales flyers, inside sales specials, and seasonal promotions.

Expanding Gardner's Territory

On separate occasions, 2 U.S. distributors had told Butch they were concerned about the future of their businesses. This led Butch to think about acquiring more territory. As he explained:

> Do I make the investment and have a $35 to $45 million company in the next 4 to 5 years? Or do I take the conservative approach and be happy with a $20 million company in 4 to 5 years?
>
> One distributor has annual sales of about $12 million. Like us, they have a primary distribution center and a branch warehouse, but their business is virtually all Iams. One of their markets is dominated by national accounts with relatively low margins. So they've had to become very efficient. We might, for example, acquire a part or all of the distributor's territory.
>
> What will an acquisition do for us? I know Rob feels there may be synergies in distribution (e.g., back-haul opportunities from major markets), information systems, and management.

Butch knew the distributors did not have to sell, thus a buyer would have to pay a premium for the business. Also, Iams would have to agree to transfer the territory to Gardner.

> Iams has been reluctant to let buyers pay premiums of more than 5% of sales. Thus, I'd buy the assets at market value plus a 5% premium, which is about 2 years of net profit.

Butch could raise the acquisition capital. The prime rate was 8%, and he was paying 1½% over prime for working capital. Equity financing could be arranged, but Butch had reservations about this.

> The bank said they'd lend me up to $1.5 million. The next option would be a private placement through D. A. Davidson (a regional investment and underwriting firm). The problem with going public is that I'd be more of an administrator, and that doesn't appeal to me. It'd take away the freedom of entrepreneurship.

Gardner's Strategic Alternatives

In April 1999, Iams retained a consulting firm to help the distributors develop their strategic planning capabilities. Iams agreed to pay half of the cost or up to $10,000 per distributor.

Gardner was the fourth distributor selected to participate. The first meeting with the consultant was scheduled for late May. As Butch explained:

> This is an opportunity for us to get a better understanding of Iams's strategy and to build our partnership with Iams. I asked the consultants to sign a confidentiality agreement promising not to disclose the contents of our discussions with Iams. They agreed.

In May 1999, as Butch and Rob were waiting for Butch's luggage to be off-loaded from the Delta flight on his return from Puerto Vallarta, Butch said:

> I'm seriously thinking about retiring to Puerto Vallarta, maybe next year. I'm okay with our mission and objectives, but we *must* define our strategies. I want to be able to leave for, say, 6 months and be confident that there will be no unpleasant surprises when I return. Where are you at on that?

Rob said, "We're meeting on Friday morning to discuss strategy." Butch decided not to attend the meeting. The management team had performed well in his absence, and he wanted to maintain the continuity of Rob's leadership. He also felt it was time for the management team to develop and implement its own strategies. The Iams consultant would not be at the meeting.

At the Friday morning meeting, several of the managers arrived with their laptop computers, giving them easy access to the corporate data. As the meeting proceeded, it was apparent that there were various views of how Gardner should position itself for the future. Rob and Glen were on performance-based compensation plans, and other members of the management team looked forward to being on similar plans. Hence, some of the views were fairly forcefully stated. Typical of many such meetings, the ideas developed spontaneously, and the managers had difficulty staying on task (**Exhibit 9**).

Just before noon Rob brought the meeting to a close with the suggestion that he and Glen develop a written statement of Gardner's strategies. The statement would be distributed to the managers before the next meeting, which was scheduled for next Friday morning. As the meeting was breaking up, Rob reiterated Butch's concerns about clearly defining the company's strategies in each of its 3 businesses. In response, someone noted how Butch's management style had changed in the last few years; and that triggered a parting discussion.

> I can remember how he used to react if he thought we were having fun. If he heard music or someone laughing, he'd come out of his office with a frown on his face. . . . He still has his desk from Sears. . . . His old office had a window that looked out over the warehouse floor. Over the years the racks gradually blocked off his view. . . . When we began the recent office renovation, he asked for an office with an outside view. . . .
>
> Butch has changed from a manager to a leader. . . . His management style has become more professional. He knew what he wanted, but he needed the assistance of someone who knew how to get it done. . . . Hiring Rob was very important. . . . He's had trouble letting others manage, but that's changing. He realizes that to pass over the management he has to pass the whole thing, and that's been difficult for him to do. . . .
>
> He isn't as involved in the day-to-day. He likes working with Don Gallagher on the catalogues and flyers. . . . He goes out and visits the customers. When the owner of the business stops to visit, that really helps us. He doesn't distinguish between the customers. He stops to talk to all of them. . . .
>
> He's been gone more lately. When he went to Mexico recently, we didn't hear anything from him. Finally, we got an e-mail saying, "I haven't heard from you guys. Is the building still there?" . . . Even though he doesn't want to talk about the business, he wants us to say: "Everything is okay, and we're still here!" . . . We even got a call from his sister in Arizona saying, "Butch hasn't heard from you guys for a while." . . .

Exhibit 9
Excerpts from the May 1999 Meeting of Gardner's Managers to Discuss Gardner's Strategic Alternatives

The May 1999, Friday morning meeting to discuss the company's strategies was held in a meeting room at the Gardner Distributing Co.'s office in Billings, Montana. Most of Gardner's managers were at the meeting. The following excerpts are from comments made by Rob Chouinard, the General Manager; Glen Brown, the Administrative Controller; Milan Cook, the Operations Manager; and Mike Hofferber, the Key Account Manager.

Rob: Our strategy this year has been to increase our pet supplies and lawn and garden sales. We've identified classes of trade, like hardware and even farm-type operations, that we've been selling to but nothing else. We've started to develop programs for them so that we can take over their pet supplies departments. We customize the programs based on the type of trade. For example, we've just set 3 Ace Hardware stores with Iams and pet supplies.

At the same time, Iams is allowing us to sell to "rural and upscale" grocery stores in areas where Iams products are not available. Once we are selling Iams to the store, we can afford to develop programs for the store in pet supplies and lawn and garden. Iams has to approve each store, and we have to move carefully. Our independents don't like this, and we've lost 2 accounts.

Glen: Lawn and garden is the future of our business! In green goods there are always going to be growers, retailers, and distributors. It won't be like pet supplies where there are big-box stores, like PETsMART and PETCO. Also there are the demographics—the aging of the population. Then, there is the institutional business—the golf courses, municipalities, hospitals, and schools. There's lots of market there!

Rob: It's getting so people will pay to have someone care for their lawn. Also there are patio gardens. We need to reach out to those small but growing markets.

Right now we're not selling lawn and garden products in the Spokane market. We need to think about that! Do we buy an existing competitor or develop our own operation there?

When you talk about soils and pots, there aren't a lot of dollars in that. It's hard to market. Everyone is talking about developing a Web page and selling from that, but getting the product in here would kill them. We're looking at using a Web page for order entry, product promotion, etc.

The rumor is that Scotts is buying Ortho. We deal with Scotts, so this should help us.

Mike: Central is not going to put a distribution center in Montana. There's not enough business. Central is closing its distribution center in Denver and consolidating its Salt Lake City distribution center. I doubt if anyone is looking at opening a lawn and garden business in Montana. There are better places to invest. If we do a good job, we won't give someone an opportunity to open up in Montana!

Rob: We are well positioned in Billings to service a very large area. We're also well positioned to defend it!

Glen: Our geography is an advantage! We can go north into Canada, which we haven't done. We can go east to Minneapolis, west to Seattle, and south to Denver and Salt Lake City. We can go into their markets more easily than they can come into ours. Our central location plus our experience with delivery in that geography gives us an advantage.

Mike: For us, the nearest regional distribution centers are located in Denver, Salt Lake City, Seattle, and Portland. Manufacturers prepay the freight to the distribution center. Thus, some products aren't profitable to truck into our area. This creates opportunities for us! An example is rock salt. Rock salt is heavy, and it is only worth $2 a bag. Albertsons doesn't want to ship it from Salt Lake City. If we can convince the manufacturer to prepay the freight to our warehouse, then it may be profitable for us to distribute it.

Rob: We are poised to buy more Iams geography. The opportunity may arise in the next 3 to 5 years. Buying more Iams geography is not that simple.

In February, we received a 3-year commitment from Iams with two 1-year renewal options. Some distributors only got 1-year renewals. That's positive!

Milan: We should be able to double our size in the next 5 years. We can do this by expanding our territory and developing a new class of dealer, which we've started to do in lawn and garden. I think we know how to go into a new market and how to develop a class of trade that wouldn't be there initially.

(continued)

Exhibit 9

Excerpts from the May 1999 Meeting of Gardner's Managers to Discuss Gardner's Strategic Alternatives (*continued*)

Glen: For me, the issue is this: Where does the company want to be longer term? We need to grow to be a viable distributor for a manufacturer—so we can be viable with Iams, Ortho, or someone else. Iams wants to be working with players who can dominate their markets, and they are realizing that takes someone like us who has some marketing competencies in their geography and some synergies that they get from some other products rather than being just a distributor.

The Iams business creates opportunities in lawn and garden and pet supplies. Lawn and garden and pet provide a lot more gross profit! If we could fill our trucks with lawn and garden and pet supplies like we do with Iams and roll them down the road, we'd be fat cats. But we can't do that, so we need Iams.

Longer term we must get the gravy business with lawn and garden and pet supplies and get our foot in the door to those markets with Iams! Iams will get us to breakeven. From there, we can expand into the lawn and garden and pet businesses.

Milan: In the last 2 years we have developed real management synergy. Three years ago everyone did a little bit of something. Now, everyone knows exactly where they're at and where the company wants to be.

Glen: Rob has taken over the marketing very effectively. That's the 1 piece we didn't have—a proactive marketing approach. Marketing is now much more a part of our business, and that ties in with our long-term strategy of combining Iams with the lawn and garden and pet businesses.

We're also developing a second layer of management and management succession.

We're putting down infrastructure! We're looking at 2 questions: What do we want to be? What does it take to do that? That's a big shift. We're preparing for what we want to be. We've done a lot of that this year.

Rob: We're changing from micromanagement to empowerment! Mike created this position. He's out working with the customers getting new business! I really feel we have the pieces in place, and we're financially sound. Our year-to-date net income is over $200,000!

Glen: That's great! But our year-to-date net cash flow is only $30,000! We need to watch that too! At this time of year we're extending our receivables and building inventory. Cash flow is more important than net income.

The Future

As Butch was leaving the office that Friday, he was reflecting on Rob's recap of the meeting.

Rob's enthusiasm is contagious! He and Mike are sure pushing Iams's "rural and upscale" grocery store strategy. It's opening opportunities in premium pet foods, pet supplies, and lawn and garden supplies. But this may be a relatively short-run opportunity, given the region's vast expanse and limited population. Moreover, Hill's is going to respond! And they're a tough competitor!

Apparently, Mike also favors purchasing, selling, and distributing products that the large, multistore retailers don't want to ship from their distribution centers (e.g., rock salt). But we must also service and expand the existing customer base.

Glen is our long-range thinker. He believes the future of the business is in lawn and garden supplies. Rob says Glen wants to develop acquisition strategies, new markets and marketing strategies, and new supplier linkages (e.g., with desirable brand names).

We have a good working relationship with Iams. We need to develop the relationship and the synergies the partnership creates across our other businesses without losing our ability to pursue new opportunities! This may be our biggest challenge!

In sum, we need to decide what businesses to grow and how to grow them. We also need to examine the possibility that one or more of our businesses may have reached maturity or may be declining. If so, then we need to decide how to retrench!

Note

T. Parker-Pope, "For You, My Pet: Why the Veterinarian Really Recommends That 'Designer' Chow," *Wall Street Journal* (November 3, 1997), p. A1.

Wal-Mart Stores, Inc.: Strategies for Dominance in the New Millennium

James W. Camerius

David Glass had recently announced that he was stepping down from his role as President and Chief Executive Officer (CEO) at Wal-Mart Stores, Inc. He stepped to the podium in early 2000 at a Kansas City convention of the company's store managers to introduce Wal-Mart's new CEO, Lee Scott, 51, to a crowd of cheering executives. "I'm not going anywhere; I'll be around to give everyone more help than they probably would like," Glass suggested. At 64 years old, he would remain Chairman of the firm's Executive Committee.

Lee Scott was only the third CEO in the entire history of Wal-Mart. Sam Walton had built the company from the ground up. During the 12 years that David Glass held the position, sales grew from $16 billion to $165 billion. Lee Scott had been personally recruited by David Glass 21 years before from a Springdale, Arkansas, trucking company to come to Wal-Mart as a manager of the truck fleet. In his years at Wal-Mart he had established himself as a leader, innovator, and team player. Over the last 4 years he served as Chief Operating Officer (COO) and Vice Chairman of the company. He was aware that there were tremendous opportunities to serve new markets with the company's stores. His management mandate was drive the company to a new level of success in domestic and international markets.

A Maturing Organization

In 2000, Wal-Mart Stores, Inc., Bentonville, Arkansas, operated mass merchandising retail stores under a variety of names and retail formats including: Wal-Mart discount department stores; SAM's Wholesale Clubs, wholesale/retail membership warehouses; and Wal-Mart Supercenters, large combination grocery and general merchandise stores in all 50 states. In the International Division, it operated stores in Canada, Mexico, Argentina, Brazil, Germany, South Korea, United Kingdom, and Puerto Rico, and stores through joint ventures in China. It was not only the nation's largest discount department store chain, but it had also surpassed the retail division of Sears, Roebuck and Co. in sales volume as the largest retail firm in the United States. It was also considered the largest retailer in the world, with sales of $165 billion in 1999. The McLane Company, Inc., a Wal-Mart subsidiary, sold a wide variety of grocery and nongrocery products to variety of retailers including selected Wal-Marts, SAM's Clubs and Supercenters. In 1999, *Discount Store News* honored Wal-Mart as "Retailer of the Century" with a commemorative issue of the periodical.

A financial summary of Wal-Mart Stores, Inc., for the fiscal years ended January 31, 1998, January 31, 1999 and January 31, 2000 are shown in **Exhibit 1**.

This case was prepared by James W. Camerius of Northern Michigan University. This case was edited for SMBP-8th Edition. All rights reserved to the author. Copyright © 2000 by James W. Camerius. Reprinted by permission.

Exhibit 1

Consolidated Statements of Income: Wal-Mart Stores, Inc.
(Dollar amounts in millions except per share data)

Year Ending January 31	2000	1999	1998
Revenue	**$165,013**	$137,634	$117,958
Net sales	**1,796**	1,574	1,341
Other income-net	**166,809**	139,208	119,299
Cost and expenses:			
Cost of sales	**129,664**	108,725	93,438
Operating, selling and general and administrative expenses	**27,040**	22,363	19,358
Interest costs:			
Debt	**756**	529	555
Capital leases	**266**	268	229
Total Expenses	**157,726**	131,885	113,580
Income before income taxes, minority interest, equity in unconsolidated subsidiaries and cumulative effect of accounting change			
Provision for income taxes	**9,083**	7,323	5,719
Current	**3,476**	3,380	2,095
Deferred	**(138)**	(640)	20
	3,338	2,740	2,115
Income before cumulative effect of accounting change, net of tax benefit of $119	**(198)**	—	—
Net Income	**$5,377**	$4,430	$3,563
Net income per common share:			
basic net income per common share:			
Income before cumulative effect of accounting change	**$1.25**	$0.99	$0.78
Cumulative effect of accounting change, Net of tax	**(0.04)**	—	—
Net income per common share	**$1.21**	$0.99	$0.78
Average number of common shares	**4,451**	4,464	4,516
Diluted net income per common share:			
Income before cumulative effect of Accounting change	**$1.25**	$0.99	$0.78
Cumulative effect of accounting change, Net of tax	**(0.04)**	—	—
Net income per common share	**$1.20**	$0.99	$0.78
Average number of common shares	**4,474**	4,485	4,533
Pro forma amounts assuming accounting change Had been in effect in fiscal 2000, 1999 and 1998:			
Net Income	**$5,575**	$4,393	$3,517
Net income per common share, basic and diluted	**$1.25**	$0.98	$0.78

Notes were deleted.

Source: Wal-Mart Stores, Inc.

The Sam Walton Spirit

Much of the success of Wal-Mart was attributed to the entrepreneurial spirit of its founder and Chairman of the Board, Samuel Moore Walton (1918–1992). Many considered him 1 of the most influential retailers of the century.

Sam Walton or "Mr. Sam" as some referred to him traced his down-to-earth, old-fashioned, home-spun, evangelical ways to growing up in rural Oklahoma, Missouri, and Arkansas. Although he was remarkably blasé about his roots, some suggested that it was the simple belief in hard work and ambition that had "unlocked . . . countless doors and showered upon him, his customers, and his employees . . . , the fruits of . . . years of labor in building [this] highly successful company."

"Our goal has always been in our business to be the very best," Sam Walton said in an interview, "and, along with that, we believe that in order to do that, you've got to make a good situation and put the interests of your associates first. If we really do that consistently, they in turn will cause . . . our business to be successful, which is what we've talked about and espoused and practiced." "The reason for our success," he said, "is our people and the way that they're treated and the way they feel about their company." Many have suggested it was this "people first" philosophy, which guided the company through the challenges and setbacks of its early years, and allowed the company to maintain its consistent record of growth and expansion in later years.

There was little about Sam Walton's background that reflected his amazing success. He was born in Kingfisher, Oklahoma, on March 29, 1918, to Thomas and Nancy Walton. Thomas Walton was a banker at the time and later entered the farm mortgage business and moved to Missouri. Sam Walton, growing up in rural Missouri in the depths of the Great Depression, discovered early that he "had a fair amount of ambition and enjoyed working," he once noted. He completed high school at Columbia, Missouri, and received a Bachelor of Arts Degree in Economics from the University of Missouri in 1940. "I really had no idea what I would be," he once said, "At one point in time," adding as an afterthought, "I thought I wanted to become President of the United States."

A unique, enthusiastic, and positive individual, Sam Walton was "just your basic home-spun billionaire," a columnist once suggested. "Mr. Sam is a life-long small-town resident who didn't change much as he got richer than his neighbors," he noted. Walton had tremendous energy, enjoyed bird hunting with his dogs and flew a corporate plane. When the company was much smaller he could boast that he personally visited every Wal-Mart store at least once a year. A store visit usually included Walton leading Wal-Mart cheers that began, "Give me a W, give me an A . . ." "To many employees he had the air of a fiery Baptist preacher." Paul R. Carter, a Wal-Mart Executive Vice President, was quoted as saying, "Mr. Walton has a calling." He became the richest man in America, and by 1991 had created a personal fortune for his family in excess of $21 billion. In 1999, despite a division of wealth, 5 family members were still ranked among the richest individuals in the United States.

Sam Walton's success was widely chronicled. He was selected by the investment publication, *Financial World* in 1989 as the "CEO of the Decade." He had honorary degrees from the University of the Ozarks, the University of Arkansas, and the University of Missouri. He also received many of the most distinguished professional awards of the industry like "Man of the Year," "Discounter of the Year," "Chief Executive Officer of the Year," and was the second retailer to be inducted into the Discounting Hall of Fame. He was recipient of the Horatio Alger Award in 1984 and acknowledged by *Discount Stores News* as "Retailer of the Decade" in December of 1989. "Walton does a remarkable job of instilling near-religious fervor in his people," said analyst Robert Buchanan of A. G. Edwards. "I think that speaks to the heart of his success." In late 1989 Sam Walton was diagnosed to have multiple myeloma, or cancer of the bone marrow. He remained active in the firm as Chairman of the Board of Directors until his death in 1992.

Corporate Governance

Exhibit 2 provides the 15 members of Wal-Mart's Board of Directors. Four are internal members: (1) S. Robson Walton, Chairman, (2) David D. Glass, Chairman, Executive Committee of the Board, (3) Donald G. Soderquist, Senior Vice Chairman, and (4) H. Lee Scott, Senior Vice Chairman.

Exhibit 2
Board of Directors and Executive Officers: Wal-Mart Stores, Inc. (January 31, 2000)

Directors	
John A. Cooper, Jr.	H. Lee Scott
Stephen Friedman	Jack C. Shewmaker
Stanley C. Gault	Donald G. Soderquist
David D. Glass	Dr. Paula Stern
Roland Hernandez	Jose Villarreal
Dr. Frederick S. Humphries	John T. Walton
E. Stanley Kroenke	S. Robson Walton
Elizabeth A. Sanders	

Officers	
S. Robson Walton Chairman of the Board	**Thomas Grimm** Executive Vice President and President and CEO, SAM's Club
H. Lee Scott President and CEO	**Don Harris** Executive Vice President, Operations
David D. Glass Chairman, Executive Committee of the Board	**John B. Menzer** Executive Vice President and President and CEO International Division
Donald G. Soderquist Senior Vice Chairman	**Coleman Peterson** Executive Vice President, People Division
Paul R. Carter Executive Vice President and Vice President, Wal-Mart Realty	**Thomas M. Schoewe** Executive Vice President and Chief Financial Officer
Bob Connolly Executive Vice President Merchandise	**Robert K. Rhoads** Senior Vice President, General Counsel and Secretary
Thomas M. Coughlin Executive Vice President and President and CEO, Wal-Mart Stores Division	**J. J. Fitzsimmons** Senior Vice President, Finance and Treasurer
David Dible Executive Vice President, Speciality Division	
Michael Duke Executive Vice President, Logistics	

Source: Wal-Mart Stores, Inc., *2000 Annual Report.*

The Marketing Concept

GENESIS OF AN IDEA

Sam Walton started his retail career in 1940 as a management trainee with the J.C. Penney Co. in Des Moines, Iowa. He was impressed with the Penney method of doing business and later modeled the Wal-Mart chain on "The Penney Idea" as reviewed in **Exhibit 3**. The Penney Company found strength in calling employees "associates" rather than clerks. Penney's, founded in Kemerer, Wyoming, in 1902, located stores on the main streets of small towns and cities throughout the United States. Early Walton 5 & 10s were on main streets and served rural areas.

Following service in the U.S. Army during World War II, Sam Walton acquired a Ben Franklin variety store franchise in Newport, Arkansas. He operated this store successfully with his brother, James L. "Bud" Walton (1921–1995), until losing the lease in 1950. When Wal-Mart was incorporated in 1962, the firm was operating a chain of 15 stores. Bud Walton became a Senior Vice President of the firm and concentrated on finding suitable store locations, acquiring real estate, and directing store construction.

The early retail stores owned by Sam Walton in Newport and Bentonville, Arkansas, and later in other small towns in adjoining southern states, were variety store operations. They were relatively small operations of 6,000 square feet, were located on "main streets" and displayed merchandise on plain wooden tables and counters. Operated under the Ben Franklin name and supplied by Butler Brothers of Chicago and St. Louis, they were characterized by a limited price line, low gross margins, high merchandise turnover, and concentration on return on investment. The firm, operating under the Walton 5 & 10 name, was the largest Ben Franklin franchisee in the country in 1962. The variety stores were phased out by 1976 to allow the company to concentrate on the growth of Wal-Mart discount department stores.

FOUNDATIONS OF GROWTH

The original Wal-Mart discount concept was not a unique idea. Sam Walton became convinced in the late 1950s that discounting would transform retailing. He traveled extensively in New England, the cradle of "off-pricing." After he had visited just about every discounter in

Exhibit 3
The Penney Idea (1913)

1. To serve the public, as nearly as we can, to its complete satisfaction.
2. To expect for the service we render a fair remuneration and not all the profit the traffic will bear.
3. To do all in our power to pack the customer's dollar full of value, quality, and satisfaction.
4. To continue to train ourselves and our associates so that the service we give will be more and more intelligently performed.
5. To improve constantly the human factor in our business.
6. To reward men and women in our organization through participation in what the business produces.
7. To test our every policy, method, and act in this wise: "Does it square with what is right and just?"

Source: Vance H. Trimble, *Sam Walton: The Inside Story of America's Richest Man* (New York: Dutton), 1990.

the United States, he tried to interest Butler Brothers executives in Chicago in the discount store concept. The first Kmart, as a "conveniently located 1-stop shopping unit where customers could buy a wide variety of quality merchandise at discount prices" had just opened in Garden City, Michigan. Walton's theory was to operate a similar discount store in a small community and in that setting, he would offer name-brand merchandise at low prices and would add friendly service. Butler Brothers executives rejected the idea. The first "Wal-Mart Discount City" opened in late 1962 in Rogers, Arkansas.

Wal-Mart stores would sell nationally advertised, well-known brand merchandise at low prices in austere surroundings. As corporate policy, they would cheerfully give refunds, credits, and rain checks. Management conceived the firm as a "discount department store chain offering a wide variety of general merchandise to the customer." Early emphasis was placed upon opportunistic purchases of merchandise from whatever sources were available. Heavy emphasis was placed upon health and beauty aids (H&BA) in the product line and "stacking it high" in a manner of merchandise presentation. By the end of 1979, there were 276 Wal-Mart stores located in 11 states.

The firm developed an aggressive expansion strategy. New stores were located primarily in communities of 5,000 to 25,000 in population. The stores' sizes ranged from 30,000 to 60,000 square feet with 45,000 being the average. The firm also expanded by locating stores in contiguous geographic areas. When its discount operations came to dominate a market area, it moved to an adjoining area. While other retailers built warehouses to serve existing outlets, Wal-Mart built the distribution center first and then spotted stores all around it, pooling advertising and distribution overhead. Most stores were less than a 6-hour drive from 1 of the company's warehouses. The first major distribution center, a 390,000 square-foot facility opened in Searcy, Arkansas, outside Bentonville in 1978.

NATIONAL PERSPECTIVES

At the beginning of 1991, the firm had 1,573 Wal-Mart stores in 35 states with expansion planned for adjacent states. Wal-Mart became the largest retailer and the largest discount department store in the United States.

As a national discount department store chain, Wal-Mart Stores, Inc., offered a wide variety of general merchandise to the customer. The stores were designed to offer 1-stop shopping in 36 departments that included family apparel, health and beauty aids, household needs, electronics, toys, fabric and crafts, automotive supplies, lawn and patio, jewelry, and shoes. In addition at certain store locations, a pharmacy, automotive supply and service center, garden center, or snack bar were also operated. The firm operated its stores with "everyday low prices" as opposed to putting heavy emphasis on special promotions, which called for multiple newspaper advertising circulars. Stores were expected to "provide the customer with a clean, pleasant, and friendly shopping experience."

Although Wal-Mart carried much the same merchandise, offered similar prices, and operated stores that looked much like the competition, there were many differences. In the typical Wal-Mart store, employees wore blue vests to identify themselves, aisles were wide, apparel departments were carpeted in warm colors, a store employee followed customers to their cars to pick up their shopping carts, and the customer was welcomed at the door by a "people greeter" who gave directions and struck up conversations. In some cases, merchandise was bagged in brown paper sacks rather than plastic bags because customers seemed to prefer them. A simple Wal-Mart logo in white letters on a brown background on the front of the store served to identify the firm. Yellow smiley faces were used on in-store displays. In consumer studies it was determined that the chain was particularly adept at striking the delicate balance needed to convince customers its prices were low without making people feel that its stores were too cheap. In many ways, competitors like Kmart sought to emulate Wal-Mart by introducing people greeters, by upgrading interiors, by developing new logos and signage, and by introducing new inventory response systems.

A "Satisfaction Guaranteed" refund and exchange policy was introduced to allow customers to be confident of Wal-Mart's merchandise and quality. Technological advancements like scanner cash registers, handheld computers for ordering of merchandise, and computer linkages of stores with the general office and distribution centers improved communications and merchandise replenishment. Each store was encouraged to initiate programs that would make it an integral part of the community in which it operated. Associates were encouraged to "maintain the highest standards of honesty, morality, and business ethics" in dealing with the public.

The External Environment

Industry analysts labeled the 1980s and early 1990s as eras of economic uncertainty for retailers. Many retailers were negatively affected by increased competitive pressures, sluggish consumer spending, slower-than-anticipated economic growth in North America, and recessions abroad. In 1995, Wal-Mart management felt the high consumer debt level caused many shoppers to reduce or defer spending on anything other than essentials. Management also felt that the lack of exciting new products or apparel trends reduced discretionary spending. Fierce competition resulted in lower margins and the lack of inflation stalled productivity increases. By 1998 the country had returned to prosperity. Unemployment was low, total income was relatively high, and interest rates were stable. Combined with a low inflation rate, buying power was perceived to be high and consumers were generally willing to buy. At the beginning of the year 2000, the United States had experienced 1 of the longest periods of economic expansion in its history.

Many retail enterprises confronted heavy competitive pressure by restructuring. Sears, Roebuck and Company, based in Chicago, became a more focused retailer by divesting itself of Allstate Insurance Company and its real estate subsidiaries. In 1993, the company announced it would close 118 unprofitable stores and discontinue the unprofitable Sears general merchandise catalog. It eliminated 50,000 jobs and began a $4 billion, 5-year remodeling plan for its remaining multiline department stores. After unsuccessfully experimenting with an "everyday low-price strategy," management chose to realign its merchandise strategy to meet the needs of middle market customers, who were primarily women, by focusing on product lines in apparel, home, and automotive. The new focus on apparel was supported with the advertising campaign, "The Softer Side of Sears." A later companywide campaign broadened the appeal: "The many sides of Sears fit the many sides of your life." Sears completed its return to its retailing roots by selling off its ownership in Dean Witter Financial Services, Discovery Card, Coldwell Banker Real Estate, and Sears mortgage banking operations. In 1999, Sears refocused its marketing strategy with a new program that was designed to communicate a stronger whole-house and event message. A new advertising campaign introduced with the slogan, "The good life at a great price. Guaranteed." In 2000, a new store format was introduced that concentrated on 5 focal areas: Appliances, Home Fashions, Tools, Kids, and Electronics. Other departments including men's and women's apparel assumed a support role in these stores.

The discount department store industry by the early-1990s had changed in a number of ways and was thought to have reached maturity by many analysts. Several formerly successful firms like E.J. Korvette, W.T. Grant, Atlantic Mills, Arlans, Federals, Zayre, Heck's, and Ames had declared bankruptcy and as a result either liquidated or reorganized. Venture announced liquidation in early 1998. Firms like Target Stores, and Shopko Stores began carrying more fashionable merchandise in more attractive facilities and shifted their emphasis to more national markets. Specialty retailers such as Toys "R" Us, Pier 1 Imports, and Oshmans had matured and were no longer making big inroads in toys, home furnishings, and sporting goods. The "superstores" of drug and food chains were rapidly discounting increasing amounts of general merchandise. Some firms like May Department Stores Company with Caldor and Venture and Woolworth Corporation with Woolco had withdrawn from the field by either selling their discount divisions or closing them down entirely. Woolworth's remaining 122 Woolco stores in Canada were sold to Wal-Mart in 1994. All remaining Woolworth variety stores in the United States were closed in 1997.

Several new retail formats had emerged in the marketplace to challenge the traditional discount department store format. The superstore, a 100,000–300,000 square foot operation, combined a large supermarket with a discount general-merchandise store. Originally a European retailing concept, these outlets were known as "malls without walls." Super Kmart, American Fare, and Wal-Mart's Supercenter Store were examples of this trend toward large operations. Warehouse retailing, which involved some combination of warehouse and showroom facilities, used warehouse principles to reduce operating expenses and thereby offer discount prices as a primary customer appeal. Home Depot combined the traditional hardware store and lumberyard with a self-service home improvement center to become the largest home center operator in the nation.

Some retailers responded to changes in the marketplace by selling goods at price levels (20–60%) below regular retail prices. These off-price operations appeared as 2 general types: (1) factory outlet stores like Burlington Coat Factory Warehouse, Bass Shoes, and Manhattan's Brand Name Fashion Outlet, and (2) independents like Loehmann's, T.J. Maxx, Marshall's, and Clothestime which bought seconds, overages, closeouts, or leftover goods from manufacturers and other retailers. Other retailers chose to dominate a product classification. Some super specialists like Sock Appeal, Little Piggie, Ltd, and Sock Market, offered a single narrowly defined classification of merchandise with an extensive assortment of brands, colors, and sizes. Others, as niche specialists, like Kids Mart, a division of Venator (Woolworth) Corporation targeted an identified market with carefully selected merchandise and appropriately designed stores. Some retailers like Silk Greenhouse (silk plants and flowers), Office Club (office supplies and equipment), and Toys "R" Us (toys) were called "category killers" because they had achieved merchandise dominance in their respective product categories. Stores like The Limited, Limited Express, Victoria's Secret, and The Banana Republic became mini-department specialists by showcasing new lines and accessories alongside traditional merchandise lines.

Kmart Corporation, headquartered in Troy, Michigan, became the industry's third largest retailer after Sears, Roebuck and Co. and second largest discount department store chain in the United States in the 1990s. Kmart had 2,171 stores and $35,925 million in sales at the beginning of 2000. The firm was perceived by many industry analysts and consumers in several independent studies as a laggard. It had been the industry sales leader for a number of years and had recently announced a turnaround in profitability. In the same studies, Wal-Mart was perceived as the industry leader even though according to the *Wall Street Journal*: "they carry much the same merchandise, offer prices that are pennies apart, and operate stores that look almost exactly alike." "Even their names are similar," noted the newspaper. The original Kmart concept of a "conveniently located, 1-stop-shopping unit where customers could buy a wide variety of quality merchandise at discount prices," had lost its competitive edge in a changing market. As 1 analyst noted in an industry newsletter: "They had done so well for the past 20 years without paying attention to market changes, now they have to." Kmart acquired a new President and Chief Executive Officer in 2000. Wal-Mart and Kmart sales growth over the period 1990–1999 is reviewed in **Exhibit 4**. A competitive analysis is shown of 4 major retail firms in **Exhibit 5**.

Exhibit 4

Competitive Sales & Store Comparison (1990–1999 Calendar Years)[1]
(Dollar amounts in thousands)

Year	Kmart Sales	Stores[1]	Sales	Wal-Mart Stores[1]
1999	$35,925,000	2,171	$165,013,000	3,989
1998	33,674,000	2,161	137,634,000	3,999
1997	32,183,000	2,136	117,958,000	3,406
1996	31,437,000	2,261	104,859,000	3,054
1995	34,389,000	2,161	93,627,000	2,943
1994	34,025,000	2,481	82,494,000	2,684
1993	34,156,000	2,486	67,344,000	2,400
1992	37,724,000	2,435	55,484,000	2,136
1991	34,580,000	2,391	43,886,900	1,928
1990	32,070,000	2,350	32,601,594	1,721

Note:
1. Number of general merchandise stores.

Some retailers like Kmart had initially focused on appealing to professional, middle-class consumers who lived in suburban areas and who were likely to be price sensitive. Other firms like Target, which had adopted the discount concept early, attempted to go generally after an upscale consumer. Some firms such as Fleet Farm and Pamida served the rural consumer, while firms like Value City and Ames Discount Department Stores chose to serve the urban consumer.

In rural communities Wal-Mart success often came at the expense of established local merchants and units of regional discount store chains. Hardware stores, family department stores, building supply outlets, and stores featuring fabrics, sporting goods and shoes were among the first to either close or relocate elsewhere. Regional discount retailers in the Sunbelt states like Roses, Howard's, T.G.& Y. and Duckwall-ALCO, who once enjoyed solid sales and earnings, were forced to reposition themselves by renovating stores, opening bigger and more modern units, remerchandising assortments, and offering lower prices. In many cases, stores like Coast-to-Coast and Ben Franklin closed upon a Wal-Mart announcement that it was planning to build in a specific community. "Just the word that Wal-Mart was coming made some stores close up," indicated 1 local newspaper editor.

Domestic Corporate Strategies

The corporate and marketing strategies that emerged at Wal-Mart were based upon a set of 2 main objectives that had guided the firm through its growth years. In the first objective the customer was featured, "customers would be provided what they want, when they want it, all at a value." In the second objective the team spirit was emphasized, "treating each other as we would hope to be treated, acknowledging our total dependency on our Associate-partners to sustain our success." The approach included: aggressive plans for new store openings; expansion to additional states; upgrading, relocation, refurbishing and remodeling of existing stores; and opening new distribution centers. For Wal-Mart management, the 1990s were considered an era in which the firm grew to become a truly nationwide retailer which operated in all 50 states. At the beginning of 2000, Wal-Mart management predicted that over the next 5 years, 60 to 70% of sales and earnings growth would come from domestic markets with Wal-Mart stores and Supercenters, and another 10 to 15% from SAM's Club and McLane. The remaining 20% of the growth would

Exhibit 5

An Industry Comparative Analysis (1999 Calendar Year)

	Wal-Mart	Sears	Kmart	Target
A. Store Comparison				
Sales (Millions)	$165,013	$41,071	$35,925	$33,702
Net Income (Thousands)	$5,377	$1,453	$403	$1,144
Net Income Per Share	$1.21	$3.83	$1.29	$2.45
Dividends Per Share	$.14	$n/a	$n/a	$.40
% Sales Change	20.0%	2.7%	6.6%	9.9%

Number of Stores:

Wal-Mart United States
Discount Stores—1,801
SAM's Clubs—463
Supercenters—721

Wal-Mart International
Discount Stores—572
SAM's Clubs—49
Supercenters—383

Sears, Roebuck and Company (all divisions)
Sears Merchandise Group
Full-line Department Stores—858
Hardware Stores—267
Sears Dealer Stores—738
Sears Auto Centers Stores—798
NTB (National Tire & Battery Stores)—310

Kmart Corporation
Big Kmart—1,860
Traditional Kmart—206
Super Kmart—105

Target Corporation
Target—912
Mervyn's—267
Department Stores—64

B. How the Stores Did

DISCOUNTERS	TOTAL SALES 2000 (millions)	LATEST MONTH Change from year earlier	COMPARABLE STORES Changes from year earlier	TOTAL SALES 2000 (millions)	YEAR-TO-DATE Changes from year earlier	COMPARABLE STORES Changes from year earlier
Wal-Mart	$14,140.0	+28.4%	+10.9%	$44,011.0	+23.6%	+6.6%
Kmart	2,770.0	+0.8	−0.8	8,195.0	+1.5	+0.0
Target	2,460.0	+17.0	+11.1	7,612.0	+8.2	+3.2
Costco	2,270.0	+13.0	+9.0	20,610.0	+16.0	+12.0
Dollar General	305.0	+17.9	+3.6	996.7	+18.1	+4.0
Ames	265.7	−6.2	+4.1	830.7	+1.8	+1.2

Sources: A. Corporate Annual Reports. *B.* Adapted from *Wall Street Journal* (February 4, 2000), p. 2B.

come from planned growth in international markets. As David Glass once noted, "We'll be fine as long as we never lose our responsiveness to the customer."

In the decade of the 1980s, Wal-Mart developed a number of new retail formats. The first SAM's Club opened in Oklahoma City, Oklahoma in 1983. The wholesale club was an idea which had been developed by other firms earlier but which found its greatest success and growth in acceptability at Wal-Mart. SAM's Clubs featured a vast array of product categories with limited selection of brand and model; cash-and-carry business with limited hours; large (100,000 square foot), bare-bones facilities; rock bottom wholesale prices; and minimal promotion. The limited membership plan permitted wholesale members who bought membership and others who usually paid a percentage above the ticket price of the merchandise. A revision in merchandising strategy resulted in fewer items in the inventory mix with more emphasis on lower prices. A later acquisition of 100 Pace warehouse clubs, which were converted into SAM's Clubs, increased that division's units by more than a third. At the beginning of 2000, there were 463 SAM's Clubs in operation.

Wal-Mart Supercenters were large combination stores. They were first opened in 1988 as Hypermarket*USA, a 222,000 square foot superstore which combined a discount store with a large grocery store, a food court of restaurants and other service businesses such as banks or videotape rental stores. A scaled down version of Hypermarket*USA was called the Wal-Mart Supercenter, similar in merchandise offerings, but with about 180,000 to 200,000 square feet of space. These expanded store concepts also included convenience stores, and gasoline distribution outlets to "enhance shopping convenience." The company proceeded slowly with these plans and later suspended its plans for building any more hypermarkets in favor of the Supercenter concept. At the beginning of 2000, Wal-Mart operated 721 Supercenters. The name, Hypermarket*USA, was no longer used to identify these large stores.

Wal-Mart also tested a new concept called the Neighborhood Market in a number of locations in Arkansas. Identified by the company as "small-marts," these green-and-white stores were stocked with fresh fruits and vegetables, a drive-up pharmacy, a 24-hour photo shop, and a selection of classic Wal-Mart hard goods. Management elected to move slowly on this concept, planning to open no more than 10 a year. The goal was to ring the Superstores with these smaller stores to attract customers who were in a hurry and wanted only a few items.

The McLane Company, Inc., a provider of retail and grocery distribution services for retail stores, was acquired in 1991. It was not considered a major segment of the total Wal-Mart operation.

Several programs were launched in Wal-Mart stores to "highlight" popular social causes. The "Buy American" program was a Wal-Mart retail program initiated in 1985. The theme was "Bring It Home to the USA" and its purpose was to communicate Wal-Mart's support for American manufacturing. In the program, the firm directed substantial influence to encourage manufacturers to produce goods in the United States rather than import them from other countries. Vendors were attracted into the program by encouraging manufacturers to initiate the process by contacting the company directly with proposals to sell goods that were made in the United States. Buyers also targeted specific import items in their assortments on a state-by-state basis to encourage domestic manufacturing. According to Haim Dabah, president of Gitano Group, Inc., a maker of fashion discount clothing which imported 95% of its clothing and now makes about 20% of its products here: "Wal-Mart let it be known loud and clear that if you're going to grow with them, you sure better have some products made in the U.S.A." Farris Fashion, Inc. (flannel shirts); Roadmaster Corporation (exercise bicycles); Flanders Industries, Inc. (lawn chairs); and Magic Chef (microwave ovens) were examples of vendors that chose to participate in the program.

From the Wal-Mart standpoint the "Buy American" program centered around value —producing and selling quality merchandise at a competitive price. The promotion included television advertisements featuring factory workers, a soaring American eagle, and the slogan:

"We buy American whenever we can, so you can too." Prominent in-store signage, and store circulars were also included. One store poster read: "Success Stories—These items formerly imported, are now being purchased by Wal-Mart in the U.S.A."

Wal-Mart was 1 of the first retailers to embrace the concept of "green" marketing. The program offered shoppers the option of purchasing products that were better for the environment in 3 respects: manufacturing, use, and disposal. It was introduced through full-page advertisements in the *Wall Street Journal* and *USA Today*. In-store signage identified those products that were environmentally safe. As Wal-Mart executives saw it, "customers are concerned about the quality of land, air, and water, and would like the opportunity to do something positive." To initiate the program, 7,000 vendors were notified that Wal-Mart had a corporate concern for the environment and to ask for their support in a variety of ways. Wal-Mart television advertising showed children on swings, fields of grain blowing in the wind, and roses. Green and white store signs, printed on recycled paper, marked products or packaging that had been developed or redesigned to be more environmentally sound.

The Wal-Mart private brand program began with the "Ol' Roy" brand, the private label dog food named for Sam Walton's favorite hunting companion. Introduced to Wal-Mart stores in 1982 as a low-price alterative to national brands, Ol' Roy became the biggest seller of all dog-food brands in the United States. "We are a (national) brand-oriented company first," noted Bob Connolly, Executive Vice President of Merchandising of Wal-Mart. "But we also use private label to fill value or pricing void that, for whatever reason, the brands left behind. Wal-Mart's private label program included thousands of products that had brand names such as SAM's Choice, Great Value, Equate, and Spring Valley.

Wal-Mart had become the channel commander in the distribution of many brand name items. As the nation's largest retailer and in many geographic areas the dominant distributor, it exerted considerable influence in negotiation for the best price, delivery terms, promotion allowances, and continuity of supply. Many of these benefits could be passed on to consumers in the form of quality name-brand items available at lower than competitive prices. As a matter of corporate policy, management often insisted on doing business only with producer's top sales executives rather than going through a manufacturer's representative. Wal-Mart had been accused of threatening to buy from other producers if firms refuse to sell directly to it. In the ensuing power struggle, Wal-Mart executives refused to talk about the controversial policy or admit that it existed. As a representative of an industry association representing a group of sales agencies representatives suggested, "In the Southwest, Wal-Mart's the only show in town." An industry analyst added, "They're extremely aggressive. Their approach has always been to give the customer the benefit of a corporate saving. That builds up customer loyalty and market share."

Another key factor in the mix was an inventory control system that was recognized as the most sophisticated in retailing. A high-speed computer system linked virtually all the stores to headquarters and the company's distribution centers. It electronically logged every item sold at the checkout counter, automatically kept the warehouses informed of merchandise to be ordered and directed the flow of good to the stores and even to the proper shelves. Most important for management, it helped detect sales trends quickly and speeded up market reaction time substantially. According to Bob Connolly, Executive Vice President of Merchandising, "Wal-Mart has used the data gathered by technology to make more inventory available in the key items that customers want most, while reducing inventories overall."

At the beginning of 2000, Wal-Mart set up a separate company for its Web site with plans to go public. Wal-Mart.com.Inc., based in Palo Alto, California, was jointly owned by Wal-Mart and Accel Partners, a Silicon Valley venture-capital firm. The site included a wide range of products and services that ranged from shampoo to clothing to lawn mowers as well as airline, hotel and rental car bookings. After launching and then closing a SAM's Club Web site, Wal-Mart had plans to reopen the site in mid June, 2000 with an emphasis on upscale items such as jewelry, housewares, and electronics and full product lines for small business owners. SamsClub.com would be run by Wal-Mart from the company's Bentonville, Arkansas, headquarters.

International Corporate Strategies

In 1994, Wal-Mart entered the Canadian market with the acquisition of 122 Woolco discount stores from Woolworth Corporation. When acquired, the Woolco stores were losing millions of dollars annually, but operations became profitable within 3 years. At the end of 1999, the company had 166 Wal-Mart discount stores in Canada and planned to open 17 new stores in fiscal 2000. The company's operations in Canada were considered as a model for Wal-Mart's expansion into other international markets. With 35% of the Canadian discount and department store market Wal-Mart was the largest retailer in that country.

With a tender offer for shares and mergers of joint ventures in Mexico, the company in 1997 acquired a controlling interest in Cifra, Mexico's largest retailer. Cifra, later identified as Wal-Mart de Mexico, operated stores with a variety of concepts in every region of Mexico, ranging from the nation's largest chain of sit-down restaurants to a softline department store. Retail analysts noted that the initial venture involved many costly mistakes. Time-after-time it sold the wrong products, including tennis balls that wouldn't bounce in high-altitude Mexico City. Large parking lots at some stores made access difficult as many people arrived by bus. In 2000, Wal-Mart operated 397 Cifra outlets in Mexico, in addition to 27 Wal-Mart Supercenters and 34 SAM's Club Stores.

When Wal-Mart entered Argentina in 1995, it also initially faced challenges adapting its U.S.-based retail mix and store layouts to the local culture. Although globalization and American cultural influences had swept through the country in the early 1990s, the Argentine market did not accept American cuts of meat, bright colored cosmetics, and jewelry that gave prominent placement to emeralds, sapphires, and diamonds even though most Argentine women preferred wearing gold and silver. The first stores even had hardware departments full of tools wired for 110-volt electric power; the standard throughout Argentina was 220. Compounding the challenges was store layout that featured narrow aisles; stores appeared crowded and dirty.

Wal-Mart management concluded that Brazil offered great opportunities for Wal-Mart, with the fifth largest population in the world and a population that had a tendency to follow U.S. cultural cues. Although financial data were not broken out on South American operations, retail analysts cited the accounts of Wal-Mart's Brazilian partner, Lojas Americanas SA, to suggest that Wal-Mart lost $100 million in start up costs of the initial 16 stores. Customer acceptance of Wal-Mart stores was mixed. In Canada and Mexico, many customers were familiar with the company from cross-border shopping trips. Many Brazilian customers were not familiar with the Wal-Mart name. In addition, local Brazilian markets were already dominated by savvy local and foreign competitors such as Grupo Pao de Acucar SA of Brazil and Carrefour SA of France. And Wal-Mart's insistence on doing things "the Wal-Mart way" initially alienated many local suppliers and employees. The country's continuing economic problems also presented a challenge. In 2000, Wal-Mart planned to expand its presence by opening 3 more SAM's Clubs in Brazil.

Because of stubborn local regulations, management felt it would be easier for Wal-Mart to buy existing stores in Europe than to build new ones. The acquisition of 21 "hypermarkets" in Germany at the end of 1997 marked the company's first entry into Europe, which management considered "1 of the best consumer markets in the world." These large stores offered 1-stop shopping facilities similar to Wal-Mart Supercenters. In early 1999 the firm also purchased 74 Interspar hypermarket stores. All of these German stores were identified with the Wal-Mart name and restocked with a new and revamped selection of merchandise. In a response to local laws that forced early store closings and forbid Sunday sales, the company simply opened stores earlier to allow shopping to begin at 7 A.M.

Wal-Mart acquired ASDA, Britain's third largest supermarket group, for $10.8 billion in July 1999. With its own price rollbacks, people greeter, "permanently low prices" and even "smiley" faces, ASDA had emulated Wal-Mart's store culture for many years. Based in Leeds,

England, the firm had 232 stores in England, Scotland, and Wales. While the culture and pricing strategies of the 2 companies were nearly identical, there were differences, primarily the size and product mix of the stores. The average Wal-Mart Supercenter in 1999 was 180,000 square feet in size and had about 30% of its sales in groceries. In contrast, the average ASDA store had only 65,000 square feet and did 60% of sales in grocery items.

The response in Europe to Wal-Mart was immediate and dramatic. Competitors scrambled to match Wal-Mart's low prices, long hours, and friendly service. Some firms combined to strengthen their operations. For example, France's Carrefour SA chain of hypermarkets combined forces with competitor, Promodes, in a $16.5 billion deal. In 1999, Carrefour dominated the European market with 9,089 locations. It was also 1 of the world's largest retailers with market dominance not only in Europe, but in Latin America and Asia as well.

Wal-Mart's initial effort to enter China fell apart in 1996, when Wal-Mart and Thailand's Charoen Pokphand Group terminated an 18-month-old joint venture because of management differences. Wal-Mart decided to consolidate its operations with 5 stores in the Hong Kong border city of Shenzhen, one in Dalian, and another in Kumming. Although management had plans to open 10 additional stores in China by the end of 2000, analysts concluded that the company was taking a low profile approach because of possible competitive response and government restrictions. Beijing restricted the operations of foreign retailers in China, requiring them, for instance, to have government backed partners. In Shenzhen, it limited the number of stores Wal-Mart could open. Planned expansion in the China market came as China prepared to enter the World Trade Organization and its economy showed signs of accelerating. At the beginning of 2000, Wal-Mart also operated 5 Supercenters in South Korea.

The international expansion accelerated management's plans for the development of Wal-Mart as a global brand along the lines of Coca-Cola, Disney, and McDonald's. "We are a global brand name," said Bobby Martin, an early President of the International Division of Wal-Mart. "To customers everywhere it means low cost, best value, greatest selection of quality merchandise, and highest standards of customer service," he noted. Some changes were mandated in Wal-Mart's international operations to meet local tastes and intense competitive conditions. "We're building companies out there," said Martin. "That's like starting Wal-Mart all over again in South America or Indonesia or China." Although stores in different international markets would coordinate purchasing to gain leverage with suppliers, developing new technology and planning overall strategy would be done from Wal-Mart headquarters in Bentonville, Arkansas. At the beginning of 2000, the International Division of Wal-Mart operated 572 discount stores, 383 Supercenters, and 49 SAM's Clubs. Wal-Mart's international unit accounted for $22.7 billion in sales in 1999. **Exhibit 6** shows the countries in which stores were operated and the number of units in each country.

Exhibit 6

Wal-Mart International Division
(1999)

Country	Stores
Mexico	460
United Kingdom	236
Canada	166
Germany	95
Brazil	16
Puerto Rico	15
Argentina	10
China	8
South Korea	5

Source: Wal-Mart, Hoovers Online.

Decision Making in a Market-Oriented Firm

One principle that distinguished Wal-Mart was the unusual depth of employee involvement in company affairs. Corporate strategies put emphasis on human resource management. Employees of Wal-Mart became "associates," a name borrowed from Sam Walton's early association with the J.C. Penney Co. Input was encouraged at meetings at the store and corporate level. The firm hired employees locally, provided training programs, and through a "Letter to the President" program, management encouraged employees to ask questions, and made words like "we," "us," and "our" a part of the corporate language. A number of special award programs recognized individual, department, and division achievement. Stock ownership and profit-sharing programs were introduced as part of a "partnership concept."

The corporate culture was recognized by the editors of the trade publication, *Mass Market Retailers*, when it recognized all 275,000 associates collectively as the "Mass Market Retailers of the Year." "The Wal-Mart associate," the editors noted, "in this decade that term has come to symbolize all that is right with the American worker, particularly in the retailing environment and most particularly at Wal-Mart." The "store within a store" concept, as a Wal-Mart corporate policy, trained individuals to be merchants by being responsible for the performance of their own departments as if they were running their own businesses. Seminars and training programs afforded them opportunities to grow within the company. "People development, not just a good 'program' for any growing company but a must to secure our future," is how Suzanne Allford, Vice President of the Wal-Mart People Division explained the firm's decentralized approach to retail management development.

"The Wal-Mart Way," was a phase that was used by management to summarize the firm's unconventional approach to business and the development of the corporate culture. As noted in a report referring to a recent development program: "We stepped outside our retailing world to examine the best managed companies in the United States in an effort to determine the fundamentals of their success and to 'benchmark' our own performances." The name 'Total Quality Management' (TQM) was used to identify this vehicle for proliferating the very best things we do while incorporating the new ideas our people have that will assure our future." In 1999, *Discount Store News* honored Wal-Mart Stores, Inc., as "Retailer of the Century" with a commemorative 200-page issue of the magazine.

The Growth Challenge

H. Lee Scott, Jr., indicated that he would never forget his first meeting with Sam Walton. "How old are you?" Walton asked the then 30-year-old Scott, who had just taken a job overseeing the Wal-Mart trucking fleet. "Do you think you can do this job?" asked Walton. When Scott said yes, Walton agreed and said "I reckon you can." More than 20 years later as Wal-Mart's new CEO, Scott was facing his toughest challenge yet: keeping the world's biggest retailer on its phenomenal roll and delivering the huge sales and earnings increases that investors had come to expect from Wal-Mart over the years. Analysts had correctly projected that Wal-Mart would surpass General Motors to be ranked number 1 in revenue on the *Fortune* 500 list 2000. The combination of growth and acquisition had caused revenue to make huge leaps every year. In 1999 it went up 20%, from $139 billion in 1998 to $165 billion. Earnings also increased in 1999 by 21%, to nearly $5.4 billion. Industry analysts noted that this growth was on top of an 18% compound annual growth rate over the past decade.

Wal-Mart Stores, Inc., revolutionized American retailing with focus on low costs, high customer service, and everyday low pricing to drive sales. Although the company had suffered though some years of lagging performance, it had experienced big gains from its move into the grocery business with 1-stop supercenters and in international markets with acquisition and new ventures. To keep it all going and growing was a major challenge. As the largest retailer in the world, the company and its leadership was challenged to find new areas to continue to grow sales and profits into the future. Lee Scott knew that an ambitious expansion program was called for to allow the company to meet these objectives.

Financial Situation

Wal-Mart's financial position is shown in **Exhibits 1, 7,** and **8.** A 5-year (2000–1996) record of financial performance of Wal-Mart is shown in **Exhibit 8**. In FY 1990, Kmart's sales were $32,070,000,000, and Wal-Mart's sales were $32,601,594,000. In FY 1991, Kmart's sales were up $35,925,000,000 (an increase $3,855,000,000 or 12.02%), while Wal-Mart's sales increased to $165,013,000,000 (an increase of $132,411,406,000 or 406.15%). Wal-Mart's sales increase was 34.347 times larger than Kmart's sale increase. Wal-Mart's FY 1999, net income was $5,575,000,000 compared with Kmart's net income of $403,000,000. Kmart had 1,860 Big Kmart stores, 105 Super Kmart Centers, and 202 Discount stores for a total of 2,167. Wal-Mart had 2,373 Wal-Mart stores, 512 SAM's Clubs, and 1,104 Supercenters, for a total of 3,989 stores.

Exhibit 7

Consolidated Balance Sheets and Operating Statements, 1998–99: Wal-Mart Stores, Inc.
(Dollar amounts in millions)

Fiscal Year Ending January 31	2000	1999
Assets		
Current assets:		
Cash and cash equivalents	$ 1,856	$ 1,879
Receivables	1,341	1,118
Inventories		
At replacement cost	20,171	17,549
Less LIFO reserve	378	473
Inventories at LIFO cost	19,793	17,076
Prepaid expenses and other	1,366	1,059
Total current assets	24,356	21,132
Property, plant and equipment, at cost:		
Land	8,785	5,219
Building and improvements	21,169	16,061
Fixtures and equipment	10,362	9,296
Transportation equipment	747	553
	41,063	31,129
Less accumulated depreciation	8,224	7,455
Net property, plant and equipment	32,839	23,674
Property under capital lease:		
Property under capital lease	4,285	3,335
Less accumulated amortization	1,155	1,036
Net property under capital leases	3,130	2,299
Other assets and deferred charges:		
Net goodwill and other acquired intangible assets	9,392	2,538
Other assets and deferred charges	632	353
Total assets	$70,349	$49,996
Liabilities and shareholders' equity		
Current liabilities:		
Commercial paper	$ 3,323	$ —
Accounts payable	13,105	10,257
Accrued liabilities	6,161	4,998
Accrued income taxes	1,129	501
Long-term debt due within 1 year	1,964	900
Obligations under capital leases due within 1 year	121	106
Total current liabilities	25,803	16,762
Long-Term Debt	13,672	6,908
Long-Term Obligations Under Capital Leases	3,002	2,699
Deferred Income Taxes and Other	759	716
Minority Interest	1,279	1,799
Shareholders' equity		
Preferred stock ($.10 par value; 100 shares authorized, none issued)		
Common stock ($.10 par value; 5,500 shares authorized, 4,457 and 4,448 issued and outstanding in 2000 and 1999, respectively)	446	445
Capital in excess of par value	714	435
Retained earnings	25,129	20,741
Other accumulated comprehensive income	(455)	(509)
Total Shareholders' Equity	25,834	21,112
Total liabilities and shareholders' equity	$70,349	$49,996

Notes were deleted.

Source: Wal-Mart Stores, Inc., *2000 Annual Report.*

Exhibit 8

11-Year Financial Summary 1990–2000: Wal-Mart Stores, Inc.
(Dollar amounts in millions except per share data)

	2000	1999	1998	1997	1996
Net sales	$165,013	$137,634	$117,958	$104,859	$93,627
Net sales increase	*20%*	*17%*	*12%*	*12%*	*13%*
Comparative store sales increase	*8%*	*9%*	*6%*	*5%*	*4%*
Other income-net	1,796	1,574	1,341	1,319	1,146
Cost of sales	129,664	108,725	93,438	83,510	74,505
Operating, selling and general and administrative expenses	27,040	22,363	19,358	16,946	15,021
Interest costs:					
Debt	756	529	555	629	692
Capital leases	266	268	229	216	196
Provision for income taxes	3,338	2,740	2,115	1,794	1,606
Minority interest and equity in unconsolidated subsidiaries	(170)	(153)	(78)	(27)	(13)
Cumulative effect of accounting change, net of tax	(198)	—	—	—	—
Net income	$ 5,377	$ 4,430	$ 3,526	$ 3,056	$ 2,740
Per share of common stock:					
Basic net income	1.21	0.99	0.78	0.67	0.60
Diluted net income	1.20	0.99	0.78	0.67	0.60
Dividends	0.20	0.16	0.14	0.11	0.10
Financial position					
Current assets	$ 24,356	$ 21,132	$ 19,352	$ 17,993	$17,331
Inventories at replacement cost	20,171	17,549	16,845	16,193	16,300
Less LIFO reserve	378	473	348	296	311
Inventories at LIFO cost	19,793	17,076	16,497	15,897	15,989
Net property, plant and equipment and capital leases	35,969	25,973	23,606	20,324	18,894
Total assets	70,349	49,996	45,384	39,604	37,541
Current liabilities	25,803	16,762	14,460	10,957	11,454
Long-term debt	13,672	6,908	7,191	7,709	8,508
Long-term obligations under capital leases	3,002	2,699	2,483	2,307	2,092
Shareholders' equity	25,834	21,112	18,503	17,143	14,756
Financial ratios					
Current ratio	.9	1.3	1.3	1.6	1.5
Inventories/working capital	(13.7)	3.9	3.4	2.3	2.7
Return on assets	9.8%***	9.6%	8.5%	7.9%	7.8%
Return on shareholders' equity	22.9%	22.4%	19.8%	19.2%	19.9%
Other year-end data					
Number of domestic Wal-Mart stores	1,801	1,869	1,921	1,960	1,995
Number of domestic Supercenters	721	564	441	344	239
Number of domestic SAM's Club units	463	451	443	436	433
International units	1,004	715	601	314	276
Number of Associates	1,140,000	910,000	825,000	728,000	675,000
Number of Shareholders	341,000	261,000	246,000	257,000	244,000

Exhibit 8

11-Year Financial Summary 1990–2000: Wal-Mart Stores, Inc. *(continued)*

	1995	1994	1993	1992	1991	1990
Net sales	$82,494	$67,344	$55,484	$43,887	$32,602	$25,811
Net sales increase	*22%*	*21%*	*26%*	*35%*	*26%*	*25%*
Comparative store sales increase	*7%*	*6%*	*11%*	*10%*	*10%*	*11%*
Other income-net	914	645	497	404	262	175
Cost of sales	65,586	53,444	44,175	34,786	25,500	20,070
Operating, selling and general and administrative expenses	12,858	10,333	8,321	6,684	5,152	4,070
Interest costs:						
Debt	520	331	143	113	43	20
Capital leases	186	186	180	153	126	118
Provision for income taxes	1,581	1,358	1,171	945	752	632
Minority interest and equity in unconsolidated subsidiaries	4	(4)	4	(1)	—	—
Cumulative effect of accounting change, net of tax	—	—	—	—	—	—
Net income	$ 2,681	$ 2,333	$ 1,995	$ 1,609	$ 1,291	$ 1,076
Per share of common stock:						
Basic net income	0.59	0.51	0.44	0.35	0.28	0.24
Diluted net income	0.59	0.51	0.44	0.35	0.28	0.24
Dividends	0.09	0.07	0.05	0.04	0.04	0.03
Financial position						
Current assets	$15,338	$12,114	$10,198	$8,575	$6,415	$ 4,713
Inventories at replacement cost	14,415	11,483	9,780	7,857	6,207	4,751
Less LIFO reserve	351	469	512	473	399	323
Inventories at LIFO cost	14,064	11,014	9,268	7,384	5,808	4,428
Net property, plant and equipment and capital leases	15,874	13,176	9,793	6,434	4,712	3,430
Total assets	32,819	26,441	20,565	15,443	11,389	8,198
Current liabilities	9,973	7,406	6,754	5,004	3,990	2,845
Long-term debt	7,871	6,156	3,073	1,722	740	185
Long-term obligations under capital leases	1,838	1,804	1,772	1,556	1,159	1,087
Shareholders' equity	12,726	10,753	8,759	6,990	5,366	3,966
Financial ratios						
Current ratio	1.5	1.6	1.5	1.7	1.6	1.7
Inventories/working capital	2.6	2.3	2.7	2.1	2.4	2.4
Return on assets	9.0%	9.9%	11.1%	12.0%	13.2%	14.8%
Return on shareholders' equity	22.8%	23.9%	25.3%	26.0%	27.7%	30.9%
Other year-end data						
Number of domestic Wal-Mart stores	1,985	1,950	1,848	1,714	1,568	1,399
Number of domestic Supercenters	147	72	34	10	9	6
Number of domestic SAM's Club units	426	417	256	208	148	123
International units	226	24	10	—	—	—
Number of Associates	622,000	528,000	434,000	371,000	328,000	271,000
Number of Shareholders	259,000	258,000	181,000	150,000	122,000	80,000

Notes were deleted.

Source: Wal-Mart Stores, Inc.

Notes

Mark Albright, "Changes in Store," *New York Times* (May 17, 1999), pp. 10, 12.

Joan Bergman, "Saga of Sam Walton," *Stores* (January 1988), pp. 129–130+.

Neil E. Boudette, "Wal-Mart Plans Major Expansion in Germany," *Wall Street Journal* (July 20, 2000), p. A21.

Chip Cummins, "Wal-Mart's Net Income Increases 28%, But Accounting Change Worries Investors," *Wall Street Journal* (August 10, 2000), p. A6.

"David Glass's Biggest Job Is Filling SAM's Shoes," *Business Month* (December 1988), p. 42.

Amy Feldman, "How Big Can It Get?" *Money* (December 1999), pp. 158+.

Johnathan Friedland and Louise Lee, "The Wal-Mart Way Sometimes Gets Lost in Translation Overseas," *Wall Street Journal* (October 8, 1997), pp. A1, A12.

Constance Gustke, "Smooth Operator," *Worth* (March 2000), pp. 41+.

Kevin Helliker, "Wal-Mart's Store of the Future Blends Discount Prices, Department-Store Feel," *Wall Street Journal* (May 17, 1991), p. B1, B8.

Kevin Helliker and Bob Ortega, "Falling Profit Marks End of Era at Wal-Mart," *Wall Street Journal* (January 18, 1996), p. B1.

"How the Stores Did," *Wall Street Journal* (May 5, 2000), p. B4.

John Huey, "America's Most Successful Merchant," *Fortune* (September 23, 1991), pp. 46–48+.

Jay L. Johnson, "The Supercenter Challenge," *Discount Merchandiser* (August 1989), pp. 70+.

Steven Komarow, "Wal-Mart Takes Slow Road in Germany," *USA Today* (May 5, 2000) p. 3B.

Clifford Krauss, "Wal-Mart Learns a Hard Lesson," *International Herald Tribune* (December 6, 1999), p. 15.

John Larrabee, "Wal-Mart Ends Vermont's Holdout," *USA Today* (September 19, 1995), p. 4B.

Louise Lee, "Discounter Wal-Mart Is Catering to Affluent to Maintain Growth," *Wall Street Journal* (February 7, 1996), pp. A1.

Louise Lee and Joel Millman, "Wal-Mart to Buy Majority Stake in Cifra," *Wall Street Journal* (June 4, 1997), pp. A3+.

Carol J. Loomis, "Sam Would Be Proud," *Fortune* (April 17, 2000), pp. 131+.

"Management Style: Sam Moore Walton," *Business Month* (May 1989), p. 38.

Barbara Marsch, "The Challenge: Merchants Mobilize to Battle Wal-Mart in a Small Community," *Wall Street Journal* (June 5, 1991), pp. A1, A4.

Todd Mason, "Sam Walton of Wal-Mart: Just Your Basic Homespun Billionaire," *Business Week* (October 14, 1985), pp. 142–143+.

Brandon Mitchener and David Woodruff, "French Merger of Hypermarkets Gets a Go-Ahead," *Wall Street Journal* (January 26, 2000), p. A19.

Emily Nelson, "Wal-Mart to Build a Test Supermarket in Bid to Boost Grocery-Industry Share," *Wall Street Journal* (June 19, 1998), p. A4.

Emily Nelson and Kara Swisher, "Wal-Mart Eyes Public Sale of Web Unit," *Wall Street Journal* (January 7, 2000), p. A3.

"Our People Make the Difference: The History of Wal-Mart," Video Cassette (Bentonville, Arkansas: Wal-Mart Video Productions, 1991).

Tom J. Peters and Nancy Austin, *A Passion For Excellence* (New York: Random House, 1989), pp. 266–267.

Cynthia Dunn Rawn, "Wal-Mart vs. Main Street," *American Demographics* (June 1990), pp. 58–59.

"Retailer Completes Purchase of Wertkauf of Germany," *Wall Street Journal* (December 31, 1997), p. B3.

Howard Rudnitsky, "How Sam Walton Does It," *Forbes* (August 16, 1982), pp. 42–44.

"Sam Moore Walton," *Business Month* (May 1989), p. 38.

Francine Schwadel, "Little Touches Spur Wal-Mart's Rise," *Wall Street Journal* (September 22, 1989), p. B1.

Sears, Roebuck and Co., *Annual Report*, Chicago, Illinois, 1999.

Kenneth R. Sheets, "How Wal-Mart Hits Main St.," *U.S. News & World Report* (March 13, 1989), pp. 53–55.

Target Corporation, *Annual Report*, Minneapolis, Minnesota, 1999.

"The Early Days: Walton Kept Adding 'A Few More' Stores," *Discount Store News* (December 9, 1985), p. 61.

Richard Tomlinson, "Who's Afraid of Wal-Mart?" *Fortune* (June 26, 2000), p. 186.

Vance H. Trimble, *Sam Walton: The Inside Story of America's Richest Man* (New York: Dutton, 1990).

Susanna Voyle, "Asda Criticised for Price Claims," *Financial Times* (December 8, 1999), p. 3.

"Wal-Mart Spoken Here," *Business Week* (June 23, 1997), pp. 138+.

Wal-Mart Stores, Inc., *Annual Report*, Bentonville, Arkansas, 2000.

"Wal-Mart's Asda Says CEO to Head Europe Expansion," *Wall Street Journal Europe* (December 3, 1999), p. 6.

"Wal-Mart Takes a Stand," *The Economist* (May 22, 1999), p. 31.

"Wal-Mart: The Model Discounter," *Dun's Business Month* (December 1982), pp. 60–61.

"Wal-Mart Wins Again," *The Economist* (October 2, 1999), p. 33.

Sam Walton, with John Huey, *Sam Walton Made in America* (New York: Doubleday Publishing Company, 1992).

Peter Wonacott, "Wal-Mart Finds Market Footing in China," *Wall Street Journal* (July 17, 2000), p. A31.

"Work, Ambition—Sam Walton," Press Release, Corporate and Public Affairs, Wal-Mart Stores, Inc.

Wendy Zellner, "Someday, Lee, This May All Be Yours," *Business Week* (November 15, 1999), pp. 84+.

Ann Zimmerman, "Wal-Mart Posts 19% Profit Rise, Exceeding Analysts Expectations," *Wall Street Journal* (May 10, 2000), p. B8.

Ann Zimmerman, "Wal-Mart to Open Reworked Web Site for SamsClub.com," *Wall Street Journal* (June 6, 2000), p. B8.

CASE 24

The Home Depot, Inc.: Growing the Professional Market (Revised)

Thomas L. Wheelen, Hitesh (John) P. Adhia, Thomas H. Cangley, and Paul M. Swiercz

On April 23, 1988, Arthur M. Blank, President and Chief Executive Officer (CEO) was presiding over a strategic planning session for new strategies for each of Home Depot's 6 regional divisions (see "Organizational Structure") for the professional contractor market. Home Depot's management estimated this market to be $215 billion in 1997. Home Depot has been concentrating on the Do-It-Yourself/Buy-It-Yourself market sector, which Home Depot management had estimated to be $100 billion in 1997. Home Depot sales were $24.1 billion in 1997. **Exhibit 1** shows the combined sales for the Do-It-Yourself/Buy-It-Yourself sector and the professional sector to be $365 billion. The heavy industry sector was treated as a separate market sector. In 1998, Home Depot had less than 4% of the $215 billion professional sector.

In early April 1998, the company's management announced a new store format. In 1998, the company planned to build 4 new smaller stores with about 25% (25,000 square feet) of the existing store size. These stores would be similar to local hardware stores or Ace Hardware stores.

The Home Depot, Inc.

Founded in Atlanta, Georgia, in 1978, Home Depot was the world's largest home improvement retailer and ranked among the 10 largest retailers in the United States. At the close of fiscal year 1997, the company was operating 624 full-service, warehouse-styled stores—555 stores in 44 states and 5 EXPO Design Center stores in the United States, plus 32 in 4 Canadian provinces (See **Exhibit 2**).

The average Home Depot store had approximately 106,300 square feet of indoor selling space and an additional 16,000–28,000 square feet of outside garden center, including houseplant enclosures. The stores stocked approximately 40,000–50,000 different kinds of building materials, home improvement products, and lawn and garden supplies. In addition, Home

This case was prepared by Professor Thomas L. Wheelen of the University of South Florida, Hitesh (John) P. Adhia, CPA, Founder of mutual fund, Adhia Funds, Inc., Thomas H. Cangley, Manager, of Raytheon Corporation and Professor Paul M. Swiercz of the George Washington University. The authors would like to thank the research assistants, Carla N. Mortellaro and Vincent E. Mortellaro, for their support. This case may not be reproduced in any form without written permission of the copyright holder, Thomas L. Wheelen. This case was edited for SMBP-8th Edition. Copyright © 1999 by Thomas L Wheelen. Reprinted by permission.

Exhibit 1
Total Market for Do-It-Yourself/Buy-It-Yourself Sector, Professional Sector, and Heavy Industry Sector

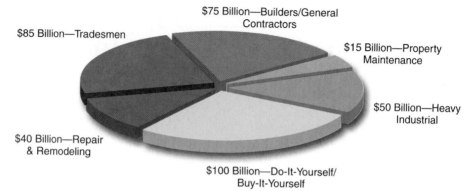

$365 Billion Market

Note: Home Improvement Research Institute, 1997 Product Sales Estimates; U.S. Census Bureau Product Sales Estimates.

Source: The Home Depot, Inc., *1997 Annual Report*, p. 3.

Depot stores offered installation services for many products. The company employed approximately 125,000 associates, of whom approximately 7,900 were salaried, and the remainder of the employees were paid on an hourly basis.

Retail industry analysts had credited Home Depot with being a leading innovator in retailing, by combining the economies of warehouse-format stores with a high level of customer service. The company augmented that concept with a corporate culture that valued decentralized management and decision making, entrepreneurial innovation and risk taking, and high levels of employee commitment and enthusiasm.

The stores served primarily the Do-It-Yourself (DIY) repair person, although home improvement contractors, building maintenance professionals, interior designers, and other professionals have become increasingly important customers.

Home Depot also owned 2 wholly owned subsidiaries, Maintenance Warehouse and National Blind & Wallpaper Factory. The company also owned Load 'N Go™, an exclusive rental truck service for their customers.

History[1]

Home Depot's Chairman, Bernard Marcus, began his career in the retail industry in a small pharmacy in Millburn, New Jersey. He later joined the Two Guys Discount Chain to manage its drug and cosmetics departments and eventually became the Vice President of Merchandising and Advertising for the parent company, Vornado, Inc. In 1972 he moved into the Do-It-Yourself home improvement sector as President and Chairman of the Board at Handy Dan/Handy City. The parent company, Daylin, Inc., was chaired by Sanford Sigoloff. He and Marcus had a strong difference of opinion over control, and 1 Friday at 5:00 P.M. in 1978, Marcus and 2 other Handy Dan top executives were discharged.

That weekend, Home Depot was born when the 3 men—Bernard Marcus, Arthur Blank, and Kenneth G. Langone—laid out plans for the Do-It-Yourself chain. Venture capital was provided by investment firms that included Inverned of New York as well as private investors. Two key investors were Joseph Flom, a takeover lawyer, and Frank Borman, then Chairman of Eastern Airlines.

Exhibit 2

Store Locations: Home Depot, Inc.

The Home Depot Canada
32 stores

Western Division
153 stores

Northeast Division
137 stores

Midwest Division
63 stores

Southwest Division
86 stores

Southeast Division
148 stores

Western Division	153
	Number
Location	**of Stores**
Arizona	**18**
Phoenix	14
Prescott	1
Tucson	3
California	**96**
Bakersfield	1
Fresno	3
Los Angeles	51
Modesto	1
Sacramento	5
San Diego	11
San Francisco	23
Stockton	1
Colorado	**10**
Colorado Springs	2
Denver	7
Pueblo	1
Idaho	**1**
Boise	1
Nevada	**5**
Las Vegas	3
Reno	2
Oregon	**7**
Eugene	1
Portland	6
Utah	**4**
Salt Lake City	4
Washington	**12**
Seattle/Tacoma	11
Spokane	1

Southeast Division	148
	Number
Location	**of Stores**
Alabama	**6**
Birmingham	3
Huntsville	1
Mobile	1
Montgomery	1
Florida	**63**
Daytona Beach/	
Melbourne/	
Orlando	10
Ft. Lauderdale/Miami/	
West Palm Beach	25
Ft. Myers, Naples	6

Ft. Walton	1
Gainesville/Ocala	3
Jacksonville	4
Pensacola	1
Tallahassee	1
Tampa/	
St. Petersburg	12
Georgia	**32**
Athens	1
Atlanta	24
Augusta	1
Columbus	1
Dalton	1
Macon	1
Rome	1
Savannah	1
Valdosta	1
Indiana	**1**
Clarksville	1
Kentucky	**3**
Lexington	1
Louisville	2
Mississippi	**1**
Horn Lake	1
North Carolina	**18**
Asheville	1
Charlotte	6
Fayetteville	1
Greensboro/	
Winston-Salem	3
Hickory	1
Raleigh	5
Wilmington	1
South Carolina	**7**
Charleston	1
Columbia	2
Greenville/	
Spartanburg	4
Tennessee	**17**
Chattanooga	2
Johnson City/	
Kingsport	2
Knoxville	3
Memphis	3
Nashville	7

Northeast Division	137
	Number
Location	**of Stores**
Connecticut	**13**
Hartford	6

New Haven	3
Danbury/Fairfield	
Norwalk	4
Delaware	**1**
Christana	1
Maine	**2**
Bangor	1
Portland	1
Maryland	**14**
Baltimore	8
Washington,	
DC area	**6**
Massachusetts	**17**
Boston	13
Southern Mass.	3
Springfield	1
New Hampshire	**4**
Manchester	1
Nashua	1
Portsmouth	1
Salem	1
New Jersey	**25**
Northern	
New Jersey	19
Southern	
New Jersey	6
New York	**32**
Albany	2
Buffalo	4
Hudson Valley	4
Johnson City	1
New York City/	
Long Island	16
Rochester	3
Syracuse	2
Pennsylvania	**20**
Allentown/	
Bethlehem	2
Harrisburg/	
Reading	3
Philadelphia	10
Pittsburgh	3
Scranton/	
Wilkes Barre	2
Rhode Island	**1**
Warwick	1
Vermont	**1**
Williston	1
Virginia	**7**
Washington,	
DC area	7

Southwest Division	86
	Number
Location	**of Stores**
Arkansas	**2**
Little Rock	2
Illinois	**1**
O'Fallon	1
Kansas	**1**
Kansas City	1
Louisiana	**9**
Baton Rouge	1
Lafayette	1
Lake Charles	1
New Orelans	5
Shreveport	1
Mississippi	**3**
Gulfport	1
Jackson	2
Missouri	**7**
Columbia	1
Kansas City	2
St. Louis	4
New Mexico	**3**
Albuquerque	3
Oklahoma	**6**
Oklahoma City	4
Tulsa	2
Texas	**54**
Auston	5
Beaumont	1
Corpus Christi	1
Dallas/Ft. Worth	21
El Paso	2
Houston	16
Lubbock	1
Midland	1
San Antonio	6

Midwest Division	63
	Number
Location	**of Stores**
Illinois	**24**
Chicago	23
Quincy	1
Indiana	**2**
Evansville	1
Hobart	1
Iowa	**1**
Waterloo	1

Michigan	**22**
Detroit	14
Flint/Saginaw	3
Grand Rapids	2
Kalamazoo	1
Lansing	1
Traverse City	1
Minnesota	**10**
Minneapolis/	10
St. Paul	
Ohio	**4**
Boardman	1
Cleveland	2
Toledo	1

Home Depot Canada	32
	Number
Location	**of Stores**
Alberta	**4**
Calgary	2
Edmonton	2
British Columbia	**8**
Vancouver	8
Manitoba	**1**
Winnipeg	1
Ontario	**19**
Kitchener	1
London	1
Ottawa	2
Toronto	14
Windsor	1

EXPO Design Center	5
	Number
Location	**of Stores**
Atlanta	1
Dallas	1
Long Island	1
Miami	1
San Diego	1

Total Stores	**624**

Source: Home Depot, Inc., *1994 Annual Report*, p. 32, and *1997 Annual Report*, p. 36.

When the first stores opened in Atlanta in 1979, the company leased space in 3 former Treasury Discount Stores with 60,000 square feet each. All 3 were suburban locations in the northern half of the city. Industry experts gave Home Depot 10-to-1 odds it would fail.

In 1980, a fourth Atlanta stored opened, and the company had annual sales of $22.3 million. The following year, Home Depot ventured beyond Atlanta to open 4 stores in South Florida and also had its first public offering at $12 a share. By early 1990, its stock had soared by 7,019% and split 8 times. In May 1995, an original share was worth $26,300.

In the early 1980s, inflation rose over 13%, and unemployment was as high as 9.5%. These were rough times for most start-up companies, but Home Depot prospered as hard-pressed shoppers sought out the best buy. The company was voted the Retailer of the Year in the home center industry in 1982 and had its first stock splits.

By 1983, Marcus was a nationally recognized leader in the Do-It-Yourself industry. New Orleans was a strong market with many homeowners and young people, so Home Depot moved in with 3 stores. Other additions were in Arizona and Florida. Two stores opened in Orlando, in the backyard of the Winter Haven–based Scotty's, and 1 more opened in South Florida. Home Depot's strong drawing power became evident as customers passively waited in long checkout lines.

In 1984, Home Depot's common stock was listed on the New York Stock Exchange. It was traded under the symbol "HD" and was included in the Standard & Poor's 500 Index. Marcus believed about the only restraint Home Depot faced that year was its ability to recruit and train new staff fast enough. However, Home Depot was soon to face other problems. In December, things briefly turned sour when Home Depot bought the 9-store Bowater Warehouse chain with stores in Texas, Louisiana, and Alabama. Bowater had a dismal reputation. Its merchandise didn't match Home Depot's, and nearly all its employees had to be dismissed because they were unable to fit into the company's strong customer service orientation.

Of the 22 stores opened in 1985, most were in 8 new markets. Going into Houston and Detroit were moves into less hospitable terrain. The company lost money with promotional pricing and advertising costs. This rapid expansion into unknown territories also took management's attention away from the other stores. The media quickly noted that Home Depot was having problems and suggested that its troubles could be related to rapid expansion into the already crowded home center business. Home Depot's earnings dropped 40% in 1985.

Marcus had to regroup in 1986. He slowed Home Depot's growth to 10 stores in existing markets, including the first supersized store with 140,000 square feet. Home Depot withdrew from the Detroit market, selling its 5 new stores. By 1987, 6 California stores and 2 Tennessee stores had opened, and the company had sales of $1 billion. In that same year, Home Depot introduced an advanced inventory management system; as a result, inventory was turned 5.4 times a year instead of the 4.5 times for 1986. The company also paid its first quarterly dividend.

In 1988, 21 stores opened, with heavy emphasis in California. For the second time, Home Depot was voted the Retailer of the Year in the home center industry.

Home Depot expanded its market beyond the Sunbelt in early 1989 by opening 2 stores in the northeast—East Hanover, New Jersey, and North Haven, Connecticut. By the end of the year, there were 5 stores in the Northeast.

The year 1989 was also a benchmark year for technological developments. All stores began using Universal Product Code (UPC) scanning systems to speed checkout time.

The Company's satellite data communications network installation improved management communication and training. Sales of the year totaled $2.76 billion, and plans were made to open its initial contribution of $6 million to the Employee Stock Ownership Plan (ESOP). On its tenth anniversary, Home Depot opened its 100th store (in Atlanta) and by the year's end had become the nation's largest home center chain.

Thirty stores opened in 1990, bringing the total to 147, with sales of $3.8 billion. The largest store—140,000 square feet—was in San Diego. To handle more volume per store,

Home Depot developed and tested a new store productivity improvement (SPI) program designed to make more effective use of existing and new store space and to allow for more rapid replenishment of merchandise on the sales floor. The SPI program involved the renovation of portions of certain existing stores and an improved design for new stores with the goal of enhanced customer access, reducing customer shopping time, and streamlining merchandise stocking and delivery. As part of SPI, the company also experimented with modified store layouts, materials handling techniques, and operations.

Home Depot continued its expansion by opening an additional 29 stores to bring the total number of stores to 174 in 1991, which generated total sales of $5.1 billion. In addition, the company's SPI program proved successful and was implemented in substantially all new stores and in selected existing stores. Home Depot also continued to introduce or refine a number of merchandising programs during fiscal 1991. Included among such programs were the introduction of full-service, in-store interior decorating centers staffed by designers and an expanded assortment in its lighting department. In 1991, management created a new division, EXPO Design Centers. The first store was opened in San Diego. EXPO Design Centers' niche was the extensive use of computer-aided design technology that the store's creative coordination used. It was targeted to upscale homeowners. These features were of assistance to customers remodeling their bathrooms and kitchens. To assist this strategy further, Home Depot offered a selection of major kitchen appliances. The product line offered was the top of the line. This allowed Home Depot to remain a leading-edge merchandiser.

From 1991 through 1995, many of the new merchandising techniques developed for the Home Depot EXPO were transferred to the entire chain. In 1994, the second EXPO store opened in Atlanta and was mostly dedicated to offering design services. The Atlanta store was 117,000 square feet, and the San Diego store was 105,000 square feet. In 1995 these stores were expanded in California, New York, and Texas. This division was expected to grow to 200 to 400 stores.

By the end of fiscal year 1992 Home Depot had increased its total number of stores to 214, with annual sales of $7.1 billion. Earlier that year, the company had begun a companywide rollout of an enlarged garden center prototype, which had been successfully tested in 1991. These centers, which were as large as 28,000 square feet, featured 6,000- to 8,000-square-foot greenhouses or covered selling areas, providing year-round selling opportunities and significantly expanded product assortment. Also during 1992, the company's "installed sales program," which it began testing in 3 selected markets in 1990, became available in 122 stores in 10 markets. This program targeted the buy-it-yourself customer (BIY), who would purchase an item but either did not have the desire or the ability to install the item. Finally, the company announced its national sponsorship of the 1994 and 1996 U.S. teams at the Winter and Summer Olympics.

During 1993, Home Depot introduced Depot Diners on a test basis in Atlanta, Seattle, and various locations in South Florida. Depot Diners were an extension of the company's commitment to total customer satisfaction and were designed to provide customers and employees with a convenient place to eat. The company continued to develop innovative merchandising programs that helped to grow the business further. The installed sales program became available in 251 stores in 26 markets, with approximately 2,370 installed sales vendors who, as independent, licensed contractors, were authorized to provide service to customers. By the end of fiscal year 1993, Home Depot had opened an additional 50 stores and sales were $9.2 billion, up by 30% from 1992.

From the end of fiscal year 1989 to the end of fiscal year 1994, the company increased its store count by an average of 24% per year (from 118 to 340) and increased the total store square footage by 28% per year (from 10,424,000 to 35,133,000). Home Depot entered the Canadian market on February 28, 1994. The company entered into a partnership with and, as a result, acquired 75% of Aikenhead's Home Improvement Warehouse. At any time after the sixth anniversary of the purchase, the company had the option to purchase, or the other partner had the right to cause the company to purchase, the remaining 25% of the Canadian company. Home Depot Canada commenced operations with 7 stores previously operated by

Aikenhead's. Five additional stores were built during fiscal 1994, for a total of 12 stores at fiscal year end. Approximately 9 additional new Canadian stores were planned for a total of 21 by the end of fiscal year 1995.

The company also made its initial entry into the Midwest by opening 11 stores in the region's 2 largest markets: Chicago, Illinois, and Detroit, Michigan. Approximately 16 new stores were scheduled for 1995, and by the end of 1998, the company expected approximately 112 stores to open.

During fiscal year 1994, Home Depot began developing plans to open stores in Mexico. The first store was scheduled to open in 1998. Although the company was already building relationships with key suppliers in Mexico, entry into the market was to be cautious and slow, paying special attention to Mexico's volatile economy. On a long-term basis, however, the company anticipated that success in Mexico could lead to more opportunities throughout Central and South America. Home Depot planned to expand its total domestic stores by about 25% per year, on average, over the foreseeable future. The international openings were to be above and beyond this figure. Management felt that its growth was optimal, given its financial and management resources.

In 1995, the company offered more private-label products. The company used the "Homer" character on all its private products and its advertisements. The first 24-hour store was opened in Flushing, New York. Ben Sharon of *Value Line* said, "[Home Depot's] ability to adopt different characteristics among regions and markets should keep Home Depot ahead of the industry in the years ahead."[2] By the end of 1995, the company had a total of 423 stores, of which 400 were Home Depot stores, 19 were Canadian stores in 3 provinces, and 4 EXPO stores.

In March 1995, *Fortune* announced that Home Depot had made its list of America's Most Admired Corporations. Home Depot ranked 8.24, or fifth overall in the competition. In 1996, Home Depot ranked second. The company ranked first for rate of return (39.0%) for the past 10 years. The top 4 companies were Rubbermaid (8.65), Microsoft (8.42), Coca-Cola (8.39), and Motorola (8.38). *Fortune* stated, "The winners chart a course of constant renewal and work to sustain culture that produces the very best products and people."[3] Over 1,000 senior executives, outside directors, and financial analysts were surveyed. Each corporation was rated in 10 separate areas.

Home Depot had encountered local opposition to locating 1 of its stores in a small community in Pequannock Township, New Jersey. A group called "Concerned Citizens for Community Preservation" mobilized to prevent Home Depot from opening a store in the town. Members of the group posted flyers and signs throughout the township. These flyers documented Home Depot's alleged "legacy of crime, traffic, and safety violations." The flyers stated, "Our kids will be crossing through this death trap," referring to Home Depot's proposed parking lot. Another flyer asked, "How will we be protected?"[4]

In July 1995, Home Depot filed a lawsuit against Rickel Home Centers, a closely held competitor based in South Plainfield, New Jersey, claiming that "[Rickel] used smear tactics in a concerted effort to block Home Depot from opening stores in Pequannock and Bloomfield, about 25 miles to the south."[5] The suit stated that Rickel had published false statements "impugning Home Depot's name, reputation, products, and services." The suit named Rickel and Bloomfield citizens' groups as defendants.

This was not the first time that citizens' groups had tried to stop a new store or development. Wal-Mart had a severe challenge when it was trying to open a new store in Bennington, Vermont. In 1997, the company opened its first store in Williston, Vermont.

On July 20, 1995, Dennis Ryan, President of CrossRoads, announced the opening of the first of Home Depot's new rural chain, CrossRoads, in Quincy, Illinois. A second store was planned to be opened in Columbus, Missouri, in January or February 1996. The target market for this chain was farmers and ranchers who shopped in smaller, rural towns across America. At that time, there were about 100 farm and home retailers, with about 850 stores and annual sales of $6 billion. A typical CrossRoads store would have about 117,000 square feet of inside retail space, plus a 100,000-square-foot lumberyard. In contrast, the average size of a Tractor Supply Company (a competitor) store was about one tenth the size of a CrossRoads store and did not have a lumberyard. Dennis Ryan said, "This really is a Home Depot just tailored to this [Quincy] community."[6]

The store carried the typical products of Home Depot. In addition, CrossRoads carried pet supplies, truck and tractor tires and parts, work clothing, farm animal medicines, feed, and storage tanks, barbed wire, books (such as *Raising Sheep the Modern Way*), and other items. Employees would install engines and tires and go to the farm to fix a flat tractor tire.[7] The company soon terminated this strategy because the stores did not generate sales and profits that Home Depot expected. The existing CrossRoads stores were renamed Home Depot stores.

By year-end 1996, the company acquired Maintenance Warehouse/America Corporation, which was the leading direct mail marketer of maintenance, repair, and operating products to the United States building and facilities in management market. The company's 1996 sales were approximately $130 million in an estimated $10 billion market. Home Depot management felt this was "an important step towards strengthening our position with professional business customers."[8] The company's long-term goal was to capture 10% of this market.

At the end of 1996, the company had 512 stores, including 483 Home Depot stores and 5 EXPO Design Centers in 38 states, and 24 stores in Canada.

In 1997, the company added 112 stores for a total of 624 stores in 41 states. Stores in the United States were 587 Home Depot stores and 5 EXPO Design Center stores plus 32 stores in 4 Canadian provinces. This was a 22% increase in stores over 1996. Two thirds of the new stores in fiscal 1997 were in existing markets. The company "continues to add stores to even its most mature markets to further penetrate and increase its presence in the market."[9]

The company planned to add new stores at a 21 to 22% annual growth rate, which would increase stores from 624 at the end of 1997 to 1,300 stores at the end of fiscal 2001. This meant the company would have to increase its associates from approximately 125,000 at the end of 1997 to 315,000 in 4 years (2001).

During 1998, Home Depot planned to open approximately 137 new stores, which would be a 22% increase in stores. The company planned to enter new markets—Anchorage, Alaska; Cincinnati and Columbus, Ohio; Milwaukee, Wisconsin; Norfolk and Richmond, Virginia; San Juan, Puerto Rico; Regina, Saskatchewan, and Kingston, Ontario in Canada; and Santiago, Chile. The company intended to open 2 stores in Santiago during fiscal 1998. To facilitate its entry into Chile, Home Depot entered into a joint venture agreement, in fiscal 1997, with S.A.C.I. Falabella, which was the largest department store retailer in Chile. The company's position on the joint venture was that it "was proving to be beneficial in expediting The Home Depot's startup in areas such as systems, logistics, real estate, and credit programs."[10]

This global expansion fit the company's stated vision to be 1 of the most successful retailers in the next millennium. According to management, "the most successful retailers . . . will be those who, among other things, can effectively profitably extend their reach to global markets."[11] Home Depot management "plans to employ a focused, regional strategy, establishing platform markets for growth into other markets."[12]

Corporate Culture

The culture at Home Depot was characterized by the phrase, "Guess what happened to me at Home Depot?" This phrase showed Home Depot's bond with its customers and the communities in which it had stores and was a recognition of superb service. Home Depot called this its "orange-blooded culture."

The orange-blooded culture emphasized individuality, informality, nonconformity, growth, and pride. These traits reflected those of the founders of the company, who within hours of being fired from Handy Dan, were busily planning the Home Depot stores to go into competition with the company from which they had just been summarily dismissed. The culture was "really a reflection of Bernie and me[sic]," said Blank. "We're not formal, stuffy folks. We hang pretty loose. We've got a lot of young people. We want them to feel comfortable."[13]

The importance of the individual to the success of the whole venture was consistently emphasized at Home Depot. Marcus's statements bear this out: "We know that 1 person can make a difference, and that is what is so unique about The Home Depot. It doesn't matter where our associates work in our company, they can all make a difference."[14] While emphasizing the opportunities for advancement at Home Depot, Marcus decried the kind of "cradle to grave" job that used to be the ideal in America and is the norm in Japan. To him, this was "a kind of serfdom."[15] Home Depot attempted to provide excellent wages and benefits, and superior training and advancement opportunities, while encouraging independent thinking and initiative.

Informality was always in order at Home Depot—"spitballs fly at board meetings"—and there was always someone around to make sure that ties got properly trimmed. When executives visited stores, they went alone, not with an entourage. Most worked on the floors in the beginning and knew the business from the ground up. They were approachable and employees frequently came forward with ideas and suggestions.

Nonconformity was evident in many different areas of the company—from the initial warehouse concept to the size and variety of merchandise to human resource practices. Both Marcus and Blank "flout conventional corporate rules that foil innovation." Training employees at all levels was 1 of the most powerful means of transmitting corporate culture, and Home Depot used it extensively. One analyst noted that Home Depot (in a reverse of the "top-to-bottom" training sequence in most organizations) trained the carryout people first: "The logic is that the guy who helps you to your car is the last employee you come in contact with, and they want that contact to be positive."[16]

Company management perception of what the customer finds on a visit to a Home Depot store is a "feel good" store. The company defined a feel good store as "a place where they *feel good* about walking in our doors, *feel good* about consulting our knowledgeable associates, *feel good* about paying a low price, and *feel good* about returning time after time."[17]

The Home Depot was built on a set of values that fostered strong relationships with its key constituencies. The company's management embraced the values of taking care of its people, encouraging an entrepreneurial spirit, treating each other with respect, and being committed to the highest standards. For the customers, management believed that excellent customer service was the key to company success, and that giving back to the communities it served was part of its commitment to the customer. Importantly, management believed that if all employees lived all of these values, they would also create shareholder value.

The Home Depot's long-term growth planning was taking place with full recognition of the importance of the company's culture to its future success. Its goal was for each associate to not only be able to explain the company's culture of respect, trust, ownership, and entrepreneurial spirit, but most importantly, to believe it and live it.

The management of Home Depot was often asked how the company had managed to grow so fast for as long as it had and still be successful, both financially and with its customers. They responded that aggressive growth required adapting to change, but continued success required holding fast to the culture and values of the company as the company grew.[18]

In addition, Home Depot recognized its role in the community, and strove to be known as a good "corporate citizen." In 1 community, a woman lost her uninsured home and teen-aged son to a fire. Home Depot's management responded, along with other residents, by providing thousands of dollars of free materials and supplies to assist in the rebuilding effort. In another incident, a community organization sponsored a graffiti cleanup, and the Home Depot store in the area donated paint and supplies to assist in the project. These were just a few of the stories that communities told about Home Depot, which also participated in Habitat for

Humanity and Christmas in April, and had provided over $10 million to help fund many community projects in the United States and Canada. The company also was active in environmental activities and promoted environmentally healthy building and home improvement practices.

Merrill Lynch stated about Home Depot's culture that its "entrepreneurial culture and heavy dedication toward customer service, combined with its large merchandise selection, has resulted in a retailer that leads its industry by almost every performance measure."[19]

Corporate Governance

BOARD OF DIRECTORS

The Board of Directors of Home Depot were as follows.[20]

Bernard Marcus (68) had been Cofounder, Chairman, and Chief Executive Officer since the inception of the company in 1978 until 1997, when he passed the title of CEO to Arthur M. Blank, and remained as Chairman. He had served on many other boards. He owned 21,842,890 shares (2.98%) of the company's stock.

Arthur M. Blank (55) had been Cofounder, President, Chief Operating Officer, and Director since the company's inception, and was named Chief Executive Officer in 1997. He had served on many other boards. He owned 12,182,614 shares (1.66%).

Ronald M. Brill (54) had been Executive Vice President and Chief Financial Officer since March 1993. He joined the company in 1978 and was elected Treasurer in 1980. He owned 872,392 shares of the company's stock.

Frank Borman (70) had been a Director since 1983. He had been a NASA astronaut and retired U.S. Air Force colonel. He was the retired Chairman and Chief Operating Officer of Eastern Airlines and presently was the Chairman of Patlex Corporation. He was a major investor in 1983 and owned 265,782 shares of the company's stock. He served on many other boards.

Barry R. Cox (44) had been a Director since 1978. For the past 20 years, he had been a private investor. He owned 1,650,243 shares of stock.

Milledge A. Hart, III (64) had been a Director since 1978. He served as Chairman of the Hart Group, Chairman of Rmax Inc., and Chairman of Axon, Inc. He served on many other boards. He owned 1,733,185 shares of the company's stock.

Donald R. Keough (71) had been a Director since April 1993. He was President and Chief Operating Officer and Director of Coca-Cola Company until his retirement in April 1993. He owned 20,304 shares of the company's stock. He served on many other boards.

John I. Clendenin (63) had been a Director since 1996. He had been Chairman and Chief Executive Officer of BellSouth Corporation for the last 5 years until his retirement in 1996 and remained Chairman until 1997. He owned 5,477 shares of the company's stock.

Johnnetta B. Cole (61) had been a Director since 1995. Dr. Cole served as President of Spelman College in Atlanta, Georgia, from 1987 until July 1997. She served on many other boards and foundations. She owned 4,803 shares of the company's stock.

Kenneth G. Langone (62) had been Cofounder and Director since the company's inception. He had served as Chairman, President, Chief Executive Officer, and Managing Director of Invened Associates, Inc., an investment banking and brokerage firm. He served on many other boards. He owned 6,850,243 shares of the company's stock.

M. Faye Wilson (60) had been a Director since 1992. She had been Executive Vice President of Bank of America NT&SA since 1992. She owned 16,743 shares of the company's stock.

The Directors were paid $40,000 per annum, of which $10,000 was in the form of restricted shares of common stock, and an additional $1,000 fee and expenses for each meeting. The Executive Committee included Messrs. Marcus, Blank, and Langone. The Audit

Committee included Messrs. Borman, Cox, Hart, and Keough. The Compensation Committee included Messrs. Borman, Clendenin, Cox, and Keough. The Human Resource Committee included Dr. Cole, Mr. Langone, and Ms. Wilson.

FRM (Fidelity) Corporation owned 55,991,937 (7.65%) shares of common stock.

TOP MANAGEMENT

Key executive officers of Home Depot, besides Bernard Marcus, Arthur M. Blank, and Ronald M. Brill, who served on the Board, were as follows:[21]

Mark R. Baker (40) has been President of the Midwest Division since December 1997. Mr. Baker first joined the company in 1996 as Vice President—Merchandising for the Midwest Division. Prior to joining Home Depot, from 1992 until 1996, Mr. Baker was an Executive Vice President for HomeBase in Fullerton, California.

Bruce W. Berg (49) has been President—Southeast Division since 1991. Mr. Berg joined the company in 1984 as Vice President—Merchandising (East Coast) and was promoted to Senior Vice President (East Coast) in 1988.

Marshall L. Day (54) has been Senior Vice President—Chief Financial Officer since 1995. Mr. Day previously served as Senior Vice President—Finance from 1993 until his promotion to his current position.

Bill Hamlin (45) was recently named Group President and continues to serve as Executive Vice President—Merchandising. Prior to being named Executive Vice President—Merchandising, Mr. Hamlin served as President—Western Division from 1990 until 1994.

Vernon Joslyn (46) has been President—Northeast Division since 1996. Mr. Joslyn previously served as Vice President—Operations for the Northeast Division from 1993 until his promotion to his current position.

W. Andrew McKenna (52) was named Senior Vice President—Strategic Business Development in December 1997. Mr. McKenna joined Home Depot as Senior Vice President—Corporate Information Systems in 1990. In 1994 he was named President of the Midwest Division and served in that capacity until he assumed the duties of his current position.

Lynn Martineau (41) has been President—Western Division since 1996. Mr. Martineau most recently served as Vice President—Merchandising for the company's Southeast Division from 1989 until his promotion to his current position.

Larry M. Mercer (51) was recently named Group President and has been Executive Vice President—Operations since 1996. Mr. Mercer previously served as President—Northeast Division from 1991 until his promotion to his current position.

Barry L. Silverman (39) has been President of the Southwest Division since July 1997. Mr. Silverman previously served as Vice President—Merchandising of the Northeast Division from 1991 until his promotion to his current position.

Bryant W. Scott (42) has been President of the EXPO Design Center Division since 1995. Since 1980, Mr. Scott has served in a variety of positions, including Vice President—Merchandising for the Southeast Division.

David Suliteanu (45) was named Group President—Diversified Businesses in April 1998. Mr. Suliteanu previously served as Vice Chairman and Director of Stores for Macy's East, a position he held from 1993 until he joined Home Depot in April 1998.

Annette M. Verschuren (41) has been President of The Home Depot Canada since 1996. In 1992, Ms. Verschuren formed Verschuren Ventures Inc. and remained there until joining Michaels of Canada Inc. in 1993 where she served as President until joining the company.

In 1997, Bernard Marcus, who had been CEO since the company's inception in 1978, passed the title to Arthur M. Blank. Mr. Blank now served as President and CEO.

Exhibit 3 shows all the officers of Home Depot.

Exhibit 3

Officers: Home Depot, Inc.

Corporate

Bernard Marcus
Chairman of the Board

Arthur M. Blank
President and Chief Executive Officer

Ronald M. Brill
Executive Vice President and
Chief Administrative Officer

Bill Hamlin
Executive Vice President
Merchandising and Group President

Larry M. Mercer
Executive Vice President
Operations and Group President

David Suliteanu
Group President, Diversified Services

Alan Barnaby
Senior Vice President, Store
Operations

Marshall L. Day
Senior Vice President,
Chief Financial Officer

Pat Farrah
Senior Vice President, Merchandising

Bryan J. Fields
Senior Vice President, Real Estate

Ronald B. Griffin
Senior Vice President
Information Services

Richard A. Hammill
Senior Vice President, Marketing

W. Andrew McKenna
Senior Vice President
Strategic Business Development

Stephen R. Messana
Senior Vice President, Human
Resources

Dennis Ryan
Senior Vice President, Merchandising

Lawrence A. Smith
Senior Vice President, Legal and
Secretary

Terence L. Smith
Senior Vice President, Imports/
Logistics

Richard L. Sullivan
Senior Vice President, Advertising

Robert J. Wittman
Senior Vice President, Merchandising

Mike Anderson
Vice President, Information Services

Ben A. Barone
Vice President, Credit Marketing

Dave Bogage
Vice President, Management and
Organization Development

Patrick Cataldo
Vice President, Training

Gary C. Cochran
Vice President, Information Services

Charles D. Crowell
Vice President, Distribution Services

Kerrie R. Flanagan
Vice President, Merchandise Accounting

Mike Folio
Vice President, Real Estate

Frank Gennaccaro
Vice President, Merchandising

Paul Hoedeman
Vice President, Information Services

Ted Kaczmarowski
Vice President
Construction/Store Planning

Bill Peña
Vice President/General Manager
International Development

William K. Schlegal
Vice President, Imports

Kim Shreckengost
Vice President, Investor Relations

Don Singletary
Vice President, Human Resources—
North American Stores

Grady Stewart
Vice President, Operations

Carol B. Tome
Vice President, Treasurer

DeWayne Truitt
Vice President
Compensation and Benefits

Gregg Vickery
Vice President, Controller

Edward A. Wolfe
Vice President, Loss Prevention

Ken Young
Vice President, Internal Audit

Midwest Division

Mark Baker
President

H. George Collins
Vice President, Store Operations

Robert Gilbreth
Vice President, Store Operations

Steven L. Mahurin
Vice President, Merchandising

Michael J. Williams
Vice President, Human Resources

Northeast Division

Vern Joslyn
President

Jeff Birren
Vice President, Store Operations

Carol A. Freitag
Vice President, Human Resources

William G. Lennie
Vice President, Merchandising

Michael McCabe
Vice President, Store Operations

Pedro Mendiguren
Vice President, Store Operations

Southeast Division

Bruce Berg
President

Tony Brown
Vice President, Store Operations

Dennis Johnson
Vice President, Merchandising

Eric Johnson
Vice President, Store Operations

H. Gregory Turner
Vice President, Store Operations

John Wicks
Vice President, Merchandising

(continued)

Exhibit 3 Officers: Home Depot, Inc. *(continued)*

Southwest Division	**The Home Depot Canada**	**Steven L. Neeley**
Barry L. Silverman	**Annette M. Verschuren**	Vice President, Sales
President	President	**Kevin Peters**
Jerry Edwards	**John Hayes**	Vice President, Logistics
Vice President, Merchandising	Vice President, Merchandising	**Ron Turk**
Frank Rosi	**Dennis Kennedy**	Vice President
Vice President, Human Resources	Vice President, Store Operations	Chief Financial Officer
Tom Taylor		**Jeffrey R. Wenham**
Vice President, Store Operations	**EXPO Design Center Division**	Vice President, Human Resources
Western Division	**Bryant Scott**	
Lynn Martineau	President	**National Blind & Wallpaper Factory**
President	**Christopher A. McLoughlin**	**David Katzman**
Terry Hopper	Vice President, Division Controller	President
Vice President, Store Operations	**Steve Smith**	**Rick Kovacs**
Ethan Klausner	Vice President, Merchandising	Senior Vice President, Merchandising
Vice President, Merchandising		**David Littleson**
Bruce Merino	**Maintenance Warehouse**	Chief Financial Officer
Vice President, Merchandising	**Jonathan Neeley**	**Steve Kaip**
Timothy J. Pfeiffer	President	Vice President, Information Systems
Vice President, Store Operations	**Jim Ardell**	**Debra Russell**
Thomas "Buz Smith	Vice President, Merchandising	Vice President, Operations
Vice President, Store Operations	**Mike Brown**	**Bob Shepard**
Greg Lewis	Vice President, Information Systems	Vice President
Division Controller	**Bill Luth**	Installation/Retail Development
	Vice President, Marketing	

Source: The Home Depot, Inc., *1997 Annual Report*, p. 36.

Organizational Structure

The official organizational structure of Home Depot (see **Exhibit 4**) was much like that of other retail organizations, but according to a human resources spokesperson, the environment was so relaxed and casual people felt like they could report to anyone. Marcus and Blank presided at the top of Home Depot's organizational chart and were supported by Executive Vice Presidents: Executive Vice President and Chief Administrative Officer; Executive Vice President of Merchandising and Group President; and Executive Vice President of Operations and Group President.

There were 3 Group Presidents, of which 2 were also Executive Vice Presidents. The other was the Group President of Diversified Businesses. These executives were supported by 13 Senior Vice Presidents (see **Exhibit 4**). The company had 21 Vice Presidents at the corporate level.

The organization was divided into 7 divisions:

1. Southeast Division,
2. Western Division,
3. Northeast Division,
4. Midwest Division,
5. Home Depot Canada Division,
6. Southwest Division, and
7. EXPO Design Centers.

Exhibit 4

Organizational Chart: Home Depot, Inc.

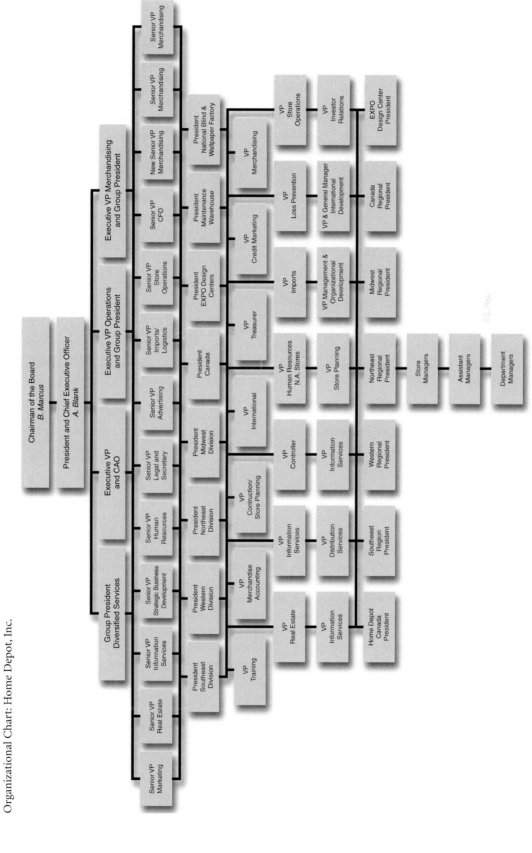

Note: This does not include the company's wholly-owned subsidiaries (1) National Blind & Wallpaper Factory and (2) Maintenance Warehouse.

Source: Company records.

Each division was headed by a President, who was supported by Vice Presidents of Merchandising and Store Operations. Under each Vice President in a division was a group of regional managers responsible for a number of stores. There were a number of Vice Presidents at the division level, some of which included Legal, Information Services, Logistics, Advertising, the Controller, and Human Resources.

At the store level, Home Depot was set up much as would be expected—with a Manager, Assistant Managers, and Department Managers. The average Home Depot store had 1 Manager whose primary responsibility was to be the master delegator. Four to 6 Assistants usually presided over the store's 10 departments. Each Assistant Manager was responsible for 1 to 3 departments. One Assistant Manager was responsible for receiving and the "back end" (stock storage area), in addition to his or her departments. The Assistant Managers were supported by Department Managers who were each responsible for 1 department. The Department Managers reported directly to the Assistant Managers and had no firing/hiring capabilities. Assistant Managers normally handled ordering and work schedules, and so on. Department Managers handled employees' questions and job assignments. In a recent change, human resource officers were made responsible for recruiting, staffing, employee relations, and management development for each division.[22]

HOME DEPOT CANADA (AIKENHEAD'S)

On February 28, 1994, Home Depot acquired a 75% interest in Aikenhead's Home Improvements Warehouse chain of 7 warehouses in Canada for approximately $161,584,000. It was a joint venture with Molson Companies, Ltd.; Home Depot served as the general partner. Stephen Bebis, a former Home Depot officer, developed the chain along the Home Depot concept. He initially served as President of this unit and was replaced by Annette M. Verschuren in 1995.

Operations[23]

The stores and their merchandise were set up so that all of the stores were very similar. The company's corporate headquarters was responsible for the "look," but individual managers could change a display or order more or less of a product if they could justify the change. The Managers within individual stores made decisions regarding their employees, such as firing and hiring, but they looked to headquarters in areas such as training. One Manager of a store in Georgia said that if he did not like a particular display or promotion, it was at his discretion to change it or drop it. The Manager went on to say that he and other store managers work hand in hand with corporate headquarters, and that if he wanted to make "major" changes or had a significant store or personnel problem, he would deal with headquarters.

During 1994, Home Depot introduced a prototype store format, which offered about 32,000 more square feet of selling space and a significantly broader and deeper selection of products and services, as well as a more convenient layout than the traditional stores. These "Type V" stores were designed around a design center, which grouped complementary product categories.

Operational efficiency had been a crucial part of achieving low prices while still offering a high level of customer service. The company was assessing and upgrading its information to support its growth, reduce and control costs, and enable better decision making. From the installation of computerized checkout systems to the implementation of satellite communications systems in most of the stores, the company had shown that it had been and would continue to be innovative in its operating strategy.

By fiscal year 1994, each store was equipped with a computerized point-of-sale system (POS), electronic bar code scanning systems, and a minicomputer. These systems provided efficient customer checkout with approximately 90% scannable products, store-based inventory management, rapid order replenishment, labor planning support, and item movement information. In fiscal year 1994, faster registers were introduced along with new check approval systems and a new receipt format to expedite credit care transactions.

Home Depot's attitude of complete customer satisfaction has led the company to constantly seek ways to improve customer service. When the company was faced with clogged aisles, endless checkout lines, and too few salespeople, it sought creative ways to improve customer service. Workers were added to the sales floor. Shelfstocking and price tagging were shifted to nighttime, when the aisles are empty. The changes were worth the expense because now employees were free to sell during the day. In an effort to ease customer crowding, Home Depot used a "clustering" strategy to locate new stores closer to existing ones.

The company also operated its own television network (HDTV). This money-saving device allowed Home Depot's top executives to get instant feedback from local managers and also allowed training and communications programs to be viewed in the stores. Management's operating philosophies and policies were more effectively communicated because information presented by top management could be targeted at a large audience. This addition had increased employee motivation and saved many dollars by making information available in a timely manner.

Home Depot was firmly committed to energy conservation and had installed reflectors to lower the amount of lighting required in a store. The reflectors darkened the ceiling but saved thousands of dollars a year in energy bills. Further, the company had pursued a computerized system to maintain comfortable temperatures, a challenge due to the stores' concrete floors, exposed ceilings, and open oversized doors for forklift deliveries. The system also had an automated feedback capability that could be used for equipment maintenance.

The adoption of the Point-of-Sale (POS) technology had improved each store's ability to identify and adapt to trends quickly. The information provided by this technology was transferred to computer centers in Atlanta and Fullerton, California, where consumer buying trends were traced. This allowed Home Depot to adjust its merchandising mix and track both buyer trends and inventory.

In 1987, the company had introduced an advanced inventory management system that allowed it to increase inventory turnover significantly, from 4.1 in 1985 to 5.7 in 1994. This let Home Depot carry $40 million less in inventory, tying up less working capital to finance it. This efficiency allowed a cost structure that was significantly lower than the competition's.

In 1994, the company introduced phone centers to serve its customers who called to inquire about pricing and availability of merchandise. Adding experienced salespeople to a phone bank to answer calls quickly and efficiently had increased weekly phone sales. Without having to respond to phone calls, the sales staff could better concentrate on serving in-store customers.

The company continued to see greater efficiency as a result of its Electronic Data Interchange (EDI) program. Currently over 400 of the company's highest volume vendors were participating in the EDI program. A paperless system, EDI electronically processed orders from stores to vendors, alerted the store when the merchandise was to arrive, and transmitted vendor invoice data.

In fiscal year 1994, stores were outfitted with Electronic Article Surveillance (EAS) detectors, which triggered an alarm if a person exited the store with merchandise that had been affixed with an EAS label that had not been desensitized at the cash register. The system was proving to be a deterrent to theft, with many stores reporting reductions in shoplifting offenses.

Home Depot continuously experimented with new operating concepts, such as CrossRoads and EXPO Design Centers. Its investment in new retail technology and its willingness to streamline operations for the benefit of the customer and employees had paid off in areas such as inventory turnover, in-stock turnover, in-stock inventory positions, querying problems, employee motivation, and information flow from the company's buyers to its store-level managers and employees.

MERCHANDISING[24]

If Home Depot's advertising strategy of creating awareness of the company's stores and encouraging do-it-yourselfers (DIYs) to tackle more at-home projects was getting people into the stores, the merchandising mix was aimed at getting people to buy. According to Marcus, "We could sell them anything . . . but we don't. We don't want the customer to think we're a discounter, food store, a toy store, or anything else, because it would confuse [them]."[25] Home Depot wanted to be thought of as the DIY warehouse, nothing less.

Advertising

The company maintained an aggressive campaign, using various media for both price and institutional policy. Print advertising, usually emphasizing price, was prepared by an in-house staff to control context, layout, media placement, and cost. Broadcast media advertisements were generally institutional and promoted Home Depot "the company," not just pricing strategy. These advertisements focused on the "You'll feel right at home" and "Everyday Low Pricing" ad slogans, name recognition, and the value of Home Depot's customer service. Although the company had grown over the years, the goal of its advertising was still to project a local flavor. The Western Division maintained its own creative department because of its different time zone and unique product mix. The company attempted to use information for the field in the various markets and put together an effective advertising campaign. The company still relied heavily on print media.

Home Depot sponsored the 1996 U.S. Summer Olympic Games in Atlanta. Through the sponsorship, Home Depot had hoped to further its ties with the home improvement customer, create sales opportunities, further differentiate itself from competitors, maintain its corporate culture, and support key businesses in the community. Home Depot began 1994 by unveiling a program to help pave the Olympic Park in Atlanta with engraved bricks, hiring athletes to work in the stores and office while they trained for the Games, and continuing a cooperative partnership with vendors in the Home Depot Olympic Family. This partnership had grown to include 29 key suppliers in the United States and 26 in Canada. Each member of the "Family" represented a specific home improvement product category and could participate in many of Home Depot's Olympic Games promotions.

The company participated in the Olympic Job Opportunities Program, in which Home Depot provided part-time jobs for 100 hopeful Olympic athletes as they trained for the Olympics. Twenty-six of the American and Canadian athletes participated in the Olympic Games and 6 earned medals. The company planned to remain a sponsor for at least the next 6 years for the Olympic Games in 2000, 2002, and 2004. The company also acted as a sponsor for the 1998 Winter Olympic Games.

Customer Target Market

Home Depot stores served primarily do-it-yourselfers, although home improvement contractors, building maintenance professionals, interior designers, and other professionals had become increasingly important customers. DIY customers continued to be the core business and made up approximately two thirds of the total home improvement segment. DIY customers bought materials for the home and installed them personally.

Due to the increasing home improvement activity, buy-it-yourself (BIY) customers began to emerge. BIY customers chose products, made the purchase, and contracted with others to complete the project or install the furnishings. Home Depot was catering to this segment by expanding its installed sales program companywide.

Home Depot also continued to target the professional business customer. It had set up a commercial credit program, provided commercial checkout lines in the stores, and had hired additional associates with experience in various professional fields.

The typical DIY customer was a married male homeowner, aged 25 to 34, with a high school diploma or some college, and had an annual income of $20,000 to $40,000. Projections through 1999 indicated that households headed by 25 to 35-year-olds with earnings over $30,000 would increase 34% to 38% by 1999. The 45 to 54 age group was earning over $30,000 and was expected to increase by 40%.

Economics

The DIY industry exhibited a demand pattern that was largely recession-proof. Because a mere 15% of Home Depot's business came from contractors, a downturn in home construction had only a modest impact on Home Depot sales. In addition, analysts pointed out that, during hard times, consumers could not afford to buy new or bigger homes; instead they maintained or upgraded their existing homes. Home improvement spending had declined in 1 recession during the past 20 years. The new strategy to penetrate the professional market might affect the company's sales more in future recessions.

Merchandising Strategy

The company's *1994 Annual Report* stated that Home Depot's goal was to be "The Do-It-Yourself Retailer." Merchandising included all activities involved in the buying and selling of goods for a profit. It involved long-range planning to ensure that the right merchandise was available at the right place, at the right time, in the right quantity, and at the right price. Success depended on the firm's ability to act and react with speed, spot changes, and catch trends early.

During 1994, Home Depot refined its merchandising function to be more efficient and responsive to customers. The new structure gave Division Managers responsibility for specific product categories, and specialists in each of these categories made sure the business lines were kept current. There were also field merchants who worked with the stores to ensure proper implementation of new programs as well as the maintenance of any ongoing programs. This approach strengthened product lines, got the right merchandise to the customers, reduced administration costs, and prepared Home Depot to expand into additional product lines.

The merchandising strategy of Home Depot followed a 3-pronged approach: (1) excellent customer service, (2) everyday low pricing, and (3) wide breadth of products.

Each Home Depot store served 100,000 households with a median income of $45,000. Of those households, 75% were owner-occupied. In 1997, Home Depot responded to the demographics of certain markets by expanding its service hours to 24 hours a day in 15 store locations.

Home Depot continued to introduce or refine several merchandising programs during fiscal 1997. Key among them was the company's ongoing commitment to becoming the supplier of choice to a variety of professional customers, including remodelers, carpenters, plumbers, electricians, building maintenance professionals, and designers. According to management, company had reacted to the needs of this group by enhancing and increasing quantities of key products for professional customers. In addition, the company was testing additional products and service-related programs designed to increase sales to professional customers, including expanded commercial credit programs, delivery services, and incremental dedicated staff.

The company's installed sales program was available, with varying services offered, in all of the company's stores. The company authorized approximately 3,500 installed sales vendors who, as independent licensed contractors, provide services to customers. This program targeted the BIY customer, who would purchase a product but did not have the desire or ability to install it.

Construction on the company's new Import Distribution Center (IDC), located in Savannah, Georgia, was completed in fiscal 1997. Built with the intention of servicing the company's stores located east of the Rocky Mountains, the IDC began shipments in April

1997, and by the end of fiscal 1997 was servicing all targeted stores. The 1.4-million-square-foot facility was staffed with approximately 600 associates. The IDC enabled the company to directly import products not currently available to customers or offer products currently sourced domestically from third-party importers. Other benefits included quicker turnaround deliveries to stores, lower costs, and improved quality control than would be possible if the products were purchased through third-party importers.

The company sponsored the "1997 National Home and Garden Show Series." Bringing together 16 of the nation's most successful consumer shows under 1 national sponsorship provided maximum exposure and support to the shows. Through this sponsorship, the company played a key role in bringing the most innovative lawn and garden, interior design, and home improvement products and services to the attention of the general public.

Home TLC, Inc., an indirect, wholly owned subsidiary of The Home Depot, Inc., owned the trademarks, "The Home Depot," and "EXPO," as well as the "Homer" advertising symbol and various private label brand names that the company uses. The company's operating subsidiaries licensed from Homer TLC, Inc., the right to use this intellectual property. Management believed that the company's rights in this intellectual property were an important asset of the company.

Home Depot was the only big-box retailer to offer a number of other exclusive, high-quality products such as Pergo® laminate flooring, Ralph Lauren® paints, and Vigoro® fertilizer. Each of these products made The Home Depot unique from its competitors and provided its customers with a better selection of products. Home Depot's proprietary products included Behr Premium Plus paints, Hampton Bay ceiling fans and lighting products, Husky tools, and Scott's lawnmowers. These proprietary products provided Home Depot customers with a quality product at a value price and often filled a needed void in the product offerings.

Following the success of Home Depot's best-selling *Home Improvement 1-2-3*™ book, the company recently released *Outdoor Projects 1-2-3*™, the company's latest how-to book sold in Home Depot stores and bookstores. For the past 3 years, Home Depot has sponsored *HouseSmart with Lynette Jennings*™, 1 of the highest-rated shows on The Discovery Channel®. The company planned to extend its reach to tomorrow's homeowners in 1998 through *Homer's Workshop*™, the first how-to, project-oriented television program for children.

Clustering Strategy

The clustering strategy had been employed to allow Home Depot's aggressive expansion program. Home Depot had intentionally cannibalized sales of existing stores by opening 2 other stores in a single market area. The short-run effect was to lower same-store sales, but a strategic advantage was created by raising the barrier of entry to competitors. It reduced overcrowding in the existing stores. It also allowed the company to spread its advertising and distribution costs over a larger store base, thereby lowering selling, general, and administrative costs. The company's 1997 gross margin was 28.1%.

Customer Service

The availability of sales personnel to attend to customer needs was 1 clear objective of the Home Depot customer service strategy.

Customer service differentiated Home Depot from its competitors. The provision of highly qualified and helpful employees, professional clinics, and in-store displays had developed into a customer service approach referred to as "customer cultivation." It gave DIY customers the support and confidence that no home project was beyond their capabilities with Home Depot personnel close at hand.

Home Depot employees went beyond simply recommending appropriate products, tools, and materials. Sales personnel cultivated the customer by demonstrating methods and techniques of performing a job safely and efficiently. This unique aspect of the company's service also served as a feedback mechanism—employees helping the next customer learn from the problems and successes of the last one.

All of the stores offered hands-on workshops on projects such as kitchen remodeling, basic plumbing, ceramic tile installation, and other activities in which customers in a particular locality had expressed interest. Offered mainly on weekends, the workshops varied in length, depending on complexity. Only the most experienced staff members, many of them former skilled craftsmen, taught at these workshops. Promotion of the workshops was done through direct mail advertising and in-store promotion.

At many Home Depot stores, customers could rent trucks by the hour through Load 'N Go™, Home Depot's exclusive truck rental service. The company also expanded a tool rental service to more stores during fiscal 1998. In addition, the company's special order capabilities should improve, due in part to the acquisition in November 1997 of National Blind & Wallpaper Factory and Habitat Wallpaper & Blinds stores, which became wholly owned subsidiaries of Home Depot. When integrated with the stores beginning in fiscal 1998, the innovative ordering systems of these companies should give Home Depot the capability to handle wallpaper and window covering special orders in a more efficient, cost-effective, and convenient manner for customers.

Pricing Strategy

Home Depot stressed its commitment to "Everyday Low Pricing." This concept meant across-the-board lower prices and fewer deep-cutting sales. To ensure this, Home Depot employed professional shoppers to check competitors' prices regularly.

One of the major reasons that Home Depot was able to undercut the competition by as much as 25% was a dependable relationship with its suppliers. The company conducted business with approximately 5,700 vendors, the majority of which were manufacturers. A confidential survey of manufacturers conducted by Shapiro and Associates found that Home Depot was "far and away the most demanding of customers." Home Depot was most vocal about holding to shipping dates. Manufacturers agreed that increased sales volume had offset concessions made to Home Depot.

Products

A typical Home Depot store stocked approximately 40,000 to 50,000 products, including variations in color and size. The products included different kinds of building materials, home improvement products, and lawn and garden supplies. In addition, Home Depot stores offered installation services for many products. Each store carried a wide selection of quality and nationally advertised brand name merchandise. The contribution of each product group was as follows.[26]

	Percentage of Sales		
Product Group	Year Ending February 1, 1998	Year Ending February 2, 1997	Year Ending January 28, 1996
Plumbing, heating, lighting, and electrical supplies	27.1%	27.4%	27.7%
Building materials, lumber, floor, and wall coverings	34.2	34.0	33.9
Hardware and tools	13.5	13.4	13.2
Season and specialty items	14.8	14.7	14.8
Paint and others	10.4	10.5	10.4
	100.0%	100.0%	100.0%

The company sourced its store merchandise from approximately 5,700 vendors worldwide, and no single vendor accounted for more than 5% of total purchases.

Average Store Profile

According to Bob Evans in the Store Planning Division of Home Depot, all of the stores were company-owned, not franchised, and most were freestanding, built to Home Depot's standards.

Home Depot owned 74% of its buildings in 1997, leasing the remainder. Marcus planned to increase that percentage. In 1989, the company had owned only about 40% of its stores. Although the company preferred locations surrounded by shopping centers, Marcus insisted that the company was not interested in being attached to a shopping center or mall. Stores were placed in suburban areas populated by members of the Home Depot target market. Ownership provided Home Depot with greater operational control and flexibility, generally lower occupancy loss, and certain other economic advantages. Construction time depended on site conditions, special local requirements, and related factors. According to Evans, depending on "if we have to move a mountain, fill a canyon, level a forest, or how many gopher turtles are in the ground that we have to relocate," building a store can take up to a year.

Current building standards were 108,000 square feet for each store itself and 16,000 to 28,000 square feet of outside selling space for the garden department. Stores did vary, however, because the company "will make the store fit the land," and many of the original stores were located in leased strip-center space. Home Depot had increased its average store size from about 97,000 to 108,000 square feet, with an additional 20,000 to 28,000 square feet of outside (garden) selling space. The average weighted sales per square foot was $406, $398, $390, $404, and $398 for 1997, 1996, 1995, 1994, and 1993, respectively. The weighted average weekly sales per operational store was $829,000; $803,000; $787,000; $802,000; and $764,000 for 1997, 1996, 1995, 1994, and 1993, respectively. Although Marcus would like to see stores averaging 120,000 square feet, Evans said that "the hundred [thousand square-foot size] is what we're building most of [sic]." Some stores had thousands of customers a week and "just get too crowded," according to Evans. Marcus had estimated that "in some cases, we have 25,000 to 30,000 people walking through a store per week."

Because of the large number of customers, older stores were being gradually remodeled or replaced with new ones to add room for new merchandise, to increase selling space for what is already there, and sometimes even to add more walking room on the inside—and more parking space.

Because merchandising and inventory were centrally organized, product mix varied slightly from store to store. Each, however, sported the Home Depot look: warehouse style shelves, wide concrete-floored aisles, end-displays pushing sale items, and the ever-present orange banners indicating the store's departments. Most stores had banners on each aisle to help customers locate what they're looking for. Regional purchasing departments were used to keep the stores well stocked and were preferred to a single, strong corporate department "since home improvement materials needed in the Southwest would differ somewhat from those needed in the Northeast."

Information Systems

Each store was equipped with a computerized point-of-sale system, electronic bar code scanning system, and a UNIX server. Management believed these systems provided efficient customer check-out (with an approximately 90% rate of scannable products), store-based inventory management, rapid order replenishment, labor planning support, and item movement information. Faster registers as well as a new check approval system and a new receipt format had expedited transactions. To better serve the increasing number of customers applying for credit, the charge card approval process time had been reduced to less than 30 seconds. Store information was communicated to the Store Support Center's computers via a land-based frame relay network. These computers provided corporate, financial, merchandising, and other back-office function support.

The company was continuously assessing and upgrading its information systems to support its growth, reduce and control costs, and enable better decision making. The company continued to realize greater efficiency as a result of its electronic data interchange (EDI) program. Most of the company's highest volume vendors were participating in the EDI program. A paperless system, EDI electronically processed orders from buying offices to vendors, alerted the stores when the merchandise was to arrive, and transmitted invoice data from the vendors and motor carriers to the Store Support Center. In addition, during fiscal 1997 the company continued to develop new computer systems to facilitate and improve product order replenishment in Home Depot stores.[27]

The Year 2000 Problem

The company was currently addressing a universal situation commonly referred to as the "year 2000 problem." The year 2000 problem related to the inability of certain computer software programs to properly recognize and process date-sensitive information relative to the year 2000 and beyond. During fiscal 1997, the company developed a plan to devote the necessary resources to identify and modify systems impacted by the year 2000 problem, or implement new systems to become year 2000 compliant in a timely manner. The cost of executing this plan was not expected to have a material impact on the company's results of operations or financial condition. In addition, the company had contacted its major suppliers and vendors to ensure their awareness of the year 2000 problem. If the company, its suppliers, or vendors were unable to resolve issues related to the year 2000 on a timely basis, it could result in a material financial risk.[28]

HUMAN RESOURCES[29]

Home Depot was noted for its progressive human resources policies, which emphasized the importance of the individual to the success of the company's operations.

Recruitment/Selection

Throughout its entire recruiting process, Home Depot looked for people who shared a commitment to excellence. Also, management recognized that having the right number of people, in the right jobs, at the right time was critical. Employee population varied greatly among stores, depending on store size, sales volume, and the season of the year. In the winter, a store could have had fewer than 75 employees and in the spring would add another 25 to 40 employees. Some of the larger northeastern stores had as many as 280 employees. Full-time employees filled approximately 90% of the positions.

When a store first opened, it attracted applications through advertisements in local newspapers and trade journals such as *Home Center News*. A new store would usually receive several thousand applications. When seasonal workers and replacements were needed, help-wanted signs were displayed at store entrances. Walk-in candidates were another source, and applications were available at the customer service desk at all times. There was no formal program to encourage employees to refer their friends for employment. At the management level, the company preferred to hire people at the Assistant Manager level, requiring them to work their way up to store Manager and beyond. Historically the company often hired outside talent for senior positions. Now that the company had grown, Home Depot believed that, whenever possible, executives should come up through the ranks, although management from the outside was occasionally brought in. To support its growing infrastructure, Steven Messana served as Senior Vice President for Human Resources.

Interviews were scheduled 1 per day per week; however, if someone with trade experience applied, an on-the-spot interview might be conducted. "Trade" experience included retail, construction, do-it-yourself, or hardware. The company tended to look for older people who brought a high level of knowledge and maturity to the position. In addition to related experience, Home Depot looked for people with a stable work history who had a positive attitude, were excited, outgoing, and hard workers.

The selection process included preemployment tests (honesty, math, and drugs). The stores displayed signs in the windows that said that anyone who used drugs need not apply. Interviews were conducted with 3 or 4 people—an initial qualifier, the Administrative Assistant in operations, an Assistant Manager, and the store Manager. Reference checks were completed prior to a job offer. More in-depth background checks (financial, criminal) were conducted on management-level candidates.

To help ensure that Home Depot selected the best qualified people, during fiscal 1997 the company designed a proprietary automated system for identifying the best candidates for store sales associate positions. This system, which had been through extensive validation testing, screened candidates for competencies and characteristics inherent to Home Depot's best sales associates. The company planned to use this system to evaluate additional positions in the future.

Retention

Employee turnover varied from store to store. In the first year of operations, turnover could run 60% to 70% but would fall below 30% in future years. The company's goal was to reduce turnover to below 20%. The major causes of turnover were students who returned to school, employees who were terminated for poor performance, and tradespeople who considered Home Depot an interim position (often returning to their trade for a position paying as much as $50,000 per year). Very few people left the organization looking for "greener pastures" in the retail industry.

Career development was formally addressed during semiannual performance reviews, with goals and development plans mutually set by employees and managers. The company was committed to promotions from within and had a formal job-posting program. Vacancy lists were prepared at the regional level and distributed to the stores. Store managers were promoted from within. Affirmative action plans were used to increase female and minority representation.

Compensation

Employees were paid a straight salary. Bernard Marcus said, "The day I'm laid out dead with an apple in my mouth is the day we'll pay commissions. If you pay commissions, you imply that the small customer isn't worth anything." Most management-level employees were eligible for bonuses that were based on such factors as a store's return on assets and sales versus budget. Assistant Managers could receive up to 25% of their base salary in bonuses, and store Managers could earn up to 50% if their stores' performance warranted. Store managers could earn $50,000 to $120,000. The typical employee earned $10 to $14 per hour.

During fiscal year 1988, the company established a leveraged Employee Stock Ownership Plan (ESOP), covering substantially all full-time employees. In 1989, the company made its initial contribution to the ESOP of $6 million, which represented about $0.05 per share. Fully funded by the company, the ESOP was established to provide additional retirement security for the employees, while simultaneously reducing taxable income and discouraging hostile takeover attempts. At February 1, 1998, the ESOP held a total of 10,161,272 shares of the company's common stock in trust for plan participants. The company made annual contributions to the ESOP at the discretion of the Board of Directors. All employees eligible for the ESOP were entitled to receive a substantial portion of their annual salary in profit sharing. Tim Sparks, 31, who started out loading customers' cars in the lot at the age of 19 and managed a store in Jacksonville, Florida, said, "My father was a peanut farmer in Alabama. Dirt poor. Where else could a son go from that to being a millionaire?"

Recognition programs emphasized good customer service, increased sales, safety, cost savings, and length of service. Badges, cash awards, and other prizes were distributed in monthly group meetings.

Communication was the key by which Home Depot perpetuated its culture and retained its people. That culture included an environment in which employees were happy and where they felt productive and secure. The company sold employees on their role in Home Depot's success—they were giving the company a return on its assets. The environment avoided bureaucracy, was informal and intense, and encouraged honesty and risk taking. Each store maintained a strong open-door policy, and a Manager would spend 2 or 3 hours discussing a concern with an employee.

Top management was equally accessible to employees through frequent visits to the stores. An in-house TV broadcast, "Breakfast with Bernie and Arthur," was held quarterly. Impromptu questions were solicited from the employees. Department Managers met with employees weekly to provide new information and solicit feedback. Worker opinions also mattered at the top. When the company planned to open on New Year's Day, the employees voted to close and prevailed. When the company wrote a check-out training manual, a store cashier from Jacksonville helped write it. Internal sales charts were posted on bulletin boards so that employees would know how their store compared with others in the area.

Training

Home Depot believed that knowledgeable salespeople were 1 of the keys to the company's success and spent a great deal of time training them to "bleed orange." Callers to the home office found that corporate executives spent most of their time in the stores training employees. "We teach from the top down, and those who can't teach don't become executives," said 1 top executive. Training costs to open a new store were about $400,000 to $500,000.

Regular employees went through both formal and on-the-job training. Classes were held on product knowledge (giving the employee "total product knowledge . . . including all the skills a trade person might have"); merchandising concepts, and salesmanship (so that they could be sure that a customer has available, and would purchase, everything needed to complete a project); time management; personnel matters; safety and security; and how to interpret the company's various internally generated reports.

Each new employee was required to go through a rigorous week-long orientation, which introduced new hires to Home Depot's culture. To ensure that employees were convinced of the company's commitment, Bernard Marcus, Arthur Blank, and Ron Brill conducted many of the management training sessions. New employees were then paired with experienced associates in the stores to gain first-hand knowledge of customer service and general store operations. They trained an average of 4 weeks before working on their own. Even then, when there were no other customers in the department, newer employees would watch more experienced employees interact with customers to learn more about products, sales, and customer service. Employees were cross-trained to work in various departments, and even the cashiers learned how to work the sales floor.

The Home Depot Television Network allowed the company to disseminate policies and philosophies, product upgrades, and so on. With the ability to target special or mass audiences, the training possibilities were endless. The fact that the programs were broadcast live, with telephone call-ins, enhanced their immediacy and made interaction possible.

According to management, Home Depot's training programs were key to arming associates with the knowledge they needed to serve customers. During fiscal 1997, the company made several changes to its human resources and training programs to prepare for and support Home Depot's future growth plans. To address the unique growth needs of its divisions, new human resources officers were responsible for areas such as recruiting, staffing, employee relations, and management development in their divisions. They were also responsible for areas such as recruiting, staffing, employee relations and management development in their divisions. They were also responsible for implementing the store training programs that take entry-level sales associates from the basics to becoming project experts and, ultimately, masters in their respective departments.

Employees

As of the end of January 1998, the company employed approximately 125,000 people, of whom approximately 7,900 were salaried and the remainder were on an hourly basis. Approximately 76% of the company's employees were employed on a full-time basis. There were no unions. The company has never suffered a work stoppage.

Industry and Competitors

RETAIL BUILDING AND SUPPLY INDUSTRY

The retail building supply industry was moving rapidly from one characterized by small, independently run establishments to one dominated by regional and national chains of vast superstores. Home Depot developed the concept of the all-in-1 discount warehouse home improvement superstore, designed to be all things to all people. The main rival to Home Depot was Lowe's, which had been replacing its older, smaller stores with new superstores. Other companies in the industry were facing the challenge by reconfiguring their stores and by targeting niche segments, but some were being forced to close stores in the face of increased competition.

In 1997, the retail building supply industry showed mixed results. The stronger companies (Home Depot and Lowe's) got stronger, and the weak struggled. The largest 2 operators, Lowe's and Home Depot, extended their dominance, especially in the Do-It-Yourself (DIY) segment of the market (see **Exhibit 5**). Small regional operators such as Grossman in the Northeast were liquidated.

In 1997, Leonard Green & Partners bought out both Hechinger and Builders Square, formerly owned and started by Kmart, in an effort to turn the 2 struggling chains into 1 profitable chain.[30]

The retail building supply industry served 2 distinct clients—the professional building contractor and the DIY homeowner. The DIY customer had grown in importance over the past few years. Home Depot's main competitors were:

- **Hechinger** was located in the mid-Atlantic states and was recently acquired by Leonard Green & Partners. Hechinger had financial problems for several years before it was acquired.

- **Lowe's** was located in 22 states with 442 stores and had recently moved into large metropolitan areas—Dallas and Atlanta. The company had developed regional distribution centers to better serve its growing markets. Lowe's 1997 sales were estimated to be $10,190,000,000 and second to Home Depot with sales of $24,156,000,000 for 1997 (see **Exhibit 5**).

- **BMC** was renamed Building Materials Holding Corporation. The company had over 50 stores in 10 western states and was focusing on the professional/contractor market segment.

- **Hughes Supply** had 310 stores, principally in Florida, Georgia, and other southeastern states. The 1997 sales were estimated to be $1,810,000,000. The company made 13 acquisitions in 1996, which added about $340 million to its sales base. After these acquisitions, Hughes was in new territories—upper New York and California. The company focused on the professional/contractor market segment (see **Exhibit 5**).

- **Wolohan Lumber** had 58 stores located in Illinois, Indiana, Kentucky, Ohio, and Wisconsin. The company strategy was to focus on the professional/contractor market segment. The 1997 sales were estimated to be $425,000,000 (see **Exhibit 5**).

Exhibit 5 provides a summary of the key information on these companies.

The industry did not have barriers to entry in the form of patents or special technology. There was a major learning curve on efficiently managing a 100,000-square-foot store. The superstore warehouses tried to serve all market segments, but they had become increasingly consumer-oriented. Because of this, smaller competitors were focusing their strategies on the professional constructor segment of the market.[31]

Exhibit 5
Retail Building Supply Industry

A. Competitors

Company	Number of Stores 2000-2002	1997		Sales in Millions ($) 2000-2002	1998	1997	1996
Homebase, Inc.	105	84		$ 1,900.0	$ 1,500.0	$ 1,465.0	$ 1,448.8
Home Depot	1,050	624		54,000.0	30,100.0	24,600.0	19,535.0
Hughes Supply	362	310		2,500.0	1,960.0	1,810.0	1,516.1
Lowe's Companies	620	442		17,500.0	11,900.0	10,190.0	8,600.2
Woloham Lumber	75	58		620.0	410.0	425.0	430.4
Industry totals and averages				$66,000.0	$42,000.0	$38,050.0	$33,287.0

Company	Net Profit in Millions ($) 2000-2002	1998	1997	1996	Net Profit Margins % 2000-2002	1998	1997	1996
Homebase, Inc.	$ 38.0	$ 24.0	$ 21.0	$ 21.4	2.0%	1.6%	1.4%	1.5%
Home Depot	2,790.0	1,455.0	1,160.0	937.7	5.2	4.8	4.7	4.8
Hughes Supply	70.0	50.0	40.0	32.5	—	2.6	2.2	2.1
Lowe's Companies	645.0	405.0	345.0	292.2	3.7	3.4	3.4	3.4
Woloham Lumber	12.5	6.0	5.0	6.7	—	1.5	1.2	1.6
Industry totals and averages	$2,310.0	$1,510.0	$1,330.0	$1,287.2	3.6%	3.6%	3.5%	3.5%

B. Industry Indicators

	2000-2002	1998	1997	1996
Sales in millions ($)	$66,000.0	$38,050.0	$33,287.0	$27,152.0
Number of stores	2,350	1,980	1,860	1,922
Net profits in millions ($)	$ 2,310.0	$ 1,510.0	$ 1,330.0	$ 1,287.0
Net profit margin (%)	3.6%	3.6%	3.5%	3.6%

Note: Figures for 1998–2002 are projections.

Source: Value Line, January 16, 1998, pp. 884, 888–892.

Eagle Hardware & Garden of Seattle, Washington, operated 24 home improvement stores. Its founder, David Heerensperger, viewed Home Depot's entry into Seattle as a "war." He said, "They are aiming for us, but we're a thorn in their side. Eagle is the first home center they haven't completely run over."[32]

Eagle's stores averaged 128,000 square feet, compared to Home Depot's 103,000 square feet. Eagle offered other services, namely, a custom-design section, free chain-cutting station, fences, and an idea center where customers could watch videotapes and live demonstrations of home improvement techniques. Heerensperger began preparing for Home Depot's onslaught 6 years ago. He came up with a design for new stores that were brighter and more elegant than Home Depot's stores. He took into consideration women customers by reducing rack-type displays.[33] Eagle was building the largest stores in the industry in the West Coast and Northwest markets. Eagle planned to maintain a managed-growth strategy.

According to Ronald Pastore, real estate expert, "Between 1992 and 1994, 55% of all new retail square footage was built by big-box retailers (like Wal-Mart and Home Depot)."[34] In 1994, these retailers accounted for 80% of all new stores.

There had been a rampant construction of new retail space over the past 20 years. The supply of retail space nationally was 19 square feet for each person, and this was more than double the level of 20 years ago. The supply had far exceeded the population in growth for the same period. Christopher Niehaus, real estate investment banker, said, "That number is too high. It needs to come down."[35] He predicts that the discount sector is heading for the "'biggest shake-out' in retailing because of overbuilding."[36] Don McCrory, real estate expert, said, "Our question is, if the big-box tenants go out of business, what do you do with the enormous box?"[37]

THE PROFESSIONAL BUSINESS SEGMENT[38]

Early in fiscal 1997, Home Depot began a formal study of the professional business customer market. The findings of this study clearly indicated that there were many opportunities to grow its presence in the pro market that fit within the company's core business. The study also indicated that many of these opportunities could be captured inside its stores.

Estimated professional business customer sales across all channels in the United States were approximately $265 billion in 1997, substantially higher than the $100 billion Do-It-Yourself market. Excluding the heavy industrial sector, the majority of which was outside Home Depot's core business, the pro market opportunities for the company totaled approximately $215 billion. Home Depot's share of this market was less than 4% in 1998.

The initial focus for growing sales in the professional market was on the professional business customer who already shopped in Home Depot stores, but also made purchases at other retail and wholesale outlets. By listening and responding to his or her needs, the company intended to make Home Depot this customer's supplier of choice.

Late in fiscal 1997, Home Depot began a test in its stores in the Austin, Texas, market designed to increase professional customer sales while continuing to serve the strong and growing Do-It-Yourself customer market.

The test in Austin included incremental associates primarily responsible for serving and building relationships with the professional business customer. Professional business customers in these stores were assisted at a Pro Service Desk to more quickly meet their product and service needs. In addition, customized services, such as enhanced ordering and credit programs and a menu of product delivery options were available to the pro customer. The test, which was to be expanded to additional stores in fiscal 1998, was helping the company to successfully develop and refine its formula for serving the professional business customer inside its stores.

There were other ways to reach the professional customer, too. During fiscal 1997, Home Depot distributed its ProBook™ professional equipment and supply catalog to professional customers across North America. The ProBook contained over 15,000 products from its stores

Exhibit 6

Professional Business Customer Market

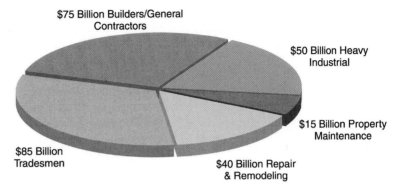

$265 Billion Market

$75 Billion Builders/General Contractors

$50 Billion Heavy Industrial

$15 Billion Property Maintenance

$40 Billion Repair & Remodeling

$85 Billion Tradesmen

Source: The Home Depot, *1997 Annual Report*, p. 4.

chosen especially for facility maintenance managers and the building trades. In addition, the company's longer term growth initiatives included exploring opportunities for serving professional customers with more specialized needs through distribution channels outside Home Depot stores.

The total professional business customer market was estimated to be $265 billion in 1997 (see **Exhibit 6**). The heavy industry with an estimated $50 billion in sales was treated as a separate sector. The professional business market ($215 billion) consisted of 4 subsectors: (1) tradesmen ($85 billion), (2) builders/general contractors ($75 billion), (3) repair and remodeling ($40 billion), and (4) property maintenance ($15 billion).

In 1996, the $215 billion professional business customer target market can be further separated by volume of expenditures. The typical Home Depot pro customer was a repair and remodel professional who purchased up to $200,000 of products annually, but tended to buy less than 10% of this amount from the company. The Home Depot planned to capture more of this customer's sales by responding to the distinct product and service needs of this professional. (See **Exhibit 7**.)

The company purchased Maintenance Warehouse as part of Home Depot's strategy to penetrate the professional market.

Exhibit 7

U.S. Professional Business Customer Profile—$215 Billion Total Target Market

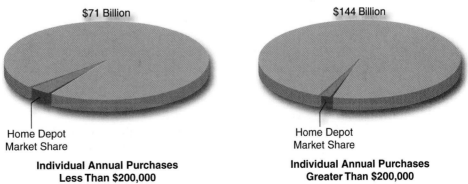

$71 Billion

$144 Billion

Home Depot Market Share

Home Depot Market Share

Individual Annual Purchases Less Than $200,000

Individual Annual Purchases Greater Than $200,000

Source: The Home Depot, Inc., *1997 Annual Report*, p. 7.

DO-IT-YOURSELF (DIY) INDUSTRY

The Home Depot occupied the number 1 position in the DIY industry with sales of $24.1 billion, more than twice its nearest competitor, Lowe's Companies. Home Depot had approximately 24% market share. Clearly the $100 billion industry was extremely fragmented. The industry remained dominated by small- to mid-sized stores, with only a handful of the top retailers operating stores about 100,000 square feet in size. The trend was clearly moving in the direction of bigger stores, however, as companies such as Lowe's and Home Depot enjoyed success with their large-store formats. As these companies continued to roll out their superstores at an aggressive rate, industry analysts expected the industry to consolidate over time, with the major retailers gaining their share at the expense of the smaller, less efficient DIY chains.

Home Depot was regarded as the premier operator in the DIY industry. The following list shows the 6 top competitors in 1996. However, based on competitors' announced expansion plans, Home Depot believed that the level of direct competition would increase to 22% of its total store base. The largest and most formidable foe facing Home Depot was the North Carolina chain, Lowe's. Since 1995, Lowe's had gone into more direct competition with Home Depot in more cities as both companies expanded. As Home Depot added more stores in Lowe's market, analysts believed that Lowe's could face increased margin pressure. Lowe's had been able to maintain its profit margin at 3.4% since 1996. Because Home Depot was more geographically dispersed than Lowe's and had a more balanced portfolio of stores, Home Depot was better able to be price competitive in these markets. The top 6 retail building supply companies in 1996 were as follows:

1. Home Depot
2. Lowe's Companies
3. Payless Cashways
4. Builders Square
5. Menard's
6. Hechinger's

Other competitors were Sutherland Lumber, Wickes Lumber, and Scotty's.

America's do-it-yourselfers spent approximately $100 billion in home improvement products in 1997, up more than 6% from the previous year. This all-important customer group was getting larger in number and more confident and capable to take on home improvement projects every year. In addition, demographic changes were taking place within the Do-It-Yourself customer group that had important implications for the future of the home improvement industry. Home Depot was positioning itself to continue to grow its share of this industry segment as these changes took place.

The rate of home ownership in the United States continued to grow as first-time buyers entered the housing market at a rapid pace and baby-boomers moved in force to more expensive homes and second homes. During 1997, existing single-family home sales reached their highest point on record, and new single-family home sales showed strong increases from the previous year. In addition, studies showed that the average age of existing homes continued to increase, and people were staying in their homes later in life. All of these trends enhanced Home Depot's opportunities to add new stores across North America as well as to increase sales in its existing stores.[39]

The $100 billion DIY market breaks into 5 market segments: (1) lumber and building materials, (2) lawn and garden, (3) plumbing and electrical, (4) hardware and tools, (5) paint and supplies, and (6) hard surface flooring. **Exhibit 8** shows their market segment shares.

HomeBase, formerly HomeClub, was acquired by Zayre Corporation, a discount retail chain, in 1986. It was consolidated with BJ's Wholesale Club and renamed Waban, Inc. Zayre spun the company off to shareholders on June 14, 1989. In July 1997, Waban spun off the com-

Exhibit 8

$100 Billion Do-It-Yourself Market

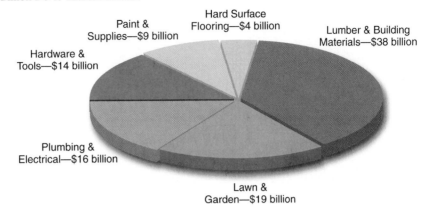

Source: The Home Depot, Inc., *1997 Annual Report*, p. 8.

pany to shareholders and was renamed HomeBase. In 1997, the company had to write off $27 million to cover store closings. The company was changing its strategy from being defensive to a more aggressive stance, such as accelerating store remodeling program. Analysts said, "This is an extremely competitive industry, and profit margins are small, so only the well-managed companies prosper and survive." He went on to say, "Look at Kmart; the company could not effectively manage Builders Square. They had to sell it off."[39]

Finance

The 10-year performance of Home Depot in selected key growth financial indicators is as follows:

Financial Indicator	Compound Growth Rate	
	5-year Annual	10-year Annual
Net sales	27.6%	32.5%
Earnings before taxes	28.3	35.6
Net earnings	27.5	36.6
Total assets	23.4	35.8
Working capital	19.9	33.6
Merchandise inventory	30.8	32.8
Net property and equipment	32.3	38.8
Long-term debt	9.1	37.9
Shareholders' equity	25.2	36.3
Capital expenditures	28.4	32.8
Number of stores	23.9	23.6
Average total company weekly sales	27.6	32.5
Number of customer transactions	23.8	27.6
Average sale per transaction	$3.00	$3.70
Weighted average sales per square foot	$1.00	$4.40

These compound growth rates had provided Home Depot shareholders with 48 consecutive quarters of growth in sales and earnings. Fiscal year (FY) 1997 was from February 3, 1997, to February 1, 1998.

Exhibit 9 shows that the average sale per transaction had increased from $33.92 in 1990 to $43.63 in 1997, or 28.7%. During the same period, average total company weekly sales had

Exhibit 9

Ten-Year Selected Financial and Operating Highlights: Home Depot, Inc.

(Dollar amounts in thousands, except where noted)

	5-Year Annual Compound Growth Rate	10-Year Annual Compound Growth Rate	Fiscal Years³									
			1997	1996¹	1995	1994	1993	1992	1991	1990¹	1989	1988
Statement of Earnings Data												
Net sales	27.6%	32.5%	$24,156	$19,535	$15,470	$12,477	$9,239	$7,148	$5,137	$3,815	$2,759	$2,000
Net sales increase—%	—	—	23.7	26.3	24.0	35.0	29.2	39.2	34.6	38.3	38.0	37.6
Earnings before taxes²	28.3	35.6	2,002	1,535	1,195	980	737	576	396	260	182	126
Net earnings²	27.5	38.6	1,224	938	732	605	457	363	249	163	112	77
Net earnings increase—%²	—	—	30.5	28.2	21.0	32.2	26.1	45.6	52.5	46.0	45.9	41.9
Diluted earnings per share ($)²,³,⁴,⁵	24.4	31.0	1.64	1.29	1.02	0.88	0.67	0.55	0.39	0.30	0.21	0.15
Diluted earnings per share increase—%²	—	—	27.1	26.5	15.9	31.3	21.8	41.0	30.0	42.9	40.0	36.4
Weighted average number of common shares outstanding assuming dilution³,⁴	1.7	4.6	762	732	717	714	711	699	662	608	574	519
Gross margin—% of sales	—	—	28.1	27.8	27.7	27.9	27.7	27.6	28.1	27.9	27.8	27.0
Store selling and operating—% of sales	—	—	17.8	18.0	18.0	17.8	17.6	17.4	18.1	18.2	18.3	17.8
Pre-opening expense—% of sales	—	—	0.3	0.3	0.4	0.4	0.4	0.4	0.3	0.4	0.3	0.4
General and administrative expense—% of sales	—	—	1.7	1.7	1.7	1.8	2.0	2.1	2.3	2.4	2.5	2.4
Net interest income (expense)—% of sales	—	—	—	0.1	0.1	(0.1)	0.3	0.4	0.3	(0.1)	(0.1)	(0.1)
Earnings before taxes—% of sales²	—	—	8.3	7.9	7.7	7.8	8.0	8.1	7.7	6.8	6.6	6.3
Net earnings—% of sales²	—	—	5.1	4.8	4.7	4.8	5.0	5.1	4.8	4.3	4.1	3.8
Balance Sheet Data and Financial Ratios												
Total assets	23.4%	35.8%	$11,229	$9,342	$7,354	$5,778	$4,701	$3,932	$2,510	$1,640	$1,118	$699
Working capital	19.9	33.6	2,004	1,867	1,255	919	994	807	624	301	274	143
Merchandise inventories	30.8	32.8	3,602	2,708	2,180	1,749	1,293	940	662	509	381	294
Net property and equipment	32.3	38.8	6,509	5,437	4,461	3,397	2,371	1,608	1,255	879	514	332
Long-term debt	9.1	37.9	1,303	1,247	720	983	874	844	271	531	303	108
Shareholders' equity	25.2	36.3	7,098	5,955	4,988	3,442	2,814	2,304	1,691	683	512	383
Book value per share ($)³	22.9	31.2	9.70	8.26	6.97	5.06	4.17	3.46	2.67	1.29	0.99	0.75
Long-term debt to equity—%	—	—	18.4	20.9	14.4	28.6	31.1	36.6	16.0	77.7	59.1	28.1
Current ratio	—	—	1.82:1	2.01:1	1.89:1	1.76:1	2.02:1	2.07:1	2.17:1	1.73:1	1.94:1	1.74:1
Inventory turnover	—	—	5.4x	5.6x	5.5x	5.7x	5.9x	6.3x	6.1x	6.0x	5.9x	5.8x
Return on beginning equity—%	—	—	19.5	18.8	21.3	21.5	19.9	21.5	36.5	31.9	29.2	23.9

Statement of Cash Flows Data											
Depreciation and amortization	32.4%	38.8%	$283	$232	$181	$130	$90	$70	$52	$34	$21	$15
Capital expenditures	28.4	32.8	1,525	1,248	1,308	1,220	900	437	432	400	205	105
Cash dividends per share ($)[3]	28.6	43.5	0.19	0.15	0.13	0.10	0.07	0.05	0.04	0.02	0.02	0.01
Store Data[6]												
Number of stores	23.9%	23.6%	624	512	423	340	264	214	174	145	118	96
Number of states	16.6	17.8	41	38	31	28	23	19	15	12	12	10
Number of Canadian provinces	—	—	4	3	3	3	—	—	—	—	—	—
Square footage at year-end	26.0	26.8	66	54	44	35	26	21	16	13	10	8
Increase in square footage (%)	—	—	23.1	21.6	26.3	33.2	26.3	26.8	24.1	27.4	26.9	33.4
Average square footage per store (in thousands)	1.6	2.6	106	105	105	103	100	98	95	92	88	86
Store Sales and Other Data[6]												
Comparable stores sales increase—%[7]	—	—	7	7	3	8	7	15	11	10	13	13
Average total company weekly sales	27.6%	32.5%	$465	$369	$298	$240	$178	$137	$99	$72	$53	$38
Weighted average weekly sales per operating store (in thousands)	2.7	7.1	829	803	787	802	764	724	633	566	515	464
Weighted average sales per square foot ($)[7]	1.0	4.4	406	398	390	404	398	387	348	322	303	282
Number of customer transactions	23.8	27.6	550	464	370	302	236	189	146	112	84	64
Average sale per transaction ($)	3.0	3.7	43.63	42.09	41.78	41.29	39.13	37.72	35.13	33.92	32.65	31.13
Number of associates at year end (actual)	26.2	29.9	124,400	98,100	80,800	67,300	50,600	38,900	28,000	21,500	17,500	13,000

Notes:
1. Fiscal years 1996 and 1990 consisted of 53 weeks; all other years reported consisted of 52 weeks.
2. Excludes the effect of the $104 million nonrecurring charge in fiscal 1997.
3. All share and per-share data have been adjusted for a 3-for-2 stock split on July 3, 1997.
4. Share and per-share data have been restated for the adoption of SFAS 128 "Earnings per Share."
5. Diluted earnings per share for fiscal 1997, including the $104 million nonrecurring charge, were $1.55.
6. Excludes Maintenance Warehouse and National Blind and Wallpaper Factory.
7. Adjusted to reflect the first 52 weeks of the 53-week fiscal years in 1996 and 1990.

Source: Home Depot, Inc. *1997 Annual Report,* first page fold-out.

increased from $72,000 to $465,000, or 545.8%. The weighted average weekly sales per operating store had increased from $566,000 in 1990 to $829,000 in 1997, or 464%. The weighted average sale per square foot had increased from $322 in 1990 to $406 in 1997, or 25.5%.

If someone had invested $1,000 on June 30, 1982, in Home Depot, on June 28, 1997, the investment would have been worth $152,479. Only 2 stocks surpassed Home Depot's performance: Keane ($321,022) and Mark IV Industries ($269,265).

Exhibits 9, 10, and **11** provide the company's 10-year selected financial and operating income highlights, consolidated statement of earnings, and balance sheet.

Exhibit 10

Consolidated Statement of Earnings: Home Depot, Inc.
(Dollar amounts in millions, except per share data)

Fiscal Year Ending[1]	February 1, 1998	February 2, 1997	January 28, 1996
Net sales	$24,156	$19,535	$15,470
Cost of merchandise sold	17,375	14,101	11,184
Gross profit	6,781	5,434	4,286
Operating expenses			
Selling and store operating	4,287	3,521	2,784
Pre-opening	65	55	52
General and administrative	413	324	270
Nonrecurring charge	104	—	—
Total operating expenses	4,869	3,900	3,106
Operating income	1,912	1,534	1,180
Interest income (expense)			
Interest and investment income	44	25	19
Interest expense	(42)	(16)	(4)
Interest, net	2	9	15
Minority interest	(16)	(8)	—
Earnings before income taxes	1,898	1,535	1,195
Income taxes	738	597	463
Net earnings	$1,160	$938	$732
Basic earnings per share	$1.59	$1.30	$1.03
Weighted average number of common shares outstanding	729	719	709
Diluted earnings per share	$1.55	$1.29	$1.02
Weighted average number of common shares outstanding assuming dilution	762	732	717

Notes:
1. Fiscal year (FY) 1997 was February 3, 1997 to February 1, 1998.
2. Notes were deleted.

Source: Home Depot, Inc. *1997 Annual Report*, p. 21.

Exhibit 11

Consolidated Balance Sheet: Home Depot, Inc.
(Dollar amounts in millions, except per share data)

Fiscal Year Ending[1]	February 1, 1998	February 2, 1997
Assets		
Current assets		
Cash and cash equivalents	$172	$146
Short-term investments, including current maturities of long-term investments	2	413
Receivables, net	556	388
Merchandise inventories	3,602	2,708
Other current assets	128	54
Total current assets	4,460	3,709
Property and equipment, at cost		
Land	2,194	1,855
Buildings	3,041	2,470
Furniture, fixtures, and equipment	1,370	1,084
Leasehold improvements	383	340
Construction in progress	336	284
Capital leases	163	117
	7,487	6,150
Less accumulated depreciation and amortization	978	713
Net property and equipment	6,509	5,437
Long-term investments	15	8
Notes receivable	27	40
Cost in excess of the fair value of net assets acquired, net of accumulated amortization of $18 at February 1, 1998 and $15 at February 2, 1997	140	87
Other	78	61
Total assets	$11,229	$9,342
Liabilities and shareholders' equity		
Current liabilities		
Accounts payable	$1,358	$1,090
Accrued salaries and related expenses	312	249
Sales taxes payable	143	129
Other accrued expenses	530	323
Income taxes payable	105	49
Current installments of long-term debt	8	2
Total current liabilities	2,456	1,842
Long-term debt, excluding current installments	1,303	1,247
Other long-term liabilities	178	134
Deferred income taxes	78	66
Minority interest	116	98
Shareholders' Equity		
Common stock, par value $0.05. Authorized: 1,000,000,000 shares; issued and outstanding—732,108,000 shares of February 1, 1998 and 720,773,000 shares at February 2, 1997	37	36
Paid-in capital	2,662	2,511
Retained earnings	4,430	3,407
Cumulative translation adjustments	(28)	2
Total shareholders' equity	7,101	5,956
Less: shares purchased for compensation plans	3	1
	7,098	5,955
Total liabilities and shareholders' equity	$11,229	$9,342

Notes:
1. Fiscal year (FY) 1997 was February 3, 1997 to February 1, 1998.
2. Company consolidated balance sheet showed **Commitments and contingencies** instead of **Total liabilities and shareholders' equity**.

Source: Home Depot, Inc., *1997 Annual Report*, p. 22.

Notes

1. This section is based on Paul M. Swiercz's case "The Home Depot, Inc." as it appears in *Cases in Strategic Management*, 4th ed., Thomas L. Wheelen and J. David Hunger (Reading, Mass.: Addison-Wesley, 1993), pp. 367–397. It is referred to as Swiercz in further citations. Any information beyond 1989 is new to this case.
2. Ben Sharav, "Home Depot," *Value Line* (July 21, 1995), p. 888.
3. Rahul Jacob, "Corporate Reputation," *Fortune* (March 6, 1995), pp. 54–55.
4. Elena Lesser and Anita Sharpe, "Home Depot Charges a Rival Drummed Up Opposition to Stores," *Wall Street Journal* (August 18, 1995), p. A-1.
5. *Ibid.*
6. Chris Roush, "Home Depot Reaches a Cross Roads," *The Atlanta Journal* (July 16, 1996), p. P6.
7. *Ibid.*
8. The Home Depot, Inc., *1996 Annual Report*, p. 5.
9. The Home Depot, Inc., *1997 Annual Report*, p. 16.
10. *Ibid.*
11. *Ibid.*
12. *Ibid.*
13. *St. Petersburg Times* (December 24, 1990), p. 11.
14. *Business Atlanta* (November 11, 1988).
15. *Ibid.*
16. *Chain Store Executive* (April 1983), pp. 9–11.
17. The Home Depot, Inc., *1995 Annual Report*, p. 3.
18. The Home Depot, Inc., *1997 Annual Report*, p. 13. This was directly quoted with minor editing.
19. *Ibid.*, p. 5.
20. The Home Depot, Inc., *Form 10-K* (February 1, 1998), pp. 8–9. The material was abstracted, *1997 Annual Meeting of Shareholders Notice*, pp. 3–6.
21. The Home Depot, Inc., *1997 Form 10-K*, pp. 8–9.
22. The Home Depot, Inc., *1997 Annual Report*, p. 35.
23. Swiercz, "The Home Depot, Inc."
24. *Ibid.*, The Home Depot, Inc., *1996 Annual Report*, p. 13, and The Home Depot, Inc., *1997 Form 10-K*, pp. 4, 10–11. Some paragraphs in this section are directly quoted with minor editing.
25. Susan Caminiti, "The New Champs of Retailing," *Fortune* (September 1990), p. 2.
26. The Home Depot, Inc., *1997 Form 10-K*, p. 3. The table is directly quoted.
27. *Ibid.*, The Home Depot, Inc., *1997 Form 10-K*, pp. 6–7. This section was directly quoted with minor editing.
28. The Home Depot, Inc., *1997 Annual Report*, p. 20. This section was directly quoted with minor editing.
29. Swiercz, "The Home Depot, Inc." and The Home Depot, Inc. *1997 Annual Report*, pp. 12–13.
30. Ben Sharav, "Retail Building Supply Industry," *Value Line* (January 16, 1998), p. 884.
31. Ben Sharav, "Home Depot," *Value Line* (July 21, 1995), p. 884.
32. Robert LaFranco, "Comeuppance," *Forbes* (December 4, 1995), p. 74.
33. *Ibid.*, pp. 74–75.
34. Mitchell Pacelle, "Retail Building Surge Despite Store Glut," *Wall Street Journal* (January 17, 1996), p. A-2.
35. *Ibid.*
36. *Ibid.*
37. *Ibid.*
38. The Home Depot, Inc., *1997 Annual Report*, pp. 6–7. The first 5 paragraphs were directly quoted with minor editing.
39. *Ibid.*, p. 80.
40. Robert Berne and William M. Bulkeley, "Kmart and Waban Consider Combining Home Improvement Chains in New Firm," *Wall Street Journal* (February 4, 1997), p. A-3.

case 25

Amy's Bread (Revised)

Paula S. Weber, Cathleen S. Burns, and James E. Weber

Introduction

Amy glanced at the clock and moaned. It was 3:30 A.M., time to get up and head to her Manhattan bakery, but she hadn't slept all night. She had a big decision to make. "No," she muttered to herself, she had a multitude of big decisions to make.

Amy muttered to herself, "There are already so many days when I feel stretched past the breaking point. There are so many demands." Amy mentally ticked them off: "Ensuring consistent quality, scheduling and training staff, ordering supplies, developing new recipes, contacting potential customers, collecting from slow-paying clients. . . the list is truly endless." Amy wondered, "If I decide to expand, can I do it successfully? Can I find another trustworthy manager, like Toy Kim Dupree, to help me manage the staff and maintain bread quality? Can I find expansion space in Manhattan? Should I close our current location and expand to a much larger space thus eliminating the need to manage 2 locations? Should I look for a location for my wholesale production or a space that would provide both retail and wholesale opportunities?" There was so much to decide. Right now though, Amy's dough starters were waiting, as were her employees. She had to get up and face another busy day at her bakery.

Amy's Bread, founded in 1992, served about 50 wholesale customers, including some of the finest restaurants, hotels, and gourmet food shops in Manhattan. Amy's Bread also had a waiting list of more than 30 wholesale customers from other quality restaurants, hotels and shops. Amy thought, "I really want to meet their needs and accept their business, but any further production expansion in my existing space is impossible. I know I can't produce 1 more loaf without hurting bread quality, which is absolutely unthinkable! We are already working 3 shifts and there is no more room for additional equipment." Amy and her Assistant Manager, Toy Kim Dupree, had commiserated, "The bakery is stretched to the limits. Dough production ranges from 1,800 to 3,000 pounds of bread per day, well over capacity for just 1,300 square feet." As Toy described, "We are like sardines making bread. Surviving in these close quarters is so difficult. Not only do we produce all of the wholesale and retail bread in this 1 location, but we also store ingredients and have a small office."

This case was prepared by Professors Paula S. Weber and James E. Weber of St. Cloud State University, and Cathleen S. Burns of the University of Missouri–Columbia. This case was edited for SMBP-8th Edition. Copyright © 2000 by Professors Paula S. Weber, Cathleen S. Burns, and James E. Weber. Reprinted by permission.

Amy worried that some of the customers on her long waiting list were on the brink of turning away. But, Amy thought, "Am I really ready to tackle a major expansion? On the 1 hand, I have worked so hard to make my dreams a reality, I can't imagine stopping now. But, can I handle an expansion and larger ongoing operations? Financially? Mentally? Physically?" Amy remembered Toy's recent comment: "Amy's Bread is finally turning a profit." The thought of an expansion and additional debt was very scary.

What Gave Rise to Amy's Bread?

AMY'S PERSONAL HISTORY

Amy was born and raised in Minnesota, where her father was a high level executive for Pillsbury and her mother was a gourmet cook with a family reputation for baking fresh breads. As a child, Amy remembered coming home from school to the smell of her mother's homemade breads wafting from the kitchen. After high school, Amy earned a degree in economics and psychology. She then moved to New York in 1984 to try her luck in the Big Apple.

Amy soon found that an office job was not for her, and that she longed to pursue a more creative career. She talked endlessly to her managers and coworkers about her dream of opening her own business. It was then that Amy began to solicit support and promises of financial backing if she were ever to start her own business. After 3 years, Amy left her white-collar marketing position to pursue her dream. She decided to attend the New York Restaurant School for culinary training. After graduating from their program, Amy landed a job as a chef for 1 of New York's most highly acclaimed French restaurants. After 2 years of very challenging work and longer hours than her marketing job, Amy escaped to Europe. Amy said, "It was there I discovered my true passion: bread baking." She backpacked around England, Italy, and France, and eventually settled in France where there are strong traditions of bread baking. Amy worked in bakeries in 3 different French towns, spending a month at each. "When I returned to New York in 1989, I was brimming with ideas and excitement about opening my own bakery," Amy recalled.

Amy spent the next 2 years as a pastry chef and bread baker for another top New York eatery. As Amy worked, she simultaneously developed recipes and business plans. Amy dreamed that someday soon she would be working for herself.

History of Amy's Bread

Amy knew that opening a bakery in New York would be extremely challenging. First, it was a highly competitive industry with low wholesale profit margins. Second, space in New York was always at a premium and renting a desirable location was going to be extremely expensive. Third, she discovered that banks would not loan her money. Banks viewed bakeries as restaurants, far too risky an investment without a prior proven track record. Amy remained undaunted. She was determined to achieve her goal of running her own business, one that sold a million dollars worth of beautiful breads each year made by employees who took pride in their work and were rewarded for their efforts. Amy had clear goals: "I wanted to be famous for making a great product and for creating a good place to work. I did not care a lot about being rich. I just want to sell beautiful breads from a cute, cozy place."

In 1992, armed with some savings, a loan from her parents, private loans from her former colleagues in the marketing profession, a good business mind, and a very determined spirit, Amy took the big step. She quit her restaurant job and opened Amy's Bread on Ninth Avenue in a tough area of Manhattan known as Hell's Kitchen. The space she found was an old storefront that had been a fish market and had been empty for 5 years. While only 650 square feet, it was still expensive, but it was the most affordable space she could find. With the help of family and friends, it still took 6 months to renovate the space, including plastering and painting. Amy installed equipment, hired and trained staff, developed a customer list, and began production.

The Key Ingredients

PERSONNEL

Amy's Bread started with a staff of 6 dedicated employees who scrubbed up used equipment, built shelves, and lent a hand as needed. Amy recalled, "I taught them bread-making techniques, and then, with little idea of what was to come, we opened for business." Amy's Bread sometimes used newspaper advertisements for attracting employees, but most responded to a "Now Hiring" sign in the bakery's window. Assistant Manager, Toy Kim Dupree, described reasons employees came to work for Amy's Bread. "Some were interested in bread baking, but many came because we offered a 5-day work week while many bakeries and restaurants have a 6-day work week. We also worked hard to create a happy, open, and friendly environment. It's what we wanted for ourselves and what we hoped to create for our employees. Our aim was to have a perfect product, but we recognized that we were dealing with human beings. Anyone who is too intense does not fit in well here. We don't have any room for prima donnas. We also tend to pay more than our competitors."

A typical employee would begin in the shaping area working to form the bread loaves. From there, they can move to baking the bread, and, finally, to the mixing of the dough. Toy described a key management challenge as "helping employees to beat the boredom of their repetitive work." Toy said, "Our most successful employees have a positive outlook, are dependable and conscientious, think on their feet, and interact well with their coworkers. We have no cubicles here!" Employees suggested solutions to management issues with Amy having the final say. As Toy described, "We all put our heads together, bringing in our separate areas of expertise. Our goals were to produce very high quality breads by hand, pay our employees a decent living wage, and ensure that our customers get good value for their money."

Over the years, Amy's Bread had experienced very low turnover. Retail staff started at $8.00 an hour and baking staff at $10.00. In fact, Amy's Bread's lowest paid employees were the cleaning staff, and they started at $7.50 an hour, well above minimum wage. Benefits were available to employees who worked more than 20 hours a week, and employees who were with the company longer than a year were eligible for a 401K plan. The majority of her employees (88%) were minorities for whom English was a second language. Training was often done by demonstration. Payroll expenses were extremely high representing over 50% of sales. With a hand-made product, it was difficult to attain any economy of scale concerning labor. New sales led to additional payroll expense.

Amy reminisced, "The first year was by far the toughest. We learned to handle dough in stifling hot weather. We had to keep going on only a few hours of sleep a day and get by without money when our customers were slow to pay. Our space was so narrow and cramped that we struggled to get racks of dough through it. However, sales were good, and sometimes all the bread was sold by noon!"

BREAD PRODUCTION

Amy surmised that "practice and patience were the keys to perfect bread and all successful bread started with quality ingredients." Amy explained, "Dough batters are very challenging. They can be too dry, too wet, not rising quickly enough, or rising too quickly. Many external elements can affect the dough including the air temperature, the temperature of the water, the timing of each step." One of the most critical aspects of the success of Amy's Bread was her devotion to sourdough starters. The starters are essentially flour, yeast, and water. Amy quipped, "The starters are the miracle ingredient that gives life to the bread."

Amy mused, "A baker's work is really never done. The demands are constant. The dough keeps rising and must be carefully watched throughout the process. The bakery operates 24 hours a day, 7 days a week. Wholesale customers want bread every day. On weekends and holidays their orders double!" Amy's Bread had a staff of 32 bread mixers, shapers, and bakers by 1998.

At about 5:00 A.M., the mixing began. Amy described the process: "We fill a large mixer with flour, water, the all-important sourdough starter, salt, and yeast. Before long, the mixer's fork kneader pulls and stretches a mass of supple dough. The dough is put aside to rest and rise slowly at a cool temperature and then divided into portions to be shaped and baked."

Every step was physically demanding and workers got sore arms and shoulders and very, very tired legs and feet. At noon the shaping of the loaves for the next day's orders began. Racks of rising dough were cut and formed. This was a totally manual process as each loaf must be hand-shaped. The bread was then left to rise again at a cool temperature so it can ferment. Finally, the loaves were baked in the early hours of the morning. After the bread was baked, it was cooled and packed for delivery by an Amy's Bread truck. Amy commented, "Smelling the bread as it comes out of the oven, seeing its golden color, feeling its texture, and enjoying its delicious flavor certainly contributes to job satisfaction!"

CUSTOMERS

Amy's original business plans called for providing breads wholesale to restaurants and hotels. She had a loyal customer in a former employer and a list of interested customers. Her location was really not the best for retail traffic. Retail business would simply be a sideline—she would sell excess loaves to people who wandered in to check out the bakery.

Slowly, but surely, Amy began earning a citywide reputation for high quality, innovative, yet consistent products. Her signature bread, semolina with golden raisins and fennel, brought Amy's Bread lots of attention. By 1996, her wholesale customer list had grown to almost 40 customers, and she was preparing about 600 pounds of dough a day just for her semolina, golden raisin, fennel bread. Her product line included approximately 50 items made from 15 different doughs. Amy's best-selling products included her semolina bread, walnut scallion bread, black olive twists, apple walnut raisin rings, and organic whole wheat bread with toasted seeds.

As Amy's business grew, she discovered a growing retail interest. The area around Amy's Bread was improving and new restaurants and coffee shops were opening. She began to bake rolls and single serving loaves specifically for retail customers. She eventually hired counter help to service the retail customers and began selling not only breakfast breads, like muffins and scones, but sandwiches to customers as well. She set up attractive window displays and added a few small tables in the front of her shop. Amy's retail business gradually grew until it represented about 25% of sales. Best-selling items for retail traffic included focaccia with rosemary, bread twists, sourdough baguettes, and country sourdough loaves. Amy noted that her staff "took great pride in serving retail customers." They told Amy, "We enjoyed hearing directly from the customers how much they enjoy the bread."

Amy commented that "wholesale is my mainstay and where the greatest volume of sales exist. However, the profit margin on retail is better than on wholesale." Amy remarked, "A critical part of my expansion decision is deciding whether the expansion should be solely for wholesale space, a combination of retail and wholesale, or purely retail." Amy felt this was a crucial issue because the use of the space really drove the location decision. Amy knew, "If I were to expand to meet my waiting list of wholesale customers only, then the facility needed to have good access to major streets with an ample truck dock for loading baked loaves, and unloading supplies and ingredients. It also could be located in a less "desirable" neighborhood. However, if retail were to be the emphasis, then I needed to find an attractive space with lots of foot traffic in a neighborhood where many people lived and worked."

COMPETITORS

When Amy's Bread opened, bread baking appeared to be a growth industry, boosted by healthful eating trends. The U.S. Department of Commerce reported that per-capita consumption of specialty breads increased 12% from 1988 to 1993. A 1992 article in *Bakery Production and Marketing* stated that key trends predicted for supermarkets in the 1990s would be the expansion of in-store bakeries as a key aspect of enhancing their outreach to customers.

In 1993, per-capita consumption of specialty breads was 23.28 pounds, which represented 30% of all bread consumption. A Gallup Poll in January 1995 showed that 71% of adults prefer bread to all other grain-based foods. Ninety percent indicated that grain-based foods were convenient and 63% thought bread was low fat. New bread chains and franchise locations were springing up every day including Stone Mill Bread Company, Panere, La Madeleine, and the original, Au Bon Pain. Perhaps the biggest of the franchise chains was the Great Harvest Bread Company, founded in 1976. In 1995, Great Harvest had 87 stores with 15 more under development, sporting a 30% annual growth rate.

Closer to home, Amy's Bread had several primary competitors for specialty breads including the Tom Cat Bakery in Queens (1 of New York's other boroughs), Ecce Panis, and Eli's Bread. They were well established and larger than Amy's Bread. They supported a client list that included famous restaurants such as the Union Square Café and gourmet grocery stores such as Balducci's and Dean & Deluca. These bakeries tended to be more mechanized than Amy's Bread utilizing equipment for dough shaping and baking.

Some of the larger commercial bakeries had folded due to competitive pressures but, at the same time, more and more small bakeries featuring specialty varieties were opened in Manhattan and the surrounding area. These microbakeries, like Amy's Bread, catered to upscale restaurants and gourmet shops that wanted to pamper their customers with the best of fresh, creative breads. Amy felt that "the secret to financial success in the bakery business was to differentiate your breads, rather than copying what everyone else made."

Amy maintained, "The keys to getting and maintaining wholesale customers are innovative and consistently high-quality breads. One of the ways I ensure high quality is by the hand-shaping and individual baking of the bread. The retail customers also want consistent quality, but they are looking for convenient locations and prompt service too. I don't focus on what my competitors charge. Occasionally I see their price lists, but I basically charge what I feel I must to cover my expenses and overhead. In fact, many of our prices have not changed since we first opened for business."

Baking Up a Success

FINANCIAL RESULTS

Shortly after her 1992 opening, Amy discovered what many entrepreneurs find to be a major roadblock: cash flow. As new entrepreneurial businesses began to flourish, more and more upfront money was needed for equipment, supplies, and staff. Typically, the customer base had not grown large enough to cover all the expenses, nor were customer accounts as current as desired, and sometimes products were not priced correctly. Amy remarked, "Soon after opening, I discovered that even if I sold every loaf I could make, my revenue would not be high enough to cover my high monthly lease and equipment rental expenses." Amy was very lucky though, when adjoining space opened up in December, and although she could not easily afford to lease the space, she also knew that she could not continue to exist without expanding. Quickly, Amy was able to borrow enough additional funds from family and friends to lease the adjoining open space. By January 1993, she was in full production in her newly expanded space.

Though the beginning months proved to be quite a struggle, Amy's Bread gradually grew. The 1998 income statement and accompanying schedules for Amy's Bread highlight her sales and profitability (see **Exhibit 1**). Amy remarked, "Since payroll expenses rise with sales, the real profits only come from economies of scale reached with fixed expenses like rent and utilities." Amy further noted, "Given the low unemployment rate, there often is a shortage of good staff available at the salaries her business could afford to pay." Amy's contribution margin on retail operations was 47% while it was only 35% for wholesale operations (see **Exhibit 2**). Other bakeries that were more mechanized experienced higher profit margins. In order to ensure the highest quality of product, Amy's Bread hand-shaped all their breads; so labor costs were much higher than other bakeries. For example, a "mechanized" bakery with sales revenue similar to Amy's Bread had only 5 employees while Amy's Bread needed 20 employees to produce the same amount of sales.

In analyzing other expenses, Amy commented, "Food cost changes usually come from flour, nuts, dairy products, and olive oil. Prices for those products are quite volatile while prices for other ingredients remain quite stable." In the mid-nineties the baking industry experienced a steep rise in the price of flour. However industry reports showed that bakeries were only able to raise their prices 5% over the same time period. In addition, restaurants, overwhelmed with sources of bread providers, were resistant to bakery industry pressures for price hikes. For quality reasons though, Amy rejected using "quick-bread" mixes where you only add eggs and oil, preferring more expensive fresh, organic ingredients and sourdough starters.

MARKETING TECHNIQUES

Amy said her most successful marketing technique was to "keep current customers happy." She noted, "Word of mouth is very powerful in the New York restaurant business." Another way that Amy had obtained new customers was by being very available to the press. Amy emphasized, "Whenever someone calls for an interview, I make the time to meet with them and make every effort to make them feel welcome. I invariably discuss what is unique about my breads and, of course, everyone receives free bread samples." Amy also commented, "The fact that I am a woman in a male-dominated industry helps ensure that my business is an interesting story." Amy also determined that "whenever there was a mention of my business in a local paper, business increased a great deal for the next 2 to 3 weeks and some of the new customers continued to return. A positive review by an outsider is better than any ad I could write." However, limited advertising was used for special events or seasonal product promotion.

Amy's Bread has been recognized by *The New York Times*, *New York Magazine*, *Modern Baking*, *Gourmet*, and *Food and Wine*, just to mention a few. Excerpts from these articles include the following:

> At her tiny, charming storefront in what used to be known as Hell's Kitchen, Amy Scherber turns out a dozen and a half sublime varieties that are anything but conventional white bread. Amy's is the candy store of bread bakeries.

> *New York Magazine*, June 1994.

> Armed with a gentle manner, modest business plan, and a genuine love for baking bread, Amy Scherber, 34, has managed, in less than 2 years, to position her bakery in the highly competitive, sometimes cutthroat, specialty wholesale bread market of New York City.

> *Modern Baking*, November 1994.

Exhibit 1

1998 Income Statement & Schedules: Amy's Bread

Income Statement

Net Wholesale Sales	$1,050,000	75%
Net Retail Sales	350,000	25%
Net Sales	**1,400,000**	**100%**
Cost of Sales	910,000	65%
Gross Margin	490,000	35%
General and Administrative Expenses	350,000	25%
Net Income before Taxes	140,000	10%
Income Taxes (40%: NYC, NY & Federal)	56,000	4%
Net Income	**$ 84,000**	**6%**

Cost of Sales

Raw Material			
Beginning Inventory	$ 4,000		0.29%
Purchases	280,000		20.00%
Total Available	284,000		20.29%
Less Ending Inventory	8,000		0.57%
Total Raw Material Used		276,000	19.71%
Labor			
Production Salaries	400,000		28.57%
Retail Salaries	50,000		3.57%
Payroll Taxes	50,000		3.57%
Total Burdened Labor		500,000	35.71%
Other Production Overhead			
Paper Supplies and Kitchen Tools	30,000		2.14%
Repairs and Maintenance	10,000		0.71%
Uniform Expenses	5,000		0.36%
Disposal	5,000		0.36%
Depreciation	40,000		2.86%
Incoming Freight	25,000		1.79%
Other Production Costs	19,000		1.36%
Total Production Overhead		134,000	9.57%
Cost of Sales		**$ 910,000**	**65.00%**

General and Administrative Expenses

Officers' Salaries	$ 50,000	3.57%
Office Salaries	100,000	7.14%
Payroll Taxes	20,000	1.43%
Group Insurance	35,000	2.50%
Delivery	10,000	0.71%
Advertising	2,000	0.14%
Bad Debts	3,500	0.25%
General Insurance	17,000	1.21%
Office Expense	5,000	0.36%
Dues and Subscriptions	1,000	0.07%
Professional Fees	13,000	0.93%
Permits	4,000	0.29%
Rent	60,000	4.29%
Telephone	6,000	0.43%
Utilities	20,000	1.43%
Entertainment	1,000	0.07%
Fees and Expenses	2,500	0.18%
Total General and Administrative Expenses	**$ 350,000**	**25.00%**

Exhibit 2

Costs and Prices by Product Line: Amy's Bread

Bread Type	Form	Gram Wt	Raw + Labor Cost	Wholesale Price	Wholesale CM	Retail Price	Retail CM
Country Sourdough	Loaf	750	$0.50	$2.00	$1.50	$3.00	$2.50
Country Sourdough	Baguette	400	$0.20	$1.00	$0.80	$1.50	$1.30
Organic WholeWheat with Toasted Seeds	Loaf	525	$0.20	$2.50	$2.30	$3.50	$3.30
Organic WholeWheat with Toasted Seeds	Doz/rolls	800	$0.80	$3.50	$2.70	$4.50	$3.70
Rye	Loaf	500	$0.35	$2.00	$1.65	$3.00	$2.65
Rye	Doz/rolls	850	$0.50	$3.50	$3.00	$4.50	$4.00
Large Sticky Buns	Bun	100	$0.20	$0.50	$0.30	$0.75	$0.55
Focaccia Rosemary	Sm Disk	150	$0.10	$1.00	$0.90	$1.50	$1.40
Focaccia Rosemary	Lg Disk	350	$0.20	$2.00	$1.80	$3.50	$3.30
Yeast-free	Loaf	400	$0.20	$0.75	$0.55	$1.00	$0.80
Potato	Loaf	400	$0.40	$2.00	$1.60	$3.00	$2.60
Semolina Raisin Fennel	Loaf	500	$0.60	$2.50	$1.90	$3.50	$2.90
Semolina Raisin Fennel	Doz/rolls	850	$1.75	$4.00	$2.25	$6.00	$4.25
Walnut Scallion	Loaf	525	$0.80	$3.50	$2.70	$4.00	$3.20
Black Olive	Doz/twists	1,000	$2.00	$7.00	$5.00	$9.00	$7.00
Apple Walnut Raisin	Ring/9 pc.	1,500	$3.00	$12.50	$9.50	$14.00	$11.00
Average			$0.74	$3.14	$2.40	$4.14	$3.40
Average without last 2 high-end breads			$0.49	$2.20	$1.71	$3.09	$2.60

Amy had other successes as well, the 1996 Zagat Marketplace Survey ranked Amy's Bread third out of 27 New York bread bakeries. "The best thing to happen to Ninth Avenue" say admirers of this "charming" bread shop filled with the aroma of "home baking"; it offers "imaginative breads to build meals around" and "consoling sticky buns"; the breads are also sold in food specialty shops around Manhattan; owner, Amy Scherber (the "Streisand of bakers") and her "friendly" staff "revere bread and it shows in every loaf" (Zagat 1996).

Other marketing techniques pursued by Amy's Bread included decorating the shop windows for every holiday. One could find large decorated heart cookies on Valentine's Day and big baskets of specialty breads on Easter. Amy regularly sent free samples of her breads to influential chefs. She donated bread to charities, taught baking classes, and appeared on TV Food Network shows. In addition, the Amy's Bread delivery truck helped spread the word as it circled Manhattan delivering bread.

Amy was not one to rest on her laurels. Amy developed a cookbook with her assistant manager, Toy Kim Dupree, which was published in 1996. This effort consumed countless hours to carefully modify recipes meant for huge batches of dough down to the 1 loaf size. It also involved having the recipes tested by untrained bakers and editing and improving the instructions. Amy had to explain her techniques so that the novice baker could understand them. Amy noted, "The cookbook project took way more of my time than I could have ever anticipated." The cookbook was a hit with bakers everywhere. Reviews of the book, as well as glowing customer comments, were posted at the Amazon.com Web site.

To add to her challenges, Amy's long-time exposure to bread and yeast had made her allergic to many basic bread ingredients. Amy said, "I have learned that if I spend too much time around the mixing of the dough, I get an itchy nose, watery eyes, and a cough. I also have to be careful to eat bread in moderation."

Because of the popularity of her Manhattan bakery and her cookbook, Amy was contacted to consult with bakeries across the country. She also made a videotape appearance on *"The Oprah Winfrey Show"* featuring successful young entrepreneurs.

Amy was also in the process of developing an Amy's Bread Web site designed primarily for marketing and public relations purposes. While they would accept online orders, Amy noted that, "bread is about freshness, impulse buying, and temptation. We do not expect much mail-order business, and truthfully, shipping expenses can often be higher than the cost of the bread."

What's Hot for the Future?

Armed with 6 years of continuing success, Amy was facing a critical decision. Should she expand or stand pat? She had a waiting list of wholesale customers, but could she stretch herself and her resources enough to expand successfully? Despite the popularity of Amy's Bread, Amy was still working long hours and earning only a modest income. Amy had managed to put away a good-sized nest egg, but it wasn't nearly enough for expansion. Armed with sales and financial projections, she began by looking for additional wholesale production space in Manhattan. Amy was looking for about 3,000 to 4,000 square feet that would essentially triple her current space. She based this requirement on her growing waiting list of potential customers, analyses of optimal production layouts, and associated projections for sales and expenses.

Amy eventually found a 6,000 square foot building on 31st Street that she felt she could afford. She also succeeded in getting a bank to agree to a $150,000 loan for her business plan. Unlike her 1992 application for a loan, Amy now had a proven track record and was interested in borrowing funds to purchase a hard asset, a building. However, her estimated budget for purchasing the building and making needed improvements was approximately $300,000. Amy's personal savings as well as the bakery business savings were not enough to make up the difference. Creative finances would be required to expand... but Amy declared, "I have managed before and will again."

While pursuing this plan, a developer contacted Amy with a new option. A lease was available on a 7,500 square foot space that was part of a block-long warehouse renovation on 15th Street. The developer's idea was to fill the space with a variety of food producers with small retail shops who sold their products at slightly reduced prices directly from the production source. The proposed market would include a fresh produce shop, flower shop, pastry shop, etc. This space was essentially an empty shell with no wiring, ventilation, plumbing, or interior walls. Amy would need to make all the leasehold improvements, but she could also choose how things were to be designed and constructed. Amy estimated that it would take 4 months to construct her store at a cost of approximately $500,000. This rental space had retail potential while the 31st Street building she could purchase was essentially a production facility only and was located in a desolate area. Amy was faced with a decision to lease space that would service both retail and wholesale customers, or to buy a space that would serve wholesale customers only.

Amy commented, "While retail is profitable, you need many locations to reach more customers and increase retail volume while wholesale business volume can be increased from just 1 location." Amy's gross sales were approximately 75% wholesale and 25% retail. The wholesale business was much more stable with advance bread orders for large, fixed amounts. Retail business depended on individual consumer buying decisions for much smaller quantities. However, an item that sold for $1.10 wholesale would retail at $1.75. This represented a price increase of 59% contrasted with an additional retail cost of only about 14% (for counter staff, table space, etc.) resulting in a projected per-item net retail gross profit margin increase of 45%. And, retail sales were for cash only.

Exhibit 3

Comparison of Buy/Lease Options: Amy's Bread
(Year 1 through year 5 only)

A. 31st Street (6,000 square feet) (Wholesale only)	YEAR 1	YEAR 2	YEAR 3	YEAR 4	YEAR 5	5-YEAR TOTAL
Projected Incremental Contribution Margin:						
Number of incremental wholesale customers from year 0	10	20	30	30		
Projected incremental contribution margin per customer	$5,712	$5,712	$5,712	$5,712	$5,712	
Projected incremental contribution margin over year 0	**$57,120**	**$114,240**	**$171,360**	**$171,360**	**$171,360**	**$685,440**
Projected Incremental Costs:						
Maintenance	($48,000)	($48,000)	($48,000)	($60,000)	($60,000)	($264,000)
Mortgage ($300,000 @12%)	($51,650)	($51,650)	($51,650)	($51,650)	($51,650)	($258,250)
Subtotal incremental fixed costs of expansion	($99,650)	($99,650)	($99,650)	($111,650)	($111,650)	($522,250)
Projected incremental margin less incremental fixed costs	($42,530)	$14,590	$71,710	$59,710	$59,710	$163,190

Assumptions for 31st Street:
Maintenance will increase $12K every 3 years.
A 12%, 10-year mortgage for $300,000 needs to
be paid. The monthly payment is $4,304.13.
During year 15, the location can be sold for $350,000.

B. 15th Street (7,500 square feet) (Wholesale & Retail)	YEAR 1	YEAR 2	YEAR 3	YEAR 4	YEAR 5	5-YEAR TOTAL
Projected Incremental Contribution Margin:						
Number of incremental wholesale customers from year 0	10	20	30	30	30	
Projected incremental contribution margin per customer	$5,712	$5,712	$5,712	$5,712	$5,712	
Projected incremental contribution margin over year 0	**$57,120**	**$114,240**	**$171,360**	**$171,360**	**$171,360**	**$685,440**
Projected Incremental Costs:						
Rent	($24,000)	($24,000)	($24,000)	($30,000)	($30,000)	($132,000)
Renovation Loan ($500,000 @ 12%)	($86,083)	($86,083)	($86,083)	($86,083)	($86,083)	($430,415)
Subtotal incremental fixed costs of expansion	($110,083)	($110,083)	($110,083)	($116,083)	($116,083)	($562,415)
Projected incremental margin less incremental fixed costs	($52,963)	$4,157	$61,277	$55,277	$55,277	$123,025

*** The 15th Street answer ONLY considers
incremental contribution margin from wholesale
customers. This location can also serve retail customers,
generating even more contribution margin.

Assumptions for 15th Street
Rent will increase $6K every 3 years. A 12%, 10-year mortgage
for $500,000 needs to be paid. The monthly payment is $7,173.55.

C. Sources of Capital for Expansion:	31st Street	15th Street
Bank Loan	150,000	150,000
Personal Loan	20,000	20,000
Bakery Savings Account	130,000	150,000
Other (includes some equity investors)	0	180,000
Total	300,000	500,000

Amy said, "I am sure the answer lies in careful financial projections for sales and associated costs, a bit of luck and a lot of passion and hard work." It was time to complete some detailed financial analysis, including cash flows to help decide the best course of action. Amy stated, "Deciding not to expand would be the only 'sure' bet. But, I'm not sure I am ready to sit back and be satisfied with what I have already accomplished. I have worked so hard to get this far, I am not sure I can turn hard-earned customers away. And, what if my business slumps because I can't meet increasing demand? Can I keep interest in my bread high if I am turning away potential customers? Should I rely on my personal insights and awareness of New York City trends?" What should Amy do? Expand or stand pat? If expand, should it be a wholesale operation only? Wholesale and retail? Retail only? Two locations or 1? (see **Exhibit 3.**)

CASE 26

Inner-City Paint Corporation (Revised)

Donald F. Kuratko and Norman J. Gierlasinski

History

Stanley Walsh began Inner-City Paint Corporation in a run-down warehouse, which he rented, on the fringe of Chicago's "downtown" business area. The company is still located at its original site.

Inner-City is a small company that manufactures wall paint. It does not compete with giants such as Glidden and DuPont. There are small paint manufacturers in Chicago that supply the immediate area. The proliferation of paint manufacturers is due to the fact that the weight of the product (52½ pounds per 5-gallon container) makes the cost of shipping great distances prohibitive. Inner-City's chief product is flat white wall paint sold in 5-gallon plastic cans. It also produces colors on request in 55-gallon containers.

The primary market of Inner-City is the small- to medium-sized decorating company. Pricing must be competitive; until recently, Inner-City had shown steady growth in this market. The slowdown in the housing market combined with a slowdown in the overall economy caused financial difficulty for Inner-City Paint Corporation. Inner-City's reputation had been built on fast service: it frequently supplied paint to contractors within 24 hours. Speedy delivery to customers became difficult when Inner-City was required to pay cash on delivery (C.O.D.) for its raw materials.

Inner-City had been operating without management controls or financial controls. It had grown from a very small 2-person company with sales of $60,000 annually 5 years ago, to sales of $1,800,000 and 38 employees this year. Stanley Walsh realized that tighter controls within his organization would be necessary if the company was to survive.

Equipment

Five mixers are used in the manufacturing process. Three large mixers can produce a maximum of 400 gallons, per batch, per mixer. The 2 smaller mixers can produce a maximum of 100 gallons, per batch, per mixer.

This case was prepared by Professor Donald F. Kuratko of Ball State University and Professor Norman J. Gierlasinski of Central Washington University. This case was edited and revised for SMBP-8th Edition. Copyright © 1984 by Donald F. Kuratko and Norman J. Gierlasinski. Reprinted by permission.

Two lift trucks are used for moving raw materials. The materials are packed in 100-pound bags. The lift trucks also move finished goods, which are stacked on pallets.

A small testing lab ensures the quality of materials received and the consistent quality of their finished product. The equipment in the lab is sufficient to handle the current volume of product manufactured.

Transportation equipment consists of two 24-foot delivery trucks and 2 vans. This small fleet is more than sufficient because many customers pick up their orders to save delivery costs.

Facilities

Inner-City performs all operations from 1 building consisting of 16,400 square feet. The majority of the space is devoted to manufacturing and storage; only 850 square feet is assigned as office space. The building is 45 years old and in disrepair. It is being leased in 3-year increments. The current monthly rent on this lease is $2,700. The rent is low in consideration of the poor condition of the building and its undesirable location in a run-down neighborhood (south side of Chicago). These conditions are suitable to Inner-City because of the dusty, dirty nature of the manufacturing process and the small contribution of the rent to overhead costs.

Product

Flat white paint is made with pigment (titanium dioxide and silicates), vehicle (resin), and water. The water makes up 72% of the contents of the product. To produce a color, the necessary pigment is added to the flat white paint. The pigment used to produce the color has been previously tested in the lab to ensure consistent quality of texture. Essentially, the process is the mixing of powders with water, then tapping off of the result into 5- or 55-gallon containers. Color overruns are tapped off into 2-gallon containers.

Inventory records are not kept. The warehouse manager keeps a mental count of what is in stock. He documents (on a lined yellow pad) what has been shipped for the day and to whom. That list is given to the billing clerk at the end of each day.

The cost of the materials to produce flat white paint is $2.40 per gallon. The cost per gallon for colors is approximately 40% to 50% higher. The 5-gallon covered plastic pails cost Inner-City $1.72 each. The 55-gallon drums (with lids) are $8.35 each (see **Exhibit 1**).

Selling price varies with the quantity purchased. To the average customer, flat white sells at $27.45 for 5 gallons and $182.75 for 55 gallons. Colors vary in selling price because of the

Exhibit 1
Paint Cost Sheet: Inner-City Paint Corporation

	5 Gallons	55 Gallons
Sales price	$ 27.45	$ 182.75
Direct material	(12.00)	(132.00)
Pail and lid	(1.72)	(8.35)
Direct labor	(2.50)	(13.75)
Manufacturing overhead ($1/gallon)	(5.00)	(5.00)
Gross margin	$ 6.23	$ 23.65
Gross profit ratio	22.7%	19.9%

variety in pigment cost and quantity ordered. Customers purchase on credit and usually pay their invoices in 30 to 60 days. Inner-City telephones the customer after 60 days of nonpayment and inquires when payment will be made.

Management

The President and majority stockholder is Stanley Walsh. He began his career as a house painter and advanced to become a painter for a large decorating company. Walsh painted mostly walls in large commercial buildings and hospitals. Eventually, he came to believe that he could produce a paint that was less expensive and of higher quality than what was being used. A keen desire to open his own business resulted in the creation of Inner-City Paint Corporation.

Walsh manages the corporation today in much the same way that he did when the business began. He personally must open *all* the mail, approve *all* payments, and inspect *all* customer billings before they are mailed. He has been unable to detach himself from any detail of the operation and cannot properly delegate authority. As the company has grown, the time element alone has aggravated the situation. Frequently, these tasks are performed days after transactions occur and mail is received.

The office is managed by Mary Walsh (Walsh's mother). Two part-time clerks assist her, and all records are processed manually.

The plant is managed by a man in his twenties, whom Walsh hired from 1 of his customers. Walsh became acquainted with him when the man picked up paint from Inner-City for his previous employer. Prior to the 8 months he has been employed by Walsh as Plant Manager, his only other experience has been that of a painter.

Employees

Thirty-five employees (20 workers are part-time) work in various phases of the manufacturing process. The employees are nonunion, and most are unskilled laborers. They take turns making paint and driving the delivery trucks.

Stanley Walsh does all of the sales work and public relations work. He spends approximately one half of every day making sales calls and answering complaints about defective paint. He is the only salesman. Other salesmen had been employed in the past, but Walsh felt that they "could not be trusted."

Customer Perception

Customers view Inner-City as a company that provides fast service and negotiates on price and payment out of desperation. Walsh is seen as a disorganized man who may not be able to keep Inner-City afloat much longer. Paint contractors are reluctant to give Inner-City large orders out of fear that the paint may not be ready on a continuous, reliable basis. Larger orders usually go to larger companies that have demonstrated their reliability and solvency.

Rumors abound that Inner-City is in difficult financial straits, that it is unable to pay suppliers, and that it owes a considerable sum for payment on back taxes. All of the above contribute to the customers' serious lack of confidence in the corporation.

Financial Structure

Exhibits 2 and **3** are the most current financial statements for Inner-City Paint Corporation. They have been prepared by the company's accounting service. No audit has been performed because Walsh did not want to incur the expense it would have required.

Exhibit 2

Balance Sheet for the Current Year Ending June 30: Inner-City Paint Corporation

Current assets		
Cash	$ 1,535	
Accounts receivable (net of allowance for bad debts of $63,400)	242,320	
Inventory	18,660	
Total current assets		$262,515
Machinery and transportation equipment	47,550	
Less accumulated depreciation	15,500	
Net fixed assets		32,050
Total assets		$294,565
Current liabilities		
Accounts payable	$217,820	
Salaries payable	22,480	
Notes payable	6,220	
Taxes payable	38,510	
Total current liabilities		$285,030
Long-term notes payable		15,000
Owners' equity		
Common stock, no par, 1,824 shares outstanding		12,400
Deficit		(17,865)
Total liabilities and owners' equity		$294,565

Future

Stanley Walsh wishes to improve the financial situation and reputation of Inner-City Paint Corporation. He is considering the purchase of a computer to organize the business and reduce needless paperwork. He has read about consultants who are able to quickly spot problems in businesses, but he will not spend more than $300 on such a consultant.

The solution that Walsh favors most is one that requires him to borrow money from the bank, which he will then use to pay his current bills. He feels that as soon as business conditions improve, he will be able to pay back the loans. He believes that the problems Inner-City is experiencing are due to the overall poor economy and are only temporary.

Exhibit 3

Income Statement for the Current Year Ending June 30:
Inner-City Paint Corporation

Sales		$1,784,080
Cost of goods sold		1,428,730
Gross margin		$ 355,350
Selling expenses	$ 72,460	
Administrative expenses	67,280	
President's salary	132,000	
Office Manager's salary	66,000	
Total expenses		337,740
Net income		$ 17,610

The Vermont Teddy Bear Co., Inc.: Challenges Facing a New CEO (Revised)

Joyce P. Vincelette, Ellie A. Fogarty, Thomas M. Patrick, and Thomas L. Wheelen

"A teddy bear is almost a 100-year-old product that has been made in every conceivable size, style, fabric, and price combined with a saturated market. Yet the teddy bear industry stands as a model of strength and durability. Every year, bear makers create and market hundreds of original models."[1]

Vermont Teddy Bear Company was founded in 1981 by John Sortino selling handsewn teddy bears out of a pushcart in the streets of Burlington, Vermont. Since this time, the company's focus has been to design, manufacture, and direct market the best teddy bears made in America using quality American materials and labor.

Until 1994, Vermont Teddy Bear experienced a great deal of success and profitability. Problems arose in 1995. Since 1995, the company has had 2 CEOs. It changed its name to The Great American Teddy Bear Company and then changed it back to The Vermont Teddy Bear Company when customers got confused. From its inception, Vermont Teddy Bear had been known for its Bear-Gram delivery service. In 1996, the company decided to shift emphasis away from Bear-Grams to other distribution channels. By 1998, the company decided to renew its emphasis on Bear-Grams. Vermont Teddy has always been proud of the fact that its teddy bears were made in America with American materials and craftsmanship. In 1998, the company changed this philosophy by exploring the offshore sourcing of materials, outfits, and manufacturing in an effort to lower costs.

Elisabeth Robert assumed the titles of President and Chief Executive Officer in October 1997 and began to cut costs and position the company for future growth. According to Robert, there were many reasons to invest in The Vermont Teddy Bear Company. "I believe that there is growth potential in this company. We are going to regain our balance this year. This is a rebuilding year. We are taking key steps to reposition the company. The move offshore is going to provide this company an opportunity to become more profitable. We will gain additional flexibility with price points. There is opportunity for us to expand from a regional brand to a national brand. While we continue to emphasize the premium teddy bear gift business, we intend to expand into larger markets. There is now a whole new opportunity for us in the corporate incentives and promotions market as well as the wholesale market. We have weekly inquiries from companies who recognize our brands. These companies would love to buy and resell our product or use our product as a corporate gift. Our growth will come not only from

This case was prepared by Professor Joyce P. Vincelette, Ellie A. Fogarty, Business Librarian, and Professor Thomas M. Patrick of the College of New Jersey, and Professor Thomas L. Wheelen of the University of South Florida. They would also like to thank Matthew Tardougno for his assistance on this project. This case was edited for SMBP-8th Edition. This case may not be reproduced in any form without written permission of the copyright holder, Thomas L. Wheelen. Copyright © 1998 by Thomas L. Wheelen. Reprinted by permission.

expansion of our radio markets but in the corporate and wholesale markets as we use offshore manufacturing alternatives to move to broader price points."[2]

According to Robert, "our competitors are the people who sell chocolates, flowers, and greeting cards. We target the last minute shopper who wants almost instant delivery."[3] Gift purchases account for 90% of the Company's sales.[4] "We thought we were in the teddy bear business," said Robert. "In fact we are in the gift and personal communications business. Our competition isn't Steiff [the German toy manufacturer]: it's 1-800 Flowers."[5]

On 1 beautiful June day in Vermont, Elisabeth Robert reflected on the enormous tasks to be accomplished. She wondered if she could successfully reposition her company and return it to profitability. Was she making the correct strategic decisions?

History: Why a Bear Company?

The Vermont Teddy Bear Co., Inc., was founded in 1981 by John Sortino. John got the inspiration for the teddy bear business shortly after his son Graham was born. While playing with his son, he noticed that Graham had many stuffed animals, but they were all made in other countries. Sortino "decided that there should be a bear made in the United States."[6]

He decided to design and manufacture his own premium-quality teddy bears. To turn his concept into reality, Sortino taught himself to sew and enrolled in drawing classes. In 1981, his first creation, Bearcho, was a bear whose thick black eyebrows and mustache resembled those of Groucho Marx. His first bear line included Buggy, Fuzzy, Wuzzy, and Bearazar, the bear with super powers. In 1982, Vermont Teddy Bear Company began limited production of Sortino's early designs using 5 Vermont homesewers. In 1983, Sortino took his operation to the streets where he sold his handmade bears from a pushcart on the Church Street Marketplace in downtown Burlington, Vermont. Four days later he sold his first bear. By the end of 1983, 200 bears were sold. He concluded from his selling experiences that customers "want bears that are machine washable and dryable. They want bears with joints. They want bears that are cuddly and safe for children. They want bears with personality."[7]

In 1984, Vermont Teddy was incorporated under the laws of the State of New York and Sortino's pushcart business had turned into a full-time job. To facilitate bear manufacturing, local homeworkers were contracted to produce an assortment of the founder's original designs. Even though the company opened a retail store in Burlington, Vermont, in 1985, the majority of the company's products were sold through department stores such as Macy's and Nieman Marcus during the 1980s. As the retail industry consolidated through mergers and store closings during the late 1980s, Sortino realized that a new market needed to be found for his bears. In search of a new customer base, Sortino turned to a local radio station and began advertising the company's products. This advertising strategy paved the way for the "Bear-Gram," where customers could send the gift of a Vermont Teddy Bear by placing an order through the company's 800 number.

The company initiated its Bear-Gram marketing strategy in 1985 in the Burlington, Vermont area. Local radio advertisements aired on WXXX in Burlington and customers called an 800 number to order the product. It was not until shortly before Valentine's Day in 1990 that the company introduced radio advertising of its Bear-Gram product on radio station WHTZ ("Z-100") in New York City, positioning the Bear-Gram as a novel gift for Valentine's Day and offering listeners a toll-free number to order from the company's facility in Vermont. The test proved to be successful, and the Bear-Gram concept was expanded to other major radio markets across the country. These radio advertisements were generally read live by popular radio personalities. John Sortino believed that the radio had been a successful medium for the Bear-Gram for several reasons. He believed that the use of popular radio personalities lent credibility to the product. In addition, because the disk jockey could give away a few bears, more air-time was spent on the product than the paid "60 seconds."[8] He also believed that radio advertising allowed for flexibility in the use of advertising copy, which could be adjusted as the company changed its marketing focus.

Due to the success of the Bear-Gram concept, Vermont Teddy's total sales of $400,000 in 1989 rose to $1.7 million in 1990 and over $5 million in 1991.[9] As sales increased, a larger manufacturing facility was needed. In 1991, the company leased and moved into a new factory space and guided factory tours began. The larger production facilities made it possible for Vermont Teddy Bear to begin producing bears in bulk and to enter into larger sales agreements with retail establishments. In 1992, *Inc.* magazine listed Vermont Teddy as the eightieth fastest growing company in the United States with sales totaling $10.6 million.[10]

Vermont Teddy Bear went public on November 23, 1993. By this time, sales totaled $17 million.[11] In 1993, the company was named the first national winner of the Dun & Bradstreet "Best of America" Small Business Award and was ranked as the fifty-eighth fastest growing company in the United States by *Inc.* magazine.[12] Also in 1993, the company was the recipient of the Heritage of New England Customer Service Award. Previous recipients of the award included L.L. Bean, Inc., Boston Beer Company, and Ben & Jerry's Homemade, Inc.[13]

In 1994, construction began on a new factory and retail store in Shelburne, Vermont, which opened for business in the summer of 1995. In 1994, *Inc.* magazine listed Vermont Teddy Bear, with sales totaling $20.5 million, as the twenty-first fastest growing small, publicly owned company in the United States and named the company "Small Business of the Year."[14]

Prior to 1994, Vermont Teddy Bear had experienced a great deal of success and profitability, with sales growth in excess of 50% for 3 consecutive years.[15] However, 1994 marked the beginning of the company's financial troubles. The company's expenses increased in accordance with its anticipated growth, but sales did not increase as rapidly.

Vermont Teddy Bear's rapid growth during the 1990s taxed the organizational structure and efficiency of the company's operations. Due to the company's declining financial situation, on June 20, 1995, the company's Founder, President, and Chief Executive Officer, John Sortino, resigned. Sortino recognized that the future success of the company "depends on the transition from an entrepreneurial company to a professionally managed organization." He further stated, "I wanted to assist the company in positioning itself for the arrival of a new CEO. I will provide guidance to the company in a consulting role, and I will retain my position on the Board of Directors."[16]

On August 2, 1995, R. Patrick Burns was appointed as President and CEO. Also in 1995 Elisabeth Robert joined the company as Chief Financial Officer. Outside observers wondered if the company could successfully make the transition to a new CEO and generate enough sales to pull itself out of debt and remain profitable.

In its attempts to turn the company around, the new management team eliminated several unprofitable marketing ventures (such as its sponsorship of a NASCAR circuit race car and driver) and reduced general and administrative cost. By 1996, the new team had generated a profit of $152,000.[17]

During the later part of 1996, Vermont Teddy Bear took on a new trademarked name, "The Great American Teddy Bear Company," in an attempt to broaden brand appeal and take advantage of national and international distribution opportunities. Even though the "Vermont" name gave good name recognition in the Northeast, the company felt that it had less impact in other parts of the country. They were wrong. Customers became confused, and Disney's entry into the personalized teddy bear gift market with their "Pooh-Grams" added to the confusion. The confusion contributed to a decrease in Bear-Gram sales. By Valentine's Day, the company returned to its established mark, The Vermont Teddy Bear Company.

Late in 1996, the new management team began to explore opportunities for growth. They believed that the emphasis of the company should shift from the Bear-Gram business to other distribution channels. Their new 5-year plan included opening new retail stores and expanding the catalog.

By 1997, retail sales were the fastest growing part of Vermont Teddy's business. Sales for the factory retail store in Shelburne for the fiscal year ending June 30, 1996, were 19% ahead of 1995.[18] It appeared obvious to top management that retail was a growing profit center for the company. The company's factory store had become a major Vermont tourist destination and had averaged 130,000 visitors a year since opening in July 1995.[19] As a result, the company became interested in high tourist traffic areas for retail expansion, hoping to duplicate this success at other retail locations.[20]

The location for the company's second retail store was North Conway, New Hampshire, a major tourist destination in both winter and summer months. The store opened in July 1996. The third retail location opened at 538 Madison Avenue in New York City in February 1997. The New York City location was chosen because it had been the number 1 market for Bear-Grams since the company began advertising on radio in 1990. The company believed that the New York store would benefit from the millions of dollars of radio advertising that the company had invested in this market. The fourth store opened in Freeport, Maine, on August 16, 1997, 2 doors down from L.L. Bean.

Fiscal 1997 was a disappointing year for Vermont Teddy. After a year of controlling costs and a return to profitability in 1996, they had set out in pursuit of revenue growth in 1997. The 1997 initiatives included an expanded catalog and the new retail stores. As part of the shift away from Bear-Grams, the company downsized their radio media buying department. The company lost money on their catalog programs, and the new retail stores were not as profitable as expected. Resources diverted to expanding secondary marketing channels, coupled with accelerating changes in the radio industry, contributed to a decline in Bear-Gram sales. The end result was a loss of $1,901,795 in fiscal 1997.[21]

Because of Vermont Teddy Bear's declining performance, R. Patrick Burns chose to step down as President and CEO in October 1997. Elisabeth Robert assumed the title of President and CEO and retained the title of Chief Financial Officer.

According to CEO Robert, "When we made the decision to expand our distribution channels in the areas of retail and catalog, our focus was on being a teddy bear category killer. We thought we were in the teddy bear business. Now what I believe is that we are in the Bear-Gram business, the gift business, and the impulse business. This is a completely different marketplace. Our competitors are the people who sell chocolates, flowers, and greeting cards. We target the last-minute shopper who wants almost instant delivery."[22] She further stated that "the primary focus of the company would return to maximizing returns in the radio Bear-Gram business, which constituted the majority of the company's annual revenue."[23]

In 1998, the management team began seriously looking at the profitability of their various retail locations. They also began looking at the catalog, intending to optimize its size and product offerings to ensure its future profitability.

Corporate Governance

As of June 30, 1998, The Vermont Teddy Bear Co., Inc., had a total of 7 Board members and 2 Executive Officers, both of whom were also members of the Board of Directors.

BOARD OF DIRECTORS AND EXECUTIVE OFFICERS[24]

The Board members, Executive Officers, and their experience and qualifications were as follows.

R. Patrick Burns (53) had been President and CEO of Vermont Teddy Bear from 1995 until 1997. He had been a Director of the company since 1995. He planned to remain active as a consultant to the company focusing on developing strategic marketing partnerships for the next 2 years. Prior to joining the company, he was the Chief Executive Officer of Disney Direct Marketing. He had also held senior management positions at J. Crew, Inc., and at L.L. Bean, Inc.

Joan H. Martin (74) was a private investor who had been a Director of the company since 1991. Martin had no business experience during the past 8 years apart from managing her private investment portfolio.

Fred Marks (70) became a Director of the company in 1987 and became its Treasurer and Chairman of the Board in 1989. He served as the company's Chief Financial Officer until January 1995 and Treasurer until 1996. Previously Marks had served as Chairman of the Board of 2 privately held companies: Selection, Ltd., a manufacturer of remote controls for computers and televisions; and Contaq Technologies, a manufacturer of ultrasonic instruments.

Elisabeth B. Robert (43), Director, Chief Executive Officer, President, Treasurer and Chief Financial Officer, joined the company in 1995 as the Chief Financial Officer replacing Stephen Milford. She was appointed a Director of the company in January 1996 and Treasurer of the company in April 1996. She assumed the titles of CEO and President from R. Patrick Burns who stepped down from the positions in October 1997. Before joining Vermont Teddy, Robert served as the Chief Financial Officer for a high-tech start-up company specializing in remote control devices, where she was also a founding partner.

Spencer C. Putnam (52), Director, Vice President, and Secretary, joined the company as its Chief Operating Officer in June 1987 and continued in this role. He had been a Director of the company and Secretary of its Board since 1989. Before joining the company, Putnam was the director of the Cooperative Education Program at the University of Vermont.

David W. Garrett (55) had been a Director of the company since 1987. He was a Vice President of First Albany Corporation, an investment banking and brokerage firm. Garrett was also President of the Garrett Hotel Group, a private hotel development and management firm and President of The Black Willow Group, Ltd., a private company which owned and operated The Point, a luxury hotel in Saranac Lake, New York.

Jason Bacon (64) became a Director of the company in 1997. He was a consultant to nonprofit organizations and a private investor focusing on real estate and securities with international perspective. Prior to his involvement with Vermont Teddy Bear, he served as a Managing Director at Kidder, Peabody & Company.

OWNERSHIP

As of June 30, 1998, there were 5,183,733 shares of the company's common stock outstanding held by 1,553 shareholders.[25] Approximately 2,551,300 shares or approximately 49.2% of the stock was owned beneficially by the current directors and officers of the company. These figures did not include options or warrants held by current directors and officers, their spouses or minor children to purchase shares of the company's Common Stock or Series B Preferred Stock.[26]

In November 1993, the company made an Initial Public Offering (IPO) of 5,172,500 shares of common stock. The stock ranged from $17.19 to $11.44 from offering to December 31, 1993. Prior to the IPO, 4,000,000 shares of common stock were outstanding and held by 9 shareholders. Ninety shares of nonvoting Series A Preferred Stock were held by shareholder Joan H. Martin. This preferred stock had an 8% cumulative dividend and liquidation value of $10,000 per share. On July 12, 1996, the company privately placed 204,912 share of Series B preferred stock. This stock was held by 12 shareholders and was not entitled to any dividends or voting rights. The 204,912 Series B shares were convertible into 482,441 shares of common stock.[27]

The following individuals owned more than 5% of the company's stock as of June 30, 1998.[28]

Beneficial Owner	Number of Shares	Percent Owned
Joan H. Martin	1,840,975	35.5
Fred Marks	600,500	11.6
Margaret H. Martin	267,000	5.2
Spencer C. Putnam	84,000	1.6
R. Patrick Burns	17,625	0.3
Jason Bacon	5,500	0.1
Elisabeth B. Robert	2,700	0.1

Notes were deleted.

Vermont Teddy has never paid cash dividends on any of its shares of common stock. The high and low stock prices for 1998 were[29]

Quarter Ending	High	Low
June 30, 1998	$1.63	$1.06
March 31, 1998	$1.63	$0.75
December 31, 1997	$2.13	$0.88
September 30, 1997	$2.56	$1.06

Company Philosophy

From its founding by John Sortino in the early 1980s until 1998, the company's focus has been to design and manufacture the best teddy bears made in America, using American materials and labor. The company believed that apart from its own products, most of the teddy bears sold in the United States were manufactured in foreign countries, and that the company was the largest manufacturer of teddy bears made in the United States. The company's Mission Statement can be seen in **Exhibit 1**.

This philosophy was modified significantly in 1998 with the company's decision to explore the offshore sourcing of materials and manufacturing alternatives in an effort to lower the company's cost of goods sold and to broaden its available sources of supply. Company customer surveys revealed that price was more important to potential customers than the "Made in America" label.[30] During 1998, the company began purchasing raw materials for bear production and some teddy bear outfits from offshore manufacturers. Vermont Teddy felt that plush materials from offshore were of better quality and less costly than those produced in the United States. They felt that importing these materials would enable them to produce a better, lower cost product and would provide the flexibility to meet a broader range of price points in response to customer needs.[31] The company planned to continue to handcraft the 15-inch "classic" teddy bear in Vermont for those customers interested in an American-made product. The new label read, "Made in America, of domestic and foreign materials."[32] The company also planned to explore opportunities to introduce new teddy bear products made offshore to their design specifications at significantly lower cost points for sale initially into the wholesale and corporate channels.

With this change in philosophy, the company was committed to understanding its potential offshore partners and to ensuring that its partners provided decent, lawful working conditions. It required that all offshore vendors sign a written statement to this effect prior to any business dealings.[33]

Exhibit 1

Mission Statement: The Vermont Teddy Bear Co., Inc.

The Vermont Teddy Bear provides our customers with a tangible expression of their best feelings for their families, friends, and associates. We facilitate, communicate, and therefore participate in caring events and special occasions that celebrate and enrich our customers' life experiences.

Our products will represent unmatchable craftsmanship balanced with optimal quality and value. We will strive to wholesomely entertain our guests while consistently exceeding our external and internal customer service expectations.

The Vermont Teddy Bear brand represents the rich heritage of the "Great American Teddy Bear" begun in 1902. We are the stewards of a uniquely American tradition based on the best American virtues including compassion, generosity, friendship, and a zesty sense of whimsy and fun.

Exhibit 2

Stakeholder Beliefs: The Vermont Teddy Bear Co., Inc.

Our customers are the foundation of our business. Exceeding their expectations *everyday* will form the backbone of our corporate culture. Zealous pursuit of "world class" customer service will build a self-fulfilling cycle of pride, partnership, team spirit, and personal commitment in every player in our company.

Our employees are our internal customers. The philosophy that applies to our external customers extends also to our internal associates. We will cultivate a results-oriented environment that encourages fairness, collaboration, mutual respect, and pride in our organization. Pro-active, positive, open-minded confrontation among well-intentioned colleagues will ensure innovation, reject complacency, and stimulate individual growth. Our company supports employee diversity and provides clear opportunities for each of us to reach our full personal and professional potential.

Our investors provide capital in good faith, and we are accountable for creating a realistic return while protecting the assets of our company. Our financial strength and profitability are essential to fulfilling all of our stakeholder commitments.

Our vendors provide a partnership opportunity for innovative product development, unsurpassed external customer service, and mutual prosperity. This is based on exceeding our customers' expectations for unique, innovative, high-quality communications and products delivered to our customers where and when they want them at a price that reinforces our reputation for perceived value.

Our community deserves our commitment to being ethically, legally, and environmentally responsible while remaining fiscally sound. We will support organizations and individuals with values similar to ours and participate actively in those enterprises that seek to improve local and world conditions for future generations. We will seek to maintain a dynamic balance between meeting our commitment to our community and maintaining the viability of our own enterprise.

Exhibit 2 details Vermont Teddy's statement of Stakeholder Beliefs. The company believed that the quality, variety, and creativity of the company's products, and its commitment to customer service, were essential to its business. Its manufacturing practices were environmentally sound. The company sought to use the best available materials for its bears. Customer service policies rivaled those of L.L. Bean. Each bear was sold with a "Guarantee for Life," under which the company undertook to repair or replace any damaged or defective bear at any time even if eaten by the family dog or destroyed by a lawn mower.[34]

Products and Services

Vermont Teddy Bear made old-fashioned, handmade, jointed teddy bears ranging from 11 to 72 inches tall, in 6 standard color selections including tan, honey, brown, and black. More than 100 different bear outfits were available for customers to outfit and individualize their bears or to emphasize certain relevant characteristics of the receiver such as policewoman, gardener, doctor, or racing car driver. Some of the more popular outfits included tutus, wedding gowns, tuxedos, business suits, and sports uniforms. Bears could also be dressed in a wide variety of outfits that personalized the bear for significant life events, such as a new baby, get well, birthdays, graduations, weddings, and "I love you." A collection of bears could also be designed for schools, sports teams, businesses, and other organizations. New "edgier" products were added in 1997 such as "Shredder, the Snowboarder Bear," targeted primarily at radio customers. As of June 30, 1998, 40% of the outfits were outsourced to overseas contractors.[35] Prices for the bears in standard outfits ranged from $40 to more than $200. Custom-made clothing was available at an additional cost.

Until 1997, bear materials were mostly American made, though mohair fur used for the premium bears came from Europe. All other fur was hypoallergenic, plush polyester. Bears were stuffed with virgin Dacron 91, a fire retardant filler for safety. Vermont teddy bears had movable joints, a feature associated with traditional, high-quality teddy bears. These joints were made from recycled Ben & Jerry's ice cream containers. In keeping with the company's attempt to produce the bears with domestic materials, the bears' eyes had come from the only eye maker left in America. Noses and paw pads were ultrasuede, also 100% American made.[36] Using American-made materials had been 1 of the methods by which Vermont Teddy Bear differentiated its products from those of its competitors. The company's 1998 move to the off-shore sourcing of raw materials represented a significant departure form the company's historical position as an American manufacturer using almost exclusively American materials.[37]

In addition to the products it manufactured, Vermont Teddy Bear sold items related to teddy bears, as well as merchandise from other manufacturers featuring the logo of Vermont Teddy Bear. It did a small amount of licensing with Tyco, Landmark, and a manufacturer of children's and women's sleepwear. Some items such as clothing, jewelry, and accessory ornaments were available primarily at the company's retail stores and through its direct mail catalog. The company also sold stuffed toys that had been manufactured by other companies, such as Gund and Steiff.[38] Vermont Teddy Bear planned to alter this strategy in 1999 to focus more attention on the sale of the company's own manufactured products, including those manufactured offshore.

In addition to manufacturing and selling bears and bear-related merchandise to individual consumers, the company's Corporate Division provided unique and original customized products for corporations. Vermont Teddy also silk-screened or embroidered bears on clothing with the customer's logo, slogan, or team name. In 1998, the company planned to offer a line of offshore-manufactured ancillary products for corporate customers and outlets such as QVC.[39] Information about products offered through the company's Corporate and Wholesale Programs could be found on the company's Web site.

Marketing Strategies and Distribution Methods

Vice President of Sales was Katie Camardo. Robert D. Delsandro was appointed Vice President of Marketing and Design in May 1998. He had been employed by The Vermont Teddy Bear Company as Creative Director since 1996 and had been responsible for developing a completely new look for the company's products, retail stores, printed promotional materials, and catalog. He was credited with creating the new "edgier" look of Vermont Teddy Bear.[40]

Although many teddy bear producers defined their product as a toy and marketed solely to children, Vermont Teddy Bear marketed its bears as an attractive gift or collectible for both children and adults. The company defined its target market as "children between the ages of 1 to 100."[41]

The company was primarily known for its Bear-Gram delivery service. Bear-Grams were personalized teddy bears that were delivered directly to recipients as gifts for holidays and special occasions. Bear-Grams were gift boxed in unique containers complete with "air-holes" for the bear. The bears were accompanied by a personal greeting from the sender.

Orders for Bear-Grams were generally placed by calling a toll-free number (1-800-829-BEAR) and speaking with company sales representatives called "Bear Counselors." Customers could also visit the company's Web site <**www.vtbear.com**> and place their orders online. "Bear Counselors" entered an order on a computer, which was part of the company's computer network of approximately 250 workstations that linked order entry with sales and accounting systems. The company had plans to upgrade, expand, and integrate its computer systems, including the purchase of an inventory control system. In 1994, the company installed a new telephone system, which improved its telemarketing operations and was designed to accommodate future growth in telephone call volume. The company strove to provide rapid response to customer orders. Orders placed by 4 P.M. EST (3 P.M. on the Internet) could be shipped the same day. Packages were delivered primarily by UPS and other carriers by next day air or ground delivery service.[42] The company also sought to respond promptly to customer complaints. The company believed that, as a result of the quality of its products and service, it had established a loyal customer base.

The company attributed its success to this direct-marketing strategy. Since 1990, when the Bear-Gram was introduced to prime-time and rush-hour audiences in the New York City market, the company had continued to rely primarily on Bear-Gram advertising. It had also continued to focus its advertising on morning rush-hour radio spots, with well-known personalities such as Don Imus and Howard Stern, promoting the bears.

For the fiscal year ending June 30, 1998, Bear-Grams accounted for 70.2% of net revenues of $17.2 million. The percent of net revenues for the company's primary distribution methods can be seen in **Exhibit 3**. Included in Bear-Gram revenues were sales from the company's Internet Web site. Other principal avenues of distribution included company-owned retail stores, direct mail catalogs, and licensing and wholesale agreements. The company's sales were heavily seasonal, with Valentine's Day, Christmas, and Mother's Day as the company's largest sales seasons.[43] For Valentine's Day 1998, more than 47,000 bears were sent out by people across the country who wished to say "I love you."[44]

During the summer of 1997, Vermont Teddy Bear Company began doing business on the Internet with a new Web site designed to inform and entertain Internet subscribers. The Web site provided a low-cost visual presence and was developed for the purpose of supporting the radio advertising of Bear-Grams. Pictures of the product and other information could be accessed. A total of 396, 000 hits to the Web site were recorded during fiscal 1998, more than double the 195,000 hits recorded during fiscal 1997.[45] By August 1998, 10 to 20% of Vermont Teddy's business was being handled online.[46] All radio advertisements were tagged with a reference to the Web site, which, in turn, provided visual support for the radio advertising and the opportunity for customers to place orders online.[47]

Since 1990, the company had extended its Bear-Gram marketing strategy beyond New York City to include other metropolitan areas and syndicated radio programs across the United States. During the fiscal year 1998, the company regularly placed advertising on a total of 44 radio stations in 12 of the 20 largest market areas in the United States.[48] **Exhibit 4** shows the company's largest markets. **Exhibit 5** shows the most frequent reasons given by customers for purchasing a Vermont Teddy Bear-Gram. The company was featured on Dateline NBC, Tuesday, December 17, 1996. Newsbroadcaster Stone Phillips interviewed R. Patrick Burns, President and CEO, on the subject of American companies that manufactured products in the United States.[49]

Exhibit 3
Primary Distribution Methods: The Vermont Teddy Bear Co., Inc.

Year Ending June 30	1998	1997	1996	1995
Bear-Grams[1]	72.0%	70.0%	75.8%	78.7%
Retail Operations	18.0%	17.7%	12.9%	9.2%
Direct Mail	9.2%	10.9%	7.2%	8.8%
Other	0.8%	1.4%	4.1%	3.3%

Note:
1. Excludes Bear-Gram revenues from retail operations.

Source: The Vermont Teddy Bear Co., Inc., *1998 Annual Report*, p. 3.

Exhibit 4

Vermont Teddy Bear's Largest Markets
(Percentage of Bear-Grams for the 12 months ending June 30)

Markets	1998	1997	1996	1995
New York City	37.8%	40.8%	35.5%	38.6%
Boston	13.4%	13.2%	9.5%	9.5%
Philadelphia	8.9%	11.6%	8.9%	7.3%
Chicago	6.5%	8.9%	7.3%	8.5%
Los Angeles	6.3%	5.8%	4.0%	3.8%

Source: The Vermont Teddy Bear Company, Inc., *1998 Annual Report*, p. 4.

In 1998, the company was planning to expand its radio advertisements into new markets including Minneapolis, Dallas, and Milwaukee and to examine opportunities to consolidate radio advertising buys through annual contracts with major stations.[50]

The company had explored additional methods to market Bear-Grams and to publicize its toll-free telephone number. In June 1993, the company's toll-free number was listed for the first time in the AT&T toll-free telephone directory. Before then, the toll-free number was not readily available to customers, except in radio advertisements. Vermont Teddy Bear also expanded its listings in metropolitan phone book Yellow Pages and initiated the use of print advertising in magazines and newspapers, as well as advertising on billboards and mass transit panels.

Vermont Teddy Bear believed that the popularity of Bear-Grams created an opportunity for catalog sales. For the fiscal year ending June 30, 1998, direct mail accounted for 9.2% of net revenues.[51] In addition, repeat buyers represented 33% of sales, giving the company an opportunity to use its customer database in excess of 1,500,000 names.[52] The company introduced its first catalog for Christmas in 1992. By 1994, catalog sales accounted for 16.7% of sales.[53] Vermont Teddy planned to prepare 3 catalogs in 1995, but the management shakeup that resulted in Patrick Burns's becoming CEO caused the company to scale back its plans. Instead it mailed just 165,000 copies of an 8-page book to previous customers. The small-size book kept up the company's presence but did not have the pages nor the product range to boost holiday sales. Quarterly sales dropped 24% below December 1994 levels.[54]

In 1996, to compensate for the decline in radio advertisement effectiveness, the company increased December 1996 catalog circulation to approximately 1 million. To increase its catalog circulation, Vermont Teddy Bear acquired additional mailing lists from prominent catalog companies, including Disney, FAO Schwarz, Hammacher-Schlemmer, Saks Fifth Avenue, and

Exhibit 5

Most Frequent Reasons for Purchasing Bear-Grams: Vermont Teddy Bear Co., Inc.
(Percentage of Bear-Grams for the 12 months ending June 30)

Reasons for Purchases	1998	1997	1996	1995
Valentine's Day	27.7%	22.1%	20.8%	19.2%
Birthdays	11.8%	11.6%	13.4%	15.9%
New Births	11.6%	10.3%	12.8%	9.9%
Get Wells	11.0%	9.7%	12.0%	10.4%
Christmas	8.4%	5.6%	8.6%	10.4%

Source: The Vermont Teddy Bear Company, Inc., *1998 Annual Report*, p. 4.

Harry & David. To strengthen its retail and catalog offerings, Vermont Teddy broadened the scope of its product line. New items included lower priced teddy bears, company-designed apparel, toys, books, and jewelry, as well as plush animals from other manufacturers such as Gund and Steiff.

Its Valentine mailing in 1997 amounted to 600,000 catalogs. Direct mail revenues increased from 1996, but they did not meet expectations due to the poor performance of rented mailing lists. In addition, the company incurred higher than anticipated costs due to the outsourcing of the order fulfillment process and was left with inflated inventories due to lower than expected sales.

During fiscal 1998, more than 15 million circulated pages were mailed to prospective customers. CEO Robert believed that Vermont Teddy's in-house list, which stood at 1.4 million names, would be a profitable future source of business. The company planned to increase the number of circulated pages during 1999, primarily though renting and exchanging of additional names from other catalogs and mailing to more names on the in-house mailing list.[55] It planned to handle all catalog fulfillment at company facilities in Shelburne. It also planned to continue to develop its own internal systems to adapt to the requirements of its catalog customers as the catalog business grew.[56]

During fiscal 1998, sales from retail operations accounted for 18.0% of net revenues.[57] Due to the continued unprofitability in its retail stores, the company reversed its retail expansion strategy in fiscal 1998. Vermont Teddy Bear's New York City retail outlet was closed to the public on December 7, 1997, due to structural problems. A sales profile for the store reaffirmed the company's core market. Bear-Grams accounted for 60 to 70% of the store's purchases—the same product that was being sold through the radio advertisements, without the overhead of New York rents.[58]

The company planned to close its retail location in Freeport, Maine, in August 1998 and its North Conway, New Hampshire, store in October 1998. CEO Robert commented, "After 2 successful holidays at Valentine's Day and Mother's Day, it is more clear than ever, that focusing on radio Bear-Grams is the right strategy. Retail apart from our highly successful factory store here in Shelburne, is not a distribution channel that fits our current business. We are in the Bear-Gram business, offering a convenient, creative and expressive gift delivery service. It makes no sense to ship out a Bear-Gram from an expensive retail store front."[59]

The Shelburne factory store had continued to be successful as the company added new merchandise. To make the store more entertaining and interactive, the company invested $100,000 in its renovation in 1996.[60] Programs such as "Make a Friend for Life," which enabled customers to stuff, dress, and personalize their own bear and "virtual" factory tours, using video and theatrical demonstrations of teddy bear making received favorable responses from customers.[61]

In November 1996, the company announced that it had joined forces with Gary Burghoff to produce a video that promoted the company's new "Make a Friend for Life" products.[62] Burghoff was known for playing the character Radar O'Reilly in the M*A*S*H television show and was famous for his relationship with his teddy bear.

Vermont Teddy Bear had also targeted children's literature as a way of generating name recognition. A children's book, *How Teddy Bears Are Made: A Visit to the Vermont Teddy Bear Factory*, was available for purchase and could be found at libraries. The company also began to publish other children's books in order to develop characters for their teddy bears.

Beginning September 1, 1997, The Vermont Teddy Bear Co., Inc., introduced nationally a line of officially licensed NFL Teddy Bears. The NFL Bear was offered in 14 different teams and wore NFL Properties' uniforms and gear, including officially licensed jerseys, pants, and Riddell helmets.[63] NFL Properties, Inc., was the licensing and publishing arm of the National

Football League. To advertise this new product, Vermont Teddy enlisted Wayne Chrebet, wide receiver for the NY Jets, and Mark Chmura, tight end for the Green Bay Packers, to be spokespeople for the NFL Teddy Bears. Chrebet and Chmura were featured in radio and print advertisements in New York and Milwaukee, respectively. The company believed that officially licensed NFL Bears would be a popular choice for sports fans, especially during the football and Christmas seasons. The company advertised the bear on sports-talk radio in metropolitan areas around the country.[64]

Vermont Teddy Bear conducted business almost exclusively in the United States. Bears could be shipped abroad, but it was very expensive. Some bears were shipped into Canada, and some radio advertising was done in Montreal. The added shipping charges, along with unfavorable exchange rates, caused price resistance to the products in Canada. In 1995, the company test marketed both the Bear-Gram and the use of the 800 number via radio advertising in the United Kingdom. Test results indicated that both were successful, but the program had to be eliminated because the company did not have the corporate infrastructure or the financial resources to support it.[65] The company had some trademarks registered in Great Britain and Japan and had discussions with companies in both of these countries. According to Robert, "These are the 2 countries that seem to have the most interest in Vermont Teddy's products."[66]

Vermont Teddy Bear's management believed that there were a number of opportunities to increase company sales. The company's strategy for future growth included increasing sales of Bear-Grams in existing markets, expanding sales of Bear-Grams in new market areas, increasing direct-mail marketing of teddy bears through mail-order catalogs and similar marketing techniques, increasing sales of premium teddy bears through wholesale channels to unaffiliated retail stores, and increasing the company's retail store sales through increased factory tours and visits.[67] Management was also interested in expanding sales through its Corporate Division.

Facilities and Operations

In the summer of 1995, in an effort to consolidate locations and improve manufacturing efficiency, the company relocated its offices, retail store, and manufacturing, sales, and distribution facilities to a newly constructed 62,000-square-foot building on 57 acres in Shelburne, Vermont. The new site was approximately 10 miles south of Burlington, the state's largest city. The new buildings were designed as a small village, the Teddy Bear Common, to promote a warm and friendly atmosphere for customers as well as employees. The new facility was estimated to have cost $7,900,00.[68] The company intended to minimize lease costs by subleasing any unused space. On September 26,1995, the company had entered into a $3.5 million commercial loan with the Vermont National Bank. Repayment of the mortgage loan was based on a 30-year fixed-principal payment schedule, with a balloon payment due on September 26, 1997.[69]

On July 18, 1997, Vermont Teddy completed a sale-leaseback transaction with W. P. Carey and Co., Inc., a New York–based investment banking firm, involving its factory headquarters and a portion of its property located in Shelburne. W. P. Carey bought the 62,000-square-foot headquarters facility and its 15-acre site, leaving the company with ownership of the additional land. W. P. Carey was not interested in acquiring the other building lots on the site due to their zoning restrictions. This financing replaced the company's mortgage and line of credit, which was about to come due on September 26, 1997.[70]

The company had a 3-year lease on 10,000 square feet of inventory space at a separate location in Shelburne for $56,000 annually.[71] The company also had the following lease agreements for its retail stores:[72]

Location	Square Footage	Annual Rent	1999 Rent Obligation	End of Lease Obligation
North Conway, NH	6,000	$ 49,608	$ 28,938	1/31/1999
New York City, NY	2,600	$300,000	$300,000	10/23/2006
Freeport, ME	6,000	$240,000	$ 25,644	8/6/1998

For in-house manufacturers, all production occurred in the Shelburne manufacturing space, which included state-of-the-art packing and shipping equipment. The plant manager was Brad Allen. Visitors and guests were given the opportunity to take guided or self-directed tours that encompassed the entire teddy bear making process. The factory tour had become such a popular tourist attraction that approximately 129,000 visitors toured the factory and retail store in fiscal 1998. Since moving to its new location in 1995, more than 390,000 visitors had toured the facilities.[73]

In 1994, when the company was looking for a new location, it purchased only the 15-acre parcel it built on in Shelburne. Then the company bought the surrounding property because it wanted some control in the kind of neighbors it would have. As of June 30, 1998, plans to sell or lease the other lots had not been successful due to stringent zoning restrictions on the site. The zoning restrictions required that less than a quarter of the space be devoted to retail, effectively ruling out any kind of direct retail or outlet mall approach, which is the kind of business that could take advantage of the visitor traffic to the teddy bear factory. The company proposed a project for this unused space involving an attempt to bring together up to 50 Vermont manufacturers in a cooperative manufacturing, demonstration, and marketing setting—a made-in-Vermont manufacturing/exhibition park. Investors expressed concerns about the capital investment requirement.[74]

Vermont Teddy Bear began using Sealed Air Corp's Rapid Fill air-filled packaging (air bags) system to protect its teddy bears from damage during shipping in 1997. Previously it had used corrugated cardboard seat belt inserts to package the bears during shipping, but found that there were drawbacks, including minor damage to the products and the high cost of postage. Sealed Air's inflatable plastic bags were lighter than the corrugated inserts resulting in savings in postage costs and the plastic bags did not damage the bears with plush fur. Vermont Teddy Bear saved $150,000 in postage costs in 1997 and could realize $30,000 to $40,000 in additional savings in 1998.[75]

Vice President of Data Processing was Bonnie West. According to CEO Robert, Vermont Teddy Bear's desktop computers were in need of updating. However, West believed the company's call centers had state-of-the-art technologies, including PC terminals and very-high-tech telephone switching equipment that allowed the company to handle significant call volume. The company also had a high-tech shipping system, including state-of-the-art multicarrier software so that if a major carrier like UPS went on strike, it could immediately make adjustments.

Human Resource Management

Vermont Teddy Bear employees were known as the "Bear People," a term that expressed management's appreciation and respect for their dedication. Beth Peters was Vice President of Human Resources. As of June 30, 1998, the company employed 181 individuals, of whom 94 were employed in production-related functions, 67 were employed in sales and marketing positions, and 20 were employed in administrative and management positions.[76] None of the employees belonged to a union. Overall, the company believed that favorable relations existed with all employees.[77]

The company supplemented its regular in-house workforce with homeworkers who performed production functions at their homes. The level of outsourced work fluctuated with company production targets. As of June 30, 1998, there were 21 homeworkers producing product for the company. Homeworkers were treated as independent contractors for all purposes, except for withholding of federal employment taxes. As independent contractors, homeworkers were free to reject or accept any work offered by the company.[78] Independent contractors allowed the company flexibility in meeting heavy demand at holiday periods such as Christmas, Valentine's Day, and Mother's Day. This relationship also allowed the homeworkers flexibility in scheduling their hours of work.

Bear Market

The teddy bear was first created in the United States in 1902. The Steiff Company of Grengen/Brenz, Germany, displayed one at a fair in Leipzig in 1903. Thomas Michton of Brooklyn, New York, was credited with creating the name "Teddy Bear" in honor of President Theodore Roosevelt. At the time of the naming, President Roosevelt had been on a well-publicized hunting trip in Mississippi while negotiating a border dispute with Louisiana. When he came up empty-handed from his hunting, his aides rounded up a bear cub for the President to shoot. His granddaughter, Sarah Alden "Aldie" Gannett, said, "I think he felt he could never face his children again if he shot anything so small. So he let it go."[79]

The incident was popularized in cartoons by Clifford Berryman of the *Washington Post*. Michton and his wife stitched up a couple of honey-colored bears and then displayed them in their novelty store window along with a copy of Berryman's cartoon.

The bears sold in a day. Michton made another stuffed bear and sent it to President Roosevelt requesting his permission to use his name. Roosevelt replied with a handwritten note: "I doubt if my name will mean much in the bear business, but you may use it if you wish." It was simply signed "T. R."[80]

Teddy bears today fall into 1 of 2 broad categories: either to a subsegment of the toy industry, plush dolls and animals, or are part of the collectibles industry. Although no one knows exactly how many teddy bears are sold each year, it is known that teddy bears accounted for 70 to 80% of the $1 billion plush toy industry in 1997.[81] "Bears sell across every season, occasion, and holiday," said Del Clark, Director of Merchandising for Fiesta, a Verona, California, maker of stuffed animals.[82] Not only have bears historically been a steady seller, but returns of teddy bears are almost nonexistent.[83]

The U.S. toy industry (including teddy bears, dolls, puzzles, games, action figures and vehicles, and preschool activity toys) was estimated to be worth $25 billion in sales and had been growing at an annual rate of more than 3%.[84] With its combination of a large demographic base of children and a population with a high level of disposable income, the U.S. toy market was larger than those of Japan (the number 2 market) and Western Europe combined.[85] Most toys that are sold in the United States were made in foreign countries. Chinese-produced toys represented about 30% of all U.S. toy sales due to inexpensive labor and favorable duty rates on imports.[86] The big toy manufacturers were buying each other's operations and those of smaller toy makers. In 1997, the number 1 toy manufacturer, Mattel (maker of Fisher-Price toys and Barbie dolls), bought Tyco Toys, formerly ranked number 3. Hasbro (maker of G.I. Joe, Monopoly, and Milton Bradley toys) was the number 2 toy maker. Some games and toys maintained popularity over time, others were passing fads. It was difficult to predict which would remain popular over time. In the 1990s, marketing appeared to be the key to success. Toy production and marketing were regularly integrated with movies and television programs. For example, Star Wars action figures and other merchandise accounted for about one third of number 3 toy make Galoob Toys' 1997 sales of $360 million.[87] Small toy makers found it difficult to compete with the multimillion-dollar marketing campaigns and the in-depth market research of companies like Mattel, although there was always an exception such as Beanie Babies.

During 1997, manufacturers' shipments of plush products rose 37.5%, from $984 million to $1.4 billion, largely as a result of the Beanie Baby craze.[88] Designed by Ty Warner, the owner of Ty, Inc., Beanie Babies had been the big sales item since 1996 when they generated sales of $250 million. The $5 toys were produced in limited numbers and sold through specialty toy stores rather than through mass-market retailers. Beanie Baby characters no longer in production fetched up to $3,000 among collectors. Some retailers reported a decline in the sales of other plush toys due to the demand for Beanie Babies.[89]

Competitors of Vermont Teddy Bear were of various types. Major plush doll manufacturers such as Mattel and Hasbro were considered competition in this subsegment of the toy industry. More direct competition for Vermont Teddy came from other bear manufacturers including Steiff of Germany, Dakin, Applause, Fiesta, North American Bear, and Gund, the leading maker of toy bears. Information about some of these direct competitors is presented in **Exhibit 6**.

In general, these competitors relied on sales though retail outlets and had much greater financial resources to drive sales and marketing efforts than did Vermont Teddy Bear. Unlike Vermont Teddy Bear, these companies depended on foreign manufacturing and sources of raw materials, enabling them to sell comparable products at retail prices below those currently offered by Vermont Teddy. In addition, small craft stores had begun to sell locally produced all-American-made teddy bears, and publications had been developed to teach people to craft their own bears.

The collectible market in bears had recently been booming with people seeking bears as financial investments. Collectible bears are those that are meant to be displayed, not drooled or spit up on by their owners. "In the past 5 to 10 years we've seen a tremendous growth in the

Exhibit 6
Competition: The Vermont Teddy Bear Co., Inc.

Steiff
High-quality bears are manufactured in Germany and the Far East. The bears are not individually customized. The company's trademark is a button sewn into the ear of each bear. Prices of Steiff bears range from $50 for a 6-inch-tall bear to several thousand dollars for a life-size model. The bears are sold in a variety of outlets from discount stores and supermarkets to high-end specialty shops and antique stores.

Gund
This mass producer of a wide range of plush animals established an Internet Web site, allowing users to view and purchase products. Bears are manufactured overseas, primarily in Korea. Appearance of the bears is different from Vermont Teddy Bears', with shorter noses and limbs. They offer a broad range of styles and prices.

Teddy Bear Factory
This is the only other American manufacturer of teddy bears. The company is located in San Francisco and highly regional in its sales and marketing efforts. Vermont Teddy Bear advertises in the San Francisco Bay area but does not consider the Teddy Bear Factory to be strong competition because of the size and because its market is so regional.

North American Bear Company
This middle-sized company manufactures all of its bears in the Orient, primarily in Korea. Appearance of the bears is different from Vermont Teddy Bears, with shorter noses and limbs. The company advertises in trade magazines and has begun to do consumer advertising. It sells to retailers in Europe and Japan and collectors and gift shops in the United States.

Applause Enterprises, Inc.
This company focuses on manufacturing plush toy versions of Sesame Street, Looney Tunes, Star Wars, Muppets, and Disney characters as well as nonplush toys. Company was formed by the 1995 merger of plush toy maker Dakin and a company founded by Wallace Berrie.

upscale bear, the limited editions, and the artist-designed bears," said George B. Black, Jr., director of the Teddy Bear Museum in Naples, Florida.[90] The "collectible" segment of the plush market generated $441 million in consumer sales for 1996, up from $354 million in 1995. Collectible plush sales for 1997 were expected to reach nearly $700 million. This would make plush 1 of the fastest growing categories in the $9.2 billion collectibles industry.[91] Collectible bears started at about $25 but could cost $1,000 or more. This number was somewhat misleading, considering that the value of a collectible bear can be in excess of $50,000. A 1904 Steiff "Teddy Girl" bear sold at a Christie's auction in 1994 for a record $171,380.[92]

Two trade magazines, *Teddy Bear and Friends* and *Teddy Bear Review*, targeted the collectibles market. These magazines tell bear collectors where they can buy and sell old bears. In 1998, major bear shows and jamborees were held in at least 25 states, as well as hundreds of bear-making retreats and workshops.[93]

The concept of Bear-Grams lent itself to 2 distinct groups of competitors. Vermont Teddy Bear competed not only with soft plush stuffed animals, especially teddy bears, but also with a variety of other special occasion greetings such as flowers, candy, balloons, cakes, and other gift items that could be ordered by phone for special occasions and delivered the next day. Many of these competitors had greater financial, sales, and marketing resources than Vermont Teddy Bear.[94]

Patents, Trademarks, and Licenses

The company's name in combination with its original logo was a registered trademark in the United States. In addition, the company owned the registered trademarks in the United States for "The Vermont Teddy Bear Company," "Bear-Gram," "Teddy Bear-Gram," and "Make A Friend For Life." The company also owned the registered service marks "Bear Counselor," "Vermont Bear-Gram," and "Racer Ted," and had applications pending to register the company's second and third company logos, "Bearanimal," "Coffee Cub," "Vermont Bear-Gram," "Vermont Baby Bear," "The Great American Teddy Bear," "All-American Teddy Bear," "Beau and Beebee," "Teddy-Grams," and "Vermont Teddy Wear."[95]

Vermont Teddy Bear also owned the registered trademark "Vermont Teddy Bear" in Japan and had an application pending to register "The Great American Teddy Bear" in Japan.[96]

Although the company had continuously used the "Bear-Gram" trademark since April 1985, its initial application to register the mark on June 13, 1990, was rejected by the U.S. Patent and Trademark Office due to prior registration of the mark "Bear-A-Grams," by another company on June 7, 1988. The company reapplied to register "Bear-Gram," and its application was approved on November 5, 1996.

The company also claimed copyright, service mark, or trademark protection for its teddy bear designs, its marketing slogans, and its advertising copy and promotional literature.

On May 16, 1997, Vermont Teddy Bear sued Disney Enterprises, Inc., for injunctive relief and unspecified damages claiming that Disney copied its bear-by-mail concept with Pooh-Grams based on Disney's Winnie the Pooh character. The complaint accused Disney of unfair competition and trademark infringement saying the Pooh-Gram is "confusingly similar" to Bear-Grams in name, logo, how it is personalized, how it is delivered, and even how it is marketed.[97] Disney introduced Pooh-Grams in its fall 1996 catalog and escalated its promotion of the product using the Internet, print, and radio advertising. Disney disagreed saying that the Vermont Teddy lawsuit was without merit because Winnie the Pooh has been a well-known Disney character for 25 years and there are all kinds of grams—mail-grams, candy-grams, money-grams, telegrams, flower-grams—not just Bear-Grams.

On September 9, 1997, Vermont Teddy announced that it had entered into an agreement to resolve its dispute with Walt Disney Co. Under the agreement, Disney will continue to offer its Pooh-Gram products and services but will voluntarily limit its use of the Pooh-Gram mark in certain advertising and will adequately distinguish its trademarks and service marks from those of Vermont Teddy Bear. Vermont Teddy in turn will be allowed to offer certain Winnie-the-Pooh merchandise for sale in its mail order catalogs but cannot offer the merchandise with its Bear-Gram program.[98]

Finance

On November 23, 1993, Vermont Teddy Bear Co., Inc., sold 1.15 million shares of stock at $10 a share through an underwriting group led by Barrington Capital Group L.P. The stock rose as high as $19 before closing the day at $16.75, an increase of 67.5% in its first day of trading. The market's reaction to the IPO signaled that investors thought the stock was undervalued at $10 and that the company had a great deal of growth potential. During fiscal 1998, the company's stock price fluctuated between $2.56 and $0.75 a share. This was an indication that investors reconsidered the growth potential of Vermont Teddy Bear.

Vice President of Finance was Mark Sleeper. **Exhibits 7** and **8** detail Vermont Teddy Bear's financial situation. Prior to 1994, Vermont Teddy Bear had experienced a great deal of success and profitability. The company's net sales increased 61% from $10,569,017 in 1992 to $17,025,856 in 1993, while the cost of goods sold decreased from 43.1% of sales to 41.8% during the same time period. Net income increased 314% from $202,601 in 1992 to $838,955 in 1993.

Sales reached a peak in 1994 at $20,560,566. This represented a 21% growth over 1993. Unfortunately profits did not experience similar growth. Had it not been for an almost $70,000 tax refund, the company would have experienced a net loss in 1994. The company's net profit fell to $17,523 after taxes in 1994 due to a substantial increase in both selling expense and general and administrative expenses. These 2 items combined for an increase of 35% over comparable figures for 1993.

In 1995, sales fell to $20,044,796. Although this represented only a 2.5% decline, this decline in sales painted a picture for the next 2 years. While sales were decreasing, selling and general and administrative expenses continued to climb. These expenses grew by 10% to $13,463,631 in 1995. These 2 items represented 67% of sales in 1996, whereas they were 53% of sales in 1993.

After 3 years of declining sales, Vermont Teddy Bear's sales grew by 4.4% in 1998 to $17,207,543. Vermont Teddy Bear experienced a loss of $2,422,477 in 1995. It returned to profitability in 1996, earning $151,953. Unfortunately that was the last profitable year for the company. Losses were $1,901,745 in 1997 and $1,683,669 in 1998. Interest expense had risen dramatically for the company from $35,002 in 1995 to $608,844 in 1998.

The company included in its quarterly report to the SEC (Filing Date: 5/14/98) that it had been operating without a working capital line of credit since July 18, 1997. On that date, the company completed a sale-leaseback transaction involving its factory headquarters and a portion of its property located in Shelburne, Vermont. This financing replaced the company's mortgage and line of credit. The company received $5.9 million from this transaction. Of this amount, $3.3 million was used to pay off the mortgage and $600,000 was used to pay off the line of credit. A $591,000 transactions cost was associated with the sale-leaseback. The lease obligation was repayable on a 20-year amortization schedule through July 2017.

On October 10, 1997, Vermont Teddy received a commitment from Green Mountain Capital L.P. whereby it agreed to lend the company up to $200,000 for up to 5 years at 12% interest. The loan was secured by security interest in the company's real and personal property. Green Mountain Capital also received warrants to purchase 100,000 shares of common stock at an exercise price of $1.00. The warrants could be exercised any time from 2 years from the date of the loan to 7 years from the date of the loan.

Exhibit 7

Consolidated Balance Sheets: The Vermont Teddy Bear Co., Inc.

Year Ending June 30	1998	1997	1996	1995	1994[1]	1993[1]	1992[1]
Assets							
Current assets							
Cash and marketable securities	$ 1,527,052	$ 441,573	$ 1,121,500	$ 1,070,862	$ 2,379,760	$ 8,561,525	$ —
Accounts receivable, trade	51,538	46,304	131,550	122,679	142,029	103,762	77,815
Inventories	2,396,245	3,302,313	1,974,731	3,042,484	4,024,247	2,425,233	1,135,940
Prepaid expenses	444,229	386,947	277,502	213,236	568,680	123,886	10,681
Due from officer	—	—	—	—	565,714	—	—
Deferred income taxes	233,203	259,016	240,585	126,393	322,106	194,082	—
Total current assets	4,652,267	4,436,153	3,745,868	4,575,654	8,002,536	11,408,488	1,224,436
Property and equipment	8,844,475	9,845,935	10,300,318	10,493,214	3,052,002	861,419	589,196
Construction in progress	—	—	—	—	3,275,527	—	—
Due from officer	—	—	—	—	128,008	128,008	102,480
Deposits and other assets	903,110	272,348	98,086	102,676	121,640	97,400	14,356
Notes receivable	87,500	95,000	95,000	190,000	190,000	—	—
Total assets	$14,487,352	$14,649,436	$14,239,272	$15,361,544	$14,769,713	$12,495,315	$1,930,468
Liabilities and shareholders' equity							
Current liabilities							
Cash overdraft	$ —	$ —	$ —	$ —	$ —	$ —	$ 148,048
Line of credit	—	550,000	—	—	—	—	—
Notes payable, bank	45,603	—	—	—	36,748	108,748	180,748
Current installments of							
Long-term debt	231,133	3,443,096	187,095	27,805	21,981	22,793	19,075
Capital lease obligations	225,738	103,759	104,146	126,306	99,901	45,604	41,795
Accounts payable	1,846,042	2,562,536	1,353,698	2,513,468	3,336,558	1,319,499	1,604,066
Accrued expenses	916,191	657,347	449,048	860,440	442,467	381,146	156,777

Income taxes payable		117,810	117,810	90,889	37,365		3,264,707
Total current liabilities	2,150,509	1,995,600	4,055,465	3,618,908	2,131,352	7,316,738	
Construction loan payable							
Long-term debt	81,401	82,411	60,408	3,252,379	3,505,812	372,999	338,317
Capital lease obligations	61,350	58,883	398,220	347,874	312,814	209,054	5,748,182
Other liabilities	958,219	—	—	204,430	84,430	—	—
Accrued interest payable, debentures							
Deferred income taxes		47,492	105,992	126,393	240,585	259,016	233,203
Total liabilities	3,251,479	2,184,386	4,620,085	7,549,984	6,274,993	8,157,807	9,584,409
Shareholders' equity							
Preferred stock $.05 par value:							
Authorized 1,000,000 shares							
Series A	—	900,000	900,000	900,000	900,000	900,000	1,044,000
Cumulative dividends at 8%							
Preferred stock $.05 par value:							
Authorized 375,000 shares							
Series B	—	—	—	—	—	10,245	10,245
Common stock, $.05 par value:							
Authorized 20,000,000 shares	200,000	258,625	258,625	258,625	258,638	258,638	259,787
Additional paid-in capital	185,868	10,073,842	10,073,842	10,073,842	10,074,595	10,565,482	10,587,316
Treasury stock at cost							
(12,000 shares)	—	—	(106,824)	(106,824)	(106,824)	(106,824)	(106,824)
Accumulated deficit	(1,706,879)	(921,538)	(976,015)	(3,314,083)	(3,162,130)	(5,135,912)	(6,891,581)
Total shareholders' equity	(1,321,011)	10,310,929	10,149,628	7,811,560	7,964,279	6,491,629	4,902,943
Total liabilities and shareholders' equity	$1,930,468	$12,495,315	$14,769,713	$15,361,544	$14,239,272	$14,649,436	$14,487,352

Note:
1. Fiscal year ending December 31.

Source: The Vermont Teddy Bear Company, Inc., *1998 Annual Report.*

Exhibit 8

Statement of Operations: The Vermont Teddy Bear Co., Inc.

Year Ending June 30	1998	1997	1996	1995	1994[1]	1993[1]	1992[1]
Net sales	$17,207,543	$16,489,482	$17,039,618	$20,044,796	$20,560,566	$17,025,856	$10,569,017
Cost of goods sold	7,397,450	7,068,549	7,309,038	9,101,028	8,619,580	7,123,930	4,555,424
Gross margin	9,810,093	9,420,933	9,730,580	10,943,768	11,940,986	9,901,926	6,013,593
Selling expenses	7,866,843	7,961,003	6,287,208	9,121,023	8,907,440	6,862,328	4,454,891
General and administrative expenses	3,031,716	2,938,251	2,954,601	4,342,608	3,311,306	2,184,500	1,266,770
Total expenses	10,898,559	10,899,254	9,241,809	13,463,631	12,218,746	9,046,828	5,721,661
Operating income (loss)	(1,088,466)	(1,478,321)	488,771	(2,519,863)	(277,760)	855,098	291,932
Interest income	26,126	53,267	41,092	192,156	248,987	27,887	2,152
Miscellaneous income	29,243	(11,973)	63,236	1,620	1,620	25,000	—
Interest expense	(650,572)	(464,768)	(441,146)	(35,002)	(24,848)	(97,810)	(91,483)
Income (loss) before taxes	(1,683,669)	(1,901,795)	151,953	(2,361,089)	(52,001)	810,175	202,601
Income tax provision (benefit)				61,388	(69,524)	(28,780)	
Net income (loss)	$(1,683,669)	$(1,901,795)	$ 151,953	$(2,422,477)	$ 17,523	$ 838,955	$ 202,601
Preferred stock dividends	(72,000)	(72,000)	—	(72,000)	(72,000)	(53,614)	—
Net earnings (loss) common shareholders	(1,611,669)	(1,829,795)	151,953	(2,350,477)	89,523	892,569	202,601
Net earnings (loss) per common share	(0.34)	(0.38)	0.03	(0.48)	(0.10)	0.19	0.05
Weighted average number of shares outstanding	5,172,475	5,160,750	5,160,583	5,160,500	5,164,057	4,210,070	4,024,140

Note:

1. Fiscal year ending December 31.

Source: The Vermont Teddy Bear Company, Inc., *1998 Annual Report.*

To reduce costs, the company closed its retail store in New York City and planned to close the Freeport, Maine, and North Conway, New Hampshire, stores before the end of 1998 because the revenue increases necessary to support the annual lease obligations would not be achievable in the short run. The company's lease obligation of $300,000 per year on the New York City store would continue until a replacement tenant was found.

On May 22, 1998, it was announced that The Vermont Teddy Bear Co., Inc., had signed a letter of intent with the Shepherd Group, a Boston-based private equity investment firm, for a proposed $600,000 equity investment with the company. The Shepherd Group invested in venture and existing small- to middle-market companies focusing on companies with high-growth potential and unique market-ready quality products and services. In return for the $600,000 investment, the Shepherd Group received 60 shares of Series C Preferred Stock as well as warrants to purchase 495,868 shares of Common Stock at $1.21 per share. The transaction was subject to final agreements and various approvals and conditions.

The Series C Convertible Redeemable Stock carried a 6% coupon, and each share was convertible into 8,264,467 shares of the company's Common Stock. The Preferred had voting rights, and the Shepherd Group was entitled to 2 seats on the company's Board of Directors.

Elisabeth Robert noted, "The additional funds will provide working capital for the company to pursue growth in the Bear-Gram channel and to maximize the benefits of importing raw materials. Additionally Tom Shepherd has strong financial and operations experience and will bring a valuable perspective to the Board of Directors. Tom's strong suit has been working with companies that have not yet realized the full potential of their brand."[99]

According to some analysts, the survival of this company was going to depend on maintaining a source of working capital, cost containment, and a rebound in sales back to their 1995 level. The company had taken an aggressive approach to ensuring survival, but this was not done cheaply. High interest rates were paid and warrants to purchase stock, at what might turn out to be a bargain price, had been issued.

Notes

1. Cynthia Crossen, "Isn't It Funny How a Bear Makes Money, Year After Year?" *Wall Street Journal* (February 17, 1998), p. B-1.
2. "Vermont Teddy President and CEO Interview," *The Wall Street Journal Corporate Reporter, Inc.* (January 21, 1998).
3. *Ibid.*
4. The Vermont Teddy Bear Co., Inc., *1997 Annual Report.*
5. Richard H. Levy, "Ursine of the Times: Vermont Teddy Bear Company Pulls Back from Catalog Sales," *Direct Marketing* (February 1998), p. 16.
6. Maria Lisa Calta, "Cub Scout," *Detroit News* (March 5, 1995), pp. 22-D, 23-D.
7. *Ibid.*
8. Phaedra Hise, "Making Fans on Talk Radio," *Inc.* (December 1993), p. 62.
9. The Vermont Teddy Bear Co., Inc., *1994 Annual Report*, p. 3.
10. The Vermont Teddy Bear Co., Inc., *Company Time Line*, Information Packet, p. 2.
11. *Ibid.*
12. *Ibid.*
13. The Vermont Teddy Bear Co., Inc., *Form 10-KSB* (June 30, 1995), p. 1.
14. *Company Time Line*, p. 2.
15. The Vermont Teddy Bear Co., Inc., Press Release (April 17, 1995).
16. The Vermont Teddy Bear Co., Inc., *1994 Annual Report* (Letter to Shareholders), p. 2.
17. *The Wall Street Journal Corporate Reporter, Inc.* (January 21, 1998).
18. "The Vermont Teddy Bear Company Roars into New York City," Vermont Teddy Bear Co., Inc., Press Release (October 9, 1996).
19. "The Vermont Teddy Posts Year-End Results, Closes Equity Deal," Vermont Teddy Bear Co., Inc., Press Release (September 29, 1998), p. 1.
20. "The Vermont Teddy Bear Company Expands Retail Activities," Vermont Teddy Bear Co., Inc., Press Release (June 20, 1996).
21. The Vermont Teddy Bear Co., Inc., *1997 Annual Report* (Letter to Shareholders), p. 3.
22. *The Wall Street Journal Corporate Reporter, Inc.* (January 21, 1998).
23. The Vermont Teddy Bear Co., Inc., *1997 Annual Report* (Letter to Shareholders), p. 3.
24. The Vermont Teddy Bear Co., Inc., *1997 Annual Report*, p. 22, and *1997 Proxy Statement* (October 28, 1997), pp. 6, 10, 21–23.
25. The Vermont Teddy Bear Co., Inc., *Form 10-KSB* (September 28, 1998), p. 10.
26. The Vermont Teddy Bear Co., Inc., *1997 Proxy Statement* (October 28, 1997), pp. 4–5.
27. The Vermont Teddy Bear Co., Inc., *Form 10-KSB* (September 28, 1998), p. 10.
28. The Vermont Teddy Bear Co., Inc., *1998 Proxy Statement* (July 23, 1998), p. 5.
29. The Vermont Teddy Bear Co., Inc., *Form 10-KSB* (September 28, 1998), pp. 9–10.
30. The Vermont Teddy Bear Co., Inc., *1997 Annual Report*, p. 4.
31. *Ibid.*

32. *Ibid.*

33. The Vermont Teddy Bear Co., Inc., *Form 10-KSB* (September 28, 1998), p. 6.

34. Calta, p. 22-D.

35. The Vermont Teddy Bear Co., Inc., *Form 10-KSB* (September 28, 1998), p. 6.

36. The Vermont Teddy Bear *Gazette* (summer 1995 edition), p. 7.

37. The Vermont Teddy Bear Co., Inc., *Form 10-KSB* (September 28, 1998), p. 6.

38. *Ibid.*

39. Levy, p. 16.

40. "Vermont Teddy Bear Appoints Vice President of Marketing and Design," The Vermont Teddy Bear Co., Inc., Press Release (May 5, 1998).

41. Calta, p. 22-D.

42. The Vermont Teddy Bear Co., Inc., *Form 10-KSB* (September 28, 1998), p. 3.

43. *Ibid.*

44. The Vermont Teddy Bear Co., Inc., "Vermont Teddy Bear Posts Quarterly Profit on Increased Revenues," Press Release (May 14, 1998), p. 1.

45. The Vermont Teddy Bear Co., Inc., *Form 10-KSB* (September 28, 1998), p. 4.

46. Jim Kerstetter, "Setting Up Mom and Pop," *PC Week On-Line* (August 24, 1998), p. 1.

47. The Vermont Teddy Bear Co., Inc., *Form 10-KSB* (September 28, 1998), p. 4.

48. *Ibid.*

49. "Vermont Teddy Bear Company to be Featured on Dateline NBC, December 17, 1996," The Vermont Teddy Bear Co., Inc., Press Release (December 17, 1996).

50. The Vermont Teddy Bear Co., Inc., *1997 Annual Report*, p. 10.

51. The Vermont Teddy Bear Co., Inc., *Form 10-KSB* (September 28, 1998), p. 3.

52. *Ibid.*, p. 5

53. The Vermont Teddy Bear Co., Inc., *1994 Annual Report*, p. 3.

54. Melissa Dowling, "Vermont Teddy Bears the Pressure," *Catalog Age* (May 1996), p. 12.

55. The Vermont Teddy Bear Co., Inc., *Form 10-KSB* (September 28, 1998), p. 5.

56. The Vermont Teddy Bear Co., Inc., *1997 Annual Report* (Letter to Shareholders), p. 4.

57. The Vermont Teddy Bear Co., Inc., *Form 10-KSB* (September 28, 1998), p. 3.

58. Levy, p. 16.

59. "Vermont Teddy Bear Announces Second-Quarter Results," Press Release (February 13, 1998).

60. The Vermont Teddy Bear Co., Inc., *1997 Annual Report.*

61. The Vermont Teddy Bear Co., Inc., *1997 Annual Report* (Letter to Shareholders), p. 4.

62. "Vermont Teddy Bear Company Joins Forces with America's Most Famous Teddy Bear Person," The Vermont Teddy Bear Co., Inc., Press Release (November 5, 1996).

63. "NFL Football Soft and Cuddly? The Vermont Teddy Bear Company Introduces Officially Licensed NFL Teddy Bears," The Vermont Teddy Bear Co., Inc., Press Release (August 27, 1997).

64. "The Vermont Teddy Bear Company Kicks Off NFL Bear-Grams," The Vermont Teddy Bear Co., Inc., Press Release (September 30, 1996).

65. *The Wall Street Journal Corporate Reporter* (January 21, 1998).

66. *Ibid.*

67. *Ibid.*

68. The Vermont Teddy Bear Co., Inc., *1997 Annual Report*, p. 13.

69. The Vermont Teddy Bear Co., Inc., *Form 10-KSB* (September 28, 1998), p. 8.

70. "Vermont Teddy Bear Refinances Factory Headquarters," The Vermont Teddy Bear Co., Inc., Press Release (July 21, 1997).

71. The Vermont Teddy Bear Co., Inc., *Form 10-KSB* (September 28, 1998), p. 5.

72. *Ibid.*

73. *Ibid.*

74. Edna Tenney, "A Teddy Bear's Modest Proposal," *Business Digest*, <webmaster@vermontguides.com> (October 10, 1997), pp. 1–3.

75. Bernard Abrams, "Switch to Air Bags Bears Watching," *Packaging Digest* (March 1998), pp. 50–52.

76. The Vermont Teddy Bear Co., Inc., *Form 10-KSB* (September 28, 1998), p. 7.

77. "Bear Necessities," *Direct Marketing Magazine* (July 1998), p. 18.

78. *Ibid.*

79. Calta, p. 23-D.

80. *Ibid.*

81. Crossen, p. B-1.

82. *Ibid.*

83. "Bullish for Bears," *The Times* (Tampa) (February 18, 1998), pp. E1–2.

84. Stuart Hampton, *Hoovers Online: Toys and Games Industry Snapshot*, 1998, p. 1.

85. J. S. Krutick, et al., "Salomon Smith Barney Toy Industry Update," *Investext Report*, number: 2715626 (June 23, 1998), p. 6.

86. Hampton, p. 2.

87. Donna Leccese, "Growth at a Price," *Playthings* (June 1998), p. 30.

88. *Ibid.*

89. The Vermont Teddy Bear Co., Inc., *1997 Annual Report*, p. 11.

90. Leccese, p. 30.

91. Calta, p. 23-D.

92. Crossen, p. B-1.

93. The Vermont Teddy Bear Co., Inc., *1997 Annual Report*, p. 11.

94. The Vermont Teddy Bear Co., Inc., *Form 10-KSB* (September 28, 1998), p. 7.

95. *Ibid.*

96. Bruce Horovitz, *USA Today* (May 27, 1997), p. B-2.

97. "Vermont Teddy Bear and Disney Settle Suit," The Vermont Teddy Bear Co., Inc., Press Release (September 9, 1997).

98. The Vermont Teddy Bear Co., Inc., *1994, 1995, 1996, 1997 Annual Reports* and *Form 10-KSB* (September 28, 1998).

99. The Vermont Teddy Bear Co., Inc., Press Release (May 22, 1998), pp. 1–3.

Guajilote Cooperativo Forestal, Honduras

Nathan Nebbe and J. David Hunger

Guajilote (pronounced wa-hee-low-tay) Cooperativo Forestal was a forestry cooperative that operated out of Chaparral, a small village located in the buffer zone of La Muralla National Park in Honduras' Olancho province. Olancho was 1 of 18 Honduran provinces and was located inland bordering Nicaragua. The cooperative was 1 result of a relatively new movement among international donor agencies promoting sustainable economic development of developing countries' natural resources.[1] A cooperative in Honduras was similar to a cooperative in the United States. It was an enterprise jointly owned and operated by members who used its facilities and services.

Guajilote was founded in 1991 as a component of a USAID (United States Agency for International Development) project. The project attempted to develop La Muralla National Park as an administrative and socioeconomic model that COHDEFOR (the Honduran forestry development service) could transfer to Honduras' other national parks. The Guajilote Cooperativo Forestal was given the right to exploit naturally fallen (not chopped down) mahogany trees in La Muralla's buffer zone. Thus far, it was the only venture in Honduras with this right. A buffer zone was the designated area within a park's boundaries, but outside its core protected zone. People were allowed to live and engage in economically sustainable activities within this buffer zone.

Guajilote in 1998 was facing some important issues and concerns that could effect not only its future growth, but also its very survival. For 1 thing, the amount of mahogany wood was limited and was increasingly threatened by forest fires, illegal logging, and slash and burn agriculture. If the total number of mahogany trees continued to decline, trade in its wood could be restricted internationally. For another, the cooperative had no way to transport its wood to market and was thus forced to accept low prices for its wood from the only distributor in the area. What could be done to guarantee the survival of the cooperative?

Operations

Guajilote's work activities included 3 operations using very simple technologies. First, members searched the area to locate appropriate fallen trees. This, in itself, could be very difficult since mahogany trees were naturally rare. These trees were found at elevations up to 1,800

This case was prepared by Nathan Nebbe and Professor J. David Hunger of Iowa State University. Copyright ©1999 by Nathan Nebbe and J. David Hunger. This case was edited for SMBP-8th Edition. Reprinted by permission. Presented to the Society for Case Research and published in *Annual Advances in Business Cases 1999*. Reprinted by permission.

meters (5,400 feet) and normally were found singly or in small clusters of no more than 4 to 8 trees per hectare (2.2 acres).[2]

Finding fallen mahogany in La Muralla's buffer zone was hampered due to the area's steep and sometimes treacherous terrain. (La Muralla means "steep wall of rock" in Spanish.) The work was affected by the weather. For example, more downed trees were available during the wet season due to storms and higher soil moisture—leading to the uprooting of trees.

Second, the cooperative set up a temporary hand-sawmill as close as possible to a fallen tree. Due to the steep terrain, it was often difficult to find a suitable location nearby to operate the hand-sawmill. Once a suitable work location was found, men used a large cross-cut saw to disassemble the tree into various components. The disassembling process was a long and arduous process that could take weeks for an especially large tree. The length of time it took to process a tree depended on a tree's size—mature mahogany trees could be gigantic. Tree size thus affected how many trees Guajilote was able to process in a year.

Third, after a tree was disassembled, the wood was either carried out of the forest using a combination of mule and human power, or floated down a stream or river. Even if a stream happened to be near a fallen tree, it was typically only usable during the wet season. The wood was then sold to a distributor who, in turn, transported it via trucks to the cities to sell to furniture makers for a profit.

Guajilote's permit to use fallen mahogany was originally granted in 1991 for a 10-year period by COHDEFOR. The permit was simply written, and stated that if Guajilote restricted itself to downed mahogany, its permit renewal should be granted automatically. The administrator of the area's COHDEFOR office indicated that if things remained as they were, Guajilote should not have any problem obtaining renewal in 2001. Given the nature of Honduran politics, however, nothing could be completely assured.

In 1998, Guajilote's mahogany was still sold as a commodity. The cooperative did very little to add value to its product. Nevertheless, the continuing depletion of mahogany trees around the world meant that the remaining wood should increase in value over time.

Management and Human Resources

Santos Munguia, 29 years old, had been Guajilote's leader since 1995. Although Munguia had only a primary school education, he was energetic, intelligent, and had proven to be a very skillful politician. In addition to directing Guajilote, Mr. Munguia farmed a small parcel of land and raised a few head of cattle. He was also involved in local politics.

Munguia had joined the cooperative in 1994. Although he had not been 1 of Guajilote's original members, he quickly became its de facto leader in 1995, when he renegotiated a better price for the sale of the cooperative's wood.

Before Munguia joined the cooperative, Guajilote had been receiving between 3 and 4 lempiras ($0.37 or 11 lempiras to the dollar) per foot of cut mahogany from its sole distributor, Juan Suazo. No other distributors were available in this remote location. The distributor transported the wood to Tegucigalpa or San Pedro Sula and sold it for 16 to 18 lempiras per foot. Believing that Suazo was taking advantage of the cooperative, Munguia negotiated a price increase to 7 to 8 lempiras per foot ($0.60 to $0.62 per foot at the July 15, 1998 exchange rate) by putting political pressure on Suazo. The distributor agreed to the price increase only after a police investigation had been launched to investigate his business dealings. (Rumors circulated that Suazo was transporting and selling illegally logged mahogany by mixing it with that purchased from Guajilote.)

Munguia: El Caudillo

After renegotiating successfully with the cooperative's distributor, Santos Munguia quickly became the group's caudillo (strong man). The caudillo was a Latin American political and social institution. A caudillo was a (typically male) purveyor of patronage. All decisions went through, and were usually made by, him. A caudillo was often revered, feared, and hated at the same time because of the power he wielded. Munguia was viewed by many in the area as an ascending caudillo because of his leadership of Guajilote.

Guajilote did not operate in a democratic fashion. Munguia made all of the decisions—sometimes with input from his second in command and nephew, Miguel Flores Munguia—and handled all of Guajilote's financial matters. Guajilote's members did not seem to have a problem with this management style. The prevailing opinion seemed to be that Guajilote was a lot better off with Munguia running the show by himself than with more involvement by the members. One man put the members' view very succinctly: "Santos, he saved us (from Suazo, from COHDEFOR, from ourselves)."

Guajilote's organizational structure emphasized Munguia's importance. He was alone at the top in his role as decision maker. If, in the future, Munguia became more involved in politics and other ventures that could take him out of Chaparral (possibly for long periods of time), he would very likely be forced to spend less time with Guajilote's operations. Munguia's leadership has been of key importance to Guajilote's maturing as both a work group and as a business. In 1998, there did not seem to be another person in the cooperative that could take Munguia's place.

Guajilote's Members

When founded, the cooperative had been composed of 15 members. Members were initially selected for the cooperative by employees of USAID and COHDEFOR. The number of employees has held steady over time. Since the cooperative's founding, 3 original members have quit; 4 others were allowed to join. Although no specific reasons were given for members leaving, they appeared to be because of personality differences, family problems, or differences of opinion. No money had been paid to them when they left the cooperative. In 1998 there were 16 members in the cooperative.

None of Guajilote's members had any education beyond primary school. Many of the members had no schooling at all and were illiterate. As a whole, the group knew little of markets or business practices.

Guajilote's existence has had an important impact on its members. One member stated that before he had joined Guajilote, he was lucky to have made 2,000 lempiras in a year; whereas, he made around 1,000 to 1,500 in 1 month as a member of the cooperative. He stated that all 5 of his children were in school, something that he could not have afforded previously. Before joining the cooperative, he had been involved in subsistence farming and other activities that brought in a small amount of money and food. He said that his children had been required previously to work as soon as they were able. As a simple farmer, he often had to leave his family to find work, mostly migrant farm work, to help his family survive. Because of Guajilote, his family now had enough to eat and he was able to be home with his family.

This was a common story among Guajilote's members. The general improvement in its members' quality of life also appeared to have strengthened the cooperative members' personal bonds with each other.

Financial Situation

No formal public financial records were available. As head of the cooperative, Santos Munguia kept informal records. Guajilote's 1997 revenues were approximately 288,000 lempiras (US $22,153). (Revenues for 1996 were not available.) Guajilote processed around 36,000 feet of wood during 1997. Very little of the money was held back for capital improvement purchases due to the operation's simple material needs. Capital expenditures for 1997 included a mule plus materials needed to maintain Guajilote's large cross-cut saws.

Each of Guajilote's 16 members was paid an average of about 1,500 lempiras (US $113) per month in 1997 and 1,300 lempiras (US $100) per month in 1996. 1998 payments per month had been similar to 1997's payments, according to Guajilote's members. Money was paid to members based on their participation in Guajilote's operations.

There was conjecture, among some workers, that Santos Munguia and his second in charge were paying themselves more than the other members were receiving. When Munguia was asked if he received a higher wage than the others because of his administrative position in the group, he responded that everything was distributed evenly. An employee of COHDEFOR indicated, however, that Munguia had purchased a house in La Union—the largest town in the area. That person conjectured, based on this evidence, that Munguia was likely receiving more from the cooperative than were the other members.

Issues Facing the Cooperative

Guajilote's size and growth potential was limited by the amount of mahogany it could produce in a year. Mahogany was fairly rare in the forest and Guajilote was legally restricted to downed trees. Moreover, with the difficulties of finding, processing by hand, and then moving the wood out of the forest, Guajilote was further restricted in the quantity of wood it could handle.

Lack of transportation was a major problem for Guajilote. The cooperative had been unable to secure the capital needed to buy its own truck; lending through legitimate sources was very tight in Honduras and enterprises like Guajilote did not typically have access to lines of credit. Although the prices the cooperative was receiving for its wood had improved, the men still thought that the distributor, Juan Suazo, was not paying them what the wood was worth. It was argued that when demand was high for mahogany, the cooperative gave up as much as 10 lempiras per foot in sales to Suazo. Guajilote could conceivably double its revenues if it could somehow haul its wood to Honduras' major market centers and sell it without use of a distributor. The closest market center was Tegucigalpa—3 to 4 hours from Chaparral on dangerous, often rain soaked, mountain roads.

A Possibility

Some of the members of Guajilote wondered if the cooperative could do better financially by skipping the distributor completely. It was possible that some specialty shops (chains and independents) and catalogs, throughout the world, might be interested in selling high quality mahogany furniture, i.e., chests or chairs, that were produced in an environmentally friendly manner. Guajilote, unfortunately, had no highly skilled carpenters or furniture makers in its membership. There were, however, a couple towns in Honduras with highly skilled furniture makers who worked on a contract basis.

A U.S. citizen with a furniture export business in Honduras worked with a number of independent furniture makers on contract to make miniature ornamental chairs. This exporter reviewed Guajilote's situation and concluded that the cooperative might be able to make and market furniture very profitably—even if it had to go through an exporter to find suitable markets. Upon studying Guajilote's operations, he estimated that Guajilote might be able to more than treble its revenues. In order to do this, however, the exporter felt that Guajilote would have to overcome problems with transportation and upgrade its administrative competence. Guajilote would need to utilize the talents of its members more if it were to widen its operational scope. It would have to purchase trucks and hire drivers to transport the wood over treacherous mountain roads. The role of administrator would become much more demanding, thus forcing Munguia to delegate some authority to others in the cooperative.

Concerns

In spite of Guajilote's improved outlook, there were many concerns that could affect the cooperative's future. A serious concern was the threat of deforestation through fires, illegal logging (i.e., poaching of mahogany as well as clear cutting), and slash and burn agriculture.

Small fires were typically set to prepare soils for planting and to help clear new areas for cultivation. Often these fires were either not well supervised or burned out of the control of the people starting them. Due to the 1998 drought, the number of out-of-control forest fires had been far greater than normal. There seemed to be a consensus among Hondurans that 1998 would be 1 of the worst years for forest fires. Mahogany and tropical deciduous forests are not fire resistant. Fires not only kill adult and young mahogany trees, but also destroy their seeds.[3] Mahogany could therefore be quickly eliminated from a site. Each year, Guajilote lost more area from which it could take mahogany.

To make matters worse, many Hondurans considered the area around La Muralla National Park to be a frontier open to settlement by landless campesinos (peasant farmers). In fleeing poverty and desertification, people were migrating to the Olancho province in large numbers.[4] Not only did they clear the forests for cultivation, but they also cut wood for fuel and for use in building their homes. Most of the new settlements were being established in the area's best mahogany growing habitats.

Another concern was that of potential restrictions by CITIES (the international convention on trade in endangered species). Although trade in mahogany was still permitted, it was supposed to be monitored very closely. If the populations of the 12 mahogany species continued to decrease, it was possible that mahogany would be given even greater protection under the CITIES framework. This could include even tighter restrictions on the trade in mahogany, or could even result in an outright ban similar to the worldwide ban on ivory trading.

Notes

1. Kent Norsworthy, *Inside Honduras* (Albuquerque: Inter-Hemispheric Education Resource, 1993), pp. 133–138.
2. Hans Lamprecht, *Silviculture in the Tropics* (Hamburg: Verlag, 1989), pp. 245–246.
3. Lamprecht.
4. Norsworthy.

The Carey Plant

Thomas L. Wheelen and J. David Hunger

The Gardner Company was a respected New England manufacturer of machines and machine tools purchased by furniture makers for use in their manufacturing process. As a means of growing the firm, the Gardner Company acquired Carey Manufacturing 3 years ago from James Carey for $3,500,000. Carey Manufacturing was a high quality maker of specialized machine parts. Ralph Brown, Gardner's Vice President of Finance, had been the driving force behind the acquisition. Except for Andy Doyle and Rod Davis, all of Gardner's Vice Presidents (**Exhibit 1**) had been opposed to expansion through acquisition. They preferred internal growth for Gardner because they felt that the company would be more able to control both the rate and direction of its growth. Nevertheless, since both Peter Finch, President, and R. C. Smith, Executive Vice President, agreed with Brown's strong recommendation, Carey Manufacturing was acquired. Its primary asset was an aging manufacturing plant located 400 miles away from the Gardner Company's current headquarters and manufacturing facility. The Gardner Company was known for its manufacturing competency. Management hoped to add value to its new acquisition by transferring Gardner's manufacturing skills to the Carey Plant through significant process improvements.

James Carey, previous owner of Carey Manufacturing, agreed to continue serving as Plant Manager of what was now called the Carey Plant. He reported directly to the Gardner Company Executive Vice President, R. C. Smith. All functional activities of Carey Manufacturing had remained the same after the acquisition, except for sales activities being moved under Andy Doyle, Gardner's Vice President of Marketing. The 5 Carey Manufacturing salesmen were retained and allowed to keep their same sales territories. They exclusively sold only products made in the Carey Plant. The other Carey Plant functional departments (Human Resources, Engineering, Finance, Materials, Quality Assurance, and Operations) were supervised by Managers who directly reported to the Carey Plant Manager. The Managers of the Human Resources, Engineering, Materials, and Operations Departments also reported indirectly (shown by dotted lines in **Exhibit 1**) to the Vice Presidents in charge of their respective function at Gardner Company headquarters.

Until its acquisition, Carey Manufacturing (now the Carey Plant) had been a successful firm with few problems. Following its purchase, however, the plant had been plagued by labor

This case was prepared by Professors Thomas L. Wheelen of the University of South Florida and J. David Hunger of the Iowa State University. Names and dates in the case have been disguised. An earlier version of this case was presented to the 2000 annual meeting of the North American Case Research Association. This case may not be reproduced in any form without written permission of the 2 copyright holders. This case was edited for SMBP-8th Edition. Copyright © 2001 by Thomas L. Wheelen and J. David Hunger. Reprinted by permission.

Exhibit 1
Gardner Company Organization Chart

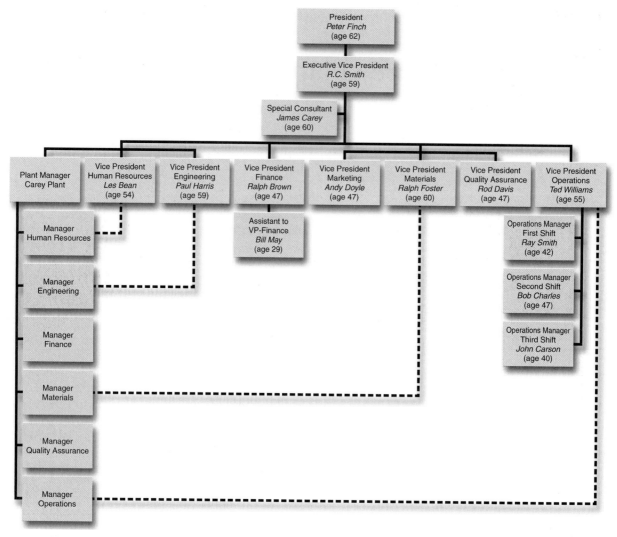

Note: Dotted lines show an indirect reporting relationship.

problems, increasing costs, a leveling of sales, and a decline in profits (**Exhibit 2**). Two years ago, the Carey Plant suffered a 10-week strike called by its union in response to demands from the new management (Gardner Company) for increased production without a corresponding increase in pay. (Although Gardner Company was also unionized, its employees were represented by a different union than were the Carey Plant employees.) Concerned by both the strike and the poor performance of the Carey Plant since its purchase 2 years earlier, Ralph Brown initiated a study last year to identify what was wrong. He discovered that the poor performance of the Carey Plant resulted not only from its outdated and overcrowded manufacturing facility, but also from James Carey's passive role as Plant Manager. Gardner's Executive Committee (composed of the President and 8 Vice Presidents) had been aware of the poor condition of the Carey Plant when it had agreed to the acquisition. It had therefore initiated plans to replace the aging plant. A new state-of-the-art manufacturing facility was being built on available property adjacent to the current plant and should be completed within a few months. The information regarding James Carey was, however, quite surprising to the

Exhibit 2

Carey Plant: Recent Sales and Profit Figures

Year	Sales	Profits
5 Years Ago	$12,430,002	$697,042
4 Years Ago	13,223,804	778,050
3 Years Ago	14,700,178	836,028
2 Years Ago	10,300,000	(220,000)*
Last Year	13,950,000	446,812

*Ten-week strike during October, November, December.

Committee. Before Gardner's purchase of Carey Manufacturing, James Carey had been actively involved in every phase of his company's operations. Since selling the company, however, Carey had delegated the running of the plant to his staff, the Department Managers. One of his Managers admitted that "He was the driving force of the company, but since he sold out, he has withdrawn completely from the management of the plant."

After hearing Brown's report, the Executive Committee decided that the Carey Plant needed a new Plant Manager. Consequently, James Carey was relieved of his duties as Plant Manager in early January this year and appointed special consultant to the Executive Vice President, R. C. Smith. The current staff of the Carey Plant was asked to continue operating the plant until a new Plant Manager could be named. Vice Presidents Brown and Williams were put in charge of finding a new Manager for the Carey Plant. They recommended several internal candidates to the Executive Vice President, R. C. Smith.

The Offer

On January 31 of this year, Smith offered the Plant Manager position of the Carey Plant to Bill May, current Assistant to Ralph Brown. May had spent 6 years in various specialist capacities within Gardner's Finance Department after being hired with an MBA. He had been in his current position for the past 2 years. Brown supported the offer to May with praise for his subordinate. "He has outstanding analytical abilities, drive, general administrative skills and is cost conscious. He is the type of man we need at the Carey Plant." The other executives viewed May not only as the company's efficiency expert, but also as a person who would see any job through to completion. Nevertheless, several of the Vice Presidents expressed opposition to placing a staff person in charge of the new plant. They felt the Plant Manager should have a strong technical background and line management experience. Brown, in contrast, stressed the necessity of a control-conscious person to get the new plant underway. Smith agreed that Gardner needed a person with a strong finance background heading the new plant.

Smith offered May the opportunity to visit the Carey Plant to have a private talk with each of his future staff. Each of the 6 Department Managers had been with the Carey Plant for a minimum of 18 years. They were frank in their discussions of past problems in the plant and in its future prospects. They generally agreed that the plant's labor problems should decline in the new plant, even though it was going to employ the same 405 employees (half the size of Gardner) with the same union. Four of them were concerned, however, with how they were being supervised. Ever since the acquisition by the Gardner Company, the Managers of the Operations, Materials, Human Resources, and Engineering Departments reported not only to James Carey as Plant Manager, but also to their respective functional Vice Presidents and staff at Gardner headquarters. Suggestions from the various Vice Presidents and staff assistants often conflicted with orders from the Plant Manager. When they confronted James Carey about the situation, he had merely shrugged. Carey told them to expect this sort of thing after an acquisition. "It's important that you get along with your new bosses, since they are the ones who will decide your future in this firm," advised Carey.

Bill May then met in mid-February with Ralph Brown, his current supervisor, to discuss the job offer over morning coffee. Turning to Brown, he said, "I'm worried about this Plant Manager's position. I will be in a whole new environment. I'm a complete stranger to those Department Managers, except for the Finance Manager. I will be the first member of the Gardner Company to be assigned to the Carey Plant. I will be functioning in a line position without any previous experience and no technical background in machine operations. I also honestly feel that several of the Vice Presidents would like to see me fail. I'm not sure if I should accept the job. I have a lot of questions, but I don't know where to get the answers." Looking over his coffee cup as he took a drink, Brown responded, "Bill, this is a great opportunity for you. What's the problem?" Adjusting himself in his chair, May looked directly at his mentor. "The specific details of the offer are very vague in terms of salary, responsibilities, and authority. What is expected of me and when? Do I have to keep the current staff? Do I have to hire future staff members from internal sources or can I go outside the company? Finally, I'm concerned about the lack of an actual job description." Brown was surprised by his protégé's many concerns. "Bill, I'm hoping that all of these questions, except for salary, will soon be answered at a meeting Smith is scheduling for you tomorrow with the Vice Presidents. He wants it to be an open forum."

The Meeting

The next morning, May took the elevator to the third floor. As he walked down the hall to the Gardner Company Executive Committee conference room, he bumped into Ted Williams, Vice President of Manufacturing, who was just coming out of his office. Looking at Bill, Ted offered, "I want to let you know that I'm behind you 100%. I wasn't at first, but I do think you may have what it takes to turn that place around. I don't care what the others think." As the 2 of them entered the conference room, May looked at the 8 Gardner Vice Presidents. Some were sitting at the conference table and working on their lap tops while others were getting some coffee from the decanter in the corner. R. C. Smith was already seated at the head of the table. Ralph Brown, sitting on 1 side of the table, motioned to May to come sit in an empty chair beside him. "Want some coffee?" Brown asked. "Good idea," responded May as he walked over to the decanter. Pouring cream into his coffee, May wondered, "What am I getting myself into?"

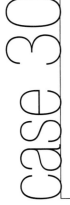

Arm & Hammer[1]: Poised for Growth?

Roy A. Cook

The arm of Vulcan, the mythical hammer-wielding god of fire, first appeared on baking soda packages produced by Cofounder Austin Church in 1867. Since then, the ARM & HAMMER™ brand has earned the confidence of 6 generations of Americans and is recognized as 1 of the nation's best known and most trusted logos.[2]

Background

For 150 years, Church & Dwight Company, Inc., worked to build market share on a brand name that was rarely associated with the company. This brand name became so pervasive that it could be found on a variety of consumer products in 95% of all U.S. households. As the world's largest producer and marketer of sodium bicarbonate-based products, Church & Dwight had until the early 1900s achieved fairly consistent growth in both sales and earnings as new and expanded uses were found for sodium bicarbonate. Sodium bicarbonate is used in many products because it can perform a variety of functions, including cleaning, deodorizing, leavening, and buffering. Although Church & Dwight may not be a household name, the company's ubiquitous yellow box of ARM & HAMMER Baking Soda is.

Shortly after its introduction in 1878, ARM & HAMMER Baking Soda became a fundamental item on the pantry shelf as homemakers found many uses for it other than baking, such as cleaning and deodorizing. It can also be used as a dentrifice, a chemical agent to absorb or neutralize odors and acidity, a kidney dialysis element, a blast medium, and a pollution control agent. It is also showing promise as a potential treatment for osteoporosis.

From the 1980s through the early 1990s, company sales, on average, increased almost 15% annually. However, the stated strategy of "selling related products in different markets all linked by common carbonate and bicarbonate technology"[3] faltered and sales growth plateaued in 1993. As the Chairman of 1 investment company said, "The only thing they had going for them [was] their uniqueness and they lost it. They made poor marketing and operating decisions that cost them a lot of money."[4]

Faced with investment community concerns and a string of disappointing financial results, Robert A. Davies III, President and Chief Executive Officer (CEO), articulated 2 key

Exhibit 1

Consolidated Statements of Income: Church & Dwight Company, Inc.
(Dollar amounts in thousands, except per share data)

Year Ending December 31	1997	1996	1995	1994
Net sales	$574,906	$527,771	$485,759	$491,048
Cost of sales	330,682	306,047	289,734	281,271
Gross profit	244,224	221,724	196,025	209,777
Selling, general, and administrative expenses	213,668	194,461	183,669	201,362
Restructuring charges	—	—	3,987	6,941
Income from operations	30,556	27,263	8,369	1,474
Equity in joint venture income	6,057	5,140	7,389	7,874
Investment earnings	1,666	1,544	1,249	655
Gain on disposal of product lines	—	—	339	410
Other income	1,320	(424)	201	209
Interest expense	(912)	(352)	(1,255)	(890)
Income before taxes	38,687	33,171	16,292	9,732
Income taxes	14,181	11,943	6,140	3,615
Net income	$ 24,506	$ 21,228	$ 10,152	$ 6,117

Source: Company records.

financial objectives for the company in 1996. The first was to raise operating margins from around 7% to 10% by 1998. The second was to achieve annual sales gains in the high single- or low double-digit range.[5] The financial picture for Church & Dwight during these transitional years from 1994 to 1997 is captured in the financial statements shown in **Exhibits 1** and **2**.

Management

The historically slow but steady course that Church & Dwight has traveled reflects top management's efforts to focus the company's activities. The ability to remain focused may be attributable to the fact that more than 50% of the outstanding shares of common stock have been owned by descendants of the company's Cofounders. Dwight C. Minton, a direct descendant of Austin Church, directed the company as CEO from 1969 through 1995. He became a member of the Board in 1965 and succeeded his father as Chairman of the Board in 1981. Although Minton remained on the Board, he stepped down as CEO and passed those duties on to the first nonfamily member in the company's history, Robert A. Davies, III.

Although Davies was a nonfamily member, he had a long history of service with Church & Dwight. He served as Vice President, General Manager of the Arm & Hammer Division, and then as President/Chief Operating Officer from 1969 through 1984. Davies continued to expand his experiences by serving as President and CEO of California Home Brands (a group of canning companies). In 1995, he returned to Church & Dwight as President of the Arm & Hammer Division to put the division "back on track."[6] Commenting on the change in leadership, Minton stated, "The effect of [Davies'] presence with us today is seen in an improved marketing focus and tighter cost structure."[7]

Many companies with strong brand names in the consumer products field have been susceptible to leveraged buy-outs and hostile takeovers. However, a series of calculated actions spared Church & Dwight's management from having to make last-minute decisions to ward off unwelcome suitors. Besides maintaining majority control of the outstanding common stock, management proposed, and the Board amended the company's charter in 1986. This amendment gave current shareholders 4 votes per share but required future shareholders to buy and hold shares for 4 years before receiving the same privilege. The Board of Directors was also structured into 3 classes containing 4 directors in each class to serve staggered 3-year terms.

Exhibit 2

Consolidated Balance Sheets: Church & Dwight Company, Inc.
(Dollar amounts in thousands)

Year Ending December 31	1997	1996	1995	1994
Assets				
Current assets				
Cash and cash equivalents	$ 14,949	$ 22,902	$ 11,355	$ 4,659
Short-term investments	3,993	5,011	5,027	2,976
Accounts receivable, less allowances of				
$1,532, $1,478, $1,304, and $912	49,566	41,837	44,427	44,404
Inventories	61,275	48,887	41,349	55,078
Current portion of note receivable	4,131	—	—	—
Deferred income taxes	9,802	11,962	11,704	10,820
Prepaid expenses	5,727	4,920	5,313	5,268
Total current assets	149,443	135,519	119,175	123,205
Property, plant, and equipment (net)	142,343	138,371	144,339	138,460
Note receivable from joint venture	6,869	11,000	11,000	11,000
Equity investment in affiliates	26,871	16,211	11,258	13,868
Long-term supply contract	2,775	3,314	3,852	4,391
Intangibles and other assets	22,713	3,556	3,556	3,556
Total assets	$351,014	$307,971	$293,180	$294,480
Liabilities and shareholders' equity				
Current liabilities				
Short-term borrowings	$ 32,000	—	$ 5,000	$ 25,000
Accounts payable and accrued expenses	92,090	93,375	86,815	72,974
Current portion of long-term debt	685	—	—	—
Income taxes payable	1,456	5,379	5,286	1,802
Total current liabilities	126,231	98,754	97,101	99,776
Long-term debt	6,815	7,500	7,500	7,500
Deferred income taxes	20,578	20,005	19,573	18,887
Deferred income	—	—	—	339
Deferred liabilities	3,786	2,392	1,595	1,176
Nonpension postretirement and postemployment benefits	14,263	14,008	13,729	12,861
Shareholders' equity				
Common stock—$1 par value	23,330	23,330	23,330	23,330
Additional paid-in capital	34,097	33,364	33,061	32,823
Retained earnings	197,622	182,069	169,438	167,901
Cumulative translation adjustments	(591)	(194)	(686)	(741)
	254,458	238,569	225,143	223,313
Less common stock in treasury, at cost	(74,568)	(72,708)	(70,501)	(69,372)
Due from officers	(549)	(549)	(960)	—
Total shareholders' equity	179,341	165,312	153,682	153,941
Total liabilities and shareholders' equity	$351,014	$307,971	$293,180	$294,480

Source: Company records.

As a further deterrent to would-be suitors or unwelcome advances, the company entered into an employee severance agreement in 1989 with key officials. This agreement provided severance pay of up to 3 times the individual's highest annual salary and bonus plus benefits for the preceding 3 years if the individual were terminated within 1 year after a change in control of the company. Change of control was defined as "the acquisition by a person or group of 25% or more of company common stock; a change in the majority of the Board of Directors not approved by the pre-change Board of Directors; or the approval by the stockholders of the company or a merger, consolidation, liquidation, dissolution, or sale of all the assets of the company."[8]

As Church & Dwight pushed more aggressively into the consumer products field, several changes were made in key management positions. The current roster of key officers along with their ages, positions, and original dates of employment are shown in **Exhibit 3**. Several of these individuals, including Davies, Bendure, Crilly, Kornhauser, Koslow, and Wilcaukas, brought extensive marketing experience to the top management team.

In addition to the many changes that had taken place in key management positions, changes also began to be made in the composition of the Board of Directors. As of July 30, 1998, the Board of Directors was expanded from 12 to 13 members. Prior to this change, 2 new Board members were added in 1992 and 1 was added in 1995. Excluding these additions to the Board, the average length of service for the 9 remaining members was 21 years. The mid-year 1998 change brought in a replacement for a retiring Director who had served for over 29 years and 1 new Board member. Four of the 5 Directors who were elected since 1992 brought significant experience in the consumer products field to the Board. They had gained these experiences from companies such as Frito-Lay, Pepsi-Cola International, California Home Brands, Diamond Crystal Salt, Lever Brothers Personal Products, Johnson & Johnson International, and McNeil Consumer Products.[9, 10]

Exhibit 3

Key Officers and Their Management Positions: Church & Dwight Company, Inc.

Name	Age	Positions	Anniversary Date
Robert A. Davies, III	62[1]	President and Chief Executive Officer	1995
Raymond L. Bendure, Ph.D.	54[1]	Vice President Research and Development	1995
Mark A. Bilawsky	50[1]	Vice President, General Counsel and Secretary	1976
Mark G. Conish	45[1]	Vice President Manufacturing and Distribution	1993
James P. Crilly	55[1]	Vice President Arm & Hammer Division	1995
Zvi Eiref	59[1]	Vice President Finance and Chief Financial Officer	1995
Dennis M. Moore	47[1]	Vice President/General Manager International Operations/Business Development	1980
Eugene F. Wilcaukas	55[1]	Vice President, President and Chief Operating Officer Specialty Products Division	1997
Leo T. Belill	57[2]	Vice President Specialty Products Division	1986
Alfred H. Falter	48[2]	Vice President Corporate Purchasing	1979
W. Patrick Fiedler	49[2]	Vice President Sales and Marketing, Specialty Products Division	1995
Gary P. Halker	47[2]	Vice President, Controller and Chief Information Officer	1977
Jaap Ketting	46[2]	Vice President—Brazil	1987
Henry Kornhauser	65[2]	Vice President—Advertising	1997
Larry B. Koslow	46[2]	Vice President Marketing Personal Care, Arm & Hammer Division	1995
Ronald D. Munson	55[2]	Vice President International Operations, Specialty Products Division	1983
Joyce F. Srednicki	53[2]	Vice President Marketing Household Products, Arm & Hammer Division	1997

Notes:
1. Executive Officers serving for such term as the Board of Directors shall determine.
2. Executive Officers serving for such term as determined and at the discretion of the Chief Executive Officer.

Source: Church & Dwight Co., Inc., *Notice of Annual Meeting of Stockholders and Proxy Statement*, 1998, p. 7.

Consumer Products

Not only had the ARM & HAMMER logo become a trusted consumer trademark, but baking soda also became synonymous with environmental safety in consumers' minds. Church & Dwight had long been known for environmental education, conservation, and products that were environmentally sound, as can be seen in the following statement:

> From nineteenth-century trading cards and "Books of Valuable Recipes" to twentieth-century print advertisements and radio and television commercials, a wide range of communication tools educated the public to the many attributes of baking soda. While the media have changed drastically since the early years, the message has been consistent: ARM & HAMMER Baking Soda is a safe, natural, pure-food product with a unique variety of applications.[11]

Church & Dwight has selected an overall family branding strategy to further penetrate the consumer products market in the United States and Canada by introducing additional products displaying the ARM & HAMMER logo. The ARM & HAMMER brand controls a commanding 85% of the baking soda market. By capitalizing on its easily recognizable brand name logo, and established marketing channels, Church & Dwight has moved into such products as laundry detergent (approximately 4% of the market), carpet cleaners and deodorizers (approximately 28% of the market), air deodorizers (approximately 13% of the market), toothpaste (approximately 7% of the market), and deodorant/antiperspirants (less than 2% of the market). This strategy has allowed the company to promote multiple products using only 1 brand name.

The strategy to move more aggressively into the consumer products arena can be traced to Dwight Minton. From the company's founding until 1970, it produced and sold only 2 consumer products: ARM & HAMMER Baking Soda and a laundry product marketed under the name Super Washing Soda. In 1970, under Minton, Church & Dwight began testing the consumer products market by introducing a phosphate-free, powdered laundry detergent, which has since been reformulated. Several other products, including a liquid laundry detergent, fabric softener sheets, an all-fabric bleach, tooth powder and toothpaste, baking soda chewing gum, deodorant/antiperspirants, deodorizers (carpet, room, and pet), and clumping cat litter have been added to the expanding list of ARM & HAMMER brands. However, in a recent move, the company departed from its previous strategy of developing new product offerings in-house by buying several well-known consumer brands such as Brillo®, Parsons® Ammonia, Cameo® Aluminum & Stainless Steel Cleaner, Rain Drops® water softener, SNO BOWL® toilet bowl cleaner, and TOSS 'N SOFT® dryer sheets from The Dial Corporation.

The company's largest selling consumer product line continued to be laundry detergent, capturing approximately 4% of the market. "Despite a virtual absence of advertising, the detergent is positioned to offer quality cleaning at a substantial discount (15–20%) to Procter & Gamble's Tide."[12] The mature $4.3 billion domestic soap detergent market was growing at less than 1% annually, but it was far from tranquil. Environmental concerns continued to increase, and competition from the introduction of innovative products intensified. During 1992 and 1993, Church & Dwight allowed its laundry detergents pricing structure to move above its targeted differential of 15–20% discount without any supporting advertising, which resulted in market share erosion. "A 10% price decrease, implemented in December 1993, effectively corrected this price relationship by the middle of 1994."[13] Although this move stopped market share loss, growth in this highly competitive segment has been elusive. New low-cost entrants such as USA Detergents and Huish Detergents have shifted the playing field to a pricing emphasis.[14]

Faced with the problems of a mature domestic market, marketers often rely on a segmentation approach to gain market share. New consumer products must muscle their way into markets by taking market share from current offerings. Church & Dwight also began to focus its attention outside the United States and Canada. The key difference in the U.S. and Canadian markets was that they were both marketing driven, whereas the markets in the rest of the world were still product driven.[15]

The company's household consumer products have traditionally been heavily promoted (but not advertised) and sold at prices below market leaders. At times, these price differentials were as much as 25%. Church & Dwight had to modify this generic strategy somewhat as it rolled out ARM & HAMMER Dental Care from regional test markets.

The task of successfully implementing a nationwide marketing campaign is not new to the company. In 1972, with Davies heading up the Arm & Hammer Division, Church & Dwight made marketing history when it introduced ARM & HAMMER Baking Soda as a refrigerator deodorizer. A national television advertising campaign and point-of-sale promotions in grocery stores were used. The outcome was accelerated growth and a 74% increase in volume over a 3-year period.[16]

The company's consumer products strategy has been focused on niche markets to avoid a head-on attack from competitors with more financial and marketing clout. In exploring new and existing markets, the common thread was to seek new uses of the basic baking soda ingredient for loyal users. To further this objective, Church & Dwight developed its own consumer research studies on trends in baking soda use for health care and household applications, identifying users by age, gender, income level, and education level.[17]

The company's most recent and aggressive entrants into the consumer products market have been its dental care products. Although it entered a crowded field of specialty products, Church & Dwight planned to ride the crest of increasing interest by both dentists and hygienists in baking soda as an important element in a regimen for maintaining dental health.[18] Church & Dwight was able to sneak up on the giants in the industry and moved rapidly from the position of a niche player in the toothpaste market (along with products such as Topol, Viadent, Check-Up, Zact, and Tom's of Maine) to that of a major competitor. In only 5 years, the company captured market share (almost 10%) and the attention of major competitors. These competitors were initially slow to react to this new category of dental care products, but they finally responded through new product offerings, heavy promotions, and price cuttings to stem market share loss.

Church & Dwight's dramatic success in penetrating the toothpaste market did not go unnoticed nor unchallenged. Both Procter & Gamble and Colgate introduced similar products. In addition, Procter & Gamble indicated that it would compete on a price basis (possibly lowering prices on baking soda toothpaste by as much as 30%) supported by heavy advertising. This fiercely competitive $2 billion market continues to attract a great deal of attention and marketing emphasis from a variety of key players, as can be seen in **Exhibit 4**.[19, 20]

Exhibit 4

Market Share of Niche Toothpaste Products

Brand	Market Share		
	1997	**1995**	**1992**
Crest	27%	30%	31%
Colgate	19	18	22
Mentadent	11	11	0
Aqua Fresh	11	8	9
ARM & HAMMER	7	7	10

Sources: Advertising Age, April 21, 1997, p. 16; Zachary Schiller, *Business Week*, August 14, 1995, p. 48; and Kathleen Deveny, "Toothpaste Makers Tout New Packaging," *Wall Street Journal*, November 10, 1992, p. B-1.

Baking soda–based toothpastes accounted for 30% of all sales in the domestic toothpaste market. This phenomenal growth continued to attract new entrants such as Unilever PLC, Chesebrough-Pond Inc. (Mentadent), and Warner-Lambert Co. (Listerine Cool Mint). "Competition remains robust, as new brands continue to appear and existing brands expand into emerging category growth segments."[21] New and expanded consumer product offerings designed to promote improved oral care continued to drive sales growth.

Baking soda's success as a toothpaste ingredient resulted in its use in many other personal care products including mouthwash, shampoo, foot powder, and deodorant/antiperspirant. In 1994, the company rolled out an entry into the fiercely competitive deodorant/antiperspirant market with a $15 million launch of an antiperspirant with baking soda. In less than 2 years, ARM & HAMMER Deodorant Antiperspirant with Baking Soda gained almost 2.5% of an approximately $1½ billion market.[22, 23] But by 1998, its market share had eased to less than 2%.

As more and more products were added to Church & Dwight's consumer lineup, the need for additional marketing expertise grew. Along with the addition of Henry Kornhauser to the top management team in 1997, Church & Dwight brought many of its marketing tasks in house. Kornhauser brought 17 years of senior management and agency experience with him to Church & Dwight. The first major project undertaken by this new in-house function was the $15 million launch of ARM & HAMMER Dental Care Gum.[24]

For the most part, Church & Dwight's entries into the consumer products market met with success. However, some products failed to meet expectations or could even be termed failures. Most notable among the company's marketing missteps were an oven cleaner and a previously unsuccessful foray into underarm deodorants. The company eventually sold off the oven cleaner line and pulled the underarm deodorant from test markets during the mid 1970s. Another potential marketing problem may be looming on the horizon. ARM & HAMMER could be falling into the precarious line-extension snare. Placing a well-known brand name on a wide variety of products could cloud its position and cause it to lose marketing pull.[25] As the company officials looked toward the future prospects for consumer products, the following strategy was stated to guide their actions: "to establish Church & Dwight as a major factor in the $7 billion household products business, primarily using our famous trademark to market middle-priced brands acceptable to the great majority of American consumers . . . . To add to this, via acquisition, other strong brand equities capable of delivering the same objectives."[26]

Specialty Products

Church & Dwight was in an enviable position to profit from its dominant niche in the sodium bicarbonate products market because it controlled the primary raw material used in its production. The primary ingredient in sodium bicarbonate is produced from the mineral trona, which is extracted from the company's mines in southwestern Wyoming. The other ingredient, carbon dioxide, is a readily available chemical that can be obtained from a variety of sources.

The company maintained a dominant position in the production of the required raw materials for both its consumer and industrial products. It manufactured almost two thirds of the sodium bicarbonate sold in the United States and, until 1995, was the only U.S. producer of ammonium bicarbonate and potassium carbonate. In 1998 the company had the largest share (approximately 60%) of the sodium bicarbonate capacity in the United States with 430,000 tons of annual capacity in addition to 11,000 tons of production capacity in Venezuela. Its closest competitor, FMC, had an estimated annual capacity of only 70,000 tons. A third competitor, NaTec, had an estimated annual capacity of 125,000 tons. In addition, 10,000 tons per year were imported from Mexico.[27, 28, 29]

The Specialty Products Division of Church & Dwight basically consisted of the manufacture and sale of sodium bicarbonate for 3 distinct market segments: performance products, animal nutrition products, and specialty cleaning products. Manufacturers use sodium bicarbonate performance products as a leavening agent for commercial baked goods; an antacid in pharmaceuticals; a chemical in kidney dialysis; a carbon dioxide release agent in fire extinguishers; and an alkaline in swimming pool chemicals, detergents, and various textile and tanning applications. Animal feed producers use sodium bicarbonate nutritional products predominantly as a buffer, or antacid, for dairy cattle feeds, and they make a nutritional supplement that enhances milk production of dairy cattle. Sodium bicarbonate has also recently been used as an additive to poultry feeds to enhance feed efficiency. Specialty cleaning products are found in blasting (similar to sand blasting applications) as well as many emerging aqueous-based cleaning technologies such as automotive parts cleaning and circuit board cleaning.

Although management has focused increased attention on consumer products, **Exhibit 5** shows the relevant contributions of consumer products and continued importance of specialty products to total sales over a 5-year period. The stated strategy for this segment is "to solidify worldwide leadership in sodium bicarbonate and potassium carbonate, while broadening our product offerings to other related chemicals . . . to build a specialized high-margin specialty cleaning business, allying carbonate technology, the ARM & HAMMER trademark and environmental position."[30]

Fluctuations in the significance of specialty products sales can be traced to a series of acquisitions, partnership agreements, and divestitures. These included the acquisition of a 40% interest in Brotherton Chemicals Ltd., a United Kingdom producer of ammonium-based chemicals; a 49% interest in Sales y Oxidos, S.A., a Mexican producer of strontium carbonate; purchase of a 40% interest in 2 Brazilian bicarbonate and carbonate-related companies; a partnership agreement entered into with Occidental Petroleum Corp. to form Armand Products Co., which produces and markets potassium chemicals; and control of National Vitamin Products Co., which specializes in animal nutrition products. Although the flurry of chemical related acquisitions appeared to have the potential for accelerating growth, management decided to divest the National Vitamin Products Company and the 49% interest in Sales y Oxidos, S.A.

Just like the Consumer Products Division, the Specialty Products Division focused on developing new uses for the company's core product, sodium bicarbonate. With this goal in mind, a Specialty Cleaning Unit (now called Specialty Cleaning Products) was formed in 1994. This unit was created "in the anticipation that, over the next few years, many of the current solvent-based cleaning products will be regulated out of existence. This new unit will use our core, environmentally friendly carbonate and bicarbonate technology in the industrial and precision-cleaning markets to build a major position both domestically and internationally."[31]

Pollution control processes at coal-fired electrical plants where sodium compounds are used to clean flue gases may open up an entirely new market for Church & Dwight's specialty products in the environmental area. The company has tested a process whereby dry injection rather than the typical wet scrubbers can be used to remove sulfur oxide and nitrogen oxides

Exhibit 5

Percentage of Net Sales

	1997	1996	1995	1994	1993
Consumer products	80	79	78	80	81
Specialty products	20	21	22	20	19

Source: Company records.

from smokestack emissions. The company is hoping that it may help to provide solutions to the country's acid rain problems. The process of dumping baking soda into incinerators of all types to neutralize various pollutants causing acid rain has been successfully tested[32] but has not been adopted on a commercial basis. Reducing sulfur dioxide from smokestack emissions also is being explored in waste incinerator applications.

To this point, utilities have opted to use lime because it is cheaper. However, lime poses disposal problems, and bicarbonate is still being considered for flue gas desulfurization because of its environmental superiority.[33] Experiments with municipalities' adding sodium bicarbonate to their water supplies to reduce lead content have proved to be very successful. Although water treatment applications are currently providing minimal revenues, the potential for future sales is enormous.

Additional opportunities are being explored for ARMEX Blast Media. This is a sodium bicarbonate-based product used as a paint stripping compound. It gained widespread recognition when it was used successfully for the delicate task of stripping the accumulation of years of paint and tar from the interior of the Statue of Liberty without damaging the fragile copper skin. It is now being considered for other specialized applications in the transportation and electronics industries and in industrial cleaning because of its apparent environmental safety. ARMEX also has been introduced into international markets.

The company launched another specialty chemical product, ARMAKLEEN, in 1992. It is an aqueous-based cleaner used for cleaning printed circuit boards. This potentially promising product may have an enormous market because it may be able to replace chlorofluorocarbon-based cleaning systems. "ARMAKLEEN, a carbonate and bicarbonate technology, is the first nonsolvent-based system for this market."[34] Sodium bicarbonate also has been used to remove lead from drinking water and, when added to water supplies, coats the inside of pipes and prevents lead from leaching into the water. This market could grow in significance with additions to the Clean Water Bill. The search for new uses of sodium bicarbonate continues in both the consumer and industrial products divisions.

International Operations

Church & Dwight has traditionally enjoyed a great deal of success in North American markets; however, less than 5% of sales are outside the United States and Canada. It has achieved full distribution in the U.S. and Canada and limited distribution in Mexico.[35] It was not until 1994 that the company entered into the United Kingdom market with its DENTAL CARE products.[36] "Moving into overseas markets will put Church & Dwight into heightened competition with major oral-care and household product marketers such as Procter & Gamble Company, Unilever, and Colgate-Palmolive Company."[37] The Specialty Products Division has established small footholds in Venezuela and Brazil. South American markets hold the promise of rapid growth and the company is also exploring opportunities in the Far East. According to Eugene Wilcaukas, Vice President, "We've been a little late in Asia. We have a strong desire to be there and the financial ability to accomplish it."[38]

The company expanded its presence in the international consumer products markets with the acquisition of DeWitt International Corporation, which manufactures and markets personal care products including toothpaste. The DeWitt acquisition not only provided the company with increased international exposure but also with much needed toothpaste production facilities and technology. Even with this acquisition, the company still derives over 96% of its revenues from the United States and Canada. Owing to the perceived limited market potential of the DeWitt product line, Church & Dwight divested the subsidiary's brands and its overseas operations but retained its U.S. toothpaste manufacturing facilities in Greenville, South Carolina.

At the same time the company was testing the international waters for its consumer products, it was also continuing to pursue expansion of its specialty products into international markets. Attempts to enter international markets have met with limited success, probably for 2 reasons: (1) lack of name recognition and (2) transportation costs. Although ARM & HAMMER is 1 of the most recognized brand names in the United States (in the top 10), it does not enjoy the same name recognition elsewhere. In addition, "[i]nternational transportation represents 40 to 45% of Church & Dwight's sales expense, versus 5 to 10% domestically."[39] However, export opportunities continue to present themselves as 10% of all U.S. production of sodium bicarbonate is exported.

Church & Dwight's Future

The company's stated mission for the 1990s was

> We will supply customers quality ARM & HAMMER Sodium Bicarbonate and related products, while performing in the top quarter of American businesses.[40]

The core business and foundation on which the company was built remained the same after more than 150 years. However, as the new management team at Church & Dwight became established and looked to the future, they had to reflect on the successes and mistakes of the past as they planned for the future. With the proper strategic moves, the future held the opportunity to once again enhance shareholder wealth of this publicly traded, but family controlled, company.

Notes

1. ARM & HAMMER is a registered trademark of Church & Dwight Company, Inc.
2. Church & Dwight Company, Inc., *1995 Annual Report*, inside cover.
3. "C&D Sees Growth Despite Competition," *Chemical Marketing Reporter* (December 11, 1989), 236, p. 9.
4. Andrea Adelson, "Arm and Hammer Names a New President," *New York Times* (February 2, 1995), p. D3.
5. Church & Dwight Company, Inc., *1996 Annual Report*, p. 4.
6. Adelson, p. D3.
7. Letter to Stockholders, November 14,1995.
8. Church & Dwight Company, Inc., *Notice of Annual Meeting of Stockholders* (1989), p. 17.
9. Church & Dwight Company, Inc., *Notice of Annual Meeting of Stockholders and Proxy Statement* (1998).
10. "Church & Dwight Company, Inc., Announces New Board Members," *Company Press Release* (July 30, 1998).
11. *Marketing Milestones: 150th Anniversary* (1996), p. 2.
12. "C&D Sees Growth Despite Competition," p. 19.
13. Church & Dwight Company, Inc., *1994 Annual Report*, p. 1.
14. Kerri Walsh, "Soaps and Detergents," *Chemical Week* (January 29, 1998), pp. 27–29
15. Pam Weisz, "Church & Dwight in Need of Next Big Idea," *Brandweek* (November 13, 1995), p. 8.
16. Church & Dwight Company, Inc., *1988 Annual Report*.
17. Carrie M. Wainwright, "Church & Dwight: Slow But Steady into Personal Care," *Drug & Cosmetic Industry* (February 1987), p. 28.
18. David Kiley, "Arm & Hammer Mixes Its Own," *Adweek's Marketing Week* (July 4, 1988), p. 3.
19. Based on information from Towne-Oller & Associates, New York.
20. Tara Parker-Pope, "Colgate's Total Grabs Big Share of Toothpaste Sales," *Wall Street Journal* (March 6, 1998), p. B3.
21. Church & Dwight Company, Inc., *1995 Annual Report*, p. 7.
22. *Brandweek* (January 31, 1994), p. 4.
23. Bear Stearns Report, 1996.
24. Judann Pollack, "Arm & Hammer Spending Soars to Back Dental Gum," *Advertising Age* (March 23, 1998), p. 49.
25. Ronald Alsop, "Arm & Hammer Baking Soda Going in Toothpaste as Well as Refrigerator," *Wall Street Journal* (June 24, 1988), pp. 2–24.
26. Church & Dwight Company, Inc., *1997 Annual Report*, p. 10.
27. "C&D Sees Growth Despite Competition," pp. 9, 19.
28. Gretchen Busch, "New Bicarb Pact Could Have Impact on Supply Picture," *Chemical Marketing Reporter* (November 30, 1992), 242 (22).
29. *Chemical Marketing Reporter* (August 22, 1994), pp. 3+.
30. Church & Dwight Company, Inc., *1997 Annual Report*, p. 13.
31. Church & Dwight Company, Inc., *1984 Annual Report*, p. 13.
32. Kathleen Deveny, "Marketing," *Wall Street Journal* (April 27, 1990), p. B-1.
33. "Lime Wins on Price," *Chemical Marketing Reporter* (August 22, 1994), p. 17.
34. Rick Mullin, "Soaps and Detergents: New Generation of Compacts," *Chemicalweek* (January 27, 1993), p. 29.
35. Riccardo A. Davis, "Arm & Hammer Seeks Growth Abroad," *Advertising Age* (August 17, 1992), pp. 3, 42.
36. "Arm & Hammer Set for Second TV Push," *Marketing* (July 7, 1994), p. 7.
37. Davis, p. 42.
38. Robert Westervelt, "Church & Dwight Takes Brazilian Stake," *Chemical Weekly* (June 18, 1997), p. 15.
39. Robert J. Bowman, "Quality Management Comes to Global Transportation," *World Trade* (February 1993), p. 38.
40. Church & Dwight Company, Inc., *1989 Annual Report*.

Tasty Baking Company

*Ellie A. Fogarty, Joyce P. Vincelette, Thomas L. Wheelen,
and Thomas M. Patrick*

Carl S. Watts, President, CEO, and Chairman of Tasty Baking Company, was filled with mixed emotions when he looked at the date on his desk calendar. October 1, 1998, meant the beginning of Phase II of his company's broad-based planned rollout of Tastykakes to the Midwestern states. Since 1991, Tasty Baking Company had pursued a growth and geographic expansion strategy to move beyond its strong regional market on the East Coast. With Phase II, Tastykake brand snack cakes would be available in a total of 47 states! Watts couldn't help but smile as he colored in Nebraska and Kansas on his map of the United States.

What took the smile away was the realization that 3 months had passed since Interstate Bakeries, the largest wholesale bakery in the United States and maker of Hostess and Dolly Madison snack cakes, had announced its plan to acquire Drake Bakeries of New Jersey, maker of popular Northeast snack cakes Yodels and Devil Dogs and Tastykake's biggest regional competitor. This time, Tasty Baking Company had not questioned the acquisition during the 90-day period allowed for challenges and the deal was finalized the previous week. In 1987, Tasty Baking Company had successfully asserted violation of anti-trust laws when it asked the Federal Trade Commission to require the divestiture of Drake Bakeries by Ralston Purina (then owners of Continental Baking Company, makers of Hostess Snack Cakes).

The snack cake industry was consolidating faster than Watts could believe. Just last year, he had hired his own consultant to investigate acquisition possibilities for Tasty Baking Company. In the snack cake industry, it was cheaper to buy than build in terms of expansion. Watts's mind was distracted: how could he and his company concentrate on geographic expansion and the related growth pains he expected and, at the same time, confront the Interstate Bakeries competition in Tasty Baking Company's most secure market?

Company History (1914–1998)

THE EARLY YEARS

The Tasty Baking Company was incorporated on February 25, 1914, in Pennsylvania. Herbert C. Morris, a Boston egg salesman, and Philip J. Baur, a Pittsburgh baker, established a bakery in North Philadelphia to produce Tastykakes. These prewrapped, single-serving, white iced cakes were named by Morris's wife, Willavene, and retailed for 10¢ at local grocers.

This case was prepared by Ellie A. Fogarty, Business Librarian, and Professors Joyce P. Vincelette and Thomas M. Patrick of The College of New Jersey, and Professor Thomas L. Wheelen of the University of South Florida. This case was edited for SMBP-8th Edition. This case may not be reproduced in any form without written permission of the copyright holder, Thomas L. Wheelen. Copyright © 1999 by Thomas L. Wheelen. Reprinted by permission.

Morris and Baur only supplied retailers with as many cakes as they thought would sell quickly. This controlled distribution kept fresh products on the shelves and avoided losses resulting from stale goods. Their basic principle to use only the freshest ingredients to make the finest possible products continues to guide the company today.

By 1918, sales exceeded $1 million and in 1923, a 6-story plant on Hunting Park Avenue was opened. By 1930, the facility had been expanded to 5 times its original size. To increase dwindling sales during the Depression, company bakers discovered they could bake 3 chocolate cupcakes from the same amount of batter normally used for 2. They packaged them together, kept the price at a nickel, and buyers thought they were getting a better bargain. During this time, Tasty Baking Company began selling its popular single-portion, rectangular pie, shaped to fit into a lunch box.

In 1951, Philip J. Baur suffered a stroke and died at the age of 66. Paul R. Kaiser, Baur's son-in-law, became President. Herbert C. Morris accepted the post of Chairman of the Board, a position he maintained until his death in 1960.[1] Tasty Baking Company began trading on the American Stock Exchange in 1965.

ACQUISITIONS AND DIVESTITURES

In 1965, Tasty Baking Company purchased Philip and Jacobs, Inc., a family graphic arts supply business founded in the mid 1880s, as part of a diversification move. At that time, Tasty Baking Company was made up of 2 separate divisions, Tastykake and Philip and Jacobs, Inc. Through subsequent acquisitions, Philip and Jacobs, Inc., grew to become 1 of the largest distributors of supplies and equipment to the printing industry in the United States. Philip and Jacobs, Inc., was spun off to Tasty Baking Company shareholders on August 1, 1993, so that Philip and Jacobs, Inc., could pursue an expansion policy and the Tastykake Division, now the only business of the Tasty Baking Company, could focus on its core business of snack cakes. Tasty Baking Company shareholders received 2 shares of Philip and Jacobs, Inc., common stock for every 3 shares of Tasty Baking Company common stock. In September 1994, Philip and Jacobs, Inc., merged with Momentum Corporation of Washington to form PrimeSource Corporation.

Continuing to grow and diversify, Tasty Baking Company acquired Buckeye Biscuit Co. in 1966. Larami Corporation, a Philadelphia toy manufacturer, was purchased in 1970. In 1976, Tasty Baking Company acquired Ole South Foods Co., a frozen dessert manufacturer. Ole South Food's operations were then discontinued in 1979.

In 1981, Philip J. Baur, Jr., son of the Tastykake founder, became Chairman of the Board. Nelson G. Harris was named President and CEO. Harris implemented a strategic planning process, the beginning of the company's 5-year plans, and explored new products and markets. Harris upgraded the factory and equipment in the plant for $40 million. He also sold off the company's extraneous businesses: Larami Corporation in 1981 and Buckeye Biscuit Company in 1986.

Owner/Operators

In 1986, as the company began its second 5-year plan, Tasty Baking Company's 460 sales routes were sold. Sales representatives were given the opportunity to purchase the exclusive right to sell and distribute Tastykake products in defined geographical territories in the Mid-Atlantic states and become independent owner/operators. However, many interested drivers were unable to obtain financing at the bank (in some cases, routes cost as much as $50,000). To assist the independent owner/operators in the purchase of the routes, the company arranged financing with a group of Philadelphia banks. Each owner/operator who elected to accept this financing signed a note for the purchase of the route and placed the route as security on the loan. In addition, Tasty Baking Company agreed that, at the bank's option, the company would repurchase any route in loan default. Selling the routes raised $16 million for the company. The owner/operators grasped this entrepreneurial opportunity and worked harder, faster, and better with a resulting increase in sales. In 1997, a route sold for 10 times its weekly sales. Five thousand dollars in weekly sales was typical of most routes. Tasty Baking Company provided financial assistance through its subsidiary, Tasty Baking Company Financial Services, Inc. As the route grew and prospered, parts could be sold to new owner/operators. Approval from Tasty Baking Company was needed before any existing routes or parts of routes were sold.

In 1995, the company was contacted by the IRS regarding the owner/operators' employee status. Tasty Baking Company treated them as independent contractors and did not pay FICA taxes on them. The IRS argued that independent contractors could take the jobs they wanted and decline the ones they didn't want. They could work for several companies at a time. This was not the case with Tasty Baking Company's owner/operators. By 1997, the dispute was resolved. Tasty Baking Company took a $1.95 million charge in its fourth quarter to cover penalties assessed by the IRS for unpaid taxes from 1990 to 1997. Tasty Baking Company now treats its owner/operators as "statutory employees" for payroll tax purposes only.[2]

Dutch Mill

In 1995, Tasty Baking Company completed its first acquisition of a competing bakery in the company's 81-year history. Tasty Baking Company, the fourth largest baking company in the United States and the Mid-Atlantic region's leading snack cake producer, purchased Dutch Mill Baking Company for $1.87 million. Dutch Mill, a New Jersey–based baker of donuts, all-natural muffins, cookies, and fat-free angel food cake, maintained an 11% market share (ranked number 3) in northern New Jersey and metropolitan New York City, the largest retail food market in the United States. Tasty Baking Company had only a 1% share of the $100 million snack cake market in New York City at the time.[3]

Carl S. Watts, who was elected President and CEO after Harris retired in 1992, stated that, "the acquisition of Dutch Mill Baking Company supplements our core strategic plan which is to build our baseline business through geographic expansion and new product development. Dutch Mill will complement our efforts quite nicely and will allow for possible sales and marketing synergies to be exchanged between the 2 brands."[4]

STRATEGIC ALLIANCES

Although the Schmidt Baking Company in Baltimore has been delivering Tastykakes along the Eastern shore of Maryland for over 40 years, the 1990s marked the beginning of an era of strategic distribution alliances for Tasty Baking Company. In 1991, when the company's management team drafted its third 5-year plan, the company was looking to geographically expand its markets.

In 1992, Tasty Baking Company formed a partnership with Kroger Stores, 1 of the nation's largest grocery chains, to distribute Tastykake products to its 1,200 supermarkets in the Southeast and Midwest. Kroger baked English muffins that Tasty Baking Company bought and distributed on its routes under the Tastykake name. In exchange, Tasty Baking Company bought 600,000 to 700,000 pounds of peanut butter annually from a Kroger subsidiary. The Kroger arrangement gave the Tastykake brand legitimacy as it established a distribution foothold in new territories. In 1993, Tasty Baking Company joined up with Merita Bakery, a division of Interstate Bakeries Corporation, to sell Tastykake cakes and pies in Florida and Georgia and in Fry's Food & Drug Stores in Phoenix, Arizona.[5]

In an attempt to penetrate the largest snack cake market, metropolitan New York City, Tasty Baking Company entered into a distribution agreement with Frito-Lay in January 1994. This marked the first time Tastykakes were delivered on a route operated by a nonbakery company. Frito-Lay, the food division of PepsiCo Inc., distributed Tasty Baking Company's snack cakes, donuts, and cookies to supermarkets, convenience stores, and other retail outlets along the company's 200 routes. However, the potato chips and other salty snacks produced by Frito-Lay had a 30-90 day shelf-life, much longer than a snack cake, which had a 4 to 7 day shelf-life. Incompatible delivery schedules led to the termination of Tasty Baking Company's agreement with Frito-Lay in 1995.

In April 1994, Tasty Baking Company negotiated a marketing agreement that made it the exclusive supplier of snack cakes to 500 Wawa convenience stores in Connecticut, Pennsylvania, New Jersey, Delaware, and Maryland, pushing out Hostess, Dolly Madison, and some other brands.

WESTWARD EXPANSION

Chicago

Tastykakes made their way into the Chicago market during the summer of 1997. In June, 187 Jewel Food Stores began offering a 10-item line of family packs shipped fresh 3 times a week via tractor trailer. Direct-store delivery was handled by the Chicago-based Alpha Baking Company with additional support by The Sell Group, a food brokerage company. Tasty Baking Company leveraged its high market share in the Philadelphia area in its negotiations with Jewel. Jewel and ACME Markets, a major grocery chain in the Northeast with whom Tasty Baking Company had an established, strong relationship, were owned by American Stores of Salt Lake City, Utah. Tasty Baking Company worked with national product people in Utah to put together the comprehensive distribution program. Tasty Baking Company picked products from its portfolio of 100 SKUs to optimize the product mix to guarantee the success of the brand over time and to ensure that the products didn't duplicate one another in icings, fillings, and form.[6]

By August 1997, Tastykakes had entered 177 of Southland Corporation's 7-Eleven convenience stores in Chicago. Tasty Baking Company was participating in 7-Eleven's Combined Distribution Center (CDC) program. In the past, the CDC concept had encountered difficulties with short shelf-life products like snack cakes, which perform significantly better with a direct-store door (DSD) system due to the relatively perishable nature of the product. Fortunately Tasty Baking Company switched to a new packaging film that had become available to extend the shelf-life of its snack cakes to 21 days from 7 to 10 days.

In January 1998, Tasty Baking Company made its Tastykakes available in all 104 Dominick's Supermarkets in Chicago. Tasty Baking Company kicked off its entry into Chicago with broadcast and print ad campaigns using radio, free-standing inserts (FSIs), and in-store media. Later, Tasty Baking Company added Eagle and Kroger Supermarkets to its account list in Chicago. By the spring of 1998, on an annual run rate, Tasty Baking Company had a 5% market share in Chicago, taking share from Hostess, the category leader.[7]

Colorado

Continuing its relationship with 7-Eleven, Tasty Baking Company entered 240-plus 7-Eleven stores from Denver and Colorado Springs to Pueblo, Fort Collins, and Grand Junction in October 1997. Tasty Baking Company supported this move with 405 spot radio ads in the Denver/Boulder metropolitan area.[8]

Ohio

Tastykakes were introduced to 100 Super Kmart, Sparkle, Heinen's, Food Centre, and other stores from Youngstown to Lorain (Cleveland area) in May 1998. Only one fourth of Tastykake's product line was selected to distribute to Ohio with the direct route sales method. Tastykake fruit pies were considered too fragile to ship and would be available only on the East Coast.[9]

West Coast

Tasty Baking Company began a rollout to the 249 Luck Stores in Southern California and Nevada in the summer of 1998. This was seen as a key market for Tastykake's Tropical Delights line of snack cakes, a refreshing tasting vanilla cake filled with guava, coconut, papaya, or pineapple filling and topped with coconut, which was targeted to the Latino consumer and those in warmer climates. Tasty Baking Company reached others on the West Coast and the Pacific Northwest through a wholesaler network with Coremark International, the number 2 wholesaler in the nation.

Midwest Expansion

In August 1998, Tasty Baking Company began Phase I of a broad-based planned rollout of its products to the Dakotas, Minnesota, Wisconsin, Michigan, Illinois, and parts of Iowa. Metz Baking Company, a major manufacturer and distributor of bread, rolls and other bakery products in the Midwest and North Central United States, distributed top-selling family packs of Tastykakes on approximately 650 of its direct-store delivery routes to grocery stores. The effort was supported with a major ad campaign including radio, consumer promotions, FSI-coupons, in-store displays, and consumer sampling. Phase II, begun in October 1998, included 300 more routes to Nebraska, Kansas, and more areas of Iowa.[10]

In 1998, Tasty Baking Company manufactured over 100 varieties of snack cakes, donuts, cookies, pies, and muffins. Independent owner/operators and distributors sold these products in 47 states, Washington D.C., and Puerto Rico. Tasty Baking Company dominated the Philadelphia market, holding 64% share of the snack cake segment.

Corporate Governance

BOARD OF DIRECTORS

Philip J. Baur, Jr., retired as Chairman of the Board on January 22, 1998, a position he had held since 1981. Mr. Baur had been a Director of the company since 1954. He was a Director of PrimeSource Corporation. Mr. Baur controlled 3%, or approximately 251,309 shares of common stock.[11] (See **Exhibit 1** for the Board of Directors and the Executive Officers.)

Carl S. Watts was elected a Director in April 1992. In 1998, he held 2%, or 130,397 shares of common stock. Watts, who started at Tasty Baking Company in 1967 as a route driver and held a variety of positions in the Sales and Marketing Department before being appointed Vice President of Sales and Marketing in 1985 and President of the Tastykake Division in 1989, was elected President and CEO and remains in that position today. On January 23, 1998, Watts succeeded Philip J. Baur, Jr., as Chairman of the Board of Directors.

No other Director or Executive Officer controlled 1% or more of the company's common stock. All Directors and Executive Officers as a group owned approximately 8% of outstanding stock.

Nelson G. Harris was elected a Director of Tasty Baking Company in April 1979, President of the company in September 1979, CEO in April 1981, and Chairman and CEO in February 1991, in which capacity he served until his retirement on May 1, 1992. Harris served as Chairman of the Executive Committee of the Board of Directors. He was a Director of American Water Works Company, Inc., and Rittenhouse Trust Company.[12]

Judith M. von Seldeneck was elected a Director in July 1991. She was the CEO of Diversified Search Companies, a general executive search firm. Von Seldeneck was also a Director of CoreStates Financial Corporation, Keystone Insurance Company, and Triple A MidAtlantic. James L. Everett, III, a retired CEO of PECO Energy Company, served as a Director of Tasty Baking Company since 1970.[13]

Exhibit 1

Board of Directors and Executive Officers: Tasty Baking Company

Board of Directors	Executive Officers
Philip J. Baur, Jr. Retired Chairman of the Board	**Carl S. Watts** Chairman, President and Chief Executive Officer
Carl S. Watts Chairman, President and Chief Executive Officer	**John M. Pettine** Vice President and Chief Financial Officer
Nelson G. Harris Chairman of the Executive Committee	**William E. Mahoney** Vice President, Human Resources
Fred C. Aldridge, Jr., Esq. Attorney-at-law	**Elizabeth H. Gemmill, Esq.** Vice President and Secretary
G. Fred DiBona, Jr. President and CEO, Independence Blue Cross	**Paul M. Woite** Vice President, Manufacturing
John M. Pettine Vice-President and Chief Financial Officer	**W. Dan Nagle** Vice President, Sales and Marketing
James L. Everett, III Retired Chairman of the Board, PECO Energy Company	**Daniel J. Decina** Treasurer and Controller
Judith M. von Seldeneck Chief Executive Officer, Diversified Search Companies	**Eugene P. Malinowski** Assistant Treasurer
	Thomas M. Lubiski Assistant Controller
	Edward J. Delahunty Assistant Secretary
	Colleen M. Henderson Assistant Secretary

Source: Tasty Baking Company, *1995 Annual Report,* p. 32.

Fred C. Aldridge, Jr., a retired senior partner of the Philadelphia law firm of Stradley, Ronon, Stevens & Young, was elected a Director in 1981. He was President of The Grace S. and W. Linton Nelson Foundation and President of Preston Drainage Company. John M. Pettine was elected a Director in April 1992. He had served as Vice President, Finance, since December 1983 and had been elected Vice President and Chief Financial Officer of the company in April 1991. Both Aldridge and Pettine were Directors of PrimeSource Corporation.[14]

G. Fred DiBona, Jr., was elected a Director in 1998. DiBona was president and CEO of Independence Blue Cross since 1990. He was also a Director of Philadelphia Suburban Corporation, Pennsylvania Savings Bank, and Magellan Health Services, Inc., and Chairman of the Blue Cross and Blue Shield Association.[15]

EXECUTIVE OFFICERS

William E. Mahoney was elected Vice President, Human Resources in December 1984. He joined the company in 1972 and served as Director of Industrial Relations and Personnel from 1982 to 1984. Paul M. Woite was elected Vice President, Manufacturing, on April 21, 1995. Woite was Manager, Maintenance Operations from May 1989 to October 1993 and Director, Engineering & Maintenance, from October 1993 to April 1995. He joined the company in 1963. W. Dan Nagle was elected Vice President, Sales and Marketing, in November 1989. He joined the company in 1984 as Director of Marketing and became Director of National Sales in 1986.[16] (See **Exhibit 1** for the Board of Directors and the Executive Officers.)

Snack Cake Industry

CONSOLIDATION

Dozens of companies, many of which operated only on a regional basis, supplied the snack cake market. That was why, until recently, the market for snack cakes had not seen a great deal of consolidation. This was primarily due to the perishability of the sweet baked goods. Because they go stale so quickly, they usually cannot be shipped over long distances and must therefore be baked near the markets in which they will be consumed. Thus national marketers had to operate multiple bakeries or use artificial preservatives in their products. As a result, economies of scale were limited—which in turn provided additional opportunities for regional and local bakeries.[17]

In the highly competitive snack cakes market, where overall growth in retail sales had been relatively flat during the early 1990s, competitors were looking for new ways to extend their marketing reach and cut their distribution expenses. One important new trend was consolidation between the leading players. For example, Interstate Bakeries Corporation (IBC) made strategic acquisitions in the 1990s to become the largest wholesale bakery in the United States. In 1995, IBC acquired Continental Baking, maker of Hostess snack cakes and Wonder Bread. In 1998, IBC acquired Drakes Bakery, maker of Yodels and Devil Dogs. IBC controlled almost 20% of the snack cake market with its powerhouse brands. In addition to acquiring brands, IBC acquired the John J. Nissen Baking Company of Portland, Maine, and swapped its Grand Junction, Colorado, bakery plus cash for Earthgrains' Massachusetts bakery. This way, IBC could manufacture its snack cakes and breads closer to its markets.

LOW-CALORIE/LOW-FAT PRODUCTS

In 1993, shoppers moved away from low-calorie, fat-free, and low-fat foods in favor of "full-flavored" foods. Manufacturers responded by reducing the number of products aimed at health- and diet-conscious consumers. During 1994, however, shoppers took their cue from the Nutrition Labeling and Education laws that became effective that May by seeking out more healthful foods. Again, food manufacturers were quick to respond. As fast as they had disappeared, a wide array of low-fat and reduced-fat products reappeared on store shelves packaged with calorie-revealing labels. These "new" products were among that year's most popular introductions.[18] By 1998, all the major snack cake brands included low- and reduced-fat varieties. However, emphasis was back on the sweet in sweet goods as snack cake companies noted a decline in the health-consciousness trend. With FDA approval of Procter & Gamble's Olestra as a GRAS (generally recognized as safe) ingredient, new possibilities existed for producers of fat- and calorie-laden foods. This no-fat fat substitute would make formulating healthy products that taste good much easier.

DEMOGRAPHICS

Demographic trends affecting the snack cakes market included the teenage market, aging baby boomers, and the increase of single-parent homes and dual-career families. These trends created a greater demand for convenient bakery snacks. The appeal of a snack cake was that it saved time and effort, came in a single-serving package, and required no preparation. The use of snack cakes and cookies tended to rise with the presence of children between the ages of 2 and 11 in the household.[19] Research showed that, on average, the under-25s buy fewer bakery products than the over-40s. Snack cake manufacturers would have to reach this younger market segment to promote sales of bakery products. Younger customers were as concerned, if not more concerned, about fat and calories. As bakers roll out better-tasting low- and no-fat snack cakes, teenagers could turn to bakery foods in large numbers.[20]

Census forecasts indicated that by 2010, Hispanics will be the largest ethnic minority in the United States. Developing foods based on ethnic preferences to satisfy new consumers became important for all food manufacturers.

NEW PRODUCTS

Breakfast products became the focus of many wholesale bakeries in the late 1990s. In 1997 and 1998, the top snack cake companies introduced branded varieties of donuts, pastries, buns, rolls, coffee cakes, muffins, cereal bars, and granola bars. Competition from in-store bakeries (ISBs), which had been making steady sales gains throughout the 1990s, caused wholesale manufacturers to secure new retail customers and prevent consumers from defecting to ISBs.

SALES OUTLETS

To make the purchase of snack cakes as easy as possible, the products were available in super-markets, convenience stores, mass merchandisers, and vending machines. The popularity of gourmet coffee helped sales in convenience stores—commuters picked up a snack cake with their coffee on the way to the office. In 1997, sales of snack cakes by outlet were: $1,344.1 million, supermarkets; $409.0 million, convenience stores; $238.9 million, mass merchandisers; and $92.5 million, vending machines. Another $495.6 million of snack cakes were sold in drug stores, mom-and-pop stores, and on military bases.[21] (See **Exhibit 2**.)

FORECASTS

Analysts in the bakery industry were watching the impact of the 1996 Farm Act on wheat production and prices. According to the law, wheat farmers no longer had to grow wheat to receive payments from the government. Farmers may decide to allocate sizable acreage to alternative crops due to market forces. Other analysts considered whether farmers would forward-integrate into milling and other aspects of food manufacturing, including baking. A more distant possibility considered was the thought that millers and bakers would backward-integrate into wheat production to ensure a supply of desired product. Gyrations in commodity prices for wheat and flour could be affected by export demand from China, the

Exhibit 2
1997 Sales by Outlets

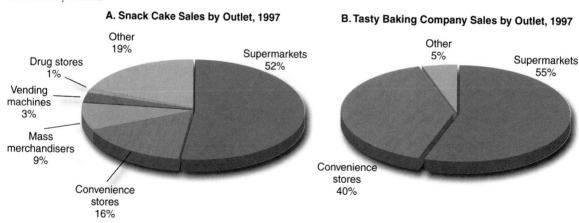

A. Snack Cake Sales by Outlet, 1997

Other 19%
Drug stores 1%
Vending machines 3%
Mass merchandisers 9%
Convenience stores 16%
Supermarkets 52%

B. Tasty Baking Company Sales by Outlet, 1997

Other 5%
Supermarkets 55%
Convenience stores 40%

Source: "Bakery Foods: Snack Cakes & Pies," *Snack Food & Wholesale Bakery* (June 1998), p. S1.

Source: Dan Malovany, "Sweet Expectations, "*Snack Food & Wholesale Bakery* (January 1998), p. 18.

world's largest importer of wheat. China's imports could expand from 50% to 100% over the next 10 years. Bakers would have to keep an eye on flour prices to see the future impact on production costs.

Competition

Tasty Baking Company characterized its competition as "everything . . . that you might consume as a snack," for example, in the summer months, ice cream and frozen yogurt or for sports fans, pretzels, potato chips, and peanuts. By 1998, Tasty Baking Company was competing with cookie, donut, and snack bar makers, as well as institutional and private label bakeries. Competition also included other regional or local bakeries and in-store bakeries. However, snack cakes accounted for over 80% of Tasty Baking Company's sales in 1997, so its most immediate competition came from other snack cake producers. The primary brands that competed with Tastykakes were Interstate Bakeries (Hostess, Dolly Madison, and Drake), McKee (Little Debbie), and Entenmann's (Bestfoods) (see **Exhibit 3**).

HOSTESS

Continental Baking Company, maker of Wonder Bread and Hostess Twinkies, was the nation's largest baker until it was acquired by Interstate Bakeries Corporation (IBC), a Kansas City, Missouri–based company and maker of Home Pride Bread and Dolly Madison snack cakes, in July 1995. Besides Twinkies, the Hostess line included Ho Ho's, Ding Dong's, Suzy Q's, assorted donuts, coffee cake, and a collection of fruit pies. The "light" product line included Twinkie Lights, Cupcake Lights, and fat-free Crumb Coffee Cakes.

DOLLY MADISON

The Dolly Madison snack cakes did not lose sales to the Hostess line once the acquisition was completed. The Dolly Madison line was targeted toward young men and convenience stores, whereas Hostess targeted kids and moms who shopped in supermarkets. In 1997, IBC's market share for Hostess and Dolly Madison snack cakes was 16% (see **Exhibit 3**).

Exhibit 3
Snack Cake U.S. Market Share, 1997

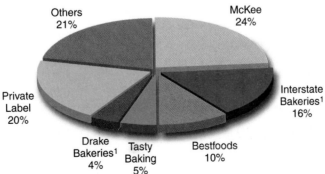

Note:
1. Drake Bakeries acquired by Interstate Bakeries in 1998.

Source: "Bakery Foods: Snack Cakes/Pies," *Snack Food Wholesale Bakery* (June 1998), p. S1.

DRAKES

IBC completed an acquisition in 1998, and Drake Bakeries, formerly owned by Culinar of Canada, increased its ownership of bakeries to 70. Drake Bakeries, maker of Yodels and Devil Dogs, competed with Tasty Baking Company for the Northeast and Mid-Atlantic region. The combination of Drake's and Hostess would give IBC a dominant market share in many of Tasty Baking Company's strong regions. In 1997, Drake's market share was 4% (see **Exhibit 3**).

LITTLE DEBBIE'S

Little Debbie's producer, McKee Foods, was a privately held, Tennessee company that marketed 60 varieties of snack cakes and 20 varieties of Sunbelt bread and cereal to 44 states. It was the number 1 snack cake in sales in 1997. Examples of Little Debbie products include Chocolate Twins, Swiss Cake Rolls, Nutty Bars, Donut Sticks, Jelly Rolls, and Marshmallow Pies. Its 1997 market share for snack cakes was 24% (see **Exhibit 3**).

ENTENMANN'S

Bestfoods, maker of Entenmann's cakes, had 10% market share in 1997 (see **Exhibit 3**). Bestfoods was a global consumer foods company that operated in 60 countries. Its best known brands included Knorr, Hellmann's, Thomas' English Muffins, and Skippy Peanut Butter.

TASTY BAKING AND OTHERS

Tasty Baking Company's market share in 1997 was 5%. Private label brands had 20% market share with the remaining 21% belonging to many small companies (see **Exhibit 3**).

Company Profile

CORPORATE STRUCTURE

In 1994, Tasty Baking Company completed a restructuring program designed to enhance the company's overall competitiveness, productivity, and efficiency. To facilitate team work and communication, departments and responsibilities in every area within the company were realigned vertically by product line rather than horizontally across lines. Previously each functional area had its own supervisory hierarchy, objectives, responsibilities, and budgets. Conflicts and turf battles resulted, and mistakes and oversights by 1 group were blamed on the other.

To break down barriers between employees in different departments, Tasty Baking Company had set up a series of programs to open communications and broadened duties to give its people more responsibility. At monthly meetings, teams of employees on a particular line were brought together to discuss costs, operations, and budgets. This resulted in broader participation in problem solving and gave the company full benefit of the innovative ideas of its employees.

CORPORATE CULTURE

Tasty Baking Company's conservative corporate culture stemmed largely from its founders, Morris and Baur. Throughout their careers, they had conducted their business honestly and ethically. Morris and Baur instilled in Tasty Baking Company a commitment to the finest ingredients, highest quality, and daily delivery of fresh products.

Tasty Baking Company was a family-oriented company, and workers were encouraged to suggest friends and family members for employment positions. This, and the fact that Tasty Baking Company tried to promote from within, contributed to a very low turnover rate. Employees' opinions were taken seriously. In 1994, Tasty Baking Company changed its award for implemented suggestions from $50 to $75, and usable ideas from workers increased 400%.[22]

Tasty Baking Company was dedicated to the community in which it operated. The Allegheny West Community Development Project, started by Tasty Baking Company in 1968, built or rehabilitated over 400 homes for low-income families in North Philadelphia.[23] The Allegheny West Foundation, run by President Ron Hinton, was started to promote stability and improvement of the local neighborhood. Tasty Baking Company was also involved in the work of the United Way, the Greater Philadelphia Food Bank, the Philadelphia Committee for the Homeless, various educational programs, and soup kitchens.

HUMAN RESOURCES

Following the example of its founders, Tasty Baking Company highly valued its employees. The company employed approximately 1,060 full-time and 100 part-time workers. The company considered its employee relations to be good. No employee of the company was represented by a union. In 1994 and 1995, Teamsters Local 115 led an 8-month organizing drive, which ended on April 5, 1995. Employees rejected the appeal to join the union in a 442 to 223 vote. In 1969, the Bakery, Confectionery & Tobacco Workers also conducted an unsuccessful campaign at Tasty Baking Company.[24]

The company participated in a funded noncontributory pension plan providing retirement benefits for substantially all employees. The Tasty Baking Company Thrift Plan permitted participants to make contributions to the Plan on a pretax salary reduction basis. The company contributed $1.00 for each $1.00 contributed by an employee up to a specified limit. The company's contribution was invested in Tasty Baking Company common stock, and participants chose from a selection of Dreyfus Corporation investment options for their contributions. The company contributed $355,077 to the Plan in 1997, $369,169 in 1996, and $370,124 in 1995.[25] Over 93% of Tasty Baking Company employees owned company shares through the 401K program.[26]

MARKETING

Because Tasty Baking Company considered its competition to be all types of snack foods, it wanted to change the company's marketing strategy. In the 1980s, the strategy developed around taste—"Nobody bakes a cake as tasty as a Tastykake!" Tasty Baking Company involved consumers, store managers, trade buyers, and the company's ad agency, the Weightman Group of Philadelphia, in a process called "Brand Planning" to gain a better understanding of its brand and how it competed in the whole universe of snack products.

Tasty Baking Company followed its products from the shelf to the home to see how they were consumed and what role the snacks played in people's lives. The results of this study, which would either revalidate the current "taste" strategy or point the company in a new strategic direction, set the course for Tasty Baking Company's next advertising campaign.[27] When taste emerged as the main reason people bought Tastykakes, the study led to the first major advertising effort since 1989.

The "Moments" campaign included three 15-second vignettes featuring family members enjoying a Tastykake together, with the popular "Nobody Bakes a Cake as Tasty as a Tastykake" jingle recorded in a variety of soundtracks including country, urban gospel, and contemporary.

Tasty Baking Company made use of strategically placed in-store displays, billboards, transit ads, product samples, business publications, newspapers, coupons, spot radio and television advertising, and sporting events to promote its products. In 1997, Tasty Baking Company spent $210,000 advertising its products. When entering new markets, Tasty Baking Company used free-standing inserts (FSIs) in Sunday newspapers, promotions, and heavy in-store sampling to generate trial of the products.

In 1989, Tasty Baking Company introduced "Tastykare," a direct marketing program to serve displaced Philadelphians who longed for Tastykakes. By calling a toll-free number, customers throughout the United States could have Tastykake products delivered via second-day air service. This service was also available on the Internet.

PRODUCTS

Tasty Baking Company produced over 100 different varieties of snack cakes, donuts, cookies, pies, and muffins (see **Exhibit 4**). The availability of some products varied according to the season of the year. The cakes, cookies, and donuts principally sold at retail prices for individ-

Exhibit 4
Tastykake Products—1998: Tasty Baking Company

Sugar Wafers	Chocolate Juniors	**Holiday Theme Varieties**
Tasty Klairs	Butterscotch Krimpets	Coconut Kandy Kakes
Brownies	Peanut Butter Kandy Kakes	Witchy Good Treats
Koffee Kakes	Creme-filled Chocolate Cupcakes	Frosty Kandy Kakes
P.B. Krunch	Chocolate Kandy Kakes	Sparkle Kakes
Jelly Krimpets	Coconut Juniors	Bunny Trail Treats
Honey Buns	Creme-filled Buttercream Cupcakes	Cupid Kakes
Whirly Twirls	Cinnamon Raisin Breakfast Buns	Kringle Kakes
Kreme Krimpies	Chocolate Cupcakes	St. Patty's Treats
Pecan Twirls	Creme-filled Koffee Kakes	Santa Snacks
Lemon Juniors	Orange Juniors	Bunny Bars
PoundKake	Chocolate Covered Pretzels	Ghostly Goodies
Bear Claws		Tasty Tweets
		Sweetie Kakes
Low Fat	**Mini Donuts**	**Pies**
Lemon Krimpets	Powdered Sugar	Apple
Apple Krimpets	Rich Frosted	Blueberry
Raspberry Krimpets	Honey Wheat	Cherry
Lemon-filled Koffee Kakes	Chocolate	Pumpkin
Apple-filled Koffee Kakes		Lemon
Raspberry-filled Koffee Kakes	**Gold Collection**	Strawberry
Creme-filled Vanilla Cupcakes	Chocolate Royale	Peach
Creme-filled Chocolate Cupcakes	Carrot Cake	Lemon-Lime
	Chocolate Chunk Macadamia Cookie	Coconut Creme

Pastry Pockets—apple, lemon, cheese
Tasty Mini Muffins—blueberry, banana nut, carrot, raisin, nut
Tastykake English Muffins—traditional, sourdough, cinnamon raisin
Tasty Mini Cupcakes—4 varieties
Kreme Bars—chocolate and peanut butter
Cookies—oatmeal raisin and chocolate chip
Snak Bars—strawberry-, lemon-, fudge-iced, oatmeal raisin, chocolate chip
Danish—cheese, raspberry, lemon
Tropical Delights—guava, papaya, pineapple, coconut

Source: Tasty Baking Company documents.

ual packages ranging from 33¢ to 99¢ and family convenience packages and jumbo packs ranging from $2.39 to $3.99. The pies sold at retail for 75¢ each.[28] Tasty Baking Company developed its best known and most loved varieties in the 1920s and 1930s—chocolate cupcakes, Butterscotch Krimpets, rectangular Tasty pies, and Kandy Kakes. These products remained the most popular items throughout the company's history.

A Tasty Baking Company analysis of snack cake consumption that focused on how sales fluctuated during certain times of the year led to the introduction of a holiday- and seasonal-themed line of products. This analysis noted the increase in home baking during the major holidays—Easter, Christmas—as well as the sharp increases in candy sales during those times of the year. To attract holiday business, Tasty Baking Company introduced Coconut Kandy Kakes for Easter. The response was very favorable, and the line was expanded. Unlike the company's traditional products, all the holiday-themed items were more targeted toward children and impulse sales. Even the wrappers were decorated to tie in with the theme. So far, the company's regular line had been cannibalized very little.[29]

Tasty Lites, a line of reduced-fat, reduced-calorie products, was introduced in 1991. To circumvent the new FDA rulings on light/lite foods, the line was renamed TastyToos in 1992. In 1995, Tasty Baking Company reengineered its ingredients and processes to retain the taste but remove the fat in its product line. Even the film used to wrap the low-fat product was changed to keep in more moisture and flavor. This new low-fat line, with less than 2 grams of fat, included 8 varieties. Although he did not cite specific sales figures, Gary G. Kyle, Director of Marketing, said sales of the new products went beyond original sales expectations. The raspberry-filled Koffee Kakes emerged as the strongest seller, followed by the Creme Filled Chocolate Cupcakes.[30]

In 1998, Tasty Baking Company's Snak Bars were the result of a reworking of the cookie bar recipe that was not performing well. The new product was 33% larger than the previous product. Tasty Baking Company added vitamins and minerals for the nutrition-conscious consumer. Snak Bars were packaged in metallic wrappers with distinctive graphics. They were targeted to men and women with busy schedules who were looking for grab-and-go snacks. The 5 varieties were strawberry-iced, lemon-iced, chocolate chip, oatmeal raisin, and fudge-iced.

Tropical Delights, or Delicias Tropicales on the bilingual packaging, were introduced first to the Puerto Rico market and later expanded to all of Tasty Baking Company's markets. Taste panels were conducted in Puerto Rico to ensure authenticity. Tropical Delights were distributed by Holsum Bakery in Puerto Rico. Varieties included coconut-topped vanilla cakes with guava, papaya, pineapple, or coconut filling. The packaging featured palm trees and tropical fruit in addition to bilingual wording of nutritional information. Although created to appeal to the Hispanic market, these refreshing cakes became popular in warmer climates and with members of Generation X.

In April 1998, 3 varieties of Danish products debuted at the Oxford facility: cheese, raspberry, and lemon. New varieties, such as blueberry or cherry, could easily be created in the future.

Also in 1998, Tasty Baking Company rolled out chocolate and peanut butter varieties of Kreme Bars, chocolate cakes filled with vanilla or peanut butter and covered with a dark or milk chocolate coating. They were sold in 12-cake Family Packs and individual 2-cake packs. In addition, Tasty Baking Company brought out premium Tasty Collection chocolate chip and oatmeal raisin cookies, the number 1 and 2 preferred varieties of cookies.

Tasty Baking Company instituted 2 new brands, Aunt Sweetie's Bakery and Snak n' Fresh, which allowed Tasty Baking Company to enter the private label, food service, and institutional marketplaces with yeast raised and other products without compromising the integrity of its Tastykake brand.

PRODUCTION

In the 1960s, Tasty Baking Company automated the production systems at its Hunting Park plant, which cut the mixing, baking, icing, wrapping, and packaging time from 12 hours to 45 minutes and the truck loading time from 5 hours to 3 minutes. From 1986 to 1990, the company's 565,000 square foot, 6-story production facility received $50 million worth of upgrades, which included a complete renovation of its Kandy Kake line and a second donut line. In 1989, the company reduced its dependence on conventional energy sources by building an on-site 3.5-megawatt co-generation system in order to run its facilities with minimal use of petroleum-based products.

The Hunting Park plant had 16 production lines (14 ovens and 2 donut fryers). Each line had its own bulk handling system, depositor, oven, icing system, metal detector, wrapper, cartoner, ink-jet coder, caser, and bar coder. Production occurred 6 days a week for 2 to 2½ shifts a day with an annual output in excess of 100 million pounds. Tasty Baking Company baked over 3.5 million individual cakes and pies each day and 2.5 million donuts every week.

In 1995, with the acquisition of Dutch Mill Baking Company, Tasty Baking Company expanded its product lines and distribution. The Dutch Mill facility produced boxed donuts, muffins, and fat-free angel food cake.

The Oxford facility operated as wholly owned subsidiary of Tasty Baking Company and allowed the company to produce the products that had been made for them by other companies. The 160,000-square-foot facility produced a variety of yeast-raised donuts, bear claws, Danish, and cinnamon or fruit-filled sweet rolls. Tasty Baking Company was investigating how to use this facility to serve the in-store bakery and food-service segment of the bakery industry. Whereas the Hunting Park facility was a multilevel maze of ingredient handling, mixing, and dedicated lines, production at the single-level Oxford plant ran in a relatively straight line that was designed for flexibility and short runs. All equipment was on wheels for quick changes.

True to its guiding principle of consistent quality and fresh products, Tasty Baking Company set up a rigorous vendor certification program. It began with a series of formal audits, starting with raw material evaluation. If the vendor's product passed this analysis, a small quantity of ingredients was used in a production run. If the ingredients met expectations, Tasty Baking Company would bring in a partial order. The vendor and Tasty Baking Company worked on the specifications together. Three consecutive trials were run before ordering a full shipment. Even after certification, virtually every raw material was analyzed from a biological, chemical, physical, and organoleptic/sensory aspect before it was accepted in production. All results were recorded in a database for monthly reports that were distributed to the purchasing department and vendors.[31]

Technicians checked cocoa samples every morning for color, flavor, aroma, fineness, moisture, and butterfat content. Surprise sampling could occur at any time. Random sampling was conducted approximately every 15 minutes on some lines.

Tasty Baking Company employed tasters to ensure the proper color, size, icing, and distribution of the filling. They also checked the aroma, the flavor release, and the quantity and quality of the flavor. One taster typically sampled 60 to 70 bites of snack cakes each day. Rejections were rare, once every few years, because the production staff had its own quality-control levels. Several times a year, a panel of 8 to 10 testers met to make sure their palates agreed and that the company's products were true to their original form.[32]

Tasty Baking Company used 3 natural preservatives in the production of its snack cakes: sorbic acid, citric acid, and potassium sorbate. According to the *Foods & Nutrition Encyclopedia*, the food industry used additives for 1 or more of the following 4 appropriate purposes:

1. To maintain or improve nutritional value.

2. To maintain freshness.

3. To help in processing or preparation.

4. To make food more appealing.

On the other hand, the following uses of food additives were considered inappropriate:

1. To disguise faulty or inferior processes.
2. To conceal damaged, inferior, or spoiled foods.
3. To gain some functional property at the expense of nutritional quality.
4. To replace economical, well-recognized manufacturing processes and practices.
5. To use in excess of the minimum required to achieve the intended effects.[33]

Sorbic acid is a food additive possessing antimicrobial benefits; it prevents food spoilage from bacteria, molds, fungi, and yeast. It is commonly used in the form of sodium sorbate or potassium sorbate. In the body, it is metabolized like other fatty acids. It is on the GRAS (generally recognized as safe) list of approved food additives when used at low concentrations. Higher concentrations were regulated by the U.S. Food and Drug Administration. Besides baked goods, sorbic acid was used in beverages, cheese, fish, jams, salads, and wine. Citric acid had been used in food preparation for over 100 years and was used as a flavoring agent in foods.[34] Tasty Baking Company complied with federal regulations concerning food additives and used proper quantities to maintain freshness in its products.

To avoid using preservatives and to expand geographically, Tasty Baking Company used a special film developed by Mobil. The high-barrier coating of Mobil BICORO 110 AXT delivered excellent moisture, oxygen, and aroma barrier characteristics as well as good seal performance for improved shelf-life. This film provided good machinability as well as excellent printing characteristics for the aesthetics needed in the increasingly competitive battle for shelf space. AXT film, first used only on low-fat products, increased the shelf-life of the product to 21 days versus 7 to 10 days and provided management with flexibility with the products. The company could extend its geographic reach because this packaging would maintain the freshness of the product. Improvements in profitability were also noticeable because fewer products needed to be discarded before reaching customers' hands. Although the cost of the film was higher, these costs were compensated by increased sales.[35]

DISTRIBUTION

Tasty Baking Company's products were available in 47 states, Washington D.C., and Puerto Rico. These products were sold primarily by 487 independent owner/operators through distribution routes to approximately 30,000 retail outlets in a 6-state region from New York to Virginia, which was the company's principal market. Tasty Baking Company also distributed its products through its strategic alliances. In addition, products were available through the Tastykare program, whereby consumers called a toll-free number to order the delivery of a variety of Tastykake gift packs.[36]

Outside of the store-door routes, Tasty Baking Company found a way to flash-freeze its baked goods without affecting quality or taste. They shipped the products frozen to retailers' warehouses where they were allowed to thaw and then coded with a 21-day shelf-life.[37]

Tasty Baking Company's strategic alliance with Merita Bakery moved Tastykake cakes and cookies into Florida and southern Georgia on the 1,200 routes Merita runs in those areas. Tastykake products were shipped frozen via tractor-trailer to 5 Kroger manufacturing/warehouse locations: Anderson, South Carolina; Columbus, Ohio; Memphis, Tennessee; Houston, Texas; and Indianapolis, Indiana. The products were sold in Kroger's 1,200 supermarkets in the Southwest and Midwest.

After signing a distribution agreement with Fry's Food & Drug Stores in 1993, Tasty Baking Company wrote to all its Tastykake customers in Arizona telling them where they could find Tastykakes. Fry's, which had originally ordered only 5 or 6 items from Tasty Baking Company, was inundated with requests from consumers and increased the number of items ordered as well as the amount of each item.[38]

Tasty Baking Company's main distribution channel was through supermarkets (55% of sales). However, the company made 40% of its sales through convenience stores. The remaining 5% came from vending machines and other channels (see **Exhibit 2**).[39]

INFORMATION SYSTEMS

Computer technology continued to revolutionize the food industry. Investment in automation was essential to remain competitive and to meet increasingly demanding customer expectations for electronic data interchange. In 1993, Tasty Baking Company made a $3 million investment in hand-held computers for the owner/operator delivery routes. By keeping track of inventory as well as credit and billing, these devices cut paperwork by hours a week and improved billing and inventory accuracy. All owner/operators were trained to use these computers, which made their operations more efficient and provided timely sales information to management. Some of Tasty Baking Company's customers indicated that in the near future they would require suppliers to have handheld computers capable of downloading inventory and billing information directly into their stores' computer system whenever a product delivery was made.[40]

In 1997, Tasty Baking Company engaged in a project to upgrade its computer hardware and software in order to improve its operating performance and avoid any potential year 2000 problems. The company expected to complete the project in 1999.[41]

Tasty Baking Company entered an agreement with Ross Systems Inc. for software and services valued at nearly $1.6 million. The licensed product, Ross' Renaissance CS Enterprise Resource Planning & Supply Chain System, helped Tasty Baking Company manage current projects as well as implement its aggressive growth plans.[42]

FINANCE

Exhibits 5 and **6** provide financial information for Tasty Baking Company. Net sales for 1997 were 8% higher than they were for 1992. Unfortunately net income dropped by 29% for the same time period. These numbers do not depict an accurate picture for Tasty Baking Company.

In 1997, several favorable events took place for the shareholders. The company moved to the New York Stock Exchange. Such a move increased the liquidity of Tasty Baking Company common stock as well as raising its profile among institutional investors. The Board of Directors increased the dividend by 7.1% and authorized a 5-for-4 stock split. These actions helped push Tasty Baking Company stock up by 75.6% in 1997.

After a lengthy legal battle, Tasty Baking Company took a pretax charge of $1,950,000 ($1,171,170 after taxes) in connection with its dispute with the IRS related to the treatment of Tasty Baking Company owner/operators for payroll tax purposes. Excluding this charge, Tasty Baking Company's 1997 net income was up by $933,000, or 15%, over 1996. This increase was due in part to increased productivity, stable commodity prices, expense control, and increased sales. Gross sales increased by 4.5% in 1997 over 1996, and net sales increased by 2% for the same time period.

Tasty Baking Company was successful in reducing its cost of sales as a percentage of net sales. This figure was 60.8%, 62.0%, and 63% for 1997, 1996, and 1995, respectively. This was brought about by improvements in manufacturing efficiencies, reduced utility costs, and product price increase. Selling and administrative expenses increased by $1,576,509 (4.1%) in 1997 due to increased advertising costs and an increase in selling expense.

Long-term debt increased in 1997 by $2,470,637 to $7,773,053 due to facility modernization. However this amount was only 55% as great as it was in 1992. Current interest expense is less than half of what it was in 1992.

Return on sales (net income/sales) remained fairly stable. It was 4.1%, 4.3%, 4.0%, and 4.1% for 1997, 1996, 1995, and 1994, respectively. Return on equity exhibited a downward trend. It was 14.6%, 16.2%, 15.7%, and 17.6% for 1997, 1996, 1995, and 1994, respectively.

Tasty Baking Company leased most of its facilities. The company contributed property to the Tasty Baking Company Pension Plan and in turn leased this property back from its employees at market rates. The company retained the option to repurchase the property at any time at its then fair market value.

In August 1995, Tasty Baking Company exchanged 578,435 shares of stock (worth $649,000) for the purchase of Dutch Mill Baking Company. The purchase price exceeded the fair market value of its assets by $303,000. This amount will be amortized on a straight-line basis over 15 years.

On July 1, 1996, Tasty Baking Company purchased a 160,000-square-foot manufacturing facility in Oxford, Pennsylvania, for $4 million. This purchase allowed Tasty Baking Company to manufacture products that had been previously made by other suppliers. This step helped Tasty Baking Company increase margins and expand new product offerings.

Exhibit 5

Consolidated Highlights of Operating Results (Unaudited): Tasty Baking Company

Year Ending December 31	1997	1996	1995	1994	1993	1992
Net sales	$149,291,974	$146,718,391	$141,831,073	$142,055,111	$137,772,730	$138,381,391
Costs and expenses						
Cost of sales	90,754,876	90,955,370	89,403,295	84,921,787	82,603,806	84,598,553
Depreciation	7,214,997	7,267,639	7,463,311	7,327,385	6,784,732	6,991,671
Selling, general and administrative	40,198,649	38,622,140	37,040,622	40,713,980	40,684,291	40,644,071
Payroll tax settlement and severance charges	1,950,000	—	—	—	—	—
Restructure charge (early retirement program 1990)	—	—	950,000	1,240,000	—	—
Interest expense	536,820	520,375	675,613	803,688	838,184	1,175,164
Provision for doubtful accounts	499,787	825,145	785,036	592,040	530,980	245,012
Other income, net	(1,607,522)	(1,742,863)	(4,901,455)	(3,164,684)	(3,262,708)	(3,414,411)
Total cost and expenses	139,547,607	136,447,806	131,416,422	132,434,196	128,179,285	130,240,060
Income from continuing operations before provision for income taxes	9,744,367	10,270,585	10,414,651	9,620,915	9,593,445	8,141,331
Provision for income taxes						
Federal	3,183,866	3,528,932	2,345,811	3,086,954	2,988,595	2,203,537
State	881,528	784,352	500,319	942,330	633,530	438,116
Deferred	(388,204)	(347,278)	1,377,541	(209,113)	284,316	477,270
Decrease in net deferred tax asset due to change in tax rate	—	—	550,868	—	—	—
Total income taxes	3,677,190	3,966,006	4,774,539	3,819,871	3,906,441	3,118,923
Income from continuing operations before cumulative effect of changes in accounting principles	6,067,177	6,304,579	5,640,112	5,800,744	5,687,004	5,022,408
Discontinued operations						
Income from spun-off subsidiary, net of income taxes	—	—	—	—	2,253,366	3,554,002
Provision for cost spin-off, net of income taxes	—	—	—	—	(804,569)	—
Cumulative effect of changes in accounting principles on spun-off subsidiary	—	—	—	—	(805,264)	—
Cumulative effect of changes in accounting principles for income taxes	—	—	—	—	1,003,507	—

Postretirement benefits other than pensions	—	—	—	—	(11,708,989)	—
Net income (loss)	$6,067,177	$6,304,579	$5,640,112	$5,800,744	($ 4,374,945)	$8,576,410
Retained earnings						
Balance, beginning of year	22,265,220	19,425,849	17,228,764	14,680,877	45,851,426	42,119,726
Dividend of P&J common shares	—	—	—	—	(22,806,526)	—
Cash dividends paid on common shares	(3,544,121)	(3,465,208)	(3,443,027)	(3,252,857)	(3,989,078)	(4,844,710)
Balance, end of year	24,788,276	22,265,220	19,425,849	17,228,764	14,680,877	45,851,426
Earnings per common share						
Increase from continuing operations before cumulative effect of changes in accounting principles	$0.78[1]	$0.82[1]	$0.92	$0.94	$0.93	$0.83
Income from spun-off subsidiary, net of income taxes	—	—	—	—	$0.37	$0.58
Provision for cost of spin-off, net of income taxes	—	—	—	—	($0.13)	—
Cumulative effect for changes in accounting principles on spun-off subsidiary	—	—	—	—	($0.13)	—
Cumulative effect of changes in accounting principles for:						
Income taxes	—	—	—	—	$0.16	—
Postretirement benefits other than pensions	—	—	—	—	($1.92)	—
Net income (loss) per common share	$0.78[1]	$0.82[1]	$0.92	$0.94	($0.72)	$1.41

Note:
1. Reflects 5-for-4 stock split.

Source: Tasty Baking Company, *1997, 1996, 1995, 1994 Annual Reports.*

Exhibit 6

Consolidated Balance Sheets: Tasty Baking Company

Year Ending December 31	1997	1996	1995	1994	1993	1992
Assets						
Current assets						
Cash	$ 748,117	$ 233,366	$ 85,104	$ 147,251	$ 141,026	$ 449,626
Receivables	18,661,411	16,962,591	18,630,903	17,574,423	17,361,496	18,304,372
Inventories	3,296,202	2,855,512	3,263,282	2,937,060	2,952,719	3,466,721
Deferred income taxes, prepayments and other	2,241,587	2,726,014	3,349,314	3,681,528	3,130,000	2,488,753
Total current assets	24,947,317	22,777,483	25,328,603	24,340,262	23,585,241	24,709,472
Property, plant, and equipment						
Land	1,267,095	1,267,095	697,987	697,987	697,987	697,987
Buildings and improvements	27,843,342	27,366,281	24,797,546	23,937,822	23,921,821	23,821,084
Machinery and equipment	120,598,909	110,715,679	101,374,855	97,366,055	93,677,286	88,446,734
	149,709,346	139,349,055	126,870,388	122,001,864	118,297,094	112,965,805
Less accumulated depreciation	(105,501,230)	(98,375,648)	(91,230,770)	(84,063,636)	(76,736,251)	(72,054,686)
	44,208,116	40,973,407	35,639,618	37,938,228	41,560,843	40,911,119
Net assets of discontinued operations	—	—	—			29,047,734
Other assets	25,163,945	23,677,474	24,334,762	24,858,106	25,358,935	17,427,948
Total assets	$94,319,378	$87,428,364	$85,302,983	$87,136,596	$90,505,019	$112,096,273
Liabilities and shareholders' equity						
Current liabilities						
Current portion of long-term debt	$29,354	$58,340	$127,720	$222,831	$185,742	$221,789
Current obligations under capital leases	543,962	587,336	513,159	455,712	426,800	373,170
Notes payable, banks	900,000	—	700,000	1,800,000	1,800,000	6,400,000
Accounts payable	4,345,944	3,963,610	4,699,747	4,075,343	5,684,555	4,800,391
Accrued payrolls and employee benefits	6,817,319	5,608,274	4,310,550	3,565,536	3,664,585	3,975,443
Accrued income taxes	—	1,474,887	—	893,111	679,028	982,997
Other	1,826,981	925,338	1,033,612	987,307	368,546	533,570
Total current liabilities	14,463,560	12,617,785	11,384,788	11,999,840	12,809,256	17,287,360

Long-term debt, less current portion	7,773,053	5,302,416	4,576,385	5,349,558	8,572,389	14,255,701
Long-term obligations under capital leases less current portion	587,156	1,131,118	1,653,134	2,166,293	2,634,101	2,929,256
Deferred income	——	——	——	3,271,268	4,642,445	6,117,343
Accrued pensions and other liabilities	11,771,540	11,203,178	13,129,760	11,691,444	11,554,424	10,721,376
Postretirement benefits other than pensions	18,129,226	18,267,013	18,620,763	19,707,364	20,049,638	——
Shareholders' equity						
Common stock, par value $.50 per share, Authorized 15,000,000 shares, issued 7,289,087 shares	4,558,243	4,555,680	3,644,544	3,644,544	3,644,544	3,554,344
Capital in excess of par value of stock	29,337,938	28,831,377	29,662,330	29,175,510	29,105,725	23,424,543
Retained earnings	24,788,276	22,265,220	19,425,849	17,228,764	14,680,877	45,851,426
	58,684,457	55,652,277	52,732,723	50,048,818	47,431,146	72,830,313
Less—Treasury stock, at cost	16,738,364	16,329,055	16,364,757	16,601,793	16,579,825	11,280,132
Management Stock Purchase Plan receivables and deferrals	351,250	416,368	429,813	496,196	608,555	764,944
Total shareholders' equity	41,594,843	38,906,854	35,938,153	32,950,829	30,242,766	60,785,237
Total liabilities and shareholders' equity	$ 94,319,378	$ 87,428,364	$ 85,302,983	$ 87,136,596	$ 90,505,019	$ 112,096,273

Source: Tasty Baking Company, *1997, 1996, 1995, 1994 Annual Reports.*

Notes

1. Tasty Baking Company, *1988 Annual Report*, p. 3.
2. Rosland Briggs, "Tasty Baking Settles 3-Year Tax Battle," *Philadelphia Inquirer* (January 16, 1998), p. C1.
3. M. B. Pinheiro, "Baked Goods Industry," *Janney Montgomery Scott Industry Report* (September 5, 1995), p. 17.
4. Kathleen M. Grim, "Tasty Baking Company Acquires Dutch Mill Baking Company, Inc.," *PR Newswire* (August 29, 1995), p. 1.
5. Julia C. Martinez, "Philadelphia's Tasty Baking Co. Considers Buying Another Bakery," *Philadelphia Inquirer* (April 23, 1994), p. D1.
6. Dan Malovany, "Sweet Expectations," *Snack Food & Wholesale Bakery* (January 1998), p. 18.
7. E. R. Katzman, "Global Food Industry," *Merrill Lynch Capital Markets Report* (April 13, 1998), p. 81.
8. "Philadelphia's Tastiest Treasures Now Appearing on Store Shelves in 7-Eleven Stores in Colorado," *PR Newswire* (October 2, 1997).
9. Michael Sangiacomo, "Tastykakes Come to Northeast Ohio," *The Plain Dealer* (May 22, 1998), p. 1B.
10. "Tasty Baking Company Continues Midwest Expansion," *Business Wire* (September 24, 1998).
11. Tasty Baking Company, *1998 Proxy Statement*, pp. 3, 8.
12. *Ibid.*, p. 8.
13. *Ibid.*
14. *Ibid.*
15. *Ibid.*
16. *Ibid.*
17. "Market for Bakery Snacks: Industry Overview," *FIND/SVP Report* (January 1995), p. 1.
18. *Standard & Poor's Industry Survey* (April 13, 1995), p. F2.
19. "Market for Bakery Snacks: The Consumer," *FIND/SVP Report* (January 1995), p. 2.
20. Carol Meres Krosky, "It's a Brave New World," *Bakery Production and Marketing* (January 15, 1996), p. 36.
21. "Bakery Foods: Snack Cakes/Pies," *Snack Food & Wholesale Bakery* (June 1998), pp. S1–21.
22. Robert Carey, "Employee Ideas Get Unboxed," *Incentive Performance Supplement* (June 4, 1995), p. 4.
23. Alan J. Heavens, "Open Door to Homeownership," *Philadelphia Inquirer* (September 24, 1995), p. R1.
24. Francesca Chapman, "Tasty Bakers Won't Go Union Route," *Philadelphia Daily News* (April 7, 1995), p. 45.
25. Tasty Baking Company, *1997 Annual Report*, p. 27.
26. Malovany, "Sweet Expectations," p. 18.
27. "Complete Competitor," *Snack Food* (July 1994), p. 27.
28. Tasty Baking Company, *Form 10-K* (1997), p. 2.
29. "Happy Holidays: Introduced New Holiday-Theme Products in Its Tastykake Product Line," *Snack Food* (July 1994), p. 28.
30. Maria Gallagher, "But Are They Tasty?" *Philadelphia Daily News* (January 31, 1996), p. F1.
31. "Fast and Fresh: Implements a Strict Quality Control Program Starting from Its Raw Materials to Final Products," *Snack Food* (July 1994), p. 35.
32. "Quality, a Matter of Taste," *The Orlando Sentinel* (September 17, 1996), p. B5.
33. *Food & Nutrition Encyclopedia,* 2nd ed. Boca Raton, FL: CRC Press, p. 10.
34. *Ibid.*, p. 2005.
35. Judy Rice, "Live Long and Prosper," *Prepared Foods* (August 1996), p. 128.
36. Tasty Baking Company, *Form 10-K* (1994), p. 2.
37. Mary Ellen Kuhn, "Bakeries on the Brink," *Food Processing* (March 1995), p. 35.
38. Paul Rogers, "Tasty Obsession," *Snack Food* (July 1994), p. 24.
39. Malovany, "Sweet Expectations," p. 18.
40. Tasty Baking Company, *1993 Annual Report*, pp. 8–9.
41. Tasty Baking Company, *1997 Annual Report*, p. 14.
42. "Ross Systems, Inc. Announces $1.6 Million Agreement," *PR Newswire* (August 7, 1997).

Redhook Ale Brewery

Stephen E. Barndt

Paul Shipman, Chief Executive Officer of Redhook Ale Brewery, knew that he needed to reevaluate his strategy and its execution. Redhook's rapid growth had ended shortly after it invested in a major increase in production capacity. Operating at about 50% of production capacity, the company suffered a net loss in 1997 that continued into 1998.

Redhook brewed only specialty beer, referred to as craft beer. Craft beer is a more flavorful, fuller bodied premium beer, follows traditional old world brewing methods, and uses high-quality materials. The company started as a microbrewery but grew continually and reached national status by the end of 1996. Shipman, one of Redhook's founders, had guided the company from a small player in 1 city to a leading position as a national competitor and aimed at dominating the craft beer segment of the domestic beer industry. The company's 3 small-batch breweries, 2 in the Pacific Northwest and 1 in the Northeast, had a combined design capacity of 575,000 barrels (each containing 31 gallons) per year of Redhook branded beer to tap a growing market for craft beer. However, growth in the craft beer market attracted attention, and competition grew from other microbreweries, brewpubs, regional specialty brewers, and from large mass-market brewers. With increased competition, 1996 saw the beginning of a downturn with a reduction in sales and profitability.

Company History

Redhook was started in 1981 by Paul Shipman, with additional investment and assistance from Jerry Jones and Gordon Bowker. Shipman, 45, with an undergraduate degree in English from Bucknell and an MBA from the University of Virginia, had worked as a marketing analyst for Chateau Ste. Michelle winery prior to starting up Redhook. Earlier, he had spent a year in Europe where he was introduced to high quality beer. Jerry Jones was an executive and consultant in the field of ski resort management. Gordon Bowker was also the founder of Starbucks Coffee Company and served Redhook as Vice President, Treasurer, and Secretary.

Shipman started Redhook with a belief that U.S. consumers would respond well to a quality European-style beer made with the best equipment and using the finest ingredients. The company's initial brewing operations were carried out in a converted transmission shop in Seattle. The company did not have a bottling line and all beer that was brewed was packaged in

This case was prepared by Professor Stephen E. Barndt of Pacific Lutheran University. This case was edited for SMBP-8th Edition. Copyright © 1998 and 2000 by Stephen E. Barndt. This case was published in the *Business Case Journal* Summer 1998, Vol. 1, No. 1, pp. 53–69. Reprinted by permission.

15.5 gallon kegs. First year production totaled 1,000 barrels and was sold to local taverns and restaurants for on-premises consumption.

Sales and production grew gradually through the mid 1980s. Redhook sold through its own distribution group and independent beer distributors. The first major increase in production occurred in 1989 when Redhook replaced its first brewery with a larger capacity, state-of-the-art brewery located in a converted electric trolley barn in Seattle. In 1993, the company acquired land east of Seattle in the town of Woodinville where it constructed a much larger brewery. The Woodinville brewery came on line in September 1994, with an initial capacity of 60,000 barrels per year. Sales remained primarily in the state of Washington but ranged throughout the Pacific Northwest and California.

Redhook consummated a long-term distribution agreement with Anheuser-Busch, the largest brewery in the United States, late in 1994. Opening the way for nationwide sales, the agreement enabled Redhook to market its products via Anheuser-Busch distributors seeking increased volume through a broader product line. As a result, Redhook was selling its beer in 48 states in 1998.

Redhook constructed a new brewery near Portsmouth, New Hampshire, to better serve the eastern United States and lower transportation costs. The Portsmouth brewery came on line in late 1996 with an initial capacity of 100,000 barrels per year. To finance its rapid growth, Redhook sold a 25% equity interest to Anheuser-Busch and, in 1995, sold 2,193,492 shares of stock in an initial public offering to end the year with 7,683,492 shares outstanding.

The Brewing Industry

The U.S. brewing industry was both highly competitive and highly regulated. Several large and many small brewers competed for the $29 billion wholesale market using brand name, distribution channel, or taste to attract consumers. The market consisted of 3 distinct segments—national, imported, and craft beer—each characterized by its own predominant marketing strategy. Brewers participating in each of the segments were subject to various government requirements in such areas as taxation; product safety, quality, and disclosure; and environmental protection.

NATIONAL BEERS

The national beer segment was the largest by far and exhibited the highest degree of consolidation in the industry. The 5 largest brewers—Anheuser-Busch, Inc., Miller Brewing Company, Adolph Coors, Stroh Brewery, and Pabst—accounted for 93% of all the domestic beer sold in the United States in 1996.[1] Anheuser-Busch was the leader with a 49% market share followed by Miller with 22%, and Coors with 10%.

Competitors in this segment brewed large batches in breweries designed for high volume production. Beers brewed for the mass market substituted more corn, rice, and other ingredients in place of barley; they were pasteurized to lengthen shelf life, but were considered less flavorful than imported or craft beers. High volume, efficient production, and inexpensive raw materials resulted in low product cost. The national brewers' branded products were widely distributed. They favored extensive advertising to capture national recognition in some cases and regional recognition in others. Advertising media used included network TV, spot TV, spot radio, magazines, or sponsored events such as sports spectaculars.

IMPORTED BEERS

Imported beer played a relatively minor role in the total U.S. market with a 7.4% market share. Competitors in this segment distributed their products widely and catered to consumers who desired a more flavorful beer.[2] Bars, restaurants, and retailers selling bottled goods often carried 1 or more imported brands such as Becks, Corona, Heineken, Labatts, Moosehead, Guinness, and San Miguel. The majority of beers imported into the U.S. were bottled in Mexico, Europe, and Canada. Extent of advertising varied from importer to importer but was generally intensive using such media as radio spots, print, and outdoor signage.

CRAFT BEERS

Craft beer, with 2.9% of the beer market, was the newest growth segment of the industry.[3] During the 1980s and 1990s, ever increasing numbers of craft brewers both created and filled a demand for distinctive flavorful beers, using high-quality ingredients brewed with European-style recipes. Some craft beers featured flavors of fruit, honey, spices, oatmeal, coffee, pumpkin, or other additives.

The market was increasingly fragmented with 1,306 craft brewers across the nation as of January 1998, up from 1,042, 803, and 540 at the end of 1996, 1995, and 1994, respectively.[4] While the number of firms was continuing to grow, the craft beer market had reached a time in its development where total demand had ceased to grow at double-digit rates. After growth in demand of about 50% in 1994 and 1995, 1996 saw 25% growth, and, in 1997, total sales only increased 5%.[5]

There were 4 categories of brewers producing craft beer. Microbreweries produced less than 15,000 barrels per year and served limited markets, usually through independent distributors and direct sales. Brewpubs were the smallest volume producers, usually brewing 2,500 barrels or less per year for consumption in the pub. Regional specialty brewers produced over 15,000 barrels per year and distributed through independent distributors both locally and in 1 or more regional markets. Contract brewers developed beer recipes and contracted with larger national or regional breweries, e.g., Strohs and Pittsburgh Brewing, for the actual brewing. Contract brewers usually marketed their branded beers regionally or nationally using independent distributors and their own advertising and promotion.

In 1997, 48 brewers each produced over 10,000 barrels of craft beer. Five contract brewers led by Boston Beer and Pete's Brewing Company each produced 15,000 or more barrels. Twenty-five regional specialty brewers produced at least 15,000 barrels. Another 10 microbrewies each produced between 10,000 and 15,000 barrels. Boston Beer Company, Pete's Brewing Company, Sierra Nevada Brewing Company, Redhook Ale Brewery, Pyramid Brewing Company, and Widmer Brewing Company all topped 100,000 barrels in 1997.[6] The relative craft beer market shares among the top 10 craft brewers in 1996 are presented in **Exhibit 1**.

Exhibit 1
Craft Brewer Market Shares

Brewer	1996 Market Share
Boston Beer	25.1 %
Pete's Brewing	8.8 %
Sierra Nevada Brewing	5.5 %
Redhook Ale Brewery	4.7 %
Pyramid Brewing	2.6 %
Widmer Brewing	2.6 %
Anchor Brewing	2.2 %
Full Sail Brewing	1.7 %
Portland Brewing	1.4 %
Spanish Peaks Brewery	1.2 %

Source: Adapted from Sarah Theodore, "Domestic Specialty Suffers Growing Pains in '97," *Beverage Industry,* January 1998, pp. 9–18.

THE MARKET FOR BEER

Adult per-capita consumption of beer declined from the early 1980s to about 30 gallons in 1997 as federal beer taxes were doubled, blue-collar jobs declined, health and fitness became fashionable, and the population aged.[7] This per-capita decline was offset by growth in the total adult population so total U.S. beer sales were relatively constant at between 185 and 190 million barrels per year. However, major differences existed among the 3 segments. Since 1995, sales of national brands declined about 5%, popular brands declined 9%; imported beer sales increased 25% to 14 million barrels; and craft beer sales increased 32% to 5.2 million barrels.[8] Taste, demand for greater variety, and a "trading-up phenomenon" were offered as reasons for the continuing growth in demand for craft and imported beer.[9] While craft beer sales were expected to continue growing, the rate of growth was expected to be lower as the market matured, and importers used larger advertising budgets and marketing skills to increase their share.

A national survey found that beer consumers who drank craft beer were more likely to be young (less than 45 years of age), to be college educated, and to have above-average incomes (greater than $50,000). Greater numbers of men than women were drawn to craft beer, although a greater share of beer-drinking women had an interest in craft beers than did beer-drinking men. Craft beer drinkers also tended to drink more than the average drinker. However, 80% of those who drank craft beer consumed less craft beer than other types of beer.[10] In addition, there were regional differences in craft beer consumption. Craft beer was most popular in the West, followed by the Northeast and Midwest. While craft beer was most popular in the upscale segment of the population, it had seen increasing popularity in middle-income households. This increased acceptance was reflected in a study that showed 19% of surveyed adults had tried craft beer in 1996, up from 13% a year earlier.[11]

COMPETITIVE PRACTICES

Imported and craft beers were aimed at beer drinkers who sought prestige products and who desired superior flavor. However, a high level of substitutability existed among the 3 classes of beer. Consequently, national brand, import, and craft beer companies competed and attempted to get the beer drinking populace to switch to their types of beer and thus increase their market share. Imported and craft beers competed head to head since both were at the premium price, distinctive flavor end of the beer spectrum.

The national brewers used extensive advertising, often through costly mass media. However, they faced the threat of restrictions on what, how, and where they could advertise as a result of political and news media concerns that drinking was harmful. They developed and relied on wide distribution through networks of wholesale distributors. These distributors sought to saturate the market by placing their products in bars, restaurants, grocery stores, convenience stores, and other outlets. They provided regularly scheduled deliveries with secured and stocked shelf space and rotated retailers' inventory to insure freshness.

Imported beers, with a much smaller market share, used selective targeted advertising and relied more on their distributors to push their higher margin product through on-site consumption and consumer retail channels. Distribution was the key for craft brewers as well, but actual methods of distribution varied depending on size of the company. For example, brewpubs selling only for consumption in their own establishments, relied on creating a pleasant atmosphere, complementary foods, and the idea that the pub itself was something special. Many of the microbreweries, regional specialty brewers, and contract brewers also had their own pubs and attempted to create a local identity using similar methods. Smaller microbreweries often distributed only kegged beer to local restaurants and bars and tried to instill a local pride in their premium beers. Larger microbreweries usually sold both kegged and bottled products by using independent distributors in a broader local or regional area. Across all craft brewers, the split between packaged (bottled) and draft (kegged) beer was 72 to 28%.[12]

Microbrewery advertising and promotion were limited and most often took the form of displays in drinking establishments; giveaways such as glasses, mugs, and coasters; and sponsorship of concerts, festivals, or seasonal events. Most regional specialty brewers and contract brewers used the same distribution and promotion strategy as the large microbreweries. Boston Beer and Pete's Brewing Company became the first exceptions when they introduced local TV advertising.

Growth of the craft beer market was noted by the large national brewers and they entered the craft segment with their own specialty beer products. Anheuser-Busch sought to have 60% of the craft beer market by 2005[13] while Miller's objective was 25% by 2000.[14] Anheuser-Busch, Adolph Coors, Miller, and Strohs all set up specialty units with separate staff to manage their new brands.[15] By the end of 1996, Miller and Strohs each had acquired control or an interest in 2 microbreweries, while Coors had 1. Anheuser-Busch had a 25% interest in Redhook and distribution alliances with both Redhook and Widmer Brewing. Brand names offered by the majors included Augsburger, Blue Moon, Celis, Elk Mountain, George Killian, Icehouse, J. W. Dundee, J. J. Wainwright, Jacob Leinenkugel, Michael Shea's, Red Dog, Red River Valley, and Red Wolf. In most cases the brands were marketed under a name other than the controlling company's name, e.g., Northern Plains Brewing (Strohs), Plank Road Brewery (Miller), and Blue Moon Brewing Company (Coors). In 1995 Anheuser-Busch alone had 7 craft-type beers that sold 650,000 barrels.[16] In addition, in 1996, Anheuser-Busch initiated a program to increase its exclusive distributor force from 40% of the total Anheuser-Busch distributors to 70%. This would reduce the incidence of competitors benefiting from the services of Anheuser-Busch distributors. While Anheuser-Busch could not use punitive measures because they could be considered to be in restraint of trade, it could encourage its distributors to voluntarily carry Anheuser-Busch products, including Redhook, exclusively. Incentives were provided to reward this exclusive distribution. Some speculated that eventually pressures would be placed on distributors to cause them to volunteer.[17] Miller and Coors also appeared to be interested in getting their distributors to devote more effort on their own specialty beers and less on microbrewery beers.[18]

In addition to pressures from major national brewers on their distributors to reduce product lines to a narrower spectrum of selected brands, the sheer number of craft and other brands in the United States overwhelmed distributors. With about 4,500 brands and ever increasing numbers of craft brewers seeking to add their brands to the market, distributors began to cull less popular brands and restrict themselves to the higher volume brands for which they could reasonably expect to secure shelf space.

Growth was a widely sought goal among craft brewers. The large contract and regional specialty brewers were moving toward national distribution. By 1996, Boston Beer had already reached all 50 states and Redhook sold in 47 states, Pete's in 40 states, and Pyramid Brewing in 27 states. A number of microbreweries were operating more than 1 brewery and several brewpubs had started chains. Starting in 1995, 7 of the largest craft brewers went public or announced a public offering to raise funds for growth; these included Boston Beer, Brandevor Enterprises, Pyramid Breweries, Pete's Brewing, Portland Brewing Company, Redhook, and Widmer Brewing.

Redhook's Objective and Business Strategy

Redhook had set an objective to be the leading craft brewer through market development into unserved regions of the nation and continued market penetration once established in a region. The company articulated a business strategy in its 1995 annual report and prospectus with 6 key elements:

1. Production of high-quality craft beers
2. Control of production in company-owned breweries

3. Operation of regional brewing facilities
4. Production economies through technologically advanced equipment
5. Strategic distribution alliance with Anheuser-Busch
6. Promotion of products within local markets[19]

Products and Production

Redhook did not pasteurize its craft beers. Not pasteurizing ensured that the flavor was not degraded, but it reduced shelf life to about 3 months.

In 1997, Redhook produced 9 different branded products and from time to time produced small batches of experimental brews that it test marketed under its Redhook Blueline label. These products were brewed and packaged in both kegs and bottles at its own operating breweries. The Fremont brewery in Seattle had a capacity of 75,000 barrels per year. The brewery was installed in an old trolley car barn under a lease with an option to buy. The company also owned and leased adjacent properties for kegging, warehousing, and other uses. This brewery was temporarily closed early in 1998. The Woodinville, Washington, brewery, constructed on 22 acres owned by the company, started with a capacity of 60,000 barrels, reached 170,000 barrels in 1995, and 250,000 in 1996. The Portsmouth, New Hampshire, brewery constructed on 23 acres of subleased land started with a capacity of 100,000 barrels to be increased in stages to 250,000. Portsmouth was chosen as a site because of its central location in a large market and the high cost of transporting kegged and bottled beer from the Northwest.

Only the highest quality malts, grains, hops, and other ingredients were purchased from a few regular suppliers at competitive prices. Alternative sources were available, if needed. The ingredients were processed in state-of-the-art automated brewing equipment designed in Europe for efficient production of small batches. The bottling line was fully integrated and automated with fast changeover capability.

As a producer of premium craft beers, Redhook emphasized quality in product formulation, brewing, and bottling. Each brewery had its own laboratory for testing product quality. In addition, the Woodinville brewery served as the focal point for quality, monitoring all breweries' production and product quality control.

Distribution

In 1994, Redhook formed a distribution alliance with Anheuser-Busch.[20] The alliance was to run for 20 years but could be terminated after 10 years under certain conditions. Under the alliance, Anheuser-Busch invested in Redhook, gaining a 25% stake in the company's equity, and made its nationwide network of some 700 wholesale distributors (44% of the nation's wholesalers) available for distribution of Redhook products. Redhook retained full control over production and marketing. Anheuser-Busch distributors in the U.S. and Mexico participating in the alliance were to be given exclusive distribution rights in their territories. Distribution agreements with Redhook's current distributors remained in effect until they expired, at which time Anheuser-Busch distributors could take over. When an Anheuser-Busch distributor for an area declined to carry Redhook products, Redhook could use a non-alliance distributor.

In accordance with the agreement, Redhook sold its beer to Anheuser-Busch and shipped the beer to the latter's distribution centers. Anheuser-Busch distributors then ordered from and paid Anheuser-Busch for the Redhook beer they received for retail distribution. While

Anheuser-Busch was paid a per-barrel fee for use of the distribution network, Redhook believed that the added cost was more than offset by efficiencies in shipping, billing, and paperwork. In addition, distributor acceptance of Redhook and its products was good.

The Redhook and Anheuser-Busch alliance was controversial. Critics found fault with the alliance, citing the belief that it would heat up the fight for shelf space and wondering if small brewers could remain independent once they became dependent on a large brewer. Jim Koch, CEO of Boston Beer Company, referred to Redhook as Budhook (a takeoff from Anheuser-Busch's Budweiser brand) after the alliance. He implied his views concerning the threat of national brewers gaining control over craft brewers in the statement:

> In the long run, the big brewers would like to dominate this part of the beer business the way they do every other part—why shouldn't they? Anheuser-Busch has stated they want to control half the beer industry. Microbreweries are naive to think that doesn't mean half the microbrew business.[21]

An even stronger statement came from another executive who said "as soon as they put you into their distribution network, they control your inventory, pricing, and own you lock, stock, and barrel."[22]

Others believed that major brewers entry into the craft beer market benefited the industry because they increased awareness of craft beer. Pete Slosberg of Pete's Brewing Company reflected this view in his statement:

> I believe any vehicle that will introduce more Americans to different beers, even if it's not our brand is a good thing. It lets drinkers know there is an alternative.[23]

Marketing and Sales

Redhook's marketing strategy emphasized distribution and didn't rely on costly media advertising. The company focused its efforts on distributor training, retailer education and support, and spread of word-of-mouth awareness through various consumer promotions. Redhook coached its distributors, worked with distributor salespeople to get greater attention for Redhook products during their sales calls, and, in cooperation with the distributors, offered incentives for the salespeople to develop new accounts. The 44 member (as of March 1, 1998) sales and marketing staff[24] conducted a number of other education and promotion programs such as

1. Distributor Tours
2. Community Gatherings
3. Marketing On-Site
4. Price Discounting
5. Company-Owned Pubs
6. Visitor Tours
7. Homepage

DISTRIBUTOR TOURS

Redhook offered distributors tours of the breweries, conducted on-site sales training, and provided sales support. The latter included providing point-of-sale materials; assistance in designing grocery store displays, stacking, and merchandising inventory; and company sales representative contact with restaurant and grocery buyers. In addition, Redhook often helped distributors in new markets by hiring a local sales representative prior to first distribution to help generate product awareness.

COMMUNITY GATHERINGS

Redhook sponsored and participated in local community gatherings such as craft beer festivals, food events, sporting events, and music and other entertainment programs.

MARKETING ON-SITE

The company promoted its products on-premises at pubs and restaurants. This included providing samples of Redhook products, consumer and retailer education, tap handles, neon signs, banners, coasters, table tents, and glassware. In addition, limited quantities of the company's Blueline label products were placed in selected establishments, providing consumers the chance to try something different and exclusive.

PRICE DISCOUNTING

Redhook selectively discounted prices to distributors and, through them, retailers. Price discounts were a direct response to price cuts by rivals in intensely competitive markets.

COMPANY-OWNED PUBS

There were 3 company-owned and operated pubs: Trolleyman Pub at the Fremont brewery, Forecaster's Public House at Woodinville, and Cataqua Public House at Portsmouth. A pleasant atmosphere with scheduled live music, a complete selection of Redhook beers, and a food menu to complement the beers were used as ways of increasing awareness of and identification with Redhook and its beer. In addition, the pubs were used as sources of consumer feedback on its Blueline and other beers.

VISITOR TOURS

Brewery tours were also used as a means of educating the public about Redhook. Tours took visitors through the brewery, showing key activities in the brewing process. More than 50,000 visitors toured the company's operating breweries in 1997.

HOMEPAGE

Redhook provided a homepage on the World Wide Web and offered classes on brewing through a program called Redhook University.[25] The homepage contained information about the company, its breweries and brewing process; its products, including Blueline offerings; live music schedules for its pubs; news about company progress; a schedule of events; and brewery tours. Redhook University classes available to the public included subjects such as homebrewing, commercial production, brewing science, and brewing history.

Human Resources

The company had 210 employees; 69 in production, 44 in marketing and sales, 15 in administration, and 82 in pubs. Fifty-seven of these worked part time. The company's salesforce was large enough to service the nationwide distributor network.

The executive group consisted of Shipman as President and Chief Executive Officer; Brad Berg, Executive Vice President and Chief Financial Officer; David Mickelson, Executive Vice President and Chief Operating Officer; Pamela Hinkley, Vice President, Sales and Marketing; and Allen Triplett, Vice President, Brewing. Berg, with a bachelor's degree in accounting from the University of Northern Iowa, had experience as a Partner in the Coopers & Lybrand accounting firm and had served in executive positions in Burlington Resources, Inc., and Holly Residential Properties, Inc. Mickelson graduated with a bachelor's degree in business from the University of Washington. He had served as a loan officer for Barclays Bank PLC and as Controller for Certified Foods, Inc., prior to joining Redhook in 1987. Hinckley joined Redhook in 1988 with a bachelor's degree in psychology from Suffolk University and several years' experience in the wine industry, first with Stevenot Winery and later as a wine buyer for a specialty food and wine retailer. Prior to joining Redhook in 1985, Triplett had earned a degree from the University of Wyoming and had studied at the Siebel Institute of Brewing and University of California at Davis. Shipman was considered to be strong in delegation to these executives and encouraged subordinates to develop their own ideas and act on them. His strategy specialist, Anthony Grasst, summed it up as follows:

> You have to be completely independent and willing to do something instinctively rather than by order. Paul believes everybody finds their niche. You either bloom or you die. It's an extraordinarily dynamic environment. You have to take risks. His attitude is: Let's do it.[26]

The management team worked in an open office where collegiality and collaboration were part of the culture. Staff participation in major decisions was common. Even the hiring process was collegial—everyone in a department had a say in who was hired.

Ownership

Anheuser-Busch was the largest Redhook stockholder with a 25% equity interest. GE Capital Redhook Investment Corporation owned 9.3% of the stock while the 3 original Co-owners, Paul Shipman, Jerry Jones, and Gordon Bowker owned 6.4, 3.2, and 2.1%, respectively. The Board of Directors consisted of Shipman and 8 outside directors, including 2 Anheuser-Busch representatives.

Anheuser-Busch's investment in Redhook was subject to a standstill agreement until November 16, 2001. Under the standstill, Anheuser-Busch and its affiliates could not own more than 25% of the common stock prior to November 16, 1999 and not more than 30% after that until November 16, 2001. Anheuser-Busch could terminate the standstill before November 16, 2001, if another individual or organization acquired or attempted to acquire 25% or more of the company's common stock before November 16, 1999, or 30% before November 16, 2001. The standstill could also be terminated in the event of a merger or consolidation agreement between Redhook and a third party.

In September 1995, Redhook's board approved a "poison pill" agreement to protect against any unwanted takeover. In the event of an uninvited takeover bid or the acquisition of 20% or more of the common stock in the open market, stockholders, other than the acquirer, could exercise 1 shareholder right per share held. Each right would allow the holder to buy $240 worth of stock for $120. In the case of a takeover attempt by Anheuser-Busch prior to November 11, 2001, the rights would not be exercisable until Anheuser-Busch bought shares to exceed the limits specified in the standstill agreement.

Financial Performance

Redhook experienced continuous growth in sales through 1996 and income through 1995. Most sales were to distributors although beer, food, and other items sold through the company's pubs contributed to total sales. Pub sales grew to $3,406,000 in 1997 from $3,372,000, $3,347,000, and $1,739,000 in 1996, 1995, and 1994, respectively. **Exhibit 2** shows that while profits were up in each year between 1991 and 1995, the profit growth in 1994 and 1995 was less than the increase in net sales and units sold. Profit in 1996 declined despite a 38% increase in sales. A net loss along

Exhibit 2

Capacity, Units Sold, Sales Revenue, and Net Income

Year	Usable Capacity (barrels)	Barrels Shipped	Change (%)	Net Sales (%)	Change (%)	Net Income (in millions)	Change (%)
1997	425,000	214,600	(4.5%)	$34,286	(8.9%)	($1,399)	(145.3%)
1996	425,000	224,700	42.0%	$35,678	38.0%	$3,086	(3.0%)
1995	245,000	158,700	69.0%	$25,894	73.0%	$3,182	50.0%
1994	135,000	93,700	27.0%	$14,929	30.0%	$2,125	6.0%
1993	75,000	73,900	49.0%	$11,484	42.0%	$2,005	59.0%
1992	75,000	49,500	46.0%	$ 8,086	34.0%	$1,260	74.0%
1991		34,000		$ 5,797		$ 724	

Source: Redhook Ale Brewery, *1995, 1996, and 1997 Annual Reports.*

with a decline in sales was incurred in 1997. Redhook attributed the reduced profits to increased competition from more craft brewers with more brands and price cutting, particularly in the saturated western states' market starting in the second half of 1996. In addition, 1996 and 1997 saw higher costs in establishing national sales and distribution along with the higher depreciation and operating costs associated with the new Portsmouth brewery. The stock market reacted to the company's growth and profit problems with a reduction in Redhook's stock price to about $6 compared to its initial public offering price of $17 and a high of over $34. **Exhibit 3** shows comparative income statements for the years 1993 through 1997.

The growth and profit slump was continued into 1998. In the first quarter of 1998, Redhook reported a net loss of $715,000. Sales volume declined 4.9% from the 1997 first quarter. On the other hand, reductions in sales, marketing, and administration resulted in a decline in selling, general, and administrative expenses of 3.8% over first quarter 1997 figures.

Exhibit 3

Income Statement: Redhook Ale Brewery
(Dollar amounts in thousands, except income per share)

Year Ending December 31	1997	1996	1995	1994	1993
Gross sales	$37,894	$39,410	$28,426	$16,209	$12,331
Less excise taxes	3,608	3,732	2,532	1,280	847
Net sales	34,286	35,678	25,894	14,929	11,484
Cost of sales	25,963	23,581	16,970	8,686	6,163
Gross profit	8,323	12,097	8,924	6,243	5,321
S, G, & A expenses	9,981	7,853	4,606	2,801	2,000
Operating income	(1,658)	4,244	4,318	3,442	3,321
Interest expense	378	—	23	130	158
Other income (expense)	93	615	678	9	40
Income before taxes	(1,943)	4,859	4,973	3,321	3,203
Income taxes	544	1,773	1,791	1,196	1,099
Income before accounting change	(1,399)	3,086	3,182	2,125	2,104
Effect of change in accounting					99
Net income	$(1,399)	$ 3,086	$ 3,182	$ 2,125	$ 2,005
Net income per diluted share	$ (.18)	$ .34	$ .44	$ .43	$ .53

Source: Redhook Ale Brewery, *1996 and 1997 Annual Reports.*

Prior to the 1995 public offering, Redhook had been largely dependent on the use of debt to finance growth. After Anheuser-Busch's 25% investment in Redhook and the company's initial public offering, use of debt decreased. **Exhibit 4** displays leverage ratios prior to and after Anheuser-Busch's investment and the initial public offering in 1995. **Exhibit 5** provides balance sheet data for 1995 through 1997.

At the end of 1997, the company had 7,687,486 shares of common and 1,289,872 shares of convertible redeemable preferred stock outstanding. All of the preferred stock was owned by Anheuser-Busch and was credited as though converted to common stock in calculating that company's share of common stock. Redhook declared an extraordinary dividend of $2.00 per share in 1994 but otherwise had not declared dividends.

The Future?

By late 1996, several conditions had intensified competition and price cutting for craft and specialty beers, including imports. First, the number of craft brewers had continued to grow rapidly. Second, the major beer companies, with their financial, marketing, and distribution strengths had gone on the offensive to try to reach a dominant position in specialty beers. Third, importers had wakened to the increased demand for flavorful, high quality beer and had marketed their well-known brands to consumers who were confused by a myriad of craft beers. Fourth, some regional markets had become saturated and others were approaching saturation. Under these conditions, some craft brewers had grown while others had lost sales. Redhook and several other brewers in the saturated Northwest market were among the latter.

Knowledgeable people, including Redhook's Shipman, suggested the craft beer segment had entered a shakeout period.[27] An increase in closures and consolidation among weaker firms was expected. Other strategic responses to the increased competition included further market development and market penetration on 1 hand and concentration on a focused market on the other. Some craft brewers were continuing their move toward regional and national distribution. A few, including Boston Beer and Pete's Brewing Company and several microbreweries were exporting beer for sale in foreign nations. Smaller microbreweries that had expanded regionally were, in some cases, retrenching and reconcentrating on their home territories where they were better known and had stronger distribution. Major brewers had added to their lines of specialty beers and were aggressively marketing them.

Exhibit 4
Redhook Ale Brewery Use of Debt

Year Ended December 31	Total Debt to Equity	Long-Term Debt to Equity	Total Debt to Total Assets
1997	.58/.25	.16/.13	.37/.20
1996	.52/.21	.10/.08	.34/.17
1995	.45/.15	.03/.02	.31/.13
1994	26.34/.33	2.99/.15	.96/.25
1993	2.0/.33	.31/.14	.67/.25

Note: Convertible redeemable preferred stock is like a debt in that it can be redeemed at its original price under certain conditions. On the other hand, the stock is fully convertible to common and has the same voting rights as common. Because of these features, each ratio is calculated in 2 ways. The first ratio treats preferred stock as a short-term liability (debt) and the second ratio treats it as equity.

Source: Redhook Ale Brewery, 1995, 1996, and 1997 Annual Reports.

Exhibit 5

Balance Sheet: Redhook Ale Brewery

Year Ending December 31	1997	1996	1995
Current assets			
Cash (& equivalent)	$ 892,165	$ 1,162,352	$24,676,600
Receivables	1,588,368	2,051,591	2,027,454
Inventory	2,815,782	2,229,376	1,340,444
Tax receivable & other	1,644,328	2,153,017	272,849
total current assets	6,940,643	7,596,336	28,317,347
Fixed assets (net)	88,761,436	86,357,559	57,799,694
Other assets	1,067,264	1,170,144	521,395
Total assets	96,769,343	95,124,039	86,638,436
Liabilities and equity			
Current liabilities			
Accounts payable	2,290,012	4,075,699	4,828,902
Accrued payroll & taxes	1,322,966	1,220,212	695,645
Refundable deposits	1,166,070	950,926	972,957
Other accrued expenses	231,816	367,025	312,948
Current long-term debt	591,759	132,554	121,659
Total current liabilities	5,602,623	6,746,416	6,932,111
Long-term debt, less current portion	9,873,973	6,190,764	1,825,339
Deferred income taxes	3,987,519	3,582,692	2,389,588
Other	40,546	52,461	35,348
Convertible redeemable Preferred stock	15,966,255	15,921,855	15,877,455
Stockholders equity			
Common stock	38,438	38,428	38,417
Paid-in capital	56,805,633	56,652,764	56,642,663
Retained earnings	4,454,356	5,938,659	2,897,515
Total stockholders equity	61,298,427	62,629,851	59,578,595
Total liabilities and equity	$96,769,343	$95,124,039	$86,638,436

Source: Redhook Ale Brewery, *1995, 1996, and 1997 Annual Reports.*

In spite of the maturity of the beer market, saturation or near saturation in the craft beer segment, and competition-induced lower prices and profit margins, some saw continued growth prospects in craft beer of up to 8% of the national market.[28] With the Anheuser-Busch distribution alliance, Redhook was well positioned to develop new markets, especially the northeast, close to its new brewery in New Hampshire. Earlier, in a 1994 meeting with August Busch III, Shipman was given a rough map of the United States and asked to "put X's where you want to build breweries."[29] Shipman was reported to have put 5 X's on the map. While only 1 new brewery had been built by the end of 1996, in an interview with the author Shipman stated

> I'm convinced that we are going to figure out the keys to success in this industry and act on them in a way that delivers the kind of success that's going to lead to building more breweries.[30]

In 1997, Paul Shipman stated his goals as

1. Continued market development and penetration in the East and other parts of the nation
2. Addressing the shortfall of growth in the West and, particularly, the Pacific Northwest by working with distributors and retailers, introducing new products, and salesmanship
3. In the longer run, growth in international markets, e.g., Japan where Redhook products were being sold through 7-Eleven convenience stores[31]

Into 1998, Redhook had not deviated from the goals and strategy developed when the industry was in a rapid growth phase in spite of the company's sales decline and overall poor performance in 1997. The only strategic change was to cut costs by temporarily closing the Fremont brewery, transferring all Western production to the Woodinville brewery. For Paul Shipman, 1998 was a time for reevaluation. Were Redhook's goals and strategy still valid and, if so, what should be done to implement them in view of the changes in growth and competition affecting the craft beer segment?

Notes

1. Sarah Theodore, "Domestic Specialty Suffers Growing Pains in 97," *Beverage Industry*, January 1998, pp. 9–18.
2. "Specialty and Microbrewery Report," *Modern Brewery Age*, May 18, 1998, pp. 12–17.
3. *Ibid.*
4. Lee Moriwaki, "Shakeout brewing," *The Seattle Times*, November 3, 1996, pp. F1, 4; David Edgar, "Craft Brewing: Fastest Growth in the Industry," *The New Brewer*, May–June 1995, p. 13; and M. Sharon Baker, "Yakima Brewing Defies Industry," *Puget Sound Business Journal*, March 27–April 2, 1998, p. 15.
5. Richard A. Melcher, "Those New Brews Have the Blues," *Business Week*, March 9, 1998, p. 40.
6. "Specialty and Microbrewery Report," pp. 12–17.
7. Sarah Theodore, pp. 9–18.
8. *Ibid.*
9. Eric Sfiligoj, "Small Wonder," *Beverage World*, May 1996, p. 72.
10. John Student, "True Brew," *American Demographics*, May 1995, pp. 32–39.
11. John P. Robinson, "Microbrews Going Mainstream," *American Demographics*, December 1996, pp. 25–26.
12. Eric Sfiligoj, p. 72.
13. Melanie Wells, "Pete's Gut-Instinct Marketing Push," *USA Today*, October 7, 1996, p. 2B.
14. Gene Muller, "Message in a Bottle," *The New Brewer*, July–August 1995, p. 13.
15. Richard A. Melcher, Sandra Dallas, and David Woodruff, "From the Microbrewers Who Brought You Bud, Coors . . . ," *Business Week*, April 24, 1995, pp. 66, 70.
16. Steve Kaufman, "Microbrewery Stocks Look to Full-Bodied Future," *The News Tribune*, April 4, 1996.
17. Maxim Lenderman, "Mind Games," *Beverage World*, September 1996, pp. 70, 72, 74.
18. Jerry Kherouch, "Even as A_B Backs Off, Small Brews Still Face Distribution Bottleneck," *Brandweek*, September 30, 1996, p. 9.
19. *Redhook Ale Brewery 1995 Annual Report.*
20. Redhook Ale Brewery, *Prospectus*, April 16, 1995.
21. Gordon Young, "Attack of the Microbreweries," <http://www.metroactive.com/features/breweries.html>.
22. Gerry Khermouch, "Micros on Majors' Menu at Taste Fest," *Brandweek*, October 31, 1994, p. 12.
23. Gordon Young.
24. *Redhook Ale Brewery 1997 Annual Report.*
25. Redhook Ale Brewery, <http://www.redhook.com>.
26. Leslie Holdcroft, "Going Public a Rebirth for Northwest Brewer," *Washington CEO*, November 1995, p. 15.
27. Lee Moriwaki, "Forecast Sinks Redhook Stock," *The Seattle Times*, December 20, 1996, p. D1.
28. Lee Moriwaki, p. F1, 4.
29. Patricia Sellers, "A Whole New Ball Game In Beer," *Fortune*, September 19, 1994, p. 86.
30. Paul Shipman, Personal Interview, May 16, 1997.
31. *Ibid.*

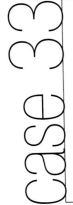

The Boeing Commercial Airplanes Group: Decision 2001

Richard C. Scamehorn

How It All Started—The Boeing Company

With the advent of World War I, Bill Boeing started The Boeing Company in 1916 in response to the military's growing interest in air power. Their first big success, during the peace between World War I and World War II, was the B-9 bomber, called the "Death Angel."

In the mid-1930s Boeing developed Project "X," later called the XB-15. Although not a success, its technology led to the development of the B-17. This heavy bomber, when viewed by the press in 1940, had so many machine guns as protective armament that 1 reporter called it, a "Flying Fortress." The name stuck and it was produced in greater numbers than any other large aircraft during World War II.

Boeing's further advancements came with jet-powered aircraft: The B-47 "Stratojet," The KC-135 "Tanker," and the B-52. The B-52 was first used by the United States Air Force during the 1950s and it remains today as the workhorse heavy bomber of the U.S. Air Force.

However, Boeing's greatest claim to fame was in commercial aircraft. Utilizing the KC-135 technology, Boeing developed the world's first successful long-range commercial jet transport—the B-707. This airplane created the "jet set." Passengers could now fly overnight from Europe to Asia or North America, or with a refueling stop, from Asia to North America. It cut the travel from Europe to North America from 5 days (by ship) to 8 hours, and across the Pacific from 10 days to 17 hours. It obsoleted entire fleets of steamships and made international travel so economical that it became a common event for both pleasure and business.

Boeing quickly followed this success with a mid-range B-727, followed by a short-range B-737. Then, in 1969, Boeing launched the era of the jumbo jets with the maiden flight of the B-747 jumbo jet from New York to Los Angeles carrying 385 passengers. With this stable of safe, reliable aircraft, Boeing dominated the world's aircraft market. McDonnell Douglas developed its jumbo jet DC-10 and Lockheed had its L-1011, but neither could challenge the B-747.

Boeing then increased its competitive advantage by "stretching" the B-747 into a B-747-SUD (Stretched-Upper-Deck) allowing 40 first-class passengers to sit in the upper level in isolated quiet. They further developed the 747-SP for ultra-long-range flights, nonstop from Sydney to Los Angeles. This was accomplished by shortening the body, removing 35 rows of seats, and using the resultant savings of weight to add additional fuel tanks for the increased

This case was prepared by Richard C. Scamehorn, Executive in-Residence Emeritus, at Ohio University. This case was edited for SMBP-8th Edition. Copyright © 2001 by Richard C. Scamehorn. Reprinted by permission.

range. The most recent design is the B-747-400, a high performance, fuel-efficient, long-range version that became the standard for long-haul, intercontinental flights. **Exhibit 1** shows the major products manufactured and sold by Boeing's 3 strategic business segments—(1) Boeing Commercial Aircraft, (2) Boeing Military Aircraft and Missile Systems, and (3) Boeing Space and Communications and (4) other units. The 2000 sales and other operating revenues for these segments were $31,171,000,000 (60.7%), $12,197,000,000 (23.8%) $8,039,000,000 (15.7%) and $758,000,000 (1.4%),[1] respectively (less accounting adjustments of $844,000,000).

A Late Entrant into the Industry

Airbus Industrie was formed on December 18, 1970 as a *Groupement d'Interet Economique* (the French term for a grouping of economic interests), with the governments of France, Germany, and Britain as partners. The private companies involved represented some of the world's best aircraft technology. They were Aerospatile (of France) with 37.9% ownership, Daimler-Benz Aerospace Airbus (of Germany) also with 37.9% ownership, British Aerospace Ltd. with 20%, and Construcciones Aeronauticas SA (CASA of Spain) with 4.2%.

With this consortium of noteworthy firms, the most advanced economies of Europe became stakeholders in Airbus Industrie, giving it commercial advantage within the European Common Market (later to become the European Union). However, the organization, or more explicitly, the lack of an organization, was dysfunctional. The partners were continuously required to agree on each business decision since the organization lacked a CEO or Managing Director who, under a corporate structure, would make such management decisions.

Airbus Industrie developed innovative features in their aircraft which were offered by neither Boeing nor McDonnell Douglas. They included:

1. A large reduction in the number of mechanical parts
2. Comprehensive built-in diagnostic test equipment
3. Reduction of maintenance
4. Reduced airframe weight
5. Better aircraft handling
6. Easier introduction of active controls
7. Simpler autoflight system interface
8. Better optimization of control functions
9. The first inflatable passenger evacuation slide with in-fuselage storage
10. The first extended twin operations (ETOPS) with airborne auxiliary power units for high-altitude engine restarts

These features were important to airlines for both safety and operational economies. In addition, Airbus Industrie created virtually identical flight decks, handling characteristics, and procedures that were shared by the A-320 family and the A-330/340 family. This commonality, covering aircraft from 120 seats to 400 seats, is possible only with the similar handling that can be achieved from a fly-by-wire control system. It leads to Cross Crew Qualification (CCQ) and Mixed Fleet Flying (MFF) and the resultant cost benefits.

CCQ enables a pilot to train for a new aircraft type with "Difference Training" instead of a new full type rating training course because the flight decks, handling characteristics, and operational procedures of CCQ-capable aircraft are so similar. Difference Training is 70% shorter than training for a completely dissimilar aircraft. As an example, when adding 4 A-330s to an existing fleet of 20 A-320s, CCQ can reduce training costs by $500,000 per additional aircraft per year.

---

1. This adds to 101.6%. The accounting differences and eliminations were $844,000,000 (1.6%) so with this subtracted—the four would equal 100.0%

Exhibit 1

Strategic Business Unit Products: Boeing Company

A. Boeing Commercial Airplanes

Alan Mulany, President / Renton, Washington

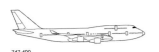
747-400

The Boeing 747-400

The 747-400 seats 416 to 568 passengers, depending on seating configuration and, with the recent launch of the Longer-Range 747-400, has a range of 8,850 miles. With its huge capacity, long range and fuel efficiency, the 747 offers the lowest operating cost per seat of any twin-aisle commercial jetliner. The 747-400 is available in an all-cargo freighter version as well as a combi model for passengers and cargo. Boeing continues to study 747 derivatives that will fly farther or carry more passengers to continue the 747 leadership in meeting the world's need for high-capacity, long-range airplanes.

Orders: 1,338[1] Deliveries: 1,261

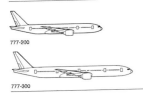
777-200

777-300

The Boeing 777-200 and 777-300

The 777-200, which seats 305 to 440 passengers depending on configuration, has a range of up to 5,925 miles. The 777-200ER (extended range) can fly the same number of passengers up to 8,861 miles. The 777-300 is about 33 feet longer than the -200 and can carry from 368 to 550 passengers, depending on seating configuration, with a range of 6,854 miles. The company recently introduced two longer-range 777s.

Orders: 563[1] Deliveries: 316

767-200

767-300

767-400

The Boeing 767-200, 767-300, and 767-400

The 767-200 will typically fly 181 to 224 passengers up to 7,618 miles in its extended-range version. The 767-300, also offered in an extended-range version, offers 20 percent more passenger seating. A freighter version of the 767-300 is available. The first extended-range 767-400ERs were delivered to Delta Air Lines and Continental Airlines in August 2000. The airplane typically will carry between 245 and 304 passengers up to 6,501 miles. In a high-density inclusive tour arrangement, the 767-400ER can carry up to 375 passengers. Boeing committed to production in September 2000 a longer-range 767-400ER. This longer-range version is the same size as the 767-400ER, but has the equivalent range of the 767-300ER.

Orders: 901[1] Deliveries: 817

757-200

757-300

The Boeing 757-200 and 757-300

Seating 194 passengers in two classes, the 757-200 is ideal for high-demand, short-to-medium-range operations and can fly nonstop intercontinental routes up to 4,500 miles. It is also available in a freighter version. The 757-300 can carry 240 to 289 passengers on routes of up to 3,990 miles.

Orders: 1,027[1] Deliveries: 948

737-600

737-700

737-800

737-900

The Boeing 737-600, 737-700, 737-800 and 737-900

The Boeing 737 is the best-selling commercial jetliner of all time. The Next-Generation 737-600/-700/-800/-900 have outsold all other airplanes in their market segment. These new 737s incorporate advanced technology and design features that translate into cost-efficient, high-reliability operations and outstanding passenger comfort. The 737 is the only airplane family to span the entire 100-to-189-seat market, with maximum ranges from 3,159 (the -900) to 3,752 (the -700) miles. The 737 family also includes two Boeing Business Jets, derivatives of the 737-700 and -800.

Orders: 4,873[1] Deliveries: 3,857

717-200

The Boeing 717-200

The 717 twinjet meets the growing need worldwide for a 100-seat, high-frequency, short-range jet, flying a maximum range of 1,647 miles. The durable, simple, ultra-quiet and clean twinjet's effective use of technology results in the lowest operating costs.

Orders: 151[1] Deliveries: 44

Boeing Commercial Aviation Services

Boeing Commercial Aviation Services

Boeing Commercial Aviation Services provides the most complete portfolio of commercial aviation support products and services in the industry. This organization is an important component in the company's total solutions approach, and offers a wide range of products and services aimed at bringing even more value to our customers. This includes spare parts, airplane modification and engineering support, and a comprehensive worldwide customer support network. Commercial Aviation Services also oversees a number of joint ventures such as FlightSafetyBoeing Training International and wholly owned subsidiaries Jeppesen Sanderson Inc., Continental Graphics and The Preston Group.

1. Orders and deliveries as of December 31, 2000.
2. Order numbers do not include options.
3. For Section D--Other Units title added by authors.

(continues)

Exhibit 1

Strategic Business Unit Products: Boeing Company (*continued*)

B. Boeing Military Aircraft and Missile Systems

Jerry Daniels, President / St. Louis, Missouri

C-17 Globemaster III

The C-17 Globemaster III is the most advanced, versatile airlifter ever made. It is capable of flying long distances, carrying 169,000 pounds of payload and landing on short, austere runways close to front lines. Since entering operational service in 1995, the C-17 has become the U.S. Air Force's premier airlifter. The United Kingdom is the C-17's first international customer.

C-17 Globemaster III

F/A-18E/F Super Hornet

The F/A-18E/F Super Hornet is the nation's newest, most advanced strike fighter, designed from its inception to perform both fighter (air-to-air) and attack (air-to-surface) missions. During 2000, deliveries continued ahead of schedule. The Super Hornet also received the 1999 Collier Trophy, and the U.S. Navy's highest possible grade for operational evaluation.

F/A-18E/F Super Hornet

Joint Strike Fighter

Boeing and the JSF One Team have developed an affordable multirole strike fighter to meet the tactical aircraft modernization needs of the U.S. Air Force, Navy and Marine Corps, and also the United Kingdom Royal Air Force and Royal Navy. Boeing is building and flight-testing two concept demonstration aircraft while also designing the operational JSF. During design and build of the aircraft, Boeing demonstrated the lean design and manufacturing processes that will keep JSF affordable for all military services. Selection of a single contractor to build as many as 3,000 of the multiservice fighters is scheduled for 2001.

JSF Preferred Weapon
System Concept

F-22 Raptor

Boeing and Lockheed Martin are developing the U.S. Air Force's next-generation air superiority fighter. The team is building nine flight-test and two ground-test aircraft, and eight production-representative test vehicles. The Raptor is meeting all performance requirements.

F-22 Raptor

F-15 Eagle

The F-15E Eagle is the world's most capable multirole fighter and the backbone of the U.S. Air Force fleet. The F-15E carries payloads larger than any other tactical fighter but retains the air-to-air capability of the F-15C. It can operate around the clock and in any weather. Since entering operational service, the F-15 has a perfect air combat record with more than 100 victories and no losses. Three other nations fly the F-15.

F-15 Eagle

AV-8B Harrier II Plus

The newest upgraded variant of the AV-8 Harrier family, the multimission Harrier II Plus adds the APG-65 radar system to the aircraft's proven vertical/short-takeoff-and-landing capabilities. A Boeing, BAE Systems and Rolls-Royce team produces the AV-8B. The Harrier II Plus was developed through a three-nation agreement among the United States, Spain and Italy.

AV-8B Harrier II Plus

T-45 Goshawk

The T-45 Goshawk aircraft is the key component of the U.S. Navy's T-45 Training System. The system includes advanced flight simulators, a computer-assisted instructional program, a computerized training integration system, and a contractor logistics support package. U.S. Navy and Marine Corps student naval aviators train in the T-45 at Naval Air Stations Meridian, Mississippi, and Kingsville, Texas.

T-45 Goshawk

V-22 Osprey

In partnership with Bell Helicopter Textron, Boeing has developed the V-22 Osprey tiltrotor aircraft. Low-rate initial production and flight testing have begun. Initial deliveries of 360 aircraft to the U.S. Marine Corps began in 1999. The U.S. Special Operations Command has 50 CV-22s on order.

V-22 Osprey

CH-47 Chinook

Preparation is under way for a new modernization program for the U.S. Army's CH-47 Chinook. The CH-47F is scheduled to enter the fleet in 2003 with several major system improvements. Under this program, Chinooks will remain in Army service at least until 2033 and will achieve an unprecedented 71-year service life. Boeing is also manufacturing CH-47SD Chinooks for international customers.

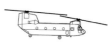
CH-47 Chinook

RAH-66 Comanche

The Boeing-Sikorsky team is developing the RAH-66 Comanche, the U.S. Army's 21st century combat helicopter. Two prototypes are in flight test. In the year 2001, the program will validate aircraft systems and prepare for development of 13 production-representative aircraft for operational test, evaluation and training.

RAH-66 Comanche

Exhibit 1

Strategic Business Unit Products: Boeing Company (*continued*)

B. Boeing Military Aircraft and Missile Systems (continued)

AH-64D Apache Longbow

AH-64D Apache Longbow

The AH-64D Apache Longbow, an advanced version of the combat-proven AH-64A Apache, is the most lethal, survivable, deployable and maintainable multimission combat helicopter in the world. In addition to multiyear contracts from the U.S. Army for 501 Apache Longbow aircraft, Boeing is under contract to deliver advanced Apache aircraft to the Netherlands, Singapore and the United Kingdom. Egypt and Israel are finalizing agreements for new or remanufactured AH-64Ds, and several other nations are considering the Apache Longbow for their defense forces.

SLAM-ER

JDAM

CALCM

SLAM-ER, JDAM, CALCM

A world leader in all-weather precision munitions, Boeing covers a wide spectrum of attack weapon capabilities. These include the Standoff Land Attack Missile Expanded Response (SLAM-ER), the Joint Direct Attack Munition (JDAM), the Conventional Air Launched Cruise Missile (CALCM), the Air-to-Ground Missile (AGM-130), and Brimstone and Harpoon missiles. Customers include all U.S. military services and the armed forces of 27 other nations. Export sales are approved by the U.S. government.

Military Aerospace Support

Military Aerospace Support

Military Aerospace Support is developing and delivering innovative products and services to reduce life-cycle costs and increase the effectiveness of aircraft and missile systems fielded around the globe. The business has a comprehensive support portfolio that includes upgrade, modification and maintenance programs; a full range of training systems and services; support systems; domestic and international logistics support services; and sustainment data and supply chain management support competencies.

C. Boeing Space and Communications

Jim Albaugh, President / Seal Beach, California

Space Shuttle

Space Shuttle

The Space Shuttle is the world's only operational, reusable and human-rated launch vehicle. Boeing builds, maintains, modifies and, as a United Space Alliance partner, operates the Shuttle system. Boeing also builds, tests and performs flight processing for the Shuttle's main engines – the world's only reusable liquid-fueled large rocket engines. Boeing-developed upgrades could enable the Shuttle to fly to 2030 and beyond.

Delta II

Delta II

Delta II has become the industry standard for reliability, on-time delivery of payloads to orbit, and customer satisfaction since its introduction in 1989. Delta II enjoys a 97-percent success rate for more than 90 launches.

Delta III

Delta III

With the successful launch of Delta III on August 23, 2000, the performance of operational Delta vehicles has nearly doubled, with demonstrated ability to place up to 3,810-kg class commercial satellites into geosynchronous transfer orbit.

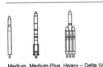
Medium, Medium-Plus, Heavy – Delta IV

Delta IV

The Boeing Delta family of rockets continues to evolve to meet launch market needs and will offer a family of launch vehicles, beginning in 2002, for nearly every payload class from 900 kg to more than 13,000 kg to geosynchronous transfer orbit. The Delta IV will bring assured and affordable access to space while lowering the per-kilogram cost of launch to orbit by up to 50 percent.

Sea Launch

Sea Launch

Boeing is part of an international consortium, including firms from Russia, Ukraine and Norway, that conducts commercial satellite launches from a mobile sea-based platform. Sea Launch successfully launched its first commercial payload in October 1999 from the equatorial Pacific. Home port is Long Beach, California.

International Space Station

International Space Station

Boeing is prime contractor to NASA for the design, development and on-orbit performance of the International Space Station. The first components were joined in orbit in 1998. In 2000 the station began hosting humans and by 2005 will permanently house up to seven crew members. Station assembly will require more than 40 U.S. and Russian launches.

(*continues*)

Exhibit 1

Strategic Business Unit Products: Boeing Company (*continued*)

C. Boeing Space and Communications (continued)

NMD Prime Contractor

Boeing is prime contractor for the National Missile Defense (NMD) program, which is designed to defend the United States from a limited ICBM attack. The multiyear, multibillion-dollar effort calls for the company to develop, test and integrate all NMD elements. The program has enjoyed several successful integrated flight demonstrations. Current plans include developing and demonstrating the system to a point at which a decision to deploy can be made within the next several years.

NMD Prime Contractor

Future Imagery Architecture

In 1999, a Boeing-led team was awarded the FIA contract from the National Reconnaissance Office (NRO) – a key element of the NRO's space-based architecture. This significant contract, which extends through 2010, confirms the leadership position of Boeing in the area of space imaging.

Future Imagery Architecture

Global Positioning System

Boeing has built a total of 40 GPS satellites. Currently, Boeing is under contract to build six follow-on Block IIF satellites with a possibility of 27 additional vehicles. Additionally, Boeing is under U.S. Air Force contract to lead the ground control segment of the GPS constellation and is competing to build the next-generation GPS Block III.

Global Positioning System

Airborne Laser

Boeing is prime contractor on the Airborne Laser program and leads a team with a $1.3-billion contract to conduct the program definition and risk reduction phase of the ABL program. This U.S. Air Force effort is intended to explore the feasibility of an airborne laser system for defense against tactical theater ballistic missiles during their boost phase. Boeing is also leading a national team on the Space-Based Laser program.

Airborne Laser

737-700 Airborne Early Warning & Control System

In 2000, a Boeing-led team was selected to develop an AEW&C system for Turkey and Australia. The program, which in Australia is known as Project Wedgetail, will utilize 737-700 aircraft to provide airborne electronic and communications systems for the Turkish and Australian defense forces. Boeing has gained significant experience on such systems through 30 years of successfully designing, developing and managing 707 AWACS and 767 AWACS systems and upgrades.

737-700 Airborne Early Warning & Control System

Boeing 376, Boeing 601, Boeing 702

With the October 2000 acquisition of Hughes Electronics' space and communications businesses, Boeing Satellite Systems is the world's largest manufacturer of commercial communications satellites. Core products include: the versatile Boeing 376 spacecraft; the Boeing 601 satellite, the world's best-selling large spacecraft; and the Boeing 702, the world's highest power satellite. Boeing Satellite Systems has launched over 190 satellites since 1963, including 12 in 2000.

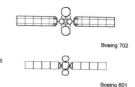
Boeing 702
Boeing 376
Boeing 601

D. Other Units

Boeing Capital Corporation   Jim Palmer, President / Renton, Washington

An asset-based leasing and lending organization, Boeing Capital Corporation manages a portfolio of more than $6 billion in assets, an amount that could grow significantly in the next five years. For more than 30 years, it has been a worldwide provider of lease and loan financing for all types of commercial and business aircraft and a wide range of commercial equipment.

Connexion by Boeing   Scott Carson, President / Kent, Washington

Connexion by Boeing℠ will effectively change the way people travel by providing high-speed, two-way Internet and live television services to aircraft in flight. Through the service, two-way, broadband (or high-data-rate) connectivity is delivered directly to airline seats, providing passengers with personalized and secure access to the Internet, company intranets and live television and audio content. Connexion by Boeing will also provide airline personnel with information that will enhance operational efficiency on the ground and in the air.

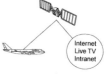
Internet
Live TV
Intranet
Connexion by Boeing

Air Traffic Management   John Hayhurst, President / Kent, Washington

Many of the world's air traffic systems are straining today to maintain efficient, reliable and convenient service, much less support the anticipated growth. Boeing is developing an air traffic management system that will dramatically increase capacity, improve safety and remain affordable for those who use the system. It will require a fundamental change to how the system operates. The Boeing approach involves defining system requirements, applying an operational concept that supports those requirements and selecting the right technology set.

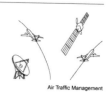
Air Traffic Management

Source: The Boeing Company, *2000 Annual Report*, pp 100–103.

This gets pilots out of the retraining program and back on flight duty faster, increasing crew productivity up to 20%. It results in total savings of over $1,000,000 per additional aircraft per year.

The Boeing 777

In the late 1980s, Airbus Industrie had launched 2 new 300-seat aircraft—the twin engine A-330 and the longer range, 4-engine A-340. The economies of Airbus' twin-engine, wide-body jumbo jet interested the world's airlines. Boeing considered the concept of introducing a double-deck version of Boeing's successful B-767, but discussions with airline executives caused them to shelve this idea.

Instead, in December, 1989, Boeing announced the B-777 project: a totally new twin-engine design with 310 to 395 seats (depending on multiple or single class configuration). This program would become Boeing's largest project since the highly successful B-747 program of the 1960s. The staggering development cost of the B-777 was budgeted at more than $6 billion.

Boeing put Philip Condit (later to become Boeing's Chairman and CEO) in charge of the exciting program. Condit utilized the previously proven concept of sharing the risk of the development costs with the major subcontractors and also introduced new features in the development of the B-777. Foremost was the inclusion of airline executive's inputs, which Boeing called "working together," into the features of the B-777. United Airlines, the first buyer of the new plane, had the largest role along with executives from 7 of the other world's airlines.

In addition, the B-777 was Boeing's first plane designed completely by computer, without the usual full-scale mock-ups to identify interferences of either mechanical or electronic components. Further, the design would also be Boeing's first to utilize state-of-the-art fly-by-wire controls instead of mechanical linkages to move the airplane's control surfaces.

By June 1995 the B-777s were operating at the world's airlines and its acceptance was typified in a British Airways report that, "It's been the most successful new aircraft ever to enter the fleet."

Unfortunately, not every aspect of the B-777 program was hailed as successful. The implementation of the computer-design program's cost was at least 50% more than Boeing's traditional hard-copy, blueprint approach.

Although a stand-alone success, critics of the B-777 program argued that it cannibalized sales from Boeing's biggest profit generator, the B-747-400. The B-747-400's nominal seating capacity was 416; about 20% larger than the B-777. These critics argued that some amount (the exact percentage had a wide range) of B-747-400s would have been sold to these customers instead without the $6 billion development cost.

From the standpoint of strategic market mix, the B-777 allowed Boeing to catch up with Airbus' A-330, but not surpass the Airbus product line (the creators of state-of-the-art fly-by-wire controls in commercial jets). As Boeing was making deliveries of the B-777s, Airbus was talking with the world's airlines about a "super-jumbo" airliner, a step beyond any existing design.

Boeing Buys Big

In December, 1996, Philip Condit announced that Boeing would acquire McDonnell Douglas Corporation. The news shocked the world's aerospace industry, wondering why Boeing would want to buy the manufacturer of the MD-11 jumbo and the smaller MD-80 jet. Pundits thought the deal would have a difficult time obtaining approval from the U.S. Justice Department and an even more difficult process obtaining approval from the European Union's Competition Commission, who had already stalled a proposed merger between American Airlines and British Airways.

After these critics examined the deal further, they realized that McDonnell Douglas' strong position in defense market products would complement Boeing's weak position. Correspondingly, Boeing's strong position in commercial airliners would complement McDonnell Douglas' weak position.

With this conclusion, approvals followed by both U.S. Justice Department and EU Competition Commission. Harry Stonecipher, McDonnell Douglas' Chairman and CEO, became Boeing's Vice Chair and Chief Operating Officer. Many thought this also was a synergistic outcome, since Stonecipher was a hands-on operational specialist, whereas Condit gave more attention to strategic events. *Fortune*, describing the relationship in Condit's own words, "He [Stonecipher] can see a hole in an operational plan from 50 yards. I, for whatever reason, can see around corners."

The acquisition was successfully completed in 1997.

A Change in the Product Line

Following the successful launch of the B-777, it became clear that the MD-11 jumbo jet was redundant and was dropped from the enlarged Boeing product line. For some time, the future of the much smaller MD-80, now restyled as the MD-95, was unclear. The MD-95 was close in seating capacity to the B-737 (although smaller), and was therefore considered as a possible competitor to the B-737, therefore, many thought that it would follow the MD-11 to oblivion.

However, as private business jets were becoming larger and more customized, Boeing announced the B-717 during the summer of 1997, a shortened version of the MD-95. It was the only business jet offering well over 100 seats, and many observers felt a business jet with such a large seating capacity would serve only a tiny niche segment. Others concluded that the only reason Boeing made this move was out of loyalty to the major risk-sharing subcontractors who had invested to keep the MD-95 program alive.

The Summer of 1997

The successful acquisition of McDonnell Douglas was good reason to break out the champagne, and there was reason to break out a second bottle! Boeing had been booking orders at a pace that elevated their backlog to a record altitude. There were 2 reasons for this.

First, the airline industry was upgrading their fleets of aircraft. With the availability of the B-767 and B-777 along with the A-330 and A-340, no airline wanted to be labeled as having an "old" fleet. They all wanted to brag to the market that they fly the most modern equipment in the industry.

Second, the price was right. Boeing's President of commercial aircraft, Ron Wooddard, believed that a newly instituted production system, called DCAC/MRM would reduce costs by as much as 25%. Based upon this, Boeing began discounting prices to customers in an attempt to achieve a publicly stated goal of 67% market share. Although it looked like the right thing at the time, it would soon develop into a classic "Hurry Up and Wait" scenario.

The Hurry Up

The onslaught of orders raised Boeing's contractual backlog to record levels (see **Exhibit 1**), and by the summer of 1997 it appeared necessary to double production output. The plan for the hot-selling B-737 was to ramp up production from 10 planes per month to 24 per month by the spring of 1998. The leviathan B-747-400, currently at 2 planes per month, was scheduled to increase to 5 per month by 1998.

In an interview with the *Wall Street Journal*, Wooddard said, "There's no doubt we are intentionally driving the system right to the ragged edge [to achieve market share]. We're nervous about everything, but we're not panicked and we're not going to miss our schedules." He further forecast that the company's total output would rise from the 1996 level of 18 planes per month to 43 per month by the spring of 1998 (the previous record output was 39 per month in 1992).

The Wait

Unfortunately, this attempt ran head-on into the unsuccessful implementation of DCAC/MRM and the result was chaos. Shortages of thousands of parts developed from Boeing's 3,000 parts suppliers. By the fall of 1997, Boeing managers said that parts shortages ranged at times from 2,000 parts up to 7,000 parts. On September 15, Boeing announced it would miss deliveries for 12 of the 36 aircraft scheduled for September delivery, including 4 of its most profitable B-747-400s.

As the situation worsened, production personnel were averaging 20% overtime each week (some were working 7 days per week). The company was planning to hire 400 workers from the McDonnell Douglas plant in Long Beach, California, some from rival Lockheed Martin Corporation, and even some from the airlines. The situation finally got so bad that production of the 2 hot sellers—the B-737 and the B-747-400—actually had to be halted for 3 weeks in October, 1997.

The outcome from this chaos was a third-quarter loss of $696,000,000. This news was followed by the announcement on October 22 that Boeing would sustain a "production disruption" charge of $2,600,000,000 against earnings. As a result, 1997 performance showed a loss.

These losses were only part of the picture. Boeing rescheduled 2 of the 4 B-737-700s for Southwest Airlines from late 1997 into 1998. In addition, deliveries of 21 B-737-700s would slip by at least 1 month. Southwest, the nation's eighth largest carrier, was the "launch" customer for Boeing's new B-737-700. This news caused Southwest Airlines, a highly successful low-cost (but high profit) airline to delay its plans to expand service to a new city by as much as 3 months.

With the exit of 1997, a flu bug was making an entrance—the Asian economic flu. Although it showed signs of development in 1997, it wasn't until 1998 that the effects started to translate into events at Boeing. The company felt its first hit when Philippine Airlines announced in January 1998 that it could not accept delivery of 4 B-747-400s, valued at about $600 million. About the same time, Thai Airlines asked for a delay in 1998 deliveries and Asiana Airlines asked that a B-777 delivery be delayed from 1998 to 1999.

The economic flu showed some additional and unusual symptoms in the Asian airline industry. Singapore Airlines, 1 of the world's most respected, asked Northwest Airlines to purchase some of their (then) surplus used aircraft. It was later determined that Asiana Airlines took the same approach. The impact on Boeing was nearly overwhelming. Just as Boeing was ramping up for a huge production expansion, airlines in Asia wanted substantial delays. At the start of 1998, 30% of Boeing's backlog was for planes bound for Asia. Industry analysts estimated that 70 to 80 aircraft scheduled for 1998 shipment could be delayed or even cancelled.

On January 23, 1998, Boeing was forced to announce that their plan to raise production (developed just 2 months earlier) to 47 planes per month was now being scaled back to about 43 per month. The difference between 47 and 43 per month would amount to about $1.5 billion in lost revenue for 1998.

Like an unwelcome nightmare, delays and cancellations increased just as Boeing was trying to increase production. By March, 1998, Boeing announced a downsizing of 8,200 jobs due to the closing of former McDonnell Douglas defense plants. This was in addition to 12,000 cuts announced the prior December.

Adding to problems was a ruling from Europe's Joint Aviation Authority. Because of the larger seating capacity of the B-737-700, the Authority had ruled the Boeing must redesign the plane's over-the-wing emergency exits. By the time Boeing came up with the necessary changes, 2 dozen B-737-700s had already been produced; it would be necessary to retrofit these planes. An additional 35 planes being built would need to be put on hold until the necessary parts were available. Boeing eked out a profit in the first quarter of 1998, but that was all. More important, because of price discounting, product margins had dropped from 11% to 4.8%.

In 1999, the cancellations and delays continued and caused a major reduction in Boeing's contractual backlog of orders. From the end of 1998 to the end of 1999, the contractual backlog shrank by $13,688,000,000 even though shipments had increased during the period by only $1,839,000,000, roughly a quarter of a year's production (see **Exhibit 2**).

The Bad News Continues

In March, 1999, the National Transportation Safety Board started considering a demand that Boeing implement extensive and expensive modifications to its B-737, the world's most popular jet aircraft. This issue stemmed from the 1994 crash of a U.S. Airways jet in which problems with the rudder controls were the prime suspect. A United Airlines B-737 crash in Colorado added to these concerns.

As Boeing developed successive generations of the B-737, they were allowed to "grandfather-in" most of the basic design concepts of the original version. The rudder control mechanism was one of those design concepts that was grandfathered. What was suspect was known as "rudder reversal": a phenomenon when the pilot pushed on the right rudder pedal the rudder would shift, not to the right (as expected) but to the left. As a result, the plane responded just the opposite of what was expected, so the pilot tended to push harder on the right rudder pedal, causing the rudder to shift further to the left. This could cause the pilot to lose control of the plane (and this was suspected to be the cause of at least 1 crash). Although the NTSB had not yet made any final directive, the preliminary conclusion did not bode well for Boeing.

In September 2000, Boeing agreed to replace the rudder control systems on all 4,000 of its B-737 aircraft. After years of opposing such a retrofit, Boeing agreed to spend an estimated $200 million to design and install a redundant, dual-valve rudder control system to replace the single hydraulic valve system originally supplied. Boeing refused to supply an additional feature of a rudder position indicator (requested by pilots), which would show the position of the rudder on the cockpit's panel.

Exhibit 2

Financial Highlights: Boeing Company
(Dollar amounts in millions, except per share data)

	2000	1999	1998	1997	1996	1995
Sales & other operating revenues	$51,321	$57,993	$56,154	$45,800	$35,453	$32,960
Net earnings (loss)	2,128	2,309	1,120	(178)	1,818	(36)
Earnings per share: diluted	2.44	2.49	1.15	(.18)	1.85	(.04)
Contractual backlog	120,600	99,248	112,896	121,640	114,173	95,448
Research & development	1,441	1,341	1,895	1,924	1,633	1,674
Capital expenditures	932	1,236	1,665	1,391	971	747
Cash & short-term investments	1,010	3,454	2,462	5,149	6,352	4,527
Customer financing assets	6,959	6,004	5,711	4,600	3,888	4,212
Total debt	8,799	6,732	6,972	6,854	7,489	5,401
Cash dividends	504	537	564	557	480	537

Source: The Boeing Company.

Strike 1

As if this were not enough, in February 2000, Boeing's white-collared engineers union, which had affiliated with the AFL-CIO, launched the first major strike in its 56-year history. The union held out for more than a month and caused the shipping delay of at least 50 aircraft. The union leader told *Fortune*, "We weren't fighting against Boeing, we were fighting to save Boeing." All this concern stemmed from the Boeing Company's culture as an engineering driven company. With no new designs slated for production, engineers were becoming redundant, and Harry Stonecipher was determined to cut costs to enhance profitability. The engineers decided to formalize their protest.

It was clear that the culture at Boeing was changing. Wall Street thought it was for the better. The engineers thought otherwise.

Strike 2

In October 2000, the Federal Aviation Administration announced the results of "special [quality] audit," held early that year of 7 of Boeing's aircraft engineering and manufacturing facilities. It found "deep-rooted" and "systemic" problems in the company's design and manufacturing systems.

The FAA conducted the audit after what it called a "series of high-visibility production breakdowns" during the fall of 1999. It included everything from aircraft engineering to the manufacturing process at Boeing plants in Seattle, Everett, Renton, Auburn, Fredrickson and Spokane, Washington, and in Portland, Oregon.

Some of the specific incidents included:

- An airline told Boeing that 2 of 16 bolts holding the vertical stabilizer onto the tail of a B-767 were not sufficiently tightened.
- Assembly line mechanics at Boeing's Everett plant (where B-747s, B-767s and B-777s are built) reported that fuel tank repairs were being made after the tanks had been inspected and that debris, such as sealant tubes and rivet guns, was occasionally left behind.
- An adhesive was applied improperly to a condensation barrier that keeps moisture from dripping onto cockpit electronics.

These, and other specifics, led the FAA to conclude that:

- Some production processes were "incomplete or overly complex."
- Work instructions were "inadequate."
- Inspections, to ensure products conformed with design, were "inadequate."
- Some rank-and-file workers were "not knowledgeable" of approved processes and procedures.

At a news conference, John Hickey of the FAA stated that, "The findings show that these were not isolated events. What we found were very deep-rooted systemic problems that, if uncorrected, could result in noncompliance [with federal regulations]."

Liz Otis, Boeing's Commercial Airplanes Groups Vice President for Quality, agreed with the audit findings. As a result, Boeing agreed to add at least 370 new positions to its own inspection system while the company and the FAA are jointly evaluating whether increased maintenance efforts are required for certain production operations.

Officials of both Boeing and the government said they expected that millions of dollars of fines and penalties might be assessed against Boeing.

Airbus Catches Up

Early in January 1998, Airbus Industrie decided to brag a little bit, announcing that they had booked 671 aircraft orders and commitments in 1997, valued at $44.2 billion. This included a record 460 firm orders valued at $29.6 billion (see **Exhibit 3**). Although Boeing was ready to announce firm orders for 524 aircraft, Airbus still saw this high level of bookings as the airline industry's endorsement of their products. Managing Director Jean Pierson said they were, "Now well on course to achieving our objective of a consistent 50% market share early in the next century."

There were inconsistencies in these calculations, as evidenced by the claims for 1996 market share: Airbus claimed 42% while Boeing was claiming 64% share. Notwithstanding this difference, it was now clear that Airbus Industrie had arrived as Boeing's equal in the aircraft manufacturing industry (see **Exhibit 3**).

Results

During the past 5 years, revenues continued to increase, but organizational difficulties caused erratic profitability and the engineers strike would limit earnings in 2000 (see **Exhibit 2**). Other trends, such as shrinking research and development expenditures demonstrated Boeing's capability to manage for improved profitability.

In addition, Boeing had the capability to support their customer's financing needs and continued to show increases in this asset on its balance sheet.

The Airbus Industrie Organization

As late as the summer of 1999, the various Airbus partners declared that, ". . . too many obstacles stand in the way of quick moves toward that goal [of incorporation]." There were reports of a major spate in 1999, when 1 partner planned to acquire a business which would impinge on another partner, and when the actions of 1 firm's government acted to the detriment of another's government. In particular, the French Government refused to relinquish its ownership stake.

This stalemate was unfortunate, since all the partners (as well as all the analysts of the industry) saw incorporation as a more effective structure to compete with Boeing. Other

Exhibit 3

Boeing vs. Airbus: Aircraft Orders
(9 months—2000)

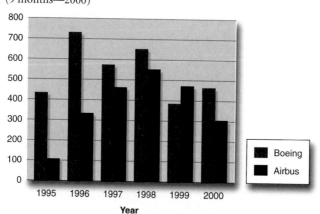

Note: Year 2000 orders are for first 9 months only.

Source: USA Today, October 19, 2000.

expected advantages were the streamlining of redundant costs. It was at this point, in the late spring of 2000, that Jurgen Schrempp, the CEO of DaimlerChrysler who had engineered the major acquisition of Chrysler by Daimler A.G., stepped into the fray. In a matter of weeks Schrempp had brought the 4 business partners to agreement. Then he achieved the master stroke by obtaining agreement from the governments of these 4 that only the French Government be allowed to retain a small stake in the new corporation.

With that agreement, on July 10, 2000, European Aeronautic Defence & Space Company—EADS for short—became a reality. As a defense contractor, EADS was repositioned to become a huge rival to Boeing and Lockheed Martin Corporation. In addition, it became a more efficient and effective competitor to Boeing's Commercial Airplanes Group.

Airbus Industrie had previously matured as a technological manufacturing consortium. Now it had matured as an organization as well, and as such was ready to break new ground.

2 Weeks Later

With the aeronautical equivalent of the "shot heard 'round the world," EADS announced it was accepting orders for the new A3XX Super Jumbo Aircraft. EADS expected such a plane to seat about 650 passengers, although a 100% coach-class configuration would well exceed 700 passengers. It would be able to carry these passengers nonstop on such popular routes as Singapore to London and Tokyo to London. Finally, the A3XX would accomplish this at a (per passenger) cost 20% less than Boeing's B-747-400.

However, this concept was not without controversy. Much of the controversy concerned the ultimate market for such an aircraft. EADS, after extensive discussions with the world's leading airlines, determined the market would be at least 1,500 aircraft. Boeing, having equally extensive discussions with many of the same airlines, concluded the market would be less than 350 aircraft. An independent analyst, Richard Aboulafia of the Teal Group, said the market would more likely be about 927 aircraft by 2019.

Furthermore, there is widespread disagreement as to the A3XX's design cost. EADS says its development will cost $10.7 billion through 2006. Independent analysts peg the cost as high as $16 billion. Many agree that even with development costs at $10.7 billion and a selling price of $225 million per aircraft, EADS would need to sell 528 planes by 2019 to break even. Sales at the Teal Group's estimate of 927 would certainly make it profitable. Sales of 1,500 would make it a bonanza (see **Exhibit 4**). Sales of 350 would make it a disaster.

Exhibit 4
A3XX Estimated Profits

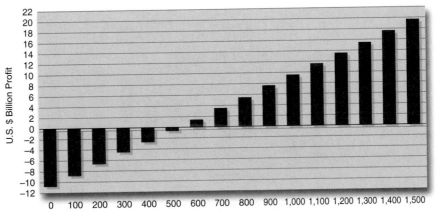

Note: Break even (B/E) at 528 units with development at costs of $10.7 billion.

To design and start construction of the A3XX, EADS would need to borrow heavily, thereby mortgaging the company against the success of the A3XX. If Boeing's market analysis was correct, EADS would probably become bankrupt. On the other hand, there was the possibility for EADS to reap a fortune in profits as well as becoming the world's premier jumbo jet manufacturer. From EADS perspective, it was a super jumbo win/lose.

On the Other Hand

Boeing's perspective was quite different. If EADS market estimates held true, it would certainly represent a major loss to Boeing. Each A3XX would represent at least 1 B-747-400 lost sale by Boeing. If Boeing's market assessment was correct, they would lose the sale of 350 B-747-400s, but then, following EADS bankruptcy, would again be the premier jet airliner manufacturer. They might even be in a position to acquire EADS (perhaps at a bargain) and thus have their cake and eat it too.

There was another possible outcome that Boeing had been studying for some time—the production of an enhanced B-747X. Such a plane would increase Boeing's seating to 522 and represent a compromise between the B-747-400 and the A3XX. The cost to develop a B-747X might be "only" $4 billion. This would lower the number required to reach breakeven as well as lower the plane's selling price to around $200 million each (see **Exhibit 5**).

Some analysts declared that Boeing had no choice but to jump in with the B-747X and compete as well as it could against the A3XX. Others claim that if Boeing's market estimate is correct, doing nothing is the correct choice. These pundits feared that EADS might achieve, more or less, sales around the A3XX breakeven. This would keep EADS in the industry as a competitor, but would probably limit sales of the B-747X to no more than its break-even point, perhaps less.

Strike 3?

In September 2000, prestigious Singapore Airlines ordered 10 A3XXs with options for an additional 15 aircraft. The list price for the A3XX might run as high as $230 million each. Although the price for this order was not announced, people close to such transactions have said that large discounts are applied for initial "launch" customers. Conventional wis-

Exhibit 5

B-747X Estimated Profit: Boeing Corporation

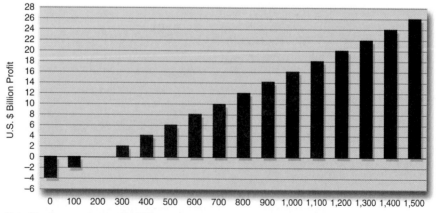

Note: Developmental cost of $4 billion.

dom estimated that the Singapore Airlines order might have been in the neighborhood of $160 million each: less than the price for Boeing's latest 416-seat current-generation B-747-400.

In November 2000, Singapore Airline's arch-rival, Qantas Airways Ltd., of Australia, announced the purchase of 18 A3XXs, valued at $3.5 billion. Although quick math calculates a unit price of $194 million each, it was not announced what, if any, spare parts, ground support equipment, or other extras were part of the Qantas order. Conventional wisdom held to the possibility of "launch" prices around $160 million.

Decision 2001

Along with the Qantas, Air France, and other orders, EADS had firm orders for 50 A3XX aircraft and had achieved the "critical mass" for a go/no-go decision. On December 19, 2000, the EADS Board of Directors formally approved the plans to develop the new super-jumbo, which was designated the A380. Specifications provided seating from 481 to 656 passengers along with a cargo version with a 150 metric ton payload. EADS announced that the A380 would take to the skies in 2006.

Notwithstanding that the stakes were extremely high and the outcome uncertain, Boeing must decide what to do about the development of a B-747X.

Financial Information

Exhibit 6 shows the consolidated statement of operations. **Exhibit 7** shows the consolidated balance sheet. Cash flows are shown in **Exhibit 8**.

Exhibit 6

Consolidated Statements of Operations: Boeing Company
(Dollar amounts in millions, except per share data)

Year Ending December 31	2000	1999	1998	1997
Sales and other operating revenues	$51,321	$57,993	$56,154	$45,800
Cost of products and services	43,712	51,320	50,492	42,001
	7,609	6,673	5,662	3,799
Equity in income (loss) from joint ventures	64	4	(67)	(43)
General and administrative expense	2,335	2,044	1,993	2,187
Research and development expense	1,998	1,341	1,895	1,924
Gain on dispositions	34	87	13	—
Net				
Share-based plans expense	316	209	153	(99)
Operating earnings (loss)	3,058	3,170	1,567	(256)
Other income (principally interest)	386	585	283	428
Interest and debt expense	(445)	(431)	(453)	(513)
Earning (loss) before income taxes	2,999	3,324	1,397	(341)
Income taxes (benefit)	871	1,015	277	(163)
Net earnings (loss)	$ 2,128	$ 2,309	$ 1,120	$ (178)
Basic earnings (loss) per share	2.48	2.52	1.16	(.18)
Diluted earnings (loss) per share	2.44	2.49	1.15	(.18)
Cash dividends per share	.59	.56	.56	.56

Exhibit 7

Consolidated Balance Sheet: Boeing Company
(Dollar amounts in millions, except per share data)

Year Ending December 31	2000	1999	1998
Assets			
Cash and cash equivalents	$ 1,010	$ 3,354	$ 2,183
Short-term investments	—	100	279
Accounts receivable	4,928	3,453	3,288
Current portion of customer and commercial financing	995	799	781
Deferred income taxes	2,137	1,467	1,495
Inventories, net of advances and progress billings	6,794	6,539	8,584
Total current assets	15,864	15,712	16,610
Customer and commercial financing	5,964	5,205	4,930
Property, plant and equipment, net	8,814	8,245	8,589
Deferred income taxes	60	—	411
Goodwill	5,214	2,233	2,312
Prepaid pension expense	4,845	3,845	3,513
Other assets	1,267	907	659
Total assets	42,028	36,147	37,024
Liabilities and shareholders' equity			
Accounts payable and other liabilities	11,979	11,269	11,085
Advances in excess of related costs	3,517	1,215	1,251
Income taxes payable	1,561	420	569
Short-term debt and current portion of long-term debt	1,232	752	869
Total current liabilities	18,189	13,656	13,774
Deferred income taxes	—	172	—
Accrued retiree health care	5,152	4,877	4,831
Long-term debt	7,567	5,980	6,103
Shareholders' equity			
Common shares, par value $5.00			
1,200,000,000 shares authorized	5,059	5,059	5,059
Additional paid-in capital	2,693	1,684	1,147
Treasury shares at cost	(6,221)	(4,161)	(1,321)
Retained earnings	12,090	10,487	8,706
Accumulated other comprehensive income	(2)	6	(23)
Unearned compensation	(7)	(12)	(17)
ShareValue			
Trust shares	(2,592)	(1,601)	(1,235)
Total shareholders' equity	11,020	11,462	—
Total shareholders' equity and liabilities	$42,018	$36,147	$37,024

Source: The Boeing Company.

Exhibit 8

Consolidated Statements of Cash Flows: Boeing Company
(Dollar amounts in millions)

Year Ending December 31	2000	1999	1998	1997
Cash flows—operating activities				
Net earnings (loss)	$2,128	$2,309	$1,120	$(178)
Adjustments to reconcile net earnings (loss)				
Share-based plans	316	209	153	(99)
Depreciation	1,317	1,538	1,517	1,354
Amortization of goodwill	162	107	105	104
In process R&D	557	—	—	—
Customer & commercial financing provision	13	72	61	64
Gain on dispositions, net	(34)	(87)	(13)	—
Changes in assets and liabilities				
Short-term investments	100	179	450	154
Accounts receivable	(768)	(225)	(167)	(240)
Inventories, net of progress billings	1,097	2,030	652	(96)
Accounts payable and other liabilities	(311)	217	(840)	1,908
Advances in excess of related costs	1,387	(36)	(324)	(139)
Income taxes payable and deferred	421	462	145	(451)
Other items	(712)	(579)	(479)	(272)
Accrued retiree health care	269	46	35	(4)
Net cash provided by operating activities	5,942	6,224	2,415	2,105
Cash flows—investing activities				
Customer & commercial financing (additions)	(2,571)	(2,398)	(2,603)	(1,889)
Customer & commercial financing (reductions)	1,433	1,842	1,357	1,025
Property, plant and equipment, net adds	(932)	(1,236)	(1,665)	(1,391)
Acquisitions, net of cash acquired	(5,727)	—	—	—
Proceeds from dispositions	169	359	37	—
Net cash used by investing	(7,628)	(1,433)	(2,874)	(2,255)
Cash flows—financing activities				
New borrowings	2,687	437	811	232
Debt repayments	(620)	(676)	(693)	(867)
Common shares purchased	(2,357)	(2,937)	(1,397)	(141)
Common shares issued				268
Stock options exercised	136	93	65	166
Dividends paid	(504)	(537)	(564)	(557)
Net cash used by financing activities	(658)	(3,620)	(1,778)	(899)
Net increase (decrease) in cash and equivalents	(2,344)	1,171	(2,237)	(1,049)
Cash & cash equivalents at beginning of year	3,354	2,183	4,420	5,469
Cash & cash equivalents at end of year	$1,010	$3,354	$2,183	$4,420

Source: The Boeing Company.

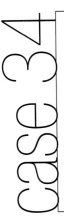

Mercedes-Benz and Swatch: Inventing the 'smart' and the Networked Organization

Eric Pfaffmann and Ben M. Bensaou

In April 1998, just a few months before the start of volume production of the new 'smart,' Mr. Meyer came out of a difficult meeting with Mr. Hoffmann, his counterpart at 1 of the key partners in the Micro Compact Car (MCC) venture. He was pacing up and down in his office overlooking a row of 'smart' prototypes brought in for testing to Renningen, Germany. In light of the evolution of his relationship with Mr. Hoffmann, he started to wonder whether cooperation with system partners in general were really working. 'Would systems partners be able to deliver in the end? What should we do if 1 system partner happened to fail us at the last minute?' What are the implications for the whole concept of a modular car and networked organization that Mercedes-Benz created jointly with the Swatch company?

Micro Compact Car: The Joint Venture

The whole adventure of the company MCC started in 1994. It was in April that Helmut Werner, then CEO of the Mercedes-Benz, and Nicolas Hayek, the CEO of SMH (Société Suisse de Microélectronique et d'Horlogerie SA), the company that made the world famous "Swatch" line of products, agreed on a rather unconventional joint venture in the automobile industry. Mercedes-Benz initially held 51% of the capital and SMH the remaining 49%. In the summer of 1997, the German partner increased its stake by SFr 75 million, now holding up to 81% of the joint venture's capital. The headquarters of MCC were located in Biel, Switzerland, the development premises in Renningen, Germany, and the production plant in Hambach, France. The marketing, sales, finance and control functions were centralized in Biel. MCC Renningen started developing the car in March 1994, the site for the plant was selected in early 1995 and inaugurated in October 1997. Volume production was scheduled for July 1998.

Mercedes-Benz owned 38.5% of MCC France, SMH 36.5%, and the French association SOFIREM (Société Financière pour Favoriser l'Industrialisation des Régions Minières) owned the remaining 25%. While MCC France invested up to FF 1.5 billion for the buildings and factory infrastructure, it was the suppliers who invested up to FF 1.3 billion for machines and tools (see **Exhibit 1**). The plant also received FF 450 million in subsidies from the European

This case was written by Eric Pfaffmann, Visiting Research Fellow at INSEAD, Doctoral Candidate at Hohenheim University, Stuttgart, Germany, under the supervision of Professor Ben M. Bensaou, Associate Professor at INSEAD. It is intended to be used as a basis for class discussion rather than to illustrate either effective or ineffective handling of an administrative situation. All names except those of senior corporate officers have been disguised. Detail financial data are not disclosed by MCC. This case may not be reproduced in any form without written permission of the 2 copyright holders. This case was edited for SMBP-8th Edition. Copyright © 1998 by INSEAD, Fountainebleau, France. Reprinted by permission.

Exhibit 1

Financial Structure of MCC

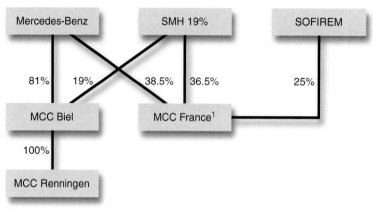

Note:

1. MCC France reports to MCC Biel

Union as a recognition for (1) its environment-friendly production system, (2) creating a new market segment, and (3) inventiveness of the concept.

'smart' was the name chosen for the new car, where *S* stands for Swatch, *M* for Mercedes, and *ART* to highlight the inventiveness of the total concept. Micro Compact Car was the name chosen for the company to evoke the revolutionary notion of a small city car. The joint venture was given extremely limited resources to carry out this experimental, yet rather ambitious, project. Under stiff financial and human capital constraints, MCC was forced from the very beginning to concentrate on the essential. "Reduce to the max" was the claim the company used to explain MCC's outsourcing strategy. What he meant was to create a new organizational form, where MCC would sit in the center and coordinate a group of key suppliers who would effectively provide more than 85% of the value-added of the 'smart.'

Mercedes-Benz

Until 1997, Mercedes-Benz AG was a wholly owned company of the Daimler-Benz group. It was the automotive division covering all vehicle segments. Following a major restructuring of the group, Mercedes-Benz as a company was dismantled. The passenger car division and the commercial vehicle division reported directly to the board of Daimler-Benz group, now comprising 5 divisions: Passenger Cars, Commercial Vehicles, Aerospace, Services, and Directly Managed Business (Rail Systems, Microelectronics, MTU/Diesel Engines). Daimler-Benz remained Germany's largest industrial company, and its vehicle divisions represent the largest divisions in terms of employees, revenues, and even profits.

Daimler-Benz was created in 1926 by 2 German automobile pioneers, Gottlieb Daimler and Karl Benz, who decided to merge their companies after World War I. Highly prosperous in the 1930s, Daimler-Benz established a strong reputation for high quality and superior engineering products. It was at the beginning of the 1960s that the company developed its image for engineering and manufacturing high quality, prestigious, and safe cars for the premium segment. This has been a key asset of the company ever since.

It was under Helmut Werner's leadership that Mercedes-Benz heavily invested in developing new passenger car models, shortening development time and significantly cutting costs. As an indication, in 1997 the company managed to launch 3 major new models: the M-Class launched first in the U.S. market, the A-Class, and the CLK. The A-Class represented for

Mercedes-Benz its first attempt to diversify away from the high end market and enter the mass market segment. These efforts in streamlining operations and strengthening innovation seemed to have paid off. In 1997, the passenger car division boasted DM 53.9 billion in revenues (up from DM 46.7 billion in 1996) and 715,000 cars in sales (up from 645,000). The car division grew by 15% when average market growth was barely 5%. The German market remained by far the most important one for Daimler-Benz taking up to 39% of total sales with 277,000 units a year, against 122,000 units for the U.S. market and 477,000 units for the whole of Europe (see **Exhibit 2**).

SMH

The SMH group was founded in 1983 as a merger between Switzerland's 2 largest companies, ASU AG (Allgemeine Schweizer Uhrenindustrie) and the SSIH (Société Suisse pour l'Industrie Horlogère). The Swiss watch industry went through a severe crisis with the entry of Japanese watchmakers and their technological innovations in quartz technology and LCD screens. Within a few years, a company like Seiko became the largest watch producers in the world. SMH response to the Japanese challenge was a technological and marketing innovation known as the Swatch. This was a tremendous success. In addition to the Swatch, SMH carries other brand names, such as Omega, Longines, and Tissot. Development and production were mainly done by ETA SA Fabriques d'Ebauche, a company established at the end of the 19th century, the technological backbone of the group's watch division (see **Exhibit 3**).

Nicholas G. Hayek was the craftsman of the company's turnaround. He was the mastermind behind the new lifestyle concept behind the Swatch. SMH was now respected as a provocative and innovative company. Check the Web page for Swatch <www.swatch.com> and you will be welcomed by the Swatch slogan: "Provocation, Innovation, Fun. Forever." In 1996, SMH sold nearly 102.5 million watches (all brand names included). It achieved CHF 2,789 million in revenues with a headcount of 16,459 employees. It has become the world's largest watchmaker.

Nicholas Hayek started to look for ways to further leverage the marketing success of the Swatch concept and the unique competence his company had in marketing and distribution. In this diversification effort, he created an automobile division. He wanted to leverage SMH's proven expertise in designing and building microelectronic propulsion systems and apply it to the automobile sector. Hayek also felt they could make a contribution toward developing environmentally friendly propulsion systems with low fuel consumption. Aware that SMH lacked the automobile expertise, he had approached a few of the key automobile

Exhibit 2
Revenues of the Daimler-Benz Passenger Cars Division by Regions

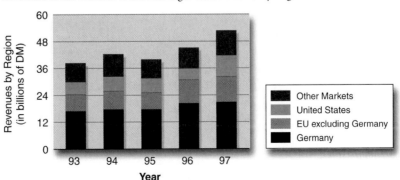

Source: Daimler-Benz Web page.

Exhibit 3

The SMH Group

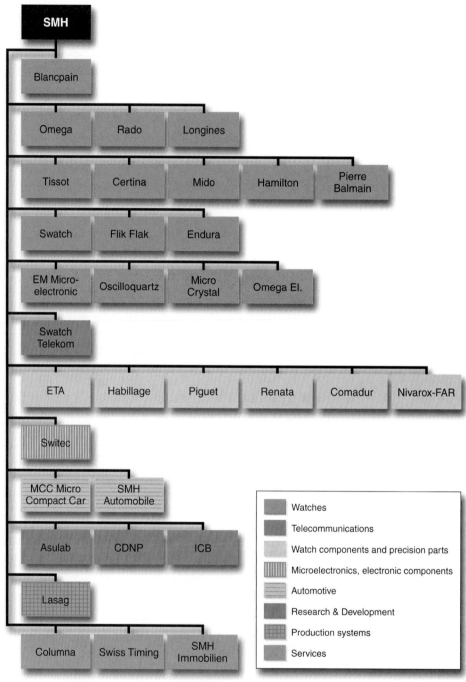

Source: Web page ETA SA Fabriques d'Ebauches.

competitors. Renault and Volkswagen declined the offer to join efforts, but Johann Tomforde, an early advocate of the city car concept within Mercedes-Benz was the one with a very receptive ear. The joint venture was signed in 1994, and SMH was expected to contribute its marketing savoir-faire to attract the younger consumer segments and to develop innovative sales concepts.

The Background of the 'smart' Concept

Two major developments triggered the search for a new car concept. First, in Germany, consumers had, since the early 1980s, become increasingly sensitive to the societal costs of individual transportation, e.g., air pollution, and energy and materials consumption. Second, individual car use was on the increase and the total number of registered cars, as well as the average number of kilometers per capita, had risen to alarming levels. In particular, the highly concentrated car park in urban areas was held responsible for negative effects on the quality of life, e.g., daily traffic jams, air pollution, living space taken by highways, shortage of parking space, and of course noise levels. There definitely was a potential market for a car that could alleviate these problems in congested urban areas. Under the strong pressure from consumer and environmentalist lobbies, governments were considering measures to restrict car pollution, control emissions, and increase taxation on fuel.

In 1990, Johann Tomforde, then heading the Mercedes-Benz strategic design and car concept department in Sindelfingen, Germany, had been working on a new concept to address these growing consumer concerns. The objective was to create a car with the following features: small size, yet maintaining a high level of passenger comfort and safety; low fuel consumption, using nontoxic, easy-to-recycle materials; and environmentally friendly production process (**Exhibit 4**). However, further market research pointed out that consumers were not ready to acquire such a city car unless it offered additional qualitative and emotional utility. Tomforde repeatedly insisted:

> The reduction of fuel consumption and emissions does not guarantee success. For potential customers, a qualitative leap must be visible, an increased utility.[1]

He pushed for a stronger marketing statement for the car, in particular an original external appearance to attract attention, a "navigation system" and customized design. The car needed to provide the customer enhanced total driving experience in order to earn acceptance of this new technology and concept of a city car. To deliver a distinct qualitative advantage, Tomforde pushed his engineers to focus on 3 concepts: the "pleasure to drive," the "mobility concept," and the concept of a customized design.

The 'smart'

What kind of car would people buy and how could you make money out of a venture like this? These were key questions for MCC. The 'smart' resulted in a significant departure from the usual product offerings from Mercedes-Benz, traditionally focused on luxury cars. The car was supposed to create its own new market in the city car segment niche. It was revolutionary in its technological innovations and the way it was designed and produced. Only 2.50 meters in length, 1.51 meters in width, but 1.53 meters high, the car was definitely designed to attract attention. The car had only 2 seats and customers could choose between 2 engines. To be on the market by October 1998, with a price tag ranging from DM 16,000 to DM 20,000, the 'smart' would be first distributed in Austria, Belgium, France, Germany, Italy, Luxembourg, the Netherlands, Spain, and Switzerland. Projected sales amounted to 130,000 units for 1999 and nearly 200,000 per year starting in 2000.

Exhibit 4

Innovations of the 'smart'

Fields of innovation	Major implementations
(1) Energy consumption	Reduced fuel consumption to below 5 liters per 100 km and reduced weight to 720 kg is achieved by innovations in the drive module; application of advanced lightweight materials; integration of functions inside technical components (e.g., the car engine).
(2) Passenger safety	Passenger safety is addressed by the interaction of the: *Tridion-frame:* Steel-faced body of the car, around which the entire vehicle is built; *Power unit:* The engine and gearbox are designed as an integrated power unit that is decoupled from the passenger compartment; *Sandwich construction:* The engine lies at the rear and underneath the passenger compartment. In event of an accident this power unit absorbs the likely return shocks to which particularly small cars are prone; *Crash box:* Security boxes that are installed in the front and in the back of the car and are able to fully absorb crashes at speeds of up to 15 km/h; *Traction and stability system (TRUST):* Electronic power management that acts on the engine and gearbox control units to keep the speed transferred to the driven wheels under surveillance and diffuse critical situations.
(3) Passenger comfort	Tridion-frame and sandwich construction maximize the available space and visibility for 2 passengers. Seats and control panels are designed according to ergonomic principles.
(4) Customized design	Modular car design allows a variety of parts that vary in color and/or material, Parts can be easily replaced. In particular Exterior "Customized Body Panel System" (CBS) consists of plastic bodywork components that cover the Tridion-frame. CBS parts can be replaced within 2 hours; Elements of the car interior such as trim panels, fittings and upholstered parts including seat upholstery.
(5) Environmental compatibility	Low emissions due to its low fuel consumption; Car parts can be recycled to a degree of 95%; Nontoxic and regenerating materials are used; Environmental friendly production methods are applied such as the powder coating of the Tridion-frame.
(6) Mobility-related services	Delivery of individualized mobility packages that go beyond the actual vehicle. Major components are the "Mobility Box" of the vehicle that offers help functions, traffic information, or assistance in finding the best way to the destination as well as a mobile phone; Decoupling of car usage and car ownership: The 'smart' is meant to be a city car for short distances. MCC therefore plans to provide 'smart' cars at airports and train stations in major European cities, as well as larger Mercedes-Benz vehicles for holiday trips.

The 'smart' would not have been a viable product in the market without some major technological innovations (see **Exhibit 4**) such as its use of new advanced light weight materials in the engine (only 59 kg, a third of the weight of comparable engines) and the body panels to improve on fuel consumption (the whole car weighs 720 kg compared to 815 kg for the Renault Twingo). In addition, the number of components in the engine turbocharger were brought down to 8 instead of the normal 18.

The 'smart' was a tiny passenger car and safety was an even more important factor. MCC wanted it to be superior to other cars of this size. Its engineers were able to use Tridion-frame technology invented by Mercedes-Benz—a steel-faced body for the car, around which the entire vehicle was designed. They also came up with the "sandwich" design where the engine is located in the rear underneath the passenger compartment. The engine and the gearbox were designed as an integrated power unit decoupled from the passenger compartment. In the event of an accident the power unit would absorb the likely return shocks to which small cars are particularly prone. Crash boxes were installed in the front and in the back of the car and were able to fully absorb crashes at speeds of up to 15 kilometers per hour.

Another key feature of the 'smart,' likely to make it a market success, was its customized design and its "mobility box" concept. Tomforde used to complain that car design has traditionally been an engineers' monologue where the only time the customer could express himself or herself was at the time of purchase. He preferred to have a dialogue and wanted to bring back the customer into the conversation. He aggressively pushed for shorter development time to allow for faster customer feedback and championed a "modular" design that would allow complete customization. Miss Dessain, for instance, would walk into a 'smart' dealership or visit the smart homepage and custom design her own vehicle. She could independently choose from 4 colors from the body panels, 2 colors from the Tridion frame, or select 1 of the special colors and many other options. In addition, she could at any time after her purchase change any of these features very quickly (e.g., body panel changes take only 2 hours) and at low cost. The "mobility box" offers individualized "mobility" packages to include car navigation services, such as help functions, traffic information and assistance, and a mobile phone.

The Networked Organization

MCC was under very tough constraints to develop and make the 'smart.' Mercedes-Benz took almost 6 years to develop the new A-Class. There was no way MCC could afford this luxury, since volume production was already scheduled to start 4 years down the road. The low target price necessary for the 'smart' to make it in the marketplace was also a fundamental challenge for the organization. Notwithstanding the fact that MCC had a limited set of financial resources provided by its 2 parent companies. The task clearly required a novel approach to product development and production, and an organizational innovation was necessary to follow suit on the innovation in the product concept. This meant developing 2 things: (1) a "modular" car design and (2) a corresponding networked organization where MCC would act as a central coordinator of a network of system partners.

THE MODULAR ARCHITECTURE OF THE SMART

The architecture of a car's design can be defined as a set of the modules and systems. A module would refer to a spatial area of the car, e.g., the cockpit, the doors, the seats, or the drivetrain. Modules are then determined in a way to facilitate the assembly process and minimize assembly and logistics costs and time. MCC defined large modules of the 'smart' that could be outsourced to system partners for development and production. The target of MCC was to optimize logistics and minimize final assembly time to a world-best of 4.5 hours.

Within the spatial modules you would find systems, e.g., the air management system, the brake system, or the wiper system. They are determined by the function they have to fulfill and the components that execute this function. As such, systems are defined by the development process. Conflicts are bound to occur between the needs of the development process and the requirements of the assembly process each time some physical component, executing a given function, is shared by multiple spatial modules. Finally, modules and systems are made of parts and components. Parts are typically technologically simple, generic, with a standardized interface and execute a standardized function, e.g., screws or oil seal rings. Components are made of parts and usually would have a distinct, stand-alone functionality.

THE MODULAR ORGANIZATIONAL DESIGN

An important consequence of the modular architecture of the 'smart' was the possibility of designing an organization where boundaries would set exactly around the technical modules. At the outset, there were 5 organizational modules: (1) the bodywork and fittings, (2) the cockpit and front-end module, (3) the chassis, (4) the drive module, and (5) the doors, flaps and roof (see **Exhibit 5**). **Exhibit 6** in addition illustrates the parallelism between the technical architecture of the 'smart' chassis and the organizational structure highlighting the interfaces between MCC and its partner suppliers.

The modular organizational design could not, however, eliminate the impact of some inconsistencies in the product architecture. For instance, to heat the interior of a car, the engine blows warm air into the passenger compartment at different temperatures depending on its own heat level. This warm airflow is also affected by other factors, e.g., the speed of the vehicle or the local weather conditions. In other words, the heating system is a cross-modular function. This implies the need for some incremental and interactive redesigns, which affect function design and module boundaries during the development process. The design of the organizational model was based on the premise of perfect modularity, whereby each system neatly fitted into its allotted module and no system cut across technical module boundaries. In

Exhibit 5

Organizational Modules of the 'smart'

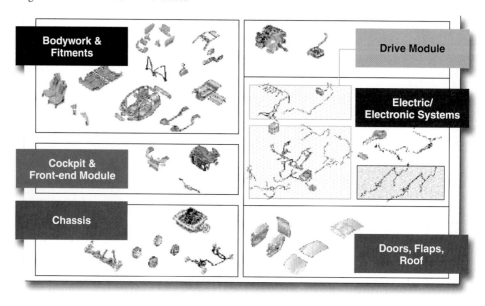

Exhibit 6
Illustration of the Isomorphic Interfirm Modular Organization for the Chassis Development and Production

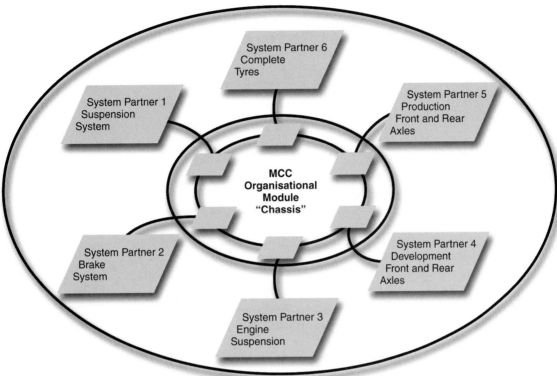

fact, perfect modularity is quasi-impossible for a car, since systems such as air-management, acoustics, or wire harnessing are inevitably cross-modular.

The integration across modules was difficult, as the technical interaction between the modules was ill defined and fuzzy. It also revealed another problem with the modular organization: cross-unit responsibility. Looking at how the "heating" function was managed showed that nobody was really responsible for the overall integration across modules. Engineers and managers, at MCC, as well as the suppliers, were more preoccupied with their modules and naturally suboptimized. Mr. Meyer explained: "I was working with Mr. Hoffmann on a consistent tolerances concept within the doors module. Of course, I did not oversee what was going on in the drive module."

After some incidents, MCC realized that given the modular design of the organization, the cross-modular functions of the 'smart' would not receive enough attention and care during the development phase. Furthermore, the organizational modularity in itself masked the danger that optimization of the entire vehicle was not promoted with the necessary rigor. The solution was to add a sixth organizational model, called "electrical connections/electronic systems" that would specifically focus on cross-modular issues. As an overlay structure, MCC also established another cross-module organization, "total vehicle optimization/vehicle testing" that would look after the systematic coordination of cross-module information flows. The managers in charge were made responsible for testing and the optimization of the entire vehicle and had the same hierarchical level as functional managers within the other organizational modules. They were to settle conflicts within MCC across the various modules.

System Partner Integration

MCC heavily relied on outsourcing from legally independent suppliers. The successful execution of the 'smart' project was therefore dependent on the level of mutual cooperation and agreement about the division of tasks and responsibilities between MCC and its system partners. Precise process definitions were developed to clarify mutual targets and facilitate coordination and adjustments between MCC and system partners. At the same time, these processes had to allow for greater flexibility and cooperation at the buyer-supplier interfaces. **Exhibit 7** summarizes the guiding principles for system partner integration.

Exhibit 7

Principles of System Partner Integration

Measures	Agreements
(1) Supplier contracts	(1) Single sourcing (2) Lifetime-contracts (3) Minimum purchasing volumes (4) Profit margins per unit (5) Obligatory target costs of each product developed by a system partner
(2) Intellectual property management	(1) MCC acquired ownership of the design concepts contained in rejected suppliers' proposals (2) MCC claimed ownership rights for patents where the underlying innovations concern the security and the competitive advantage of the 'smart,' regardless of whether they were developed by suppliers or by MCC (3) Patents that are based on generic product and process innovations are registered by the supplier who developed them. The property rights remain exclusively theirs
(3) Fundamental guidelines	(1) MCC controls the entire process chain (2) Supplier companies invest in production equipment, machines, and tools and operate their business on their own behalf according to the development and production contracts (3) MCC provides plant surfaces and industrial services (4) MCC is responsible for the general context conditions that ensure that suppliers could smoothly execute their tasks
(4) Organizational structure	(1) System partners should set up and maintain a project organization that mirrors the organization of MCC. (2) System partners must assign function managers and project managers for the duration of the entire project. (3) System partners locate their offices on the development premises of MCC during particular development stages
(5) Control of information flows	(1) Open-books calculation (2) Development protocol (3) Conflict management

CONTRACTUAL ARRANGEMENTS

The relationships between MCC and its system partners were based on contracts and rules to which all participants had to agree. The contracts spelled out the rights and duties of system partners and the formal agreements on intellectual property management. The rules defined the fundamental project guidelines, the project organization, and transparency between MCC and system partners. Contracts were separately negotiated with each system partner and were not based on the standard contract schemes provided by the Association of German Automobile Industry (VDA). The contracts stipulated exclusivity rights for the suppliers, e.g., single sourcing principle for MCC, but also expected system partners to assume some of the project's business risk, for instance, by prefinancing of system and module development as well as tools. Contracts also stipulated an obligatory target price that served as the reference for the assessment of any cost deviations likely to occur in later stages of the development process.

INTELLECTUAL PROPERTY RIGHTS AGREEMENTS

Intellectual property rights was a critical issue for both sides. MCC wanted to avoid supplier companies exploiting innovations developed for 'smart' with other customers. This would clearly affect the market attractiveness of the 'smart.' MCC therefore decided in some cases to acquire all ownership of the design concepts, even for rejected suppliers' proposals. Rejected suppliers would receive a lump sum compensation upon demand. MCC did not engage in any joint patent registration with any system partner. It would quickly become a source of dispute.

PROJECT ORGANIZATION

The fundamental guidelines were called "smart alliance" and in simple terms allocated the basic responsibilities and obligations between MCC and the suppliers. MCC was the smart project leader and played the role of the focal company in a broad network of tight buyer–supplier relationships (even though suppliers assumed part of the risk of the project). Modifications brought to components during the development phase or completion of the quality control of the assembled vehicle needed approval and supervision from MCC.

System partners should develop a 3-layer project hierarchy for development and production parallel to the hierarchical structure within MCC, with its function managers, then project managers and finally the board of directors on top. In addition, system partners had to assign function managers and project managers for the duration of the entire project. This should provide the channel for lateral communication between MCC and system partners and clearly identified who would be the contact person responsible for the 'smart' project within each organization. Furthermore, suppliers had temporary desks in Renningen and were asked to produce/assemble their systems at the very assembly plant MCC built in France for the 'smart.'

CONFLICT MANAGEMENT MECHANISMS

Conflicts during the project were anticipated and unavoidable. The basic channel for interfirm conflict resolution was provided by the project organization and its lateral communication bridges. For example, Mr. Meyer of MCC was not quite satisfied with some tolerance calculations for the doors' module that his system partner counterpart, Mr. Hoffmann, had just sent him. He went to talk to him directly. "If I had talked directly to his boss, the project manager, Mr. Hoffmann would have felt bad and thought the customer was complaining to his boss about him personally." The procedure prescribed by MCC required that conflicts should be resolved at the level they occur.

Transparency, also conceded by MCC, was instrumental in reducing conflict and supported smooth interactions and trust building in the relationships. Mr. Meyer explained: "We agreed with most system partners on 'open-book calculations' to provide each other with the most relevant data." MCC guaranteed purchasing volumes to the suppliers and gave them access to its market research data from which they could gain confidence in estimated sales volumes themselves. The same applied for the composition of the target price to which system partners were committed.

THE ROLE OF DEVELOPMENT PROTOCOLS

A major tool to control the information flows between MCC and system partners was the so-called "development protocols." These included all product-relevant data and were interactively updated during the course of the 'smart' development. A system partner would get access only to the data relevant to their own development responsibilities and could not see the protocol for other suppliers. In fact, knowledge about the smart was distributed between MCC and the system partners according to the predetermined task assignments and responsibilities. On the other hand, system partners would disclose only 'smart'-related knowledge to MCC, which was, of course, only a fraction of their own knowledge base.

Nevertheless, it was still not possible to force mutual transparency with contracts. Mr. Meyer's experience was that: "Transparency on the side of system partners depends very much on the supplier you deal with. It also depends on the personal relationships you have built with component managers at the suppliers." He also admitted that the degree of transparency varied during the different stages of the project.

Partner Integration During the Development Process for the 'smart'

The concept of the 'smart' and of the organization of MCC were quite revolutionary ideas in the car business and required a fundamental departure from the traditional ways of designing and producing a car. It was critical to develop the proper management processes to deal with the unique aspects of the technical architecture of the 'smart'—the internal modular project organization as well as the external network of system partners. The smart project was broken down into 3 phases: (1) concept development, (2) concept realization, and (3) full production (see **Exhibit 8**). Not surprisingly, the most time-consuming phases of the project were concept realization and production. Each phase consisted of a set of subprocesses that dictated "what to do when" and how to reach the planned targets. Each phase corresponded to a different team composition within MCC's modular organization. The teams reflected the nature of the major tasks to be accomplished at each development stage and the corresponding domains of expertise required.

CONCEPT DEVELOPMENT

There were distinct phases during the concept development of the 'smart': (1) strategic product planning, (2) procurement marketing, and (3) concept competition.

Strategic Product Planning

Some strategic product planning activities had been carried out by Mercedes-Benz and SMH prior to the foundation of MCC. However, the major work load was carried out when MCC took up its work around April 1994. The main objective was to develop an initial definition of the development protocols. These protocols were to reflect the basic concept requirements of the 'smart,' of which the most important one was to determine how much customers were ready to pay for the car.

Exhibit 8

Structure of the Development Process

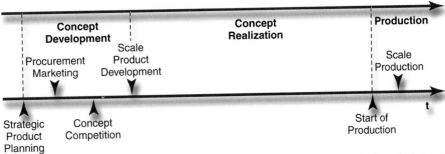

Note: Exhibit 8 indicates the time duration of each phase (except for strategic product planning and scale production), but should not be interpreted as an exact time schedule. Also, the starting and termination times of distinct development phases tend to overlap. Therefore, Exhibit 8 should be seen as an approximate representation of the development process structure.

This target price was the basis for the calculation of the cost structure for the whole vehicle and for prospective system partners. The procedure estimated how much customers were willing to pay for the key functionalities of the 'smart' value proposition to the market. Each key utility was given a price tag, then each function was translated in terms of its constituent physical components. The result gave the maximum cost allowed for each component. This latter task was typically delicate, as most key functions can be implemented in different ways, with different combinations of components, and required the participation of the most experienced component managers, purchasing specialists as well as benchmarking experts.

In the first half of 1994, Mr. Meyer was heavily solicited for his long experience in door design and his knowledge of the related upstream component markets. This analysis represented the very first contact newly founded MCC had with external supplier and in particular the first contact Mr. Meyer had with Mr. Hoffmann.

Procurement Marketing

The procurement marketing phase also started in spring 1994 and partly overlapped with strategic product planning. During this phase, MCC preselected up to 6 to 8 potential system suppliers. Those who passed this initial screening were invited to take part in a concept competition and were asked to propose concept studies for their specialty system, or module, on the basis of the customer price targets defined during the strategic planning phase. This was the first time in the 'smart' project that MCC tapped suppliers' creativity and the specialized knowledge they had developed in the domain of their expertise. The quality of a supplier's concept study, even though very important, was not the only key factor in MCC's evaluation. MCC also looked at other factors related to the supplier's general performance, e.g., company size, turnover, plant locations, certificates, and references.

Benchmarking and purchasing specialists and component managers supported by controllers would be working together to determine which companies could deliver on the creativity required in their new roles within the MCC networked organization. Suppliers were indeed expected to develop from scratch feasible and innovative product concepts within the domain of their expertise. The burden on them in terms of conceptual complexity and creativity was different from what was usually expected in the traditional way of making cars. They were used to developing products around preexisting blueprints or physical components. The system partner's financial stability was also essential to guarantee that it could make the needed investments.

Mr. Meyer admitted:

> Mr. Hoffmann's company was very promising. They had an excellent reputation for quality in processes and products. Their financial foundation was solid. My colleagues in the doors selection team were also very positive. I have to say that in the beginning I was not sure they would be able to deliver feasible door solutions without receiving precise specifications from us. This was a sensitive issue for us because door development had always been done inside. One of my former colleagues in the Mercedes-Benz purchasing department knew this supplier and strongly recommended them to us. This made a difference, and finally Mr. Hoffmann's company was invited to join the concept competition.

CONCEPT COMPETITION

In June 1994, MCC began the concept competition phase to determine who would be their "dancing partners." MCC gave those companies invited to the competition a first development protocol, which provided them with the basic description of the product they were asked to deliver. The specifications included the external measurements of the item, its design, the interfaces with other physical components as well as its functional and crash-resistance requirements. In addition, suppliers received the detailed target costs for their parts and the outline of the development contract.

Each candidate was required to present its concept proposal to MCC within a couple of months. Once all proposals were received, MCC started the most critical task, i.e., the evaluation and final selection of system partners and their concepts. The evaluation team included component managers, benchmarking specialists, purchasing agents, and controllers.

The evaluation scheme developed by MCC assessed the product concepts with respect to their technical and economic aspects and included both quantitative and qualitative dimensions. In particular, they were assessed against the original marketing and technological targets of the 'smart.' The "weight reduction" target, for instance, was assessed by converting the manufacturing costs of a module into a price-per-kilogram factor and then estimating the weight of the total car. A concept solution with a lower manufacturing price but a heavier weight than competing solutions would be handicapped by its price-per-kilogram factor. Mr. Meyer was pleased:

> Mr. Hoffmann and his colleagues did very well in this respect. Their door concept had the lowest price per kilogram and seemed to be the most appropriate solution for the complex doors of the smart. This further confirmed my trust in them. After the final assessment was completed, they were given a contract offer.

CONCEPT REALIZATION

When this phase started in April 1995, the 'smart' project significantly increased in size and cost. System partners had allocated human and financial resources to the project and were actively involved in implementation. The first peak in the interaction between MCC and its system partners took place at the beginning of the concept realization phase when concepts had to be translated into products and when MCC asked its partners to locate their project teams at MCC's development facilities in Renningen.

Engineers from both sides were starting to cooperate. First of all, they had to learn how to interact and coordinate across their firm boundaries. This was not easy for them. They had to develop and get accustomed to new rules of conduct. It took about 1 year for MCC to get people inside and outside on the same wavelength. Their cooperation centered around the sequential fulfillment of all functions and the related target costs agreed upon. Neither the system partners nor MCC had earlier blueprints to work from. Components and the production equipment, e.g., dies and tools, had to be built from scratch. The main documents on which system partners and MCC-module teams based their development activities were the development protocols.

Optimization of product functions at the concept realization phase often implied some design changes for supplier components. Yet agreeing on design changes was one of the most difficult parts of managing relationships in the network. Design changes opened the door to price negotiations. All system partners had signed a contract in which target prices and function execution were set in writing, and suppliers were entitled to demand a price increase only when they delivered a functionality at a higher level of performance than the contracted target value. Conversely, if they underperformed in a functionality, their price would drop below the stipulated target costs.

Conflicts were common as it was difficult to determine whether a design change would bring an increase or decrease in function performance. Typically system partners would insist that the design changes provided some improvement in functionality.

This was where the organization structures and conflict management mechanisms were put into action, as experienced by Mr. Meyer and Mr. Hoffmann when they had to develop consistent tolerances. As Mr. Meyer explained:

> Tolerances have to be defined for the doors and the frame into which the doors will be installed in such a way that these tolerances compensate each other and guarantee integration. At the beginning, the tolerances worked out by Mr. Hoffmann and his team did not fit. I already got on quite well with him, and found him to be a nice person, but I had difficulty explaining to him what I really needed from him. I would make suggestions but he would come up with his own proposals.

Clearly, managing coordination and conflicts within the network required some elaborate and transparent evaluation scheme. MCC used the concept of "value-analysis," similar to the process used for the determination of customer target prices. With this technique MCC would examine whether supplier solutions deviated from stipulated target values. This would apply to supplier products as well as development and production processes.

As indicated in **Exhibit 9**, design changes could be initiated by either a system partner or an MCC module team, but the supplier had to work out an appropriate solution. MCC com-

Exhibit 9
The Interface between MCC and System Partners during Concept Realization

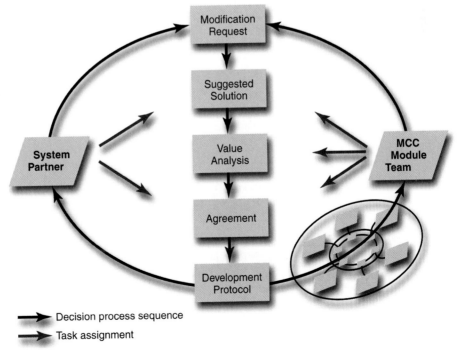

ponent managers could nevertheless make suggestions, the supplier had the discretion to accept or refuse. If no agreement could be reached, MCC would conduct detailed value analyses on costs and functions and eventually system partners and MCC had to agree upon a solution (which could also imply further changes). The changes were then included in the development protocols with which both MCC and its partners had to comply. Any revisions would become the basis for the next phase of improvements and changes.

PRODUCTION

The production phase was scheduled to start in July 1998. The manufacturing and assembly process at the Hambach plant in France was characterized by a quasi-dissolution of the boundaries between MCC and its system partners (see **Exhibit 10**). There was a risk for MCC components managers, for example, experiencing some conflict in their role. They had been in direct contact with the supplier on a daily basis, they knew most about the supplier problems, and they could identify with the interest of the supplier instead of enforcing MCC positions.

Which supplier would be asked to manufacture at the new Hambach plant and which ones would be asked to produce and ship from their existing factories? Determining factors included the specificity of the deliveries to the 'smart,' the potential for economies of scale, the

Exhibit 10

Organization of the Collaborative Production Process

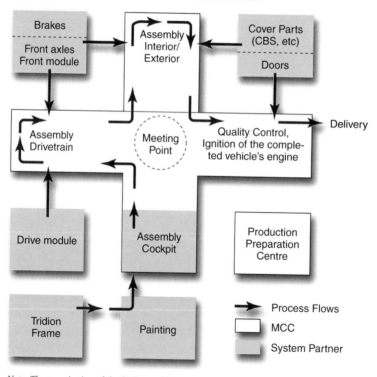

Note: The organization of the final assembly process corresponded to the modular product and organization architecture of the 'smart.' As Exhibit 10 indicates, MCC performed the core assembly that took the form of a cross, or in the term of MCC, a "plus." The core assembly of MCC was the focal point of the production plant. The cross was surrounded by the system partners who were self-dependent for the manufacturing and assembly of the modules. The cross shape of the assembly line allowed the system partners to be correctly located on the assembly line for the installation of their modules. As can be seen in Exhibit 10, "the assembly process followed the product," beginning with the welding of the car body, and moving on to the painting of the frame. The next assembly steps were "engagement" of the car body and cockpit, the installation of the drive module, front module, brake system, and exterior as well as interior system-modules. The assembly process of the 'smart' was completed by quality control and the ignition of the completed vehicle's engine.

level of additional investments required, and the complexity of the logistics. For instance, the body of the 'smart' and the Customized Body Panel System (CBS) were completely 'smart'-specific, so no prior manufacturing facilities existed. Manufacturing the car body and the CBS-parts away from Hambach and delivering them JIT to the final assembly plant would have significantly increased the complexity of the logistics and costs. Conversely, system partners for engines, axles, and seats had no intention of setting up new manufacturing facilities at Hambach. They integrated the additional production volumes into their existing facilities and could realize scale economies.

Full production was to start in a few months, but for Mr. Meyer there were some fundamental questions left to answer, in particular if the 'smart' project is a financial success. Does the approach really achieve the desired results in terms of innovativeness, lead times, and costs? In the long run, wouldn't the networked organization approach destroy an automobile company's ability to initiate and integrate innovation? Would MCC be able to maintain its focal position in the network even without the backing of Mercedes-Benz? In fact, MCC as system integrator did not build and maintain technical knowledge about products and processes. This was done by supplier companies. What could and what should Mr. Meyer do if Mr. Hoffmann does not deliver?

Note

1. Johann Tomforde, "smart—Vom Designkonzept eines urbanen Kompaktfahrzeugs bis zum Aufbau eines Unternehmens für individuelle Mobilität." Lecture at the conference "Automobil-Design—Visionen für die Zukunft des Automobils" (Essen, Germany: November 28/29, 1996), p. 7 (Translation by the authors).

A.W.A.R.E.

John K. Ross III and Eric G. Kirby

It was a typically beautiful morning in central Texas as Sherry stood at the office door watching the bustle of activity in the arena. It was just before the first client arrived and Bobby, the Lead Instructor, and several volunteers were getting Duke ready for Cindy. Duke was a 1,000-pound horse that would be led from his stall, groomed, tacked, and then would provide Cindy an hour of physical and emotional therapy. Cindy was a beautiful 9-year-old girl with cerebral palsy who used a small walker and leg braces to walk and would, for a short time, allow Duke to be her legs—and her friend.

With a grin and a bang, Cindy opened the screen door to the office and entered as fast as she could. Sherry turned to help her put on her helmet, and within minutes Cindy was being assisted into the arena and onto the mounting blocks where Bobby and Duke waited. Cindy's smile grew wider as she approached Duke and carefully climbed the mounting blocks. With the help of Bobby and the volunteers, Cindy lifted 1 leg up and over the saddle, and she was ready to ride. After carefully leaving the mounting blocks Cindy excitedly said "Walk on" and Duke, Cindy, Bobby, and the volunteers began an hour of intense physical therapy, which for Cindy would seem to pass like minutes and would be the highlight of her week.

History

This was A.W.A.R.E. (Always Wanted A Riding Experience). Located in San Marcos, Texas (30 miles south of Austin), A.W.A.R.E. was a not-for-profit therapeutic horseback riding center under the provisions of Section 501(c)3 of the U.S. Internal Revenue Service. Cathy Morgan founded A.W.A.R.E. in October of 1986 using her personal horse, 4 horses borrowed from friends, and a small arena borrowed from another friend. Cathy was a certified special education teacher and horse-riding expert. For years she had dreamed of combining her love for special children and horseback riding. There was a ready clientele for her specialized type of therapy and growth occurred quickly.

The authors wish to thank the fine people at A.W.A.R.E. for their cooperation and assistance. Although A.W.A.R.E. is real, the names used in this case have been changed. This case was prepared by Professors John K. Ross III and Eric G. Kirby of Southwest Texas State University. This case was edited for SMBP-8th Edition. Copyright © 2000 by John K. Ross III and Eric G. Kirby.

Horseback riding as physical and emotional therapy began in Europe, probably in the 1600s. The modern therapeutic benefits were not realized until Liz Hartel of Denmark won the silver medal for dressage at the 1952 Helsinki Olympic Games—despite having paralysis from polio. Within a short period of time, medical and equine professionals had begun riding centers for rehabilitation purposes in England and then in North America by the 1960s. The first professional organization, North American Riding for the Handicapped Association (NARHA), was formed in 1969 for educational purposes and later to accredit active centers. Today, the number of NARHA-affiliated centers totals more than 550, providing more than 30,000 individuals with riding experiences <www.narha.org>.

Within 2 years of founding A.W.A.R.E., Cathy had moved to a larger outdoor arena with 9 stalls and lights for night riding. By then she had found 3 additional riding experts to become instructors and was soon "riding" clients from 9:00 A.M. until 9:00 P.M. She was charging $10 for a 1-hour riding lesson and providing scholarships (discounted rates or free-of-charge) for some clients. A small Board of Directors, comprised of Cathy's acquaintances, had been formed and they provided some assistance. For the most part they were not a strong Board, being comprised of well-meaning individuals who were not members of the community's "movers and shakers" and not particularly savvy at running a business. Cathy was able to continue offering the therapeutic riding services, but, as in many small not-for-profits, cash flow was a continual problem. In fact, some weeks her instructors did not get paid until a client paid.

In 1992 Cathy began a letter-writing campaign for donations to help support A.W.A.R.E. with operating expenses, to provide scholarships, and to move to a covered arena. Their facilities were unusable when it rained, at which time the arena turned into a quagmire. Additionally, riders and volunteers were suffering from the heat and sun during the long Texas summers when afternoon temperatures in the 100s were not uncommon. The fund-raising campaign paid off when 2 locally owned corporations joined together and donated 20 acres with a covered arena, worth about $250,000. For the next year Cathy and a group of volunteers worked to refurbish the land and arena to meet NARHA accreditation standards.

During that same time A.W.A.R.E. put on a successful fundraiser dinner-dance-auction which netted approximately $19,000, and Cathy decided to return to teaching. The Board searched to replace Cathy but was unable to successfully find a long-term Executive Director. After 2 Executive Directors left within a short time because of the long hours, hard work, and meager salary, 1 of the volunteers, Sherry Ross (a local CPA who was working as a full-time volunteer), took over the functions of Executive Director and began exercising tight fiscal control of the operation.

Current Situation

A.W.A.R.E. was located on the donated property 7 miles south of San Marcos, approximately one-quarter mile off of an interstate highway, and directly behind 1 of the country's largest outlet malls. Recently the property across the street had begun to be developed into an upscale residential community. A.W.A.R.E. had 13 horses, over 100 clients per session (a 16-week period of time equivalent to a university semester), an unpaid Executive Director, 2 full-time paid instructors, 4 part-time paid instructors, and over 200 volunteers per session. A typical day began when Yvonne (who lived in a mobile home on the A.W.A.R.E. property as part of her salary) fed the horses at 7:00 A.M. Classes then began sometime after 8:00 A.M. and continued throughout the day, ending around 9:00 P.M.

For a typical lesson, the instructor began preparations 30 minutes prior to its start by reviewing previous lessons and goals for that client, organized aids (toys for fine motor skills, etc.), then assisted the volunteers as they groomed and tacked the horse. Once the client arrived they donned a helmet and mounted their horse. During the lesson, 1 volunteer would be the "horse handler" and also had responsibility for observing and controlling the horse. One or 2 other volunteers would walk beside the horse as "sidewalkers" (spotters) for safety reasons and to interact with the client. The instructor then guided the class, leading the client through a series of activities designed to focus on verbal, gross or fine motor skills, balance, flexibility, or some other specific goal. Frequently these activities were disguised as games or play and may have included singing, interactions with other riders, and other "fun" activities. All of this was accomplished while the client was sitting, lying, or standing on the horse's back. At the conclusion of the hour lesson, the client was dismounted and returned with the instructor to the office area, returned his or her helmet, and talked briefly with the instructor. The volunteers untacked the horse and returned it to its stall. The instructor would then make notes about the current lesson in the client's file for future reference. Up to 6 clients may have ridden in a group lesson and been supervised by 1 instructor.

The Executive Director was also an instructor and, with the help of the Lead Instructor, performed all of the office work necessary to keep A.W.A.R.E. operating. This included preparing financial records, correspondence, payroll, schedule preparation, and the like. To begin a typical semester session, A.W.A.R.E. must contact previous riders to confirm continuing riding, select others who might want to ride from a waiting list, advertise for volunteers and conduct volunteer training, schedule lesson times that match both rider and instructor needs, perform routine maintenance on the facilities, and so forth. The workload was very heavy and the Executive Director generally worked 60 to 70 hours per week. **Exhibit 1** shows the current organizational structure for A.W.A.R.E.

The Lead Instructor typically worked 40 to 50 hours per week and the 1 other full-time instructor worked a 40-hour week (both were paid about $10/hour). All other instructors were part time and were paid $8.00 per hour. Instructors had to be trained in the dual disciplines of horsemanship and physical therapy. A.W.A.R.E. would not ride a client unless a physician had approved horse riding as a beneficial therapy and the instructors had been able to provide not just a pony ride, but a therapeutic riding experience. The instructors continuously supported each other with ideas to improve their lessons and the sharing of knowledge about instructional pedagogy. Additionally, A.W.A.R.E. supported instructors attending specialized conferences on therapeutic horseback riding. However none of the instructors were certified physical therapists.

Exhibit 1
Organizational Structure

The Board of Directors for A.W.A.R.E was comprised of 6 volunteers from the local community and included 2 physicians, a university business professor, the wife of the local newspaper editor, the spouse of a local prominent lawyer, and a local businessperson. Although the Board members were good, well-intentioned individuals, the Board, as a whole, was not strong. They had put on 2 successful fund-raising events and seemed prepared to attempt another. However, the average tenure of the current Board member was well over 5 years, which was much too long to remain effective in a not-for-profit such as A.W.A.R.E. With only 6 members, the work of the Board could be demanding, and burnout could occur.

A.W.A.R.E. had a very good reputation in the local community as a well-run, efficient, and caring organization. The staff and volunteers were active in community affairs, A.W.A.R.E. received funds from the United Way, participated in local and state equestrian Special Olympics (where their riders generally took home most of the gold medals), and cooperated with other not-for-profits in local events. A.W.A.R.E. also had an excellent reputation amongst the equestrian community throughout the state.

Financials

When A.W.A.R.E. was located in a small arena, the majority of the expenses concerned involved payroll and horses. These were still the 2 largest expense items, however, maintenance and upkeep on the much larger facility had increased expenses dramatically. Additionally, expenses from several other items, like insurance, taxes, and veterinary care, had also increased drastically. Revenues came almost entirely from client fees, supplemented by donations. (See **Exhibits 2** and **3**.)

The contributors of the land placed a stipulation that for the first 5 years, only therapeutic horseback riding was to be allowed on the property. That time had now expired; however,

Exhibit 2

Balance Sheet: A.W.A.R.E.

Year Ending December 31	1999	1998	1997	1996	1995
Assets					
Current assets					
Checking and savings	$ 17,336	$ 20,229	$ 20,312	$ 8,608	$ 19,961
Accounts receivable	(864)	(1,189)	(659)	(362)	(187)
Total current assets	16,472	19,040	19,653	8,246	19,774
Fixed assets					
Buildings and land	265,419	265,000	265,000	265,000	265,000
Horses	10,551	10,850	7,550	4,401	4,400
Equipment	32,486	31,485	18,622	27,195	28,073
Accumulated depreciation	(85,195)	(70,622)	(24,087)	(22,034)	(11,329)
Total fixed assets	223,261	236,713	267,085	274,561	286,144
Total Assets	$239,733	$255,753	$295,738	$282,808	$305,918
Liabilities and equity					
Liabilities					
Current liabilities	$ 157	$ 0	$ 0	$ 0	$ 124
Total liabilities	157	0	0	0	124
Equity					
Retained earnings	239,576	255,753	295,738	282,808	305,794
Total equity	239,576	255,753	295,738	282,808	305,794
Total liabilities and equity	$239,733	$255,753	$295,738	$282,808	$305,918

Note: Rounding errors on total.

Exhibit 3

Profit and Loss Statement: A.W.A.R.E.

Year Ending December 31	1999	1998	1997	1996	1995
Ordinary income/expenses					
Income					
Rider fees	$ 50,097	$49,703	$44,894	$28,863	$42,184
Donations	10,670	12,716	8,056	4,051	6,579
United Way	7,653	423	5,550	3,982	3,924
Other income	4,095	1,451	3,275	4,367	25,089
Total income	72,515	64,293	61,775	41,263	77,767
Expenses					
Hay and feed	5,097	5,832	6,094	8,866	1,685
Facility maintenance	2,555	2,015	1,229	1,214	1,602
Insurance	3,294	1,875	1,900	1,864	1,265
Payroll	38,381	29,615	22,780	26,194	31,057
Other expenses	37,938	25,034	26,053	17,074	27,156
Total expenses	87,265	64,371	58,056	55,212	62,765
Net ordinary income	(14,750)	(78)	3,719	(13,949)	15,002
Other income/expenses					
In-kind donations	3,960	2,500	7,400	0	350
Net other income	3,960	2,500	7,400	0	350
Net income	$(10,790)	$ 2,422	$11,119	$13,696	$15,352

no other revenue sources had been attempted. Clients were charged $25.00 for a 1-hour riding session with 1 of A.W.A.R.E.'s instructors. A modified fee could be charged for group lessons and some clients were given scholarships. Hippotherapy, horseback riding with a certified physical therapist (PT), billed out as physical therapy and is covered by insurance. Currently, a local physical therapist brings a group of her clients to A.W.A.R.E. once a week. A.W.A.R.E. charges only their regular riding fees and the PT bills the insurance companies at her regular rates.

Decision Time

Sherry, still standing at the door to the arena, frowned as she began to ponder several recent events that had placed A.W.A.R.E. in a precarious position. She was worried about, and unsure of, both the short-term and long-term viability of the organization. Over the past several years, the summer session had been very profitable for A.W.A.R.E. During the summer, a diagnostic camp for children was run by a national social organization that had brought 12 to 14 riders per day as part of their planned activities. This cash flow paid the summer salaries for the instructors, bought a year's supply of hay for the horses, and allowed A.W.A.R.E. to net around $7,000 for the summer. The camp informed A.W.A.R.E. only weeks before the summer session was to begin that they were not participating this summer. The loss of cash flow could severely impact both the summer and fall programs. The loss of additional future revenues could force A.W.A.R.E. to scale back operation significantly.

Cash flow will also be impacted when Sherry steps down as Executive Director. Sherry had been the volunteer Executive Director for over 6 years and a medical condition was forcing her to retire. It would be expensive to replace her with a paid Executive Director (a typical salary range might be $36,000 per year) and an additional full-time instructor.

While these problems can be overcome, Sherry was worried about the future. What will A.W.A.R.E. be in 5 to 10 years? Will it even be in existence, operating as it does now, or be something completely different? What was best for the short- and long-term viability of A.W.A.R.E.? As volunteer Executive Director, Sherry realized there was a number of alternatives ranging from closing A.W.A.R.E. to the creation of a nationwide network of similar programs. More realistically, A.W.A.R.E. could offer profit-generating activities such as riding camps for well children or perhaps hold another fund-raiser and hire a new Executive Director. Other options might include partnering with the local hospital or other not-for-profits in the surrounding area. Sherry did realize that due to the success and proximity of the outlet mall, the current property could be sold for about $750,000.

When Cathy Morgan first began A.W.A.R.E., she envisioned the eventual development of an entire therapy complex with staff physicians, live-in clients, and extensive therapy programs. However, Cathy was no longer with the program, and Sherry was unsure what direction A.W.A.R.E. should take or how to get there.

References and Sources for Additional Information

North American Riding for the Handicapped Association: <www.narha.org>

San Marcos Home Page: <ci.san-marcos.tx.us>

San Marcos Chamber of Commerce: <www.sanmarcostexas.com>

Case Index